# 20-GAME LOSERS

### EDITED BY BILL NOWLIN AND EMMET R. NOWLIN
#### ASSOCIATE EDITORS: BOB LEMOINE, LEN LEVIN, AND CARL RIECHERS

Society for American Baseball Research, Inc.
Phoenix, AZ

20-Game Losers
Edited by Bill Nowlin and Emmet R. Nowlin
Associate Editors: Bob LeMoine, Len Levin, and Carl Riechers

Copyright © 2017 Society for American Baseball Research, Inc.
All rights reserved. Reproduction in whole or in part without permission is prohibited.

ISBN 978-1-943816-59-0
(Ebook ISBN 978-1-943816-58-3)

All photographs are courtesy of the National Baseball Hall of Fame and Library, except the following:
Detroit Public Library: 86
Diamonds in the Dusk: 57, 58, 71
Find-A-Grave.com: 23
Library of Congress: 24, 29, 89, 102, 106, 127, 150, 182, 195, 197, 211, 213
Bill Nowlin: 48, 167, 250
public domain: 113, 188, 222, 229, 232

Original cover art for SABR by Ronnie Joyner
Book design: Gilly Rosenthol

Society for American Baseball Research
Cronkite School at ASU
555 N. Central Ave. #416
Phoenix, AZ 85004
Phone: (602) 496-1460
Web: www.sabr.org
Facebook: Society for American Baseball Research
Twitter: @SABR

# CONTENTS

1. INTRODUCTION ...................... 1

2. 20-GAME LOSER, PROFILES OF THE 20-LOSS SEASONS ............ 2
   by David E. Skelton

3. THE VANISHING 20-GAME LOSER ... 13
   by Barry Mednick

## PLAYER

4. STEVE ARLIN ........................ 16
   by Gregory H. Wolf

5. BILL BAILEY ......................... 22
   by Eric Frost

6. GEORGE BAUMGARDNER ........... 27
   by Joe Schuster

7. BOOM-BOOM BECK ................. 34
   by Paul E. Doutrich

8. GEORGE BELL ....................... 39
   by John Struth

9. BILL BONHAM ...................... 45
   by Joel Rippel

10. ED BRANDT ......................... 50
    by C. Paul Rogers III

11. BUSTER BROWN .................... 56
    by Mark S. Sternman

12. HARRY BYRD ........................ 61
    by Armand Peterson

13. GEORGE CASTER ................... 69
    by Chris Rainey

14. JOHN COLEMAN .................... 74
    by Justin Mckinney

15. CLIFF CURTIS ....................... 85
    by Alan Drude

16. ART DITMAR ........................ 94
    by David E. Skelton

17. GUS DORNER ...................... 100
    by Paul Hofmann

18. CECIL FERGUSON ................. 105
    by Jeff Findley

19. DANA FILLINGIM .................. 111
    by Niall Adler

20. SAM GRAY .......................... 118
    by Gregory H. Wolf

21. DAN GRINER ....................... 125
    by Gregory H. Wolf

22. GUY HECKER ....................... 131
    by Bob Bailey

23. RANDY JONES ..................... 135
    by Alan Cohen

24. VERN KENNEDY .................... 142
    by Joel Rippel

25. HENRY KEUPPER .................. 147
    by Emmet R. Nowlin

26. BRIAN KINGMAN .................. 152
    by Chad Moody

27. DON LARSEN ....................... 159
    by Charles F. Faber

28. MIKE MAROTH ..................... 165
    by Barbara Mantegani and Dave Raglin

# CONTENTS

29. AL MATTERN .................................. 175
    by Bob LeMoine
30. JIM MCCORMICK ............................ 181
    by Chris Rainey
31. STONEY MCGLYNN .......................... 186
    by Steve Schmitt
32. HARRY MCINTIRE ........................... 192
    by John Struth
33. JACK NABORS ................................ 199
    by Stephen V. Rice
34. ROLLIE NAYLOR ............................. 204
    by Phil Williams
35. SUNNY JIM PASTORIUS ................... 209
    by Glen Sparks
36. ORLANDO PEÑA ............................. 216
    by Joel Rippel
37. SCOTT PERRY ................................ 221
    by Phil Williams
38. FRED SANFORD .............................. 227
    by Warren Corbett
39. JACK SCOTT .................................. 231
    by Skip Nipper
40. GEORGE ALLEN SMITH .................... 236
    by Jeff English
41. JIM TOBIN ..................................... 240
    by Gregory H. Wolf
42. CLYDE WRIGHT .............................. 248
    by Paul E. Doutrich

## HALL OF FAMERS WHO LOST 20 OR MORE GAMES IN AT LEAST ONE SEASON

43. 20-GAME LOSERS POPULATE THE BASEBALL HALL OF FAME .............. 255
    by Bill Nowlin
44. STEVE CARLTON ............................. 258
    by Cosme Vivanco
45. JACK CHESBRO .............................. 266
    by Wayne McElreavy
46. JOHN CLARKSON ............................ 2721
    by Brian McKenna
47. CANDY CUMMINGS .......................... 284
    by David Fleitz
48. PUD GALVIN .................................. 288
    by Charles Hausberg
49. JESSE HAINES ................................ 301
    by Gregory H. Wolf
50. WALTER JOHNSON ........................... 308
    by Charles Carey
51. TIM KEEFE .................................... 313
    by Charlie Bevis
52. TED LYONS ................................... 325
    by Warren Corbett
53. RUBE MARQUARD ........................... 331
    by Joe Wancho
54. JOE MCGINNITY .............................. 339
    by Don Doxsie
55. PHIL NIEKRO ................................. 346
    by Tom Hufford

# CONTENTS

56. HANK O'DAY ................................... 354
    by Dennis Bingham

57. OLD HOSS RADBOURN ................ 368
    by Brian McKenna

58. EPPA RIXEY ................................... 380
    by Jan Finkel

59. ROBIN ROBERTS .......................... 383
    by C. Paul Rogers III

60. RED RUFFING ............................... 400
    by Warren Corbett

61. AMOS RUSIE ................................. 405
    by Charles F. Faber

62. ED WALSH ..................................... 411
    by Stuart Schimler

63. JOHN MONTGOMERY WARD ....... 415
    by Bill Lamb

64. MICKEY WELCH ............................ 424
    by Bill Lamb

65. VIC WILLIS .................................... 431
    by Daniel R. Levitt

66. CY YOUNG ..................................... 435
    by Bill Nowlin and David Southwick

67. A STAFF WITH FOUR 20-GAME
    LOSERS ......................................... 444
    by Bill Nowlin

68. CHICK FRASER .............................. 445
    by Mike Lynch

69. KAISER WILHELM ......................... 452
    by Gregory H. Wolf

70. VIC WILLIS .................................... 449
    by Daniel R. Levitt

71. IRV YOUNG .................................... 460
    by Will Anderson and Bill Nowlin

72. 20-GAME LOSERS IN THE MINOR
    LEAGUES ....................................... 466
    by Bill Nowlin

73. CHRIS ARCHER - NEARLY A
    20-GAME LOSER IN 2016 ............. 470
    by Bill Nowlin

74. THE PROTECTION MYTH ............. 472
    by Warren Corbett

75. CONTRIBUTORS ........................... 475

# 20-GAME LOSERS

## INTRODUCTION BY BILL NOWLIN

**YOU HAVE TO BE A VERY GOOD** pitcher to lose 20 games in one season. Why would a manager keep putting you out there to pitch, time after time, if you didn't have a chance to win the game?

In fact, as it happens, more than 25 percent of the pitchers in the National Baseball Hall of Fame are pitchers who lost 20 or more games in a single season. One of them even lost 20 or more games for 10 years in a row!

The names in this book are often well-known names. There were three years that Cy Young lost more than 20 games. Other 20-game losers were Steve Carlton, Walter Johnson, Phil Niekro, Robin Roberts, and Red Ruffing, to name a few.

For this book, we wanted to include a variety of pitchers who lacked SABR biographies, and we have included more than 35 who fit that brief. We've also included every one of the 23 Hall of Famers who are 20-game losers. We've also included Mike Maroth and Brian Kingman, the two most recent pitchers to have this distinction, and Jack Nabors, who had a 1-20 season. You will find Guy Hecker, whose record of 52-20 constituted the best winning percentage of any 20-game loser.

And we featured one woebegone pitching staff which had *four* 20-game losers, all in the same season.

This is not a small population we had to draw from—some 499 pitchers have had seasons in which they lost 20 or more games. Stratospheric earned-run averages were not to blame. Only two of the 499 had an ERA over 6.00. Having an exemplary ERA didn't exempt you from losing 20 games—consider these ERAs for some of the players in the book for their 20-game-losing seasons: Ed Walsh (1.27), John Montgomery Ward (1.74), the aforementioned Hecker (1.80), Jim McCormick (1.85), and half a dozen more with ERAs under 2.00.

We could go on and on, but suffice it to say this take on pitching records offers plenty of quirks to explore. Thanks to the 53 members of SABR who combined their efforts to create a truly fascinating book—if we do say so ourselves.

# 20-GAME LOSER: PROFILES OF THE 20-LOSS SEASONS

## BY DAVID E. SKELTON

**IT HAS BECOME ALMOST AS RARE AS** the major-league Triple Crown, and even more so than its statistical opposite of a pitcher winning 20 games in a single season. Since 1980, there has been only one pitcher who lost 20 games in a single season—21 to be exact—and there is no reason to think baseball will see another such season in the foreseeable future. It has become baseball's equivalent of Bigfoot: seemingly rumored to exist, but impossible to see.

Historically, it didn't used to be this way. Prior to 1980, baseball saw a fairly regular sprinkling of pitchers with at least 20 losses per season. The roster of said pitchers was remarkably diverse: from the pitcher who approached the mound with the expectation of sinister, scary music, to the later Hall-of-Fame inductee.

As opposed to delving into the reasons for this paucity (of which there are many), the research herein has instead focused on the unique circumstances surrounding many of these past 20-game losers. This research has been limited to the period from 1920 to the present—a time when the 20-loss season was not rare, but not as pervasive as the preceding period when, for example, from 1900-20, there was an average of five or more pitchers logging 20 losses per season (with a high of 14 such pitchers in 1905). Therefore, unless otherwise cited, the statistical "leaders" noted in the 20-loss/season category are limited to the last 92 years. Barring an unlikely rash of any future 20-loss seasons, these statistics will likely stand for many years to come.

For purposes of capturing the 20-loss "achievement," the following categories have been established: The Deserved, The Repeat Offenders, Dr. Jekyll and Mr. Hyde, The Unjustified, Miscellaneous, and The Teammates.

As described below, these categories are not intended as "hard" boundaries. A pitcher slotted in "The Repeat Offenders" column could easily slide two categories later (Phil Niekro, for instance), or justifiably be listed under two separate columns (Dick Ellsworth: The Deserved and The Repeat Offenders). The intention herein is not to pursue a thorough analysis of the 20-loss season as much as establish a sorting for purposes of relating the rather interesting events, statistical anomalies and, in some instances, ironies that helped lead these pitchers into such an exclusive club.

Furthermore, at no point in these brief statistical summaries should the reader perceive intent to belittle or denigrate the pitchers cited. In fact, it is often to the contrary, as any hurler who accumulated as many as 20 losses had to have had a certain level of confidence from his manager to have taken the mound so regularly. As will be seen, these same 20-loss "victims" were often the staff aces hurling for some rather pathetic teams.

Staff ace or not, the pitchers and their stories tell an interesting tale.

## THE DESERVED

In deference to the above-referenced "cue the sinister scary music" there are certainly some pitchers whose particular season appears to beg 20 losses. Notwithstanding the success achieved in other years, they include (in no particular order):

### Mike Maroth, Detroit Tigers (2003)

Mike drew the Opening Day assignment for the Tigers to start the 2003 season, and the 3–1 loss to the visiting Minnesota Twins would seemingly portend the ominous season ahead for both Maroth and the Tigers. The team went on to establish an American

League record for losses in a season—one shy of the post-1900 low mark set by the expansion New York Mets in 1962—while Maroth went on to etch his name in the long list of pitchers with 20 losses.

The Tigers were in the midst of a 12-year drought of consecutive losing seasons, and in 2003 management moved to reverse this trend with a full scale youth movement (every starting pitcher was less than 27 years old). Still the team flailed evidenced by A.L. season lows in categories such as team batting average and runs scored (one of the few categories in which they did lead the league was with errors—138—33 more than the league average). Maroth's scant nine wins led the Tigers staff, but he might have avoided the sizable number of losses if he had garnered more offensive support—in 14 of the 21 losses, the team scored three or fewer runs.

Conversely, a 5.73 ERA—more than a run higher than the league average—did little to further his cause. Adding insult to injury, Maroth led the league in earned runs allowed, and shared the dubious distinction of most home runs allowed with two other hurlers. Amongst his 20-loss brethren in the entire history of baseball (including the years before 1920), Maroth has the fewest number of complete games pitched (one), and the highest total of home runs allowed per nine innings (1.6). With such homely numbers, the determination is that Maroth "deserved" the 20-loss season, and is therefore "inducted" herein.

### Pedro Ramos, Minnesota Twins (1961)

San Luis Pinar del Rio saw its share of heavy fighting during the rebellion that ousted Cuban dictator Fulgencio Batista.[1] Although he never participated in the fighting, native son Pedro Ramos may have felt he'd had his own experience with combat "shell shock," for over the course of three seasons, he led the American League in home runs allowed—and it was during one of these years that he also joined the ranks of the 20-loss season.

Pedro Ramos flirted with a 20-loss season often before reaching the inglorious threshold. While pitching for the lowly Washington Senators 1958–60, Ramos managed to twirl 18, 19, and 18 losses respectively. It apparently took the team's relocation to Minnesota in 1961 for him to finally achieve 20 losses. Perhaps unsurprisingly, Ramos led the American League in losses over each of the referenced four seasons.

In joining his 20-loss brethren, Ramos shares two distinctions with Mike Maroth: he was the Opening Day starter for his team in 1961 and he led the league in home runs allowed. Unlike Maroth, he set a pace for gopher balls that far outdistanced that year's second-place finisher, Gene Conley (39–33).

Ironically, two potential scenarios that did not come to fruition might have prevented Ramos from reaching 20-losses in 1961.

The 18-loss season that Ramos endured in the preceding season could be blamed in large part on the lack of offensive support he received from his teammates. Ramos produced a nice 3.45 ERA in 1960 (league average: 3.87), while his team could only muster an average of less than 1.5 runs per game in 15 of his 18 losses. Frustration finally boiled over, and he "demanded to be traded to another club, preferably the Yankees."[2] One can only surmise that had such a trade occurred, and Ramos found himself pitching for the power-laden offense that included Mickey Mantle and Roger Maris, he would not have attained the 20-loss threshold the following season (no matter how many gopher balls he served up).

On a completely separate front, Ramos and his fellow native Cubans nearly sat out the entire 1961 season. After the Cuban rebellion, the International League withdrew its Havana franchise, and in the latter part of 1960 there was much speculation that, in retaliation, "Fidel Castro won't let Cuban players come to the United States [in 1961]."[3] Obviously, had Castro delivered on this perceived threat and prevented the Cuban players from playing, Ramos would not have been around to twirl his 20 losses.

But play he did, and not for the Yankees. His ERA increased by an additional one-half run, and he would lead the league in base hits allowed while serving up the aforementioned league-leading 39 home runs. Such ugly numbers "award" Ramos the distinction of joining Mike Maroth in induction to the "deserving" category.

### "Honorable" Mention: Don Larsen, Baltimore Orioles (1954)

Far more famous for being the only pitcher to twirl a perfect game in World Series competition, two years earlier Larsen was a part of the humble franchise that relocated from St. Louis to Baltimore in 1954. A team in the midst of 14 consecutive non-winning campaigns (they managed to secure a .500 season in 1957), the move to Maryland did little to turn their fate around as the team lost 100 games for the second straight season.

An anemic offense contributed to the malaise as the club garnered only 52 home runs throughout the 1954 season (a mere three more than the N.L. champion Ted Kluszewski's 49 dingers the same year). Larsen could arguably be slotted in the "Unjustified" category due to this lack of offensive support. Fairly or not, he is slotted here for the unique record he holds among the roster of 20-loss pitchers: Larsen's .125 winning percentage (3–21) is the lowest mark registered for the period researched from 1920 forward, and eighth lowest all-time.

Unlike the fate that befell Pedro Ramos, Larsen would be traded to the New York Yankees at the conclusion of the 1954 season, and attain a certain level of success over five seasons that included the aforementioned perfect game. Then, on December 11, 1959, Larsen was traded once more to the Kansas City Athletics, where he again posted an incredibly low winning percentage during the 1960 season: .091 (1–10).

Thus, for attaining the lowest winning percentage in modern major league history—with a sizable assist from his teammates' feeble offensive skills—Larsen's 20-loss season places him in the "deserved" category.

There are certainly many other pitchers who could conceivably belong in this problematic grouping with Messrs. Maroth, Ramos, and Larsen, but some of these have carved out a category all to themselves.

### THE REPEAT OFFENDERS

The all-time list is extensive, and includes such notables as Cy Young and Walter Johnson, as well as Pud Galvin, Tim Keefe, and Old Hoss Radbourne (each a HOF inductee). The period from 1920 forward includes its own share of HOF notables such as Phil Niekro, Ted Lyons, Red Ruffing, and Eppa Rixey. The category that captures such worthy hurlers is that of "The Repeat Offenders," defined as those who have on more than one occasion lost 20 or more games in a single season. There are 17 such pitchers since 1920 (three of whom actually span the period from 1917–25), not all of whom stand out as prominently as the HOF inductees above, but many of these have an interesting back-story all the same.

### Phil Niekro, Atlanta Braves (1977, 1979) Wilbur Wood, Chicago White Sox (1973, 1975)

Excluding the remarkable season that lefty Mickey Lolich had with the Detroit Tigers in 1971—45 games started, while completing 29 of those—it is not surprising that Phil Niekro and Wilbur Wood are the only pitchers since 1923 to take the mound in a starting role 43 or more times in a single season (in large part due to the lack of arm strain sustained by a knuckleball hurler). In so doing, both former 20-game winners (on numerous occasions) also posted two 20-game losing seasons while pitching for their respective sub-.500 clubs. In fact, during a four-year stretch in each of their careers (Niekro, 1976–79; Wood, 1971–74), they would personally account for over 27 percent of his team's total victories. With these similar characteristics, Niekro and Wood are consigned together in the "Repeat Offenders" category.

Much as a knuckleball is baffling to a hitter, the two 20-loss campaigns that Niekro posted appear just as mystifying. Niekro accumulated these two seasons while pitching for a dreadful Braves team that finished last in the N.L.'s Western Division four years in a row. One such season was accompanied by 21 wins, truly an amazing win total considering the fact that he led or tied the league lead in some rather dubious categories—41 home runs allowed, 113 walks allowed, 311 hits allowed, and 11 hit batsmen (Niekro would also rank second to Vida Blue in earned runs allowed). Conversely, the other, more "deserving" 20-loss season (an ERA that rose to a non-career-like 4.03) saw Niekro lead the league in some of the same dubious categories—although yielding a much lower (26) home run total—while winning five fewer games. Taken all together, it appears that a combination of pitching for a poor-performing team, and a tendency toward yielding the gopher ball (Niekro is fourth all-time in career home runs allowed) provide the ingredients necessary for this Hall of Fame inductee to also find entry into the "Repeat Offenders."

Unlike Niekro, fellow knuckler Wilbur Wood did not pitch for a last-place team during his 20 loss seasons—though it was often very close. In the two 20-loss campaigns (in 1974 Wood was one loss shy of three consecutive 20-loss seasons) the White Sox finished fifth in a six-team division. Like his fellow knuckler, pitching for a poor-performing cast contributed mightily to one of the two 20-loss seasons as his teammates could muster a total of only 18 runs in 15 of those 20 losses. Still further evidence that these two should be forever linked in the "Repeat Offender" category is their remarkably similar statistical lines during each of their 20-loss seasons:

|             | W-L   | ERA  | and | W-L   | ERA  |
|-------------|-------|------|-----|-------|------|
| Wilbur Wood | 24–20 | 3.46 | and | 16–20 | 4.11 |
| Phil Niekro | 21–20 | 3.39 | and | 16–20 | 4.03 |

Still, these two do not stand alone in common pairing, as evidenced by the following:

**Paul Derringer, St. Louis Cardinals and Cincinnati Reds (1933); Cincinnati Reds (1934)**
**Red Ruffing, Boston Red Sox (1928, 1929)**
**Bump Hadley, Chicago White Sox and St. Louis Browns (1932); St. Louis Browns (1933)**
**Roger Craig, New York Mets (1962–63)**

It is remarkable to lose 20 games in each of two separate seasons. What may be even more noteworthy is to have done so in consecutive years, for that is exactly what Messrs. Derringer, Ruffing, Hadley, and Craig achieved. Even more extraordinary is the fact that two of these four pitchers would, at an early stage in their careers, lose at least 47 games over the course of two campaigns and still go on to earn Hall of Fame consideration (and, in one instance, induction).

Few players have launched their major-league careers as successfully as Paul Derringer did in 1931—leading the N.L. with a .692 winning percentage (18–8) while helping the St. Louis Cardinals to a World Championship. Unfortunately, the team would plummet to a second division finish the following season, and Derringer's sophomore year followed suit (11–14, 4.05 ERA). A rocky start in 1933 precipitated a multi-player trade that sent Derringer to the Cincinnati Reds, a fate that foretold the two consecutive 20-loss seasons, as the Reds were in the midst of a nine-year drought that included five last-place finishes.

Arriving in Cincinnati with an 0–2 mark, Derringer went on to lose an additional 25 games—one has to go back to 1905 to find a pitcher with more than 27 losses in a single season—followed by 21 losses in 1934. Amazingly, Derringer accumulated these losses with ERAs of 3.30 and 3.59 in 1933 and 1934, respectively (while allowing an incredibly low four home runs in 1933). The anemic Cincinnati offense tells the entire story as it managed only 25 runs in 30 of the 48 losses Derringer sustained over that two-year period. Fortunately, Derringer's (and the Reds' fate overall) would take a more positive turn, and he would go on to garner MVP consideration in five of the next six seasons. Derringer's later success notwithstanding, the 1933–34 campaigns serve to earn him consideration in the "Repeat Offenders" category.

Derringer's counterpart in regard to receiving Hall of Fame consideration (and, in this instance, induction) is Red Ruffing. A 39–93 career mark at the age of 24 would hardly seem conducive to such a later honor. Ruffing accumulated 25 and 22 losses in 1928 and 1929 seasons, respectively. Similarities to Derringer do not end with HOF consideration though, for much as Derringer struggled with some very bad Cincinnati clubs, Ruffing pitched for some incredibly horrible Boston Red Sox teams.

The angst of January 3, 1920 is considerably lessened by the 2004 and 2007 championship seasons, but it is still capable of invoking the wrath of Red Sox' fans worldwide. That was the day Babe Ruth was sold to the New York Yankees, and the sale contributed largely to the franchise's tailspin over the following 14 seasons. Ruffing joined the Sox in the teeth of this long descent and a league-low team batting average for nine consecutive seasons (1922–30) contributed to the lack of offensive support that garnered Ruffing 25 and 22 losses. Not discounting the fact that 20 losses for any pitcher is often the result of a certain team-wide ineptitude, Ruffing did not help his cause when leading the league in earned runs surrendered during both the 1928 and 1929 campaigns.

While the Red Sox continued a slow crawl out of perpetual second-division league occupancy (including last-place finishes in nine of 11 seasons), Ruffing would be spared a portion of this fate when traded to the New York Yankees early in the 1930 season. The trade contributed largely to the resurrection of Ruffing's career, as he went on to win an average of more than 16 games over the course of 13 seasons, including four consecutive 20-win campaigns. Still, just as Ruffing's latter success mirrors Derringer's as far as helping to turn his career around, the two 20-loss campaigns of Ruffing serve as induction as a "Repeat Offender" as well.

Roger Craig never attained the success that Messrs. Derringer and Ruffing achieved, ending his career with only a .430 winning percentage. Nearly 50 percent of his career 98 losses was accumulated while pitching two seasons for the hapless expansion New York Mets, and perhaps one name more than any other illustrates the frustration Craig experienced in two consecutive 20-loss seasons: Roy Sievers!

On July 19, 1963, Craig took the mound in Connie Mack Stadium against the Philadelphia Phillies sporting a 2–15 record. Having lost 24 games in the Mets' inaugural season the year before, Craig was well on his way to two consecutive 20-loss seasons. But the 15 losses did not tell the whole story of Craig's valiant efforts coming into this game, as seven of those losses were games where he gave up only eight earned runs combined! On this night, the 33-year-old righty was working on a masterful three-hit shutout when, with one out into the ninth, Phillies' left fielder Tony Gonzalez hit a triple to right, followed promptly by a Roy Sievers home run that resulted in a heartbreaking 2-1 loss for Craig.

Sadly, Craig's demise at Sievers hands was not limited to this game alone. A month and a day later, Craig took the very same mound and again threw goose eggs into the ninth. With two outs and his team trailing 1-0, Sievers stepped to the plate and deposited the fourth pitch into the stands to tie the game (from which the Phillies prevailed in extra innings).

These two games seemingly capture the essence of what it was like to play for the Mets during Craig's two-year stretch: not enough offense (last in team batting average), a porous defense (most unearned runs allowed), and an unreliable pitching staff (last in team earned run average). "Can't anybody here play this game?" lamented Manager Casey Stengel, but as evidenced by the games cited above, another Stengelese quotation seems more appropriate to Roger Craig: "You make your own luck. Some people have bad luck all their lives."[4]

Yet if bad luck can be defined as being unfortunate enough to be traded from a contending team to a near-perennial cellar-dweller, then Bump Hadley is as unlucky a pitcher as Casey Stengel might have ever encountered. Hadley began his major-league career with the then-successful Washington Senators—a unique phrase if ever there was one—and posted a respectable 58–56 record over the course of five seasons. A sequence of two trades in less than five months would place Hadley into the starting rotation for the lowly 1932 St. Louis Browns, where a far less successful 38–56 mark would be sustained over three long campaigns—including consecutive 20-loss seasons, 1932–33.

Not that Hadley seemed to help his own cause. Over the course of these two consecutive 20-loss endeavors he uncharacteristically led the American League in both earned runs and walks allowed (marks that would surely make Hadley eligible for the "Deserved" category). Yet, unlike "Deserved" Pedro Ramos, who unsuccessfully sought to be traded to the power-laden Yankees, Hadley found himself with the Bronx Bombers toward the end of his career. During this five-year stint, Hadley would again achieve respectable numbers (49–31) to complement his earlier success with the Senators.

Ironically, Hadley posted two of the four consecutive 20-loss seasons sustained by Browns' pitchers between the years 1931–34. The mantle of continuity would be raised by a pitcher who, since 1920, stands alone in the "Repeat Offender" category.

## Bobo Newsom, St. Louis Browns (1934); Detroit Tigers (1941); Philadelphia Athletics (1945)

A tall righty from Hartsville, South Carolina, Bobo Newsom pitched 20 years in major-league ball while logging time with nine different franchises. Jumping into the big leagues permanently in 1934 (after posting a 30-win season the year before with Los Angeles of the Pacific Coast League), Newsom would experience three 20-loss seasons while coming remarkably close to losing 20 games in at least two additional years. Thrice a 20-game winner (and a four-time American League All-Star), the combined 60 losses over three seasons accounted for over 27 percent of Newsom's career total of 222 losses.

Newsom didn't waste any time accumulating his first 20-loss season. St. Louis Browns' manager Rogers Hornsby inserted Newsom into the starting rotation in his first full season—he'd made six appearances with two teams over the course of four years prior to his rookie campaign with the Browns—and he responded favorably, leading the team in wins, ERA, complete games, saves, strikeouts, and innings pitched. Unfortunately, twirling for a pitiful Browns' club, he also led the American League in losses with his first 20-loss campaign. Subsequent 20-loss seasons would mirror Newsom's rookie endeavor, as he would be among the team leaders in some of the very same categories while pitching for the Detroit Tigers and Philadelphia A's in 1941 and 1945, respectively.

The most remarkable aspect herein is how close Newsom came to two additional 20-loss seasons. In his sophomore endeavor, Newsom opened the season with an 0–6 mark when he was sold by the Browns to the similarly inept Washington Senators. Newsom would go on to post a respectable 11–12 mark with the Senators, for an accumulation of 18 losses for the season. Yet, that does not tell the whole story: Newsom missed the entire month of June, resulting in an estimated eight fewer opportunities to have lost two additional games, enough to have attained a fourth 20-loss endeavor.

Then, in 1942, Newsom found himself back with the Senators after a 20-loss campaign with the Detroit Tigers the year before. By August 23, Newsom stood at 17 losses with more than a month to go. A week later, Newsom would be sold to the pennant contending Brooklyn Dodgers where he would fall one loss short of the "coveted" 20-loss campaign. One is left to speculate that had Newsom remained with the second division Senators through the month of September, he might have accumulated the three additional losses necessary to attain a fourth 20-loss season.

For purposes of bringing closure to the "Repeat Offenders" category, the 10 remaining pitchers who posted at least two 20-loss campaigns since 1920 are below. Of distinct note are three pitchers who inexplicably garnered MVP consideration during these particular seasons:

| Pitcher | Team | Year |
|---|---|---|
| **Eppa Rixey** | Philadelphia Phillies | 1917, 1920 |
| Jesse Barnes^ | Boston Braves | 1917, 1924 |
| Sad Sam Jones | Boston Red Sox | 1919 |
| | New York Yankees | 1925 |
| Jack Scott | Boston Braves | 1920 |
| | Philadelphia Phillies | 1927 |
| Slim Harriss | Philadelphia A's | 1922 |
| | Boston Red Sox | 1927* |
| **Ted Lyons** | Chicago White Sox | 1929, 1933 |
| Hugh Mulcahy | Philadelphia Phillies | 1938*, 1940* |
| Murry Dickson+ | Pittsburgh Pirates | 1952* |

|  | Philadelphia Phillies | 1954 |
|---|---|---|
| Al Jackson | New York Mets | 1962, 1965 |
| Dick Ellsworth | Chicago Cubs | 1962, 1966 |

*garnered MVP consideration; BOLD indicates a Hall of Fame inductee.*

^ *Barnes holds a unique distinction among his 20-loss brethren—losing 20 games for the same team twice, while hurling for another club in between.*

+ *Dickson's removal from the starting rotation after August 25 likely spared him a third 20-loss campaign in 1953. Had he done so, it would have qualified him as the only pitcher since 1907 with three consecutive such seasons, last accomplished by Boston Beaneaters/Doves hurler Irv Young (Kaiser Wilhelm posted a major-league career three-peat in 1908, but his streak was interrupted by two minor-league campaigns in 1906–07). Overall, there have been 34 pitchers who have posted a 20-loss three-peat, most of whom did so in the 19th century—including 10 consecutive 20-loss seasons posted by Hall of Fame inductee Pud Galvin.*

## DR. JEKYLL and MR. HYDE

This category is reserved for those pitchers who, for one reason or another, managed to win 20 games in a particular season, only to turn around and lose 20 in the following campaign (or vice versa). Evidence provided of this about-face is symptomatic of such a Jekyll-and-Hyde performance, thereby capturing this unique designation.

### Luis Tiant, Cleveland Indians (1968: 21–9, 1969: 9–20)

The year 1968 would be a watershed year for pitching, the dominance of which would result in a mere six major-league batters managing to achieve a meager .297 average while seven hurlers posted an ERA of less than 2.00. Tiant was among that select few, capturing his first of two career American League ERA titles with a minuscule 1.60 (barely edging out teammate Sam McDowell's 1.81), while also pacing the league in shutouts with nine. Tiant posted a deceptive 21–9 record which could easily have been enhanced with a little more offensive support, as he did not reckon in three decisions where he pitched a total of 19 innings while giving up a collective eight hits and two runs. With such sterling numbers, it is remarkable to realize that, although Tiant secured Cy Young Award consideration three times throughout his career, 1968 was not one of those occasions. Denny McLain's 31-victory year had much to do with that.

The anemic offensive output in the major leagues ushered in a number of rule changes for the 1969 season—a smaller strike zone and a reduced mound height. These new rules brought about the desired effect as the major leagues witnessed a spike of nearly 20 percent more runs scored per game. Tiant's numbers suffered accordingly as he led the major leagues in such dubious categories as home runs and walks allowed while tying the major-league mark for losses with 20. Although it is easy to blame this about-face on the newly implemented rule changes, no other pitcher suffered such a dramatic turnaround, thereby granting the anointment of Tiant as an inductee to the Jekyll-and-Hyde category.

### Dick Ellsworth, Chicago Cubs (1962: 9–20, 1963: 22–10)

On September 2, 1963, a ground-ball out induced by Chicago Cubs closer Lindy McDaniel resulted in the final out of a 7–5 victory for the visiting team, insuring McDaniel's teammate Dick Ellsworth a 20th win (the first such season for a Cubs hurler since 1945). Ellsworth went on to post a career-high 22 victories and a second-place finish in pursuit of the ERA crown (2.11), while pacing the Cubs to their first winning season in 17 years—an 82–80 mark that still resulted in a poor seventh-place finish. The club's success—meager as it was—was largely attributable to the efforts emanating from the mound as the pitching rotation witnessed a dramatic turnaround from the prior season. Spared a last place ranking for team ERA by the expansion New York Mets in 1962, the Cubs would post a second-best team ERA of 3.08 during the following season.

Yet pitching was not often a source of pride for this Windy City bunch, and the team could again be thankful for the existence of the newly inducted New York Mets in sparing them a last place finish in 1962 while chalking up 103 losses (Mets: 120 losses). Again, Ellsworth paced the team, though this time in a losing effort with a team-high 20 losses (incidentally, Ellsworth and teammate Don Cardwell joined the roster of top nine pitchers for the most losses in the National League in 1962, while the remaining seven came from the two expansion teams—the Mets and the Houston Colt .45s). Furthermore, if Ellsworth's name appears familiar, he was included in the roll call of "Repeat Offenders" when he added a 22 loss season to his Cubs resume during the 1966 campaign. Still, the 20 loss/22 win seasons of 1962–63 respectively earn Ellsworth induction into the category of "Dr. Jekyll and Mr. Hyde."

### Steve Carlton (1972: 27–10, 1973: 13–20)

When one examines Carlton's 27 wins in 1972 vs. his 20 losses in 1973, one question arises: how could he possibly win 27 games? Carlton toiled for the last place Philadelphia Phillies during this Jekyll-and-Hyde phase of his career, producing a herculean effort from the slab. Incredibly, the 27 wins tell only part of the story as his teammates marshalled only seven runs in eight outings where he did not figure in the win—a smattering of runs in even half of those eight games might have ushered Carlton into the select company of pitchers who've reached the 30-win threshold. A sterling 1.97 ERA was accompanied by 310 strikeouts—a figure reached by only five other pitchers since 1972—and a major-league leading 30 complete games. The 27 victories made up an astonishing 46 percent of the club's total of 59 wins. Such numbers resulted in the first of four career Cy Young Awards while also garnering Carlton MVP consideration.

The 1973 season saw Carlton return to mere mortal status as his ERA rose to 3.90 (not far removed from the major-league average of 3.75) while leading the staff in games started (40), complete games (18), and strikeouts (223). Although Carlton's overall stats were decidedly different, the Phillies' offensive malaise remained intact (even though the lineup featured major components of the 1980 Championship team—specifically Mike Schmidt, Greg Luzinski, Bob Boone and Larry Bowa), exemplified by the fact that in 14 of Carlton's 20 losses, the Phils were only capable of mustering a total of 12 runs! Arguably, this lack of offensive support could easily qualify "Lefty" for the "Unjustified" category, but other qualified candidates have relegated this Hall of Famer to "Dr. Jekyll and Mr. Hyde" instead.

Before considering the next group, the following reflects all other pitchers who have had a 20-win/20-loss season (or vice versa) in consecutive years. Some we've seen already while others will be seen again:

### 20 WIN / 20 LOSS SEASONS

| Pitcher | Team | Year | Record |
|---|---|---|---|
| Joe Oeschger | Boston Braves | 1921 | 20–14 |
| | | 1922 | 6–21 |
| Bobo Newsom | Detroit Tigers | 1940 | 21–5 |
| | | 1941 | 12–20 |
| Alex Kellner* | Philadelphia Athletics | 1949 | 20–12 |
| | | 1950 | 8–20 |
| Murry Dickson | Pittsburgh Pirates | 1951 | 20–16 |
| | | 1952 | 14–21 |
| Larry Jackson | Chicago Cubs | 1964 | 24–11 |
| | | 1965 | 14–21 |
| Mel Stottlemyre | New York Yankees | 1965 | 20–9 |
| | | 1966 | 12–20 |
| Stan Bahnsen | Chicago White Sox | 1972 | 21–16 |
| | | 1973 | 18–21 |
| Wilbur Wood | Chicago White Sox | 1972 | 24–17 |
| | | 1973 | 24–20 |
| | | 1974 | 20–19 |
| | | 1975 | 16–20 |
| Jerry Koosman | New York Mets | 1976 | 21–10 |
| | | 1977 | 8–20 |

*Kellner's 20-win performance was posted during his rookie year, but he fell short of the Rookie of the Year Award when placing second to Roy Sievers (he of the aforementioned Roger Craig infamy). Although his career would stretch another nine seasons, Kellner would never repeat the success of his debut season.*

## 20-GAME LOSERS

### 20 LOSS / 20 WIN SEASONS

| Pitcher | Team | Year | Record |
|---|---|---|---|
| Eddie Rommel | Philadelphia Athletics | 1921 | 16–23 |
| | | 1922 | 27–13 |
| Dolf Luque | Cincinnati Reds | 1922 | 13–23 |
| | | 1923 | 27–8 |
| **Ted Lyons** | Chicago White Sox | 1929 | 14–20 |
| | | 1930 | 22–15 |
| Paul Derringer* | Cincinnati Reds | 1933 | 7–27 |
| | Total—STL/CIN | 1934 | 15–21 |
| | | 1935 | 22–13 |
| Randy Jones+ | San Diego Padres | 1974 | 8–22 |
| | | 1975 | 20–12 |
| | | 1976 | 22–14 |

**BOLD** indicates a Hall of Fame inductee

* Derringer is the only pitcher since 1920 to have a 20-win season preceded by two consecutive 20-loss campaigns.

+ Jones is the only pitcher since 1920 to have two consecutive 20-win campaigns on the heels of a 20-loss season.

### THE UNJUSTIFIED

Of the 97 20-loss campaigns since 1920, nearly one-third (31) were hurled by a pitcher whose earned run average was less than either the circuit or major-league average (and often both) for a particular season—going a long way toward explaining why a team would trot their pitcher out so frequently while the losses continued to accumulate. As the term implies, this category attempts to capture the stories of those pitchers who, while posting better-than-average numbers, unjustly accumulated 20 losses. Much like Carlton, Niekro, and others aforementioned, these pitchers were all victims of anemic run support, making it seemingly impossible to avoid the debit ledger. For example:

### Jerry Koosman, New York Mets
### (1977: 8–20, 3.49 NL/MLB avg: 3.91/4.00)

Deservedly, the 1962 expansion New York Mets are held up as one of the most inept teams in the history of the game, but they can claim at least one positive distinction: a slightly greater offensive output than their 1977 counterpart:

| Category | 1962 Mets | 1977 Mets |
|---|---|---|
| Batting Average | 0.240 | 0.244 |
| Home Runs | 139 | 88 |
| Runs Scored | 617 | 587 |

It was in the midst of such offensive malaise that Jerry Koosman took the mound 32 times, giving up more than four earned runs on only four of those occasions. His meager eight wins would, sadly for the team as a whole, be among the team's top three season leaders. Adding insult to injury, the Mets offense would muster only 19 runs scored in 16 of the 20 losses. Little did he know that this production would appear like an offensive avalanche to the next pitchers on our list.

### Phil Niekro, Atlanta Braves 1979
### 21–20, 3.39 NL/MLB avg:
### 3.73/4.00 HR allowed: 41

Pedro Ramos, Minnesota Twins 1961 11–20, 3.95 AL/MLB avg: 4.02/4.03 HR allowed: 39 *NOTE: he of the aforementioned "Deserved" category is included here amongst this unique niche.*

### Murry Dickson, Pittsburgh Pirates 1952
### 14–21, 3.57 NL/MLB avg:
### 3.73/3.70 HR allowed: 26

### Eddie Rommel, Philadelphia Athletics 1921
### 16–23, 3.94 AL/MLB avg:
### 4.28/4.03 HR allowed: 21

As unique as this niche may be, there were other pitchers (or groups of same) who carved their own indelible mark.

### MISCELLANEOUS

Perhaps no 20-loss profile would be complete without identifying the two pitchers who lost 20 in a season and never wore a major-league uniform again.

| Pitcher | Team | Year | Record |
|---|---|---|---|
| Dick Barrett | Philadelphia Phillies | 1945 | 8–20 |
| Gordon Rhodes | Philadelphia A's | 1936 | 9–20 |

Relegated to the minors in 1946 and 1937 respectively, neither Barrett nor Rhodes (with a combined total of 13 years in the major leagues) would ever see another opportunity to return.

They nearly were joined in this unique group by Roy Wilkinson (4–20; Chicago White Sox, 1921), but a mere four appearances in 1922 separates him from this pair. Still, Wilkinson, along with Joe Oeschger (6–21; Boston Braves, 1922) managed to carve their own special place in the archives: as the only pitchers to lose 20 while starting so few games—23! [Spoiler alert: they both sustained many of the losses coming out of the bullpen.]

In a complete reversal to the fortunes of Barrett and Rhodes are the two pitchers who accompany Bobo Newsom by entering the major leagues with a 20-loss campaign:

| Pitcher | Team | Year | Record |
|---|---|---|---|
| Clay Kirby | San Diego Padres | 1969 | 7-20 |
| Bill Wight | Chicago White Sox | 1948 | 9-20 |

Then there is the 20-loss campaign disguised as the sophomore jinx. In a case eerily similar to that which befell Alex Kellner a mere three years earlier, Harry Byrd did secure Rookie of the Year honors after the 1952 campaign, only to fall to 11–20, 5.51 ERA in his follow-up endeavor. Ultimately he bounced between five different clubs in hopes of regaining his debut success, but was relegated to the minor leagues in 1957 from which he never returned.

Lastly is the statistical blurb of Pat Caraway (10–24; Chicago White Sox, 1931). Accompanied by a 6.22 ERA, Caraway holds the dubious distinction of maintaining the highest earned run average in the 20th Century among his 20-loss brethren.

## THE TEAMMATES (and other additional TEAM-WIDE analyses)

There have been only 97 20-loss campaigns since 1920. What is of particular note is that, in more than 15 percent of those instances, that pitcher had a teammate putting up similar numbers in the loss column:

| Year | Team | Pitcher | Record |
|---|---|---|---|
| 1973 | Chicago White Sox | Wilbur Wood | 24–20 |
| | | Stan Bahnsen | 18–21 |
| 1965 | New York Mets | Jack Fisher | 8–24 |
| | | Al Jackson | 8–20 |
| 1962 | New York Mets | Roger Craig | 10–24 |
| | | Al Jackson | 8–20 |
| 1936 | Philadelphia Phillies | Bucky Walters | 11–21 |
| | | Joe Bowman | 9–20 |
| 1934 | Cincinnati Reds | Si Johnson | 7–22 |
| | | Paul Derringer | 15–21 |
| 1930 | Boston Red Sox | Milt Gaston | 13–20 |
| | | Jack Russell | 9–20 |
| 1920 | Boston Braves | Jack Scott | 10–21 |
| | | Dana Fillingim | 12–21 |
| 1920 | Philadelphia Athletics | Scott Perry | 11–25 |
| | | Rollie Naylor | 10–23 |

To even the casual observer between 1920 and 1945, Philadelphia could often be a brutal city in which to follow baseball (particularly when owner/manager Connie Mack was in the midst of one of his many iterations of "house-cleaning" associated with the Athletics). This seemed doubly so when it came to the 20-loss campaign, as the Phillies or their other-league counterpart would make it a semi-regular practice.

For example, when Perry and Naylor posted their 20-loss efforts jointly, Phillies pitcher Eppa Rixey posted his own 11–22 mark. A year later, in 1921, Eddie Rommel lost 23 games for the Athletics while the Phillies George Smith matched him with a 4–20 record.

When in 1936 teammates Walters and Bowman accounted for 41 losses between them, the A's were able to counter with their own Gordon Rhodes (whom we visited earlier). Then in 1945, in lieu of actual teammates, the two franchises that shared the same Shibe Park (later named Connie Mack Stadium) would each have a pitcher who shared the same 8–20 mark—Bobo Newsom, A's; Dick Barrett, Phillies.

It almost goes without saying, but since 1920 these two franchises—one of which residing in Oakland these many years—outpace all others in the number

of 20-loss campaigns by one of their hurlers to this day:
- 14: PHI/KC/OAK Athletics
- 13: Philadelphia Phillies
- 10: BOS/MIL/ATL Braves
- 9: Chicago White Sox

## CONCLUSION

The 20-loss season has been visited upon a variety of pitchers—from the youngster ushered thereafter out of baseball, to the eventual Hall of Fame inductee. Besides just "getting there," many of these hurlers had an interesting sidebar in reaching that dubious threshold, a sidebar worth the telling.

It bears repeating that at no point herein was there intent to denigrate or belittle the accomplishments of the pitchers cited. In fact, just the opposite, as the author found a whole new appreciation of many of these pitchers—Wilbur Wood or Bobo Newsom, for example—while researching this material.

Still, if this extensive profile accomplishes nothing else, it is the desire that these 20-loss campaigns, seemingly forgotten in the midst of other (sexier?) statistical endeavors, are not consigned to the waste bin of time.

## ACKNOWLEDGEMENTS

The author would like to thank Bill Nowlin for both his assistance and encouragement to this endeavor. Further thanks is extended to Clifford Blau for his diligence in fact-checking the narrative.

*An earlier version of this article was published in the Baseball Research Journal. (Spring 2013).*

All data drawn from www.Baseball-reference.com

## NOTES

1  "Rollicking Ramos No Joke to Swatters," *The Sporting News*, May 3, 1961.

2  "Pedro Wins Spurs as One-Half of Nat Sunday Slab Punch," *The Sporting News*, June 1, 1960.

3  "Will Castro Bar Cubans From Playing in U.S.?," *The Sporting News*, October 12, 1960.

4  www.baseball-vault.com/casey-stengel-quotes.html

# THE VANISHING 20-GAME LOSER

BY BARRY MEDNICK

**ON SEPTEMBER 29, 2016, CHRIS** Archer of the Tampa Bay Rays took the mound with a record of 8 wins and 19 losses. Facing the possibility of a 20-loss season, Archer pitched 6⅔ innings and beat the Chicago White Sox, 5-3. He never trailed in the game. And once again, the major leagues avoided having a 20-game loser.

The last pitcher to start a game with 19 losses and lose the game was Mike Maroth, who notched his 20th loss of the season on September 5, 2003, as Toronto defeated his Detroit Tigers, 8-6.

The last pitcher before Archer to start a game with 19 losses and avoid a 20th loss was Albie Lopez, who tossed a three-hit, complete-game shutout in Milwaukee on October 5, 2001.

In fact, the 20-game loser is now as rare as the pay telephone or the service station attendant who washes your windshield. Mike Maroth is the only man to lose 20 games in one season over the course of the last 36 years. But there was a time when 20-game losers were as common as knotholes in the outfield fence, when it was even possible to lose 20 games with an earned-run average below 2.00, when even men who would later enter the Hall of Fame lost 20 games. For the first decade of the twentieth century, the combined 16 major-league teams averaged 7.5 such hurlers a season. In the 45-year period from 1901 to 1945, only four seasons failed to produce a 20-game loser, and one of those was in 1918, when the number of games played were reduced due to World War I.

What changed? Despite the longer season introduced in the 1961 expansion, the shift to a near-universal five-man rotation, the rise of relief specialists, the reduction in the number of complete games because of pitch counts, and the enhanced minor-league affiliations that allow teams to demote players in midseason have contributed to the dearth and possible extinction of the 20-game loser. Even teams with more than 100 losses are able to spread the responsibility across a larger staff.

Like many 20-game losers, Archer was a good pitcher on a bad team. He had the most innings pitched and was second in wins and earned-run average for the 68-94 Rays. Many of the 20-game losers led their team in wins, ERA, or innings pitched, and several led in all three categories. For example, in 1952, Murry Dickson lost 21 games but topped the Pirates' staff with 14 wins, 277⅔ innings pitched, and a 3.57 ERA. That year, the Pirates lost 112 games, and Dickson took credit for one third of their victories.

### Five-man rotation

The 1903 Philadelphia AL team featured four pitchers who each started over 20 games. The rest of the staff combined for five starts. The 1975 Yankees had five pitchers who each started at least 20 games. The rest of the staff combined for only three starts. Although these are extreme examples, they demonstrate the shift from a pitcher starting every fourth day to one starting every fifth day.

The graph below shows the average number of pitchers per team who started at least 20, 25, and 30 games from 1901 to 2016. The data demonstrate a slight upward trend over time. Injuries, trades, and managerial decisions obscure the strict rotation that most teams have used. Doubleheaders, more common in the past, often require the use of an additional pitcher who would not otherwise start a game. Seasons shortened by war or strikes represent the anomalies.

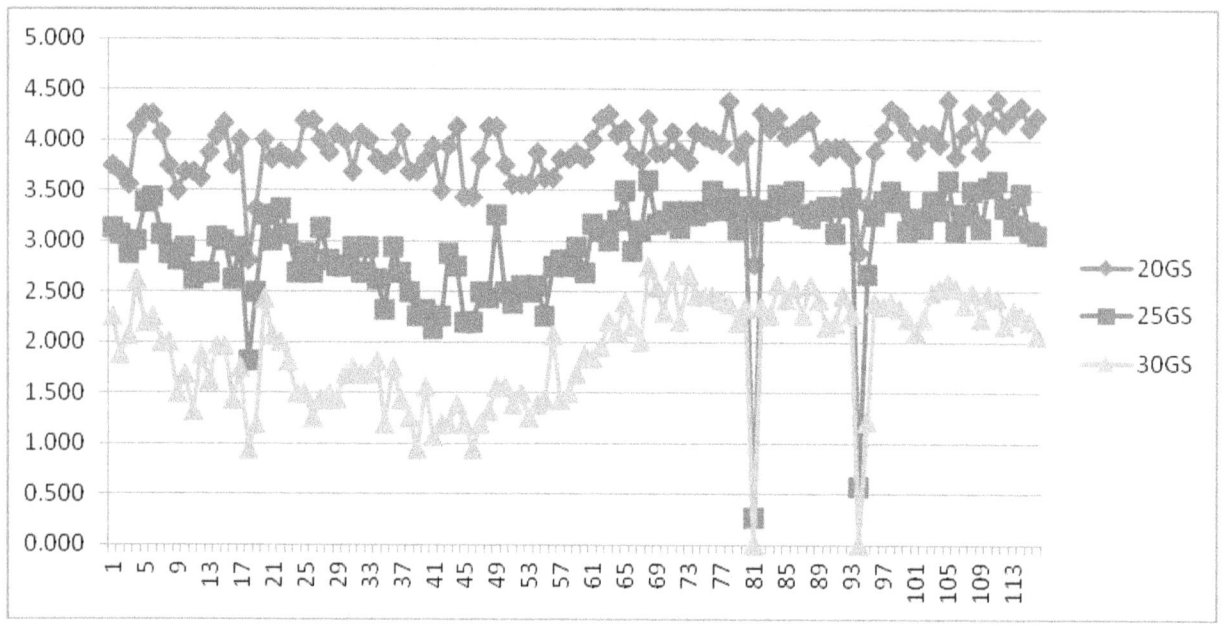

If we remove the years with fewer than 150 games and average the results over decades, the trend is clearer. The number of pitchers who started at least 30 games has increased by almost one per team. The number of games is fixed at 162. With a four-man rotation, a pitcher might get 40 starts and about 28 decisions a year. With the five-man rotation, a pitcher gets 32 starts, which leads to about 22 decisions per year.

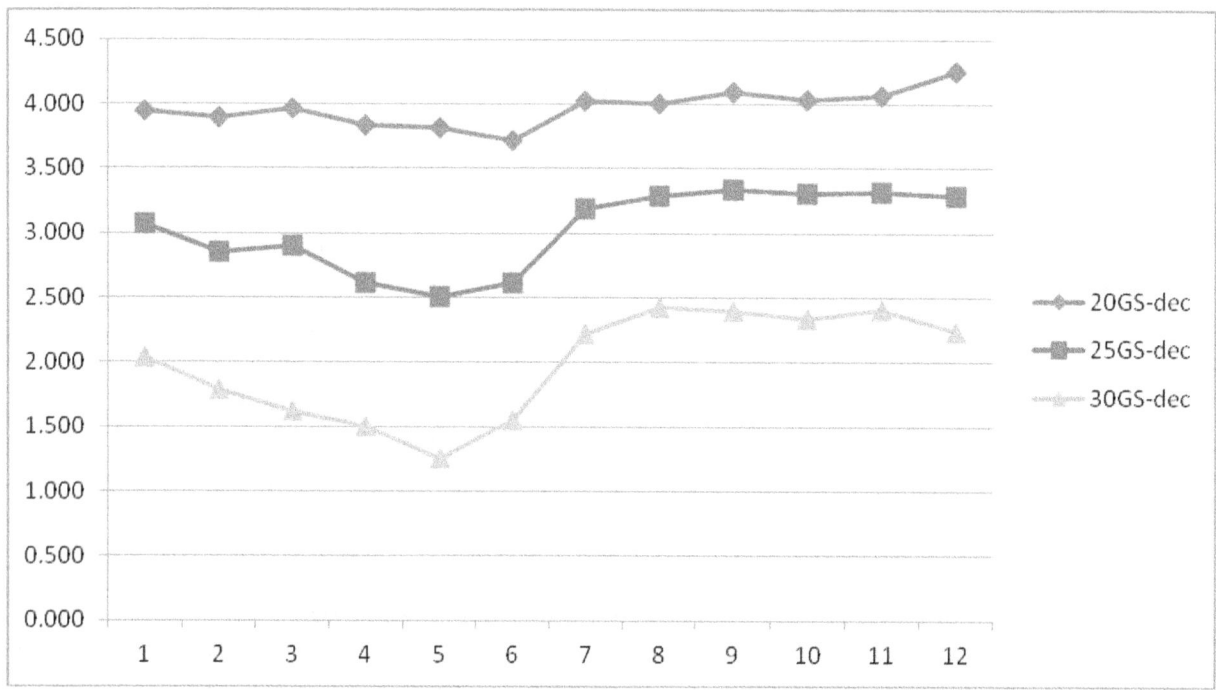

Fewer starts translate to fewer decisions, making it harder to lose 20 games in a season.

# 20-GAME LOSERS

## Relief specialists

In 1903, complete games were the norm, and almost all starters performed some relief. However, only Harry Howell pitched 10 games in relief, and he started 15. By 1984, 38 percent of all pitchers who started at least 10 games did not pitch at all out of the bullpen, and 54 percent of pitchers who relieved in at least 10 games never started.

| Year | Started at least 10 games | Did not relieve | Relieved at least 10 games | Did not start |
|------|---------------------------|-----------------|----------------------------|---------------|
| 1903 | 45                        | 4               | 1                          | 0             |
| 1984 | 155                       | 59              | 187                        | 102           |

The shift to relief specialists meant that relievers were earning a significant number of decisions, which reduced the number of candidates for 20-game-loser status.

## Complete games

Nineteenth century star Will White started 402 games and completed 98 percent of them. Every team in 1901 had at least 107 complete games. In 2016, all teams combined for 83 complete games, and Chris Sale led the majors with six complete games. Blame the emphasis on pitch counts and the increased concerns about how high workloads can shorten a pitcher's career. Teams now spend a great deal of money on closers, set-up men, and left-handed relief specialists for key moments of the game in the late innings. A manager now has many options and many excuses to remove a starter from the game even though the team is ahead and the starter is pitching well.

Fewer complete games mean fewer losses.

A managerial rule of thumb is to not remove a pitcher until he gives up five runs. However, in 2016, 42 percent of all starting pitchers were sent to the showers even though they had not given up five runs and the team was leading at the time. It has become more difficult for a starter to earn a loss once his team has the lead.

## Minor-league affiliations

One hundred years ago, minor-league teams operated independently. Players were sold to higher-level teams. Today, most minor-league teams are affiliated with a major-league club. The parent club provides the players and moves players from one team to another as desired. So a pitcher who is performing poorly at the major-league level may be demoted and replaced by a promising rookie during the season.

The Boston NL team of 1901 used only five pitchers the entire season. Today, it is not uncommon for a team to use more than five pitchers in a single game. As a result, pitchers who are piling up losses may find themselves reduced to limited roles or demoted. In 2016, almost two-thirds of all major-league pitchers also spent time in the minor leagues. In 1901, that figure was less than one-fifth.

## SOURCES

Baseball-reference.com.

Mednick, Barry, and Herman Krabbenhoft. "Twenty Game Losers –1961-1987," *Baseball Quarterly Reviews*, Volume 2, Number 4 (1987).

Mednick, Barry. Research presentation "Twenty Game Losers," 1987 SABR national convention, Washington, D.C.

Neft, David S., & Richard M. Cohen. *The Sports Encyclopedia: Baseball*, 6th edition (New York: St. Martin's Press, 1987).

Petriello, Mike. "Archer restores value with strong second half," mlb.com, November 10, 2016. m.mlb.com/news/article/208476454/chris-archer-restores-value-in-second-half/.

# STEVE ARLIN

## BY GREGORY H. WOLF

**RIGHT-HANDED PITCHER STEVE ARLIN** always knew there was more than baseball. After leading The Ohio State University to two consecutive berths in the College World Series and a national title in 1966, he brokered an unusual professional baseball contract that permitted him to pursue a degree in dentistry in the spring and early summer. Dr. Arlin eventually became the sport's most famous dentist during his six-year career in the majors (1969-1974), spent mostly with the moribund, cellar-dwelling San Diego Padres, whose ineptitude as an expansion team was surpassed by only the New York Mets. Arlin also has the dubious distinction of leading the NL in losses in consecutive seasons. "It was more than a little frustrating," said Arlin of playing for such terrible teams, and he recalled how sportswriters often joked that he "ought to sue the team for malpractice."[1]

Stephen Ralph Arlin was born on September 25, 1946, in Seattle, Washington, to Ralph Wampler and Darlene (Mahns) Arlin. His grandfather, Harold Wampler Arlin, was the world's first salaried baseball broadcaster, for KDKA in Pittsburgh, where he made history by announcing the game on August 5, 1921, between the Philadelphia Phillies and Pirates at Forbes Field, as well as the first football game about two months later. By the time Steve started elementary school, the Arlins had relocated from the Pacific Northwest to Lima, Ohio, located about 170 miles west of Cleveland, where his father worked as an electrical engineer. Steve starred on the hardwood and diamond at Shawnee High School in Lima, and also played American Legion ball in the summers.

Arlin attended Ohio State on a baseball scholarship and became one of the most dominant pitchers in college baseball history. A two-time All-American, Arlin led the Buckeyes to the College World Series as a sophomore in 1965 (freshmen were not eligible for varsity athletics at the time). He emerged as the hurling star of the double-elimination tournament, setting a series record by fanning 20 in a complete-game 15-inning, 1-0 shutout of Washington State.[2] The Buckeyes ultimately lost to the Sal Bando- and Rick Monday-led Arizona State Sun Devils in the championship; however, Arlin was named to the all-tournament team. He paced the NCAA with 165 strikeouts (including 31 in the CWS) in 141 innings and victories (13), tied with ASU's Jim Merrick, and was named the National College Pitcher of the Year.[3] Despite Arlin's well-publicized intentions to return to OSU for his junior year, the Detroit Tigers hoped to change his mind by offering him a reported $80,000 bonus after selecting him in the 23rd round of the inaugural amateur draft in June. Arlin did not take the bait and was back in Columbus in the fall. Described as the "greatest one-man show ever seen in the College World Series," Arlin led the Buckeyes to their first (and as of 2016) only CWS baseball title, in 1966.[4] He pitched in five of his team's six games, twice defeated the number-one-ranked University of Southern California, finished the tournament with 28 strikeouts in 20⅔ innings while yielding just two runs and five hits, and was named the tournament's most outstanding player. In his two-year varsity career, he set Buckeye records for victories (24-3) and strikeouts (294), both since broken. He was subsequently inducted to the OSU Athletic Hall of Fame (1976), the College Baseball Hall of Fame (2008), and the Omaha College World Series Hall of Fame (2014).[5] In 2004 Arlin became the first baseball player in OSU history to have his number (22) retired.

Arlin was primed for the next stage of his career, which began when the Philadelphia Phillies selected him with the 13th pick of the first round of the amateur draft (secondary phase) in June. Enticed by a reported $105,000 bonus, believed to be the Phillies' largest-ever at the time, Arlin signed on June 22, 1966, at a ceremony at his parents' house in Lima.[6] Scout

Tony Lucadello, who had followed Arlin since his prep days, was credited with the signing. Arlin picked up an additional bonus that December when he married Susan Lynn Blazer from Upper Arlington, outside Columbus, Ohio. Together they had two sons.

Arlin's three-year stint in the Phillies' farm system was anything but smooth. After raising eyebrows with the Bakersfield Bears in the Class-A California League (116 strikeouts in 110 innings) in 1966, he earned a look-see at the Phillies spring training in 1967, but by the end of March the young hurler was back in Columbus enrolled in dental school at OSU. Consequently, he missed most of spring training and reported to Reading in the Double-A Eastern League in mid-June. This arrangement ruffled feathers in the Phillies organization, especially among coaches who questioned the hurler's commitment to baseball. Among Arlin's few highlights was a seven-inning no-hitter for Reading, but that came with the caveat of 10 walks.

Arlin possessed a heater in the low 90s and a knee-buckling curve, but struggled with control, and failed to live up to the Phillies expectations. His obligation to dental school limited him to a dismal 5-15 record and just 161 innings with 100 walks in 1967-1968, while he worked his way up to Triple-A San Diego (Pacific Coast League).

While Phillies brass blamed the time Arlin missed in spring training and the early season for his failure to develop into a bona-fide starter, Arlin had a different perspective. "Philadelphia mishandled me in the minor leagues," he told sportswriter Bill Ballew.[7] Arlin explained how pitching coaches, especially Al Widmar, changed his pitching mechanics so that he could throw even harder, but the results were catastrophic. "They turned my whole motion around," he said. "They made me turn my butt toward the plate more. When I finished the motion, I'd fall off to first base instead of always finishing in good defensive position. So I actually did everything in the major leagues without the good curveball."[8]

The book closed on Arlin in Philadelphia on October 14, 1968, when the San Diego Padres selected him with the 57th pick in the expansion draft. "There's no telling how good Arlin might be if he gets a full spring training behind him," said Padres GM Eddie Leishman.[9] Like the Phillies, the Padres would have to wait to find out. Skipper Preston Gomez seemed to lose interest in the 23-year-old hurler when he chose dental school over spring training. When Arlin finally reported to the big-league club in mid-June of 1969 for his first competitive baseball of the season, Gomez was unimpressed. "[Arlin] doesn't look like a ball player," Gomez said of the sandy-haired youngster with glasses. "I thought he was some kid Eddie (Leishman) had sent down to pitch batting practice."[10] Arlin's debut on June 17 in the second game of a doubleheader against the Los Angeles Dodgers probably didn't change Gomez's mind. Arlin yielded an RBI single, a wild pitch, a walk, and a three-run homer to the first three batters he faced. Two weeks later Arlin (11 earned runs and nine walks in 10⅔ innings) was back in Columbus, but this time it was a demotion to the Jets, the Pittsburgh Pirates' affiliate in the Triple-A International League (the Padres launched a Triple-A team the next season). Arlin's 2-5 slate with 4.73 ERA did not warrant a September call-up.

Graduating from dental school in June 1970, Dr. Arlin reported to the Salt Lake City Bees in the PCL. Predictably, he struggled as he worked himself into shape, posting a 5-7 record with a dismal 6.10 ERA in 87 innings. With the Padres en route to their second straight last-place finish in the NL West, Arlin was recalled on September 4. Bombed in his first outing (11 baserunners and four runs in a 3⅔-inning no-decision), Arlin shocked the Padres with a masterful seven-hit shutout with just one walk against the Atlanta Braves on September 23 for his first big-league victory. "He has a major-league arm," cooed pitching coach Roger Craig. "There's no reason why he can't be a big winner."[11]

In late February of 1971 Arlin reported to Yuma, Arizona, to participate in his first complete spring training as a professional. He admitted that missing spring training every season affected his development. "I'd come in pretty far behind everybody," he said. "I never really did get into shape."[12] However, Arlin had no apologies for his decision to attend dental school. "I never thought about doing it differently," he told sportswriter Ron Rapoport, "All the people want is production. I understand that. I wanted school behind me."[13]

Widely expected to join the starting rotation, the 25-year-old Arlin impressed Gomez with his poise, demeanor, and approach to the game. "He's the kind of pitcher who learns from his mistakes," said the Cuban-born skipper. "He hasn't pitched that much in pro ball, but he has the maturity that some of our others pitchers lack."[14] Hurling for the major leagues' worst offense (3.02 runs per game) and the NL's second most porous defense proved more challenging than expected for the cerebral Arlin. He lost 11 of his first 13 decisions. (Both victories were shutouts.) Then he suddenly hit a groove over a 14-start stretch from June 30 to September 3, going 7-5 and posting a 2.43 ERA in 107⅓ innings.

Arlin's future looked bright, and never did it shine brighter than on July 25 in the second game of a doubleheader against the future World Series champion Pittsburgh Pirates at San Diego Stadium. Nursing a 2-0 lead with two outs in the ninth and a runner on, Arlin induced the eventual major-league home-run leader, Willie Stargell to foul off seven successive pitches on a 3-and-2 count before walking him. Unfazed, he ended the game by whiffing the next batter, pinch-hitter Roberto Clemente, to complete a three-hit shutout. The Padres finished with the NL's worst record (61-100) for the third straight season, but their young pitching staff emerged with the NL's third-best team ERA (3.22), which produced a "note of optimism about the future," suggested Padres beat writer Paul Cour.[15] While 23-year-old Clay Kirby (15-13, 2.83 ERA, 231 strikeouts) and Dave Roberts (14-17, 2.10 ERA) garnered most of the attention Arlin posted nine wins (all by complete game), a team-best four shutouts, and a respectable 3.48 ERA in 227⅔ innings. He was also a tough-luck loser, leading the NL with 19 defeats; in 13 of those the Padres scored two runs or less; in four more, they scored three runs.

Eleven games into the 1972 season, Preston Gomez was fired for what beat writer Phil Collier described as the "defeatist complex" permeating the clubhouse.[16] Into the void stepped Padres coach and first-time skipper Don Zimmer, who vowed to make his club better prepared mentally. If anything, the Padres took a step back. The Padres were once again the lowest-scoring team in the NL (3.19 runs per game), while their promising pitching corps finished with the second-worst team ERA in the league. That toxic mix produced another last-place finish in the NL West. Arlin gave Zimmer his first of 885 wins as a manager by outdueling red-hot Steve Carlton on April 29 in San Diego. He tossed a stellar five-hitter to beat the Phillies, 4-0, and exact a measure of revenge against the organization that gave up on him. He spun another shutout (a four-hitter against the New York Mets' Jerry Koosman at Shea Stadium) in his next start, part of a career-long 19⅓-scoreless-inning streak. Sports pages had a field day with Arlin's dentist title. "Dr. Arlin Pastes Pirates in the Teeth," and "Padres Pitching Dentist Numbs Bucs," following his masterful two-hit blanking of the Pirates on June 18, were typical of the kinds of headlines about the hurler's accomplishments.[17] That victory inaugurated an eight-start stretch during which Arlin did his best Nolan Ryan impression. He yielded just 33 safeties in 71 innings, tossed three two-hitters and a one-hitter, and surrendered just one hit in a career-long 10-inning outing in an eventual 14-inning Padres victory over the Mets. Bad luck sometimes followed Arlin even when he won a game. One strike from a no-hitter against the Phillies on July 18, Arlin yielded what sportswriter Bruce Keidan of the *Philadelphia Inquirer* described as a "bad hop" single to Danny Doyle.[18] "I beeped it up for him," said Zimmer, who had mysteriously ordered third baseman Dave Roberts to play shallow to guard against a bunt.[19] Noticeably aggravated and shocked, Arlin balked facing the next batter, Tom Hutton, whose subsequent RBI single ruined the shutout, though Arlin still won the game. Sporting an impressive 2.80 ERA despite an 8-11 record, Arlin was widely expected to be named to the NL All-Star squad, but was snubbed. "I can't believe there are nine pitchers in the league better than Steve," said Roger Craig incredulously.[20] After the All-Star break, Arlin was plagued by the same shoulder pain that bothered him the previous season. At one point he had lost 14 of 15 decisions, including 10 in a row, and ultimately finished the season with 10 wins and a major-league-most 21 defeats (as well as an NL-most 122 walks and 15 wild pitches). He lost seven one-run games; in 19 of the losses, the Padres scored three runs or less (31 total runs).

Given his 20-41 career record after the '72 campaign, it's no surprise that the competitive Arlin expressed his frustration publicly. "[I find this] very difficult to live with," he replied when asked about losing 21 games. "I felt at the time of the All-Star break, I was one of the better pitchers in baseball."[21] Arlin's career highs in innings (250), starts (37), complete games (12), and strikeouts (159) could not soothe his disappointment. "I'm in a profession in which the object is to win, and all I do is lose."[22]

Arlin might have wished that offseason rumors about his trade to the Boston Red Sox in a multiplayer transaction involving Red Sox Reggie Smith and Rico Petrocelli had proved to be true. When the Padres got off to a horrible start in 1973, players were "close to rebellion" against skipper Zimmer, the coaching staff, and the front office.[23] Arlin, pounded in his first five starts (5.40 ERA), was shunted to the bullpen for six weeks, during which time he and his teammates were jolted by a statement from the Padres' majority owner, entrepreneur-banker C. Arnholt Smith. With his bank on the verge of failure,[24] Smith agreed to sell the club to a consortium led by Joseph Danzansky, a Washington, DC, grocery-store magnate who intended to relocate the club to the nation's capital. "All of us were in a state of shock," said Arlin, "and depressed the rest of the season."[25] With the staff in shambles, ultimately finishing 11th in the NL in team ERA (4.16), Arlin rejoined the rotation and enjoyed some unexpected success. After tossing a three-hit shutout against the Houston Astros in the Astrodome on June 30, Arlin blanked the Dodgers on two hits five days later in Los Angeles to complete a surprising sweep on the division leaders. While Zimmer further alienated his player by calling the sweep a "1000-to-1 shot," Arlin took aim at everyone but the players in a postgame tirade.[26] "I want to make a splash for this team," he said. "We play in a town where no one recognizes us. You never see our pictures hanging in a bar. ... All that's written about is the move to Washington."[27] Arlin tossed his third shutout in four starts, beating the Chicago Cubs, 1-0, at Wrigley Field on July 17, but struggled thereafter for the lowest-scoring and worst defensive team in the majors. Despite his finishing with a team-high 11 victories (and 14 losses), Arlin's 5.10 ERA (in 180 innings) was the highest among qualified starters in the NL as the Padres lost 102 games and once again finished last in the West Division. Just days before the season concluded, Arlin cast doubts about his future. "I know my attitude has been brutal," he admitted. "I don't think I ever want to play another season like this. For the first time in my life, my favorite sport has not been fun for me."[28]

On December 11, 1973, all 11 NL club owners approved Smith's sale of the Padres to Danzansky. The club was slated to play its home opener on April 4, 1974, at RFK Stadium.[29] Topps Baseball Card Co. even printed cards showing Padres players with

"Washington Nat'l Lea." as the team affiliation. But the dream of baseball in Washington was fleeting as legal battles soon halted the sale. Smith, under investigation for embezzlement and being sued for breaking the San Diego Stadium lease, changed course and sold the club to Ray Kroc, billionaire founder of McDonald's, who promised to keep the team in San Diego.

The mood at the Padres' spring training in Yuma was noticeably more optimistic in 1974. John McNamara had replaced Zimmer as pilot, and Bill Posedel, former pitching coach/guru of the Oakland A's, was coaxed out of retirement. Kroc's deep pockets also helped as the king of burgers signed aging slugger Willie McCovey and former All-Star second sacker Glen Beckett. Arlin, however, was not a happy camper. His personal nemesis, Buzzie Bavasi, was still the general manager, and their relationship was toxic. "He spent more time belittling his players than building them up," said Arlin scornfully.[30] Throughout the offseason, Arlin had demanded a trade, and then ridiculed Bavasi in the press for not honoring his wish. "I couldn't take it anymore," said Arlin about the losing.[31] Compounding the problem was Arlin's sore shoulder, ultimately diagnosed as a torn rotator cuff. "I should have been on the disabled list the rest of the season," said Arlin after he retired.[32] He finally got his wish on June 15, when the Padres sold him to the Cleveland Indians in a waiver transaction for two players to be named later. (Cleveland sent pitchers Brent Strom and Terry Ley six days later to complete the trade.) The Indians harbored few expectations for the beleaguered hurler, whose 1-7 record and 5.91 ERA had earned him a demotion to the Padres bullpen. Arlin made only 10 starts for the Tribe, notched just two victories, and posted a whopping 6.60 ERA in 43⅔ innings before his ailing rotator cuff made it impossible to throw.

"I felt like in 1975 I'd win 15 games," said Arlin candidly years after his playing days were over.[33] His shoulder felt fine after six months of rest in the offseason, but Arlin chose to retire instead. "I don't need any more hassles," he said when asked why he had not reported to the Indians' spring-training facility in Sarasota.[34] With a 34-67 career record, including 11 shutouts, and a 4.33 ERA in 788⅔ innings, Arlin quit baseball at the age of 29. (He batted .139 with 32 hits.) He enjoyed great success against Willie Stargell (.185, 5-for-27), Joe Torre (.167, 3-for-18) and Dave Concepcion (.095, 3-for-21); but was lit up by Bob Watson (.464, 13-for-28), Ralph Garr (.459, 17-for-37), and Garry Maddox (.423, 11-for-26).

Unlike many athletes, Arlin did not worry about transitioning to life away from sports. Baseball's most famous dentist established a private practice in San Diego, where had practiced for more than 25 years and retired in 2004.

Arlin died on August 17, 2016, at the age of 70. He was survived by his wife, Robin, and his sons, Scott and Steve, from his first marriage.

"He had a great arm, great stuff," remembered former Padres teammate and 1976 Cy Young Award winner Randy Jones. "Probably wasn't the best command in the world, but on the days he had good command he was lights out. He just loved to compete. He did things the right way and he had an edge on him. It was a lot of fun to watch him compete and I learned a lot from him."[35]

## SOURCES

In addition to the sources noted in this biography, the author also accessed Arlin's player file and player questionnaire from the National Baseball Hall of Fame, the *Encyclopedia of Minor League Baseball*, Retrosheet.org, Baseball-Reference.com, the SABR Minor Leagues Database, accessed online at Baseball-Reference.com, and *The Sporting News* archive via Paper of Record.

## NOTES

1. Bill Ballew, "Steve Arlin: Ohio State Star May Have Been Best Ever in College Ranks," *Sports Collectors Digest*, September 23, 1994: 141.
2. Associated Press, "Ohio State Whiz Hurls Big Shutout," *Tallahassee* (Florida) *Democrat*, June 11, 1965: 12.
3. United Press International, "Sports Greats Trek to Columbus For TD Club Banquet," *Daily Times* (New Philadelphia, Ohio), January 20, 1966: 14.
4. Bob Williams, "Buckeyes Bag Bunting as No. 1 College Team," *The Sporting News*, July 2, 1966: 2.
5. See "Baseball: Steve Arlin Elected to Hall of Fame," OhioStatebuckeyes.com, ohiostatebuckeyes.com/sports/m-

6. Allen Lewis, "Arlin Given Reported $105,000 by Phillies," *The Sporting News*, July 9, 1966: 15.
7. Ballew: 140.
8. Ibid.
9. Paul Cour, "Padres Join List of Big Bidders for Phils' Allen," *The Sporting News*, December 7, 1968: 44.
10. Paul Cour, "Dental Student Arlin Curing Padre Bullpen Pain," *The Sporting News*, July 12, 1969: 18.
11. Paul Cour, "Dentist Arlin Could Fill Padres' Mound Cavity," *The Sporting News*, November 28, 1970: 48.
12. Ron Rapoport, "Getting Arlin on Ball Field Tougher Than Pulling Teeth," *Los Angeles Times*, March 24, 1971: III, 3.
13. Ibid.
14. Paul Cour, "Dentist Arlin Wins Padres' Mound Berth," *The Sporting News*, April 10, 1971: 37.
15. Paul Cour, "Sharp Pitching Pierces Padres' Gloom," *The Sporting News*, August 14, 1971: 11.
16. Phil Collier, "New Boss Cracks Downs on Bumbling Padres," *The Sporting News*, May 13, 1972: 17.
17. Charley Feeny, 'Dr. Arlin Pastes Pirates in the Teeth," *Pittsburgh Post-Gazette*, June 19, 1972: 12; Bob Smizek, "Padres Pitching Dentist Numbs Bucs," *Pittsburgh Press*, June 19, 1972: 24.
18. Bruce Keidan, "Doyle Ruins Arlin's No-Hitter in 9th," *Philadelphia Inquirer*, July 19, 1972: 25.
19. Ibid.
20. Phil Collier, "Low-Hit Gems Are Arlin's Specialty," *The Sporting News*, August 5, 1971: 17.
21. Furman Bisher "A Dentist in the House?" *The Sporting News*, October 14, 1972:10.
22. Ibid.
23. Phil Collier, "Buzzie, Players, Discuss Mutiny Report," *The Sporting News*, May 19, 1973: 13.
24. Smith was majority owner of United States National Bank in San Diego. When the bank collapsed in 1973, it was the largest bank failure in US history. v25    Phil Collier, "Padres Preach New Gospel With Kroc's Blessing," *The Sporting News*, April 6, 1974: 3.
26. Ross Newhan, "Dodgers' Skid at Six, 3-0, on Arlin's 2-Hitter," *Los Angeles Times*, July 6, 1973: III, 1.
27. Ibid.
28. UPI, "Padres No Longer Located," *Times Standard* (Eureka, Californian), October 1, 1973: 10.
29. Jake Russell, "San Diego Padres Were Once So Close to Moving to DC, They Had Uniforms Made," *Washington Post*, June 16, 2016.
30. Bob Nold, "Arlin Determined to Show Bavasi," *Akron* (Ohio) *Beacon-Journal*, July 4, 1974: C5.
31. Ballew, 141.
32. Ibid.
33. Ibid.
34. Tom Callahan, "Trying Spring for Dr. Allen," *Cincinnati Enquirer*, March 9, 1975: 4C.
35. Jeff Sanders, "Former Padres RHP Steve Arlin Dies at 70," *San Diego Union-Tribune*, August 22, 2016.

# BILL BAILEY

## BY ERIC FROST

**SEVERAL THINGS ARE MEMORABLE** about the career of pitcher Bill Bailey, but unfortunately, almost none of those things would be considered pleasant memories. Most notably, Bailey established a major-league record by experiencing 10 consecutive losing seasons in his 11-year career. Even among the group of pitchers known as 20-game losers, Bailey might be considered something of an overachiever: He was saddled with the 20-loss label once in the Federal League and twice in the minor leagues. It would be easy to overstate Bailey's struggles as a professional pitcher, but he was largely a victim of dumb luck, having to spend much of his career on poor teams, and pitching in an era where a complete game was the norm.

William Franklin Bailey was born in Fort Smith, Arkansas. His parents were William Fuller Bailey of Walker County, Georgia, and the former Leeky Elvira Corn of North Carolina. His mother moved to Walker County before marrying her husband, and the couple came to Fort Smith just prior to Bill Bailey's birth on April 12, 1888. The elder William F. Bailey died in 1897 and Mrs. Bailey married John U. McLean, a county court clerk, in 1898. The family seems to have moved between Arkansas and Texas a couple of times during Bailey's childhood. Leeky McLean (who was listed as L.E. McClane on her 1951 death certificate) long outlived her son and was a widow at the time of her death.[1]

Bailey lived in Houston at the time he entered professional baseball as an 18-year-old with the Beaumont Oilers in 1906.[2] Bailey finished the South Texas League season with an 11-9 record, splitting the year between Beaumont and the Austin Senators. For the first couple of years of Bailey's statistics, there is no indication that the slender left-handed pitcher (5-feet-11 and 165 pounds, according to Baseball-Reference.com) might become known for his hard luck in both the major and minor leagues.

In fact, Bailey was actually a 20-game winner in 1907, finishing 22-11 with Austin before signing with the St. Louis Browns. A typed document in Bailey's file at the Baseball Hall of Fame indicates that he received what seems like a modest increase in pay upon his promotion; he had been earning $100 per month with Austin and he pulled in $150 per month as a rookie major leaguer. At 19, he was the youngest major-league player that season, and he finished 4-1 with five starts in six games.

After Bailey lost a close game for the Browns against Washington, sportswriter J. Ed Grillo of the *Washington Post* wrote, "Bill Bailey is a very deliberate young man. He is not in any hurry about delivering the ball to the plate and acts as though he might make a good pitcher though he still lacks considerable experience."[3]

The 1908 Browns finished 83-69, but despite an ERA of 3.04, Bailey ended up with only a 3-5 record in 22 games, including 12 starts. Bailey was scheduled to start the 1909 season with the Pueblo Indians. An April 2 column in the *Wichita Eagle* said that with his acquisition, the Pueblo team was one solid player away from being a contender. However, a separate column in the same issue of the paper announced that the Browns were recalling Bailey to the major leagues.[4]

By July 1909, the *St. Louis Post-Dispatch* suggested that Bailey had been pitching to hold on to his job before throwing well in a tough 10-inning loss on July 16.[5] Bailey finished the year 9-10 in 32 games despite a 2.44 ERA. The 1909 Browns slid to a 61-89 record and they finished below .500 almost every year until the early 1920s, long after Bailey's association with the team had ended.

A December 1909 article in the *Cincinnati Enquirer* expressed mild concern about Bailey's frailty, but it said that if he kept in shape over the winter, he would likely be a star among American

League pitchers. "His fast ball has a jump on it possessed by mighty few lefthanders; his curve ball is a thing of beauty, and last year he developed a move holding the base runners to the sacks, which would play a prominent part in his work," the article said.[6]

Reality wasn't as kind to Bailey. With the hapless Browns in 1910, Bailey had a 3.32 ERA, but opposing teams scored almost as many unearned runs as earned runs against him, and he ended up with only three wins to go with 18 losses. After the season, Bailey's name was included in some trade talks between St. Louis and Detroit. Ultimately, the teams could not agree to a deal, so Bailey remained on the Browns.[7]

When Bailey struggled in a few games for the 1911 Browns, the team traded him to the Montgomery Billikens of the Southern Association in exchange for Del Pratt. The deal worked out well for St. Louis; Pratt became the team's everyday second baseman from 1912 to 1917.

Bailey also did well at Montgomery, finishing 17-6 with a 1.50 ERA and tying a single-game league record in early September by striking out 14 batters.[8] The Montgomery squad was previously known as the Climbers, but Bailey was one of five players named Bill, and the Billiken doll was popular in the United States at the time, so the name stuck, at least for that season.[9]

In 1912, Bailey spent most of the season with the Providence Grays of the International League, going 14-18, and he was hit hard in three major-league appearances with the Browns. He stayed with Providence all year in 1913, improving his won-lost record to 19-15 and lowering his ERA significantly to 3.46.

In 1914, Bailey was with the Grays for most of the season. Earning an 11-8 record by August, Bailey was said to have met with several team executives from the Federal League during a road trip to Buffalo, New York. The Federal League was attempting to compete with the established major leagues by enticing players under contract to "jump" to the new league. Bailey signed with the league's Baltimore Terrapins.[10]

It must have been exciting to watch Bailey pitch for Baltimore in 1914. He had a much higher walk rate (4.8 per nine innings) and strikeout rate (9.2 per nine innings) than anyone else in the Baltimore rotation. He had an average ERA (3.08) and finished 7-9 despite pitching 10 complete games in 18 starts. The 1914 Terrapins finished in third place with an 84-70 record.

Bailey's defection indirectly led to the demotion of young Boston Red Sox pitcher Babe Ruth, the only time in Ruth's major-league career that he was sent to the minor leagues. Ruth was a promising prospect, but there was not much room on the Boston pitching staff. Red Sox owner Joseph Lannin also owned the Grays, who, unlike the Red Sox, were still in their pennant race. After Bailey jumped to the Federal League and Providence pitcher Red Oldham went to the major leagues, Grays fans were becoming restless. In response, Lannin sent Ruth, the highly publicized rookie, to Providence.[11]

Bailey returned to the Terrapins for the 1915 season. He didn't pitch as well as he had the year before, finishing with a 4.63 ERA, but his 6-19 record would have almost certainly been better with another franchise. The Terrapins finished 47-107, scoring

almost 100 fewer runs than they had the year before. Bailey was not alone in his pitching misfortune. The previous season's ace, Jack Quinn, finished with a 9-22 record this time around despite a 3.45 ERA. George Suggs, a 24-game winner the year before, had an 11-17 record with a 4.14 ERA. Even future Hall of Famer Chief Bender, who jumped to the Terrapins for 1915, was 4-16 despite a 3.99 ERA.

Late in the season, Bailey was sent to the Chicago Federals in exchange for Dave Black.[12] He had much better luck there, finishing with a 3-1 record and three shutouts in five games. The single loss with Chicago placed Bailey in the 20-loss category for the first time in his professional career. After the Federal League folded in 1915, the Chicago Whales were merged with the Chicago Cubs, but Bailey was released by the Cubs before he appeared with them.[13]

Bailey ended up pitching for Toledo of the American Association in 1916 and part of 1917, and he appeared rather uneventfully with New Orleans of the Southern Association in late 1917 and early 1918. When the Detroit Tigers called on Bailey in June 1918, he gave up 10 runs in a one-inning relief appearance.[14] The Tigers still gave Bailey a few chances as a starting pitcher that year, but combined as a starter or reliever he gave up nearly six earned runs per game, ending his run with Detroit.

In 1919, Bailey was pitching for the Beaumont Oilers when he walked 185 batters, setting a Texas League record.[15] He threw 50 games that year. Though his complete-game total is not available, we know that Bailey earned 45 decisions, finishing with a 24-21 won-lost record. He spent the 1920 season with Beaumont again; the team's nickname changed from the Oilers to the Exporters. He had another strong season, turning in an 18-16 record with a 2.58 ERA.

With the Exporters in 1921, Bailey compiled a 7-10 record with a 2.69 ERA. This was enough to pique the interest of several major-league clubs, and the St. Louis Cardinals obtained him in a June trade for Jakie May (who went on to a long big-league career), a player named George Scott, and cash. The Cardinals also acquired Brooklyn pitcher Jeff Pfeffer around the same time. For much of the year, the Cardinals had

relied on heavy offense, so they made the trades to stabilize their pitching staff.[16]

In Bailey's debut for the Cardinals, he pitched a 10-inning complete game, but he lost the game on his own throwing error.[17] He saw action in 19 games for the 1921 Cardinals, but only six of them were starts. He gave up nearly 12 hits per nine innings, and he finished with a 2-5 won-lost record and a 4.26 ERA.

Bailey's last major-league season was 1922. He pitched 12 games for the Cardinals, and for the first time in his major-league career, he did not start any games. His 0-2 record gave him a 38-76 major-league record. His career ERA ended up at 3.57. His last season in the big leagues made him the first pitcher with losing records in 10 consecutive seasons. No pitcher had that many consecutive losing seasons until Ron Kline in the 1960s.[18]

The 1923 season was a rough one for Bailey. He had stints with two teams in separate leagues and he gave up more than five earned runs per nine innings during his time with each team. He was 9-18 for the Houston Buffaloes. Sixteen of Bailey's losses with Houston were consecutive, tying a consecutive-loss record for Texas League pitchers.[19]

In August of that year, Bailey was traded to the Omaha Buffaloes of the Western League in exchange for Tex McDonald, a veteran infielder whose last shot at the major leagues had ended with the shutdown of the Federal League eight years earlier.[20] Though Bailey's ERA was still high for Omaha, his luck seems to have improved, as he had an 8-5 record for the team. Still, the five losses with Omaha took him well over the 20-loss threshold for the season.

Bailey pitched for Omaha again in 1924 and 1925. He continued to earn large numbers of decisions, finishing 23-15 and 17-19, respectively. Between Bailey and left-handed pitcher Harvey Harris, Charles Brill of the *Daily Oklahoman* described Omaha as heading into the 1926 season with the best pitching staff in the Western League.[21] However, Bailey was out of baseball before the regular season started because of multiple episodes of intestinal bleeding.[22]

Bailey had become ill for the first time while Omaha's team was training in Orange, Texas.[23] He was admitted to Baptist Hospital in Houston. Wink Goff, a player on the Houston Buffaloes, donated blood for a lifesaving transfusion.[24] On March 30, 1926, one day after Bailey was admitted to the hospital, newspaper reports said that he was near death but that there was still some hope for improvement.[25]

At least one benefit game was held for Bailey in the Western League.[26] His health rallied for several months, but he returned to the hospital that fall and he died on November 2, 1926, just before he was to receive another blood transfusion.[27] He was buried at Forest Park Lawndale Cemetery in Houston.

Little is known about Bill Bailey's personal life. Genealogical research indicates that he married Texas native Elise Villiepique (sometimes listed as Sunshine Elise Villiepique) on January 8, 1924, and that they had a son, Thomas Street Bailey, in 1912. No divorce records could be located, but Villiepique's 1954 death certificate, which lists Thomas S. Bailey as the informant, indicates that she had lived in Dallas for more than 40 years.[28] Villiepique was widowed by Daniel Ruggles, an editor for the *Dallas Morning News*.[29] Thomas Bailey died in 2000.

## SOURCES

In addition to the sources cited in the Notes, the author made extensive use of the major-league and minor-league statistics at Baseball-Reference.com. Unless otherwise noted, the statistics came from this source.

## NOTES

1. Certificate of Death: L.E. McClane, Texas Bureau of Vital Statistics. We were unable to determine the occupation of William Fuller Bailey.
2. "Beaumont Here Today," *Houston Post*, May 10, 1906: 3.
3. J. Ed Grillo, "Rally Just in Time," *Washington Post*, September 26, 1907: 8.
4. "Pueblo Won't Get Pitcher Bailey," *Wichita Eagle*, April 2, 1909: 7.
5. James Crusinberry, "Bailey Wins New Life in Major League," *St. Louis Post-Dispatch*, July 17, 1909: 6.
6. "Don't Quit if First Act Is Poor," *Cincinnati Enquirer*, December 26, 1909: 2.
7. "Baseball Flashes From Meetings in New York," *New Castle (Pennsylvania) News*, December 15, 1910: 11.
8. "Bill Bailey, Billiken, Equals Strikeout Mark," *Times-Democrat (New Orleans)*, September 4, 1911: 7.
9. Richard Worth, *Baseball Team Names: A Worldwide Dictionary, 1869-2011* (Jefferson, North Carolina: McFarland, 2013), 192.
10. "Bill Bailey Hurdles From Providence Grays to Terrapins," *Rochester Democrat and Chronicle*, August 9, 1914: 25.
11. Robert W. Creamer, *Babe: The Legend Comes to Life* (New York: Simon & Schuster, 1992), 91, 92.
12. "Bill Bailey Is Traded Off," *Washington Herald*, September 18, 1915: 9.
13. "Pitcher Bill Bailey Is Released by Cubs," *St. Louis Star and Times*, April 10, 1916: 10.
14. "Tigers Take Bad Beating From Fohls," *Detroit Free Press*, June 30, 1918: 17.
15. Individual Records, Texas League, milb.com/content/page.jsp?sid=l109&ymd=20100316&content_id=8811502&vkey=history.

16 "Pfeffer and Bill Bailey Bolster Card Hurling Staff," *Houston Post*, July 5, 1921: 11.

17 "Chicago Next Stop of Bucs," *Pittsburgh Press*, June 25, 1921.

18 Donald Dewey and Nicholas Acocella, *The New Biographical History of Baseball* (Chicago: Triumph Books, 2002), 16.

19 Individual Records, Texas League.

20 "Omaha Gets Bill Bailey," *St. Louis Post-Dispatch*, August 2, 1923: 25.

21 Charles Brill, "Rates Omaha to Finish One, Two or Three in Race," *Des Moines Register*, April 7, 1926: 12.

22 Ibid.

23 "Bill Bailey Dies at Houston Tuesday," *Dallas Morning News*, November 3, 1926.

24 "Bailey Won't Play Anymore," *Mount Carmel News*, April 17, 1926.

25 "Bill Bailey, Veteran Major Southpaw, Near Death," *Minneapolis Morning Tribune*, March 30, 1926: 14.

26 "Catcher Lowry to Join Demons," *Des Moines Register*, June 2, 1926: 9.

27 "Bill Bailey, Colorful Baseball Character, Dies," *Alexandria* (Louisiana) *Daily Town Talk*, November 4, 1926: 4.

28 Certificate of Death: Elise Ruggles, Texas Bureau of Vital Statistics.

29 "Daniel G. Ruggles, 66, Former Editor, Dies," *Dallas Morning News*, September 21, 1953.

# GEORGE BAUMGARDNER

## BY JOE SCHUSTER

IN MANY WAYS GEORGE Baumgardner could have become the hero of a kind of baseball fairy tale: He came to the St. Louis Browns in 1912 as a 20-year-old right-handed pitcher after playing only two seasons of Class-D ball in the mountains of his native West Virginia, someone who, the story goes, had honed his skills by throwing rocks at squirrels and who kept in shape by cutting wood. He also had considerable talent. His manager compared his fastball to Walter Johnson's and one writer said his curve "broke like a streak of lightning."[1] In his debut in April of that year, Baumgardner bested the Chicago White Sox and future Hall of Famer Ed Walsh 4-1, striking out seven and allowing only three hits. He was even better in his next outing, also against the White Sox, when he shut them out for 15 innings and struck out 10 in a game that ended in a 0-0 tie. Sportswriters across the country, including Grantland Rice, began predicting he would become one of the premier pitchers in the game.

However, whatever talent Baumgardner had, he was also what one writer called "the high nut" of baseball, someone who liked to jump onto and off moving trains, spontaneously hop on stage, uninvited, to sing in movie theaters and perform magic on street corners, and preferred his salary in $1 bills since it made him feel richer.[2]

For a few years, as long as Baumgardner seemed to possess promise, those stories were, for the most part, humorous asides to a career that seemed on the verge of greatness. In the end, however, his eccentricity got in the way of his ability and he became the butt of public jokes and cautionary tales. After a solid 1914 season in which he posted the only winning record of his career, 16-14, and helped the Browns to a respectable (for them) fifth-place finish, he came to camp for 1915 out of shape. The team sent him to Louisville in the American Association before the season was even a month old—or at least tried to, since he refused to report, choosing to go home to West Virginia rather than face the embarrassment of demotion to the minor leagues. He came back for 1916 but after eight innings over four games the Browns let him go. Baumgardner's major-league career ended with a lifetime record of 38-49, his chief claim to fame being his inclusion in the ignoble club of pitchers who lost 20 games in a season when he went 10-20 in 1913.

George Washington Baumgardner was born on July 22, 1891, in Barboursville, West Virginia, then a village of around 400 people near the Ohio border, roughly 15 miles from Huntington. He was the second youngest of 10 children of Charles Baumgardner, a carpenter, and his wife, Frances, a laundress.[3]

If one is to judge by the newspaper accounts from Baumgardner's time in baseball, he was generally perceived as a naïve country boy; his formal education ended after the seventh grade at Barboursville PS #2.[4] One story described him as "not versed in the finer points of the world's ways" and reported that he was so unschooled that he was never ever able to actually sign his name to his contracts but could only mark them with an "X."[5] (Although this last detail gives us insight into the way in which the press viewed Baumgardner, it is apocryphal as the Baseball Hall of Fame archives hold two contracts bearing his signature.[6]) Another story made much of the fact that Baumgardner never left his home state until he joined the Browns.[7] Another reported that he perfected his pitching by throwing stones at squirrels, trying to kill them.[8] Yet another mocked him for not knowing that the American League was one of two major leagues since, when a reporter asked his opinion of his opponent for his debut, Ed Walsh, he reportedly replied, "What I want to know … if this Walsh is such a great pitcher, why ain't he drafted by the National League?"[9] Still other stories made much of the fact that Baumgardner did not know he should eat the spears and not the stalks on a piece of asparagus and that when he bought a rubber raincoat in New York he was so fascinated by the novelty of it that he wore it even on sunny days.[10]

Despite his naïveté, Baumgardner was, by many accounts, a natural talent on the diamond.

While the records of his life in baseball before he joined the Browns are scarce, it appears that Baumgardner's first professional experience was with the Huntington Blue Sox of the six-team, Class-D Virginia Valley League in 1910, playing under a manager named Cy Young. (Although many sources today report that the Hall of Fame pitcher helmed Huntington that year, at least one newspaper account from that time makes plain that the team's skipper was actually a different person with the same name.[11])

While the writer was not able to find Baumgardner's statistics for that season—Baseball Reference, the *Spalding* and *Reach* guides, and the Baseball Hall of Fame archives offer only the final league standings but no individual records—brief game accounts throughout the season give evidence of his effectiveness. One reports Baumgardner struck out 14 in a July 4 game and "had [Ashland-]Catlettsburg at his mercy."[12] The following month, he recorded the only no-hitter in the league that season, also against Ashland-Catlettsburg; afterward, a reporter dubbed him the "premier twirler" for his team, which finished the year with the best record in the league.[13] In October, Baumgardner faced major-league competition for likely the first time when the Pittsburgh Pirates came to Huntington for an exhibition game, but the Pirates "hit freely" against him, scoring eight runs on 14 hits, five of them for extra bases.[14]

Baumgardner stayed with Huntington the next year, as the Virginia Valley League added two teams and became the Mountain States League. Once again he pitched well; by mid-June his record stood at 11-1—and he received more national attention for his one loss than he did for any of his victories, since newspapers across the country picked up the story because the defeat came in a June 8 game against Charleston in which he and opposing pitcher Dick Niehaus each tossed no-hit ball through 10 innings, Charleston finally winning in the 11th when Baumgardner gave up a run on three hits. A bit more than a week later, on June 18, on the recommendation of scout Billy Doyle,[15] the Browns signed him to a contract for 1912.[16] However, they allowed him to finish the season with Huntington.[17] He ended the season leading the league in strikeouts (292) while finishing tied for the most victories (24) and for the fewest runs allowed per nine innings (1.98).

When Baumgardner first showed up for the Browns training camp before the 1912 season, the team reportedly had small expectations for him. He was young and by most accounts green, a 20-year-old right-handed pitcher with only two seasons of Class-D ball on his résumé. Though the official record lists him at 5-11 and 178 pounds, he reportedly gave the team the impression that he was frail.[18] According to one account, the Browns did not allow him to him face any hitters until one day manager Bobby Wallace noticed the speed of his pitches as he threw to catcher Paul Krichell.[19] Even as he took the mound to face Browns hitters in an intrasquad game, however, the team still remained skeptical as they had yet see him throw anything but fastballs. Team scout and former player Monte Cross said, "I was a little afraid he did not own a change of pace. He used a side arm delivery entirely and I feared he couldn't control a curve ball."[20]

In that workout, on March 22, however, Baumgardner turned in an outing that led the *St. Louis Post-Dispatch* to declare him the "newest sensation," adding that he "monopolized the spotlight for a full half-hour and was the recipient of what was probably the most lavish praise ever heaped upon the head of a bush league pitcher." According to the story, Baumgardner "served up the most deceptive assortment of breakers ever seen on the local diamond" as his teammates watched in awe.[21] It was after this workout that Wallace compared him to Johnson.

Baumgardner made his major-league debut in the team's fourth game of the season, against Chicago in White Sox Park on April 14, the same day the passenger liner *Titanic* struck the iceberg that sank it.

Opposing him, Ed Walsh was already regarded as one of the premier pitchers in the game—he'd notched 100 victories over the previous four years—but on that Saturday afternoon, Baumgardner was, according to the *Chicago Tribune*, better, pitching "as neatly as Cy Young or Rube Waddell might have done it in their palmy days … [working] with splendid control … able to cut the ball across any portion of the plate except the middle."[22]

In his next outing, the 0-0, 15-inning tie in his home debut six days later, also against the White Sox, his pitching again earned praise: "Baumgardner was a wonder. … His delivery is almost unfathomable. … And his control is excellent."[23] Newspapers across the country began talking about him with enthusiasm. The *Washington Post* declared Baumgardner "sensational"[24] while the *Arizona Republic* suggested he was "the pitching sensation of the current baseball season."[25] Grantland Rice mentioned him in a column five days after the extra-inning tie game:

"'Fanatic' suggests that we add Larry Cheney, of the Cubs, and George Baumgardner, of the Browns, to the list of budding slabmen with the stuff. Consider them added, with bells attached and the laurel tied on. Both have arrived and delivered."[26]

Even when he lost eight of his next nine decisions, the press's admiration for Baumgardner was not shaken as writers attributed his record more to the Browns' inept play rather than his lack of ability. Referring to him as a "speed demon," the *Post-Dispatch* wondered what his record would have been had he "been backed up [by] the [pennant-winning] Red Sox?"[27] When he went 9-5 over the rest of the season, to close out 11-13, observers declared, "Great things are expected of George Baumgardner … next season."[28]

However, the season also brought suggestions that Baumgardner's eccentricity might get in the way of his ability: After his second start, the 0-0 15-inning game, he left the team for nearly three weeks. St.

Louis newspapers explained his absence by saying he had gone back to West Virginia to take care of his mother, who had fallen ill.[29] But a newspaper in West Virginia suggested that he had returned to Barboursville because he was homesick; the story reported he had his manager's permission and that he would rejoin the Browns the following weekend to start against the Tigers.[30] However, his next start would not come until nearly a week after that.

Later that year, on a road trip in Boston, Baumgardner missed the team train for New York. When he finally met up with the Browns, manager George Stovall, who had replaced Wallace on June 2, chided him for "loafing," but Baumgardner defended himself, saying, "I got lost in that bloody town. Never saw so many crooked streets in all my life."[31] Stovall assigned outfielder Willie Hogan as Baumgardner's keeper when the team was on the road.

When the season ended, Baumgardner went back home to Barboursville, where he bought his mother a house with money he'd set aside from his salary with the Browns. He performed a song-and-dance act to earn extra cash, while doing strength training by cutting trees.[32]

In January 1913, Baumgardner agreed to his contract with the Browns at what was reported as a "substantial boost" in his salary. When he returned it, Stovall predicted that he would "develop into one of the star pitchers in the … league," saying that his speed and control would "combine with the experience he had gained the past year [and] he will prove a valuable man for the team."[33]

Stovall's projection that Baumgardner would be valuable to the Browns proved prophetic in a way, as he was something of a workhorse for a bad team. He led them in games started (31), innings pitched (253⅓) and complete games (23); all of those totals ranked among the top 10 in the league. His other statistics were not so good: he went 10-20 with a 3.13 ERA that was among the highest among American League pitchers with 200 or more innings. He also led the league's hurlers in most hits allowed, 267.

Despite his record, Baumgardner became a prime target of the "outlaw" Federal League. The Browns fired Stovall as manager and, after he hooked up with the Kansas City Packers, he set his sights on acquiring the pitcher for the fledgling league. For the next year, the Browns and Packers engaged in a tug-of-war over the rights to Baumgardner. Starting in the fall of 1913, newspapers gave conflicting reports: Baumgardner had signed with the Packers; Baumgardner was "loyal" to the Browns.[34] The conflict came to a head when Stovall, claiming Baumgardner had agreed to jump to the Federal League, threatened to go to court to seek an injunction preventing Baumgardner from playing for the Browns that season when the pitcher decided to stay with St. Louis.[35]

In the end, there was no injunction and Baumgardner signed a contract with the Browns paying him $3,000 for the season.[36] That year, he turned in what was his best season with the Browns, going 16-14 with an ERA (2.79) that ranked in the top half of the league among hurlers with more than 150 innings pitched. Again, when the year ended, the Federal League set its sights on landing him and the Browns found themselves having to court the pitcher when he refused to sign his contract at first. The bone of contention was that Branch Rickey, who had taken over as manager after the team had fired Stovall, had several times mentioned that he would consider trading Baumgardner, who preferred to stay in St. Louis, and he insisted he would not sign unless the team promised it wouldn't trade him.[37] It may also have helped that his contract for 1915 gave him a substantial raise by the day's standards, to $4,200.[38] Perhaps more than his record of the season before, the increase in his salary came about because he had scored highly on an arcane "cardiac test" that Rickey had devised and which, according to Rickey, measured in a mathematical way a player's competitiveness and coolness under pressure.[39]

As it turned out, Baumgardner's performance over the next two years make plain that the test returned flawed results, at least in his case, as he pitched only 30⅓ innings in 1915 and 1916 combined.

He reportedly showed up in camp in 1915 in such bad shape that one sportswriter referred to him as a "class Z" pitcher and suggested he would not be ready to pitch in league competition until sometime in May.⁴⁰ His condition was made worse when he was struck in the head by a line drive by Dee Walsh while pitching batting practice; he lay unconscious for half an hour.⁴¹ (In a gibe at Baumgardner, the writer added, "Had the blow landed on a vulnerable spot the result might have been very serious."⁴²)

Not surprisingly, then, Baumgardner got off to a miserable start. He made his first appearance on April 15, entering the game in the third with the Browns trailing the White Sox 9-0; he pitched the final seven innings, surrendering seven runs on 10 hits and three walks, though only four of the runs were earned. The next time out, on April 24, he pitched the final inning of a 4-1 loss. Because he surrendered only one hit and no runs, Rickey decided Baumgardner was ready to start; he did the next day, and he pitched well, allowing only one run on four hits; but the Browns were shut out and he took the loss. The press, however, looked on it optimistically:

"Though he lost ... much praise is due George Baumgardner, the erratic speed ballist ... for the wonderful pitching [he] exhibited Sunday. 'Baumy' hurled a beautiful game and deserved better luck. ... [The] news of Baumgardner's return to form will doubtless cheer [Rickey]."⁴³

Rather than being the beginning of his return to the form the Browns expected of him, however, the game was the last time Baumgardner was effective on the mound. Over the next two weeks he pitched in four more games, all in relief, throwing a total of 6⅓ innings, allowing seven runs on 14 hits and six walks. With the Browns in last place, already 10½ games out of first place by May 10, Rickey decided to clean house and tried to send Baumgardner to the minor leagues. He refused and went home to West Virginia instead.⁴⁴

There, Baumgardner latched on with a local semipro team and at least one report claimed he had gotten into shape and that his pitches seemed to have the same pop and movement; however, rather than taking any initiative to contact the Browns, Baumgardner waited for them to call. "I am waiting to hear from them. ... I ain't much at letter writing, they don't need to expect any word from me."⁴⁵

Rickey offered Baumgardner a chance to come back to the Browns for 1916 but before spring training ended, the Browns gave him his release. He persuaded them to let him stay with the team by saying he would pay his own expenses as he tried to get into shape.⁴⁶ The team finally gave him a contract calling for $75 a month and he became the focus of much derision after that, as Memphis in the Southern League offered him a contract calling for $200 a month, but he declined, saying, "Nobody would see me if I went to Memphis."⁴⁷ One article that mocked him for his lack of financial acumen added, "George Baumgardner ... is all puffed up like a pouter pigeon because he has signed a new contract with the Browns. All of which only proves how easy it is to get Baumgardner all puffed up."⁴⁸

He appeared in only four games for the Browns in 1916, pitching eight innings, before the team released him for what would turn out to be the last time. He picked up with Little Rock of the Southern Association, which welcomed him enthusiastically: Describing him as a "graceful pitcher" who "works hard but doesn't show it on the surface," team President Robert G. Allen predicted that Baumgardner would "burn up this league."⁴⁹

However, it later came out that Baumgardner had reported to the team with a "strained and dislocated nerve in his back that [caused] him pain every time he [threw] the ball."⁵⁰ After only five games, he surrendered to the pain and went back to West Virginia "to get the old soup bone ready for next year."⁵¹ There, he experimented briefly with trying to become a southpaw.⁵²

Baumgardner returned to Little Rock for 1917 (as a right-handed pitcher) and threw a combined no-hitter with teammate Tom Phillips in the season opener but was bombed his next time out, surrendering 20 hits and eight runs, and then pitched inconsistently after that. After he appeared in 15 games, going 3-5 with a 5.14 ERA, the eighth-worst among pitchers with 70 innings or more, the team let him go, ending his professional career, though at least one newspaper story says that he played independent semipro baseball in West Virginia for a time.[53]

Baumgardner joined the US Army in early 1918, training at Camp Shelby in Mississippi. While he was there, he reportedly married a woman named Nellie Dietz, whom newspaper accounts of the marriage described as an "artist's model."[54] They eventually divorced.[55] He eventually ended up in France where, in 1919, he reportedly was a sergeant in the 150th Infantry.[56]

Two years later, Baumgardner signed a contract with Joplin of the Class-A Western League, but there are no records that he ever appeared in a game with them.[57]

At the time of the 1930 census, Baumgardner was living with a brother in Barboursville and working as a laborer in the building industry.[58] The 1940 census also shows him living with his brother, but does not report an occupation; his World War II draft card, which he filed in 1942, also leaves blank the space for employment.[59] Baumgardner died from a heart attack due to a coronary occlusion on December 13, 1970.[60] His obituary in the *Huntington Herald-Dispatch* says he was an active member of the Veterans of Foreign Wars and was survived by one of his sisters and several nieces and nephews.[61]

## SOURCES

In addition to the sources cited in the Notes, the author also consulted Ancestry.com, Baseball-Reference.com, and Retrosheet.org.

## NOTES

1 "Pick Up Baumgardner," *Huntington* (Indiana) *Press*, June 20, 1913: 6.

2 "Baumgardner Rube's Successor; 'High Nut' of Baseball," *Akron Beacon Journal*, January 11, 1915: 9.

3 Year: 1900; Census Place: *Barboursville, Cabell, West Virginia*; Roll: 1756; Page: 3B; Enumeration District: 0001; FHL microfilm: 1241756; Year: 1910; Census Place: *Barboursville, Cabell, West Virginia*; Roll: T624_1678; Page: 3B; Enumeration District: 0007; FHL microfilm: 1375691.

4 George W. Baumgardner player questionnaire on file in A. Bartlett Giamatti Research Cernter of the National Baseball Hall of Fame and Museum

5 "Allen Could Not Get Pitcher Baumgardner and Now George Signs to Play for Only $75," *Arkansas Democrat* (Little Rock), June 9, 1916: 13.

6 George Baumgardner contracts for 1914 and 1915, Giamatti Research Center.

7 "Baumgardner Not Yet Old Enough to Cast His First Vote," *Pittsburgh Post-Gazette*, May 5, 1912: 20.

8 "G. Baumgardner and Chapman Join Team," *Arkansas Democrat*, July 27, 1916: 7.

9 "Baumgardner Rube's Successor."

10 Louis Lee Arms, "George Baumgardner, Brownies' Mound Artist, Is Worthy Successor to Waddell and Raymond," *Washington Times*, January 1, 1915: 10.

11 "Hard Hitters Are Wanted for Team," *Paducah* (Kentucky) *Sun Democrat*, July 27, 1910: 4.

12 "Virginia Valley League," *Cincinnati Enquirer*, July 5, 1910: 13

13 "Virginia Valley League," *Cincinnati Enquirer*, August 15, 1910: 8.

14 "Leach's Barnstormers Make It Four Straight," *Pittsburgh Daily Post*, October 14, 1910: 9.

15 "Scout Who Discovered George Baumgardner Is Signed by Cleveland," *St. Louis Post-Dispatch*, November 22, 1912: 18.

16 "Another Hurler for Browns," *Indianapolis News*, June 19, 1911: 10.

17 "New Battery for Browns," *Washington Post*, July 7, 1911: 8.

18 "Pick Up Baumgardner."

19 Ibid.

20 W.J. O'Connor, "Browns' Advisory Board Discovers New 'Wonder' in Pitcher Baumgardner," *St. Louis Post-Dispatch*, March 23, 1912: 7.

21 Ibid.

22 Sam Weller, "Youngster Stars in Defeat of Sox," *Chicago Tribune*, April 15, 1912: 13.

23 "Browns Tie White Sox in 15 Inning Game," *St. Louis Post-Dispatch*, April 21, 1912: 21.

24 "Sox and Browns in 15 Rounds Without Score, *Washington Post*, April 21, 1912: Sports-1.

25 "George Baumgardner of the St. Louis Browns Is the Pitching Sensation of the Current Baseball Season," *Arizona Republic* (Phoenix), June 2, 1912: 10.

26 Grantland Rice, "Bingles and Bunts," *Washington Times*, April 25, 1912: 15.

27 Clarence Lloyd, "Johnson Shares Pitching Honors With Joe Wood," *St. Louis Post-Dispatch*, November 13, 1912: 15.

28 "Baseball Aftermath," *Pittsburgh Press*, November 11, 1912: 12.

29 "Cobb's Vicious Slide Puts Out Browns Star Catcher," *St. Louis Post-Dispatch*, May 6, 1912: 7.

30 "Baumgardner Was Real Homesick," *Huntington Herald Dispatch*, April 30, 1912: 2.

31 "Geo. Baumgardner, Bug, Has Keeper to Pilot Him in Larger Cities," *Lansing* (Michigan) *State Journal*, September 17, 1912: 8.

32 "Heat Waves From Radiator League," *Wilkes-Barre Record*, December 2, 1912: 9; "Short Snappy Sportlets," *El Paso Herald*, January 22, 1913: 9; W.J. O'Connor, "Hedges May Balk Detroit's Plan to Release High," *St. Louis Post-Dispatch*, January 31, 1913: 16.

33 "Baumgardner Has Signed," *Pittsburgh Press*, January 13, 1913: 19.

34 Clarence F. Lloyd, "Baumgardner Is Loyal to Browns, Rickey Declares," *St. Louis Post-Dispatch*, November 26, 1913: 7; "Mystery of the Jumping Quintet Still Unsolved by Browns' Owner, *St. Louis Post-Dispatch*, January 10, 1914: 6.

35 "Stovall's Failure to Land Brownies Means Legal Fight," *St. Louis Post-Dispatch*, March 12, 1914: 19.

36 George W. Baumgardner 1914 Contract.

37 Harry F. Pierce, "Baumgardner Will Not Sign a Contract With Browns Until Team Reaches Camp at Houston," *St. Louis Star and Times*, November 12, 1914: 14.

38 George W. Baumgardner 1915 Contract.

39 W.J. O'Connor, "Cardiac Test Applied to All Browns; Austin Fails," *St. Louis Post-Dispatch*, January 8. 1915: 14

40 Harry F. Pierce, "Brownies Are Not Enthusiastic Over Opening of Season," *St. Louis Star and Times*, April 13, 1915: 11.

41 L.C. Davis, "Sport Salad," *St. Louis Post-Dispatch*, April 9, 1915: 16.

42 Ibid.

43 John M. Quinn, "Brilliant Return of Baumgardner Brings Promise," *St. Louis Star and Times*, April 26, 1915: 10.

44 Harry F. Pierce, "Ordered to Report to Louisville Club, Baumy Balks," *St. Louis Star and Times*, May 11, 1915: 13.

45 Billy Evans, "Looking Them Over," *Philadelphia Inquirer*, March 7, 1916: 12.

46 "Baumgardner Pays His Way," *St. Louis Post-Dispatch*, April 9, 1916: 35.

47 "Baumgardner Not Best Businessman on Earth," *Twin City Daily Sentinel* (Winston-Salem), June 21, 1916.

48 "All Could Not Get Pitcher Baumgardner."

49 "George Baumgardner," *Daily Arkansas Gazette* (Little Rock), July 27, 1916: 8.

50 "Baumie Pitches Well, Jake Hits Homer, Rain Helps," *Daily Arkansas Gazette*, August 2, 1916: 6.

51 "Baumgardner Going Home to Plan 1917 Coup," *Arkansas Democrat*, August 21, 1916: 7.

52 "George Baumgardner Is Now a Left-Hander, *St. Louis Star and Times*, March 21, 1917: 13.

53 "Baumgardner Is Out," *El Paso Herald*, October 6, 1917: 14.

54 "Cannon Balls, Wedding Bells for Baumgardner," *Daily Arkansas Gazette*, February 18, 1918:6.

55 George W. Baumgardner Certificate of Death, on file with the A. Barlett Giamatti Research Center at the National Baseball Hall of Fame and Museum

56 "An Old Friend," *Arkansas Democrat*, March 27, 1919: 11.

57 "Baseball Notes," *Galena* (Kansas) *Evening Times*, May 14, 1921: 3.

58 Year: 1930; Census Place: Barboursville, Cabell, West Virginia; Roll: 2528; Page: 9B; Enumeration District: 0001; Image: 427.0; FHL microfilm: 2342262

59 Year: 1940; Census Place: Barboursville, Cabell, West Virginia; Roll: T627_4397; Page: 14B; Enumeration District: 6-1; The National Archives at St. Louis; St. Louis, Missouri; *Draft Registration Cards for Fourth Registration for West Virginia*, 04/27/1942 - 04/27/1942; NAI Number: 563733; Record Group Title: *Records of the Selective Service System*; Record Group Number: 147

60 George W. Baumgardner Certificate of Death

61 "George Washington Baumgardner," *Huntington Herald-Dispatch*, December 14, 1970: 6.

# WALTER "BOOM BOOM" BECK

## BY PAUL E. DOUTRICH

**WALTER WILLIAM BECK LOOKED LIKE** a pitcher. At least that's what Casey Stengel thought. "When you see a guy as big and strong and who looks like an athlete, then watch him throw without the slightest suggestion of strain, you just gotta go for him."[1] Beck stood 6-feet-2 and weighed 200 pounds with broad shoulders and a barrel chest. In Memphis, where he pitched from 1930 through 1933, they called him "Big Train" because his stature and his effortless, sweeping side-arm pitching motion reminded fans of the great Walter Johnson. "His fastball is a 'sneaker' because he throws it with so little effort."[2] Of course, Beck didn't have Johnson's speed. Instead he mixed "a corking fastball, good curve and a change of pace … and he appears to know how to pitch."[3] By the time he joined the Brooklyn Dodgers in 1933, "I learned that I could pitch better ball if I let the rest of the team do part of the work."[4]

Beck grew up in Decatur, Illinois, where his father, an avid baseball fan, worked as a carpenter. Playing on local semipro teams after graduating from high school, Walter eventually caught the eye of a St. Louis Browns scout. In 1924, at the age of 20, he began his professional career with the Browns. However, during three seasons (1924, '27, '28), he pitched in only 20 games for St. Louis. Instead, Beck spent most of his time playing for numerous minor-league teams. Finally released by the Browns after the 1928 season, he pitched for three teams the following year. In 1930 he joined the Memphis Chickasaws of the Southern Association. There he became a star, winning 62 games during the next three seasons, including 27 in 1932.

The Dodgers were excited about adding Beck to their 1933 roster. The previous season, Brooklyn had finished third in the National League, nine games behind the pennant-winning Chicago Cubs. While the team hit at a .283 clip, third best in the league, Dodgers moundsmen were among the worst in the league. The once reliable Dazzy Vance had slumped for the second year in a row. By the time the 1933 campaign began, he was sitting in the St. Louis Cardinals bullpen. With the exception of 20-game-winner Watson "Watty" Clark, the rest of the Dodgers staff mirrored Vance's disappointing performance. As a whole they combined for the second worst earned-run average in the league. Team manager Max Carey left no doubt that in 1933 he intended to rebuild his pitching staff. Walter Beck became an integral part of that plan.

Almost as soon as the Dodgers gathered in Miami for spring training, baseball people began touting Beck's potential. None was more effusive than Jim Nasium, who wrote in *The Sporting News*, "(Beck) is the bright and shining hope of this Dodger pitching staff. … He will be one of the pitching finds of the year in the National League."[5] Other writers were impressed by Beck's talent on the mound but also "his obvious intelligence and poise on and off the field."[6] Acknowledging his homey demeanor and conscientiousness, the writers and his teammates dubbed him "Elmer the Great."[7] It was a nickname he carried throughout the season. Most importantly, "(he) has won the unqualified approval of Manager Max Carey."[8]

As early as the third day of spring training the Dodgers manager had slotted his newcomer into the team's starting rotation. Teaming him up with Ray Benge, whom the Dodgers had acquired from the Philadelphia Phillies over the winter, Clark, and young Van Lingle Mungo, who had been impressive late in the previous season, Carey thought he had his pitching problems solved.

The Dodgers' season started with a win in Philadelphia. The next day Beck made an impressive National League debut. Supported by seven Dodgers runs, he held the Phillies to seven "measly" hits and a single marker. Only in the fourth inning did the home team mount a threat. Catcher Spud Davis led off with a single. Hal Lee followed with another single and both runners moved up a base when Lefty O'Doul in left field misplayed the ball. With runners on second and third, no one out and the score 1-1, "Beck pitched superbly," striking out two men and getting the third out on a grounder to escape from the jam.[9] Phillies manager Burt Shotton was particularly impressed, commenting, "I've seen young sensations come up and blow that ball past the hitter but that kid pitches with his head."[10]

Beck's first win was the beginning of a productive two weeks. Though his team struggled, he continued to impress. In his first four starts he lost only once (a 2-1 squeaker to the Boston Braves), giving up just one earned run per game. Four days later he evened the score masterfully, shutting out the Braves, 1-0, for his fourth victory. *The Sporting News* exclaimed, "Beck was easily the outstanding member of the pitching staff for the first ten days of the season.... Beck is the best young Brooklyn pitcher unveiled since Dazzy Vance."[11]

The weeks that followed were not as successful. Dodgers hitters continued to slump while the pitchers faltered. For Beck, the problems began with a 13-4 drubbing by Dizzy Dean and the St. Louis Cardinals. In his next start, against Cincinnati, he failed to get a single out, giving up five first-inning runs. By the end of May Beck had won only one more game while losing four times and giving up more than 10 earned runs per nine innings during the four-week stretch. Meanwhile, the Dodgers were hitting at a paltry .238 clip and scoring only 3.5 runs per game.

June was no better. Aside from a win against Pittsburgh, Beck's only complete game in more than a month, he lost four more times while his earned-run average continued to soar. Midway through the month, he hit bottom with an embarrassing 15-4 loss to the cellar-dwelling Phillies in which he gave up six runs in less than two innings.

Everyone agreed that Beck's problem was his loss of control, particularly control of his fastball, and that "when this freshman side-armer can't throw to his 'spots' he might as well be pitching with his left arm."[12] The source of the problem, however, became a well-explored mystery. Since spring training some had warned about the side-arm "bugaboo." "Those side arm guys can never throw straight two days in succession," wrote a *Brooklyn Eagle* scribe.[13] Others suggested that the problems arose because Beck was not getting enough work. A week later, there were complaints that he was getting too much work. In mid-June an unnamed "veteran ball player" observed that Beck "doesn't work into a sweat before he starts on hot days.... All his best work was done in the chill of April."[14] Beck's lack of concentration was another proposed source of the problem. Critics began calling him a "two-out pitcher," citing several games Beck had lost games because he allowed opponents to have big innings after he had retired the first two batters.[15]

In mid-June, manager Carey decided to experiment with his young pitcher by periodically using him in relief. Twice in 10 days Beck wrapped relief stints around his starts. However, because the Dodgers staff was overworked and "tottering," especially after the June 16 trade of Watty Clark to the Giants, the experiment lasted for only two weeks. Despite the ongoing struggles, the one thing no one questioned was Beck's confidence. After an ugly loss to the Reds, Carey assured everyone, "He still thinks he's good."[16]

Beck's and the Dodgers' travails continued into July. The young hurler started the month with a complete-game victory over the Cubs, but it proved to be his last win for six weeks. His most discouraging effort came on July 23. After coasting through eight innings, he gave up four ninth-inning runs in an 8-5 loss to the Giants.[17] Meanwhile his team briefly sank into the National League cellar before scratching its way back to sixth by the end of the month. Finally, in early August a former Memphis teammate, Joe Hutchinson, observed, "He's pitching too much underhand. He's always had more stuff when he throws underhand but his sidearm control is much better and he's practically unhittable that way."[18] Evidently through the course of the grueling season and responding to tough National League hitters, Beck had inadvertently become more of a submarine-style pitcher than a side-armer. By raising his release point, he regained the control he needed to win. The adjustment worked.

In late July, the Dodgers began a seven-week period in which they played 19 doubleheaders, thus putting additional pressure on an already exhausted pitching staff. Despite the workload, Beck began again to show the talent that had excited Dodgers fans three months earlier. On August 13, employing his rejuvenated side-arm style, he ended his five-game losing streak in an 11-0 romp over the Braves. He went on to win two of his next three games. Though he won only twice more during the rest of the season, "Beck's record over the six-week stretch is amazing. Somehow he managed to salvage five victories. But in the six defeats, the Dodgers supported him with a total of just four runs."[19] Additionally, during that six-week stretch he gave up just over 2.5 earned runs per game.

Beck's season ended with another frustrating loss, his 20th of the season, to Boston. His teammates were able to score only a single run while committing four errors that allowed all four Boston runs to score. Despite Beck's dismal 12-20 won-lost record, manager Max Carey was satisfied with his pitcher's season. "I think the experience he's gotten taking a regular turn on the mound this year for us will make him a consistent winner next year," the manager said.[20] Certainly Dodgers fans hoped that Carey's prediction would become a reality.

Encouraged by Carey's words, Beck was anxious to continue in 1934 what he had started late in the 1933 season. However, when the 1934 season opened, his manager was gone. After a slew of unpopular trades, tensions with his players, and two years close to the National League cellar, Carey had lost the confidence of both fans and the club's ownership. Instead they preferred Carey's colorful coach, Casey Stengel. Immediately the new manager let it be known that his primary challenge was his pitching staff. When assessing his pitchers, Stengel listed Van Lingle Mungo as his ace, but "then his voice starts sputtering weakly, something like a dying phonograph record.

Benge, Beck, and (Ownie) Carroll didn't supply the sort of pitching that lifts a club into the first division."[21] Additionally, Stengel was worried that Beck had lost velocity on his fastball, something that Beck himself acknowledged.

Stengel's concern grew throughout spring training. To compensate for his loss of velocity and trouble pitching to left-handed hitters, Beck attempted to develop a knuckleball. It did not work. He was regularly pounded by the opposition, and even on the few occasions when he did pitch well, he was smacked around by left-handed hitters. Meanwhile the Dodgers manager focused on a couple of rookies or possible trades that would bring an experienced pitcher to Brooklyn. Just a few days before the season opener, Stengel remained "extremely dissatisfied with the Brooklyn pitching staff."[22] Fortunately for Beck, there remained few alternatives and largely because he had a year under his belt, he was penciled in as the fourth man in the Dodgers rotation.

The season started well for "Elmer the Great." Though his first start ended in a tie, he held Boston to

a single run through seven innings. However, the next six weeks did not go as well. He lost four times, gave up over 12 earned runs per game, and only once did he survive as many as four innings. Assessing Beck in early June, *Brooklyn Eagle* writer Tommy Holmes lamented: "Beck's performances have been worse than anybody thought they could be."[23] In early June Beck was demoted to the bullpen. For a month he pitched well in relief. In six appearances he gave up only six runs in 14 innings and seemed to have recaptured some of his former effectiveness. As a reward, Stengel decided to give Beck a start in the second game of a July 4 doubleheader against Philadelphia. It became a fateful decision.

Beck's first start in more than a month didn't last long. Facing only eight Phillies, he gave up three hits, walked three and allowed three runs in only two-thirds of an inning. Stengel had seen enough. Anticipating Beck's reaction, Stengel remained in the dugout and instead instructed his catcher, Al Lopez, to inform Beck that his afternoon was over. Meanwhile, from the dugout Stengel waved in a relief pitcher.[24]

As expected, Beck was furious. Rather than handing the ball to Lopez "(Beck) threw perhaps the best fast ball he has thrown this season up against the right field fence."[25] The ball hit the tin façade with a thunderous boom. Meanwhile, several feet away, right fielder Hack Wilson was dozing with his back to the field. When he heard the boom off the wall, Wilson instinctively rushed to retrieve the ball, turned and fired a perfect strike to second. The crowd howled at the sequence. Soon after, an amused reporter labeled Beck "Boom Boom" and for the rest of his life Elmer the Great was known as Boom Boom Beck.

A week later Stengel gave Beck a chance for redemption with a start in the second game of a doubleheader against the last-place Cincinnati Reds. This time Beck gave up six runs in two innings. The loss was his sixth of the season and helped swell his earned-run average to just over one run per inning pitched. Soon after, with "a so-called speed ball (that) was going faster fence-wards … than it was going up to the plate," Beck was sent to Albany in the International League.[26] Used as both a starter and in relief, he continued to flounder. In late September Albany returned him to Brooklyn.

By the time Beck pitched again, the Dodgers were locked in sixth place with just four games left in their season. Playing his fourth doubleheader in five days, Stengel decided to start two of his most disappointing pitchers, Beck and Leslie Munns. To their manager's amazement, both won. In the second game, Beck pitched magnificently, limiting Philadelphia to just four hits and winning 10-1. After the sweep, Stengel reported: "The world is upside down."[27] However, despite the performance, no one was surprised when in early November the Dodgers released Beck. He had ended the season with a 7.42 earned-run average and a 2-6 won-lost record.

Not ready to end his career, Beck joined the Mission Reds in the Pacific Coast League. For the next three years he pitched for the Reds, winning 52 games while losing 61. When the club folded in 1938, Boom Boom moved on to two other Pacific Coast League teams in 1938, the Hollywood Stars and the Seattle Rainiers. He was 7-10 combined with a fat 6.67 earned-run average. For most, such a season would signal a further slide into minor-league obscurity, but not for Boom Boom Beck.[28]

In 1939 Beck's Memphis manager, Jimmy "Doc" Prothro, was hired to manage the Philadelphia Phillies. Among the worst teams in major-league history, the Phillies at the time were in the midst of five consecutive 100-loss seasons, finishing each season 50 or more games behind the pennant winners and at least 15 games out of seventh place. From 1939 through the 1942 season, Beck was one of the regulars on the Phillies staff. Initially used as both a starter and a reliever, by 1943, his final year with Philadelphia, he came out of the bullpen exclusively. During those five years, he won 12 games while losing 33.

Beck's major-league career ended three years later after brief stops in Detroit, Cincinnati, and Pittsburgh. After four more years in the minor leagues, his professional playing days ended with the Toledo Mud Hens in 1950. In 1957 he returned to the major leagues as the pitching coach for another bedraggled staff, the Washington Senators, where he remained for three seasons. Like the Phillies during Beck's playing days, the Senators were considered one of the worst teams in the major leagues, with an equally bad pitching staff. Beck's last decade in professional baseball was spent as a part-time scout for the Senators and minor-league pitching coach for the Milwaukee/Atlanta Braves.

Throughout the last two decades of his life, Beck's passion for baseball and his gift for gab made him a popular speaker wherever baseball fans gathered. His colorful tales were sprinkled with stories about the many players, both well-known and not, whom he had encountered during his years in the game. In those 20 years he earned a comfortable living from his investments and he became an avid golfer. Neither a hip replacement in 1975 nor three years later the death of his wife of 49 years, Pearl, slowed him down much. Until his death on May 7, 1987, Walter "Boom Boom" Beck remained a local celebrity in his Decatur, Illinois, home, a devoted golfer, and a captivating story-teller.

## NOTES

1. Tommy Holmes, "Casey Stengle (sic) Another Ready to Go in Big Way for Boy From Decatur," *Brooklyn Eagle*, March 1, 1933: 19. "When you see a guy as big and strong and who looks like an athlete, then watch him throw without the slightest suggestion of strain, you just gotta go for him."
2. Tommy Holmes, "'Big Injun Me,' Beck's First Idea: Wanted to Strike 'Em All Out," *Brooklyn Eagle*, March 15, 1933: 22.
3. Jim Nasium, "Brooklyn's 1933 Hopes Rest on Improved Pitching Staff," *The Sporting News*, March 9, 1933: 3. Jim Nasium was the nom de plume of Edgar Forrest Wolfe, a sportswriter and cartoonist based in Philadelphia.
4. Tommy Holmes, "Dodgers' New Hurler Soon Learned He Wasn't the Whole Team," *Brooklyn Eagle*, March 15, 1933: 22.
5. Jim Nasium, "Brooklyn's 1933 Hopes."
6. Thomas Holmes, "Manager of the Dodgers Clings to His Five-Man Starting Idea," *Brooklyn Eagle*, March 5, 1933: 36.
7. "Training Camp Notes," *The Sporting News*, March 23, 1933: 2.
8. *New York Times*, March 3, 1933: 20.
9. Stan Baumgartner, "Beck Thwarts Phil Hitters; Frederick Thumps at 1.000 Clip," *Philadelphia Inquirer*, April 15, 1933: 13-14.
10. Harold Parrott, "Beck of the Dodgers Impresses With His Nerve in Pitching to Sluggers," *Brooklyn Daily Eagle*, April 15, 1933: 10.
11. *The Sporting News*, April 27, 1933: 3.
12. Harold Parrott, "Juggled Lineup Fails on Attack for Carey After Hurlers Crack," *Brooklyn Daily Eagle*, June 5, 1933: 19.
13. Harold Parrott, "Walter's Wild Spree Predicted by Cards as Dodgers Go Wooly," *Brooklyn Daily Eagle*, May 3, 1933: 22.
14. Harold Parrott, "Beck Like a Groundhog, Routed Thrice in the Sun: Clark's Case Alarming," *Brooklyn Daily Eagle*, June 14, 1933: 18.
15. Harold Parrott, "Record Puts Rookie of Carey's Twirling Staff in Freak Role," *Brooklyn Daily Eagle*, June 30, 1933: 21.
16. Harold Parrott, "Blow-Up in Row," *Brooklyn Daily Eagle*, May 13, 1933: 12.
17. Harold Parrott, "With Shaute Showing Need for Rest, Carey Must Have Pitchers," *Brooklyn Daily Eagle*, July 24, 1933:18. The *Eagle* said reliever Joe Shaute was the losing pitcher, but other sources, including Retrosheet.org and Baseball-reference.com, give Beck the loss.
18. Harold Parrott, "Carey Predicts Beck Will Be Consistent Winner on Mound in 1934," *Brooklyn Eagle*, August 30, 1933: 18.
19. Harold Parrott, "Shut Out Ball Beck's Best Effort; Defeat His Lot," *Brooklyn Eagle*, September 30, 1933: 10.
20. Harold Parrott, "Carey Predicts."
21. Tommy Holmes, "It Will Be Do or Die for Dear Old Casey," *The Sporting News*, March 8, 1934: 1.
22. Tommy Holmes, "Dodgers May Offer Braves Cuccinello," *The Sporting News*, April 5, 1934: 1.
23. Tommy Holmes, "Boston Uses Brooklyn as Stepladder to Gain Higher Standing Rung," *Brooklyn Daily Eagle*, June 3, 1934: D1.
24. Rex Spires, "'Boom Boom' Beck Had a Gift of Gab," *Decatur (Illinois) Herald and Review*, August 2, 1987: 50. This was a story Beck told many times after he retired. However, in his accounts he made it to the second inning before being lifted for a relief pitcher. The *Philadelphia Inquirer* box score credits him with only two-thirds of an inning.
25. Thomas Holmes, "Dodgers Win, Then Slaughtered," *Brooklyn Daily Eagle*, July 5, 1934: 13.
26. *The Sporting News*, August 9, 1934: 8.
27. Tommy Holmes, "World's Upside Down, Says Shocked Stengel as Munns, Beck Win," *Brooklyn Daily Eagle*, September 25, 1934: 18.
28. Forrest R. Kyle, "Reserve Clause? Old-Timers Wanted Only a Chance to Play," *Decatur Review*, January 23, 1970: 13. Of his time in the Pacific Coast League, Beck later claimed: "I sent DiMaggio and Williams to the majors."

# GEORGE BELL

## BY JOHN STRUTH

**GEORGE "FARMER" BELL ENTERED** pro baseball later in life. He was 29 when he first toed the rubber with the Amsterdam-Johnstown-Gloversville Hyphens of the New York State League in 1904. Before that he had made a name for himself as an amateur player in South Central New York. Making an immediate impact with the team, he found himself in Brooklyn by 1907. Though his career was short, he had a positive impact on the Brooklyn team. After baseball he served in the US Army, returned to farming, then managed a lodge for many years. All the while, he remained close the game he loved.

George Glenn Bell was born on November 2, 1874, in Greenwood, New York. He was the second son of three born to Sylvester and Emma Bell. Sylvester Bell, born in 1845, was a Civil War veteran who fought with the 189th New York Infantry. He was wounded in action on March 31, 1865.[1] Upon mustering out in 1865, he returned to farm life. He married Emma Bardwell in 1870 and had three sons with her. Emma died in August 1879, at the age of 28. A little over a year later Sylvester married Electa "Lettie" Rude. They had five children, three sons and twin daughters. Greenwood, in western New York on the border with Pennsylvania, was farm country. Sylvester labored as both a farmer and house painter. George worked on the family farm from an early age. Somewhere he picked up a love for baseball. Bell began playing for local sandlot teams and into his adulthood gained a reputation as an excellent pitcher.

In 1898 Bell married Claudia Elizabeth Bush. By 1900 the couple had moved to Union, Pennsylvania, purchased land and began farming. Throughout that period, Bell continued to play baseball in his native New York. He and Claudia had their first child, Freda Jae Bell, on February 14, 1903.

Throughout this period, Bell continued to dominate the amateur baseball scene in the New York and Pennsylvania countryside. All that changed in 1904. Howard Earl, manager of the Amsterdam-Johnstown-Gloversville Hyphens of the New York State League, recruited Bell to pitch for his team.[2]

Bell, then 29, made an immediate impact. In 1904, his first season with the Hyphens, Bell notched 17 wins, including a no-hit game. (The next season the Hyphens were renamed the Jags.) Bell followed with 25 wins in 1905. That season the Jags were fighting for the pennant and Bell was handed the ball on the final day of the season. He pitched both ends of the doubleheader against Utica, winning both and clinching the pennant for his team.[3]

In 1906 Bell plied his trade with Altoona in the Tri-State League. There he led his team in wins, with 23, while losing 16. The Mountaineers finished fourth in a six-team division with a 64-62 record, 10½ games back.[4]

"Farmer" Bell stood 6-feet tall and weighed between 190 and 210 pounds. He batted and threw right-handed. He got his big break in 1907, when he was called up by Brooklyn. At the ripe age of 32, he was pitching in the major leagues for the first time. On February 7, the *Brooklyn Daily Eagle* announced, "Bell has all the ear-marks of a star, and it is the belief in the local camp that the former Tri-State Leaguer will prove the best pitcher Brooklyn ever had."[5]

Patsy Donovan, the Brooklyn manager, asserted that the 1907 Superbas would be a much better team than the 1906 version. He was especially high on his pitching staff. Wrote one sportswriter, "He believes he has a first-class corps with Doc Scanlon, Elmer Stricklett, Harry McIntyre [McIntire] and Jim Pastorious as the regular boxmen ... and also feels confident that Bell, a new twirler, will pan out well."[6]

Bell fashioned a promising season, pitching in 35 games, starting 27, and posting a 2.25 earned-run average in 263⅔ innings. His 2.25 ERA was the best of his career. Despite those figures, his record was 8 wins and 16 losses. He also pitched two tie games. Bell's record was as much a reflection on the futility of the Brooklyn club as it was an indictment of him.

The *Brooklyn Eagle* was not averse to pointing that out. On April 25, the *Eagle* reported on Bell's 13-inning performance in a 1-1 tie with Boston, "Bell deserves a lot of sympathy, but he made it apparent nevertheless that he is a star."[7] On May 15 Bell gained his first major-league win, defeating St. Louis 10-0, surrendering five hits and a walk. The *Eagle* announced, "George Bell registered his first victory. He should have had three."[8]

Bell continued to pitch well until late July, when he evidently tired. Throughout August and September, he made several relief appearances and his starts were spotty. On August 25, the *Eagle* wrote, "George Bell has figured as a trial horse quite frequently of late, went to the rescue, but while he checked the opposition, the home batters could do very little with Karger's [Ed Karger] southpaw shots."[9]

Perhaps best summing up Bell's season, the *Eagle* wrote on September 26, "George Bell lost a tough game yesterday, 3 to 1. … Both boxmen were in rare form, and had not Jordan and Levine bunched sad miscues in the seventh inning the big twirler would have applied the whitewash."[10]

The 1908 season was not a good one for Bell, professionally or in his personal life. He finished the campaign with a 4-15 record. Bell pitched in 29 games, starting 19. He did not pick up his first victory until July 12. His ERA was 3.59 in 155⅓ innings. Coverage of his season reflected his struggles, though not without irony. In one account, the *Eagle* wrote, "George pitched good ball. It was not as good as the article handed out by one "Slats" Beelee, however, and the backing the Brooklyn nine gave George was not good. … The result was to be expected."[11] That result was a 3-1 loss to Boston.

After a loss to New York on September 9 the *Eagle* observed, "[H]is habit of winding himself into a huge a knot when delivering the ball, and in the process of disentanglement was so slow and painstaking that the men on bases had a dozen yards start on the ball."[12]

Most poignantly, Bell lost his infant child during the season. As the tragedy unfolded, Bell arguably pitched the most brilliant game of his career. Leading up to that start, Bell had been in manager Donovan's doghouse. He was being used sparingly because of weight and conditioning concerns.[13] On July 31 Bell was scheduled to start against Pittsburgh. Shortly before the game was to begin, he received a telegram informing him that his infant child was gravely ill and not likely to survive.

As it turned out, there was no transportation immediately available for Bell to get home. Wrote the *Eagle*, "Rather than having him sitting around worrying about the situation, Manager Donovan suggested that Bell go in and pitch the game, and Bell agreed to do it."[14] Bell pitched Brooklyn to a 2-0 victory, outdueling Irv "Young Cy" Young. His sacrifice bunt in the third inning helped set up the first run of the game. The *Eagle* concluded, "He left last night in ample time, accompanied not only with the sympathies of his comrades, but with their congratulations, as well. For no pitcher, even with his mind clear of trouble, ever performed a better's day work.[15]

Bell was absent from the team over the next two weeks. Upon his return to Brooklyn he did not pitch effectively for the remainder of the season. Compounding his ills, he was struck on the pitching arm by a batted ball on September 2 and missed his next two starts.[16]

Bell's 1909 season began with a new-look Brooklyn team. Harry Lumley had been hired to manage the team. One of his first acts was to drop several players who had "exhausted the limits of their usefulness to Brooklyn."[17]

Bell pitched well out of the gate. He defeated Philadelphia in his home opener, 7-3, on May 5. After he beat Philadelphia in his next start, the *Eagle* said, "Brooklyn won it because Bell pitched another of his surprisingly fine games. …"[18] Continuing his winning ways, Bell defeated Pittsburgh 2-0 on May 19. The *Eagle* wrote that he pitched "masterly ball."[19]

After his fast start, Bell continued his good season through July. After he shut out Chicago 1-0 on July 17, the *Eagle* correspondent wrote that Bell was "pitching the best ball of his career."[20]

In August, Bell's performance, while adequate, fell off a little. Still he continued his mastery over a very strong Pittsburgh nine, defeating the Pirates 4-1 on August 5. After a loss to Cincinnati on September 28, the *Cincinnati Enquirer* observed, "George Bell, who has gained in weight, until he has some trouble in getting around at his former speed, was easy for the fourth placers, who bunched their long hits on him and won solely on their merits, earning all their runs."[21]

Whether that observation was based on fact or reputation, it's easy to believe that the strain of a full season had begun to affect Bell's performance. The fact that he struggled with weight and conditioning issues throughout his career adds to the likelihood that the *Enquirer's* observation was accurate.

In the end, 1909 proved to be Bell's most productive season. In 33 appearances, he started 30 games, completing 29. He fashioned a 16-15 record. Bell tossed six shutouts, and had an ERA of 2.71 over 256 innings pitched. Still he was nearing 35 and was battling a return of weight issues as he looked forward to the 1910 season.

There was talk of a trade in the works between Brooklyn and Chicago. The Cubs were good but lacked pitching. Brooklyn wanted to shore up its infield defense. As spring training moved along, the names bandied about were Harry McIntire, Nap Rucker, and Bell. Rucker was highly thought of by Brooklyn, and was their best and youngest pitcher. In the end, McIntire was traded to the Cubs for three infield prospects.

Based on their spring training, the Superbas were excited about their prospects of moving up in the standings. A Georgia newspaper wrote, "Big George Bell will play the roll (sic) of iron man this season with the Brooklyn Superbas. Bell pitched great last year. And Manager Dahlen thinks he will be another [Christy] Mathewson, if he is given plenty of work."[22]

Bill Dahlen was Brooklyn's third manager in three seasons. In addition to trading McIntire for infield prospects from the Cubs, Brooklyn brought up a 21-year-old outfielder, Zack Wheat. The Superbas were positioned for the modest goal of cracking the "upper" division by year's end.

Right from Opening Day, Dahlen kept his promise to use Bell often. Rucker was hit hard by Philadelphia in a 6-2 loss. Bell relieved in the sixth and completed the game. The *Eagle* reported, "Bell stopped the bingling while he tarried."[23] Throughout May, Bell pitched well, without luck. The *Eagle* wrote, "George Bell appears to be Harry McIntire's logical successor as the champion hard luck pitcher in the league. He lost some tough ones … but yesterday's was the limit."[24]

That trend continued through June, July, and August. Late in August Bell and Dahlen got into a row during a game he pitched against Pittsburgh. Through 11 innings the game was tied, 3-3. In the 12th, after a single and strikeout, Dahlen came to the mound and "instructed [Bell] to pass Clark [Fred Clarke] and Wagner [Honus Wagner]. … Bell did not like the plan, and he told his manager. But he had to obey instructions."[25] The *Eagle* man noted, "It was needless to say that Dahlen was mad after it was over

and George Bell was just angry. Indeed, the two had some hot words before they left the field."[26]

Reporters covering the Superbas sympathized with Bell's plight early on. However, as the season persisted, subtle comments of a more critical nature were presented for its readers' consumption. For example, on June 26 the paper wrote, "Both Bell and [Al] Mattern pitched admirably and received gilt-edged support. Bell, however, had his usual one bad inning."[27] After a 3-2 loss to Pittsburgh in August, the paper said, "George Bell was on the mound for Brooklyn, and although pounded for twelve hits, he managed to keep them pretty well scattered until the 7th."[28]

By September, Bell began to show signs of fatigue. Throughout much of the month, he pitched poorly, losing to Boston, St. Louis, and Philadelphia, all second-division teams. On September 28, Bell shut out Pittsburgh, 2-0. The *Eagle* reported, "George Bell did the trimming, and in quite an artistic style. Behind Bell the Superbas played snappy baseball in every department."[29]

Finally, on October 12, the last day of the season, Brooklyn played a doubleheader against Boston. In the first game, Bell pitched eight innings, allowing one run on six hits. He left with the score tied. Rube Dessau came in relief and promptly conceded eight runs. That game represented a perfect microcosm of Bell's season.

Bell, statistically, had his most impressive season. He pitched in 44 games, starting 36. In 310 innings pitched he had an ERA of 2.64. Bell completed 25 games with four shutouts. His record was 10 wins and 27 losses, with a WAR (wins above replacement) of 4.6, the best of his career.

Bell started 1911 with the same bugaboo that had persisted throughout much of his major-league playing career, weight. On New Year's Eve, the *Eagle* reported, "Bill Dahlen, manager of the Superbas, in pursuance of the Black Hand propaganda issued the other day, is planning a hustling campaign with the object in view of starting his athletes right for the season. ... George Bell attracted the attention of the cheerful leader, who declares that the Academy Corner farmer was so far beyond the limit in avoirdupois last season as to have been able to challenge for the heavyweight wrestling title."[30]

As might be expected, Bell's 1911 season was plagued by injury and illness. He missed time in May due to illness, and on his return, he was not effective through several starts. Box scores indicate that he was relegated to the bullpen, with spot starts throughout June and early July. Bell sprained his ankle and was out from mid-July through late August. Ironically, on April 12 the *Eagle* had written, "George Bell has reported for opening of the season in the best shape ever ... and if hard work will accomplish anything, George will be a top-notcher."[31]

Through April Bell pitched well, winning twice and losing twice and keeping his team in every game. After he shut out the Phillies on the 29th, the *Eagle* wrote, "It was peaches and cream for George Bell, and he fairly reveled in the going."[32] The article did go on to reference "our own fat boy," so weight was still an issue.

Bell then missed nearly two weeks with flu-like symptoms. On his return in mid-May, his pitching fell off. On the 23rd the *Eagle* wrote, "Bell started like a house afire, but burned out in the fourth and died down in the fifth."[33]

While Bell did defeat Chicago 1-0 on May 17, his overall performance led to demotion to the bullpen. The day he pitched so well against Chicago, trade rumors surfaced of a deal between New York and Brooklyn that would have sent Bell and Jake Daubert to New York for Fred Merkle, Art Devlin, and an unnamed outfielder. That trade rumor was quickly denied by Superbas owner Charlie Ebbets, who remarked, "it would be an excellent trade for New York."[34]

Throughout June and early July, Bell made only two more starts. He continued to be hit hard. In mid-July he hurt his ankle. Recovery was slow. On his return to the mound on August 20, Bell was shellacked by Pittsburgh, giving up seven runs in 7⅓ innings. On August 25, the *St. Louis Dispatch* wrote, "George Bell ... has been of little value to his team this season because of illness. He is probably done for the season."³⁵ And so it was!

On September 21 Bell was released. On the 25th the *Altoona Tribune* reported, "Baseball fans will be grieved to know of the release of the veteran pitcher, George Bell, of the Brooklyn club, to the Toronto club of the Eastern league. Bell was a member of the Superbas for five years, being one of team's pitching mainstays until the present season. He was bothered by a bad foot for the greater part of the season. … It refused to mend and Bell became practically worthless as a pitcher."³⁶ Bell refused to accept the assignment and went home for the season. His season record was 5-6. He pitched in 19 games, starting 12. He completed six, with two shutouts. Bell pitched 101 innings and compiled an ERA of 4.28.

Bell pitched four seasons in the minor leagues before hanging up his spikes. He pitched with Newark in the International League from 1912 until his release during the 1914 season. For two of those seasons, he pitched relatively effectively, crafting 10-4 and 10-11 records, with low ERAs. In 1914, Bell's final season there, he was 1-4 before his release in August. He then joined the Keene, New Hampshire, club in the Twin Mountain League, a semipro team.³⁷

Bell finished his professional career in 1915. The *Wilkes-Barre Record* made note, "George Bell, the former Brooklyn and Newark hurler, has been signed by Syracuse. The *Syracuse Journal* man refers to Bell as a "promising youngster" who is being sent to Syracuse for further seasoning. Gee whiz; smoke up! Bell is already so well-seasoned the he is full of weather cracks."³⁸ That season, at age 40, Bell crafted a 12-7 record with two clubs, Syracuse in the New York State League and Warren in the Interstate League.

Bell continued to play an active role in local baseball, pitching for and managing several semipro clubs in rural Pennsylvania and New York. In 1916 he managed the St. Mary's team of Altoona.³⁹ In 1921 he was managing and pitching for the Blossburg club.⁴⁰

In 1918 Bell enlisted in the Army. The *Pittsfield Post-Gazette* wrote, "One of baseball's almost forgotten figures, George Bell, formerly with Brooklyn, is still pitching. Bell, though aged 40 [actually 43], enlisted some time back in the Army and is now stationed at Fort Slocum, New York. He pitches on one of the fort teams and still does a good job of it. When Bell enlisted, he tipped the scales at 220 pounds. He now weighs 173 and says he never felt better in his life."⁴¹

By 1914 Bell owned four farms in Pennsylvania.⁴² In addition to maintaining a connection to baseball and farming, in 1925 Bell and his wife purchased and ran a summer and hunting lodge in Stony Creek, New York.⁴³

By 1935 Bell was spending part of the year living with his daughter in the Jackson Heights section of Queens in New York City. Through an acquaintance, he got in touch with the National League office and requested a lifetime pass to ballgames. In the back-and-forth correspondence he was notified that he did not meet baseball's criteria of 10 major-league seasons to be eligible for the pass. He was informed that if any changes to that protocol were made, he would be notified.⁴⁴

Bell died at the Bronx Veterans Hospital on December 25, 1941, of pyelonephritis, secondary to chronic uremia. It seems likely that his residence in Jackson Heights corresponded with his illness and treatment. He was buried in New York State, but after his wife died he was interred beside her in Lakeland, Florida.

In the end, Bell's major-league career lasted five seasons. His Achilles' heel throughout his career was conditioning, specifically his weight. His weight problems came up frequently throughout his five Brooklyn seasons. It got him in the doghouse with one manager, and led to special efforts by two others at "extra conditioning." His weight struggles, by all account, affected his performances. Bell finished his career with a 43-79 record. His ERA of 2.85 was near the league average. Of the 160 games Bell pitched in, he started 124. He completed 92 games, 17 of those by shutout.

One can speculate that had Bell begun his career at an earlier age and kept himself in shape throughout, he could have crafted a good career. The fact is that he acquitted himself well in four of the five seasons he pitched in the majors, all in his 30s. The last season was spoiled by illness and injury. In fact, he pitched a couple more seasons at the minor-league level, and did well. But what-ifs are just that. Still, in the end he could hold his head high and know he belonged in the major-league pitching fraternity.

## NOTES

1 *Report of the Adjutant-General*, 124. Bell, Sylvester. Found in dmna.ny.gov/history/reglist/civil/rosters/Infantry/189th_Inf_CW_Roster.pdf. Sylvester Bell was wounded at Boydton Plank Road, Virginian, during the Appomattox Campaign. In the New York State Adjutant-General Report he is listed as 20 years old, though he could not have been more than 19.

2 *Fulton County Baseball and Sports Hall of Fame Induction Biography: George Bell*, Gloversville, Fulton County, New York, emerydesigns.net/Hall_of_Fame/george.bell.html.

3 *Wilkes-Barre Record*, February 6, 1912: 19.

4 checkout.bigcartel.com/2176336/orders/LKLA-969960.

5 *Brooklyn Daily Eagle*, February 7, 1907: 10.

6 *Pittsburgh Press*, February 10, 1907: 18.

7 *Brooklyn Daily Eagle*, April 25, 1907: 24.

8 *Brooklyn Daily Eagle*, May 15, 1907: 22.

9 *Brooklyn Daily Eagle*, August 25, 1907: 35.

10 *Brooklyn Daily Eagle*, September 26, 1905: 23.

11 *Brooklyn Daily Eagle*, May 15, 1908: 22.

12 *Brooklyn Daily Eagle*, September 10, 1908: 20.

13 *Tacoma Daily News*, August 18, 1908: 9.

14 *Brooklyn Daily Eagle*, July 31, 1908: 18.

15 Ibid.

16 *Brooklyn Daily Eagle*, September 2, 1908: 18.

17 *Cincinnati Enquirer*, January 10, 1909: 10.

18 *Brooklyn Daily Eagle*, May 11, 1909: 22.

19 *Brooklyn Daily Eagle*, May 20, 1909: 20.

20 *Brooklyn Daily Eagle*, July 18, 1909: 43.

21 *Cincinnati Enquirer*, September 28, 1909: 4.

22 *Marion* (Georgia) *Daily Mirror*, March 31, 1910: 6.

23 *Brooklyn Daily Eagle*, April 21, 1910: 23.

24 *Brooklyn Daily Eagle*, May 5, 1910: 21.

25 *Brooklyn Daily Eagle*, August 26, 1910: 18.

26 Ibid.

27 *Brooklyn Daily Eagle*, June 26, 1910: 53.

28 *Brooklyn Daily Eagle*, August 13, 1910: 18.

29 *Brooklyn Daily Eagle*, September 29, 1910: 25

30 *Brooklyn Daily Eagle*, December 31, 1910: 21.

31 *Brooklyn Daily Eagle*, April 12, 1911: 27.

32 *Brooklyn Daily Eagle*, April 29, 1911: 25.

33 *Brooklyn Daily Eagle*, May 23, 1911: 25.

34 *Brooklyn Daily Eagle*, May 17, 1911: 6.

35 *St. Louis Dispatch*, August 25, 1911: 8.

36 *Altoona Tribune*, September 25, 1911: 10.

37 *Watertown* (New York) *Daily Times*, August 12, 1914: 6.

38 *Wilkes-Barre Record*, April 29, 1915: 9.

39 *Altoona Tribune*, February 28, 1916: 14.

40 *Wellsboro* (Pennsylvania) *Agitator*, August 24, 1921: 2.

41 *Pittsburgh Post-Gazette*, September 16, 1918: 8.

42 *Jersey Journal* (Jersey City, New Jersey), January 19, 1914: 7.

43 Baseball Hall of Fame Library, player file for George Glenn Bell.

44 Baseball Hall of Fame Library, player file for George Glenn Bell. Correspondence of June 13, 1935, Fred Jacklitsch to Ford Frick; Bill Brandt to George Bell, June 20, 1935; George Bell to Bill Brandt, June 24, 1935; Bill Brandt to George Bell, July 6, 1935.

# BILL BONHAM

## BY JOEL RIPPEL

**AFTER BEING DRAFTED THREE TIMES** and not signing, Bill Bonham was not drafted after his senior season at UCLA.

"I really didn't have a great record with UCLA," Bonham said. "Too, I think a lot of clubs thought I had a bad attitude."[1]

Bonham eventually signed a free-agent contract with the Chicago Cubs. Less than a year later, the 6-foot-3 right-handed pitcher was in the major leagues.

Bonham, who was born in Glendale, California, was raised in the Pacoima neighborhood in the northern San Fernando Valley of Southern California. After his senior season at Francis Poly High School, when he earned second team All-East Valley League honors, he was selected in the 31st round of the June 1966 amateur draft by the California Angels.

Bonham opted to attend Los Angeles Valley College and was drafted again by the Angels before his freshman season started. He was selected in the fourth round of the secondary phase of the January 1967 draft.

Bonham again turned down the Angels and pitched two seasons for Los Angeles Valley. As a sophomore in 1968, he had a couple of standout performances. On March 16 he struck out the first nine hitters he faced and finished with a school-record 20 strikeouts in a 3-2 victory over Santa Monica. On April 10 he pitched a no-hitter and struck out 18 in a 1-0 victory—and scored the winning run in the bottom of the ninth—over L.A. Pierce. In 67⅓ innings that season, he struck out a team-record 88 batters.

After the season, Bonham was drafted again when the Baltimore Orioles selected him in the 31st round of the June 1968 amateur draft. Bonham turned the Orioles down and enrolled at UCLA.

In 1969 Bonham helped the Bruins earn their first berth in the College World Series. The UCLA team, which included future major leaguer Chris Chambliss, went 42-10-1 in the regular season and took a 13-game winning streak into the College World Series, in which they were winless.

In his senior season, Bonham earned the team's pitcher award, winning four games with a 2.60 ERA while striking out 110 in 82⅔ innings. After going undrafted in June, he signed with the Cubs for a $2,000 bonus.

Bonham made his professional debut with Huron (South Dakota) of the Class-A Northern League. In 18 games, he was 3-3 with six saves and a 3.00 ERA. In 39 innings, he struck out 69.

In December the Cubs announced that Bonham would be invited to 1971 spring training as a nonroster player. Bonham took advantage of the opportunity and caught the attention of manager Leo Durocher.

On March 21 he pitched four scoreless innings against the Milwaukee Brewers, which all but clinched a spot on the Cubs roster. The outing was his second in a row of four shutout innings.

"He's going back to Chicago, unless a train runs over him, God forbid, bit my tongue," Durocher said.[2]

Bonham made his major-league debut against the St. Louis Cardinals on April 7, in the second game of the season. He entered the game in the top of the fourth inning, with two runners on, none out, and the Cardinals leading 6-0. He walked the first two hitters he faced and then gave up a two-run single to the next hitter. After issuing another walk, Bonham was replaced.

On April 18 Bonham made his first start, going 3⅔ innings in an 8-1 loss to the Giants in San Francisco. Over the next 24 days, he made just two relief appearances (April 23 and May 9) and on May 13 he was optioned to Tacoma (Pacific Coast League). He had pitched in five games and was 0-1 with an 8.44 ERA.

"This will give him a chance to pitch," observed Durocher. "It was not doing him any good sitting on the bench here all the time."[3]

Two days after being sent to Tacoma, Bonham picked up a victory in relief in an 8-7 victory over Portland. In three weeks at Tacoma, he appeared in eight games (11 innings) and was 2-1 with four saves and a 2.45 ERA. The Cubs recalled him on June 3.

Bonham picked up his first major-league victory on June 17, pitching three shutout innings in the Cubs' 7-6, 10-inning victory over the Cardinals in St. Louis. For the season he was 2-1 with a 4.65 ERA in 33 games.

In his second spring training with the Cubs, Bonham wasn't quite as impressive as when he was a rookie in 1971, and was the final roster cut before the season started. Bonham was optioned to Wichita (American Association), where he was solid as a starter.

On April 28 Bonham pitched a one-hitter in the Aeros' 2-0 victory over Indianapolis. Less than two weeks later, he threw another one-hitter in Wichita's 2-0 victory over Oklahoma City. After going 10-4 with seven complete games and three shutouts in 18 starts, Bonham was recalled by the Cubs on July 17.

On July 21, he started and went seven innings in the Cubs' 11-3 victory over the Astros in Houston. He made three more starts, but for the rest of the season was primarily used as a reliever. He was 1-1 with a 3.12 ERA and four saves in 19 appearances with the Cubs.

Bonham stuck with the Cubs for good in 1973. He was used as a spot starter and reliever. His 44 appearances included 15 starts (and three complete games) and six saves.

Bonham had a solid spring in 1974 with a 2.86 ERA and was named the Cubs' Opening Day starter. At Wrigley Field on April 9, Bonham pitched his first career shutout, a four-hitter in a 2-0 victory over the Philadelphia Phillies. But it would turn out to be a long season for Bonham and the Cubs.

Bonham's second victory didn't come until May 12. A loss to the Padres on June 18 dropped his record to 4-10. But between June 23 and July 18, Bonham pitched well, going 5-1 in seven starts to improve his record to 9-11. Then he won just 2 games and lost 11 over the final 2½ months of the season. On September 20 in St. Louis, Bonham allowed five runs in four innings in a 5-2 loss to the Cardinals. The loss was his 20th of the season.

Bonham finished with an 11-22 record and a 3.86 ERA in 44 appearances (36 starts and a career-high 242⅔ innings). He had 10 complete games, among them two 1-0 losses, a 2-0 loss and two 2-1 losses. The Cubs, who were 77-84 in 1973, were 66-96 in 1974.

"When I pitched badly I lost," said Bonham, "and when I pitched good, I lost some of those games, too. For a while, it seemed it didn't make any difference how I pitched. I didn't get much in the way of results. It's an unsuccessful thing to lose that many games and it makes you feel like a failure. It's tough to digest 20 losses. But I try to look at the other aspects. I got a lot of innings in. I picked up a lot of experience.

"When you lose 22, you've got something wrong. I have to change something, but I don't really know what it is. I'm going to have to keep working hard until I find the answer."[4]

Bonham was one of three 20-game losers in the National League in 1974. Randy Jones and Steve Rogers were the others. There were two 20-game losers in the American League, Mickey Lolich and Clyde Wright.

Bonham and the Cubs showed improvement in 1975. He was 13-15 with a 4.71 ERA. In his 36 starts, he had seven complete games and two shutouts as the Cubs improved to 75-87. In 1976 Bonham was 9-13 with a 4.27 ERA in 31 starts.

The 1977 season was the first in which Bonham was used exclusively as a starter. After beating the Padres 10-5 in Chicago on August 6, he was 10-10. But the victory was his last of the season. Over the final seven weeks of the season he made eight starts and went 0-3. For the season, he was 10-13 with a 4.36 ERA in 34 starts.

After the season Bonham asked to be traded, because he "felt a change of scenery might him turn around a career that has been a disappointment to him."[5] And on October 31 the Cubs obliged, trading him to the Cincinnati Reds for veteran pitcher

Woodie Fryman, minor-league pitcher Bill Caudill, and cash.

Bonham, who was 53-70 in six seasons with the Cubs, said, "I'm not leaving with any animosity. I wanted to leave only to help Bill Bonham pitch the way he hasn't yet pitched. This is a new direction for me. The fans of Chicago have been great, and the Cubs management has been the same. I asked to be traded to one of five clubs, and Cincinnati was my first choice. I thank (Cubs GM Bob) Kennedy for accommodating me."[6]

Bonham got off to a good start with the Reds in 1978, winning his first seven decisions before suffering his first loss on June 12.

His second start of the season was a 12-3 complete-game (his only one of the season) victory over the San Francisco Giants in Cincinnati. Five days later, he pitched into the ninth inning of an 8-2 victory over the Dodgers in Los Angeles to improve to 3-0. After that outing, Bonham experienced discomfort in his elbow, and was sidelined for four weeks.

"Last year I had some stiffness in my arm that cost me a starting assignment, but I pitched regularly after that," Bonham said. "This soreness is different."[7]

Bonham returned to the mound on May 12, when he took a shutout into the seventh inning and combined with Paul Moskau to beat the Philadelphia Phillies, 3-0. After a no-decision on May 17, he and Pedro Borbon combined to shut out the Braves, 10-0, in Atlanta, on May 22.

Bonham, who improved to 5-0 with that victory, admitted after the game how much the elbow injury had scared him. "I knew I hurt the elbow really bad," he said. "And, at the time, I was afraid I wouldn't pitch again. I really worried a lot. Then I realized I was overreacting, putting pressure on myself."[8]

At that point, Bonham said, he told himself, "I am a Christian. God gave me the ability to pitch. If he wants me to, I will. So after that I was able to relax."[9]

On July 7 Bonham improved to 9-2, allowing just one run and striking out seven in 6⅔ innings in a 2-1 victory over the San Francisco Giants in Cincinnati. But then he was sidelined again because of discomfort in his elbow. After a month on the sidelines, Bonham returned on August 6 and allowed one run in five innings (with no decision) in the Reds' 3-1 victory over San Diego.

Back-to-back losses in August dropped Bonham's record to 9-4. He earned his 10th victory (6-3 over the Astros in Houston) on September 4 and 11th (6-3 over the Giants in Cincinnati) on September 9. On September 14, he allowed four runs in 5⅓ innings in an 8-1 loss to the Padres in San Diego. It was Bonham's final outing of the season, which saw him go 11-5 with a 3.53 ERA. He didn't have a shutout, but he combined with relievers on four occasions for shutouts.

On September 27 Bonham had surgery on his right elbow in Los Angeles, where Dr. Frank Jobe "removed loose bodies and bone spurs from his right elbow and transplanted the ulnar nerve."[10]

Bonham was able to open the 1979 season in the Reds' rotation—the number 2 starter behind Tom Seaver. His first start of the season was a no-decision; he allowed two runs in seven innings in a 4-2 loss to the San Francisco Giants.

After his second start, a 4-2 victory over San Diego, Bonham experienced stiffness in his right shoulder and was sidelined for three weeks.

He made his next start on May 6, going just three innings in the Reds' 17-5 victory over the Houston Astros. After giving up four runs in the first inning, Bonham pitched two scoreless innings before being removed because he had thrown 65 pitches.

After going six innings (a no-decision) in his next start, Bonham was in the rotation the rest of the season. He made 29 starts, going 9-7 with a 3.79 ERA.

But heading into spring training in 1980, there were some lingering issues for Bonham.

"He was still experiencing stiffness in his forearm," Reds manager John McNamara said. "However, Dr. Frank Jobe assured him he'd be all right and could start working out after the first of the year. Last year we had to handle Bonham with kid gloves because he was coming back after elbow surgery. I'm hoping that won't be the case this year."[11]

Bonham opened the 1980 season in the starting rotation. In his first outing, on April 12, he went 6⅔ innings with no decision in a 5-4 victory over the Atlanta Braves. A week later, he got his first victory of the season, allowing four hits and one run in a 6-1 victory over the Braves. But in his third start, Bonham retired just one of the seven hitters he faced and allowed five runs in a 7-1 loss to the Cubs.

That was Bonham's last outing for two months. In mid-May he was placed on the 21-day disabled list. After rejoining the Reds, on July 26 he went five innings and teamed with reliever Tom Hume for a 5-1 victory over the New York Mets. It was his final major-league appearance.

Six days after the victory over the Mets, Bonham was scratched from a start against the Phillies after he experienced pain in his right shoulder. He returned to the disabled list. He was reactivated in September but did not pitch. In his abbreviated season, four appearance, he was 2-1 with a 4.74 ERA.

On October 28, 1980, Bonham underwent shoulder surgery in Los Angeles. Dr. Frank Jobe removed "a chronic bursa" from Bonham's right shoulder.[12]

A month after the surgery, Bonham, his wife, and Hume and his wife were staying at the MGM Grand Hotel and Casino in Las Vegas, when the hotel was devastated by a fire.

The Bonhams and the Humes were in their rooms on the 24th floor when the fire broke out shortly after 7 A.M. After being awakened by shouts, "the Humes quickly aroused the Bonhams, who occupied an adjoining room, and the two couples headed for the fire exit stairway, aware they were 24 floors away from safety. As they descended, the smoke became denser. It became unbearable when they reached the 16th floor. All the guests who jammed the stairway then turned around and headed for the rooftop."[13]

About 1,000 people were rescued from the rooftop. The blaze, one of the worst hotel fires ever in the United States, claimed 85 lives, 75 from inhalation.

Recovering from the shoulder surgery, Bonham was optioned to Triple-A Indianapolis at the start of the 1981 season. In early June, a week before the major-league season was halted by the players strike on June 12, the Reds recalled Bonham and placed him on the disabled list. During the strike, he worked

out in Cincinnati, throwing a simulated game every fifth day.

"I've been throwing all of my pitches—fastball, slider, curve and changeup—and haven't experienced any discomfort," Bonham said. "That's what I tried to do in spring training and after the Reds sent me to Indianapolis at the season's start. But when I tried to get into the groove, my arm was too sore."[14]

In July Bonham was sent to Indianapolis on a 20-day rehabilitation assignment. But in late August, Bonham, who was in the final year of a four-year contract, was released by the Reds.

Bonham continued working out in the offseason and was invited to spring training by the Reds in 1982 on a conditional basis. He was one of the surprises of spring training for the Reds and battled Mike LaCoss and Charlie Liebrandt for the fifth spot in the Reds' rotation.

On March 23 he pitched five scoreless innings in a 6-2 exhibition victory over the Detroit Tigers. Five days later, on the 28th, he had his worst outing of the spring, allowing five runs in three innings. "After today's performance, I am sure it will be hard to break camp with the team," Bonham said, "I'd like to take a little more time. I'm not ready to start, at least not ready to start every fifth day."15

Manager McNamara said, "He threw the ball pretty well. He just got hit, that's all. He threw some pretty good curve balls. As far as giving up the runs, that does not concern me. He's not missing out of the strike zone by much. Before, he was all over the place. Most of the pitches he missed with were down. If you're going to be wild, it's best to be wild down."16

When the Reds announced their regular-season roster, they said Bonham would remain at their minor-league complex in Tampa.

In late June, Bonham signed a minor-league contract and was assigned to Indianapolis. Manager George Scherger said Bonham was "up to 80 pitches per workout and we are all encouraged he can pitch again."17 The optimism was short-lived. Bonham made his first start on July 2, going four innings in a 5-3 loss to Louisville. He allowed two runs in the first inning but then threw three shutout innings. He threw 66 pitches—34 in the first inning.18

Five days later Bonham was scheduled to start against Oklahoma City but was scratched because of a sore arm. On July 9 the team announced that Bonham had returned to his home in California. His playing career was over at the age of 33.

Bonham spent parts of 10 seasons in the major leagues, going 75-83 with 11 saves and a 4.01 ERA in 300 appearances (214 starts). He had four shutouts among 27 complete games. In parts of six minor-league seasons, he was 17-9 with 10 saves and a 3.25 ERA in 52 appearances. He struck out 227 in 216 innings.

Bonham worked as a roving minor-league pitching instructor in the Houston Astros organization for several seasons. After that, he helped his wife run a boutique in the Southern California coastal town of Solvang.

## SOURCES

In addition to the sources cited in the Notes, the author also consulted Baseball-Reference.com, milb.com, and retrosheet.org. When contacted in May of 2017, Bonham politely declined to speak about his career.

## NOTES

1 Earl Lawson, "Father-Critic Finds Little Fault With Reds' Bonham," *The Sporting News*, May 6, 1978: 9.

2 George Langford, "Cubs Rookie 'Wings' Way Toward North," *Chicago Tribune*, March 22, 1971: C2.

3 George Langford, "Bonham Optioned; Cubs Get Newman," *Chicago Tribune*, May 14, 1971: C4.

4 Jerome Holtzman, "Bonham Spots Light Beam in 22-Loss Season," *The Sporting News*, October 26, 1974: 18.

5 Richard Dozer, "Caudill Seen as Gem in Cub Future," *The Sporting News*, November 19, 1977: 48.

6 Ibid.

7 Earl Lawson, "Seaver's Slump Has Reds 'Concerned,'" *The Sporting News*, May 13, 1978: 19.

8 Earl Lawson, "Reds Fire Away With BBs—Bonham and Bair," *The Sporting News*, June 10, 1978: 8.

9 Ibid.

10 Earl Lawson, "Foster Swung More, Connected Less in 78," *The Sporting News*, October 14, 1978: 36.

11 Earl Lawson, "Keystone No. 1 Question for Reds," *The Sporting News*, February 9, 1980: 38.

12 "Caught on the Fly," *The Sporting News*, November 15, 1980: 59.

13 Earl Lawson, "'God Was Watching,' Says Grateful Hume," *The Sporting News*, December 20, 1980: 47.

14 Earl Lawson, "Reds: Bonham's in Trim," *The Sporting News*, August 1, 1981: 37.

15 Wire services, "Bonham's Stock Takes a Plunge," *Richmond* (Indiana) *Palladium-Item*, March 29, 1982: A5.

16 Ibid.

17 "Bill Bonham Signs," *Indianapolis Star*, June 28, 1982: 23.

18 David Knight, "Birds Use Their Free Tickets," *Indianapolis Star*, July 3, 1982: 26.

# ED BRANDT

BY C. PAUL ROGERS III

**FOR THE FOUR YEARS FROM 1931** through 1934 Edward Arthur Brandt, largely forgotten today, was one of the top left-handers in the National League. Toiling for the mediocre Boston Braves, Dutch, as he was called by his teammates, reeled off victory totals of 18, 16, 18, and 16 and was a big reason why the Braves were at or above .500 in three of those seasons, cracking the first division in 1933 and 1934. The 6-foot-1, 190-pound Brandt was anything but an overnight success and in fact was something of a reluctant big leaguer. As a youngster coming up, he suffered from an inferiority complex and homesickness that led him to jump his minor-league club on more than one occasion and head back to his comfortable surroundings of Spokane, Washington. But with the help of people like Bill McKechnie, Brandt persevered and pitched in the big leagues for 11 years.

Brandt was born on February 17, 1905, in Spokane, one of eight children. His parents were August Brandt, born in Illinois with his occupation listed as a tinner, and the former Magdelena "Maggie" Heintz, who was born in Germany. Young Ed took to baseball at an early age and pitched his Grant Grammar School team to three school championships. He graduated to Lewis and Clark High School and continued his spectacular success, three times striking out 21 batters in a game. He quit school, however, when he got an offer to pitch for the Willys-Overland team in the Spokane City League. To support himself when he wasn't pitching, Brandt got a job in a sawmill, but quit after a friend got his hand tangled up in a saw and lost a finger, concluding that there must be a better job for an aspiring pitcher.[1]

Brandt's success pitching for Willys-Overland led to an offer from the Seattle Indians of the Pacific Coast League in the fall of 1922, when he was just 17 years old. He reported to spring training with the Indians, who trained in San Jose, California, in 1923. He soon became homesick and convinced he couldn't compete at that level, jumped the club, and returned home to Spokane. But Seattle persisted and persuaded Brandt to report to the Aberdeen Grays of the Class-D South Dakota League to gain some confidence. After a couple of good outings there, he again became plagued with self-doubt and headed home again to Spokane, shortly before the league folded on July 17.[2]

Brandt later said, "I knew I would win ballgames in the semipro league, but I also knew I would be a failure in Organized Baseball."[3]

He managed four appearances for Seattle in 1924 before returning home and pitching exceptionally well in the Spokane City League. Brandt remained much more comfortable pitching at the semipro level and toiled for town teams in Tonasket, Washington, and Wallace, Idaho, while making five appearances for Seattle in 1925. A Braves scout saw him in Wallace and wanted to sign him but he was under contract to Seattle and apparently failed to meet the Braves team in Chicago as promised, so Boston passed on him. In 1925, while pitching semipro ball for Baker, Oregon, he unknowingly pitched a game against a team that included Chick Gandil, one of the banned Black Sox from the 1919 World Series. Although Gandil was playing under an assumed name, Brandt found himself on Organized Baseball's ineligible list.[4]

Seattle managed to get Brandt reinstated in 1926 and he appeared in four games for the Indians, going 2-0 with a 3.43 earned-run average in 21 innings. The following year, at age 22, he began to show his potential, winning 19 games against 11 losses with a 3.97 ERA in 261 innings for a third-place Seattle club. Late in the year, the Boston Braves purchased his contract for $20,000, but Brandt balked, demanding part of the purchase price. When he didn't get it, he again jumped the club and went home to Spokane.

With no other recourse, Brandt reported to the Braves for 1928 and stuck with the club out of spring training.[5] He made his major-league debut on April 15, starting the third game of the year against the Brooklyn Robins at Ebbets Field. He pitched an eight-inning complete game, losing a pitcher's duel to Watty Clark by a 3-2 score. Brandt was about two months past his 23rd birthday. He won his first big-league game four days later on April 19 against the Giants in the Polo Grounds, relieving Joe Genewich to start the fourth inning with the Braves trailing 5-2. Boston came back to tie it, 8-8, in the ninth and won it with a run in the 10th inning to give Brandt the win. He pitched seven relief innings in all, allowing three runs on four hits.[6]

That performance earned Brandt a start a week later and he did not disappoint, hurling a masterful two-hit shutout against the Robins to win 4-0. As with many young left-handers, his control was not his strong suit. He walked five while striking out only one.[7] After a rough outing against the Giants on April 29, Brandt pitched all 11 innings of a 5-4 extra-inning win against the Pirates in Forbes Field to bring his record to 3-2. After some indifferent starts, he again righted himself with two consecutive complete game victories in late May, 3-1 over the Phillies and 4-1 over Brooklyn, to bring his record to 5-5. He threw another complete game on June 8 to beat the Pirates 9-5 and go 6-5 with an earned-run average of 3.61.[8]

Brandt, however, then ran into tough sledding and lost six decisions in a row to drop his record to 6-11 and raise his earned-run average to almost 5.00. A complete-game 3-1 win against the Cubs on July 25 broke the skid, but then Brandt lost six of seven to fall to 8-17. It didn't get any better. After a 9-2 complete-game win over Brooklyn on September 5 in which he scattered 13 hits, he lost his final four starts to fall to 9-21 for his rookie campaign. His 20th loss occurred on September 21 against the Cincinnati Reds by the score of 3-2. Brandt's final earned-run average in 1928 was 5.07 in 225⅓ innings. He completed 12 out of 32 starts and relieved six times for 38 total appearances.

The Braves as a team managed only 50 wins against 103 losses to finish in seventh place, 44½ games out of first. Star second baseman Rogers Hornsby, who batted .387 to lead the league, had taken over as manager of the club in mid-May from Jack Slattery.[9] Under Hornsby's tutelage the team went 39-83. Hornsby disliked pitchers and was notoriously tough on them throughout his career; thus, one can surmise that the sensitive Brandt did not exactly flourish under the Rajah. In fact, Brandt was 4-16 after Hornsby became manager.

Braves owner Emil Fuchs decided to manage the team himself in 1929 and while the team won six more games than in 1928, it sank to the basement, 43 games behind the pennant-winning Cubs. Fuchs used Brandt more sparingly, due in part to Brandt's missing almost the month of May with an injury and to his indifferent success. For the year he won 8 while losing 13, but his earned-run average rose to an unsightly 5.53 in 167⅔ innings. Still, he managed to complete 13 of his 21 starts.

Fuchs brought in future Hall of Famer Bill McKechnie to manage the club in 1930. McKechnie had a great reputation for his ability to handle pitchers, but had no early success in turning Brandt around. While the club improved to 70 wins and finished in sixth place, 22 games out of the pennant, Brandt suffered with a sore arm for much of the season and scuffled to a 4-11 record. His earned-run average (5.01) was not much improved. McKechnie used Brandt primarily as a long man out of the bullpen, but he did start 13 games, completing four.

After his first three big-league campaigns, the 25-year-old Brandt's record stood at 21 wins against 45 losses. He was regarded "as a mystery man ... [who] seemed to have everything a pitcher needed to win except confidence."[10]

At some point, probably during spring training in 1931, McKecknie had a conversation with Brandt in which he asked the lefty, also known as Big Ed for his tall frame, what he liked to do in the winter. Brandt said he liked to hunt, to which McKechnie said, "Then you'd better make up your mind that you're a major-league pitcher and not just a semipro star. If you don't, you'll be scratching the year 'round on a job in a sawmill or a tin shop. Get me?"[11]

Brandt had undergone surgery for a chronic sinus condition over the winter, so whether it was McKechnie's admonition or better health or both, he started the 1931 season like a house afire, winning his first eight starts, all complete-game victories. Although he cooled off a little once the dog days of summer arrived, Brandt still finished the season with 18 wins and 11 losses for a team that won only 64 games and finished in seventh place, 37 games out of the lead. His 2.92 earned-run average was third lowest in the league and his 23 complete games were second-most. He topped off his career year by being named to Babe Ruth's mythical All-American baseball team[12] and even finished 10th in National League MVP voting.

Under McKechnie, the Braves improved to .500 and fifth place in 1932 with a 77-77 record. Brandt again was the workhorse of the staff, leading the team in wins while also finishing at .500 with a 16-16 record in 254 innings. His earned-run average jumped by a run to 3.97 and he gave up more hits, 271, than innings pitched. He completed 19 of 31 starts and tossed two shutouts.

Brandt returned to his 1931 form in 1933, again posting 18 wins against 14 losses as the Braves improved to an 83-71 record to finish in the first division, only nine games behind the pennant-winning New York Giants.[13] He could again claim to be, along with Carl Hubbell, one of the top two left-handers in the National League. His 2.60 earned-run average was fourth lowest in the league while his 23 complete games were the third most and his 288 innings were fourth highest.

Brandt pitched in tough luck early in 1933 and his 5-3 loss to the Pirates on June 18 dropped his record to 4-8, even though his earned-run average stood at 2.77. But from there he went 14-6, benefiting from better run support as he continued to pitch well. During one stretch Brandt won six decisions in a row, including a four-hit shutout against the Cincinnati Reds on July 2. He finished the season by winning four of five starts, including another four-hit shutout of the Reds on September 19.

Brandt was one of the best hitting pitchers in the National League during his career and in 1933 had his best year at the plate, batting .309 with 30 hits in 97 official at-bats. He was a good-enough hitter to be used as a pinch-hitter several times during his career, which ended with his batting average at a more than respectable .236.

In 1934 Brandt had another solid year, finishing at 16-14 for a Braves team that again finished in fourth place, with a 78-73 record. He threw 20 complete games among his 28 starts, fifth most in the league, and finished with a respectable 3.53 earned-run average in 255 innings. He threw a two-hit shutout against the Cubs in May, a three-hit shutout of the Pirates in July, and whitewashed the Giants in August on another two-hitter.

The Braves' 1935 season began with a lot of hoopla as the team signed the 40-year-old Babe Ruth. Brandt pitched the season opener on April 16 and defeated Giants ace Carl Hubbell, 4-2, as the Babe smashed a home run and a double and made a great running catch in left field.[14] But Ruth was at end of the line and on June 2 announced his retirement, as the wheels were coming off the bus both for the Braves and for Brandt.[15] The team fell off the cliff to a 38-115 record, finishing in the basement, 61½ games out of the lead and 26½ games out of seventh place. The team lost 15 in a row on the road in July and then went 2-28 from mid-August to mid-September.[16]

Brandt didn't help rescue the Braves as his earned-run average rose to 5.00 in 174⅔ innings and he won only five of 24 decisions. On April 27 he beat the Dodgers 4-2 to bring his record to 2-1 for the young season. He then lost seven in a row. On June 30 Brandt defeated the Phillies 9-3 in a complete-game 12-hitter to bring his record to 5-8. It was his last win of the season as, plagued by a sore arm,[17] he lost 11 consecutive decisions to finish the year 5-19.[18]

With nothing to lose, the Braves cleaned house after their disastrous '35 campaign and on December 12 dealt Brandt and utilityman Randy Moore to the Brooklyn Dodgers for second baseman Tony Cuccinello, catcher Al Lopez, and pitchers Ray Benge and Bobby Reis.[19] The Dodgers were entering their third season with Casey Stengel at the helm and had finished 29½ games off the lead in fifth place in 1935. The trade didn't help much as the club slipped to seventh in 1936, 20 games under .500.

Brandt was in effect the Dodgers' number-three starter, behind Van Lingle Mungo and Fred Frankhouse, who had come over from the Braves in a separate deal. Brandt started the year slowly and after a 5-3 loss to the Cubs on July 21, saw his record fall to 3-10. But with better run support, he won eight of his final 11 decisions to finish with an 11-13 record. He threw 12 complete games in 29 starts and ended with a respectable 3.50 earned-run average in 234 innings.

Brandt showed his moxie and impressed at least one sportswriter when he was felled by a first-inning line drive struck by Johnny Moore of the Phillies in a meaningless game at the Baker Bowl on August 5. He staggered to his feet, and although initially wobbly, finished with eight shutout innings to win the game 7-3.[20] In Brandt's last start of the year, he pitched 12 innings against the Phillies in a no-decision that the Dodgers lost in the 13th, 4-2. One headline the next day was titled "Brandt Closes Luckless Year with Dodgers."[21]

Brandt's strong finish convinced the Pittsburgh Pirates to acquire him after the season in a trade for southpaw pitcher Ralph Birkofer and infielder Cookie Lavagetto. The Pirates had finished in fourth place the previous two seasons under manager Pie Traynor and were looking for pitching help to bolster a lineup that had hit a robust .286 in 1936 to tie for the league lead. It was a chance for Brandt to pitch for a contender as well as for a club that could provide run support.

Brandt won his first three starts as the Pirates got off to a fast start in 1937, winning 11 of their first 14 games. But plagued by lack of run support, his old bugaboo, and a sore arm, he lost his next five decisions to fall to 3-5 as the Pirates settled into third place. Brandt, who was known to drink and carouse a bit, also managed to get cross-ways with strait-laced manager Traynor. As a result, there was speculation that Traynor did not use Brandt as much as he might have during Brandt's tenure with the club.[22]

Brandt continued to be inconsistent in '37 but pitched a sparkling two-hit shutout against his old team, now called the Boston Bees, on July 30 in a game the Pirates won 1-0 with a run in the bottom of the ninth.[23] He similarly defeated the Reds 1-0 on September 9 in a game the Pirates also won in the bottom of the ninth on an Arky Vaughn triple and a single by Bill Brubaker.

For the season, Brandt won 11 and lost 10 in 176 innings with a solid 3.11 earned-run average. He started 25 games, completed seven, and appeared eight times in relief as the Pirates finished in third place with an 86-68 record, 10 games off the pace.

After the season, it was revealed that Brandt had secretly gotten married during the season on August 5 in Wheeling, West Virginia. It was reported that the newly married couple was spending the offseason on Brandt's ranch near Libby, Montana.[24]

The 33-year-old Brandt returned to the Pirates for the 1938 season but was plagued by arm trouble early in the year and missed three weeks in late June and early July. He was used as a spot starter, with 13 starts, and in relief, with 11 appearances. Brandt was still capable of throwing a gem and shut out the Phillies 8-0 on July 19 for his second win of the year. But for the year he was inconsistent and finished 5-4 with a 3.46 earned-run average in only 96 innings for a Pirates team that was in the pennant race all year and finished in second place, only two games behind the Cubs, their hearts broken by Gabby Hartnett's famous homer in the gloamin'.

Brandt reported to spring training with the Pirates in 1939 in San Bernardino, California. However, he was abruptly given his unconditional release by Traynor on March 23 for "breaking training rules." According to Traynor, Brandt didn't arrive at the team hotel the night before "until a little before breakfast time."[25] Five days later Brandt signed with the Hollywood Stars of the Pacific Coast League.[26] He began the season with the Stars but again encountered arm problems. After going 2-3 in six appearances, he was again released, effectively ending his professional baseball career.[27]

After baseball, Brandt returned to Spokane and then for a time ran a dude ranch and hunting lodge that he had purchased in Montana. He spent about six months in the Army in 1942 and 1943 and was a private in the 41st Armored Regiment stationed at Camp Polk, Louisiana, where he was listed as a physical director.[28] He was apparently discharged because of his age and again returned to Spokane to work in the local war industry. He subsequently purchased a tavern in nearby Clayton but continued to live in Spokane.[29] He was granted a divorce from his wife in August 1944.[30]

Shortly before midnight on the evening of November 2, 1944, Brandt and his fiancée were involved in a minor traffic accident as they prepared to return to Clayton from Spokane. As Brandt talked on the street to the driver of the other car, he was struck and fatally injured by another car that was traveling about 40 miles per hour.[31] He was just 39 years old.

Ed Brandt's lifetime major-league record was 121 wins against 146 losses with a 3.86 earned-run average. Although he finished 25 games under .500, it is important to remember that he toiled for second-division teams for the bulk of his career and was uniformly considered a hard-luck pitcher during his playing days.[32] From 1931 through 1934, he was considered one of the elite left-handers in the National League, finishing among the league leaders in innings pitched, complete games, and shutouts. During those years, he averaged 17 wins a campaign and put together a 68-55 record for Braves teams that finished no better than fourth place. Not bad for a reluctant major leaguer who for many years thought he could never succeed in Organized baseball.

## SOURCES

The author would like to thank Greg Ivy for his genealogical research help for this biography.

## NOTES

1. Harry T. Brundidge, "Ed Brandt Won Belated Success After Prolonged Battle," *The Sporting News*, November, 19, 1931: 7.

2. Lloyd Johnson and Miles Wolff, eds., *The Encyclopedia of Minor League Baseball* (Durham, North Carolina: Baseball America, Inc., 2d ed. 1997); Brundidge: 7.

3. John E. Spalding, *Pacific Coast League Stars, Volume II* (Manhattan, Kansas: Ag Press, 1997), 46.

4. Brundidge: 7; Tommy Holmes, "Ex-Brave Signs With Flatbush Club," unidentified clipping dated January 24, 1936, from the Ed Brandt clippings file, National Baseball Library.

5. Brundidge: 7.

6. The Giants' lineup featured Hall of Famers Bill Terry, Edd Roush, Freddie Lindstrom, and Travis Jackson as well as Lefty O'Doul, who many believe should be in the Hall of Fame.

7. He had also walked five in his first appearance, but also struck out five.

8. Two of the runs scored by the Pirates were unearned.

9. The 1928 Braves not only had Hornsby at second, but had future Hall of Famer George Sisler playing first base.

10. "And then suddenly the big left-hander was off to the races," Holmes.

11. Brundidge: 7.

12. Harold "Speed" Johnson, *Who's Who in Major League Baseball* (Chicago: Buxton Publishing Co., 1933), 89.

13. Ben Cantwell had his career year in 1933 and could lay claim as the ace of the Braves staff. He went 20-10 with a 2.62 earned-run average in 255 innings. By 1935 Cantwell had slipped to an

# 20-GAME LOSERS

    unsightly 4-25 record. Cantwell's lifetime record was 76-108, although his career earned-run average was a respectable 3.91.

14  Harold Kaese, *The Boston Braves—An Informal History* (New York: G.P. Putnam's Sons, 1948), 231.

15  Al Hirshberg, *The Braves—The Pick and the Shovel* (Boston: Waverly House, 1948), 49-62; Mitchell Conrad Stinson, *Deacon Bill McKechnie—A Baseball Biography* (Jefferson, North Carolina: McFarland & Company, 2012), 154-58.

16  Gary Caruso, *The Braves Encyclopedia* (Philadelphia: Temple University Press, 1995), 56-57; Jonathan Weeks, *Cellar Dwellers—The Worst Teams in Baseball History* (Lanham, Maryland: Scarecrow Press, 2012), 91-102.

17  Holmes.

18  He did pitch in some tough luck, losing two games by 3-2 scores, one by a 2-1 count, and one 1-0 game.

19  While the trade seemed to favor the Braves, it largely involved players who seemed to be on the downside of their careers. Dan Daniel, "Brooklyn Given Brandt and Moore in Big Deal," *New York World-Telegram*, December 13, 1935.

20  The Old Scout, "Pirates Aided by Acquisition of Ed Brandt," unidentified clipping dated December 7, 1936, from the Ed Brandt clippings file, National Baseball Library.

21  Edward T. Murphy, "Brandt Closes Luckless Year with Dodgers," unidentified clipping dated September 25, 1936, from the Ed Brandt clippings file, National Baseball Library. Hugh Mulcahy pitched all 13 innings for the Phillies. He earned his first major-league victory when Chile Gomez hit a two-run single in the top of the 13th and Mulcahy followed with a scoreless bottom half of the inning.

22  James Forr and David Proctor, *Pie Traynor—A Baseball Biography* (Jefferson, North Carolina: McFarland & Company, 2010), 148, 169.

23  Al Todd doubled to lead off the ninth, moved to third on a bunt hit by Pep Young, and scored on a fly ball by Red Lucas to end the game.

24  Unidentified clipping dated October 7, 1937, from the Ed Brandt clippings file, National Baseball Library.

25  Brandt was released even though it left the Pirates with only one left-handed pitcher, rookie Ken Heintzelman. "Pirates Release Brandt, Veteran," unidentified clipping dated March 23, 1939, from the Ed Brandt clippings file, National Baseball Library. Traynor reportedly sat in the hotel lobby until 3 A.M. waiting for Brandt and teammate Russ Bauers to come in for the evening before giving up and going to bed. Forr and Proctor, 173-74.

26  Unidentified clipping dated March 28, 1939, from the Ed Brandt clippings file, National Baseball Library.

27  "Hollywood Club Releases Ed Brandt," unidentified clipping dated May 3, 1939, from the Ed Brandt clippings file, National Baseball Library.

28  Unidentified clipping dated January 21, 1943, from the Ed Brandt clippings file, National Baseball Library.

29  "Crash Fatal to 'Lefty' Brandt," *Spokane Spokesman-Review*, November 3, 1944: 15.

30  Unidentified clipping dated August 31, 1944, from the Ed Brandt clippings file, National Baseball Library.

31  Brandt was struck by a car driven by First Lieutenant Louis Sanchez, who was convalescing at the Fort Wright Hospital from battle fatigue after more than 50 missions over Germany as a bombardier. He had won the Air Medal and Distinguished Flying Cross and may have been suffering from what we would now call post traumatic stress syndrome. On the night of the accident Sanchez was being followed by a patrol car because of his speeding and erratic driving. No alcohol was involved, however. "Question Raised in Brandt Death," *Spokane Spokesman-Review*, November 3, 1944: 14.

32  Murphy, "Brandt Closes Luckless Year with Dodgers"; The Old Scout, "Pirates Aided by Acquisition of Ed Brandt" ("For eight years the husky left-hander has been tossing 'em in for light scoring teams."); Letter to the Editor of *The Sporting News* from J. Roberson dated June 1, 1933, from the Ed Brandt clippings file, National Baseball Library (Ed Brandt is "the greatest pitcher in the National League" and "the champion hard luck pitcher in the game today," and would win 25 games with a better-hitting team).

# BUSTER BROWN

## BY MARK S. STERNMAN

**FAMILY, FRIENDS, AND TEAMMATES** could easily have called Charles E. Brown "Charlie Brown" instead of Buster Brown. Given that he would own the worst career winning percentage (.331) for a pitcher with a minimum of 150 decisions, a name that long after his death would have recalled the perpetually defeated *Peanuts* comic-strip character would have suited Brown.

In *Leviathan*, the English philosopher Thomas Hobbes opined, "Life is nasty, brutish, and short." Sadly, these six words well encapsulate the professional career and truncated life of Buster Brown, a slightly-below-average hurler who had the dual misfortune of toiling for truly terrible teams before his untimely death at the all-too-abbreviated age of 32.

Born in Boone, Iowa, on August 31, 1881, Brown stayed closed to home by attending Ames Agricultural College, now known as Iowa State University, where he went 14-0 as a sophomore.[1] He pitched no-hitters against Coe College, striking out 16, and against Grinnell College with 14 strikeouts.[2] Described by his alma mater "as an exceptional pitcher and captain of the 1905 team,"[3] Brown mixed baseball business with collegiate pleasure by playing university ball during the school years and pro ball during the summers. He pitched for semipro Onawa (Iowa) in 1902, in the Three-I League for the 1903 Rock Rapids (Iowa) Islanders, and in the Western League for the 1904 Omaha Rangers.[4]

The St. Louis Cardinals bought Brown from Omaha in the summer of 1904 and had high hopes for the young righty. Going into the 1905 season, a member of the St. Louis front office claimed that Brown would "make some … batters think [Christy] Mathewson is doing the pitching before the season is half gone."[5]

Brown, "the former handler of the expectoration pellet," had other ideas and received permission to delay reporting until June 1 so he could finish the college term.[6]

The Cardinals occupied sixth place in the National League standings when Brown made his major-league debut, on June 22, 1905. The circumstances seemed favorable: St. Louis hosted Boston, which languished in seventh place and would send Vic Willis and his 1-11 record to the mound. Brown hit hard and got hit hard. He tripled in his first at-bat but gave up eight runs on 11 hits in six innings of toil. Brown "sustained all of the blows familiar to the big gunners, got rattled just like a veteran, fired [pitches] squarely over the plate, indicating the experience of a trained boxman when about to go for a jaunt in his airship."[7] It was a damning description in the early days of manned flight.

Brown recovered after this subpar start to enjoy a promising rookie campaign.[8] Although he had an 8-11 record, his .421 winning percentage bettered the team's .377 mark. Of the five St. Louis pitchers who pitched in more than 20 games, Brown had the lowest ERA at 2.97. He also tied for the team lead with three shutouts, and finished, despite his delayed start, fourth on the squad in WAR.

Brown had a similar second season, winning eight games again (although losing 16 this time). He set career highs in complete games (21) and strikeouts (109). Facing the Cubs in Chicago in a year when the West Siders would go 116-36, Brown gave up only three hits in a 15-inning complete-game 4-2 victory. Brown survived eight walks and a wild pitch in the win. He held the Cubs hitless after the fifth inning.[9]

Over the course of 1906, Brown yielded just two home runs and even hit one himself, an inside-the-park job on a "long hit between centre and right fields"[10] in an 11-2 loss to the Giants. Brown walked five and threw two wild pitches, a typical outing in a campaign that saw him issue the fourth-most walks in the NL and throw the most wild pitches. Brown struggled with his control throughout his career.

The results of this game notwithstanding, in the 1906 offseason New York Giants manager John McGraw was "hot after" Brown; according to rumor, he was willing to give Joe McGinnity to St. Louis for Brown and [catcher Mike] Grady.[11] The deal looked lopsided given that McGinnity had just gone 27-12, the eighth time in eight seasons that he had won at least 21 games, but the Iron Man at the age of 35 had little left. St. Louis supposedly rebuffed the exchange, wanting both cash and players for Brown.[12]

St. Louis had overplayed its cards. Brown got off to a terrible start in 1907, with a 1-6 record and a relatively high 3.39 ERA (nearly a full run above the league average of 2.46). On June 10, St. Louis traded Brown to the Philadelphia Phillies for left-handed pitcher Johnny Lush.[13] In its first issue after the trade, *The Sporting News* featured Brown on its front page and captioned a photo of him by noting that his "lack of control is a great handicap to have, but if he succeeds in overcoming this weakness, he will rank higher. ... He has been charged with sulking during his career as a Cardinal and has several times expressed his desire to enter the services of another team."[14]

Although badmouthed on the way out of St. Louis by unnamed sources who accused him of being "too nervous to stand a hard game ... and a weakling,"[15] Brown found freedom in Philadelphia, where his 9-6 record and 2.42 ERA would have served as personal bests if they could have stood apart from his subpar St. Louis statistics. Capping off a happy campaign, Brown announced after the 1907 season that he would marry Nina Myers of Onawa, Iowa.[16]

Brown pitched in only three games in relief in 1908 but did get married; a postseason brief notes that he and his wife would return from Philadelphia to Prairie City, Iowa.[17] Brown saw little more action in 1909 than he had the previous year; through mid-June, he had appeared just seven times, with only one start. Used in mop-up situations, Brown for the Phillies in 1908 and 1909 had no decisions. Granting its unwanted man freedom, Philadelphia on July 16, 1909, swapped Brown, Lew Richie, and Dave Shean to the Boston Doves for Johnny Bates and Charlie Starr. Boston manager Harry Smith welcomed his new pitcher, saying he expected Brown to be a winner for the Doves. "Brown has loads of stuff, but lacks control, owing to idleness," Smith noted.[18]

While defying Smith's prediction with a 4-8 record, Brown proved a valuable member of the Boston staff, a sad-sack assortment of 15 pitchers, none of whom had a winning record. Brown yielded just 7.9 hits per nine innings, the best mark on the team among the regular starting pitchers. Despite joining the team midway through the season, Brown finished third on the awful 45-108 club in WAR.

In 1910, Boston remained in last place despite winning eight more games than the prior year. Brown easily led the team in WAR and had a fine 2.67 ERA in a year when the NL as a whole had a 3.02 mark. Brown set a career high in games pitched with 46, ranking him in a four-way tie for third in the league, and in innings with 263. But in this, his best season, Brown went just 9-23 (just trailing his teammate Cliff

Curtis in this dubious category; Curtis had a 6-24 record).

One of Brown's nine wins came on May 26 when he stifled the defending World Series champion Pittsburgh Pirates on a complete-game, four-hit effort in a 4-1 Boston road victory. The *Boston Globe* reported that Brown's "delivery proved puzzling to the champs."[19] Perhaps his most painful defeat came against a man to whom he had once been crazily compared, Christy Mathewson.[20] Facing Big Six and the Giants, a first-division club, Brown through eight innings had yielded just one hit and enjoyed a 3-0 lead. But New York rallied for a trio in the ninth to tie the score; an error in the 14th sparked a five-run rally that led to a frustrating 8-3 loss for Brown. The *Globe* concluded, "While Brown was effective with his slow ball, he failed to put on the extra speed and at the close was outpitched by the wonderful Mathewson. … Brown pitched one of the prettiest games seen at the park in a long time, and but for a slip in the last ditch would have a good one on the [one and] only Matty."[21]

In 1911, Boston bottomed out with a 44-107 record, helped in part by a 14-game losing streak suffered by Brown after he had pitched brilliantly on Opening Day to beat Brooklyn. After this strong start, a Boston correspondent optimistically opined, "Brown has the makings of a first-class box artist. With a strong club behind him I think he would prove to be one of the best twirlers in the league."[22]

Alas, Boston had a terribly weak club with "a very error-prone defense."[23] Fred Tenney managed the Rustlers; his career winning percentage as a skipper, .334, only slightly eclipsed that of Brown, his most-used pitcher. Brown lost to Philadelphia on April 19 and kept on losing through July 28 against Pittsburgh, a streak he finally broke by beating St. Louis on August 2, Boston's first win after dropping 16 straight games. Over the last two-plus months of the season, Brown got even wilder but proved tougher to hit; his 7-4 record over the closing stretch appears even more impressive in comparison with Boston's 37-103 mark over the rest of the season.

### 1911: A Tale of Three Seasons[24]

|  | W-L | IP | H | BB | K | WP | HBP | R | RA |
|---|---|---|---|---|---|---|---|---|---|
| April 12 | 1-0 | 9 | 5 | 3 | 3 | 0 | 0 | 1 | 1.00 |
| April 19- July 29 | 0-14 | 137⅔ | 167 | 60 | 48 | 4 | 6 | 111 | 7.26 |
| August 2- October 9 | 7-4 | 94⅔ | 84 | 54 | 27 | 2 | 4 | 48 | 4.56 |

Completing a four-year stretch in which he went just 25-64, Brown bottomed out in terms of winning percentage in 1912 by taking just four of 19 decisions although for the only season in his career he struck out more batters than he walked (68-66) and had a career-best WHIP of 1.259. He pitched a one-hitter against Philadelphia on May 27[25] before suffering through another months-long winless streak beginning with his next appearance. Brown went 0-11 from May 31 through September 10. He earned his final win on September 14, 1912, in game two of a doubleheader against St. Louis. In a complete game, Brown gave up only eight hits while leading both teams with three hits of his own, including two doubles, as Boston won 11-2.

Even after four frustrating seasons, Brown had high hopes for 1913. After signing his contract, Brown penned a letter, writing, "I hope this will be our banner year … and I have a feeling that … the team will be much stronger than it was last year."[26] Boston did go from 52 wins in 1912 under Johnny Kling to 69 wins in 1913 under George Stallings, but Brown did not contribute. He pitched just twice, both times in long relief in April home games that the Braves easily lost.

Unwittingly, Brown helped the 1914 Miracle Braves triumph. On May 1, 1913, Boston traded Brown and $4,000 to Toronto of the International League.[27] The Braves received Dick Rudolph, who in 1914 alone won three more games for Boston than Brown won in his 139 games pitched in the Hub (Rudolph's 28 wins included 26 in the regular season, and Games One and Four of the World Series sweep of Philadelphia).

Brown would not live to see the miracle. He died on February 9, 1914, at the age of 32 "after an operation for a growth under his arm."[28] His death certificate lists the cause of his death as acute lymphangitis with a contributing factor of dilation of the left ventricle of his heart.[29]

## NOTES

1 "Buster Brown, 'Losing Ways" diamondsinthedusk.com/uploads/articles/153-img2-BROWN_Buster.pdf (accessed March 1, 2017).

2 "Charles E. Brown, Pitcher of the St. Louis National Club," *Sporting Life*, May 11, 1907: 1.

3 "Diamond Reflections: Cyclones in the Majors," add.lib.iastate.edu/spcl/exhibits/baseball/majors.htm (accessed March 1, 2017).

4 Diamonds in the Dusk credits Brown with a 27-15 record, 107 strikeouts, and 63 walks in 1904. Baseball Reference lists Brown with 28 games pitched (and 63 walks) that season.

5 Wm. G. Murphy, "St. Louis Sayings," *Sporting Life*, February 25, 1905: 8.

6 Wm. G. Murphy, "St. Louis Siftings," *Sporting Life*, March 11, 1905: 2.

7 "Brown Bounced," *Boston Globe*, June 23, 1905: 8.

8 "Brown of St. Louis, with his strength and two months' experience, has developed into one of the stars." "National League News," *Sporting Life*, September 16, 1905: 3.

9 "Spuds Drop Two but Retain Lead," *Chicago Tribune*, May 31, 1906: 11.

10 "Easy Win for Giants," *New York Times*, June 17, 1906.

11 Wm. F.H. Koelsch, "Metropolitan Mention," *Sporting Life*, December 22, 1906: 10.

12 "National League News," *Sporting Life*, December 29, 1906: 7; "New Year Notes," *Sporting Life*, January 5, 1907: 10; "National League News," *Sporting Life*, February 23, 1907: 5.

13 St. Louis also received $5,000, according to "Local Jottings," *Sporting Life*, June 22, 1907: 7.

14 "Charles E. Brown," *The Sporting News*, June 15, 1907: 1.

15 "An Odd Handicap," *Sporting Life*, July 6, 1907: 5.

16 "Buster Brown to Marry," *The Sporting News*, December 12, 1907.

17 "The Phillies' Winter Quarters," *Sporting Life*, October 31, 1908: 5.

18 "National League Notes," *Sporting Life*, July 31, 1909: 9.

19 "Boston Wallops Groggy Pirates," *Boston Globe*, May 27, 1910: 7.

20 The two did have similar builds. Brown stood an even 6 feet tall and is listed as weighing 180; Mathewson had an extra inch and 15 more pounds.

21 "New York Wins, 8 to 3, in 14th," *Boston Globe*, July 7, 1910: 6.

22 A.H.C. Mitchell, "Boston Briefs," *Sporting Life*, April 22, 1911: 5.

23 Tom Ruane, "The Deadball Era's Worst Pitching Staff," retrosheet.org/Research/RuaneT/bsn1911_art.htm (accessed March 21, 2017).

24 Data compiled from "The 1911 BOS N Regular Season Pitching Log for Buster Brown," retrosheet.org/boxesetc/1911/Kbrowb1020091911.htm (accessed March 21, 2017). Small discrepancies exist between the sums of some of these daily results as compared to Brown's seasonal records.

25 "The Phillies were unable to connect with the curves of 'Buster' Brown … and that tells the reason for their whitewash." Brown went seven scoreless innings, striking out eight and giving up just one hit, according to the box score and game story at "See Both Teams Win in Philadelphia," *Boston Globe*, May 28, 1912: 7. Retrosheet has Philadelphia getting two hits off Brown. See retrosheet.org/boxesetc/1912/B05272PHI1912.htm.

26 "Brown Sixth Brave to Sign," *Boston Globe*, December 24, 1912: 7.

27 Diamonds in the Dusk credits Brown with a 13-13 record, 228⅓ innings pitched, 80 strikeouts, and 94 walks for Toronto in 1913. Baseball Reference has no data on Brown's Toronto time.

28 "W.M. Tackaberry's Toronto Topics," *Sporting Life*, April 4, 1914: 13.

29 The death certificate comes from the National Baseball Hall of Fame and Museum's file on Brown. Thanks to Reference Librarian Cassidy Lent of the Hall for scanning the Brown file.

# HARRY BYRD

## BY ARMAND PETERSON

**HARRY BYRD HIGHWAY RUNS WEST** from US 401 for about five miles along South Carolina Route 34/151, and past Darlington Raceway, NASCAR's first paved superspeedway. The 1.25-mile egg-shaped oval, built in 1950, is a shrine for stock-car racing comparable to what Wrigley Field is for baseball. Many racing fans visiting the Darlington Raceway Stock Car Museum probably ask, "What did Harry Byrd drive?" or "Who was Harry Byrd?"

Byrd was, in fact, a Darlington native and the American League Rookie of the Year in 1952, when he had a 15-15 record for the Philadelphia Athletics, and compiled a 3.31 ERA in 228⅓ innings. He was a local boy who made good, but returned home after his professional career was over. He compiled a lifetime record of 46-54 in seven seasons in the major leagues, and 120-129 in 12 seasons in the minor leagues.

Harry Byrd was born on February 3, 1925, in Mont Clare, South Carolina, an unincorporated village about seven miles northeast of Darlington. He was the youngest of six children—two girls and four boys—born to James Curtis Byrd Sr. and Annie Tuttle Byrd. His father, like most folks in Mont Clare, made a living as a laborer in logging and pulp lumber operations, and raised chickens for food and extra income. Later he became a superintendent in a sawmill.

Mont Clare had a grammar school for grades one to seven, with two teachers. Harry and a group of nine or 10 boys with ages in an approximate four-year range learned to play baseball together at the school. They played ball all the time. One of the boys later explained that the only two things to do at recess were see-saw or play baseball. "After all," he said, "the interest span for see-sawing is very limited for boys that age."[1] The boys started playing games with nearby villages when they were about 10 years old. Harry was chosen as the pitcher because he won the team's long-throw contest. There were no official leagues, and games were arranged on an ad-hoc basis. The coach drove the players to away games in a wagon towed behind his car.

Harry enrolled at Darlington St. John's in eighth grade. He started logging with his father when he was 12 years old, and the hard labor turned him into an imposing physical specimen, with wide shoulders and well-developed muscles. He played football and baseball at St. John's High School. As a junior Byrd pitched St. John's to the 1942 State Class-A Championship. Legendary Columbia High School coach H. B. Rhame called Byrd "the best high school pitcher he had ever seen."[2] Five players from the old Mont Clare youth team were on the squad—Harry, his older brother, Wesley, Tom Tyson, Robert Richardson, and Tom Kleven.

Later in 1942 Harry's father moved the family to Pelzer, South Carolina, probably to take a job in textile mills that were booming to fill wartime orders. Pelzer was an unincorporated village in northern Anderson County, just south of Greenville. Harry pitched for the Pelzer Bears town team and a Junior American Legion team from Greenville in the spring of 1943. He graduated with the Pelzer High School Class of 1943 on May 24, and enlisted in the Army on June 8. He was assigned to an airborne division, but then was transferred to the 567th Anti-Aircraft Battalion, which arrived in Europe on December 20, 1944. Byrd was discharged on February 3, 1946, and returned to his family, now back in Mont Clare. He still had the desire to play baseball. "There wasn't much time to play ball in the Army," he declared. "I played a little softball now and then, but it didn't do anything for me. I began to wonder whether I'd be able to pitch again."[3]

He did not have to wait long to find out. Johnny Stokes, Darlington County sheriff and Harry's Legion coach, had alerted Philadelphia Athletics scout Ira Thomas about Byrd back in 1941 and 1942.

Thomas signed the burly right-hander shortly after he came home, and the A's assigned him to their Martinsville (Virginia) farm team in the Class-C Carolina League.

Byrd had a 15-12 record for sixth-place Martinsville, but had control problems all year. He walked 108 batters in 236 innings, and finished with a 4.77 ERA. Harry returned to Mont Clare after the season, and worked in local logging operations, a practice he maintained throughout his baseball career. (Major-league sportswriters later frequently referred to him as a "lumberjack" or "woodsman.") He also met Mary Lee Lyles, a girl from nearby Hartsville. They were engaged before Harry returned to baseball in early 1947, and were married in October.

Byrd spent the next two seasons with Savannah (Georgia), the A's farm team in the Single-A Sally (South Atlantic) League. He had solid, but unspectacular results: 16-13, with a 5.56 ERA in 1947, and 15-15, with a 4.09 ERA in 1948. He continued to have control problems and was overshadowed by other young pitchers in the A's organization: Lou Brissie, Carl Scheib, Alex Kellner, and Bobby Shantz. Brissie was 24 years old in 1948, Byrd and Kellner were 23, while Shantz was 22, and Scheib only 21.

Savannah sold Byrd to Buffalo of the Triple-A International League in October 1948. It is unclear whether the Athletics had given up on him, or felt they had too many young pitchers in their organization, or if they simply wanted to give him experience in a tougher league. (They owned no farm teams above Class A.)

Byrd got off to a good start in the Buffalo spring training camp in Waxahachie, Texas. Bisons manager Paul Richards called Byrd the best rookie pitcher in his training camp, and Byrd said Richards taught him how to pitch. "Before he took hold of me, I was just a thrower. I still had a lot of rough spots, understand, but after three weeks under Richards I felt I had a chance to go somewhere in baseball."[4] The relationship was strained when Harry learned his father had suffered a heart attack. He asked the team for a leave to go home to care for his father's 400 chickens. Team officials figured Byrd was just homesick and refused

his request. Byrd went home anyway, and Buffalo suspended him. Byrd later regretted his decision. "I was a fool to leave the Buffalo team in spring training," he said in a 1952 interview. "But I could think only of my father at the time. He recovered, and is in fairly good health now. But that season almost wrecked me."[5]

Back home in Mont Clare, Byrd contemplated quitting Organized Baseball, and soon began pitching for his old Legion coach, Johnny Stokes, with nearby Hartsville in the semipro Palmetto League. When Buffalo offered to reinstate Byrd, Stokes talked him into accepting. He was optioned in mid-August to Savannah, where he had a subpar 2-8 record with a 4.67 ERA in 54 innings of work.

Byrd was still under contract with Buffalo, which had moved its 1950 spring-training base from Texas to Avon Park, Florida. He was brought to the A's camp in West Palm Beach early in spring training to pitch batting practice and impressed Hall of Famer Mickey Cochrane, who had just been hired as one of the team's coaches. "He's big and fast," Cochrane said. "He's strong and has a good fastball. His curve is fair, but getting better. I think he's a helluva prospect."[6] Thanks to sore arms by three expected starting pitchers—Alex Kellner, Dick Fowler, and Joe Coleman—the Athletics purchased Byrd's contract from Buffalo and he found himself on the Opening Day roster.

Byrd's first major-league game was forgettable. He entered the game in the top of the ninth inning against Boston at Shibe Park on April 21, with the Athletics trailing 4-1, and gave up a grand slam to Vern Stephens. He was optioned to Buffalo in June after making six short relief appearances. Byrd struggled to a 4-9 record with the last-place Bisons. His 6.75 ERA (in 108 innings) was the highest in the International League for pitchers who worked more than 100 innings.

Nevertheless, the Athletics placed Byrd on their 1951 spring-training roster. He saw little action once spring-training games began and was optioned to Single-A Savannah once again, but was encouraged by advice given to him during training camp by the A's new pitching coach, future Hall of Famer Charles "Chief" Bender. "It was the Chief who encouraged me to throw side-arm, my natural style," Byrd said in a 1952 interview.[7] He had been a side-armer growing up, but professional pitching coaches had drilled him on throwing straight overhand. "He needed to wind up in order to get anything on the ball up top," Bender recalled. "But I noticed that when he threw from down near his chest, he had speed to burn."[8] Byrd had a solid season at Savannah, with an 18-14 record and a 3.59 ERA in 248 innings pitched. He thrived on the heavy workload.

The Athletics seemed to have the nucleus for a strong team coming into spring training in 1952. After finishing above .500 three seasons in a row, 1947-1949, they had a miserable 52-102 record in 1950, but in 1951 under new manager Jimmy Dykes, their first new manager in 50 years, the team finished 18 games better at 70-84. First baseman Ferris Fain led the league in batting with a .344 average, outfielder Gus Zernial led the league with 33 home runs and 129 RBIs, and Bobby Shantz became the team's ace starter with an 18-10 record.

Byrd felt good about his season at Savannah, was in good shape after an offseason of hard physical labor in a sawmill, had a good relationship with A's pitching coach Chief Bender, and was looking forward to reporting to 1952 spring training. He was given more chances to pitch in early exhibition games than he had in 1951 and made the Opening Day roster.

Byrd was used sparingly early in the season. He impressed Dykes with a six-inning relief job against Washington on May 10 when he came in to replace an injured Morrie Martin. Dykes rewarded Byrd with a start against the Browns at St. Louis on May 14, but he lasted only three innings, and didn't get another start until May 27. Byrd came through with a complete-game 7-3 victory—his first major-league win—over the Red Sox at Boston, and Dykes put him in the starting rotation for the rest of the season. The team was 31-37 at the All-Star break, and in sixth place. Shantz was 14-3 and almost single-handedly keeping the team competitive. Byrd was 5-7 overall, but 4-5 as a starter.

The A's were 48-38 after the break and finished the season in fourth place. Shantz continued his brilliant season with a 10-4 second-half record, while Byrd was 10-8. Byrd was a workhorse, starting 19 games, relieving in three others, and pitching 155⅔ innings … and asking for more work. "I've been lucky, I guess," Byrd drawled. "Never had a sore arm. My arm's been tired, understand, but never sore. Luck, I guess."[9]

Byrd started five games with only two days' rest. Two came late in the season. He beat Boston on August 28, giving up three earned runs in eight innings, and on August 31, in the same series in Philadelphia, he shut out the Red Sox 2-0. Then, on September 3 he pitched a one-hit shutout to beat the Yankees, 3-0.

Byrd finished the season with a 15-15 record. He could have been 17-13, but he lost 1-0 at Cleveland on September 11 and 1-0 at New York on September 21. His ERA at the All-Star break was 4.46 in 72⅔ innings pitched, but his second-half ERA was 2.78, bringing his season's average down to 3.31. Byrd gave a lot of credit for his success to Bobo Newsom, the 19-year veteran pitcher the A's signed in June after his release from the Washington Senators. Newsom was from Hartsville, just a few miles down the road from Darlington, and the two had a lot in common. "I never could have done it without Newsom," Byrd volunteered. "He helped me a lot. Bobo was the first to notice that I was rearing back so far that I was letting go of the ball too soon."[10]

The A's had a lot to feel good about—Ferris Fain won his second consecutive batting title with a .327 average; Gus Zernial had another good year, with 29 home runs and 100 RBIs; and Bobby Shantz was voted the league's Most Valuable Player.

Byrd and his family shared a home with Everett "Skeeter" Kell (younger brother of future Hall of Famer George Kell) and his family during the season. A's officials suggested he should stay in Philadelphia over the winter to cash in on his reputation, but he moved back to Darlington. "Can't do it," he said. "You can't go huntin' or fishin' in Philadelphia like you can down home."[11] More than 200 local supporters attended the Darlington Lions Club "Harry Byrd Night" on October 13. Chamber of Commerce president Kenneth James presented Byrd with a repeating shotgun from the Lions Club. "I hope your eye is as keen on partridge as it is on home plate," he said.[12]

In late November the Baseball Writers Association of America announced they had voted Byrd the 1952 American League Rookie of the Year. Byrd tallied nine votes to eight for catcher Clint Courtney of the Browns and seven for catcher Sammy White of the Red Sox. (Three writers from each city in the league served as the electors.) It was a mild surprise. *The Sporting News* had selected Courtney as Rookie of the Year in its September 24 edition, but it was the third year in a row its choices differed from the official BBWAA voting.

A reporter from nearby Florence caught up to Byrd and his wife, Mary Lee, at a cold Friday-night high-school football game on November 21 to ask him about the award. He wrote that "There probably wasn't a more surprised man in Darlington yesterday than Harry Byrd. He still wore that dazed look late last night, hours after he had been informed of his selection as the American League's 'Rookie of the Year' for 1952."[13] Byrd said he didn't think he had a chance to win the award, but seemed more interested in the game between bitter rivals Darlington and Hartsville. Asked what immediate plans he had, Byrd said he had a deer hunt Saturday morning and would be hunting squirrels in the afternoon … just like many other men in the area.

Byrd changed his offseason plans a little, however, and decided to do a little less work in the sawmill. In August he had speculated that the hard physical labor tightened up his muscles too much. "But next winter I think maybe I'll quit a month earlier, and do a lot of runnin'. I've always been slow gettin' started, and I believe maybe all that sawin' may tighten me up. I know I've always had trouble gettin' loose."[14] Probably because of the reduced hard physical labor, Byrd came into spring training overweight. Byrd claimed it was only 10 pounds, but manager Jimmy Dykes said it was 20 or more. Harry's weight was a sore spot between the two all season.

The A's figured their starting pitching would be strong, and general manager Art Ehlers had made a big trade in December to bolster their offense. The A's traded their two-time batting champ Ferris Fain and minor-league infielder Bobby Wilson to the Chicago White Sox for Eddie Robinson, a three-time All-Star who had 29 HRs and 117 RBIs in 1951 and 22 HRs and 104 RBIs in 1952, Joe DeMaestri, and Ed McGhee.

The A's closed out April at 7-6, a far cry from their disastrous 1-8 start in 1952. Manager Jimmy Dykes took advantage of two open dates and three rainouts to start his aces Shantz and Kellner in 10 of the team's first 17 games. Byrd started three times. The team was 10-7 and in third place after a doubleheader sweep of Chicago on May 3, but then lost seven straight and fell to seventh place. They would remain in sixth or seventh the rest of the season.

Byrd hit bottom on May 10 when he failed to complete the second inning in an eventual 8-0 loss to the Senators. He was 1-4 at the time, with a 6.30 ERA, but steadily improved his record to 9-10 and a 4.20 ERA at the All-Star break. Byrd was a consistent arm for Dykes on a pitching staff full of injuries, including 1952 AL MVP Bobby Shantz, who tore a tendon in his shoulder on May 21. Alex Kellner missed parts of June with shoulder soreness, then fractured a finger on his left hand on August 26 and was lost for the season. Carl Scheib had persistent arm troubles and started only eight games all season

Thus, Dykes had to look for number one and two starters as well as number four. The one constant was Harry Byrd, strolling to the mound every three or four days, sometimes less. Dykes started Byrd three times with two days' rest in the second half, and once, on September 2, with only one day of rest after a short, four-inning start on August 31.

Byrd beat the Indians 9-3 on July 18, his first start after the All-Star break, pulling his record even at 10-10. But then his season imploded. He lost nine games in a row, and started five others during that streak where he had no decision. He finally broke the streak with a 2-0 shutout of the Browns on September 13. The A's were in collapse, as well, with a 5-22 record from August 15 to September 9.

Byrd suffered his 20th loss in his last start of the season, on September 22 when the Yankees knocked him out of the box with six runs in 1⅔ innings. He finished with an 11-20 record and a 5.51 ERA in 236⅔ innings pitched. His second-half record was 2-10, with a 7.46 ERA.

It is fair to ask why Dykes kept writing Byrd's name in the starting lineup. One answer is that he had no choice—the injuries to Shantz, Kellner, and Scheib left him no other options. Another answer is that Dykes and the Athletics still believed that Byrd had major-league stuff. Other teams in the league believed it, too. As soon as the season ended, the league's scribes began speculating on possible trades, frequently mentioning Byrd. The New York Yankees had an aging pitching staff: Allie Reynolds (36 years old), Vic Raschi (34), Eddie Lopat, (35), and Johnny Sain (35). Byrd was the Yankees' first choice in the trading marketplace, but Boston, Chicago, and Cleveland were also seriously interested in him, if for no other reason than to keep him away from New York.

There were big changes in the A's front office on November 2 when Art Ehlers left to become general manager for the new owners of the St. Louis Browns, who were moving the franchise to Baltimore. Connie Mack's sons Roy and Earle quickly took control of the team and signed infielder Eddie Joost to replace Jimmy Dykes as manager. Dykes was offered a front-office job, but negotiated a release and soon was made manager of the Orioles.

Joost was realistic about the team's future. "I see no first-division possibilities as we now stand. We have to make some changes—and we will. We'll trade anybody except Bobby Shantz and maybe Harry Byrd. ..."[15] He voiced the majority opinion on Byrd, saying that "most people agree that few—if any—have as much on the ball as Byrd."[16]

However, the Athletics and Yankees announced a big 13-player trade on December 16. The A's sent Byrd, Eddie Robinson, Tom Hamilton, Carmen Mauro, and Loren Babe to the Yankees in exchange for Vic Power, Bill Renna, Don Bollweg, John Gray, Jim Robertson, Jim Finigan, two additional players to be named later, and $25,000.[17] A's beat writer Art Morrow wrote that obtaining Byrd and the slugging Robinson practically guaranteed another pennant for Casey Stengel: " 'Twas the week before Christmas, chuckled New Yorkers, and Santa Claus dropped in early at Yankee Stadium."[18]

The Yankees dismissed worries about Byrd's physical condition. "Byrd is a good, strong pitcher," Stengel said. "He wasn't in the best of physical shape much of last season, but did not have a sore arm. He's experienced and strong and should be a topflight pitcher."[19]

The Yankees brought Byrd to New York for a physical in early January. Ordinarily, players are permitted to take physicals in their hometowns, but the team wanted to talk to him about his conditioning. Byrd tried to downplay his weight, insisting that working in a sawmill after the season had already brought his weight down 10 pounds, from 218 to 208. When asked in an interview if he gained weight because he had lost interest over the A's poor season, Dan Daniel wrote, Harry protested. "No, it wasn't that. Not exactly."[20] When asked to clarify, Byrd said, "I don't want to say what it was."[21]

Byrd's reticence and awkwardness gave him a bad reputation with the press, even though his temperament could simply have been the natural result of his rural upbringing. The front-page story in the January 6, 1954, issue of *The Sporting News* reported on rankings of players on each team by major-league writers. There were 44 categories, ranging from "fastest runner" to "best dressed" to "best all-around athlete." Byrd was cited as "most temperamental," "least cooperative with writers," and "worst dressed."[22] Others were more forgiving. In November 1957, for example, Detroit general manager John McHale claimed many bad reputations were overexaggerated. "We found that with Byrd. Nobody wanted him a year ago because of reports on his behavior. … He gave us less trouble than anyone on the club."[23]

Byrd later laid the blame on Jimmy Dykes for pitching him too much in batting practice and making him run too much during the 1953 season. Dykes made a sharp reply. "He wasn't in shape and I was determined to get him in shape. Too many players are satisfied today to coast along. They don't have enough drive. I did Byrd a favor and he doesn't know it. In fact, he asked to pitch batting practice. Now he blames it on the manager, claims it was too much. That's the bunk."[24]

The Yankees sold longtime ace Vic Raschi to the Cardinals on February 23, 1954, opening a spot for Byrd in the rotation. Tom Morgan was also expected to compete for a starting job after spending a year and a half in military service.

Byrd had bad luck while losing his first three starts. He gave up only three earned runs in 17 innings pitched, but the Yankees did not score a run when he was on the mound in those games. He finally won his first game on May 9, pitching seven innings in a 7-4 victory over the Athletics, but tore a muscle in his side in a game on May 14 and sat out two weeks. Then he was plagued several times by attacks of hives, caused by a reaction to some antihistamine shots. Byrd had a 4-5 record, with a 3.96 ERA in 61⅓ innings pitched, at the All-Star break, and had become a spot starter. Six of his 11 starts had been in doubleheaders, when extra starting pitchers were required.

Byrd pitched a complete-game shutout to beat Detroit 6-0 on July 18, his first start after the All-Star Game. In his next start, on July 22, he pitched another complete game to beat Chicago, 11-1. Both games, not surprisingly, were in doubleheaders, but he had worked his way back into the starting rotation. On August 28 he started and pitched six innings in a 4-2 win against Detroit, bringing his overall record to 9-7. Since the All-Star Game he had started nine games, completed four, with a 2.05 ERA and a 5-2 record. At the time the Yankees were 88-40 and 3½ games behind Cleveland, and appeared to be on their way to winning at least 100 games for the first time since 1942.

But Harry made only two appearances the rest of the season. Rookie Bob Grim, on his way to a 20-6 record and Rookie of the Year honors, and Whitey Ford each started five of the team's final 26 games. Byrd's fate with the Yankees was foretold when Tommy Byrne, a regular starter for the Yankees in 1949 and 1950, was purchased from Seattle of the Pacific Coast League on September 3, and started five games in September.

Byrd was not surprised when he found that he was traded to Baltimore in a multiplayer deal on November 17, 1954. Harry and Jim McDonald, Willie Miranda, Hal Smith, Gus Triandos, Gene Woodling, and four players to be named later were sent to the Orioles in return for Billy Hunter, Don Larsen, Bob Turley, and four players to be named later. Byrd said he was happy to be traded. "Not that I'm sore at the Yankees or at Casey Stengel or at the organization," he said. "It's not that. It's just that I have to pitch regularly to be effective and I didn't get that chance to pitch regularly with the Yankees."[25]

Byrd started well at Baltimore in 1955, beating the Senators 3-0 on April 23 with a three-hit shutout, but the Orioles placed him on waivers and Chicago picked him up on June 15. He shut out the Senators again, giving up only four hits in a 7-0 win on June 23, but was not very effective the rest of the season. His combined record was 7-8, with 20 starts and a 4.61 ERA in 156⅓ innings pitched.

Chicago traded Byrd to Detroit on May 15, 1956, along with Bob Kennedy and Jim Brideweser in exchange for Fred Hatfield and Jim Delsing. He had pitched only 4⅓ innings in three games at the time. Detroit sent him to their Charleston farm team in the Triple-A American Association, where he spent the rest of the season. Used as a starter there (21 of 24 games) his record was 8-9, with a 4.06 ERA.

Byrd decided to play with Centauros de Maracaibo in Venezuela's four-team Occidental League over the winter to build up his arm strength. The league played a 57-game schedule from December 1956 to February 1957. Byrd had an 11-7 record with a 2.36 ERA for the third place (28-29) Centauros, and got a lot of work, pitching 156 innings.[26]

Detroit assigned Byrd to Charleston again in 1957. After several games he was sent down to the Tigers' Birmingham farm team in the Double-A Southern Association. He was recalled by the Tigers in late June, and pitched two innings in relief only hours after he joined the team in Washington. Although he was a starting pitcher at Charleston and Birmingham, he became a short reliever in Detroit. He pitched in 37 of the team's 89 remaining games, and had a 4-3 record and a 3.36 ERA in 59 innings pitched.

Byrd appeared to be a key man in Detroit's bullpen plans for 1958. He was placed on the Detroit 40-man roster in January, but was the last man cut in spring training and returned to Birmingham. In July, Detroit sold the 33-year-old's contract to Omaha (a Cardinals farm team) in the Triple-A American Association. "Youth has the right of way in the Tigers' farm system," said an article in *The Sporting News*. "When veteran Righthander Harry Byrd was sold by the Birmingham Barons (Southern) to Omaha (American Association), it was announced here [Detroit] that the move was made to give young pitchers more work. Byrd, whose bull-pen work was vital in the Tigers' fourth-place finish last season, had an 8-11 mark at Birmingham."[27]

Harry never made it back to the big leagues. He had an 8-16 record for Miami in the Triple-A International League in 1959, and pitched for Miami and for Portland (Oregon) of the Triple-A Pacific Coast League in 1960. He retired in 1961, after pitching in 21 games for Portland and Hawaii in the PCL.

When it was over, Byrd returned to his roots back in Darlington, where he worked, hunted, and fished with folks he grew up with. He was active in the local VFW, hunters' clubs, and several baseball alumni organizations, and was a member of the Wesley Memorial United Methodist Church. He returned to work in the lumber business and eventually worked for more than 10 years as a foreman with the R.E. Goodson Construction Company, whose origin was building roads for logging operations. He played some more baseball, too, as player-manager for the Darlington Rebels in the semipro Border Belt League (consisting of eight towns on either side of the South Carolina/North Carolina border).

Harry died after a short illness on May 14, 1985. He left behind his wife, Mary Lee, and two daughters, Pamela and Vicky.

## SOURCES

In addition to the sources listed in the notes, the author consulted baseball-reference.com, newspaperarchive.com, newspapers.com, and retrosheet.org, as well as:

Cobb, Bill, and Gene Welborn. *Memories of Pelzer 1881-1950* (Bountiful Utah: Family History Publishers, 1995).

Johnson, Lloyd, and Miles Wolff, eds. *The Encyclopedia of Minor League Baseball* (Durham, North Carolina: Baseball America, 1997).

"A History of the 567th Battalion." 567thbattalion.com, accessed June 1, 2017.

Anderson County Library, Anderson, South Carolina 29621.

Baseball Hall of Fame Library, Cooperstown, New York, player file for Harry Byrd.

Darlington Historical Commission, Darlington, South Carolina 29532.

Hennepin County (Minnesota) Library: Ancestry Library Edition; ProQuest Historical Newspapers, the *New York Times*; and ProQuest Newsstand.

## NOTES

1   Arthur Richardson, "How Harry Byrd Came to Be a Major League Pitcher," *Darlington News & Press*, September 27, 1990: One-C.

2   "Statistics About Darlington Class A Baseball Champs of South Carolina," *Florence* (South Carolina) *Morning News*, May 31, 1942: 5.

# 20-GAME LOSERS

3   Edgar Williams, "1953's for the BYRD!," *Baseball Digest*, November 1952: 21.

4   Williams: 22.

5   Ibid.

6   Art Morrow, "Wyse Posts First Win—Gets Connie to Up Pay Terms," *The Sporting News*, April 12, 1950: 16.

7   Art Morrow, "Hats Off," *The Sporting News*, September 17, 1952: 22.

8   Ibid.

9   Art Morrow, " 'Get Lost for Awhile,' Dykes Tells Bobby in Effort to Ease Tension on A's Ace," *The Sporting News*, August 20, 1952: 9.

10  Art Morrow, "Dotted Line Dash of Athletics Finds Bobo Out in Front," *The Sporting News*, October 8, 1952: 8.

11  Williams: 23.

12  Arthur Strickland, "Harry Byrd Honored by Darlington Friends," *Florence* (South Carolina) *Morning News*, October 14, 1952: 9.

13  Bob Weirich, "Surprised Byrd Says, 'Who, Me?' at AL Rookie-of-Year Selection," *Florence Morning News*, November 22, 1952: 1.

14  Morrow, " 'Get Lost for Awhile.' "

15  Art Morrow, "Joost Plans Player Changes, Few Rules," *The Sporting News*, November 25, 1953: 3.

16  Ibid.

17  Daniel, "Champs Now Eyeing Turley or Larsen in Oriole Trade," *The Sporting News*, December 23, 1953: 9.

18  Art Morrow, "A's Given Eight, Including Power, Bollweg and Renna," *The Sporting News*, December 23, 1953: 9.

19  Dan Daniel, "Champs Now Eyeing Turley."

20  Dan Daniel, "Byrd, First Yank to Sign, Denies He's Overweight," *New York World-Telegram and Sun*, January 14, 1954.

21  Ibid.

22  C.C. Johnson Spink, "The Low-Down on Majors' Big Shots," *The Sporting News*, January 6, 1954: 1-2.

23  Watson Spoelstra, "Swap Sewed Up by McHale in Frank's Absence in Cuba," *The Sporting News*, November 27, 1957: 7.

24  " 'Byrd Out of Shape,' Snaps Dykes to 'Overwork' Charge," *The Sporting News*, March 10, 1954: 20.

25  Van Newman, " 'Great to Be Yank, But Not Once-a-Week Kind!'—Byrd," *The Sporting News*, February 16, 1955: 13.

26  Olaf E. Dickson, "Dickens, Hoskins Occidental Loop Bat, Hill Leaders," *The Sporting News*, February 20, 1957: 30.

27  "Byrd Sale Points Up Bengal Emphasis on Kids in Chain," *The Sporting News*, July 16, 1958: 17.

# GEORGE CASTER

## BY CHRIS RAINEY

**GEORGE CASTER WAS A "GAY AND** delightful fellow who went laughing through the summers, doing what was asked of him as well as he could."[1] He was the ace and backbone of the Philadelphia Athletics pitching staff in 1937 and 1938 despite losing 19 and 20 games respectively in the two seasons. He tossed 513 innings those two seasons, tantalizing batters with a dancing knuckleball and a mixture of curves and fastballs. The Athletics won 107 games those two summers and Caster accounted for 28. He also absorbed 39 losses. The A's won about 35 percent of their games; Caster's winning percentage was .418.

The Caster family had slowly worked their way across the United States. George's great-grandfather was born in Ohio, his grandfather in Iowa, and his father in South Dakota. George Jasper Caster was the first child born to Ira Brinton Caster and Catherine (Corbett) Caster when he joined the family in Colton, California, on August 4, 1907. He would be joined later by a sister, Catherine, and a brother, John. Ira was a grocery-store proprietor. He also served occasionally as a deputy sheriff in San Bernardino County. Caster's mother had musical talent as a singer and whistler. She was active in the society activities of the area as both a performer and a hostess. Caster attended local schools and graduated from Colton High School. He then enrolled in San Bernardino Community College and attended the University of Southern California briefly.

Colton was a major junction on the railway system in California. During the 1920s its population nearly doubled to 8,000. The community supported a wide range of baseball teams; there was a local league as well as semipro teams that toured. Caster first appeared in box scores as a 19-year-old. Early in his career he made it known that he was a workhorse and would take the hill as often as his team needed. Playing in a winter league in 1927 for a team called West Coast Theatre, he pitched in both ends of a doubleheader against teams named L.A. Nippons and Torrance Merchants. He was pulled after six innings of the first game, but watched his team come back for a 9-7 win. Then he pitched a complete-game victory in the nightcap.

The next spring, Caster pitched for the Colton Cement Dusters before joining the Colton Merchants in a winter league. By this time, news of his talent had spread throughout California and he had signed a contract to join the San Francisco Mission Reds of the Pacific Coast League in 1929. That winter he played baseball, attended college, and played basketball for an independent team. In mid-February of 1929 he left for spring training with the Mission Reds and some early tutelage from manager Wade Killefer.

Caster was a right-handed thrower and hitter. He stood 6-feet-1-inch and weighed 180 pounds. After a month with the Missions, he was farmed out to the San Bernardino Padres in the newly formed Class-D California State League. His manager, former major-league outfielder Rube Ellis, recognized Caster's talent and made him the ace of the staff. Caster responded by leading the league in wins and winning percentage as well as strikeouts. He became a fan favorite because he "has a 'fast' ball and shows more zip on his twisters than any other hurler."[2]

The league disbanded in mid-June with the Padres in third place. Caster was one of the players elevated to the Reds roster. In 84 innings, he posted a 5-4 mark with a 4.71 ERA. Caster earned his first PCL win on June 20, when he relieved football great Ernie Nevers. Caster got one out to close the ninth and saw his team rally to win the game. The Reds made the playoffs in 1929 for the only time in their 12-year history, but lost to the Hollywood Stars.

In the offseason, on November 6, 1929, Caster married Daisy Jeanne Herlinger. She was a native of Colorado who had moved to San Bernardino and graduated from high school there a year after Caster left Colton High School. The couple had no children.

In 1930, Caster got off to a shaky start, losing his first start and following that with a rocky relief appearance. He righted himself and won three straight starts before a couple of rough outings shattered his confidence. He spent about a month in relief before he was returned to the rotation in early June. Three losses and a no-decision coupled with control issues forced the Reds to option Caster to the Globe Bears in the Class-D Arizona State League on July 6.

Caster continued to be inconsistent with Globe. The *Arizona Republic* credited him with a 6-7 regular-season mark for the playoff-bound Bears.[3] The Bears swept Phoenix in the first round as Caster tossed a complete-game victory in the second match-up. He lost the opener of the finals with the Bisbee Bees and then was hammered in a relief appearance. A scheduling disagreement led to a forfeit win for Bisbee to end the playoffs. Caster returned to the Bay Area and made six starts for the Missions, winning the last two. He closed out the season on the coast with an 8-10 mark and a 5.48 ERA.

Caster came to training camp in 1931 intent upon improving his craft. Wildness had eroded his confidence in 1930 and he worked on both his control and his mindset in tight situations. He had to learn to work out of jams, especially in late innings. He was put to an early test on March 16 in an exhibition game with the Detroit Tigers. He entered the game in the sixth and the Missions quickly put him in a hole by making two errors. Caster surrendered some runs, but kept his composure and finished the game. Mission rallied for an 8-6 win.

In 1930 Caster walked 78 in 128 innings. In 1931 he walked 79, but worked 236 innings. The Missions struggled to an 84-103 finish and just missed the cellar. Caster posted a 13-17 record. His season high points came on May 31, when he shut out Sacramento on four hits, and July 5 and September 8, when he tossed complete-game victories and hit home runs. He was scouted by the Pirates in July and the Phillies in September, but neither team made an offer.

Caster held out briefly in 1932, but reported to the Missions' training camp in Woodland, California, in excellent shape. He pitched a March 24 exhibition against the Chicago Cubs in San Francisco which the Missions won 11-4. The Missions were destined to finish in last place with a 71-117 record despite Ox Eckhardt's league-leading .371 batting average. Despite the positive start, Caster's season quickly turned sour. He did not record a win until April 29. An ankle injury and a bout with a dead arm made him ineffective.

On July 5, after Caster allowed four first-inning runs and retired only one batter, the Missions released him. He was quickly signed by Los Angeles. He lasted less than two innings in his first and only start for the Angels. In July and August, he made nine relief appearances before he was released along with Fred Haney and Homer Summa on September 1. He closed out the season with a 3-9 record.

The *San Francisco Chronicle* wrote on January 21, 1933, that Caster had been signed by the Seattle Indians. The writer offered that Caster had the ability, but that he "works so hard that he loses his stuff. If he had better poise and learned how to conserve his strength he could win in this league."[4]

The Indians opened the season poorly and were in last place at 4-10 before Caster saw much action. He got his first start on May 7 and lost to Portland. Nine days later he faced Oakland and beat the Oaks 11-5, helping his own cause with two doubles. On June 10, he blasted a three-run homer and pitched a complete-game 11-4 win over Hollywood. But the losses piled up faster than the wins. For the season, Caster went 12-19 for the Indians, who finished last in the PCL at 65-119.

The 1934 season opened on a bright note when Caster beat San Francisco 4-1, but that was his high point with the Indians. They sold him to Portland on May 5. Caster's game came together with the Beavers. He posted his finest ERA in the Pacific Coast League at 3.40, which led the team. He surrendered 9.46 hits per nine innings, by far his lowest total in the six seasons in the PCL. Connie Mack and the Athletics came calling and Caster went east along with Jack Wilson on September 6.

Caster made his major-league debut on September 10, 1934, in Cleveland. He had gone to a no-windup delivery and used it when he faced the Tribe's power trio of Earl Averill, Hal Trosky, and Joe Vosmik. He held the trio of .300 batters without a hit on his way to a 9-6 win. Roy Mahaffey pitched the ninth inning after Caster was touched for three runs in the eighth. At the plate, Caster poked a couple of singles and drove in two runs. Four days later he took on the Browns in St. Louis. He tossed a complete game but lost 5-2. On September 19 he went 10 innings in Chicago to beat the White Sox 5-3. He closed out his rookie season with two relief appearances, winning one and losing one. In 37 innings, Caster posted a 3.41 ERA to go with his 3-2 record. He batted .267 with 4 RBIs.

Caster's 37 innings put him 10th on the staff in work. At 26, he was the fourth oldest pitcher on the staff. The Athletics had finished fifth in 1934 and prospects looked good for 1935. Mack returned sluggers Jimmie Foxx and Bob Johnson, kept his infield intact, and added rookie Wally Moses to the outfield. But the pitching staff took a nosedive. Only Johnny Marcum and Roy Mahaffey put up better numbers in 1935 than in 1934. Sugar Cain and Joe Cascarella went from a combined 21 wins to just one and were both dealt. Bill Dietrich's ERA skyrocketed.

Caster took on the role of mop-up man in 1935. He appeared in 25 games and worked 63⅓ innings. Only four times did he find himself in an Athletics victory. At the close of the season he got his only start and gave up eight runs to Cleveland in a 10-0 loss. He finished 1-4 with a 6.25 ERA.

Caster returned to the Portland Beavers in 1936. There he was united with veteran catcher Earle Brucker. In their early sessions, Brucker was unimpressed with Caster's fastball or curve. "Is that all you got?" he asked. "What do you use for a change of pace?" Caster said he had a knuckleball, but catchers did not like him using it. "You throw it," Brucker said, "If I can't catch it, I'll run it down."[5]

With his pitching repertoire complete, Caster went on to his finest season. He won 25 games to lead the league and led in strikeouts with 234. The Beavers finished in first place and then won eight of nine playoff games to clinch the title. Caster netted three of the playoff victories to give him 28 wins for the year. He pocketed over $3,000 in prize money. Brucker and Caster joined the Philadelphia Athletics for 1937.

Caster began 1937 by ruining the April 23 Ladies Day in Washington. Before 15,000 spectators, he tossed a nifty four-hitter and won 7-1. He followed that performance with four complete games in his next five outings and found himself the ace of the Athletics staff. He posted a 12-19 record with a 4.43 ERA. His wins and ERA were both second on the team. He completed 19 of his 33 starts and tossed three shutouts. The first of those was against Cleveland on June 27. The 10-0 win snapped a personal six-game losing streak.

The following year, 1938, Caster stepped up his performance as the Athletics fell into the cellar. He went 16-20, throwing 20 complete games. Caster's ERA of 4.35 was more than a point below the team's total and below the league average, too. He tossed two shutouts. Only Bobo Newsom and Red Ruffing had more complete games and only Newsom worked more innings. Caster accomplished all this for a team that managed only 53 wins. His overall WAR of 5.0 was the best on the team.

Caster earned the honor of starting on Opening Day in 1939 and responded with a four-hit shutout of Washington. That would be the high point of a season in which he was plagued with arm troubles. He missed two weeks in May and June and then was shelved from July 9 to September 11. When he came back late in the season he was relegated to relief duties. He posted a 9-9 mark.

The 1940 season proved to be an even greater struggle for Caster. He dropped his first four decisions before earning a win in relief. He proceeded to lose seven more starts before finally earning a win in a June 26 complete game. He posted two wins in July on his way to a dismal 4-19 record. His ERA ballooned to 6.56. On November 16, he was picked up on waivers by the St. Louis Browns.

Caster continued his struggles in 1941 with the Browns by winning only 3 of 10 decisions and posting an ERA of 5.00. Luke Sewell took over as Browns manager in late May. Caster was given the role of game finisher and would never start another game in the majors. The statistic of a save did not exist in the 1940s, but baseball historians have added the statistic retroactively. Caster embraced his new role and became one of the game's best relievers. In 1942 he had an 8-2 record with five saves. His ERA was a sparkling 2.81. He followed that up with a 6-8 mark and eight saves in 1943. His ERA of 2.12 was the second best in the league for pitchers with more than 10 innings. His eight saves tied him with Johnny Murphy for fourth.

The Browns won the pennant in 1944 and Caster played a major role. His 12 saves tied him for the league lead. He had a 6-6 record and an ERA of 2.44.

Writer Frederick G. Lieb called him simply "the best relief pitcher in the majors."[6] Caster did not see any action in the World Series. In 1945 Caster struggled and was placed on waivers with a 6.89 ERA. The league-leading Detroit Tigers took a chance and claimed him on August 8. He immediately paid dividends by going 4⅓ and 4⅔ innings to earn victories on August 11 and 12. He suffered two rough outings versus the Yankees when he surrendered 10 runs in 8⅓ innings. Without those two outings, his ERA would have been 2.51; as it was, it soared to 3.86. With Detroit, he won five of six decisions and saved two games.

Caster saw action in Game Six of the World Series. With one out in the fifth, he relieved Virgil Trucks, who had surrendered four runs. He stranded two runners by getting Andy Pafko to pop up to third and striking out Bill Nicholson. The Tigers claimed the title in Game Seven and Caster added a nice bonus to his salary.

Caster had been eligible for military service throughout the war years. He was a member of the Naval Reserve and had been cleared for submarine duty. In the offseason, he worked in the Long Beach shipyards, which earned him a 2-B classification in 1944. However, he was still called for induction in 1944, but was not taken. It is unknown why he was never called to service.[7]

Caster returned to the Tigers in 1946. He recorded five saves and a 2-1 record, but with an ERA of 5.66 and at age 38, his career was near an end. He was released and in 1947 played for Hollywood and San Diego in the PCL. His season and career ended in a collision on a California highway. In 1950, he sued the driver and won a settlement, claiming the accident injured his pitching arm. In 1949 he was appointed manager of the Riverside Dons in the Class-C Sunset League. He was fired on September 11 after the team bus broke down 50 miles from a game in Las Vegas. Caster, in the eyes of the team president, did not do enough to get the team to the ballpark.

Caster retired from baseball and became a machinist with Douglas Aircraft. He was attending the company Christmas party on December 18, 1955, when he succumbed to a major heart attack. He was interred in the Sunnyside Mausoleum on the grounds of Forest Lawn Cemetery in Long Beach, California.

## SOURCES

In addition to the sources cited in the Notes, the author also relied on Baseball-Reference.com.

## NOTES

1 Red Smith, "Views of Sport," *Seattle Daily Times*, December 22, 1955: 25.

2 *San Bernardino County Sun*, May 29, 1929: 12.

3 *Arizona Republic*, September 2, 1930: 11.

4 "Charley Hall Sends Hurler to Missions," *San Francisco Chronicle*, January 21, 1933: 12.

5 Red Smith, "Views of Sport," *Seattle Daily Times*, December 22, 1955: 25.

6 Frederick G. Lieb, "Yank Jinx Big Threat to Browns," *The Sporting News*, June 8, 1944: 1.

7 His military information was on his HOF questionnaire filled out by Daisy Caster.

# JOHN COLEMAN

## BY JUSTIN MCKINNEY

**IT TAKES A SPECIAL KIND OF TALENT** for a pitcher to lose 20 games in a season. The pitcher has to pitch both poorly enough to lose, but well enough that he keeps getting chances to pitch. If losing 20 games takes talent, how much more talent does it take to lose 48 games in a season? That is the case of the ill-fated Jack Coleman, who in 1883 became the biggest loser in baseball history.

John Francis "Jack" Coleman was born to Irish immigrants John and Mary Coleman, though both his birthdate and birthplace are up for debate. Baseball-reference.com lists Coleman as having been born on March 6, 1863, in Saratoga Springs, New York. The original source of this information is a December 23, 1893, *New York Clipper* profile of Coleman.[1] However, the 1880 census shows Coleman being born in Illinois circa 1860. To complicate matters further, Coleman's death certificate provides a birth year of 1855 and a birthplace of Chicago. Based on contemporary accounts from his playing days and the census records, the 1860 birth year and Chicago birthplace seem most likely.

John was the fourth child born to the family. Coleman's father died when John was young; Mary was listed as a widow and seamstress on the 1870 census. The Coleman family had emigrated from Ireland to Canada and eventually settled in Chicago between 1857 and 1859. Young John was listed as a druggist on the 1880 census and alternately as a clerk in the 1880 Chicago city directory. Coleman's baseball career began around this time, when he appeared with the Acmes, a top Chicago amateur club.[2]

The first murmurings of Coleman's potential as a pitcher began in 1882, with the Peoria Reds, one of the top semipro clubs in the Midwest. The Reds would join Organized Baseball the following year in the fledgling Northwestern League. Coleman drew notice when he struck out 37 men in two games against a Chicago amateur team.[3] He was courted by the Fort Wayne Golden Eagles in September 1882, along with his catcher, Frank Ringo.[4] Coleman is also credited with having attended or played for Syracuse University in 1882, but this appears to be untrue.[5]

Coleman and his catcher Ringo were in high demand and signed with the newly formed Philadelphia Phillies in November 1882. The Phillies were set to join the National League for the 1883 season. The duo was recommended to Phillies President Al Reach by the legendary Cap Anson, who had practiced with the pair in Chicago.[6] This signing was not without controversy as Peoria Reds manager Charles Flynn indicated that the battery were reserved by the Peoria Reds for 1883 and claimed that the Phillies had stolen Coleman and Ringo.[7] The dispute was eventually resolved, as Reach claimed that neither Coleman nor Ringo had signed with Peoria for the coming season.[8] The fledgling Northwestern League gave up its claim to the players, seemingly to avoid conflict with the more powerful National League.

Coleman joined the Phillies for their first round of spring practice in late March. The club played the first exhibition game in franchise history at Philadelphia's Recreation Park on April 2, 1883, against the amateur Ashland club from Manayunk, Pennsylvania. The young pitcher was up to the task and he no-hit the Ashlands and struck out 13 batters. The Phillies won by a final score of 11-0. The *Philadelphia Times* commented that Coleman "seems to have mastered all the known curves, and besides, has a slow, drop ball."[9] Reach and manager Bob "Death to Flying Things" Ferguson must have thought they had a great find in the right-hander. The Phillies and Coleman continued their strong play with three straight wins against local amateur clubs and two wins in Baltimore against the American Association Orioles. On April 16, over 6,000 people were in attendance to watch Coleman pitch against the rival Philadelphia Athletics. The eventual pennant-winning Athletics were no match for Coleman's "low drop ball" and "very deceptive" delivery and the Phillies took the game by a score of 8-1.[10] The club did not use Coleman again until April 26, when he was in the pitcher's box for the club's first loss of the exhibition season, 10-2 to the Athletics.

The Phillies and Coleman began their first major-league season on May 1 in Philadelphia, facing off against Charles "Old Hoss" Radbourn and the Providence Grays. Coleman pitched well and the Phillies staked him to a 3-0 lead going into the top of the eighth inning. Coleman unraveled and allowed four runs on a walk to Radbourn and hits by Jerry Denny, Barney Gilligan, Jack Farrell, and Paul Hines. The Grays held the lead and won, 4-3. This was the start of a losing trend for both Coleman and the Phillies. It was the first loss of Coleman's major-league career and the first of more than 10,000 losses for the Phillies, baseball's losingest franchise.

The following day, Coleman lost 4-1 to Radbourn's Grays. He was back in the box again on May 4 for an 11-10 loss to Charles Buffinton and the Boston Beaneaters. Coleman started seven of the Phillies' first eight games. He was spelled by right-hander Jack Neagle, who garnered the first regular-season win in Phillies' history on May 14 in Chicago. Coleman got his first career win the following day in Detroit, with a 10-inning, 4-3 victory over the Wolverines. On May 28, he outdueled future Hall of Famer Pud Galvin in an 11-inning, 3-2 victory in Buffalo. By the end of May, the Phillies had a dismal record of 4-16 and Coleman had started 15 games.

Despite the club's poor record, Coleman pitched quite well at times. He won back-to-back games for the first time in mid-June. On June 12, he defeated Jim McCormick and the Cleveland Blues 4-3 in 12 innings and followed it up with his first career shutout, a 2-0 victory over Galvin and the Bisons, on June 14. Two days later, on June 16, Coleman defeated the legendary "Pud" for the third time, 4-2. While Coleman was showing great potential, the Phillies were plagued by their inability to find a capable second pitcher. Jack Neagle was let go after a 22-4 shellacking by Buffalo on June 15. Rookie Edgar Smith was given a trial on June 20, but was clearly overmatched in a 29-4 blowout in Boston.

With this futility it is no wonder that Coleman started the next seven straight games. This included his second shutout, a 4-0 victory over Charlie Sweeney in Providence on June 26. Rookie right-hander Art Hagan was signed to spell Coleman and the duo alternated pitching duties throughout the summer. Coleman's seeming dominance over Galvin ended in July, when he was battered by the Buffalo Bisons to the tune of a 21-6 loss on July 17 and a 25-5 demolition on July 19. It was clear that Coleman was exhausted, but due to the club's small roster, the overworked right-hander was also used in center field and left field on his offdays. He was showing promise as a left-handed hitter and he would finish the year with a .234 batting average with 32 RBIs. On August 4, Coleman pitched a 6-0 shutout in Detroit over Stump Weidman and downed future New York Gothams star and future Hall of Famer Smiling Mickey Welch 7-3 on August 9.

The club then lost 14 straight games, including Hagan's disastrous 28-0 loss to Providence on August 21 that led to his release. The newly acquired veteran Blondie Purcell broke the losing streak with two straight wins on September 3 and September 7. Despite the abysmal record of the Phillies, Coleman's pitching was garnering positive reviews. *Sporting Life* described him as "a very quiet lad, a fair batter and a promising young pitcher."[11] Around this time, the American Association's Cincinnati Red Stockings were reportedly interested in acquiring Coleman, but Phillies' President Al Reach turned down the offer for the twirler.[12]

Coleman's final victory of the 1883 season came in a 14-8 victory over Buffalo on September 19 in Philadelphia. This win would be his 12th of the year and his fourth over Galvin and the Bisons. Coleman made his final start in a 9-3 loss to Detroit on September 21 and he made one more relief appearance, on September 26. The Phillies' inaugural season mercifully closed on September 29. The club finished a dismal 17-81, 46 games behind the first-place Beaneaters.

The young hurler experienced perhaps the most unique rookie season in all of baseball history. He finished with a record of 12-48, an ERA of 4.87, and 159 strikeouts. Using modern statistics it is possible to contextualize Coleman's performance. While his ERA+ of 63 was considerably below average, Coleman was greatly hindered by the porous Phillies' defense. The first-year franchise put up one of the most dismal defensive performances in history. The club committed 639 errors in 99 games, almost 100 more than the next worst team, while its .553 defensive efficiency rating remains the worst mark in National League history.[13] Coleman's FIP (Fielding Independent Pitching) was 3.34, a mark good for 12th in the league ahead of such established stars as Mickey Welch and Fred Goldsmith. Despite the pitcher's relative effectiveness, the dismal team defense ensured that Coleman set multiple single-season records that will never be equaled. Apart from the record 48 losses, he set records for most hits allowed, 772, and most earned runs, 291. Remarkably, Coleman's 538⅓ innings pitched were only good for a distant third place on the leaderboard behind the legendary workhorses Galvin and Radbourn.

The Phillies thought enough of Jack Coleman to place him on their reserve list after the season. In the offseason, Jack returned to his native Chicago. In February 1884, he competed in a handball match for a purse of $50. Coleman was described by the *Daily Inter Ocean* as "a well-known athlete and reputed to be a hard hand ball hitter."[14] On March 2, the *Philadelphia Times* reported that he was training with veteran outfielder Jack Remsen in a Chicago gymnasium.[15] At 5-feet-9 and 170 pounds, Coleman was reputed to be a great wrestler and very strong. He was an early fitness enthusiast in a time when many of his contemporaries eschewed offseason workouts. In 1890, *Sporting Life* described Jack's training regimen, noting that he "always had a penchant to show a huge forearm and biceps and a back full of hard knotty muscles, and accordingly haunted a gymnasium through the winter and swung clubs in the summer."[16]

The 1884 Phillies would be managed by one of the game's legendary figures, Harry Wright. Wright was the mastermind and star of baseball's first professional team, the 1869 Cincinnati Red Stockings. He would go on to manage baseball's first professional dynasty, the 1872-1875 Boston Red Stockings of the National Association. His presence was enough for the *Philadelphia Times* to declare optimistically: "History will not repeat itself this year, so far as the Philadelphia Club is concerned, if the prestige gained by the new manager amounts to anything."[17]

Coleman entered the 1884 season on a high note. The Phillies, led in part by Coleman's pitching and timely hitting, had taken the second annual city series from the rival Athletics, six games to five. However, Coleman's role as number-one starter was being usurped by 21-year-old rookie phenom Charlie Ferguson. Before his untimely death in 1888 at age 25, Ferguson had established himself as baseball's greatest all-around player. Wright was determined not to overuse either man by the standards of the times, so he alternated Ferguson and Coleman in the pitcher's box. Coleman was in left field for the Phillies' 13-2 Opening Day victory over Detroit on May 1. The next day Coleman pitched a three-hit, 3-0 shutout over Detroit. Things were looking up when the club won again on May 3 over the Chicago White Stockings, giving the Phillies' their first-ever three-game winning streak.

This brief flurry of success was short-lived. On May 5, Coleman was hit hard in a 12-7 loss to Chicago's Larry Corcoran. He rebounded with a 12-1 win over Buffalo on May 12, but lost his next five starts to close out the month. In late May, the Phillies added the hard-throwing Jim McElroy to spell Coleman. Jack, not surprisingly, based on his usage thus far in his career, was now suffering from a lame arm. The Phillies continued to use him in center field despite his arm troubles. It was a different time: There was no disabled list in 1884 and unless a player was physically crippled, he was expected to play. By the time Coleman returned to pitching for a 16-6 blowout loss to the New York Gothams on June 10, the once promising Phillies were now 9-24.

Coleman's right arm was well enough by late June that he had resumed regular pitching duties. The results continued to be lackluster, however, and Coleman's health came into question again. After a 7-1 loss to Detroit on July 9, in which he was described as being "out of condition and having little speed,"[18] the overworked hurler was removed from regular pitching duties. In just his second season, his pitching career seemed in jeopardy. Wright would give Coleman three more starts that summer, culminating with a 9-4 loss in New York on August 13. The following week, Coleman and his personal catcher, Ringo, were both released. Ringo had hit a dismal .132 in 26 games for the Phillies. The *Daily Inter Ocean* commented on Coleman's release, chiding the Philadelphia management for overusing the young pitcher in the spring by having him pitch 19 consecutive games against the Athletics, which left him unable to "make a creditable showing in the box."[19] While the claim that Coleman pitched 19 straight exhibition games was fabricated, the damage done to Jack's right arm through the Phillies' abuse was very real.

Coleman and Ringo were not out of work long, as the Philadelphia Athletics of the American Association came calling and signed the battery in late August. After his arrival with the Athletics, Coleman was used in the outfield almost exclusively, despite fielding an abysmal .743 in 24 games. This was down from the already subpar .844 fielding average he had in 27 games in the outfield with the Phillies. Manager Lon Knight evidently was not confident in his new acquisition's arm health and used Coleman to pitch only twice the rest of the season, 6-2 losses to the St. Louis Brown on September 7 and October 9.

Coleman's final numbers for 1884 were below average. He went 5-17 with a 4.72 ERA in 175⅓ innings, just about as well as his rookie season but in far fewer innings. He hit .230, including a meager .206 in 28 games with the Athletics, while notching his first two career home runs. His arm injury, poor fielding in the outfield, and mediocre hitting would seem to suggest his major-league career was on the rocks. The Athletics must have seen something in spite of his poor performance. In late December, it was reported that Coleman would be the club's starting center fielder and change pitcher for the 1885 season.[20]

The Athletics' optimism was rewarded when on March 15, 1885, the *Philadelphia Times* reported that "Coleman has fully recovered the use of his arm and promises to do good service for the Athletics this season."[21] Jack was given the role of starting right fielder while his pitching appearances became increasingly sporadic. He would make just three starts and five relief appearances all season. The Athletics leaned heavily on the veteran Bobby Mathews as their number-one pitcher, which lessened the need for Coleman to pitch. In addition, Jack was still suffering from arm troubles; the June 24, 1885, issue of *Sporting Life* reported that "Coleman is not anxious to pitch. He says he can pitch a straight ball all day long, but as soon as he tries to curve his arm becomes lame."[22]

Fortunately for the Athletics and for Coleman's career prospects, he turned out to be a very good hitter and his pitching ability was no longer his main attribute. While he remained a below-average fielder, finishing the year with an .844 fielding percentage against the league average for right fielders of .879, he did have 23 outfield assists, good for fourth in the league. *Sporting Life* noted that "Coleman has shown great improvement as a right fielder since he first assumed the position and his batting is great."[23] Near the end of the season, Jack "badly strained a ligament near the elbow" during practice and it was feared he would be permanently disabled.[24] The injury caused him to miss the final few games of the season and it was speculated that a permanent move to first base might be in his future.

Despite the injury, the former pitcher ended the 1885 season entrenched in the American Association leader board. In 96 games, he hit .299, good for eighth in the league. He added a .345 on-base percentage (10th), a .415 slugging percentage (10th), and a .760 OPS (ninth). He also added three home runs and was sixth in the American Association with 70 RBIs. His 133 OPS+ was good for 11th in the circuit. Despite Coleman's strong hitting, the Athletics finished the season with a 55-57 record and a distant fourth-place behind the dynastic St. Louis Brown Stockings.

The 1885 season was the best year of Jack's professional career and also brought significant changes to his personal life. He was married to Maggie, a Philadelphia native, in the fall and he spent his first-ever offseason in Philadelphia, relocating from his native Chicago. The *Philadelphia Times* reported in March 1886 that the former pitcher turned outfielder was training along with Joe Quest, Orator Shafer, Fred Corey, Jack O'Brien, and Jocko Milligan in a Philadelphia gymnasium. Jack was described as being "in excellent condition and his arm is now under perfect control."[25] It was suggested that Coleman would be expected to resume pitching duties in 1886 as well. The resuscitation of Coleman's right arm was seemingly becoming a yearly concern.

The rumors of a move to first base proved unfounded; Jack opened the 1886 season as the starting right fielder for the Athletics. The proclamations of his return to the pitcher's box proved mostly untrue: His only start of the season was a 5-1 victory over Cincinnati on July 5. In July, a well-known Philadelphia physician, Dr. Seth Pancoast, boasted that he could heal Coleman's right arm with a months-long treatment, though it is unclear if this offer was ever taken up.[26] It was apparent that despite these rumblings about Coleman's pitching abilities, the Athletics saw his primary value as a hitter and used him as their number-three or cleanup hitter for the majority of the season. The breakout hitter of 1885 was slowed somewhat in 1886. Coleman's batting average slumped to .246, with a meager .296 on-base percentage. While his average dropped by 53 points, he maintained his power with 16 triples and 65 RBIs in 121 games. The Athletics were not impressed with his play and released Coleman in September.

The rival Pittsburgh Alleghenys, on their way to a strong second-place finish, quickly snapped Coleman up and installed him in left field. His bat was rejuvenated and he closed the season with a flourish, hitting .349 with 9 RBIs in 11 games for the Pittsburgh club. He became a fan favorite along the way for his heavy hitting. His overall season numbers appear quite modest: a batting line of .254/.302/.355 with 74 RBIs and 29 stolen bases. In the context of the 1886 American Association season, however, his numbers were quite good. He completed the season with an above-average OPS+ of 108. His 17 triples were good for second place in the league, while his 74 RBIs were seventh.

Coleman returned to Philadelphia for the off-season, where the *Philadelphia Times* noted he was a "daily visitor to the gymnasium."[27] In November 1886, it was announced that Coleman and the Pittsburgh Alleghenys would become the first team to move from the American Association to the National League. The Alleghenys were one of the founding members of the Association, but despite a strong second-place finish in 1886, manager Horace P. Phillips was quick to cite the club's shabby treatment in the Sam Barkley affair as a prime reason for the club's jump to the National League.[28] That affair involved St. Louis Brown Stockings second baseman Sam Barkley, who was put up for sale by St. Louis. The second baseman signed with both the Baltimore Orioles and the Pittsburgh Alleghenys in the spring of 1886. As a result of signing with both clubs, Barkley was suspended by the American Association, while its officials tried to determine which club had the rights to Barkley.[29] Eventually it was resolved that Barkley would join the Alleghenys, but the aftermath left a bitter taste in the mouth of manager Phillips and his team.

The coming of the 1887 season brought the now-annual announcement in the media that Coleman would return to the pitcher's box. Jack's prospective return to pitching was reportedly motivated by the drastic rule changes that both the National League and American Association agreed to for 1887. The pitching distance remained 50 feet, but pitchers were now encouraged to start at the back of the pitchers' box, making the true pitching distance 55 feet 6 inches. Meanwhile five balls would constitute a walk, down from six, and in the most galling change, it was announced that that batters would get four strikes instead of three. In January 1887, Coleman announced his intentions to pitch under the new rules and the Alleghenys were reportedly eager to comply.[30]

Coleman signed for a salary of $1,500 for the 1887 season.[31] Despite his strong hitting, this salary placed him as one of the lowest paid players on the club, with the newly acquired former Cleveland Blues and Chicago White Stockings ace Jim McCormick commanding the largest salary on the club at $3,000.[32] In late March, Coleman arrived in Pittsburgh filled with "confidence and vigor"[33] to begin training with the club. Despite his confidence, it was reported in early April that his arm was "still too weak to permit his pitching this year in old-time form."[34] In lieu of Coleman's return to pitching, it was predicted confidently that he would be "the patient man of the club this season as he makes every effort to secure a base on balls or a sure hit."[35] His speed also garnered attention when it was reported that he was the fastest man on the club, able to run the bases in 16 seconds.[36] In mid-April, multiple reports suggested that Coleman's arm was nearing full strength, but evidently the Alleghenys were not in agreement, and 1887 was the first year of his professional career in which he did not pitch.

With a strong rotation buoyed by his old rival, the indefatigable Pud Galvin, the hard-throwing left-hander Ed Morris, who won 41 games in 1886 as a 23-year-old, and 31-game winner Jim McCormick, the Alleghenys seemed like a strong pennant contender. The promise of the 1887 season would soon disintegrate into a tragic, tumultuous, and frustrating one for the Alleghenys. In July, veteran first baseman and team leader Alex McKinnon, batting .340 and in the midst of a career year was diagnosed with typhoid. He died on July 24. Left-hander Morris struggled to adapt to the new league and won only 14 games, while veteran McCormick, with over 4,000 innings under his belt, would struggle along to a 13-23 record in his final major-league season. Meanwhile, without McKinnon, the Alleghenys lineup was one of the league's weakest, with Fred Carroll, Bill Kuehne, and Coleman being the only above-average hitters.[37] The local media also blamed the club's failures on dissension and booze, as the so-called "California clique" of Tom Brown, Carroll, and Morris was seen as a toxic and debaucherous force on the club's morale.[38] The team limped to a 55-69-1 record, good for sixth place, a far cry from their second-place finish in the American Association the previous year.

Despite the team's struggles, Coleman turned in his third consecutive strong hitting season, with a slash line of .293/.337/.396 and a 109 OPS+. He chipped in two home runs, 54 RBIs, and 25 stolen bases. He also showed drastic improvement in the field, as he fielded .899 against a league average of .883 for right fielders. *Sporting Life* commented on his much improved defense, noting, "It is hard to realize to see his field work here that it is the same Coleman."[39] The *Philadelphia Times* even listed Coleman as the league's best defensive right fielder on July 10.[40] This was a remarkable turnaround from his poor fielding of the previous two seasons and a testament to his strong work ethic and adaptability. Coleman culminated his strong year, by becoming a father for the first time, when his son John Francis Coleman Jr. was born in Philadelphia on September 29, 1887.

Despite playing for the rival Alleghenys, Coleman remained a popular figure in Philadelphia. The local papers made frequent reference to his numerous friends in town and how well supported he was by his old hometown. As a show of gratitude, he was presented with a $225 diamond pin by the Philadelphia faithful on July 4.[41] In the summer Coleman joined the Eagle Social Club with several other major leaguers including his old teammates Blondie Purcell, Cub Stricker, and Orator Shaffer. The Eagles would be a great help to Jack in the offseason of 1887, when he came down with an undisclosed illness. The November 16, 1887, issue of *Sporting Life* reported that the Eagles had offered him assistance while he was bedridden with an illness during the previous weeks.[42] In mid-December, it was reported the Coleman was still sick but improving rapidly. On December 24, the *Pittsburgh Post* reported that Coleman was planning to retire due both to his illness and family pressure to quit, but also conceded that the threat might just "mean that John wants an increase of salary."[43]

Coleman's retirement threat proved to be short-lived. The January 11, 1888, *Sporting Life* reported that "Coleman, who attempted to play the mother-don't-want-me-to-play-ball-any-more racket on Pittsburg, has returned to the fold and signed to play with the Smoky City team next year."[44] It was reported that Jack would play first base in the coming year since the Alleghenys had signed former Chicago White Stocking and future evangelist Billy Sunday to man right field. Despite this potential rivalry, Coleman and Sunday would become lifelong friends.[45] Coleman continued working out daily at the gymnasium in the offseason and in March it was reported that he was once again "doctoring his elbow in hope that he may one day be able to pitch again."[46] Alleghenys manager Horace Phillips reported that while Coleman's arm was improving to the point that he could now throw overhand, he would not be able to pitch due to pain in his elbow.[47] It was rumored in early April that Louisville, Baltimore, Washington, and Indianapolis were all angling for Coleman's release from the Alleghenys. Pittsburgh would not budge and despite spraining his ankle in early April in an exhibition game, Coleman was in the lineup when the season opened on April 20 against Detroit.

Somewhat surprisingly given the offseason rumors of a move to first base, Coleman was slotted in right field. It soon became evident that he was not fully recovered from his offseason illness. Both his hitting and fielding suffered in the first month of the season, and the Pittsburgh papers suggested that Irish-born outfielder Jocko Fields might take over in right if the poor play continued. The *Pittsburgh Press* asserted that Coleman's poor play was caused by a blood-purifying medication that had impaired his eyesight and caused general weakness.[48] Coleman's demise was seemingly temporary; by the end of May he had regained his batting eye with a string of multi-hit games.

Coleman continued his streaky play all season long, with the local papers alternating between calling for his release and celebrating his return to form. At one point the *Pittsburgh Press* called him the weak point of the Pittsburgh outfield and lamented that he could no longer throw.[49] Despite these complaints about Coleman's defense and his poor arm, he still finished the season with 20 outfield assists in 91 games and a .928 fielding average against a league average of .902. Jack also saw time at first base, backing up future Hall of Famer Jake Beckley, who made his major-league debut in June. Coleman ended the year with his weakest hitting season since becoming a position player with a slash line of .231/.285/.274. In late September, Coleman reportedly made an offer of $1,000 to wrestle any man in the National League in a catch-as-catch-can wrestling match.[50] Silver Flint, the Chicago catcher and a close friend of Coleman's accepted the offer, but it is not known if a match ever took place.[51]

Despite his poor play and the criticism of the Pittsburgh newspapers, Coleman was reserved in October by the club. In December, Coleman's fighting prowess was tested when he fought a mysterious Englishman after a debate about the "relative merits of base ball and cricket."[52] Coleman turned out to be no pugilist and was knocked down by his foe, ending the fight. Jack resumed baseball activities and participated in an indoor baseball game in Philadelphia on

New Year's Day 1889. In mid-January, he departed for Hot Springs, Arkansas, to train with teammate Fred "Sure Shot" Dunlap and Detroit Wolverines pitcher Pete Conway.[53] Despite his best efforts to maintain his condition, Jack's time with the Alleghenys was coming to an end. On April 26 he was given his 10-day release by manager Horace Phillips, as the club chose to keep pitcher-outfielder Al Maul for his ability to pitch occasionally.[54]

Fuming over his release and his poor treatment by the local press, Coleman wrote to *Sporting Life*, where he lamented the press's criticism of his throwing arm and put up a $100 bet to any man on the club who could outthrow him.[55] He received multiple offers from minor-league clubs, but was reportedly considering joining a touring wrestling troupe in lieu of any major-league offers.[56] In mid-May, the Philadelphia papers strangely began to agitate for the Athletics to sign Coleman as a pitcher. This was unusual because Coleman had not pitched regularly since 1884 and the primary reason for his release from Pittsburgh was his inability to serve as a change pitcher. But Coleman was diligently practicing his pitching with Athletics catcher Jack Brennan, hoping for a trial with the club.[57] The hard work paid off on May 27, when Coleman was signed on trial by the Athletics. Reports of his rejuvenated right arm seemed to prove true when he debuted for the Athletics by pitching a 6-1 complete-game victory over Cincinnati on May 30. The *Philadelphia Inquirer* wrote that Coleman "pitched a remarkable game … (and) had perfect command of the ball."[58] Coleman had adopted a now-antiquated underhand pitching style to compensate for his arm troubles.[59] The prodigal right-hander's triumphant return to pitching continued on June 6, when he defeated the last-place Louisville Colonels, 16-3. On June 20 against Columbus, Coleman made his only appearance of the season in the outfield when he replaced Harry Stovey in the fourth inning. Showing his rust, the left fielder made a crucial three-run error in the eighth inning that contributed to the As' 7-6 defeat.

In July, when the A's traveled west, Coleman was left at home and rumors of his release swirled.[60] He remained with the club and next appeared on the mound in a 23-10 exhibition loss to the Atlantic Association's Jersey City Skeeters on July 22.[61] This poor result perhaps explains why Athletics manager Billy Sharsig was reluctant to use Coleman in the pitcher's box despite his initial success. The Athletics were a strong club, had little use for Coleman in the field, and did not trust his health enough to use him regularly as a pitcher, even as the club struggled to find pitching. He returned to the pitcher's box in early September, losing 8-3 to Kansas City on September 2. He defeated Kansas City 12-6 on September 4 in a seven-inning game for what would be his final major-league victory. He made his last start for the Athletics on September 9, lasting just two innings in a 10-7 loss to Louisville. In early October, Coleman was released and announced that he would sue the Athletics for his remaining salary.[62] His final record was 3-2 in five starts with a 2.91 ERA, but his health remained an issue as he sought out his next major-league opportunity.

On January 2, 1890, the *Pittsburgh Dispatch* reported that Coleman might return to the Phillies, where he began his career in 1883. The article said that he had suffered from malaria in 1889, which explained his long absence from the Athletics. By October, the normally 170-pound pitcher was down to 138 pounds.[63] But thanks to his workout regimen of "daily exercise, using dumbbells and Indian clubs," he was now up to 188 pounds and experiencing "no pain in his pitching arm."[64] The Phillies' rumors proved fruitless, so Coleman went to Hot Springs to work out with the Cleveland National League club.[65] Failing to garner a major-league job, he joined the Toronto Canucks as an outfielder and pitcher at a reported salary of $2,100.[66] He hit .280 in 49 games and was 11-3 as a pitcher. This prompted the Alleghenys to take an interest. The club, decimated by defections of nearly all of its top players to the rival Players League, was on its way to a miserable 23-113 record and a place on the list of worst major-league teams of all time. Desperate for pitching, the Aleghenys signed Jack on July 14 and he made his first appearance the following day in an 8-4 complete game loss to the Phillies. He started in right field on July 17 and was on the mound on July 18 in a 17-7 loss to Brooklyn. This was his final major-league appearance. He was released the next week. He actively sought another job, but found no takers for the remainder of the season.

The demise of John Coleman's major-league career could possibly be traced directly to his overuse in 1883. Quite commendably, he was able to recast himself as a solid hitter and rapidly improving outfielder. He kept himself in great physical condition and overcame two serious illnesses to resume his career. However, Coleman never seemed able to let go of his hunger to pitch, though his right arm never recovered fully. Neither the Athletics nor the Alleghenys ever seemed entirely comfortable with him as a position player.

With Coleman's major-league career now over, he embarked on the second phase of his career, as a minor-league journeyman. He applied for the Toronto manager's job in 1891, but was unsuccessful.[67] In June 1891, he signed to play first base for Lebanon, Pennsylvania, of the Eastern Association. He was released after hitting just .213 in 28 games. He was quickly signed by Omaha of the Western Association, but his batting eye had not returned and he was let go after hitting a meager .191 in 16 games.

Never one to be counted out, Coleman rebounded in 1892, hitting .342 while splitting time between Danville and Lebanon of the Pennsylvania State League. He followed up with another strong season in 1893, hitting .295 in 70 games split between York, Harrisburg, and Scranton. He also went 23-12 as a pitcher. He was reported to have signed with King Kelly's Allentown team in 1894, but he did not appear with the club.[68]

Coleman remained a prominent figure in Philadelphia sporting circles during this time. In early 1895, he was rumored to be taking up a wrestling career, with his former teammate Fred Dunlap as a financial backer.[69] It is not clear if Coleman played baseball either professionally or semiprofessionally in 1895 or 1896. In 1897 he made his return to professional baseball. He began the year pitching for the Bristol, Pennsylvania, club and eventually joined the Philadelphia Athletics of the Atlantic League. He hit .242 in 32 games, primarily playing first base. His arm was finished, though, as he went 0-3, allowing 21 runs in 15 innings of work.

Coleman's professional baseball career was over, though he would continue to play semipro baseball throughout Pennsylvania. After over a decade of living in Philadelphia, Coleman also became something of a nomad. He does not appear on the census in 1900 or 1910, perhaps because he was moving around so much. He was reported to be living in Harlem in 1899[70] and was said to have a good position in Pittsburgh in 1901.[71] His release from the Homestead, Pennsylvania, semipro club was noted in the May 4, 1903, issue of the *Pittsburgh Daily Post*.[72] Around this time, his son, John Francis Coleman Jr., was also beginning a baseball career. He played for various teams in the low-level minors from 1906 to 1910 and he was reported to be a protégé of Connie Mack.[73]

Coleman was back in Philadelphia in 1908 looking for work as an umpire.[74] In 1909, it was reported that he was set to inherit $250,000 after the death of his brother Michael, though it is unclear if he ever received the money.[75] On February 9, 1910, The *Gazette Times* reported that Coleman, now living in McKeesport, Pennsylvania, was being considered as the referee for the James J. Jeffries-Jack Johnson heavyweight championship bout.[76] The article noted that Coleman had assisted Jeffries in his preparations to fight James J. Corbett back in 1900 and the two had remained friends. Coleman did not end up refereeing the fight and by 1912, he was living in Detroit.

A profile in the *Detroit Free Press* saw Coleman lamenting the easy life of current major leaguers. He boasted of pitching in 13 straight exhibition games on one spring-training trip and that it did not bother him at all.[77] Coleman's claim is apocryphal. In 1883 and 1884, he shared pitching duties for the Phillies in the spring. His claim that the overwork didn't bother him also is problematic; after pitching 538 innings in 1883, he battled severe arm problems for the remainder of his career and never returned to full-time pitching duties in the major leagues.

Coleman remained in Detroit for the remainder of his life. He found work in a bowling alley. He died on May 31, 1922, at the approximate age of 62 after being hit by an automobile.[78] He was survived by his son John Jr. and three daughters.

John Coleman's career was a fascinating one with many facets. While he is almost singularly remembered for the remarkably futility of his rookie season in 1883, he deserves praise for reinventing himself as a hard-hitting and steady-fielding outfielder. He was also one of the earliest players to adopt a dedicated fitness regimen and by all accounts was a good teammate and stable figure in an era when such men were not common.

In 1908, John Coleman was quoted in *Sporting Life*: "The dead are soon forgotten. In fact, most of us are lucky if we are not forgotten while we are alive."[79] This sentiment is a fitting eulogy for Coleman, who continued to persevere in his pursuit of diamond glory long after his major-league career was over. Let us not forget about John Coleman, who was much more than just baseball's biggest loser.

## SOURCES

In addition to the sources cited in the Notes, the author also consulted Baseball-reference.com, Familysearch.org, Genealogybank.com, LA84.org, Newspapers.com, Retrosheet.org, and SABR's Biographical Project

## NOTES

1 "John F. Coleman," *New York Clipper*, December 23, 1893.
2 "Charles Getzein, Pitcher of the Detroits," *New York Clipper*, October 6, 1888.
3 "John F. Coleman," *New York Clipper*, December 23, 1893.
4 "The Golden Eagles Still Soar," *Fort Wayne* (Indiana) *Sentinel*, September 15, 1882.
5 The Syracuse University Archives has no record of Coleman attending the school. Mary O'Brien, Syracuse University Archives, email to the author, April 27, 2017.
6 "Coleman and Ringo," *New York Clipper*, January 27, 1883.
7 "Base Ball," *Fort Wayne* (Indiana) *Daily News*, February 8, 1883.
8 "O.K.," *Cincinnati Enquirer*, February 18, 1883.
9 "The Philadelphias First Contest," *Philadelphia Times*, April 3, 1883.
10 "Playing Ball in the Rain," *Philadelphia Times*, April 17, 1883.
11 "League Pitchers," *Sporting Life*, September 3, 1883.
12 "Looking for a Pitcher," *Sporting Life*, September 17, 1883.
13 "BASEBALL: A History of Team Defense (Part I of II)," *Baseball Crank*, June 2, 2011, baseballcrank.com/archives2/2011/06/baseball_a_hist.php.
14 *Daily Inter Ocean* (Chicago), February 3, 1884.
15 "Base Ball Notes," *Philadelphia Times*, March 2, 1884.
16 "A Player's Career," *Sporting Life*, December 27, 1890.
17 "The Philadelphia Club," *Philadelphia Times*, March 23, 1884.
18 "Philadelphia Beaten," *Philadelphia Times*, July 10, 1884.
19 "Other Games," *Daily Inter Ocean*, August 21, 1884.
20 "Base Ball," *Philadelphia Times*, December 28, 1884.
21 "Base Ball Notes," *Philadelphia Times*, March 15, 1885.
22 "Notes and Comments," *Sporting Life*, June 24, 1885.
23 "Notes and Comments," *Sporting Life*, August 5, 1885.
24 "Notes and Comments," *Sporting Life*, October 7, 1885.
25 "The Ball Players," *Philadelphia Times*, March 14, 1886.
26 "The Local Season," *Sporting Life*, July 28, 1886.
27 "Base Ball Notes," *Philadelphia Times*, November 14, 1886.
28 "Hustling Horace Talks," *Philadelphia Times*, November 28, 1886.
29 "Sam Barkley," *BR Bullpen*, baseball-reference.com/bullpen/Sam_Barkley.
30 "Base Ball Notes," *Philadelphia Times*, January 9, 1887.
31 "Notes and Comments," *Sporting Life*, August 3, 1887.
32 Ibid.
33 "More Players Arrive," *Pittsburgh Post*, March 24, 1887.
34 "Notes and Comments," *Sporting Life*, April 6, 1887.
35 "Base Ball Notes," *Pittsburgh Post*, April 9, 1887.
36 "Base Ball Gossip," *Philadelphia Times*, April 24, 1887.
37 As measured by today's OPS+ statistic.
38 "Anson's Great Work," *Pittsburgh Post*, July 9, 1887.
39 "Philadelphia News," *Sporting Life*, July 6, 1887.
40 "Base Ball News," *Philadelphia Times*, July 10, 1887.
41 "Base Ball Notes," *Philadelphia Times*, July 4, 1887.
42 "Pittsburg Pencillings," *Sporting Life*, November 16, 1887.
43 "Coleman May Retire," *Pittsburgh Post*, December 24, 1887.
44 "Washington Whispers," *Sporting Life*, January 11, 1888.
45 "Auto Victim Diamond Star Back in 80's," *Detroit Free Press*, June 1, 1922.
46 "Base Ball Briefs," *Pittsburgh Press*, March 15, 1888.
47 "Base Ball Briefs," *Pittsburgh Press*, March 6, 1888.

## 20-GAME LOSERS

48 "Sporting," *Pittsburgh Press*, May 8, 1888.

49 "Sporting," *Pittsburgh Press*, June 22, 1888.

50 "League Notes," *Chicago Tribune*, September 17, 1888.

51 "Base Ball Notes," *Philadelphia Times*, September 30, 1888.

52 "Philadelphia Pointers," *Sporting Life*, December 26, 1888.

53 "Base Ball Notes," *Philadelphia Times*, January 6, 1889.

54 "Coleman Released," *Pittsburgh Dispatch*, April 27, 1889.

55 "A Blast From Coleman," *Sporting Life*, May 8, 1889.

56 "Notes and Comments," *Sporting Life*, May 22, 1889.

57 Ibid.

58 "John Coleman Pitches a Winning Game for the Athletics," *Philadelphia Inquirer*, May 31, 1889.

59 "About Coleman's Pitching, *Pittsburgh Dispatch*, June 1, 1889.

60 "Sporting Notes," *Pittsburgh Post*, July 8, 1889.

61 "The Athletics Done Up, *Philadelphia Inquirer,* July 23, 1889.

62 "Ball Notes," *Wilkes-Barre* (Pennsylvania) *News*, October 5, 1889.

63 "May Sign Coleman," *Pittsburgh Dispatch*, January 2, 1890.

64 Ibid.

65 "Sporting Notes," *Chicago Inter Ocean*, April 3, 1890.

66 "Base Ball Briefs," *Philadelphia Times*, April 28, 1890.

67 "Toronto Tips," *Sporting Life*, March 14, 1891.

68 "Glints From the Diamond," *Scranton Tribune*, April 19, 1894.

69 "Sporting Notes," *Pittsburgh Press,* January 5, 1895.

70 "New York News," *Sporting Life*, November 18, 1899.

71 "Pittsburgh Points," *Sporting Life*, August 3, 1901.

72 "Pirates Here All This Week," *Pittsburgh Post*, May 4, 1903.

73 "Off to Join Danville," *Philadelphia Inquirer*, March 28, 1908.

74 "Local Jottings," *Sporting Life*, June 20, 1908.

75 "Local Jottings," *Sporting Life*, September 25, 1909.

76 "Pittsburgh Bettors Get a Hard Bump," *Pittsburgh Gazette Times,* February 9, 1910.

77 "Old Timer Thinks Present Day Stars Have an Easy Life," *Detroit Free Press*, January 19, 1912.

78 "Auto Victim Diamond Star Back in 80's," *Detroit Free Press*, June 1, 1922.

79 "Wise Sayings of Great Men," *Sporting Life*, June 27, 1908.

# CLIFF CURTIS

## BY ALEX DRUDE

"YOU CAN'T WIN 'EM ALL." IT'S SAID with a shrug, a human acknowledgement that nobody goes undefeated, that nobody is perfect, that even if you do everything possible sometimes you will lose.

The origin of this phrase could be Connie Mack after the 1916 Philadelphia A's went 36-117. But it could also be from Cliff Curtis, one of the most hard-luck pitchers to ever throw a ball in a major-league game.[1] In 1910-11 with the Boston Doves, Curtis lost a major-league record 23 consecutive decisions (since broken by Anthony Young), and didn't win a game in 28 consecutive starts, also a record (now a three-way tie with Matt Keough and Jo-Jo Reyes).

Born in Delaware, Ohio, on July 3, 1881, Clifton Garfield Curtis almost certainly got his middle name in honor of a fellow Ohio native, President James A. Garfield, shot by an assassin the day before. (The president lived in agonizing pain for several months before dying in September.) Such a patriotic addition makes sense for Cliff considering that his father, Albert, was a Civil War veteran who became a tinsmith and then sold used goods.[2]

The third of six children, Cliff grew up playing baseball and was good at it. With brother Bert as his catcher, they played for many area teams.[3] Big for his time—topping out at 6-feet-2 and listed at 180 pounds—he was often the tallest player on his teams and played center for the Delaware High School basketball team.[4] But baseball was his sport, and he signed his first pro contract in 1902, appearing in a few games for the Columbus team, 30 miles from home, in the new American Association. His mother, Emogene, died that same year over the winter.[5]

Curtis got a full season with the Central League's Fort Wayne (Indiana) team in 1903, and threw two no-hitters while winning 27 games for the league champs.[6] The Cleveland Naps drafted him and it seemed like a charmed start, the Ohio boy given a chance to play for an Ohio major-league team.[7]

Unfortunately for Curtis, this was the beginning of a pattern in his major-league path—so close, and yet so far. The Naps sold him to the American Association's Milwaukee Brewers with an option to buy him back after the season. Over the next four years he pitched well enough to get drafted or have his option get picked up, and then returned to the Brewers before getting any chance with the major-league club. Part of it was control problems. One time a *Milwaukee Journal* write-up punned that he gave up so many free passes "one would think he was a railway president."[8]

Milwaukee newspapers reported that Curtis had a second job for a few years as head baseball coach at Ohio Wesleyan College in his hometown of Delaware, but that doesn't match up with Ohio Wesleyan's records,[9] which list a "Ben Davis" as 1905's head coach and "Bert Curtis," which could also have been his brother, for 1906.[10] In addition, Curtis didn't miss an Opening Day with Milwaukee.

On January 4, 1908, Cliff's father, Albert, died, and never saw his son pitch in a major-league game.

Just over four months later, on May 8, 1908, Curtis threw the first no-hitter at Milwaukee's Athletic Park in front of 5,500 fans. In the top of the first, Indianapolis's Cy Coulter lined one right into Curtis's stomach, but he recovered and got the out. Curtis was also helped by a good catch in the seventh by Danny Green and a diving stop by Rabbit Robinson for the first out in the ninth. After the final out the crowd tried to give Curtis a celebratory ride on their shoulders around the diamond but he ran to the clubhouse to avoid it.[11] Toward the end of the season he was drafted by the Philadelphia A's but Connie Mack sold him back to Milwaukee.[12]

While he waited for some team from the majors to give him a chance, Curtis did not become bitter or angry. He was cheerful, friendly, and well-liked throughout his time playing ball and into retirement. Though not an alcoholic like so many players of the time, he was not afraid to have a beer and enjoy himself. He played poker with the fellows, and won a fine diamond-and-sapphire stickpin that he had made into a ring and eventually gave to his daughter.[13]

Off the field, at some point Curtis took up embroidery. In between starts, in hotel rooms and train waiting rooms, and going from city to city and ballpark to ballpark, Cliff Curtis made fine, colorful tablecloths that his family treasured.[14]

When the Brewers visited Kansas City in July 1909, Milwaukee won the Sunday game and so did Curtis, but those were two different games. Curtis was not scheduled to pitch in the series and instead pitched for National League star and holdout catcher Johnny Kling's team in the outlaw Inter-City League, using the name "Ellison." Curtis was recognized and the game was played under protest, but he pitched anyway and won 5-4 in 13 innings. Milwaukee manager John McCloskey feigned innocence, saying he gave Curtis the day off and didn't know what he was up to. There were no apparent repercussions for Curtis's day as an outlaw.[15]

In mid-August, Curtis was sold to the Boston Doves of the National League. He finally made his major-league debut on August 23 at the South End Grounds in Boston against the Chicago Cubs. He was given a chance after starting pitcher Lew Richie was roughed up by the defending World Series champions, giving up seven hits and seven runs in 1⅓ innings.

Curtis's fortunes in Milwaukee were already known. *Chicago Tribune* writer I.E. Sanborn called him "hard luck Curtis" and failed to mention it was his first major-league game. Curtis gave up three hits, a sacrifice, and four more runs before finally ending the inning with the Cubs ahead 11-0.

Sanborn wrote that for the next seven innings, "Curtis, despite poor control, pitched pretty good baseball and held (Frank) Chance's men without a run, although they were taking a crack at anything he put up to them for a while." While Sanborn's box

score notes a hit for Curtis, the *New York Times* does not.[16] But both show that he scored one of Boston's late runs to make the final 11-6. Both newspapers said the game was poorly played, with Sanborn going so far as to call it "Farce Comedy."[17]

Curtis made his first start that Friday against Cincinnati, and pitched a three-hitter, but three errors allowed the Reds to score three of their four runs. With the score tied in the ninth, Curtis led off the inning with a single. Two sacrifices moved him to third and Dave Shean knocked in the rookie for the winning run and his first-ever major-league victory.

His next start was against the Pittsburgh Pirates in the first game of a September 2 doubleheader. The eventual World Series champions had beaten Boston 16 straight times that season. But Curtis baffled the Pirates, not allowing a hit into the seventh, when Honus Wagner opened with a clean single but was thrown out trying to stretch it into a double. Curtis finished the 1-0 gem by leaving the tying run on second in the ninth.

Despite not getting called up until late August and pitching in only 10 games, Curtis was the WAR

(Wins Above Replacement) leader for the 1909 Doves with a 3.5. Curtis officially finished 4-5 in 10 games. (He was given the loss for his first game, even though under modern scoring rules it would go to Richie.) He threw two shutouts in 83 innings, allowing 13 earned runs (17 total) for a 1.41 ERA. The only Doves pitcher that season to win more than seven games was left-hander Al Mattern, second in team WAR with a 3.3 and a 15-21 record.

Early in the 1910 season, when the Doves opened a series in Cincinnati on May 21, Curtis was not there. He went home to marry Florence Elizabeth Van Sickle.[18] He returned on May 24 and threw a four-hit shutout against the Reds. "Cliff Curtis, of the Beantowners, upset the old fallacy that honeymoons are bad for pitchers. He made the Reds eat out of his hand, and he didn't serve 'em anything but goose eggs in all styles!"[19]

In front of a very big crowd in Boston in the first game of a doubleheader on June 8 against the champion Pirates, again Curtis stifled them, throwing a two-hit shutout and improving to 7-6.

That was Curtis's last victory for nearly a year.

After losing six straight, Curtis held a one-run lead in Pittsburgh on July 19 in the ninth inning, but an error by shortstop Bill Sweeney allowed the tying run to score. Still on the slab in the bottom of the 11th, Curtis uncorked a wild pitch and since the wall behind home plate was 75 feet away, Vin Campbell scored the winning run from second.[20]

After a loss in Chicago, Curtis next pitched in Brooklyn at Washington Park. He didn't allow a run in nine innings, but Superbas starter Cy Barger didn't allow the Doves to score either. In the bottom of the 11th, Curtis gave up his third hit of the game, a leadoff double by Jake Daubert. After a walk, a perfectly placed bunt and a hard chopper to first, Curtis had lost his 15th of the year and his ninth straight. He got a save (retroactively) against Cincinnati on August 3, but since a save isn't a "decision," his personal losing streak continued.

For loss number 20 of the season (and 14th in a row), the Doves and Pirates were tied, 3-3, in the seventh when Pittsburgh scored five runs, the big blow being a three-run homer by first baseman John Flynn.

On August 29 in Cincinnati Curtis gave up two runs in the bottom of the eighth and the game was called a tie due to darkness. He got another save on September 3 against Brooklyn. On September 20, Curtis got just one out as the Pirates scored five runs, sending him to his 24th loss of the year and 18th in a row. Curtis made his final start of the year against Philadelphia, allowed the tying run in the sixth and the game was called after seven once again because of darkness.

Curtis's 24 losses didn't even lead the league, and the 18-game personal losing streak was never mentioned. (His official 6-24 mark is the only time anyone has ever finished with that record.[21]) In fact, Curtis was called one of the best pitchers Boston had despite giving up a league-leading 154 runs (99 earned). "(Al) Mattern, Curtis and (Sam) Frock did the best work and this trio practically carried the pitching burden most of the season."[22]

Curtis was still considered trade material, and rumored to be headed to the Cubs for an unhappy Joe Tinker.[23] But nothing happened, and the 1911 season started badly for Curtis. He made his season debut against the Phillies in the fourth game of the season at the South End Grounds on April 15, promptly hurt his arm and left after just one inning.[24] Big Jeff Pfeffer pitched the rest of the way and beat a rookie in his major-league debut named Pete Alexander in 10 innings.

Curtis's next appearance was in relief in Brooklyn's home opener, and he pitched 3⅓ innings in relief to get his third career save. A week later Curtis got another start against the Phillies in the Baker Bowl. Again, he was staked to an early lead, but then he gave up two two-run home runs to Hans Lobert and lost his 19th straight game.

Another week passed before Curtis's next appearance, this time in the ninth inning of a 7-7 game with the Reds. Curtis matched zeroes with Harry Gaspar for six innings until he allowed a game-winning RBI by Dick Hoblitzell in the 15th to make it 20 straight defeats.

Curtis opened a series against Pittsburgh on May 13 and gave up five runs in the eighth to lose again. He started the final game of the series on the 17th and was still pitching in the 10th inning when Pittsburgh scored two runs for a 6-4 lead. Boston got two of its own to continue the game. Curtis stayed in as well. In the 12th an error by the normally surehanded Buck Herzog allowed the go-ahead run to score, and this time the Rustlers could not respond, sending Curtis to his 22nd straight loss.

On May 22, Herzog homered in the fourth to give Boston a 1-0 lead over the Cardinals, but Curtis allowed three runs in the top of the fifth and that was it for scoring. Curtis had opened the season 0-5 and hadn't won a game since the prior June 8.

Curtis next took the mound on May 26 against Brooklyn. The Rustlers scored two in the bottom of the first and never trailed. Curtis even singled, scored a run of his own, and threw a two-run, six-hit complete game, a 7-2 victory. Boston's 14-game losing streak was over, but more importantly so was Curtis's, mercifully, at 23 straight games.

No mention was made of the end of the losing streak or the relief Curtis must have felt. Instead, it was simply: "Curtis kept the visitors' hits well scattered and was given good support."[25] Newly acquired third baseman Harry Steinfeldt, best known for being the fourth man in the famed Chicago Cubs' Tinker-to-Evers-to-Chance infield in the early 1900s, was also singled out for being a welcome addition.

On June 8 in St. Louis, Curtis got only partway into the third before being replaced. Manager Fred Tenney started him again the next day against Slim Sallee, who is still considered one of the best pitchers in Cardinals history despite playing for them when they were at their worst. Sallee blinked first, walking Curtis in the third. Two batters later, Tenney drove him in and for a long time it looked as if that would be the difference. But in the bottom of the eighth Ed Konetchy tripled and scored, Steve Evans singled and scored, and just like that, Curtis dropped to 1-8. In exactly one calendar year (for his 23-game losing streak had started after the two-hit shutout against Pirates on June 8, 1910) he was 1-26. And that was the last game Cliff Curtis ever pitched for Boston.

The very next day, June 10, 1911, Curtis was traded to the defending National League champion Chicago Cubs. The Cubs had been in the World Series four of the last five years, winning back-to-back titles, but were now part of a three-team race with the Giants and Phillies. In addition, first baseman-manager Frank Chance was nearing the end of his injury-plagued career, so Chicago needed help.

Curtis was not the centerpiece of the deal. That honor went to Cubs catcher Johnny Kling, still considered one of the best backstops in franchise history. The last time the Cubs hadn't won the pennant was 1909, when Kling ran a pool hall in his home town of Kansas City (and Curtis pitched for his outlaw team).

The eight-player trade was billed as a steal for Chicago. "There is no doubt at all that the Chicago people managed to get what they wanted and compelled the Boston club to give up material they wished to keep. A pretty way, indeed, to weaken the weak and strengthen the strong."[26]

That included their new pitcher. "Cliff Curtis always pitched good ball for a losing team and Chance figures that he will brace up the Cubs' twirling department, which is none too strong."[27] That a guy who had just gone 1-26 in the last 365 days was lauded like that tells you about how closely statistics were followed in 1911.

After three games with Chicago, Curtis went home. On July 28, 1911, Florence Curtis gave birth to their only child, Mary Florence Curtis.[28]

Curtis rejoined the Cubs in early August. In his first game, he relieved German-born rookie Reggie Richter in the third inning of the series opener against the Cardinals. Curtis pitched a scoreless inning and the Cubs scored five in the bottom of the frame to take the lead, Curtis even singling and scoring to help Chicago to a 7-3 lead. After another scoreless frame, Chance put in Mordecai "Three-Finger" Brown. Brown pitched the last five innings for the (retroactive) save, and Cliff finally had his first and only win for Chicago.

Chance swapped Curtis to Philadelphia for Jack Rowan on August 18. Rowan appeared in exactly one game for Cubs before being sold to Louisville.

Undaunted, "Pitcher Cliff Curtis has reported to acting-manager (Red) Dooin in better shape than he has ever been in his career."[29] He made his Phillies debut on August 25 against the Reds at the Baker Bowl. Curtis's new team staked him to a three-run lead in the bottom of the first, but he ended up with a no-decision after allowing the tying run in the top of the ninth.

After an inning of mop-up duty on Labor Day, Curtis got his second start for Philly the next day, and baffled Brooklyn the entire game, not allowing a hit until the bottom of the seventh, when Zack Wheat doubled. Curtis even singled and drove in a run in the 6-0 complete-game two-hitter for his third win of the year. He now had one victory for each team he had played for, and finished the season 4-11.

Curtis, Boston Nationals

Curtis returned to Ohio and his new family for the winter. He sent in his contract for 1912 in time for spring training in Hot Springs, Arkansas. There, "Messrs. (team owner Horace) Fogel and (manager) Dooin are paying close attention to the baths at Hot Springs. Mr. Fogel obtained the services of Dr. E.H. Ellsworth, one of the best physicians at the resort, and he gives individual directions to each player. This physician declares that pitchers Alexander and Curtis came to him just in time, for they showed malarial symptoms."[30]

Escaping from malaria, Curtis was 2-4 when he took the mound at the Baker Bowl for the second game of a doubleheader against Brooklyn on June 28. In the second inning, Zack Wheat hit a hard chopper back to the mound and Curtis had no time to react. The ball hit him square in the face and knocked him unconscious.[31] Nowadays he would not be allowed to pitch until his concussion was gone, but Curtis pitched five days later in Boston on his 31st birthday and made it only through two innings.

During some downtime in Boston, one can safely assume Curtis was having beer and playing poker in the Copley Square Hotel room of one-time Phillies owner and manager Bill Shettsline, now the team's business manager, with manager Red Dooin and second baseman Jimmy Walsh. Shettsline's room was directly below current owner Horace Fogel. In the days before air conditioning, the only relief for the July heat was an open window with a large awning over it to try to get some sort of breeze. A lighted cigar stump came out of the window of Fogel's room and landed on the awning of Shettsline's window, which caught fire. The blaze quickly spread to the curtains and threatened to take over the entire room. All four men sprang into action. Shettsline and Dooin put the fire out, while "players Walsh and Curtis … threw more water over Charley Dooin than on the blaze."[32]

Hopefully not due to throwing water in his manager's face, Curtis was placed on waivers and on July 10 was claimed by Brooklyn, his fourth team in two years. "Pitcher Cliff Curtis, just claimed from Philadelphia by Brooklyn, has been a baseball nomad.

He has seen service with Chicago, Boston, Phillies and now he goes to Brooklyn. He has never been anything more than a prospect."[33]

In the long history of the Dodgers, five of their six worst years by winning percentage come between 1904 and 1912. The 1912 team is the sixth-worst Dodgers team, and this is the team Cliff Curtis now found himself on, some 30 games behind New York but still ahead of St. Louis and Boston.

Curtis made his Superbas debut five days later in Pittsburgh, in the bottom of the eighth of a tie game against Hank Robinson, a second-year Pirates lefty. Both threw zeroes for five innings, and the game stretched into the 13th. In the bottom of that inning Curtis walked Honus Wagner. When first baseman Dots Miller bunted, Wagner surprised every Brooklyn player by not just taking second, but also third. Two batters later, Alex McCarthy singled him in and Pittsburgh won, 4-3. Curtis started his Brooklyn career just the same way it had seemed to go everywhere else. The loss even dropped the Superbas into seventh place, behind St. Louis, where they would stay.

After not making it out of the second inning in his first two starts, Curtis picked up a five-inning save in his home debut at Washington Park. On August 10 against the Pirates, Cliff started but Pittsburgh led 5-1 going into the bottom of the sixth. The Superbas then scored five off Marty O'Toole to take the lead. Curtis was pinch-hit for during that inning, and Eddie Stack pitched three innings of two-hit ball for the save. Curtis finally had his first win in a Brooklyn uniform.

After two more wins, his game against Philadelphia on September 28 was the same old story. "Cliff Curtis twirled eight innings of the second game, which he should have won. Four of the five Quaker runs were helped along by Brooklyn errors."[34] Instead he dropped to 5-12 for the seasons and 3-7 with Brooklyn.

In his final game of the year, he pitched a complete game against the Giants, who had already clinched the pennant by a wide margin, and won it when the Superbas scored four in the sixth and four in the eighth. It was the last game Brooklyn ever won at Washington Park, as owner Charlie Ebbets was building a new place in Flatbush. It would be ready for 1913, and he was trying to build a winning team to complement his brand-new ballpark.

Curtis knew this, and likely figured out his age (31) and his inability to win were going against him. He sent in his signed 1913 contract before the end of December.[35]

The next spring, Curtis did not pitch in the very first game at Ebbets Field, an exhibition win over the Yankees, nor did he throw in the first official game, a loss on Opening Day to the Phillies. He made his debut there on April 21, and the Superbas had yet to score an official run at their new ballpark. First baseman Jake Daubert scored the first run in the park for the home team while Curtis pitched the ninth and did not get a decision as Brooklyn lost to Philly 2-1.

The next day in Boston, Curtis pitched a complete-game seven-hitter, allowing just one earned run in the 8-3 victory. He even singled in a run on his own behalf.

Brooklyn finally got a win at Ebbets on April 26, over the Giants, and Curtis got to start at home on May 5. He threw eight innings of two-run, seven-hit ball, but was pinch-hit for in the bottom of the inning as Brooklyn rallied to tie the score and won in the 10th on a walkoff single by second baseman George Cutshaw.

Four days later, Curtis relieved Eddie Stack in the third and got his first victory at Ebbets Field in a 7-5 win. He was now 2-0 for the first time in his major-league career and the surprising Superbas were tied for first with the Phillies.

On May 13 it was a similar story. Curtis came in for Frank Allen in the third against Cincinnati, gave up just five hits and didn't allow a run the rest of the way for a comeback win, Brooklyn's fifth in a row. On the 16th Curtis gave up three runs in the top of the first to St. Louis, two of them on an Ed Konetchy home run. But Brooklyn scored five times in the next four innings to take the lead, Curtis hung on to move to 4-0, and the Superbas were still tied for the league lead.

Then things began to go wrong. On May 22, it was raining hard even before the game with Pittsburgh began, but umpire Bill Klem told both teams to take the field as scheduled. Curtis got the start against the Pirates' Wilbur Cooper, and no runs were scored in the first four innings. In the top of the fifth, the Pirates loaded the bases with nobody out. At that point, the crowd in the bleachers, likely small to start with, left their open seats and rushed the field. They had likely been asking to move to the covered grandstand and were being denied. To avoid a forfeit Superbas management quickly allowed them to move to the mostly empty covered grandstand. Already in trouble with the bases full, Curtis then walked Max Carey, forcing in Chief Wilson for the first run of the game. Curtis got out of it but Brooklyn could do nothing against Cooper. A short time later as the downpour showed no signs of stopping, so Klem called the game and Brooklyn protested, but Klem's word was law.[36]

His best day in a Brooklyn uniform came on June 26 during a doubleheader in Philadelphia as the Superbas tried to stave off a slide into the second division. It was a hot one and Nap Rucker, Brooklyn's ace, was on the hill. In the 13th inning, tied 2-2, Rucker singled but then had to leave the game.[37] The Superbas didn't score and Curtis, scheduled to pitch the second game anyway, was called in. He pitched a scoreless two innings and when Brooklyn scored three in the top of the 14th, he came away with the victory.

Brooklyn manager Bill Dahlen, one of his old teammates in Boston, then sent Curtis back out to start game two as scheduled. Matched up against another old teammate, Pete Alexander, Curtis gave up single runs in the fourth and seventh, while the Superbas scored two off Alexander in the sixth and two more in the ninth for a 4-2 victory. Cliff Curtis had won two games in one day. The papers went nuts for the feat, with *Sporting Life* declaring it hadn't been seen since "the days of Joe McGinnity."[38]

By the time early August rolled around, however, Curtis knew he would be sent to the Newark Indians of the International League no later than August 20.[39]

As Charlie Ebbets owned both the Superbas and the Indians, the exchange seems like a mere formality today.

But at the time there was immense pride in "home town" ball teams, no matter what level of ball they played. In August 1913, the Indians were running away with the International League, seemingly on the way to their first pennant since joining the league in 1902.[40] Also, across the country in the progressive labor movement of the time, trusts and syndicates and monopolies were under fire in every industry, from steel to railroads to baseball. To keep above suspicion, Ebbets had to let Brooklyn fail (when the deal was announced the Superbas were 25 games out of first) while Newark succeeded for as long as possible. Once there was no way Newark could lose and no way Brooklyn could win, no one would complain about transferring players. Thus, the agreed-upon exchange date was August 20, when a month remained in the International League season.[41]

Curtis took the mound for the second game of the doubleheader against the Cardinals at Ebbets Field on August 16, 1913, knowing it was probably his last game in the major leagues. A friend to all on the club, no doubt the other players wanted to send him out on top.

In a time when one home run a game was a rare occurrence, the Superbas hit four. Curtis's batterymate, rookie catcher William Fischer, hit his first career home run in the third inning, a three-run blast. Casey Stengel, playing center that day, hit a solo shot in the sixth. And shortstop Bob Fisher, who hit only 11 home runs in a seven-year career, had two, in the seventh and the eighth, and he tripled as well. Even Curtis went 3-for-4. He went the full nine in the 14-5 pasting, and walked away with the most run support he ever got in a major-league game.

The trade was made official on August 19 as several Newark players were transferred to Brooklyn.[42] Curtis's manager in New Jersey was his first manager and one-time catcher on the Boston Doves, Englishman Harry Smith. Despite being all but assured of the pennant, Newark then began to falter and Curtis could not help stem the tide. In his first game at Baltimore, on September 1, he was shelled in a 12-2 loss. On the 6th in Providence he was shelled again. He pitched a two-run, four-hit game on the 13th in Jersey City but lost. He then won his next two games, including the one that finally clinched the pennant, a complete game against Jersey City on September 20.[43] It was the first time Curtis had pitched on a pennant winner since 1903 in Fort Wayne.

Curtis went on a barnstorming tour to Cuba with most of the Superbas that fall and returned to Newark for 1914.[44] And the tough baseball luck that dogged Curtis continued, for Brooklyn fired manager Bill Dahlen after 1913 and replaced him with Wilbert Robinson, the former Giants pitching coach. Every Giants pitcher for more than a decade had been tutored by Robbie. The list includes Mathewson, McGinnity, Jeff Tesreau, Rube Marquard, and Al Demaree, all stars during the Giants' long run at the top of the National League. What could Robinson have done if Curtis remained on the staff? Maybe nothing, for Curtis was already 32. Even if Uncle Robbie had been able to turn Cliff's career around, it would have been for only a year or so, and Robinson was trying to turn an entire franchise around.

Curtis went 16-12 for Newark in 1914 as the Indians slipped to fifth place. He then went back to Ohio and threw three full seasons for the Columbus Senators, the first pro team he ever played for. The Senators finished last in 1915, seventh in 1916, and in 1917 Curtis's one-time Cubs teammate Joe Tinker bought into the team and installed himself as manager. Tinker, welcomed back into Organized Ball when the Federal League folded, managed the Senators to fourth place in 1917, and at age 36 Curtis went 10-7 in his final full year in pro ball. He pitched a few games for Columbus and St. Joseph, Missouri, in 1918 before finally hanging up the spikes.

After retiring Curtis was an avid fan of the Cleveland Indians, the team that first drafted him in 1903, and a fine amateur bowler.[45] He moved his family to nearby Utica, Ohio, and ran a Ford dealership for more than 20 years.[46] He also coached the Utica High baseball team to several league championships.[47]

Perhaps the best indication of how Curtis was thought of in baseball comes through in how his family was treated by his former teammates after Cliff died at home on April 22, 1943, from a heart attack after fighting an out-of-control grass fire.[48] Daughter Mary remembered her mother, Florence, calling the Yankees hotel every time they came to Cleveland when their manager was Casey Stengel, Cliff's teammate in Brooklyn. Casey always gave them the best seats, right behind the Yankees dugout, and would spend time with the Curtis family. Curtis's grandson remembered as a 12-year-old sitting in the Yankees dugout for close to an hour, talking ball with Stengel.[49]

"I don't give a damn what his record was," his grandson said about him. "Everybody says he was a great guy and that's what's important."[50]

## SOURCES

In preparing this biography the author relied on Dennis Pajot's history of the early Milwaukee Brewers teams for Curtis' minor-league years. Game descriptions were taken from original scans of *Sporting Life* and the *New York Times*. Season and career statistical information and other statistics are from Baseball-Reference.com and Retrosheet.org.

## NOTES

1   Paul Dickson, *The New Dickson Baseball Dictionary* (New York: Harcourt, Brace & Company, 1999), 547.

2   Ancestry.com, 1900 US Census.

3   *Marion* (Ohio) *Daily Star*, April 23, 1943.

4   Ibid.

5   FindAGrave.com, Emogene L. Westfall Curtis.

6   Chuck McGill, Minor League No-hitters, docs.google.com/spreadsheets/d/1deBSHdsKaYaoBObQqY-f12dTaCv6k8vIxjhomWRrlLQ/edit?authkey=CL_3m-cC&authkey=CL_3m-cC&pref=2&pli=1#gid=0; Dennis Pajot, *1904 Milwaukee Brewers*, 16. (Pajot's research is at sabr.org/research/1902-1919-milwaukee-brewers-files); Rudolph H. Horst, "Central League," *Spalding's Official Baseball Guide 1904*, 194-197.

7   Horst.

8   Pajot, *1904 Milwaukee Brewers*, 25.

9   Pajot, *1905 Milwaukee Brewers*, 8; *1906 Milwaukee Brewers*, 9.

# 20-GAME LOSERS

10  *Ohio Wesleyan University 2017 Baseball Media Guide*, 36.

11  Pajot, *1908 Milwaukee Brewers*, 19.

12  Pajot, *1909 Milwaukee Brewers*, 9.

13  "Family of Record Holder Wants to See Met Hurler Win, *Ellensburg* (Washington) *Daily Record*, June 25, 1993.

14  Ibid.

15  Pajot, *1909 Milwaukee Brewers*, 40.

16  *New York Times*, August 24, 1909.

17  I.E. Sanborn, "Champs and Doves in Farce Comedy," *Chicago Tribune*, August 24, 1909.

18  *Marion* (Ohio) *Daily Star*, May 23, 1910.

19  Ren Mulford Jr., "Mulfordisms," *Sporting Life*, June 4, 1910: 2.

20  Clem's Baseball Reference, Forbes Field dimensions, andrew-clem.com/Baseball/ForbesField.html.

21  Bill James and Rob Neyer, *The Neyer-James Guide to Pitchers* (New York: Simon & Schuster, 2004), 477.

22  "1910 National Teams: The Boston Team," *Sporting Life*, October 22, 1910: 11.

23  "National League Notes," *Sporting Life*, November 26, 1910: 17.

24  "Philadelphia at Boston," *Sporting Life*, April 22, 1911: 8.

25  "Brooklyn at Boston," *Sporting Life*, June 3, 1911: 9; *New York Times*, May 27, 1911.

26  J.C. Morse, "Changes in the World of Baseball," *Baseball Magazine*, September 1911.

27  "Big Mid-Season Deal!" *Sporting Life*, June 17, 1911: 1.

28  "National League Notes," *Sporting Life*, August 19, 1911: 24.

29  "National League Notes," *Sporting Life*, September 2, 1911: 15.

30  "Local Jottings," *Sporting Life*, March 16, 1912: 6.

31  "Brooklyn at Philadelphia," *Sporting Life*, July 6, 1912: 11.

32  "Local Jottings," *Sporting Life*, July 13, 1912: 5.

33  "Local Jottings," *Sporting Life*, July 20, 1912: 3.

34  "Philadelphia at Brooklyn," *Sporting Life*, October 5, 1912: 9.

35  "National League News in Short Metre," *Sporting Life*, December 14, 1912: 8.

36  "Pittsburgh at Brooklyn," *Sporting Life*, May 31, 1913: 10.

37  Abe Yager, "In the Race Again," *Sporting Life*, July 5, 1913: 5.

38  Ibid.

39  "International Items," *Sporting Life*, August 9, 1913: 15.

40  "Close of the Season," *Sporting Life*, September 27, 1913: 12.

41  Abe Yager, "Loyal to Organized Ball," *Sporting Life*, August 2, 1913: 5.

42  "Brooklyn Announces Player Deals," *Sporting Life*, August 23, 1913: 7.

43  "Jersey City at Newark," *Sporting Life*, September 27, 1913: 12.

44  Abe Yager, "Brooklyn Briefs," *Sporting Life*, October 4, 1913: 18.

45  Ibid.

46  *Marion Daily Star*, April 23, 1943.

47  Ibid.

48  "Family of Record Holder Wants to See Met Hurler Win."

49  Ibid.

50  Ibid.

# ART DITMAR

## BY DAVID E. SKELTON

**IN 1955 THE KANSAS CITY ATHLETICS** coaching staff "observed [rookie right-hander Art] Ditmar during spring training and prophesied that he was destined for distinction on the mound."[1] This bright assessment was echoed three years later by New York Yankees manager Casey Stengel, who said, "I believe ... Ditmar could grow into one of the big pitchers in the majors. ... [T]he first thing he must develop is the realization that he is as good as he is, and that he has so much in him."[2] This latter appraisal seemingly explains the Old Perfessor's decision to start Ditmar in Game One of the 1960 World Series. Though his choice has been roundly condemned by armchair managers through the years, the decision did little to remove the label of invincibility that once surrounded the hard-throwing hurler.

Arthur John Ditmar was born on April 3, 1929, the second of three children of George Edward and Caroline Dorothy (Huysman) Ditmar, in the Boston suburb of Winthrop, Massachusetts. He was the great-grandson of German immigrant Henry V. Ditmar, who arrived in the Bay State in the first half of the nineteenth century. In 1855 Henry married Isabella Logan, an Irish immigrant, and they raised six children to adulthood. Their youngest son, Francis "Frank" Ditmar, pursued a career as a house painter in Boston and in 1891 married Massachusetts native Mary Canavan. This union produced five children, the youngest of whom was Art's father, George. In the 1920s George launched a career in sales and married Caroline. After the birth of their children the family moved to the other end of the state, settling in Pittsfield, Massachusetts.

The children attended Pittsfield High School, which has produced a large list of accomplished alumni including actress Elizabeth Banks and All-Star shortstop Mark Belanger. Art and his elder brother George established their own credentials at Pittsfield High on both the hardwood court and diamond field.[3] Though he played some outfield, Art was primarily a pitcher. He posted a 14-2 record for the Pittsfield Generals and was captain of the baseball team his senior year. (He also excelled in American Legion baseball but was discouraged from playing football for fear of injuring his arm.) In 1947 scouts from the St. Louis Cardinals, Pittsburgh Pirates, and Philadelphia Athletics swarmed after Ditmar pitched a one-hit gem during a tournament in Johnstown, Pennsylvania. He was invited to Philadelphia's Shibe Park for a tryout under the watchful eye of Athletics skipper Connie Mack. After graduating from high school in 1947, Ditmar spurned an athletic scholarship to the University of Mississippi to sign a $1,000 bonus contract with Athletics scout and former minor-league hurler Richard "Lefty" Lloyd.[4]

In 1948 Ditmar was assigned to the Moline/Kewanee (Illinois) A's in the Central Association (Class C). Among the most durable pitchers in the league, the 19-year-old placed among the league leaders in appearances (33) and innings pitched (193). This was accompanied by a large yield in walks (108) that contributed to a pedestrian record of 9-9, 3.68. The next year Ditmar was promoted to the Savannah Indians in the South Atlantic League (Class A). Initially projected as a starter, he was moved to the bullpen after right-hander Harry Byrd, who was expected to compete in the majors, failed in spring training and was assigned to the Indians. Ditmar made occasional starts and on June 16, 1949, he delivered a four-hit shutout against the Charleston Rebels. More importantly, he lowered his walk ratio by nearly 30 percent to finish with a record of 7-6, 2.85 in 142 innings. The Rebels fell victim again the following season when Ditmar tossed another shutout on April 24, 1950, while surrendering just one hit. The win was the first of his minor-league career-high 13 as he anchored the Indians staff alongside fellow

right-handers Duke Simpson and Kelly Swift. But Ditmar was unable to build upon this success by 1953, when he was drafted into the US Army during the Korean War. He did not see combat and spent a portion of his service at Camp Atterbury, Indiana, where his teammates included future major-league hurlers Frank Lary and Tom Brewer.

On April 26, 1953, Ditmar made his return among the professional ranks with the Ottawa A's in the Triple-A International League. It did not go swimmingly. With the exception of a four-hit shutout against the Toronto Maple Leafs in May, he struggled with his control through most of the season en route to a record of 2-13, 5.30. Optioned to Savannah in July, Ditmar rebounded with a perfect 7-0 posting that included a three-hit shutout of the Augusta Rams.[5] The abrupt turnaround captured the imagination of the pitching-poor Philadelphia Athletics and Ditmar was selected among the September call-ups though he did not make an appearance. During the offseason Ditmar was added to the club's 40-man roster.

The following spring Ditmar competed with three others for the club's fifth-starter role. Though he fell short in this competition, his strong Grapefruit League campaign earned the 25-year-old a spot on the parent roster. On April 19, 1954, Ditmar made his major-league debut in Washington's Griffith Stadium in relief of lefty starter Morrie Martin. Entering in the sixth inning against the Senators tasked with protecting a 3-1 lead, Ditmar walked the first batter he faced, slugger Roy Sievers, before retiring the side. Far less success ensued in the seventh when a throwing error by A's first baseman Don Bollweg led to two unearned runs. The game remained tied into the ninth when Ditmar surrender a walk-off homer to leadoff hitter Eddie Yost.

After a dismal appearance on May 3 against the Chicago White Sox — a game in which few Philadelphia pitchers shone in a 14-3 blowout — Ditmar pitched eight strong innings of relief over three appearances to earn his first major-league start. Facing the Senators on May 21, he was lifted after the first inning after surrendering five hits and two walks to the first eight batters. A similar fate awaited Ditmar in Boston 10 days later when a three-run homer by Ted Williams in the first and a bases-loaded walk in the second made for a very short outing. On June 12 Ditmar was optioned to Ottawa. Though he struggled with a sore arm in Ottawa, his 6-12 record was deceptive as he received little run support from the offensively inept last-place club.

Recalled by the Athletics in September, Ditmar drew a September 19 start at home against the Yankees. Following a leadoff single by second baseman Gil McDougald he held the Bombers hitless through 4⅔ innings before wriggling out of a bases-loaded jam in the fifth. He did not figure in the decision. Ditmar got a second start a week later in Yankee Stadium. In the meaningless season finale, Stengel fielded a unique lineup with center fielder Mickey Mantle at short and catcher Yogi Berra at third. The future Hall of Famers handled their posts flawlessly as the Yankees captured a slim 3-2 lead through four innings before the A's offense — a generally ineffective lot throughout the season — opened for three runs in the fifth. Though lifted after 5⅔ innings, Ditmar earned his first major-league win while also collecting the last victory for the Athletics as a Philadelphia-based club.

Ditmar's sparkling 1955 debut in Kansas City (four innings of two-hit relief against the White Sox on April 22) combined with less-than-promising April outings from righty Arnie Portocarrero prompted Ditmar's slide into the Athletics rotation. In his first start, against the Senators on May 1, he gave up five runs in the first inning and was yanked before the Athletics took a commanding lead. He quickly rebounded and over the next 19 days began "to justify [his] prospective star rating"[6] with strong back-to-back outings in Boston and Chicago. The latter performance was particularly rewarding as Ditmar held the White Sox to just one hit through 8⅔ innings and earned his first career shutout. Though he encountered difficulties throughout the season — a 9.62 ERA in his team-leading 12 losses[7] — Ditmar won four of his last five decisions to finish with the club lead in wins (12), complete games (7), innings (175⅓), and strikeouts (79). "I can thank several people for this," Ditmar said. "One in particular is [coach] George Susce, who helped me with the sinker ball. It has become my best pitch."[8] During the offseason the club spurned an aggressive attempt by the White Sox to acquire Ditmar in a multiplayer swap while Athletics manager Lou Boudreau expressed his opinion that Ditmar would "be a fixture for the next seven or eight years."[9]

Except for a strong performance against the Detroit Tigers on March 27 — a two-hit gem he shared with veteran righty Lou Kretlow — Ditmar struggled through much of Athletics' 1956 spring training. Despite the setbacks he was tabbed in a poll of nationwide scribes as the most likely Kansas City hurler to win 20 games in 1956; as it turned out, they had the number in the wrong column. Initially Ditmar appeared poised to prove the scribes correct when he tossed a one-hitter against the White Sox on April 21 in a 15-1 blowout. (A decent hitter, Ditmar collected two hits, one of which came when the Athletics scored a then-major league record 13 runs in the second inning, all the runs scoring with two outs). Less than three weeks later he collected his second career shutout by scattering seven hits against the Orioles in Baltimore. Yankees assistant GM Bill DeWitt ranked Ditmar among the AL's best flamethrowers and the interest from New York only intensified after the righty tossed another shutout on May 27 against the Tigers.

But Ditmar's season turned on a 7-2 loss to the Orioles on June 17, the first of four consecutive defeats. A month later he began a dismal string by losing 11 straight starts including two heartbreaking losses to Washington and Cleveland during which he surrendered only two earned runs in 18⅓ innings. In nearly one-third of his season-long 34 starts, the Athletics' anemic offense scored less than two runs. Ditmar posted a record of 6-17, 5.09 over his last 30 appearances en route to a major-league worst 22 losses. He led the AL with 125 earned runs yielded. Despite these homely numbers, Ditmar continued to draw considerable interest from major-league clubs throughout the offseason, including particularly aggressive pursuits from the Boston Red Sox and Cleveland Indians. On February 19, 1957, over the objections of Boudreau, he was sent to the Yankees with former AL MVP left-hander Bobby Shantz in a multiplayer swap. "Ditmar is the ace of the deal as far as we are concerned," said Yankees GM George Weiss, who had a history of success turning around former 20-game losers Fred Sanford and Don Larsen.[10] A dismayed Ted Williams predicted a 20-win season for Ditmar while Indians GM Hank Greenberg bitterly declared, "It must be nice to have a farm club in your own league."[11]

But the Splendid Splinter's 20-win prediction was not in store for Ditmar. In his first three starts in the 1957 season, Ditmar surrendered 27 hits and 9 runs over 15⅓ innings that prompted Joe King to write in *The Sporting News*, "[He's] as easy to hit as a Class D rookie with a straight ball."[12] Far more success was found working from the bullpen, where Ditmar posted a 6-1, 1.75 ERA record in 35 relief appearances. He continued to earn occasional starts throughout the season, including a 4-3 win against the White Sox on June 13 in which a wild pitch sent Chicago's Larry Doby sprawling and precipitated a 28-minute bench-clearing rhubarb. Ditmar was fined $100 for the errant throw.

Beginning at the season's one-quarter mark, the Yankees initiated a 75-38 run to easily capture their 23rd AL flag, providing Ditmar with his first postseason experience. On October 3 he entered the fourth inning of Game Two of the World Series against the Milwaukee Braves trailing 4-2 with no outs and a runner on third and induced two infield popups and a grounder to short to stem the bleeding. Before being lifted in the seventh for a pinch-hitter, he surrendered just a bunt single over four innings to keep the Yankees close in an eventual 4-2 loss. A week later Ditmar added to his scoreless string with two innings of one-hit pitching in Game Seven. When the Series ended in seven-game defeat, he was the only Yankees pitcher to go unscored upon (more than one inning) in the fall classic.

In 1958 Ditmar extended his World Series scoreless string another 3⅔ innings after narrowly dodging a return to Kansas City. Having started the season in the bullpen, Ditmar was initially packaged alongside veteran outfielder Harry Simpson in a June 15 trade for A's pitchers Duke Maas and Virgil Trucks until, at the last minute, the parties agreed upon righty Bob Grim instead. (This was after Ditmar chipped in with teammates Mickey Mantle, Don Larsen, Tom Sturdivant, and Jerry Lumpe to purchase an eight-year-old sedan to carpool from their New Jersey homes to Yankee Stadium.) Ditmar was moved into the Yankees rotation to spell injury-plagued righty Tom Sturdivant. On July 23 he carried a three-hit shutout into the ninth against the Tigers before a string of singles forced him to settle for a 16-4 win. Two complete game wins in August lifted Ditmar's record to 8-2, 2.50 before he was moved back to the bullpen following a 1-5 slide. On September 14 Ditmar secured the final out in the pennant-clinching 5-3 win over the Athletics. He finished with a record of 9-8, 3.42 in 139⅔ innings.

On October 8 Ditmar appeared in Game Six of the 1958 World Series in relief of a struggling Whitey Ford. Entering the second against Milwaukee trailing 2-1 with one out and the bases loaded, Ditmar induced perennial All-Star shortstop Johnny Logan to fly out to left on the first pitch. When Andy Pafko attempted to tag up, left fielder Elston Howard threw a strike to catcher Yogi Berra to end the inning. Ditmar held the Braves to two hits over the next three innings before being lifted for a pinch-hitter in an eventual 4-3 Yankees win. The next day he earned his only championship ring when New York outlasted Milwaukee in Game Seven.

During the offseason the Yankees turned away numerous offers for Ditmar. This decision proved prescient when the righty, in the wake of reigning Cy Young Award winner Bob Turley's 1959 struggles, became one of the staples in the Yankees rotation. "[The sportswriters] don't say much about this Ditmar," Stengel said. "[B]ut he is one pitcher who never says my arm is no good. ... he is a manager's kind of ball player."[13] With the exception of a fifth-inning homer by Rocky Colavito on May 1, Ditmar threw seven innings of perfect baseball in an eventual 4-2 loss to the Indians.[14] Six weeks later he surrendered a first-inning run before shutting down the White Sox on two hits in a 5-1 complete-game win. But his finest performance of the season came on August 28 when Ditmar delivered a two-hit shutout against the Senators while helping his own cause by driving in three runs and connecting on his second (and last) career homer, a solo blast off righty Camilo Pascual. By season's end Ditmar had posted a major-league-best 1.030 WHIP over a career-high 202 innings. A respectable 13-9 record might easily have been better but too often Ditmar received little or no support from his Yankees teammates—he compiled a 1.94 ERA in nine of his 25 starts but had four losses and five no-decisions to show for it.

In 1960 the emergence of 1959 International League pitcher of the year Bill Short, combined with unexpected challenges Ditmar encountered in spring training, relegated the veteran right-hander to the bullpen at the beginning of the season. Despite not making his first start until May 8, Ditmar became the workhorse of the Yankees staff, leading the club with 200 innings and 15 wins. Though he surrendered a club-record 25 homers, he also placed among the league leaders in ERA (3.06), winning percentage (.625), and WHIP (1.255). "He is a pitcher you can start against anybody," Stengel exclaimed as the season drew to a close.[15]

This was perhaps the Old Perfessor's mindset when he selected Ditmar to start Game One of the 1960 World Series against the Pittsburgh Pirates. (Future HOF lefty Whitey Ford might have gotten the start, but he was winless in four consecutive postseason starts dating back to 1957, and had struggled with arm problems throughout the season.) On October 5 Ditmar took the mound in Pittsburgh's Forbes Field and absorbed a 6-4 loss after retiring just one batter while yielding a leadoff walk, a double, and two groundball singles to center. "The Pittsburgh infield was like pavement," said the sinkerball artist. "[E]verything that was hit on the ground went through the infield like a shot."[16]

Despite this difficult outing, Ditmar was the starter for Game Five at Yankee Stadium, where he had a superb 10-2, 2.29 record during the season.[17] Unfortunately for the Yankees, the results were approximately the same when Ditmar yielded three runs (one earned) on three hits in 1⅓ innings. Meanwhile, two shutouts delivered by Whitey Ford in the club's losing cause contributed to accusations that Stengel had mismanaged the staff, accusations that led to the skipper's dismissal five days after the Series ended.

In 1961 Ditmar reported to spring training early "to avoid the weak arm which handicapped [him] at the outset in 1960."[18] This strategy paid immediate dividends in April with two wins in two starts but yielded far less success in May—0-2, 5.14 over six starts. In June Ditmar and fellow veteran Bob Turley, who was suffering a similar fate, were removed from the rotation in favor of Bill Stafford and rookie Rollie Sheldon. On June 14, in a move to add another left-hander to the rotation, the Yankees traded Ditmar and rookie corner infielder Deron Johnson to the Athletics for Bud Daley. (At the time of the trade Ditmar was serving as the club's interim player representative; he was replaced by Ford.)

Exemplified by the addition of 18-year-old high school grad Lew Krausse to the rotation in June, Kansas City was in the throes of a youth movement; in 1961 the A's had little incentive to use Ditmar as anything more than a spot starter. Over 16 appearances (four starts) beginning July 4 he struggled through a 6.56 ERA and finished the season with a record of 2-8 in 108⅓ innings (his fewest innings pitched since his 1954 debut in Philadelphia).

Throughout the season sportswriters trying to understand Ditmar's precipitous drop in 1961 frequently chalked it up to a sore arm—something the veteran righty vigorously denied. He would not be as fortunate in 1962. In spring training Ditmar hurt his arm but was able to persevere sufficiently to grab a spot in the Athletics rotation. He made four starts through May 12 but struggled with his control. On May 19 Ditmar took the mound in Washington's D.C. Stadium and surrendered three runs and six hits in 2⅔ innings. It proved to be his last major-league appearance. Six days later he was released. In June, Stengel, who was managing the expansion New York Mets, arranged a tryout for Ditmar but nothing came of this. He secured a stint with the Yankees' Richmond affiliate in the International League but was released on July 5 after just two weeks. Determined to make his way back to the majors, Ditmar got permission to work out with the Yankees through the fall and joined the club as a nonroster invitee the following spring. But when he did not make the club in 1963, he retired.

On October 1, 1956, Ditmar married Missouri native Mary Jane Creel, a Trans World Airlines hostess four years his junior. The union produced four children (three boys and one girl) before dissolving in divorce in 1970. During these years Ditmar attended American International College in Springfield, Massachusetts, in the offseason and earned a bachelor's degree in 1962. He remained at AIC in pursuit of his master's degree while coaching the college's basketball and baseball teams. (Major-league catcher Fran Healy was one of his players.) Around 1971 Ditmar married Dianne Meara, a professor at AIC, and moved to Cleveland suburb of Brook Park, Ohio, where he became the city's director of parks and recreation. In 1986 he retired to a life of golf, tennis, and leisure in Myrtle Beach, South Carolina.

During the 1980s the Anheuser-Busch Brewing Company spun a Budweiser television commercial that incorporated the famous Bill Mazeroski homer in the 1960 World Series. The original NBC radio broadcast had incorrectly identified Ditmar as the pitcher who surrendered the Series-ending blow. (One report suggests he was warming up in the bullpen when the drive was struck.) When the audio was replayed more than 20 years after the fact, Ditmar sued the brewing company for $500,000, claiming "the commercial held him up to 'undeserved ridicule, humiliation and contempt.'"[19] A U.S. district judge threw out the case.

Throughout his playing career Ditmar was a frequent speaker at Chamber of Commerce and sports jamboree functions and, in 1960 at the annual Sportswriters Alliance Gold Key dinner in Hartford, Connecticut. In at least two years he also spent the offseason barnstorming in New England and Canada. In retirement he was a frequent participant at autograph shows and Old Timer's Games and in 2015 he was inducted alongside West Springfield native Vic Raschi into the Western Massachusetts Baseball Hall of Fame.

Ditmar concluded a nine-year major-league career with a record of 72-77, 3.98 in 1,268 innings, a far cry from the expectations of the Athletics coaches in 1954. But with the exception of two fine seasons in the Bronx, his pedestrian record can be attributed in part to the second-division clubs for whom he played.

## SOURCES

The author wishes to thank SABR members Bill Mortell and Rod Nelson, chair of the SABR Scouts Committee, for their valuable research. In addition to the sources cited in the Notes, the author also consulted Ancestry.com and Baseball-Reference.com, and an interview with Art Ditmar conducted by Irv Berman, July 10, 1992.

## NOTES

1. "Kaycee Can See Improvement in A's—Particularly in Pitching," *The Sporting News*, June 1, 1955: 6.
2. "Not-for-Sale Sign Pinned on Ditmar, Casey's Prize Pupil," *The Sporting News*, December 24, 1958: 4.
3. The Philadelphia Athletics showed interest in signing George before he suffered an arm injury in college.
4. A second source indicates that scout Dutch Brennan signed Ditmar.
5. Another source suggests eight wins.
6. "Kaycee Can See Improvement."
7. Ditmar also placed among the league leaders in yield of homers (23), earned runs (98), wild pitches (7), and HBP (7).
8. "Lou Labels Ditmar as Dandiest Kaycee Mound Discovery," *The Sporting News*, October 5, 1955: 17.
9. Ibid.
10. "Ditmar Seen as Key Player in Yank-A's Deal," *The Sporting News*, February 27, 1957: 5.
11. "Yankee Trades Also Help A's," *The Sporting News*, June 26, 1957: 12.
12. "Yanks Collect Early Dividends on Their Ditmar, Shantz Deal," *The Sporting News*, May 15, 1957: 11.
13. "Perfessor Praises Ditmar; Manager's Kind of Player," *The Sporting News*, February 18, 1959: 7.
14. Of the 17 home runs Ditmar yielded in 1959, four were struck by Colavito, all on first pitches.
15. "Casey Tosses Bouquet to Lion-Hearted Hurlers," *The Sporting News*, September 7, 1960: 7.
16. Rich Marazzi and Len Fiorito, *Baseball Players of the 1950s: A Biographical Dictionary of All 1,560 Major Leaguers* (Jefferson, North Carolina: McFarland, 2003), 93.
17. Dan McHale, "Bill Stafford," SABR Biography, accessed August 8, 2016. (sabr.org/bioproj/person/0a22d550).
18. "Front-Liners Drill at Yank Kiddie Camp," *The Sporting News*, February 22, 1961: 10.
19. "Ditmar Suit Rejected," *The Sporting News*, October 24, 1988: 42.

# AUGUSTUS ADOLF "GUS" DORNER

BY PAUL HOFMANN

**WHILE ONLY ONE MAJOR-LEAGUE** pitcher has lost 20 games in a single season during the twenty-first century, the now dubiously recognized feat did not carry the same stigma a century ago. In fact, during the 1901-1910 decade, 12 different pitchers for Boston's National League entry produced 18 seasons of 20 or more losses. Among them were Hall of Famer Vic Willis; 20-game winners Irv Young, Togie Pittinger, and Chick Fraser; and eight other lesser known hurlers including Augustus Dorner.

Gus Dorner was a 5-foot-10, 175-pound right-hander who compiled a 35-69 lifetime record with a 3.37 ERA over a six-year major-league career that spanned 1902-1909 and included stops in Cleveland, Cincinnati, and Boston (NL). A hard-luck loser who played for poor teams and received little run support, Dorner joined the fraternity of major-league pitchers who lost 20 or more games in a season when his name appeared in the loss column a National League-leading 26 times in 1906.

Augustus Adolf Dorner was born on August 18, 1876, in Chambersburg, Pennsylvania, a rural town in the south-central region of the state. Located just north of the Mason-Dixon Line, the town was made famous as a stop on the Underground Railroad. Gus was the youngest of five children (four boys and one girl) born to Peter and Mary (Helfrick) Dorner.[1] Peter immigrated to the United States from Darmstadt, Hesse, Germany. After arriving in the United States, he served in the Union Army and later worked as a boot and shoemaker in Chambersburg. With the exception of the time he spent away for baseball, Gus was a lifelong resident of Chambersburg.

The family's connection to Chambersburg dates to the early part of the 19th century. In 1816 Mary Blattner, Dorner's maternal grandmother boarded a ship bound for the United States with her parents and four siblings. The voyage was an eventful one that turned tragic for the family. The ship became disabled and was blown off course. After weeks at sea, provisions were exhausted and Mary's father and two sisters died of starvation. The ship then drifted into a field of ice and where its sides were crushed before sinking. While the surviving members of the Blattner clan, including Mary, were saved they did not have the money to pay for their passage on the ship that rescued them. Mary, along with her sister and mother, were sold to Mr. Henry Etter, a Chambersburg resident, for $400.[2] Mary was bound out as a housekeeper to another family in the area and granted her "freedom" when she was 18 years old. She later married John Helfrick. The couple had five children, three of whom lived to adulthood, including Dorner's mother Mary.[3]

While little is known about Gus's early years and education, like many of his contemporaries in Chambersburg, he worked on the family farm while growing up. At the age of twelve he fell from the loft of his father's stable and landed on a hay wagon. His left shoulder was seriously injured and the physician who was called to attend to him removed several pieces of bone and stitched up his badly lacerated shoulder.[4] Fortunately, the injury was not to his throwing shoulder.

As a young man he worked as a cattle dealer.[5] It was around this time that he became acquainted with Henry "Pat" Rollins, a fellow resident of Chambersburg and a fellow parishioner at Corpus Christi Catholic Church.[6] Rollins was born in Washington, D.C., in 1860 and started his 19-year minor- and independent-league baseball career with Chambersburg of the Keystone Association in 1884.

The association with Rollins opened doors for Dorner. Upon the recommendation of the 40-year-old catcher, Dorner was signed by the

Decatur Commodores of the Illinois-Indiana-Iowa League for the 1901 season. He pitched with the Commodores for two seasons before being acquired by the Cleveland Bronchos in September of 1902.

On September 17, 1902, Dorner made his major-league debut with Cleveland when he faced off against Wiley Piatt at the Chicago White Sox' South Side Park III. While his inaugural major-league start was far from a masterpiece—he gave up 10 hits and walked four—the right-hander pitched well enough to earn a complete-game victory. He breezed through the first six innings without yielding a run to the White Sox before a single run in the seventh and five in the eighth evened the game at 6-6. The Bronchos regained the lead with a single run in the ninth and Dorner held off the White Sox in the ninth to earn a hard-fought 7-6 victory.[7] He also contributed with the bat and enjoyed a 3-for-3 afternoon with a sacrifice hit and a double, the only extra-base hit of his major-league career. Dorner, who batted right-handed, was not much of a threat at the plate and finished his career with a .149 batting average.

Ten days later, Dorner started the season finale at Detroit's Bennett Park and bested Win Mercer and the Tigers, 2-0 to earn his first career shutout. (This was Mercer's final major-league appearance. Tragically, he committed suicide in January of 1903.)

For Dorner, the future seemed bright. He finished his four-game late-season stint with the Bronchos with a 3-1 record, four complete games, and a 1.25 ERA. His effort marked the first time in the modern era that a pitcher with at least 20 innings pitched recorded an ERA lower than his WHIP (1.278).[8] From a statistical perspective, it appeared that Dorner factored prominently into the team's future. This, however, did not prove to be the case.

Dorner did not make his first start of the 1903 season until May 9 and appeared in only 12 games for Cleveland, now known as the Naps. Though he tossed a pair of shutouts in June, his season was plagued with fits of wildness and inconsistency. On May 23 he established a Cleveland franchise record when he came on in relief of Addie Joss and issued 11 walks in a 4-2 loss to the Philadelphia Athletics at Cleveland's League Park.[9] The 11 free passes continue as of 2017 to stand as a team record.

Dorner's record stood at 3-5, with a career-worst 4.52 ERA, when on August 17, 1903, he was traded to the Columbus Senators of the American Association. The Naps swapped Dorner and utility infielder Billy Clingman for a 22-year-old infielder named Terry Turner, who was batting an impressive .310 for the Senators. Turner went on to set the Cleveland franchise record for games played.[10] Dorner, on the other hand, began the process of working his way back to the major leagues. He appeared in 15 games with the Senators during the balance of the 1903 season and finished with a 7-7 record.

The right-hander returned to the Senators rotation in 1904. The season was the beginning of a special time in Columbus baseball history and a period of great personal success for Dorner. He had a breakout season in Columbus with 18 wins and 10 defeats. His victory total ranked second on the team behind former major leaguer John Malarkey's 24 wins as the Senators planted the seeds of what would become the American Association's first dynasty.

In 1905 the Senators were the class of the American Association field. Dorner led a triumvirate of 20-game winners with a league-leading 29 victories. Fellow right-handers Heine Berger (25) and Bucky Veil (21) also eclipsed the 20-win plateau, while 40-year-old Bill Hart came out of retirement at midseason to notch 12 victories.[11] The superlative pitching staff was complemented by veteran major-league catcher Jack Ryan, and the Senators roared to a 100-52 record and the first of three consecutive American Association crowns.[12]

Dorner's feats in Columbus drew national attention. When asked by a reporter what he credited his success to, he replied, "I attribute my success to condition as much as anything else. I try to keep myself in the best possible physical and mental shape all the time. The former is accomplished by abstinence from liquor, good hours, and plenty of work; the latter by refraining from worry."[13] He also cited studying batters' tendencies and his mastery of the spitball. "I have worked hard to get control and to perfect the spit ball. I use the spit ball a great deal, mixing it with speed and curves. I have also developed a side arm ball which has been useful to me."[14]

Dorner's comments provided insight into the type of pitcher he was. He relied on finesse and deception more than blazing speed. For his career he averaged only 2.72 strikeouts per nine innings. Despite his 11-walk outing in 1903 and other occasional fits of wildness, Dorner averaged 3.26 walks per nine innings during his major-league career. Like most of his contemporaries, he was not opposed to pitching inside. In his three full big-league seasons, 1906-1908, Dorner ranked first (17), second (15), and third (15) in hit batsmen among National League pitchers.

After Dorner's retirement, an unknown baseball scribe offered a retrospective view of his career that also characterized the right-hander as a crafty, tough-luck pitcher.

> Dorner smeared slippery elm saliva on every ball he threw; his curves did not break over an inch or so, but in his long career in the major and minor leagues a player can not be found who ever hit one of his benders the way he thought he wanted it to go. The 'stuff' on the ball, its rotation in other words, gave it queer "english" off the bat, and his endeavor to never throw two balls alike in any game precluded any tendency of his opponents to study his style. … His sale to Boston, then a trailer, discounted his efforts when his teammates fell down in fielding their positions, and he was beaten time after time by wild throws, errors of judgment and boneheads.[15]

After the 1905 season, the Senators sold Dorner's contract to the Cincinnati Reds. The hurler's stay with the Reds was short-lived; two games. His lone start with the club came on May 2, a 4-1 loss to Vic Willis and the Pittsburgh Pirates. Dorner was 0-1 with a 1.20 ERA when he was sent to the Boston Beaneaters on May 10, 1906, to complete a deal for fellow 20-game loser Chick Fraser.[16] Despite logging a 2.67 ERA with the Reds, Fraser finished 1906 with a 10-20 mark. It was the only time in major-league history that a pair of 20-game losers were traded for each other in the same season.

After joining the offensively-challenged Beaneaters, Dorner managed to win only eight games while dropping 25, largely due to an anemic offense that averaged only 2.68 runs per game. He was not the only Boston pitcher to be victimized by a lack of run support. Dorner was joined on the list of 20-game losers that season by teammates Irv Young (16-25), Vive Lindaman (12-23), and Big Jeff Pfeffer (13-22) as the Beaneaters finished with a woeful record of 49-102, in last place 66½ games behind the pennant-winning Chicago Cubs. They were only the second team in major-league history, following the 1905 Beaneaters, to have four pitchers lose 20 or more games in one season — a feat that is not likely to be duplicated

Dorner returned to the Boston team, now known as the Doves, in 1907 and tied Patsy Flaherty for the team lead in victories. He pitched a team-leading 271⅓ innings and finished 12-16 with a 3.12 ERA — more than half a run lower than his 1906 ERA. He also finished the season with a 1.000 field-

DORNER
Pitcher, Boston N. L.

ing percentage, a vast improvement over 1906, when he made 10 errors. Overall, it was his most consistent season in the major leagues.

Despite coming off his most successful season in the majors, Dorner demonstrated his eccentric side when he visited hospitalized batterymate Sam Brown in December of 1907. Brown had had an appendectomy. While visiting the light-hitting catcher, Dorner had a conversation with the doctor who performed the operation. The doctor explained to Dorner how the appendix, a useless organ, interfered with a man's "habits."[17] Dorner was so impressed with the doctor's explanation that he convinced himself removing his appendix would improve his performance on the mound. To that end, he had his appendix removed that day.

Any competitive advantage Dorner enjoyed from the removal of his appendix during the offseason was presumably purely psychological. While he filled the role of the Doves' number-three starter and pitched 216⅓ innings, his record dipped to 8-19 and his ERA rose to 3.54. While Dorner did throw a career-high three shutouts, he finished the season dropping his last five decisions.

The 1909 season was Dorner's last in the major leagues. He pitched in five games for the Doves and finished 1-2 with a 2.55 ERA and one save—the lone save of his big-league career. On May 17 Dorner appeared in his final major-league contest and 11 days later the Doves sold his contract to the American Association's Kansas City Blues. He finished the season with a 9-18 record for the Blues.

Dorner's likeness on the Blues is included in the highly collectible, landmark 1909-1911 T-206 baseball card set. A typesetting error resulted in a very limited number of Dorner's cards being printed as "Dopner." The variation is considered one of the rarest in the T-206 set. One of these error cards fetched more than $6,500 at auction in May of 2012.[18]

Dorner returned to Chambersburg at the end of the 1909 season and married Ruth Viola Karper at Corpus Christi Catholic Church on January 11, 1910.[19] An announcement of the nuptials painted Dorner as a financially conservative, if not frugal, individual. "Gus has been saving his pennies for several years, at least all the pennies that he didn't put into Chambersburg, Pa., real estate, and has a comfortable sum to lay back upon."[20] Following their vows, the couple enjoyed a modest honeymoon in Philadelphia prior to the start of the 1910 season. The newly married couple was fortunate to stay relatively close to family and friends during Dorner's final two seasons in professional baseball.

In 1910 Dorner pitched for the Wilkes-Barre Barons of the New York State League. Now an elder statesman at age 33, he went 12-6 and helped the Barons finish on top of the league. He spent the 1911 season, his final in Organized Baseball, with the Harrisburg Senators of the Tri-State League and finished with a 4-5 record. On June 11, 1911, Dorner and his wife welcomed the arrival of their only child, Paul Augustus Dorner.

Dorner's baseball career now behind him, the family returned to their roots in Chambersburg and settled at 101 West King Street, a few blocks from what was Mary Ritner's boarding house, where John Brown stayed and prepared his raid on Harpers Ferry during the summer and fall of 1859.[21] Dorner briefly managed the Chambersburg Maroons of the Class-D Blue Ridge League in 1915, served as an umpire in local independent leagues, and worked at Schaal's Garage in Chambersburg.[22]

On March 13, 1928, Ruth, Dorner's wife of 18 years, suffered an embolism and died. While she had been suffering from flu-like symptoms for nearly three months, her passing was unexpected.[23] Coincidentally, she died one day after the death of her older brother, Harvey Karper, and the two were buried next to each other in Chambersburg's Cedar Grove Cemetery. Now a widower, Dorner dedicated his remaining years to his parish and civic engagement.

Dorner was a practicing Catholic who attended Mass regularly at Corpus Christi Catholic Church. He was a member of the Holy Name and St. Vincent DePaul societies of the parish, held membership in the Knights of Columbus and the Elks, and was a charter member of the Franklin Fire Company.[24] Dorner was the driving force behind Franklin

County's effort to acquire a fire truck to serve Chambersburg and its surrounding areas. Dorner traveled throughout the region to raise the money necessary to bring fire service to the rural community, and in 1933 the fire department took possession of its first Rural Community Pumper.[25]

On June 15, 1954, Dorner's life took another unexpected turn when his 42-year-old son, Paul, suffered a heart attack and died.[26] After that Dorner's health declined steadily. He suffered a stroke in October 1954 and another in May of 1955. On May 4, 1956, Augustus Dorner died at the age of 79 after an illness that had hospitalized him since February of that year. He was buried next to his son in Corpus Christi Cemetery.[27]

## SOURCES

In addition to the sources cited in the Notes, the author also relied on Baseball-reference.com and Retrosheet.org.

## NOTES

1. United States Census, 1880.
2. George Wolf, "A White Slave," *Valley Spirit* (Chambersburg, Pennsylvania), September 20, 1894.
3. Paul Ruda, personal correspondence, March 30, 2017.
4. "Cumberland Valley Items," *Harrisburg Telegraph*, June 22, 1889.
5. United States Census, 1900.
6. Paul Ruda, personal correspondence, March 30, 2017.
7. "Spiders Win Out: Game Taken, However, Only After Stubborn Fight by Champions," *Washington Times*, September 8, 1902: 4.
8. "Pitchers With a Lower ERA Than WHIP," retrieved from valueoverreplacementgrit.com.
9. "Single Game Records," retrieved from cleveland.indians.mlb.com.
10. Scott Turner, "Terry Turner," SABR BioProject.
11. A writeup on milb.com has his record at 11-5. See milb.com/milb/history/top100.jsp?idx=59.
12. Bill Weiss and Marshall Wright, "Top 100 Teams." Retrieved from milb.com.
13. "Spitball Doesn't Hurt This Whip," *Pittsburgh Press*, August 20, 1905: 22.
14. Ibid.
15. "The Place-Hitters Are Coming to the Fore." *Muskogee* (Oklahoma) *Times-Democrat*, April 1, 1912: 1.
16. Chick Fraser was a four-time 20 game loser, in 1898 and 1904-1906.
17. "Diamond Appendices to Go: Pitcher Dorner in Favor of Cutting Out Useless Organ," *Scranton Republic*, December 27, 1907: 1.
18. Robert Edward Auctions, "1909-1911 T206 Gus Dorner—Dopner Variation—RARE! ("1 of 1")," Retrieved from robertedwardauctions.com.
19. "Gus Dorner Takes a Wife," *The News Journal* (Wilmington, Delaware), January 13, 1910: 6.
20. "Gossip of the Ball Players," *Ada* (Oklahoma) *News*, January 22, 1910.
21. Paul Ruda, personal correspondence, March 30, 2017.
22. Paul Ruda, personal correspondence, April 25, 2017.
23. Ruth Dorner, Certificate of Death.
24. "Augustus Dorner," *The News-Chronicle* (Shippensburg, Pennsylvania), May 18, 1956: 21.
25. Franklin Fire Company History. Retrieved from www.sta4.com.
26. Paul Dorner, Certificate of Death.
27. Augustus Dorner, Certificate of Death.

# CECIL FERGUSON

### BY JEFF FINDLEY

ON OCTOBER 1, 1906, CECIL Ferguson delivered a solid pitching performance for the New York Giants, shutting down the St. Louis Cardinals in the back end of a doubleheader, 2-0. The nightcap was a scheduled five-inning affair, and as noted in the *New York Times,* "the St. Louis team was completely at the mercy of Ferguson, making only two safe hits."[1]

The start was the first of Ferguson's rookie season and major-league career. Under the tutelage of manager John McGraw, Ferguson had previously been used exclusively as a "rescue pitcher," a role fulfilled for the Giants in 1905 by Claude Elliott, when Elliott was credited with six saves (This statistic was first adopted by the major leagues in 1969, but baseball researchers have calculated many statistics retroactively.)

Ferguson posted a major-league-leading seven saves in 1906 after being acquired in August 1905 by the Giants from Louisville of the American Association for a player to be named later. That trade was finalized in April 1906, when New York sent Elliott to Louisville and, in effect, traded one "rescue pitcher" for the other.

The onset of the 1906 season was a cold, wet spring training in Memphis in March, which included a bout of diphtheria for Giants ace Christy Mathewson. But high expectations traveled north as the Giants, World Series champions in 1905, arrived in New York to play some preseason exhibition games at the Polo Grounds. The next day, the *New York Times* summed up McGraw's hopes for Ferguson:

"McGraw is enthusiastic over the showing of the young Ferguson, whom he secured from Louisville in exchange for Claude Elliott. He believes the young fellow has all the attributes of a successful pitcher, and lacks only experience to whip him into such shape that he will be able to take his turn with the rest of them. He is cool headed, it is said, and ought to make good soon, though the entry of a young pitcher into major league company is the most precarious speculation known to baseball. The younger Mathewson [a comparison to Christy] has not done so well, although he has the physique to develop into a first-class man, and with careful tuition and training ought to do something. He is too young yet to expect very much of him, being only 18 years of age."[2]

In actuality, Ferguson was 22 years old at the time, but with no official major-league experience, he was relatively unknown and certainly unproven. That would change.

Cecil Benoni Ferguson was born on August 27, 1883, in Ellsworth, Indiana, the second of four sons of Ellis Ferguson, a farmer, and Catherine (Trublood) Ferguson. (His birthplace was not the town of Ellsworth in Dubois County that now sits underneath the Pakota Reservoir, but rather the small town of Ellsworth in Vigo County that is now known as North Terre Haute.[3]

As a boy growing up in Ellsworth, Ferguson was considered one of the area's finest all-around high-school athletes, playing fullback on the Terre Haute High School football teams that went unbeaten in 1901 and 1902.[4] Before graduating from high school, Ferguson signed a pro baseball contract with Terre Haute's 1902 Class-B Three-I League team, the Hottentots, but was released in June.[5] Subsequently, he spent the summer of 1902 with the Lansing Senators of the Class-D Michigan State League, until the league disbanded in August.

The following season, still just 19 years old, Ferguson signed with the South Bend Greens of the Central League, a rival of the Terre Haute team that had cut him loose the previous year. The acquisition wasn't without contention, as league President George W. Bement had to rule in a dispute between South Bend and Terre Haute over the rights to Ferguson.[6] Bement ruled in favor of South Bend, and

Ferguson rewarded the Greens with a solid season, leading them to a close second-place finish behind Fort Wayne. The final standings were actually disputed by his club, and despite multiple claims that results were inaccurate and percentages miscalculated, Fort Wayne was officially proclaimed the champion by President Bement. The teams played a postseason series of no consequence to the standings or the championship, but a side bet was arranged by the players on each side. South Bend won three games with one tie, with Ferguson's arm accounting for one of the victories.

In consideration of his strong showing in 1903, Ferguson, who had earned $150 monthly, returned his contract unsigned for the 1904 season with a request that his salary be raised to $200. The strategy didn't work, however. Central Baseball League managers were attempting to lower salaries throughout the league; Ferguson eventually signed for $125 monthly and rejoined the Greens for the 1904 season.[7]

His showing in 1904 continued to rate him a solid prospect, and although South Bend finished a distant third in the standings, Ferguson's contribution continued to be of notice. The *Fort Wayne Evening Sentinel* ran a feature in June 1904 headlined "A Young 'Phenom' Who Delivers the Goods," and noted that "Ferguson is a good man and looked upon generally as big league timber as soon as he is a little better seasoned."[8]

In late July, George Tebeau, president of Louisville Colonels of the American Association, purchased four players from South Bend. Ferguson was among them, and joined the Louisville team on September 8, four days before the close of the Central League season. The Colonels swept both ends of a doubleheader against Toledo on September 11, with Ferguson striking out nine in a 7-2 victory in the nightcap that was called after five innings because of darkness.[9]

The following season, 1905, again with Louisville, Ferguson appeared in 43 games for the Colonels, posting a 14-18 record with 313 innings pitched. Although he lost more games than he won, he continued to be noticed despite his team's futility.[10] Ferguson, identified as a prospect by the Giants' McGraw, finished the season with the Ohio Works club of Youngstown, awaiting his ascent to the major leagues as the Giants finalized a deal with Louisville.

The Giants had five established starters, Ferguson joined the team in 1906 with limited fanfare. As noted earlier, his only start late in the schedule was a quality one, but McGraw used him almost exclusively as a reliever throughout the season. In an early appearance in June, Ferguson gave up 14 hits in seven mop-up innings, after the Giants starter surrendered 11 runs in the first inning of a 19-0 loss to Chicago.[11] But the appearance proved to be an anomaly, and although not an accredited statistic at the time, Ferguson's seven saves led the league, and he posted a respectable earned-run average of 2.58 over 52⅓ innings in his rookie season.

Ferguson was used as a starter in early 1907, and posted a 3-1 mark through his first four games. But a poor outing on June 24 against the Boston Doves included five hits, four walks, and two wild pitches in the first three innings of a 10-8 loss. Ferguson did not start another game as a Giant. For the season, he again posted a respectable earned-run average of

FERGUSON, BOSTON NAT'L

2.11, but he appeared in only 15 games and posted a single save. Not only did New York finish 25½ games behind the Cubs in the final standings, but McGraw, who earlier considered sending Ferguson back to the minor leagues to improve his control,[12] now sought greater changes. On December 13, 1907, McGraw traded Ferguson along with Frank Bowerman, George Browne, Bill Dahlen, and Dan McGann to Boston for Al Bridwell, Tom Needham, and Fred Tenney. Ferguson would wear a Boston Doves jersey in 1908, a team name adapted from the Dovey brothers (George and John), who now owned the club formerly known as the Beaneaters.

If not for the St. Louis Cardinals in 1907, Boston would have finished in last place in the National League. The infusion of new players moved the Doves up a spot in 1908, and Ferguson was placed in the regular rotation, starting 21 games and completing 13. On June 12, in a home win over Cincinnati, he put together perhaps his greatest performance to date. Jack Ryder of the *Cincinnati Enquirer* described it as follows:

"It was a desperate contest all the way. The Reds played cleaner ball on the defense than the Doves, and have not lost their aggressive spirit, but they were perfectly powerless in the hands of Ferguson. The big fellow had 'em winging for fair. Any twirler who can hold our famous sluggers to two stingy hits is going some and is entitled to a prominent place in the baseball hall of fame. Fergy had the Ganzel group completed dazzled. He used speed, curves and a tantalizing slow ball copied after Dr. Coakley's, and not one of his brands was hittable. His wide curve especially was an awful fooler, and the best batters on the team were deceived over and over again into standing calmly by and letting good ones split the plate without offering at them. At other times they were caught in the act of swiping wildly at balls a foot or two from the plate. Whether they struck or did not strike it was all the same, for Fergy had them either way."[13]

Five days later, Ferguson walked four in 1⅓ innings in a 14-4 loss to Pittsburgh. It was reported that he snapped a ligament in his arm, and he was sent to the prominent therapist and healer Bonesetter Reese in Youngstown, Ohio, for treatment.[14]

Whether rest or treatment made the difference, Ferguson's first game back, on July 27, resulted in a 6-0 complete-game victory over Cincinnati, and he followed that performance with another complete game, scattering five hits in a 14-0 drubbing of Chicago on August 1. The Doves were 16 games out of first place by this point, with no hope of competing for the pennant. Ferguson won five more games before the season was over, and finished the year with an 11-11 record and another effective ERA of 2.47.

After the moderate success of the 1908 season, 1909 looked promising for Ferguson, who was still only 25 years old when the season began. An Opening Day start resulted in a 9-5 victory over Philadelphia, and the optimism was further validated early in the season when Boston traveled to New York and Ferguson stymied his former mates with a complete-game, two-hit shutout in a 10-0 thrashing at the Polo Grounds. The *New York Times* recapped the domination in this fashion: "It may have been indicated above that the Giants were defeated at the Polo Grounds yesterday afternoon. They made no runs themselves, but the Doves raced across the home plate so fast and so often that the afternoon papers disagreed as to how many tallies they did really make. One paper said nine. Most of the others said ten."[15]

With the victory in New York, Boston was first in the standings, and Ferguson was 2-1 in the young season. But the Doves lost 10 of Ferguson's next 11 starts, and on June 25 occupied the National League cellar, 27 games behind the Pirates.

Ferguson rallied in his subsequent two outings, tossing back-to-back shutouts against Philadelphia, 1-0 and 4-0. But the Doves were a hapless bunch, and Ferguson was 1-11 in his next 12 starts. His final start, on September 13, against the Giants ended in a 4-4 tie after 13 innings, called due to darkness. With 23 games remaining on Boston's schedule, Ferguson had seen his last start in 1909. Overall, he started 30 games, with 19 complete games. Boston won only 45 games, with Ferguson taking the loss in over half of those, and the Doves finished 65½ games behind the pennant-winning Pittsburgh Pirates. His final record was 5-23, with a 3.73 earned-run average.

With the disappointing season behind him, Ferguson was reported to be retiring, and announced in February 1910 that he was going into the grocery business in Ellsworth (North Terre Haute).[16] But the plan was abandoned, and he signed with Boston in March for another season.[17]

The 1910 season saw a decline in the Doves' utilization of Ferguson. He did complete 10 games among 14 starts, and although he posted a respectable 7-7 record, his innings pitched declined by more than 100 from the year before. Boston again finished last in the National League, losing 100 games.

Despite the statistical mediocrity displayed by Ferguson and the lackluster results of the Doves in general, Ferguson was credited with having perhaps the most peculiar assist made in the 1910 season, as noted in multiple newspapers, including the *Brazil Times*, a newspaper based just outside Indianapolis:

"The play came up late in the season in a game against Brooklyn and resulted in a victory for the Boston team. At least it prevented the Brooklyn team from taking the lead, and as Boston afterwards won the game, the chances are the play turned the tide.

"Ferguson was pitching. Both teams had been hitting hard and making many runs and Fergy was thrown in to save the day with a runner on third base and one out. He pitched well enough, but in spite of his efforts the batter drove a fly to Miller, who was over in deep left center. The runner held his base and the batter tore around first to race to second on the throw to the plate. Ferguson went over on the line between shortstop and the catcher, being ready to catch the ball and throw to second base in case he decided there wasn't a chance to catch the runner going home. He decided at the last minute that Miller's throw was good enough to catch the runner at the plate, and dodged quickly into a stooping position to let the ball go to Harry Smith, who was catching. But in dodging Fergy miscalculated the shoot of the ball, which darted downward, cracking him on the top of the head. Instead of losing the game, the accident won it, as the ball caromed perfectly off the pitcher's pate into Smith's hands and the runner was out at the plate by a foot.

"As Fergy came to the bench Manager Fred Lake cruelly remarked: 'I'm glad to see you using your noodle at last.'"[18]

Ferguson used his "noodle" again during the off-season. He was denied a $500 bonus from the Doves for winning half his games, the Doves claiming two of the 14 games were exhibitions. Ferguson appealed to the National Commission, which ruled in his favor, noting that the contract clause in relation to the bonus made no stipulation about what games he was to pitch. The Boston Club was ordered to pay the bonus.[19]

Meanwhile, George Dovey had died in 1909, and John Dovey and his partner sold the club to William Hepburn Russell, who renamed the team the Rustlers for the 1911 season.

Ferguson again announced he was leaving baseball for good in 1911, to remain in the plumbing supplies business which occupied his offseason hours, unless the new Boston management gave him his figure.[20] He ultimately signed his contract, and his first appearance was a start on June 4 at Cincinnati. It was a disaster. Ferguson gave up six runs without registering an out in a 26-3 embarrassment. A week later, in Chicago, Ferguson gave up seven more runs (five earned) in a 20-2 loss to the Cubs. The newly characterized Rustlers already occupied the bottom position in the standings, 19½ games out.

Ferguson pitched respectfully in a June 22 relief appearance, holding the Giants to four runs in 7⅔ innings in an 8-7 victory.

A 5-0 loss on June 26, and a brief appearance in a loss to Cincinnati on July 6 were final gasps of Ferguson's diminishing major-league experience. One final start on July 21, a 7-5 loss at home to Pittsburgh in which Ferguson allowed 11 hits in eight innings, would end the once promising career with a less-than-stellar 29-46 record.

Although not specifically noted as affecting Ferguson's baseball exploits, his father, Ellis, was kicked over the heart by a horse in early June and died in July, the final month of Ferguson's major-league career.[21]

His performance ineffective, Ferguson was sold by the Rustlers to Memphis of the Southern Association in late July. But Ferguson refused to report, staying in Boston and working out in hopes the Rustlers would recall him. He never saw action with Boston or any other major-league team the remainder of the schedule, and finally reported to Memphis for the 1912 season, when he fashioned a 9-18 record.[22]

One final sale, with Memphis shipping Ferguson to Venice (California) of the Pacific Coast League, closed out Ferguson's days in professional baseball. His statistics showed a 1-6 record in 10 starts, but the season wasn't without a colorful anecdote. In a start against Los Angeles, Ferguson was knocked unconscious by another ball to the head, the scenario described in the *Los Angeles Times* as follows:

"This brings us down to the nerve-racking round — the one in which Elliott [catcher] came near committing homicide on the head of Cecil Ferguson. Howard opened the second half with a sharp single over second. He started to steal on the next pitch. Elliott winged the ball on a line toward second with the speed of a Mauser bullet. Ferguson stooped to avoid the throw, and turned his head. The ball struck him on the cerebellum and caromed out to Carlisle in deep left.

"No one saw the direction of the ball, and Howard rushed to the plate unmolested. Ferguson staggered and slowly toppled back. He lay stretched into the middle of the diamond unattended until after Howard had scored.

"The water bucket was rushed to the center, and a few applications of the cool contents brought Fergy back to his feet. The crowd, which had been looking on with something akin to horror, greeted his return to consciousness with a round of applause, while the official scorer charged Elliott with an error and an attempt to commit manslaughter.

"Cecil, being a game individual, held his aching head with his left hand and resumed pitching with his right. He was plainly groggy, and walked [Billy] Page. Billy swiped second, and Elliott, thoroughly unnerved, sent him along to third with a throw into centerfield, Ferguson flopping on his stomach to make sure of saving his head."[23]

Despite a few appearances with Evansville back in the Central League in 1914, Ferguson was enrolled at the Kirksville (Missouri) Osteopath School with plans to become a physician. He coached the school's 1914 baseball team; it won every game on its schedule, and he was re-elected baseball mentor for the following season.[24]

Ferguson completed his studies, and emerged as Dr. Cecil Ferguson, developing into a prominent physician for athletic injuries, primarily as an arm specialist. Working as a "bone-setter" in Terre Haute, he treated athletes from the University of Illinois football team, including Red Grange.[25]

Ferguson ultimately moved his practice to Miami, Florida, and treated such prominent players as Lynwood (Schoolboy) Rowe[26] and Johnny Mize.[27]

A feature on Ferguson in 1942 summarized his contribution this way:

"You don't see his name in a box score or on a club roster, but Dr. Cecil Ferguson has played a bigger role in the baseball pennant races in recent years than many a headliner of the game.

"Dr. Ferguson, a Miami osteopath, is a 'Mr. Fix-It' of the sports world. He is described by Guy Butler of the *Miami Daily News* as the nearest approach yet to Bonesetter Reese, the famous old miracle man of sports who 'could fix anything from concussion to athlete's foot.' Himself a former pitcher for the New York Giants and Boston Braves, Dr. Ferguson in recent years has patched up some of the game's greatest stars, including such luminaries as Bob Feller, Carl Hubbell, Gabby Hartnett and Johnny Mize, not to mention scores of top-notchers in other sports.

"Dr. Ferguson confides that it was none other than the great Reese who gave him that start. While still pitching, he went to Reese to have a kink in his arm fixed, became interested in Reese's methods and later worked 18 months under him before starting out for himself."[28]

Despite his lackluster career after initially showing so much promise, Ferguson found great notoriety treating the quality of athlete he once aspired to be.

Ferguson had three brothers, all of whom became accomplished in life, two also becoming physicians. His youngest brother, Ralph, preceded Cecil in Miami, and the two practiced together before dissolving the partnership in 1931, when both brothers decided to operate independently.[29]

Denzil, the third of four Ferguson brothers, was a longtime Vigo County coroner who was followed in his career by his son, Denzil Jr.[30]

Leslie, the oldest brother, owned a downtown men's clothing store in Terre Haute and was the Vigo County recorder.[31]

While on a fishing trip, Ferguson suffered a heart attack near Montverde, Florida, and died at the age of 60 on September 5, 1943. He and his wife, Caroline (Lutz), who together raised two sons (William and Cecil Jr.), are buried in Woodlawn Park North Cemetery and Mausoleum in Miami.[32]

## SOURCES

In addition to the sources cited in the Notes, the author also accessed Retrosheet.org and Baseball-Reference.com.

## NOTES

1. "Giants Take Two Games," *New York Times*, October 2, 1906.
2. "Giants Come Home for Real Baseball," *New York Times*, April 7, 1906.
3. Pakota Reservoir Interpretive Master Plan 2009, Indiana Department of Natural Resources, in.gov/dnr/parklake/files/SP-Patoka_Lake_IMP2009.pdf, April 22, 2017.
4. Wabash Valley Visions & Voices Digital Memory Project, "Cecil Ferguson," visions.indstate.edu:8888/cdm/singleitem/collection/vchs/id/271/rec/1, May 2, 2017.
5. I.-I.-I. League Affairs, "A Protest Against Defiance of a National Board Award," *Sporting Life*, June 28, 1902: 5.
6. "Latest News from All Over the Central League," *Fort Wayne Journal-Gazette*, April 25, 1903: 2.
7. *Sporting Life*, March 5, 1904: 5.
8. "A Young 'Phenom' Who Delivers the Goods," *Fort Wayne Evening Sentinel*, June 9, 1904: 2.
9. Associated Press, "Colonels Take Both Games," *Muncie (Indiana) Star Press*, September 12, 1904: 3.
10. "Good Records in Baseball," *Louisville Courier-Journal*, December 31, 1905: 29.
11. "Giants Badly Beaten," *New York Times*, June 8, 1906: 7.
12. "May Release Giant Twirler," *St. Louis Post-Dispatch*, August 2, 1907: 7.
13. The Reds' Batting Slump Comes Along With Bells On," *Cincinnati Enquirer*, June 13, 1908: 3. "Dr. Coakley" presumably was Andy Coakley of the Philadelphia Athletics.
14. "National League News," *Sporting Life*, June 27, 1908: 9.
15. "Boston Finds Weak Giants Easy Victims," *New York Times*, April 28, 1909: 10.
16. "Diamond Chips," *Richmond (Indiana) Palladium and Sun-Telegraph*, February 12, 1910: 2.
17. "No Grocery for Fergy," *Brazil (Indiana) Daily Times*, March 16, 1910: 3.
18. "In the World of All Sports," *Brazil Daily Times*, December 28, 1910: 3.
19. "National League Men in Session," *New York Times*, December 14, 1910: 14.
20. "Big League Gossip," *Washington Herald*, April 9, 1911: 17.
21. "Races in Four Baseball Leagues," *Baltimore Sun*, June 8, 1911: 12.
22. "Sport Chat and Like O'That," *Zanesville (Ohio) Times Recorder*, October 7, 1911: 10.
23. Harry Williams, "Tigers Take Fuzzy Game," *Los Angeles Times*, September 11, 1913: 25.
24. "Palaver for the Fans," *Evansville (Indiana) Press*, June 19, 1914: 8.
25. "Ferguson a Bone-Setter," *Brooklyn Daily Eagle*, November 20, 1924: 27.
26. "Doctor Studies Rowe's Arm," *Des Moines Register*, March 17, 1934: 6.
27. "Mize Goes to Sidelines," *St. Louis Post-Dispatch*, March 6, 1942: 34.
28. Wayne Oliver, "Dixie Sports Huddle," *Asheville (North Carolina) Citizen-Times*, June 20, 1942: 10.
29. Dorothy Felker, "Surf Club's Easter Ball Finale of Winter Events," *Indianapolis Star*, April 5, 1931: 40.
30. Wabash Valley Visions & Voices Digital Memory Project, "Cecil Ferguson," visions.indstate.edu:8888/cdm/singleitem/collection/vchs/id/271/rec/1, June 4, 2017.
31. Ibid.
32. findagrave.com, Cecil B. "George" Ferguson.

# DANA FILLINGIM

## BY NIALL ADLER

**DANA FILLINGIM USED THE WET** pitch to his advantage from 1912 to 1928, as one of the last legal spitballers in the majors. His 47-73 overall record in the majors was as deceptive to the passing eye as the spitball was to an opposing batter. The right-hander won 20 games twice in the minors and once lost 20 games in the majors. He also won a 19-inning major-league game. He was a good pitcher on some bad teams. He used every advantage he could to get the win.

Dana Fillingim was born into Scotch-Irish and English ancestry on November 6, 1893, in Columbus, Georgia, the son of Alabama natives Henry and Terah (Fort) Fillingim.[1] He was the third of four brothers, the others being Henry (1881), Roscoe (1888), and Leon (1899).[2] He attended the Gordon Institute in Barnesville, Georgia, for four years.

Fillingim is said to have learned the spitball either at the Gordon Institute[3] or in working with Chicago White Sox hurler Ed Walsh.[4]

According to major-league umpire Bill Finneran, "seldom has a finger heaved such an effective spitter."[5]

According to his wife, Ava, her husband never had much of a curveball, and "the spitball acts like it's been rolled off the end of a table." When throwing the spitter overhand, his would break straight down. From a side-arm delivery, his spitter would break to either side.[6]

Dodger spitballer Bill Doak explained the pitch this way in 1961: "The spitter spun forward toward the plate. The fastball spins backward toward the mound. A liberal application of saliva on a spot about the size of a half-dollar formed the "launching pad." The two middle fingers rested on this spot. The thumb and outside fingers gripped the dry portion. The throw was the same motion as the fastball, but because of the wet surface, the ball left the two middle fingers first instead of last, giving it the down break."[7]

To further deceive batters, Fillingim pitched with a hesitation delivery, something copied by left-hander Johnny Cooney. "Fillingim slipped as he was about to deliver the ball. Fillingim recovered his equilibrium, got the ball across the plate and (Johnny) Cooney noticed that the batter was off-balance."[8]

Fillingim's "football knee," which slipped out of place when extended, would also cause concern for some teams to sign him.[9] It would eventually end his career, but not until 1928.

The spitball did have its disadvantages, discovered by basestealer Max Carey. Fillingim could not hold runners on, as the spitball was even harder for the first baseman to handle.[10]

Fillingim began his professional career in Albany, Georgia, in 1912, pitching in two games in the South Atlantic League.[11] He turned to the Empire State League and Cordele, Georgia, in 1913 for whom he went 15-10. On July 23, 1913, he pitched the front end of back-to-back no-hitters—Fillingim for nine innings followed by Cleo "Kid" Wilder's for seven in game two.[12]

A rival in high school in 1912, Wilder combined with Fillingim to go 31-20. The rest of the staff was 12-16, as Cordele dropped into last place in second-half standings.[13] Cordele was the first of many bad teams of which Fillingim was a part. The Empire State League disbanded in 1913. Cordele, the league's smallest city, became part of the Georgia State League in 1914.[14]

Fillingim would pass on his spitball to Eastman, Georgia, native John Vaughn, a fellow pitcher in the Georgia State League. Vaughn became a sought-after semipro spitballer in Akron, Ohio.[15]

In 1914 Fillingim split time between Cordele, where he was 16-6,[16] and the Atlanta Crackers in the Southern Association, to whom he was sold on August 20 and for whom he went 2-2.[17]

After four minor-league seasons Fillingim finally got the attention of the majors in 1915 while pitching for Charleston. In August he was sold to the last-place Philadelphia Athletics for $650[18] and was known as a spitball pitcher with a "fine curve and a good break to his fast one."[19] Fillingim was in the midst of a 14-5 record.

He made his major-league debut on August 2, 1915, at home against Cleveland, going seven innings, giving up four runs on eight hits. He did walk eight. News reports noted, "[A]lthough he was beaten he showed enough to warrant another chance.... [W]ildness was responsible for three of the four runs made by Cleveland and his lack of control was probably due to stage fright. After the third inning Fillingim pitched well and three of the hits secured by the Indians would have been outs with good fielding."[20]

In his next start, on August 7, he had "plenty of stuff" but gave up three runs over the first four innings against Ty Cobb's Tigers,[21] and a month later, on September 7, squandered a 2-1 lead by giving up five runs in the sixth against Washington. His career with the Athletics was brief, 0-5 for the 109-loss Athletics.

Fillingim returned to Charleston in 1916 and produced a 20-7 season. On May 12 he pitched a no-hitter against Montgomery[22] and racked up nine wins in a row.[23] Still the property of Connie Mack's A's, he struck out a rare 13 against Albany in May.[24]

At 14-4-1, Fillingim was sold to the Cleveland Indians in June where for three weeks he "viewed the scenery in Cleveland. ... (Manager Lee) Fohl let Dana warm up daily, but never used him."[25] He took his services to Columbus in July, going 2-5 with a 2.34 ERA,[26] and returned to Charleston to start August and finish the season.[27]

Fillingim joined the Indianapolis Indians in 1917 and at the age of 23 had his most successful season at 20-9 with a 2.34 ERA, which included an American Association championship.

There was high praise for the right-hander as one newspaper noted that he "appears to have lots of confidence and courage as well as a fine assortment of pitching stuff."[28] He stood at 5-feet-8 and weighed 182 pounds, "in other words all muscle." From his previous stints, "Folks in Albany who have seen him perform in the Sally League ... say he is one of the best pitchers ever developed in this part of the country." As with anyone, he longed to return to the majors.[29]

Fillingim debuted with Indianapolis with a four-hit shutout over St. Paul on May 5, 1917, hurling six no-hit innings.[30] By mid-June he was leading the American Association with a 7-1 mark and a 1.31 ERA as the Indians built a six-game lead over Columbus.[31] New York Giants scout Herman Schaefer took notice in July.[32] At 10-2 he was getting "quite a bit of attention from big league scouts."[33] The Phillies drafted him and then returned him at the end of the season because of a bum knee.[34]

Fillingim closed out 1917 by putting the Indians up 3-1 in the "Minor League World Series" with the International League's Toronto club, beating them 5-3, himself collecting three hits and getting the game-winning RBI.[35]

The eventual ban on the spitball reached the American Association in 1918. It was noted that some of the best pitchers in the league were dependent on the "freak delivery."[36] Only pitchers Jake Northrop and Fillingim pitched past 1920.

Without the spitter, Fillingim looked to develop a curveball, but was unsuccessful[37] and was traded to the Boston Braves in May for Clarence Covington and Calvin Crum. "His work has been made ineffective by the ban placed on the moist ball (in the American Association)," a newspaper commented.[38]

His first appearance for Boston, on May 9, featured four Braves errors, but seven assists by their newest pitcher in a 3-1 loss to Brooklyn.[39] Five days later he pitched a six-hit shutout against the eventual pennant-winning Cubs and followed that up with an 11-0 win over St. Louis, when he didn't allow a runner past second base.[40] He went on to win four straight decisions after losing his debut.

How good were young Fillingim's first four starts of seven or more innings with one earned run or less allowed? When Matt Harvey did it with the Mets at the age of 24 in 2013, just Fillingim and Ernie

Wingard (1924 St. Louis Browns) had done it so young.[41]

For the Braves, Fillingim, along with Bunny Hearn and Hugh Canavan, comprised a "promising bunch of young pitchers" behind older ace Art Nehf.[42]

The 1918 season also saw the U.S. continue to draft able-bodied men, including major leaguers. (The Braves sent 13 men into service.)[43]

On June 12 Fillingim's ERA plummeted to 0.29 over his first 62 innings after he beat Pittsburgh spitballer Roy Sanders, 1-0. He led the NL with four shutouts.

On June 22 he beat the Phillies 8-4, a team that passed on him because of that bad knee.[44] At that point Fillingim was 7-2 and the Braves were playing on borrowed time, improving to 29-28, in third place, nine games out. Fillingim enlisted in the Naval Reserve in early July.[45] With players leaving for the service, Boston would go 24-43 the rest of the way and Fillingim in limited action finished 7-6.

In half a season, 10 of Fillingim's 13 starts were complete games, in half as many starts as Nehf (28 complete games in 32 starts) or Pat Ragan (15 in 30). He finished the shortened year 7-6 with a 2.23 ERA, the lowest of any of the five Boston starters with 100-plus innings.

Serving in the Navy in Newport, Rhode Island, Fillingim and former big leaguer Toots Schultz provided the pitching[46] and Fillingim went 20-0 on a team featuring teammates Ray "Rabbit" Powell and catcher Walter Tragesser and outfielder Walter Rehg.[47] He was discharged in December without seeing action overseas.[48]

Fillingim returned from the service and worked at a Macon, Georgia, hotel in the offseason and returned as "one of the mainstays in the box" for the Braves.[49] Fillingim, Nehf, and Dick Rudolph were the set starters, as manager George Stallings had high hopes, while others stated that the Braves were a "hopeless organization."[50] They were right. Boston ended up sixth, losing 82 games..

Fillingim was used sparingly to start 1919, as he saw his ERA rise to 4.79, taking four losses as a starter. He did not win his first game until July 21, when he pitched six no-hit relief innings against St. Louis.

From there Fillingim started 13 of his final 17 games (nine complete games). In August and September alone he had a 2.98 ERA, but went just 3-8. He finished 6-13 with a 3.38 ERA as the Braves scored two runs or less in nine of his starts (0-8). The durable starter also pitched 15-, 11-, and 10-inning complete games, winning two of them.

Three years removed from winning 20 in the American Association, the opposite occurred in 1920 when Fillingim went 12-21 with a 3.11 ERA for the 90-loss Braves.

It was the dawn of the final legal spitballers in the majors, as 17 spitball pitchers, including Fillingim, were allowed to use that pitch until each retired.[51] By December 1920, the pitch became illegal for everyone else not grandfathered in.[52]

Fillingim had to overcome malaria prior to the start of the 1920 season.[53] He was considered one of the "best members of the twirling staff," as his control and spitball led to his success.[54]

In game three of the season Fillingim was the lucky recipient of a 19-inning win over Brooklyn on May 3, in which he gave up one unearned run in a 2-1 win. Brooklyn had played a 26-inning tie a few days before. He started the year with four straight complete games (and a 2-2 record). It took until late May for Fillingim to recover from that long outing, in the process losing three straight.[55]

At the end of June both the Braves (28-28) and Fillingim (7-8 with a 2.22 ERA) were respectable. Boston would go 36-62 the rest of the way and Fillingim followed at 5-13 as one of the "hardest luck pitchers we have seen in moons and many moons."[56]

Showing late-season grit on September 6, Fillingim "pitched his best game of the season," holding the third-place Giants to two hits in a 1-0 win.[57]

He completed 22 of his 31 starts that season, but Boston scored two or fewer runs in 20 of those starts (2-18 record). Never a strikeout pitcher, Fillingim was also one of only eight pitchers to strike out the Pirates' George Cutshaw, who finished with nine punchouts all season.[58]

Both Fillingim and Boston had a bounce-back year in 1921. The Braves finished fourth (79-74) and Fillingim was 15-10 with a 3.45 ERA.

A stiff arm all spring pushed the spitballer into the bullpen to start, as he had an 8.38 ERA through May 1.[59] But five straight wins turned the season around. He was 10-4 on July 18 and the Braves were 47-33 and six games back. But the Braves of old reappeared, as Boston played .438 ball the rest of the way and Fillingim was 5-6 with a 3.72 ERA.

Despite everything, Fillingim was one of seven NL pitchers to score three shutout victories.[60] The spitballers slowly faded as 17 became 15 and the lively ball proved troublesome. The top three spitballers, Burleigh Grimes, who would become the last legal spitballer; the Indians' Stanley Coveleski; and the White Sox Urban Faber relied on what was known as a fastball spitter. Fillingim was considered "runner-up of spitball honors" in the NL behind Grimes.[61]

With better-than-average hopes, Boston again faltered in 1922 as the Braves had another 20-game loser, Oeschger (6-21). Oeschger, Fillingim (6-9), Rube Marquard (11-15), and Hugh McQuillan (5-10) were expected to "win a majority of their games,"[62] but Boston lost 98 games.

Fillingim never recovered from a poor start in 1922 as his ERA ballooned to 5.92 on April 29 and he finished with a 4.54 ERA. After 33 complete games in 1920 and 1921, Fillingim had just five in '23 after wrenching his knee on July 10 while trying to field a bunt in the seventh inning against the Cubs. He did not pitch again that season.[63]

To try to get right for 1923, Fillingim was the only veteran pitcher to head to Hot Springs, Arkansas, on February 15. It was a schedule that saw 21 games of exhibition play primarily for the Braves rookies.[64]

The 100-loss Braves used Fillingim out of the bullpen, where despite a 1-9 record and 5.20 ERA, he had a 3.14 ERA out of the pen, combing for 100⅓ innings. Eight of his nine losses came when he was a starter.

Fillingim was due to pitch for Beaumont in the Texas League in 1924, one of the few leagues left that allowed the spitball. Because of his knee he wore a shoe with exceptionally high spikes and in one March game it got caught on the pitching rubber. He was helped from the field[65] and was lost for the season. His salary was still paid by Beaumont for the 1924 season. The club got its money back when Fillingim was sold to the Phillies after the season.[66]

Fillingim's time in Beaumont was not a total loss; it was where he met his wife, Ava Eugenia Fort, 10 years his junior.[67] The couple married in Tuskegee, Alabama, in March 1926 and they had their only child, Merle Eugenia, in 1927.[68]

Fillingim was one of a few former major leaguers looking for another shot with the Phillies, who had lost 96 the year before. He survived until May but Elmer Smith, Walter "Duster" Mails, Vean Gregg, and Ralph Shinners did not get that far.[69]

In five games in April and May, Fillingim went 1-0 with a 9.64 ERA, winning his last major-league game his first time out, pitching 1⅔ shutout innings in relief against Brooklyn on April 23.

Through an unknown transaction, he returned to Beaumont, where he won his debut on May 21.[70] Despite a high ERA, in August Fillingim was still considered one of the aces of the Texas League.[71] He won seven of the Exporters' 19 wins en route to a last-place finish at 19-55.[72] He finished 7-15 with a 5.73 ERA.

In one final attempt at the majors, Fillingim wrote to Reds owner Garry Herrmann with help of Ohio newspaper publisher James M. Cox. New Reds manager Jack Hendricks had known Fillingim in Indianapolis. The Reds declined his request because of his age, record, and knee.[73]

Back in Beaumont in 1926, Fillingim went 15-8 with a 3.54 ERA at the age of 32 before being sent to San Antonio for the 1927 season. There he pitched to a respectable 12-10 record with a 3.38 ERA, but San Antonio finished seventh of eight.

By the time of the 1927 season there were six spitballers left in the majors from the original 17.[74]

Fillingim opened San Antonio's 1928 season, his last professionally, against Cuban spitballer Oscar Tuero, who also found a home in the Texas League.[75] Fillingim went 7-10 with a 3.84 ERA before being released in August when he had "no plans for the immediate future."[76]

Six years after Fillingim hung up the spikes, Grimes won his 270th major-league victory in 1934 as the last legal spitballer in the majors.[77] Bucking the trend, the Pacific Coast League implemented the spitball as a way to draw fan interest.[78]

Fillingim moved to Alabama, where he would live out his life.[79] He worked as an inspector for the Alabama Beverage Control Board.[80] After his death from heart disease on February 3, 1961, his wife, Ava, noted in 1962 that it was harder for pitchers with the emphasis on offense. "My husband, Dana," she said, "had the finest spitball pitch ever thrown and it ought to be returned to the game."[81] Dana Fillingim was buried in Tuskegee Cemetery.

## NOTES

1. Some newspaper accounts said Fillingim was one of the first Greek-Americans in major-league history, but there is nothing in his recorded family history to indicate that this is correct.
2. Jones Family History earljones.net/aqwg8565.htm#262642.
3. Charles Faber, *Spitballers: The Last Legal Hurlers of the Wet One* (Jefferson, North Carolina: McFarland and Company, Inc., 2006), 174-79.
4. "Pitcher doesn't have a chance—Ave Fillingim," *Daily Republican* (Monongahela, Pennsylvania), August 17, 1962: 9.
5. Ed Cunningham, "Rudolph and Fillingim Hurl Braves to Victory," *Boston Herald*, April 5, 1920: 8.
6. "Pitcher Doesn't Have a Chance—Ave Fillingim."
7. Frank Hyde, "Frankly Speaking," *Post-Journal* (Jamestown, New York), November 14, 1961. chautauquasportshalloffame.org/bedientcaldwell1961.php.
8. "Cooney Tells of Hesitation Pitch," *Longview* (Texas) *News Journal*, February 3, 1943: 8.
9. George Biggers, "Play the Game," *Indianapolis Star*, June 26, 1918: 10.
10. Lester Biederman, "Carey Remembers When Ball Players Stole Bases," *Austin* (Minnesota) *Daily Herald*, May 5, 1959: 11.
11. Faber, 174-179.
12. "Fillingim Has Seen Rare Feat," *Pittsburgh Press*, May 16, 1918: 22.
13. Empire State League history on sabr.org/research/empire-state-league-south-georgia-baseball-1913.
14. Faber, 174-79.
15. Mark Price, "Ptooey! Akron Pitcher's Spitball a Moist Memory From the 1920s," *Akron Beacon Journal*, June 9, 2013. ohio.com/news/local/local-history-ptooey-akron-pitcher-s-spitball-a-moist-memory-from-1920s-1.404689.
16. "Fillingim Has Seen Rare Feat."
17. Faber, 174-179.
18. Faber, 174-179.
19. "Proposed Baseball Deals Should Be Stopped by League Presidents," *Philadelphia Evening Public Ledger*, August 3, 1915: 10.
20. Ibid.
21. "Detroit Hammers Fillingim Hard in Early Periods," *Philadelphia Evening Public Ledger*, August 7, 1915: 11.
22. "No-Hit; No-Run Game," *Charlotte News*, May 12, 1916: 13.
23. "Ninth Victory Without Defeat Dana Fillingim Adds Another to His List," *Columbia* (South Carolina) *State*, May 20, 1916: 5.
24. "Mack's Farm Hands Are Doing Well in the Minors," *Pittsburgh Press*, May 18, 1916: 27.

# 20-GAME LOSERS

25 "Fillingim Has Seen Rare Feat."

26 Faber, 174-179.

27 CE Collins "Sports Snapshots," *Arkansas Democrat*, August 2, 1916: 9.

28 "Notes of the Game," *Indianapolis Star*, March 27, 1917: 14.

29 Ralston Goss, "Mixing 'em Up," *Indianapolis Star*, March 16, 1917: 10.

30 Ralston Goss, "Fillingim and Swilling Shine in 2-0 Victory," *Indianapolis Star*, May 6, 1917: 47.

31 Statistics, *Indianapolis Star*, June 23, 1917: 8.

32 Robert Read, "Fillingim's Work Drawing Attention of New York Giants," *Indianapolis Star*, July 10, 1917: 11.

33 "Fillingim a Slab Star in the A.A.," *Oklahoma City Times*, July 24, 1917: 11.

34 "Wickland to Get Chance in Big Show," *Indianapolis Star*, September 25, 1917: 10.

35 "One More Victory and the Minor League World Series Belongs to Indianapolis," *Indianapolis Star*, September 30, 1917: 44.

36 *Capital Times* (Madison, Wisconsin), March 19, 1918: 6.

37 George Biggers "Fillingim Is Traded to Braves for Two Players," *Indianapolis Star*, May 5, 1918: 19.

38 "Braves Get Fillingim," *Des Moines Register*, May 5, 1918: 25.

39 "Marquard's First Win a Classy Pitching Feat," *Brooklyn Eagle*, May 10, 1918: 20.

40 John Hallahan, "Braves Batter Down Cards With Heavy Fire," *Boston Herald*, May 19, 1918: 12.

41 Ben Hoffman, "A Met Approaches Rarefied Air," *New York Times*, April 23, 2013. nytimes.com/2013/04/24/sports/baseball/mets-pitcher-harvey-already-has-a-historically-strong-start.html.

42 "New Hurlers Help Braves. Stallings Has Been Fortunate in Picking Up Winning Staff. Dana Fillingim," *Kansas City Star*, June 4, 1918: 8.

43 "Blow to Jawn's Hopes," *Baltimore Sun*, May 23, 1919: 12. *The Sports Encyclopedia of Baseball* (2004) lists 16 Braves players.

44 Jim Nasium, "Moran's Discard Humbles Phillies," *Philadelphia Inquirer*, June 23, 1918: 14.

45 "Fillingim New Shutout King," *Cincinnati Post*, June 13, 1918: 8.

46 "Our Navy, the Standard Publication of the U.S. Navy, Volume 12," *Our Navy*, September 1918: 71.

47 "An Obituary of Ray 'Rabbit' Powell," *Newport* (Rhode Island), *Daily News*, October 30, 1962: 14.

48 "Rowland May Go as Sox Manager," *Watertown* (New York) *Daily Times*, December 20, 1918: 8

49 "Braves' Boss in Columbus; Likes Grounds Announces That Gowdy, Maranville and Dana Fillingim on Braves," *Columbus Daily Enquirer*, February 18, 1919: 2.

50 "Braves better Than in 1914," *St. Louis Dispatch*, April 15, 1919: 26; NE Boston Brown, "National Look Weak, Lack New Materials," *Arizona Republic*, April 23, 1919: 7.

51 "The Last Legal Spitball Pitchers," Not Another Baseball Blog notanotherbaseballblog.wordpress.com/2012/09/15/the-last-legal-spitball-pitchers.

52 *St. Louis Post-Dispatch*, December 15, 1920: 19.

53 Ed Cunningham, "Rudolph Not Worrying Over Spitball Ruling," *Boston Herald*, March 5, 1920: 11.

54 "South Represented by Boston Brave Players," *Charleston* (West Virginia) *Daily Mail*, March 30, 1920: 3.

55 Ed Cunningham, "Leslie Man Plans to Hang Up uniform," *Boston Herald*, May 18, 1920: 14.

56 Burt Whitman, "Rabbit Acts Rabidly, but Will Stay With the Tribe," *Boston Herald*, July 7, 1920: 9.

57 Ed Cunningham, "Braves and Giants Take Turns Shooting Blanks," *Boston Herald*, September 7, 1920: 11.

58 "Cutshaw Is a Second Keeler, Struck Out Nine Times," *El Paso Herald*, January 29, 1921: 11.

59 "Braves Battle Giants Twice," *Boston Post*, April 19, 1921: 16.

60 "Hornsby Repeats as First Place Hitter in Nationals," *The Evening Journal* (Wilmington, Deleware), October 8, 1921: 11.

61 Urban Faber, "Wet Ball Artists Are Fading," *Appleton* (Wisconsin) *Post-Crecent*, June 23, 1922: 10.

62 Robert Maxwell "Acquisition of Larry Kopf by the Braves Rounded Out Defense of Powerful Team," *Brooklyn Daily Eagle*, March 29, 1922: 22.

63 "Watching the Scoreboard," *Muskogee* (Oklahoma) *Times-Democrat*, July 11, 1922: 8.

64 *Bridgeport* (Connecticut) *Telegram*, February 10, 1923.

65 "Downfall Cause Was Shoe Spike," *Altoona Tribune*, March 20, 1924: 8.

66 "Steers Stopped at Beaumont by Dana Fillingim's Spitball Delivery," *Dallas Morning News*, May 22, 1925: 16.

67 "Pitcher Doesn't Have a Chance—Ava Fillingim" *Monongahela* (Pennsylvania) *Daily Republican*, August 17, 1962: 9.

68 Jones family history.

69 Norman Brown, "The Year of the Big Comeback for Them," *Kingsport* (Tennessee) *Times*, March 19, 1925, 7.

70 "Steers Stopped at Beaumont by Dana Fillingim's Spitball Delivery," *Dallas Morning News*, May 22, 1925: 16.

71 *Dallas Morning News*, August 21, 1926: 12.

72 "Texas League," *The Sporting News*, September 24, 1925.

## 20-GAME LOSERS

73  Faber, 174-179.

74  "Spitball Hurler Fast Passing," *Wisconsin Rapids* (Wisconsin) *Daily Tribune*, January 11, 1927: 5.

75  "Exporters Play Buffs," *Galveston* (Texas) *Daily News*, April 13, 1927: 5.

76  "Fillingim Draws Release From Grizzlies," *Dallas Morning News*, August 4, 1928: 9.

77  Faber, 174-179.

78  William Ritt, "Spying on Sports," *Sedalia* (Missouri) *Democrat*, March 8, 1934: 10.

79  *Anniston* (Alabama) *Star*, July 5, 1942: 2.

80  Baseball Hall of Fame player questionnaire.

81  *Monongahela* (Pennsylvania) *Daily Republican*: 9.

# SAM GRAY

## BY GREGORY H. WOLF

**"I HAVE NEVER SEEN A RECRUIT** pitcher with a more deceptive hook," gushed syndicated sportswriter (and AL umpire) Billy Evans about rookie right-hander Sam Gray of the Philadelphia A's in 1924.[1] Gray rode his impressive curveball to a 10-year career, the final six with the St. Louis Browns. Three years after winning 20 games for a surprising third-place club in 1928, the durable workhorse lost 24 contests, tied for the most in the majors, as the Brownies slid into baseball oblivion for most of their remaining two-plus decades in the Gateway City.

Samuel David Gray was born on October 15, 1897, in Howe, a small farming community of about 500 residents in Grayson County, Texas, about 60 miles north of Dallas.[2] His parents, James Alonzo "Lon" and Eugenia (nee Bell) Gray, were originally from Tallapoosa, Alabama (and first cousins), married around 1888, and had settled three years later in the northeastern part of the Lone Star State to become farmers, probably focusing on cotton and wheat. At this time, Grayson County was home to the largest cottonseed-oil mill in the world.[3] The Grays had at least eight children (six sons and two daughters), of whom Sam was the sixth.[4] He attended Hack Berry school, a one-room schoolhouse, but quit in his early teens to work on the family farm. His big interest was baseball, and he apparently played with his brothers any time he could. By the time Gray was in his late teens, he was a member of a town team in nearby Van Alstyne (population about 2,000).

Like many young men across the country, Gray's life took an expected turn with America's involvement in World War I. He was drafted, mustered in on March 28, 1918, and subsequently assigned to the 3rd Trench Mortar Battalion, Coastal Artillery Corps of the US Army, stationed at Fort Jacinto in Galveston.[5] On July 14 the battalion embarked to France, via Liverpool, and arrived in Le Havre, France, on July 31. Private Gray was stationed at two different trench-warfare and artillery schools, but the war concluded before the 3rd Battalion experienced active combat. On January 5, 1919, he and his fellow soldiers departed for the United States aboard the USS Montana.

Gray was restless when he returned to the bucolic landscape of Howe, where he was expected to follow the footsteps of his brothers and become a rancher. Gray had other plans and sought refuge in the most common source of entertainment available, baseball. Possessing a strong right arm and a good batting eye, he played on semipro teams in Van Alstyne and in Sherman, the county seat with 15,000 residents, and the economic and cultural center of the region. According to one report, Gray was called the "pride of Grayson County" and had a reputation of "picking off" sparrows in trees with cheap baseballs.[6] Gray's career in professional baseball was a product of good timing and fateful location. In 1921 the Texas-Oklahoma League (Class D) was relaunched. Gray's semipro club in Sherman, which had had a team in the first incarnation of the league (1911-1914), became one of the revived circuit's six teams. Gray blazed a trail for the cellar-dwelling Lions, posting an 11-11 record and fanning a league-best 237. Transferred to Paris in 1922, Gray needed no knowledge of French to overpower opposition en route to a 23-4 record and another strikeout crown (219) while leading the Snappers to the Texas-Oklahoma League title. Meanwhile Gray had been purchased by the Detroit Tigers on scout George Leidy's recommendation.[7] He split the 1923 campaign with two Class-A clubs in the Texas League, Beaumont and Fort Worth, to which the Tigers released him outright. Gray caught the attention of former Philadelphia A's catcher Ira Thomas, who was managing the A's affiliate in the league, the Shreveport (Louisiana) Gassers.[8] Based on Thomas's recommendation, Connie Mack, owner and manager of the A's, selected Gray from Fort Worth in the annual Rule 5 draft in September.[9]

In 1924 Gray reported to the A's spring training camp in Montgomery, Alabama. Since capturing four AL pennants and three World Series championships in a five-year span (1910-1914), the A's had gone through a rough time with nine consecutive losing seasons, including seven straight in the cellar. However, the Tall Tactician's club looked to be on the rise in 1924 with the addition of a rookie hitting phenom, Al Simmons from Milwaukee in the American Association, and the continued development of a pair of stalwarts, pitcher Eddie Rommel, two years removed from leading the majors with 27 wins, and young slugger Joe Hauser. Into this fray stepped 26-year-old Gray, who defied expectations and made the club. His debut, in the A's season opener against the Boston Red Sox at Fenway Park, was an unmitigated disaster. Gray was torched for five hits and six runs (all earned) while retiring just one batter in a 12-0 loss. Confined to mop-up duty the next five weeks, Gray made his first start on the biggest stage in American sports, Yankee Stadium, in the second game of a doubleheader on May 31. Despite yielding what the *New York Times* described as one of Babe Ruth's "longest home runs of his career, possibly the longest," Gray "fooled the Yankees completely."[10] He tossed a complete-game seven-hitter to pick up his first victory, 5-3. June proved to be another calamity for the recruit hurler (10 earned runs in just 7⅓ innings), but Gray found his stride in July, winning three consecutive starts, capped off by making the Chicago White Sox look like "feeble old men" (in the words of Irving Vaughan of the *Chicago Tribune*) in an impressive four-hit shutout.[11] While the A's (71-81) moved up a slot to finish in fifth place, Gray turned in a sturdy campaign (8-7, 3.98 ERA in 151⅔ innings).

Gray's 1925 season alternated between phases of extreme success, frustration, and tragedy. He began the campaign by winning a career-best eight consecutive starts. "[Gray's] headed for stardom," gushed Philadelphia sportswriter James C. Isaminger, who compared his pitching to a forest fire destroying everything in its path.[12] Included in that stretch were consecutive shutouts of the Yankees, which earned Gray the title of "public nuisance" bestowed by New York scribe James R. Harrison.[13] "[Gray] rewrote 'The Elegy in a Country Churchyard' with a curveball," wrote Harrison, invoking the immensely popular eighteenth-century poem after the pitcher's five-hit whitewash in Yankee Stadium.[14] Ira Thomas, who had rejoined the A's as a coach, was widely credited with Gray's emergence as one of the circuit's best hurlers. Gray's eighth victory proved costly, however. With the A's in first place, Gray was hit on the right hand by a pitch from George Blaeholder of the St. Louis Browns on May 21 and broke his thumb. Upon Gray's return four weeks later, he managed to win his ninth straight decision and also suffer his first defeat in three erratic starts before tragedy struck, threatening to derail his season. His wife, Alice (née Cobb), whom he had married the previous spring, died unexpectedly.[15] Gray missed three weeks in July tending to funeral matters in Texas. While the A's high-priced and much ballyhooed acquisition from the Baltimore Orioles in the International League, Lefty Grove, struggled, the A's were in a tight pennant race with the Washington Senators. Mack relied heavily on Gray, Rommel, and dependable veteran Slim Harriss, all of whom meshed well with rookie catcher Mickey Cochrane. Often pitching on short rest, Gray faded in August and September, splitting his final 12 decisions (with a high 4.61 ERA), as the A's lost 30 of their final 54 games to finish in a distant second place. Gray's season (16-8, 3.27 ERA in 203⅔ innings) left many wondering what would have been had he not missed seven weeks.

It is difficult to determine when Gray acquired the moniker "Sad Sam"; however, by 1926 its use was common in newspapers. The epithet originated from Gray's appearance, and not from his mental state even though he had plenty of reasons to be sad. Gray had a pronounced brown tan from the Texas sun, and a weatherbeaten, prematurely wrinkled face with skin often described as leathery. Punctuated by his deeply-set dark eyes, Gray gave the impression of being sad, though his disposition was the exact opposite. He was considered a jovial, affable player, a well-liked teammate, and popular with fans. Standing about 5-feet-11 and weighing just about 165 pounds, Gray had a lithe, wiry body; contemporary reports suggested he didn't necessarily give the impression of a ballplayer. Throughout his baseball career, the real-life cowboy returned to his hometown, where he raised cattle, goats, and especially sheep. As expected, his hobbies were hunting and fishing, and playing in amateur baseball games in the balmy autumnal weather of northeast Texas.

Described as the "slickest 'hook' ball pitcher in the league," Gray based his emergence as a bona-fide ace on his deceptive curveball.[16] "A curve is always harder to hit than a fastball," said Gray in *Baseball Magazine*.[17] "I pitch a curve with three speeds. Fast, medium and slow," each of which, he noted, had its own kind of break. "Sometimes my curve will break a good deal more than a foot. I particularly like a slow curve," continued Gray about his pitch of choice to sluggers.[18] Although Gray might not have had the natural stuff like Grove, nor was he overpowering like Brooklyn's Dazzy Vance, he compensated for any perceived shortcoming with a pronounced cerebral approach to the game. His repertoire also included a solid heater with good movement and an effective change of pace. "Batting is timing," said Gray, "and if a batter is crossed up on the amount of time he's got, he's isn't like to 'get hold' of the ball."[19] He altered release points from overhand to side-arm, and occasionally dropped to a submarine style. Syndicated sportswriter John B. Foster described Gray's motion as "easy, frictionless shoulder action. [He] lets the ball go with so little perceptible effort."[20]

For the first time in more than a decade, the A's began the season considered among the challengers for the AL pennant. Expectations in 1926 were equally high for Gray, whom teammate "Bucketfoot Al" Simmons, lauded as the "toughest man to hit in the league."[21] The 28-year-old Texan, however, mysteriously struggled to find his rhythm. He was yanked after just 2⅓ innings in his first start, lost his first three decisions, and pitched erratically (he failed to make it through the fourth inning in five of his first 13 starts) After a laborious outing on July 3 against lowly Boston, yielding nine hits and five runs (three earned) but earning the victory, Gray was shunted to the bullpen. Mack, whose club came with 5½ games of the front-running Yankees in July, desperately searched for an effective combination of hurlers, seven of whom started at least 10 games. Reserved for long relief, mop-up duty, and an occasional start over the last three months of the season, Gray (11-12, 3.64 ERA in 150⅔ innings) was the odd man out, especially after the midseason acquisition of Howard Ehmke (in exchange for Harriss), who won 12 of 16 decisions.

Gray picked up a figurative win in late August 1926 when he married Texan divorcée Myrtle Thompson, mother of a young son, Dickie. However, Gray was collared with the loss about eight years later when the couple divorced.

Despite their third-place finish the previous season, the A's were seen as a viable threat to derail the Yankees' quest for another pennant in 1927. The club's strong suit was its pitching staff, which paced the AL in team ERA (3.00) and was anchored by

Grove, who captured his first of a record nine ERA crowns. It was déjà vu for Gray all over again. He was bashed in Gotham City by the Bronx Bombers (nine hits, six runs in three innings) in his first start, on April 13, and never got on track. With a dismal 8.22 ERA after an implosion in Detroit on May 12, Gray was relegated to the bullpen, having lost Mack's confidence. Given the club's surfeit of pitchers (workhorses Grove and Rube Walberg, the 43-year-old ageless wonder Jack Quinn, Ehmke, and Rommel), it was no surprise when the runner-up A's shipped Gray to the Browns for outfielder (and former A's player) Bing Miller on December 13.

The *St. Louis Post-Dispatch* described the Browns' acquisition of Gray as the final step in a massive "house cleaning" project.[22] After a disastrous 59-94 season in 1927, their second consecutive seventh-place finish, Browns owner Phil Ball had traded or sold nine players. Most prominent among them were their two-time .400 hitter, 34-year-old first baseman George Sisler, fresh off his fifth 200-hit season in seven years (sold to the Washington Senators); an aging slugger, outfielder Ken Williams (sold to the Boston Red Sox); and flychaser Harry Rice and pitcher Elam Vangilder (traded to the Detroit Tigers for left fielder Heinie Manush and first sacker Lu Blue). The Browns, suggested the *Post-Dispatch* in a positive evaluation of the rebuilding project, "[are] not going to win any pennant in 1928, nor even for several years, [but] they have taken a forward step."[23]

Skipper Dan Howley expected Gray to become the ace of a staff that had the worst team ERA (4.95) in the AL in 1927. Tabbed to start Opening Day, Gray scattered six hits over 8⅓ innings to defeat the Tigers at Navin Field on April 11. After Gray's four-hit shutout against the Cleveland Indians at League Park on May 2, sportswriter L.C. Davis of the *Post-Dispatch* praised the club's new star in one of his kitschy ditties: "You're the Brownies' pitching ace, Sammy Gray. In our hearts you've won a place, Sammy Gray. Quite a number you have won, And now your record is five and one."[24] Poems aside, Gray kept winning. He notched his 10th victory of the season, a career-longest 12-inning complete game to defeat Boston 2-1 in Sportsman's Park on June 10. It was Gray's third extra-inning, distance-going victory in eight starts, and pushed the Browns one game over .500 (26-25), though well behind the streaking Yankees (39-9). Described by the *Post-Dispatch*'s J. Roy Stockton as "one of the hardest working athletes in the business," Gray became the first Browns hurler to win 20 games since Urban Shocker in 1923 when he overcame three errors contributing to three unearned runs to beat Detroit, 5-4, on September 2.[25] Six days later Gray's season came to a premature conclusion in his next start, also against Detroit, a line drive off Harry Heilmann's bat fractured the index finger on his left hand. Coincidentally, Gray also hit his first of two career home runs in that game. The 30-year-old hurler finished fifth in the league in three categories, wins (20), complete games (21), and innings (262⅔) while posting the eighth-best ERA (3.19). Gray and teammate General Crowder (21-5), a right-hander who won eight consecutive decisions in the last five weeks of the season, became the first set of Browns hurlers to notch 20 wins in the same season since the franchise's maiden campaign in the Gateway City, in 1902, when Jack Powell (22) and Red Donahue (22) turned the trick.

Despite coming off a third-place finish, the Brownies got no respect when their spring training opened in West Palm Beach in 1928. "Their performance," opined beat writer John E. Wray in the *Post-Dispatch*, "is generally considered an accident."[26] It was just the eighth winning campaign in franchise history as a charter member of the AL. (The club was founded as the Milwaukee Brewers in 1901, and moved to St. Louis after just one season.)

"Thirty sees a pitcher at his prime, so far as endurance and strength is concerned," said Gray, now 31, in *Baseball Magazine*. "He ought to improve in control and knowledge of the batter for several years after that."[27] In a self-fulfilling prophecy, Gray picked up where he left off the previous season, winning the 1929 season opener on April 16 with a complete-game five-hitter against the White Sox in front of only 6,000 fans on a cold, damp day at Sportsman's Park.[28] He ended the month by winning his fourth straight start, a 10-inning complete game against the Tigers, 3-2, in the Motor City. The Browns (45-28) proved to be one of the surprises of the first half of the season, tied on July 7 with the Yankees in second place, 8½ games behind the A's. Then they hit a brick wall, losing almost twice as many as they won the rest of the season to finish 79-73, good for fourth place. Dapper Dan Howley once again leaned heavily on Gray, whose season mimicked the club's. Gray led the majors in innings (305), paced the AL in starts (37), finished second in compete games (23) and fifth in victories (18). That number would surely have been higher had he received better run support. In 11 of his 15 losses, the Browns scored just 11 total runs. Gray also tied teammates Crowder (17-15) and Blaeholder (14-15), and Boston's Danny MacFayden for the AL lead with four shutouts.

Bill Killefer, Howley's pitching coach the last three campaigns, took over as Browns skipper in 1930. "[Our] staff," he boasted as spring training got underway, "ranks with the best in the league."[29] Killefer had good reason to be optimistic as the club had finished third in team ERA the previous season; however, signs of trouble quickly emerged in Florida. Gray held out and did not report until mid-March. Crowder was equally upset with his contract from the cash-strapped club as the Great Depression, precipitated by the stock-market crash the previous October, tightened its grip across baseball. Starting his third straight season opener, Gray was belted for eight hits and five runs and lasted just five innings in a 6-3 loss to the Tigers in Detroit. His season soon veered out of control. He lost his first nine decisions before notching his first victory on June 8, almost two months into the season. Five days later the Browns shipped Crowder and their best offensive weapon, Heinie Manush, who had batted .378 and .355 in his two seasons with the Brownies, to the Senators for Goose Goslin. By that time St. Louis was battling Detroit for seventh place, though well in front of a horrible Boston team. Gray, sidelined by arm problems for six weeks beginning in early August, was crushed by Philadelphia in his return on September 21 (seven runs in 6⅓ innings), then ended the season by surrendering 10 earned runs (for the second time in four starts) and 14 hits in five innings in a brutal loss to Cleveland to finish the season with a dismal 4-15 record. Labeled a "prize flop" by sportswriter John M. Foster, Gray posted the highest ERA in the AL (6.28 in 167⅔ innings, though well below the unfathomable 7.71 of the Philadelphia Phillies' Les Sweetland).[30] The "Year of the Hitter," during which the AL set a new league record in runs per game (10.8), took its toll on the Browns. After five winning seasons and finishing in the first division seven times in the 1920s, the Browns (64-90), with an AL-worst 5.07 team ERA, finished in sixth place to inaugurate a dismal decade in which they averaged 95 losses per season.

The *St. Louis Post-Dispatch* reported that the "most interesting and satisfying sight" in the Browns 1931 spring training was Gray, who seemed to have overcome the chronic arm problems that had limited him to just 167⅔ innings the previous season.[31] Gray looked shaky in his season debut (a complete-game 14-hit victory against Detroit, 6-4), but Killefer counted on him and 20-game winner Lefty Stewart to have a chance to crack the first division. In his best impression of a Jekyll and Hyde act, Gray had an atrocious June (0-5, 9.99 ERA in 33⅓ innings), followed by his best stretch in two years, winning five of six decisions with a 2.80 ERA in 54⅔ innings from July 1 to July 26 to improve his record to 9-11. Propelled by Gray, the Browns (42-49) were one of the hottest teams in baseball, having won 25 of 39 games, and seemed poised to make a move. However, both Gray and the Browns slumped miserably thereafter. The Browns won only 21 more games all season (42 losses), and struggled to score enough runs (4.27) to compensate for a porous defense, which committed 87 errors, and a pitching staff that surrendered 5.78 runs per game in those 63 contests. In a nightmarish combination of bad luck, poor run support, and dreadful pitching, Gray lost his next 11 starts, finishing with an 11-24 record, tied with Pat Caraway of the Chicago White Sox for the most losses in the majors. Gray paced the majors with 37 starts; his 5.09 ERA (in 258 innings) was the fourth highest in the AL.

Expected to form with Stewart and Blaeholder the backbone of the Browns staff in 1932, Gray tossed a five-hit shutout against the White Sox at Comiskey Park in his season debut. Six days later he blanked the South Siders on three hits at Sportsman's Park. Another three-hitter, his third shutout in eight starts, took place on May 16 against the Senators in Washington. With an impressive 3.09 ERA Gray looked like the 1928-29 vintage pitcher. But he struggled in his next two starts (10 earned runs in 4⅓ innings) sandwiched around three relief appearances, and was relegated to the bullpen. By that time the Browns had acquired workhorse Bump Hadley from the White Sox. En route to making a career-high 52 appearances (second most in the AL), Gray occasionally made a spot start, the last of which occurred in the final home game of the season, on September 18. Gray's performance, suggested St. Louis sportswriter James M. Gould, caused "more enthusiasm among the fans than has been shown at a Brownie game in the last three months."[32] Probably "pitching for another chance" with the club in 1933, continued Gould, Gray tossed a 10-inning complete game with a career-high 10 strikeouts to defeat the Yankees, 2-1.[33]

After logging 206⅔ innings in 1932, Gray was plagued by a sore arm in 1933, and spent most of the season in the bullpen, making only six starts. On August 17 he was sent in a waiver transaction to the Senators, but was returned six days later, as reported by the *Post-Dispatch*, when Gray informed the Senators' brass of his arm miseries.[34] Gray's honesty infuriated recently hired Brownie skipper Rogers Hornsby. Just days before the 1934 season opened Gray was given his unconditional release by the club after an argument with the Rajah.

Within months after his release, the 36-year-old Gray was fighting for his life. According to Associated Press reports, he was attempting to catch on with the Milwaukee Brewers of the American Association when he came down with abdominal pain, necessitating hospitalization and an "emergency operation."[35] With rapidly deteriorating health and his weight down to 117 pounds, Gray was a "shadow of his former self," wrote the *St. Louis Post-Dispatch*.[36] *The Sporting News* reported in December that the former 20-game winner had been transferred to a veterans hospital in Muskogee, Oklahoma, where he had been treated for "liver troubles."[37]

Gray recuperated and returned to his ranch in northeastern Texas, but his professional baseball career seemed over. He pitched in various semipro leagues, and attempted a brief comeback in 1936 with the Dallas Steers in the Class-A Texas League, but lasted just one game. Defying expectation, Gray returned to Organized Baseball as a 40-year-old player-manager with Class-C Texarkana in the East Texas League in 1938. He won 10 games and logged 185 innings while leading the Liners to a second-place finish. Named player-manager of the Welch (West Virginia) Miners of the Class-D Mountain State League in '39, Gray concluding his active playing career in a blaze of glory. Old enough to be the father of his players, Gray was the best hurler in the circuit, posting a 16-7 record and capturing the ERA crown (3.03 in 205 innings). When he was replaced as skipper after a second-place finish, Gray returned to his ranch in Grayson County.

In parts of 10 big-league seasons, Gray went 111-115 with a 4.18 ERA in 1,951⅓ innings. He completed 101 of 231 starts among his 379 appearances, and tossed 16 shutouts. He won 72 games and tossed in excess of 1,000 innings in the minors.

Gray remained in the Van Alstyne area for the remainder of his life. On April 16, 1953, Sam Gray died at the age of 55 at the VA Hospital in McKinney, Texas. The cause of death was carcinoma of the brain. He was survived by his third wife, Jewell Waynie (Hodgins) Gray. After a funeral service, Gray was buried at Van Alstyne Cemetery.

## SOURCES

In addition to the sources cited in the Notes, the author also accessed Gray's player file and player questionnaire from the National Baseball Hall of Fame, the *Encyclopedia of Minor League Baseball*, Retrosheet.org, Baseball-Reference.com, the SABR Minor Leagues Database, accessed online at Baseball-Reference.com, and *The Sporting News* archive via Paper of Record.

## NOTES

1. Billy Evans, "Connie Has a Star in Moundsman Gray," *Reading* (Pennsylvania) *Times*, September 11, 1924: 6.
2. Most sources give Gray's place of birth as Van Alstyne; however, Gray provided Howe as his birthplace and home in a questionnaire provided by *Baseball Magazine*. Document in player's file, Baseball Hall of Fame.
3. "Grayson County," Texas State Historical Association. tshaonline.org/handbook/online/articles/hcg09.
4. According to US Census Reports of 1900, 1910, and 1920 accessed via ancestry.com.
5. Joe Hartwell, "History of the 3rd Trench Mortar Battalion, C.A.C," Rootsweb, freepages.military.rootsweb.ancestry.com/~cacunithistories/3d_Trench%20Mortar%20BTN.html. Gray's military service is based on Hartwell's history.
6. "Gray First Drew Notice by Picking Off Sparrows." *St. Louis Daily Globe Democrat*. Undated article, player's Hall of Fame file.
7. Norman E. Brown, "The Fanning Bee Hive," *Pittsburg* (Kansas) *Daily Headlight*, March 8, 1923: 12; "Sam Gray, Athletic Castoff, Had Banner Year with Browns." [Unattributed article, dated 1928, player's Hall of Fame file].
8. "Gray First Drew Notice by Picking Off Sparrows."
9. United Press, "Majors Draft Star Bushes," *Evening Journal* (Wilmington, Delaware), October 9, 1923: 10.
10. "Yankees Split Even; Break Tie for Lead," *New York Times*, June 1, 1925: S1.
11. Irving Vaughan, "Sox Getting Awful; Lose Pair to Macks," *Chicago Tribune*," July 17, 1924: 17.
12. *The Sporting News*, May 7, 1925: 3.
13. James R. Harrison, "Miller's Home Run Wins for Athletics," *New York Times*, May 4, 1925: 23.
14. Ibid.
15. Sam Gray's Wife Died of Injuries," *Shamokin* (Pennsylvania) *News-Dispatch*, July 11, 1925: 4.
16. Norman E. Brown, "He's Like Matty and Alec," *Olean* (New York) *Evening Herald*," June 6, 1925: 7.
17. F.C. Lane, "They'll Never Get His Goat," *Baseball Magazine*, September 1929: 455.
18. Ibid.
19. Ibid.
20. John M. Foster, "Sam Gray, Pitcher, Is Season's Find," *Harrisburg* (Pennsylvania) *Telegraph*, May 6, 1925: 17.
21. "Great Things Expected of Sam Gray," *Los Angeles Times*, March 14, 1926: 54.
22. J. Roy Stockton, "Deal Bringing Sam Gray to St. Louis for Bing Miller Completed Housecleaning," *St. Louis Post-Dispatch*, December 16, 1927: 48.
23. "Browns Made Rapid Strides Toward Rebuilding, Consensus of Meeting,*" St. Louis Post-Dispatch*, December 16, 1927: 48.
24. L.C. Davis "Sport Salad," *St. Louis Post-Dispatch*, May 5, 1928: 10.
25. J. Roy Stockton, "Gray Secures 17th Victory in Beating the Red Sox," *St. Louis Post-Dispatch*, August 8, 1928: 15.
26. John E. Wray, "Schang Joins Browns and Assesses He Will Be Active Again," *St. Louis Post-Dispatch*, March 4, 1929: 26.
27. Lane.
28. J. Roy Stockton, "Sam Gray Pitches in Fine Form; Manush Smashes 3- Bagger," *St. Louis Post-Dispatch*, April 16, 1929: II, 1.
29. "Killefer Says Browns Will Be 'Up There,'" *St. Louis Post-Dispatch*, February 15, 1930: 7A.
30. John. M. Foster, "'Dutch' Henry, White Sox 'Pitcher' Headed for Loss record," *San Bernardino* (California) *County-Sun*, August 1, 1930: 18.
31. "Batting Power to Decide Open Positions in Lineup of Bill Killefer's Browns," *St. Louis Post-Dispatch*, February 28, 1931: 6.
32. James M. Gould, "Sam Gray Sporting It as Browns End Home Season," *St. Louis Post-Dispatch*, September 19, 1932: 13.
33. Ibid.
34. "The Story of an Honest Pitcher," *St. Louis Post-Dispatch*, August 20, 1933: 16.
35. Associated Press, "Sam Gray Finds Club Owner With Plenty of Heart," *Moberly* (Missouri) *Monitor-Index*, June 21, 1934: 6.
36. "Sam Gray, a 'Very Sick Man,' Thinks He Can Make a Comeback," *St. Louis Post-Dispatch*, December 16, 1934: 42.
37. *The Sporting News*, December 13, 1934: 1.

# DAN GRINER

## BY GREGORY H. WOLF

**IN HIS FIRST FULL SEASON IN THE** majors, Dan Griner lost a big-league-most 22 games with the moribund St. Louis Cardinals in 1913. But few probably gave him a hard time for that dubious feat because "Big Dan," a chiseled 200-pound former football player, didn't take kindly to insults. He KO'd three teammates the following season and was a permanent fixture in skipper Miller Huggins' doghouse until the Cardinals discarded him in early 1916. With the St. Paul Saints in American Association the next two seasons, Big Dan became Cinder Dan as Griner transformed himself into one of the most notorious emery-ball pitchers in Organized Baseball. After brief return to the big leagues with the Brooklyn Robins in 1918, Griner jumped to a shipbuilders league to avoid the draft, and then spent his final six seasons in the minors.

Donald Dexter Griner was born on March 7, 1888, on the family farm in a rural, sparsely populated area, then simply known as Civil District 15, located in western Hickman County, in middle Tennessee. He was the first child of William and Margaret (Lawson) Griner, native Tennesseans of German and English stock, who, according to various US Census reports, had two younger children (Park and Mary), but also suffered the loss of three others in childbirth or soon thereafter. The elder Griner was a veteran of the Civil War, and served in the 9th Tennessee Cavalry Battalion in the Confederate Army.

Little is known about Dan's youth, but one aspect is sure. He was a big, rugged kid who liked the outdoors and had a predilection for sports. By at least 1908, Griner was playing baseball on local amateur and semipro teams in nearby Centerville, the county seat, located about 60 miles southwest of Nashville. By that time he was also a student at the Mooney School in Murfreesboro, 75 miles east of Centerville. W.D. Mooney founded the college-preparatory academy in 1901 with a special emphasis on educating the children of poor former Confederate veterans. The influential pedagogue was also instrumental in the organization and development of high-school athletics in the state in an era when there were very few public high schools, save for those in larger cities like Nashville, Memphis, or Chattanooga.

Griner was something of a wunderkind, whose name regularly graced the pages of local newspapers for his athletic prowess. He was a standout pitcher and was a member of Mooney's track and field state championship team in 1911, specializing in the 12-pound hammer throw, shotput, and discus.[1] His best sport might have been football. The *Tennessean* described the 6-foot-1, 200-pounder as one of the best prep players and tackles in the country, and seemed confident that he would attend Vanderbilt University, then a national gridiron powerhouse.[2]

Financial obligations forced Mooney to transfer the boarding school to Harriman, in the rolling hills of far Eastern Tennessee, by late 1910, and Griner's accomplishments continued to grow. He spent the summers in Centerville pitching in semipro leagues, but his big break may have come in 1912 when Mooney played a series of exhibition baseball games against the University of Tennessee, Knoxville.

By the late spring of 1912, Griner had signed a professional contract with the Cleveland (Tennessee) Counts in the six-team Class-D Appalachian League, which had been founded the previous year. The 24-year-old Griner overpowered the opposition, wining nine of his first 10 decisions and attracting the attention of big-league scouts. According to *Sporting Life*, M.R. "Bill" Armour, scout for the St. Louis Cardinals, outbid the Boston Braves, and signed Griner on June 15, with delivery to the team the following spring.[3] Six weeks later, the Redbirds paid an additional premium for Griner's immediate delivery to the club.

A perennial also-ran, the Cardinals were coming off a surprising winning season in 1911 (75-74), their first in 10 years, but had been floundering for most of 1912, and desperately needed pitching. Griner debuted on August 17 in the first game of a doubleheader against Boston at Robison Field on the north side of the Gateway City. In relief of the team's best hurler, Slim Sallee, Griner hurled three shutout innings, yielding just one hit and fanning two. His performance, and especially appearance, had a marked effect on the *St. Louis Post-Dispatch*, which described him as a "massive, broad-shouldered product of the Tennessee hills" and noted humorously that the recently arrived southpaw had to borrow a discarded uniform and cap that barely fit him.[4] "Big Dan," as he became to be known, finished his abbreviated rookie campaign with a 3-4 slate, and logged 54 innings.

*Sporting Life* hailed Griner as a future star and praised his "assortment of foolers, confidence and change of pace."[5] Consequently, the newspapers also considered the Cardinals to be one of the league's dark horses in 1913. Feisty second baseman Miller Huggins replaced Roger Bresnahan as player-manager, and tabbed Griner to start the season opener. Griner used his "mystifying" underhanded curve to fan a career-best nine in a complete-game victory over the Chicago Cubs, 5-3, at Wrigley Field.[6] With a "bewildering cross-fire" delivery, Griner completed nine of his first 12 starts, winning five of 11 decisions.[7] Sportswriter W.J. O'Connor of the *Post-Dispatch* gushed that "It's time that somebody should print a life-sized picture of Daniel Griner ... under a bold black caption: The find of 1913."[8] Griner showed "flashes of cleverness," opined sportswriter William A. Phelon, but hit a brick wall after tossing his first of 11 career shutouts, an 11-hitter against Chicago on June 24 and tallying the game's sole run after his triple. That victory improved his record to 7-9 (3.44 ERA), but thereafter Griner lost 13 of 16 decisions while yielding almost as many runs (84, 75 earned) as innings pitched (88⅓).[9]

The Cardinals (51-99) had the worst record in baseball in a miserable season in what had been a mostly forgettable existence since their admission to the NL in 1892. Griner (10-22) led the majors in losses and most hits per nine innings (11.2), while posting the second highest ERA in baseball (5.08 in 225 innings), exceeded only by teammate Pol Perritt's (6-14) 5.25. To top it off, *Sporting Life* claimed Griner's "chief fault" was his "super-extensive wind-up" which made it easy for runners to steal bases.[10]

Undeterred by 22 losses, Griner held out in 1914. He had joined the Baseball Players Fraternity, an early attempt to organize professional ballplayers, the previous campaign, and was exploring his options, which were suddenly more enticing with the rival Federal League set to inaugurate play in 1914.[11] He was actively courted by several FL teams, most notably the Pittsburgh Rebels. Schuyler Britton, Cardinals president, recognized the threat the upstart circuit posed to his club and other players, like Sallee and Dots Miller, and inked Griner to a contact in mid-March.

Despite an abbreviated spring training, Griner looked sharp in the Redbirds' season opener, tossing a complete-game five-hitter to beat the Pittsburgh Pirates, 2-1, at Robison Field in St. Louis. Soon thereafter, Griner proved to be one of Huggins' biggest headaches. On April 23 he and teammate Lee Magee got into a fight; Griner was suspended and missed the Redbirds' two-week Eastern road swing. In Huggins' doghouse, Griner pitched primarily in long relief in May, but made additional headlines for his pugilistic tendencies. He decked another teammate, catcher Ivey Wingo, and then scored his third knockout when he landed a combination on Ted Catcher's face, sending the backup flychaser to the hospital for stitches on May 27.[12] *Sporting Life* labeled Griner sarcastically the "great white hope," then an immediately recognizable epithet that boxing promoters used to describe Caucasian challengers to Jack Johnson, the first African-American heavyweight champion.[13]

Griner antagonized opponents, as well. He often pitched with what the *Post-Dispatch* described as "exasperating deliberation," walking around the mound and conferring with his catcher instead of rearing back and rifling the ball to the catcher as was customary.[14] Griner developed a reputation as one of the slowest workers in baseball, with nine-inning games lasting well over two hours in an era when the overwhelming majority were concluded in less than two hours.

Griner also had his fair share of bad luck in 1914. From July 27 to August 7 he tossed four consecutive complete games, yet lost each in walk-off fashion despite pitching the best ball in his career. He yielded just two unearned runs (eight earned) in 33 innings for a 0.55 ERA, while the Cardinals tallied just one run. "Pitcher Griner Ought to Sue Huggins Cardinals for Non-Support," ran a humorous headline in the *Post-Dispatch*.[15] In a hard-to-fathom decision, Huggins shuttled his snake-bitten right-hander back to the bullpen. After Griner suffered yet another tough-luck loss on September 25 to the New York Giants, 3-1, St. Louis sportswriter, L.C. Davis, known for his penchant for poetry, penned a short ditty, "Dan Griner lost another game, for which he wasn't much to blame. A passed ball scored the winning run, and Daniel lost it, three to one. It looks like the jinx is riding Dan, and marked him for an also ran. Against the fates he cannot buck, as [teammate] Hub Perdue hogged all the luck."[16]

Griner thumbed his nose at Dame Fortune in his final start of the year, a three-hit shutout of the Cubs. He concluded the campaign with a 9-13 record (2.51 ERA in 179 innings) as the Cardinals' NL-best team ERA (2.38) helped secure the team's best finish (third place) thus far in its 23 years in the NL.

Huggins and his problem-child Griner were at loggerheads before spring training even opened in 1915. Griner had married Grace Martin, originally from Chambersburg, Pennsylvania, the previous December in Hot Springs, Arkansas. Instead of reporting to Hot Wells, Texas, with his teammates, Griner remained in the resort city and worked out on his own, and possibly also with the Boston Red

Sox, who also trained there. By May, Huggins had had enough of the increasingly unpopular Griner. "It is a well known fact that Griner and several of his teammates do not get along," noted one insider.[17] The Cardinals apparently had agreed in principle to a trade with Cincinnati, shipping Griner to the Reds in exchange for their headache, pitcher Phil Douglas, who had been suspended because of his drinking problem.[18] Griner put the kibosh on that plan when he spun a two-hitter against the Philadelphia Phillies on May 19, facing the minimum 27 batters for just his second win of the season, both by shutout. Huggins rued his decision. Griner (5-11, 2.81 ERA in 150⅓ innings), once again in the role of swingman for most of the season, came down with arm problems and pitched only twice in the final seven weeks of the season, as the Cardinals (72-81) fell back into their customary position in the second division.

"I intend to take Griner South for another trial," said Huggins as the Cardinals prepared for spring training in the Texas heat in 1916. "Some persons think he has no winning attitude. I will not rush him. If his arm doesn't come around … I intend to ship him to the minors."[19] Hug kept his word. When active rosters were reduced to 23 players on May 15, Griner became the headache of Mike Kelley, skipper of the St. Paul Saints in the Double-A American Association.

Griner proved to be an effective yet unspectacular pitcher over the next two seasons with the Saints, posting a combined 32-25 record and logging in excess of 500 innings. He also emerged as one of the most notorious emery-ball pitchers in the league. One report described him and former big leaguer Cy Falkenburg, now with the Indianapolis Indians, as the circuit's "most prominent exponents of pitching camouflage."[20] Griner had been accused, during his stint with the Cardinals, of throwing occasionally a spitball, legal at the time, as were other freak pitches, like the mud ball, shine ball, and emery ball. The American Association, renowned as a veritable proving grounds for such dastardly pitches, enabled Griner to forge his craft. "[Griner] smeared rosin on one side and shined it on the other," said former big leaguer Joe Tinker, who managed the Columbus (Ohio) Senators in the AA in 1917 and 1918. "[The pitch] could curve around a corner. I found the old emery board in Griner's glove, and made him throw his glove out, but he pasted the emery on his belt or some other place where I couldn't find it, and the delivery was just as crazy."[21]

The Brooklyn Robins, coming off a dismal seventh-place finish but just one season removed from their first pennant, took a chance on Griner by acquiring him in a waiver transaction from the Cardinals around December 1, 1917. Skipper Wilbert Robinson's club had just lost two of its primary starters, Leon Cadore (13-13) and Sherry Smith (12-12), to Uncle Sam and the military as part of America's increased involvement in World War I, and sorely needed pitching. After several relief appearances, Griner made his first start on May 6, holding the Philadelphia Phillies hitless for 8⅔ innings at Ebbets Field. Gavvy Cravath, en route to pacing the NL in home runs for the fifth time in six years, broke up the no-hitter with a line-drive single. Griner settled for a one-hitter, but unlike his only other one (against the Boston Braves on July 30, 1914, at the South End Grounds in Boston), he won. It also proved to be his last victory in the big leagues, as he lost his next five starts. Soon thereafter, Griner jumped ship, literally.

Shipyard leagues, as SABR member Jim Leeke explained in *The National Pastime*, flourished during the years of World War I.[22] Concentrated on the East Coast, these leagues became attractive to some major leaguers after General Enoch Crowder, provost marshal of the US Army, announced a "work or fight" decree in early June 1918. However, the decision to work but continue to play baseball on the weekend, was not without consequences. "Any big-league player who sought a shipyard job in 1918 heard abuse from many fans and sportswriters," wrote Leeke.[23] Some players, most notably Shoeless Joe Jackson, sought employment at a shipyard and played on a company team to avoid the draft. So, too, did Griner, who went AWOL from the Dodgers after his last appearance, on June 8, and took a job at a munitions plant and pitched for Standard Shipbuilding of Staten Island.

Griner led his club to the league title, and then lost to Jackson's team, Harlan & Hollingsworth, champion of the Delaware River League, in the finals of the Atlantic Coast Shipyard championship. Few were sorry to see Griner go when the Superbas announced his reinstatement and transfer back to the St. Paul Saints for the 1919 season. "He gave the Shipyard League a bad smell," opined C. Stewart Wart. "Griner's removal from our midst bodes well for a cleaner slate."[24] Spitballs, emery balls, and the like were illegal in the circuit, but that did not stop Griner from relying on them, even after he had been suspended on several occasions.

During Griner's absence, the American Association had made headlines at its winter meetings in January 1918 by becoming the first professional baseball league to ban doctored pitches, in a concerted effort to increase scoring. "We put an end to all freak deliveries," said league President Thomas J. Hickey triumphantly.[25] Pitchers were apparently unfazed by the potential fines, and became more ingenious in their subterfuge. So successful were they in hiding foreign substances and objects that, according to one report, not one pitcher had been fined in the first two years of the ban.[26] Into this mix returned Griner, known as "Cinder Dan" to some for his use of coarse embers to scuff or shine a ball.

In his most successful season in Organized Baseball, Griner (21-14, 3.14 ERA in 321 innings) teamed with Dick Niehaus (23-13, 2.67, 307) to lead the Saints (94-60) in 1919 to the first of four American Association championships in six seasons. Griner reached the apex of his career in the Little World Series, which pitted the Saints against the Vernon Tigers, champion of the Pacific Coast League. Griner tossed three complete-game victories, and did not yield an earned run (two unearned) in 27 innings, but the Saints lost the series in nine games with all contests played at Maier Park, the Tigers' home field a few miles south of Los Angeles. Throughout the season, Griner plotted with teammates to conceal his nefarious tools of the trade; at other times, he openly flouted the rules. "[Griner] kept a handful of cinders back of the knoll," read one report, "and at intervals applied them to the ball" in full view of the umpire.[27] Griner's batterymate, Marty Berghammer, revealed years later how he and Griner worked in tandem. "When Dan got a new ball," said Berghammer, "he would always throw it to me. I had a piece of emery sewed inside of my glove, and it was a very simple matter to give the pill a twist and roughen [it up]."[28]

Griner did not parlay his success into another shot in the big leagues. After the 1919 season, the majors banned the spitball and its unholy brethren, with a provision that each team could name two pitchers who would be permitted to continue throwing them. The 32-year-old hurler remained with the Saints in 1920, going 16-13, as skipper Kelley's squad (115-49) captured another American Association flag. St. Paul lost the Little World Series to manager Jack Dunn's Baltimore Orioles (110-43), who had secured their second of seven consecutive International League titles.

Released by St. Paul early in the 1921 season, Griner worked his way down the minors like so many other players of the era. After a season with the St. Joseph (Missouri) Saints in the Class-A Western League, he pitched briefly for the Cleveland Manufacturers in the Class-D Appalachian League, and then served as pitcher-manager for the Fulton (Kentucky) Railroaders in the Class-D Kentucky-Illinois-Tennessee (KITTY) League in 1922-23.

At the age of 35, Griner concluded his 13-year professional baseball career. In parts of six big-league seasons, he posted a 28-55 record and 3.49 ERA in 673⅔ innings. He batted .237 on 52 hits.

Griner drifted away from baseball in retirement. According to his player's questionnaire from the Baseball Hall of Fame, he attended Florida Southern College, and subsequently worked as a medicine salesman. On June 4, 1950, Griner died of an apparent heart attack at the age of 62 in Bishopville, South Carolina. He was survived by his second wife, Lucille (Parrott) Griner, originally from South Carolina, whom he had married in 1935. Griner was buried in the Bethlehem Methodist cemetery in Bishopville.

## SOURCES

In addition to the sources cited in the Notes, the author also accessed Griner's player file and player questionnaire from the National Baseball Hall of Fame, the *Encyclopedia of Minor League Baseball*, Retrosheet.org, Baseball-Reference.com, the SABR Minor Leagues Database, accessed online at Baseball-Reference.com, and *The Sporting News* archive via Paper of Record.

## NOTES

1 "Mooney Wins Track Meet With Only Four Men," *Tennessean* (Nashville, Tennessee), May 14, 1911: 17.

2 *Tennessean*, November 29, 1911: 10.

3 *Sporting Life*, June 22, 1912: 3.

4 "Pitcher Griner, in Hand-Me-Down Suit, Performs Like a John," *St. Louis Post-Dispatch*, August 8, 1912: 4, 1.

5 *Sporting Life*, April 26, 1913: 9.

6 Ibid.

7 W.J. O'Connor, "Griner Pitches a Good Game and Cards Beat Cubs," *St. Louis Post-Dispatch*, April 13, 1913: 4, 1.

8 W.J. O'Connor, "Griner Looks Like a Find," *St. Louis Post-Dispatch*, June 5, 1913: 16.

9 William A. Phelon, "The Great 1913 Campaign and How It Looks To a Non-Combatant," *Baseball Magazine*, August, 1913: 24.

10 *Sporting Life*, August 2, 1913: 10.

11 "What Players Ask For. Long List of Demands," *San Francisco Call*, October 29, 1913: 1. See also "Baseball Players Fraternity," *Baseball Magazine*, October 1914: 89-92.

12 W.J. O'Connor, "Griner Lands on Catcher; Ted Lands on Hospital List," *St. Louis Post-Dispatch*, May 28, 1914: 22.

13 *Sporting Life*, March 20, 1915: 17.

14 "Cardinals Blank Dodgers; Huggins Outfit Now in Third," *St. Louis Post-Dispatch*, June 14, 1914: 4, 1.

15 "Pitcher Dan Griner Out to Sue Huggins' Cardinals for Non-Support," *St. Louis Post-Dispatch*, August 4, 1914: 14.

16 L.C. Davis, "Sport Salad," *St. Louis Post-Dispatch*, September 26, 1914: 8.

17 "One Good Game Blocks Trade of Dan Griner," *Pittsburgh Press*, May 22, 1915: 15.

18 Ibid.

19 W.J. O'Connor, "Huggins to Keep Only 2 Catchers for 1916 Season," *St. Louis Post-Dispatch*, February 4, 1916: 16.

20 "Banishment of the Trick Ball Stuff Is Pleasing," *Pittsburgh Post-Gazette*, January 6, 1918: 25.

21 " 'Shine Ball' No Mystery; Just the Emery Made Over," *Brooklyn Daily Eagle*, September 30, 1917: 38.

22 Jim Leeke, "The Delaware River Shipbuilders League, 1918," *The National Pastime*, 2013. sabr.org/research/delaware-river-shipbuilding-league-1918.

23 Ibid.

24 C. Stewart Wart, "After the Whistle Has Blown," *The Morse Dry Dock Dial* (New York), March 1917: 17.

25 "Banishment of the Trick Ball is Pleasing."

26 "Pitcher Griner Violates Antispitball Order and Escapes Ump's Reprimand," *Lead* (South Dakota) *Daily Call*, September 24, 1919: 6.

27 Ibid.

28 Manning Vaughan, "Putting 'Em on the Pan," *Milwaukee Journal*, December 5, 1929: III, 5.

# GUY HECKER

## BY BOB BAILEY

**GUY HECKER HAS BEEN REGARDED** as the best combination of hitter and pitcher during the nineteenth century.[1] In a major-league career that lasted from 1882 to 1890 he won 175 games and compiled a .282 batting average. But when one looks at his year-by-year record, two seasons stand out. Fittingly, one was as a hitter and one was as a pitcher.

Guy Jackson Hecker was born April 3, 1856, to Thomas and Lucinda Hecker near Youngsville, Pennsylvania, in Warren County. Guy was the eldest of two brothers (Charles was a year younger), and his father worked as a laborer in Warren County. Guy was born three years prior to Edwin Drake drilling the first successful oil well in nearby Titusville, Pennsylvania, in 1859. This event set off an oil boom in the area during the 1860s, and Thomas Hecker relocated his family up the Allegheny River to the prosperous town of Oil City in Venango County where he became the Superintendent of Streets for the borough of Venango.

Guy Hecker, who threw and batted right-handed, was a regular on the ball fields of Oil City and in 1877 landed a spot on his first professional team in Springfield, Ohio. He returned to Oil City after one season to marry and entered the business world while still playing in the amateur and semipro ranks in and around Oil City. In 1879 a young pitcher joined the team who would play a key role in getting Hecker to the majors. The pitcher was Tony Mullane, who won 284 games in his own major-league career. Mullane became friendly with Hecker in his only season with Oil City, and when Tony joined the 1882 Louisville Eclipse in the newly formed American Association, he convinced the Louisville management to sign Hecker as a first baseman and backup pitcher just before the start of the 1882 season.

In Hecker's first big-league season he hit .276 in 78 games and split 12 decisions as a pitcher. The six-foot, 190-pounder split his major-league time as a pitcher (336 games) and first baseman (322 games) and spent 75 games in the outfield. The highpoint of his 1882 season came on September 19 when he threw the second no-hitter in American Association history, against the Alleghenys of Pittsburgh. He missed having the first no-hitter by a week when his teammate Mullane no-hit the Cincinnati club.

Mullane moved on to St. Louis in 1883 and Hecker became Louisville's top pitcher. He posted a 28-23 record while pitching 469 innings. As a hitter he continued to hit in the .270s. In 1884 he exploded as a pitcher and began to develop as a major-league hitter. He raised his batting average to .297 and slugged at a .430 clip. But in the pitcher's box Hecker was the dominant pitcher in the American Association. He set the American Association single-season records for wins (52), innings pitched (670 2/3 in 1884), and complete games (72). He completed the pitcher's triple crown by leading the Association in ERA (1.80), and strikeouts (385). Only two other pitchers in major-league history have won as many as 50 games in a season. A year after Hecker's 52-win season, John Clarkson won 53. But Hecker's real misfortune was that the all-time single-season wins record was set the same season Hecker won 52, as Charley Radbourn won 59 for Providence in the National League. Hecker's 52-20 record in 1884 included a game against Washington in June in which he struck out the first seven batters he faced, and a one-hitter against St. Louis in August.

But records were not something players or fans thought much about in the 1800s, and Hecker opened the 1885 campaign ready to continue his mastery of the American Association. However, after a game on April 21 he complained of a sore arm. He tried to pitch though the arm trouble and had flashes of his old brilliance. There were various conjectures as to the cause of his troubles, including the enforcement of the rule requiring a pitcher to keep his delivery below his shoulder level. But no medical cause was ever announced, and Hecker compiled a 30-23 record in 480 innings pitched. His decline concerned the Louisville management enough that they purchased the contract of a young lefty from Chattanooga, Tom (Toad) Ramsey, late in the season. Hecker's decline as a pitcher was matched in the batter's box as his average dropped to .273 and his slugging average dropped nearly 100 points to .337.

Over the winter Hecker did two things. He allowed his arm to rest, and he opened the Hecker Supply Company in Louisville. During the 1885 season he had indicated his dissatisfaction with his salary, and it had been rumored that he was seeking his release from Louisville. It is probable that, instead of a higher salary, someone in the Louisville management agreed to help finance Hecker's sporting goods company to keep him in Louisville. By January he was on the road hawking sporting goods across the South. The combination of resting his arm and starting a new business allowed him to miss much of the team's preseason training routine. He never liked playing in cold weather and blamed the 1885 preseason for some of his arm troubles.

The 1886 season started well for Hecker as he was named team captain and won his Opening Day start with a three-hitter against Cincinnati. But within a week of that win he was diagnosed with an inflamed nerve in his right arm. Some on the Louisville team thought his pitching days were over. Through May he pitched about once a week and had compiled a 3-4 record. Most of the pitching load fell to Ramsey, who was 38-27 in 588 2/3 innings for the season. As Ramsey's status with the team grew, he became more at odds with Hecker. Ramsey said that Hecker was jealous of Ramsey's success and it would be good for the team if Hecker were released.[2] An anti-Hecker clique grew, and Guy was soon replaced as team captain. But the dissension on the club continued. Hecker's reputation as a gentleman and Ramsey's as a hard drinker got prominent play in the local press. In the midst of this turmoil, Hecker found himself off to the best hitting season of his career. Hitting .417 in June, he raised his season's average to .341.

But Hecker's immediate problem was his arm. He tried corn plasters and massages. He tried rest and a lighter pitching load. In July he finally found a treatment that helped. Twice daily he would soak his arm in "electric-baths" at the *Courier-Journal* press room.[3] He was so convinced of the benefits of this early "electronic-stimulation" treatment that he carried a galvanic battery on road trips. Hecker was back and he began pitching as well as he hit. Starting in July he won 11 straight games enroute to a 26-23 pitching record.

During this period of rejuvenation, Hecker had the greatest hitting day any pitcher has ever experienced in the majors. In the second game of an August 15 doubleheader with Baltimore Hecker won the game as the starting pitcher while hitting three home runs and three singles with seven runs scored. His 15 total bases was a major-league record at the time, as was his three-homer game as a pitcher (matched by Jim Tobin in 1942). His seven runs scored remain the major-league single-game record by any player.

As his contribution in the pitcher's box resumed, his batting was the best of his career. In July he hit .379. He upped that to .500 in August and found himself on top of the batting leaders list with a .378 average starting September. With the temperatures turning cooler Hecker's average began to drop, and he closed the season with a .342 average. It took several weeks for the American Association office to announce the final averages and crown the season's batting champ. When they did in November, standing atop the league was New York's Dave Orr with a .346 average followed by Hecker and Caruthers at .342 and Browning and Tip O'Neill of St. Louis at .339. But many decades later, as statisticians researched and corrected baseball records for the publication of the *Baseball Encyclopedia*, the revised averages put Hecker's .342 at the top of the list followed by Browning (.340), Orr (.338), Caruthers (.334), and O'Neill (.328). So Guy Hecker did not win the American Association batting title in 1886 but, as it turns out, he did post the highest batting

OLD JUDGE CIGARETTES  Goodwin & Co., New York.

average. Subsequent research has found that Hecker's league-leading average in 1886 was actually .341. In 1886 Guy Hecker appeared in 49 games with 378 plate appearances. Modern readers may question Hecker's eligibility for a batting championship but during the 19th century no league had any rules for minimum games, plate appearances, or at-bats for eligibility for the batting title.

In correspondence with David Nemec, author of the *Great Nineteenth Century Baseball Encyclopedia* and *The Rules of Baseball*, he states that "the best that can be said is that in every season the winner was at least a reasonable choice (if not always a correct one)."[4] So someone in the league office assessed the final numbers and chose the champion based on whatever criteria seemed appropriate at the time. Nemec notes that in 1883 the American Association announced Tom Mansell as the batting champion "until media derision forced it to go with [Ed] Swartwood." In the 1887 *Reach's Official American Association Base Ball Guide* Hecker makes the list as Reach used a 20-game standard to be included in the publication. The 1887 *Spalding Guide* does not include Hecker as they used a 100-game standard.

After 1886 Hecker showed a rapid decline as both a hitter and a pitcher. Although his batting average in 1887 could be seen as a lusty .366, during that one season walks counted as hits. Without the 31 walks he hit .319 on a comparable basis with 1886.[5] His pitching record fell to 18-12. There are two reasons given for his pitching decline. Having averaged over 500 innings pitched for four seasons could have ended his effectiveness. But 1887 also saw a shrinking of the pitcher's box. Hecker's pitching style included making a "hop, skip, and jump winding his arm beautifully about his head" to deliver a pitch.[6] Having to change his pitching style to accommodate the smaller pitching area could also have contributed to his decline.

By 1889 the Louisville team that had been a first-division team in the early years of the American Association was now a perennial tail-ender. Undercapitalized and beset by seemingly annual ownership changes, the team sunk to a 27-111 record in 1889. Things took a particularly bad turn after the parsimonious Mordecai Davidson took over control of the club. Davidson squeezed what money he could out of the franchise, even naming himself manager for a brief period. When he instituted a series of fines for errors and poor play, the players began to revolt. After one payday where several players owed the club money due to fines and only one player received a full paycheck, they issued an ultimatum: either the fines were returned or they would refuse to play. Davidson refused and on June 14, 1889, Guy Hecker was one of six Louisville players to participate in the first major-league strike when they refused to take the field in Baltimore. The players returned the next day when the American Association agreed to mediate the dispute.

Most of the dispute was resolved with new ownership in August, but Guy Hecker's Louisville run was about over. Pete Browning played his last game that season for Louisville in early September, and on September 17 Guy Hecker was released with a month to go in the season. The new management had decided to develop a younger team, and there was no place for the hero of 1884 and 1886.

Hecker left the American Association with his name high on several career pitching category lists. His Association record included 173 wins (third), 15 shutouts (eighth), 1,078 strikeouts (fourth), 322 pitching appearances (second), and 137 losses (first).

In 1890 he replaced Ned Hanlon as the manager of the National League's Pittsburgh club. But this was the year of the Players League revolt and Hecker presided over a ragtag bunch that lost 113 games. Over the next two seasons he was player-manager for Fort Wayne in the Northwestern League and Jacksonville in the Illinois-Indiana League. He returned to Oil City in 1893 to enter the oil business but kept active in baseball by managing the local team for several seasons. The locals called the independent team "Hecker's Hitters."

Guy Hecker died at the age of 82 on December 3, 1938, in Wooster, Ohio. He had settled in Wooster to operate a grocery store after leaving Oil City. At the time of his death the strong right arm that produced 52 major-league wins in 1884 was almost useless as a result of injuries suffered in an automobile accident in 1931. He was buried in Wooster Cemetery.

## SOURCES

In addition to the sources cited in the notes, the author also relied on:

Nemec, David. *The Beer and Whiskey League* (New York: Lyons & Burford, 1994).

Thorn, John, Pete Palmer & Michael Gershman, eds., *Total Baseball, 7th ed.* (Kingston, New York: Total Sports Publishing, 2001).

*Louisville Commercial*

*Louisville Times*

*Oil City* (Pennsylvania) *Derrick*

*The Daily Record* (Wooster, Ohio)

## NOTES

1. L. Robert Davids, ed. *Great Hitting Pitchers* Cooperstown: Society for American Baseball Research, 1979).

2. *Courier-Journal* (Louisville, Kentucky), May 25, 1886; *Courier-Journal*, June 2, 1886 (include both references)

3. *Courier-Journal*, July 3, 1886

4. E-mail from David Nemec to author, October 1, 2015.

5. Depending on the standard used, one could find a batting average as high as .403: 149 hits and walks / 407 PA = .366 BA; 149 hits and walks / 370 AB = .403 BA; 118 hits / 370 at-bats = .319 BA.

6. *Courier-Journal*, June 21, 1886.

# RANDY JONES

## BY ALAN COHEN

*"It happens every time. They cheer him even before he throws a ball. It's the way he comes across. He's a humble person, the underdog making good. People can relate to him. He's not that big in stature (6 feet, 180 pounds) and he is not overpowering on the mound. Randy's the common man's pitcher."*
—John McNamara, 1976[1]

*"If I was a pitcher, I'd be embarrassed to go out to the mound with that kind of stuff."*
—Mike Schmidt, 1976.[2]

*Not overpowering is putting it mildly. His assortment of junk was frustrating to the best of the hitters in the National League. Switch-hitting* Pete Rose *after, at one point, going 4-for-29 against Jones, decided to try his luck left-handed. After a frustrating effort on June 30, 1976 where Rose went 0-for-3 with a walk, Rose said "Left-handed, right-handed, cross-handed, he still gets you out."*[3]

*"I'd lose something in the fifth or sixth inning of a lot of those games," he remembers. "It was a tough year. I lost a lot of confidence by the second half of the season. People said it takes a good pitcher to lose 20 games, but I never bought that."*
– Randy Jones, reflecting on his 1974 season.[4]

**RANDALL LEO JONES WAS BORN ON** January 12, 1950, in Fullerton, California. His father, Jim, was a plant superintendent for a large agricultural company. Randy graduated from Brea-Olinda High School and attended Chapman University in Orange, California. In his senior year of high school, he went 8-2 with a 0.91 ERA and 110 strikeouts. He was named to the Irvine League All-Star team, and was the starting pitcher in the Orange County Prep All-Star game. At Chapman, during this first two varsity seasons, he played for coach Paul Deese. In his freshman year, his fastball was impressive. But on a pitch to the plate that season, he stumbled off the mound and pulled some tendons. Thereafter, he got by on junk. In 1970 Chapman was rated number 1 in the NCAA's College Division. After an impressive win against USC in his sophomore year, he said, "I was confident. I challenged their hitters. I threw my fastball and slider over the plate, daring them to hit the ball. They didn't."[5] Jones went 11-4 as a sophomore with a 1.75 ERA, and was named second team All-American.

Jones married his high-school sweetheart, Marie Stassi, on October 10, 1970. They had two children, Staci, born in January 1975, and Jami.

After his sophomore and junior years, Jones played summer ball for the Glacier-Pilots of Anchorage in the Alaska Baseball League. The team, managed by Paul Deese, participated in the National Baseball Congress tournament in Wichita, Kansas, in 1970. Jones pitched a complete game in the semifinals to advance his team to the finals.[6] After the 1971 season in Alaska, the Glacier-Pilots returned to Wichita and, in the final game, Jones pitched the team to a 5-4 win over the Fairbanks Goldpanners. The game wasn't decided until the bottom of the ninth inning when Anchorage tallied the winning run off Fairbanks pitcher Dave Winfield.[7] It capped off a season during which Jones went 14-1 with three wins in the National Baseball Congress tourney.[8] Deese and Jones remained lifelong friends and eventually Deese, a successful businessman, counseled Jones on his post-baseball business ventures.

By Jones's senior year, with the zip out of his fastball, and most of the scouts looking the other way, he was effective nonetheless. Under coach Bob Pomeroy, Jones went 11-4 with a 1.42 ERA during the regular season. In the NCAA District Eight Tournament he shut out Cal State on a three-hitter, prompting opposing coach Al Matthews to say, "He wasted his fastball and made us hit his breaking pitches."[9]

Although his fastball was nonexistent by the end of his four years at Chapman, Jones emerged with a degree in business, planning to go into real estate if he couldn't continue in baseball. However, one scout did keep his eye on the young Jones. Both Marty Keough and Cliff Ditto of the Padres noticed that he could be a success. Keough said, "He threw strikes. He got a quick breaking ball and he got people out."[10] He was drafted in the fifth round by the San Diego Padres in 1972, and signed for a bonus estimated at $3,000.

Jones began his pro career in 1972 with the Tri-City Padres in the Northwest League. It was a short stay; he pitched in only one game before being promoted to Alexandria, Louisiana, in the Texas League. He went 3-5 with a 2.91 ERA and returned to Alexandria the next season. After going 8-1 in 10 starts with the Aces to start the 1973 season, Jones was called up to the Padres in June, never to return to the minor leagues. The key to his success that season was a sinkerball he learned from Padres minor-league pitching instructor Warren Hacker.[11] Hacker "showed me how to place my fingers differently and how to apply pressure with them," Jones said.[12] The lefty went 7-6 with a 3.16 ERA in 20 games for San Diego that year.

The next year, 1974, Jones was 8-22 (with a 4.45 ERA) in 40 games, and he led the National League in losses. It was a tough season. As the losses mounted, Jones said, "With any luck, my record could be 14-9 instead of 7-16. When you get people to hit the ball on the ground and the ball consistently finds a hole, it isn't bad luck—it's no luck at all."[13] Seventeen of his losses were by two runs or less. As the season wore on and the losses mounted, he was dispatched to the bullpen in September and four of his last five appearances were in relief, including a two-inning save against the San Francisco Giants on September 24. However, in his final appearance of the season, two days later against the Los Angeles Dodgers, he faltered and was charged with four runs in 2⅔ innings as Los Angeles won, 5-2, in 10 innings. It was Jones's 22nd loss and the 100th loss for the Padres, who finished last in the NL West.

After working with pitching coach Tom Morgan, Jones altered his mechanics and found success in 1975. He said Morgan "made some fundamental changes in my delivery; now my body is doing all the work, my arm isn't getting tired. I feel like I could pitch forever. It's incredible."[14] And some days, he seemingly had to pitch forever, since the team still wasn't giving him much in the way of run support.

On May 19 Jones outdueled John Curtis of the St. Louis Cardinals, pitching a 10-inning one-hitter that ended when the Padres' Johnny Grubb hit a homer in the bottom of the 10th. The next high point of the season came on July 3 against Cincinnati. He took a perfect game into the eighth inning when Tony Perez reached second on an error by shortstop Hector Torres. Showing the wisdom of former Dodger pitcher Billy Loes, Jones said that "he lost it in the stadium lights. That was obvious to me."[15] Two batters later, Bill Plummer broke up the no-hitter and shutout with a double that scored Perez, knotting the game at 1-1. Jones was prepared to pitch into the night. "I had made up my mind that they would have to drag me out of there. If [manager John] McNamara wanted to remove me, he would have had to tie me up."[16]

Although Jones could eat up the innings, he did not eat up the clock. He dispensed with the Pirates using only 68 pitches in a May 24 shutout, and defeated the Astros 6-1 in 1:37 on August 6. He won 20 games that year, led the NL with a 2.24 ERA, and was selected for his first All-Star Game, where he picked up a save. He finished second to Tom Seaver in the Cy Young Award balloting and was named the National League Comeback Player of the Year.

Jones's success continued into 1976. For his performance in 1975, San Diego owner Ray Kroc increased his pay from $24,500 to $65,000. Jones went 16-3 in the season's first half (an All-Star break win total that no one as of 2017 has equaled). His celebrity status was such that the Padres attendance figures more than doubled when he pitched. After the great

start, there was speculation that he could be the next 30-game winner, but he took everything in stride. "There's no sense thinking about number 30 until you've won 29," he said. "A good start isn't necessarily an indication of what's going to happen for the whole season. I've had success taking games one at a time and omitting everything else from my mind. Guys get in trouble when their minds get astray and they start thinking way ahead."[17]

Despite his great performance in 1975, Jones did not get national hype until the night of June 9 when the Mets were in San Diego with their Cy Young ace Seaver, and 42,972 fans came to see their hero Jones. His achievements were well known to the home folks, who turned out in droves to see Randy. The game was scoreless for four innings before the Padres scored single runs in the fifth, sixth, and eighth innings to win, 3-0. Jones's record went to 11-2, as he scattered seven hits, struck out four, walked none, and sent the folks home in 2:10.

In one stretch, from May 17 to June 22, Jones tied a 63-year-old National League record by going 68 consecutive innings without issuing a walk. During that stretch, he faced 265 batters. The record had been set by Christy Mathewson of the New York Giants in 1913. On June 22, after striking out San Francisco's Darrell Evans to tie the record, he had received a standing ovation from the crowd of 29,940. The ovation continued as Jones came to bat in the seventh inning with the score tied 2-2. He singled and, with one out, came home on Tito Fuentes' two-run homer. Jones's streak ended when he walked Giants catcher Marc Hill leading off the eighth inning. The count went to 3-and-2 and Hill fouled off two pitches before taking a sinker for ball four. "Before I let it go, I knew it was going to be a ball," Jones said. "My arm was too far behind my body. I was pushing, I was too anxious."[18] There was no further scoring, and the 4-2 victory extended Jones's record for the season to 13-3. The win put the Padres into second place, a half-game ahead of the Dodgers, and kept San Diego within five games of the league-leading Reds.

For the second consecutive year, Jones pitched in the All-Star Game. He started, and his appearance was vintage Jones. In his three innings, seven of the outs were on groundballs. There was one foul popup and one strikeout. Jones was the winning pitcher when the NL won the game, 7-1. After the All-Star Game, his numbers trailed off a bit. He also came very close to tragedy. On the evening of August 4, the Padres returned home from Atlanta after a game in which Jones lost 1-0, putting his record at 18-6. Driving home from the airport, possibly at a speed faster than that of his fastball, Jones failed to negotiate a curve near his home and, as his wife said, "The telephone pole was sitting in the front seat."[19] A passing driver took Jones to the hospital. His only injuries were cuts to his face and neck. Lucky to be alive and with more than 30 stitches, Jones was back on the mound on August 10 at New York's Shea Stadium, losing a 5-4 decision to Jerry Koosman. In all, he was 4-8 after the accident, largely due to lack of support. In his last six losses of 1976, the Padres scored three runs or less, and they were shut out twice. Nevertheless, Jones finished the season with a 22-14 record, and a 2.74 ERA. Never known for the speed of his pitches, he struck out just 93 despite leading the league with 315⅓ innings pitched.

Jones started 40 games that season and had 25 complete games, both league highs. And he worked in a hurry. His games on average lasted little more than two hours. On August 27, when he shut out the Expos 2-0, he sent the folks home in 1:38. On September 19, in the first game of a doubleheader at Houston, Jones completed the game (a 3-2 loss) in 1:42. His quickest outing was on July 20, when he shut out Philadelphia 3-0 in 1:31. And his sinker was working to perfection. As pitching coach Roger Craig said, "It isn't so much as how much it sinks as when it sinks. It sinks late. It looks good on top of the plate and then sinks under the bat after the batter's committed himself."[20]

In 2016, reflecting on that 1976 season and the crowds that came to cheer him on, he said, "I had never seen anything like it; I don't know that anybody in San Diego had. Our ballclubs in those days weren't very good. (They had never had a winning season before 1976.) We had talent, but we didn't have consistency. But the boys really seemed to step up on the days I pitched, and the fans really got behind me."[21]

He also commented, "Everybody is mystified that I could complete 25 games. You have to remember that I completed 25 games and I didn't average 100 pitches in those games. I'd throw 89, 88, 92 pitches in a nine-inning game. That was philosophically how I approached the game. I went out in the first inning and I wanted to throw three pitches. I definitely tried to get the third one on the first pitch."[22]

But 1976 was Jones's last year as an elite pitcher. In his last start, he felt a tear in his forearm. He had severed the nerve attached to his biceps tendon. Jones had surgery after the 1976 campaign to repair a nerve injury, but never again had a season above .500. "It was years of futility and frustration," he recalled in 1998.[23]

Jones won just six games in 1977 but they included a vintage performance against the Phillies on May 4 in San Diego, his only complete game of the season. He pitched against Jim Kaat and won 4-1 in a mind-boggling 1:29 to bring his record at the time to 2-4. Of the 27 Phillies outs, 19 came on groundballs. Not everyone was happy about the swiftness of the game.

Ted Giannoulas (a/k/a The San Diego Chicken) said, "That game took money out of my pocket because as an hourly wage worker back then making $4 an hour, I could only put down an hour and a half on my time card. So I made $6 on that game, then they took out taxes. For the rest of the year, I would swear the names Randy Jones and Jim Kaat under my breath."[24] But after that single major success, Jones's ERA still stood at 4.85. His record for the season wound up at 6-12 with an ERA of 4.58.

Jones began the 1978 season slowly. After winning his first decision against Atlanta, on April 20, he was ineffective in his next two starts, finishing April at 1-2. He recorded his first shutout of the season on May 10, defeating Chicago 1-0. In a season marked by inconsistency, Jones lost four games in June but came back to win three games in July. His second shutout of the season, a 1-0 win over the Dodgers on August 1, put his record at 9-9. The Padres had a disappointing season. They fell out of contention early and, despite a winning record of 84-78, finished in fourth place, 11 games behind the division champion Dodgers. Jones bounced back from a terrible 1977 to record two shutouts and seven complete games, His season's record was 13-14 with a 2.88 ERA.

Hopes were high in the spring of 1979. Manager Roger Craig said, "He's got his confidence back. I think he'll have a big year. Randy will win three or four more games because Fred Kendall is catching him again. He trusts Kendall and that's important because he never shakes off a pitch. Randy is the only good pitcher I've ever seen who doesn't shake off his catcher's signs."[25] Pitchers are notorious for bragging about their hitting, but on May 13, 1979, Jones had a stolen base that was the first theft by a pitcher in the then 11-year history of the San Diego franchise. It came at home in the third inning against Mike Scott of the Mets. He had reached on an error by Scott and manager Craig, with Gene Richards at the plate, put on the hit-and-run play. Richards swung and missed and Jones got into second ahead of the throw from Mets catcher John Stearns.[26] It was his only career stolen base. He tired in the eighth inning and did not factor in the decision as the Padres won in extra innings. Jones's 1979 season pretty much mirrored 1978, as he went 11-12, but his ERA rose to 3.63. There were no shutouts, but he did complete six games, as the Padres dropped to 68-93 and finished in fifth place in the NL West.

In the spring of 1980, things were looking up for Jones. He was 4-2 and coming off three consecutive complete-game shutouts when he faced the Pirates on May 21 in the first game of a doubleheader. He took a 3-0 lead into the bottom of the fourth inning but then the troubles started again. During the inning he felt a pain in the right side of his ribcage. "I tried to compensate by throwing with my arm instead of my body, and strained the nerve in the arm again," Jones said. "My fingers went numb. Damn, it was frustrating."[27] He remained in the game until the bottom of the sixth inning, and was not involved in the decision. Pitching in pain for the balance of the season, Jones won only one of his last 12 decisions and had a 5.32 ERA during that stretch. For the season, he was 5-13 with a 3.91 ERA.

After the 1980 season, Jones was dealt to the New York Mets for a pair of prospects, Jose Moreno and John Pacella. He won eight games over two seasons with the Mets before retiring. The 1981 season was a disaster. He lost his first five decisions, but it was a team effort: Of the 36 runs he allowed in his first eight starts, only 20 were earned. The Mets were challenged when it came to fielding groundballs. Jones's only win came on May 31 against the Cubs. He allowed one run in 6⅓ innings of his 6-1 victory. For the strike-shortened season, Jones was 1-8 with a 4.85 ERA.

Jones's first appearance of 1982 indicated that things would be different from 1981. During the off-season, he had done a great deal of running and he came to spring training in great shape. New Mets manager George Bamberger gave Jones the ball on Opening Day and he beat the Phillies and Steve Carlton, 7-2 at Veterans Stadium. Jones pitched the first six innings, scattering four hits and allowing only one run. The over-anxious Phillies were swinging at bad pitches and three of the outs were on easy comebackers. After the win, he said, "I had good concentration and, believe it or not, I warmed up on the mound (in chilly 41-degree weather). My sinker began to come around in the second inning and I got a lot of important outs with it. I had excellent concentration. My mental approach today was perfect."[28] One week later, at Shea Stadium, Jones triumphed again over the Phillies, 5-2, in the Mets' home opener.

Things were looking up for Jones and for the Mets, who were coming off five straight losing seasons. The signs outside had said, "The Magic is Back" since 1980. But was it? Jones got off to a great start, winning six of his first eight decisions. On May 10 he hurled his first complete game since 1979, beating the Padres 3-2 and reducing his ERA to 2.60. On May 18, against Cincinnati at Shea Stadium, he got his fifth win though he was charged with four runs in seven-plus innings. After his sixth win, a four-hit shutout at Houston on May 23, the Mets were in second place with a 23-18 record, 1½ games behind the National League East-leading Cardinals.

But Jones was only 2-2 at home, and Shea Stadium had been a nemesis to him over the years. It all began in 1973 when, in his major-league debut on June 16, he entered the game in relief and yielded his first major-league hit, a home run by an aging Willie Mays, and continued through his time with the Mets. In 1982 he won at home only once after May 23, and his record sank from 6-2 on May 23 to 7-10 at the end of the season. His ERA rose from a low of 2.60 on May 10 to a disturbingly high 4.60 at the end of the season. On the road in 1982 he was 4-2 with a 2.37 ERA, but he was 3-8 at home with a 7.47 ERA. As Jones's fortunes got worse, so did those of the Mets. After the good start, they finished the season in sixth place in the NL East with a 65-97 record. The Mets had several young guns coming up through the minors and Jones, hoping to catch on with another club, was released, on his own request, after the season.[29] He was philosophical when he said, "A manager can't use a pitcher who can't win at home and I understood when Bamberger took me out of the rotation."[30]

When 1983 rolled around, Jones went to spring training with the Pirates as a nonroster invitee. He was released on March 27.

For his career, Jones was 100-123 with an ERA of 3.42. He had 73 complete games, of which 19 were shutouts.

After his playing days were over, Jones returned to San Diego, where he became a fixture. His residence in Poway is about 25 miles north of San Diego. He tended to the string of car washes he had opened during his days with the Padres. His other business pursuits revolved around food; he started in his sister's catering business, became a food broker, and eventually opened his own barbecue stand at the ballpark. He also did pregame and postgame shows.[31] In his time as a food broker for AGS Foods, he traveled to military food services operations, mixing business with pleasure. In addition to making sales calls, he conducted baseball clinics for children of military personnel.[32]

Jones's number was 35 retired by the Padres in 1997, and two years later he was a member of the first group inducted into the Padres Hall of Fame. He remained, as of the end of the 2016 season, the Padres' leader in starts, complete games, shutouts, and innings pitched.

Jones also worked with young pitchers. He had put an ad in the local newspaper offering to give pitching lessons to youngsters, and had 35 students. In 1990, a 12-year-old saw the ad and his folks gave Jones a call. "I remember vividly the four, five years we spent in the backyard with Randy," said 2002 Cy Young Award winner Barry Zito. "When I did something incorrectly, he'd spit tobacco juice on my shoes, Nike high tops we could barely afford, he's spitting tobacco juice on them." In his teaching, it was Jones's goal that his best students "that showed a burning desire" would be shown his Cy Young trophy. What Zito learned from Jones was "the mental side, never giving in."[33]

Jones also worked with the Padres Volunteer Team, which was launched in February 2015 to help nonprofits, including the USO, for which in September 2015 the group put together 300 "we care" packages for US military families.[34]

He threw out the ceremonial first pitch at the 2016 All-Star Game in San Diego. In November 2016, years of tobacco use caught up with Jones and he was diagnosed with throat cancer. He started treatments at Sharp Hospital the following month, and completed his treatment on February 1, 2017. To thunderous applause, he threw out the first pitch on Opening Day 2017 in San Diego. When he was tested on May 1, he was hoping to be given a clean bill of health.[35] The following day, the call came from his doctor: he was cancer-free. "To say I'm cancer-free today will give somebody else a little hope," he commented. "If they have any hopes, don't doubt it. You've got to put the work in, but the process works."[36]

## SOURCES

In addition to the sources cited in the Notes, the author used Baseball-Reference.com, the Randy Jones player file at the National Baseball Hall of Fame Library, and the following:

Broderick, Pat. "Former Padre Still Pitching … Food This Time," *San Diego Business Journal*, September 22, 1997: 8.

Denman, Elliott. "Jones Returns to Top of Heap," *Asbury Park* (New Jersey) *Press*, May 23, 1982: B3.

Shaw, Bud. "You've Got to Believe in Jones Now," *Philadelphia Daily News*, April 9, 1982: 93.

## NOTES

1. Ron Fimrite, "Uncommon Success for a Common Man," *Sports Illustrated*, July 12, 1976.
2. Dave Distell, "Fans Flocking to See Randy Jones," *Los Angeles Times*, June 24, 1976.
3. Ibid.
4. Al Doyle, "Former Cy Young Award Winner, Randy Jones," *Baseball Digest*, August 2001: 64.
5. Al Carr, "Randy Jones—The 'Vow Boy' of Chapman's Baseball Varsity," *Los Angeles Times*, May 7, 1970: III-14.
6. Merrill Cox, "Anchorage, Peck Here, Peck There, Colorado Tumbles," *Wichita* (Kansas) *Eagle*, August 30, 1970: 6F.
7. Bob Stewart, "Pilots Win Alaskan '71 Rush for NBC Gold," *Wichita* (Kansas) *Eagle*, September 1, 1971: 17.
8. Andy Williams, "City Pays Tribute to National Champions," *Anchorage Daily News*, October 11, 1971: 9.
9. "CHCS Down to Last Strike," *Hayward* (California) *Daily Review*, May 26, 1972: 27.
10. Dave Anderson, "Randy Jones Wins Without Fastball," *New York Times*, June 10, 1976: 49.
11. Jack Murphy, "The Best of Seasons for Randy and Marie," *San Diego Union*, July 6, 1975: H-1.

# 20-GAME LOSERS

12  "Randy Jones Wins Without Fastball."

13  Phil Collier, "Pittsburgh Surges by Pirates, 7-3," *San Diego Union*, August 10, 1974: C-1.

14  Murphy, "The Best of Seasons for Randy and Marie."

15  Ibid.

16  Ibid.

17  Distell.

18  Phil Collier, "Jones Notches 13th, Ties N.L.'s No-Walk Record," *San Diego Union*, June 23, 1976: C-1.

19  Jack Murphy, "Randy in Stitches; the Padres Aren't Laughing," *San Diego Union*, August 6, 1976: C-1.

20  Jack Flowers, "Randy Jones: Shades of Denny McClain, Dizzy Dean," *Pensacola* (Florida) *News Journal*, June 24, 1976: 1-C.

21  Jeff Sanders, "'Crafty Left-Hander Had It All Working—Randy Jones Wins 1976 National League Cy Young Award," *San Diego Union-Tribune*, March 13, 2016: S-7.

22  Kirk Kenney, "Rush Hour (and a Half)—Forty Years Ago Today Padres Beat Phillies in a Mere 89 Minutes—Unthinkable Today," *San Diego Union-Tribune*, May 4, 2017: S-1.

23  Paul Gutierrez, "Catching Up With Randy Jones," *Sports Illustrated*, August 3, 1998.

24  Kenney.

25  Murphy, "Glory Was Sweet; Randy Craves Encore," *San Diego Union*, March 11, 1979: H-1

26  United Press International, "Jones's Stolen Base First by Padre Pitcher," *Lexington* (Kentucky) *Herald*, May 14, 1979: B-4.

27  Dick Young, "Ready to Play Some Hardball," *New York Daily News*, February 6, 1981.

28  Hal Bodley, "Phillies Can't Keep Up With Mets' Jones," *Wilmington* (Delaware) *Morning News*, April 9, 1982: C-1.

29  Russ Franke, "Jones Makes a Pitch for More Major Fun," *Pittsburgh Press*, February 23, 1983: D2.

30  Charley Feeney, "When Randy Jones Was a Met, Shea Was Just No Place Like Home," *Pittsburgh Post-Gazette*, February 21, 1982: 10.

31  Gutierrez.

32  Doyle.

33  "Former Cy Young Pitcher Helped Develop Zito Into Award Winner," *Hamilton* (Ontario) *Spectator*, November 8, 2002: E05.

34  Stephanie R. Glidden. "Volunteers Pitch in to Help Get Care Packages to Our Military," *San Diego Business Journal*, September 28, 2015: 41.

35  Dennis Lin, "Randy Jones Visits Padres Camp; Hopes to Be Declared Cancer-Free," *San Diego Union-Tribune*, March 23, 2017.

36  Jeff Sanders, "Padres Report—An Emotional Jones Says Cancer Is Gone," *San Diego Union-Tribune*, May 3, 2017: S-5.

# VERNON KENNEDY

BY JOEL RIPPEL

**IN THE SPRING OF 1992, AT THE AGE** of 84, Vernon Kennedy was still competing athletically.

At the Missouri Senior Olympics, Kennedy took part in the discus, long jump and shot put. He won a gold medal in the discus, captured a bronze in the long jump, and finished fourth in the shot put.

Kennedy's success at that track and field competition shouldn't have come as a surprise. As a 20-year-old college student, he won the decathlon at the prestigious Penn Relays.

Kennedy, who was born Lloyd Vernon Kennedy on March 20, 1907, in Kansas City, Missouri, was a gifted all-around athlete at Central Missouri State Teachers College (Warrensburg, Missouri). In football, he was a three-time all-conference player (as a 6-foot, 175-pound tackle). In track and field, he helped the Mules win four consecutive conference titles. At the 1927 conference meet, he took first place in five events (shot put, javelin, pole vault, discus, and long jump).

On April 29, 1927, in Philadelphia, Kennedy won the grueling 10-event decathlon competition (which took eight hours to complete) with a Penn Relays record of 7,236 points. He took first in three events and tied for first in a fourth en route to his record-setting performance.

Kennedy, played 25 seasons of professional baseball, but didn't play intercollegiate baseball at Central Missouri; the school didn't field a varsity baseball team until 1956. But Kennedy, who graduated from Central Missouri in 1929 with a bachelor's degree in education (he majored in history), found time to develop his baseball talents by playing town-team ball.

In the summer of 1930, a scout for the Philadelphia Athletics saw Kennedy, a right-hander, strike out 16 in a game, and offered him a contract. Kennedy signed and began his professional career with Burlington of the Class-D Mississippi Valley League. Kennedy went 6-5 with a 4.18 ERA in 16 appearances for Burlington.

Burlington sold Kennedy's contract after the 1930 season and the Pirates brought Kennedy to spring training in 1931 and 1932. Kennedy said that in those two years he was the "forgotten man"—ignored by everyone.[1]

Kennedy split the 1931 season between Hazleton of the Class-B New York-Pennsylvania League and Wichita of the Class-A Western League. He made 12 appearances for each team—going 2-5 with a 6.38 ERA for Hazleton and 2-3 with a 5.40 ERA for Wichita.

In 1932 Kennedy traveled with the team to Pittsburgh out of spring training, but made no appearances for the Pirates and was released in May.[2]

Kennedy signed with St. Joseph of the Western League and went 13-13 in 29 appearances. After the season, the club did not file a reserve list and Kennedy became a free agent. He signed with Oklahoma City of the Class-A Texas League. In his first seven games, Kennedy said, the team scored only three runs, and he lost all seven games.[3]

Kennedy regrouped to finish with a team-high 15 victories (and 18 losses) and a 3.49 ERA. After the season, the A's purchased his contract and he went to spring training with the team in 1934.

In the final days of spring training, the A's elected to keep Alton Benton, who had been a teammate of Kennedy's in Oklahoma City, over Kennedy for the final pitching spot on the roster. On April 9, the A's returned Kennedy to Oklahoma City. But by the end of the 1934 season, Kennedy was in the big leagues. He went 17-18 with a 3.15 ERA with Oklahoma City, and his contract was purchased by the Chicago White Sox in September.

On September 18, 1934, at the age of 27, Kennedy made his major-league debut. He started and pitched 7⅓ innings in a 6-0 loss to the Athletics in Chicago.

Kennedy singled in his first major-league at-bat. (A decent hitter, he had a .244 batting average in his 12-year major-league career.)

Five days later, on the 23rd, Kennedy made his second start, against the Cleveland Indians in Chicago. He pitched a complete game, allowing seven hits, in a 2-1 loss to the Indians. He also started Chicago's season finale, on September 30 in Cleveland. He went three innings and got no decision. In the three appearances, Kennedy was 0-2 with a 3.72 ERA.

After their 53-99 record and last-place finish in 1934, the White Sox were looking for pitching help in 1935, and Kennedy made the club out of spring training. He wasn't used much in the first six weeks of the season, making just two starts (both no-decisions) and three relief appearances. On May 31, Kennedy made his third start and pitched a complete game, allowing just one earned run, in a 6-2 loss to Cleveland in Chicago.

Eight days later, Kennedy earned his first major-league victory by outdueling Elden Auker and the defending American League champion Detroit Tigers, 3-2. He allowed the Tigers just five hits. Kennedy won five of his next seven starts (with one no-decision) to improve to 6-2.

On August 25, Kennedy pitched a complete game in a 6-1 loss (only three earned runs) to the New York Yankees. Two days later, he pitched two innings of relief to save a 4-3 victory over the Yankees in Chicago.

On August 31, Kennedy provided more relief to the overworked White Sox pitching staff (four doubleheaders in the previous six days). He took a 9-7 record into his start against the Cleveland Indians in Chicago and he pitched the first no-hitter in the American League since 1931. Kennedy aided his own cause with a bases-loaded triple in the sixth inning that gave the White Sox a 5-0 lead (the eventual final score).

With one out in the ninth, Cleveland's leadoff hitter, Milt Galatzer, hit a line drive to left that threatened the no-hit bid but Al Simmons made a diving catch. Kennedy walked the next hitter, Earl Averill—his fourth walk of the game—to bring Joe Vosmik to the plate. Kennedy got Vosmik, a career .307 hitter who batted .348 with 216 hits, 47 doubles, and 20 triples in 1935, to look at a called third strike.

"I didn't know I was pitching a no-hitter until the start of the ninth inning," Kennedy said. "Then the boys told me, and I was limp as a rag when I walked off the mound after throwing that inside pitch for the third strike on Vosmik."[4]

Kennedy said luck was with him and he praised Simmons for his diving catch on Galatzer's smash.[5]

In his next start, Kennedy allowed four earned runs in six innings in a 6-2 loss to the Red Sox in Boston on September 8. In the final month of the season, Kennedy was 1-4 in September to finish the season with an 11-11 record and a 3.91 ERA. He completed 16 of his 25 starts. The White Sox, who had lost 99 games in 1934, improved to 74-78 in 1935. The White Sox were 60-56 on August, but lost 22 of their final 36 games to finish in fifth place.

The 1936 season, Kennedy's second full season in the major leagues, was filled with highlights. He went 21-9 with career highs in starts (34), complete games (20), and innings pitched (274⅓), and was named to the American League squad for the All-Star Game. Kennedy was one of five players on the 22-player American League roster whom manager Joe McCarthy didn't use in the National League's 4-3 victory in Boston.

Kennedy earned his 20th victory on September 9. Pitching on three days' rest, he pitched 13 innings to outduel Rube Walberg and Lefty Grove in a 3-2 victory over the Red Sox in Chicago. Kennedy allowed 10 hits and walked six (he walked a career-high 147 in 1936), but the Red Sox left 14 runners on base. Kennedy won his next start but lost his last two decisions and finished 21-9. The White Sox rose to third place with an 81-70 record.

On Opening Day of 1937, April 21, in St. Louis, Kennedy was roughed up by the Browns. He allowed 14 hits and 11 earned runs in 4⅓ innings in the Browns' 15-10 victory. Kennedy regrouped to win three of his next four decisions and finished the season with a 14-13 record (and a career-high 114 strikeouts) as the White Sox improved to 86-68 with another third-place finish.

After the season, Kennedy was traded by the White Sox to the Detroit Tigers in a six-player swap. He was considered the key to the deal, which at least one writer call unpopular with the press and fans in Detroit.

"Opinion in Detroit is overwhelmingly one of protest against the trade. Here and there are defenders of (Tigers player-manager) Mickey Cochrane, who made the deal solely to get Kennedy, but a majority sentiment of press and public holds that the Tigers weakened the team in the wholesale shift," wrote Sam Greene in *The Sporting News*.[6]

Kennedy got off to a good start with the Tigers. In his first start, against his former teammates on April 20, Kennedy pitched 6⅔ innings with no decision in a 5-4 loss to the White Sox in Chicago. But he went 10-4 in the first 2½ months to earn his second All-Star Game berth. As in 1936, Kennedy did not get into the game (in Cincinnati, won by the National League, 4-1). Kennedy was just 2-5 over the final 2½ months of the season to finish 12-9.

After a fourth-place finish (84-70) in 1938, Kennedy and the Tigers got off to a slow start in 1939. On May 13 in St. Louis, he took the loss in the Browns' 5-3 victory. The loss dropped Kennedy to 0-3 and the Tigers to 7-15. After the game the Browns and Tigers completed a nine-player trade, which included both starting pitchers from the day's game. Kennedy joined the Browns and among the four players received by the Tigers was Bobo Newsom.

Over the remainder of the 1939 season, Kennedy started 27 games for the Browns (with 12 complete games), winning 9 and losing 17. Including his 0-3 record in four starts for the Tigers before the trade, Kennedy finished 9-20.

On September 12 in Philadelphia, Kennedy, who was riding a four-game losing streak, allowed three runs to the A's in the bottom of the first inning and was pinch-hit for in the top of the second. The 9-1 victory for the A's was Kennedy's 20th loss and dropped the Browns to 36-97. Three days later, Kennedy started and went eight innings in the Browns' 9-5 victory over the Senators in Washington for his ninth victory of the season. The Browns finished the season with a 43-111 record.

The Browns and Kennedy showed improvement in 1940. He went 12-17 in 32 starts (18 complete games) as the Browns finished in sixth place with a 67-87 record.

Kennedy opened the 1941 season with three consecutive losses before winning two of his next three starts to improve to 2-4. On May 15, two days after the second anniversary of his trade to the Browns, Kennedy was sent to the Washington Senators in exchange for catcher Rick Ferrell. Kennedy went just 1-7 in 17 games (7 starts) for the Senators to finish the 1941 season with a 3-11 record. After the season his contract was purchased by the Cleveland Indians.

Kennedy went 4-8 for the Indians in 1942 (12 starts) but rebounded with a 10-7 record for the Indians in 1943—his best season since 1938. He began the 1944 season with the Indians, going 2-5 in

10 starts. On July 28 his contract was purchased by the Philadelphia Phillies. Kennedy was 1-5 the rest of the season. On June 10, 1945, Kennedy (0-3 thus far) was traded to the Cincinnati Reds for rookie infielder Wally Flager.

Kennedy made what turned out to be his final major-league appearance on September 27, 1945, at the age of 38. He pitched eight innings and allowed three earned runs, in the Reds' 7-4 loss to the Cubs in Cincinnati. The loss dropped Kennedy to 5-15 for the season — 5-12 with the Reds, who finished seventh with a 61-93 record. After the season, Kennedy pitched for a team of NL players who played an eight-game series against a group of AL players.

Kennedy went to spring training with the Reds in 1946, but was released on March 20 — his 39th birthday. But he wasn't finished with professional baseball — he pitched in the minor leagues for nine more seasons.

After being let go by the Reds, Kennedy signed with the San Diego Padres of the Pacific Coast League. In 1946 he was 18-13 with a 2.92 ERA for team that finished 30 games under .500 (78-108). Kennedy returned to the Padres in 1947, going 9-15 with a 4.11 ERA (the Padres were 79-107).

Before the 1948 season the Padres traded Kennedy to the Hollywood Stars of the Pacific Coast League. At 41, he was 9-12 with a 3.93 ERA for the Stars, who were 84-104. In January of 1949, the Stars sold Kennedy's contract to Dallas of the Texas League.

With a 6-4 record and a 2.54 ERA for Dallas, Kennedy was traded to the Minneapolis Millers of the American Association at the end of May. He told the *Minneapolis Tribune*, "I've had a pretty long career, (and) was ready to hang 'em up, but now I'd like to see it extended."[7]

Even though he was in his 20th professional season, Kennedy said he was virtually the same weight when his career began. "In the 20 years I've been pitching," he said, "I haven't varied over three or four pounds from 175. I've always believed in clean living and I preach it to youngsters. Keeping in shape will do more to help a fellow than anything else."[8]

Kennedy went 3-3 with a 7.15 ERA in 20 games, all in relief, with the Millers. Released after the season, he wasn't ready to end his career. In early 1950, Kennedy advertised his services in *The Sporting News*:

"Ex-major leaguer, now a free agent, wants pitching job with Class AA or higher baseball league. Would consider job throwing batting practice in majors. Vernon Kennedy, Mendon, Mo."[9]

Kennedy didn't find a job in Organized Baseball in 1950. But in February of 1951, *The Sporting News* reported: "Vernon Kennedy, former big-league hurler who played with a St. Joseph (Mo.) semi-pro team last season, is returning to organized baseball this year as a relief pitcher for Oklahoma City (Texas League)."[10]

Kennedy, who had pitched for Oklahoma City in 1933 and 1934, spent the next three seasons with Oklahoma City. In 1951 he was 9-7 with a 2.64 ERA in 54 games and in 1952 he was 11-4 with a 2.23 ERA in 42 games. He pitched in the Texas League all-star game in 1952. In 1953 he was 4-4 with a 4.44 ERA in 44 games. All of his appearances were in relief except for one start in 1953.

Kennedy spent the 1954 and 1955 seasons with Beaumont of the Texas League. In 1954 he was 3-4 in 16 games. By opening the 1955 season with Beaumont, he became the oldest player in Texas League history. *The Sporting News* noted, "A check by Bill Ruggles, league statistician, has disclosed that pitcher Vern Kennedy of Beaumont is the oldest active pitcher in all league history. The ex-major leaguer observed his 48th birthday, March 20, making him one year older than Herschel (Jackie) Reid was when he last pitched for Shreveport and Fort Worth in 1941."[11]

Kennedy was 1-1 in 14 appearances before being released by Beaumont at the end of May. In all, he had won 128 games and lost 129 in 14 minor-league seasons. For his 25-year professional career, he was 232-261.

But Kennedy still wasn't done pitching. A month after leaving Organized Baseball, Kennedy pitched in an amateur game in which he was overshadowed by his daughter, according to *The Sporting News*, which wrote:

"Fifteen-year old Carol Kennedy proved a pitcher in the finest tradition in a one-inning relief appearance for the Salisbury (Mo.) Merchants against the Jefferson City Tweedies in Salisbury, June 28. The daughter of ex-major league pitcher Vernon Kennedy, Carol hurled the ninth inning and retired the side without being scored on to clinch a 10-3 victory. She walked two batters but caught the game-ending pop fly. Her dad, a veteran of 24 years in professional baseball, hurled the seventh and eighth innings and allowed one run."[12]

Kennedy next spent 12 years teaching driver's education in Missouri. In 1951 his alma mater, Central Missouri State, established the Vernon Kennedy Award, to be presented annually to the school's outstanding male athlete. In 1954 Central Missouri named its football field Vernon Kennedy Field. In 1955 Kennedy was inducted into the Missouri Sports Hall of Fame and in 1992 he was a member of the inaugural class for the Central Missouri Athletic Hall of Fame.

Kennedy, 85 years old, died on January 28, 1993, in an accident at his home in Mendon, Missouri. The roof of a smoke-house he was dismantling collapsed on him, killing him instantly, according to the Chariton County coroner.[13] The president of his alma mater called him "a remarkable man."[14]

Kennedy was survived by wife Maud, a daughter, a son, two grandchildren, six-great grandchildren, three brothers and a sister.

## SOURCES

In addition to the sources cited in the Notes, the author also consulted Baseball-Reference.com, milb.com, mosportshalloffame.com, Retrosheet.org, and ucmathletics.com.

## NOTES

1. Bill Dooly, "Mack's New 'Big Three'—Mahaffey, Cain and Marcum!" *The Sporting News*, March 29, 1934: 3.
2. Ibid.
3. Ibid.
4. "Enters Hall of Fame," *The Sporting News*, September 5, 1935: 1.
5. Ibid.
6. Sam Greene, "Detroit Fans Deride Cochran for Swapping Walker to Dyke," *The Sporting News*, December 9, 1937: 1.
7. Halsey Hall, "It's a Fact," *Minneapolis Tribune*, June 4, 1949.
8. Ibid.
9. *The Sporting News*, February 8, 1950: 24.
10. "Caught on the Fly," *The Sporting News*, February 21, 1951: 23.
11. "Rough Night for Mel McGaha," *The Sporting News*, May 4, 1955: 31.
12. 'Diamond Dust," *The Sporting News*, July 6, 1955: 37.
13. Cathie Burnes Beebe, "Vern Kennedy Dies; Was Pitcher, CEMO Star," *St. Louis Post-Dispatch*, January 30, 1993.
14. Ibid.

# HENRY KEUPPER

## BY EMMET R. NOWLIN

A TALL LEFT-HANDED PITCHER, Henry Keupper pitched seven years in professional baseball, but just one year in the majors—1914, when he was 8-20 for the last-place St. Louis Terriers of the short-lived Federal League.

Henry John Keupper was born on June 24, 1887, in Staunton, Illinois. Staunton, the second largest city in Macoupin County, has always been a small town, with a population of about 2,200 in 1890.[1] In southern Illinois, it is about 35 miles northeast of St. Louis.

Henry "Hank" Keupper was born the youngest of six siblings. He had two sisters, Mary and Lillian, and three brothers, Hubert, Hugo, and Edward. His parents, Henry Sr. and Mary (Kowans), were German-born. Mary came to the United States in 1881 and Henry then or the year before. They married in June 1881 in Menard, Illinois.

In 1900 Hank's father was employed as a mine manager in Gillespie, Illinois, and his mother worked as a mine clerk. Hank attended the Staunton and Gillespie public schools and graduated from high school in Gillespie. After high school he pitched semipro ball for one year.

In March 1907 it was reported that Peoria Distillers manager Frank Donnelly had signed Keupper for the 1908 season.[2] This was Keupper's first foray into the minor leagues, and he was one of the youngest players on the team, with a reported salary of $125 per month.[3] The 1908 Distillers finished sixth the Class-B Three-I (Illinois-Indiana-Iowa) League. That season was one of only two in which Keupper was able to win more games than he lost. He appeared in 35 games and ended the year with 15 wins and 14 losses.

Keupper was reported drafted by one of the New York major-league ballclubs, and was "regarded in [the Three-I League] as a sure comer."[4]

In the offseason, Keupper and teammate Roland Wolfe went to Douglas, Arizona, with "several other Three-I League players at the end of the season." The two Distillers remained there and ran street cars.[5]

Keupper began the 1909 season back with the Distillers, appearing in 16 games with a record of 4-7. He spent the second half of the season with the Indianapolis Indians in the Class-A American Association, for whom he was 3-4 in 20 games under manager Charles Carr. On February 7, 1910, Carr traded Keupper to the Nashville Volunteers of the Class-A Southern Association for pitcher John Duggan.

In 1910 the Keupper family was living in Herrin, Illinois. Hank's father still was employed as a mine manager. His mother had become a dealer in grain.

Henry wasn't the only ballplayer in his family. His brother Hugo was a catcher in at least three known seasons, 1910 for the Clinton (Illinois) Champs, and in 1913 and 1914 for the Bloomington Bloomers. The two brothers were teammates in 1913. (Newspaper articles from April and May 1912 show Hugo Keupper quitting Bloomington due to homesickness, and Henry pitching well.)[6] The 1910 census shows another brother, Hubert, as a ballplayer.

In April 1910 both Henry and Hugo reported to manager Joe Keenan in Bloomington, Illinois. The Springfield newspaper reported, "Hugo and Henry Keupper … also came in yesterday. They are pitcher and catcher, and the fame of the Keupper boys battery is known all over southern Illinois. They made a great showing in the [offseason] Trolley league last year."[7]

The brothers were assigned to different teams, Hugo to Clinton and Henry to Nashville, managed by Bill Bernhard. The Vols needed a left-hander, and Bernhard was impressed with Keupper's work in spring training.[8] Keupper posted a record of 12-16 in 35 games. One highlight was the August 18 game against visiting Memphis. Keupper pitched a 1-0 shutout, giving up only "three scattered singles";

Nashville scored its only run in the first inning.[9] In at least one game, May 5 in Birmingham, Keupper played right field.

The 1910 Southern League batting champion was Shoeless Joe Jackson of the New Orleans Pelicans, near the start of his career. In a series between Nashville and New Orleans, Keupper made the New Orleans paper briefly as one of the pitchers who feared Jackson at the plate: "In the Nashville series Keupper started by walking Jackson twice in one game on purpose. Another time he tried to walk Joe and Joe reached out and got one for a fly. Bill Viebahn did the same stunt, and both [Charlie] Case and Bernhard walked Jackson purposely in Sunday's game."[10]

Keupper began the 1911 season with Nashville. On September 3 the Southern Association's Chattanooga Lookouts purchased his contract. Five days later, he beat Atlanta, 3-1, the only run coming on a solo homer. Chattanooga became a Detroit farm club, and it was reported in mid-September that Keupper would "revert to Nashville or to some other club."[11] On September 20 Keupper was included on the list of players reserved by Nashville for the 1912 season.

In February 1912 it was reported that the Class-B Bloomington Bloomers had purchased his contract from Nashville.[12] In the 1912 season Keupper was 14-19 for the Three-I League team. For Nashville and Chattanooga, Keupper earned a salary of $200 per month, and for Bloomington in 1912 and 1913 he was paid $150 a month.

Keupper began the 1913 season with Bloomington, as did his brother Hugo, who was offered a contract by manager Harry Syfert. Hugo caught in 70 games and hit for a .234 batting average. As a batter, in 54 at-bats, Henry hit for a .259 average, notably winning his own game on July 3 against Danville with a 10th-inning double.

Henry worked in 27 games and posted a record of 11-9 before he jumped his contract to join the Federal League. The *Chicago Tribune* reported, "Bloomington directors received word today that pitcher Henry Keupper, one of the most effective members of the staff, who has been on leave of absence, joined the St. Louis Federal league team and was playing under the name of King."[13]

A United Press dispatch dated August 14, 1913, reported that Bloomington "is after the scalp of the new Federal League, and would have that body outlawed by the National Commission." The brief notice continued, "The complaint has been filed with the Commission by the local club that the St. Louis Federals are playing Henry Keupper, who jumped after signing a contract to play with the local team."[14]

Another paper reported on August 18, "Another player has jumped the Bloomer ranks. Hugo Keupper is the latest to pull the kangaroo stunt. Keupper, who is just a fair backstop, departed from Bloomington early Saturday morning, and is thought to have signed with the St. Louis Federal club, of which team his brother, Hank, is a member."[15]

The Bloomington club suspended Keupper for his jump to the St. Louis Feds. "The return of Keupper to Bloomington by the Feds would be a fortunate thing for the local club," the *Duluth News-Tribune* wrote, "as Keupper was one of the most effective members of the staff."[16]

Pitching for the Terriers, managed for most of the season by Mordecai "Three Finger" Brown (Brown was fired with 38 games to play and was replaced by Fielder Jones), Keupper made his major-league debut on April 19 in the Terriers' fourth game of the season, and pitched a complete-game 9-2 victory over the Indianapolis Hoosiers. He scattered six hits and struck out two, but walked 10 batters. Three thousand fans braved a frigid day at Handlan's Park to see the game. The cold "had considerable effect on Keupper's pitching," wrote the *St. Louis Post-Dispatch*. "He grew wild at times and in all handed out 10 passes. Four of these came in one round and resulted in the two runs scored by the Hoosiers."[17]

Four days later the two teams played again, at Indianapolis, and Keupper shut out the Hoosiers, 3-0, on five hits, this time only walking one batter. The 16,000 spectators saw a 0-0 game through the first eight innings. In the top of the ninth, St. Louis took a 1-0 lead and then Keupper drove a double to left field, scoring two more runs.

Keupper's third outing was not as good. Hosting the Brooklyn Tip-Tops in the first game of a May 2 doubleheader, Keupper gave up eight hits and four runs in four innings of work before being replaced. Brooklyn beat the Terriers 4-3, and Keupper had his first loss of the season.

It should be noted that decisions on pitchers' losses in games where more than one pitcher worked for a team were made in ways other than we employ today. As Tom Ruane of Retrosheet has written, "Official scorers often used their own idiosyncratic and inconsistent judgment back then when determining winners and losers."[18] As a result, some databases today show Keupper with differing numbers of losses.

Tracking Keupper's wins and losses throughout the season is a difficult task. In researching newspapers of the day, one comes across numerous mentions of a Keupper playing baseball. For instance, the May 6 *Daily Illinois State Register* reported two games involving a Keupper—a game between Quincy and Dubuque in which "Pitcher Keupper had the losers completely at his mercy" and a game in Bloomington against Decatur, in which Keupper was the catcher.[19] Hugo was the catcher, and the other Keupper was their brother, Hubert.

On May 7 at St. Louis, Henry Keupper yielded 13 runs (six earned) in a 15-7 loss to the Pittsburgh Rebels. Eight errors contributed to his defeat. More than once, errors may have cost Keupper a game. On May 25 in Baltimore, his teammates committed seven errors, accounting for three unearned runs in a game Keupper lost 6-3.

Keupper beat Brooklyn on May 16 in a 5-3 complete game, but in a game at Pittsburgh he was pummeled for 10 earned runs on 14 hits, but only one base on balls.

In the month of May his record was 1-5. On May 4 the Terriers were in first place with a record of 11-5. After a strong start, the team steadily declined throughout the season. Keupper lost seven consecutive games between May 21 and June 13. By June 23, he had a record of 3-10.

On August 7, with an apparent record of 5-11, Keupper beat Pittsburgh 2-1, the first of three consecutive wins, the latter two in long relief.

St. Louis switched managers before the game of August 22, Fielder Jones taking over for Brown. This prompted some optimism. "The Terriers have been instilled with new life by their new boss, Fielder Jones, and it is certain that there will be no easy sailing in the Mound City," the *Kansas City Star* wrote. "In [Dave] Davenport, [Bob] Groom, and Keupper the Terriers have three corking hurlers."[20] The team was in seventh place at the time, and never improved its position. Under Jones, the Terriers were 12-26.

Keupper's most heartbreaking loss of the season was perhaps his 10-inning, 2-1 defeat on August 26 to the Chicago Whales. The 10 innings were the most he pitched in any game in the majors.

On September 5 Keupper won his eighth and final game of 1914, improving his record to 8-17 with $3\frac{1}{3}$ innings of three-hit, scoreless relief against the Kansas City Packers. His 18th loss came on September 16 in Buffalo, a complete-game 7-3 defeat. His 19th was in Baltimore on September 29, when the Terrapins scored eight runs off him and St. Louis lost, 8-1.

Keupper became a 20-game loser in his final game, on October 6 at Federal League Park in Indianapolis. He gave up one run in the third inning and two in the fourth. The Terriers scored one in the top of the seventh, but Keupper was hit for three runs in the bottom of the seventh, two of them on Benny Kauff's two-run home run. Each team scored one run in the eighth and St. Louis scored twice in the top of the ninth, but lost, 7-4, and Keupper had loss number 20.

Because Indianapolis won the game and Chicago lost two, the Whales lost their half-game lead in the Federal League standings. The win over Keupper gave the Hoosiers the lead they needed in the standings and two days later Indianapolis won the pennant.

Unfortunately for Keupper and his team, the St. Louis Terriers ended up in last place. Only two of their pitchers won more games than they lost. The *Philadelphia Inquirer* reported Bob Groom with a final record of 12-20 and Keupper with a final record

of 9-18.²¹ As indicated above, our current understanding shows them both with 20 losses.

The St. Louis team released Keupper after the season. Keupper wanted to play again in 1915 and reported back to the Bloomington club on April 13, hoping for an opportunity to make the team. In a story headlined "No Place for Federal Castoff," the *Washington Evening Star* reported: "In a decision handed down by J.H. Farrell, a secretary of the National Association of Minor Leagues, Henry Keupper, Bloomington, Illinois, pitcher, who in 1913 joined the St. Louis Federals and who after having been released by Manager Fielder A. Jones asked to be reinstated in the Bloomington Club, is prohibited from playing with any club of organized ball. Keupper is the first released Federal League player to attempt to get reinstatement."²² The *Pawtucket Times* headlined the story "Farrell Condemns Keupper To Life Of Wanderer."²³ American League president Ban Johnson had written a letter to the National Commission on April 13, enclosing a very brief clipping from the *Chicago Tribune* reporting that Keupper was requesting reinstatement; Johnson wrote, "Under no circumstances should this man be permitted to return to organized baseball."²⁴

Hubert Keupper pitched in the Three-I league for Quincy in 1915 but Henry remained banned, "with the outlaw brand on him," despite Bloomington's efforts to have him reinstated.²⁵ The *Rockford* (Illinois) *Register Gazette* reported that he joined an independent team at Henry, Illinois.²⁶ The Chicago White Sox scheduled a game against the Henry team for July 21, but White Sox manager Pants Rowland learned that the club was "harboring a contract jumper from organized ball in the person of Henry Keupper."²⁷

In January 1916 Secretary Farrell of the NAPBL announced that Keupper and a few dozen other Federal League jumpers were made free agents "as a result of the recent peace pact."²⁸

Keupper played with the Henry team for a year and a half and it was reported on July 13, 1916, that he would rejoin Bloomington at Peoria that day.[29] However, as late as August 23 he was reported playing with the Henry Greys.

In 1920 Keupper was living in Lake Creek, Illinois, working as a coal miner. In 1930 he was living in Johnston City, Illinois. There Keupper worked as a "machine runner" in a coal mine, and his wife Amy as a dry-goods saleswoman. Two years later, in February 1932, Keupper was "running a coal cutting machine at Royalton mines. He lost a finger from his left hand which was crushed."[30]

In the early 1940s he worked as a merchant in Shawneetown, Illinois, running a retail variety store. He also owned an orchard in Pittsburg, Illinois.

In October 1945, Keupper was appointed postmaster of Saline-Woodford, Illinois.

Keupper died of a heart attack on August 14, 1960, in Marion, Illinois. He was cremated and the remains were interred at Lakeview Cemetery in Johnston City.

## NOTES

1. macoupinctygenealogy.org/history/staunton.html.
2. "News Notes," *Sporting Life*, March 9, 1907: 14.
3. Salary information found in Keupper's player file at the National Baseball Hall of Fame.
4. "Indiana-Illinois-Iowa," *Sporting Life*, January 23, 1901: 8. This article reported that he was drafted by the New York American League club, but a February 6, 1909, article in the same publication listed him as drafted by the New York Giants.
5. "Street Car Men in Arizona," *Daily Illinois State Register* (Springfield, Illinois), December 13, 1908: 15.
6. See "Vogel Reports to Dick Smith," *Daily Illinois State Register*, April 12, 1912: 10, and "Danville Drops Two to Bloomers," *Daily Illinois State Register*, May 31, 1912: 10.
7. "III League Teams Satisfying Fans," *Daily Illinois State Register*, April 13, 1910: 3. Confusingly, the October 23, 1911, *Daily Illinois State Journal* mentioned a "Herman Keupper" as having a tryout with Bloomington, pitching in 1911 in the Trolley League in southern Illinois, and signing with Peoria for 1912.
8. "Weeding Out at Nashville," *Sporting Life*, April 23, 1910: 12.
9. "Nashville 1, Memphis 0," *Arkansas Gazette* (Little Rock), August 19, 1910: 8.
10. Ham, "Sporting Chat," *New Orleans Item*, August 30, 1910: 8.
11. W.G. Foster, "Chattanooga to Be Detroit Farm," *Atlanta Constitution*, September 17, 1911: E3.
12. "News Items Gathered From All Quarters," *Sporting Life*, February 17, 1912: 12.
13. "Is Keupper Playing in 'Fed'?" *Chicago Tribune*, August 5, 1913: 11.
14. United Press, "Three-Eye Club Is After the Federals," *Cincinnati Post*, August 14, 1913: 6.
15. "Versatile Views," *Daily Illinois State Register*, August 18, 1914: 5.
16. "Farrell Forbids Springfield to Play with Feds," *Duluth News-Tribune*, March 10, 1914: 8.
17. "Keupper Makes It Three Out of Four for Terriers Over Champs," *St. Louis Post-Dispatch*, April 20, 1914: 12.
18. Tom Ruane, email to Bill Nowlin, September 10, 2016. For a number of reasons involving historical record-keeping and changing definitions of what constitutes a win or a loss, there were differences in wins and losses as reflected on Retrosheet and Baseball-Reference.com at the time this article was written. Both Tom Ruane of Retrosheet and Pete Palmer were consulted regarding the number of Keupper's wins and losses.
19. "Smashing Attack Wins for Gems," *Daily Illinois State Register*, May 6, 1914: 10.
20. "First Division the Goal," *Kansas City Star*, September 1, 1914: 8.
21. "Cobb and Daubert Retain Their Championship Crowns," *Philadelphia Inquirer*, October 11, 1914: 7.
22. "No Place for Federal Cutoff," *Washington Evening Star*, April 16, 1915: 20.
23. *Pawtucket Times*, April 17, 1915: 6.
24. Letter from Ban Johnson to August Herrmann of the National Commission, April 13, 1915. Thanks to Dan Levitt for providing a copy of this correspondence.
25. "Some Three-I Gossip," *Daily Register-Gazette* (Rockford, Illinois), May 21, 1915: 5.
26. "Our League and Others," *Daily Register-Gazette*, June 1, 1915: 5.
27. "Rowland Balks," *Salt Lake Telegram*, July 18, 1915: 16.
28. "Many Fed Players Made Free Agents," *The Oregonian* (Portland), January 20, 1916: 18.
29. "Close Decisions," *Morning Star* (Rockford, Illinois), July 13, 1916: 9.
30. *Evansville Courier and Press*, February 9, 1932: 18.

# BRIAN KINGMAN

## BY CHAD MOODY

**PITCHER BRIAN KINGMAN COMPILED** an 8-20 record with the 1980 Oakland Athletics. Prior to 1980, instances of pitchers losing 20 games in a season occurred with great regularity. After Kingman's 20-loss season, however, his place in baseball lore was cemented for 23 long years until it finally happened again. The stinging effects of Kingman's 20-loss season contributed to the premature end of his once-promising big-league career, and also lingered for years in his post-baseball life. Over time, however, Kingman began to accept—and even embrace—his place in baseball infamy.

Brian Paul Kingman was born of English and German descent on July 27, 1953, in Los Angeles.[1] His father, Paul, was an accountant, and his mother, Cecile, was a homemaker. Older siblings Dolores, Cordelia, and John rounded out the family. Kingman did not inherit his love for the game from his parents; neither his father nor his mother was a baseball fan.[2] Instead, he traced his interest in baseball back to the first Los Angeles Dodgers game he attended as a child. He recalled, "Attending that game made a tremendous impression on me. It wasn't just the game itself, it was being in the middle of 30,000 to 40,000 cheering people, mostly adults, who were invested in the outcome of the game." From that initial experience, Kingman's love for the game quickly blossomed. "My parents made me attend church every Sunday, but by the age of 9 or 10 I decided that baseball was my religion," he once wrote. "Koufax and Drysdale might as well have been gods, and Vin Scully, the Dodgers radio voice the high priest. Each game was like a sermon."[3]

Because of his father's lack of interest in sports and relatively advanced age (Kingman was born when his father was in his mid-40s), Kingman was not afforded the opportunity to participate in organized baseball as a preteen. "It wasn't a fit for [my father's] schedule," he explained.[4] Baseball therefore had to wait until his teenage years. In addition to playing American Legion baseball for the West Los Angeles Post team, Kingman developed his skills on the University High School baseball team in Los Angeles. The Los Angeles City Section interscholastic league was highly competitive, helping to develop several future major-league stars during that era, including Eddie Murray, Ozzie Smith, and Robin Yount.[5] The right-handed Kingman—who also played high-school football—excelled on the mound during his high-school senior year in 1971, posting a 1.89 ERA and being named to the All-Western Second Team.

After graduating from high school, Kingman continued both his education and baseball at Santa Barbara City College. His pitching talent did not go unnoticed while playing for the Vaqueros. On June 5, 1973, Kingman was drafted by the California Angels in the 12th round of the June Amateur Draft, but did not sign, choosing instead to remain in college. Upon attaining an associate degree, Kingman enrolled at the University of California, Santa Barbara. In addition to pursuing his bachelor's degree he played varsity baseball for the Gauchos, and was fourth in strikeouts (38 in 49 innings) in the Pacific Coast Athletic Association in 1974. During the summer of '74, Kingman continued to work at his pitching craft by playing for the semipro Calgary Jimmies of the former Alberta Major League. He was very effective for Calgary, leading the club to a championship in dramatic fashion by winning both games of a doubleheader. Although statistics for his season with the Jimmies are uncertain, it is believed that Kingman finished with an 8-2 record and nine complete games.[6]

The following year was an important one for Kingman both personally and professionally. On a personal level, he completed his studies at UCSB, attaining a bachelor's degree in psychology and sociology. Shortly thereafter, Kingman became a professional baseball player when he was signed by Oakland Athletics scout Phil Pote as an amateur free agent on June 18, 1975. Oakland assigned him to the Boise A's of the Class-A short-season Northwest League. Used primarily as a starter at Boise, Kingman had a solid first professional season, finishing the year 4-6 with a 3.89 ERA and five complete games. The highlight of Kingman's inaugural minor-league campaign came on August 26, when the 6-foot-2, 200-pound hurler tossed a three-hit shutout with 11 strikeouts against the Eugene Emeralds — the only time the Northwest League-champion Emeralds were shut out all season.

Seeing promise in the 22-year-old, the Athletics promoted Kingman to the Double-A Chattanooga Lookouts of the Southern League in 1976. He spent the entire season in Chattanooga and excelled. On June 6 Kingman came within one out of a seven-inning no-hitter against Charlotte before having it broken up by a single. Reflecting on his strong start to the season, Kingman recalled, "I was 8-3 halfway through the season, had a moving fastball in the mid-90s, and good command of a sharp-breaking slider. If it weren't for the fact that the A's were a team with several established veteran pitchers, I would likely have been called up to the big leagues at that time."[7] He also ended the year in fine fashion, posting a 2.64 ERA while finishing second in the league in wins (14), fourth in innings pitched (184), and seventh in strikeouts (101). Kingman was a strong candidate for a September call-up to the big-league club when rosters were expanded, but tore a tendon in his elbow late in the minor-league season, ending any hopes he had of joining the Athletics.[8]

Based on his performance at Chattanooga, Kingman was promoted to the Triple-A San Jose Missions of the Pacific Coast League, where he spent the entire 1977 season. The elbow problems he suffered at the end of the prior season lingered throughout the year in San Jose, causing Kingman to miss eight weeks of the season. He remembered, "I spent a lot of time in doctors' offices, getting cortisone shots and on the disabled list." The injury adversely affected his performance on the mound. "I was no longer able to throw in the mid-90s, and there was no bite to my slider," noted Kingman.[9] In 16 appearances for the Missions (mostly as a starter), he finished the season with a disappointing 3-6 record and 7.80 ERA. Kingman underwent elbow surgery to repair the damage during the offseason.[10]

Unable to throw a ball until the following spring training after his successful surgery, Kingman found himself on the disabled list for the first nine weeks of the 1978 season. Although he rehabbed with Oakland's Triple-A club in Vancouver, Kingman was sent to the Modesto A's of the Class-A California League when he was finally able to take the mound in live games. Kingman admitted, "It was psychologically hard to find myself in A ball two years after being close to making the big leagues. Watching my teammates from Chattanooga move on to Triple A and the big leagues was hard as well. I felt like I was going backwards."[11] In addition to having to work hard to physically rehabilitate his injured elbow, Kingman also had to relearn to how to pitch. "I became a different pitcher by necessity. The velocity and movement on my fastball were diminished, and a curveball replaced my slider," he recalled.[12] Finding inspiration in the lyrics from the then-current hit song "Baker Street" by Gerry Rafferty, Kingman persevered through this difficult time, and ultimately found his form.[13] Although he finished the season in Modesto with a modest 2-2 record in 10 appearances (nine as a starter), he boasted a 2.37 ERA with 43 strikeouts in 38 innings pitched.

After his bounce-back season in 1978, Oakland gave Kingman another chance at the Triple-A level for the 1979 season, this time with the Ogden A's of the Pacific Coast League. At the same time as Kingman was carrying an impressive 7-2 record at Ogden into late June, the parent club in Oakland was mired in an awful season. With both injuries and poor performance plaguing their pitching, Oakland decided to call up the promising 25-year-old to bolster their struggling staff. On June 28, 1979, Kingman made his first major-league appearance, getting the start against the Royals in Kansas City. After some early jitters (he allowed three walks and had two wild pitches after two innings), he settled down, one-hitting the Royals into the sixth inning. He left the game after 5⅔ innings with a 5-4 lead, but ultimately received a no-decision. Kingman continued as a member of the Athletics' starting rotation for the rest of the season, and had several notable moments along the way: He tossed a complete game against the California Angels in only his second big-league start, got his first big-league win in July at Yankee Stadium, and picked up his first big-league shutout in September against the Chicago White Sox. All told, Kingman showed great promise in his rookie campaign. After a three-hit complete-game victory against the Detroit Tigers in August, Tigers manager Sparky Anderson said of Kingman, "That kid had good stuff. I was told that the A's had four or five good young pitchers and it's obvious that he's one of them."[14] Attributing his success to the new pitching approach he adopted while recovering from his elbow injury, Kingman explained, "I'm a pitcher instead of a thrower now."[15] He finished the year with five complete games and a 4.31 ERA in 18 appearances (17 starts). And aside from little-used teammate Alan Wirth, Kingman compiled the only winning record (8-7) on an Oakland team that finished the season with a dreadful 54-108 record. This juxtaposition was a harbinger of things to come for Kingman, though not in a positive way.

In an attempt to inject some life in his foundering club and improve its attractiveness for a potential sale, owner Charlie Finley hired fiery Billy Martin to manage the Athletics for the 1980 season.[16] Martin quickly installed "Billy Ball" in Oakland, which was a demanding strategy that took advantage of speed, fundamentals, and an aggressive style of play. Martin's Billy Ball also employed an aggressive approach to his pitching staff, which was returning all five of the primary starters from the prior season: Rick Langford, Mike Norris, Matt Keough, Steve McCatty, and Kingman. It was rumored that Martin's longtime pitching coach, Art Fowler, recognizing the largely untapped talent in these young hurlers, immediately went to work to take the staff to the next level by instructing them in the finer points of throwing spitballs.[17] Kingman later confirmed this, acknowledging, "Spitters? We were definitely throwing them. I know I tried a few."[18] Along with pushing rules to the limits, Martin pushed his starters to their physical limits due to a suspect bullpen, expecting the starters to pitch deep into every game.[19] The results of Martin's unique approach were immediate and effective, with the Athletics rocketing to an early-season 16-9 first-place start in the American League West before cooling off.

Although Kingman did not enjoy quite the same success as his rotation mates from a wins-and-losses perspective as the season progressed, his 7-11 record in early August was not particularly concerning, especially considering that his ERA at the time was a solid 3.34. And the cerebral Kingman—noted for being an ardent chess player and a reader of scholarly materials while on road trips—was also considered by many to have had the best "stuff" of the Oakland starters. Despite this, things began to take a turn for the worse for Kingman. Losing his next eight consecutive starts to give him 19 with 13 games remaining on the schedule, Kingman had to cope with the real possibility of a 20-loss season. He also had to cope with the effects of a hostile manager Martin, whom he once called a "tyrant."[20]

Dysfunction between the two had begun earlier in the season, when Kingman asked Martin for permission to get married during the All-Star break. Although Martin reluctantly allowed it, he did so while warning him to not let it affect his performance on the mound. Soon after marrying his wife, Diane (whom he had met in spring training in Arizona), Kingman began his extended losing streak. This provoked increasing ire from Martin, who was intolerant of losing. On several occasions, Martin was heard using foul language while vociferously castigating Kingman during visits to the mound.[21] Kingman said, "The thing is, Billy likes to yell when he loses and I was losing the most and I don't like to be yelled at."[22] Martin's abrasive style coupled with the losing began to take its toll, with Kingman recalling, "Instead of looking forward to my next start, I began to dread it."²³

Shortly after Kingman's 19th loss, despite their strained relationship, Martin sympathetically asked him if he wanted to avoid taking the mound in the final two weeks of the season. Kingman declined the offer. "I was a young player doing the macho thing. I was thinking, 'What would he think if I said no?' I didn't want him to think I was a wimp," Kingman later explained.²⁴ On September 25 Kingman was inserted into a game against the White Sox in a relief role for the first time all season due to an injury to teammate Keough. Entering the game in the second inning, he pitched into the top of the eighth inning without allowing an earned run. With the score tied 4-4, Kingman loaded the bases on his first three batters in the eighth, and was removed from the game. His replacement on the mound, Dave Beard, allowed the White Sox to take a 6-4 lead after two inherited runners scored on a single by Mike Squires that proved to be the game-winner. Although Kingman allowed only two earned runs in his 5⅔ innings of work, he was tagged with his 20th loss of the season. He appeared in two more games before the end of the season, picking up a win in a start against the White Sox and narrowly avoiding another loss in an unexpected relief role in extra innings against the Milwaukee Brewers in Oakland's final game of the year (while hungover from a celebration of the team's last road game of the season the night before).²⁵ Kingman finished the 1980 season with an 8-20 record, making him the most recent 20-game loser, replacing Phil Niekro, who had lost 20 a year earlier. With Oakland finishing the season at 83-79, Kingman became the first 20-game loser on a winning team since 1922.

Statistically, the 20 losses could be largely attributed to a hard-luck year for Kingman. His 3.83 ERA and 1.38 WHIP were both lower than league average and strikingly similar to those of fellow rotation member McCatty, who finished the season with a 14-14 record. Additionally, Kingman's ERA was nearly identical to that of 1980 20-game winner Dennis Leonard of the Kansas City Royals. Perhaps most revealing, Oakland scored a paltry average of 2.87 runs in Kingman's starts—in stark contrast to the 4.55-per-game run support the other Oakland starters received that season—and scored three runs or less in 70 percent of his starts, including five shutouts. And excluding an anomalous start in late April in which the A's scored 11 runs, Kingman's run support dropped to an even more meager 2.59 per game.

Despite his difficult 1980 season, Kingman found himself back in the Athletics' same starting rotation—dubbed the Five Aces—at the beginning of the 1981 campaign.²⁶ The team started the season with an impressive 11-0 record, with Kingman also performing well in the early going. He allowed only two earned runs in his first 22⅓ innings, and eventually carried a fine 2.72 ERA after 11 starts into the June baseball strike. Once play resumed in August, however, Kingman was sent "sulking" to the bullpen by his "nemesis" Martin after a couple of shaky starts, further aggravating their already poor relationship.²⁷ He regressed from that point, finishing the season with a 3-6 record in 18 games (15 starts) and an ERA that had ballooned to 3.95. And although Oakland advanced past the AL Division Series and into the

AL Championship Series, Kingman saw action in only one postseason game, pitching poorly in a brief relief stint in a 13-3 ALCS loss to the New York Yankees.

After struggling in spring training in 1982, Kingman was assigned to the Tacoma Tigers of the Triple-A Pacific Coast League to start the season to keep sharp until manager Martin converted from a four- to a five-man rotation. After originally refusing to report to Tacoma and asking to be traded, Kingman relented, and pitched reasonably well there in eight starts.[28] He was recalled in June; however, the lingering effects of the demotion to Tacoma caused further crumbling of Kingman's relationship with Martin. This manifested itself in a late-night altercation between the two outside a Kansas City hotel while on a late-June road trip.[29] Although Kingman's roster position with the big-league club survived this ugly incident, his performance on the mound suffered. Kingman finished the season with a 4-12 record and a 4.48 ERA in 23 games (20 starts).

Kingman got a much-needed change of scenery in 1983, when he was traded to Boston in January, acquired on the recommendation of Red Sox pitching coach Lee Stange, who worked with him while in the Athletics organization. "He can pitch," Stange said. "He has an exceptional curveball, as good as anyone here. He got into trouble in Oakland, but it wasn't entirely his fault. He didn't get along with Billy [Martin] and lost some of his confidence."[30] After accepting an assignment to the Red Sox' Triple-A affiliate in Pawtucket, however, Kingman was released in a cash-saving move before the regular season.[31] In May he was signed as a free agent by the San Francisco Giants and assigned to the Phoenix Giants of the Pacific Coast League. After starting the season in Phoenix with a 2-0 record, Kingman joined the big-league club in June.[32] Upon compiling a 7.71 ERA and 2.36 WHIP in three games with San Francisco, he was sent back to Phoenix, where he finished out the season with a 6-6 record and a 5.53 ERA in 25 games (14 starts).

Kingman was back with Phoenix for the entire 1984 season, pitching primarily out of the bullpen. Although he finished the year with an innocuous 5-5 record in 30 games, Kingman nursed lower-back injuries and posted a disappointing 6.37 ERA and 1.71 WHIP.[33] Hating the game and unwilling to continue fighting the ever-present "loser label," Kingman retired from professional baseball at age 31. "A stigma is hard to get rid of in baseball," opined former Oakland rotation mate Keough of Kingman's situation. "We are not a fast traveling business. We give labels, and they stick."[34]

Kingman settled in Phoenix. He began selling real estate, and then soon found more permanent employment working for a check-cashing company to help support his wife, Diane, and two young sons, Matthew and Alex.[35] It was here in 1992 that Kingman—disgruntled after not receiving a desired promotion—got caught and convicted of a phony check-cashing scheme against his employer, wiping out his assets and causing him to struggle to pay the bills by delivering newspapers and managing a convenience store.[36] Another misstep occurred later in that same year, when Kingman—facilitating dealings between an art broker friend and a father-son team from Las Vegas who possessed a Picasso painting—was arrested by the FBI for trafficking in stolen art in a "sting operation too hokey for a TV movie of the week."[37] Although the federal charges were dropped in the convoluted case when the painting was found to be bogus, Kingman was sentenced to 60 days in county jail, all the while maintaining his innocence. "I still think it was the silliest case I'd ever heard of," he said.[38] Kingman rebounded from these troubles, however, and eventually became the owner of a financial-services business. As of 2016 he worked for a regional distribution company, and has found the game once again, after previously thinking that "he had enough of baseball."[39] After not having thrown a ball for nearly a quarter-century, in the late 2000s Kingman was persuaded by former high-school and college teammates to join the Arizona Men's Senior Baseball League, where he "rediscovered the joyful innocence of playing baseball."[40] He was still playing in the league as of 2016, even after battling through two knee replacements.[41]

The negative effects of being a 20-game loser lingered with Kingman for years after he left the game, especially after the passing of each season with no pitcher matching that total. He resorted to packing away the memorabilia from his baseball career. "It brought back bad memories. For five years I didn't look at it. It was too painful," Kingman explained.[42] Even his children had to deal with classmates calling their father "a loser."[43] However, as his research revealed the good company he was in as a 20-game loser (the list includes numerous Hall of Famers, Cy Young Award winners, and All-Stars), Kingman began to come to terms with his place in history—even embracing it. "At the time I took it real hard. There is no question it shortened my career. But my feelings have changed 360 degrees," he said.[44] "At least I've been able to take something that once caused me pain and actually come to enjoy it. If we can do that with all kinds of things in life, think how much better off we'd all be. If you can have fun with something that caused you pain, it means you've conquered it."[45] As other pitchers approached possible 20th losses over the years, Kingman began employing a voodoo doll in an attempt to prevent his infamous feat from being overtaken. "Right now I'm the answer to a trivia question. But whenever anyone loses 19, I'm on trivia death row," he once quipped.[46] On September 5, 2003, however, Kingman's 23-year run as "The Last of the 20-Game Losers" ended as Detroit Tiger Mike Maroth suffered his 20th defeat of the season in an 8-6 loss to the Toronto Blue Jays. Upon having his place taken in the annals of baseball, the witty and self-deprecating Kingman commented, "Maybe I'll get a shot to make a comeback next year."[47]

## ACKNOWLEDGMENTS

The author wishes to thank Brian Kingman and Gary Trujillo for their research assistance.

## SOURCES

In addition to the sources noted in this biography, the author accessed Kingman's file from the library of the National Baseball Hall of Fame and Museum in Cooperstown, New York; Ancestry.com; Baseball-Reference.com; Newspapers.com; and Retrosheet.org.

## NOTES

1. Although Kingman's birth year is popularly reported as 1954, he was in fact born in 1953 as confirmed by State of California birth records and Kingman himself in email correspondence with the author on June 15, 2017.

2. Brian Kingman, email correspondence with author, November 22, 2016.

3. Brian Kingman, "The Love of Baseball—From the Eyes of an 8-Year-Old Through Sandy Koufax to the Major Leagues," *Arizona Men's Senior Baseball League Newsletter*, Issue 2.

4. Kingman email correspondence, November 22, 2016.

5. CIF Los Angeles City Section, "Notable Alumni," cif-la.org/apps/pages/index.jsp?uREC_ID=49068&type=d&pREC_ID=119529, accessed November 17, 2016.

6. Jay-Dell Mah, Western Canada Baseball, "Major Leaguers & Western Canada Baseball," attheplate.com/wcbl/major-leaguers_2.html, accessed November 17, 2016.

7. "The Love of Baseball."

8. Ibid.

9. Gary Trujillo, Coco Crisp's Afro, "Brian Kingman Interview Part 1… The Minor Leagues," cococrispafro.wordpress.com/2014/04/03/brian-kingman-interview-part-1-the-minor-leagues/, accessed November 17, 2016.

10. Associated Press, "Rookie Right-Hander Doesn't Miss Plate," *Santa Cruz Sentinel*, August 22, 1979.

11. "Brian Kingman Interview Part 1."

12. "The Love of Baseball."

13. "Brian Kingman Interview Part 1."

14. "Rookie Right-Hander Doesn't Miss Plate."

15. Ibid.

16. G. Michael Green and Roger D. Launius, *Charlie Finley: The Outrageous Story of Baseball's Super Showman* (New York: Walker Publishing Company, 2010), 290-292.

17. Bill Pennington, *Billy Martin: Baseball's Flawed Genius* (Boston: Houghton Mifflin Harcourt, 2015), 354.

18. Ron Fimrite, "Whatever Happened to the Class of '81?" *Sports Illustrated*, September 10, 1984.

19. Ibid.

20. Ibid.

21. Nancy Finley, *Finley Ball: How Two Baseball Outsiders Turned the Oakland A's Into a Dynasty and Changed the Game Forever* (Washington: Regnery History, 2016), 209.

22. "Whatever Happened To The Class Of '81?"

23. Gary Trujillo, Coco Crisp's Afro, "Brian Kingman Talks About His Career and His Troubles With Billy Martin."

24　Mel Antonen, "Kingman May Lose Distinction as Loser," *USA Today*, August 25, 2003.

25　Gary Trujillo, Coco Crisp's Afro, "Brian Kingman Interview… Part 4," cococrispafro.wordpress.com/2014/04/19/brian-kingman-interview-part4/, accessed November 17, 2016.

26　"The Amazing A's and Their Five Aces," *Sports Illustrated*, April 27, 1981.

27　"Whatever Happened to the Class of '81?"

28　United Press International, "Brian Kingman Can Relax Now. When You Are Pitching Well …" July 7, 1982, upi.com/Archives/1982/07/07/Brian-Kingman-can-relax-nowWhen-you-are-pitching-well/1060394862400/, accessed November 17, 2016.

29　Associated Press, "Oakland A's in Turmoil," *Greenville* (South Carolina) *News*, July 6, 1982.

30　Associated Press, "Kingman Welcomes Shot With Red Sox," *Galveston Daily News*, February 28, 1983.

31　David Fink, "Sports Briefing," *Pittsburgh Post-Gazette*, March 28, 1983.

32　Associated Press, "Giants Not Pretty but Still Win," *Santa Cruz Sentinel*, June 2, 1983.

33　Bob Cohn, "Lackluster Phoenix Felled by Edmonton," *Arizona Republic*, July 12, 1984.

34　"Kingman May Lose Distinction as Loser."

35　Ibid.

36　Michael Kiefer, "Brian Kingman's Blue Period," *Phoenix New Times*, July 7, 1994.

37　Ibid.

38　Thomas McShane and Dary Matera, *Stolen Masterpiece Tracker: The Dangerous Life of the FBI's #1 Art Sleuth* (Fort Lee, New Jersey: Barricade Books, 2006), 234-248; Michael Kiefer, "Take Me Out to the Exercise Yard: Netted in a Stolen-Art Sting, Brian Kingman Goes From the Big Leagues to Big House," *Phoenix New Times*, December 8, 1994.

39　Britten Gerrard, MSBLNational.com, "Kingman, Cripe Still Playing After All These Years," msblnational.com/TOR-Desert-Classic-Entry/Blog/2013-Desert-Classic-a-Huge-Success.htm, accessed November 17, 2016.

40　"The Love of Baseball."

41　Kingman email correspondence, November 22, 2016.

42　"Kingman May Lose Distinction as Loser."

43　Jeffrey Zaslow, "Lessons From Some Losers: Detroit Tigers Are Moving On," *Wall Street Journal*, September 30, 2003.

44　Jerome Holtzman, *The Jerome Holtzman Baseball Reader* (Chicago: Triumph Books, 2003), 4. At times people come up with expressions that should not be taken too literally.

45　Jayson Stark, "'King' Won't Be Forgotten," ESPN.com, espn.com/mlb/columns/story?id=1611581&columnist=stark_jayson, accessed November 17, 2016.

46　Glenn Kaplan, "Brian Kingman, Pitcher," *Sports Illustrated*, October 7, 2002.

47　"'King' Won't Be Forgotten."

# DON LARSEN

## BY CHARLES F. FABER

**HE IS A BUNDLE OF CONTRADIC-**tions, this imperfect man who pitched a perfect game. Don Larsen disdained training rules and had a mediocre major-league career; yet he pitched the greatest game in World Series history. He married out of a sense of duty; yet he refused to support his wife and baby daughter. He kept his marriage secret as long as he could, preferring to be viewed as a carefree bachelor. He loved the night life; yet he was living out his retirement years (as of 2015) in a quiet village in northern Idaho, far from the crowded bars of his youth. This man who turned down college scholarships because he didn't like to study, the same man who had to be compelled by a court order to support his family, auctioned off one of his most prized possessions to raise money to support his grandchildren's college education. Don Larsen is truly a bundle of contradictions.

Don James Larsen was born on August 7, 1929, in Michigan City, on the shores of Lake Michigan in extreme northwestern Indiana. He was the second child and only son of Charlotte and James Larsen. During his childhood his mother worked as a waitress in a restaurant, His father, son of Norwegian immigrants, was a watchmaker in a retail jewelry store. Years later Don Larsen remembered, "My first introduction to baseball was watching my father play sandlot ball."[1] When he was 4 years old Don started playing baseball with his father. James encouraged Don in his childhood ambition to become a professional baseball player. However, the youngster showed more talent in basketball than baseball. As a freshman, Don made the Michigan City High School basketball team.

In 1944 Don moved with his family to San Diego, where his mother worked as a housekeeper in a retirement home and his father became a jewelry salesman. At Point Loma High School Don became a star in basketball and baseball. He made the All-Metro Conference basketball team and received several scholarship offers to play college basketball, which he declined. He said, "I was never much with studies, and I didn't really have an interest in going to college and studying my life away."[2] Art Schwartz, a scout for the St. Louis Browns, saw Larsen pitching for an American Legion team and offered him a contract. He signed for an $850 bonus.

The Browns sent the 17-year-old right-handed pitcher to Aberdeen in the Class-C Northern League. Larsen pitched two seasons for the Pheasants, winning four games in 1947 and 17 in 1948. He started the 1949 season with the Globe-Miami Browns in the Class-C Arizona-Texas League and was promoted in midseason to Springfield in the Class-B Three-I League. Another promotion came in 1950, as he moved from the Wichita Falls Spudders in the Class-B Big State League to the Wichita Indians in the Class-A Western League. He was described by Bob Turley, one of his teammates in both the minors and majors, as a "fun-loving guy who liked to go out and have a beer or two and talk to people in bars."[3]

In 1951 Larsen was drafted into the US Army. He spent two years during the Korean War in noncombat roles. After basic training at Fort Ord, he was sent to Hawaii. When an officer learned that Larsen was a professional baseball player, he assigned him to a Special Services unit at Fort Shafter. He pitched and played first base for an Army team during 1951 and 1952. Corporal Larsen was discharged in 1953 and went to spring training in 1953 on the roster of the San Antonio Browns. After several good pitching performances, he was promoted to the big-league Browns. "I'll never forget how excited I was when I found out I made the club," he said. "It was like Christmas in springtime."[4]

The 23-year-old stood 6-feet-4 and weighed 215 pounds. His teammates gave him the nickname Gooney Bird. Writer Lew Paper said it was because of his protruding ears, pear-shaped body, and long, dangling arms.[5] Another writer, Peter Golenbock, said the nickname was bestowed because of Larsen's antics.[6]

Larsen made his major-league debut on Saturday, April 18, 1953, in the first game of a doubleheader against the Detroit Tigers at Briggs Stadium. The first batter he faced, Harvey Kuenn, touched him for a single, but he settled down and pitched shutout ball for five innings. He was knocked out of the box in the sixth, as the Tigers scored three runs to take a 3-2 lead. However, the Browns rallied to win the game, 8-7, with Larsen receiving no decision. He collected his first major-league win at Connie Mack Stadium on May 12, pitching 7⅔ innings and giving up one earned run in the Browns' 7-3 win over the Philadelphia Athletics.

The Browns moved to Baltimore in 1954. That season Larsen led the league in losses with 21, while winning only three games, but fortunately for him two of the wins were over the New York Yankees, and Yankees manager Casey Stengel remembered those two wins. Larsen did not honor the midnight curfew set by the Browns. His motto was, "Let the good times roll. You give the best you can on the field. Who cares what you do afterwards, as long as you show up and do well."[7] Jimmy Dykes, his manager in Baltimore, said, "The only thing Don fears is sleep."[8]

During the season Larsen met the future Vivian Larsen, a 27-year-old telephone operator in Baltimore. At the end of the season he intended to break off the affair, but Vivian called him in California and told him she was pregnant. Abortion was out of the question. Larsen suggested she put the baby up for adoption. She refused. Vivian was determined to keep the baby. Larsen then did what he thought was the honorable thing. They were married on April 23, 1955. Don insisted that the marriage be kept secret; he was marrying her only for the sake of the child. Three months later he left her with no intention of returning because he was not ready to settle down and preferred "a life of free and easy existence."[9]

Larsen was traded to the New York Yankees on November 17, 1954, in a huge transaction involving 17

players. He reported to spring training in 1955 with a sore shoulder and was soon sent down to the Yankees' farm club in Denver. He won 9 of 10 decisions for the Bears and after four months in the Triple-A American Association, he was recalled to New York. Between New York and Denver he had won 18 games that year, against only three losses. One of his teammates said, "He probably had a lot more ability than 95 percent of all the pitchers in baseball, He was a good hitter. He could run the bases. He could field the ball. But he was a lazy type."[10]

The Yankees won the American League pennant in 1955 and faced the Brooklyn Dodgers in the World Series. The Dodgers were playing in Brooklyn's eighth World Series. They had seven losses to show for their first seven attempts. The Ebbets Field faithful were hoping for a different outcome in 1955. The Dodgers were a powerful club, featuring four future Hall of Famers—Roy Campanella, Pee Wee Reese, Jackie Robinson, and Duke Snider—plus perennial all-star Gil Hodges and former Rookies of the Year Jim Gilliam and Don Newcombe. The Yankees won the first two games, but Brooklyn took Game Three.

Larsen started Game Four for the Yankees and did not fare well. Although staked to a 3-1 lead, he gave up a leadoff home run to Campanella in the fourth inning. Larsen then walked Carl Furillo, and Hodges hit a two-run homer to put the Dodgers ahead. In the fifth inning Gilliam led off with a walk and stole second while Reese was batting, At this point Stengel replaced Larsen with Johnny Kucks, who gave up a single to Reese and a three-run homer to Snider, one run of which was charged to Larsen. When Yankees were unable to catch up, Larsen was tagged as the losing pitcher, with a line for the game of five earned runs on five hits and two walks.

Brooklyn won Game Five to go ahead in the Series, three games to two. New York evened it up by taking Game Six. The Series came down to Game Seven. Johnny Podres pitched a masterpiece, shutting out the Yankees, 2-0, thereby earning Brooklyn its first-ever world championship.

Larsen was thrilled to have pitched in the Series: "I had stretched beyond my childhood dreams by playing for the Yankees in the World Series. Even though we lost the championship to the Dodgers, I was thankful to have been even been there in the first place."[11]

Larsen's appetite for strong drink and exuberant night life did not diminish. Mickey Mantle said of him, "Don had a startling capacity for liquor. Larsen was easily the greatest drinker I've known and I've known some pretty good ones in my time.[12] During spring training 1956 Larsen wrecked his brand-new Oldsmobile by driving it into a St. Petersburg telephone pole at 4 or 5 o'clock one morning. He admitted that he had been drinking at several bars earlier in the night and said he had fallen asleep at the wheel.

His teammates thought Larsen was a bachelor, a devil-may-care playboy.[13] They were shocked to learn of his secret marriage. Although Don and Vivian did not live together, she had moved to New York, attempting to collect some child-support money. On July 16, 1956, Justice Henry Greenberg of the Bronx Superior Court awarded Vivian $60 a week from Don in support of herself and their daughter, Caroline Jean.[14] Don didn't deliver. Living the high life that he enjoyed can be very expensive in New York City. He was having trouble making ends meet.[15] He certainly didn't have any spare cash to spend on a wife or child. He even asked the Yankees' traveling secretary, Bill McCorry, for an advance on his World Series share: "I've got to get home to California when this is over, and I don't have a nickel."[16] McCorry promised to deliver the cash if the Yankees won.

In October Vivian filed a complaint over Larsen's failure to pay child support. (He had made four payments, then stopped paying.) He owed $420, for seven weeks in arrears at $60 per week.) Vivian's lawyer, Harry Lipsig, said, "While this baseball hero is enjoying the luxuries of life and the plaudits of the public, he is subjecting his 14-month-old baby girl and his wife to the pleasures of a starvation existence."[17] Bronx Superior Court Justice Sam H. Hofstadter filed a filed an order requiring the Yankees, Larsen, and Baseball Commissioner Ford Frick to show cause why his World Series share should not be seized by the Bronx Supreme Court.[18]

The court order was in Larsen's locker when he took the mound in Yankee Stadium and pitched the most incredible game in World Series history. The Yankees had won the pennant for the second straight year in a streak that was to yield four consecutive flags. They faced the defending World Series champion Brooklyn Dodgers.

The Dodgers won Game One at Ebbets Field behind the pitching of Sal Maglie. Larsen pitched briefly in Game Two. He faced only 10 batters, six of whom reached base safely, one on a base hit, one on an error, and four by means of walks. Larsen was charged with four unearned runs. The Dodgers won a slugfest. The Series then moved to Yankee Stadium. The home team won Games Three and Four to even the Series at two games apiece. Given Larsen's poor performances in the 1955 fall classic and Game Two of the present match, there was little reason to expect him to start another game in the Series.

On the night before Game Five, Larsen went out for a few beers with Arthur Richman, a sportswriter for the *New York Daily Mirror*. Before midnight they headed back toward Larsen's hotel apartment. During the cab ride Larsen told Richman, "I'm gonna beat those guys tomorrow. And I'm just liable to pitch a no-hitter."[19] It was typical Larsen bluster. Actually, he had no idea he was going to pitch. Stengel had not yet announced the starting pitcher for the next day's game. Following the Yankees custom at the time, whenever the starter had not been determined the night before, in the morning coach Frankie Crosetti would place the warm-up ball for the day's game in one of the starting pitcher's shoes.[20]

Earlier that evening Herman Carey, father of Yankees third baseman Andy Carey, entered a novelty shop on Times Square that printed fake newspaper headlines. He purchased two. One read "Larsen Pitches No-hitter." The other stated "Gooney Birds Pick Larsen to Win Fifth Game." He returned to the hotel and taped the one about the no-hitter to the door of Larsen's room. Then he had second thoughts. He didn't want to risk jinxing the pitcher. So he shredded the paper and disposed of it. He kept the other one, without showing it to Larsen at the time.

It turned out that the fake headlines were prescient. To the surprise of most of the Yankees, manager Stengel chose Larsen to start Game Five. The pitcher arrived at the ballpark early in the morning of October 8, saw the ball, and learned he would be the starting pitcher.[21] He took a whirlpool bath and a cold shower, and had a rubdown.[22] He lay down for a short nap in the clubhouse.[23] Larsen was opposed by the tough Sal "The Barber" Maglie. Both men were at the top of their games. Using his new no-windup delivery, Larsen was unhittable. Maglie was almost as good, retiring the first 11 batters in a row until Mantle hit a solo blast in the fourth inning. By the end of the sixth inning it began to dawn on viewers that they might be watching history in the making. In keeping with baseball superstition, nobody on the Yankee bench mentioned a possible no-hitter, but surely it was on everybody's mind.

Larsen said he knew he was pitching a no-hitter, since every pitcher knows when he is throwing one. He said, "I tried to engage in conversation with some of our players on the bench during the game, but they all avoided me like the plague.[24]

Larsen mowed the Dodgers down, through the seventh, eighth, and into the ninth inning. He retired the first two batters in the ninth. Up came Dale Mitchell to pinch-hit for Maglie. Larsen's first pitch was a ball, high and outside. Next came a slow curve over the plate for a called strike. Mitchell swung at another curve and missed for strike two. He fouled off a fastball. Then he took a quarter-swing at a fastball that seemed to some to be eye-high.[25] Umpire Babe Pinelli called him out. Don Larsen had pitched the first no-hitter in World Series history. Not only was it a no-hitter, but it was a perfect game — no hits, no runs, with no one reaching base.

"Damn," said sports reporter Dick Young. "The imperfect man just pitched a perfect game."[26]

Shirley Povich of the *Washington Post* wrote, "The million-to-one shot came in. Hell froze over. A month of Sundays hit the calendar. Don Larsen today pitched a no-hit, no-run, no-man-reach-first game in a World Series."[27]

The *San Francisco Chronicle* wrote about "madcap Don Larsen, a carefree soul who breaks automobiles, likes bright lights, reads comic books…and is just about the last person in baseball who might be expected to pitch a perfect game."[28]

Larsen sent $420 to Harry Lipsig to give to his wife and daughter. "This man is still no hero," the lawyer said. "In these proceedings, he has brazenly suggested when his daughter was born she was immediately to be given out for adoption."[29]

The Dodgers won Game Six, but the Yankees took Game Seven and again reigned as baseball's world champions.

One month after Larsen's perfect game, he and Vivian divorced.

In 1957 Larsen got off to a poor start, but improved toward the end of the season, winding up with a commendable 10-4 record. The Yankees won the pennant again. In the World Series against the Milwaukee Braves, Larsen won one and lost one. In Game Three he relieved Bob Turley in the second inning and pitched well throughout the game, getting credit for the win as the Yankees prevailed, 12-3. In Game Seven Larsen was the starting pitcher, but was knocked out of the box in the third inning. With one out and a man on base, shortstop Tony Kubek made an errant throw to second base on a grounder hit by Johnny Logan. Eddie Mathews then doubled, and Larsen was out of the game. Lew Burdette pitched a shutout for his third win of the Series. The Braves were world champions for the first time since the Miracle Braves of 1914.

On December 7, 1957, Larsen married Corrine Bruess, a 26-year-old flight attendant from Minnesota, whom he had met on a flight out of Kansas City. This marriage endured. Apparently Corinne brought some much-needed stability to his life. The union produced one son, Scott, born October 5, 1962.

Both New York and Milwaukee repeated as pennant winners in 1958. Larsen started two games in the 1958 World Series. In Game Three he pitched shutout ball until relieved by Ryne Duren in the eighth inning and received credit for the win in the Yankees' 4-0 victory. In Game Seven Larsen was removed in the third inning with one out and two Braves on base and the Yankees leading, 2-1. Bob Turley erased the Braves threat and was credited with the win as the Yankees won the game, 6-2, for their 18th triumph in the fall classic.

The Yankees slipped to third place in the 1959 standings and Larsen had a losing record at 6-7. On December 11, 1959, he was traded, along with Hank Bauer, Norm Siebern, and Marv Throneberry, to the Kansas City Athletics for Joe DeMaestri, Roger Maris, Kent Hadley, and Gerry Staley.

Larsen had very little success in Kansas City, losing 10 out of 11 decisions. The A's sent him down to Dallas-Fort Worth in the Triple-A American Association, where he won two of three decisions, earning another shot at the majors. He appeared in only eight games for the A's before being traded with Andy Carey, Ray Herbert, and Al Pilarcik to the Chicago White Sox for Wes Covington, Stan Johnson, Bob Shaw, and Gerry Staley. He had a combined 8-2 record for the two clubs.

Soon he was on the move again. On November 30, 1961, Larsen was traded with Billy Pierce to the San Francisco Giants for Bob Farley, Eddie Fisher, Dom Zanni, and Verle Tiefenthaler. In the City by the Bay, Larsen became a full-time reliever, winning five games and saving 10. The Giants finished the regular season tied for first place with the Los Angeles Dodgers. In the deciding game of the three-game playoff for the pennant, Larsen relieved Juan Marichal in the eighth inning and received credit for the win, as the Giants won their first championship after their move to the West Coast. In Game Four of the 1962 World Series against the New York Yankees, Larsen picked up a win, even though he pitched only one-third of an inning. He entered the game in the bottom of the sixth inning, with two outs, runners on first and second, and the game tied, 2-2. Larsen walked Yogi Berra to load the bases and then induced Tony Kubek to ground out, ending the inning. In the top of the seventh, Larsen was lifted for a pinch-hitter, as the Giants took a lead they did not relinquish.

In 1963 Larsen had a 7-7 record with four saves for the Giants. The much-traveled pitcher was sold to the Houston Colt .45's on May 20, 1964, and was traded less than a year later to the Baltimore Orioles for Bob Saverine and cash. He won only one game for the Orioles before being released on April 11, 1966. He spent much of the next three seasons in the minors, toiling for clubs in Phoenix, Dallas-Fort Worth, Tacoma, and San Antonio.

Before the 1967 season began, the Chicago Cubs signed Larsen as a free agent. He pitched only four innings for the Cubs. His final major-league appearance came on July 7, 1967, at Houston's Astrodome in an 11-5 Cubs loss. He entered the game in the sixth inning and pitched two innings, giving up one run and one base on balls. On the last pitch the 37-year-old Larsen threw in the major leagues, Jim Wynn flied out to Billy Williams in left field to end the seventh inning. Larsen was removed for a pinch-hitter in the eighth inning, and his major-league career was over.

After retiring from baseball, Larsen worked for about 25 years as a salesman for the Blake, Moffett & Towne Paper Company in the San Jose area. When he retired from this occupation, he, Corinne, and Scott moved to the shores of Hayden Lake, not far from Coeur d'Alene in Idaho's scenic Panhandle, about 100 miles from the Canadian border. "I like Idaho because it's peaceful and quiet," Larsen said.[30]

Don's son, Scott, as of 2015 was a maintenance technician for an aerospace company in Idaho. Scott and his wife, Nancy, gave Don two grandsons, Justin and Cody. Don, his sons, and grandsons enjoy trout fishing and frogging together, hunting by spotlights in the cool of a northern Idaho morning.[31]

In 2012 Larsen announced that he was retrieving the uniform he had worn when pitching the perfect game. He had loaned it to the San Diego Hall of Champions, but he intended to auction off his most prized possession to raise money for his grandchildren's college educations. He listed it with Steiner Sports Marketing for an online auction that ran from October 8 to December 2 at steinersports.com. "I really don't know what it's worth," Larsen said. "But what I do know is that in terms of historic importance, my uniform is a part of one of the greatest moments in the history of sports. I have thought about that perfect game, more than once a day, every day of my life since the day I threw it."[32]

The auction attracted 22 bids. The uniform sold for $756,000. The winning bidder was Pete Seigel, CEO of Gotta Have It, a New York City gallery that collects and displays pop-culture memorabilia. Seigel said that Larsen's uniform would be a welcome addition to a collection of Yankees memorabilia that his company was building.[33]

Three-quarters of a million dollars is surely enough to pay Justin and Cody's college expenses. There may be enough extra cash to enable the Larsen family to take their hoped-for trip to Alaska.

## NOTES

1. Don Larsen and Mark Shaw, *The Perfect Yankee: The Incredible Story of the Greatest Miracle in Baseball History* (Champaign, Illinois: Sagamore Publishing, 1996), 37.
2. Lew Paper, *Perfect: Don Larsen's Miraculous World Series Game and The Men Who Made It Happen* (New York: New American Library, 2009), 12.
3. Paper, 13.
4. Larsen and Snow, 77.
5. Larsen and Snow, 1.
6. Peter Golenbock, *Dynasty: The New York Yankees 1949-1964* (Mineola, New York: Dover Publishing, 201), 292.
7. Paper, 13.
8. Paper, 14.
9. Paper, 17.
10. Paper, 14.
11. Paper, 15.
12. Paper, 16.
13. Paper, 17
14. Ron Rembert. "Baseball Immortals: Character and Performance On and Off the Field," in Peter Carino, ed., *Baseball/Literature/Culture Essays* (Jefferson, North Carolina: McFarland, 2004), 139.
15. Roger Kahn. *The Era, 1948-1957, When the Yankees, the Giants, and the Dodgers Ruled the World* (New York: Ticknor and Fields, 1993), 331.
16. Paper, 17.
17. Ibid.
18. Rembert.
19. Paper, 5.
20. Don Larsen, "The Game I'll Never Forget." *Baseball Digest*, October 2003: 54.
21. Ibid.
22. Kahn, 332.
23. Paper, 6.
24. Larsen, *op. cit.*, 55-56.
25. Kahn, 332.
26. Ibid.
27. Ibid.
28. Larsen and Shaw, 209.
29. Ibid.
30. Larsen, 56.
31. *Newark Star-Ledger*, October 9, 2012.
32. *New York Times*, May 26, 2012.
33. New York *Daily News*, December 6, 2012.

# MIKE MAROTH

## BY BARBARA MANTEGANI AND DAVID RAGLIN

**MIKE MAROTH MAY BE BEST KNOWN** for being the last pitcher to lose 20 games in a season (as of this writing in 2017), but there was much more to his career than what happened in 2003. He toiled for one of the worst teams in history, the 2003 Detroit Tigers that went 43-119, but just as that team turned the corner in 2006, due in part to his strong start, Maroth's career was derailed by an arm injury. Maroth handled the fate of going 9-21 in 2003 with grace and class and deserved a better fate. He will certainly be remembered by Tigers fans for his willingness to "take one for the team."

Michael Warren Maroth was born in Orlando, Florida, on August 17, 1977, to Bill and Charlotte Maroth. Bill builds exhibits for companies to use in conferences and seminars and Charlotte works in the administrative offices of the Orange County public schools, a position that she has held for a number of years.[1] Mike grew up in Orlando, and in high school pitched on the baseball team at William R. Boone High School, graduating in 1995. He was a slight, 145-pound kid who did not have a very good fastball, but he earned the chance to play at the University of Central Florida (UCF). His freshman year, the school bought him his books—that was his scholarship.[2]

Despite the modest investment in him by the school, Mike came into his own at UCF, lettering all three years he played there.[3] He grew bigger and threw harder as his college career progressed. A reliever most of his first two seasons, he became a starter his junior year. That season was tough for Mike, who came down with mononucleosis and missed a month during the season. He came back at the end of the season, though, and in his last game as a Knight Maroth, pitching in the Atlantic Sun Tournament, went into the eighth inning having given up only two hits and one run to Jacksonville State in a game ultimately won by UCF. That start was especially important to Maroth's career because it showed the scouts that he was healthy and it was his last start before the draft. While pitching at UCF, he built a relationship with Craig Cozart, at first a teammate and later a coach for UCF. Even once Maroth became a professional pitcher, he would have Cozart help him with his mechanics over the winter.[4]

Maroth must have impressed Luke Wrenn, a scout with the Boston Red Sox, with his performance with UCF, as the Red Sox drafted him in the third round after his junior year, the 85th pick overall. He signed on July 5, 1998, for a $225,000 bonus[5] and was sent to the Red Sox farm team in the Gulf Coast League. He only pitched in four games there, making, two starts and two relief appearances, but did not allow a run. That convinced the Red Sox to move him up to their short-season Class-A club in the New York-Penn League, the Lowell Spinners, in August. Maroth continued to pitch well at the higher level; in six starts, he threw 31 innings and struck out 34 men while walking 13 on the way to a 2.90 ERA. Twice, he struck out eight men in a game: on August 8 versus Pittsfield and August 29 versus Auburn.[6]

Maroth's fine 1998 season earned him the chance in 1999 to jump over low-A ball and go right to the high-A Sarasota Red Sox in the Florida State League. That league was more of a challenge to the young professional, as Maroth's ERA jumped to 4.04 in 20 games (19 starts), for Sarasota. His strikeout rate dropped to 5.2 men per nine innings (64 strikeouts in 111 1/3 innings). As July ended, the Boston Red Sox had more pressing matters on their minds than the development of the young lefty. They were in a battle with the division-rival Toronto Blue Jays for the wild card slot, half a game behind Toronto, and they decided they needed some depth for their pitching staff. The Detroit Tigers were 17 1/2 out of first place and were willing to play for the future. The Tigers sent Bryce Florie, (a veteran pitcher probably best known for later taking a line drive to the face off the bat of

Ryan Thompson of the Yankees in 2000) to the Red Sox for Maroth and assigned Maroth to their club in the Florida State League, the Lakeland Tigers.

Maroth made three starts for Lakeland before being moved up to the Tigers' Double-A team in the Southern League, the Jacksonville Suns. He returned to the Suns for the 2000 season but the beginning of the season did not go well for the 22-year-old. Maroth started the year 0-9 with a 6.36 ERA in his first 11 starts,[7] but turned it around in his 12th start as the calendar moved into June: "My 12th start I pitched a nine-inning shutout. And there really wasn't that much difference between my 11th start and my 12th. I knew what was going on. But I told myself 'I'm just going to go out there and pitch.' Instead of pressing, I just pitched."[8] It must have worked, for he went 9-5 with a 2.62 ERA after that for the Suns, who made it to the Southern League championship series before losing to the West Tennessee Diamond Jaxx, three games to two.[9] *Baseball America* magazine named Maroth the Tigers' 15th best prospect after the season.[10] In January 2001, Mike and Brooke Maroth got married. Maroth credits Brooke for instilling in him the religious belief that became a very important part of his life.[11]

Maroth pitched in 2001 for the Toledo Mud Hens, the Triple-A club of the International League, and did not have a very good season, posting a 4.65 ERA in 24 games, 23 starts, for the Mud Hens, with a strikeout rate of only 4.3 per nine innings and a 1.26 strikeout-to-walk ratio. A left shoulder strain sent him to the disabled list in August for the first time in his career. Maroth said, "I didn't do bad. I didn't do well [in 2001]. I was 7-10, with a 4.65 ERA. I knew that in the offseason I'd continue to work hard. I didn't want to press, but I wanted to keep working. I knew I was close. I worked on strengthening my shoulder."[12]

Maroth was a new pitcher for Toledo in 2002. While hitters batted .302 off him in 2001, they only hit .201 off him in 2002.[13] His ERA dropped to 2.82. Maroth credited the improvement in part to a new pitch, a back-door slider, "I'm able to throw it off the end of the plate and have it come back over for a strike. It has been a real successful pitch for me."[14]

On June 8, 2002, Maroth got the news every player dreams of: he was going to the big leagues. Maroth made his major-league debut that night for the Tigers, starting against the Philadelphia Phillies at Comerica Park. "It was definitely the longest day as I sat in the hotel room, waiting. Finally, it came. I was praying for the peace only God can give. I asked God to help me focus on pitching. I had been pitching all my life. I was just going to be doing the same thing I'd always done, only the surroundings were different. I didn't want to get caught up in who I was facing. The first inning was rough. I threw a lot of balls. I definitely had a little case of the jitters. I threw a double play ball with the bases loaded to get me out of that first inning. I got through the second inning, still with a little of the jitters, and then the next five innings were fine."[15]

Maroth's recollection of the start of the game was right. Jimmy Rollins welcomed Maroth to the major leagues with a line-drive single. After Marlon Anderson flew out to right, Bobby Abreu singled and Pat Burrell walked to load the bases. Fortunately for Maroth, he induced Jeremy Giambi to hit into a double play and escaped the first inning without surrendering a run despite 12 of his 17 pitches being balls. In the second, the Phillies threatened again with two singles, but Maroth again kept them off the scoreboard. In the next five innings, Maroth only allowed three more hits and a walk, and he departed the game after seven shutout innings. Unfortunately, the Tigers managed to post only one run, and after the bullpen gave up two runs in the eighth, the Tigers lost 2-1. Maroth made his second start six days later. While his first start was against the middling Phillies in Detroit, his second start threw him into the cauldron, facing the defending World Series champion Arizona Diamondbacks in Phoenix, with Curt Schilling on the mound. Schilling came into the game with a 12-1 record and a 2.79 ERA, but Maroth got the best of him that night. Maroth did not allow a baserunner until Greg Colbrunn led off the fifth inning with a single. Colbrunn was erased on a double play and

Maroth faced the minimum 18 batters through six innings. Maroth allowed a run in the seventh but got out of it and stayed in the game until a leadoff single and walk to start the ninth. Both runners eventually scored but Maroth and the Tigers won the game, 6-3.

"He doesn't know who I am," Maroth said about Schilling, "but hopefully he does now. A lot of great things happened in this game."[16] Schilling did now know who Maroth was, "He pitched a great game," Schilling said afterwards. "I got outpitched—that was the long and short of it."[17] Diamondbacks manager Bob Brenly noted, "He kept the ball from the middle of the plate all night long, had terrific command, and didn't make any mistakes."[18] Maroth's catcher that night, Brandon Inge, noted, "He has good sink on his fastball. If they swing, that's fine, because they'll hit a groundball. If they don't swing, that's even better, because he'll be ahead 0-1. I know he has a long ways to go, but he's smart. He knows what he's doing. At the plate, too, it turns out. He made better contact than I did."[19] Inge was referencing Maroth's fifth-inning single, a grounder through the infield off Schilling, Maroth later scored. Maroth's reaction to the hit was, "I fouled off a pitch my first time up and was happy enough with that."[20]

Four of Maroth's first five major-league starts were against National League clubs, since he was called up during an extended period of interleague play that used to occur before the leagues reorganized. The exception was his fourth start, against the Kansas City Royals, which was also the first game he got hit hard, giving up five runs in 2 2/3 innings. His sixth start came on short notice; Jeff Weaver was supposed to start but he was traded to the New York Yankees that day. Instead, Maroth got the nod against his former organization, the Boston Red Sox. Unfortunately, the Sox had five runs in after seven batters and Maroth was out of the game in the third inning. "I feel bad for the guy who went in," Nomar Garciaparra said of Maroth, "I'm sure he wasn't expecting to pitch and probably got a call this morning saying, 'By the way, you're starting.' That would be tough for anybody."[21]

Maroth's best start in 2002 arguably was on August 9 versus the Baltimore Orioles. Maroth went 8 1/3 innings without allowing a run, striking out three and walking one. He was pulled after a single with one out in the ninth, but Juan Acevedo induced a double play to end the game.

Maroth finished his rookie season with a 4.48 ERA in 21 starts, a little above the American League average of 4.46. The Tigers, meanwhile, continued their slide to irrelevance, finishing the 2002 season at 55-106, 10 1/2 games worse than their 2001 mark of 66-96. Six games into the 2002 season, the Tigers fired general manager Randy Smith and manager Phil Garner.[22] During that season the Tigers traded their then-top starter, Weaver, and after the season, the Tigers lost their team leaders in runs, runs batted in, and saves, with no replacements in sight. With Weaver and Mark Redman (traded to the Marlins for a package that included future Tiger starter Nate Robertson) gone from the 2003 roster, Maroth had the best ERA among the returning starters and so he received the Opening Day assignment. And yet the feeling was that as bad as 55-106 was, 2003 might be worse.[23]

And as feared, the worst was yet to come, both for the Tigers and their young lefty. Maroth pitched well on opening day, allowing only two runs in seven innings, but the Tigers lost 3-1. The two runs came on a second-inning Dustain Mohr home run, which ironically would not have been a home run in Comerica Park the year before. The Tigers had brought in the left-field wall from 395 to 370 feet by moving the bullpens to left field, and Mohr's home run hit the old left-field wall. Maroth's reaction to the home run was, "That's last year; the fence is where it is now. If I start looking at that, and thinking that all of the balls that go over it would have stayed in the park last year, then it's just going to get into my head. I can't worry about that stuff. The fence is where it is now and I've just got to pitch."[24]

After the Opening Day disappointment things went further downhill. The left-hander started the season with nine losses in his first 10 starts, with one no-decision. During that span Maroth did not pitch as poorly as his record would suggest, being knocked out once in the second inning, and pitching into at least the sixth in seven of the 10 games. His strikeout to walk ratio was a solid 2.5 to 1, and his ERA of 5.73 was not great, but was certainly good enough to have won a few games on a better ball club. The loss that gave Maroth an 0-9 record dropped the Tigers to 9-32.

After getting a win in five of his next 10 starts Maroth and the team hit another by-now-expected rough streak. As the losses mounted, Maroth was given the option to leave the rotation but he declined.[25] Maroth's record stood at 6-19 after another disappointing loss on August 30 against the division rival White Sox, which was also the team's 100th loss of the season.

Six days later, September 5, 2003, Maroth was scheduled to take the mound against the Blue Jays in Toronto, which put him in line for that dreaded 20th loss, which had not happened in the major leagues since Brian Kingman had lost 20 games for the Athletics in 1980. Earlier in the day, Maroth found out that his grandmother had passed away, which could have given him an excuse to skip that start, but Maroth took the mound. Kingman attended the game in Toronto with a voodoo doll he had brought to four other games where the starting pitcher was in line for his 20th loss and where all four avoided that dreaded result.[26]

Unfortunately for Maroth, the luck of the voodoo doll ran out that night. The Tigers staked Maroth to a two-run lead before he took the mound, but Toronto tied it up in the second. The Tigers got three in the third but the Jays came back with two in the third inning. Toronto started off the fourth with four hits and three runs before manager Alan Trammell pulled Maroth with the Tigers down, 7-5. The Blue Jays got one more that inning and the Tigers answered with one in the sixth inning, but that was it for the scoring. Toronto won 8-6 and Mike Maroth had lost his 20th game of the season.

Maroth said after the game, "I have no regrets about the way I pitched tonight. I went out there with everything I had. I didn't pitch well, but at least I can sleep good knowing that I gave it everything I had. Mentally, I was fine…I'm a strong person. I'm going to overcome this. I know that. Hopefully, next year and the rest of this year I'll be able to prove that."[27]

Maroth credited his religious beliefs for helping him get through that season. "I don't know how I would have handled it without Christ in my life. When guys go through struggles, some break down. I really don't know how I would have handled it. My focus was spending time in the Word. I knew that God knew how much He could put on my plate, and I would be able to handle. So I knew He wasn't going to take me overboard….[The media] were just asking, 'How are you doing this?' They were asking more about my character and the way I was carrying myself…People watched me, wanting to see how I was going to react. Most of my teammates knew I was a Christian. They wanted to see how I'd handle it."[28]

All season as the L's piled up, Maroth earned the respect of the media and his teammates. He didn't duck into the trainer's room to avoid the press and he answered all the media's questions. Teammate Eric

Munson said, "I pull for all of my teammates, but I probably root for Mike more than anybody because of what he went through and the way he handled it."[29] Another teammate, Dmitri Young, said the night Maroth lost his 20th game, "He's dealing with a lot right now.... He's a better man than most of us. For him to come out here and forget about everything and pitch for the team, I felt I failed him."[30]

Neither Maroth nor the Tigers gave up on the season. In his next start, he pitched six shutout innings against Kansas City. With six games to go in the season, the Tigers were 38-118 and seemed assured to at least match, if not break, the record for losses in a season, 120, set by the 1962 New York Mets. Maroth pitched the next game and although he gave up six runs, five earned, in five innings, the Tiger bats exploded for a 15-6 win. The Tigers won three of the next four games, including two walkoff wins. The second of those was the second-to-last game of the season, a game the Tigers won in the bottom of the ninth after falling behind 8-0 in the fifth inning.

Maroth drew the start in the last game of the season, the game where it would be determined if the Tigers would tie the Mets' record. Maroth shut out the Twins for the first four innings as the Tigers held on to a 1-0 lead. The Twins got two runs off Maroth in the fifth inning to go up 2-1 but the Tigers tied it in the bottom of the inning before scoring seven in the sixth inning to seal the win.

The Tigers had won five of the final six games to avoid setting the record for the most losses in a season. After the game, Maroth said the difference was that, "There were stretches this year when we tried not to lose. The past six times we went out there to win."[31] Maroth also gave credit to the Tigers fans, "We've heard so much about this city and its die-hard fans, and we got a taste of it. They could have heckled us, or not even come out. But they came out and supported us. We fed off that."[32]

Maroth did have quite a few sleepless nights following the season, but it had nothing to do with baseball. His and Brooke's first child, Nolan Maroth, was born on October 29, a month and a day after Maroth's season-ending win.[33]

The Tigers promised to made changes for the 2004 season. Owner Mike Ilitch vowed, "I am going to do what I feel is necessary to field a good team. I am going to go out and sign free agents."[34] The Tigers signed second baseman Fernando Vina and outfielder Rondell White on December 19, starting pitcher Jason Johnson on December 29, and traded for shortstop Carlos Guillen on January 8. The biggest move came on February 6, when 10-time All-Star catcher Ivan "Pudge" Rodriguez, just off winning a World Series championship with the Florida Marlins, signed a four-year $40 million contract with the Tigers.

Maroth was thrilled with the additions and the contributions they made early in the season. "That just totally eliminated the thoughts of last year — it's a totally different team. The guys we picked up are quality, veteran players — guys that are going to be able to come in and get the job done right away and they've done that. That's the difference this year. The young guys that are still here have a year of experience under their belt and are playing better. We still have a long way to go, but I feel we're better than our record shows."[35]

Johnson, who had gone 10-10 with a 4.18 for Baltimore in 2003, was named the 2004 Opening Day starter, with Maroth following him in the rotation. Maroth won that start, a far cry from 2003, throwing five innings and allowing three runs. Maroth's best game of the season was on July 16, when he shut out the New York Yankees on one hit, a double by Gary Sheffield in the fourth inning. Maroth worked both sides of the plate, in contrast to other recent starts where he had focused more on the outside part of the plate. The Yankees' Jason Giambi said, "He was throwing strikes — inner half and outer half. He wasn't really throwing anything over the middle of the plate. You might get a changeup one time at 82, and the next time at 85. He was locating his fastball just under my hands." Maroth followed up that start with a month of solid pitching, winning five starts in a row (with two-no decisions) between mid-July and mid-August.

Maroth finished the 2004 season with a 11-13 record and a 4.31 ERA, a big improvement over 2003's

9-21 record and 5.73 ERA. Maroth led the Tigers' pitching staff in Wins Above Replacement as calculated by Baseball Reference (bWAR) with 3.2, trailing only Rodriguez and Guillen in total bWAR on the team. The Tigers improved by 29 games to 72-90 and finished out of the American League Central Division cellar.

There was hope that the Tigers would improve again in 2005, especially after the signing of right fielder Magglio Ordonez and closer Troy Percival. However, the Tigers did not have a good season and actually finished a game worse in 2005 (71-91) then they did in 2004. Maroth won a career-high 14 games and finished with a .500 record, but his ERA rose to 4.74.

His best start of the season was on Sunday August 14. In the second game of a doubleheader against the Kansas City Royals, Maroth got within one out of a shutout. However, the Tigers had scored only one run, so with a runner on first and two out and the Royals' right-handed slugger, Mike Sweeney, coming to the plate, manager Alan Trammell brought in Fernando Rodney to get the final out.

After the season, the Tigers fired Trammell, who had been the Tigers manager since 2003. Maroth was a favorite of Trammell's and he was saddened to hear the news. "Sorry to hear that. I had prepared myself for whatever the decision was. I wanted Tram back, though. I think he has the makings of a good manager. But it's their decision."[36]

Both Tigers General Manager Dave Dombrowski and Maroth felt that the Tigers were getting close to putting together a strong team. Nobody, though, anticipated how great the 2006 season would be for the team, and sadly, Mike Maroth's physical problems also came out of the blue. For Maroth, the spring started ominously with a tender elbow that caused him to be held out of a spring training start. New Tigers manager Jim Leyland called it "precautionary," and Maroth resumed preparing for the 2006 season.[37] Maroth's first start of the season was at Texas where he allowed only one run in 5 1/3 innings.

However, Maroth's elbow problem flared up during the Texas start and he did not start again for nine days. Maroth threw seven scoreless innings against Cleveland in that game, with his elbow feeling fine. He said later, "I went out and threw a lot better than I thought I would. It was a huge improvement from [two days earlier]. It was a question mark going into the weekend. Once I get through this, I should be OK."[38]

The Tigers were off to a decent start, with a 7-5 record after Maroth's win, heading into the final game of a series at home against Cleveland before a long west coast trip. The Tigers limped through that game, getting wiped out by the Indians, and in what became a legendary tirade, Leyland let his team have it. Afterwards, Maroth said, "Jim's an experienced manager, and he knows what he's doing. We lost 10-2 today, and that's not pretty. The whole game, overall, didn't look good. He got upset with us. A manager's job is to get the most out of his players every day."[39] (It would seem that the tirade might have worked, since the Tigers went 6-2 on the road trip, won 12 of their next 15 games, and were 19-9 on May 3).

Maroth's elbow felt fine and he made his next seven starts on schedule. He and the Tigers were off to a great start. After eight starts, Maroth had a 5-2 record with a 2.45 ERA and the Tigers, coming off 12 losing seasons in a row, were 28-14, tied for both first place and the best record in baseball, with the Chicago White Sox.

Maroth's next start was against the Kansas City Royals. Mike faced only seven hitters, with six of them getting hits, including home runs from the last three men he faced before being pulled by Leyland. Maroth went on the disabled list the next day and eight days later, Dr. Lewis Yocum performed arthroscopic surgery on Maroth's left elbow, removing four bone chips. "I could feel [the elbow] locking up. We had an idea of what it could be, but until we could find out for sure, we had to go out there and have some tests that revealed the chips. I had to make a choice of pitching through it or having surgery. Dr. Yocum said that he wouldn't recommend surgery unless he absolutely had to do it. So, obviously, he felt like without it, it would be really tough to get through the year."[40]

Maroth recovered through the summer and returned to the field with four minor-league rehabilitation starts for the Toledo Mud Hens starting on August 9. He returned to the Tigers on September 6, making four relief appearances and posting a 9.53 ERA in 5 2/3 innings. Maroth was left off the Tigers' postseason roster, but he watched the postseason games from the bench as the team went on to win the American League pennant before dropping the World Series to the St. Louis Cardinals in five games. "I enjoyed it a lot more than I thought I would. When I found out I wasn't going to be on the playoff roster I didn't know how I was going to take it. But it was definitely a great experience. It was almost like I was looking at it from the outside but still being part of it. Because I didn't have to get ready for the games, I could take it all in. I got to see it all. I got the dugout perspective, which was nice. But it's a lot better out on the mound."[41]

In 2007 Maroth was counted on to be in the rotation, in part to fill the hole left by the injury to fellow left-hander Kenny Rogers, who went 17-8 with a 3.84 ERA in 2006 and was the winning pitcher in the only game the Tigers won in the World Series. After the World Series Rogers had surgery on his left shoulder to remove a blood clot and would not be available for the first half of the 2007 season.[42] The Tigers won Maroth's first seven starts (with Maroth getting credit for the win in three of them), despite a 4.69 ERA. Maroth did not start for 11 days after the last of those seven games, but it was the flu, not an arm injury, that sidelined him.[43]

On June 18, at RFK Stadium in Washington, DC, Maroth made his last start as a Detroit Tiger against the woebegone Nationals. The Tigers staked him to a 9-1 lead, six runs coming in the fifth inning (thanks in part to a Maroth double off the wall), but in the bottom of the sixth inning a single, a triple, an error on a weak grounder to shortstop, another single, and a walk caused Jim Leyland to remove Maroth from the game. Maroth still wound up with the victory in the Tigers 9-8 victory. The Tigers had Rogers and Nate Robertson returning from injuries soon, and 22-year-old fireballer Andrew Miller also had two good starts, so Maroth was the odd man out. After the game, Leyland said, "You're going to be looking at lots of [changes in the pitching staff] in the next week or so,"[44]

Four days after his start in Washington, Maroth was traded to the St. Louis Cardinals for a player to be named later [pitcher Chris Lambert]. During the announcement of the trade, Dave Dombrowski, who had been shopping Maroth around the league, said, "You don't find finer people than Mike or Brooke Maroth." Dombrowski and Leyland were glad that the destination was St. Louis, a well-regarded franchise that had a rotation spot for Maroth.[45]

Maroth heard about the trade when he got a call from Dombrowski after taking his family to the Atlanta Aquarium. Maroth said, "I wasn't that shocked. I would have loved to stay in Detroit. But it sounds like I'm going from one class organization to another."[46] In an interview soon after the trade, Maroth talked about continuing his extensive charitable work in St. Louis. "We want to be servants. I've been given a platform in baseball that allows me to do things like this. I want to take full advantage of it. It is part of our faith."[47]

That was not a surprise given what both Mike and Brooke Maroth had done while with the Tigers. Maroth's extensive charitable work led him to be the Tigers' nominee for the Roberto Clemente Award in 2005 and 2006.[48] An example of that work; after hearing from her husband about all of the food left in the clubhouse after games, Brooke contacted an organization called "Rock and Wrap it Up," that donated leftover food from concerts to shelters. The Maroths helped the program expand into baseball with an organization called "Sports Wrap."[49] Now, Sports Wrap works with 74 major-league professional sports teams to donate leftover concession and clubhouse food to feed the needy.[50] The Maroths were honored by Congresswoman Jo Ann Emerson of Missouri with the 2004 Bill Emerson Award for their work with Rock and Wrap it Up.[51]

Maroth's father, Bill, had multiple sclerosis, which led the Maroths to become active in the fight against that disease. They sponsored the "Strike Out MS

Bowling Spectacular" event that raised more than $47,000, and the "National MS Society Night" at Comerica Park in 2006.[52] Maroth also was active assisting disabled veterans and promoting literacy in the community.[53] Maroth gave Brooke credit for her commitment. "She does more behind the scenes than I do. She does not get enough credit. It's a team effort between her and I. It's not just me."[54]

Maroth pitched very well in his Cardinals debut, allowing only one run in 7 1/3 innings while picking up a hit and stolen base against the Mets, but the Cardinals lost the game, 2-1. Maroth did not make it into the sixth inning in any of his next four starts and he was sent to the bullpen. After two ineffective outings, Maroth was sidelined with what was termed a mild case of elbow tendonitis.[55] On September 6, 2007, Maroth returned to start against the Pittsburgh Pirates but lasted only 1 2/3 innings. He made five relief appearances the rest of the way, with his final big league appearance coming on September 24, 2007, a scoreless seventh inning against the Milwaukee Brewers at Miller Park. Maroth's big-league career ended on a force out at second off the bat of Ryan Braun. Maroth was released by the Cardinals on October 23, 2007.[56]

After interest was shown by the Florida Marlins and Colorado Rockies, Maroth signed a minor-league deal with the Kansas City Royals on February 8, 2008. Unfortunately, Maroth developed a stiff left shoulder and did not make the big league club.[57] He was sent to the Royals' Triple-A farm club in Omaha and made three starts that lasted 4, 2, and 2 1/3 innings. The Royals released him on April 30, 2008, and he had left shoulder surgery soon after that. After recovering from the surgery, Maroth said, "My arm feels really strong. I've already seen signs of a difference in how free my arm feels when I throw a ball."[58]

Maroth signed a minor-league contract with the Toronto Blue Jays for 2009 but tore the meniscus in his left knee two days into spring, which scuttled his chances of making the team. On March 14, 2009, Maroth faced the Tigers at Joker Marchant Stadium in Lakeland, Florida, and allowed four earned runs and seven hits in 2 2/3 innings in his only spring training appearance. Maroth was released by the Blue Jays on March 27, and then had surgery on the knee.

After recovering from the surgery, Maroth tried in vain to sign with a club, finally signing with the Indios de Mayaguez in the Puerto Rico Baseball League. After going 3-0 with a 2.60 ERA in eight appearances, he was signed to a minor-league contract by the Twins in January of 2010.[59] He was sent to the Twins' Triple-A club, the Rochester Red Wings, where he made 10 appearances before elbow problems sidelined him again. He had surgery to remove bone spurs, but in January of 2011 he decided to retire. Maroth told Fox Sports's Jon Paul Morosi that, "I gave it everything I had. I feel confident that I'm making the right decision. I'd love to keep playing, but I realize that I don't have it in me. I have no regrets. I put forth all of the effort possible to continue to play, but I believe my body just can't do it anymore."[60]

Maroth became the pitching coach of the Tigers' high-A farm team, the Lakeland Flying Tigers, in 2012. After three years in Lakeland, Maroth became the pitching coach of the Tigers' Triple-A team, the Toledo Mud Hens. At the conclusion of the 2015 season, it was announced that Maroth would not be back with Toledo. It was rumored that he would become the pitching coach for the Tigers' Double-A team, the Erie Seawolves.[61] However, in late in September 2015, Maroth was named the Atlanta Braves' Minor League Rehabilitation Pitching Coordinator, a position that he still holds.[62] That job is based in Orlando, Florida, where Maroth makes his home.

## SOURCES

In addition to the sources indicated in the Notes, the authors relied on Baseball-Reference.com.

## NOTES

1   Conversation between authors and Mike Maroth on July 5, 2017.

2   Bruce Biesenthal, "Steady on the Mound," *The Goal*, November 2002. http://www.thegoal.com/events/maroth/maroth.html, accessed June 3, 2017.

# 20-GAME LOSERS

3 University of Central Florida Baseball Record Book, 2017, http://ucfknights.com/documents/2017/5/31/UCF_Baseball_Record_Book.pdf, accessed June 4, 2017

4 High Point Panthers Baseball website http://www.highpointpanthers.com/coaches.aspx?path=baseball&rc=872, accessed June 3, 2017

5 baseballamerica.com/statistics/players/cards/21156/mike-maroth/spring accessed on June 3, 2017.

6 *2007 Detroit Tigers Information Guide* (Detroit: Detroit Tigers, 2007), 131.

7 *2007 Detroit Tigers Information Guide* (Detroit: Detroit Tigers, 2007), 131.

8 Biesenthal, "Steady on the Mound."

9 *The Sporting News Baseball Guide 2001* (St. Louis: The Sporting News, 2001), 466.

10 *2007 Detroit Tigers Information Guide* (Detroit: Detroit Tigers, 2007), 131.

11 TheGoal.com. http://www.thegoal.com/players/baseball/maroth_mike/maroth_m.html, accessed on June 3, 2017

12 Biesenthal, "Steady on the Mound."

13 *2007 Detroit Tigers Information Guide* (Detroit: Detroit Tigers, 2007), 132.

14 John Wagner, "Fifth Third Fans Inspire Maroth," *Toledo Blade*, May 5, 2002. http://www.toledoblade.com/Mud-Hens/2002/05/05/Fifth-Third-fans-inspires-Maroth.html, accessed on June 3, 2017.

15 Biesenthal. "Steady on the Mound."

16 Tom Gage, "He beats Schilling for first big-league victory, singles," *Detroit News*, June 16, 2002.

17 Biesenthal, "Steady on the Mound."

18 Ibid.

19 Gage, "He beats Schilling for first big-league victory, singles."

20 Ibid.

21 Bob Hohler, "Moving on Sox Weave Way Past Maroth and the Tigers," *Boston Globe*, July 7, 2002

22 Associated Press, "Tigers 0-6 Start Seals Garner's Fate," April 8, 2002, http://static.espn.go.com/mlb/news/2002/0408/1364856.html, accessed on June 3, 2017.

23 Albert Chen, "5 Detroit Tigers Even for a team that lost 106 games last season, the worst may be yet to come," *Sports Illustrated*, https://www.si.com/vault/2003/03/31/340606/5-detroit-tigers-even-for-a-team-that-lost-106-games-last-season-the-worst-may-be-yet-to-come, accessed June 3, 2017.

24 Matt Markey, "New Beginnings, Familiar Endings," *Toledo Blade*, April 1, 2003, http://www.toledoblade.com/Pro/2003/04/01/New-beginning-familiar-ending.html, accessed on June 3, 2017

25 George Cantor, *The Good, the Bad, & the Ugly: Detroit Tigers* (Chicago: Triumph Books, 2008), 24-25.

26 Associated Press, "Maroth Handed His 20th Loss," September 6, 2003, http://articles.latimes.com/2003/sep/06/sports/sp-tigers6, accessed on June 3, 2017.

27 Ibid.

28 Christian Broadcast Network, "Mike Maroth: A Pitcher of Faith," http://www1.cbn.com/sports/mike-maroth%3A-a-pitch-of-faith, accessed on June 3, 2017.

29 Associated Press, "Maroth's Many Sleepless Nights," March 14, 2014, http://reds.enquirer.com/2004/03/14/red2maroth.html, accessed on June 3, 2017.

30 "Maroth Handed His 20th Loss."

31 Tom Gage, "Tigers Stay Out of Record Book," *Detroit News*, September 29, 2003.

32 Bob Wojnowski, "Tigers Victory Spares Infamy," *Detroit News*, September 29, 2003.

33 "Maroth's Many Sleepless Nights."

34 John Wagner, "Tigers Notebook: Ilitch Vows to Make Changes," *Toledo Blade*, September 29, 2003, http://www4.toledoblade.com/Pro/2003/09/29/Tigers-notebook-Ilitch-vows-to-make-changes.html, accessed on June 3, 2017.

35 "Simply Baseball Straight From the Source: Mike Maroth," http://z.lee28.tripod.com/sbnsstraightfromthesource/mikemaroth.html, accessed on June 3, 2017.

36 Tom Gage, "Maroth Can Take or Leave Rodriguez," *Detroit News*, October 4, 2005.

37 Billfer. "Maroth's Elbow", http://www.detroittigersweblog.com/2006/03/maroths-elbow/, accessed on June 3, 2017. Quoting Danny Knobler's blog

38 Lynn Henning, "Maroth: Leyland is Doing His Job," *Detroit News*, April 18, 2006.

39 Ibid.

40 Jim Hawkins, "Maroth Visits Clubhouse," *Oakland Press*, June 5, 2006, http://www.theoaklandpress.com/general-news/20060605/maroth-visits-clubhouse, accessed on June 3, 2017.

41 Jim Hawkins, "Maroth's First Start is a Good One," *Oakland Press*, March 2, 2007, http://www.theoaklandpress.com/general-news/20070302/maroths-first-start-is-a-good-one, accessed on June 3, 2017.

42 Ron Parker, "Maroth Must Pick Up Slack," *Detroit News*, March 31, 2007.

43 Jim Hawkins, "Maroth Taken Deep Three Times in Loss," *Oakland Press*, May 23, 2007.

44 Jim Hawkins, "Shakeups to Come After Another Close Call," *Oakland Press*, June 19, 2007.

45  Lynn Henning, "Trade Settles Rotation," *Detroit News*, June 23, 2007.

46  Ibid.

47  Joe Strauss, "Maroth is Much More Than the Day's Boxscore," *St. Louis Post-Dispatch*, July 15, 2007.

48  http://mlb.mlb.com/news/press_releases/press_release.jsp?ymd=20050907&content_id=1200581&vkey=pr_mlb&fext=.jsp&c_id=mlb and http://mlb.mlb.com/news/press_releases/press_release.jsp?ymd=20060906&content_id=1648763&vkey=pr_mlb&fext=.jsp&c_id=mlb, accessed on June 3, 2017.

49  JoAnn Emerson, "Congratulations to Brooke and Mike Maroth," *Congressional Record*, July 7, 2004, https://www.congress.gov/crec/2004/07/07/CREC-2004-07-07-pt1-PgE1299.pdf, accessed on June 3, 2017.

50  https://www.rockandwrapitup.org/sports-wrap

51  JoAnn Emerson, "Congratulations to Brooke and Mike Maroth."

52  MS Connection, newsletter of the Michigan Chapter of the National Multiple Sclerosis Society, October 2006

53  http://detroit.tigers.mlb.com/mlb/components/official_info/community/clemente_2005/bios/maroth_mike.jsp, accessed on June 3, 2017.

54  Joe Strauss, "Maroth is Much More Than the Day's Boxscore."

55  Brian Walton, "Maroth Released by Cardinals," *Cardinal Nation*, October 25, 2007, http://www.scout.com/mlb/cardinals/story/694455-maroth-released-by-cardinals, accessed on June 3, 2017.

56  Associated Press, "Cardinals Release LHP Maroth," *USA Today*, October 23, 2007, https://usatoday30.usatoday.com/sports/baseball/2007-10-25-1530556607_x.htm, accessed June 3, 2017.

57  http://www.rotoworld.com/recent/mlb/3480/mike-maroth

58  http://www.rotoworld.com/recent/mlb/3480/mike-maroth

59  John Shipley, "Minnesota Twins Pitcher Mike Maroth Has Lost Valuable Time to Injuries," *St. Paul Pioneer-Press*, March 4, 2010, http://www.twincities.com/2010/03/04/minnesota-twins-pitcher-mike-maroth-has-lost-valuable-time-to-injuries/amp/, accessed on June 3, 2017.

60  Jon Paul Morosi. "Mike Maroth, Who Lost 20 Games But Kept Dignity, Retires", January 26, 2011, http://www.yardbarker.com/blog/mlbbuzz/article/mike_maroth_who_lost_20_games_but_kept_dignity_retires/4037633, accessed on June 3, 2017.

61  Lynn Henning, "Mike Maroth Will Note Be Back as Mud Hens Pitching Coach," *Detroit News*, September 14, 2015, http://www.detroitnews.com/story/sports/mlb/tigers/2015/09/14/mike-maroth—back-mud-hens-pitching-coach/72269784/, accessed on June 3, 2017.

62  Atlanta Braves Press Release. "Braves Announce Mike Maroth as Minor League Rehabilitation Pitching Coordinator," September 25, 2015, http://m.mlb.com/news/article/151571454/braves-announce-mike-maroth-as-minor-league-rehabilitation-pitching-coordinator/, accessed on June 3, 2017; conversation between authors and Maroth, July 5, 2017

# AL MATTERN

## BY BOB LEMOINE

**"THE STRANGER TRUDGED ALONG** the tracks in the bright June sunlight," wrote Bill Vanderschmidt of the *Rochester Times-Union* in 1955, "heading towards the point where the shadow of the West Rush depot threw a patch of shade across the rails."[1] The stranger was sent from Al Buckenberger, manager of the Rochester (New York) Beau Brummels. He was looking for 23-year-old semipro pitcher Al Mattern, who was working as a station agent on the "Peanut Line" of the New York Central Railroad. They grabbed the trolley to Rochester, and Mattern began his professional baseball career.[2]

Al Mattern may have had the talent to win 20 games, but we'll never know. Instead, he's remembered as a 20-game loser, a feat he accomplished once and almost twice. That's easy to do considering the teams he played for. He pitched five major-league seasons with the Boston National League team that changed names from the Doves to the Rustlers and finally to the Braves. Whatever they were called, Boston had three straight last-place finishes from 1909-1911, going a combined 142-315, which gave Mattern plenty of opportunities to lose. Still, the left-handed spitballer was also Boston's ace, winning a third of its games in 1909, a feat that the Hall of Fame recognized him for. It certainly wasn't for his 36-58 career record. When Mattern was done pitching to home plate, he pitched deals on Buicks to his neighbors back in the same little hamlet in western New York where spent his entire life.

Alonzo Albert Mattern was born on June 16, 1878, on a farm, in West Rush, New York, to John and Christine (Keyes) Mattern, who had emigrated from Germany.[3] The 1892 New York State census lists John Mattern as a laborer. Albert grew up with three older sisters and seven older brothers.[4] At the time of the 1900 census, he was living at the home of his brother Joseph and listed as working as a freight agent. His brothers were known for playing baseball and working on the railroad. Four of the Mattern brothers, Fred, Charles, William, and Lewis, were longtime railroad men in the area.[5] Mattern, who in baseball "reached the highest fame of his family,"[6] graduated from Avon High School in 1900 and pitched all of the games for the baseball team that season.[7] Avon is about 15 miles south of Rush.

Mattern, known as Dutch, played semipro baseball around the area. One of his catchers during that period was future New York State Supreme Court Justice William F. Love.[8] Buckenberger's Rochester team was in the Eastern League, the equivalent of the modern Triple-A International League, and Mattern joined them in June.[9] In his first professional game, he got a lot of run support as Rochester beat Worcester 27-6.[10] After pitching in just three games, Mattern was sent to Binghamton of the Class-C New York State League in July.[11]

On September 18, 1901, Mattern married Julia Burger, of Rochester, New York.[12] The couple had met during their school years.[13]

Mattern pitched in 1902 for the Canandaigua, New York, semipro team, and later rejoined Rochester. He won one game and lost two for the Bronchos.[14] He spent 1903 with the Caledonia, New York, semipro team.[15] In March of 1904, Mattern, "the East Rush telegraph operator who was given a trial by Rochester a couple of seasons ago," drew interest from New Bedford of the New England League.[16] Apparently he never pitched for New Bedford, and instead stayed at the semipro level, pitching for the Phelps, New York, team.[17]

Mattern pitched most of the 1905 season for Rochester. "Mattern, the southpaw, is beginning to let himself out," wrote the *Democrat and Chronicle* early in the season. "He has lots of speed and some very puzzling curves. It is a reasonable presumption that he will be one of the regular pitchers."[18] Mattern pitched in eight games and won seven in 1905. His season ended early when he was spiked in the hand in a collision with his first baseman.[19] He also played briefly for the Wilkes-Barre Barons of the New York State League (Class B), and the Indianapolis Indians of the American Association (Class A), possibly on short-term agreements by Buckenberger.

Mattern began the 1906 season with the Montreal Royals of the Eastern League. He pitched poorly in a return to Rochester on July 4. "It seemed too bad to treat the young man so heartlessly, especially in the neighborhood of the stomping ground of his youth," wrote the *Democrat and Chronicle*. Rochester prevailed 7-1.[20] He fell to 2-9 with Montreal with a 4.41 ERA. Later that month, Mattern was sold to the Holyoke, Massachusetts, club of the New England League.[21] At the end of the season, he pitched and lost two games for the Livonia, New York, semipro team against the African-American Cuban Giants.[22]

Mattern played for Holyoke of the Connecticut State League in 1907, having a strong 16-7 record for the pennant winners. "With an easy delivery and plenty of shoots," wrote the *Springfield Republican*, "'Matty' began to fool the heaviest hitting clubs and has been regarded as one of Holyoke's strongest pitchers."[23] His impressive work caught the eye of the Boston Doves of the National League, who purchased him for the 1908 season.[24] Not feeling that the young lefty would get into enough games, team president George Dovey sold him to the Trenton (New Jersey) Tigers of the Tri-State League "with the understanding that at the end of the season he was to have first chance to buy him back," wrote the *Trenton Evening Times*.[25] Mattern finished 20-21, and returned to Boston in September. He also worked on the side selling fruits and vegetables, and made $1,800.[26]

Mattern made his major-league debut at the South End Grounds in Boston on September 16 against the Chicago Cubs, the eventual World Series champions. "Rarely has a minor league pitcher created better impression than did Mattern yesterday," wrote the *Boston Herald*. "He was self-possessed at all times even under fire. … He used all kinds of benders and had a very puzzling slow ball."[27] Mattern al-

lowed the Cubs only one run on two hits with four strikeouts in eight innings before being lifted for a pinch-hitter. Chicago won 5-0. Mattern "looks like the real goods unadulterated and no phoney," wrote the *Boston Journal*.[28] On September 22, despite giving up 11 hits, Mattern shut out St. Louis, 7-0. He finished the season 1-2 with a 2.08 ERA in five games pitched, three being starts.

Mattern worked the farm over the winter months. He "pulls potatoes out of the ground up around Rochester during the winter, and dollars out of the people at the same time," wrote the *Boston Journal*.[29] In 1909 he was ready to be one of Boston's regular starting pitchers.

Mattern pitched a 5-1 win over Brooklyn on April 17, giving Boston a 3-0 start to the season. There were probably some ecstatic Boston fans dreaming about the World Series, but the Doves would end the season 65½ games behind pennant-winning Pittsburgh. On May 8 Mattern pitched a one-hitter in a tight 2-1 victory over New York, the run scoring on a walk and a steal of second in which Boston catcher Frank Bowerman threw the ball into center field, where

Boston outfielder Ginger Beaumont overthrew third base. Such was life pitching for the 45-108 Doves. On May 31 Mattern again dominated Brooklyn with a 1-0 shutout.

In one of the most interesting games of the season, against New York on July 26 at the South End Grounds, Mattern opposed the Giants' Red Ames. Each pitcher surrendered two runs in the first inning, then Boston tied the score 3-3 in the seventh. The game was ruled a 3-3 tie due to darkness at after 17 innings, with both starting pitchers still on the mound.[30] On July 2 Mattern shut out Philadelphia, 3-0. He closed out the season with a 3-1 win over Philadelphia again, giving him his 15th win, or one-third of Boston's total wins (45). At 15-21, Mattern was Boston's best pitcher, despite giving up 142 runs (tied for league high), 100 earned runs, and 108 walks in his 316⅓ innings pitched. His 2.85 ERA, although common in the Deadball Era, still represented how well he pitched with little run support behind him. The Doves as a team batted a woeful .223 and committed a league-high 340 errors for a pitiful .948 fielding percentage.

The team finished the 1909 season as a train wreck, then had a literal train wreck at the beginning of the 1910 season. While traveling in Kentucky at night during spring training, the Boston Special collided with a coal car parked on the tracks. The engineer was killed, and Mattern and other players carried his body from the wreckage.[31] The team recovered, and Mattern "pitched mighty fine ball" over eight innings on Opening Day in Boston, a 3-2 victory over New York in 11 innings.[32] He capped off the month by shutting out Brooklyn 1-0 on five hits on April 29, and did it again a week later (May 5) in Brooklyn. On June 4 Mattern went the distance in a 1-0 win in 12 innings over the Cubs' Three-Finger Brown. He threw a five-hitter against St. Louis on June 15 in a 2-0 Boston win and a three-hitter at Brooklyn on July 26 in a 2-1 win. Mattern shut out Cincinnati twice in three days: 5-0 and 4-0 on August 3 and 5. His final two starts, however, were forgettable, with 11-0 and 17-9 losses. Mattern came close to having back-to-back 20-loss seasons, finishing 16-19 with a 2.98 ERA. He was easily Boston's best pitcher. His 51 appearances led the National League, as did his six shutouts. Boston was again in the cellar at 53-100.

At the 1910 census, Mattern, wife Julia, and 7-year-old son Emmett lived in a home they owned in Rush. Albert is listed as a "Ball Player" for the "Boston BBC." Julia "attends every game played at the South End Grounds," the *Boston Journal* noted, "and follows every play as scientifically as the most expert fan." Emmett came to his father's games at the South End Grounds and warmed him up "wearing a big mitt and receiving easy pitches."[33]

A dreadful Boston team got even worse in 1911, as the club, now called the Rustlers after new owner William Russell, fell to 44-107, and Mattern's strong arm was no more. His record fell to 4-15 with a ballooned ERA of 4.97 in 186⅓ innings pitched. Mattern

Merry Christmas and Happy New Year To All

MAKE THIS CHRISTMAS LAST FOR THOUSANDS OF MILES

A BUICK FOR CHRISTMAS

## A. A. MATTERN

was on the mound on June 28 in the Polo Grounds in New York, newly rebuilt after a devastating fire in April. He pitched a strong game but lost to Christy Mathewson 3-0. Mattern didn't make a start between July 1 and August 1, or any at all after September 14. He hoped for a return to form in 1912, but it seemed his arm was done. He was pulled after four ineffective innings against Philadelphia on April 13, and again after just 2⅓ innings at Philadelphia on April 19. He had barely gotten used to the team's new nickname, Braves, when he was sold to Montreal, now part of the International League.[34] Mattern rebounded, finishing 17-10 in 248⅔ innings pitched. He also spent the 1913 season with Montreal, where on June 3 he allowed three hits in a shutout of Buffalo.[35] His 1913 season overall was 12-14.

Mattern spent the early part of 1914 with Montreal, but at the end of May was sold to Newark, also of the International League.[36] He spun a four-hit shutout over Baltimore on July 17.[37] His season has a fascinating story. On September 14 Mattern was pitching the second game of a doubleheader against Providence. With Newark trailing by two runs in the seventh inning, Mattern drew a walk, and a single sent him to second. The Providence manager brought a 19-year-old pitcher in to try to stop the rally. This pitcher had been a rookie for the Boston Red Sox earlier in the year and had been sent to Providence to finish the season. Babe Ruth was coming in to try and save the game, but instead, Mattern and three others scored to beat the Babe, who had also pitched and lost 2-0 to Newark in game one.[38]

It was reported that Mattern had signed with the Cincinnati Reds in 1915, but no further information was found on why he never pitched for them.[39] His name appears in some box scores for the Buffalo team of the International League.[40] Various accounts mention Mattern pitching for Newark until 1917, but no evidence of this was found.

Later in 1915, Mattern returned to the semipro circuit and pitched for the LeRoy, New York, team and struck out 14 batters in a game.[41] He also played for a Mount Morris team as well as other "towns of similar width and thickness," wrote the *Democrat and Chronicle*.[42]

For the next decade or more, Mattern pitched for various semipro teams around New York state, including the Maltops of the Rochester City League in 1916,[43] and the Husky Farmers of Honeoye Falls in 1926.[44] It was there that Mattern and son Emmett, who was then a catcher at Union College, formed a father-son battery. The old pitcher "has lost some of his speed, critics say today," noted the *Ogdensburg Republican-Journal*, "but the brainwork which made him famous in the big-time circuit still is in evidence, and he still baffles opposing batters."[45]

The 1920 census listed Mattern working as a "produce merchant." Mattern also owned the A.A. Mattern Auto Agency in West Rush, selling Buicks out of a barn on his family property. You had to battle the chickens in the yard if you wanted to get a good look at the lone car he had on display.[46] The *Democrat and Chronicle* did a full-page feature of Rush in its June 19, 1955, issue. A prominent picture is one of Mattern standing at the crossroads of Rush and West Rush. The article describes Rush as the opposite of its name. "Life is calm and placid there, moving in a serene, even way of long standing," wrote Bill Beeney. "One of Rush's most prominent citizens, and he still lives in West Rush, is Al Mattern, the baseball pitcher who performed with the Boston Braves with considerable success circa 1915. West Rush, a tiny hamlet about three miles from the village of Rush, is a sleepy little crossroads area."[47]

Over 100 former professional and semipro players from the area turned out to Al Mack's Rush Inn on February 20, 1955, to honor Mattern on his 50th anniversary of entering professional baseball.[48] "Al Mattern may not achieve a niche in Baseball's Hall of Fame at Cooperstown," the *Democrat and Chronicle* reported, "but a photograph of the former Boston National League ace, portside pitcher in uniform will adorn the walls of the national pastime's shrine." A picture of Mattern was placed in a gallery of notable records, his being winning a third of Boston's victories (15 of 45) in 1909. A letter was read from Sid Keener, Hall of Fame director, in which he recalled "that it was an exceptional mound feat, considering that Boston then was the Patsy losing club of the National League." Mattern received several souvenirs from the Hall of Fame, and the evening involved cutting a cake adorned with miniature baseball bats, and a trophy highlighting his baseball career.[49]

Al Mattern died on November 6, 1958, at the age of 80 in West Rush and was buried in the Pine Hill cemetery in Rush. He was survived by Julia, Emmett, and a brother.

## SOURCES

In addition to the sources identified in the notes, the author also benefited from Susan Mee, Rush town historian, the Rush Public Library, and Al Mattern's file from the Baseball Hall of Fame Library.

## NOTES

1. Bill Vanderschmidt, "Mattern Recalls Heyday of Honus Wagner, Matty," *Rochester* (New York) *Times-Union*, February 9, 1955: 51.

2. There are some problems identifying when this story would have taken place. Vanderschmidt's column was written in 1955 when Mattern was honored on the 50th anniversary of the start of his professional baseball career, which would put his first year in 1905. However, we know Mattern pitched for Rochester from 1901-1903. According to Jim Mandelaro and Scott Pitoniak in *Silver Seasons: The Story of the Rochester Red Wings* (Syracuse, New York: Syracuse University Press, 1996), 11-14, Buckenberger managed the Rochester team, called the Bronchos, from 1899-1901. The team nickname was changed to Beau Brummels in 1903. Buckenberger returned as manager in 1905. Perhaps Mattern's first years were considered a trial period, or he pitched only in exhibition games, or maybe in recalling events 50 years later, these early games were forgotten. In any event, accounts seem to point to 1905 as his start in professional baseball. Perhaps when Buckenberger returned as manager in 1905, he remembered Mattern and sent someone to the train depot to find him. The story seems likely to have happened in 1905 and Mattern's previous stints were either ignored or forgotten.

3. Retrosheet.org and baseball-reference.com give Mattern's birthdate as June 16, 1883, but June 16, 1878, is the date on his death certificate. All found obituaries give his age at the time of his death in 1958 as 80.

4. "Albert Mattern, Former Baseball Player, Succumbs at Home in Rush," *Honeoye Falls* (New York) *Times*, November 13, 1958: 1.

5. "Mattern Family Men Serve Railroad Over Long Period," *Honeoye Falls Times*, April 27, 1944: 5.

6. "The Mattern Boys Played Baseball and Railroaded," unknown article sent to the author by Jacqueline DeCook, great-niece of Al Mattern.

7. "Baseball at Avon," *Rochester Democrat and Chronicle*, March 1, 1901: 13.

8. "Contemporary of Wagner. Al Mattern Hurled Here," *Rochester Democrat and Chronicle*, November 7, 1958: 24.

9. "There's No Lack of Excellent Material," *Rochester Democrat and Chronicle*, January 27, 1901: 23; "Mattern Here at Last," *Rochester Democrat and Chronicle*, June 20, 1901: 15.

10. "First Place in Easy Reach," *Rochester Democrat and Chronicle*, June 23, 1901: 22.

11. "Greminger Now Leads the Others," *Rochester Democrat and Chronicle*, July 22, 1901: 11.

12. "Mattern-Berger," *Rochester Democrat and Chronicle*, September 19, 1901: 13.

13. "Wives of the Ball Players," *Boston Journal*, August 22, 1911: 5.

14. *Rochester Democrat and Chronicle*, June 13, 1902: 15.

15. "Mt. Morris 7, Caledonia 0," *Rochester Democrat and Chronicle*, September 17, 1903: 15.

16. "Local Players Soon to Depart Elsewhere," *Rochester Democrat and Chronicle*, March 30, 1904: 15.

17. *Rochester Democrat and Chronicle*, June 26, 1904: 23.

18. "Buckenberger's Bronchos in the Blue Grass of Kentucky," *Rochester Democrat and Chronicle*, April 6, 1905: 22.

19. Alfred Henry Spink, *The National Game: A History of Baseball, America's Leading Out-door Sport, from the Time It Was First Played Up to the Present Day, With Illustrations and Biographical Sketches* (St. Louis: National Game Publishing Co, 1911), 144.

20. "Buckenberger's Band Trounces Royals in Two Sharp Contests," *Rochester Democrat and Chronicle*, July 5, 1906: 14.

21. "Royals Ship Mattern," *Rochester Democrat and Chronicle*, July 28, 1906: 14.

22. *Rochester Democrat and Chronicle*, September 22 and September 30, 1906.

23. "Holyoke Wins Pennant," *Springfield* (Massachusetts) *Republican*, September 15, 1907: 14.

24. "Mattern for Tenney's," *Boston Herald*, August 4, 1907: 6.

25. "Sporting News. Trenton Secures Great Left-Hander From Boston," *Trenton* (New Jersey) *Evening Times*, March 19, 1908: 2.

26. "Sidelights on the Game," *Brooklyn Daily Eagle*, August 4, 1909: 18.

27. "Mattern Is Great While He Is In," *Boston Herald*, September 17, 1908: 5.

28. "Champions Beat Doves but Pitcher Mattern Gives Them Big Scare," *Boston Journal*, September 17, 1908: 8.

29 "Boston Nations Will Cavort Over Diamond Today," *Boston Journal*, March 8, 1909: 9.

30 "Doves and Giants in 17-Inning Tie," *Boston Journal*, July 27, 1909: 1.

31 Fred J. Hoey, "Martel Lauded as Train Wreck Hero," *Boston Journal*, April 8, 1910: 1, 11.

32 "Sweeney and Shean Humble the Giants," *Boston Journal*, April 15, 1910: 11.

33 "Wives of the Ball Players," *Boston Journal*, August 22, 1911: 5.

34 "Pitcher Mattern is Sold to Montreal Club," *Boston Journal*, April 22, 1912: 8.

35 "Leading Citizen of Rush Is Too Much for Clymer's Head," *Rochester Democrat and Chronicle*, June 4, 1913: 21.

36 "Hustlers Give Montreal No Time to Get Steadied," *Rochester Democrat and Chronicle*, May 27, 1914: 23.

37 "Double Play Puts Kibosh on Birds in Final Turn at Bat," *Rochester Democrat and Chronicle*, July 18, 1914: 15.

38 "Poor Lo Strews Tacks in Road to Pennantville," *Rochester Democrat and Chronicle*, September 15, 1914: 18.

39 "Reds Sign Mattern," *Pittsburgh Post-Gazette*, May 15, 1915: 15.

40 "Upsetting Blow to Herd Conceit in the Seventh," *Rochester Democrat and Chronicle*, May 12, 1915: 23.

41 "Mattern with Semi-Pros," *Rochester Democrat and Chronicle*, August 22, 1915: 31.

42 "Al Mattern is Signed to Work in City League," *Rochester Democrat and Chronicle*, July 9, 1916: 24.

43 Ibid.

44 "Husky Farmers Wallop Jockeys," *Canandaigua* (New York) *Daily Messenger*, July 13, 1925: 6.

45 "Father and Son Battery on Ball Team," *Ogdensburg* (New York) *Republican-Journal*, July 12, 1926: 2.

46 From Jacqueline DeCook, great-niece of Al Mattern. Email correspondence with the author, August 2, 2016.

47 Bill Beeney, "The Towns Around Us: Indian Villages Once Dotted Rush Area," *Rochester Democrat and Chronicle*, June 19, 1955: 5C.

48 As noted above, his professional career technically began with Rochester in 1901.

49 "Al Mattern Honored; Photo in Hall of Fame," *Rochester Democrat and Chronicle*, February 21, 1955: 24.

# JAMES MCCORMICK

## BY CHRIS RAINEY

**JAMES MCCORMICK AMASSED 265** victories from 1878 to 1887 in the National League and the Union Association. He possessed an excellent fastball and was one of the earliest pitchers to master the curveball. His repertoire also included a "drop" ball. Many fans believe he is an overlooked candidate for the Hall of Fame. Baseball-Reference, for instance, has a Hall of Fame Monitor ranking that gives McCormick 194 points. (A "likely" Hall of Famer would have approximately 100 points.[1]) Because McCormick pitched from less than 60 feet 6 inches and was prohibited from throwing overhand for half his career, he has not been given serious consideration.

McCormick was a husky (5-feet-11 and 225 pounds in his prime), "lovable fellow with many admirable qualities."[2] With the Cleveland Blues from 1879 to 1882, he was the "club's premier pitcher and the idol of baseball fans everywhere."[3] Despite the accolades, McCormick lost 128 games in that span while winning 127. The 128 losses were the most by any pitcher over four consecutive seasons.

McCormick was the son of James and Rosa (Lawry) McCormick. They were both born in Ireland, but moved to Scotland in search of a better life. James, called "Jimsy" by friends to avoid confusion with his father and later his son, was born in Glasgow on November 3, 1856. He was the third of six children, four born in Scotland and two in the United States. The family came to America in 1865 after hostilities had ceased in the Civil War. They settled in Paterson, New Jersey, where the father worked as a shoemaker and his mother as a housekeeper. McCormick had minimal schooling, possibly through the sixth grade. In the 1870 census he was listed as a cotton-mill worker when he was 13 years old.

Paterson was a hotbed for baseball. As a teenager, McCormick played with future Hall of Famer Mike "King" Kelly, along with future major leaguers Blondie Purcell, Edward "The Only" Nolan, and John "Kick" Kelly, on a team called the Keystones.[4] Pitcher Nolan left the club in 1876 to join the Columbus Buckeyes, an early minor-league franchise. McCormick, with his red mustache and blue eyes, took over as pitcher. The Buckeyes recruited McCormick in 1877. When they disbanded in September, he was picked up by the Indianapolis Blues. Indianapolis joined the National League in 1878 and McCormick became the change pitcher for the flamethrowing Nolan. McCormick's first major-league appearance came May 20 against the Chicago White Stockings. The Blues dropped the game to Cap Anson's men by a 3-1 score and banged out only one hit in support of McCormick.

McCormick weathered injuries to make 14 starts and post a 5-8 record. On July 11, in a game against Boston, he broke a small bone in his forearm[5] and was sidelined all of August. The *Indianapolis News* opined, "It is doubtful he will ever be enabled to pitch a ball again."[6] Reports of McCormick's demise were premature because he was back in the box on September 3. His luck was no better as he broke a finger fielding a grounder. A plucky competitor, he took his spot on September 7 against Milwaukee and won 15-6. Indianapolis lost money in 1878 and failed to make the final payroll. McCormick reportedly lost $300 in salary.[7]

The franchise was shifted to Cleveland for 1879 and retained the Blues moniker. McCormick was originally supposed to be the change pitcher for left-hander Bobby Mitchell.[8] Mitchell had slightly more experience than McCormick and as a left-hander he would be unique to the opposing batters. The Boston Red Stockings had the only other lefty in the league to see regular work, change pitcher Curry Foley. McCormick's early-season performance was so impressive that he won the number-one spot. But Cleveland featured the league's worst team batting, on-base, and slugging averages. Coupled with a below-average fielding percentage (.889) makes a 27-55 team won-lost mark no surprise. McCormick went 20-40 and appeared in the box for 546⅓ innings with a 2.42 ERA. His ERA was seventh in the league and ahead of three number-one pitchers. His 40 losses tied him with George Bradley of last-place Troy. Mitchell went 7-15, but with an ERA of 3.28.

After the season McCormick returned to Paterson and opened a saloon. He stayed in the business for more than 30 years with varying degrees of success. He also joined King Kelly and others on a New York all-star team. Perhaps the time he spent in that city led one anonymous baseball insider to suggest that "McCormick's great ambition is to have a saloon in New York like Clapp and Lynch (catcher and pitcher from various teams in and around New York)."[9] There is no evidence that McCormick ever expanded beyond Paterson. He became a member of the Elks and remained an active member his whole life.

Many publications have listed McCormick as the "manager" of the Cleveland Blues. In those days a team manager was more the business leader than the leader on the field. The team captain was more likely to handle the lineup and substitutions. The manager for Cleveland in 1879 was Joe Mack. According to numerous entries in the *Cleveland Leader*, shortstop Tom Carey was team captain. In 1880 Mack and Carey moved on to other baseball endeavors. Early speculation was that Fred Dunlap or Orator Shafer would earn the captain's role. The team executive committee, headed by Ford Evans and Charles H. Bulkeley, named McCormick the captain on April 13.[10]

Cleveland revamped its roster, adding Shaffer, Dunlap, Pete Hotaling, Ned Hanlon, and Frank Hankinson to join holdovers McCormick, Bill Phillips, Jack Glasscock, and Doc Kennedy. The team batting average improved 19 points and the fielding totals were near the top of the league. With this added support, McCormick fashioned a 45-28 (the team record was 47-37) mark in 657⅔ innings. He led the league in wins, complete games, and innings pitched, and finished fifth in ERA and second in strikeouts. The team took third place, 20 games off the pace set by Chicago. Modern-day statisticians give McCormick a WAR (wins above replacement) of 10.4—far above any of his competitors.

The National League increased the pitching distance to 50 feet in 1881, but maintained the release point below the waist. McCormick chose to step down as team captain, and third baseman Mike McGeary was the choice of president Evans. McGeary's tenure ended on May 19 and John Clapp took over as captain. McCormick was the workhorse again, leading the league in complete games while going 26-30. His backup was "The Only" Nolan.

In 1882 McCormick led the league with 36 wins as well as complete games and innings. His pitching WAR of 11.2 surpassed his 1880 season, but Cleveland still finished fifth. Partway through the 1882 season, the National League changed the pitching rules to allow the ball to be released below the shoulder.[11]

In 1883 five of the eight teams in the National League dropped the practice of a number-one man coupled with a "change" pitcher. They instead went to a two-man rotation with a third pitcher on the roster.

Cleveland brought in Hugh "One Arm" Daily to pair with McCormick. Daily went 23-19 in 378⅔ innings. McCormick was 28-12 in 342 innings. Their third pitcher was Will Sawyer, who went 4-10 in 141 innings. The lighter workload agreed with McCormick. He led the league in winning percentage (.700) and ERA (1.84).

The Union Association was formed in 1884 to compete with the National League and the American Association. Suddenly there were 28 major-league franchises that lasted more than 50 games and 5 that dropped out along the way. America's baseball talent was spread exceptionally thin and teams paid the price for their talent. Daily was an early signee with the Union Association. Cleveland replaced him with two rookies, John Harkins and Sam Moffet, to join McCormick in the box. The roster was also thin in the outfield and the trio of McCormick, Harkins, and Moffet made 67 appearances in the outfield. McCormick, who normally batted eighth or ninth, was elevated to the fifth spot in a lineup that struggled offensively.

McCormick suffered bouts with a lame arm that made him worry about his future. His catcher, Fatty Briody, had squandered all of his money and entertained thoughts of jumping leagues to help his finances. Briody, McCormick, and Jack Glasscock offered to be bought out by ownership with the intent of changing leagues. Cleveland management refused but looked into selling them to another team. It all came to a head in August.

On August 8 McCormick, Briody, and Glasscock met with officials of the Cincinnati Union Association club. The trio signed contracts to jump to the new league with a $1,000 bonus per man. Glasscock and Briody signed $1,500 contracts while McCormick signed for the same $2,500 he was making in Cleveland.[12] In a bizarre twist, the trio played an exhibition game for Cleveland against Grand Rapids about an hour after inking their Cincinnati contract. This arrangement was made possible by the friendship of manager Charlie Hackett with Cincinnati president Justus Thorner.[13] The Blues replaced the trio of defectors with players from the Grand Rapids squad after the game.

Briody summed up the decision to jump by saying, "I presume we will be blacklisted, but we have been playing ball for glory long enough. It is now a matter of dollars and cents."[14] Nine players were blacklisted during 1884, including the Cleveland trio. After the season, owner Henry Lucas of the Union Association St Louis Maroons convinced National League owners that admitting his team to the league would be a money-making proposition for all of them. Lucas also campaigned to remove the players from the blacklist and instead have them pay a fine. The owners agreed, and two levels of fines, $500 and $1,000, were created. The Cleveland players all were placed at the $1,000 level. All three played in 1885, but how the fine situation was handled is uncertain.

On August 10 McCormick took the box for Cincinnati against the league-leading St. Louis Maroons and came away with a 7-4 victory. He joined the Outlaw Reds (also known as the Cincinnati Unions) with the team in fourth place. Over the next 42 games they would climb to second, but still finish 21 games behind the Maroons. McCormick was in top form and posted a 21-3 record. The team went 35-7 over the last stretch of games. Glasscock and Briody contributed glowing statistics. Glasscock hit .419 and Briody .337. McCormick had posted a 19-22 mark in Cleveland. His combined workload with both teams made his WAR an astounding 14.5, tied for 10th best pitching value of all time. McCormick appears three times on the list of the 100 highest single-season pitching WAR's in the majors. Only Walter Johnson (7), Kid Nichols (4), Cy Young (4), and Tommy Bond (4) have more.[15]

McCormick joined Providence in 1885 as the third pitcher behind Hoss Radbourn and Dupee Shaw. He was given a contract for $2,500, which was extravagant considering that he was used only four times in 10 weeks. He had a 1-3 mark when Cap Anson contacted the Grays about his services. The White Stockings needed a partner to team with John Clarkson. The Grays announced McCormick's release on July 10 and then swapped him to Chicago for George Van Haltren and $2,000.

McCormick proved to be the perfect partner for Clarkson, who fashioned a 53-16 record (13.1 WAR). McCormick was 20-4 with the league's eighth best ERA (2.43). The White Stockings won the pennant by two games over New York and faced the American Association champions from St. Louis in the postseason. The seven-game series ended in a tie, three wins for each squad and a tie game. McCormick posted a 3-2 mark in the series. McCormick earned a lifelong fan in manager Cap Anson, who called him "one of the best men … that ever sent a ball whizzing across the plate."[16]

McCormick was paired with Paterson buddy Mike Kelly on the White Stockings. When the buddies returned to New Jersey they were given a parade that wound through the streets of the city. After the politicians feted them before an adoring crowd, "they drank all night in David Treado's saloon."[17] McCormick and Treado became partners in the saloon/café business soon after.

Over the winter the National League owners tightened their belts and established a maximum salary of $2,000. McCormick was not pleased with a drop in pay, so owner Al Spalding wrote up a contract to cover the difference. If McCormick abstained from "malt or spirituous liquor" from mid-March to the end of October he would be given a $350 bonus. If Chicago won the league championship he would receive another $150.[18]

McCormick got off to a fantastic start on way to a 31-11 mark. However his performances became more and more erratic in the second half. By the time the postseason rolled around he was complaining of arm troubles and rheumatism. In his only start against St. Louis in the postseason, he was pounded, 12-0, and surrendered two home runs to Tip O'Neill as St. Louis won the series, four games to two.

In December when the White Stockings sent out contracts for 1887, they did not extend offers to McCormick, Kelly, Ned Williamson, Silver Flint, and George Gore. That quintet plus Billy Sunday had been noted for their fondness for alcoholic beverages. Sunday had realized his problem and made a well-publicized life change. As the story unfolded over days in the *Chicago Tribune* and other newspapers, the details emerged that Spalding had special bonus contracts with all five of the players. He had Pinkerton detectives follow them and make reports on their temperance habits. Based upon the Pinkerton findings, he called the players together during the season and fined them $25 apiece. This also cost McCormick his $350 bonus.

"After that they were just as bad and I am sorry to have to admit they were in no condition to play the Browns," Al Spalding said.[19] In January Spalding was still fuming about McCormick's performance in the postseason. Of McCormick's claim of rheumatism, he said, "Rheumatism! Bah! It was drink and nothing but drink. … He drank about as much as all the rest of them put together."[20]

None of the players got their bonus money from Spalding and when Flint and Williamson eventually re-signed, they had temperance clauses in their contracts. Gore signed with New York, and Kelly moved on to Boston. After much speculation as to where he would play, McCormick signed with the Pittsburgh Alleghenys and was teamed with Pud Galvin and Ed Morris. McCormick signed for $2,500 and took nearly two weeks to get into shape before making his first appearance on May 13. He dropped a 3-2 decision to Indianapolis. More losses followed, including a 16-12 loss to New York in which he surrendered 28 hits and allowed 10 runs in the last two innings. His arm was still working into strong condition and he was unwilling to cut loose and throw his best heat. After a winless May, he finally beat Chicago on June 9. Pittsburgh finished the campaign with a 55-69 record. McCormick was 13-23, Morris 14-22, and Galvin 28-21. Only on rare occasions did McCormick show the skill he had in earlier times.

Nevertheless, Pittsburgh harbored hopes that McCormick would return in 1888. *Sporting Life* mentioned his name in nearly every edition. There was even a suggestion that McCormick wanted a three-year deal at $4,000 a year. What the front office did not know was that McCormick's wife, Jennie, was ill with consumption (tuberculosis). She died on August 21, 1888, at the home in Paterson. When Cap Anson heard the news, "his stern and rigid mind became at once sympathetic in the extreme." Anson remarked, "(T)hat is the greatest loss poor Mac can suffer. … God only knows what I would do were I to lose my wife."[21] King Kelly left his Boston teammates and went to Paterson to console McCormick. Kelly had a local florist make a tremendous floral wreath and then served as a pallbearer at the funeral. McCormick was left to raise a son, James, and daughter, Francis, on his own.

McCormick juggled his domestic duties with the saloon business until 1916, when he retired. He came down with a liver illness and lived with James, a police patrolman, in Paterson, for nearly a year before being admitted to the hospital. He died there on March 10, 1918.[22] When informed of his death, evangelist and former teammate Billy Sunday said, "He was one of the best pals I ever had."[23] He was buried in the Elks Plot of Laurel Grove Memorial Park in nearby Totowa, New Jersey.

## SOURCES

My sincere thanks to Bruce Bardarik at the Paterson library for providing important background. Also a tip of the hat to Eric Miklich as noted below.

## NOTES

1. baseball-reference.com/players/m/mccorji01.shtml. Scroll down to near the bottom of the page and see the "Hall of Fame Statistics" section.
2. Alfred C. Cappio, "Paterson's Jim McCormick," *Bulletin of the Passaic County Historical Society*, Vol. 5, No. 5, October 1961: 80-86. This excellent work has far too many anecdotes to relate here. This is the source of the nickname "Jimsy." See also W.R. Rose, "All in a Day's Work," *Cleveland Plain Dealer*, March 13, 1918. Reports on his size vary at 5-feet-10 and 5-feet-11 with a weight from 210 to 225.
3. W.R. Rose.
4. Peter M. Gordon, "King Kelly," SABR BioProject, sabr.org/bioproj/person/ffc40dac.
5. "McCormick Breaks a Bone in His Arm and the Bostons Score an Unearned Victory," *Indianapolis News*, July 12, 1878: 4.
6. *Indianapolis News*, August 24: 4.
7. *Indianapolis News*, October 24, 1878: 1.
8. William McMahon, "James McCormick," *Nineteenth Century Stars* (Cleveland: SABR, 1989), 85.
9. "Talks and Thoughts," *Cleveland Plain Dealer*, August 16, 1884: 2.
10. "In and Outdoor Sports," *Cleveland Leader*, April 14, 1880: 1.
11. 19cbaseball.com. This website is maintained by SABR member Eric Miklich and is used here for the various rule changes during McCormick's career. Eric was kind enough to advise me through emails in August 2016.
12. "Baseball Players Desert," *New York Tribune*, August 8, 1884: 2. The *Philadelphia Times*, October 23, 1887: 14, used figures of $800 for Briody, $1,200 for Glasscock and $1,600 for McCormick.
13. *Cincinnati Enquirer*, August 9, 1884: 2.
14. Ibid.
15. baseball-reference.com/leaders/WAR_pitch_season.shtml. Accessed on September 4, 2016.
16. McMahon.
17. Al Del Greco, "The Silk City and Big Jimsey," *Paterson Morning Call*, July 6, 1967: 20.
18. "Only Temperance Men: President Spalding Will Have No Others Next Year," *Chicago Tribune*, December 2, 1882: 2.
19. Ibid.
20. "Chicago Ball Men," *Philadelphia Times*, January 16, 1887: 11.
21. "McCormick's Great Loss," *Pittsburgh Daily Post*, August 22, 1888: 6
22. "Famous Old-Time Ballplayer Dead," *Paterson Morning Call*, March 11, 1918: 3.
23. "Sunday Offers Tribute to Dead Pal of Old Days," *Chicago Tribune*, March 11, 1918: 1.

# ULYSSES SIMPSON GRANT "STONEY" MCGLYNN

## BY STEVEN SCHMITT

**ULYSSES SIMPSON GRANT "STONEY"** McGlynn pitched one full season in the major leagues at age 35 and lost 25 games for the cellar-dwelling St. Louis Cardinals. But he set National League records for work—innings pitched, batters faced, and complete games—while winning 14 games and completing 33 starts. For more than 30 years, McGlynn was called the "Iron Man of Baseball" for his durability as a semiprofessional, minor-league and major-league pitcher who pitched both ends of doubleheaders and extra-inning marathons that produced glorious victories and agonizing defeats.

He was born on May 26, 1872, in Lancaster, Pennsylvania, one of eight children of Anthony (1825-1874) and Anna E. McGlinn (1834-1906). His father served as a Union infantry private in the Civil War and worked as a carpenter in Lancaster. McGlynn's grandfather, Anthony McGlinn Sr., was a mortician in the city. Anna Elisabeth was born in Charleston, South Carolina, and raised the children.[1]

"Grant" broke into baseball at the age of 15, earning $10 as an emergency catcher for Easton of the Pennsylvania State League, later signing for $125 a month. He caught for his high-school team in Carlisle, Pennsylvania, and played catcher, shortstop, and third base for Cumberland Valley, a Pennsylvania-based semiprofessional team. In 1895, McGlynn played shortstop and third base for Harrisburg in the Pennsylvania State League. When he pitched the first of 399 games over a five-year period, McGlynn struck out 22 batters in an astounding victory.[2]

On September 12, 1895, McGlynn married Bertha Bousum at Harrisburg, Pennsylvania. They had one son, Charles G. (1903-1975), a star pitcher for the Manitowoc Vans of the Lake Shore League in the 1920s and early 1930s who became director of purchasing at Mirro Aluminum Co. of Manitowoc, and two daughters—Ida, who worked for the local M&M Printing Company, and Marguerite, a member of the Cobb's Musical Comedy Co. in Prairie du Chien, Wisconsin.[3]

Little is known about McGlynn's career until 1899, when he pitched for the Susquehannas against Elizabethtown on June 4.[4] In April 1900, the *Harrisburg Telegraph* reported that McGlynn was "considered one of the best all-round ball players in this city, and has a number of offers to play with amateur teams."[5] McGlynn pitched for the Harrisburg Athletic Club for the next two seasons. In 1902, McGlynn played right field and first base for Lancaster until the Pennsylvania League folded in May. On July 20, he pitched for Harrisburg, losing 6-5. On August 22, McGlynn returned there as the opposing pitcher for the Chester, Pennsylvania, club, "enthusiastically greeted by his hosts of friends among the fans," and defeated his old club, 10-4.[6]

In 1903, McGlynn joined the York (Pennsylvania) Penn Parks of the independent Tri-State League. From 1904 through 1906, he won 94 games and lost 37. In 1904, McGlynn posted a 30-11 record and shut out Harrisburg, 1-0, on June 11, enduring hoots, jeers, the blasting of tin horns, and shouts through megaphones from a hostile crowd (perhaps upset over his defection to Chester two years earlier). His mother, a full-blooded Cherokee, cheered and clapped from the grandstand and McGlynn kept his eye on her throughout. "The shouts and jeers from the bleachers and grand stand didn't worry her," the *Harrisburg Telegraph* reported. "She wanted her son to win the game and he did."[7]

The Penn Parks won Tri-State titles in 1904 and again in 1906, when McGlynn won 36 and lost 10. On July 3, 1906, the *Philadelphia Inquirer*, reporting on McGlynn's 4-3 win for York over Lancaster, observed, "The iron man again proved his worth."[8]

McGlynn had repeatedly rejected offers to sign with Joe Cantillon's Washington Senators and refused to report to the Shreveport Pirates of the Southern League in 1905 and 1906 because of his contract with the York club. In the summer of 1906, McGlynn took $1,000 from the Class-D Steubenville Stubs of the Pennsylvania-Ohio-Maryland League. In the September 15 issue of *Sporting Life*, Washington correspondent Paul W. Eaton announced that the Senators had signed McGlynn but Shreveport invoked its contract with McGlynn and sent him to the St. Louis Cardinals. At age 34, McGlynn's major-league career began.

McGlynn pitched six complete games for the Cardinals from September 20 to October 7 and posted a 2-2 record. (Two games ended in ties.) A *Sporting Life* scribe wrote that McGlynn was "the oldest young blood that ever broke into the National League. 'Stony' shows his years in his face but not in his arm. He says he feels better now than he ever did and is good for ten years of active service."[9] On October 7, McGlynn pitched an 11-inning, 3-3 tie with the National League champion Chicago Cubs, seeking their 117th victory.

McGlynn considered quitting the game after becoming a police officer in York in November 1906, but he resigned and reported to the Cardinals' spring-training camp at Houston on March 1 after a brief holdout. "I got into Houston at four in the morning," McGlynn recalled years later. "I woke (Cardinals manager John J. McCloskey) and told him, 'Your iron man is here.' He bawled me out for having missed two weeks of training."[10]

"Stoney McGlynn is regarded by (McCloskey) as one of the greatest pitchers in the country," the *St. Louis Post Dispatch* reported, "and in pinches he is invincible."[11] In 1907, McGlynn led the National League with 352⅓ innings, 39 starts, 33 complete games, and 1,426 batters faced. Of course, McGlynn also led the league in losses (25), hits allowed (329), earned runs allowed (114), and bases on balls (112). On April 27, he lost a 12-inning game to the eventual world champion Cubs, allowing just three singles in the first six innings.[12] On June 3, McGlynn pitched two complete games in a doubleheader, winning the first game, 1-0, in 10 innings but losing the second, 5-1.[13] "McGlynn might have pitched a dozen doubleheaders and won them in the Punktown League," the *Post-Dispatch* opined, "but in the National, where the brand of ball is a bit different, he should have been satisfied with his opening triumph."[14]

McGlynn had his share of "blowups" in the late innings and made wild throws that cost games, but many defeats came from a lack of offensive support or poor defense. Still, McGlynn was the Iron Man. On July 28, he pitched a 10-inning, 1-0 shutout in the first game of a doubleheader with Brooklyn. On August 10, he beat Boston, 3-2, pitching with a broken left index finger suffered in an August 6 exhibition game against Burlington (Iowa). In winning four of his last eight decisions, McGlynn beat the Cubs, 7-2, on September 1 at the West Side Grounds and pitched all 14 innings of a 4-4 tie with the Cubs on September 11 at Chicago. He finished with a 14-25 record and a 2.91 ERA.

In January 1908, rumors flew about McGlynn returning to the York police force, buying his release from St. Louis or pitching in an outlaw league. The Cardinals also explored trading him for another Iron Man, Joe McGinnity of the New York Giants. They also coveted veteran infielder Hans Lobert of the Cincinnati Reds, who released two pitchers in hopes of acquiring McGlynn, but Lobert refused to go to St. Louis.[15]

McGlynn stayed in shape roller-skating during the winter months and McCloskey told writers that McGlynn and Bugs Raymond were ready for the season. The 1908 season proved otherwise. McGlynn managed one victory against six defeats, completing four of six starts and making 10 relief appearances. He worked only 75⅔ innings and faced only 316 batters. His iron-man work had apparently turned him into a rusty piece of scrap metal.

Instead, McGlynn became a record-setting Iron Man for the Milwaukee Brewers of the Class-A American Association in 1909. Reunited with manager McCloskey, McGlynn tossed a record 14 shutouts, won 27 of 48 decisions and worked 446 innings as Milwaukee won 90 games and finished second, 2½ games behind the Louisville Colonels. On May 9, McGlynn blanked the Colonels, 6-0. Eleven thousand fans filled Milwaukee's Athletic Park stands or sat four-deep in the outfield. A 2-0 shutout of Minneapolis on May 28 gave the first-place Brewers a four-game lead over Louisville. In early June, McGlynn took "an enforced vacation" because of a hip injury and a stomach disorder, then returned June 30 to win three straight games in one week, including two more shutouts, one of them a one-hit gem at home against the Colonels.[16]

On July 21, McGlynn beat Louisville twice in one day, 9-1 and 3-2, to put the Brewers within one game of first place. "I suppose that the people back home will jump on McCloskey for overworking me," McGlynn said. "Overworking, nothing, why when I am feeling good I could work every day and Mac never has to force me into a game." McGlynn believed four or five days' rest caused pitchers' arms to stiffen up. He claimed never to have had a sore arm because of his practice of putting his prize pitching tool under a hot shower until it turned red.[17]

On September 15, McGlynn pitched both games of a doubleheader against hard-charging Louisville, winning 5-2 and losing, 1-0. He started the next day but twisted an ankle on the pitching rubber in the first inning and left the game. He returned on the 20th and blanked Indianapolis, 1-0. Despite McGlynn's courageous work, the Brewers lost 16 of their last 21 games and finished second.

In January 1910, McGlynn signed with the Brewers for an undisclosed pay raise but the Iron Man slumped to 16-21 and Milwaukee won just 76 games. A June 1 article in the *Green Bay Press-Gazette* observed, "'Stoney' worked too hard in 1909, evidenced by the rough start in 1910."[18] He had spent the offseason doing roller-skating stunts

on the vaudeville circuit. After Milwaukee's April 6 exhibition victory at the University of Illinois, he performed at the Orpheum Theater in Champaign with pitcher Hippo Hammond, who sang baritone. Despite strong showings against the University of Illinois and Marquette University in spring training, McGlynn did not get the Opening Day starting assignment. Instead, Ralph Cutting ("another McGlynn," according to McCloskey), beat St. Paul, 2-1.[19] Cutting, 21-game winner Bill Schardt, and newcomer Jack "Rube" Gilligan pushed McGlynn into a spot starter-reliever role.

McGlynn did not win his first game until April 28, when he beat eventual league champion Minneapolis, 3-2 in 10 innings. He pitched a 12-inning shutout at St. Paul on May 22, blanked Indianapolis on May 31, and hurled another 1-0 shutout of Columbus June 19 for his seventh victory.

McGlynn ended July losing two consecutive starts and endured hoots from home fans when he made an August 6 relief appearance. He rebounded in September, "steady as a Grand Avenue cop," beating Kansas City, 3-1 on September 4.[20] Five days later, McGlynn fanned 11 St. Paul Saints in a 3-2 victory and beat them in relief the next day, driving in the winning run.[21]

In 1911, McGlynn won 22 games for player-manager Jimmy Barrett. The *Milwaukee Sentinel* reported that McGlynn "was as strong as a piece of twelve inch armor plate and he is never out of condition. The wing will probably retain all its strength and keenness for years."[22] McGlynn shut out Indianapolis, 4-0, April 14, striking out eight, but did not win again until May 12, when he beat first-place Minneapolis, 5-2.[23] It seemed all over for McGlynn when he was removed from an 11-5 defeat on May 16 and lost his next two starts. Not so. The Iron Man returned June 6 and tossed a two-hit, 1-0 shutout at St. Paul.[24] On June 13, the "galvanized wonder" blanked Indianapolis, 6-0, and the June 14 *Indianapolis Star* account read, "Nay, nay, Pauline! Stoney McGlynn, the imperial steel man, is not ready for the scrap heap just yet."[25]

McGlynn abruptly left the team on June 23 after he missed a turn because of an apparent illness and the Brewers docked him several days' pay.[26] On July 2, he returned and won both ends of a doubleheader at Columbus and won his next two starts. From July 14 to July 31, Stoney won six of seven decisions.[27] A six-game losing streak ended on September 17 with another Iron Man performance. McGlynn won both games of a doubleheader from Indianapolis, 3-2 and 4-3.[28] After another double win over Louisville on September 26, newspapers across the country crowed about the "Stone Man of old." On October 2, only darkness after four innings prevented McGlynn from claiming another twin bill over St. Paul at Milwaukee.[29]

On November 1, Barrett resigned as manager and Hugh Duffy took the reins. Stoney lost 8-1 at Toledo on April 11, 1912, made two relief appearances and was cut loose. The *Indianapolis News* reported McGlynn's release on April 30 as "the passing of one of the greatest pitchers that ever worked (in the American Association)."[30]

In May, the Brewers sold McGlynn to Mobile of the Southern Association but McGlynn instead moved to Manitowoc, Wisconsin, where he pitched for the Lake Shore League semiprofessional club. He was selected as the number 2 pitcher on the Lake Shore All-Stars, having signed with McCloskey's Ogden (Utah) Canners of the Class-D Union Association but not reporting.[31]

Manitowoc skipper Jack Herzog expected McGlynn to sign with McCloskey's Salt Lake City club (Union Association) for 1913 after the Skyscrapers bought Stoney's contract from the Brewers. McGlynn spurned the offer, saying the salary would not cover his losses for moving west.[32] He changed his mind, arrived in Salt Lake on July 31 and beat Great Falls, 4-2, on August 1, belting a three-run home run that landed 100 feet beyond the outfield fence.[33] "Salt Lake at last has a baseball hero," the *Salt Lake City Herald-Republican* beamed. In mid-August McGlynn made four relief appearances in five days and regularly saved victories for the Skyscrapers, who were in a virtual tie with Great Falls (Montana) on September 6. The following day, McGlynn started, was removed in the fifth with the score tied, and Salt Lake lost to its rivals, 10-5. The lack of pitching depth cost the 75-47 club a pennant.

In 1914, the Brewers cut all ties with McGlynn, who returned to Manitowoc. On June 28, he pitched a 12-inning shutout against Sheboygan at the Manitowoc Fair Grounds that ended in a scoreless tie because of darkness. On August 16, McGlynn hurled another doubleheader against Sheboygan, winning the nightcap with a 2-0 shutout. The following season, McGlynn joined McCloskey at a new outpost—El Paso of the Rio Grande Association (the Union Association folded in 1914). He won seven of his first eight decisions but finished 9-9.

In March 1916, McGlynn became pitching coach for the University of Illinois and pitched for Manitowoc's Lake Shore League team that summer. He pitched his final game on September 2 and decided to retire and devote his energies to coaching college teams. In 1918 he applied to be an umpire in the American Association but learned there were no openings, so he umpired in the Lake Shore and Fox River Valley Leagues and in 1923, the new Wisconsin State League.[34] In 1920, he became part owner of the Manitowoc Vans when manager John F. "Jack" Herzog retired. His son, Charles G., referred to as Stoney in the local newspapers, pitched for the club, firing eight no-hit innings in a Manitowoc victory on June 22.[35] Young Charlie led Manitowoc to the 1928 Lake Shore title with a 16-6 record and once fanned 18 pitching for Sturgeon Bay of the Cherry League in 1924.[36] Like father, like son.

The elder McGlynn continued to umpire through the 1920s, coached his employer's baseball team, the Aluminum Goods Co., in 1926, and became an executive as president of the eight-team Tri-State Amateur Circuit in 1928. The league included Manitowoc and seven other teams, mostly from southeastern Wisconsin and the Fox River Valley.[37]

He also became a hero. A lifeguard at Manitowoc's South Side bathing beach, McGlynn and a companion rescued two boys whose makeshift wooden raft had gone adrift from a strong west wind. A Northwestern Railroad switching crew saw the boys in peril and notified McGlynn, who boarded a rowboat from the beach and brought the boys to safety.[38]

In October 1931, "Stoney" McGlynn pitched his final game, an exhibition tilt at Milwaukee's Borchert Field, formerly Athletic Park. Seven years later, McGlynn attended a Milwaukee Brewers game at the same park and told their 23-game winner Whitlow Wyatt, "I hope you not only tie my record, lad, but go out and crack it," referring to the 14 shutouts McGlynn tossed in 1909.[39] The Iron Man once said he could get $60,000 in 1930s dollars for his pitching skills. But baseball was more than money to someone who gave it all and more for good teams and bad. And he gave back to his new-found Manitowoc community right up to his death on August 26, 1941, at age 69. Fifty decisions and a losing record in the majors (17-33) do not measure this man, whose likes will never be seen again.

## SOURCES

In addition to the sources cited in the Notes, the author also consulted Baseball-Reference.com, Newspapers.com, and the *El Paso Herald*.

## NOTES

1 "Ulysses Simpson Grant 'Stoney' McGlynn," Find a Grave Memorial. McGlynn/Ulysses%20Simpson%20 Grant%20_Stoney_%20McGlynn%20(1872%20-%201941)%20 -%20Find%20A%20Grave%20Memorial.html. Accessed June 6, 2017; Ancestry.com. Headstones Provided for Deceased Union Civil War Veterans 1861-1904. Ancestry.com. Headstones Provided for Deceased Union Civil War Veterans 1861-1904. ancestry.com/interactive/1195/MIUSA1879_113705- 00044?pid=66415&backurl=http://search.ancestry.com/cgi-bin/ sse.dll?indiv%3D1%26db%3DCivilWarHeadstones%26h%3D 66415%26tid%3D%26pid%3D%26usePUB%3Dtrue%26usePU BJs%3Dtrue%26rhSource%3D60525&treeid=&personid=&hi ntid=&usePUB=true&usePUBJs=true. Accessed June 5, 2017; Lancaster County Directory, 1869-70, Anthony McGlinn. Ancestry.com; Pennsylvania Death Certificates, 1906-1964, Anna Elisabeth McGlinn. Ancestry.com.

2 "Penn'a League," *Sporting Life*, June 24, 1901: 13; *Sporting Life*. May 31, 1902: 9; "Penn Park Took 'Em Both." *York (Pennsylvania) Daily*, August 26, 1903: 5.

3 Obituaries—McGlynn. *Manitowoc Herald-Times*, July 18, 1975: 3; "Engagement of Young People Is Announced," *Manitowoc Herald-Times*, January 2, 1923: 8.

4 *Harrisburg Telegraph*, May 31, 1899: 5.

# 20-GAME LOSERS

5 *Harrisburg Telegraph,* April 24, 1900: 2.

6 *Harrisburg Daily Independent,* August 23, 1902: 7.

7 "Five Out of Seven Lost to York." *Harrisburg Telegraph,* July 6, 1904: 9.

8 *Philadelphia Inquirer,* July 3, 1906.

9 "McGlynn No Youth," *Sporting Life,* October 20, 1906: 13.

10 Sam Levy, "'Iron Man' Told Whit About Arm," *Manitowoc Herald-Times,* August 30, 1938: 8.

11 "Nie's Column," *St. Louis Post-Dispatch,* March 8, 1907: 14.

12 "Long Game Away," *St. Louis-Post Dispatch,* April 28, 1907: 36.

13 "June 3, 1907: Stoney McGlynn's Iron Man Pitching Performance in Cincy," in *On This Day in Cardinal Nation — Preserving the Rich History of the St. Louis Cardinals,* June 3, 2015. onthisdayincardinalnation.com/2015/06/june-3-1907-stoney-mcglynn-has-iron-man.html. Accessed February 22, 2017; "Reds Get Even Break," *Cincinnati Enquirer,* June 4, 1907.

14 "St. Louis Players Burn Up American Association," *St. Louis Post-Dispatch,* June 5, 1907: 14.

15 "National League News," *Sporting Life,* January 4, 1908: 3; Ren Mulford Jr., "National League News. In Grave Peril," *Sporting Life,* January 18, 1908: 3; "Chicago Chat. Condensed Dispatches," *Sporting Life,* May 30, 1908: 2;

16 Manning Vaughan, "M'Glynn Holds Night Riders to One Hit," *Milwaukee Sentinel,* July 1, 1909: 10.

17 *Milwaukee Journal,* July 24, 1909. See also Dennis Pajot's The Milwaukee Brewers 1902-1919, file on the 1909 Milwaukee Brewers, page 10 at sabr.app.box.com/s/aimiuho6ardjpm-cfupfkkddf20al48gd/1/5669640185/46000535385/1. Accessed February 8, 2017.

18 "Too Much Work Hurts Pitchers, *Green Bay Press-Gazette,* June 1, 1910: 7.

19 "Brewers Win From Collegians, 6 to 2," *Milwaukee Sentinel,* April 7, 1910: 8; "Brewers Take First Game from St. Paul," *Milwaukee Sentinel,* April 14, 1910: Home Edition: 2.

20 Manning Vaughan, "Macmen on Top in Two Games," *Milwaukee Sentinel,* September 5, 1910: 2.

21 Manning Vaughan, "Late Rally Gives Brewers 3-2 Win," *Milwaukee Sentinel,* September 10, 1910: 6; "Brewers Win Half of Doubleheader," *Milwaukee Sentinel,* September 11, 1910: Part 2, Sporting: 1.

22 Manning Vaughan, *Milwaukee Sentinel,* March 12, 1911: 6.

23 H.G. Copeland, "M'Glynn Deceives Burke's Sluggers," *Indianapolis Star,* April 15, 1911: 10; Fred R. Coburn, "Millers Are Again Beaten by Milwaukee," *Minneapolis Star Tribune,* May 13, 1911: 20.

24 "Another 'Dry' Victory," *Kansas City Times,* May 17, 1911: 10; "McGlynn in Form," *Coshocton* (Ohio) *Morning Tribune,* June 7, 1911: 2; *Milwaukee Sentinel,* June 7, 1911: 6.

25 "Jinx? No, Just S. M'Glynn Again," *Indianapolis Star,* June 14, 1911: 8.

26 "M'Glynn Leaves the Milwaukee Team," *Louisville Courier-Journal,* June 24, 1911: 11.

27 Dennis Pajot. *Milwaukee Brewers 1902-1919.* 1911 Milwaukee Brewers; "M'Glynn Wins Close Contest," *Indianapolis Star,* July 15, 1911: 8; "Iron Man Humbles Burke's Redskins," *Indianapolis Star,* August 1, 1911: 8.

28 "M'Glynn is Victor in Doubleheader," *Indianapolis Star,* September 18, 1911: 8.

29 "Colonels Lose Two More Games," *Louisville Courier-Journal,* September 27, 1911: 7; "Sunday Marks Close of Association; Game of Horse Play," *Eau Claire* (Wisconsin) *Leader,* October 3, 1911: 3.

30 "McGlynn Passes From A.A.," *Indianapolis News,* April 30, 1912: 12.

31 "Baseball Notes," *Frederick* (Maryland) *Post,* June 1, 1912: 6; "Little Bits of Baseball," *Pittsburgh Press,* June 7, 1912: 26.

32 "Stoney M'Glynn Refuses to Come to Salt Lake," *Salt Lake Herald-Republican,* March 21, 1913: 8.

33 "Stoney M'Glynn's Pitching and Homer Wins 4 to 2 Game," *Salt Lake Herald-Republican,* August 2, 1913: 10.

34 "Stoney McGlynn Named Umpire in Lake Shore League," *Sheboygan Press,* June 28, 1919: 3; "McGlynn Will Umpire in New State League," *Manitowoc Herald-Times,* April 13, 1923: 9.

35 "Herzog to Quit Baseball, Sells Out Franchise," *Sheboygan Press,* April 24, 1920: 3; "Pitched Good Game," *Wausau Daily Herald,* June 23, 1920: 2.

36 "Bits of Sports Gossip," *Manitowoc* (Wisconsin) *Herald-Times,* October 2, 1928: 6; "McGlynn Fans 18, Allows 3 Hits," *Manitowoc Herald-Times,* May 31, 1924: 9.

37 "Stoney McGlynn is President of Amateur Loop," *Capital Times* (Madison, Wisconsin), April 7, 1928.

38 "Stoney McGlynn in Boat Saves Drifting Pair," *Manitowoc Herald-Times,* July 25, 1928: 1.

39 Sam Levy.

# HARRY MCINTIRE

## BY JOHN STRUTH

**HARRY MCINTIRE PLAYED PROFES**-sional baseball from 1900 through 1913. After spending five years in the minor leagues, he ascended to the major leagues with Brooklyn in 1905. Over the next five seasons McIntire toiled in futility with Brooklyn. In 1910, he was traded to the Chicago Cubs. Though pitching in a diminished role, he had his greatest success there, including making a World Series appearance in 1910. A decent-hitting pitcher and spitball specialist, "Handsome Harry" once pitched no-hit ball for 10⅔ innings before losing 1-0 in 12 innings. More ignominiously, McIntire had the unenviable distinction of losing 20 or more games in a season three times in his career, all with Brooklyn. After baseball, McIntire lived a vagabond life of a professional golfer, scout, gambler, and idle fisherman.

John Reid "Harry" McIntire was born in Detroit on January 11, 1878.[1] Further confusing matters, his last name was variously spelled McIntire or McIntyre throughout and after his playing career.

Research found no early census records or other early documentation about McIntire's childhood, except for a newspaper article published in 1910.[2] In that article, McIntire described his early childhood and discovery of baseball. His recollections went to his youth, when he expressed an interest in being a locomotive engineer or priest. He became fascinated by baseball at a young age, participating in pickup games anywhere he could.[3]

McIntire played his first organized baseball at the Brothers' School in Dayton, Ohio. He described his first position as, "back up for the catcher and very proud to chase balls that went past him."[4] Taking an interest in pitching, he worked with one of the priests to practice his craft. He noted that one of the great lessons he'd learned was that "keeping cool and never losing the temper was a better way of winning than pitching curves."[5]

McIntire said that when he graduated and began looking for work, a friend told him that the YMCA team in Kankakee, Illinois, was looking for a pitcher. McIntire pitched for the team for a couple of summers, honing his craft.[6] In 1900, at 22, he played his first season of professional baseball, for Danville, Illinois, of the Central League. Full pitching statistics aren't available for that season, but Baseball-Reference credits McIntire with 47 games played.

McIntire played part or all of five seasons in the minor leagues. After Danville he pitched for the 1901 Toledo Mud Hens in the Western Association. That team finished in third place, with a 78-60 record, six games out of first place. McIntire pitched in 25 games and also played in the outfield. For the season, McIntire batted .313 in 176 at-bats, with 12 doubles, 3 triples, and 9 home runs.

On the move, McIntire played for three teams in the Southern Association in 1902, Shreveport, Nashville, and Memphis, pitching in 16 games (4-7) and playing 25 in the field.

In 1903 and 1904 McIntire stayed in Memphis, compiling records of 20-15 and 19-8 respectively. His batting statistics fell off however, with batting averages of .185 and .215. He caught the attention of the Brooklyn Superbas, who signed him after the 1904 season.

McIntire began his career inauspiciously, making his debut in a relief appearance on April 14, 1905. He was shellacked for six runs in four innings pitched. On the 18th he made his first start, facing Boston. Though he lost the game, he allowed just two runs, both unearned, in eight innings pitched.

Next, McIntire pitched two gems, blanking Boston 4-0 on the 22nd and then defeating the Giants 3-2 on the 26th. Of the latter game, the *Brooklyn Eagle* correspondent wrote, "Harry McIntire was the hero of it all. It took a mighty swipe of the ball to bring him fame, but he was equal to it."[7] In that game McIntire defeated Joe "Iron Man" McGinnity. This was made into a big deal in Brooklyn, whose team had not defeated McGinnity the season before. So glorious was the victory that in the *Eagle* an aspiring poet wrote:

> The score stood one to nothing when the
> Giants came to bat,
> But a lightning sort of rally soon slightly
> Altered that.
> So when the Brooks came to the plate and
> Ritter got his base
> No one supposed that McIntire was even
> In the Race.
> There was blood in Harry's optic as he
> whaled the ball with wrath
> And wings on Ridder's pedals as he flew
> around the path.
> "The score is tied!" the rooters yelled, "now
> beat 'em at the wire."
> And Lumley made a star of
> McIntire.
> That's why all things are bright, although
> it's raining here to-day.
> And joy and jest are unconfined, the fans
> are blithe and gay.
> The "Iron Man," the only one, was beaten
> Out, you see.
> For the first time by our warriors, since
> 1903.[8]

Unfortunately for McIntire, April 26 marked the apex of his season. He followed his winning performance with a loss to Philadelphia on May 2. On the 9th, McIntire pitched a no-decision versus the Cincinnati Reds and he defeated the Pirates on the 13th. McIntire did not win again until June 30, though he didn't pitch badly. On June 7 he was defeated by the Reds, 5-4. The *Eagle* wrote, "Starring in their exclusive sketch, 'Beaten at the Finish,' the Superbas lost the opening spiel with the Reds."[9]

On June 30 McIntire defeated the Giants, 6-5 and on July 4 he defeated Boston, 2-1. The *New York Tribune* reported, "The feature of the afternoon game was McIntire's home run drive to centre field in the third inning. With the hit, he practically won his own game."[10] Another prolonged slump ensued.

On July 29, the *Eagle* reported, "Opposed to [Deacon] Phillippe at the start was McIntire, but the Pirates jumped all over him, and after two innings of dreadful bombardment he was removed."[11] Compounding McIntire's erratic pitching was the awful fielding of his teammates. On September 7, he was defeated by Philadelphia 5-4. The *Eagle* reported, "McIntire was opposed by [Bill] Duggleby and there was little to choose between the pair, but the support of the latter was much more steady. Five errors were charged against the Brooklynites."[12]

By season's end McIntire had lost 25 games, winning 8. In 40 games pitched, he started 35, completing 29 and pitching 308⅔ innings with a 3.70 ERA. His 101 walks and 20 hit batters (a league high) portended a wild streak he maintained through his career.

Such was the futility of Brooklyn baseball that 25 losses still earned McIntire the 1906 home opening start. And he pitched well enough to win, except that he didn't, losing to Boston 2-0. He struck out 10 and surrendered six hits in a complete-game performance. Throughout April McIntire pitched well but was winless. Sloppy play continued to mar his performances, though he also was not immune to it himself. Of a loss to New York on April 20, the *Eagle* correspondent wrote, "McIntire's muff at the plate started the champions mauling with a couple of runs they should never have scored. … [He] can blame nobody but himself for the one-sided aspect of the score."[13]

After his slow start, McIntire won about as much as he lost from May onward. On May 30 the *Eagle*, reporting on his 2-0 victory over the Pirates, wrote, "Harry McIntire, who was credited with yesterday's victory in Pittsburgh, kept up his superb form by holding them down to four scratched hits."[14]

Continuing his strong pitching, on August 1 versus the Pirates, McIntire put on a remarkable performance in a losing effort. The *Eagle* reported:

> "Local base ball history fails to parallel the game played

by the Brooklyns and Pittsburgs at Washington Park yesterday. Thirteen innings in which only one run was scored and where the losing pitcher held the visitors without a solitary hit for nearly eleven innings, is a performance that will take its place at the top of the remarkable events of the national sport. Harry McIntire was the unfortunate twirler who holds the distinction of pitching a no-hit game for ten and two-thirds innings and still suffering defeat.

Followers of base ball are not surprised over McIntire's misfortune in losing the best game of his career. He has been known as the champion hard luck pitcher since he broke into the league. Not long ago, he held Chicago down to no hits in eight innings and lost out in the ninth on one single."[15]

That day, McIntire pitched 13 innings, losing 1-0 when his no-hit game was broken up by Claude Ritchey.

By season's end McIntire had completed a second successive 20-loss season, this time finishing 13-21, despite a solid ERA of 2.97. He pitched in 39 games, starting 31 and completing 25 over 276 innings.

McIntire continued his hard-luck pitching through the 1907 season. On August 24 he started against St. Louis. Wrote the *Eagle*, "Harry McIntire handicapped himself at the start of the first game by a sensational stop of a terrific liner from [Bobby] Byrne which he beat down and threw to first in time. The drive broke a small bone in Mac's left hand, but he did not pay any attention to it."[16] He missed several starts, and perhaps it was a blessing in disguise as McIntire's season did not end in another 20 losses.

By season's end McIntire finished with a record of 7-15 in 28 games. His ERA was a career-best 2.39. Even outside Brooklyn people took notice of McIntire's plight. On October 6, the *Chicago Tribune* noted, "The pitchers who deserve the hard luck laurels for losing games after holding their opponents … are [Nat] Rucker, [Elmer] Stricklett and McIntyre."[17] (All three pitched for Brooklyn.)

While McIntire was thought of as a hard-luck pitcher, by 1908 his losing record found increasing critical notice locally. Of On June 24 the *Eagle* wrote, "Both sides used two pitchers, Harry McIntire being the first to retire, and [Lew] Moren following soon after. McIntire was an open book to the visitors, who … recovered their slugging abilities."[18] On the 30th the *Eagle* reported, "The Giants took kindly to the slants of McIntire. … Manager [Patsy] Donovan very promptly and properly chased Handsome Harry to the clubhouse."[19]

Even in victory the *Eagle* correspondent took a swipe at McIntire when he wrote, after a 6-2 defeat of Cincinnati, "McIntire was in good form, being steadier than usual."[20] Despite the results, McIntire was pitching effectively. In fact, by midsummer he boasted, "I'll pitch another no-hit game before the season is over."[21] That was not to be. The 1908 season was the third 20-loss season in McIntire's four years with Brooklyn. While his record was an anemic 11-20, he pitched four shutouts, and his retrospective WAR (Wins Above Replacement) was a career-best 3.2.

Early in the 1909 season McIntire helped Brooklyn defeat a pesky Boston nine. The *Pittsburgh Sun* wrote, "Brooklyn put an end to Boston's winning streak this afternoon through the excellent twirling of McIntire and some timely hitting by the men behind him. … Additional credit is due McIntire because some of the fielders … played raggedly in the afternoon."[22] But his season record was 7-17, and his ERA rose to 3.63.

McIntire spent January 1910 visiting Texas. During a stay in El Paso, a local paper reported that he attracted attention at the local bowling alley and the YMCA, where the memory of Christy Mathewson and his checker playing was still fresh, and he 'rolled 'em down the other alley, pally,' until the pin boys had paralysis in their arms. …"[23]

The article went on to discuss the coming season. McIntire may have had an inkling of changes; the paper reported, "Being sewed up in a contract with Brooklyn, he does not know yet what his immediate future will be. 'I may be traded, retained or sold by Brooklyn,' he says. 'It all depends on the outcome of

the meeting in New York as to which of the National League teams I play with next season.' Judging from his record of last year, the man from Babybuggyville is due to make good. ..."24

About the same time, new Brooklyn manager Bill Dahlen was sanguine about his team's prospects. Dahlen said, "I don't really believe that I hope to look for a championship team this year. My sole ambition is to give Brooklyn a winning team. ... Do I think I have a good pitching department? Of course it could be made stronger; but I am satisfied. I bank on Rucker and McIntire."25

Despite Dahlen's hopes, on April 9 McIntire was traded to the Cubs for three minor-league prospects, Tony Smith, Happy Smith, and Bill Davidson. "Brooklyn has figured in several deals in major league baseball, but the trade arranged yesterday by Manager Dahlen appears to be the best that has ever been pulled off," wrote the *Eagle*. "... While Brooklyn has undoubtedly made a trade that will be of great benefit to the local team, still Harry McIntyre will be greatly missed, not only by the club but by the local fans. Of all the hard luck twirlers that Brooklyn ever had, Handsome Harry had more than his share last season and even before that."26

Another newspaper opined, "Charles W. Murphy, president of the Chicago Cubs, gave Tony Smith, Happy Smith and Davidson, three promising youngsters, for McIntyre, the Brooklyn pitcher, just because the twirler always has had the Buffalo sign on Pittsburg. One report says Murphy gave $7,000 to boot. Shows how bad Chicago wants to beat Pittsburg."27

McIntire did not disappoint. While not spectacular, he fashioned a good season. Writing of McIntire's 1-0 victory over Pittsburgh, the *El Paso Herald* reported on April 28, "The best piece of news was the performance of Harry McIntyre with the Cubs. In the one to nothing game with Pittsburg, Harry worked the well-oiled machine. ... His work against the world champs was spoken of in the telegraphic reports of the game as brilliant and it looks as if Harry was due to lose the title of the hard luck pitcher of the major leagues."28

Soon McIntire may have felt as though he was back in Brooklyn. On May 12, he lost to New York, and while he surrendered five runs in seven innings, the Cubs backed him with seven errors.

On September 29, McIntire defeated Boston 8-3. Wrote the *Chicago Tribune*, "Chicago Cubs crept nearer the inevitable today. ... McIntire was selected to do the honors and held the Doves safe after a bad start. ..."29

Chicago won the pennant going away, with a 104-50 record, 13 games in front of the second-place New York Giants. They met the Philadelphia Athletics in the World Series and lost in five games. McIntire was moved to a bullpen role in the Series and made two appearances. In Game One he relieved Orval Overall in the fourth inning and pitched five innings of one-hit ball, surrendering one unearned run. Philadelphia won, 4-1. In Game Three, he relieved Ed Reulbach in the third inning. He was hit hard and in one-third of an inning he gave up four runs, taking the loss.

On a pitching staff featuring Mordecai "Three Finger" Brown, King Cole, Overall, and Reulbach, McIntire held his own. Because the Cubs were so deep in pitching, he was not called on to pitch an extravagant number of innings. McIntire finished the season with a 13-9 record with a 3.07 ERA in 176 innings pitched (19 starts). For McIntire, enjoying his first winning record in the majors and pitching in the World Series must have felt very satisfying.

Then 33, McIntire entered the 1911 season hopeful for more. He started off positively. On April 18, the *Chicago Tribune* wrote, "One of the pleasing features of the game was the pitching of Harry McIntire. He showed more yesterday than he showed at any time last year. He looked as good as he ever did when he was about the only star on the Brooklyn club. He had his old side arm delivery, was hooking over curves, shooting fast ones … all with the ease and grace of a master of the game."[30] McIntire pitched a complete game in his first start, on April 17, giving up only two unearned runs on six hits in a 7-2 victory.

Throughout the year McIntire pitched adequately and was winning consistently, but getting into games more sporadically than in the past. His season record was 11-7. However, he pitched in only 25 games, the fewest of his career to date. He started 17 games and had a 4.11 ERA.

McIntire's 1912 season consisted of four appearances. It was alleged that he came into camp out of shape. However, in his April starts he pitched well. On April 12, he lost to Cincinnati 3-2 in 10 innings. The *Tribune* wrote, "Up to the tenth innings McIntire outpitched [Rube] Benton by considerable. The Reds were able to get only five hits off the side arm spitter."[31] On April 25 he defeated the St. Louis Cardinals, 5-2. On May 2, McIntire lost to Pittsburgh 6-0, surrendering four runs in 2⅔ innings. In that same series, he slugged a pinch-hit triple.

By June 21 McIntire had been sold to Milwaukee of the American Association; his major-league career appeared to be over. However, McIntire never appeared with Milwaukee, and Milwaukee rescinded the deal because McIntire was not in shape.[32]

For Chicago McIntire's won-loss record was 1-2. He did not give up. He worked hard to get in shape over the winter.

Joe Tinker became the Cincinnati manager in 1913. According to the *Pittsburgh Press*, he brought several Cubs teammates with him to Cincinnati, in part to be with familiar faces. One invitee to spring training was McIntire.[33]

McIntire made the team, and came north. However, his stay was brief, He made one appearance with the Reds, pitched one inning, allowed three runs and took a loss. Shortly afterward he was released.

After his baseball career, McIntire nearly disappeared, but not entirely. He settled first in Louisiana, and then Florida. Applying for a passport in 1919, he noted that he had been residing in Hammond, Louisiana, for four years. His stated reason for making the application was to scout ballplayers in Cuba. It is unknown with which team he may have been affiliated.

In the 1920 US Census, McIntire still listed Hammond as his home. He stated that he was married, and listed his occupation as ballplayer.

Insight is gained about McIntire in a 1970 correspondence between Wilbur S. McIntire, Harry's nephew, and Colonel Jack W. Rudolph. The nephew wrote,

> "I suppose that you would have to consider John Reid (McIntire) definitely a 'loner.' Many of the years of his life were unknown to his immediate family. It can be said that he never 'worked a day in his life.' To a great extent he made his way by gambling. For instance in the late '30's, I was playing with a band … at the Eagles picnic grounds near Dayton, on which was situated a private gambling club. … I had occasion, without good cause, to visit the establishment. Upon entering the door, here was my Uncle John, running a roulette wheel. (Out of Chicago).
>
> "At one time he was engaged by one of the 'sugar kings' to fly with him to Cuba to participate in a poker game. The stakes in

this game were the highest in the history of this country. The family tells that he came back to the U.S. with $60,000.

"I do know that sometime near 1940 he married an extremely wealthy widow from Louisiana. During this time, or prior to 1938, he was a pro in golf and gave lessons in Florida. You can see the information is very vague."[34]

It appears that McIntire married twice. In his World War I draft registration form, dated September 12, 1918, he identified Mrs. Nellie McIntire as his next of kin. It does not appear that he had children.[35] McIntire was survived by two brothers Will and Frank, and a sister, referred to as Mrs. Walter Payne.[36] After his death, on January 9, 1949, his estranged family took care of his burial in Dayton, Ohio. They were the ones who listed his birthday as January 11, 1879, and birthplace as Dayton.[37]

John Reid McIntire was an enigma to many. His nephew's sketch paints the picture of a restless soul, on the fringe of society. But his steady residences in Louisiana and Florida belie that perception. Perhaps he was not constituted to work 9 to 5. Because of his estrangement from family, the picture of McIntire painted by his nephew should be taken cautiously.

McIntire played professional baseball in all or part of 14 seasons, nine in the major leagues. In five seasons with Brooklyn he established a record of futility hard to imagine, losing 20 or more games in three of those years. Labeled a hard-luck pitcher, McIntire performed at or slightly better than the league average over his career. A testament to that is his winning record in the two full seasons he pitched for a stronger club in Chicago. Ironically, he enjoyed that success during a time of diminishing skill.

Standing 5-feet-11 and weighing in at 180 pounds, he threw right-handed and was best known for his side-arm spitball. McIntire finished his career with a 71-117 record. He compiled a 3.22 ERA in 1,650 innings pitched. Over his career he had 17 shutouts.

## NOTES

1. It is often reported that McIntire was born in Dayton, Ohio, on January 11, 1879. However, he consistently described his birthdate as January 11, 1878, in the census, and on passport application and draft registration forms. See, for instance, passport application, January 11, 1919, Louisiana, county of Tangipahoa. The purpose of application was, "To look over ground for securing ball players" in Cuba. He also consistently described his birthplace as Detroit, Michigan, in those same documents.
2. "His Career Was Accidental," *Huntington Park* (California) *Daily Signal*, October 11, 1910: 7.
3. Ibid. Searches for more information on McIntyre's family turned up a John R. McIntire (carpenter contractor) and a John K. McIntire (insurance agent) in the Dayton area. It is not clear if either (or perhaps another person) was Harry McIntire's father.
4. Ibid.
5. Ibid.
6. Ibid.
7. *Brooklyn Daily Eagle*, April 27, 1905: 11.
8. "Baseball Notes," *Brooklyn Daily Eagle*, April 27, 1905: 11.
9. *Brooklyn Daily Eagle*, June 8, 1905: 10.
10. *New York Tribune*, July 5, 1905: 11.
11. *Brooklyn Daily Eagle*, July 30, 1905: 43.
12. *Brooklyn Daily Eagle*, September 8, 1905: 10.

13 *Brooklyn Daily Eagle*, April 21, 1906: 10.

14 *Brooklyn Daily Eagle*, May 30, 1906: 3.

15 *Brooklyn Daily Eagle*, August 2, 1906: 3.

16 *Brooklyn Daily Eagle*, August 25, 1907: 35.

17 *Chicago Tribune*, October 6, 1907: 35.

18 *Brooklyn Daily Eagle*, June 24, 1908: 22.

19 *Brooklyn Daily Eagle*, June 30, 1908: 20.

20 *Brooklyn Daily Eagle*, September 18, 1908: 20.

21 *Brooklyn Daily Eagle*, August 4, 1908: 3.

22 *Pittsburgh Sun*, April 20, 1909: 7.

23 "Big League Pitcher Visits the City," *El Paso Herald*, January 11, 1910: 4.

24 Ibid.

25 "Manager Bill Dahlen Predicts a Successful Season for Brooklyn Infants," *Pittsburgh Press*, February 7, 1910: 12.

26 *Brooklyn Daily Eagle*, April 10, 1910: 16.

27 *Donaldsonville* (Louisiana) *Chief*, May 21, 1910: 7.

28 *El Paso Herald*, April 28, 1910: 5.

29 *Chicago Tribune*, September 30, 1910: 12.

30 "McIntire Shows Real Class," *Chicago Daily Tribune*, April 18, 1911: 22.

31 *Chicago Tribune*, April 13, 1912: 8.

32 "McIntire's a Brewer," *Elyria* (Ohio) *Chronicle Telegram*, June 21, 1912: 6.

33 "Harry McIntire Will Be Tried by the Reds," *Pittsburgh Press*, January 26, 1913: 20

34 Baseball Hall of Fame library, player file, correspondence between Wilbur S. McIntire and Col. James W. Rudolph, June 8, 1970.

35 Draft registration, September 18, 1918.

36 Baseball Hall of Fame file, John Reid McIntire, correspondence between Col. Jack W. Rudolph and librarian Mrs. Joseph "Frances" Casey, Winchester Community Library, April 15, 1970.

37 search.ancestry.com/cgibin/sse.

# JACK NABORS

## BY STEPHEN V. RICE

**IN 1916 STAN COVELESKI OF THE** Cleveland Indians and Jack Nabors of the Philadelphia Athletics played their first full season in the major leagues, and each pitched more than 200 innings. They had similar ERAs — 3.41 for Coveleski and 3.47 for Nabors — but while Coveleski's won-lost record was 15-13, Nabors' record was abysmal: 1-20. Cleveland won half its games that year, while Philadelphia compiled the worst record (36-117) in major-league history from 1900 to 2014. Compared with the 1916 Indians, the 1916 Athletics scored 29 percent fewer runs and committed 35 percent more errors. Charlie Grimm, who roomed with Nabors during this inglorious season, said:

> "Do you think that [Nabors' losing] turned him to brooding, made him sour or a bad companion? Not at all. Nabors was the cheeriest individual you could ever find. He was happy because he was in the major leagues and going around the circuit in princely style. After losing game after game, many of which were lost by evil support, he never complained, but just took it as a matter of course."[1]

Herman John "Jack" Nabors was born on November 19, 1887, in Montevallo, Alabama. He was the fourth of nine children born to farmer James Crow Nabors (1858-1933) and Sarah M. (Foster) Nabors (1860-1944).[2] Jack pitched for amateur teams near Montevallo, and for industrial teams in Walker County, Alabama, that "would pay him if he pitched and won."[3] The lanky right-hander stood 6-feet-3 and weighed 185 pounds.

In 1914 Nabors received a tryout with the Selma (Alabama) River Rats of the Class-D Georgia-Alabama League.[4] The next year he pitched for two other teams in the league. After a brief stint with the Talladega (Alabama) Tigers, he spent the remainder of the season with the Newnan (Georgia) Cowetas, named for the Coweta Indians. One of his Newnan teammates was a southpaw from Atlanta named Bill Terry; 15 years later, Terry hit .401 for the New York Giants. The 27-year-old Nabors, with a 12-1 record, and the 16-year-old Terry, with a 7-1 record, led Newnan to the 1915 pennant. During one stretch Terry threw 46 consecutive scoreless innings, including a no-hitter on June 30,[5] but it was overshadowed by Nabors' achievement on June 15: a 13-inning no-hitter in a 1-0 victory over Talladega, with 11 strikeouts and no walks. Two men reached base on errors, but one was thrown out trying to steal second base, so Nabors faced only 40 batters in 13 innings.[6] *Sporting Life* and the *New York Times* reported his gem.[7]

After the season ended on July 14, the Newnan team represented Gastonia in the Western North Carolina League, which began its season on July 26.[8] Terry went with his teammates to Gastonia,[9] while Nabors headed to Philadelphia. According to the *Philadelphia Evening Ledger*, Nabors was sought by every major-league team, and "after a spirited bidding contest, the Athletics got him for what is said to be the highest price [$500] ever paid for a Class D minor league player."[10]

The Athletics won four pennants in five seasons from 1910 to 1914, but after the 1914 season the famous "$100,000 infield" was broken up: In December second baseman Eddie Collins was sold to the Chicago White Sox for $50,000. Third baseman Home Run Baker held out for the entire 1915 season and was sold to the New York Yankees in 1916 for $37,500. Mired in seventh place in early July 1915, Connie Mack sold shortstop Jack Barry to the Boston Red Sox for $10,000.

Eddie Plank and Chief Bender had signed with the Federal League. Mack had sold Herb Pennock and Bob Shawkey. What remained of the pitching staff was a ragtag collection of youthful and erratic hurlers. Mack was desperate for help when he acquired Nabors from the deep bushes. Normally, a Class-D star might advance to Class B, or maybe Class A, but Mack immediately pressed Nabors into service with the major-league club. It was quite a leap. Mack said:

> "I have never in my life seen a ballplayer as green as he was when he joined us. Ordinarily I would have passed him up at once, but he naturally interested me. I have had plenty of green ones, but he was the limit. I took a liking to the youngster because he realized that he knew absolutely nothing about the game. All he could do was throw the ball. He did not even know how to wind up, much less have a delivery which was permitting him to get the maximum amount of speed out of his pitches. The curve ball he used was of the back-lot variety and no one had shown him what to do with it or his fast ball. I was first attracted to the youngster because of his wonderful natural fast ball."[11]

Nabors made his major-league debut on August 9, 1915, in Philadelphia against the Chicago White Sox. He pitched a complete game and lost, 8-4. He was wild (seven walks and one hit batsman) and allowed 12 hits. The Athletics made six errors, including two by Nabors. The White Sox learned quickly that he did not know how to field his position, with "six of the first seven hits credited against him being safe bunts that were beaten out, while the other one was a hit that [first baseman Stuffy] McInnis fielded and Nabors forgot all about covering first."[12] Mack said, "I felt sorry for the lad when the opposing team started bunting on him. Nabors was tied into knots and if they had not taken pity on him they would have been beating out bunts yet."[13] Nabors pitched in 10 games for the Athletics in 1915 and posted a 0-5 record with a 5.50 ERA. The Athletics finished the season in last place with a 43-109 record; however, the nightmare had just begun.

### The 1-20 Season

Mack and the Philadelphia coaches had a chance to work with Nabors at spring training in 1916. Nabors showed "great improvement" and was "the talk of the Mack camp."[14] *Sporting Life* reported that he "probably has more natural ability than any man on the staff, but Nabors is so awfully green that he will not be of much use this year. At the present time Mack plans to send him to the mound regularly, believing that there is no better way to learn than by profiting by mistakes. He does not expect Nabors to show much until late in the season, but will not farm him out, as he wants to school this lad himself."[15] Mack admitted, "The season of 1916 is going to be an experimental one with the Athletics."[16]

Mack rewarded Nabors' progress by letting him start the season opener against the Boston Red Sox at Fenway Park on April 12, 1916. The Red Sox, with Babe Ruth on the mound, won the game, 2-1. Nabors impressed Mack by allowing no runs and two hits in his four innings of work against the defending world champions. Bullet Joe Bush took the loss for Philadelphia. The following is a chronology of the games in which Nabors received a decision:

# 20-GAME LOSERS

- 0-1, April 18, at New York: Nabors got his first loss of the season in a 4-2 game. Shawkey pitched for the Yankees and held the Athletics to six hits.
- 1-1, April 22, versus Boston: Nabors defeated the Red Sox, 6-2. He was a "surprise"[17] and "performed eloquently."[18] However, it would be the only victory of his major-league career.
- 1-2, April 28, at Washington: Nabors had a comfortable 6-3 lead but was wild in the ninth inning, and the Senators came back to win, 7-6.
- 1-3, May 9, versus Detroit: Nabors was removed after one inning, having surrendered five runs on four hits and three walks. The Tigers won, 16-2. The *Philadelphia Evening Ledger* reported that Nabors "appears to have lost confidence."[19] He was sidelined for the next two weeks due to illness.[20] Mack said that once Nabors got going, he would be a star.[21]
- 1-4, May 27, at Washington: Nabors allowed three hits in seven innings but lost, 3-1, to Walter Johnson and the Senators. The *Washington Post* noted that Johnson was hit harder than Nabors.[22] The *Philadelphia Evening Ledger* reported that Nabors "gave the wonderful Johnson a great battle and showed enough to clinch a regular turn on the mound."[23]
- 1-5, June 16, at Detroit: The Athletics committed six errors, including one by Nabors, and lost the game, 4-3. Nabors allowed no earned runs in seven innings.
- 1-6, June 24, at Boston: Through eight innings, Nabors had a one-hitter and was ahead 2-1. In the ninth inning, Harry Hooper and Hal Janvrin singled for the Red Sox and were on third base and second base, respectively, with one out, when Dick Hoblitzell flied out to short left field. Hooper tagged up and headed for home, and would have been out at the plate, but rookie catcher Mike Murphy dropped the ball and Hooper scored the tying run. Janvrin advanced to third base on the play. Tillie Walker then stepped to the plate. Murphy, "whose heart was broken by the misplay, allowed Nabors' first pitch [to Walker] to shoot through his hands, strike his protector and then bound away off toward the Red Sox bench, while Janvrin danced home" with the winning run.[24]
- 1-7, June 29, versus New York: Nabors was removed after giving up three runs in the first inning. Shawkey pitched a shutout as the Yankees won, 5-0.
- 1-8, July 3, versus Boston: Nabors allowed two earned runs in eight innings, but lost, 6-4.
- 1-9, July 8, versus Detroit: Nabors "pitched a great game"[25] but was defeated, 3-2.
- 1-10, July 13, versus St. Louis: Nabors threw five innings and allowed two runs, as the Browns earned a 7-3 victory. He "twirled good ball"[26] but was stuck with another loss.
- 1-11, July 21, versus Cleveland: The Indians hit Nabors hard and won, 7-2.
- 1-12, July 27, at St. Louis: Nabors pitched a six-hitter but lost, 3-2.
- 1-13, August 1, at Chicago: Nabors allowed one earned run, but the White Sox prevailed, 3-0. Mack said he was satisfied with Nabors' work,[27] despite his woeful won-lost record.
- 1-14, August 8, at Detroit: The Tigers pounded Nabors for 16 hits and won, 9-0. Ty Cobb got four hits. It was Philadelphia's 20th consecutive loss. Mack said, "But all that time, by these hard knocks, my boys were getting just the experience necessary to season them. ... Nabors will be one of the best a year from now with a little seasoning."[28]
- 1-15, August 14, at New York: Nabors allowed two earned runs but lost, 4-3. At one point, he retired 20 batters in a row "with a fine display of what is technically known as 'the stuff.'"[29]
- 1-16, September 1, at Washington: Nabors allowed one earned run but lost, 3-1, to Walter Johnson and the Senators.

- 1-17, September 4, at Washington: Nabors pitched a six-hitter but lost, 2-0.
- 1-18, September 7, versus Boston: Nabors threw a four-hitter and allowed no earned runs but lost, 2-0. "Nabors was a puzzle to the champions, and only for a bad error by [Val] Picinich in the fourth inning he would not have been scored on."[30]
- 1-19, September 14, at Cleveland: Nabors gave up five earned runs in seven innings in a 9-1 Indians victory.
- 1-20, September 28, versus Washington: The Senators won, 4-1, as Nabors allowed two runs in eight innings.

Clearly, Nabors performed far better than his record indicates. He was handed several tough-luck losses. He had raw talent and was a work-in-progress as a pitcher and as a fielder. He led major-league pitchers with 13 errors during the season.

Postscript

Before spring training in 1917, Mack intended to keep Nabors in the starting rotation,[31] but after spring training, Mack said, "Nabors has been a disappointment to me and I am not counting upon him."[32] Mack did not say why he was disappointed, but presumably, Nabors pitched poorly in the spring. The day before Mack expressed this, Hal Phytz of the Warren (Pennsylvania) Times Mirror wrote that Nabors "must show more to be numbered among the chosen."[33]

Nabors' major-league career ended in late April when he was traded to the Indianapolis Indians of the American Association. Indianapolis sent him to the Denver Bears of the Western League. He pitched a three-hit shutout against Wichita (Kansas) on June 2; a no-hitter against Sioux City (Iowa) on July 22; and a two-hit shutout against Omaha on August 9.[34] However, he lost his last seven decisions of the season and ended up with a 9-17 record for the Bears.[35]

In the spring of 1918 Nabors declared that he was ready to serve in the Army during World War I. He said, "Every man owes a duty to his country and should allow nothing to interfere between him and his performance of it," he said. "I am glad to have the chance to do my bit with the rest of the red-blooded Americans."[36] That summer the Army sent Nabors to Camp Dodge, Iowa, and he pitched for the camp baseball team.[37] In the winter he came down with a severe case of the flu during the influenza pandemic of 1918-1919. He never pitched again and spent his remaining years "in and out of a sick bed."[38] He died of tuberculosis on October 29, 1923, in Wilton, Alabama, at the age of 35.

Nabors was a tragic figure in baseball history. Under different circumstances, he might have had a fine career. Instead he lives on in the record books with an ignominious career record of 1-25.

## NOTES

1. *Philadelphia Inquirer*, July 28, 1936.
2. Joel C. DuBose, ed., *Notable Men of Alabama: Personal and Genealogical, Volume 1* (Atlanta: Southern Historical Association, 1904); findagrave.com.
3. *Anniston* (Alabama) *Star*, September 8, 1968.
4. Baseball Hall of Fame file.
5. *Atlanta Constitution*, July 1, 4, and 8, 1915.
6. *Atlanta Constitution*, June 16 and August 2, 1915. Art Decatur was the opposing pitcher in Nabors' 13-inning no-hitter and allowed only six hits in the game. Decatur pitched in the National League from 1922 to 1927.
7. *Sporting Life*, June 26, 1915; *New York Times*, June 16, 1915.
8. *Gastonia* (North Carolina) *Gazette*, July 16, 1915.
9. *Gastonia Gazette*, July 30, 1915.
10. *Philadelphia Evening Ledger*, July 13, 1915. The record amount paid by the Athletics to acquire Nabors was $500, according to the A's ledgers at the DeGolyer Library, Southern Methodist University.
11. *Philadelphia Evening Ledger*, March 14, 1916.
12. *Philadelphia Inquirer*, August 10, 1915.
13. *Philadelphia Evening Ledger*, March 14, 1916.
14. Ibid.
15. *Sporting Life*, March 25, 1916.
16. John G. Robertson and Andy Saunders, *A's Bad as It Gets: Connie Mack's Pathetic Athletics of 1916* (Jefferson, North Carolina: McFarland, 2014).
17. *Philadelphia Evening Ledger*, April 24, 1916.
18. *Washington Evening Star*, April 23, 1916.
19. *Philadelphia Evening Ledger*, May 11, 1916.

## 20-GAME LOSERS

20  *Philadelphia Evening Ledger*, May 18 and 20, 1916.

21  *Pittsburgh Press*, May 26, 1916.

22  *Washington Post*, May 28, 1916.

23  *Philadelphia Evening Ledger*, May 29, 1916.

24  *Boston Daily Globe*, June 25, 1916.

25  *New York Sun*, July 9, 1916.

26  *Philadelphia Evening Ledger*, July 14, 1916.

27  *Scranton* (Pennsylvania) *Republican*, August 5, 1916.

28  *Charlotte* (North Carolina) *News*, August 27, 1916.

29  *New York Tribune*, August 15, 1916.

30  *Boston Post*, September 8, 1916.

31  *Sporting Life*, February 17, 1917.

32  *Reading* (Pennsylvania) *Times*, April 10, 1917.

33  *Warren* (Pennsylvania) *Times Mirror*, April 9, 1917.

34  *El Paso* (Texas) *Herald*, June 4, 1917; *Wichita* (Kansas) *Daily Eagle*, July 23, 1917; *Wichita* (Kansas) *Beacon*, August 10, 1917.

35  *Wichita Beacon*, August 18 and November 23, 1917.

36  *Indianapolis News*, April 2, 1918.

37  *Spalding's Official Base Ball Guide*, 1919.

38  *Anniston Star*, September 12, 1968.

# ROLLIE NAYLOR

## BY PHIL WILLIAMS

**IS ROLLIE NAYLOR THE UNLUCKIEST** pitcher in baseball history? Pitching for the then-hapless Philadelphia Athletics from 1917 through 1924, he amassed a 42-83 career record and an ERA+ of 101. Through 2016, more than 800 pitchers with at least 100 decisions to their credit have earned an ERA+ of at least 100. (With this retrospectively-calculated statistic, anything over 100 is considered better than average.) None have a winning percentage as low as Naylor's .336.[1] But the diligent, well-humored right-hander seemed impervious to adversity. After all, Naylor pitched with the sight of only one eye.

Roleine Cecil Naylor was born on February 4, 1892, in Krum, a small Texas town some 45 miles north of Dallas and Fort Worth. He was the seventh of James and Laura (Whalen) Naylor's eight children. His parents farmed for a living. One day, as a teenager, while his mother gave him a haircut, Rollie whittled a piece of wood into a toothbrush. Somehow he slipped and stuck himself in his right eye with the stick. A permanent loss of sight resulted.[2]

The first four Naylor brothers—Art, Taylor ("Dick"), Fredric, and Jerry—all played baseball. In 1913 they facilitated Rollie's professional debut with several teams in the Class-D Texas-Oklahoma League. First he twirled for the Ardmore, Oklahoma, squad that Art managed.[3] Then Jerry caught his efforts with the Durant, Oklahoma, team.[4] Finally, he landed in Hugo, Oklahoma, where it was Dick's turn to catch his pitching.[5]

In 1914, Rollie pitched for Bartlett in the Class-D Middle Texas League. He remained with Bartlett until the middle of the 1915 season, when the league went belly-up. Houston of the Class-B Texas League grabbed him. The "tall right-hander with a world of blazing speed and an occasional hook" won his first two games with the Buffaloes.[6] But Naylor soon struggled, and finished his Houston stint with a 2-7 record.

Houston did not reserve Naylor for the 1916 season.[7] Another Texas League team, the Waco Navigators, picked him up. Waco quickly farmed him out to the McAlester (Oklahoma) Miners of the Class-D Western Association.[8] Naylor emerged as one of the circuit's finest pitchers, going 19-11 and leading the league with 228 strikeouts.[9]

Meanwhile, in Philadelphia, the once-proud Athletics achieved a 36-117 mark in 1916. Connie Mack drafted with renewed determination that fall.[10] For $500, he took a flyer on Naylor.[11] The newcomer arrived in the Athletics' Jacksonville training camp in March 1917 and started well, but was then "walloped unmercifully."[12] Mack farmed him out to New Haven of the Class-B Eastern League, managed by former Athletic Danny Murphy. Naylor excelled in Connecticut, leading the league with 18 victories. Mack recalled him that September.

On September 14, 1917, Naylor made his major-league debut, in Washington. He allowed five hits and five walks while going the distance in a 2-1 victory over the Senators. Over the next several weeks, Naylor made another four starts. In 33 innings with Philadelphia in 1917, Naylor went 2-2 with a sterling ERA of 1.64 (ERA+ of 169). Although the Athletics landed in the cellar for the third straight season, their 55-98 record represented a 19-game improvement from their 1916 nadir. Naylor provided hope that the Mackmen might continue their climb back to respectability.

But by November 1917, Naylor was in the Army. Contemporary reporting indicated he "saw plenty of action" and "the heaviest kind of fighting" in France.[13] He seems to have served with the 65th Coast Artillery Corps.[14] Naylor mentioned the 65th in a 1918 letter to his father and, two years later, with his American Legion membership.[15] Naylor returned to

the States in March 1919, and a month later rejoined the Athletics.

The 27-year-old rookie stood 6-feet-1 and weighed 180 pounds. "A quiet, religious sort of fellow," Naylor smiled "from sunrise to sunset."[16] He employed a "cork-screw, pivot delivery."[17] From the onset of his major-league career, Naylor possessed "a cracker-jack slow ball which breaks something on the order of Matty's famous fade-away with his zip."[18] But instead of Christy Mathewson's screwball, this pitch was later identified as a forkball.[19] At first, Naylor's offspeed offerings seemed secondary to his fastball and curveball, but they emerged as his primary weapons later in his career.[20]

During Naylor's absence, fueled by an outstanding debut from pitcher Scott Perry, Philadelphia inched forward again in the war-shortened 1918 season, finishing with a 52-76 record. But in 1919 the Athletics immediately regressed. By June 5, the team was 6-24. Naylor, reacquainting himself with major-league play, had seen limited action in six games and claimed an ERA of 6.75.

The team continued to flounder, eventually landing in the cellar with a 36-104 record. But Naylor emerged as the steadiest piece of an unfortunate starting rotation. From June 29 through August 1, he lost nine straight games. In these affairs, Philadelphia was shut out four times, and Naylor's ERA was 3.18. Naylor finished with a 5-18 record, but led the team with 204⅔ innings pitched. His 3.34 ERA (and ERA+ of 101) was the best among staff regulars.

On September 7, 1919, the Athletics journeyed to New Haven to play a Sunday exhibition game. With Naylor pitching, Philadelphia won 4-1.[21] Gertrude Donavan, "a well-known concert singer" and a New Haven native, sat in the stands.[22] A year later, she and the pitcher were married.

In December 1919, Mack informed Philadelphia sportswriter James Isaminger that, over the past several seasons, he possessed "concrete evidence of cases where other managers sent their players to members of his team and filled their ears with tales of how much more money they would be drawing if they could get away from the Athletics."[23] To dissuade halfhearted efforts from tempted players, Mack responded forcefully: "Hereafter we will not sell or trade any player on our team who is of use to us or any other big league club."[24] Thus, when White Sox manager Kid Gleason offered "almost" $25,000 for Naylor that offseason, he was rebuffed.[25]

Another early-season swoon doomed the 1920 Athletics. By July 6, after losing 27 of the previous 28 games, the team was 30½ games off the American League pace. Suspensions and desertions abounded. "Philadelphia is crying for good baseball," Isaminger wrote of the damage afflicted on the city's sports psyche by the Athletics and Phillies.[26] The Mackmen concluded the 1920 season with a 48-106 mark.

Naylor persevered. From May 24 through July 3, he lost 11 games in a row. Amid this misery, over 18 days in June, he threw five consecutive complete games, in which he allowed only 10 earned runs. Naylor finished the 1920 campaign with a 10-23 record. His ERA of 3.48 (and ERA+ of 115) suggests a quality pitcher toiling for a poor team. Tigers President Frank Navin, reportedly "sweet on" Naylor, dangled outfielder Ira Flagstead and cash as trade bait for the pitcher that offseason.[27] Mack again passed.

In 1921 Naylor struggled with injuries early on. Two months into the season, he had pitched less than 20 innings. In midseason, for several weeks he returned to top form. On July 12, at Detroit, he kept the Tigers at bay for 15 innings before yielding a triple and sacrifice fly in the 16th, and losing 2-1.[28] Nine days later, at Chicago, he suffered another 2-1 extra-inning loss, when Bibb Falk launched a homer into the right-field bleachers to lead off the 14th.[29] But soon after this stretch, his troubles returned. Naylor went 3-13 in 1921, with a 4.84 ERA (and an ERA+ of 92). Isaminger opined that "Naylor has been a big disappointment and whether he returns is matter of doubt."[30]

Mack did send Naylor a contract that winter but, after the pitcher's poor showing, it included a pay cut. Naylor balked. Mack, noting that the club had substantially raised Naylor's salary after his fine 1920 showing, argued that a reduction was justified after his mediocre 1921 season. If Naylor had a beef, Mack suggested, he should take it up with Commissioner Kenesaw Mountain Landis. Naylor promptly wrote the judge. Landis, undoubtedly anxious not to set any precedent on arbitrating salary squabbles, kicked the matter to AL President Ban Johnson. Naylor, sensing his fight was up, signed the contract.[31] Occasional business differences aside, all indications suggest the pitcher and the manager held each other in high esteem.

Possibly to combat arm problems, Naylor modified his motion in 1922. "Last year he was more of an overhand pitcher," Mack explained, "Now he's throwing them side arm and he has a better change of pace."[32] On April 12 in Boston, Naylor started the season opener. In the fourth, behind 1-0, he loaded the bases with none out. Mack pulled him, and the Athletics went on to win 3-2.[33] After this inauspicious beginning, Naylor went on to post a 10-15 record, with a 4.73 ERA (an ERA+ of 90). The Athletics, driven by Eddie Rommel's 27-13 season, finally escaped the cellar with a 65-89 seventh-place finish. "The crowds this season are much bigger than last year," Isaminger noted that May, "and old-time enthusiasm is being stirred."[34] When the 1922 season concluded, attendance at Shibe Park topped the 400,000 mark for the first time since 1913.

Naylor "works hard to win and he never utters a peep when the breaks go against him," a Philadelphia sportswriter observed as the 1923 season dawned.[35] That spring, fortune finally smiled back at the "smiling hurler."[36] In his first 10 starts, Naylor pitched eight complete games, and possessed an 8-1 record with a sparkling 2.20 ERA. On Saturday, June 16, before taking on the Indians at home, the Athletics sported a 29-21 record, and stood only three games behind the Yankees. With an overflow crowd expected at Shibe Park, ropes were laid out beyond the outfield lines. Naylor, not scheduled to start, shagged flies. Then he tripped over one of the ropes, damaging ligaments in his left leg.[37] For the next four weeks, he was sidelined. By the time he returned, other injuries had riddled the Athletics. The team was under .500 and out of the race.

"Rollie was never his self after that," an onlooker noted.[38] After he returned in July, his performance was pedestrian. Naylor concluded the 1923 season with a 12-7 record and a 3.46 ERA (an ERA+ of 119). The Athletics finished 69-83 and climbed another rung in the standings to sixth place. The next season, Naylor began badly, going 0-5 in 10 games with a 6.34 ERA (an ERA+ of 68). On June 28, 1924, with Philadelphia languishing in last place, Mack traded Naylor and Paul Strand to Toledo for Bill Lamar. For the remainder of the season—indeed for almost a decade to come—the Athletics played winning baseball.

With the Mud Hens in 1924, Naylor went 4-10. The next season, he spent time with four clubs. In May, New Haven purchased him from Toledo.[39] Later that month, Seattle picked up the hurler, only to sell him to Mobile after two months. Naylor spent the entire 1926 season with Mobile. The Bears released him that August, and the pitcher returned home to Oklahoma to twirl for Tulsa for the next two seasons. His "tantalizing slow balls" helped the Oilers win the Class-A Western League pennant in 1927, and the circuit's playoffs in 1928.[40] Naylor was then signed by Toronto as a free agent. But he was soon back in the Western League, pitching—and scouting—for Pueblo in 1929 and 1930.[41] His professional pitching career concluded with the Fort Smith Twins of the Class-C Western Association in 1931.

Naylor then turned to umpiring. He began with the Eastern League in 1932. But that circuit soon folded, and Naylor caught on with the Western League. In 1936 he joined the Texas League's staff, where he remained until he concluded his officiating career with the American Association in the 1943 season.

Gertrude died suddenly in the early 1930s, along with a baby; the couple had no other surviving children. Sometime later that decade, possibly from his travels as a Western League umpire, Naylor met Pauline (Vanora) Lyon, in Des Moines. The two soon married. From her first marriage, Pauline had a daughter, Maxine.[42]

After umpiring, Naylor lived in Fort Worth, where he sold men's clothing before retiring in 1960. Baseball friends often visited, and he closely followed Texas League action. But he was characteristically modest about his major-league career, finding greater satisfaction in playing catch with Maxine's children than in reciting past glories. On June 18, 1966, Rollie Naylor died from a heart attack. Pauline, Maxine, and five step-grandchildren survived him. He was buried in the Odd Fellows Cemetery in Denton, Texas.

## SOURCES

In addition to the sources noted in this biography, the author also accessed Naylor's file from the National Baseball Hall of Fame, the *Encyclopedia of Minor League Baseball*, and a number of sites such as ancestry.com, baseball-reference.com, chroniclingamerica.loc.gov/newspapers, genealogybank.com, newspapers.com, and retrosheet.com.

The author is grateful to Joe Hartwell for his insights toward the 65th Coast Artillery Corps, and especially to Ron Sanders (the pitcher's step-grandson) for sharing his knowledge of Rollie Naylor's life.

## NOTES

1. From baseball-reference.com's play index, 1876 through 2016. Immediately ahead of Naylor on this list, with a career winning percentage of .370, is his teammate, Scott Perry.

2. Ron Sanders, telephone interview with the author, March 8, 2017. Naylor, on his World War I draft registration card (available via ancestry.com), wrote: "lost eyesight of right eye." Also, for an elderly Athletics fan recalling Naylor's loss of sight, see Edgar Williams, "Woman's Memories of Old-Time Baseball," *Philadelphia Inquirer*, January 24, 1993. This fan recalled Naylor having a glass eye which, per Sanders, is not accurate: he did not lose his right eye, just its sight.

3. "Raising Baseball Money," *Daily Ardmoreite* (Oklahoma), February 26, 1913; "More Players Here," *Daily Ardmoreite*, March 26, 1913; "Ardmore Loses Another Game," *Daily Ardmoreite*, April 17, 1913; "Three Straight to Texarkana," *Daily Ardmoreite*, April 30, 1913.

4. "Durant 11, Bonham 10," *Bonham* (Texas) *Daily Favorite*, June 7, 1913.

5. "Friday's Results," *Daily Ardmoreite*, July 27, 1913.

6. "Three in a Row From the Giants," *Houston Post*, June 24, 1915.

7. "Twenty Players Are in Navigators' Camp," *Dallas Morning News*, March 12, 1916.

8. "Broncs Take Fast Game From Navs," *Waco Morning News*, April 9, 1916; "Kike's Komment," *Fort Worth Star-Telegram*, September 16, 1916.

9. *Sporting Life*, January 6, 1917, 10.

10. Norman Macht, *Connie Mack: The Turbulent & Triumphant Years, 1915-1931* (Lincoln: University of Nebraska Press, 2012), 60-87.

11. T.H. Murnane, ed., *Spalding's Official Guide of the National Association of Professional Base Ball Leagues, 1917* (New York: American Sports Publishing Company, 1917), 25.

12. "Baseball's Two Highest-Priced Performers Will Exhibit Wares in Diamond Classic This Fall," *Philadelphia Evening Public Ledger*, September 17, 1917.

13. "Another Recruit Reports to Mack," *Philadelphia Inquirer*, April 4, 1919; James C. Isaminger, "Phils Will Try Out Much Young Talent," *The Sporting News*, March 20, 1919: 1.

14. Naylor's headstone indicates he served with the 162nd Depot Brigade. During World War I depot brigades served as staging areas for men coming from or going to specific units. If he indeed served with the 65th Coast Artillery Corps, it is quite possible he passed through the 162nd. For background on the 65th, see Joe Hartwell, "The History of the 65th Artillery, C.A.C. 1917-1919," freepages.military.rootsweb.ancestry.com/~cacunithistories/65th%20Arty.html, accessed March 9, 2017.

15 "City News and Views," *Daily Ardmoreite*, March 1, 1918; "Many Branches of Service Are Represented in Legion Membership," *Daily Ardmoreite*, November 7, 1920.

16 J.C. Kofoed, "Stove League Stories," *The Sporting News*, January 31, 1924: 6; "Buds From Rose Field," *Philadelphia Evening Public Ledger*, March 20, 1917.

17 "Recruit Pitcher of Macks Hands Nationals Defeat," *Washington Herald*, September 15, 1917.

18 Ibid.

19 "Mrs. Naylor Is Also a 'Fork' Ball Twirler," *Mount Carmel* (Pennsylvania) *Item*," June 13, 1923.

20 "Billy Evans Says," *Jersey City Journal*, July 18, 1923.

21 "Connie Mack's Team Beats New Haven in Sunday Contest," *Bridgeport* (Connecticut) *Times and Evening Farmer*, September 8, 1919.

22 J.C. Kofoed, "Stove League Stories," *The Sporting News*, November 30, 1922: 6; "Mrs. Naylor."

23 James C. Isaminger, "Tampering With His Players Must Stop," *The Sporting News*, December 11, 1919: 1.

24 Ibid.

25 James C. Isaminger, "Connie Nails Yarn by Gotham Scribes," *The Sporting News*, January 22, 1920: 1.

26 James C. Isaminger, "Shibe Park Setting Record for Homers," *The Sporting News*, May 27, 1920: 1.

27 Harry Bullion, "Peace Reigns as Baseball Chiefs Gather," *Detroit Free Press*, December 10, 1920; "Nationals Sign New Agreement," *Philadelphia Inquirer*, December 15, 1920.

28 For a game account, see "Tiges Win Longest Battle of Season," *Detroit Free Press*, July 13, 1921.

29 For a game account, see I.E. Sanborn, "Falk's Homer in 14th Nets Faber Victory No. 20," *Chicago Tribune*, July 22, 1921.

30 James C. Isaminger, "This Sounds Like Annual Tale That Connie Mack Has to Tell," *The Sporting News*, December 1, 1921: 1.

31 "Landis Refuses to Help in Settling Salary Scrap Between Mack and His Men," *Philadelphia Inquirer*, February 12, 1922; James C. Isaminger, "Fletcher Returning to Play Second Base for Phillies," *The Sporting News*, February 23, 1922: 1.

32 Edwin J. Pollock, "Naylor's Work Pleases Connie," *Philadelphia Evening Public Ledger*, April 19, 1922.

33 For a game account, see Ed Cunningham, "Athletics Defeat Red Sox, 3 to 2, in Opening Game at Fenway Park," *Boston Herald*, April 13, 1922.

34 James C. Isaminger, "Different Tune on Shibe Park Homers," *The Sporting News*, May 18, 1922: 1.

35 "Shibe Park Flashes," *Philadelphia Inquirer*, April 25, 1923.

36 "Tigers Send Johnny Kerr to Omaha Leaving but Two Extra Infielders," *Detroit Free Press*, June 10, 1923.

37 "Jinx Hits Mack's Title Contenders," *Harrisburg Telegraph*, June 18, 1923.

38 "Strand and Naylor Traded to Toledo," *Philadelphia Inquirer*, June 29, 1924.

39 "Rollie Naylor Back With New Haven Club," *Springfield* (Massachusetts) *Republican*, May 7, 1925; "Naylor Found for Blows in Pinches," *Springfield* (Massachusetts) *Republican*, May 11, 1925.

40 "Tulsa Wins Flag Playoff From Rivals," *Des Moines Register*, October 2, 1928.

41 Walter E. Dobbins, "State League Notes," *Lincoln* (Nebraska) *Evening Journal*, August 5, 1930.

42 Details of Naylor's family life from Ron Sanders, telephone interview with the author, March 8, 2017.

# SUNNY JIM PASTORIUS

## BY GLEN SPARKS

**THE NUMBERS LOOK AS GLOOMY AS** an April rainout. Sunny Jim Pastorius compiled a career won-loss mark of just 31-55 in four seasons with the Brooklyn Superbas. That equated to a modest .360 winning percentage. He endured 20 losses in 1908.

During one awful streak, Pastorius lost a team-record 15 straight games. The left-hander posted a humbling 5-29 record in his final two campaigns. Brooklyn, having seen enough, released him, effectively ending his major-league career.

Grim stuff, right? But wait. The story of Sunny Jim's baseball life is not simply one of hanging curveballs, bases on balls, and tough defeats. Pastorius enjoyed many big moments while on the pitcher's mound. The 5-foot-10-inch, 165-pound hurler with a mop of dark hair went a respectable 26-26 in his first two seasons. He did this for teams that finished a combined 38 games below .500 and 90 games out of first place. He even led the Superbas in wins one year. Yes, Sunny Jim had some talent. He posted a career 3.12 ERA over 727 innings, completed 57 games, and tossed 10 shutouts.

James Washington Pastorius was born on July 12, 1881, in Pittsburgh, the son of Robert and Martha Jane "Jenny" (Woods) Pastorius. Young Jim grew up in a brawny city that flexed its industrial muscle. The Edgar Thomson Steel Works had opened near the Monongahela River in 1872. Soon enough, business tycoon Andrew Carnegie merged Thomson and other companies into US Steel. Pittsburgh, already famous as an iron maker, would soon be known as America's Steel City. Robert Pastorius was employed as a puddler, working with molten iron, an occupation known for producing a short life expectancy. Robert (1844-1882) died the year after James was born. James appears to have been the youngest of six children born to Robert and Jenny.

At a young age, Jim Pastorius worked as a laborer in a Pittsburgh mill, according to the 1900 census. He began his professional baseball career in 1902 with the Albany Senators of the Class-B New York State League. He pitched there from 1902 through 1905 and appeared in 122 games. (He probably acquired the "Sunny Jim" nickname about this time. Jingle writer Minnie Maud Hanff invented morose Jim Dumps and happy-go-lucky Sunny Jim in 1902 to advertise Force, a new wheat-bran cereal. One bowl of Force and Jim Dumps turned into Sunny Jim. Figures of Sunny Jim appeared in magazines, on billboards and trolley cars, and elsewhere.)[1]

Among Pastorius's best efforts with Albany: He knocked off the Amsterdam-Gloversville-Johnstown Jags 7-1 on July 27, 1905. Sunny Jim struck out eight and walked just one in going the distance. Losing hurler Frank McPartlin gave up 13 hits and all seven Albany runs. According to *Sporting Life*, "Pastorius had the locals completely at his mercy, while McPartlin's riddles were easily solved by the Senators."[2] Sunny Jim earned a promotion to Brooklyn in the spring of 1905.

The Superbas needed help. They had suffered through a franchise-worst record of 48-104 in 1905, settling into last place, 56½ games behind the pennant-winning New York Giants. Right fielder Harry Lumley led the team with a .293 batting average and seven home runs. William "Doc" Scanlan went 14-12 on the mound with a 2.92 ERA to anchor the pitching staff. Ned Hanlon, Brooklyn's manager since 1899 and known by some as Foxy Ned, lost his job after that sorrowful season. Owner Charles Ebbets hired Patrick "Patsy" Donovan, a native of Queenstown, Ireland, as the team's new skipper.

A 24-year-old Pastorius pitched his first major-league game on April 15, 1906, against the Boston Beaneaters. Irving Melrose Young opposed Sunny Jim. A left-hander like Pastorius, Young was in his second year in the majors. He had gone 20-21 for Boston in 1905. Some reporters had taken to calling Irv Young "Cy the Second," and "Young Cy" after the great hurler Denton True "Cy" Young. (Irv Young never quite lived up to his nickname. He went 63-95 in six big-league seasons.)

It was a soggy Sunday afternoon in Brooklyn. The bad weather kept attendance down to about 5,000 fans at Washington Park. Pastorius made it through five innings. He gave up a run in the second inning and two apiece in the fourth and fifth. Young allowed a solo home run to Lumley in the fourth and two tallies in the ninth. The *Brooklyn Daily Eagle* described Lumley's homer as "a perfect drive, straight as a bird's flight out of sight."[3] The Superbas lost 5-3 and dropped to 0-4 in the young season. A tough-minded reporter called Pastorius "something of a disappointment," but added, "Still with the slippery ball, he was greatly handicapped, and it is well to suspend judgment on his abilities until a better day."[4]

The young pitcher responded. He beat the Cincinnati Reds 4-1 on May 23 in Brooklyn and "was remarkably steady throughout."[5] Sunny Jim allowed just five hits, fanned three and walked one. Only one Reds player reached base after the first inning. According to Jack Ryder of the *Cincinnati Enquirer*: "As the confident Reds were about to reach out and grab a seventh victory, a youth with a name that sounds like a patent medicine got in their way and blocked them off."[6] Ryder added: "The young giant (Pastorius) is a southpaw who belonged in Brooklyn last year but needed some more of that valuable article known as experience. … It will be a long time before he has to go back for more."[7]

Pastorius lost 4-1 on June 15 to his hometown Pittsburgh Pirates. A *Daily Eagle* writer blamed the defeat on tired Superbas bats, though, not Sunny Jim. "'Lefty' Pastorius twirled well enough to win ordinarily, but Donovan's men have lost their batting eyes lately," the *Eagle* opined.[8] Claude Ritchey drove in two Pittsburgh runs. Jim Nealon banged out a double and a triple, both times with two strikes against him. "Later, Pastorius got revenge by striking him out on a wide offshoot," according to the *Eagle*. "Barring some lightning fielding, the game was devoid of thrill and was over in eighty-two minutes."[9] Brooklyn dropped to 21-33.

The 1906 Superbas finished in fifth place with a 66-86 mark, 50 games behind the powerhouse Chicago Cubs (116-36). On the upside, it was an 18-game improvement for them over the previous season. Lumley batted .324, while first baseman Tim Jordan knocked 12 home runs (the most in the National League) and drove in 78 runs. Once again, Scanlan topped the team in wins, going 18-13. Pastorius ended up 10-14 (a .417 winning percentage) with a 3.61 ERA in 211⅔ innings. He pitched in 29 games, started 24, and completed 16. Pastorius fanned 58 and walked 69.

Pastorius apparently spent some time in the off-season getting medical attention. Doctors straightened a ligament in his back, making him "much better on his feet in the pitching box" and "much better than formerly at picking up bunts."[10]

In early March of 1907, Pastorius, along with several teammates, boarded the steamship Comanche in Manhattan, bound for the Superbas' spring-training camp in Jacksonville, Florida. Some players, though, opted to travel by train. At least one newspaper report speculated that the sea air might be more fit for sailors than for ballplayers. "The club management, however, seems to think that the innovation will be a pleasing one and be very helpful to the health of the men," the writer concluded.[11]

Apparently no player suffered from lingering seasickness or any other malady after the three-day ocean voyage. By late March, the Superbas had enjoyed "more than two weeks of good, honest practice behind them" and were "probably more advanced than any other club in the league."[12] Brooklyn team treasurer Henry Medicus liked the team, especially its pitching staff. "(George) Bell and (Nap) Rucker look especially good to me, while Pastorius is wonderfully improved," he said.[13] Medicus predicted that with a good start "I don't think anyone can stop us."[14] He reported, with an air of optimism that shines like the Florida sun, "We have as good a chance for the pennant as anybody."[15]

# 20-GAME LOSERS

It didn't work out that way. The Superbas did not get off to a good start. Really, they did not get off to a bad start, either. No, the Brooklyn Superbas of 1907 got off to a disastrous start. They were 1-16-1 after their first 18 games. That probably ended any talk of future pennant glory.

Brooklyn began the season by losing its first four games. It was Pastorius who put finally put the Superbas into the win column. He shut out the New York Giants, 3-0, on April 18 at Washington Park. Pastorius surrendered just two hits in a pitchers' duel with Luther "Dummy" Taylor, a deaf-mute from Kansas who would win 116 games in the big leagues. Brooklyn broke through with two runs in the seventh and one in the eighth. "It was a pitcher's battle all the way," reported the *Daily Eagle*, "with Pastorius going like a well-oiled bit of machinery."[16]

Pastorius pitched many other fine games. He beat the Boston Doves (the former Beaneaters) 7-1 in the opening game of a doubleheader on May 28 in Boston. Pastorius gave up a solo homer to Clarence "Ginger" Beaumont in the first inning and blanked Boston the rest of the way. He scattered eight hits. "The weather was intensely cold" and "Pastorius was in excellent form."[17] Pastorius helped Brooklyn sweep a doubleheader against the Philadelphia Phillies on June 22 at Washington Park. He allowed one run on six hits as the Superbas won 5-1. He "pitched brilliantly and the Phillies were fortunate to avoid a shut out," the *Daily Eagle* boasted.[18]

Pastorius scattered 11 hits on July 19 in a lopsided win at home against the Cincinnati Reds. Brooklyn managed just two more hits than the Reds, but the Superbas made them count. They led 4-0 after two innings and won 8-1. "Jimmy Pastorius shines resplendently," the *Daily Eagle* announced in a subhead.[19] Pastorius even added three hits of his own. He struck out two Cincinnati batters and walked one. "Pastorius took things easy after his Superbas

had secured a safe lead, depending on his fielders to pull him out," the *Daily Eagle* reported.[20]

Brooklyn played nearly .500 baseball after that debacle of a beginning and finished 65-83, in fifth place, 40 games behind the first-place Chicago Cubs. Lumley led the team with 9 home runs and 66 RBIs. Pastorius fashioned a 16-12 won-loss record. At one point, he was 11-5 (.688 winning percentage) before going 5-7 down the stretch. It was his best season in the majors. The 25-year-old led the team in wins and posted what was a career-low ERA (2.35). He set career highs for innings pitched (222), complete games (20), and shutouts (4). Pastorius started 26 games and relieved in two others.[21]

Pastorius surely hoped to build on that solid 1907 campaign. However, not much went right for the pitcher or the team in '08. The Superbas mostly struggled and finished just 53-101 (.344). They ended the season in seventh place. It was Brooklyn's worst showing during the Sunny Jim Pastorius era.

Brooklyn's record stood at a modest 15-26 on June 6, following an 8-2 drubbing by the Reds. The Superbas had lost three straight games and eight out of 10. Pastorius took the ball on June 8. Cincinnati scored three early runs, and that was enough. Brooklyn managed just two tallies. The sloppy Superbas committed five errors. After the last out, "the gloom that pervaded the directors' office after the game could hardly be penetrated."[22] How could the Superbas turn things around? The *Daily Eagle* reported that Ebbets would not sell any player, "but was ready to make any swap calculated to strengthen the outfit."[23]

The losing also started to wear on Pastorius. The Pittsburgh Pirates' Albert "Lefty" Liefeld beat him 2-0 on July 21. Pittsburgh scored one run in the first inning and another in the fifth. "Jim never faltered, but kept right on working," the *Post-Gazette* reported. "Yet when he realized the game was slipping away from him for good, he began to show signs of uneasiness and irritation."[24] Pastorius did not care for the umpiring. In the eighth inning, he was called out on strikes and "entered a vigorous protest." Later, he showed his disapproval of ump Bob Emslie's judgment by "chewing the rag" continuously. "All the same," the writer decided, "he pitched a great game."[25] (The *Post-Gazette* referred to Sunny Jim as the "South Side glass worker," apparently hinting at an offseason career in his hometown.[26])

Pastorius hooked up again with Irv Young, now with the Pirates, for an epic duel on August 22, 1908. Young Cy and Sunny Jim put up goose eggs for 16 straight innings. According to the *Daily Eagle*, they "worked like Trojans and seemed to grow stronger as the minutes sped away."[27]

Pittsburgh scored the winning run with two outs in the 17th inning. Young had singled and raced to third on a Roy Thomas base hit. Pastorius walked Tommy Leach to load the bases. Danny Moeller knocked a ball over second base, bringing home Young. Pastorius scattered 11 hits, Young gave up nine. Brooklyn dropped to 40-68.

Pastorius took the mound September 26 in the second game of a doubleheader against the Chicago Cubs. His won-loss record stood—or had slumped to—a humble 3-19. The Cubs won the first game of the double dip, 5-0, behind Ed Ruelbach, who struck out seven batters. Ruelbach, playing the role of workhorse, also started the second game. Chicago scored a single run in the third inning following a Johnny Kling hit and an error by Tommy McMillan. The Cubs added two runs in the eighth. Ruelbach walked with two out, and Jack Hayden singled to put runners on first and second. Johnny Evers followed with a liner to center field. Brooklyn outfielder Al Burch's throw sailed away from Joe Dunn, allowing both runners to score.

Pastorius gave up the three runs and five hits, struck out two, and walked three in picking up the loss. "While Reulbach was puzzling the Superbas, (Irving "Kaiser") Wilhelm and Pastorius were doing their best with the poor support which was accorded them. Ed Reulbach was the whole procession yesterday afternoon."[28] Reulbach pitched a total of 18 innings, gave up no runs, nine hits, and two walks, and struck out 11.

The *Daily Eagle* praised the Superbas' fan support: "For a tail-end team, the crowd of close to 15,000

PASTORIUS, BROOKLYN

shows how popular the national game is in this borough. There was considerable enthusiasm, and as both teams pulled off some remarkable fielding stunts, there was ample opportunity to applaud."[29]

Sunny Jim Pastorius, who lost 15 consecutive games at one point, managed to win his final start of the year. Brooklyn nipped Boston 3-2 on October 2. Boston scored both its runs in the third inning on an error by Al Burch and led 2-1 going into the eighth inning. In that late frame, Brooklyn's Tim Jordan doubled home John Hummel to tie the score and raced home on Tommy Sheehan's base hit. "Pastorius had one of his good days, and outside of that (third) inning, the Bostons were neatly blanked."[30] Pastorius allowed seven hits, struck out four, and gave up a walk. He ended the season with a 4-20 record. The pitcher completed 16 games, blanked two teams, and had a 2.44 ERA.

Jordan led the Brooklyn offense in '08 with 12 homers (the most in the NL) and 60 RBIs. He didn't get much help. Brooklyn batted just .213 as a team. No major-league team has ever hit fewer doubles than the 110 the Superbas got in 1908. (The 2008 Texas Rangers hold the major-league record for most doubles in a season, 376. The 1930 St. Louis Cardinals own the NL record with 373.)[31] On the mound, Rucker led the team with 17 wins. He lost 19, though. The Superbas nearly had four 20-game losers in 1908. Besides Pastorius, Wilhelm (16-22) and Harry McIntire (11-20) also reached that mark. Maybe not surprisingly, Ebbets fired Donovan as manager after three seasons and hired Lumley to run the team.

The 1909 Superbas, though, did not look much different from Brooklyn teams of the recent past. They didn't make a run at the pennant, won just 55 games, lost 98 and ended up in sixth place, 55½ games behind the pennant-winning Pirates. This would be Pastorius's final season in the big leagues.

Not much went right for Sunny Jim in 1909. He won just one of 10 decisions and finished with a sky-high ERA of 5.76 in 79⅔ innings. He did, however, pitch one of the best games of his career. Pastorius nearly no-hit the Philadelphia Phillies on July 28 at the Baker Bowl. Philadelphia catcher Leon "Doc" Martell broke up the no-no with a one-out triple in the ninth inning and with Brooklyn ahead, 4-0. The hit annoyed infielder George McQuillan so much that he "threw his glove in the air and jumped on it when it came down."[32]

Pastorius, who walked four, got the final two outs and kept the shutout. He secured his first and only win of the season. The Philly fans had been rooting for Pastorius as the opposing pitcher took the mound in the ninth. "A cry of disappointment went up from the stands when Martell made the hit," the *Eagle* reported.[33]

Pastorius struggled in many of his starts. He allowed nine free passes and eight runs in a 9-1 loss to the Pirates on August 3. Pastorius, the *Pittsburgh Daily Post* decided, "gave the wildest exhibition seen here in years."[34] A few weeks later, on August 23, the St. Louis Cardinals lit up Pastorius, again by a 9-1 score, in the second game of a doubleheader at Washington Park. The Cards scored four runs in the first inning; the home crowd, unsympathetic toward their pitcher's woes, began yelling "Take him out!"[35] The *Eagle* sympathized with Pastorius. "Pitchers are only human, although the baseball fan doesn't seem to realize it," the newspaper opined.[36]

During his final campaign, Pastorius allowed 58 walks in 79⅔ innings, or 6.6 per nine innings. To make matters worse, he surrendered 91 hits. His WHIP that season soared to 1.870, the highest of his career by far. Brooklyn released the 28-year-old to the Louisville Colonels in the American Association on August 28. He later pitched for the Kansas City Blues and the Milwaukee Brewers, also in the American Association, before being let go in 1911.[37]

At the time of his 1918 registration for the World War I draft, Pastorius was employed as a machinist's helper, but by 1920 he had found work as a county roads inspector. Pastorius spent more than 20 years with the Allegheny County Highway Department and worked his way up to foreman. He kept active in baseball by helping young ballplayers who lived on Pittsburgh's south side. Pastorius suffered from diabetes and died on May 10, 1941, at St. Joseph's Hospital in Pittsburgh, at the age of 59 due to complications from an infection of the veins leading to venous thrombosis.[38] He had been sick for about six weeks. Divorced at the time of his death, Pastorius left behind one son, Dr. George J. Pastorius, plus a brother and a sister. Sunny Jim is buried in the city's South Side Cemetery.

The name of Sunny Jim Pastorius popped again in 1987. Pitcher Rick Honeycutt was suffering through a miserable season for the Los Angeles Dodgers. He lost 11 straight games at one point. The question began to circulate in newspapers: Would Honeycutt break Pastorius's all-time Dodgers record for most consecutive losses? Alas, with that dubious streak still intact, the Dodgers traded Honeycutt to the Oakland A's in August. Sunny Jim's record was safe.

## SOURCES

In addition to the sources cited in the Notes, the author also consulted Baseball-Reference.com and the Pastorius player file at the National Baseball Hall of Fame.

## NOTES

1. Eileen Margerum, "A Case for Sunny Jim: An Advertising Legend Revisited," *The Journal of Salem State College*, Fall 2001/Spring 2002.
2. *Sporting Life*, Volume 45, No 23, 1905.
3. *Brooklyn Daily Eagle*, April 16, 1906: 6.
4. Ibid.
5. *Cincinnati Enquirer*, May 24, 1906: 4.
6. Ibid.
7. Ibid.
8. *Brooklyn Daily Eagle*, June 16, 1906: 8.
9. Ibid.
10. *Washington Evening Star*, March 31, 1907: 62.
11. *Pittsburgh Press*, March 4, 1907: 12.
12. .*Pittsburgh Press*, March 27, 1907: 18.
13. Ibid.
14. Ibid.
15. Ibid.
16. *Brooklyn Daily Eagle*, April 19, 1907: 22.
17. *Brooklyn Daily Eagle*, May 29, 1907: 20.
18. *Brooklyn Daily Eagle*, June 23, 1907: 58.
19. *Brooklyn Daily Eagle*, July 20, 1907: 12.
20. Ibid.
21. The Superbas team was not, as it may be evident, always superb. Founded originally as an American Association club in 1884, the Brooklyn Base Ball Club was known by several unofficial nicknames throughout its history. Some called them the Atlantics or Grays and by 1888 the team was referred to the Grooms or Bridegrooms. The Superbas moniker became fashionable starting in 1899 when Brooklyn won the National League championship. The Superbas repeated that feat in 1900, and the team nickname stuck, at least for a while. Another name that was common (ca. 1895) was Trolley Dodgers, later shortened to Dodgers. They were known as the Robins, for their manager Wilbert "Uncle Robbie" Robinson from 1914 to 1931. The club has been officially known as the Dodgers since 1932, and the name was first inscribed on their uniforms beginning in 1933. But as Brooklyn fans could have told you, the team was also referred to as "Dem Bums." See John Thorn, ed., *Total Baseball* 6th Ed. (New York: Total Sports, 1999), 34-35; "Brooklyn Dodgers," baseball-reference.com/bullpen/Brooklyn_Dodgers; "Dodgers Uniforms and Logos," losangeles.dodgers.mlb.com/la/history/uniforms_logos.jsp.
22. *Brooklyn Daily Eagle*, June 9, 1908: 22.
23. Ibid.
24. *Pittsburgh Post-Gazette*, July 22, 1908: 9.

25 Ibid.
26 Ibid.
27 *Brooklyn Daily Eagle*, August 23, 1908: 42.
28 *Brooklyn Daily Eagle*, September 27, 1908: 49.
29 Ibid.
30 *Brooklyn Daily Eagle*, October 3, 1908: 20.
31 baseball-almanac.com/rb_2b2.shtml.
32 *Brooklyn Daily Eagle*, July 29, 1909: 18.
33 Ibid.
34 *Pittsburgh Daily Post*, August 4, 1909: 7.
35 *Brooklyn Daily Eagle*, August 24, 1909: 18.
36 Ibid.
37 Jim Pastorius's Hall of Fame player file.
38 Commonwealth of Pennsylvania Certificate of Death.

# ORLANDO PEÑA

## BY JOEL RIPPEL

**ORLANDO PEÑA WAS A TYPICAL** youth in Cuba in the early 1950s. He was crazy about baseball. As a teenager, he played baseball in Havana with a group of friends who included future major leaguers Jackie Hernandez, Marcelino Lopez, and Zoilo Versalles.[1]

Peña was born Orlando Gregorio (Quevara) Peña in Victoria de las Tunas, Cuba, on November 17, 1933. Victoria de las Tunas is the capital of Las Tunas Province in east-central Cuba about 400 miles from Havana.

Before turning to baseball as a teenager, Peña worked as a butcher in his father's supermarket. (He had scars on his fingers to remind him of his first job.) He went on to play professional baseball for nearly two decades.[2]

In 1955 Peña and 286 others attended a tryout camp in Havana conducted by the Cincinnati Reds. He was one of three players signed by the Reds out of the camp. He got no bonus and was assigned to Daytona Beach of the Class-D Florida State League for $175 a month.

Peña won 21 games with a 1.96 ERA for Daytona Beach and earned all-star honors. For 1956 the Reds assigned him to High Point-Thomasville of the Class-B Carolina League. There he went 19-12 with a 2.42 ERA to help the Hi-Toms earn the league title.

After winning 40 games in his first two professional seasons, Peña moved up to the Triple-A International League in 1957. As a spot starter (12 starts) and reliever for the Havana Sugar Kings, he was 12-10 (tying for team lead in victories) with a 2.76 ERA. On the next to last day of the season, pitching in relief against the Miami Marlins, Peña was struck in the face by a line drive, but x-rays revealed no fractures.

In 1958 Peña went to spring training with the Reds, one of 22 pitchers in camp. He opened the season with Havana. Used again as a spot starter and reliever, Peña was 11-10 with a 3.27 ERA and four shutouts. The Reds brought him up in late August.

On August 24, 1958, Peña made his major-league debut, in relief against the Los Angeles Dodgers at LA Memorial Coliseum. After allowing a single to Gino Cimoli to lead off the bottom of the eighth inning, Peña retired the next six hitters and was the winning pitcher when the Reds rallied in the ninth to grab a 6-5 victory.

Over the final month of the season, Peña made nine relief appearances, allowing just one earned run in 15 innings. He was 1-0 with three saves and a 0.60 ERA.

After pitching in 25 games in the Cuban League over the winter, Peña reported to spring training with the Reds in 1959. He solidified his bid to make the Opening Day roster by tossing a complete-game five-hitter in a 4-1 exhibition victory over the St. Louis Cardinals on March 25. Peña allowed just four earned runs and 21 hits in 26 innings in four exhibition appearances.

Peña indeed stuck with the Reds; one columnist wrote that Peña was his "dark-horse nominee for rookie of the year."[3] Peña made eight starts and 38 relief appearances in 1959, going 5-9 with five saves and a 4.76 ERA. San Francisco's Willie McCovey was a unanimous choice as the Rookie of the Year.

Peña didn't make the Reds' Opening Day roster in 1960. He opened the season with Havana (which was relocated by the International League to Jersey City on July 7). Peña went 13-11 with a 3.30 ERA in 37 appearances (29 starts) to earn a September recall by the Reds. Peña was 0-1 with a 2.89 ERA in four appearances over the final two weeks of the season.

Peña spent the entire 1961 season in the International League. He opened the season with Jersey City but in July was traded to the Toronto Maple Leafs with cash for pitcher Ken Johnson. Peña was 12-8 with a 3.75 in 41 appearances for the two teams. In November, the Reds, who still controlled Peña's contract, sold him to Toronto.

Peña opened the 1962 season with Toronto, which now had a working agreement with the Milwaukee Braves. He was 9-9 with a 3.12 ERA in 24 appearances for the Maple Leafs. He made 19 starts (with 10 complete games and five shutouts) before the Braves traded him to the Kansas City Athletics on August 3, 1962.

The Athletics, who were managed by Hank Bauer and in ninth place (46-61) at the time of the trade, moved Peña into the starting rotation immediately.

On August 5 Peña made his American League debut, pitching a complete-game six-hitter in Kansas City's 5-2 victory over the Cleveland Indians. Cleveland's runs were solo home runs by Al Luplow and Tito Francona. Peña helped his own cause with an RBI single. He picked up his second victory with a five-hitter in a 12-1 victory over the Twins in Minnesota on August 24. Five days later, Peña tossed his first major-league shutout, allowing three hits in a 6-0 victory over the Los Angeles Angels in Kansas City. Over the final two months of the season, Peña was 6-4 with a 3.01 ERA in 13 appearances.

Peña and the Athletics got off to a good start in 1963. He won three games without a loss in the first month (including a 5-0 shutout of the Baltimore Orioles). Peña's fourth victory, 11-3 over the Cleveland Indians on May 1, was a four-hitter.

Peña lost his next five decisions, but his five-hitter in a 9-3 victory over the Washington Senators on May 31 evened his record at 5-5. In June he and the Athletics both struggled. Peña went 0-5 as the Athletics won just 9 of 30 games.

Peña's losing streak reached eight games before he beat the Baltimore Orioles, 2-1, on July 19. Peña won his next two decisions to improve to 8-13 but then lost his next six decisions to drop to 8-19 on August 25.

On August 31 he earned his ninth victory with a 7-0 shutout of the Angels in Kansas City, and he won his next two starts to improve to 11-19.

On September 14 Peña lasted just one inning in the Athletics' 6-4 loss to Boston in Kansas City. He allowed four runs in the first inning (including three on a home run by future Hall of Fame manager Dick Williams) in his 20th loss of the season.

Six days later, Peña outpitched 20-game-winner Jim Bouton in the Athletics' 4-3 victory over the Yankees in New York.

Peña finished the season with a 12-20 record and a 3.69 ERA for the Athletics, who finished in eighth place (73-89).

In 1964 the Athletics dropped to last place with a 57-105 record. Peña led the pitching staff with 12 victories. He was 12-14 with a 4.43 ERA in 40 appearances (32 starts). In 219⅓ innings, Peña had a career-high 184 strikeouts.

Peña and the Athletics struggled at the start of the 1965 season. A 5-4 loss to the Chicago White Sox on May 18 dropped his record to 0-6 with a 6.88 ERA and the Athletics to 7-23. That was Peña's last start for the Athletics. He pitched out of the bullpen before being claimed on waivers by the Detroit Tigers on June 23. Peña, who had made 82 starts for the Athletics since August of 1962, would start only three more games in the major leagues.

After being acquired by the Tigers, Peña went 4-6 with four saves and a 2.51 ERA in 30 relief appearances. In 1966 he made 54 relief appearances for the Tigers (pitching 108 innings). He was 4-2 with seven saves and a 3.08 ERA.

Peña opened the 1967 season with the Tigers, but on May 6 he was sold to the Cleveland Indians. With the Indians, he made 48 appearances (one start), and was 0-3 with a team-high eight saves and a 3.36 ERA.

Peña did not make the Indians' Opening Day roster in 1968. He was optioned to Portland of the Triple-A Pacific Coast League and it would be two years before he returned to the major leagues. Peña was 3-6 with a 2.75 ERA in 27 appearances for Portland when his contract was sold on July 9 to the league rival Seattle Angels. With the Angels he was 4-0 and he finished the season with a 7-6 record and 2.80 ERA in 56 games.

In September 1968 Peña's contract was purchased by the expansion Kansas City Royals. Over the winter, Peña pitched in the Puerto Rican League, going 4-7 with a 1.97 ERA for league champion Santurce. Peña spent the 1969 season with the Royals' Omaha farm team in the revived American Association. He went 9-3 with a 4.34 ERA for the Royals, who won the league playoffs.

After the 1969 season, Peña pitched for Magallanes in the Venezuelan League. On November 16, the day before his 36th birthday, he had a memorable outing as he went the distance in a 1-1 game that was stopped by rain in the 15th inning. The next day, Peña who hadn't returned to Cuba since the Castro revolution in 1960, flew to Miami to meet his mother, who had been allowed to emigrate from Cuba. Peña rejoined Magallanes and helped the Navigators win the Caribbean World Series.

That performance gave Peña hope that he could stick with the Royals in 1970. Instead, he was released the day before Opening Day and was taken on as one of two batting practice pitchers for the Royals. Nick Willhite, who had spent parts of five seasons in the major leagues, was his left-handed counterpart.

"I had a good winter season in Venezuela, so I thought I had a chance of making the Royals," Peña said. "I knew it would be tough. Then when I saw all of those young guys, I knew I had problems. This organization is going with young guys.

"I talked everything over with my wife. [Manager] Charlie Metro explained how I could help the Royals. This is a beautiful organization to work for."[4]

In early June the Pittsburgh Pirates came to Kansas City for an exhibition game. Peña threw batting practice as usual. The next day he signed a free-agent contract with the Pirates, who were looking for bullpen help in their bid for the NL East Division title. Peña went 2-1 with two saves and a 4.78 ERA in 23 appearances for the Pirates before being released in late August.

In March of 1971, the 37-year-old Peña signed a minor-league contract with the Baltimore Orioles and spent time with the Orioles in camp. He opened the season with Miami of the Class-A Florida State League and in his first appearance of the season, pitched a 2-0 shutout victory over Key West. With a 9-4 record and a 0.70 ERA (nine earned runs in 115 innings), Peña earned a promotion to Rochester of the International League. With Rochester, he was 2-1 with five saves and a 2.45 ERA in 11 appearances. He also made five appearances with the Orioles in August, going 0-1 with a 3.07 ERA.

The four teams Peña played for in 1971 all won titles: La Guaira (Venezuela), Miami (its third straight Florida State League title); Rochester (which won the International League title and the Little World League Series); and the Orioles (the American League pennant). After the season, Peña, who pitched winter ball for 20 consecutive seasons, returned to the Venezuelan League.

Peña spent the entire 1972 season in the minor leagues again, splitting his time between Miami and Rochester. At 38, he had arguably his best season in Organized Baseball.

He started the season with Miami again, going 15-3 with five shutouts, seven saves, and a 1.38 ERA. In 10 appearances with Rochester, Peña was 7-0 with a 0.96 ERA. His combined season totals: 22-3 with a 1.25 ERA and 187 strikeouts in 180 innings.

That season earned Peña a nonroster invitation to spring training with the Orioles in 1973 and he pitched his way on to the squad. Peña was used sparingly by the Orioles over the first two months of the season, going 1-1 with a save and a 4.03 ERA in 11 appearances (including two starts). On June 15 the Orioles sold Peña's contract to the St. Louis Cardinals. He pitched well for the Cardinals: 4-4 with a 2.18 ERA in 42 relief appearances. His six saves were second on the club (behind fellow Cuban Diego Segui's 17).

Peña returned to the Cardinals in 1974, going 5-2 with a save and a 2.60 ERA in 42 appearances. On September 5 the Cardinals traded him to the California Angels for pitcher Rich Hand. In four appearances for the Angels over the final month of the season, Peña pitched eight shutout innings and recorded three saves. His three saves led the team (which had only 12 saves in a 68-94 season).

The 1974 season was the 11th in which Peña had pitched for two or more teams in the same season. Angels general manager Harry Dalton had an explanation for the many moves by Pena (18 teams in 20 professional seasons):

"For about eight years now people have thought that Orlando's arm was about to die and most clubs haven't wanted it to happen while he was on their roster. So whenever they have to make room, the old man is the first to go.

"But used right, Peña has proved he can still do a job. And he's a good guy to have on a club. When he was released by Pittsburgh I signed him (Dalton was then with Baltimore) and sent him to our Miami club as a player-coach and he was great with our young pitchers. He's simply a professional pitcher."[5]

In early March of 1975, Angels manager Dick Williams said that Peña was one of two relief pitchers assured of a spot on the Angels' Opening Day roster. In his 20th spring training, Peña acknowledged the rumors that he threw a doctored ball.

"Well," he said, "maybe I've thrown a few at various times. But then with the new spitball rules it's a little tougher, although there's no real way for the umpires to detect it. I throw a forkball, too, and it acts the same way as a spitter (dipping sharply at the plate). No, I don't mind if they accuse me of it because it makes the hitter worry a little more."[6]

Peña's major-league career ended in 1975, when he was released by the California Angels on May 5. The release came four days after he was the losing pitcher in the Angels' 11-10 loss in 13 innings to the Royals in Kansas City. Peña was 0-2 with a 2.13 ERA in seven appearances at the time of his release.

In his 14 big-league seasons, Peña was 56-77 with 40 saves and a 3.71 ERA in 427 appearances. He made only 93 starts in the big leagues—77 of them in his three seasons (1962-1964) with the Kansas City A's.

But Peña, who was 41, wasn't done pitching. After being released by the Angels, he signed a minor-league contract with the Oakland A's. After throwing three days of batting practice in Oakland, he was assigned to Tucson of the Pacific Coast League. Over the rest of the season, Peña went 2-6 with a 6.27 ERA in 21 appearances for the Toros.

In 1979 the Inter-American League, with franchises in Miami, Caracas, Santo Domingo, San Juan, Maracaibo (Venezuela), and Panama, was formed and classified as a Triple-A league. Roberto Maduro, the former owner of the Havana Sugar Kings, headed the league.

Peña was named the pitching coach for the Miami team, which was managed by Davey Johnson. Early in the season, Johnson was forced to leave the leave to seek medical attention for back problems. While he recovered from surgery, Peña and Hal Breeden were interim co-managers.

The league was short-lived. On June 17 the Panama and San Juan clubs folded. On June 30 the remaining four teams folded. Miami, with a 51-21 record, was in first place when the league shut down. Peña made one appearance on the mound for the Amigos, pitching six innings (allowing just one earned run), at the age of 45.

Over 13 minor-league seasons, Peña compiled a 148-91 record with a 2.75 ERA in 451 games (210 starts).

Soon after the Inter-American League folded, Peña went to work as a scout for the Detroit Tigers. He had an immediate impact.

In the first week of June of 1980, Commissioner Bowie Kuhn lifted the embargo on signing Cuban refugees. Peña and the Tigers led the way to the signing of Cubans. Peña signed three players — Eduardo Cajuso, Barbaro Garbey, and Roberto Salazar — to minor-league contracts. Cajuso and Salazar did not rise above Class A, but Garbey, whom Peña had discovered in a refugee camp at Fort Indiantown Gap, Pennsylvania, reached the majors with the Tigers in 1984. Garbey spent parts of three seasons in the major leagues during his career, which spanned 15 seasons (including seven in Mexico).

Peña worked for the Tigers through 1986, and then went to work for the Chicago White Sox as a scout and roving pitching coach.

In June of 1989, the White Sox summoned Peña to work with struggling pitcher Melido Perez.

Peña "tried to work the kinks out of Perez's forkball delivery. (Peña had learned to throw the forkball from Pirates great Elroy Face in the 1950s.) After working with Perez, Peña traveled to Sarasota, Florida, to work with first-round draft pick Jack McDowell, who had been sent to the minors after going 5-10 with the White Sox the previous season.[7]

Peña continued to work as a scout for the White Sox into the 1990s.

Peña is a member of the Caribbean Baseball Hall of Fame, which honors players primarily from the Caribbean Series. He pitched in four Caribbean Series.

## SOURCES

In addition to the sources cited in the Notes, the author also consulted Baseball-Reference.com, milb.com, and Retrosheet.org.

## NOTES

1. Patrick Reusse, "Versalles Was Our Early Hero; Shortstop Had a Real Love of the Game," *Minneapolis Star Tribune*, June 10, 1995: 1C.
2. Associated Press, "Orlando Pena Back Again After 17 Baseball Years," *Iowa City Press-Citizen*, April 21, 1972: 17.
3. Dick Young, "Young Ideas," *The Sporting News*, April 8, 1959: 20.
4. Joe McGuff, "Metro Goes to Bat for Sunken Bases," *The Sporting News*, May 2, 1970: 18.
5. Ross Newhan, "Orlando Pena: Does He or Doesn't He?" *Los Angeles Times*, March 18, 1975: G1.
6. Ibid.
7. Bill Jauss, "White Sox Notes," *Chicago Tribune*, June 18, 1989: B4.

# SCOTT PERRY

## BY PHIL WILLIAMS

**CONTROVERSY AND CONTRAST DE-** fined Scott Perry's brief major-league career. In 1918, his first full season, the Boston Braves and Philadelphia Athletics battled for his services, exposing the increasing inability of Organized Baseball to govern itself in the pre-commissioner era. Philadelphia retained Perry, and he produced a memorable rookie effort, becoming one of only seven pitchers in the twentieth century to win 20 games with a last-place team. But Perry's desire to pitch for the cellar-dwelling Athletics soon waned. In 1920, his final full season, he lost 25 games. Only three pitchers since have tasted as much defeat in a single campaign.

Officially, Herbert Scott Perry was born on April 17, 1891, in Denison, Texas. But later in life he claimed 1892 as his birth year and Corsicana, Texas, as his birthplace.[1] He likely had a hard-scrabble youth. By 1900 his mother, Sallie, headed the household, with his father apparently gone from the picture. As a young man, Scott did not spoke of his schooling, but claimed to be "a mighty good ditch digger."[2]

Perry made his professional debut in 1910, pitching for the Western Association's Tulsa Oilers.[3] He hoped to stick with the Western League's Wichita Jobbers in 1911, but before the season began, they optioned him to Hastings of the Nebraska League. The Wichita squad relocated to Pueblo in midseason, recalled Perry, and he finished the campaign in Colorado. The team returned to Wichita in 1912, and Perry was a staff workhorse for the next two seasons.

Contemporary accounts described the right-hander as "a tall, rangy youth" and a "big blond Adonis."[4] Nicknamed "Rope," he stood 6-feet-1 and weighed "better than 175 pounds without an ounce of surplus flesh on his body."[5] Perry became a family man, marrying Beulah, with son Scott Jr. and daughter Marmette soon arriving.

"They just fussed around with me for years," Perry later recalled of his convoluted career path.[6] Wichita dealt him to Louisville in June 1914. Perry was back with Colonels for the 1915 season, but clashed with manager Jack Hayden and jumped the team that May. Hayden responded by dealing him to the St. Louis Browns on a trial basis. Perry made his major-league debut on May 13, 1915, starting against the Athletics. He lasted two innings. St. Louis returned Perry to Louisville, which sold him to the Atlanta Crackers.[7]

Perry prospered in Atlanta, winning 40 games over the next two seasons. After the 1916 Southern Association campaign ended, Atlanta sold him to the Cubs. Per the deal's terms, Chicago put $2,000 on the barrelhead, with a remaining $4,000 due if the recruit lasted through the next Opening Day.[8] Perry pitched impressively that September. Chicago reserved him for the coming season.

But during 1917's spring training, new Cubs manager Fred Mitchell concluded that Perry was expendable. On April 10, a day before the season launched, Chicago wired Atlanta manager Charlie Frank that the pitcher was being returned. Perry instead stayed put, and signed on with the American Steel and Wire company team in Joliet.

Frank sold his AWOL pitcher to Cincinnati in another conditional and backloaded deal, with the bulk due if Perry remained with the Reds past June 1.[9] He went east, pitched poorly in four games, and was cast back to Atlanta before the larger payment came due. A week later Frank again dealt him, this time to the Boston Braves. The Braves would pay $500 for a 30-day trial, and another $2,000 if Perry was kept past this span. Perry clashed with Braves manager George Stallings and saw no game action. American Steel and Wire sent an offer. Perry jumped on June 17, 1917.

America had entered the World War two months earlier, and in the country's industrial hubs, semipro ball prospered as never before. For Perry and his young family, it provided more stability than bouncing between major-league trials, or along the rails on a minor-league circuit. For $190 a month, he pitched every Sunday for the company team. During the week he supplemented this income by driving a company truck and twirling for other semipro teams.[10]

Meanwhile, the Crackers sought the entire $2,500 of the deal, asserting no responsibility for Perry's desertion. The Braves claimed the deal nullified, as Perry had bolted only 17 days into the 30-day trial. In August 1917 baseball's National Commission reached a compromise decision: Boston owed Atlanta the $500 trial cost. In rebuffing Atlanta's claim for the additional $2,000, the Commission acknowledged the Braves' purposeful inaction: "The Boston Club did not formally or informally perfect its title to the player beyond the trial term."[11]

It seemed the affair was settled. But the Commission's chairman, Reds owner Garry Herrmann, sowed the seeds for future controversy with off-the-record, and contradictory, communications. Herrmann "gave the Boston club his promise that it should have prior claim to Perry's services in case that player desired to return to Organized Ball" if the Braves paid the Crackers the remaining $2,000 within 13 days (the remainder of the 30-day trial). Simultaneously, he "authorized" Atlanta "to give employment to or dispose of the player."[12] Atlanta reserved Perry for the coming season.

As the 1918 campaign neared, Perry decided to return to Organized Baseball. He approached Atlanta, which signed him.[13] Frank enjoyed a close relationship with Athletics manager Connie Mack, and players commonly shuttled between the two teams.[14] Catcher Cy Perkins, hoping to stick with Philadelphia after two seasons in Atlanta, recommended Perry to Mack. The managers worked out a deal. Mack offered —and Perry accepted — a $1,800 salary for the season.[15] Neither Mack nor Perry was aware of Herrmann's private promises to Boston.

Perry possessed an easy side-arm motion that reminded contemporaries of Jack Powell and Walter Johnson. He effectively mixed and disguised four-seam fastballs, curves, and offspeed pitches. Having

SCOTT PERRY
P-Phila. Athletics

conquered wildness over his minor-league apprenticeship, he confidently pitched inside. "It seemed certain that he was knicking or scuffing the ball," noted Hugh Fullerton, admiring his breaking stuff. When all else failed, Perry deviated from his side-arm motion; against Babe Ruth, he employed an underhand delivery.[16]

The once-proud Athletics had finished in the AL cellar for three consecutive seasons. Mack threw Perry into action, and the newcomer responded with several excellent complete-game efforts as the 1918 season began. In Boston on April 16, Perry lost a 1-0 pitching duel to Carl Mays. Six days later, in Washington, he bested Johnson, 5-1, for Philadelphia's first victory. On April 26 Perry pitched no-hit ball for six innings before eventually losing, 2-1, to Dutch Leonard and Red Sox.

The next day, the Braves filed a claim for Perry with the National Commission. Stallings dubiously asserted that he had been unaware of Perry's whereabouts until his third start. The Commission—consisting of Herrmann, AL President Ban Johnson, and NL President John Tener—was expanded to include minor-league executives John Farrell and Robert Baugh. On June 12 the body voted to award Perry to Boston. Herrmann, Tener, and Farrell formed the majority opinion; Johnson and Baugh dissented.

Johnson promptly advised the Athletics' chief to seek an injunction in court against the Commission's ruling. Mack needed little prodding to take on Stallings; the Braves' brutal bench-jockeying of the Athletics in the 1914 World Series remained fresh in his memory. Dismissing Stallings' offers to accept a lesser player than Perry, Mack received his injunction in a Cleveland common pleas court on June 17.

The affair was one of the 1918 season's lead stories. *The Sporting News* labeled the Braves' opportunism "a lamentable lack of sportsmanship" while questioning the "surprising lack of sense of logic and justice" in the Commission's ruling.[17] Fullerton noted that Mack had "broken the strongest unwritten law in baseball, which is that no owner shall carry any baseball case into a court of law."[18] Ernest Lanigan suggested that Perry had become "the Dred Scott of baseball."[19] The analogy seemed less apt regarding the pitcher's freedom, and more so in suggesting that baseball's federal government was increasingly incapable of settling differences between individual teams.

Mack held the upper hand. Boston had no contractual claim to Perry, and Organized Baseball did not want its practices exposed. Court follow-ups were kicked down the road as the larger issue of America's involvement in a world war consumed baseball. Tener stated that he regarded the National Commission as irrelevant given Mack's actions, then resigned in early August. Johnson faced revolt in AL ranks as an early end to the 1918 season was effected.

Perry finished the campaign with the most successful season in his uneven career. His 20-19 record enabled Philadelphia to improve its record from 55-98 in 1917 to 52-76 in the shortened 1918 season. Only Johnson, Stan Coveleski, and Mays won more games than Perry. Only Johnson and Coveleski topped his 146 ERA+ (calculated retrospectively). Mack paired pitchers with catchers to form lasting batteries, and for each of Perry's 36 starts, Perkins caught him.[20] As Philadelphia sportswriter James Isaminger noted, Perry became a fan favorite: "Every time he walks to the tee it is a signal for a wild demonstration."[21]

As the season wound down, Johnson helped settle the controversy between the Braves and Athletics. In October Mack paid Boston $2,500, as attorneys asked the court to dissolve the injunction. It was "a nominal sum," Isaminger suggested, as "Perry is worth more than ten times that amount."[22]

Perry wasn't unaware of his value. After the National Commission awarded him to Boston, Stallings reportedly sent the pitcher an offer for $4,000. Perry shared the offer with Mack, who suggested that better pay was forthcoming. After he won his 20th game, Mack gave him a $500 bonus. In the offseason, Perry sought $4,000 for the coming 1919 season. He settled for a lesser, unspecified amount.[23]

Mack hoped that 1918's gains signaled light at the end of a painful rebuild. In February 1919 he announced that "I will never again sell another player, although not unwilling to make an advantageous deal. The policy of the Athletics is to acquire strength rather than take it away."[24] But a month into the new season, the Mackmen again occupied the cellar. Perry, despite a 2.35 ERA, was 0-6. He grew frustrated with the defensive play behind him, particularly that of second baseman Red Shannon.[25] By July 14, with an 18-52 mark, Philadelphia was halfway to another 100-loss finish.

Chicago led the race, with New York and Cleveland a handful of games back. It was a pre-trade-deadline era, and all three teams sought to bolster their staffs for the stretch run. The pitching market's linchpin was Carl Mays, who peevishly deserted the Red Sox on July 13. Indians president James Dunn started negotiations with the Boston Red Sox, but was told to back off by Johnson. The Yankees ignored the AL chieftain and struck a mostly-cash deal for Mays on July 29. Dunn thus turned his focus upon Perry. Boston also inquired, hoping to replace the lost Mays. But the White Sox, with Eddie

Cicotte and Lefty Williams starting over half of the squad's games, proved the most aggressive.[26]

Mack held firm: "They all want Perry but I am not selling to any club now in the fight for the championship."[27] "I offered Connie Mack $25,000 in real money for Pitcher Scott Perry," sighed White Sox manager Kid Gleason, "but Mack wouldn't listen to the offer."[28] Johnson voided the Mays deal. But the Yankees, using as a model Mack's actions to keep Perry, went to court, and successfully retained Mays. Another fracture appeared in baseball's hierarchy. The Yankees, Red Sox, and White Sox opposed Johnson; the other five AL magnates, including Mack, supported his actions.

Isaminger reported that contending teams directly approached Perry during the 1919 season. Their pitch: If he "eased up" he could earn his release or a trade, "and then 'join a real team and get the money.'"[29] Certainly Perry saw that Mays had tested the boundaries of player independence, and been rewarded. Accustomed to jumping, and perhaps believing he could force Mack's hand by doing so, Perry quit the Athletics on August 12. "I can have a better time playing ball around with teams that are trying to win their games, and I guess maybe I can make a living that way, too," he said.[30] Perry left behind a 4-17 record with Philadelphia. He also left behind a suspension for violating club training rules. For Perry was also tempted by drink.

With his family in tow, Perry wound up in Franklin, in northwestern Pennsylvania's rough-and-tumble oil country. After Franklin's semipro season ended, he stayed in town, working in the tailoring business. But after news reached him of the Ruth deal struck between Boston and New York, Perry reconsidered: "I don't see anything in the papers about them paying $125,000 for a tailor. Guess I better go to bat and see what I can do about getting some of this coin."[31] He settled his differences with Mack, was reinstated by the National Commission, and signed a $5,000 contract to pitch with the Athletics in 1920.

Perry beat the Yankees on Opening Day, 3-1. But from that point, both his season — and Philadelphia's — went downhill. The Athletics again finished last, with a 48-106 mark. Perry finished 11-25. Mack, wrote one Philadelphia reporter, was not always "particularly enthusiastic" about Perry's efforts.[32] But he also twirled for the worst hitting and fielding team in the league. Perry achieved an ERA+ of 111, and threw 16 complete games in which he allowed three earned runs or less.

Offseason rumors suggested that Perry might be part of a package deal with either the Yankees or Senators.[33] But nothing came of either, and he was back in Philadelphia for the 1921 season. Not until May 2, when he beat Washington, did he produce a quality start. Perry promptly celebrated too much, and Mack suspended him for 10 days. "There is nothing vicious or wrong with him," Isaminger suggested, "but [he] is easily led by friends."[34] Upon his return, after a couple of appearances in Cleveland, the Indians offered the Athletics two players and $25,000 for Perry.[35] Mack turned the deal down. Perry lost against visiting Boston on June 1. Then he left for Franklin. "I had many chances to trade him and get a lot of money," Mack lamented, "and now he's gone."[36]

Perry would also have regrets. The National Commission was no more. In its place stood a less accommodating Kenesaw Mountain Landis, who had just set a precedent that Perry could not ignore. In 1920, another Athletics pitcher, Walt Kinney, went over to Franklin. In March 1921, Kinney applied for reinstatement. Landis suspended him for five years.

Franklin baseball was buoyed by gambling interests, and subject to boom and bust.[37] It also mostly consisted of a rivalry with nearby Oil City. This "Two-Team League" collapsed in July 1921. Perry signed on with a Hornell, New York, team. Then came stops in Trenton, Erie, and lesser outposts.

Beulah and the children left for California in 1922, not to return.[38] Perry was arrested on a larceny charge in 1924.[39] Two years later, he came back to Organized Baseball, after Philadelphia dealt his title to Dallas. Perry pitched in a handful of Texas League games late in the 1926 season, a few more in 1927, then was released "because he loved his 'likker' too much, and refused to stay in good condition."[40] He finished the 1927 season, and his time in professional baseball, with the Piedmont League's High Point (North Carolina) squad. As late as 1932, for a Kerrville, Texas, team, Perry twirled semipro ball.

After baseball, Perry cooked and washed dishes in Colorado and Missouri. On October 27, 1959, he died from bronchopneumonia. Scott Perry was buried in Woodlawn Cemetery in Independence, Missouri.

## SOURCES

In addition to the sources noted in this biography, the author also accessed Perry's file from the National Baseball Hall of Fame, and a number of sites such as ancestry.com, baseball-reference.com, chroniclingamerica.loc.gov/newspapers, genealogybank.com, newspapers.com, and retrosheet.com.

## NOTES

1   Perry's death certificate indicates 1891 and Denison. In the 1900 census, 1892 is listed as his birth year. In his 1917 draft card, he provided both 1892 and Corsicana. In both 1921 and 1957, he wrote to Corsicana newspapers, claiming the city as his birthplace: "Corsicana Boy Is Pitching for Athletics," *Corsicana Daily Sun*, May 26, 1921; Talmadge Canant, "Comments by Canant," *Corsicana Daily Sun*, April 24, 1957.

2   "Jobbers to Leave for Their Homes," *Wichita Beacon*, September 26, 1912.

3   "Tulsa Pitcher Is Sold to the Cubs," *Tulsa World*, August 27, 1916, mentions Perry being with Tulsa in 1909. But accounts in 1910 papers suggest that he was with the club then. See for example: "Adios, Senators! Adios," *Guthrie* (Oklahoma) *Daily Leader*, July 25, 1910. Also box scores in *Guthrie Daily Leader*, June 8, 1910; *Dallas Morning News*, July 12, 1910; *Topeka Daily Capital*, July 16, 1910.

4   "Kaws Scored 1st Win Over Pueblo," *Topeka Daily Capital*, June 30, 1911; "Jobbers Staged Another Batfest," *Wichita Beacon*, May 14, 1913.

5   "Despain Beginning to Get Worried by His Hoodoo," *Rocky Mountain News* (Denver), March 20, 1911.

6   Sid C. Keener, "Athletics' Star Pitcher Covered Considerable Territory Before He Landed," *Cleveland Plain Dealer*, July 6, 1919.

7   Harry F. Pierce, "Ordered to Report to Louisville Club, Baumgardner Balks," *St. Louis Star and Times*, May 11, 1915; "Notice for Perry," *St. Louis Star and Times*, May 15, 1915; Harry F. Pierce, "Rickey Will Recall Pitcher Perry Who Hurled No-Hit Game," *St. Louis Star and Times*, July 20, 1915.

8   Norman Macht, *Connie Mack: The Turbulent & Triumphant Years, 1915-1931* (Lincoln: University of Nebraska Press, 2012), 138.

9   "Notes of the Game," *Cincinnati Enquirer*, May 21, 1917.

10  Keener, "Athletics' Star Pitcher"; "Semi-Pros and Amateurs," *Chicago Examiner*, June 19, 1917; "Scott Perry May Win Under Connie Mack," *Pittsburgh Press*, April 7, 1918.

11  For an overview of this controversy, see Macht, *Connie Mack: The Turbulent & Triumphant Years*, 139-141. For the ruling's text, see "National Commission Decisions," *The Sporting News*, August 9, 1917. For contemporary assessments of this decision see James C. Isaminger, "Quaker Fans Whoop Up for Mackmen," *The Sporting News*, May 9, 1918; "The Astounding Perry Case," *The Sporting News*, June 20, 1918.

12  August Herrmann, "National Commission's Work," *1918 Reach Official American League Guide*, 57-60.

13  Joe Vila, "Big Rumpus Likely Over Perry Case," *Philadelphia Inquirer*, June 20, 1918.

14  Al Weinfeld, "Crackers Break Just as Spurt Is Expected," *The Sporting News*, June 21, 1917.

15  Macht, *Connie Mack: The Turbulent & Triumphant Years*, 141.

16  On Perry's pitching style, see James Crusinberry, "Perry Checks Braves 2-0; Wortman Swats Win in 11th," *Chicago Tribune*, September 15, 1916; James Crusinberry, "Seventeen Straight to Giants; Tinkers Again Victims, 5-0," *Chicago Tribune*, September 23, 1916; Jim Nasium [Edgar Wolfe], "Rube Oldring Has Charge of Athletics," *Philadelphia Inquirer*, April 4, 1918; Ernest J. Lanigan, "Failed to Finish His First Battle," *Pittsburgh Press*, July 7, 1918; Hugh S. Fullerton, "Yanks Give Local Fans Rare Treat by Manner They Defeat Athletics," *New York Evening World*, April 29, 1919; Keener, "Athletics' Star Pitcher"; "Perry Does Not Fear Bat of Babe Ruth," *Cincinnati Post*, March 23, 1920.

17  "The Astounding Perry Case."

18  Hugh Fullerton, "Giants Needed Everything, Including Luck, to Win," *New York Evening World*, June 18, 1918.

19  Lanigan, "Failed to Finish."

20  On this tendency of Mack's, see Phil Williams, "Philadelphia Athletics Batterymates, 1901-1914," *The Inside Game: The Official Newsletter of SABR's Deadball Era Committee*, June 2015.

21  James C. Isaminger, "Tener Believes His Stand Is Right One," *The Sporting News*, July 18, 1918.

22  James C. Isaminger, "For Harmony Sake Mack Gives Up Cash," *The Sporting News*, October 24, 1918.

23  On salary matters, see "No Huge Sum for Hurler," *Pittsburgh Press*, April 17, 1919; Macht, *Connie Mack: The Turbulent & Triumphant Years*, 166; "After Debating with Mack, Scott Perry Signs Contract," *Boston Herald*, February 7, 1919.

24  James C. Isaminger, "Connie Makes His Annual Promises," *The Sporting News*, February 27, 1919.

25  James C. Isaminger, "Sentiment Cuts a Figure with Connie," *The Sporting News*, July 3, 1919; James C. Isaminger, "Connie Nails Yarn by Gotham Scribes," *The Sporting News*, January 22, 1920.

26 For a recent accounting of the Mays affair, see Steve Steinberg and Lyle Spatz, *The Colonel and Hug: The Partnership That Transformed the Yankees* (Lincoln: University of Nebraska, 2015), 110-117. For contemporary reports, see Gibby [pseud.], "The Morning Hatchet," *Pittsburgh Daily Post*, July 30, 1919; "Yankees Get Mays, Pay Heavy Price," *St. Louis Post-Dispatch*, July 31, 1919; Henry P. Edwards, "Dunn Went to Limit to Get Star Hurler to Strengthen Indians," *Cleveland Plain Dealer*, December 25, 1919.

27 "White Sox Offer for Scott Perry is Turned Down," *Chicago Tribune*, July 29, 1919.

28 "Baseball Gossip," *Pittsburgh Press*, August 8, 1919.

29 James C. Isaminger, "Tampering With His Players Must Stop," *The Sporting News*, December 11, 1919; James C. Isaminger, "Phillies Give New Sign of Being Alive," *The Sporting News*, January 15, 1920.

30 " 'We're Through,' Says Perry, Also Speaking for Rogers," *Philadelphia Evening Public Ledger*, August 14, 1919.

31 "Scott Perry Signs With Philadelphia," *Pittsburgh Post-Gazette*, January 12, 1920.

32 "A's Home to Play Foes from West," *Philadelphia Evening Public Ledger*, May 11, 1920.

33 "Huggins After Dugan," *New York Times*, December 2, 1920; "Rumors Griff Offers Rice and Judge for Mackmen," *Washington Post*, December 18, 1920.

34 James C. Isaminger, "Macks at Top Form as They Start West," *The Sporting News*, May 12, 1921.

35 "Cleveland Makes Athletics Good Offer for Perry," *Washington Times*, May 23, 1921; James C. Isaminger, "A Place in History if Not in Standing," *The Sporting News*, June 9, 1921.

36 Robert W. Maxwell, "A's Wallop 7 Homers, Make League Record and Win from Tigers," *Philadelphia Evening Public Ledger*, June 4, 1921.

37 James C. Isaminger, "Not Much to Cheer About From Philly," *The Sporting News*, August 28, 1919.

38 On Perry's family leaving, see "Scott Perry to Play Next Year with Babcocks," *Olean* (New York) *Times Herald,* December 12, 1922. Future census records also support this split.

39 "Scribbled by Scribes," *The Sporting News*, April 24, 1924.

40 "Athletics Buy Pitchers," *Brooklyn Daily Eagle*, September 19, 1926, 39; Moulton (Ty) Cobb, "Sporting News," *The Eagle* (Bryan, Texas), May 23, 1927.

# FRED SANFORD

## BY WARREN CORBETT

**"YES SIR, IT'S GREAT TO BE A YANKEE,"** Fred Sanford said.[1] Making it even greater, he was traded from the nearly bankrupt St. Louis Browns to the pinstriped promised land.

Presented with the opportunity of a lifetime, Sanford flopped.

After the right-hander had lost 21 games for the Browns in 1948, the Yankees paid $100,000 plus three players to acquire him. The consensus opinion was that he could win 15 or 20 in New York and return the club to its rightful place on top of the standings. It didn't happen; the deal made Sanford the Yankees' "$100,000 lemon" and ruined his career.

John Frederick Sanford was born on August 9, 1919, in Garfield, Utah, a mining town of a few dozen homes built by the Utah Copper Company just outside Salt Lake City. It is now a ghost town, but during Sanford's childhood the fathers worked in the mine or the smelter while the children splashed in the swimming hole known as Bare-Bum Beach and, if they dared, climbed Hundred Foot Cliff. Fred was one of three sons and four daughters of Frederick Charles Sanford and the former Mary Alice Unsworth, immigrants from England.

Sanford pitched for a Junior American Legion team that won back-to-back state championships, and in semipro ball around Salt Lake City. He earned a tryout with the Pacific Coast League San Diego Padres in 1938, but the club kept him around for six weeks with only one appearance before handing him his release. The next year a Yankees scout told him he didn't throw hard enough to make it in pro ball. After Sanford defeated the bearded House of David barnstorming team, Browns scout Jacques Fournier signed him to a $110-a-month contract with the Browns' Class-C affiliate in Youngstown, Ohio.

At 6-feet-1 and around 200 pounds, blond and blue-eyed, "Sandy" looked the part of a pitcher. He rose through the farm system in fits and starts. With the top farm club in Toledo in 1942, he recorded complete-game victories in exhibitions against the Yankees and Tigers. The next year he finished 13-9 and earned a September call-up. In three relief appearances for the Browns, he gave up just two runs in 9⅓ innings.

Sanford had married his high-school girlfriend, Bonnie Elaine Brown, in 1941, and she was pregnant with the first of six children. Impending fatherhood didn't keep him from being drafted after the 1943 season. "I was in an outfit where you had to dig in the mud and do real soldiering," he recalled.[2] He served more than two years in the Army field artillery with the 41st Infantry Division, surviving combat in New Guinea and the Philippines, and winding up with the occupation troops in Japan after the war ended.

Returning home in time for spring training in 1946, Sanford learned that the Browns prohibited families from joining the players in Anaheim, California. He rebelled, telling a reporter, "I didn't see my wife and kids for two years while I was serving in the Pacific theater, and I intend to see something of them now."[3] Sent back to Toledo for his third year at the highest minor-league level, he led the American Association with a league-record 154 strikeouts, posting a 2.74 ERA with a 15-10 record.

Called up in September, Sanford arrived with a bang. In his first start he shut out the Yankees on five singles. A week later he blanked the White Sox on four hits without allowing a runner to reach third base. His season ended sourly when he was torched for seven runs in four-plus innings in his final start, but he looked like a welcome ray of hope for the seventh-place Browns.

This Fred Sanford was no junk dealer. He featured a pitcher's meat and potatoes: fastball, curve, changeup. He opened the 1947 season in the bullpen, but moved into the rotation in June. He beat the

Yankees, 4-3, in his first start, then beat them again a week later by the same score.

On July 27 Ted Williams broke up a tie game with a booming two-run homer off Sanford in the sixth. Two batters later Boston's Jake Jones topped a dribbler up the third-base line. As it rolled foul, Sanford threw his glove at the spinning ball. By rule, Jones was awarded a triple that traveled all of 60 feet. The Browns protested that the ball was dead because it was foul, but umpire Cal Hubbard said the rule made no such exception. Sanford acknowledged that he had suffered a brain cramp because he was still seething over the Williams home run. As the Browns lost 95 games and finished last, Sanford compiled a creditable 3.71 ERA, but a 7-16 record.

He was the Opening Day starter in 1948. Facing the Cleveland Indians, he walked the leadoff batter and gave up two hits in the first inning, but escaped with only one run scoring. When the first two batters singled in the second, manager Zack Taylor relieved him. "It's not his arm that gets him into trouble, it's his head," Taylor said. "If he opens the game with anything other than perfect control he seems to worry about getting the ball over the plate and he's just an ordinary pitcher."[4]

One sportswriter called Sanford "the barrel-chested, strong-armed ace of the Brownie staff."[5] The team again was going nowhere, heading for 94 defeats and a sixth-place finish. Sanford lost his 19th game on September 15. With more than two weeks left in the season, the club made no effort to protect him from a 20th loss. He took his regular turn, splitting four more decisions to finish 12-21, leading the league in losses. Taylor said, "I probably could have saved him five or six games with good relief pitchers."[6] Good hitting would have helped, too; the Browns scored no more than two runs in 12 of Sanford's defeats.

With all that, Sanford was a below-average pitcher in 1948. He recorded a 4.64 ERA and gave up 19 home runs, third most in the league. AL batters hit .279 against him, he walked more than he struck out, and he completed only nine of 33 starts.

The Browns, as usual, were practically broke. A year earlier they had tapped the Red Sox for a reported $375,000, dealing away slugging shortstop Vern Stephens and pitchers Jack Kramer and Ellis Kinder. Now they turned to the AL's other big bankroll, the Yankees.

New York general manager George Weiss said the Browns offered him a choice among three pitchers. He consulted several of his leading players, including Joe DiMaggio and Tommy Henrich, and picked Sanford. St. Louis threw in catcher Roy Partee in return for the Yankees' third-string catcher, 23-year-old Sherman Lollar, pitchers Red Embree and Dick Starr, and—most important—$100,000.

The Yankees were betting big that Sanford was the arm they needed to bounce back from a third-place finish. The new manager, Casey Stengel, said he went to sleep that night dreaming of a pennant. The next morning he learned that the defending champion Indians had acquired pitcher Early Wynn and former batting champ Mickey Vernon from Washington. "The Yankees went to bed pennant winners and woke up in second place," Stengel said.[7]

Sanford was working in the Salt Lake City police garage when he got news of the trade. He said he wasn't surprised, because several Yankees had told him he would be joining them next year. His first move: go on a diet. He had ballooned to more than 225 pounds, and wanted to drop below 200. Arriving in spring training hungry, the $100,000 man told a reporter, "I can pitch well enough to justify the deal. That is, I can pitch successfully for the kind of club I'm with now."[8]

The Yankees opened the 1949 season without DiMaggio, who had surgery to remove a bone spur from his heel. Even so, the team won its first four games. In his first start, on April 23 at Boston, Sanford fell behind, 2-0, but the Yankees exploded in the fourth to give him a 6-2 lead. He gave it right back. Sanford surrendered a double, walked two, and shortstop Phil Rizzuto threw away a groundball. Then Boston's Vern Stephens hammered a grand slam to put the Red Sox up, 7-6.

Stengel pulled Sanford from the game and didn't give him another start for more than a month. The manager, in his first year, was trying to live down his reputation as a loser and a clown, and was under pressure to lead the Yankees back to the World Series. With another team, with a more secure manager, Sanford might not have been on such a short leash. But with the Yankees under Stengel, it was win now or else.

Sanford never regained his manager's confidence. Most of his 11 starts came against tail-end teams or in doubleheaders when the club needed an extra arm, and most of his relief appearances were in mop-up roles, when the Yankees had fallen behind. He pitched fairly well, with a 3.87 ERA, but in only 95⅓ innings. Even after winning three September starts to bring his record to 7-3, he was a spectator at the World Series as New York defeated Brooklyn in five games.

"I tried too hard," he said. "I pressed every time I worked until August."[9] Stengel voiced a charitable view: "Maybe he is one of those fellows who can't adjust overnight when traded from a second division [team] to a pennant contender. I know he was a disappointment during the first half of the season, but he improved considerably later, and if you look up the records you'll see he did well in September."[10]

Stengel gave him 10 starts in the first half of 1950, mostly against the league's weak sisters. Sanford completed only two, with a 5.10 ERA, and went back to the bullpen. He left the team around September 1 when his father got sick and died. After he returned, he pitched just once as the Yankees charged from behind to claim another pennant. Again, he sat out the Series.

With a 4.55 ERA and 5-4 record, Sanford was "the forgotten man of the Yankee pitching staff," according to the *New York Times*'s James P. Dawson.[11] His name cropped up in offseason trade rumors, but no deal materialized. The next spring he vented his frustration: "I cannot do myself or the Yankees any good pitching 113 innings. I want to pitch 250. I cannot maintain condition sitting around. Nor am I gaited for sitting and thinking. That's no good if, nearing 32, you haven't made a place for yourself."[12]

"I would be delighted to pitch him as often as he said he should pitch," Stengel said. "But if Fred gives me a couple of poor outings, what am I to do?"[13] Sanford pitched just 11 times for New York in 1951 before he was not only forgotten, but gone.

At the June 15 trading deadline, the Yankees shipped Sanford to Washington with veteran reliever Tom Ferrick and Triple-A pitcher Bob Porterfield for lefty Bob Kuzava. The *Washington Post* greeted the newcomers with a sarcastic headline: "Nats Pick Up Three Losers From Yankees."[14]

"I was convinced Sanford could help us, and all our good hitters agreed," Yankee GM Weiss said later. "He was just a flop with us, that's all."[15] Emblematic of what Stengel thought of him, he started only three games against New York's main challengers, Boston and Cleveland. Sanford's 4.18 ERA and 12-10 record in two-plus seasons stamped him in Yankees history as the "$100,000 lemon."

Sanford and Ferrick were throw-ins in the trade. Porterfield was the man Washington manager Bucky

Harris wanted; the right-hander had pitched for him when Harris was managing New York. Porterfield became the Senators' ace for the next four years.

In Sanford's first start for Washington, he held the Indians to one run in 7⅓ innings and won a spot in the rotation. But after seven starts his ERA stood at 6.57. The Senators shuffled him back to the Browns in a waiver deal. He fell apart in his return to St. Louis, walking 23 batters in 27⅓ innings with a 10.21 ERA. That was below even the Browns' standards, and they traded him to Portland of the Pacific Coast League after the 1951 season. His big-league career was over at 32.

Sanford pitched for two years in Portland before a sore shoulder forced him to retire in the spring of 1954. Returning home to Salt Lake City, he picked up his offseason job as a deputy sheriff and criminal investigator. He later worked as a production-control specialist for the Hercules Powder Company, a manufacturer of explosives for the military.

Fred and Bonnie were married for 70 years and raised five children; another died in infancy. Fred Sanford died at 91 on March 15, 2011. Bonnie died less than two months later.

## SOURCES

In addition to the sources cited in the Notes, the author also consulted:

Familysearch.org.

"Sanford, J. Fred." Obituary in the *Salt Lake Tribune*, March 27, 2011. genealogybank.com/doc/obituaries/obit/13644C78AC6A6068-13644C78AC6A6068, accessed July 17, 2016.

Sanford, John Frederick. Player questionnaire (1964) in his file at the National Baseball Hall of Fame library, Cooperstown, New York.

Wadley, Carma. "Memories of a Company Town." *Deseret News* (Salt Lake City), August 12, 2005. deseretnews.com/article/600155105/Memories-of-a-company-town.html?pg=all, accessed July 17, 2016.

## NOTES

1 Dan Daniel, "Sanford Goes Hungry to Feast on Wins," *The Sporting News*, March 16, 1949: 3.

2 Frederick G. Lieb, "Big Fred's Blanks Make Brownie Fans Blink," *The Sporting News*, October 2, 1946: 9.

3 "Ex-GI Sanford Balks at Browns' Ban on Families," *The Sporting News*, February 14, 1946: 6.

4 Dent McSkimming, "Sanford, Prospective Gibraltar of Browns' Mound Staff, to Get Plenty of Work, Taylor Says," *St. Louis Post-Dispatch*, May 3, 1948: 4B.

5 Ray Nelson, "A's Beat Browns for Ninth in Row and Regain First Place," *St. Louis Star-Times*, May 12, 1948: 22.

6 W.J. McGoogan, "Browns Swing 5-Player Deal With Yankees, Drop Out of Trade Mart," *St. Louis Post-Dispatch*, December 14, 1948: 2B.

7 Shirley Povich, "This Morning," *Washington Post*, December 15, 1948: 17.

8 Daniel, "Sanford Goes Hungry."

9 Daniel, "Sanford Thinks Sanford Fills Casey's Bill," *New York World-Telegram*, March 6, 1950, in Sanford's file at the National Baseball Hall of Fame library, Cooperstown, New York.

10 "Sanford Becomes 15th Yank to Sign," *New York Times*, February 1, 1950: 35.

11 James P. Dawson, "Sanford Seeking Role as Starter," *New York Times*, February 26, 1951: 34.

12 Daniel, "Sanford 'Mystery' Solved by Fred—'I Can Win if They Let Me Pitch," *The Sporting News*, March 7, 1951: 4. As usual, Daniel "cleaned up" the quotes.

13 Ibid.

14 "Nats Pick Up Three Losers From Yankees," *Washington Post*, June 16, 1951: 13.

15 "Weiss Would Like to Forget '48 Deal for Fred Sanford," *The Sporting News*, February 8, 1956: 13.

# JACK SCOTT

## BY SKIP NIPPER

**IN THE 1922 WORLD SERIES AGAINST** the New York Yankees, New York Giants manager John McGraw called on little-known Jack Scott to start Game Three. A right-handed knuckleballer, Scott held the opposition to four hits in a complete-game shutout, 3-0. Even Babe Ruth had a hard time with the 6-foot-2, 199-pound thrower, grounding out three times. It appeared Jack was on his way to stardom. But his career would be highlighted by a sequence of highs and lows.

During the summer, the Giants had signed Scott, who was cast adrift by the Cincinnati Reds in May with a sore arm that was "shot to pieces." Through the previous winter, Scott had not only suffered a bad arm, but also watched a warehouse on his farm go up in smoke.[1] When the Reds gave up on him, Scott approached McGraw in the lobby of the Giants' hotel when they next visited Cincinnati. The conversation that followed let the manager know how sincere, yet bad off, the pitcher was.

"My name is Jack Scott," he said. "(Reds manager Pat) Moran fired me. But I'm not through. I know that I can come back and that I can cure my arm. All that I want is a chance to prove it."

"All right. Get back to New York and work out at the Polo Grounds," said McGraw, "I'll look you up when we come back."

"Could I have the carfare?" Scott asked, "I'm broke."[2]

He hurried to New York and the Polo Grounds, even working out with the Yankees (who shared the Polo Grounds with the Giants), and when the Giants returned, McGraw added him to the roster. Scott was also treated by specialists as promised,[3] and he did everything he could to revitalize his arm. He worked his way into the pitching lineup, and between August 1 and October 1 accumulated an 8-2 won-lost record.

McGraw heaped praise on his new star after his World Series performance against the Yankees. "His presence there gave me a real thrill," the manager said. "That spirit wins many a ball game."[4]

On top of his World Series half-share amounting to $2,225.50,[5] Scott earned some additional income by joining a barnstorming tour through Pennsylvania with teammates Rosy Ryan and Dave Bancroft. He injured himself in one of the games, even though McGraw had urged him to take it easy. Scott sought permission from McGraw to play in additional games on the West Coast, but the manager denied his request.

Jack's mother, expecting to meet her son at the train station upon his return to North Carolina, gave an account of what Scott should be doing in the off-season. "Manager McGraw told Jack to stay at home and rest up this winter, taking good care of his arm."[6] "I had rather hunt duck down home," said her son.[7]

The Giants won the pennant again in 1923. Scott and Rosy Ryan led the team with 16 victories, but a repeat performance in the World Series was not to be; Scott had a loss as the Yankees won the Series in six games. In Game Four (after striking out Babe Ruth in the first inning), Scott allowed three earned runs in the second inning before being replaced, and was charged with the loss. The next day he pitched two innings of relief in what turned out to be his last postseason game.

Scott was one of a handful of pitchers to have twice lost 20 games in a major-league season, and also lost 20 with the Toledo Mud Hens. But highlight performances before, between, and after his distinction as a "repeat offender"[8] more aptly define Scott's character and abilities.

John William Scott was born on April 18, 1892, to Emma and James Scott. His family owned a tobacco and fruit farm in Ridgeway, North Carolina. Jack was raised on the farm and attended Ridgeway High School. Between chores and school, he played baseball.

"He has been playing ball since he was a little boy, and I remember how boys used to come to the house to get him for games in different parts of the county," recalled his mother.[9]

Noted for both his pitching and hitting, Scott played for his hometown Ridgeway team, and in 1911 joined the nearby Warrenton club.[10] On September 11, he struck out 15 Warren High School batters in an 8-0 shutout.[11]

He continued playing in the area[12] before being given a tryout with the Durham Bulls (Class-D North Carolina State League). He showed up in time for the first day of practice on March 12,[13] and so impressed manager James Kelly that he was named the starter in an exhibition contest against the Philadelphia Phillies on March 24. The day before the game, the *Durham Morning Herald* described his pitching style:

"Judging from the appearance of Scott he is a bit slow but to see this fellow heave a ball over the home plate a batter has got to have his eyes peeled."[14]

Manager Wild Bill Donovan and his Providence Grays of the International League were training in Durham, and Donovan agreed to umpire the game. With a crowd of 2,500 looking on, Scott kept the major-league club spellbound for eight innings until Phillies manager Red Dooin inserted himself as a pinch-hitter in the bottom of the ninth, trailing 4-3. With one on and two out, he rapped a double to tie the score. Catcher Mickey LaLonge stepped up and slapped another double, driving in his skipper with the winning run.[15]

Two weeks later, Scott was in the hospital for an unexplained reason. His condition was described as serious enough that he had been "off his diet for several days" and he had a new sobriquet: "Lonesome."[16]

With no reference to his illness, Scott was back pitching for Ridgeway once again. By season's end, he was back with Durham. According to the *Durham Herald Leader* at season's end, "Pitcher 'Lonesome' Scott leaves this morning for his home in Ridgeway, N.C. This big fellow has not done a great deal of work during the season, but the manager believes that he has the stuff and has been letting him season a while,

and absorb some of the tactics of the professionals from the bench."[17]

Scott would return to Durham, but not right away. In 1914 he signed with Roanoke Mills in the semipro Roanoke Valley League as a pitcher and outfielder. In his first appearance, against a team from Rosemary, he struck out 16 in the first seven innings, holding the opposing team to two hits. When the game went into extra innings, Scott continued to pitch until his team scored a run in the 12th to win. Scott struck out 21 and issued no walks.[18]

On July 30, 1914, Scott tossed a three-hitter against Roanoke Rapids (with all the hits coming in the first three innings) and struck out 16. He batted cleanup and scored twice.[19] Roanoke Mills won, but no season for Scott can be found.[20]

Scott signed with Durham again in August,[21] put up mediocre numbers, soon was sold to last-place Greensboro. His sporadic performance continued. On September 8 he lasted 1⅓ innings against Winston-Salem, allowing seven hits and seven runs.[22] In March of 1915, he was released by Greensboro.[23]

Scott appears to have spent the 1915 season with Roanoke Rapids, a semipro team in the Tri-Town League that included two other teams, Franklin and Emporia. He pitched and hit well as his team won the league championship."[24]

Scott began the 1916 season with Portsmouth (Class-C Virginia League), where he was described as "a big 200-pounder, with wonderful speed."[25] In five games he was 3-0 before moving to Macon (Class-C South Atlantic League). There he produced an 8-12 record before being purchased by Pittsburgh and reporting to the club on August 25. Called on to pinch-hit in his first two appearances, both at Forbes Field, he walked on September 6 and struck out three days later.

In his major-league pitching debut, on September 19, Scott relieved Elmer Jacobs in the fourth inning against the Giants at the Polo Grounds. Pitching the rest of the way in the Giants' 9-2 triumph, Scott gave up six runs, including a two-run homer by Benny Kauff.

Earlier, on the 11th, Scott started in an exhibition game in Binghamton, New York. Fighting a bad cold, he gave up seven hits in six innings. The Pirates lost 6-5 and *Pittsburgh-Post Gazette* sportswriter Charles J. Doyle gave Scott a less than glowing tribute:

"Scott had a dandy curve ball working, but he put it too close to the batter's groves [sic]. He held the Binghamton boys to seven hits, but many of these safe swats came at critical times."[26]

Manager Jimmy Callahan sent Scott home about 10 days before the season ended. The *Pittsburgh Press* wrote, "Pitcher Jack Scott, who has done the pitching in batting practice for a couple of weeks, and practically ever since the club went on the road, went home last night. He will winter at Ridgeway, N.C. Jack is big and husky, has a lot of stuff and is a good prospect. ... He has provided a lot of fun for the other players. He is witty and is a big favorite. All the players say he is sure to make good."[27]

A few days later, the Pirates released Scott to Macon of the Class-C South Atlantic League).[28] He started the 1917 season with two wins, two losses, and a tie before the club folded. Scott quickly signed with Nashville of the Class-A Southern Association.[29]

Before making his debut, on May 25, Scott paid a visit to the Macon city clerk and filled out his draft registration card. On May 29 he pitched his first game for the Vols, losing to the New Orleans Pelicans, 2-1.

Scott continued to show great promise; by late July he had given up only 27 earned runs in 124 innings in earning nine wins against six losses. His victories included a one-hitter against Mobile and a two-hitter against the Pelicans.

Nashville sportswriter Blinkey Horn was effusive, if somewhat obscure, in describing Scott's progress with the Vols: "Unfurling his fallaway forking backed up with an unusual amount of diamond courage, Sally [yet another nickname] Scott got down to box business without regard for his critics until now he has soared to a commanding heighth. No slabber ever broke in against greater handicaps than Scott."[30]

On August 14, the day Scott defeated Mobile to improve his record to 12-9, his draft board in Ridgeway called him home for examination and possible induction into the armed forces. The next day, the Boston Braves wired Nashville President Clyde Shropshire saying they would purchase Scott if he avoided military service. The only other requirement was that Scott "display major league slabbing ability."[31] Scott did not receive military orders, and joined the Braves on August 16. In three starts and seven appearances for the Braves, he was 1-2.

Scott had to sit out the 1918 season after his arm was burned in a gasoline explosion while he was cranking his car.[32] Back with the Braves in 1919, he finished with a 6-6 record.

In 1920 Scott won 10 games but lost 21, in the first of his two major-league seasons with that many defeats. His final loss came at the hands of the Phillies on October 2 in Boston, a 4-2 loss in 11 innings. Scott gave up only eight hits but the Braves made four errors behind him.

Scott led National League pitchers with 47 appearances in 1921. His record improved to 15-13, but he hurt his arm again. His sensational 1922 World Series pitching performance could not have been predicted.

In February 1922 the Braves sent Scott to Cincinnati for aging pitcher Rube Marquard and infielder Larry Kopf. In May the Reds released Scott, the Giants signed him, and his World Series heroics soon followed.

Scott was suspended in May of 1923 for skipping a trip to Boston. Though he had a strong season (16-7, 3.89 ERA), in January of 1924 he was placed on waivers and offered to Louisville, which declined.[33] Eventually he was traded to Toledo along with catcher Alex Gaston for pitcher Joe Bradshaw,[34] although the Giants recalled Scott on September 17 to report once the American Association season ended.[35] For the Mud Hens he was 20-20, albeit with a good 3.25 ERA.

At age 33 Scott returned to lead the Giants with a 3.15 ERA in 1925. His won-lost record was 14-15. In 1926 he led the National League in appearances with 50, but after a 13-15 record he was traded on January 9, 1927, to the Phillies in a three-team transaction also involving the Brooklyn Robins, who sent pitcher Burleigh Grimes the Giants.

The Phillies depended on Scott to anchor their staff. On June 19, 1927, he pitched complete games in both ends of a doubleheader at Cincinnati's Redlands Field.[36] He won the first game, 3-1, but lost the nightcap, 3-0. He walked only one batter in 17 innings. His final loss of the year came on September 27 at the Baker Bowl when the Giants slugged him for six hits and three runs in 1⅓ innings. He led the league in appearances with 48, and finished 9-21.

On December 14, 1927, the Phillies sold Scott to Toledo, his second ride with the Mud Hens. He fashioned a respectable 13-9 record in 1928 before John McGraw took another chance with him. The *Brooklyn Daily Eagle* lauded the acquisition: "Jack is a hunk of a citizen and he ought to be able to stand lots of double duty."[37] He pitched in 16 games (three starts) and had a 4-1 record and 3.58 ERA as the Giants finished second to the St. Louis Cardinals. Back with the Giants again in 1929, he was 7-6.

Relegated to the second team through 1930 spring training,[38] the 39-year-old Scott pitched sparingly, and when the season began, he was on the Toledo roster for the third and last time. He pitched in only 13 games and was 5-3. His last season as a professional was 1931, when he split time between Toledo and Wilkes-Barre (Class-B New York-Pennsylvania League).

Released by the Mud Hens, Scott went to Wilkes-Barre on July 25 and asked Barons manager Mike McNally for a job, offering to pitch a "free game." "If I suit you, sign me up," Scott said. "If I don't, you won't have to pay me."[39] Scott won a job, and posted a 6-3 record for the Barons in his final season in Organized Baseball.

A left-handed hitter, Scott had a respectable .275 batting average in 12 seasons in the majors. He won 103 games and lost 109, with a 3.85 ERA in 1,814⅔ innings pitched. Twenty-game losses were offset by great memories for the hard-luck pitcher.

Scott returned to his family's tobacco and fruit farm in North Carolina, and served as Warren's police chief for 30 years.[40] When he died on November 30, 1959, in Duke University Hospital at the age of 67, he was undergoing emergency stomach surgery and suffered a massive hemorrhage.[41] He is buried in Fairview Cemetery in Warrenton.

For some, Scott's legacy is having lost 20 games twice in the majors and once in the minor leagues. But Jack would recall his special moment in baseball annals when he won a World Series game over the Yankees and future Hall of Famer Waite Hoyt.

"That was my greatest game," Scott recalled years later. "I had an easy time with Babe Ruth. I fed him an assortment of slowballs, fastballs and curves. The only time he reached base against me was when he got his foot in the way of a slowball and [he] was waved to first as a hit batsman."[42]

The highs that come with strikeouts, shutouts, and World Series victories countered Scott's homesickness, personal loss, arm trouble, and 20-loss seasons. But he knew his place in baseball history.

## SOURCES

In addition to the sources cited in the Notes, the author consulted ancestry.com, baseball-reference.com, newspapers.com, and findagrave.com.

## NOTES

1 "1922 Yankees Go Home," thisgreatgame.com/1922-baseball-history.html, retrieved February 18, 2017.

2 Robert F. Kelly, "Quit Is Not Jack Scott's Middle Name," *Association Men*, April 1923: 362.

3 "Scott, in Great Comeback, Brings Warren Fame," *Warren Record* (Warren County, North Carolina), October 13, 1922: 3.

4 "Scott's Father Saw Him Stage Comeback in World's Series," *Binghamton* (New York) *Press and Sun-Bulletin*, October 10, 1922: 19.

5 *Chicago Tribune*, October 10, 1922: 22.

6 "Scott," *Warren Record*.

7 "Rather Hunt Duck Than Tour the World, Pitcher Scott Says," *Warren Record*, November 10, 1922: 1.

8 David Skelton, "20-Game Losers," *Baseball Research Journal*, Volume 42, Issue 1 (2013): 111.

9 "Scott," *Warren Record*.

10 "Base Ball Items," *Warren Record*, July 21, 1911: 7.

11 "Base Ball Season Ends," *Warren Record*, September 15, 1911: 7.

12 "Scott," *Warren Record*.

13 "Ten Players Have Reported," *Durham* (North Carolina) *Morning Herald*, March 18, 1913: 3.

14 "The Durham Bulls to Play Philadelphia," *Durham Morning Herald*, March 23, 1913: 7.

15 "Pair of Doubles Saved Phils' Scalp," *Philadelphia Inquirer*, March 25, 1913: 13.

16 "Local Happenings," *Durham Morning Herald*, April 15, 1913: 3.

17 "Honoring the Bulls," *Durham Morning Herald*, September 4, 1913: 1.

18 "Roanoke Valley League Games," *Roanoke Rapids* (North Carolina) *Herald*, July 17, 1914: 1.

19 "Roanoke Valley League Games," *Roanoke Rapids Herald*, July 31, 1914: 1.

20 "Exit Roanoke Valley League," *Roanoke Rapids Herald*, September 11, 1914: 4.

21 "Grounds Too Wet for the Ballgame," *Durham Morning Herald*, August 5, 1914: 2.

22 "Twins Take the One That Put Victory on the Ice," *Twin City Daily Sentinel* (Winston, North Carolina), September 9, 1914: 6.

23 "Farrell's Decisions," *Atlanta Constitution*, March 14, 1915: 5B.

24 "Roanoke Rapids Wins Pennant," *Roanoke Rapids Herald*, August 27, 1915: 1.

25 A.H. Trent, "The Virginia League," *Sporting Life*, April 27, 1916: 22.

26 Charles H. Doyle, "Pirates Drop Loose Contest to Binghamton," *Pittsburgh Post-Gazette*, September 12, 1916: 8.

27 "Pitcher Scott Is Sent To His Home," *Pittsburgh Press*, September 21, 1916: 32.

28 "Pitcher Jack Scott Released by Pirates," *Pittsburgh Press*, September 28, 1916: 28.

29 "Blinkey" Horn, " 'Sally' Scott, Pitcher From Macon Club, Signed by Vols," *Nashville Tennessean*, May 26, 1917: 10.

30 Horn, "Do Figures Lie? Lay Before You Record of Scott and Meador," *Nashville Tennessean*, July 28, 1917: 8.

31 Horn, "Braves Agree to Price on Scott if He Avoids Draft," *Nashville Tennessean*, August 16, 1917: 8.

32 Kelly, 361.

33 "Pitcher Scott Is Waived Out of Majors by Giants," *Rochester Democrat and Chronicle*, January 10, 1924: 28.

34 "Bradshaw Sold to Giants," *Portsmouth* (Ohio) *Daily Times*, January 18, 1924: 23.

35 "Giants Recall Scott," *Brooklyn Daily Eagle*, September 17, 1924: 24.

36 "This Day in All Teams History June 19," nationalpastime.com/site/index.php?action=baseball_team_search&baseball_team=All+Teams&fact_Month=06&fact_Day=19, retrieved February 1, 2017.

37 "New York Clubs Still Keep Their Pitching Faith," *Brooklyn Daily Eagle*, August 22, 1928: 26.

38 "McGraw Uses Mailed Fist on Roush, *Brooklyn Daily Eagle*, March 26, 1930: 22.

39 Ed Kelly, "Kel-e-Graphs," *Scranton Republican*, July 28, 1931: 15.

40 Paul Batesel, *Major League Baseball Players of 1916: A Biographical Dictionary* (Jefferson, North Carolina: McFarland, 2007), 133.

41 "Former Major Leaguer Dies," *Burlington* (North Carolina) *Daily Times-News*, December 1, 1959: 16.

42 "Necrology," *The Sporting News*, December 9, 1959: 24.

# GEORGE ALLEN SMITH

## BY JEFF ENGLISH

ON APRIL 4, 1919, BOSTON'S BABE Ruth stepped to the plate to lead off the second inning of an exhibition game against the New York Giants at Plant Field in Tampa, Florida. Journeyman right-hander George Smith was on the mound for the Giants, hoping to stick for his third stint with the club after finishing the previous season an eight-game winner — two each for Cincinnati and the Giants and four as a Brooklyn Robin. With the count three balls and a strike, Smith unleashed a fastball to the Red Sox slugger, who responded with a mighty swing. Few if any of the reported 4,200 onlookers in attendance would soon forget what transpired, as the ball left Ruth's bat on a line to right-center field. Fleet-footed Giants right fielder Ross Youngs was forced to abandon his chase as the ball sailed well beyond the field's outer marker, finally kicking up some dust when it landed on the far side of a race track beyond the field. Those who witnessed it called it the longest ball they ever saw struck, and today a historical marker claiming "Babe's Longest Homer" places the distance of the blast at 587 feet. While both the distance and the claim itself remain subjects of debate, the blast might best be viewed as a preseason indicator that Ruth was about to transform the game with a record-setting 29 home runs during the season. But absent from the marker is any reference to the man who made Ruth's feat possible, the tall, lanky Smith who was, as it turned out, not long for the Giants roster. He went on to make just three regular-season appearances before a trade in May sent him to Philadelphia.

George Allen Smith signed with John McGraw's New York Giants on June 27, and made his major-league debut as a Giant against the St. Louis Cardinals on August 9, 1916, fresh off the campus of Columbia University, where he had earned the moniker Columbia George. He'd been seen as a potential "star" by the *New York Times* as early as his junior year. Noting an April 1915 game in which he struck out 17 Wesleyan batters, the newspaper reported, "It is not Smith's intention to go into professional baseball."[1]

When he ultimately did sign a pro contract, Columbia coach Andy Coakley predicted that Smith would have "a successful career as a big leaguer."[2] The 6-foot-2 Smith, listed at 163 pounds, had a reputation as quiet and bookish off the field, but on the field, "he was an implacable enemy of anybody who wore the uniform of the opposing ball club.[3]

In the first game of the signing day's doubleheader, Smith pitched a scoreless inning while striking out two, and after two more brief appearances in relief, won his first career start on September 13 against the Cincinnati Reds. It was in the second game of a doubleheader, and Smith worked 5⅓ innings. (He would have to wait two years before earning his second victory.[4]) The *Times* noted, "His debut was a howling success. … He had a world of speed and a curve as round as a barrel hoop. Smithie will do."[5]

McGraw was greatly impressed by Smith early on, comparing him to the legendary Christy Mathewson. "Smith, to me, is the Matty of this generation."[6] McGraw compared Smith's poise, aloofness, and delivery to those of Mathewson and added, "Never before have I seen a young pitcher in whom I have as much confidence as I have in Smith."[7]

In nine appearances in 1916, Smith worked a total of 20⅔ innings, and was 1-0 with a 2.61 earned-run average.

In 1917, he trained with the Giants in Texas and pitched 36⅓ innings in 14 regular-season games with a record of 0-3 and a 2.84 ERA. On July 10, he was farmed out to Rochester (International League) for a couple of months, returning to pitch in the Giants game on September 20. He had gotten in a lot of work during his weeks with Rochester, and was 8-11 (2.33) in 178 innings.

Matty to send Smith back, saying he never intended to let him go and that the deal was made without his knowledge. And Matty, according to reports from St. Louis, is going to fall for it and let Smith return to the Giants."[9] On June 27, Smith returned to the Giants.

He earned just two wins in five decisions with the Giants before again finding himself on the move, this time to the Brooklyn Robins, whom Smith rewarded with a loss and then four complete-game victories through September 2.[10] The war-shortened regular season ended on Labor Day in 1918. It was the last year in which Smith enjoyed more wins than losses.

The *Brooklyn Daily Eagle* later reported the Cincinnati sojourn as a loan: "McGraw lent Smith to Cincinnati this season. … Afterward New York reclaimed him. Now New York has turned him over to Brooklyn."[11] And on September 4, the paper reported that Smith was back with the Giants for the third time: "Cincinnati turned him back to New York, which then loaned him to Brooklyn for the rest of the campaign. Smith beat the Phillies in Philadelphia on Labor Day in the last game of the season. His return to the Giants is not due to failure with the Superbas. On the contrary, New York demanded that Brooklyn make the transfer because Smith had shown very promising form with Brooklyn."[12]

On December 12, it was reported nationally that the Giants had traded Smith and first baseman Walter Holke to Brooklyn for Jake Daubert. The trade was apparently never consummated.

Smith closed out 1918 by marrying Eva Senst of Port Chester, New York. The marriage took place in secret, and the couple did not announce their nuptials until New Year's Day.[13] News accounts of the marriage indicate that Smith was already teaching mathematics in Greenwich during the offseasons.[14]

Smith was born on May 31, 1892, in Byram, a neighborhood in the town of Greenwich, Connecticut, the only child of Max and Sadie Allen Smith, who had been married for two years.[8] Max Smith had emigrated from Germany as a child in 1869. Byram was notable as home to Byram Quarry, which supplied stone for the construction of the Brooklyn Bridge and the base of the Statue of Liberty. Max Smith owned a restaurant in Greenwich, so George had the opportunity to excel in the classroom as well as on the field.

Two years removed from the campus at Columbia, Smith began his 1918 season as a 25-year-old member of the Cincinnati Reds pitching staff, having been purchased from New York on May 2. There he worked under manager Christy Mathewson His stay in Cincinnati was brief and his contributions modest, and by the end of June the Giants had reacquired Smith and his 2-3 won-lost record (4.07 ERA). It was a bizarre scenario, as reported by the *Cincinnati Post*: "The Reds took Smith on a deal that gave New York no strings on him. But, now that New York is shy on pitchers, John McGraw has appealed to

Smith dropped two decisions in his three appearances with the Giants to open the 1919 season before the May 18 trade that sent him and infielder Ed Sicking to the Philadelphia Phillies in exchange for pitcher Joe Oeschger.[15] He made 19 starts for the Phillies, posting a 5-11 mark and a 3.22 ERA. The Phillies finished last in the standings, 47½ games behind the pennant-winning Reds, with no pitcher winning more than eight games. His 13 combined losses were eighth worst in the league, and the eight home runs he surrendered were the second most allowed among National League pitchers. Despite a subpar performance on the field, George had good reason to celebrate late in the season. On September 2, his wife, Eva, gave birth to their only child, a son they named George A. Smith Jr.

Smith enjoyed his finest season in 1920, winning 13 games for the Phillies and manager Gavvy Cravath. He pitched 11 complete games and yielded a league-high 10 home runs. His 43 appearances placed him sixth in the league. Among his strongest performances were a 13-inning complete-game win against Brooklyn on May 2, and three weeks later, an 11-inning win against the same club. Despite Smith's contributions, Philadelphia finished last in the league for the second season in a row, 30½ games behind first-place Brooklyn. His own record was 13-18 (3.45).

That 1920 season proved to be the high-water mark of Smith's career, and he struggled mightily in 1921 to approximate its modest success. With Philadelphia now being managed by Bill Donovan, Smith began the year with eight losses before gaining his first victory in a complete-game win at Cincinnati on June 18. He went on to win just three more games while losing a league-high 20 for a Phillies team that finished in the cellar with a record of 51-103. After 87 games, Donovan had been replaced as manager by Kaiser Wilhelm. The Phillies won 25 games under Donovan and 26 under Wilhelm.

Smith somehow managed a shutout against the Boston Braves for his final win of the season on August 12, despite allowing 12 hits and a walk with just two strikeouts. He yielded 10 or more hits in 13 appearances during the season, including 20 on two occasions. Philadelphia, scoring the fewest runs in the league while posting the highest team ERA, ended the 1921 campaign 43½ games behind the pennant-winning New York Giants. Smith's ERA was 4.76, to go with his 4-20 record. He'd eaten up some innings (221⅓), but allowed 303 hits and walked 52 batters.

Smith began his 1922 season with a one-sided loss to the Brooklyn Robins, who would eventually account for six of his 14 losses that season. After June 29, he was used mostly in relief, with four scattered starts. The Phillies saw fit to put Smith on the mound on 42 occasions, 10th most among National League pitchers. In return, he gave them five wins and served up a career-worst 16 home runs, third most among his peers. His seven wild pitches placed third in the league, and on at least one occasion contributed to a fist fight with an opposing team.

Smith faced the New York Giants on April 25 and May 7 and hit Giants outfielder Ralph Shinners with a pitch in each contest. Facing the Giants again on June 29, Smith surrendered six earned runs over seven innings before having his day called for him. In his biography of Giants manager John McGraw, author Charles C. Alexander recounts what happened next:

"George Smith, just lifted for a pinch-hitter, walked past on his way to the visitors' dressing room and met a shower of McGraw's choicest obscenities. Smith swung at McGraw and missed, whereupon Shinners rushed between them and took a right to the jaw for his troubles. As Smith and Shinners rolled on the ground, McGraw tried to land a blow on the Phillies pitcher, only to miss and cut Shinner's cheek. By then players from both bullpens had arrived to break it up. Commissioner Landis was present, but from his box behind first, he complained, he hadn't been able to see much of the fracas."[16] A later newspaper report said, "They carried Shinners to a hospital, and it was several months before he was ready for action again."[17]

The following February, Philadelphia traded Smith to the Brooklyn Robins for left-hander Clarence Mitchell. Brooklyn manager Wilbert Robinson had been impressed by Smith early on, and never forgot him. He hoped he could get something more out of Smith than had the demoralized Phillies.[18] In 25 appearances for the Robins in 1923, Smith recorded three wins against six losses. All three wins came within an 11-day span in July, including a 10-inning, complete-game effort on the 28th against the Cincinnati Reds in which he allowed just a single run. It was Smith's final victory in the big leagues. He was released outright to Indianapolis on February 14, 1924.

With his major-league opportunities having dried up by 1924, Smith managed a 3-5 record in 43 games with the Indianapolis Indians of the Double-A American Association, and led the semi-pro Wilton Farmers to the Norwalk (Connecticut) City Championship.[19]

When his playing days were over, the bookish "Columbia" George Smith took to teaching mathematics full-time at Greenwich High School, where he had taught in the offseason since 1919. He retired as the department head in 1957.

His athletic exploits not forgotten, in 1961 Smith was a member of the inaugural class of honorees of the Greenwich Old Timers Athletic Association. Joining him were J.B. Conlon, Tony Manero, Jack Dempsey, Gene Tunney, and George M. Weiss. The dinner held in their honor marked the first time Dempsey and Tunney found themselves seated together since their controversial rematch for the heavyweight title, won by Tunney in 1927.

At the dinner, Smith was asked about the fastball he fired to Ruth all those years ago at Plant Field in Tampa. "I can still see Ross Youngs running back and looking up in the air under that one," he recalled.[20]

After a long illness, George Smith died in Greenwich at the age of 72 on January 7, 1965. He is buried at Greenwood Union Cemetery in Rye, New York. His final major-league record was 39-81, with a 3.89 ERA. (His obituary in the *Washington Post* said it had been 4-81.[21])

## SOURCES

In addition to the sources cited in the Notes, the author also relied on Ancestry.com, Baseball-Reference.com, and Smith's player file from the National Baseball Hall of Fame.

## NOTES

1. "Many Stars Among College Pitchers," *New York Times*, May 9, 1915: S1.
2. "Giants Get Collegians," *Washington Evening Star*, June 28, 1916: 18.
3. Frank Graham, "Smith Was a Hard Fighter," *New York Sun*, August 14, 1936.
4. He was not the same George Smith, a 3-year old colt, who won the Kentucky Derby at Churchill Downs in May 1916.
5. The *Times* also explained to local readers, "He is the lad who used to pitch for Nicholas Murray Butler's uptown school for boys and girls." See "Giants Give One to Their Guests," *New York Times*, August 10, 1916: 6.
6. "McGraw Finds Second Christy Mathewson," *Charlotte Observer*, August 24, 1916: 8.
7. Ibid.
8. Byram was apparently once known as East Port Chester. (Port Chester, New York, was a town just over the state line from Connecticut.
9. "What Sort of Deal Is This?" *Cincinnati Post*, June 22, 1918: 6.
10. It was widely reported in mid-July that Smith had been traded to the Boston Braves for pitcher Bunny Hearn on June 14. In fact, the Smith in question was infielder Jimmy Smith.
11. "George Smith Joins Superbas," *Brooklyn Daily Eagle*, August 3, 1918: 4.
12. "Smith Back With Giants," *Brooklyn Daily Eagle*, September 4, 1918: 18.
13. *Columbia Alumni News*, Vol 10, no. 21, March 14, 1919.
14. "Pitcher Smith Was Secretly Married," *Harrisburg* (Pennsylvania) *Patriot*, January 3, 1919: 9.
15. "Joe Oeschger Traded," *Philadelphia Inquirer*, May 19, 1919: 14.
16. Charles C. Alexander, *John McGraw* (Lincoln: University of Nebraska Press, 1988), 240.
17. "Bean-Ball Spoils Career of Much Touted Rookie Star," *New Orleans States*, May 1, 1926: 9.
18. Norman E. Brown, "Perseverance Finally May Bring Success to Pitcher George Smith," *Augusta* (Georgia) *Chronicle*, March 5, 1923: 6.
19. thehour.com/wilton/article/Wilton-s-baseball-past-put-on-display-11121817.php. Baseball-Reference.com has Smith on the roster of the St. Petersburg Saints of the Class-D Florida State League, but it must have been for a very brief tenure, as no statistical data is provided. The league disbanded on August 8.
20. Graham.
21. "George Smith Dies, Pitched for Phillies," *Washington Post*, January 9, 1962: C2.

# JIM TOBIN

## BY GREGORY H. WOLF

**NO ONE CONFUSED PORTLY RIGHT-** hander Jim Tobin with hard-throwing contemporaries like Bob Feller, Johnny Vander Meer, or Hal Newhouser. "Tobin's fast ball could not break a pane of glass," opined sportswriter Arthur Daley in the *New York Times*. "He has two pitches — slow and slower. ... He is the most tantalizing gent on the mound in all baseball."[1] But that wasn't always the case. Tobin suffered a severe shoulder injury in 1939 that jeopardized his career. Cast off by the Pittsburgh Pirates, "Old Ironsides" emerged with the lowly Boston Braves as one of the era's best knuckleballers. Over a four-year stretch (1941-1944) he completed 100 of 125 starts, posted a misleading 56-66 record, and tossed a no-hitter. He was also a threat at the plate. In 1942 he belted three homers in one game, the only hurler in modern history to accomplish the feat. Known for his prickly personality, Tobin was out of the major leagues after the 1945 campaign even though he was seemingly at the height of his career.

James Anthony Tobin was born on December 27, 1912, in Oakland, California, the second of three sons born to Richard John and Hannah "Annie" (O'Leary) Tobin. Both of his parents were born in Ireland, immigrated to the United States in the first decade of the twentieth century, and married around 1910. Richard found work in Oakland street-car system, moving up from trackman to foreman. The Tobins resided in the eastern part of city, where Richard Jr., Jim, and youngest son Jackie were introduced to baseball on local sandlots. (Jackie also had a long career in Organized Baseball, spending 1945 with the Boston Red Sox as an infielder.)

Given his short, stocky size as a youth, Tobin often played catcher. He eventually shed the tools of ignorance as a member of the baseball team at Roosevelt High School and began concentrating on pitching. A growth spurt added seven inches onto his frame by the time he graduated in 1931, transforming Tobin into a rugged 6-foot, 175-pounder with an intimidating presence on the mound.

Tobin's trek to the big leagues started in 1931 at a baseball school and tryout camp sponsored by the Oakland Oaks of the Pacific Coast League. The 18-year-old impressed the brass enough to earn a contract and assignment to the Bisbee Bees in the Class-D Arizona-Texas League the following year. Tobin won nine of 11 decisions before the league disbanded in late July. Unclaimed by the Oaks, Tobin returned to Oakland and hurled in semipro circles, where he caught the attention of Bill Essick, a super-scout for the New York Yankees whose signees included Lefty Gomez and Joe DiMaggio.[2] On Essick's recommendation, the Yankees signed Tobin.

Tobin's four seasons in the Yankees' farm system were marked by success and increased frustration as he moved up the ladder. He spent most of the 1933 campaign with the Wheeling Stogies in the Class-C Mid-Atlantic League and earned a late-season promotion to the Binghamton Triplets in the Class-A New York-Penn League. A 15-10 slate for Binghamton in 1934 moved Tobin up another notch to Oakland, where he began the next season with the Oaks, just a step removed from his dream. *The Sporting News* described the hurler as a "lively, young, all-around prospect [who] gains as much praise for his batting and utility work as for his hitting."[3] The paper also noted Tobin's free-for-all spirit, which would eventually characterize his relationship with all the big-league teams he played for. "[Tobin's] lack of seriousness was regarded as a defect and he was constantly warned that he never would succeed."[4]

A knee injury limited Tobin to just 23 appearances and an 11-8 record in 1935 with the Oaks, but the Yankees thought enough of him to add him to their 40-man roster. Had Tobin not required an appendectomy, he would have been at the Yankees' spring training in 1936. The now 23-year-old, who proudly called himself the "Mighty Tobin," responded with his best season in Organized Baseball in 1936 (16-8 and 230 innings) with the Oaks.[5] He also regularly pinch-hit and occasionally played first base, producing a .261 batting average in 153 at-bats.

Tobin arrived at the Yankees' spring camp in St. Petersburg, Florida, in 1937 with a chip on his shoulder. Rooming with former Bay Area prodigy and budding superstar DiMaggio, Tobin clashed with George Weiss, the director of the Yankees farm system, and especially manager Joe McCarthy, who, according to sportswriter Dan Daniel, considered Tobin "more clown than pitcher."[6] "The Yankees had a lot of fine pitching in 1937," said Tobin, "and I did not get, maybe did not warrant, great attention."[7] But when the Yankees optioned him to the Newark Bears in the International League, Tobin balked, returned home to Oakland, and threatened to quit baseball altogether. The Yankees blinked first and sold him to the Pittsburgh Pirates on April 14, less than a week before the regular season started. "If you keep trying, fighting, it all comes out in the wash," said Tobin in what could pass as his personal motto.[8]

If Tobin was frustrated with McCarthy, he must have been livid with Pirates manager Pie Traynor, who installed the hurler at the far end of the bench. Tobin tossed a scoreless inning of relief in his debut on April 30, then did not pitch again until May 31, when he picked up the win in a sloppy four-inning relief outing (three runs and five walks) in the second game of a doubleheader against Cincinnati. By the end of August, Tobin, sporting a miserable 6.10 ERA in only 31 innings, seemed destined for the minors before emerging in what Pittsburgh sportswriter Charles J. Doyle called a "blaze of victories."[9] Beginning with a four-hitter against the Reds in the second game of a twin bill on September 8, Tobin tossed six consecutive complete games, winning five of them and yielding just eight earned runs in 54 innings (1.33 ERA) to conclude his rookie season as the hottest pitcher in baseball.

In 1938 Tobin arrived at the Pirates' spring training in San Bernardino, California, brimming with confidence, which swelled following complete-game victories in his first two starts in the season. Pittsburgh sportswriter Les Biederman reported that Tobin worked closely with pitching coach Johnny Gooch, who changed his motion to a more overhand delivery in order to conceal his pitches.[10] The Pirates would "sink or swim," opined Doyle, with a core of young and relatively inexperienced hurlers, including Bob Klinger, a rookie; Tobin and Ross Bauers, beginning their second full seasons; and third-year speedballer Cy Blanton.[11] After treading water through May, the Pirates began swimming a 4x100 relay. On June 15 Tobin tossed the first of his 12 career shutouts by blanking the league-leading New York Giants on five hits at the Polo Grounds. A month later, on July 14, he relieved Blanton to start the ninth and hurled three hitless innings to earn the victory against the Brooklyn Dodgers at Ebbets Field and push the Bucs into first place. In what the *Pittsburgh Post-Gazette* called a "sensational" performance, Tobin gave the Pirates yet another emotional lift by tossing 11 scoreless innings of relief to beat the Boston Braves in the first game of a doubleheader on July 24.[12] The surprise team of baseball, the Pirates seemed primed to capture their first pennant since 1927. Tobin's shutout on September 22 as part of a doubleheader sweep at Ebbets Field maintained the Pirates' 3½-game lead in a fierce race with the Chicago Cubs. "My mother could manage the Yankees and win a pennant," said an indignant Tobin, his sights already set on facing his former tormenter McCarthy in the World Series.[13] And then the bottom fell out. The Pirates lost seven of their final 10 games, and the Cubs won 11 of 13, punctuated by Gabby Hartnett's "Homer in the Gloamin'" against the Bucs at Wrigley Field on September 28. Tobin lost his last three starts, but was hardly to blame. They took place in a six-day stretch, the final two coming on one and two days' rest, to end a disappointing season with a team-high 14 victories and a sturdy 3.47 ERA in 241⅓ innings.

Tobin's 1939 campaign started with a holdout during spring training and got worse as the season commenced. The stubborn hurler clashed with skipper Traynor about staying in games, and their relationship turned toxic. While the Pirates struggled to play .500 ball, Tobin suffered a wrenched back and injured his shoulder in a wild head-first slide trying to stretch a single into a double against the St. Louis Cardinals on July 9.[14] The injury proved much more debilitating than expected, and was indeed career-altering. Tobin, who had hurled inconsistently even before the mishap, made only seven more appearances and landed on the disabled list twice, finishing with a disappointing 9-9 slate and a 4.52 ERA in 145⅓ innings. The Pirates won just 23 of their final 69 games, a noteworthy collapse that Smoky City sportswriter Havey Boyle attributed to the "crumbling pitching staff."[15] Injuries to Tobin, moundmates Bauers and Bryant, and outfielder Johnny Rizzo, coming off a productive rookie season (111 RBIs), as well as down seasons by All-Stars Arky Vaughn and Lloyd Waner, contributed to the Pirates' worst season since 1917. The clubhouse was rife with tension, with players openly questioning Traynor, who was fired at season's end. Tobin was widely seen as one of the instigators of the unrest. His days as a Pirate seemed numbered when hard-nosed Frankie Frisch was named manager and promised a more disciplined club. On December 6 the Pirates sent Tobin along with cash to the Boston Braves for starter/reliever Johnny Lanning.[16]

Tobin joined the Braves, a perennial second-division team, at their spring training facility in Bradenton, Florida, but noticed that something was horribly wrong. "I found that my arm hurt every time I tried to put something on a pitch."[17] He abandoned his fastball, curve, and occasional screwball and transformed himself into a soft-tossing knuckleballer. "I had been fooling around with the pitch for years,"

said Tobin, "[but] did not use it in competition."[18] Now it became a necessity to salvage his career. Less than a week before the season commenced, Tobin slipped while fielding a bunt on a wet infield during an exhibition game against the Washington Senators at Griffith Stadium on April 11 and tore ligaments in his knee.[19] Sidelined for 3½ months, Tobin debuted for skipper Casey Stengel's club on July 27, tossing two hitless innings of relief against the Pirates at Braves Field. After getting rocked in his first start, a week later (seven runs in three innings), in a loss to the Reds, Tobin completed nine of 10 starts, winning six of them. He concluded the season by holding the Giants to two hits over seven scoreless innings of relief to earn his seventh victory and lowered his ERA to 3.83 in 96⅓ innings for the seventh-place Tribe.

Tobin's late-season success raised the ante in 1941. Once called the "Rock of Gibraltar" by Boston sportswriter Howell Stevens as much for his husky frame as for his unflappable presence on the mound, Tobin unexpectedly struggled while opponents teed off on his flat knuckler.[20] With a 2-4 record and 5.27 ERA, Tobin was relegated to mop-up duty in June and fared no better. "Jim was pitching for his job," suggested beat reporter Jack Malaney when he took the mound in the second contest of a July 4 twin bill against the Philadelphia Phillies in Boston.[21] Ignoring rumors of his imminent trade or demotion to the minors, Tobin responded with a gem, a two-hit shutout, to commence what Howell Stevens described as "one of the most astounding" pitching stretches in recent Braves history.[22] Tobin, whom the Boston press playfully called Abba Dabba and Shamus (a nod to his Irish descent), as well as Old Ironsides, completed 17 of 18 starts with a stellar 2.27 ERA in 174⅓ innings. In the only start he didn't complete, Tobin hurled 12 innings of one-run ball against Cincinnati at Crosley Field; it was also the fourth time he tossed at least 10 innings during that stretch. While Malaney gushed that Tobin's performance "placed him on a footing with any pitcher in the league,"[23] Howell noted that his knuckleball was the "deadly poison" that killed batters in their tracks.[24] The Braves finished in seventh place, but Tobin, who completed 20 of 26 starts and finished with a 12-12 record, was a beacon of hope on an otherwise dismal staff.

After some initial tribulation, Tobin's mastery of the knuckler in 1941 drew comparisons to other knuckleballers, such as longtime Giant Freddy Fitzsimmons, then with the Dodgers, the Senators' Dutch Leonard, and the White Sox' Ted Lyons. "My knuckler ... floats," Tobin, who did not go into a full windup, said a few years later. "It breaks a couple of ways certain days better than others. To be at its best, the knuckleball should be pitched into the wind. Then it does strange pranks. To make a knuckleball effective, you have to pitch it low; get it high and hanging, and you are murdered."[25] Abba Dabba wasn't exaggerating: On 23 occasions in his last five seasons, he gave up at least 12 hits in a game.

Tobin captured the hearts of the Braves faithful with his knuckler. "It's not only a tough pitch to hit but also to describe," noted catcher Ray Berres, Tobin's teammate on the Pirates and Braves. "From the stands it looks like Tobin can't get away with that kind of slow stuff for more than three innings. But when you're up there hitting, you see it wave and dance like a butterfly or a piece of cardboard in the wind."[26]

Even umpires were impressed with the tricks Tobin's knucklers performed. Veteran umpire Bill Stewart recounted an embarrassing situation one time when he was certain a Tobin knuckler would be high and inside. "I've never in my life seen a ball break and dart downward over the plate as that one did," said Stewart. "I yelled 'Ball — Strike,' then blushed," confusing both the batter and Tobin.[27]

Tobin overcame a nagging strain to his Achilles tendon in 1942 spring training to fashion a complete-game victory against the Phillies in his debut on April 15. He added another chapter to his growing list of accomplishments by socking a two-run homer, his first as a Brave, and only the third in his career. Though he had been used as a pinch-hitter in his big-league career thus far, he was not yet known as one of the best hitting pitchers in baseball. But that quickly changed. On April 22 he whacked three more hits and mesmerized the Dodgers for 11 scoreless innings with knuckleballs described poetically by sportswriter Arthur E. Patterson as looking like a "cross between a grapefruit and a bean bag, with a bit of dead cod thrown in," only to yield four tallies in the 12th and lose, 4-0.[28]

Three days after defeating the Phillies in a route-going outing on May 9 and collecting two more hits, Tobin walloped a pinch-hit home run in a loss to the Chicago Cubs at Braves Field. The next day, May 13, featured what Howell Stevens of the *Boston Post* considered "one of the most astounding feats of baseball history."[29] En route to a complete-game five-hitter against the Cubs, Tobin belted three consecutive home runs and drove in four runs in a 6-5 victory. While Fred Knight of the *Boston Traveler* described it as an "adjective-exhausting feat,"[30] Jerry Nason of the *Boston Globe* wrote that Tobin "went absolutely berserk with the bat and with piledriving power" to become the first big-league pitcher to clout three round-trippers in one game since Guy Hecker of the Louisville Colonels in the American Association in 1886.[31] Irving Vaughan of the *Chicago Tribune* was impressed, too, musing, "[Tobin's] bat was nothing short of terrifying."[32] Despite Tobin's exploits on the mound and at the plate, the Braves were a terrible team and finished in seventh place for the fourth consecutive season. Old Ironsides was a workhorse, leading the majors with 28 complete games (in 33 starts) and 287⅔ innings, with 12 victories but also 21 losses. When his knuckleball was fluttering, he seemed unbeatable, posting a 2.06 ERA in his victories compared with 4.76 in his losses. Then again, the Braves provided little support, scoring three runs or fewer in 19 of his 21 defeats, leading Stevens to lament that Tobin had been dogged by "cruel luck" all season long.[33]

Braves fans were buzzing when interim skipper Bob Coleman, who had replaced Casey Stengel (sidelined for two months with a broken leg), guided the club to a 14-8 start in 1943. That early-season success, however, was an aberration as the Braves "proved utterly lacking in offense," wrote Malaney about the lowest scoring team in baseball.[34] The pitching, on the other hand, Malaney suggested, was "one of the reasons why Boston's fans [didn't] entirely give up."[35] In his most consistent season, Tobin completed 24 of 30 starts en route to a 14-14 record while missing several turns in July with a leg injury. On June 26 he baffled the Giants with a knuckler that Gotham sportswriter Harry Cross described as "travel[ing] so slowly that it looked as big as a balloon when he reached the plate."[36] Tobin tossed a six-hitter to defeat aging Carl Hubbell, off whom he whacked a monstrous home run over the grandstand roof in the Polo Grounds. On July 4 Tobin took revenge against Pirates manager Frankie Frisch, whom he held responsible for his banishment from the Pittsburgh club, by shutting out the Bucs, 13-0, collecting three hits, including a home run, and scoring three times. Tobin, described as "more of a home run threat … than any other member of the team," even had a one-game tryout at first base to inject some pop into an anemic offense that hit only 39 round-trippers that season, including Tobin's pair.[37] But Abba Dabba's floaters were more important to the club than his long balls. Reflecting on Tobin's season, sportswriter Ken Smith quipped that the rotund hurler "drives managers to distraction with his slow knuckler."[38] Tobin (250 innings and a career-low 2.66 ERA) formed with Al Javery (17-16 with a big-league-most 303 innings), Nate Andrews (14-20 and a staff-best 2.57 ERA in 283⅔ innings), and Red Barrett (12-18, 255 innings) the most durable mound quartet in baseball.

Tobin's future with the Braves appeared murky as the 1944 season got underway while World War II claimed the services of more and more ballplayers. Recently reclassified 1-A, Tobin was expected to report to Army basic training at any point, but that call never came. Tobin was almost unhittable in his first three starts, which took place over a nine-day span. After a tough-luck three-hit, 2-1 loss to the Giants, Tobin held the Phillies hitless for 5⅓ innings, settling for a one-hit shutout. Against the Dodgers at Braves Field, Tobin needed only 98 pitches and 90 minutes to pitch the big leagues' first no-hitter since St. Louis Cardinal Lon Warneke's in 1941, and he also smacked a home run.[39] Sportswriter Jerry Nason of the *Boston Globe* gushed that Tobin sent a "torrent of 'butterfly' pitches dipping, fluttering, and staggering across the plate" to mesmerize Dodgers hitters.[40] Braves president and part-owner Bob Quinn was as excited as his players were. "It was one of the most intelligent games I ever saw pitched," he told sportswriter Ed Rumill of the *Christian Science Monitor*.[41] "[Tobin] had good hitters like Dixie Walker, Augie Galan, and Mickey Owen looking foolish, waving their bats wildly and missing by two feet."[42] Tobin claimed his success was the result of throwing his knuckler side-arm to righties instead of overhand.[43] Another no-hitter followed on June 22, albeit an abbreviated five-inning no-no against the Phillies that was called for darkness, but it was nonetheless Tobin's fourth shutout in just over two months. Playing for the lowly Braves, second-class citizens even in Red Sox-crazy Boston, hardly afforded Tobin the kind of national notoriety he might have gotten had he played for a contender. But when St. Louis Cardinals hurler George Munger was summoned to the Army just days before the All-Star Game, Tobin was chosen to take his place, and joined teammates Andrews and Javery on the National League staff. Back at Forbes Field, but now on a national stage, Tobin tossed a 1-2-3 ninth in the NL's 7-1 victory. Tobin fired complete-game victories in his first two starts after the midsummer classic, including tying his career longest game with a 14-inning outing against the Cubs in the first game of a twin bill on July 22 to improve his record to 11-10 and lower his ERA to 2.24. The Braves limped to another second-division finish in Coleman's first full season as skipper, and Tobin was much less effective in the final 2½ months, during which his ERA almost doubled. He finished with a career-best 18 wins, with 19 losses, and once again led the majors with 28 complete games, and a sturdy 3.01 ERA in 299⅓ innings.

After an acrimonious contract dispute and late arrival at spring training, Tobin tossed a complete game and knocked in two runs in a 13-5 trouncing of the Giants in his 1945 season debut. The burly 32-year-old took his turn, often on two and three days' rest, but was the last man standing of the pitching staff's big four. Javery and Andrews were sidelined with injuries and Barrett had been traded to the Cardinals for three-time 20-game winner Mort Cooper, who went down with arm problems. While the Braves played .500 ball as late as July 21, the clubhouse was racked with tension and dissent. Tobin's frustration mounted after he tossed six consecutive complete games in a 24-day stretch in July, winning just one despite a 2.15 ERA in 50⅓ innings. Tobin, whom sportswriter Jack Malaney considered "too outspoken" in his critique of the team and management, was finally seen as expendable and was sold to the Detroit Tigers in a waiver transaction on August 9.[44]

Suddenly on a team with pennant aspirations, Tobin let loose with a tirade against the Braves. "I was never happy in Boston," he claimed. "You fought yourself dizzy ... and you finished down in the dumps. [Losing] beats your brains out."[45] He saved his sharpest words for Braves president John Quinn, who saw Tobin as the root of the clubhouse problems: "Imagine accusing a man who has given what I had to the Boston ball club, of being the chief of a lot of jakes, the big bad wolf."[46]

Tobin's debut with the Tigers was "spectacular," gushed Motor City sportswriter Sam Greene.[47] In the first game of a doubleheader against the Yankees on August 12, Tobin hurled three innings of relief and blasted a three-run walk-off round-tripper in the 11th inning to emerge as a hero in front of more than 50,000 fans at Briggs Stadium. Cast in the role of swingman, Tobin posted a 4-5 slate (3.55 ERA in 58⅓ innings) as the Tigers, on the last day of the season, secured their first pennant since 1940 and their fourth in 12 years. Led by 25-game winner Hal Newhouser, the Tigers overcame a two-games-to-one deficit to win the 1945 World Series against the Chicago Cubs. Tobin made just one appearance in the fall classic, yielding two runs in three innings of relief in a 9-0 Game One drubbing in Detroit.

Tobin's career in the big leagues came to an abrupt conclusion when the Tigers released him before spring training in 1946 after failing to find a trading partner. In parts of nine seasons, Abba Dabba posted a 105-112 record, completed 156 of 227 starts, and compiled a 3.44 ERA in 1,900 innings. He walloped 17 home runs and drove in 102 runs while batting .230.

After dividing the 1946 season with the Seattle Rainiers and the San Francisco Seals in the PCL, splitting 20 decisions as a swingman, Tobin hung up his spikes. "I never had the urge to stick around baseball after I was through as a player," said Tobin, who almost held true to those words. He retired to Oakland, where he had spent the offseasons throughout his baseball career. He and his wife, Agnes (Caslin) Tobin, whom he met in Pittsburgh and married in September 1937, raised two daughters, Connie and Patricia.[48] Tobin was coaxed out of retirement briefly to pitch for the Oaks in 1948 and 1949 (12 total appearances) and then again in 1950 by former batterymate Al Todd, who managed the Memphis Chickasaws. But it was obvious that Old Ironsides was no longer emotionally invested in the game. Tobin spent the remainder of his life working primarily as a barkeep and owned a tavern for six years.

Suffering from heart problems in his 50s, Tobin died at the age of 56 on May 19, 1969, at Providence Hospital in Oakland. He had suffered a heart attack following vascular surgery and was buried at the Holy Sepulchre Cemetery in Hayward, California.[49]

## SOURCES

In addition to the sources noted in this biography, the author also accessed Tobin's player file and player questionnaire from the National Baseball Hall of Fame, the Encyclopedia of Minor League Baseball, Retrosheet.org, Baseball-Reference.com, the SABR Minor Leagues Database, accessed online at Baseball-Reference.com, and *The Sporting News* archive via Paper of Record. Special thanks to Bill Mortell for his assistance with genealogical research.

## NOTES

1 Arthur Daley, "Sports of the Times. Tobin the Tantalizer," *New York Times*, September 1, 1943: 31

2 "Caught on the Fly," *The Sporting News*, January 23, 1936: 2.

3 "Minors Worth Watching," *The Sporting News*, May 23, 1935: 5.

4 Ibid.

5 Ibid.

6 Dan Daniel, "Over the Fence," *The Sporting News*, September 29, 1938: 4.

7 Dan Daniel, "From Second Flight to Flag Contender," *The Sporting News*, September 13, 1945: 4.

8 Ibid.

9 Charles J. Doyle, "Traynor Calls for Pitch-Out on Number of Hurlers," *The Sporting News*, November 18, 1937: 1.

10 Les Biederman, "Gooch's Handling Real Story," *Pittsburgh Press*, May 1, 1938: III, 1.

11 Charles J. Doyle, "Bucs Bids to Cards and Phils Revealed," *The Sporting News*, June 23, 1938: 3.

12 "Tobin's Hard Luck Ends in Brilliant Exhibition," *Pittsburgh Post-Gazette*, July 25, 1938: 21.

13 United Press, " 'I'll Show That McCarthy' Tobin's War Cry for Series," *Pittsburgh Press*, September 22, 1938: 23.

14 Les Biederman, "Bucs Outlook Bright as Club Goes on Road," *Pittsburgh Press*, July 10, 1939: 20.

15 Havey Boyle, "Mirrors of Sport," *Pittsburgh Post-Gazette*, September 8, 1939: 16.

16 Though many fans were dismayed about the trade of Tobin, a bona-fide starting pitcher, for a swingman with a 20-25 record in parts of three seasons, Pittsburgh papers reported after the transaction that the Pirates had tried to move Tobin earlier. It had appeared that he would be demoted to Syracuse in the International League in partial payment for pitcher Johnny Gee before the deal for Lanning came through.

17 United Press, "I'll Show That McCarthy.'"

18 Dan Daniel, "From Second Flight to Flag Contender."

19 Associated Press, "Tobin Hurt as Nats Top Bees, 5 to 4," *Pittsburgh Post-Gazette*, April 12, 1940: 18.

20 Howell Stevens, "Bees Looking More Like Ready Honey," *The Sporting News*, April 4, 1940: 10.

21 Jack Malaney, "Braves Get Braver on Tobin's Twirling," *The Sporting News*, August 7, 1941: 5.

22 Howell Stevens, "Jim Tobin on Verge of Release Last Summer, Soared Back as Winning Moundster for Braves on His Butterfly Ball," *The Sporting News*, November 20, 1941: 3.

23 Jack Malaney, "Braves Get Braver on Tobin's Twirling."

24 Howell Stevens, "Jim Tobin on Verge Of Release Last Summer."

25 Daniel, "From Second Flight to Flag Contender."

26 Herbert Goren (The Old Scout), "Tobin Defies Hitters With Knuckler," *New York Sun*, May 15, 1942.

27 Frank C. True, "Freak Plays, Foolers for Fans, Toughest to Tag by Men in Blue," *The Sporting News*, June 1, 1944: 9.

28 Arthur E. Patterson, "Tobin Limits Brooklyn to 4 Hits In 11 Innings, Then Errs Afield," *New York Herald-Tribune*, April 23, 1942.

## 20-GAME LOSERS

29 Howell Stevens, "Jim Tobin Slams Three Home Runs," *Boston Post*, May 14, 1942: 16.

30 Fred Knight, "Probing Reveals Tobin, Lombardi on Home Run Diet," *Boston Traveler*, May 14, 1945: 24.

31 Jerry Nason, "Tobin Hits 3 Homers, New Pitchers' Mark," *Boston Globe*, May 14, 1942: 1.

32 Irving Vaughan, "Tobin Blasts 3 Circuit Drives," *Chicago Tribune*, May 14, 1942: 23.

33 Howell Stevens, "Al Javery Big Jive Man of Braves," *The Sporting News*, August 20, 1942: 18.

34 Jack Malaney, "Junked Junket Just Another Jolt for Joe," *The Sporting News*, October 7, 1943: 14.

35 Jack Malaney, "Jave Puts Jive Into Hub Fans With 1-Hitter," *The Sporting News*, September 23, 1943: 14.

36 Harry Cross, "Boston Hands Hubbell First Loss of Year," *New York Herald-Tribune*, June 27, 1943.

37 Jack Malaney, "Hurling Helps Braves When Batting Caves," *The Sporting News*, August 5, 1943: 14.

38 Ken Smith, " 'Get Some Slowball Slickers,' Ott's Highball to Giants' Scouts," *The Sporting News*, January 6, 1944: 3.

39 Ed Rumill, "Tobin Great Pitcher for 90 Minutes," *Christian Science Monitor*, April 28, 1944: 9.

40 Jerry Nason, "Tobin Hurls No-Hitter, Homers Against Brooklyn," *Boston Globe*, April 28, 1944: 1.

41 Rumill, "Tobin Great Pitcher for 90 Minutes."

42 Ibid.

43 Stan Baumgartner, "What's Tobe Got That's New? Merely Sidearm Knack of Slinging Knuckler," *Philadelphia Inquirer*, May 4, 1944.

44 Jack Malaney, "Sale of Tobin Shocks Boston," *The Sporting News*, August 16, 1945: 14.

45 Dan Daniel, "From Second Flight to Flag Contender."

46 Ibid.

47 Sam Greene, "Basement Boys Give Steve Two Big Dividends," *The Sporting News*, August 16, 1945: 6.

48 *Daily Courier* (Connellsville, Pennsylvania), January 18, 1938: 15.

49 Jim Tobin's Certificate of Death. Player's file, Baseball Hall of Fame, Cooperstown, New York.

# CLYDE WRIGHT
## An Angel Who Lost 20 Games as a Brewer

BY PAUL E. DOUTRICH

**JEFFERSON CITY, TENNESSEE, IS A** small farm town at the western foothills of the Great Smoky Mountains. Clyde Wright was born there on February 20, 1941. During the 1940s and '50s, when he was a boy, life in Jefferson City revolved around family, friends, chores, and school. For Clyde, family meant mom, dad, his five brothers, and his sister. Living on a farm, there were always cows to milk, hogs to feed, fields to work, or neighbors to help, but the Wright boys usually found time to have a little fun: baseball, football, or fishing at either Cherokee or Douglas lakes. It was a world that rarely extended beyond Knoxville, 30 miles down "the four lane," Route 11.[1] Even college for Clyde was at the hometown school, Carson-Newman. This was the world that Clyde Wright knew growing up and the world that taught him his work ethic and fair-minded, easygoing outlook.

Wright's ascent to the major leagues was swift. In June 1965 he was a senior at Carson-Newman College pitching his hometown college team to the National Association of Intercollegiate Athletics (NAIA) championship. A year later he was on the mound for the California Angels pitching in his major-league debut against the Minnesota Twins. In both cases he won impressively. The NAIA championship game against the University of Nebraska-Omaha took 13 innings before Carson-Newman could scratch out a 3-2 win. In the game Wright struck out 22, a Carson-Newman record that, as of 2017, still stood. He was chosen the tournament's most valuable player.

Selected by the California Angels in the sixth round of the 1965 draft, the major leagues' first free-agent draft, Wright spent his summer pitching in Davenport, Iowa, for the Quad City Angels, an A-level team in the Midwest League. The young hurler proved to be one of the few bright spots on the team. Though Quad City finished 17 games beneath .500, Wright compiled an impressive 7-2 record with a 1.99 earned-run average. It was good enough to earn him a promotion the following season to the El Paso Sun Kings in the Double-A Texas League. Starting the season with eight consecutive wins, he quickly became the team's ace. Then on June 10, he was called up to the Angels. Despite the call-up, that evening he went out and beat the Arkansas Travelers, 2-1, for his ninth victory.[2] The next morning he was on a plane to Chicago to join his new team.

Five days after having beaten Arkansas, Wright was penciled in to start the first game of a doubleheader against Harmon Killebrew, Tony Oliva, and the rest of the reigning American League champion Minnesota Twins. His mound opponent, Jim Kaat, would chalk up 25 wins during the season.

A wiry 6-foot-1 180-pound southpaw, Wright as a collegian did it all. A right-handed batter though he threw left-handed, he was one of his college team's leading hitters and a dominant pitcher who won 32 of the 37 college games he pitched.[3] As a professional he was never an overpowering pitcher who racked up strikeouts. Instead he relied on precise control and stealth. His method was to move his pitches around, change speeds, and hit his spots. On the mound he considered the white part of home plate the hitter's part. The black part was his part. His goal was to keep hitters off balance, outthink them. He preferred to get an out with one pitch instead of five or six. Later in the southpaw's career Reggie Jackson maintained, "Clyde Wright is one of the best in baseball today. He knows how to pitch."[4] Others came to share Jackson's opinion comparing him to Whitey Ford and Warren Spahn.

Wright's major-league debut was spectacular. The young hurler sliced through the first 10 hitters he faced and held the powerful Twins to just four hits. Only once did he have any problems. Already up five runs in the fifth inning, he gave up a pair of doubles that accounted for half of the Twins' hits and their only run in the game. From there on he sailed to an easy 8-1 win, his first in the major leagues. After the game his manager, Bill Rigney, gushed: "It was the best start in the majors I've ever seen." Catcher Bob Rodgers chimed in: "He did it so easy, it was effortless. ... He was Mr. Cool."[5] Only new teammate Rick Reichardt had any criticism. "He was great, but we've got to do something about the name Clyde. From now on, he's Skeeter Wright."[6] And from then on during his major-league career he remained Skeeter Wright.[7]

During the next eight weeks Wright remained part of the Angels starting rotation, winning three more games, including a shutout against the Senators, while losing five. Though his earned-run average climbed to 3.52 after a home loss to Minnesota on August 10, he consistently pitched up to his manager's expectations. After the game with the Twins, Wright left the team to serve his summer obligation in the National Guard. When he returned in early September, he was relegated to the bullpen, making only one more start in 1966. He ended his first major-league season with four wins against seven defeats and a 3.74 ERA. By most standards, while not spectacular, it had been a respectable rookie year for the young left-hander.

Wright's National Guard obligations also affected the beginning of his 1967 season. In early October, shortly after his rookie season, he began five months of active military service. He did not return until the following March and arrived to spring training late. He was among those pitchers who were expected to vie for the place in the California rotation vacated when Dean Chance was traded to Minnesota. Instead, Wright came to camp well behind his teammates. Consequently, two weeks before the season opener, he was one of two pitchers (Fred Newman was the other) sent to the Angels' minor-league camp so they could get more work. Team officials assured fans that Wright was expected to be back with the parent club before season began. That did not happen.[8]

Wright spent the first two months of the 1967 season with Triple-A Seattle in the Pacific Coast League. As he had the previous season at El Paso, he began his minor-league stint with a flourish. By June 10, when the Angels recalled him, he had become Seattle's ace with an 8-4 record. Once back on the parent club, he immediately staked a claim to a spot in the starting rotation. Teaming up with reliever Minnie Rojas, Wright breezed through his first three starts, winning two while Rojas won the other. In each he pitched the first seven innings and then watched while Rojas finished the games off. By the end of June he had established himself as the Angels' fifth starter. Unfortunately for Wright, manager Bill Rigney employed a four-man rotation, which meant that Wright was used primarily as a spot starter.

In August, with the Angels in a five-team pennant race, Wright's season was again interrupted by his National Guard obligation. When he returned a month later, the Angels had fallen six games off the pace and out of the race. Resuming his spot-starter role, he finished the season with solid starts against the Orioles and the Yankees and a couple of good relief appearances. The team, however, finished fifth in the American League. Wright ended his second major-league season with a 5-5 record and a 3.26 earned-run average.

Eager to improve his status in 1968, Wright joined fellow Angels hurler Jack Hamilton for offseason conditioning. Having completed only one of his 11 starts in 1967 (Hamilton had completed none of his 20 starts), Wright's goal was to build endurance and strength using an Exer-Genie Exerciser. The Exer-Genie is a hand-held isometric device developed by NASA to help astronauts maintain muscle while in space. In the late 1960s many professional and college athletes had begun to use it.[9] For Wright, the results seemed immediate. In his first start of the season he went nine innings, beating the Senators, 6-1. Manager Rigney raved, "That contraption is an absolutely incredible thing. ... Wright has never been faster than he was Wednesday."[10]

The rest of the season did not go as well. Despite his apparent new endurance and strength, Wright remained a spot starter and relief pitcher throughout 1968. He started only 13 games and relieved in 28. All of his six losses and only four of his 10 wins came as a starter. Along the way he had several notable games, including a shutout over the White Sox, his only other complete game, but it was not a satisfying year for him. Meanwhile the Angels floundered near the bottom of the American League, finishing only 1½ games ahead of the cellar-dwelling Senators.

The following year Wright's evolving role as a reliever grew. Manager Rigney made it clear even before the season started that he intended to use Wright primarily in relief. With several young arms to assess, the Angels manager limited Wright's innings during spring training, giving the lefty little chance to compete for a starting slot.[11] Once the season began, Wright was summoned sporadically, rarely going more than two innings. His starts were few and far between. The first came on May 4 and he did not start another game for two months. The low point was August 5 against the Yankees. With two on and two out in the bottom of the ninth and the Angels up 2-0, he was called in to get the last out. Instead he served up a home run. It was the sixth of his eight losses that season. Equally disheartening, he won only a single game, saved none and finished with a 4.10 earned-run average on one of the worst teams in the major leagues. After the season the Angels considered trading Wright but had no takers. It appeared that his days with the Angels might be just about over.

Three circumstances between the end of the 1969 season and the beginning of the 1970 season transformed Wright's career. One of those circumstances was the result of playing winter ball in Puerto Rico. Teammate Jim Fregosi, who was managing the Ponce team in the Puerto Rican league, persuaded Wright to pitch for him. He also suggested that Wright work on another pitch to add to his fastball-curveball repertoire. The solution was a screwball. By the time spring training started, Wright had perfected the pitch. He could throw it at various speeds and with the same precision with which he threw his other

two pitches. Wright's screwball transformed him on the mound.

The second circumstance actually began during the previous season. On May 27, 1969, manager Bill Rigney was fired and replaced by Lefty Phillips. While Phillips continued Rigney's method of handling the Angels pitching staff, during the following winter he made it clear that Wright would get his chance in the starting rotation. "(Wright) came off a 10-6 season in '68 and he just never got a chance last spring. … I know that the man has a lot of talent more than just one-game talent. Look what he did in Puerto Rico for Jim Fregosi. … No, right now Wright is my man. He'll have to show me he CAN'T do the job."[12] Clearly the attitude about Wright's place on the team had changed.

The third, and perhaps most important, factor in Wright's transformation was a new level of self-confidence. After the discouraging 1969 season, "I had to do something to regain my self-respect."[13] So he agreed to play in Puerto Rico. "It was a winter for mental health. Pride came back and with it confidence."[14] But it almost didn't happen. After losing his first two starts, one by a 10-1 score, Wright was ready to leave and so discouraged that he began considering retiring from baseball altogether. "(Fregosi) told me not to get down on myself and to stay."[15] From that point on, Wright's winter and career turned around. He perfected his screwball, and finished the winter with a stellar 11-5 record and a real opportunity to be part of the Angels' 1970 starting rotation.

The 1970 season started inauspiciously for Wright. Though he won his first outing, it was not impressive. He went only six innings and gave up four earned runs against the Royals. The second game, a loss to the White Sox, was a bit better. Then things started to fall in place. He went nine innings in a 7-1 win against the Royals and followed with another complete-game win over the Brewers. By June he had seven wins and three weeks later had already equaled his career-high 10-win total.

The high point of the season came on July 3. Before the game that night, Wright was inducted into the NAIA Hall of Fame. The game was against the Athletics, arguably the best power-hitting team in the American League. As he warmed up, Wright told pitching coach Norm Sherry, "If I can hold 'em to two runs tonight, we can win." Sherry responded by telling Wright that "Roger Craig (Sherry's former teammate) used to have the philosophy that every time he went out he'd pitch a no-hitter. Then when a team got a hit he'd say that it would be a one-hitter."[16] Wright liked the thought and carried it with him to the mound. Twenty-nine batters and 98 pitches later he had accomplished something that Craig never had. He had pitched a no-hitter, the second in Angels history and the first in Anaheim Stadium. For his work that night he became part of a second hall of fame.

The success continued for Wright. Eleven days after his no-hitter, with a 12-6 record, he took the mound in the All-Star Game. Entering the game in the 11th inning, he had the dubious distinction, an inning later, of being the losing pitcher on a play that lives on in All-Star Game history. With two out and Pete Rose on second, Wright gave up a single to Jim Hickman. Trying to score from second, Rose ferociously slammed into catcher Ray Fosse. The collision, which Wright watched from just a few feet away, effectively ended Fosse's budding career.

Through August Wright kept racking up wins while maintaining an earned-run average below 3.00. Not even his two-week National Guard service slowed him down. Instead, he was flown in to pitch the two games he otherwise would have missed. He lost the first and won the second. By the end of August he had 18 wins. On September 16 he beat Minnesota for his 20th win and finished the season 22-12. His 2.83 ERA was the third best in the American League. He was chosen as *The Sporting News* Comeback Player of the Year.

During the following two seasons Wright further established himself as one of the better pitchers in the American League. Though he lost one game more than he won (16-17) in 1971, in several ways his season was comparable to his 22-win season. Most notably, he kept his earned-run average beneath 3.00. It was a season that began with great expectations for the team but quickly fell apart. On the mound the staff, led by Wright and a young flamethrower, Nolan Ryan, looked solid. Combined with an offense that included the 1971 batting champion, Alex Johnson, the Angels were expected to compete with Oakland for the American League West championship. However, a string of injuries and a season-long battle between Johnson and manager Phillips destined California to a losing season, 25½ games back of the Athletics. Before the next season began, both Johnson and Phillips were gone. Shoulder problems and a sore ankle slowed Wright early in 1972 but he finished the season with a respectable 18-11 record and a 2.98 earned-run average on one of the worst teams in the American League.

Success on the baseball diamond brought Wright a degree of local notoriety. Some suspected that Wright, an attractive bachelor making a "handsome salary" in a city of movie stars, might become the next in a line of conspicuous Angels playboys that had started with pitchers Bo Belinsky and Dean Chance.[17] Wright in most ways, despite his gregarious nature, remained the same easygoing country boy he had been when he left Jefferson City. Aside from his characteristic "Tennessee twang," he typically maintained a low profile, preferring to blend in rather than stand out. Of course, he did savor some of the benefits of his success. He bought a comfortable home near the ballpark; relished the city's nightlife, and was often seen escorting a stunning blonde model, Vicki Holloway (they later married and had five children).[18] An avid golfer, he also became a frequent participant in celebrity golf tournaments.

Wright came into the 1973 season as the fourth-winningest southpaw in the American League over the previous three seasons. His place in the starting rotation was secure, but his future with the Angels was not. During the winter Bobby Winkles had replaced Del Rice as the team's manager and immediately began rebuilding the team. By the time of the season's first pitch, Winkles had traded or released almost half of the 1972 roster. Wright's work during the coming season would determine whether or not he would be part of the team's long-term plans. It didn't take long before doubts about Wright's place with the Angels became a reality. Hampered by a back problem, he didn't get his first win until mid-May, then struggled through the rest of the season, finishing with a dismal 11-19 record. Additionally, a prickly relationship with manager Winkles further soured Wright's chances of returning with the Angels. Two weeks after the season ended he was traded to Milwaukee in a 10-player exchange.

As bad as the 1973 season had been for Wright, 1974 was worse. His new manager, Del Crandall, initially listed him as the third man in the team's rotation. Healthy again and buoyed by a good spring training, Wright got off to a fast start, winning his first three outings and going nine innings in two of them. Then his season fell apart. He lost five of his next six starts, failing to get past the fourth inning in half of them. The worst, however, was yet to come. In mid-July Wright began a personal seven-game losing streak during which he gave up 6.17 earned runs per game. In the final two games of his streak he lasted a total of only three innings and was battered for 10 runs. The losing streak ended his days as a Brewers starter. In mid-August Crandall announced that through the rest of the season Wright would be used in relief exclusively.[19] The Brewers manager lifted his edict only once. In late September, Wright was given a final start against Detroit. He came into the game with 19 losses and left in the sixth inning with his 20th loss and the highest earned-run average in his career, 4.46.

The start against Detroit was Wright's last as a Brewer. On December 5, 1974, he was traded to Texas for pitcher Pete Broberg. It was a trade that Wright welcomed. In addition to his substandard performance on the mound, his relationship with Crandall had deteriorated steadily as the season wore on. "We just didn't see eye to eye." He complained that "Crandall went around asking guys if they liked me. … He asked them, 'How come you play bad behind Clyde? Don't you like him?'" Wright claimed that the only reason he was given his last start was because "Crandall thought I had a chance to lose my 20th game." Crandall countered: "(Wright) is trying to put the monkey on somebody else's back. He's trying to disguise his own failings with a smokescreen rather than accept that he had a bad year."[20]

Texas offered Wright yet another fresh start. Manager Billy Martin hoped that the acquisition would plug a left-handed hole in the starting rotation. Minimally, Wright would fortify the relief staff. Martin imagined the possibility of another 20-win season for his new southpaw.[21] Wright shared Martin's enthusiasm. With the addition of a knuckleball, he was ready for another comeback, proposing, "[S]ome people win it (Comeback Player of the Year Award) and say they never have to win it again. I'll take it every other year if that's the way it has to be."[22]

Unfortunately for Wright, the comeback didn't happen. He was used primarily as a starter through the first two months of the season, then he worked out of the bullpen and as a spot starter. He ended the season with a 4-6 record and a 4.44 earned-run average. The following spring he returned to the Rangers with hopes of redemption; but on April 2, he was released, thus ending his major-league career with 100 wins, 111 losses, and a 3.50 earned-run average.

While major-league teams were done with Wright, he wasn't done with professional baseball. Within two months of his release he was pitching for the Yomiuri Giants in Japan's Central League alongside the great Japanese slugger Sadaharu Oh. He spent the next three baseball seasons with the Giants, winning 22 games and losing 18. As with other Americans playing in Japan, Wright was paid well and felt appreciated by fans and teammates, but had problems adjusting to the daily training regime and the team's management. Comparing his new team with his major-league teams he lamented: "Conditioning—that's all they think about. … Spring training is four times as tough as in the States. … They go to the park at 10 and finish at 4:30 and then run 3½ miles back to the hotel."[23] While conditioning was grueling, management was a constant irritation. From his first day on a Japanese mound through his last appearance, Wright regularly collided with team executives over everything from playing time to living conditions. For his antics he was immediately dubbed "Crazy Righto" by his handlers, and "Crazy Righto" he remained for three years.

Away from the ballpark, language and cultural issues effectively isolated many of the American players. Frequently Wright filled those empty hours at bars with fellow Americans. Two of his favorite drinking companions were Charlie Manuel and former Angels teammate Roger Repoz. The threesome's escapades added another dimension to Wright's "Crazy" nickname but also led him to alcoholism. In 1978, upon returning from his final season in Japan, he said, "My wife (Vicki) said either I stop drinking or she was leaving me."[24] He sobered up.

After ending his career as an active player, Wright remained in the baseball world through his relationship with the Angels, whom he considered "my second family."[25] He maintained close friendships with numerous former teammates. In 2013 he was selected as 55th on the top 100 all-time Angels players list. Game days typically found him operating Clyde Wright's Tennessee BBQ and entertaining fans with colorful baseball stories. When not at the stadium he worked to promote the Angels in other ways ranging from charity golf tournaments to drug and alcohol awareness lectures. In 1980 he founded the Clyde Wright Pitching School. Among his notable trainees were two future major leaguers, his son Jaret Wright and Kyle Hendricks. Slowed briefly by a heart bypass in 2013, Wright later returned to the golf links, gardening at the home he bought shortly after coming to Anaheim, and enjoying time with his grandchildren. He remained a popular figure with Angels fans.

## NOTES

1 William Endicott, "A Big League Pitcher Comes Home Humbly," *Los Angeles Times*, October 29, 1970: 1.

2 Special Report, "Wright Called Up by Angels," *El Paso Herald-Post*, June 11, 1966: 6.

3 John Wiebusch, "Winter Restores Wright's Pride," *Los Angeles Times*, March 19, 1970: 69.

4 Staff, "Wright Still Seeks Public Appreciation," *Los Angeles Times*, April 5, 1973: 182.

5 John Hall, "Youngster Wins Debut 8-1: Angels Take a Pair," *Los Angeles Times*, June 16, 1966: 46.

6 "Youngster Wins": 49.

7 John Hall, "What Is a Clyde?" *Los Angeles Times*, September 7, 1970: 65. Four years later Hall restated his claim about Reichardt's role in dubbing Wright "Skeeter." Instead he attributed the sobriquet to team trainer Freddie Frederico.

8 "Angels Send Fred Newman to Holtville," *Los Angeles Times*, March 28, 1967: 33.

9 Exer-Genie/history.com.

10 John Wiebusch, "Exer-Genie Works," *Los Angeles Times*, April 26, 1968: 116.

11 John Wiebusch, "Winter Wins Restore Wright's Pride," *Los Angeles Times*, March 18, 1970: 69.

12 John Wiebusch, "Phillips Admits Angels Have Some Problems," *Los Angeles Times*, February 25, 1970: 100.

13 "Winter Wins": 100.

14 Ibid.

15 Ibid.

16 John Wiebusch, "No-ooo-ooo-ooo-Hitter," *Los Angeles Times*, July 4, 1970: 34.

17 Dave Distel, "Angels' Wright Takes Tobacco Road to Success," *Los Angeles Times*, April 5, 1973: 182.

18 Ross Newhan, "Wright Hopes for Another Comeback Award in Texas," *Los Angeles Times*, December 25, 1974: 74.

19 Associated Press, "Brewers have won 5 of last 6 games," *Fond Du Lac* (Wisconsin) *Commonwealth Reporter*, August 19, 1974: 22.

20 Associated Press, "Disagreements Caused Trade, Says Wright," *Tennessean* Nashville), December 7, 1974: 19.

21 Associated Press, "Martin Says Club Rates as Favorite," *San Antonio Express*, April 1, 1975: 36.

22 Ross Newhan, "Wright Hopes for Another Comeback Award in Texas," *Los Angeles Times*, December 25, 1974: 79.

23 William Chapman, "Players Work Up a Sweat in the Land of the Rising Sun," *Honolulu Star-Advertiser*, July 15, 1978: 47.

24 Marcia C. Smith, "Wright Loves to Tell an Old Angel's Story," *Orange County Register"* October 24, 2011.

25 Ibid.

# 20-GAME LOSERS POPULATE THE BASEBALL HALL OF FAME

## BY BILL NOWLIN

**THESE DAYS IF A PITCHER LOSES 20** games in a single season, he might not have much of a job the following year. For more than one reason, most managers wouldn't send a guy out there who already had 18 or 19 losses. A pitcher would only rarely have the opportunity to lose 20 games. That's why since 1980 there's been only one pitcher who has lost 20. Mike Maroth was 9-21 in his sophomore season for the 2003 Detroit Tigers but was kept on board and had a couple of good years in '04 and '05.

Of the 74 pitchers currently honored in the National Baseball Hall of Fame, 21 are 20-game losers. That's 28.4 percent. How could it be that more than 25 percent of the pitchers in the Hall have lost 20 or more games in a season? Doesn't that seem to defy reason? Isn't it counterintuitive?

Several of them were "repeat offenders"—they didn't have just one bad season in which they lost 20 games. They had more than one.

In fact, Pud Galvin lost 20 or more games for 10 years in a row!

The 20-game losers who are in the Hall of Fame:

**Steve Carlton**—13-20 in 1973, the year after his 27-10 season in 1972. Carlton lost 19 in 1970. He was six times a 20-game winner.

**Jack Chesbro**—Over a six-year stretch, he averages 25.5 wins per season. In 1905 he won "only" 19, falling just that one W short of six years in a row of winning 20 or more. His 41 wins in 1904 (he was 41-12) almost, but not quite, got the New York Highlanders to the American League pennant. His 20-loss season in 1908 was the last year he had more than five decisions, and the last year in which he recorded a win. Teammate Joe Lake lost 22.

**John Clarkson**—Clarkson lost 21 games for Chicago in 1887 (but he won 38) and 20 games for 1888 (when he won 30). Including those two seasons, he was a 20-game winner for eight years in a row, and two of them were stupendous seasons (53-16 in 1885 and 49-19 in 1889). He started 70 of his team's 113 games. Teammate Jim McCormick (20-4) was another 20-game winner that year, but there were seven seasons in which the UK-born McCormick lost 20 or more, twice losing 30 and once (in 1879) losing 40.

**Candy Cummings**—Cummings had a short six-season career. He lost 20 for the New York Mutuals in 1872 (but won 33) and he lost 26 for the Philadelphia Whites in 1974 (he won 28). Generally considered the inventor of the curveball, he may have been the most "lightweight" major leaguer, listed as 120 pounds.

**Pud Galvin**—From 1879 through 1888—10 seasons in a row—Galvin never lost fewer than 22 games. No other pitcher lost 20 or more games for 10 years in a row, getting hired year after year. In back-to-back seasons of 1883 and 1884, Galvin won 46 games each year.

**Jesse Haines**—In his first full season for the Cardinals, he was 13-20 despite a very good 2.98 ERA. He later had three 20-win seasons, and was overall 210-158 (3.64) and 3-1 over the course of four World Series. He was voted into the Hall by the Veterans Committee in 1970.

**Walter Johnson**—Universally acclaimed as one of the best pitchers in baseball history, Johnson had six seasons in a row in which he won 20 or more games. (In fact, he averaged 29 wins over that stretch.) And in the season he lost 20 (1916), he won 25. There followed three more seasons of 20 or more wins—for an overall span of 10 consecutive 20-win seasons, and then — just for good measure — he added a couple more later in his career, helping the Senators win back-to-back pennants in 1924 and 1925. All told, Johnson won 417 games with a career 2.17 ERA.

**Tim Keefe** — The pride of Cambridge, Massachusetts, Keefe was a 20-game loser three years in a row, with a fourth such season later on in 1886 (a year in which he won 22 games more than the 20 he lost). Six years in a row, he won 32 or more games (1883-1888.)

**Ted Lyons** — Ted Lyons pitched in parts of 21 seasons for the Chicago White Sox. He was twice a 20-game loser (1929 and 1933), but thrice a 20-game winner (1925, 1927, and 1930).

**Rube Marquard** — Coming off three consecutive seasons of 23 wins or more (1911-1913, all three seasons seeing his New York Giants in the World Series), Marquardt lost 22 in 1914 — despite a 3.06 earned-run average that year that was just marginally better than his 3.08 career ERA.

**Joe McGinnity** — Iron Man McGinnity began his career with eight consecutive seasons winning 20 or more games. Only twice did he lose that many, in his 1901 season (26-20) with Baltimore and his 31-20 season with the Giants in 1903. He had a career 2.66 ERA.

**Phil Niekro** — A master of the knuckleball, the elder of the two Niekro brothers pitched in 24 major-league seasons, winning 318 games with a 3.35 ERA. In 1977 he lost 20 games and in 1979 he lost 20 games. He had three seasons when he won 20 or more — 1969, 1974, and the just-mentioned 1979 (he was 21-20). He was a five-time All-Star and won four Gold Gloves.

**Hank O'Day** — O'Day pitched in only seven seasons and in just one of them — his last — did he have a winning record. In three of his first five seasons he lost more than 20 games. How did a guy with a 73-110 career record get into the Hall of Fame in the year 2013? He was voted in as an umpire. O'Day umpired 3,984 major-league games over the course of 35 years.

**Old Hoss Radbourn** — Radbourn started 64 percent of his team's games when he pitched for the 1884 Providence Grays; his record that year was 59-12. He'd improved on his 49-25 season the year before, the first of his four 20-game-loss seasons. He won 309 games in 11 seasons, averaging 28 wins a year.

**Eppa Rixey** — Eppa Rixey pitched eight years for the Phillies and 13 years for the Cincinnati Reds. His 21- and 22-loss seasons both came for Philadelphia. After his 11-22 year in 1920 (he'd been 22-10 just the year before), the Phils traded him to the Reds for Greasy Neale and Jimmy Ring. He then added three more 20-win seasons to his résumé.

**Robin Roberts** — Robin Roberts won 20 or more games for the Phillies six seasons in a row, 1950 through 1955. He won "only" 19 in 1956. And then he bore a 10-22 season, his 20-loss campaign (in a year the Phillies finished 77-77.)

**Red Ruffing** — In 1928 and 1929 Ruffing lost 25 and 22 games respectively for the Boston Red Sox. He sort of had two careers — he was 36-96 in seven seasons for the Red Sox, hardly Hall of Fame material. But after Boston traded him to the Yankees (for Cedric Durst), he built a 231-124 career that embraced four consecutive 20-win seasons (1936-39).

**Amos Rusie** — "The Hoosier Thunderbolt" pitched nine seasons of nineteenth-century baseball. In more than half of them (five seasons), he lost 20 or more games (twice more than 30 games), but at the same time he won 20 or more games in eight of the nine seasons — every one but his rookie year. From 1891 through 1894, he won 32 or more games.

**Ed Walsh** — Big Ed Walsh followed up his 24-18 season in 1907 with a spectacular 40-15 season in 1908, and back-to-back 27-win seasons in 1911 and 1912. The year he lost 20 was 1910, when he was 18-20 and yet led the league with a 1.27 ERA (the fifth year in a row his ERA was under 2.00).

**John Montgomery Ward**—In 17 seasons, Ward played over 1,500 games as a position player. In the first seven of those seasons, he pitched in 293 games (winning 164). Ward's first seasons (1878-1880, for Providence) saw him average 36 wins a year. His 1880 season resulted in a 39-24 record.

**Mickey Welch**—Welch's rookie year, with the Troy Trojans in 1880, saw him put up a record of 34-30. He put together nine 20-plus-win seasons, mostly with the New York Giants, and four 20-loss campaigns. His best season was 1884, when his record was 44-15.

**Vic Willis**—Pitching for the Boston Beaneaters from 1898 to 1905, Willis had three 20-win seasons but also three 20-loss seasons. In 1905 he was 12-29 and he was traded to the Pittsburgh Pirates for Dave Brain, Del Howard, and Vive Lindaman. He reeled off four 20-win seasons and never lost more than 13.

**Cy Young**—Last but by no means least, Cy Young won 511 major-league games, with a staggering 749 complete games out of 815 games started. In 22 years he compiled an ERA of 2.63. He was a three-time 20-game loser, twice in the nineteenth century with the Cleveland Spiders (both times he won more games than he lost) and once in the twentieth with the dismal 1906 Boston Americans. Fifteen times he was a 20-game winner, and five of those years, he was a 30-game winner.

A remarkable group of pitchers, ranging from the nineteenth century into the latter years of the twentieth. It just goes to show you can lose 20 games—and sometimes quite a bit more—but still make it to the National Baseball Hall of Fame.

# STEVE CARLTON

### BY COSME VIVANCO

**THE 1980 SEASON WAS A BANNER** year for Steve Carlton. Lefty, as he was universally known around the league, led all National League pitchers with 24 wins. He was the major-league leader in strikeouts with 286. He struck out 10 or more batters in 11 games. Carlton led all pitchers in WAR (Wins Above Replacement) with 10.2. Baltimore Orioles pitcher Steve Stone led all pitchers in wins with 25, but Carlton won the 1980 National League Cy Young Award by an overwhelming margin and finished fifth in the NL MVP voting behind his teammate Mike Schmidt. After his historic 1972 campaign (27 victories for a Phillies team that won only 62 games and finished in the NL East basement), Carlton's next three seasons had been marred by mediocrity. But with a renewed focus, he established himself as one of the game's top pitchers during the period 1976-1980. During those seasons he won 20 games or more three times, and won the NL Cy Young Award twice. Carlton was the best left-handed pitcher in the game.

Baseball is an apt metaphor for life. It's incredibly complex, with many facets that make sense. And there are also plenty of maddening aspects that are excruciatingly difficult to wrap your head around. The one tendency that is most striking about the game is how unfair it can be at times. Just imagine that you were a participant in a simple trade to benefit both parties, one solid player for another. Yet, as the years go by, you wind up being another player on the bench, an answer to a trivia question in some seedy bar, and—the final touch—a footnote in history.

This must have been what Rick Wise felt if he watched television on the evening of October 21, 1980, as Steve Carlton was charged with the awesome responsibility of pitching the Philadelphia Phillies to their first-ever World Series title. The journey to the doorstep of immortality was an improbable one. The Phillies established themselves as the top club in the National League East from 1976 to 1978, only to lose in the NLCS all three years. In Game Five of the 1980 National League Championship Series, Philadelphia fought back from a 5-2 deficit to clinch the pennant in front of a raucous Houston Astrodome crowd. In Game Five of the 1980 World Series, the Phillies scored two runs off Kansas City Royals relief ace Dan Quisenberry in the top of the ninth inning to go up 4-3 and win the game, thus sending the Phillies back home up three games to two in the Series, with Carlton ready to go.

Where would the 1972 Phillies have been without Carlton? That question may have been answered on the night of October 21, 1980, when Carlton pitched seven solid innings and Phillies fans finally saw their team win its first World Series. Without Lefty the Philadelphia Phillies of his era would be somewhere between here and parts unknown.

Steve Norman Carlton was born on December 22, 1944, in Miami, Florida, the only son of Joe Carlton, an airline maintenance worker, and his wife, Anne. As a boy Steve liked to hunt. One time, while he was rabbit hunting in the Everglades, his rifle jammed so he picked up a rock and from 90 feet away hit a rabbit in the head. He was also known to knock off a line of birds hanging from telephone wires with just a handful of rocks. Once Carlton flung an ax toward a quail that had taken shelter between the branches of an oak tree. With incredible precision, he sliced the head off the bird.

During his teenage years, Carlton became a big believer of the teachings of Eastern philosophy, in particular the writings of Paramahansa Yogananda, who believed that greatness in life can be achieved through meditation. The teachings of the Yogananda and other philosophers played a crucial role in Carlton's maturation process as a big-league pitcher.

At North Miami High School, Carlton played baseball and basketball. A basketball forward who

could outjump most centers, he could also throw a football 75 yards. He had no plans beyond high school and had little to no interest in academia, nor did he have a desire to attend a major university. Even as a young baseball player he showed the signs of the enigmatic superstar that puzzled many throughout his career. His concentration swirled around what was in front of him rather what was around him. In his senior year of high school, Carlton was good enough on the pitching mound that he decided to quit the basketball team and focus solely on baseball.

In October 1963, while attending Miami Dade College, Carlton signed a $5,000 bonus contract with the St. Louis Cardinals. For Rock Hill of the Class-A Western Carolinas League in 1964, he compiled a record of 10-1 with an ERA of 1.03 and struck out 91 batters in 79 innings. In midseason Carlton was promoted to advanced Class-A Winnipeg (Northern League) and then to Double-A Tulsa. Overall, he won 15 games. In 1965 he made the Cardinals roster out of spring training and on April 12, 1965, Carlton made his major-league debut, against the Chicago Cubs at Wrigley Field, facing one batter in a relief role and walking him.

The young left-hander had a very introverted personality, but there was a tinge of brashness to it. One day as catcher Tim McCarver stood shaving in front of a mirror, Carlton walked up behind him, tapped him on the shoulder and said, "You need to call more breaking balls behind in the count."[1] With shaving cream halfway around his face, McCarver looked up at his new teammate and was incredulous as he felt that a young nobody would call him out in front of his teammates. "Who are you to tell me to call more breaking balls behind in the count?" McCarver said. "What kind of success have you had to tell me that?"[2]

The pairing of McCarver and Carlton was quite interesting. McCarver had a knack for getting close to pitchers, but Carlton was a very stubborn pitcher who would make up his mind beforehand. McCarver was also known to be very headstrong, and the two would often butt heads. McCarver would eventually become Carlton's personal catcher for the Phillies during the late 1970s.

Carlton saw little action for the Cardinals in 1965 and spent the early part of the 1966 season at Triple-A Tulsa, going 9-5, with an ERA of 3.59. On July 25, the Cardinals summoned Carlton to pitch in an exhibition game during the Hall of Fame festivities in Cooperstown. Facing the defending American League champion Minnesota Twins, the 21-year-old impressed the Cardinals by pitching a complete game and striking out 10 as the Cardinals won, 7-5. Six days later, on July 31, he was in a Cardinals uniform, starting against the Los Angeles Dodgers. In four innings of work he struck out one, walked two, and gave up two runs. On August 5 Carlton started again and got his first major-league victory, over the New York Mets. He tossed a complete game, striking out one, walking three, and yielding only one run. By the end of the season he had made nine starts and won three games. The next season Carlton became a vital piece of the Cardinals rotation, winning 14 games, losing 9, and posting an ERA of 2.98. On September 20 Carlton struck out 16 batters and pitched a complete game, but wound up the loser as St. Louis lost to Philadelphia, 3-1, at Connie Mack Stadium. The 1967 Cardinals won the pennant and the World Series, beating the Boston Red Sox in seven games. Carlton started Game Five, pitched six innings, giving up three hits and one unearned run, and took the 3-1 loss.

The most dominant force on the successful Cardinals teams of the 1960s was pitcher Bob Gibson. He was the most competitive and most feared pitcher of his era. He saw the battle between a pitcher and batter as a simple act of survival. Sandy Koufax was Picasso, but Bob Gibson was the Terminator. And Steve Carlton wanted to be just like him. Carlton watched Gibson go about his daily business. How he conducted himself on the mound. From Carlton's point of view, the pitching mound was Bob Gibson's office. No one dared to walk into his office. "Steve learned more from Gibson than he did from anybody," said Tim McCarver. "The way he went about his independent selection of pitches. His refusal to listen to meetings because nobody could pitch like he could."[3]

In 1968 Carlton won just 13 games (he lost 11) but was 8-4 at the end of June and was named to his first All-Star team. His mentor, on the other hand, dominated the league with a minuscule ERA of 1.12. In that year's World Series, Carlton pitched four innings in relief, giving up three earned runs and seven hits as the Detroit Tigers came back from a three-games-to-one deficit to beat the Cardinals.

During an exhibition game in Japan after the season, Carlton decided to test the pitch that was an effective part of Gibson's arsenal. He would do so against the greatest player in the history of Japanese baseball, Sadaharu Oh. "I had been fooling with a pitch in Japan, after Sadaharu Oh hit two home runs off me, I figured what the heck," Carlton said. "I threw Oh, a left-handed hitter, the slider. When he backed away and the ball was a strike, I knew I had something."[4]

With a new pitch added to his repertoire, Carlton's 1969 season was his best so far. He won 17 games, losing 11. He had 210 strikeouts 236⅓ innings. Carlton lowered his ERA from 2.99 the previous season to 2.17. His WAR (Wins Above Replacement) was 6.8. He made his second All-Star team. On September 15 he set a major-league record by striking out 19 in a nine-inning game against the visiting New York Mets. Carlton, however, lost the game, 4-3. After the 1969 season, Carlton believed that he earned his way into the conversation as one of the game's elite pitchers and wanted to be compensated fairly. He asked for a raise in his salary from $26,000 to $50,000 for 1970. The Cardinals had a different view and Carlton missed a significant part of spring training. Then he led the National League with 19 losses (he won 10 games) and his ERA jumped dramatically to 3.73. On May 21 in Philadelphia he struck out 16 Phillies but lost the game, 4-3.

Carlton's mechanics were off in 1970. He had taken a break from the slider, the pitch that brought him to the precipice of superstardom. There are conflicting tales as to why he stepped away from the pitch, but one story that sticks out is that the Cardinals cajoled Carlton into not throwing the slider for fear it might hurt his curveball.[5]

One of the most important people to enter Carlton's life was a night watchman who was known to people as "Briggs." During the 1970 season, he was sending Carlton four or five letters a week. Briggs was concerned that Carlton's lackluster performance on the mound was due to poor concentration. So he sent him letters that contained snippets of writings from Nietzsche and Schopenhauer. Carlton was aware of the work of the two philosophers but never applied their theories to baseball. One can suggest that for a fan to send his favorite player five letters a week is a strange individual, but Carlton viewed Briggs as anything but strange. He was a spiritual guide who understood that the key to solving the riddle that is a major-league hitter is to develop a mind free from distraction.

With a newfound concentration and focus, Carlton produced his first 20-win season in 1971. A look at the numbers, though, suggests that he had only slightly improved from his mediocre 1970 campaign:

1970: 10-19, 3.73 ERA, 193 strikeouts, 109 walks, 4.2 WAR, 1.372 WHIP, 13 CG

1971: 20-9, 3.56 ERA, 172 strikeouts, 98 walks, 4.1 WAR, 1.365 WHIP, 18 CG

In 1971 Carlton made his third All-Star team. A notable highlight of the season was a 12-strikeout performance against the Los Angeles Dodgers on June 22. Eleven days later he walked 10 batters in a start against the San Francisco Giants. After the season, he again asked for a raise. This time the asking price was for $65,000 per year. Gussie Busch, the Cardinals owner, offered $60,000. Carlton decided to hold out. His holdout, combined with teammate Curt Flood's refusal to accept a trade to the Philadelphia Phillies after the 1969 season, and the ensuing litigation deeply angered Busch, who felt he had no other alternative but to defend his principle—that he was the owner of the club and had the final say on policy, no matter how unpopular it might be. Thus, he ordered that Carlton be traded.

Carlton was traded to the Philadelphia Phillies for right-handed pitcher Rick Wise on February 25, 1972. The trade didn't cause an earthquake around the league. Wise had won 75 games to that point in his big-league career while Carlton had won 77. Wise walked fewer batters while Carlton struck out more. Carlton held the major-league record for strikeouts in a nine-inning affair but Wise also had a notable historic performance on June 23, 1971, when he pitched a no-hitter and slugged two home runs against the Cincinnati Reds. McCarver remarked that the deal was "a real good one for a real good one."[6] However, Carlton was incensed that the Cardinals would trade him to Philadelphia. He was so angry that he called the head of the Players Association, Marvin Miller, and asked him what could be done about the deal. Miller gave Carlton two options—accept the deal or retire. Carlton decided to accept the trade.

Carlton set a personal goal of 25 victories that year. He began to throw the slider again. In his second start of the 1972 season, in a battle between student and teacher, Carlton got the best of his former mentor, Bob Gibson, by tossing a three-hit shutout against the Cardinals. He began the season 3-0. On April 25 he had a 14-strikeout performance against the San Francisco Giants, and on May 7 he struck out 13 Giants and upped his record to 5-1. But he then lost five games in a row and on May 30 his record was 5-6. Then Carlton went on a tear, pitching in 19 games with 15 wins and four no-decisions, and on August 17 his record was 20-6. In this stretch, he posted a WHIP of 0.932, and struck out 8.2 batters per nine innings. He hurled five shutouts and tossed 15 complete games.

On October 3 Carlton's complete-game victory against the Chicago Cubs in Wrigley Field made his season record 27-10. The Phillies finished with a record of 59-97, which made them the cellar dwellers in the National League East. Carlton's ERA for his remarkable campaign was 1.97. He tossed 30 complete games and hurled eight shutouts. Carlton struck out 310 batters and walked 87 in 346⅓ innings. His WHIP was 0.993 and his WAR was 12.1. Teammate Don Money, a third baseman, posted the second highest WAR on the club, a paltry 1.9.

The most impressive stat from Carlton's 1972 season was 46 percent—he accounted for 46 percent of the Phillies victories. Carlton was a one-man wrecking crew for the Phillies. Not only was he a maestro on the mound, but he was pretty handy with the stick as well. On April 19 he had two hits off his mentor and former teammate Bob Gibson, as the Phillies beat the Cardinals, 1-0. On July 23 the Phillies beat the Dodgers 2-0 on a two-run triple by Carlton. And on September 28 Carlton had a single and an RBI double as the Phillies defeated the Pittsburgh Pirates, 2-1.

Carlton was the unanimous choice for the 1972 NL Cy Young Award, and he also finished fifth in the MVP voting behind Cincinnati Reds catcher Johnny Bench.

Pittsburgh Pirates slugger Willie Stargell offered the best metaphor to describe Carlton in 1972: "Sometimes I hit him like I used to hit Koufax, and that's like drinking coffee with a fork."[7]

Historic pitching seasons typically come in the context of a club soaring to championship heights. Lefty Grove, Bob Gibson, Sandy Koufax, and Greg Maddux all had such seasons. Carlton's incredible season was remarkable for many reasons, but the most extraordinary aspect was that while the Phillies were an abysmal failure on a daily basis, he succeeded whenever he got the opportunity. Baseball is a sport centered on the psychology of how players handle failure. Steve Carlton was surrounded by a disastrous Phillies team but he managed extremely well by establishing himself as the best pitcher in the game. He took the ideas put forth by Bob Gibson and turned them into poetry during the summer of '72.

There was hope that Carlton would deliver an encore performance of his record-breaking 1972 campaign. He started the 1973 season 4-2, but by August 26 he was 11-16 with an ERA of 3.90. There were no memorable highlights to speak of in 1973, but there were a number of lowlights. His best game was a four-hit shutout with 12 strikeouts against the San Diego Padres on May 26. Carlton probably was suffering a tired arm. In '72 he pitched in 346⅓ innings, the most in his career. After a mediocre 1973, some wondered if he had been a one-season wonder.

Carlton stopped talking to reporters in 1973. Later he would say that speaking to reporters disrupted his concentration and it affected his performance. He never stopped talking to the Philadelphia radio crew, but when he spoke it was only about subjects other than baseball. The silence was so deafening that Braves announcer Ernie Johnson remarked, "The two best pitchers in the National League don't speak English: Fernando Valenzuela and Steve Carlton."[8]

In 1976, Carlton finally found the right mental balance on the mound and won 20 games for a Phillies team that won its first of three straight division titles. He collaborated with trainer Gus Hoefling, who believed in the philosophy that your body is your temple. Under Hoefling's guidance, Carlton incorporated a grueling training regimen that included martial arts, meditation, and stretching his left arm in a container of rice. Carlton sought to become devoid of emotion. He believed that emotion was subjective and the training was designed to remove any form of distraction that could disrupt his concentration on the mound. The Phillies organization went so far as to build him a $15,000 "mood behavior" room next to the clubhouse. Carlton would sit in this soundproof room and sit on an easy chair staring at a painting for hours. On days off, his teammates would catch Carlton performing martial arts exercises to keep up with his strength training.

On October 9, 1976, Carlton pitched in his first postseason game since the sixth game of the 1968 World Series, as he took the mound for Game One of the NLCS against the Cincinnati Reds. He gave up five runs, four of them earned, struck out six, and walked five in seven innings of work as the Phillies lost 6-3 to Cincinnati. The Reds swept all three games.

In 1977 Carlton won 23 games, made his sixth All-Star team, and won his second Cy Young Award. On August 21, 1977, he struck out 14 as the Phillies beat the Houston Astros, 7-3. Four starts later, Carlton again struck out 14 as the Phillies defeated the Cardinals, 11-4. However, in the 1977 NLCS he was anything but super. In 11⅔ innings of work, including the loss that clinched it for the Dodgers in Game Four, Carlton gave up nine earned runs and had an ERA of 6.94.

In 1978, Carlton produced a 16-13 record for a Phillies team that won its third straight division crown. In 1979, the Phillies fell to fourth place in a tough National League East, but Carlton had a good year. He posted an 18-11 record and made the All-Star team for the seventh time. He pitched two one-hitters. The second was against the Mets on the Fourth of July. The next start, he struck out 14 in a complete-game victory over the Giants.

In 1980 Carlton finally established himself as one the great pitchers in the game. In a year that saw the Phillies fight their way to a World Series title, Carlton produced many incredible highlights. In his fourth start of the year, he pitched a one-hitter against the Cardinals. In his two consecutive starts against the San Diego Padres he struck out 22 in 16 innings. In the 1980 postseason, Carlton went 3-0 with a 2.30 ERA. In the second game of the World Series, against the Kansas City Royals, he gave up 10 hits but struck out 10 and got the win. Carlton returned for Game Six and handcuffed the Royals, 4-1, to help seal the Phillies' first World Series title.

In the strike-shortened 1981 season Carlton finished third in the Cy Young Award voting behind Dodgers rookie left-hander Fernando Valenzuela.

The next season, 1982, was another banner year for Carlton as he became the first pitcher to win a fourth Cy Young Award. He led all major-league pitchers with 23 wins. He was the leader in strikeouts with 286. He tossed six shutouts and completed 19 games.

In 1983 Carlton posted a record of 15-16 and led the National League in strikeouts with 275 as the Phillies won the National League pennant. In his only World Series appearance, Carlton struck out seven in 6⅔ innings as the Phillies lost Game Three to the Baltimore Orioles, 3-2.

From 1982 to 1984, Carlton competed with Nolan Ryan for the top spot on the all-time strikeout list. The mark to beat was the 3,509 strikeouts of Walter Johnson. Ryan tied the mark on April 27, 1983. With his 3,526th strikeout on June 7, 1983, Carlton surpassed Ryan as the strikeout king. The 1983 season ended with Carlton at the head of the list with 3,709 strikeouts to Ryan's 3,677. (Eventually Ryan caught up to Carlton and took over as the all-time strikeout king by a considerable margin.)

On September 23, 1983, Carlton went eight innings and got victory number 300, defeating the Cardinals, 6-2. He struck out 12 and picked up his 15th win of the season. By 1985, his skills had diminished considerably. He found himself on the disabled list for the first time in his career with a strain in his rotator cuff. When Carlton was released by the Phillies on June 24, 1986, he was 18 strikeouts short of 4,000. Ten days later he signed with the San Francisco Giants. On August 5 Carlton became the second pitcher to record 4,000 strikeouts as he fanned Eric Davis of the Cincinnati Reds. But his brief tenure with the Giants was mostly unsuccessful, and he was released on August 7, two days after the record strikeout. He went 1-3 with the Giants with a 5.10 ERA. In his only win, he pitched seven shutout innings against the Pirates.

Carlton announced his retirement but it was short-lived. He finished the 1986 season with the Chicago White Sox, going 4-3 with a 3.69 ERA. The White Sox did not offer him a contract for 1987, so he signed on with the Cleveland Indians, where he made history with teammate Phil Niekro as they became the first teammates with 300 wins each to appear in the same game.

The combination was broken up on July 31, 1987, when the Indians traded Carlton to the Minnesota Twins. On August 8, 1987, he got his 329th and final victory as the Twins defeated the Oakland A's, 9-2. When the Twins won the World Series that year, the team made a customary visit to the White House to receive congratulations from President Reagan. In the photo that was taken of the occasion, all of Carlton's teammates were listed by name but he was listed as an unidentified Secret Service agent.[9]

Carlton pitched his final major-league game against the Indians on April 23, 1988. He allowed eight earned runs in five innings of work and was the losing pitcher. Carlton was released by the Twins on April 28 after four games (0-1, 16.76 ERA).

Carlton sought work from another team but found no takers. No one wanted to take a chance on a pitcher who was beyond the twilight of his career. The New York Yankees offered him the use of their training facilities but no spot on their spring-training roster for 1989. He believed that there was a conspiracy by the Twins organization to prevent from ever pitching again. "The Twins set me up to release me by not pitching me and other owners were told to keep their hands off. Other teams wouldn't even talk to me. I don't understand it," Carlton said in a 1994 interview.[10] There was no conspiracy. No collusion between teams. Big-league GMs saw what everybody else had seen. Steve Carlton was done.

Carlton retreated to Durango, Colorado, with his wife, Beverly, whom he married in 1965, and spent time riding motorcycles and dirt bikes. He was an avid skier, and devoted hours to poring over his Eastern metaphysical books. His sons Steven and Scott were already grown and living in different states.

And yet, Lefty believed he could still pitch on a major-league level.

In 1994 Carlton was elected to the Baseball Hall of Fame in his first year of eligibility with 96 percent of the vote. For a man who refused to entertain reporters' questions for many years, he called a press conference on the day he was elected. For 45 minutes Carlton spoke at great length on numerous subjects including fear. Prior to his formal enshrinement, Carlton made some controversial comments to writer Pat Jordan in which he declared that the last eight US presidents up to that point were guilty of treason, that AIDS was created by the government to eradicate society of gays and blacks, and that the world was being ruled by the Elders of Zion and Jewish bankers. Carlton's teammate and closest friend Tim McCarver defended him against charges that he was an anti-Semite. "He is a very complicated person and has a hard time being human," said McCarver.[11]

The psychology of Steve Carlton the big-league pitcher was one of pure determination to perfect his craft. He turned a simple game of toss between catcher and pitcher into a mental game of chess within himself. When Carlton finally ended his freeze-out of the press, many were confused by the bizarre nature of his comments, but it shouldn't have come as a surprise. Because of the flawed nature of his introverted personality, Carlton gave the press what he thought they wanted to hear instead of chatting with them on a more personable level. To the press he was a goofy former big-league pitcher content with living a life of isolation in the mountains. To many baseball fans, he was an artist. No one knew the real Steve Carlton.

Nevertheless, when he delivered his Hall of Fame acceptance speech on July 31, 1994, he was greeted enthusiastically by many Phillies fans who had come to pay homage to a man who had provided them with endless amounts of joy during their summers.

In 1998 Carlton and his wife, Beverly, were divorced after 33 years of marriage. That year he was ranked number 30 by *The Sporting News* among the 100 Greatest Baseball Players. The next year he was a nominee for the Major League Baseball All-Century Team. With his jersey number 32 already retired by the Phillies in 1989, Carlton received another honor as the club unveiled a statue of him outside Citizens Bank Park in 2004.

As of 2017 Carlton was living in Durango. He had reduced his public appearances to charity golf outings and taking part in ceremonial first pitches at Phillies games, the most notable being in 2008, when he tossed out the traditional first pitch prior to Game Three of the World Series between the Phillies and Tampa Bay Rays.

In his 24 years as a major-league pitcher, Carlton finished with a record of 329-244. His career ERA was 3.22. He struck out 4,136 batters, good enough for fourth place on the all-time list. Carlton is the major-league record holder (as of 2017) for pickoffs with 144. He pitched six one-hitters, and started 69 consecutive games in which he pitched at least six innings.

In an interview with Roy Firestone, Carlton was asked, "Why do you think you were put on this earth?"

"To teach the world how to throw a slider," Carlton replied.[12]

He was pretty darn good at it.

## SOURCES

In addition to the sources cited in the Notes, the author also consulted Baseball-reference.com, Stevecarlton.com, and the following:

Fimrite, Ron. "Eliminator of the Variables," *Sports Illustrated*, April 9, 1973: 82-89.

## NOTES

1 youtube.com/watch?v=zbdsGyn2J3I: Steve Carlton: The Early Years.

2 Ibid.

3 youtube.com/watch?v=jq7fSzT3yHM: *Steve Carlton: ESPN Sportscentury*: Original airdate March 1, 2004.

4 Steve Wulf, "Steve Carlton," *Sports Illustrated*, January 24, 1994: 48.

5 joeposnanski.com/no-53-steve-carlton/.

6 *The Sporting News*, March 11, 1972: 38.

7 *The Sporting News*, August 26, 1972: 6.

8 Wayne Stewart, *The Gigantic Book of Baseball Quotations* (New York: Skyhorse Publishing Inc., 2007), 166.

9 Steve Wulf, "Scorecard," *Sports Illustrated*, November 9, 1987: 13.

## 20-GAME LOSERS

10  Pat Jordan, "Thin Air: In the Mountains with Steve Carlton, Armed Conspiracist," Deadspin.com, thestacks.deadspin.com/thin-air-in-the-mountains-with-steve-carlton-armed-co-478492324.

11  Murray Chass, "Was Silence Better for Steve Carlton?," *New York Times,* April 14, 1994: B15.

12  youtube.com/watch?v=R7xsdUOEnvg: Steve Carlton: Slider.

# JACK CHESBRO

## BY WAYNE MCELREAVY

DESPITE A SENSATIONAL 1904 season in which he won 14 straight games and set modern records with 41 wins and 48 complete games, Jack Chesbro is best remembered for the wild pitch he tossed to score Boston's pennant-clinching run on the final day of the season.

Broad-shouldered with a sandy complexion, Chesbro normally carried 180 pounds on his 5-feet-9 frame. Before mastering the spitball, he relied on an excellent fastball, which he delivered with a straight-over-the-top motion.

He was born "John D. Cheesbro" on June 5, 1874 in Houghtonville, a village in North Adams, Massachusetts, the fourth of five children of shoemaker Chad Brown and Martha Jane (Fratenburgh) Cheesbro. He would eventually write his name as "Chesbro," but he never legally changed it from the birth spelling. The family name was pronounced "Cheez-boro," but he became known as "Chez-bro" early in his major-league career. Throughout his youth, family members called him "Chad."

After starring for amateur teams, Chesbro and three other locals, including future big-league teammate Art Madison, moved to Middletown, New York in 1894 to play for the Asylums, a team representing the state mental hospital. While he did work with patients, his primary purpose was to pitch for the ball club. His pitching skills were honed by Asylums catcher Pat McGreevy who, noting Chesbro's long fingers, predicted great success for the pitcher. Chesbro also acquired the nickname "Happy Jack" while working at the hospital after a patient noted his cheery disposition and friendly grin.[1]

Joining the professional ranks with Albany of the New York State League in 1895, Chesbro went 5-1 before the club folded on May 20.[2] He joined Johnstown of the same loop and went 2-9 before the league itself folded on July 6. He then hooked on with Springfield of the Eastern League, but was released after seven games. Despite a 2-1 record, he allowed 22 walks and 39 hits with only six strikeouts in 32 innings. He then pitched semipro ball in Cooperstown, New York.

In 1896, Chesbro started the season with Roanoke of the Virginia League. Though that club folded on August 20, Chesbro had last pitched for them June 22 finishing with an 8-11 record. He then spent the remainder of the summer pitching in Cooperstown.

Chesbro signed with Richmond of the Atlantic League in 1897. He was 16-18 then went 23-15 in 1898 en route to the league championship. At season's end, he was drafted by Baltimore's Ned Hanlon, but Hanlon moved to Brooklyn, Baltimore was nearly contracted and Chesbro never signed.[3] Back with Richmond in 1899, he began the season 17-4 before being sold on July 7 to Pittsburgh for $1,500.[4] He posted a sub-par 6-9 record with 59 walks and 28 strikeouts.

On December 8, 1899 Chesbro, Paddy Fox, Art Madison, John O'Brien, and cash were traded to Louisville for 12 players, including Honus Wagner. The Louisville club was dissolved with Chesbro and the three others assigned to Pittsburgh in March as the NL reduced from 12 to eight teams.

With just half a season of major-league experience under his belt, Chesbro refused to accompany the team south for spring training in 1900, though he later reported for duty.[5] His absence from spring training and threats to retire would become an almost annual event. He improved to 15-13 with a second-place club in 1900 then was 21-10 in 1901 and 28-6 in 1902, pacing the league in shutouts each year for pennant winners. He also led the National League in wins and winning percentage in 1902.

Before the 1902 season ended, word had spread that Chesbro had already signed to jump to the American League in 1903.[6] He was not allowed to participate in a postseason series of games at the

Pittsburgh ballpark in which the players split the receipts. Weeks later he took part in an all-star tour of the west coast. Pitching against Sacramento December 13, he took a 13-1 beating as he watched his opponent, Elmer Stricklett, hold the all-stars to three hits off a newly-developed spitball.[7]

Chesbro was declared property of the New York American League franchise under the major-league peace agreement of 1903.[8] Though the press referred to the team as the "Greater New Yorks" and "Highlanders," this was the beginning of the storied Yankees franchise and Chesbro became their first great pitcher.

Because Chesbro did not report to the team until April 1, he missed a spring training series in which New York faced Stricklett, who was now with New Orleans. Nonetheless, he led fourth-place New York to a 21-15 mark. He reported earlier the next spring. Though Stricklett was now property of the White Sox, their paths would cross. After playing an exhibition series with Chicago, New Orleans requested the loan of a pitcher for their next series against New York.[9] When Stricklett became the pitcher on loan, Chesbro studied how the spitter was thrown and set out to master it.[10]

New York manager Clark Griffith disliked the spitball, and catcher Jim McGuire didn't like catching it. After beginning 1904 at 4-3 through May 7, McGuire agreed to catch the spitter, and Chesbro was given permission to use the wet one as his primary weapon. He won his next 14 starts.[11] Becoming an amazing workhorse, Chesbro would complete 48 of his 51 starts and relieve in four others while amassing a staggering 454 2/3 innings pitched. Twenty-eight of his starts were with less than three days of rest.

While the spitter is usually cited as the main reason for his remarkable season, Chesbro also began using another pitch. He developed a "slow ball," which McGuire and umpire Bill Carpenter said was the best they had ever seen.[12] He had also reported to camp weighing 163 pounds as opposed to his usual 180.[13]

New York trailed Boston by a half-game entering a five-game season-ending series against Boston. The original schedule called for four games, but New York owner Frank Farrell rented his ballpark to Columbia University for a football game.[14] Boston willingly accepted the offer to transfer the October 8 game to Boston, which also allowed the clubs to make up a rainout from June 29.[15]

Pitching on two days' rest, Chesbro beat Boston for his 41st win to put New York a half-game up with four to play. Griffith's plan was to have Chesbro remain in New York to rest for the double-header on the final day, October 10. However, Chesbro showed up at the train station with the approval of Farrell. He talked his way into a start with no days' rest and was knocked out of the box for only the third time all season as New York suffered a 13-2 loss. Cy Young hurled a 1-0 shutout in the second game to put Boston up by a game and a half with two to play. New York would need to sweep on the final day to take the flag.

In the final-day showdown, Chesbro started the first game. Making his eighth start in 15 days, he had a 2-0 shutout through six innings. The game was halted when he came to bat in the third inning so friends from North Adams could present him with a fur coat and hat. When play resumed he promptly tripled for one of his two hits on the day.

Aided by two errors, Boston scored twice in the seventh to tie. Lou Criger led off the Boston ninth with a single and advanced to third on two outs. With a 2-2 count on Freddy Parent, Chesbro made his famous wild pitch, allowing Criger to score. Though Parent singled on the next pitch, Chesbro would be remembered as the man who lost the pennant on a wild pitch. Bill Dinneen held New York in the bottom half as Boston clinched the pennant. The gravity of the wild pitch was magnified when Ambrose Puttmann blanked Boston in the second game.

Chesbro talked of retiring during the offseason, then weeks later claimed he had developed a new pitch that would revolutionize baseball in 1905.[16] Calling it the jump ball, he claimed it was different from the riser, because it took an abrupt jump rather than a steady rise. He declared he would take one tour around the league before using it as he had yet to master it.[17] He was so confident of his new pitch that he revealed the secret of throwing the spitter.

His tour around the league was derailed by three weeks of inactivity due to a sore arm.[18] Chesbro denied the problem was the spitball despite arm miseries of other pitchers who had adopted the wet one.[19] Upon switching to the spitball almost exclusively, Chesbro had changed his delivery from over-the-top to a round-house fling. He also stayed north during spring training to coach Harvard and reported to New York weighing 200 pounds. Regardless, he claimed his trouble was due to malarial fever developed from the cold he caught while pitching in the rain on opening day.[20]

After struggling to a 19-15 record in 1905, Chesbro decided to forego coaching Harvard in order to report to spring training on time in 1906.[21] He won 23 games but lost 17 and led the league in earned runs allowed. When his contract for 1907 arrived in the mail, he mailed back his intention to retire to tend to his business interests.[22] He had bought a farm in Conway, Massachusetts at the turn of the century. He also owned a sawmill and timber land. He was making more money on the farm than on the ballfield.[23]

In March Chesbro said he'd sign for the same salary as 1906, citing a figure of $8,500.[24] However, that would have given him a hefty raise. Two weeks into the season, he sought out Griffith at the Boston hotel and signed a deal. Griffith left coach/catcher McGuire with Chesbro with orders for them to report to the club in a week.

Chesbro was a mediocre 10-10 in 1907 followed by a 14-20 mark for a last-place club in 1908. Amid rumors he was to be farmed to Indianapolis in 1909, he said he would retire rather than be disgraced. He skipped spring training and refused to report to New York causing the National Commission to place him on the ineligible list. He was reinstated May 24, but he was out of shape. One newspaper described him as being "decidedly fat."[25]

After making only nine appearances with an 0-4 record, Chesbro was waived September 11 to the Boston Red Sox.[26] Under the terms of the agree-

ment, Boston had until May 1 of the following year to decide whether to keep him or return him to New York. He made just one appearance for Boston, losing to New York in first game of a doubleheader on the final day of the 1909 season.[27] It was his last major-league game.

The Red Sox announced in January 1910 that Chesbro would be returned.[28] New York had no plans for him on the major-league roster, but he would not report to the minors, which again caused him to be placed on the ineligible list.[29] He stayed on his farm and pitched nearby semipro Whitinsville to a championship.[30]

Chesbro coached Massachusetts Agricultural College (now the University of Massachusetts) in 1911 and continued to pitch for semipro clubs.[31] He met with New York owner Farrell and new manager Harry Wolverton about a comeback in 1912.[32] Wolverton agreed to take a look at him, but before leaving for camp he reconsidered and released Chesbro. Wolverton felt he had enough prospects and was not a believer in comebacks.

Deciding to pay his own way to Hot Springs, Chesbro thought he could catch on with another club. The National Commission granted his request for reinstatement as a free agent.[33] He worked out with Brooklyn and Pittsburgh, but both passed on him.[34] He returned to Conway and continued to pitch and coach semipro teams. He was still making occasional mopup appearances at age 53 in 1927 for South Deerfield, Massachusetts.

Chesbro pitched from a big-league mound one last time September 11, 1922 at Braves Field, tossing a couple of innings in an old-timers game sponsored by the *Boston Post* to benefit Boston Children's Hospital.[35] Old friend Clark Griffith signed him as a coach with the Washington Senators in 1924.[36] However, when Al Schacht was hired June 1 to be reunited with coach and fellow clown Nick Altrock, both Chesbro and Ben Egan were trimmed from the coaching staff.[37] Chesbro was out of organized baseball for good.

Jack Chesbro died November 6, 1931 on his Conway chicken farm. He had climbed a hill to determine the problem with a water pipeline when he succumbed to a heart attack.[38] He is buried in Conway's Howland Cemetery. He was survived by his wife, the former Mabel Shuttleworth, a Conway resident he had married in 1896. The couple had no children.

In *The Politics of Glory*, Bill James illustrated how Chesbro's career numbers (198-132 W/L, 2.68 ERA) were similar, and probably poorer, than his Pittsburgh teammates Sam Leever (194-100, 2.47), Deacon Phillippe (189-109, 2.59), and Jesse Tannehill (197-117, 2.80.) Primarily on the basis of one fantastic season, Chesbro is the only one of the quartet to receive baseball's highest honor — election to the Hall of Fame. He was selected by the Old-Timers Committee in 1946.

The wild pitch haunted Chesbro for the remainder of his life. Despite his remarkable season, he was constantly asked about the pitch that lost the pennant. Years later, Clark Griffith blamed Red Kleinow for missing the pitch, which he claimed passed the 5'7" Parent about neck high. Kleinow, who had become the regular catcher partially due to Jim McGuire's trouble handling the spitter, had died in 1929 and apparently never publicly commented on the issue. Shortstop Kid Elberfeld said that Kleinow could not have caught the pitch with a crab net.[39] Contemporary accounts indicate the ball sailed high over Kleinow's head and struck the press stand on the fly.

Chesbro's widow produced numerous articles and letters in 1939 indicating the wild pitch should have been scored a passed ball. When the *New York Journal-American* published her story, she considered the matter closed and her husband vindicated.

## SOURCES

In addition to the sources cited in the Notes, the author consulted an array of government records in Conway and North Adams, Massachusetts and Franklin County, Massachusetts.

On the pronunciation of Chesbro's name, he spoke with grandnephew John S. Chesbro Sr. (October 24, 2004) Deane Lee, author of the townhistory of Conway (October 27, 2004), and Jack Ramey of the Conway Historical Society on the same date, as well as Larry Chesebro', a distant relative, on September 4, 2000 and January 11-12, 2003;

Others helpful in learning more about Chesbro's life were Merritt Clifton, Bess Kemp, Walter Phillips, and Tom Shieber.

Various other articles, unknown newspapers but probably *The Sporting News*, from *The Sporting News* player file.

Grayson, Harry. *They Played the Game* (New York: A. S. Barnes and Company, 1945).

James, Bill & Rob Neyer. *Neyer/James Guide to Pitchers* (New York: Simon & Schuster, 2004), 56.

Lieb, Frederick G. *Boston Red Sox* (New York: G. P. Putnam's Sons, 1947).

MacFarlane, Paul, ed., *Daguerreotypes of Great Stars of Baseball* (St. Louis: The Sporting News, 1981), 52.

Spink, J. G. Taylor, letter to S. C. Thompson, February 17, 1959 regarding Chesbro's 1904 record. Repository: Chesbro file, *The Sporting News*

Trachtenberg, Lee. "If It Ain't Broke, Don't Fix It," *Yankees Magazine*, December 24, 1987.

## NOTES

1   Thanks to Bob Mayer for information on the Asylums and Albany clubs, January 17, 2010.

2   Ernest J. Lanigan, *Knickerbocker News*, February 2, 1951.

## 20-GAME LOSERS

3 *Washington Post*, October 26, 1898: 8.

4 *Washington Post*, July 8, 1899: 8, and July 10, 1899: 8.

5 *Chicago Daily Tribune*, March 20, 1900: 9.

6 *New York Times*, September 7, 1902: 12.

7 *Washington Post*, December 23, 1902: 8. For the boxscore, see *The Sporting News*, December 27, 1902: 7.

8 *New York Times*, January 11, 1903: 10.

9 *The Sporting News*, April 2, 1904: 1.

10 *The Sporting News*, March 19, 1904: 2.

11 *Washington Post*, July 8, 1904: 8.

12 *Los Angeles Times*, August 2, 1904: A3.

13 *New York Times*, March 24, 1904: 6.

14 *Washington Post*, August 28, 1904: S3.

15 *Washington Post*, October 2, 1904: S1.

16 *Chicago Daily Tribune*, November 20, 1904: A1.

17 *Los Angeles Times*, January 31, 1905: 113, and *Washington Post*, February 19, 1905: S10.

18 *Washington Post*, April 30, 1905: S1.

19 *Washington Post*, May 9, 1905: 9, and *Washington Post*, May 16, 1905: 9.

20 *Washington Post*, June 4, 1905: S1.

21 *Washington Post*, December 24, 1905: S1.

22 *New York Times*, February 23, 1907: 10, and Washington Post, February 23, 1907: 8.

23 *New York Times*, March 20, 1907: 7.

24 *Washington Post*, March 21, 1907: 9.

25 *Washington Post*, May 25, 1909: 9.

26 *Washington Post*, September 12, 1909: S1.

27 *New York Times*, October 3, 1909: S1.

28 *New York Times*, January 16, 1910: S2.

29 *Washington Post*, February 5, 1909, p. 8, and *Washington Post*, February 13, 1909: 8.

30 *Washington Post*, September 11, 1910: M5.

31 *Washington Post*, March 20, 1911: 8.

32 *Washington Post*, February 3, 1912: 8.

33 *New York Times*, March 21, 1912: 9.

34 *New York Times*, March 13, 1912: 9.

35 *New York Times*, September 12, 1922: 17, and *Washington Post*, September 12, 1922: 14.

36 *Washington Post*, February 7, 1924: S1, and *Washington Post*, March 3, 1924: 15.

37 *Washington Post*, June 2, 1924: 17.

38 *North Adams Evening Transcript*, November 7, 1931.

39 *The Sporting News*, February 19, 1942: 4.

# JOHN CLARKSON

## BY BRIAN MCKENNA

**MORE THAN A FEW CONTEMPORARY** baseball insiders viewed John Clarkson as the finest pitcher of the 19th century. He won 30 or more games in a season six times, including two of the top four all-time totals, 53 in 1885 and 49 in '89. In the 10-year period between August 1884 and July 1894, he amassed 327 victories in the National League, and then retired at the age of 33. Clarkson was recognized as half of the "$20,000 Battery," so called for the price Boston paid for the pitcher and King Kelly. Perhaps more recognize his name because he spent much of the last four years of his life in mental hospitals. Some even claim that the crazed former ballplayer mutilated his wife. Seemingly the Hall of Fame forgot his name entirely, overlooking his contributions until 1963.

John Gibson Clarkson was born on July 1, 1861, in Cambridge, Massachusetts, to a Scottish-born father, Thomas G. Clarkson, and an Irish-born mother, Ellen M. (Hackett) Clarkson. John had two younger sisters, Isabella and Helena, and four younger brothers, Arthur, Thomas, Walter, and Frederick. Arthur and Walter, also pitchers, followed John into the majors, as did two cousins from his mother's side of the family, Mert and Walter Hackett.

In contrast to most big leaguers of the era, John was born into a family of means. His father owned a prospering jewelry and watchmaking business in Boston. John attended local schools and trained in the jewelry business as a teenager. He was also attracted to baseball, perhaps influenced by a watchmaking coworker of his father's and one of professional baseball's founding fathers, Harry Wright. At his high school, the Webster School, John made the baseball team as a catcher in 1878. During the season, he also made his debut in the pitcher's box. After high school he worked in the family trade and attended the local Comer's Business School. Because Clarkson hailed from the Harvard University area, false reports throughout his career said he was a graduate of the university. He was not, but his brothers Walter and Frederick did, and played baseball there.

Starting in 1880, John played amateur ball for the Beacons of Boston for a little over two years. He also played for the Hyde Park club at times. Clarkson was one of the Beacons' star hitters and eventually developed into the club's leading pitcher. The team played all comers, including major-league clubs, and Clarkson soon gained a reputation as one of the area's leading hurlers. During his Beacon days he received some pitching tips from Boston Red Stockings pitcher Tommy Bond. In late April 1882, the Beacons played the Worcester Ruby Legs of the National League in an exhibition contest. Worcester manager Freeman Brown signed Clarkson soon after the game to help solidify his rotation, which had been a little shaky against some college squads that April.

A few days later, on May 2, 1882, 20-year-old Clarkson made his major-league debut, in a home game against Boston. It was the second game of the season, on a very cold and windy day that kept the crowd to only 400. Though he was hit hard, Clarkson pulled out an 11-10 victory, helped by a couple of doubles of his own. He started again three days later but lost to Hoss Radbourn and the Providence Grays, 17-2. The reviews after the contest were stinging, for example: "With Clarkson as pitcher today, the Worcesters were beaten by the Providence team with the utmost ease, they batting Clarkson for fourteen singles and two two-baggers in the sixth and seventh innings."[1] On the 11th, he pitched better but lost again, 4-0, to Tim Keefe of the Troy Trojans. The rebound was noticed: "Clarkson pitched for the Worcesters and was quite effective, no earned runs being scored off his pitching."[2] In three games he pitched, opposite three of the toughest hurlers of the early professional era, Bobby Mathews (Boston), Radbourn, and Keefe, he fared adequately if unspectacularly. Unfortunately, his shoulder was ailing and he was released before the end of the month, within a week or so of his final game. It appears that he sat idle the rest of the season.

After the 1882 season, Arthur Whitney, a Boston-Worcester area player, took over the Saginaw, Michigan, club of the Northwestern League. Whitney contacted Clarkson over the winter and signed him to a contract. At first Clarkson filled a utility role, playing every position but catcher. The club directors were unimpressed and soon discussed releasing the young player. Whitney then installed him on the mound and those thoughts dissipated. The move proved a success. Clarkson appeared in 21 games as pitcher for the club; his record is unknown, but the team challenged for the championship all season, falling just two games short of the title. Clarkson credited Whitney with turning his career around and solidifying his spot in professional baseball. Specifically, Whitney helped convert Clarkson to an overhand pitcher, spending hours working on his motion behind the team's hotel and at the ballpark. The overhand style was just about to become legal in the National League.

Clarkson returned to Saginaw in '84, posting a season that earned him accolades throughout the industry. In 45 games and nearly 400 innings pitched he accrued a 34-9 record with nine shutouts and a stunning 388 strikeouts and a 0.64 ERA—all by the middle of August. He hit .306 as well. He was regularly fanning upward of 10, 15 and even 19 batters a game. In five games pitched between June 30 and July 14, Clarkson racked up 73 strikeouts. This caught the eye of major-league managers. In early August, pitchers Jim McCormick and Jack Glasscock, along with catcher Fatty Briody, jumped the Cleveland National League club for Cincinnati of the Union Association. Manager Charlie Hackett tried to sign Clarkson to fill the void but the deal fizzled. Then, on August 14, the Northwestern League ousted the Saginaw club for nonpayment of dues and the club disbanded.

Now a free agent, Clarkson fielded offers from Boston, Chicago, and Cincinnati but signed with Cap Anson of the White Stockings around August 24. His first game with the club took place three days later, a 5-3 loss to Hoss Radbourn. The *St. Louis Globe-Democrat* wrote of Clarkson after the game, "His pitching is very effective ... He is a good fielder and his playing today showed him to be a valuable addition to the nine."[3] Clarkson appeared in 14 games for the White Stockings, posting a 10-3 record. On September 30, he struck out seven straight New York Gothams batters, and 13 in all.

Clarkson, a 5-foot-10, 155-pound right hander, threw the three basic pitches, fastball, curve, and changeup. He relied heavily on curves, especially his drop curve, one that fell sharply, from a 12 o'clock to 6 o'clock angle. He could throw a sweeping rising curve as well. Billy Sunday said that Clarkson "could put more turns and twists into a ball than any pitcher I ever saw."[4] Teammates said he could put so much English on a billiard ball with his big hands that it would circle the entire table. Clarkson's fastball was a riser, generally sailing up through the zone. He liked to keep the batter off-balance, delivering the ball from a variety of arm angles, most often from sidearm, and trying to work the element of surprise. The *Brooklyn Eagle* wrote of his delivery, "Clarkson, of Boston, faces second base first, then quickly whirls around and throws the ball over the plate, startling the batter."[5] He wore a large, shiny belt buckle that he tried to shine in the batter's eyes. Umpires routinely had him remove it. Excellent fielding complemented his pitching talents. *Sporting Life* wrote, "Clarkson fields his position better than any other League pitcher."[6]

Clarkson possessed a good deal of pitching speed, but that wasn't his dominant weapon. Wrote the *Chicago Daily Inter Ocean*, "Clarkson is able to pitch every other day for the reason that instead of adopting (Amos) Rusie's method of firing the ball at the catcher with cannonball speed, he depends entirely upon head work, change of pace, and the fielders back of him. In this way Clarkson saves his arm, and is still ready for the finish."[7] Clarkson did in fact strike out a great many batters, but that wasn't his goal. He much preferred to cut down on his pitch count by having the batter put the ball in play for his fielders

JOHN CLARKSON.

terrific, and he could throw any curve. However, his favorite ball was a drop something like the spitball of today, although he delivered it without the ointment necessary nowadays."[10] The *Chicago Tribune* noted more reasons for his success: "John Clarkson was a great pitcher, because he was a student of the game and relied upon his strategy and control rather than his physical strength, which never was great. He was naturally an athlete, possessed of plenty of speed, but used it in moderation and was of the style of pitchers represented in later years by (Clark) Griffith. Clarkson was one of the first to develop the 'jump' ball and as the pitching distance then was shorter than it is today he was able to use it with deadly effect. That, in connection with the drop curve which Clarkson also had perfectly under control, made him the best of his day."[11]

Part of Clarkson's strategy was to regularly pitch around the best hitters in the game. . One such example was against New York in 1885: "Clarkson pitched for us and showed more good judgment and foresight than I have ever seen any pitcher display in a ballgame. In the first inning, for instance, with (Orator) O'Rourke and (Roger) Connor—the heaviest batters in the League — ... Clarkson sent them to first on called balls, and as a result caught O'Rourke napping at second, while Connor and (Buck) Ewing went out a moment later in a double play. ... In taking no chances against the heavy-hitting abilities of Connor and O'Rourke, Clarkson proved his ability to use his head as well as his hands in his work."[12]

Clarkson was also fortunate to work with some of the best catchers of the day. With Chicago, Silver Flint caught 148 of his games. King Kelly worked as the backstop in 73 of Clarkson's games with both Chicago and Boston. Charlie Bennett (119 games) and Charlie Ganzel (43) worked behind the plate in the bulk of his outings with Boston. Chief Zimmer (57 games) did the same with Cleveland. Years later Zimmer called Clarkson the greatest of all pitchers—and Zimmer caught Cy Young for nearly a decade.

Chicago White Stockings manager Cap Anson said that Clarkson "was peculiar in some things,

to do their job. Moreover, he was a master at working to a batter's weakness and at keeping him guessing. Sam Thompson, an outfielder with Detroit and Philadelphia, said, "I faced him in scores of games and I can truthfully say that never in all that time did I get a pitch that came where I expected it or in the way in which I guessed it was coming."[8] Cap Anson said, "In knowing exactly what kind of a ball a batter could not hit and in his ability to serve up just that kind of ball, I don't think I have ever seen the equal of Clarkson."[9]

Clarkson's forte was his control; he put the ball where he wanted. Teammate Fred Pfeffer, an infielder, defined this ability: "I stood behind him day in and day out, and watched his magnificent control, as confident of success, especially in tight places, as I would have been with the United States army behind me. There was Clarkson's long suit—he was master of control. I believe he could put a ball where he wanted it nine times out of ten. He had everything any pitcher ever had as well. His speed was something however, and in order to get his best work you had to keep spurring him along, otherwise he was apt to let up, this being especially the case when the club was ahead and he saw what he thought was a chance to save himself."[13] Anson added, "Many regard him as the greatest, but not many know of his peculiar temperament and the amount of encouragement needed to keep him going. Scold him, find fault with him, and he could not pitch at all. Praise him and he was unbeatable."[14] Anson suggested that Clarkson was deeply affected by razzing and would falter on the mound amid abuse. Some of these broad accusations, though, don't seem to match up with the record books or day-in/day-out contemporary accounts.

Clarkson started 1885 coaching the pitchers at Dartmouth. He continued to train college squads throughout his baseball career and into retirement. It was a part of his winter conditioning. The only year he took off from coaching was 1886 and that was because of his impending marriage. He coached Harvard pitchers from 1887 to 1892. In 1890 he also worked with the hurlers at the Boston Athletic Association. In 1893 and '94 he worked out the staff at Yale. In '94 he also trained the Union College pitchers in Schenectady, New York. The following year he worked for the University of Michigan.

His talents went beyond baseball. In March 1885, Clarkson refereed a boxing match in Hanover, New Hampshire. It was a championship bout between a minor leaguer named Harmon and a Professor Craig. On train trips and in hotels throughout spring training and during the season starting in '85, Clarkson and King Kelly entertained their teammates with song.

By any measure Clarkson was the National League's most valuable player in 1885. He started 70 games, finishing all but two, and posted a 53-16 record in 623 innings. Those 53 victories are the most in a season after Hoss Radbourn's 59 the previous year. Clarkson tossed 10 shutouts and struck out 308 batters. All the numbers mentioned other than the loss total led the league.

From June 1 to 24, 1885, Clarkson won 13 consecutive games. On June 20, he shut out Buffalo, 5-0, on a one-hitter. It was one of his ten straight victories over Buffalo that season. Clarkson pitched a no-hitter on July 27, a 4-0 win over Providence and Radbourn. The *Sporting Life* wrote, "Clarkson's work in the box last week was really remarkable. In one game he disposed of the Providence club without a hit…In another but four hits were made on him in fourteen innings and in the Philadelphia game also but four hits were made off him—a total of but eight hits in thirty-two innings. Wonderful."[15]

Chicago took the pennant by two games over New York that season; the rest of the league was at least 30 games behind the White Stockings. In the postseason championship series, the White Stockings tied the St. Louis Browns of the American Association, 3-3-1. Many modern researchers consider the postseason series that began in 1884 to be the first World Series, but the tie that year goes a long way at viewing the 19th-century postseason contests as mere exhibitions.

After the season, Clarkson barnstormed in St. Louis before returning to Chicago for the winter. He stayed in Chicago to split the distance with his girlfriend, Ella Moorhead McKenna. Ella, from Detroit, was born in May 1860. They met when he was with Saginaw. On March 4, 1886, the couple married. She traveled with the club that spring to Hot Springs, Arkansas, and back. Over the years she attended many games. It's probably good that she did since Clarkson attracted more than his share of women to the park. He was a good-looking Irishman with dark hair and bluish-gray eyes. And he was a bit of a dandy when it came to his attire, as the *Sporting Life* noticed: "All of the Chicago players dress well off the field but Clarkson is the bright particular dude of the team. He is very scrupulous about his dress, and there is considerable of the English in his style."[16] The *Detroit Free Press* said, "His uniform was always immaculate, his linen always possessed the fresh-from-the-laundry touch, he was always smoothly shaved, his manners were always faultless."[17] He also wore a silk handkerchief on the outside of his uniform.

In 1886, Clarkson won 36 games in 55 starts, striking out 313. On August 14 he defeated St. Louis, 5-2, for the 17th consecutive time, a record that still stands. Four days later, he fanned 16 Kansas City batters to set the club record. On August 23, Clarkson tossed a one-hitter over Detroit, losing a no-hitter in the eighth inning on a controversial hit by Deacon White. Chicago won the pennant by 2½ games over Detroit. Again the White Stockings faced the St. Louis Browns of the American Association in the postseason. This time St. Louis won, four games to two. Clarkson was 2-2 in four starts, winning Games One and Three. The series is memorable for the sixth and final game, a contest regarded as one of the finest of the era. Clarkson took the mound with his club down three games to two and took a 3-0 lead into the eighth inning, hoping to tie the series. However, the Browns pushed across three runs to even the score. In the 10th, St. Louis outfielder Curt Welsh tried to steal home. He was seemingly caught but Clarkson's pitch to King Kelly went astray and Welsh scored the winning run. Clarkson had apparently crossed up his catcher. It was known as the "$15,000 Slide" because of the winner-take-all agreement between the clubs. The Chicago players were drinking heavily during the series, some showing signs of drunkenness while on the field. Clarkson may not have been drinking during the day, but he was tearing it up at night. It was said that he was slotted to start Game Five but couldn't because of a hangover. It was the only time in seven tries that an American Association club won the postseason series between the two leagues.

Over the winter, Clarkson worked out daily with fellow Cambridge native Tim Keefe. The two pitchers were concerned about the new rules in 1887 that shrank the pitcher's box and lengthened the pitching distance to 55 feet 6 inches. It had been 50 feet when Clarkson debuted in 1882. Clarkson was also concerned about the loss of his catcher, King Kelly, who had been sold to Boston for $10,000. These matters didn't deter Clarkson, though; he led the league in most pitching categories again in 1887, amassing a 38-21 record in 59 starts. Detroit won the pennant, however. Clarkson defeated the Wolverines nine times, the most by one pitcher over an eventual pennant winner. As the end of the season neared, Clarkson negotiated a $200 bonus if the club finished in second place; but the White Stockings fell to third. After another fine year, he wanted a significant boost in income; he also wanted out of Chicago; more specifically, he wanted to play near his home. He declared, "My home is in Boston, and all the domesticities I have center there. I am anxious to have a house of my own, and to fit it up as a permanent residence."[18] As the season ended he met with club president Al Spalding and told him so, asking for a trade to Boston, and later sending follow-up letters reaffirming his desire. Clarkson's family was also pushing him to leave baseball and join the family jewelry business. (Another rumor, neither proved nor disproved, claimed that Clarkson and the White Stockings' shortstop, Ned Williamson, had had a falling-out and Clarkson vowed to never play with him again.)

Spalding had his own plans; he was having a fire sale. After getting the cash for Kelly, he was offering any of his men for the right price. He set the menu: $10,000 for Clarkson; $7,500 for Ned Williamson; $5,000 for Fred Pfeffer; $2,500 each for Mark Baldwin, Jimmy Ryan, and Dell Darling. The owner declared: "There is no player so good but that his equal can be found."[19]

Clarkson wanted a salary close to that of Bob Caruthers, a pitcher for St. Louis, who was making a reported $4,500. The *Sporting Life* took the pitcher's side: "Clarkson has pitched more games in the last two years than any other pitcher in the country. No wonder he feels sore when he considers that he is not paid as much as many players who are playing with weaker clubs and only pitch once a week or once in two weeks."[20] Clarkson also cited Henry Boyle, a pitcher for Indianapolis, who made $500 more than he did with a weaker team in a smaller market, with a lighter workload and less success.

Clarkson, or more likely some friends, approached Boston Beaneaters president Arthur Soden and asked him to work a trade. Soden offered the White Stockings $7,500 as early as September 1887. It wasn't enough; Spalding was holding out for more. Part of Spalding's negotiating stance was to declare that the club would rely on Gus Krock and George Van Haltren on the mound for the coming season if

Clarkson chose to hold out. Clarkson was equally as adamant, in fact more so. In December he declared, "You can depend upon it that I will not play in the Chicago club next year under any circumstances. … I think it is about time that I should have something to say where I shall play. I will remain in Boston and work at my trade. I mean just what I say. I will not play in Chicago under any circumstances."[21] He threatened to sit out the season and join the family business if not traded. Spalding shot back that he would simply blacklist the player if he didn't report in the spring.

By February 1888, the entire White Stockings squad had signed except for their disgruntled ace. The deal was finally brokered on April 3, just before the exhibition season began. The *Boston Globe* headlined, "HE IS OURS: Ten Thousand Dollars for Another Beauty."[22] Clarkson was reunited with his backstop King Kelly; the pair was now known as the "$20,000 Battery." Two days later, on the 5th, 4,500 Boston fans showed up to see the battery in action, a high turnout for a blustery spring-training game in New England. The high dollar sales for the two players led in part to mounting dissatisfaction among players. A lot of money was being thrown around between the owners, but the reserve clause was helping to hold down salaries and personal freedoms as well. The prevailing players union, the Brotherhood of Professional Baseball Players, was busy solidifying its ranks in response to the disgruntlement. Clarkson joined his colleagues, pledged his support to the Brotherhood in early 1889, and paid his dues. Oddly, he did so at the urging of Boston Beaneaters director William Conant, who believed that the other men would play better behind him during the season if he did. According to *Boston Globe* sportswriter Tim Murnane, "The pitcher promised at the time that he would never hurt the Boston club."[23]

Clarkson started on Opening Day 1888, not ceding a hit until the sixth inning, and Boston won its first nine games, five of which were credited to their new ace. In all, he went 33-20 with a league-leading innings total (483 1/3) again. The club, though, finished in fourth place, 15½ games out.

Clarkson was appointed temporary captain in April 1889 amid fighting between the club directors, on the one hand, and player-manager John Morrill and King Kelly, who presented separate issues, most involving his alcoholism. Morrill was sold to Washington, where he became manager, and Jim Hart was brought in to manage the Beaneaters. It looked to be a bright year indeed. After spending all that money for Kelly and Clarkson, Boston tapped the failing Detroit Wolverines for Charlie Bennett, Dan Brouthers, Charlie Ganzel, and Hardy Richardson. The club went 18-4 in May to take a 3½ game lead in the standings. Clarkson didn't lose his second game until June 10, by which point he was 15-2. In the first game of a doubleheader on June 22 in Pittsburgh, Clarkson shut out the Alleghenys 5-0, allowing only five hits and striking out 12. In the seventh inning of the second game he was ejected while sitting on the bench. Pittsburgh manager Fred Dunlap noticed that Clarkson was signaling to his teammate, pitcher Bill Sowders, and informed the umpire. On July 12, Clarkson was pulled for some extra rest in the fifth inning despite leading 10-0 and tossing a no-hitter. Reliever Sowders gave up just one hit the rest of the way in the 13-1 defeat of Pittsburgh. On September 16, the Beaneaters started a 15-game road trip to finish the season. They stood a half-game behind the New York Giants in the standings. Clarkson and the club directors agreed that he'd pitch every game down the stretch for some extra compensation. Clarkson actually started 13 of those games, taking two games off, but that was done in consultation with club officials. It was a tactical error; the pennant slipped out of Boston's hands.

For the first time in major-league history, the pennant came down to the final day of the season (October 5). The Beaneaters were facing Pittsburgh, and the Giants were playing the Cleveland Spiders. Clarkson and Boston manager Jim Hart made waves by offering the Cleveland battery $1,000 if they defeated New York. The money would come from a previous promise by the *Boston Globe* to reward the local club if it copped the pennant. New York in turn offered a suit of clothes to the Pittsburgh players if they stopped the Beaneaters. Henry Chadwick, for one, found this all distasteful. Clarkson lost to Pittsburgh, 6-1, and New York defeated Cleveland to take the championship by one game over the Beaneaters. As would be the case for decades to come, the contenders played an uneven number of games: New York finished at 83-43; Boston, at 83-45. Drinking may have cost the club the pennant, as more than a few of the men imbibed heavily as the season and summer moved to a close. Clarkson won the pitching Triple Crown, leading the league in wins (49), strikeouts (284), and earned run average (2.73). He tossed eight shutouts. The 49 wins are the fourth highest total in major-league history. In the five seasons from 1885 to 1889, Clarkson posted a 209-93 record with 295 complete games, 2,716 innings pitched, and 1,365 strikeouts. For all this work and success Clarkson wasn't even listed among the top 20 earners of 1889 according to the *Spalding Guide*. He wanted his big payday.

With the growing unrest among players, 1889 was a contentious year. As the summer wore on, the players firmed up plans to organize a league of their own. The new league, the Players League, would operate in 1890 as a third major league, pulling most of the top players from the National League. The two leagues would compete head-to-head in virtually every National League city. Clarkson was hedging his bets on the new league, though. He was listed as a member of its Boston entry and had signed an agreement to sign a contract, though not an actual contract. He was also one of the first to purchase stock in the new Boston club. However, he soon started backtracking. After an interview with him, the *Chicago Tribune* called Clarkson "a shining mark in his profession, a Brotherhood man, and a signer with the rest of the Boston team to the agreement which now binds the players to the National Players' League."[24] But Clarkson added: "I shall also consult my own interests, do the best I can, and do not consider the agreement which I signed binding on me other than a promise that I would go with the other men if such a step is consistent and legal. … I am with the boys, and if it is for my best interests to go with them I shall do so. But I am not bound. The League people are entitled to a good deal of consideration at our hands."[25] His Brotherhood colleagues didn't see it the same way. Like the other ballplayers, Clarkson had agreed with and supported the union, attended meetings and voted. He even nominated King Kelly for an office. However, as the plans actually came into fruition, he needed to reevaluate his commitment. He was concerned that the new league wasn't well funded or organized and that it would fail, leaving the men to "scramble for old positions and loss of the best part of a season's earnings."[26]

Soon after the Brotherhood solidified its plans at a meeting on November 4 in New York, Clarkson departed with many of his teammates on a California barnstorming trip. In late November, Kelly headed to San Francisco to meet the Boston players and gain their signatures for the coming season. He was worried about some of the comments made by Clarkson and Hoss Radbourn; they seemed to be pulling away from the union. "Mike Kelly, who is deputed by the Brotherhood to sign players, arrived in the city yesterday," a press service report said. "He is rather disappointed at not being able to secure John Clarkson. Clarkson has been offered by the Brotherhood the same salary as he was getting from the League and Kelly offered to give him $500 out of his own pocket, but it wasn't enough."[27] Clarkson wanted more money, stating that he "must in justice to myself and family earn my money while I can."[28] Certainly this additional quote didn't win any friends: "I am looking out for myself as usual, and ain't bothering myself a great deal about anyone else."[29]

In secret, Clarkson started trading telegrams with Beaneaters owner Arthur Soden, and a deal was worked out. Soden said, "We paid John Clarkson $25,000 for three years. For simply signing his name to a contract we paid him $10,000. This is the largest salary that has ever been paid to a baseball player."[30] It was in fact a lot of money; no one had been guaranteed $25,000 before. Clarkson made the best deal possible, financially speaking. The pitcher also agreed to act as an agent for the Boston club. Soden gave him carte blanche to re-sign as many men as possible. He talked Pop Smith and Charlie Ganzel into re-signing with the club and approached several others, including Hardy Richardson and even Kelly. Clarkson also sent telegrams to and later visited Charlie Bennett's residence and signed him up as well.

Naturally this was in violation of the agreement Clarkson had made with the Brotherhood and most of his teammates and friends around the league. It wasn't received well, many believing that he previously sat in on their meetings solely to report back to Soden and the League. Fred Pfeffer recalled, "I never saw such a change in a man in my life. When I last saw him before that he was as strong a Brotherhood man as could be found and dwelt at length on the prospects of the Players League. Then he became an icicle. It chilled me through to hear him talk and I walked away from him."[31] Someone discovered that Clarkson was working as an agent for the League and sent a telegram to John Morrill, a secretary of the Brotherhood, in San Francisco. It read: "Clarkson is a traitor and is working for Soden. Show this to the boys and watch Clarkson."[32] He wasn't treated well after that and had a strained relationship with many for months to come, even years. For the rest of the barnstorming trip, many shunned Clarkson, blasting him for his duplicity. Kelly, once a good friend, apparently was among them. Their friendship never recovered.

On December 18, the Brotherhood met again to firm up the new league. The members expelled Clarkson and 14 others, officially blacklisting them. On January 11, 1890, the men returned to Chicago from San Francisco. The *Chicago Tribune* wrote, "The Brotherhood sentiment was strong in all excepting Clarkson, who did not move about with the others."[33] Hardy Richardson took the opportunity to publicly blast the pitcher, calling him out for his double-agent activities and disloyalty to his colleagues. The two didn't speak for many months. (One story during this period was that Ella Clarkson talked her husband into staying in the National League because the Boston directors offered her free tickets to games for herself and any friends.)

Boston dropped to fifth place in 1890 despite 26 wins from Clarkson. On April 19, he won 15-9 over Brooklyn even though he himself committed 10 errors, which were actually wild pitches. Sloppily, there were a total of 35 errors in the contest. The Players League folded after only one season and the men funneled back to their old teams. During the negotiations Monte Ward declared, "The talk of refusing to play with (Jack) Glasscock, (Jerry) Denny, Clarkson, or any of the deserters from our ranks is all bosh. Of course it is a bitter pill, but for the sake of peace and harmony we will swallow it."[34] That was merely the face of the union speaking publicly; the friction did not go away. Many of the men had issues with Clarkson and he was treated rudely and shunned by some for the rest of his career. Some observers claimed that a few of his teammates slacked off while Clarkson was on the mound, the very thing Conant, the Beaneaters director, feared previously. King Kelly for one refused to return to Boston, instead jumping to the American Association, in part because he didn't want to play with Clarkson and Charlie Bennett.

Both Clarkson and Kid Nichols won at least 30 games for the Red Stockings in 1891 and the club captured the pennant by 3½ games over Chicago. Clarkson presented a new look for 1892, shaving off his trademark mustache for a season or so. He started off shakily, posting an 8-6 record through 16 games. On May 6, he went toe-to-toe with Cincinnati and opposing pitcher Elton "Icebox" Chamberlain for 14 scoreless innings, giving up only four hits but walking six. Chamberlain surrendered only three hits and a walk. "Six times during the game for Boston and four for Cincinnati would a base hit have decided the contest," the *Boston Globe* wrote the next day.[35] The game was called at the beginning of the 15th inning "on account of the sun," as the umpire Jack Sheridan declared that it was beating in the batters' and pitchers' eyes. A sore arm kept Clarkson off the mound from May 15 to 25. On the 26th, he defeated Louisville 7-0 but lost a no-hitter with two outs in the ninth when Hughie Jennings placed a single. With a young Kid Nichols developing into an ace, Arthur Soden was looking to shed the expensive Clarkson but was a little hesitant to do so since he was still under the three-year contract for which the club had given him a significant signing bonus. Regardless, on June 30, 1892, Clarkson, whose record was 8-6 at the time, was given his unconditional release. The dismissal had as much to do with cutting costs as it did with Clarkson's shaky start and questions about the health of his arm. With the merger of the National League and American Association, only one major league operated in 1892. The owners were thus in a position to tighten their belt. They would soon implement system wide payroll cuts and institute a salary cap.

Cleveland owner Frank Robison wanted Clarkson, but his co-owners didn't. Robison pressed and got his way. It added to a rift among them though, which wasn't resolved until Robison bought the others out later in the summer. The Spiders signed the free agent on July 5. The payroll cuts hit just as Clarkson joined the Spiders; every man was required to sign a new contract at a lower rate. Clarkson's days of being the staff ace were over in Cleveland; that distinction belonged to the speedballer Cy Young. Clarkson did well, winning 17 games for the club and proving that his arm was holding up by pitching a total of 389 innings. He won his first game for the Spiders on July 9, an 8-2 victory over Tim Keefe. On September 21, he claimed his 300th major-league win, a five-hitter over Pittsburgh that the Spiders pulled out in the ninth inning, 3-2. Cleveland finished in second place, 8½ games behind Boston. Since there was only one major league, the top two teams faced off in a championship series. Boston won the series, five games to none, with one tie. Clarkson lost both of his starts. In Game Five, he blew a six-run lead and lost, 12-7.

Before the 1893 season, the pitching rubber was pushed back another five feet to the current distance of 60 feet 6 inches. It signaled the beginning of the end of Clarkson's effectiveness. Though only 31 years old, he couldn't adjust adequately and won only 24 more games in 53 starts. He did, however, log the innings once again, a total of 445 2/3. Cleveland gave Clarkson a contract for $2,500, which was actually $100 over the salary cap. It was also $200 more than Cy Young was making. That didn't sit well with Young, and the club had to renegotiate with its ace. The next season, 1894, couldn't have started any worse for Clarkson. He planned a camping trip near Kansas City with his good friend and former batterymate Charlie Bennett. On the trip in early January, Bennett carelessly hopped off the train to speak with a friend. He slipped, fell under the wheels and lost parts of both legs.[36] The scene was bloody and horrifying. Clarkson was dramatically affected. He was already drinking heavily toward the end of his career, and the incident didn't help matters. Clarkson stayed with his friend for over a month, returning home on February 19 to take over the Yale pitching staff. He helped organize a benefit for the catcher later in the year.

Throughout his time in Cleveland, Clarkson clashed with his teammates and was said to be unhappy. Many of them were staunch Brotherhood supporters. A cynic might claim that some didn't play their best when he was on the mound. Cy Young, who wasn't a part of the Brotherhood struggle, later acknowledged Clarkson's help in refining his game. According to Young's biographer Reed Browning, "Clarkson showed Young how to improve his curve ball, advised him on ways to sharpen control, and prodded him to think about pitching strategy."[37] All these were lessons he had been imparting to college pitchers for years. Moreover, "Young declared unequivocally that Clarkson had helped him become a better pitcher."[38]

On July 12, 1894, Clarkson made his final major-league appearance, in a 20-10 shellacking by Philadelphia. The next day he was traded to Baltimore for another aging pitcher, Tony Mullane. Orioles manager Ned Hanlon was happy to make the trade for the pennant run, declaring, "Clarkson has not been satisfied in Cleveland and will show his appreciation of the change of base by demonstrating that he is still one of the best pitchers in the business. He has, beyond doubt, the easiest delivery of all the pitchers. His coolness in trying circumstances is proverbial. I have made many deals in my effort to build up a team, but none which gave me more satisfaction that when I traded Mullane even up for Clarkson."[39] The *Washington Post* was a little less enthusiastic about the repercussions of the trade: "It is an open secret that Clarkson has been dissatisfied in Cleveland and anxious to get away, while Mullane is never satisfied anywhere, so neither team has much the worst of the bargain."[40] The *Boston Globe* saw little for the Orioles to gain: "Perhaps John Clarkson may do better in Baltimore than Cleveland. But that remains to be seen. His work this season is decidedly of the passé order."[41] To Hanlon's dismay, Clarkson refused to join the Orioles, returned home to Bay City, Michigan, and retired. Mullane appeared in four games for Cleveland and was done as well.

For his career, Clarkson inserted a 328-178 win-loss record into the books and nearly 2,000 strikeouts. Before the mound was pushed back to 60 feet 6 inches in 1893, he fanned the second most batters, behind Tim Keefe. Clarkson failed to complete only 33 of his 518 starts. He also knocked 24 home runs, a number by far the most of any 19th century pitcher and a record that lasted for decades.

In September 1894, John and Ella Clarkson purchased a cigar store and manufactory at 103 Center Avenue in Bay City. They later opened a wholesale business on Fifth Avenue and a retail establishment in the Phoenix area. In 1904 they opened another cigar enterprise at Sixth and South Sherman Streets in Chicago. The latter three businesses proved unsuccessful. The decade after leaving baseball was for the most part spent managing his four business enterprises. John's brother Arthur moved to Bay City to help run the businesses after his professional baseball career ended. He initially worked as a clerk in the cigar store and then took over operations at the Phoenix location. Later, he opened a clothing store a few doors down from the cigar shop. During this time, John made infrequent trips to Boston to visit friends and family and to Detroit to check in with Charlie Bennett and Ella's family.

On the baseball end, Clarkson established, organized, managed, and occasionally pitched for an independent, amateur Bay City club in 1895. He tried to place a Bay City franchise in the Interstate League for 1897, but it was a no-go. Also in '97, Ban Johnson, president of the Western League, wired Clarkson offering the ex-pitcher a job as an umpire. Clarkson had actually worked four games during his major-league career, three of them behind the plate. However, he replied, "Many thanks, but I am out of baseball for good."[42] Through the rest of the decade, though, Clarkson teased reporters about a possible return to the majors but it was ultimately in jest. As late as 1904, a *Chicago Journal* writer wrote that Clarkson "looks as strong and agile today as he did fifteen years ago."[43]

In March 1905, Clarkson, then in his early 40s, was listed as the vice president of the Michigan State League and was set to manage the Bay City franchise. In May, Ella and Arthur summoned John's father to Bay City for a family conference. John had been in a "bad way for several months."[44] They decided to confine him to the Oak Grove Sanitarium in Flint, Michigan, for the "treatment of mental disorders," a nervous breakdown combined with depression and possibly paranoia which was certainly exacerbated by his excessive drinking.[45] He was said to live in the past more than the present, often recalling his baseball days as if they were yesterday. As the *Sporting Life* noted at the time of his death, "He seemed to have no memory at all for things of today, but talked clearly and lucidly of matters connected with the past."[46] King Kelly would have been surprised. He once described Clarkson as "a quiet, modest gentleman, and does less talking about baseball than any player in the country."[47] Clarkson returned home briefly in December 1905 but was soon transferred to the Eastern Michigan Asylum in Pontiac. At the time reports declared, "There are no hopes that his condition will improve." He had "completely broken down mentally and physically."[48]

After three months in Pontiac, his father brought him to the McLean Psychiatric Hospital in Waverly, Massachusetts, near the family home in Cambridge in March 1906. At the time Thomas Clarkson told reporters, "John is in a bad way, and he has been for the last two years.... Physically he is as well as he ever has been and this, of course, gives us encouragement.

His mind wanders back to the old baseball days. His wife … came on with him and is now at our home. When he became sick she ran his business for some time, but is now closed out."[49]

Ella moved in with her in-laws. Clarkson remained, for the most part, at McLean except for occasional furloughs during holidays and such. His family visited often. Eventually he lived with his wife and parents for stretches at a time. A report from Cambridge in February 1908 claimed that Clarkson "is looking well."[50] He was living with his family and often visited friends in Boston. He was even seen as a spectator at a ballgame that October. John was supposedly doing well at the end of the year. Ella visited Bay City and told reporters that her husband was improving and perhaps might leave McLean. That was perhaps wishful thinking. The truth is that the doctors saw little long-term hope for her husband.

In January 1909, Clarkson was living with his parents at their home on Wave Way Avenue in Winthrop, Massachusetts. He became ill with pneumonia and was readmitted to McLean. Both lungs were overtaken by the illness; Clarkson lapsed into a coma and died on February 4 at the age of 47. The death certificate listed the cause of death as lobar pneumonia of six days' duration. It also noted that Clarkson had suffered from a general paralysis for the past several years. John Clarkson was buried in the family plot at Cambridge Cemetery. He rests not far from Tim Keefe.

Unfounded rumors persist that Clarkson killed his wife. The fact is that after his death, she returned to Bay City and helped Arthur Clarkson in business. Bay City erected a ballfield soon after John's death and named it in his honor. In 1963 one of the top pitchers of the 19th century was finally inducted into the National Baseball Hall of Fame.

Too often reviewers have projected Clarkson's psychological problems at the end of his life back into his playing career. There may indeed have been some clues, but a lot has been read into little things, and too much has been interjected into the story long after the fact. Too many have taken liberties with supposed clues of mental instability during his playing career. There are no hints of significant mental difficulties in contemporary accounts before his entering a sanitarium, which, by the way, was more than a decade after his retirement from the game. Later claims that he was a loner, high-strung, moody, and depressed both on and off the mound were exaggerated in an effort to signify underlying troubles. Clarkson was calm and collected on the mound; he was noted as so time and again. He may have disliked being singled out for razzing at times but that is not abnormal. He may have needed coaxing at times but isn't baseball history littered with stories of catchers and managers giving pitchers pep talks? It's amazing how a pitcher can be so successful year in and year out, month-in and month-out and some claim he was still prone to "wilt" or "wither" on the mound.

Cap Anson made several comments about Clarkson's temperament at or near the end of the pitcher's life that some have used to trace his mental difficulties back as far as two decades before he actually was institutionalized. It's perhaps telling that these quotes don't show up in Anson's book *A Ball Player's Career*, which was published in 1900 before Clarkson had his breakdown. Anson chose to add these characterizations only after Clarkson's difficulties became known publicly. In the book, Anson talks about Clarkson needing encouragement throughout the game to keep him focused, but nowhere does he mention anything about the pitcher's fragile temperament.

It is clear, though, that Clarkson was a heavy drinker throughout his career. If it didn't start with the White Stockings, it certainly blossomed then. Quite a few of his teammates were heavy drinkers, including close friends George Gore, Billy Sunday, Jim McCormick, King Kelly, and Ned Williamson. There were also plenty of men to drink with on the Boston nine, Hoss Radbourn for one. Certainly whatever trials Clarkson had in his later life, he exacerbated them with two decades of alcohol abuse. Billy Sunday, who left baseball in part to escape the drinking influence, attributed Clarkson's health problems to smoking: "Cigarettes broke down his health. I have known him to smoke eight to ten boxes of them in a day. I used to room with John. The water would be stained with nicotine when he'd take a bath."[51]

Notes

There is no relation between the author and Mrs. John Clarkson, the former Ella McKenna.

There is a persistent story that John Clarkson threw a lemon to the plate during one game to demonstrate to umpire Jack Kerins that it was too dark to continue play. The story suggests that Kerins called the pitch a strike, thus proving Clarkson's point. No date or even year is ever identified in the claim, suggesting that it has never been verified. Kerins was a substitute umpire for only one game in the National League, on September 6, 1888. At the time, Kerins was living in Indianapolis, his birthplace. The game he umpired pitted Pittsburgh against Indianapolis and didn't involve Clarkson. The story was introduced into lore by John McGraw at the time of the publication of his book *My Thirty Years in Baseball*. In an accompanying piece distributed by the Christy Walsh Syndicate in January 1923, McGraw claimed that the pitcher was "Clarkson, I think." In the story the catcher was Wilbert Robinson. While it's not impossible that those two were batterymates at some point during some postseason or preseason, it's more likely that the pitcher was merely misidentified 30 years later. If the lemon story in fact has merit and Kerins and Clarkson were participants, it surely would have taken place during an exhibition contest.

## SOURCES

Ancestry.com

*Atchison Champion*, Kansas, 1892.

*Atchison Daily Globe*, Kansas, 1887, 1888, 1894.

*Baltimore Sun*, 1887, 1889, 1909.

Baseballlibrary.com.

*Bay City Journal*, Michigan, website Bjmi.us.com.

*Bay City Times*, Michigan, 1909.

*Bay City Tribune*, Michigan, 1895, 1909.

*Boston Advertiser*, 1880-81, 1887, 1888, 1890, 1893.

*Boston Globe*, 1887-94, 1905, 1908, 1909.

*Brooklyn Eagle*, 1909.

*Cedar Rapids Evening Gazette*, Iowa, 1885.

*Cincinnati Enquirer*, 1892.

*Cleveland Herald*, 1883.

*Daily Picayune*, New Orleans, 1887.

*Daily Review*, Decatur, Illinois, 1905.

*Detroit Free Press*.

Egan, James M. Jr. *Baseball on the Western Reserve: The Early Game in Cleveland and Northeast Ohio, Year by Year and Town by Town 1865-1900* (Jefferson, North Carolina: McFarland, 2008).

Familysearch.com.

*Fitchburg Sentinel*, Massachusetts, 1881.

Fleitz, David L. *Cap Anson: The Grand Old Man of Baseball* (Jefferson, North Carolina: McFarland and Company, Inc., 2005).

*Hartford Courant*, 1909.

Ivor-Campbell, Frederick, Robert L. Tiemann, and Mark Rucker, eds. *Baseball's First Stars* (Cleveland: The Society for American Baseball Research, 1996).

James, Bill, and Rob Neyer. *The Neyer/James Guide to Pitchers: An Historical Compendium of Pitching, Pitchers, and Pitches* (New York: Simon and Schuster, 2004).

Kusmierz, Marvin, "John Gibson Clarkson (1861-1909)," *Bay City Journal* website, September 2002.

*Los Angeles Times*, 1894.

*Lowell Sun*, Massachusetts, 1905, 19'09.

*Milwaukee Journal*, 1885.

*Milwaukee Sentinel*, 1884-86, 1889-90, 1894.

Morris, Peter. *A Game of Inches: The Stories Behind the Innovations That Shaped Baseball, The Game on the Field* (Chicago: Ivan R. Dee, 2006).

*New York Times*, 1889-94.

Pearson, Daniel Merle. *Baseball in 1889: Players vs. Owners* (CITY, Wisconsin: Popular Press, 1993).

*Reno Evening Gazette*, 1906.

*Rocky Mountain News*, Denver, 1887.

SABR Batterymates Project.

Society for American Baseball Research. *The SABR Baseball List and Record Book* (New York: SABR, 2007).

*The Sporting News*, 1887.

*Washington Post*, 1885, 1888-95, 1904, 1907.

## NOTES

1 "Providence-Worcester," *Inter-Ocean* (Chicago), May 6, 1882: 4.

2 "Troy 4, Worcester 0," *Chicago Tribune*, May 12, 1882: 6.

3 *St. Louis Post-Dispatch*, August 28, 1884: 8.

## 20-GAME LOSERS

4. Elijah P. Brown, *The Real Billy Sunday: The Life and Work of Rev. William Ashley Sunday, D.D. The Baseball Evangelist* (Dayton, Ohio: Otterbein Press, 1914), 41.
5. "Base Ball Players Busy," *Brooklyn Daily Eagle*, November 25, 1888: 10.
6. "Notes and Comments," *Sporting Life*, October 21, 1885: 3.
7. "Sporting Odds and Ends," *Inter-Ocean*, July 22, 1891: 3.
8. John Clarkson, National Baseball Hall of Fame, baseballhall.org/hof/clarkson-john Date accessed January 4, 2017.
9. Jonathan Fraser Light. *Cultural Encyclopedia of Baseball* 2nd Ed. (Jefferson, North Carolina: McFarland, 2005), 198.
10. "Current Gossip of the Sporting World," *Harrisburg* (Pennsylvania) *Daily Independent*, February 9, 1909: 2.
11. "Clarkson, $10,000 Pitcher, Is Dead," *Chicago Tribune*, February 5, 1909: 10.
12. Harry Clay Palmer [Remlap], "From Chicago," *Sporting Life*, October 7, 1885: 5.
13. Adrian Constantine Anson, *A Ballplayer's Career: Being the Personal Experiences and Reminiscences of Adrian C. Anson* (Chicago: Era Pub Co, 1900), 130.
14. Harvey Frommer *Old Time Baseball: America's Pastime in the Gilded Age* (Lanham: Maryland: Taylor Trade Pub, 2005), 125.
15. "Notes and Comments," *Sporting Life*, August 5, 1885: 5.
16. "Notes and Comments," *Sporting Life*, July 14, 1886: 5.
17. Quoted in Fleitz, David L. *Ghosts in the Gallery at Cooperstown: Sixteen Little-Known Members of the Hall of Fame* (Jefferson, North Carolina: McFarland and Company, Inc., 2004), 112.
18. *Chicago Herald* story which ran in the *Freeport Journal-Standard* (Freeport, Illinois), October 14, 1887: 4.
19. "Doings on the Diamond," *Wilkes-Barre Sunday Morning Leader*, September 11, 1887: 6.
20. "Notes and Comments," *Sporting Life*, October 11, 1887: 3.
21. "Clarkson Dead Set Against Chicago," *Chicago Tribune*, December 10, 1887: 2.
22. "He is Ours," *Boston Globe*, April 4, 1888: 1.
23. Tim Murnane, "Conant After Omaha," *Boston Globe*, September 24, 1889: 5.
24. "Warring Baseballists," *Chicago Tribune*, November 12, 1889: 3.
25. Ibid.
26. "Nothing But a Name," *Evening Star* (Washington, D.C.), November 8, 1889: 7.
27. "Kelly in San Francisco," *Omaha Daily Bee*, December 4, 1889: 1.
28. "Chicago's Backers," *Sporting Life*, November 20, 1889:5.
29. Quotation found in unidentifiable newspaper clipping.
30. Philip E. Shirley, "Alas, Poor Yorick!" *Sporting Life*, April 14, 1906: 9.
31. "Out-Door Sports," *Lawrence Daily Journal* (Lawrence, Kansas), February 12, 1890: 4.
32. "Triumvir of Traitors," *Saint Paul Globe*, (Minnesota) December 10, 1889: 5.
33. "Brotherhood Men Here," *Chicago Tribune*, January 12, 1890: 7.
34. "All In favor of Peace," *New York Times*, October 10, 1890: 3.
35. "Not a Run Scored," *Boston Globe*, May 7, 1892: 5.
36. "Bennett's Recovery Assured," *Boston Globe*, January 19, 1894:2; "Cut a Hot Pace," *Boston Globe*, February 20, 1894: 2.
37. Reed Browning, *Cy Young: A Baseball Life* (Amherst: University of Massachusetts Press, 2000), 29.
38. Ibid.
39. "Clarkson Will Join the Baltimores," *New York Times*, July 16, 1894: 8.
40. "Sporting News and Comment," *Washington Post*, July 16, 1894: 6.
41. "Base Ball Notes," *Boston Globe*, July 17, 1894: 2.
42. "Clarkson Would Not an Umpire Be," *Chicago Tribune*, June 15, 1897: 4.
43. Cited in the *Denver Post* article "May Still Be a Good One," March 17, 1904: 7.
44. "Base Ball Notes," *Washington Post*, May 12, 1905: 4.
45. "Needs A Rest," *Boston Globe*, May 7, 1905: 25.
46. "Clarkson's Passing," *Sporting Life*, February 13, 1909: 6.
47. Mike "King" Kelly, Michael J. Kelly, Gary Mitchem, and Mark Durr, *Play Ball: Stories of the Diamond Field and Other Historical Writings about the 19th Century Hall of Famer* (Jefferson, North Carolina: McFarland and Company, Inc., 2006), 62
48. "John Clarkson Failing," *Boston Globe*, December 12, 1905: 7.
49. "Alas, Poor Yorick!" *Sporting Life*, April 14, 1906: 9.
50. "National League News," *Sporting Life*, February 29, 1908: 3.
51. Homer A. Rodeheaver, *Twenty Years with Billy Sunday* (Nashville, Tennessee: Cokesbury Press, 1936), 50. Cited in "A Short History of Baseball and Tobacco," in Peter Carino, ed., *Baseball/ Literature/Culture: Essays 2004-2005* (Jefferson, North Carolina: McFarland, 2006), 128.

# CANDY CUMMINGS

## BY DAVID FLEITZ

**CANDY CUMMINGS, AT FIRST GLANCE,** appears to be one of the least qualified pitchers in the Baseball Hall of Fame. His major-league won-lost record is usually listed as 21-22, because most career totals begin with the formation of the National League in 1876. Cummings earned his stardom in amateur play during the late 1860s and in the National Association, precursor to the National League, in the early 1870s. He enjoyed great success, but threw his last major-league pitch when he was only 28 years old. However, Cummings, despite his short career, was one of the most influential pitchers in baseball history. He was selected for Cooperstown immortality because he, according to most baseball historians, was the man who invented the curveball.

William Arthur Cummings, called Arthur by his family and friends, was born in Ware, Massachusetts, on October 17, 1848. He was the second child of William Cummings, a dry goods merchant, and his wife Mary, a homemaker, who moved the family to Brooklyn, New York, when Arthur was two years old. The family grew to include 12 children and appears to have been well off, because Arthur's parents sent him to a boarding school in Fulton, New York, in his teenage years.

Cummings was an enthusiastic baseball player, and an outing with some friends in 1863, when he was 14 years old, gave Arthur the idea that changed the course of his life. He and a group of boys amused themselves at a Brooklyn beach one day by throwing clamshells into the ocean. The flat, circular shells could be easily made to curve in the air, and the boys managed to create wide arcs of flight before the shells splashed into the water. "We became interested in the mechanics of it and experimented for an hour or more," recalled Arthur in his later years. "All of a sudden, it came to me that it would be a good joke on the boys if I could make a baseball curve the same way."[1] This seemingly passing thought started Cummings on a quest that took much of his time and energy for the next four years.

Throwing underhanded with his arm perpendicular to the ground, as stipulated by the rules at the time, Arthur practiced diligently and experimented with different grips and releases in an effort to find the secret of the curveball. In so doing, he made himself into an outstanding young pitcher in spite of his physical limitations. He grew to be about 5-feet-9 as an adult, but he never weighed more than 120 pounds at any time in his life. Even in that era, nearly a century and a half ago, he was small for an athlete. He also had small hands, usually a severe handicap for a pitcher. Arthur excelled on the mound anyway, perhaps due to the practice he gained from his pursuit of the elusive curveball.

In 1865, after Arthur graduated from the Fulton school, he joined the Star Junior amateur team of Brooklyn and posted an incredible 37-2 record. Later that year he was invited to join the Brooklyn Excelsior Club, one of the best amateur nines in the New York area. He soon became the team's leading pitcher, and was so dominant that people started calling him "Candy," a Civil War-era superlative meaning the best of anything.

In 1867, after four years of frustration, he found success with the curveball for the first time. He discovered that he could make the ball curve in the air when he released it by rolling it off the second finger of his hand, accompanied by a violent twisting of the wrist. Though it appears that Jim Creighton, a New York amateur pitcher, threw a ball with a quick jerk of the wrist in 1861 and 1862, Cummings was the one who combined it with the rolling motion from the fingers to maximize the amount of spin imparted on the ball.

Candy Cummings demonstrated his breakthrough in a game against Harvard College. "I began to watch the flight of the ball through the air and distinctly

ARTHUR CUMMINGS, Pitcher of the Star Club, Brooklyn, N. Y.

saw it curve," wrote Cummings many years later. "A surge of joy flooded over me that I shall never forget. I felt like shouting out that I had made a ball curve. I wanted to tell everybody; it was too good to keep to myself."[2] All day long, Harvard batters flailed helplessly at the new pitch. The secret of the curveball was his, and for several years afterward Cummings was the only pitcher in the nation to claim mastery over the pitch.

The curveball made the 120-pound Cummings the most dominant pitcher in the country. He threw a pitch that none of the batters had ever seen or practiced against, and only when other pitchers learned to throw the curveball would batters learn how to hit it. Any pitcher who sought to copy Candy Cummings would need months, if not years, of steady practice of the type that Cummings had already accumulated. This gave Cummings a gigantic head start upon his competitors and made for an advantage that perhaps no other pitcher has ever enjoyed in the history of the game.

The varsity nine of the Brooklyn Stars signed Candy as their featured pitcher in 1868. The Stars billed themselves as the "championship team of the United States and Canada,"[3] and with Cummings on the mound they were able to make good on that boast for the next four seasons. One source states that from 1869 to 1871, Cummings posted records of 16-6, 17-9, and 17-13 in top-level amateur play, and won many more in exhibitions against other outstanding ballclubs. In 1871, influential baseball writer Henry Chadwick named Candy Cummings the outstanding player in the United States, the closest thing at that time to a Most Valuable Player award.

The National Association began play in 1871 as the nation's first professional circuit. Cummings remained with the Stars that season, but his skills were in such demand that he was besieged with offers. He signed contracts with three different Association clubs before the 1872 season started, but in mid-February the Association awarded Cummings to the New York Mutuals and made the pitcher a professional for the first time. Cummings pitched every inning for the Mutuals that year, posting a 33-20 record and helping the New York team to a fourth-place finish. He led the Association in games, complete games, and innings pitched. Candy struck out only 45 men all year, but strikeouts were exceedingly rare then, and he finished second in the league in that category.

For the next several years Candy Cummings pursued increasingly generous financial offers with different teams in the National Association. In 1873 he signed with Baltimore, where he shared the pitching chores with Asa Brainard. Candy posted a 28-14 record as Baltimore finished a strong third. The 1874 campaign found the 25-year-old veteran in Philadelphia playing for the Whites, and once again pitching every inning of every game. He posted a 28-26 record with a mediocre ballclub, but made national headlines on June 15, 1874, when he struck out six Chicago White Stockings in a row.

By the 1874 season, other pitchers began to make up ground on Cummings by developing curveballs of their own. Bobby Mathews, Cummings' successor on the Mutuals, began throwing the pitch after learning it from Cummings. Alphonse Martin of the Troy Haymakers also threw a curve at about this time, though Martin later claimed that he had thrown it in amateur play in 1866, a year before Cummings. The controversy over the origin of the tricky pitch had already begun, with several rivals challenging Candy Cummings' claim to preeminence in newspaper articles across the nation. Cummings, proud of his discovery, was keenly protective of his status as the inventor of the curveball, and for the rest of his life he zealously defended his claim against all doubters.

In 1875 Cummings landed on his fifth team in five years, the Hartford Dark Blues. The 1875 season was longer than previous campaigns, so the Hartford club divided the pitching load between Cummings and 19-year-old Tommy Bond, who played right field for the first eight weeks of the campaign while learning the curveball from Cummings. Bond mastered the pitch by mid-season, and by July he and Cummings provided an effective one-two punch for the Dark Blues. Hartford finished in third place as Cummings went 35-12 and pitched seven shutouts. Bond posted a 19-16 log and batted .273 as an outfielder.

Hartford joined the new National League in 1876. Cummings, for the first time in six years, stayed with his previous team and returned to the Dark Blues, but at the age of 27 he began to slow down. Tommy Bond pitched so well early in the season that he became Hartford's main starting pitcher, pushing one of baseball's most celebrated stars to the sidelines. Candy pitched 24 games in 1876 with a 16-8 record, while Bond went 31-13 in 45 games as Hartford finished third in the new league. On September 9, 1876, in the first scheduled doubleheader in National League history, Cummings pitched two complete-game victories over Cincinnati.

Candy declined to sign a National League contract that winter, instead joining the Live Oaks of Lynn, Massachusetts, in the new International Association. That winter, Cummings attended the convention that created the new player-controlled league, and the other delegates elected him as the first president of the circuit. However, Cummings did not stay long with the Live Oaks. He left the team in late June and signed with the Cincinnati Red Stockings of the National League, though he remained president of the International Association for the balance of the season. In Cincinnati, with a worn-out arm and a weak team behind him, Cummings won only five of the 19 games he pitched.

At the age of 28, Candy Cummings came to the end of the line. Other pitchers had learned to throw the curveball, and by 1877 batters had figured out how to hit it. Cummings, with his slender frame and small hands, no longer threw a curve well enough to fool the batters, and his arm was sore from 10 years of top-level amateur and professional play. He pitched briefly in the International Association in 1878, but soon dropped back to the amateur and semipro ranks. Later that year he returned to his hometown of Ware, Massachusetts, where he learned the painting and wallpapering trade. He played ball sporadically until 1884, when he moved to Athol, Massachusetts, and opened his own paint and wallpaper company, which he operated for more than 30 years. He and his wife, the former Mary Augusta Roberts, whom he married in 1870, raised five children.

For the next several decades, Cummings passionately defended his status as the inventor of the curveball. He wrote dozens of articles and letters to editors defending his claim and refuting those, such as former Chicago White Stockings pitcher Fred Goldsmith and others, who claimed authorship of the pitch. His efforts paid off; by the early 1900s, such influential baseball men as Albert G. Spalding, player-turned-writer Tim Murnane, and *Sporting News* founder Alfred H. Spink had thrown their support to Cummings as the creator of the curve. By 1908, when Cummings wrote an article for *Baseball Magazine* titled "How I Pitched the First Curve," his reputation was secure. Today, most baseball historians credit Cummings as the first man to make a ball curve in flight and also as the first to use the pitch successfully under competitive conditions.

Cummings retired from his paint and wallpaper business in the late 1910s, and in 1920 the widowed 72-year-old moved to Toledo, Ohio, to live with his son Arthur. William Arthur Cummings died in Toledo on May 16, 1924, and was buried in the Aspen Grove Cemetery in Ware, Massachusetts. Fifteen years later, on May 2, 1939, a special committee elected Candy Cummings and five other 19th century players to the Hall of Fame.

## SOURCES

In addition to the sources cited in the Notes, the author also consulted:

Spalding, Albert G. *Base Ball: America's National Game,* new edition (San Francisco: Halo Books, 1991).

*The Scrapbook History of Baseball* (Indianapolis: Bobbs-Merrill, 1975).

*New York Clipper,* July 8, 1871.

*New York Journal,* January 8, 1912.

*New York Times,* August 22, 1883, September 29, 1900.

The Candy Cummings file, National Baseball Library, Cooperstown, New York.

## NOTES

1. W. A. Cummings, "How I Pitched the First Curve," *Baseball Magazine,* August 1908.
2. Ibid.
3. Marty Appel and Burt Goldblatt, *Baseball's Best: The Hall of Fame Gallery* (New York: McGraw-Hill, 1980), 119.

# PUD GALVIN

## BY CHARLES HAUSBERG

REFLECTING ON THE LIFE AND career of Pud Galvin, a writer commented that a proper accounting of Galvin's achievements "would be a task of time and would … require a volume in size almost equal to the dictionary."[1] Galvin pitched for 17 years during a career that spanned three decades, four major leagues, and countless changes to the rules governing pitchers. He threw the first perfect game on record and was the first pitcher to reach 300 career wins in the major leagues; but his accomplishments came before the existence of the term "perfect game," and in an age that had no sense of the meaning of 300 career victories.

Galvin's longevity and durability also set him apart, as no other pitcher of his era matched his 6,003⅓ innings pitched, 705 pitching appearances, 646 complete games, 365 wins, and 310 losses.[2] An early practitioner of a highly effective pickoff move that baffled baserunners and left opposing captains and managers contesting its legality, Galvin was also arguably the best defender at the position.

Galvin was a star and a fan favorite for his combination of athletic prowess and kind temperament. He was admired for being consistently "cool, collected," and "self-reliant" on the field,[3] as well as humorous and quick to smile. His three frequently-used nicknames reflect these characteristics. He may have been called Pud because of his ability to turn batters into pudding, or from, his pudgy physique.[4] He was presumably called "The Little Steam Engine" because he was small but powerful, and he was called "Gentle James" or "Gentle Jeems" for his kind demeanor.

Despite his historic statistics and traits, as well as numerous exceptional single-game performances, Galvin was largely forgotten after his death in 1902. He spent his best years in Buffalo and his salad days in Pittsburg,[5] small markets with poor teams. Unlike several other prominent players, Galvin did not win championships in the major leagues or play in big markets like New York, Boston, and Chicago, so his achievements were not as well remembered as those of his peers. One of Galvin's best seasons came in the lesser-known International Association, and his other two strongest showings, in 1883 and 1884, fell under the long shadow of Charles "Old Hoss" Radbourn's dominant two-year run of pitching, the best of the century. Perhaps the greatest consequence of Galvin's relative obscurity was an unduly late induction into the Baseball Hall of Fame. While a few of his equals and many worthy but less accomplished players were elected to the Hall soon after its establishment in 1936, Gentle Jeems was not inducted until 1965.

James Francis Galvin was born on Christmas Day in 1855 or 1856 in St. Louis, Missouri. He was born to Irish immigrants who lived in the Kerry Patch, a section of the city so named because many of its initial settlers hailed from County Kerry in southwestern Ireland, an area devastated by the Great Irish Famine of 1845-1849. Galvin's parents were likely part of this large emigration. Inhabitants of the Kerry Patch, located in the northern part of St. Louis, settled the area as squatters since they did not have rights to the land. The district was essentially a concentration of shacks, and was known for particularly tough living conditions and frequent violence. Its inhabitants consisted primarily of laborers, and young James, in preparation for a blue-collar life, received training as a steamfitter. However, his life went in a different direction as a result of his ability to play baseball.

By the time of his first known appearance in baseball, in 1874, the right-handed James would have grown into his short, stocky, and strong body. Standing approximately 5-feet-8, weighing in at about 190 pounds in his prime, and wearing size 9 shoes, he had a compact and solid frame, broad shoulders, and strong core and lower body that befitted the power pitcher he would become. He gained weight as he aged, apparently weighing as much as 250 pounds by 1894. Contemporary accounts were unkind about his appearance: he was often described as "short" and "fat." Some reports also pointed out his broad shoulders and small neck. Sam Crane, the player-manager of the Buffalo Bisons in 1880, recalled that "Jimmy's bull neck sunk into his wide spread of shoulders like the head of a mud-turtle into its shell."[6] Galvin kept his dark hair short and sported a full mustache.

In contrast to his substantial body, Pud had small hands, which did not allow him to throw a curveball. Instead, he featured a speedy fastball, the occasional offspeed pitch, and pinpoint control. During a gathering with friends in 1890, attended by a sports reporter, a member of the group showed his hands, damaged playing baseball as a young man. Galvin responded: "Why, if I was worth $10,000 to-day, and could spare it, I would give that amount for your hands if an exchange were possible. From the time I went into base ball I have always been handicapped by my hands, which are too small. I never saw the day yet when I was able to span an ordinary base ball. My fingers are too short to enable me to get grip enough on the ball to pitch a deep curve, so that I have been compelled to depend more on drops, straight balls and the different artifices known to pitchers to deceive the batter."[7]

Galvin's inability to throw a curveball may have been a blessing in disguise, as he perfected a simple approach to pitching that yielded consistent results. Watching Tony Mullane struggle while throwing breaking pitches one day in 1886, Galvin remarked, "Just watch them slug Tony with his ups and downs, while I keep right on winning with my little old straight-ball delivery."[8] Additionally, Galvin's limited repertoire may have been a factor in his longevity during an era in which pitchers had very short careers, because his arm did not sustain the stress of throwing hard breaking pitches.

Galvin also relied on good defense and a devastating pickoff move. He was one of the premier fielding pitchers of the era, consistently recognized for his fielding prowess in the press. His pickoff move was extraordinarily effective and incontrovertibly the most successful of the 19th century. Incorporating a shift of weight and a deceptive movement of the head and shoulders, Galvin had almost complete control over a baserunner's fate. His move was described as "a jumping-jack movement" in which "he always looks as if he were just ready to deliver the ball. He starts with a half-drop of his legs and forward movement of his body without removing one foot from the box. The runner takes a good lead off first. Then, with a smile that is childlike and blank, the veteran shoots the ball over to first and catches his man."[9] Another account noted that Galvin's pickoff move "consists of bringing his arm to the rear as if about to pitch and bending his head as though ready to deliver the ball; then, instead of giving the ball an inshoot over the plate, he fires it to first, apparently without looking."[10] This deceptive body movement was followed by an accurate throw to the base. Sam Barkley, first baseman and Galvin's teammate in Pittsburg in 1886 and 1887, said that Galvin never threw a ball "out of my reach on either side, too low to scoop or any higher than my knee."[11]

The success of the move prompted frequent arguments from the opposing teams. Some players complained that the move was a balk, most prominently John Montgomery Ward and Cap Anson. The latter, a sometime victim of the move, was particularly vocal on several occasions, taking particular issue with Galvin's shoulder movements. During the summer of 1888, Anson said that Galvin's "delivery is plainly illegal under the existing rules." Galvin's manager that season, Horace Phillips, responded that his star pitcher "always has his shoulders squarely planted and the ball in sight. It's the peculiarity of the movement that deceives you. Why nearly every prominent pitcher in the country has tried to copy that little nod of his before he throws the ball."[12] Buck Ewing concurred: "You notice that funny, false motion of his that can't really be called a balk. He fooled me so badly one day that I never even attempted to get back to first base."[13] Galvin's pickoff move was only seldom called a balk by umpires, with the exception of the 1890 Players League season, when Frank Brunell, the league's secretary-treasurer, apparently instructed umpires to outlaw his move and others like it.

Galvin was so good at catching runners napping on the basepaths that he picked off three Brooklyn players in one inning on September 23, 1886. In the third, he walked Bill McClellan, Jim McTammany, and George Smith to load the bases. He proceeded to pick off Smith at first base, followed by McClellan at third, who was caught "with his trousers at half mast." Finally, he picked off McTammany at second to end the inning. Thanks to his pickoff move, Galvin got himself out of a tough inning and led his team to an 8-2 victory.[14]

In another instance, the highly skilled Galvin seemed able to successfully pick off a runner at will. While jawing with Cap Anson in a game against Chicago in late August 1887, Galvin apparently asked Anson, "Do you want to see me catch a man?" Anson dared him to do it, so Galvin strutted to the pitcher's box and walked Jimmy Ryan on purpose. After Ryan arrived at first base, Galvin picked him off almost immediately. Anson was furious, while "Galvin almost split his side laughing" after his successful demonstration.[15]

Pickoffs were not quantified then as they are now, so a precise count of Galvin's successes is impossible to recover. His reputation and the surviving accounts, however, indicate that he had no equal when it came to holding and picking off runners. Galvin's move was the envy of the league. Pitchers tried in vain to duplicate it, and every catcher desired this skill in his pitcher. Buck Ewing said, "If I had Galvin to catch, no one would ever steal a base on me. That fellow keeps them glued to the bag."[16]

Galvin's playing career was characterized by a steady rise in achievement that peaked in 1883 and 1884, followed by an unusually long, very gradual decline. His period of decline was longer than that of most 19th-century careers. His career included many notable moments, colorful stories, and dominant seasons. Galvin was first recorded playing baseball in 1874 at the age of 17 as a member of the Turner Club of St. Louis. He also appeared as a member of other clubs in St. Louis, including the Empire Club in 1875 and the Niagara club in 1874 and 1875. Galvin made his major-league debut for the St. Louis Brown

Stockings of the National Association on May 22, 1875, to fill in for primary starting pitcher George Bradley, who hadn't pitched since May 8, possibly due to illness. After Galvin pitched three games and won two between May 22 and May 27, Bradley regained his health and returned to the pitcher's box on May 29. Galvin made only four more starts during the year and one relief appearance. Altogether he played in 13 games, pitched in eight games (seven starts, all complete games), and played all three outfield positions when not pitching.

The Brown Stockings joined the new National League for the 1876 season, but Galvin did not stay with the team. Instead, he spent the year with the St. Louis Red Stockings (Reds), a club that was in the National Association in 1875, but unaffiliated in 1876. Its 1876 roster had several holdovers from 1875, including Frank Sylvester "Silver" Flint, who would go on to become one of the 19th century's prominent catchers. While the complete record of Galvin's play that season is hard to recover, he turned in three exceptional performances. The first was a no-hitter against the National League's Philadelphia club on July 4 in an exhibition game. The other two happened on the same day, August 17, 1876, during a tournament held in Ionia, Michigan. Galvin threw the first recorded perfect game in baseball history, against the Cass Club of Detroit in an 11-0 victory. This feat was accomplished before the term "perfect game" was in the baseball lexicon, but the *Ionia Sentinel* clearly spelled out the performance, leaving no doubt about the achievement: "The Cass boys did not make a base hit or reach first base during the game. Each man of the club batted three times and each was put out three times."[17] Galvin's feat was all the more impressive because he threw a no-hitter earlier that day against the Mutuals of Jackson, Michigan, in which the defense behind him committed three errors. Galvin's accomplishments should not be taken lightly because they were not recorded in the major leagues, as the Cass Club and the Mutuals of Jackson were competitive and talented professional teams.

In 1877, Galvin joined the Allegheny Club of Pittsburg in the new International Association. Not considered a major league by baseball historians, the International Association is sometimes seen as the first minor league in baseball history, but the idea of a minor league is a later conceit. At the time it was simply a second professional league in cities not represented by teams in the National League. In 1877 teams were based in Guelph, Ontario; London, Ontario; Pittsburg; Rochester; Manchester, New Hampshire; Columbus; and Lynn, Massachusetts. Candy Cummings was the president of the league, and many other notables played in the league during its brief history (1877 until 1880), including Mike "King" Kelly, John Montgomery Ward, Mickey Welch, and Ned Hanlon. On April 30 Galvin recorded the league's first shutout, against Columbus. He threw another shutout in an exhibition victory against the Boston Red Stockings on May 2 in Pittsburg. He gave up one hit and hit a home run, possibly the first ball hit out of Pittsburg's Union Park, to score the game's only run.[18] By all accounts, Galvin's 1877 season was a success, but his statistics are difficult to recover.

Galvin's 1878 season, the first full year of his career for which a nearly complete record is readily available, proved to be historic. Now pitching for the Buffalo Bisons, a new team in the International Association, he dominated the league, winning an astounding 72 games. After a subpar season as members of the League Alliance in 1877, the Bisons fielded an entirely different roster, cutting ties with John Montgomery Ward, Larry Corcoran, Jack Glasscock, Doc Bushong, and others. In 1878, the Bisons played 116 games, and went 81-32 with three ties. Galvin pitched in 101 games, completing 96 of them and compiling a 72-25 record with three ties. He threw 17 shutouts, and went 10-5 against National League teams. He pitched every inning of the team's first 23 games and went the distance in 22 consecutive contests between September 2 and October 4. The last three games of this stretch included a 12-inning victory over the Boston Red Stockings on October 2, and a 13-inning victory over Providence of the National League the next day. It is estimated that Galvin threw at least 895 innings. Although never a consistent hitter, he did have some power throughout his career, hitting one of the team's two home runs in 1878. Aside from Galvin's superior pitching, he and four teammates, Davy Force, Joe Hornung, Steve Libby, and Bill McGunnigle, were awarded medals by the *New York Clipper* for the best fielding averages in the league. The 1878 Bisons were the International Association champions, finishing one game ahead of the Syracuse Stars.

Galvin's trickery and excellent pickoff move were already well-developed in 1878. On July 27 he and Libby executed the hidden-ball trick to perfection to fool Candy Cummings of the Cleveland Forest Citys in a 3-0 victory. In the third inning, Cummings was on base after hitting a single when his teammate Salisbury hit a popup to Libby at first. After Libby caught the ball, he faked a throw back to Galvin and kept the ball. Galvin then got in the box and readied himself to pitch. When Cummings started his lead, Libby tagged him for the third out of the inning. On August 19, behind Galvin, the Bisons defeated the

Chicago White Stockings 4-2 in 13 innings. Galvin picked off five runners. Galvin's historic 1878 season demonstrated that he was an ace capable of pitching almost every day.

After its championship season in the International Association, Buffalo joined the National League for the 1879 season, Galvin found himself back in the "major leagues" for the first time since 1875. He picked up where he left off in 1878, continuing his workhorse ways by pitching in 66 of the team's 79 games, amassing 593 innings and winning 37 games with six shutouts. Despite this strong effort, the team finished in third place.

In October 1879, after the season was over, Galvin joined a "picked nine" consisting primarily of players from the Cincinnati Red Stockings, including King Kelly, on a tour to California that also included John Clapp, Cal McVey, Davy Force, Pete Hotaling, and Jack Rowe. The team toured California with the Chicago White Stockings and played against California clubs as well as each other. *The San Francisco Chronicle* reported that both the picked nine and the White Stockings beat the California clubs with ease, with fans being most interested in seeing the two visiting teams play each other. The teams toured California for 12 weeks, with the players arriving on October 5 and leaving on December 19. By the end of the tour, King Kelly was a member of the Chicago White Stockings and Pud Galvin's future was uncertain.

Galvin likely remained in California after his fellow players left in order to try to negotiate a raise with the Bisons by threatening to play the 1880 season in California. When the Bisons called his bluff, Pud signed with the Athletic Club of San Francisco, of the California League (formerly called the Pacific Coast League), in which each team was set to play 30 League Games. In February, the California League adopted its constitution, which included clauses to make players honor their team commitments. In the words of the *San Francisco Bulletin*, "the player is bound by such iron-bound and copper-fastened rules as will make it exceedingly difficult for him to break his contract."[19] Galvin's teammates with the Athletics included future major leaguers Cliff Carroll and Jerry Denny, and the team was captained by former major leaguer Tom Carey. Galvin began the season with the team, but after the Buffalo club got off to a poor start behind pitchers Tom Poorman and Bill McGunnigle, it reached out to Galvin in the second week of May and he accepted it contract offer to come back to Buffalo, along with an advance of $300.

Galvin left San Francisco, apparently under an assumed name, to head for Cincinnati to meet up with the Buffalo club. He did not get very far before he was apprehended because the Athletic Club made it known that he was breaking his contract after receiving his next month's pay. The Athletic Club's owners requested that Galvin be brought back to San Francisco. However, according to reports issued on May 15, Gentle Jeems had escaped without a trace—the San Francisco papers suggested that he used some of the money from his two paychecks to bribe the authorities. Galvin made it to Cincinnati successfully and was the winning pitcher for the Bisons on May 22. It was Buffalo's fourth win against seven losses. By July the California League officially expelled Galvin from the League, a purely symbolic gesture.

Charley Foley (likely Curry Foley, future Galvin teammate and the first player on record to hit for the cycle) shared an exciting and certainly overblown version of Galvin's departure from San Francisco with the *New York Clipper*: "The directors [of the Buffalo Club] induced Galvin's wife to use her influence toward bringing him back. Galvin was telegraphed for, but the manager of the San Francisco team would not let him go, and they even threatened to have him arrested should he attempt to leave San Francisco. Galvin asked for his release, and, when refused it, he left for the East. He took a train out of the city some little distance and then left it and walked about twenty-three miles, which brought him into the State of Nevada. In walking across the desert Galvin's shoes were nearly burned off his feet. He joined the Buffalo Club in Cincinnati where he related to his old comrades his thrilling adventures."[20] After Galvin returned to the Bisons, the *Buffalo Express* celebrated his return with a poem:

*Could we let our pitcher stay
In the Golden City?
Could our boys without him play?
No, 'twould be a pity.
So we pressed our rightful claims
And we won back our Gentle
James*[21]

Unfortunately, there was not much to celebrate after Galvin's return. He went 20-35, primarily because of his team's lack of offense. The team finished in seventh place, going 24-58. They lost consistently; their longest winning streak reached only three games. One notable low point in Galvin's season came on June 17, when he was on the losing end of John Montgomery Ward's perfect game for the Providence Grays. Galvin also made the last out in the game. Another disappointment for the team came in the form of the struggles of a young position player who performed so poorly that he was released after appearing in only six games that season—Charles Radbourn. One can only imagine how the team's fortunes would have changed if it had retained Radbourn and seen him develop into the pitcher that he became. In the days of two-man pitching staffs, the Galvin-Radbourn combination would have been a dominant force.

One highlight came on July 16, 1880, when Galvin beat the Providence Grays and pitcher John Montgomery Ward 1-0 in 14 innings. In completing the shutout, Galvin stranded a runner on third base to end the game. Later in the season, Galvin threw the first major-league no-hitter by a road pitcher on August 20 against Worcester. This was the sixth no-hitter in major-league history. The Buffalos won 1-0 on a very rainy day in front of only 91 spectators. The rainy conditions made the game ball—one ball was used for the entire game—mushy and difficult to hit hard. One record of the game stated that the ball became "a leather bag filled with jelly."[22] This was certainly a factor in the Worcester batters' failure to hit Galvin's pitches with any authority. While some may feel that the foul weather detracts from Galvin's feat, this point of view ignores the difficulties of pitching and fielding a mushy, possibly lopsided ball in difficult weather. Not only was Galvin able to throw a no-hitter, but he did not allow any runs despite his team's six errors. He was also able to maintain his usual good control, not giving up a single base on balls.

Before the 1881 season, the Buffalo ownership significantly improved the team with the addition of Dan Brouthers, Jim O'Rourke, and Deacon White. However, it was still only able to finish in third place, a disappointment for the star-studded roster. Galvin went 28-24, throwing five shutouts and completing 48 of his 53 starts, continuing to be a workhorse for his team. After the regular season ended, the Bisons played exhibition games, including a three-game series against the Philadelphia Athletics in Philadelphia. Galvin no-hit the Athletics in the final game of the exhibition series, on October 11, giving up two walks and having two men reach base on errors.

Buffalo cranks saw their club finish in third place again in 1882. Continuing as the team's primary starter, Galvin went 28-23, starting 51 games and throwing three shutouts, both lows for him as a Bison up to that point. He accomplished a notable feat on July 4, when he won two games in one day for the second time in his career. During the season, Galvin agreed to what Harold Seymour and Dorothy Seymour Mills called an "optional" contract with the Pittsburg Alleghenys of the American Association that seemingly secured his services for the 1883 season. Charlie Bennett and Ned Williamson agreed to similar contracts with the Alleghenys, and all three men ended up deciding to remain in the National League. The Alleghenys took Bennett to court to try to force him to play for them in 1883, but the court ruled in favor of Bennett, determining that such "optional" contracts were only preliminary agreements. Thus, Galvin was allowed to stay with Buffalo in 1883.[23] By December, Galvin had been banned from the American Association, his second blacklisting since 1880.

The Bisons were fortunate that Galvin did not go to Pittsburg, for he began his two-year peak in 1883. He started 75 games, completing 72 of them and pitching 656⅓ innings. He won 46 games and had an ERA of 2.72. These four statistics were all career highs, or tied with career highs. Despite this Herculean effort, the team finished in fifth place, in part because their change pitcher, George Derby, started 13 games and lost 10 of them. In 1883 Galvin faced three other Hall of Fame pitchers, and went 3-3 against Mickey Welch, 1-1 against John Montgomery Ward, and 3-2 against Hoss Radbourn, including a defeat of the Providence pitcher in the final game of the season. At the plate, Galvin hit his first major-league home run in 1883.

Galvin had the best season of his career in 1884, but the year did not have an auspicious beginning. He started 1-4, and then injured himself on May 10 in Providence after losing a game to Radbourn on May 9. Galvin hurt himself picking up his suitcase at Providence's Narragansett Hotel, possibly the result of pitching in the cold without his sweatshirt the day before. The strain or muscle pull jeopardized his season. He returned to Buffalo and missed the next eight games, hoping that the rest would allow him to start the home opener in Buffalo on May 21.

Galvin returned to top form after the time off. All in all, he ended up starting 72 games, completing 71 of them. He went 46-22 with three ties, and threw 12 shutouts, with a 1.99 ERA. He topped 600 innings for the second consecutive year. He started the team's home opener, and the Bisons defeated the visiting Detroit Wolverines, 12-3. Galvin was especially tough on the Wolverines during an August series in Detroit August 2 to 8. On August 2 Galvin pitched a shutout, allowing one hit (a single), with seven strikeouts and no walks. On the 4th he no-hit the Wolverines while striking out nine and not surrendering any bases on balls. After two days of rainouts, Galvin pitched another shutout on August 7, giving up only three hits. The following day the teams played a doubleheader, with Galvin getting the start in the second game. He proved more hittable in this game, giving up eight hits. However, he pitched 12 innings without surrendering an earned run and striking out 16 Wolverines without any walks. Detroit scored an unearned run in the 12th inning to win the game. In the series Galvin pitched in four games, throwing 39 innings without giving up an earned run. He surrendered 12 hits and struck out 36 without any walks. After this historic run, the *Detroit Free Press* called Galvin the " 'Maud S' of the diamond," after the record-setting racehorse who was the first to run a mile in under 2 minutes, 10 seconds, on August 2, 1884.[24]

September 9, 1884, saw Galvin turn in another significant performance, when he ended Radbourn's personal 18-game winning streak, and Providence's 20-game streak. Galvin led his team to a 2-0 victory that ended with an exciting double play in the bottom of the ninth inning. Jim Lillie, Buffalo's right fielder, caught a difficult fly ball hit by Radbourn and threw the ball to second base to double off Cliff Carroll, who thought the ball would drop. One newspaper later wrote that "the whole country had been looking … to accomplish the defeat of Radbourn and the Grays,"[25] and it was Galvin who finally accomplished this feat. "Base ball enthusiasts are indebted to James Galvin," wrote another paper after he ended the winning streak, which some had grown tired of.[26] At season's end, Providence won the championship and Buffalo finished in third place.

Galvin's magnificent seasons in 1883 and 1884 were two of the best seasons of the 19th century, but they were overshadowed by the accomplishments of Radbourn, who won 48 and 59 games in 1883 and 1884, respectively, for the Providence Grays. In 1884, Radbourn also led the Grays to the National League championship and the unofficial championship of professional baseball after a postseason series victory over the American Association champion New York Metropolitans. In 1884, Radbourn's ERA was a minuscule 1.38, and his 18-game winning streak was an extraordinary feat. Thus, Galvin had the bad luck of peaking at the same time as Radbourn, who played on a better team than the Buffalo Bisons.

Galvin's 1883 and 1884 seasons took their physical toll. He would never pitch more than 450 innings or win more than 29 games for the rest of his career. His career began its long, steady decline in 1885, when he turned in a subpar season. His decline is remarkable because it lasted eight seasons, indicating that he remained a competitive pitcher and valuable player. In 1885, Galvin injured himself in a collision with Cap Anson on June 19. During a stretch of 24 games, he briefly managed the team, but the team went 7-17. By the middle of July, with his pitching record 13-19, he was sold to the Pittsburgh Alleghenys of the American Association. One of Buffalo's directors said, "The public demanded a change. Both the press and the audiences were growing irritable. We couldn't lose any more games if a pitcher were taken from the grand stand."[27] This was quite an insult to Galvin, who had pitched very well for the team since 1878 and had two of the best pitching seasons of the century in 1883 and 1884. The notion of cutting a star pitcher at the first sign of decline reflects the 19th-century reality of the unsustainable workloads given to ace pitchers as well as the inclination to part ways with star players at the first sign of trouble in order to make money from their sale.

Although different amounts were cited, it seems that Pittsburgh paid $1,500 or $2,000 for "The Little Steam Engine." His replacements in Buffalo pitched poorly, and fans stopped coming to the park. On September 17 team Josiah Jewett sold the Bisons franchise to the Detroit Wolverines for $7,000. Detroit wanted only Brouthers, Richardson, White, and Rowe, but Jewett insisted that they take the entire franchise. The Bisons finished the season with amateurs and players that Detroit didn't want to keep on its roster. Thus ended the presence of the Bisons in the National League. Buffalo would be a major-league city for only one more season, when it hosted the 1890 Buffalo Bisons in the ill-fated Players League.

Pittsburg hoped that Galvin would lead them to the American Association championship, although St. Louis had a considerable lead over them at the time. The Alleghenys surely disappointed by Galvin's performance. He appeared in only 11 games, going 3-7 before an arm injury ended his season in the second inning of a game against Louisville on August 26. He told a sportswriter that he thought his career was over and went to Buffalo to be treated by his doctor. Galvin made one more appearance that year, on September 18, and lost to New York in a terrible outing in which he could not complete four innings. The Alleghenys finished in third place.

Galvin returned from the injury and remained with Pittsburg in 1886, and stayed with the club after it joined the National League in 1887. His career in Pittsburg was unspectacular from 1885 to 1889, except that he continued to pitch while most of the pitchers he came up with in the 1870s had retired or switched positions long ago. In 1887, on a very bad team, he won 28 games, just over half of the team's 55 victories, which was a rare feat after teams began playing more than 120 games each year. In 1889 he logged over 300 innings for the final time and had an ERA above 4.00 for the first time in his career. The statistics indicate that this was Galvin's worst season, but he played the role of spoiler on the last day of the season when he beat Boston to deprive the Beaneaters of a first-place finish and preventing John Clarkson from winning his 50th game of the season.

Galvin joined the new Players League for the 1890 season, thus aligning himself with the large contingent of players unhappy with the treatment they received from National League and American Association magnates. He was not the most fervent supporter of the Brotherhood of Professional Ball Players, noting to reporters that he had never felt particularly ill-treated by ownership during his career. However, he showed his solidarity to the new league when he refused lucrative offers to jump back to the National League. At the end of his career, he did not have much to lose by siding with the Brotherhood. He played for the Pittsburg Burghers under player-manager Ned Hanlon and turned in another unspectacular season in 1890, going 12-13 in 217 innings pitched with a 4.35 ERA. He played relatively sparingly and not particularly well in 1890, his second-worst year by the numbers.

Galvin spent the 1891 season back in the National League with the Pittsburg club, pitching effectively in 246⅔ innings with a 2.88 ERA. At 35, he began the 1892 season in Pittsburg, but was sold to the St. Louis Browns after appearing in 12 games. He was headed back to the city of his birth. Shortly after his sale, he pitched a home game against Pittsburg and won. According to a report from Pittsburg, the local fans following the game from Pittsburg rooted for him even though he was pitching on the other team:

"Pittsburgers are intensely loyal to the home club and want to see them win every game if possible, but on this occasion, no sooner was it announced that Galvin was pitching than the people, with scarcely an exception, began to 'pull' for him," a reporter wrote. "Our representatives were not in such a position that they could well afford to lose games, but that seemed to concern the crowd little as long as Galvin won the games. The incident is really unique. It shows how much more popular the man is than the club, and what a vast mistake it was to release him."[28]

Galvin appeared in 12 games for St. Louis before the season ended. He had a respectable season, with a 2.92 ERA., but logged only 188 innings. It was his final season as a player, with the exception of brief comeback attempts.

Midway through the 1892 season, fans and members of the media offered assessments of Galvin's career, properly guessing that it would be his final season. Galvin's longevity, practically unheard of in the era of two-man pitching staffs, impressed followers of the game. *Sporting Life* summarized a letter from a fan from Louisville:

"A Louisville crank … figures that the veteran pitcher, Galvin, has pleased and displeased 800,000 people in his 17 years pitching, has traveled 112,000 miles or about four and a half times the circumference of the earth, has taken part in about 500 games in which on average 35 men went to the bat per game, and that four balls were pitched to each. That will make a total of 70,000 throws and balls pitched by Galvin. But during a large part of Galvin's career seven balls instead of four sent a man to first base. That runs the total up to, perhaps an even 100,000, and these balls have traveled 2000 miles, and in pitching these 100,000 balls Galvin expended sufficient strength to carry them 30,000,000 feet, or about 6000 miles."[29]

After the 1892 season Galvin attempted to extend his career. Potential comebacks were mentioned in newspapers as late as 1899, the last earnest attempt apparently came in 1894, when he played for the Buffalo Bisons of the Eastern League. At this point, Galvin was quite out of shape, weighing around 250 pounds. He pitched poorly in three games for the Bisons and was released. In his final at-bat he hit a home run, an appropriate way to cap off an extraordinary career. There were rumblings of later attempts to come back to the game, but whether he actually played in any more games is not known.

Before his brief stint in the Eastern League, on the evening of January 2, 1894, and into the early hours of January 3, Galvin and two friends encountered unexpected trouble with the law in Cleveland, where they were visiting a sick friend. After seeing their friend, they went to a bar, where a tailor named H.W. Hubbard introduced himself to the group. Shortly after leaving Hubbard's company, the group was arrested for stealing a $250 diamond pin and $125 gold watch from the tailor. Galvin and friends were jailed overnight, where they shared cells with miscreants and pestilent insects. The men went before a judge the next day expecting to have to plead their case, but the judge dropped the charges because there was no evidence against them. The angry group sought out Hubbard to demand an explanation for his false accusation, but Hubbard's friends and police protected him. Galvin and his friends vowed to sue Hubbard, but it is unclear if they ever pursued litigation.

Galvin filled his post-playing days with a variety of jobs. He was a National League umpire for the 1895 season, received mixed reviews, and did not enjoy the job. His experience resembled that of most other umpires in the 19th century—it was unpleasant and thankless work. Galvin, like most umpires, did not last very long, and did not return the next season. He is also recorded as a pipe-layer, contractor, and saloon owner in Pittsburg after his playing days ended. His saloon was unsuccessful because he did not have great business acumen. One anecdote says he had the largest bar in the Pittsburg and employed nine bartenders at one point. Subsequently, each of the nine bartenders opened his own business, while Galvin's saloon failed. His status as a saloon owner allowed him to pitch in an exhibition game between bartenders on October 1, 1896. By that time his skills had diminished so much that he pitched poorly, giving up 20 hits.

By the turn of the century, Galvin and his family were living in poverty. He had married Bridget Griffin in 1878 and had 11 children. Newspapers joked that he had enough children to field his own baseball team. His health declined sharply beginning in late 1901, and on March 7, 1902, at the age of 45, Galvin died in Pittsburgh of "catarrh of the stomach," also known as chronic stomach inflammation or chronic gastritis. His wife and six of his children survived him. Because of the family's limited finances, an event, including boxing and music, was held to raise money for his wife and children. A 1908 article quoted Dave F. Kerr, who claimed an instrumental role in Galvin's sale to Pittsburg in 1885, as bemoaning Galvin's inability to save money: "Pity the old man wouldn't heed. He drew a big salary and was one of the most popular players of his age, but his fame finally fled. You can talk about your pitchers, but to me Galvin looked one of the best men of his period. Change of pace, etc., made him a corker. The Little Steam Engine made a fortune for the ball clubs, but his bit frittered away despite the efforts of his good wife, who tried hard to induce her good-natured husband to lay up some cash for stormy times."[30] Galvin's family neither saw long-term financial support from his baseball career nor did they see him play the game very often. His daughter Marie said, "We had nine boys and two girls in the family, and there was so much to be done at home that we didn't get very many chances to see my father pitch."[31]

Galvin's death at a young age, tragic in its own right, was also a factor in his relatively quick fade from the consciousness of baseball fans and historians. Another factor was the greater star power of other pitchers in his era due to impressive single-season achievements, play on winning teams, or play in bigger cities. Galvin was outshined in his era by pitchers who were more dominant for short stretches of time, like Hoss Radbourn, or who played on winning teams or in bigger cities, like John Clarkson and Tim Keefe. After his death Galvin was increasingly forgotten as Americans became enamored with pitchers in the Deadball Era like Cy Young, Christy Mathewson, and Walter Johnson. However, at least one fan, M.G. Nowak of Milwaukee, who lived during Galvin's era, reminded the readers of *Sporting Life* about Galvin's accomplishments. In January 1906, while the country was captivated by Christy Mathewson's three shutouts in the 1905 World Series, Nowak pointed out that Galvin was able to reach similarly legendary heights during that historic series against Detroit in August 1884.[32]

As the 20th century progressed, Galvin continued to fade from the consciousness of baseball fans and historians. After the establishment of the Baseball Hall of Fame, the Old-Timers Committee, which was formed in 1939 to elect 19th- and early 20th-century baseball figures into the Hall of Fame, ignored Galvin. In 1939 five players were elected by the committee, but not Galvin. In 1945 ten players were elected, but Galvin was not one of them. Eleven players were elected in 1946, including many with achievements far less impressive than Galvin's, while Gentle James was ignored. The Old-Timers Committee voted sporadically until its name was changed to the Committee on Baseball Veterans in 1953. The new name produced the same results: It continued to ignore Galvin for more than a decade.

A cause for optimism appeared in the late 1940s in the form of Joseph M. Overfield, a Buffalo baseball historian who took a special interest in Galvin. A title researcher and later vice president at the Monroe Abstract Corporation (later Monroe Abstract and Title), he discovered his passion for baseball history in the late 1940s when he discovered a financial report about the 1878 Buffalo Bisons while conducting records research. This began a lifetime of research, writing, and service related to Buffalo baseball and its biggest star in the 19th century, Pud Galvin. Overfield wrote several articles beginning in 1953, as well as a small book of records and statistics called *Buffalo Bison Sketch Book*, also published that year. He was an early member of SABR, joining in 1972, and was recognized with a "SABR Salute" in 1986. He published his magnum opus, *The 100 Years of Buffalo*

*Baseball*, in 1985 and continued working with SABR and the Buffalo Baseball Hall of Fame until his death in 2000.

Overfield recognized the significance of Galvin as he discovered documents and images of early Buffalo baseball clubs and read 19th-century newspapers. He contacted Galvin's descendants and started a campaign to get him inducted into the Hall of Fame, which was successful in 1965. Overfield took great pride in leading the successful effort, and Galvin's two living children, Walter and Marie, were grateful to see their father recognized. Three generations of relatives attended the ceremony. Walter, 78 years old at the time of the induction ceremony, spoke at the event and said, "I thank you for remembering him. You waited a long time to catch up with the old gent."[33]

With the publication of Roger I. Abrams' *The Dark Side of the Diamond: Gambling, Violence, Drugs and Alcoholism in the National Pastime*, in 2007, Galvin became 21st-century news. He was given the title of baseball's first user of performance-enhancing drugs. Abrams found an article in the *Washington Post* from August 14, 1889, that said:

"Galvin was one of the subjects at a test of the Brown-Séquard elixir at a medical college in Pittsburgh on Monday. If there still be doubting Thomases who concede no virtue in the elixir, they are respectfully referred to Galvin's record in yesterday's Boston-Pittsburg game. It is the best proof yet furnished of the value of the discovery."[34]

In that game Galvin pitched a two-hit shutout and was uncharacteristically successful at the plate. Abrams takes the article at face value, connecting Galvin's participation in the trial with his success in the following game, in the process defying the long-held and correct notion that correlation does not imply causation.

The Brown-Séquard elixir was invented in 1889 by Charles Brown-Séquard, a French-American doctor. The elixir, which was injected, was based around extracts from guinea-pig and dog testicles and was apparently the first known modern treatment that contained testosterone. Abrams thus relates the elixir to the anabolic steroids that we know of today and ties Galvin to cheating and performance-enhancing drugs.

Abrams, however, fails to take into account the primitive nature of the Brown-Séquard elixir, which made it biologically ineffective according to scientific research published in 2002. The only possible benefit for Galvin, therefore, would have been a placebo effect. Moreover, the instance cited by Abrams appears to have been isolated. Abrams' association of Galvin's one-time use of the Brown-Séquard elixir in 1889 with modern-day steroid use is further undermined because the elixir was not banned by professional baseball. It is anachronistic to look back at Galvin's one-time use of this elixir and consider it performance enhancement, cheating, or unethical behavior. Still, national news outlets and websites publicized and excerpted Abrams' work, thus helping to slightly tarnish Galvin's reputation and legacy.

James "Pud" Galvin was one of the most important pitchers in the history of early baseball, performing significant single-game feats and recording major career milestones. His longevity in an era of two-man pitching staffs is remarkable, and his 1878, 1883, and 1884 seasons are among the most dominant seasons in 19th-century pitching. His career is also defined by his status as a fan favorite in Buffalo and Pittsburgh. His posthumous reputation has taken several turns: He was initially forgotten, then recognized with induction into the Baseball Hall of Fame in 1965, and most recently associated with performance-enhancing drugs in 2007. Galvin led an eventful and historic career, and he continues to be significant figure more than a century years after his death. The continuing expansion of the baseball research community and increasing access to unmined 19th-century newspapers should continue to sharpen the perception of Galvin and will bring to light untold dimensions and chapters of his baseball legacy that will eventually fill a dictionary-length biography of one of the 19th century's greatest pitchers.

Special thanks to James Overfield, Freddy Berowski, Howard Henry, and Tim Wiles.

## SOURCES

In addition to the Sources cited in the Notes, the author also consulted

Ancestry.com, Baseball-reference.com, Retrosheet.org, and the following newspapers:

*The Bee* [Washington, DC], *Buffalo News, Binghamton Press, Boston Evening Transcript, Chicago Tribune, Cincinnati Enquirer, Cleveland Herald, Daily Inter Ocean* [Chicago], *Daily Mail and Empire* [Toronto], *Daily True American* [Trenton, New Jersey], *Dubuque Sunday Herald, Jackson* (Michigan) *Citizen Patriot, Mansfield* (Ohio) *Daily Shield, New York Times, New York World, Philadelphia Inquirer, Pittsburg Dispatch, Providence Morning Star, The Sporting News, Toronto Daily Mail,* and *Washington Post.*

Abrams, Roger I. *The Dark Side of the Diamond: Gambling, Violence, Drugs and Alcoholism in the National Pastime* (Burlington, Massachusetts: Rounder Books, 2007)

Achorn, Edward. *Fifty-Nine in '84: Old Hoss Radbourn, Barehanded Baseball, and the Greatest Season a Pitcher Ever Had* (New York: HarperCollins Publishers, 2010).

Appel, Marty. *Slide, Kelly, Slide: The Wild Life and Times of Mike "King" Kelly, Baseball's First Superstar* (Lanham, Maryland: Scarecrow Press, Inc., 1996).

Cash, Jon David. *Before They Were Cardinals: Major League Baseball in Nineteenth-Century St. Louis* (Columbia, Missouri: University of Missouri Press, 2002).

Casway, Jerrold. *Ed Delahanty in the Emerald Age of Baseball.* (Notre Dame, Indiana: University of Notre Dame Press, 2004).

Cook, William A. *The Louisville Grays Scandal of 1877: The Taint of Gambling at the Dawn of the National League* (Jefferson, North Carolina: McFarland & Co., 2005).

Cussons, Andrea J., Chotoo I. Bhagat, Stephen J. Fletcher, and John P. Walsh "Brown-Séquard Revisited: A Lesson from History on the Placebo Effect of Androgen Treatment," *The Medical Journal of Australia* Vol. 177, No. 11 (2002).

Dacus, Joseph and James William Buel. *A Tour of St. Louis: Or, The Inside Life of a Great City* (St. Louis: Western Publishing Company, 1878).

Dickson, Paul. *The Dickson Baseball Dictionary.* 3rd ed. (New York: W.W. Norton & Company, 2009).

Fleitz, David L. *Cap Anson: The Grand Old Man of Baseball* (Jefferson, North Carolina: McFarland & Co., 2005).

Fleitz, David L. *The Irish in Baseball: An Early History* (Jefferson, North Carolina: McFarland & Co., 2009).

Hershberger, Richard. "The Evolution of the 'Perfect Game,'" in *Base Ball: A Journal of the Early Game* Vol. 4, No. 2 (Fall 2010).

Hetrick, J. Thomas. *Chris Von der Ahe and the St. Louis Browns* (Lanham, Maryland: Scarecrow Press, Inc., 1999).

Ivor-Campbell, Frederick, Robert L. Tiemann, and Mark Rucker, eds., *Baseball's First Stars* (Cleveland: Society for American Baseball Research, 1996).

McNeil, William F. *The Evolution of Pitching in Major League Baseball* (Jefferson, North Carolina: McFarland & Co., 2006).

Morris, Peter. *Baseball Fever: Early Baseball in Michigan* (Ann Arbor, Michigan: University of Michigan Press, 2003).

Morris, Peter. *A Game of Inches: The Story Behind the Innovations That Shaped Baseball* (Chicago: Ivan R. Dee, 2010).

O'Loughlin, Michael C. *Missouri Irish: Kansas City, St. Louis & Trails West* (Kansas City, Missouri: Irish Genealogical Foundation, 2007).

Overfield, Joseph M. "A Memorable Year—1884, A Memorable Performer—Jim Galvin," in *Baseball Research Journal: Eleventh Annual Historical and Statistical Review of the Society For American Baseball Research* (Cooperstown, New York: Society for American Baseball Research, 1982).

Overfield, Joseph M. *Buffalo Bison Sketch Book—Containing the Records of Buffalo Baseball Teams 1878 to Date* (Buffalo: Kelly Letter Service, 1953).

Overfield, Joseph M. *The 100 Seasons of Buffalo Baseball* (Kenmore, New York: Partners' Press, 1985).

Overfield, Joseph M. "The 1878 Buffalo Bisons: Was It The Greatest Minor League Team Of The Game's Early Years?" In *The Empire State of Baseball* (Albany, New York: Northeastern Chapter of the Society for American Baseball Research, 1989).

Putzel, Max. *The Man in the Mirror: William Marion Reedy and His Magazine* (Columbia, Missouri: University of Missouri Press, 1998).

Roer, Mike. *Orator O'Rourke: The Life of a Baseball Radical* (Jefferson, North Carolina: McFarland & Co., 2005).

Ward, John Montgomery. *Base Ball: How to Become a Player* Reprint. (Cleveland: Society for American Baseball Research, 1993).

St. Louis Irish History—The Kerry Patch. http://home.earthlink.net/~lilirish/KerryPatch.htm

This Game of Games. http://thisgameofgames.blogspot.com

## NOTES

1. *Pittsburg Gazette*, March 8, 1902.
2. The numbers cited are Galvin's "major-league" statistics. He pitched at least 1,000 innings in leagues not recognized as "major leagues." Galvin's career innings mark ranks second all-time behind that of Cy Young.
3. *Sporting Life*, September 8, 1886.
4. Ed Koszarek, *The Players League* (Jefferson, North Carolina: McFarland & Co., 2006), 130.
5. The city's name was spelled "Pittsburg" in the nineteenthth century.
6. *New York Journal*, January 12, 1912.

# 20-GAME LOSERS

7. *Pittsburg Press*, January 12, 1890.
8. *Sporting Life*, September 8, 1886.
9. *Williamsport* (Pennsylvania) *Sunday Grit*, June 14, 1891.
10. *Ludington Daily News*, May 24, 1888.
11. *Sporting Life*, August 31, 1895.
12. *Pittsburg Press*, August 21, 1888.
13. Article in Galvin's Hall of Fame player file
14. *Brooklyn Eagle*, March 8, 1942
15. *Sporting Life*, August 31, 1887.
16. Article in Galvin Hall of Fame File
17. *Ionia Sentinel*, August 25, 1876.
18. William A. Cook notes that the game may have actually been a no-hitter.
19. *San Francisco Bulletin*, February 11, 1880.
20. *New York Clipper*, February 9, 1889.
21. Poem in the *Buffalo Express*, date unknown. Quoted in Joseph M. Overfield, "'Gentle Jeems' Jim Galvin: Buffalo's First Superstar," *Bisongram*, February/March 1993, 27.
22. *Buffalo Commercial Advertiser*, August 21, 1880.
23. Harold Seymour and Dorothy Seymour Mills, *Baseball: The Early Years* (New York: Oxford University Press, 1960), 142-3.
24. Quoted in *Sporting Life*, January 6, 1906.
25. *Providence Evening Bulletin*, July 12, 1928
26. *Evening Telegram*, Providence Rhode Island, September 10, 1884
27. *New York Times*, July 14, 1885.
28. *Weekly Herald* [Baltimore], July 3, 1892.
29. *Sporting Life*, August 13, 1892.
30. *Sporting Life*, September 26, 1908.
31. Article from 1965 in unknown newspaper in Galvin Hall of Fame file.
32. *Sporting Life*, January 6, 1906.
33. Article, presumably from 1965, in unknown newspaper. Galvin Hall of Fame File.
34. Quoted in Abrams, 107.

# JESSE HAINES

### BY GREGORY H. WOLF

**THE ONLY ST. LOUIS CARDINAL TO** play on the first five National League pennant winners in franchise history (1926, 1928, 1930, 1931, 1934), Jesse "Pop" Haines was a 26-year-old "rookie" when he debuted for the Redbirds in 1920. He was a three-time 20-game winner and pitched for the Cardinals for 18 consecutive seasons before retiring at the end of the 1937 season at the age of 44 as the big leagues' oldest player. With 210 wins, he was elected by the Veterans Committee to the Baseball Hall of Fame in 1970.

Jesse Joseph Haines was born on July 22, 1893, in Clayton, Ohio, near Dayton, the youngest of the five children of Elias and Althea Haines. Five years later his father, an auctioneer and carpenter, moved the family to a farm in Phillipsburg, five miles from Clayton. For the remainder of his life, Jesse called the small Midwestern town home. "I played baseball from the time I can remember," Haines said. "[We] played with a hard rubber ball, a dime bat, and a quarter glove."[1] Haines pitched on his grammar school team, quit school after the eighth grade in 1907 to become a well driller with his oldest brother, and started to pitch for the town team in Phillipsburg, the All-Stars. "I had ambitions to become a professional," said Haines."[2] All big leaguers were heroes. We collected those little cards with pictures of ballplayers on them," he recalled. "Those cards were about the only way we ever got to see what a player looked like."[3] Raised by "honest, wholesome, God-fearing" parents who objected to playing baseball on the Sabbath, Jesse hid his uniform in a neighbor's corncrib to pursue his passion.[4] In Dayton, about 20 miles southeast of Phillipsburg, the fair-skinned, blond-haired Haines played semiprofessionally for Standard and later National Cash Register in 1912, and then for Lily Brew in 1913 when he was invited to pitch one game (a ten-inning, complete-game loss) for the Dayton Veterans of the Class B Central League.

In his first full season of professional baseball in 1914, the 21-year-old Jess, as he was known during his playing career, embarked on a grueling and frustrating six-year odyssey which included injuries and league closings with stops at at least eight minor-league teams, tryouts with major-league clubs, and a return to semipro ball before securing a permanent spot on the St. Louis Cardinals in 1920.

Signed by player-manager Harry Martin of the Fort Wayne Railroaders in the Class B Central League for a salary of $135 per month in 1914, Haines pitched just twice before breaking his finger in batting practice.[5] Shunted off to the Saginaw Ducks in the Class C Southern Michigan League, Jess won 17 games, logged 258 innings and led the Ducks to the league title by pitching a ten-inning complete game in the final of the championship series.[6] "In the minor leagues you were lucky to get paid at all," said Haines, whose salary dropped to $115 per month with the Ducks.[7] "But I wanted to play so badly that the salary meant but little to me."[8] Back with Saginaw in 1915, Haines got off to a good start and tossed a no-hitter against the Flint Vehicles in June.[9] When the league disbanded on June 29, Haines was signed by the Detroit Tigers. On the Tigers roster for two months but not seeing action in an official game, Haines was strictly a batting-practice pitcher and may have suffered from diphtheria, causing weakness.[10] Frustrated by his lack of playing time, Haines often credited Ty Cobb with giving him inspiration to forge ahead with his career. "Say, kid, you've got something on that fastball. It's hard to follow and some day they're going to reading about you," the Georgia Peach reportedly told him.[11]

Expecting an invitation to the Tigers' spring training in 1916, Haines was disappointed to be assigned to the Springfield (Illinois) Reapers in the Central League. He won 23 games for Springfield, prompting rumors that he'd be called up to the Tigers. In the offseason he was sent to the Denver Bears of the Class A Western League, but was unexpectedly returned to Springfield to start the 1917 season.[12] Described as a "star pitcher" by *Sporting Life*, Haines notched 19 wins in 1917, but found himself in limbo again when the league folded at the end of the season.

Haines may have experienced his most taxing season in professional baseball in 1918. Signing with the Topeka Kaw-nees of the Class A Western League (the team relocated during the season 170 miles to the southwest in Hutchinson, Kansas, and was known as the Salt Packers), Haines pitched for Johnny Nee, his former manager during his one-game career with Dayton in 1913. With a 12-4 record in midseason, Haines was purchased by the Cincinnati Reds. He reported to manager Christy Mathewson's team and made his major-league debut against the Boston Braves on July 20 at Redland Field. In relief of Pete Schneider with bases loaded and no outs in the fifth inning, Haines put out the fire and surrendered five hits and one run over five innings in an 8-3 defeat.

Released by the Reds shortly after his promising debut, Haines returned to Phillipsburg and contemplated quitting baseball. George Textor, player-manager of Agathon Central Steel, a semipro team in Massillon, Ohio, persuaded Haines to join his team.[13] An "unconquerable twirler" for Agathon, Haines parlayed his success into a contract with the Tulsa Oilers in the Class A Western League. With an unsightly 5-9 record and 4.19 ERA, he was sold by Tulsa in midseason to the Kansas City Blues of the Double-A American Association. Haines won 21 of 26 decisions in a remarkable turnaround to his season, indeed his career. The "best pitcher" in the league,[14] Haines drew the interest of a number of big-league teams despite breaking his ankle against Indianapolis on September 4.[15]

"St. Louis Put Over the Real Big Deals," reported *The Sporting News* about the Cardinals acquisition of Haines.[16] The perpetually cash-strapped Redbirds, who had enjoyed just three winning seasons since 1900, were a team in transition at that time. Branch Rickey took over as manager of the club in 1919 and borrowed $10,000 from local banks to take a chance on Haines. Stepping down as team president in 1920 when Sam Breadon purchased majority ownership in the team, Rickey remained at the helm but realized that the Cardinals could never compete financially with the richer teams. Consequently, he developed baseball's first farm system, and Jess Haines was the last player he ever bought.

Though Haines is remembered as a knuckleball pitcher, he began his career as a fastball-curveball pitcher. In his first start with the Cardinals, on April 17, 1920, the 26-year-old rookie held the Pittsburgh Pirates scoreless for 12 innings at Robison Field in St. Louis before giving up three runs in the 13th inning and losing the game, 3-0. He won the first of his 210 games for the Cardinals on May 6 when he shut out the Reds in St. Louis. (The Cardinals moved to Sportsman's Park on July 1, 1920.) Durable, the big, 6-foot, 190-pound Haines, started 37 games, completed 19, and led the NL with 47 appearances. "Hard-luck Haines" concluded the season with his career-high 20th loss in an epic duel with Pete Alexander at Cubs Park in Chicago on October 1. After surrendering two runs in the first five innings, Haines tossed 9⅔ consecutive no-hit innings (from the seventh to the 16th) before giving up a one-out run in the 17th to lose, 3-2. Alexander pitched a career-best 17-inning complete-game to earn the victory. Haines finished the season with a career-high 301⅔ innings for the 75-79 Cardinals.

"I soon found out I would have to have something [besides a fastball and curve], if I wanted to stick around long," said Haines, who followed up his promising rookie year by going 18-12 in 1921 and 11-9 in 1922 with an ERA slightly above league average each season.[17] With his fastball losing effectiveness and his hits per nine innings steadily rising, Haines began working on a knuckle ball. He credited Philadelphia A's pitcher, Eddie Rommel, the first big leaguer to use the knuckleball extensively, for teaching him the pitch. Unlike Rommel, who gripped the pitch with tips of his index and middle fingers, Haines gripped the ball with the first knuckles on his index and middle fingers with the ball resting against the inside of his ring finger.[18] The result was a hard knuckler that came straight down and did not flutter like Rommel's. "[My knuckler] acted like a spitball," said Haines. "I had very good control of it and threw it from different positions."[19] Even though Haines developed calluses on his knuckles because of the friction the ball caused, his knuckles had a tendency to bleed.

Adding the knuckleball to his pitching arsenal in 1923, Haines had his best season to that point. After finishing in third place in 1921 and tied for third in 1922, the Cardinals slipped to fifth at 79-74 in '23, but it was no fault of Haines. He led the team in wins (20), innings (266), complete games (23), and ERA (3.11). He celebrated his 30th birthday by shutting out the Reds on four hits en route to completing 11 of his next 16 starts and winning ten of them.

The Cardinals and Haines took sudden and unexpected steps backward in 1924. Despite a potent offense with Jim Bottomley and Rogers Hornsby (who batted .424), the Redbirds limped to a sixth-place, 65-89 record primarily due to poor pitching. In 31 starts Haines won just 8 games, lost 19, and notched a 4.41 ERA, well over the league average. Teams batted .309 against him. The following season, on a better Cardinals team, Haines won 13 of 27 decisions but his ERA rose to 4.57, and he started just 25 times.

Ironically, Haines pitched his only big-league no-hitter during his worst season. On July 17, 1924, he held the Boston Braves hitless at Sportsman's Park in a 5-0 win. It was the first no-hitter in St. Louis baseball history since George Washington Bradley pitched the first one for the St. Louis Brown Stockings in 1876, the inaugural season of the National League. "I had almost perfect control," said Haines of his game. "There was nothing special about my speed. I started as I always do — trying the corners with my curve on the outside to right-handed hitters and keeping the fast one close to the handle of the bat."[20]

A quiet, conscientious, humble, and serious person, Haines neither smoked nor drank, and eschewed the night life. He preferred life in the small town to the hustle and bustle of the big city. During the offseason, he lived with his wife, Carrie (Weidner) Haines, a Phillipsburg resident whom he married in 1915. They had one child, a daughter, Juetta Lou, born in 1925. For many years, Haines operated an auto garage with one of his brothers.

Easygoing off the field, Haines was described as a "clean sportsman, who has never taken advantage of a rival batter with an intimidating cranial shot."[21] But he was also a fiery and fierce competitor who took losing hard. Throughout his career, he was known for chewing out teammates for mental lapses, careless throwing errors, or a perceived lackadaisical approach to the game. Haines's hard-nosed attitude, his dedication to the game, and his desire to win impressed the equally competitive Hornsby, who took over the helm of the Cardinals in 1925 when Rickey was replaced as the field manager after 38 games.

By 1926 sportswriters and fans began to wonder whether the 32-year-old Haines had lost it. His fastball lacked zip, his knuckleball vanished, and he was no longer considered the staff ace.[22] But Hornsby was committed to Haines and named him to start the second game of the season, at home against the Pirates on April 14. When Pirates catcher Earl Smith hit a liner back to the mound leading off the third

inning, it hit Haines on the instep near his right ankle. Haines fell to the ground, was removed from the game, and the team feared his ankle was broken. X-rays proved negative, but Haines pitched sporadically over the next nine weeks with only one start and 11 relief appearances. Led by Flint Rhem and Bill Sherdel, the Cardinals remained in the pennant race and were tied with the Pirates a half-game behind the Reds when Haines rejoined the starting rotation on June 19. In a dramatic return, Haines shut out the Braves on seven hits. Over the next three months he anchored the Cardinals' staff and was arguably the hottest pitcher in the NL, posting 10 wins and completing 13 of 18 starts with three shutouts in one of the best stretches of his career. After a nerve-racking race with the Pirates and Reds, the Cardinals, who played their final 24 games on the road, captured their first pennant despite losing five of their last seven games.

Haines attributed his new-found success and rebirth in 1926 to two pitches. "Thought I had [the knuckler] in 1923, but it eluded me the next years. Not until midsummer 1926 did the mystery of it come back to me," he said. "And then I started to throw a slow ball. That helped me as much as the knuckler."[23]

Haines's pitching in the 1926 World Series against the overwhelming favorite New York Yankees has been overshadowed by Babe Ruth's baserunning blunder (he was caught stealing in the ninth inning of Game Seven of a 3-2 game to end the Series) and by Pete Alexander's dominating performance (two complete-game victories, and his famous save in Game Seven). After pitching an inning of scoreless relief in Game One, Haines limited the Bronx Bombers, blanked only three times during the regular season, to just five singles in a dominating shutout in Game Three, wining 4-0. In the fourth inning, Haines belted a two-out, two-run homer, his first since 1920, and one of four in his career. Given the start in Game Seven, Haines held the Yankees to two runs over 6⅔ innings. With his knuckles bleeding so profusely that he had a difficult time gripping the ball, Haines surrendered eight hits and issued five walks before giving way (with the bases full) to Alexander, who preserved Haines's victory for the Cardinals' first World Series championship.

With a cerebral approach to pitching, Haines altered his pitching motion and delivery as he aged. When he pitched semipro ball in Massillon, his delivery was described a "deceptive" and his pitches were faster than they seemed.[24] "I was wild for years," said Haines, "wilder than Bill Hallahan ever was" (referring to his Cardinals teammate nicknamed Wild Bill[25]). Haines was a strict overhand pitcher when he arrived in St. Louis, but Rickey suggested he alter his motion to overcome bouts of wildness.[26] Consequently, he began to pitch side-arm to three-quarters. His short, rhythmic delivery put little stress on his shoulder and arm, and undoubtedly helped him play until after his 44th birthday.

The world champions experienced a tumultuous offseason. Hornsby, involved in a contract dispute, was traded in late December to the New York Giants for second baseman Frankie Frisch and pitcher Jimmy Ring. Haines held out, demanding a "substantial increase in salary," reportedly a $5,000 increase to $12,500.[27] After signing in time to participate in spring training in Avon Park, Florida, the 33-year-old began the season by tossing a two-hit shutout against the Cubs in Chicago, and won his first five starts, all complete games. Haines led the league with 25 complete games and six shutouts (both career bests), and was used only twice in relief all season. On three occasions he tossed extra-inning complete-game victories (13 innings against the Cubs on June 21 and the Reds on September 26, and 11 innings against the Pirates on August 12) en route to 300⅔ innings. He also set personal bests with 24 wins and a 2.72 ERA. With the 40-year-old Alexander (21-10), Haines formed the most formidable pitching duo in the NL, but it was not enough to overcome the Pirates, who won the pennant by 1½ games over the Redbirds.

Under new manager, Bill McKechnie (the team's fourth different Opening Day skipper in as many years), the Cardinals got off to a slow start (10-11) in 1928 before the offense, led by MVP Bottomley (31 HRs, 136 RBIs, .325 BA) and Chick Hafey (27, 111, .337), woke up. Continuing his success from

1927, Haines hurled ten complete games in his first 12 starts. By the end of July it appeared as though the Redbirds would run away with the pennant, but after a poor August (14-13) they were in a tight race with the New York Giants, who went 25-8 during September. At his best when the Cardinals needed him the most, Haines pitched complete games to win his last eight starts and help lead the Cardinals to their second pennant. Completing 20 of 28 starts, Haines won 20 games and notched a 3.18 ERA. In a rematch of the 1926 World Series, the Yankees swept the Cardinals, defeating 21-game-winner Bill Sherdel in Games One and Four, Alexander in Game Two, and Haines in Game Three. Given a two-run lead after one frame, Haines surrendered a towering solo home run to Lou Gehrig in the second inning and then a two-run inside-the-park home run to him in the fourth. Haines was undone by two errors by his catcher that led to three unearned runs in the sixth inning, and departed after six innings having surrendered six hits and three walks during a 7-3 defeat.

Haines's 1929 season was a study in contrasts. A complete-game win against the Reds on May 20 gave him his 14th consecutive win over two seasons. Notching his ninth victory of the season on June 22, Haines appeared headed to a third consecutive 20-win season, but then encountered the worst slump of his career. He won just four more times, posted an unfathomable 8.00 ERA over his final 84⅓ innings, lost control of his knuckleball and his spot in the rotation. The Cardinals pitching staff, the oldest in the major leagues, fell apart. Sherdel (10-15, 5.93), Haines (13-10, 5.71), and Alexander (9-8, 3.89) seemed to be on their last legs. In disarray all season, with three different skippers, the reigning pennant winner finished in fourth place.

By the start of the 1930 season, newspapers began making more references to Haines's age. "[Haines] has gone rapidly downhill" said an Associated Press report;[28] "[Haines] slip[s] out of star class," announced another headline.[29] Gabby Street, the Cardinals' fifth different Opening Day skipper in the last six years, still had confidence in his 36-year-old starter. Given five or more days of rest in 15 of his 24 starts, Haines rebounded to post 13 wins (tied with 36-year-old spitballer Burleigh Grimes, a newcomer to the Cardinals and his roommate, for second on the team) and led the team with 14 complete games. Sluggish almost the entire season, the Cardinals caught fire, going 44-13 the last two months of the season. In fourth place on Labor Day, 6½ games out of first, they overtook the Cubs, Brooklyn Robins, and Giants in the final two weeks of the season in an exciting four-team race. Reminiscent of 1928, Haines pitched his best at the most crucial time of the season, winning his last six decisions (in seven starts). Haines enjoyed his final dramatic moment on the national stage against Connie Mack's heavily favored Philadelphia Athletics in Game Four of the World Series in St. Louis. Facing Lefty Grove, the era's best pitcher, with the Cardinals down two games to one, the big right-hander tossed a complete-game four-hitter (all singles). In the third inning Haines tied the game with an RBI single in the remarkable 3-1 victory. However, three days later, the A's won Game Six to claim their second consecutive championship.

Throughout his career, Haines was a fast worker on the mound. His victories over Grove and the A's and his shutout of the Yankees in 1926 lasted just 1:41. "You get the heebie-jeebees if you are out on the mound too long," said Haines, who rarely had discussions with his catcher during a game. "When you take too long pitching, you think about pitching one way and then change your mind. And then you end up not doing it either way you planned."[30]

Three weeks in the thermal waters at Hot Springs, Arkansas, prior to camp must have worked wonders on Haines's creaking body. He began the 1931 season by winning five of his first six starts with four complete games. But when he was hit in the right wrist on June 9 by a line drive from the Robins' Babe Herman, he missed a month. Returning to the starting rotation on July 10, he won six of eight starts, including two shutouts and four complete games, and notched an impressive 1.65 ERA in 60 innings, enabling the Cardinals to run away with the pennant. He won 12 of 15 decisions, but his season, indeed his career, took a drastic turn when he injured his right shoulder on

September 5 against the Pirates. Out for the remainder of the season and missing the Cardinals' stunning upset of the heavily favored A's in the World Series, Haines was never the same after the injury. It was his last season as predominantly a starter.

Haines's shoulder injury appeared to signal the end of his career. He logged just 85⅓ innings in 1932 in 20 appearances (10 starts) and struggled. But he returned in 1933 and transformed himself into a valuable reliever and occasional starter for the remainder of his career. From 1933 to 1936, he averaged 31 appearances (9 starts) and 105 innings per year, but his importance to the Cardinals extended far beyond his pitching. He was like a stern father-figure to a cast of new young players, among them hurlers Dizzy and Paul Dean, and Tex Carleton, and sluggers Joe Medwick and Johnny Mize. Teammates began calling him "Pop" because of his age, and papers often referred to him as "Papa Jess." Above all, Haines had the respect of his teammates. He harkened back to a time before Rickey and Breadon had transformed the Cardinals into the National League's most consistent team.

The Cardinals won their fifth pennant in nine years in 1934. The Gas House Gang, one of baseball's most enduring teams, was led by player/manager Frankie Frisch and a host of scrappy, rough, hard-nosed players like Medwick, Ripper Collins, Leo Durocher, Pepper Martin, and the Dean brothers. The team's brash personality was in stark contrast to Pop's more austere and staid approach to baseball. Haines led the team with 31 relief appearances (he started six times) and provided veteran leadership. In the Cardinals' exciting World Series championship over the Detroit Tigers, Haines pitched just once, two-thirds of an inning of mop-up duty in Game Four loss. In his World Series career, Haines won three of four decisions and posted a minuscule 1.67 ERA.

The Cardinals under Rickey and Breadon had a reputation of getting rid of their star players at the first sign of age or slippage, but they kept Haines well past his peak years. "I could have earned $4,000 or $5,000 more with the Giants or Cubs in my best years," said the intensely loyal Haines, "but then I don't think I would have lasted as long as I have."[31] Haines returned for his 18th conecutive season with the Cardinals in 1937, at the time an NL record for longest continuous service with one club. In a gesture of respect and recognition of Haines's career, Bill Terry, manager of the NL All-Star squad, named him an honorary coach of the team. Haines was pressed into the starting rotation after the All-Star Game and tossed a complete-game six-hitter to defeat Brooklyn on July 23, one day after his 44th birthday. In his next start he hurled another complete-game victory against the Dodgers. They were the final two wins in his career. "It's not my arm that's given up on me. It's my legs," he said. "After four or five innings they start wobbling."[32] By mutual agreement, the Cardinals released Haines at the end of the season.

"Old Jess" retired with 210 wins, 158 losses, 208 completes games, and 3208⅔ innings pitched in his 19-year big-league career. He won 107 games in his seven-year minor-league career.

In 1938 Haines was the pitching coach for the Brooklyn Dodgers, skippered by Burleigh Grimes. He returned to Phillipsburg the following year and served as the Montgomery County auditor for 28 years before retiring.[33] A country gentleman and farmer at heart, Haines did not miss the bright lights of the city or excitement of the stadium. "They'd never get my name on a baseball contract (today)," Haines said in retirement. "As much as I loved the game—loved to walk out there and challenge the hitters—I just couldn't take all that big-city noise."[34]

Haines received baseball's highest honor in 1970 when he was elected by the Veterans Committee to the Baseball Hall of Fame. However, his election is now seen as controversial. Frankie Frisch was the chair and major voice of the Veterans Committee during a notorious period in the early 1970s. Supported by Bill Terry and two sportswriters, Fred Lieb and J. Roy Stockton, Frisch successfully led efforts to have former teammates (Dave Bancroft, George Kelly, Haines, Chick Hafey, and Ross Youngs) enshrined. Historians have since then questioned the credentials and Hall-worthiness of these players.

After a long bout with cancer, Jesse Joseph Haines died at the age of 85 on August 5, 1978, in Dayton. He was buried at Bethel Cemetery in his hometown of Phillipsburg. Once asked to explain his longevity, Haines had a simple answer: "Get eight hours of sleep every night, watch what you eat, lay off the alcohol, and throw the ball where you're looking."35

## SOURCES

Jesse Haines player file at the National Baseball Hall of Fame, Cooperstown, New York

Ancestry.com

BaseballLibrary.com

Baseball-Reference.com

*New York Times*

Retrosheet.com

*The Sporting News*

## NOTES

1. Harry Brundidge, "Jesse Haines, Cardinal Pitcher, Used to Hide His Ball Suit in Corncrib," *St. Louis Star*, June 12, 1926, 3.
2. Ibid.
3. Ed Rumill, "They never get Jesse Haines to sign today," *Christian Science Monitor*, September 13, 1972 [no page number]. Jesse Haines player file at the National Baseball Hall of Fame.
4. Ibid.
5. "The Central League," *Sporting Life*, December 20, 1913, 15; Ernest Lanigan "Baseball Beginnings. Jesse Joseph Haines" (Associated Press), unnamed, undated publication, Jesse Haines player file at the National Baseball Hall of Fame.
6. *Sporting Life*, October 31, 1914, 15.
7. Rumill.
8. Eugene F. Karst, director of information, "Jess Haines Had Another Great Year," St. Louis Cardinals press release, January 15, 1928. Jesse Haines player file at the National Baseball Hall of Fame.
9. *Sporting Life*, July 17, 1915, 63.
10. Unnamed article with no date and page, Jesse Haines player file at the National Baseball Hall of Fame.
11. Ibid.
12. John H. Farrell, "Official Notice of Players Signed, Released, and Suspended in All Leagues of the National Association," *Sporting Life*, November 11, 1916, 9.
13. *Massillon (Ohio) Evening Independent*, August 10, 1918, 10.
14. *The Sporting News*, February 19, 1920, 2.
15. *Hutchinson (Kansas) News*, September 4, 1919, 3.
16. *The Sporting News*, February 19, 1920, 2
17. Eugene F. Karst, director of information, St. Louis Cardinals Press Release. 1929. Jesse Haines player file at the National Baseball Hall of Fame.
18. Neil Russo, "Batters Knuckled Under to Haines and Schultz," September 6, 1964, Jesse Haines player file at the National Baseball Hall of Fame.
19. Ibid.
20. Billy Evans, "Hitless Hero Says Good Control Gave Him Record Game," *Olean (New York) Times*, September 17, 1924, 7.
21. *The Sporting News*, January 18, 1934, 6.
22. The Old Scout, "Pitcher Haines Runs Up Record in Long Service," November 6, 1936. Jesse Haines player file at the National Baseball Hall of Fame.
23. Eugene F. Karst, director of information, St. Louis Cardinals Press release, 1928. Jesse Haines player file at the National Baseball Hall of Fame.
24. *Massillon Evening Independent*, August 19, 1918, 7.
25. Brundidge.
26. Ibid.
27. World Series Pitching Star Hold Out for Redbirds," (Associated Press), unnamed, undated publication. Jesse Haines player file at the National Baseball Hall of Fame.
28. "Chances of St. Louis Cards for Pennant Are Not so Hot," *Burlington (North Carolina) Daily News*, March 13, 1930, 10.
29. Philip Martin, "In the World of Sports," *McIntosh County Democrat* (Checotah, Oklahoma), January 13, 1930, 10.
30. *The Sporting News*, February, 1968, 31.
31. Paul Thomas Dix, " 'Pop' Haines Satisfied with 25-Years' Work" (United Press), November 6, 1936. Jesse Haines player file at the National Baseball Hall of Fame.
32. Bill Corum, "Jesse Joseph Haines Come Up to Forty-four and Looks Back 18 Years," *New York Journal-American*, July 19, 1937, Jesse Haines player file at the National Baseball Hall of Fame.
33. *The Sporting News*, February, 19, 1977, 38.
34. Rumill.
35. Mike Eisenbath, *The Cardinals Encyclopedia* (Philadelphia: Temple University Press, 1999), 201.

# WALTER JOHNSON

## BY CHARLES CAREY

ON AUGUST 2, 1907, A YOUNG MAN later described by Frank Graham as "beyond doubt, the greatest pitcher that ever scuffed a rubber with his spikes"[1] made his big-league debut for the Washington Senators, losing a 3-2 decision to the pennant-bound Detroit Tigers. The great Ty Cobb admitted his fastball "made me flinch" and "hissed with danger."[2] By the time he hung up his spikes 20 years later, Walter Johnson had recorded statistics which seem beyond belief — 417 wins and 279 losses, 3,509 strikeouts, 110 shutouts, 12 20-win seasons, 11 seasons with an earned run average below 2.00, and what seems almost incomprehensible a century later, 531 complete games in 666 starts. But, as superlative as his pitching record was, in Shirley Povich's words, "Walter Johnson, more than any other ballplayer, probably more than any other athlete, professional or amateur, became the symbol of gentlemanly conduct in the heat of battle."[3]

Walter Perry Johnson traveled a circuitous and improbable route to his major-league debut and subsequent stardom. He was born November 6, 1887, on a farm in Allen County, Kansas, the second of six children of Minnie (Perry) and Frank Edwin Johnson. As a child, he helped his parents scratch out a living on their 160-acre farm and found time for hunting and fishing, which became his lifelong passions. Other than occasional schoolyard pickup games, baseball had no place in his early life.

At the turn of the century, Frank Johnson was forced to give up his farm as a result of the persistent Kansas droughts. The family moved into the town of Humboldt, where Frank worked at odd jobs and Walter attended the eighth grade. At this time, Minnie's parents and siblings were all moving to the oil fields of Southern California, attracted by the good weather and plentiful jobs. After years of poverty in Kansas, a move to the Golden State seemed very appealing to Frank and Minnie. They joined the migration in April 1902, settling in Olinda where Frank found work with the Santa Fe Oil Company as a teamster.

Working on the Kansas farm and in the oil fields, Walter developed a strong, muscular, 6-feet'1 frame which eventually filled out to 200 pounds. At 16, he gained his first baseball experience with a sandlot team. Shortly afterward he started his first game against adults, pitching for a semipro team sponsored by the local oil company. Soon he was a permanent member of the oil company team, and was so impressive that a reporter commented, "Johnson was presented as a high school kid, but he is certainly a graduate in the science of delivering the ball."[4]

The unorganized baseball action of Southern California continued year-round, pitting town teams, company teams, and barnstorming teams against one another. During the winter, the rosters were augmented by major and minor leaguers who needed to pick up some extra cash. Over the next three years, it was in this environment that young Walter honed his pitching skills, if indeed they needed honing.

As Johnson readily admitted, his gift for pitching was not of his own doing, but God-given: "From the first time I held a ball," he explained, "it settled in the palm of my right hand as though it belonged there and, when I threw it, ball, hand and wrist, and arm and shoulder and back seemed to all work together."[5] His signature pitching motion was unique — a short windmill-style windup followed by a sweeping sidearm delivery. During the first part of his career he relied almost exclusively on a fastball (he developed a good curve around 1913) which inspired Ring Lardner to comment, "He's got a gun concealed on his person. They can't tell me he throws them balls with his arm."[6]

In April 1906, a former teammate arranged a job for Walter with Tacoma in the Northwestern League. After one exhibition outing, Walter was released, but another ex-teammate landed him a job playing for the Weiser (Idaho) team in the semipro Southern Idaho League. In Weiser, he was paid $90 a week, ostensibly to work for the local telephone company, but actually to play baseball on weekends. There was plenty of time to enjoy hunting and fishing in the nearby mountains during the week. Pitching until July for Weiser, Johnson racked up a 7-1 record, then returned to his California home.

It wasn't until after Walter returned for a second season in Weiser and was on his way to a 14-2 mark that his pitching prowess came to the attention of major-league baseball. "The Weiser Wonder" posted a 0.55 ERA while striking out 214 batters in 146 innings. Manager Joe Cantillon of the Washington Senators began receiving telegrams touting Johnson's feats and the wire services were spreading far and wide the story of the young pitcher's string of 77 scoreless innings, which included back-to-back no-hitters. Finally, Cantillon sent an injured catcher, Cliff Blankenship, west on a scouting trip. Blankenship persuaded the young phenom to accept a Washington contract. The 19-year-old was so reluctant to accept the offer that he demanded a train ticket to return home to California in case he didn't make good, and insisted on wiring his parents to obtain their permission to sign.

On July 22, 1907, a large crowd came to the Weiser depot to see him off. As Johnson said goodbye to his pals, there were tears in his eyes. A group of appreciative Weiser fans had tried to convince him to stay, offering to set him up with a cigar store on the town square. Johnson thanked them, but declined the offer. "You know how you are at 19," he explained later. "You want to see things."[7]

The team to which Walter Johnson reported had never finished higher than sixth in the American League, but their highly touted youngster was an immediate success. After Johnson's debut game against the Tigers, Detroit hurler Bill Donovan called him "the best raw pitcher I have ever seen."[8] The rookie posted a 1.88 ERA in 110 1/3 innings, but it wasn't enough to save the Senators from a 49-102 mark, 43½ games behind Detroit.

Walter's presence in Washington's rotation made scant difference during the next two seasons. After improving to seventh place in 1908, the woeful Nats returned to the cellar in 1909, finishing 42-110, 56 games out of first and 20 games behind the seventh-place St. Louis Browns. This is not to say that Johnson pitched badly, although he must have been extremely disappointed with his 13-25 won-lost mark in 1909. His 2.22 ERA that year was better than average, and his 164 strikeouts ranked second in the league. In 1908, Walter recorded one of the greatest pitching performances of his life over the Labor Day weekend. With his pitching staff in shambles, manager Cantillon sent the sturdy Johnson to the mound in New York for three consecutive starts over a four-day period. Walter didn't disappoint, shutting out the Highlanders on six, four, and two hits, in a feat that electrified the baseball world.

In 1910, with Johnson posting a 25-17 record with a 1.36 ERA and 313 strikeouts, the Washington team improved to seventh place. This marked the beginning of a 10-year run of 20-victory seasons for the big right-hander, who acquired the nicknames of "The Big Train" for the blinding speed of his fast ball, and "Barney," after race car driver Barney Oldfield, for his flamboyant motoring habits. During this decade, the Senators achieved some degree of respectability, finishing second in 1912 and 1913. In 1918, they were closing in on the Red Sox and Indians when the government's "work or fight" order brought the curtain down on the baseball season on Labor Day with Washington four games out, in third place.

Washington's improved performance during the second decade of the twentieth century was due mostly to Walter Johnson's pitching. This can be illustrated by a breakdown of its won-lost record into games where Walter was awarded the decision and games won or lost by other pitchers:

Johnson: 265-143, .650
Others: 490-594, .452
Total: 755-737, .507

That Johnson recorded as many losses as he did was due to the mediocre quality of his team's batting and fielding. This lack of support is reflected by the fact that he holds major-league records for number of 1-0 wins (38) as well as losses (26).

Walter's peak years were 1912-13, when he went 33-12 and 36-7, winning a Chalmers automobile as American League MVP during the latter year. He was now admired all over America not only for his pitching exploits and his fierce competitiveness, but also for the modesty, humility and dignity with which he conducted himself, never arguing with umpires, berating his teammates for their errors, brushing back hitters or using "foreign substances" on the baseball. At a time when many ballplayers were ruffians and drunkards, Walter was never in a brawl and didn't patronize saloons.

During the summer of 1913, Walter Johnson met the love of his life, Hazel Lee Roberts, the daughter of Nevada's congressman. They renewed their acquaintance when Walter returned from Kansas in 1914 and their romance soon became the talk of Washington society. The couple was married June 24, 1914, with the Chaplain of the U.S. Senate officiating. Their marriage was blessed with six children, of whom five lived to adulthood.

Walter's string of 20-win seasons was broken in 1920 when a combination of a bad cold, a sore arm, and pulled leg muscles limited him to an 8-10 mark in only 21 appearances. He did pitch his first and only no-hitter in the big leagues, on July 1 against the Red Sox. Although his health returned in 1921 and he posted a 17-14 record, tragedy struck when Frank Johnson died of a stroke in July and two-year-old daughter Elinor died from influenza in December. Burdened with the memories of these tragedies, Walter and Hazel sold their farm and moved away from Coffeyville, eventually making Bethesda, Maryland, their year-round home.

Johnson decided to make 1924, his 18th major-league season, his last hurrah, and planned to become the owner of a team in the Pacific Coast League following the season. But Washington owner Clark Griffith finally had assembled a team worthy of its

pitching ace, and the Senators captured their first American League pennant. A rejuvenated Walter Johnson was the key to their victory and was the league's MVP, delivering a 23-7 record and leading the league in wins, ERA, strikeouts and shutouts.

Facing John McGraw's New York Giants in the opening game of one of the most dramatic World Series of all time, Walter pitched well but lost 4-3 in 12 innings at Griffith Stadium. Perhaps still tired from that 165-pitch effort, he turned in a lackluster performance in the fifth game, losing 6-2 in the Polo Grounds. The Senators were now one game away from elimination and it looked as though Walter Johnson might never have another chance at World Series glory.

In the sixth game, however, Washington rallied for a 2-1 win behind Tom Zachary to set the stage for the seventh game. On a beautiful Indian summer afternoon, as the Giants and Senators battled to the finish, an ovation echoed across Griffith Stadium when Johnson headed for the bullpen in the sixth inning. In the top of the ninth, manager Bucky Harris, who had just singled in two runs to tie the score at 3-3, called the Big Train in to pitch. He handed him the ball with the words, "You're the best we've got, Walter. We've got to win or lose with you."[9]

Walter didn't disappoint his manager, or his millions of fans, holding the Giants scoreless for four innings, pitching his way into and out of one jam after another. Twice, after giving intentional walks to Ross Youngs, he fanned major-league RBI champ George Kelly. Washington secured its only world championship in the bottom of the 12th inning, when Muddy Ruel scored on an Earl McNeely ground ball that hit a pebble and bounced over the head of Giants third baseman Fred Lindstrom.

Following his World Series triumph, Johnson traveled to California, visiting his boyhood home in Olinda, pitching an exhibition game against Babe Ruth, visiting Hollywood movie studios and trying to wrap up ownership of a PCL team. After the purchase fell through, he decided to return to Washington for yet another big-league campaign. 1925 was a superb season for Washington. The Senators won the pennant handily and Walter delivered his final 20-win season while setting a record for the highest batting average by a pitcher, .433. But 1925's World Series turned out to be the exact opposite of the 1924 triumph. After Walter notched 4-1 and 4-0 wins, disaster struck in the seventh game on a muddy, rainy day in Pittsburgh. In a game which should never have been played, Walter and his team went down to a 9-7 defeat.

After 1927, his final season, Walter Johnson managed for a year at Newark in the International League, then returned to Washington, where he served as manager for four seasons. He also managed at Cleveland from 1933-35, where he was constantly under attack by the local press. Although his managerial style was criticized as too easy-going, it should be noted that his teams had an overall winning percentage of .550.

The biggest tragedy of Walter's later years, though, was Hazel's death at age 36 on August 1, 1930, apparently the result of exhaustion from a cross-country drive during one of the hottest summers on record. After he lost the woman he idolized, a cloud of melancholy descended over the rest of Johnson's life, darkening what should have been tranquil, happy years of retirement on his Mountain View Farm in the Maryland countryside.

During his later years, Walter kept busy on the farm, served as Montgomery County commissioner, was brought back by the Senators in 1939 as their broadcaster, and made an unsuccessful run as a Republican for a seat in the U.S. Congress. On June 12, 1939, along with such other greats as Babe Ruth, Ty Cobb, and Honus Wagner, Johnson was inducted into the newly-created Baseball Hall of Fame in Cooperstown, New York. During World War II, he made several brief playing appearances in war bond games, including serving up pitches to Ruth in Yankee Stadium.

After an illness of several months caused by a brain tumor, Walter Johnson died in Washington at age 59 on December 10, 1946, and is buried next to Hazel at Union Cemetery, in Rockville, Maryland.

Note: This biography originally appeared in David Jones, ed., *Deadball Stars of the American League* (Washington, D.C.: Potomac Books, Inc., 2006).

## SOURCES

In addition to the sources in the Notes, the author also consulted:

Lane, F. C., "At Coffeyville with Walter Johnson." *Baseball Magazine*, April 1915.

Thomas, Henry W. "The Weiser Wonder," (Walter Johnson in Idaho), in *Grandstand Baseball Annual* (Downey, California: Joseph M. Wayman, 1995).

Thomas, Henry W. and Charles W. Carey, "The California Comet—Walter Johnson in the Golden State," *Grandstand Baseball Annual*, 1995.

## NOTES

1   Frank Graham, *Baseball Magazine*, February 1947.

2   J. Conrad Guest, "Ty Cobb talks about the greatest pitcher he ever faced," Detroit Athletic Co., at:https://www.detroitathletic.com/blog/2013/01/02/ty-cobb-talks-about-the-greatest-pitcher-he-ever-faced/

3   Shirley Povich, *Washington Post*, December 12, 1946 - two days after Johnson's death.

4   Henry W. Thomas, *Walter Johnson, Baseball's Big Train* (Arlington, Virginia: Phenom Press, 1995), 12.

## 20-GAME LOSERS

5 National Baseball Hall of Fame site, http://baseballhall.org/hof/johnson-walter

6 Chris Jensen, *Baseball State by State: Major and Negro League Players, Ballparks, Museums* (Jefferson, North Carolina: McFarland, 2012), 106.

7 James E. Odenkirk, "**Seven—Come Eleven,**" *The Journal of the Emeritus College at ASU*. **https://emerituscollege.asu.edu/sites/default/files/ecdw/EVoice10/7come11.html**

8 Wild Bill Donovan, quoted in *Washington Post*, August 3, 1907.

9 National Baseball Hall of Fame site, http://baseballhall.org/hof/johnson-walter

# TIM KEEFE

## BY CHARLIE BEVIS

ONE OF THE GREATEST PITCHERS IN 19th-century major-league baseball, Tim Keefe won 342 games and still ranks among the top 10 pitchers in lifetime victories. He was known for his change-of-pace pitch, which he used to establish a still-standing major-league record of 19 consecutive victories in 1888. "No more graceful, skillful and strategic pitcher ever tossed a ball over the plate to the bewilderment and dismay of opposing batsmen," one writer wrote of Keefe in 1890.[1] In addition to his pitching prowess, Keefe was also a leader in the Brotherhood of Professional Base Ball Players, which led a revolt of National League ballplayers to form the ill-fated Players League in 1890.

Timothy John Keefe was born on January 1, 1857, to Irish immigrants Patrick and Mary (Leary) Keefe, who at the time of his birth resided in Cambridge, Massachusetts.[2] However, Tim was actually born in neighboring Somerville, probably at the home of a maternal relative.[3] One of seven children, he had one older brother (Daniel) and five younger sisters (Katherine, Mary, Margaret, Ellen, and Anne). Tim's father worked as a carpenter to support the family. By 1870 his father moved the family from Cambridge to Somerville, to the Inman Square neighborhood that straddles the town line between Cambridge, the location of prestigious Harvard University, and working-class Somerville.[4]

Where Keefe received his early education is unclear. By age 13 he and his older brother were listed as students in the 1870 federal census, presumably attending the Somerville public schools. Keefe likely attended Somerville High School in the footsteps of his older brother.[5] Whether or not Keefe graduated from high school is unknown.

After his schooling, Keefe, like his father, worked as a carpenter.[6] According to Keefe family legend, Tim's father encouraged his son to learn mathematics and science, to be more of an engineer than just a simple carpenter, and disliked his forays into baseball.[7] But Keefe kept at baseball, playing for local amateur teams and steadily working his way up the ranks. In 1877 he devoted more time to baseball than to carpentry when he played for the Our Boys team, based in Boston, which played a schedule during the week, not just on Saturdays, that ranged from college and independent professional teams to the Boston team in the National League.

An incident in the fall of 1877 helped to shape Keefe's attitude about professional baseball in relation to making a living as a carpenter, while also establishing his strong feelings about labor-management relations. Keefe had worked 11 days between October 26 and November 8 to build a house on a lot of land on Springfield Street in Somerville, for which he had a verbal agreement to be paid $22 for labor and materials. When the property owner, who lived in Cambridge, took advantage of the Somerville carpenter and refused to pay him, Keefe sued him and filed a mechanic's lien on the property.[8] Keefe decided that if it took these lengths to collect wages as a carpenter, he would be just as well off as a professional baseball player. It was also one of the last times that Keefe acknowledged himself as "Timothy J. Keefe of Somerville," as indicated in the land-lien recording. He moved out of his family's house in Somerville, became an itinerant ballplayer, and aspired to be a landowner in the more respected town of Cambridge.

In 1878 Keefe became a full-time professional ballplayer with the team based in the town of Westboro, about 25 miles west of Boston, where he played third base and outfield and occasionally pitched.[9] When the team relocated to the town of Clinton midway through the 1878 season to use its new ballfield, Keefe stayed on. He played in the inaugural games staged at the site of today's Fuller Field in Clinton, which Guinness World Records recognizes as the oldest baseball diamond in continuous use.[10]

Keefe played for four teams during the 1879 season. He began with Clinton, but when the team relocated to Natick in June 1879, Keefe left the team. He wasn't out of work long. Keefe caught on with the Utica, New York, team in the National Association, an East Coast league with teams that spanned geographically from Massachusetts to Washington, D.C. In mid-June Utica was on a road trip through Massachusetts and was seeking a new pitcher to reverse its losing ways. After Keefe pitched Utica to victory in an exhibition game in Boston against Harvard University, Keefe became the team's new pitcher.[11] When the Utica team disbanded in mid-July, Keefe joined the New Bedford, Massachusetts, team in the same circuit, which was managed by Jim Mutrie. After debuting in the pitcher's box on July 22 with a victory over Brockton, Keefe became New Bedford's regular pitcher. However, by mid-September, New Bedford was one of just four remaining teams in the National Association, in which the Albany, New York, team had edged the Washington Nationals for first place. Keefe left the New Bedford team to join the Albany team and pitched two games at the tail-end of its 1879 season.

Keefe was Albany's chief pitcher in 1880 in the three-team National Association, where he compiled a 7-9 league record, and pitched in numerous exhibition games against major-league teams, before Albany disbanded in early July. He made his major-league debut as an umpire in Boston on July 21. Once again, Keefe wasn't unemployed for long, as the Troy team in the National League, just ten miles upriver from Albany, signed him. Keefe was victorious in his major-league debut on August 6, 1880. In this era of one-man pitching staffs, Keefe spelled pitcher Mickey Welch for a dozen games the rest of the 1880 season, compiling a 6-6 record with a delivery the *Troy Daily Times* called "very deceptive, hard to hit, and full of curves."[12]

Because Keefe had experienced unlimited mobility in his first three years of full-time professional baseball, he expected to parlay his brief time with Troy into a better deal with another major-league team. However, the National League ballclub owners had agreed to implement the reserve clause for the 1880 season. It allowed each club to protect five players each season from jumping to another team. Keefe was one of the five players on Troy's reserve list for the 1881 season.[13] Because he was reserved, Keefe was compelled to accept Troy's salary offer of $1,500 for the 1881 season and couldn't negotiate to play for other teams.[14] When Troy reserved Keefe again for the 1882 season, he tried to hold out for more money, but had to settle for the same $1,500 salary. "I was considered a robber because I held out for $2,100," Keefe recalled later in life about being one of the earliest holdouts in baseball history.[15] With his 1877 mechanic's-lien experience fresh in his mind, Keefe embarked on a decade-long quest for increased fairness to players in baseball contracts, which culminated in his involvement with the Brotherhood of Professional Base

Ball Players in 1885 and the formation of the Players League in 1890.

For the 1881 and 1882 seasons, Keefe and Welch split Troy's pitching duties, which then still required an underhand delivery; Buck Ewing and Bill Holbert alternated at catcher. Keefe had more opportunities to pitch in 1881, since a rule change that year moved the pitcher 50 feet from home plate, from 45 feet, which encouraged managers to use a two-man pitching staff. Keefe had an undistinguished pitching record with the mediocre Troy team, 18-27 in 1881 and 17-26 in 1882, over an 84-game schedule.

As one of the smallest cities by population in the National League, Troy was forced out of the National League after the 1882 season to make room for a team in the far more populous New York City. In September 1882, viewing the probable disbanding of the Troy franchise, various ballclubs from the American Association and the National League made offers to the better Troy players, such as Keefe and Ewing, for the 1883 season, which the *Troy Daily Times* regularly reported to readers. When it became public that the National League owners, at their league meeting on September 22, had voted to expel Troy, the imminent demise of the Troy franchise set off a flurry of rumors. Ewing was the prize, as he was considered the best catcher in the league. He enticed a $2,800 salary offer from the Detroit ballclub, and eventually signed for $3,100 with owner John Day of the New York ballclub in the National League that was in essence replacing Troy.[16]

With Day outbidding other owners for the services of Ewing, Keefe was able to negotiate a hefty salary increase for himself by deftly playing Day against both the Troy management and other bidders. As the *New York Herald* reported in mid-October, "The [Troy] players have been coquetting, however, to a considerable extent, holding off from signing with the various managers, and thereby increasing the bidding by saying that they intended remaining in Troy, while at the same time they declined signing with that club."[17] Keefe no doubt relished his final interaction with the Troy club at an October 10 meeting at which management agreed to his salary demand, but he then refused to sign a contract to that effect and left the meeting.[18] Three days later the *Troy Daily Times* reported that several Troy players had signed with the New York City team.[19] Keefe signed with Day for a $2,800 salary, nearly double his Troy salary, which was good for both the 1883 and 1884 seasons.

Day wound up obtaining New York City ballclubs in both the National League and American Association, so he had Jim Mutrie split up the signed players between the two teams. Day already had John Ward as the primary pitcher for the National League team, so Mutrie made Mickey Welch the change pitcher there while Keefe was assigned to the Metropolitans team that Mutrie would manage in the American Association. Welch later said that the decision to allocate pitchers was based on the fact that Welch pitched better to catcher Ewing, the key Troy player, while Keefe was best with Holbert.[20] Keefe may have volunteered to play for the Metropolitans, to reunite with Mutrie from their days at New Bedford and to pitch to batters who had never seen his delivery before. Also, in the fall of 1882, the American Association and National League didn't recognize each other's reserve clause, so in theory Keefe had greater flexibility for future salary negotiations with the Metropolitans (although that changed in February 1883, partially as a result of Day's signing of Ewing and Keefe). By early November, Keefe was firmly affixed to the Metropolitans roster in the American Association.[21]

Mutrie paired Keefe with Jack Lynch as the Metropolitans' two-man pitching rotation in 1883, for the lengthened 98-game schedule, and in 1884, when the schedule was expanded again, to 112 games. Keefe, who had been a mediocre pitcher with Troy, blossomed with the Metropolitans. He racked up impressive pitching records of 41-27 and 37-17 during his two years with the Metropolitans, including a league-leading 359 strikeouts in 1883. In 1884 Keefe led the Metropolitans to the American Association pennant, before they faced the National League champion Providence Grays in a best-of-three-games World Series. Keefe lost both of the first two games, then umpired the third, inconsequential game.

With his $2,800 salary with the Metropolitans, Keefe earned far more than he'd ever make as a carpenter. He began to wear tailored suits, to emulate a well-heeled Cambridge citizen, which distanced himself from the blue-collar background of his father, a carpenter, and his brother, a plumber. He taught himself subjects to compensate for his lack of a college education, studying accounting to understand business and shorthand to take good notes of meetings. In New York he was exposed to the theater and other social activities of wealthy people that he could never experience in ethnically stratified Boston, which provided few such opportunities for those of Irish ancestry.

Keefe's performance with the Metropolitans led Day to hatch a plan to reunite Keefe with his former Troy teammate Mickey Welch as the pitchers for the 1885 season on his National League team, to be managed by Mutrie. Day orchestrated a ruse to transfer Keefe and teammate Dude Esterbrook from Day's American Association team to his National League team by having Mutrie take them both on a boat trip to Bermuda. On the ship Mutrie gave both players their ten-day release from their contracts with the Metropolitans, and then 11 days later signed them to National League contracts.[22] Day and Mutrie had to hide the two players from the other major-league teams because at the time the ten-day release worked like today's waiver wire, so any team could acquire the player's contract during that 10-day period before the player was freed from the reserve clause and could negotiate with other teams.

In signing with Day's National League team, Keefe seems to have negotiated a three-year contract, since he received the same $3,000 salary for each of the 1885, 1886, and 1887 seasons. Given his performance in 1885 and 1886, he almost certainly would have desired to dicker with Day about an increased salary, but there is no public record of such activity as there would be in his salary-negotiation attempts just a few years later. Keefe also likely received a sizeable salary advance in 1885 from his future earnings, since he began to invest in real estate at this time. Keefe cautiously dipped his toe into the real-estate market by investing $2,000 into a mortgage on a property in his hometown of Somerville, whose owner was required to repay the $2,000 plus interest within one year or the property would revert to Keefe.[23]

Keefe made his New York City debut in the National League on April 24, 1885, with the team now known informally as the Giants, which had six future Hall of Fame players (Keefe, Welch, Buck Ewing, Roger Connor, John Ward, and Jim O'Rourke). Behind Keefe's 32-13 pitching mark, the New York Giants made a run at the National League pennant, but finished in second place behind the champion Chicago team, led by John Clarkson, a Cambridge native.

Transferring to the New York Giants changed Keefe's life in many ways, most notably situating him as a teammate of John Ward, who had recently graduated with a law degree from Columbia College. Ward led the players' revolt against the National League owners, which began with the establishment of the Brotherhood of Professional Base Ball Players in October 1885; at the group's first meeting in November 1886, Ward was named president and Keefe was selected to be secretary-treasurer.[24] Ward often characterized the negotiation plight of the professional baseball player as no better than that of livestock or slaves. Given Keefe's early experiences in Troy with baseball negotiations, he completely agreed with that assessment. Although he was now well paid, Keefe still fought for the rights of the average ballplayer.

Keefe had his finest National League season in 1886, when he led the league with 42 wins, 62 complete games, and 535 innings pitched, as the league expanded its schedule to 126 games. The key to his pitching success was his brain, not his brawn. Throughout the 1880s, Keefe successfully adapted to continual rule changes that modified how and from where pitchers could throw the ball, lowered the number of balls a batter needed for a walk, and elongated season schedules.

"Keefe is said to be one of the most scientific pitchers in the country—that is, he uses his head as well as his hands while in the box," the *Boston Globe* commented in 1885, adding that Keefe had the lowest ratio of hits per nine-inning game in the league.[25] Keefe had similar speed and the curveball of other pitchers, but deception set him apart from the other top pitchers of the era. "His strength, however, was in deceiving the batsman," the *New York Tribune* explained. "His real effectiveness lay in his change of pace. He could pitch a speedy ball with the same preliminary movements as he used with a slow cut-curve; consequently the batsman never knew just what kind of a ball to expect when he was pitching."[26]

"Change of pace for pitchers was important in those days," Keefe said decades later. "It was then, as now, largely a case of outguessing the batter."[27] In this regard, he gave a lot of credit to his catcher, Buck Ewing. "People who followed the game say that I was a pretty good pitcher myself. Well, anybody could pitch if Ewing was catching them," Keefe believed. "He knew how to steady a pitcher, knew all the points of the batsmen in the league and used those points to great advantage. He was always constantly up to the many tricks of the game and never forgot a weakness of his opponents."[28]

Besides pitching at different speeds, Keefe threw with different arm motions, often side-arm and underhand (submarine style, in today's parlance) even though the overhand delivery had been legalized in 1884. He also made liberal use of the entire pitcher's box, throwing from different angles (not simply straight on to the batter) and taking multiple steps before releasing the ball, not always pitching from a set position. Keefe was a master of the multistep hop, skip, and jump delivery, which he described in 1888 as combining "plenty of speed and strength and a series of gymnastics to terrify the batter," in which "the pitcher had the batter completely at his mercy."[29] As Keefe recalled later in life, "We were pitching from a 50-foot distance then, and honestly, I sometimes used to wonder how they even hit us, with those advantages which we had."[30]

Midway through the 1886 season, Keefe purchased a piece of land in Cambridge that totaled 29,950 square feet (about three-quarters of an acre) on the northerly side of Cambridge Street, between Irving Street and Trowbridge Street.[31] Keefe paid $2,000 cash and financed the remainder of the $5,614.50 purchase price with a mortgage taken back by the seller, Mary Brown, wife of Frank Brown of Baltimore. The land, about one-quarter mile from Harvard and across the street from the estate of Frederick Rindge, seemed to Keefe to be ripe for development.[32]

After he purchased this land in Cambridge, newspaper accounts almost always referred to Keefe or his family as being from Cambridge, not from his real home in Somerville at 54 Springfield Street. For example, in the summer of 1887, the *New York Times* reported that "Keefe, of the New-Yorks, has gone to Cambridge, Mass., where his father died yesterday."[33] Patrick Keefe actually died in Somerville and had lived in Somerville for nearly 20 years.[34] Keefe, who was born in Somerville and had resided there since he was a boy, likely perpetuated the myth that his home was in Cambridge, since this highbrow address was far more prestigious than working-class Somerville. This myth helped to support his persona as the gentlemanly "Sir Timothy," the nickname he acquired around 1888 based on his unflappable demeanor and desire for fairness. The "from Cambridge" line also made for good association with another great nineteenth-century pitcher, John Clarkson, who truly hailed from Cambridge.

In 1887 a rule change required Keefe to abandon the "hop, skip, and jump" delivery by pitching from a fixed position, with the "pitcher compelled to keep both feet on the ground and face the batter before delivering the ball," and keep his right foot on the back line of the pitcher's box and allowed to take only one step forward.[35] Other rule changes were instituted that year to reduce the advantage of the pitcher, such as needing four strikes for a strikeout (up from three) and five balls for a walk (down from six), and allowing a hit batsman to take first base. Batters also were credited with a base hit for a walk that year. While the new rules stifled the success of many pitchers that year, Keefe adapted by focusing more on his scientific approach to deceiving the batter.

Keefe followed up his fantastic 1886 season with a solid 35-19 record in 1887, which included one tie game that generated some everlasting fame. On August 20 Keefe held a 5-3 New York lead in the top of the ninth inning when Philadelphia loaded the bases with no outs. Pitcher Dan Casey, the next hitter, "then raised the crowd to its feet by hitting safely to right, bringing in McGuire and Irwin" to tie the game.[36] When the Giants failed to score in the bottom of the ninth, the game ended 5-5. Thus began the inspiration for baseball's most famous poem, contend Jim Moore and Natalie Vermilyea, authors of the book *Ernest Thayer's "Casey at the Bat": Background and Characters of Baseball's Most Famous Poem*. Moore and Vermilyea postulate that Thayer, then living in San Francisco, read about Casey's exploits in *The Sporting News*, which included the phrase "Casey was at the bat," and modeled the pitching character in his poem after Keefe.[37]

Keefe and many of the Giants (including John Ward, who had married actress Helen Dauvray during the 1887 season) participated in a postseason baseball tour in the fall of 1887, which began in New Orleans and culminated in San Francisco, where Thayer did interview the Giants and cover several of their games for the *San Francisco Examiner*. One game in particular seemed to draw Thayer's attention, the November 26 game against Stockton, which the Giants won, 26-0. Men named Billy Cooney and Dan Flynn played for Stockton that day. Cooney and Flynn were the exact names of two characters in Thayer's poem, published in June 1888.[38]

During the winter of 1888, a New York writer wrote about Keefe's dissatisfaction with the reserve clause that held him captive to the Giants: "It is true that Keefe has been made uneasy by the unbusinesslike and you may say dishonest policy of other club officials. He has said to Mutrie: 'Jim, I think it is not right to compel me to stay in New York and play ball for the money I get from the New York Club, when I have been offered one and one-half times more salary to pitch in another League city as soon as I get my release.' That is all Tim will say, but it is enough. He has been approached by some one in whom he has faith and whom he knows talks with authority. The sum he has been offered is at least $7,500 a season. It is not at all strange, therefore, that Keefe grows restless and talks about the slavery of pitching seven months for $3,000."[39]

Keefe was in no hurry to rejoin the Giants for the 1888 season, as he held out for a higher salary in his contract negotiations with Giants owner John Day. That spring Keefe made his first appearance as a college baseball coach, at Amherst College.[40] In the late nineteenth century, professional baseball players were college baseball coaches only in the sense that they trained players before the season. The student who was captain of the college team was effectively the coach, since he negotiated the team's schedule and made the playing decisions.

Keefe wanted $4,500 to play for the Giants in 1888, a 50 percent increase over his $3,000 salary each of the previous three years; Day offered him a $4,000 salary.[41] The *New York Herald* reported that "Keefe went to his home in Cambridge, Mass., yesterday" to contemplate Day's $4,000 offer.[42] It was during this holdout that Keefe once let it slip that he didn't live in Cambridge, as the *Herald* wrote, when he told a Boston writer that he had "found a telegram from Mr. Day, which had been received at my home in Somerville."[43] Keefe seemed determined to sit out the season if he didn't get what he thought was a fair price for his services: "I might have to wait a long time. They might not send for me this season. I am not trying to play any bluff. When I get my business affairs fixed up and the weather is warmer we will fix it up if they want me, and I will jump in."[44] Keefe held out until May 1 when he finally agreed to Day's $4,000 offer.[45]

Despite the late start, Keefe led the National League with 35 wins and 335 strikeouts during the 1888 season. One reason for his success was that the league expanded to a 140-game schedule that year. This forced Mutrie to use a three-man pitching rotation, which provided Keefe with more rest between starts. A second reason was that Keefe had started to court Clara Helm, a wealthy socialite and the sister of Ward's wife, whom he had met on the train trip from California to the East Coast in February 1888. During his holdout in April, newspapers had falsely reported that the two were to soon wed; Keefe blushingly contradicted the marriage rumor.[46] Clara was a frequent spectator at the Polo Grounds during the 1888 season, often observed "gazing intently" at her boyfriend's effort on the baseball diamond.[47]

The highlight of the 1888 season for Keefe was a 19-game winning streak from June 23 to August 10. This win streak remains the major-league record (through the 2012 season), now shared by Keefe with Giants pitcher Rube Marquard, who tied the record in 1912. On August 14, Keefe was defeated by Chicago in his quest for a 20th consecutive win. Later that evening Keefe and many of the Giants attended a theater show where DeWolf Hopper recited publicly for the first time Thayer's poem "Casey at the Bat."[48]

In the midst of his record winning streak, Keefe defeated Philadelphia on July 28, when for the first time the Giants wore all-black uniforms with white lettering on the shirts.[49] Although later derided as "funeral clothes," the new togs were then called "Nadjy uniforms," based on a popular comic opera then playing in New York City in which one actress wore a "black bat" dress that had splashes of white on an all-black background. Keefe is often said to have sold the uniforms to the Giants, which can't be documented, but he may have pitched the idea for them to the Giants. The Nadjy uniforms were certainly a spark for the new sporting goods firm of Keefe & Becannon, which Keefe started in January 1889.[50]

The Giants won the 1888 National League pennant and played the St. Louis Browns of the American Association in a postseason World Series that fall. Keefe won four games (the first, third, fifth, and eighth games) to propel New York to victory in the best-of-10-games match. After winning the series, Ward participated in Chicago owner Albert Spalding's world tour that winter along with a number of other ballplayers. However, after Ward's ship had left San Francisco for Hawaii, the National League owners announced a fixed salary-classification structure (maximum $2,500) that they proposed to implement without input from the Brotherhood, which would depress salaries and eliminate contract negotiations. Keefe, who was still in New York City opening up his sporting goods store, was thrust into being the Brotherhood spokesperson while Ward was overseas.

After again coaching the Amherst College nine during March 1889, Keefe conducted his second holdout in as many years prior to the 1889 season. This time, though, he presented a better case that he had viable alternatives to pitching for the Giants. Newspapers noted that he was busy getting the Keefe & Becannon sporting goods business off the ground. He also leaked details of his real-estate investment, some of which the newspapers exaggerated. "Another cause for this independence, it is said, is the sudden increase in value of some property owned by Tim at Cambridge, Mass.," the *New York World* reported. "Recently the town officials decided to erect a public library and selected as a site for it the ground owned by Tim … [who] when offered a fair price for the property refused the offer. He had refused several others since, the last being $30,000. Tim, it is said, holds off for $50,000 and is confident of obtaining that sum."[51]

By 1889 the library in Cambridge was already under construction across the street from Keefe's property on Cambridge Street, on land donated by Frederick Rindge; what could possibly inflate the $5,614 purchase price of Keefe's land were two new high-school buildings that were to be built partially on other Rindge land, but which needed further land acquisitions.[52] Cambridge English High School and the Manual Training School were both built in 1892 but, unfortunately for Keefe, the town planners decided not to expand north of Cambridge Street to acquire land for the new public high schools.

Keefe wanted a $5,000 salary to play for the Giants during the 1889 season, but Day offered him only $4,000, the same level as the previous season. "Yes, it is true that I have asked for an increase," Keefe told newspaper reporters. "I have played good ball for the New York Club, the organization has made money, and I do not think that my demands are unjust. … If my terms are not agreed to I will attend to my sporting goods business and give up the diamond until matters are arranged to my satisfaction."[53] Day responded, "Keefe is a nice gentleman and a clever ball player, but I don't think that his services or those of any other baseball player are worth more than my [$4,000] figure."[54]

Two weeks into the 1889 season, Keefe and Day were still at loggerheads in their salary negotiation. On May 9 newspapers reported that Keefe said he'd accept $4,500, but not Day's offer of $4,000.[55] That day, with all four Giants pitchers either injured or sick, Buck Ewing pitched in the game against Boston. New York won, but clearly Keefe's services were needed. Day caved in and offered Keefe the proposed $4,500 compromise.[56] Keefe accepted and pitched his first game on May 10.

Keefe produced only 28 wins in 1889, as he missed a seventh straight 30-win season during a year of many distractions. His Brotherhood activities sapped some energy, including the meeting on July 14 at which the Brotherhood quashed an earlier plan to stage a strike and instead hatched a new plan to form a competing Players League for the 1890 season. Keefe also shed his bachelor days when he married Clara Helm on August 19, 1889, in Worcester, Massachusetts.[57]

Despite the many distractions during the 1889 season, the Giants won a second straight National League pennant and met Brooklyn of the American Association in the World Series that fall. Mutrie had overused Keefe down the stretch in order to edge Boston in the neck-and-neck battle for the pennant, with Keefe nailing a victory on the last day of the season to clinch the title. However, a tired Keefe was ineffective in the opening game of the 1889 World Series, and only pitched briefly in relief in one other appearance, as Ed Crane started five (and won four) of the eight meaningful games in the Series to lead the Giants to victory over Brooklyn.

In November 1889 the Brotherhood announced the formation of the Players League to compete with the National League. Keefe and most of the Giants players joined the New York team in the Players League, which was financed by Edward Talcott, Cornelius Van Cott, and Edwin McAlpin. Keefe and Ewing were the player representatives on the club's board of directors.[58] Keefe's sporting goods firm, Keefe & Becannon, was awarded a three-year contract to supply the official Players League baseball, which became known as The Keefe Official Ball.[59] Keefe & Becannon also supplied uniforms and equipment to many of the Players League teams. Keefe's firm made a huge bet that the league would succeed, calling the firm in its advertisements "Outfitters to the Players' National (Brotherhood) League and Manufacturer of The Keefe Official Ball."[60]

While Keefe was intellectually committed to the Players League movement, he wasn't entirely committed financially. In mid-December 1889, Keefe transferred ownership of his real-estate property in Cambridge to his mother.[61] This move ensured that creditors couldn't reach this asset for legal judgments against him (or his firm Keefe & Becannon, which was a partnership, not a corporation) if the Players League failed. Six days after Keefe transferred his real-estate property to his mother, the New York Giants served papers on Ward as they pursued a legal injunction to stop Ward (and by implication Keefe and the other confederates) from jumping to the Players League and thus enforce the reserve-clause aspect of his National League contract.

Among a lot of nasty name-calling and legal action, the Players League fought for spectators with its National League counterparts. Keefe had an uninspiring season with the Players League Giants. He secured his 300th career victory on June 4, although to no fanfare at the time. His season ended prematurely when he broke the index finger on his pitching hand on August 19. He tried to pitch on September 8, but lasted only one inning.

Almost all teams in both leagues lost money. The competition in New York City financially crippled Day of the Giants, as he lost tens of thousands of dollars and was nearly bankrupt. While the Giants of the Players League came close to breaking even, Talcott and the financial backers took advantage of Day's precarious financial situation and quickly negotiated a deal after the season ended. They agree to merge the two teams with the resulting team to play in the National League and the Talcott faction, not Day, in charge. With the flagship New York team abandoning the Players League, the league itself soon imploded and ceased to exist by January 1891.

Keefe was in serious financial difficulties after the collapse of the Players League. Since Keefe & Becannon was a partnership, Keefe was responsible for his share of the firm's unpaid debts. The firm had lost money on the first year of the contract to supply baseballs to the Players League, but expected to make it up in the next two years. The firm was also owed money by the teams that had bought uniforms and equipment. Creditors soon sued the firm and its two partners for unpaid bills. After the firm of Keefe & Becannon was officially dissolved in July 1891, a receiver paid off its obligations at cents on the dollar.[62]

During the winter of 1891, Keefe re-signed with his old team, the New York Giants of the National League, for the 1891 season. Ever the negotiator, Keefe held out for his $4,500 salary paid in 1890, but settled for a reduction to $3,500 for the season.[63] However, the Giants used Keefe sparingly during the first half of the 1891 season and he was released in July; he then signed with the Philadelphia team.

In the winter of 1892, Keefe returned to college coaching and began a stretch of six straight winters coaching the Harvard baseball team to help its pitchers prepare for the coming season.[64] Harvard was just a quarter-mile from his property in Cambridge, and about a mile from his parents' home in Somerville where he stayed when not in New York City.

Keefe pitched his last major-league game on August 15, 1893, and was released by Philadelphia the next day. The lengthening of the pitching distance to 60 feet 6 inches reduced the effectiveness of the 36-year-old pitcher. He obviously left on good terms, since he umpired Philadelphia's game on August 17. Upon his retirement as a ballplayer, Keefe was the career leader in strikeouts with 2,564 (a record broken by Cy Young in 1908) and had the second-most career victories with 342, just behind Pud Galvin.

By 1894 Keefe continued to suffer financial strain following the Players League debacle, which was compounded by the nation's severe economic depression. To raise money, Keefe sold off the majority of his still-undeveloped Cambridge property (albeit in his mother's name) and retained just a small corner lot on the Trowbridge Street side of Cambridge Street.[65] Reluctantly, Keefe returned to baseball to work as an umpire, a move he regretted. "I did not like umpiring," he later acknowledged. "Did you ever see a man who did?"[66]

Keefe served as a National League umpire from August 3, 1894, to July 6, 1896. He hoped that he could add value to baseball through his integrity and vast knowledge of the game. Instead the ballplayers gave him little respect on the diamond, arguing and complaining about any call that didn't go their way. The fans at the ballpark weren't much better, as Joe Vila of the *New York Sun* recounted in a tale of abuse that Keefe once had to endure when he umpired at the Polo Grounds: "In a grilling battle between the Giants and the Bostons, however, Keefe, absolutely honest, made several close decisions against the New Yorks. Before the game ended Keefe was the target for a volley of abuse. He was hooted and hissed and finally a mob tried to handle him roughly as he made his way to the dressing room. Believe me, boys, Keefe actually broke down and wept. The admirers of former days had turned against him in less than two hours."[67]

After an incident in St. Louis in July 1896, Keefe telegraphed his resignation to the league president, saying: "My sole reason for leaving the field yesterday and for then and there determining to sever my connection with the national game forever is that base ball has reached a stage where it is absolutely disgraceful. ... The continual senseless and puerile kicking [by the ballplayers] at every decision has been infinitely trying to me and I have been considering for some time whether I had not better resign."[68]

Keefe found more respect as an umpire in the Eastern League, where the players were more intent on advancing to the National League than showing up an umpire. He served as a minor-league umpire from August 1896 to September 1897.

The last straw for Keefe with baseball was a snub by Harvard, when the school did not renew its baseball coaching relationship with him for the 1898 season. Harvard instead opted to use the services of Boston Nationals pitcher Ted Lewis, a Williams College graduate. As *Boston Herald* writer Jake Morse reported in his column in *Sporting Life*, "It was a radical change on the part of the Harvard Athletic Committee to appoint a young pitcher like Ted Lewis in place of Tim Keefe, who has been coach at Harvard for so many seasons."[69]

Keefe became a recluse following his snubbing by Harvard. During the summer of 1899 one writer noted, "One rarely hears the name of Tim Keefe mentioned now. The former great pitcher seems to have dropped entirely out of sight and sound."[70] Indeed, over the next quarter-century until his death, Keefe stayed out of the public eye with only rare exceptions.

Keefe chose family over baseball. In 1898 his brother Daniel, a member of the Massachusetts militia, was involved in the Spanish-American War; with a wife and three young children, Keefe's brother could no longer look after their widowed mother. Keefe built two multifamily houses on the remaining piece of land he owned on Cambridge Street in Cambridge, one house at 1653 Cambridge Street and the other at 89 Trowbridge Street.[71] His mother (who technically still owned the property) and his two older sisters, Kate and Mary, moved from Somerville to live in one of the apartments in the house at 1653 Cambridge Street.[72] Keefe, who divided his time between New York City and Cambridge, earned an income from renting apartments in the multifamily buildings. After his mother died in 1909, Keefe moved into the house on Cambridge Street with his sisters, who both never married. By 1910 Keefe was also single, having divorced his wife, Clara.[73] He and his wife did not have any children.

While Keefe remained out of public view, his name carried on in corrupted versions of the poem "Casey at the Bat" that began appearing in about 1900 in a number of anthologies of humorous verse. These versions of Thayer's poem substituted the line "He signaled the pitcher" with "He signaled to Sir Timothy," and more specifically indicated Keefe through the change of the term "the writhing pitcher" to "the New York pitcher."[74]

In February 1906, Keefe consented to an interview to discuss former teammate Buck Ewing, who was critically ill at the time and would die later that year. According to Keefe, Ewing was "the greatest all around ballplayer, I would say without hesitation, that the game has ever produced."[75] Beyond his extensive remarks about Ewing as a ballplayer and leader (he credited Ewing as the reason why Giants won the pennant in 1888 and 1889), Keefe said: "Well, I try to keep up with baseball fairly well. I run in to Boston occasionally to see a game on the American League grounds ... but I can't see really, for the life of me, that the players of today excel those of the period just before the Brotherhood broke up. It seems to me that was the most prosperous time that the game has ever known. Certainly there are no better batters today than there were then."[76]

In July 1912 New York Giants pitcher Rube Marquard tied Keefe's record for 19 consecutive victories. However, as Marquard approached the 19-win threshold, there was no mention of Keefe's name, since most baseball observers believed Marquard was chasing a record of 20 wins set by Pat Luby in 1890. After the fact, Luby's streak was found to be only 17 wins, and only then was Keefe's name thrust into the spotlight as the rightful record holder.[77] If Keefe had an opinion about Marquard tying his record, he did not share it with any baseball writer for publication.

In 1928, *Boston Globe* sportswriter Ford Sawyer ran across Keefe at a Red Sox game at Fenway Park, where "the 70-year-old real estate owner is unknown to the vast majority of the thousands who are urging on their Boston favorites."[78] Keefe, who now regularly attended ballgames once a week, told Sawyer that baseball was "fundamentally the same old game" as back in the 1880s, and that he particularly liked to watch Ty Cobb.

Tim Keefe died on April 23, 1933, in Cambridge and is buried in Cambridge City Cemetery.

In 1936, at the time of the first BBWAA election for the Baseball Hall of Fame, Keefe's pitching exploits for the New York Giants in the 1880s were largely forgotten, as he received just one vote on the

78 ballots cast for the 19th-century stars component of the initial Hall of Fame class.

Keefe was more famous in the 1930s as the mythical pitcher in "Casey at the Bat," since Dan Casey did promotions to further his titular fame from the poem's title. At a "Casey Night" in May 1938, the 76-year-old Casey took swings at a minor-league game in Baltimore. He missed the first two serves from Rogers Hornsby, the former major-league star who was Casey's foil as the pitcher, but on the third pitch he stroked a hit to left field, rather than strike out as his namesake had done in Thayer's poem. As for his success, Casey said, "Hornsby didn't have as much on the ball as Tim Keefe did" back in that inspirational August 1887 game.[79]

In 1964 Keefe was enshrined in the Baseball Hall of Fame by the Veterans Committee. Since he had no children, several nieces and nephews, the children of his younger sister Ellen, represented him at the induction ceremony.[80]

A sign honoring Keefe today adorns Tim Keefe Square in Cambridge, at the corner of Cambridge and Trowbridge Streets, in front of the house at 1653 Cambridge Street where Keefe had lived for the last two decades of his life.

## SOURCES

In addition to the Sources cited in the Notes, the author also consulted Ancestry.com. Baseball-Reference.com, and McNeil, William. *The Evolution of Pitching in Major League Baseball* (Jefferson, North Carolina: McFarland, 2006).

## NOTES

1. *Sporting Life*, May 31, 1890.
2. The *Cambridge Directory* for 1857 lists the Keefe family as living on Columbia Street, near Hampshire Street. The 1860 federal census (Series M653, Roll 508, Page 324) lists the Keefe family as living in the working-class Cambridgeport section of Cambridge.
3. Birth records for 1857 in the Massachusetts State Archives (Volume 106, Page 204).
4. The 1870 federal census (Series M593, Roll 631, Page 396) lists the Keefe family as living in Somerville, but associates no street names with respondents. The *Somerville Directory* lists the family in 1873 as living at Columbia Street, near the marsh, and in 1877 at 68 Concord Avenue. The 1880 federal census (Series T9, Roll 546, Page 339) lists the Keefe family as living at 52 Springfield Street in Somerville, which is located about 50 yards from the Cambridge town line.
5. His brother Daniel "received his education in full at the Somerville grammar and high schools," according to a 1901 biography. See Charles Winslow Hall, *Regiments and Armories of Massachusetts: An Historical Narration of the Massachusetts Volunteer Militia, with Portraits and Biographies of Officers Past and Present* (Boston: W.W. Potter, 1901), 52-53.
6. *Somerville Directory*, 1877. Keefe also reported his occupation as cabinetmaker in the 1880 federal census (Series T9, Roll 805, Page 344), even though he was a professional baseball player by that time.
7. Lee Allen, "Cooperstown Corner," *The Sporting News*, April 4, 1964.
8. Land record dated November 30, 1877, at the Middlesex South Registry of Deeds (Book 1458, Page 103).
9. "The Clintons of '78," *Boston Globe*, March 24, 1889.
10. Karen Nugent, "Heirloom Diamond: Clinton Ball Field Crowned as World's Oldest," *Worcester Telegram*, October 4, 2007.
11. *Boston Globe*, June 14, 1879.
12. *Troy Daily Times*, August 19, 1880.
13. Minutes of the National League meeting held on October 5, 1880.
14. All pre-1890 salary figures are from the National League report reprinted in *Sporting Life* on April 5, 1890.
15. Ford Sawyer, "He Pitched 19 Straight Wins," *Boston Globe*, May 27, 1928.
16. Roy Kerr, *Buck Ewing: A Baseball Biography* (Jefferson, North Carolina: McFarland, 2012), 34-35.
17. *New York Herald*, October 13, 1882.
18. *Troy Daily Times*, October 11, 1882.
19. *Troy Daily Times*, October 14, 1882.
20. John Kieran, "When They Were the People," *New York Times*, January 25, 1938.
21. *New York Clipper*, November 11, 1882.
22. *New York Times*, March 27 and April 13, 1885.
23. Land record dated March 13, 1885, at the Middlesex South Registry of Deeds (Book 1696, Page 197).
24. Bryan Di Salvatore, *A Clever Base-Ballist: The Life and Times of John Montgomery Ward* (New York: Pantheon Books, 1999), 175, 189.
25. *Boston Globe*, October 14, 1885.
26. "A Declining Baseball Star: Timothy J. Keefe, Once the First Pitcher Among Baseball Players," *New York Tribune*, October 4, 1891.

27  Sawyer, "He Pitched 19 Straight Wins."

28  Philip Shirley, "A Chat with Keefe," *Sporting Life*, February 24, 1906.

29  T.J. Keefe, "Curves or Liners: The Vexed Question in Base Ball Circles, *Boston Globe*, October 21, 1888.

30  Sawyer, "He Pitched 19 Straight Wins."

31  Land record dated July 26, 1886, at the Middlesex South Registry of Deeds (Book 1759, Page 132).

32  G.M. Hopkins map of Cambridge, 1886.

33  *New York Times*, July 9, 1887.

34  Death records for 1887 in the Massachusetts State Archives (Volume 383, Page 213); *Somerville Directory*, 1873 to 1887.

35  Keefe, "Curves or Liners."

36  *New York Times*, August 21, 1887.

37  Jim Moore and Natalie Vermilyea, *Ernest Thayer's "Casey at the Bat": Background and Characters of Baseball's Most Famous Poem* (Jefferson, North Carolina: McFarland, 1994), 209.

38  Moore and Vermilyea, *Ernest Thayer's "Casey at the Bat,"* 221.

39  *Sporting Life*, February 9, 1888.

40  *Boston Globe*, March 12, 1888.

41  *Sporting Life*, April 18, 1888; *New York Times*, April 20, 1888.

42  *New York Herald*, April 20, 1888.

43  *Boston Globe*, April 24, 1888.

44  *Sporting Life*, April 25, 1888.

45  *New York Times*, April 27, 1888.

46  *Boston Globe*, April 24, 1988.

47  "Ladies Who Love the Game," *New York World*, May 6, 1888.

48  *New York Times*, August 15, 1888.

49  *New York Times*, July 29, 1888.

50  The Nadjy uniforms were highlighted in a Keefe & Becannon advertisement in *Sporting Life*, March 20, 1889.

51  "Twirler Tim Is Rich," *New York World*, January 14, 1889.

52  "The Rindge Gifts," in *The Cambridge of 1896* edited by Arthur Gilman (Cambridge: Riverside Press, 1896).

53  *New York Times*, April 18, 1889.

54  Ibid.

55  *New York Times*, May 9, 1889.

56  *New York Times*, May 10, 1889.

57  Marriage records for 1889 in the Massachusetts State Archives (Volume 399, Page 480). The marriage was not publicly revealed until four days later when it was reported by newspapers on August 23.

58  *New York Times*, December 10, 1889.

59  *Sporting Life*, December 17, 1889.

60  *Sporting Life*, June 28, 1890.

61  Land record dated December 17, 1889, at the Middlesex South Registry of Deeds (Book 1947, Page 522).

62  *New York Herald*, July 19, 1891.

63  *Sporting Life*, March 21, 1891.

64  *Harvard Crimson*, January 16, 1892.

65  Land record dated March 19, 1894, at the Middlesex South Registry of Deeds (Book 2259, Page 228).

66  Shirley, "A Chat with Keefe."

67  Joe Vila, "Without Mercy is the Average Partisan Base Ball Fan," *Sporting Life*, April 13, 1912.

68  *New Haven Register*, July 9, 1896.

69  *Sporting Life*, November 13, 1897.

70  *Sporting Life*, July 8, 1899.

71  G.W. Bromley & Co.'s *Atlas of Cambridge* shows the property as undeveloped in 1894, but with two houses on it in 1900.

72  The 1900 federal census (Series T623, Roll 656, Page 5) lists Keefe's mother and sisters, along with three boarders who were law students at Harvard, but not Keefe himself. Keefe could not be located within the 1900 census.

73  Keefe reported his marital status as divorced in the 1910 federal census (Series T624, Roll 596, Page 142), He reaffirmed this status in both the 1920 census (Series T625, Roll 707, Page 230) and the 1930 census (Series T626, Roll 916, Page 8).

74  Martin Gardner, *The Annotated Casey at the Bat: A Collection of Ballads About the Mighty Casey* (New York: Clarkson Potter, 1967), 24; *Boston Globe*, September 25, 1917.

75  Shirley, "A Chat with Keefe."

76  Ibid.

77  *Sporting Life*, July 13, 1912.

78  Sawyer, "He Pitched 19 Straight Wins."

79  *Washington Post*, May 20, 1938.

80  Harold Kaese, "Keefe Fanned Mighty Casey," *Boston Globe*, February 9, 1964.

# TED LYONS

## BY WARREN CORBETT

**TED LYONS IS REMEMBERED AS THE** "Sunday pitcher" who started only once a week for much of his career. He made the most of his workdays, finishing nearly three out of four starts with more complete games than any other contemporary pitcher. Forget won-lost record, Lyons said: "A good pitcher is a pitcher who has the ability to go the distance in a lot of games, and to hold opposing clubs to low scores and infrequent hits."[1]

Lyons never played in the minors; he spent his entire career with the Chicago White Sox, who posted a winning record only five times in the 21 years that he wore their uniform. Lyons was one of the most popular players in the team's history, friendly to all and a clubhouse cutup except on the days he pitched, when he never shaved and his teammates knew to stay out of his way.

Theodore Amar Lyons was born on December 28, 1900, in Lake Charles, Louisiana, and grew up on a farm in the heart of Cajun country. He started playing baseball with a rolled-up sock and a broomstick. At 16 he weighed only 135 pounds and had to choke halfway up on his Joe Jackson-model bat. He soon grew bigger. When the Philadelphia Athletics spent spring training in Lake Charles, manager Connie Mack promised to pay the teenager's way through college if he would sign with the A's. "For all he knew," Lyons remarked later, "he might have been paying for an eight-year course—he didn't know whether I was dumb or smart."[2] Lyons turned down the offer.

At Baylor University in Waco, Texas, he earned four varsity letters each in baseball and basketball, plus two in track. The baseball coach told him to forget about pitching and play the outfield. Lyons didn't take that advice, either. He became the team's pitching star. "I studied one term of law and then came to realize I had a little better fastball and curve than I did a vocabulary," he said.[3] (Lyons once said he went to Baylor on a trombone scholarship, but lost his scholarship when someone stomped on his trombone during a fight. That sounds like one of his trademark tall tales.)

In the spring of 1923 the White Sox trained in Seguin, Texas. When several of the big leaguers dropped by Baylor's ball field, Lyons pitched to catcher Ray Schalk. Schalk recommended the young right-hander to manager Kid Gleason. The Sox signed him for a $1,000 bonus as soon as he graduated in June. He spent $428 of his windfall on a new Ford Model-T.

Lyons joined the White Sox in St. Louis. On July 2 he sat in the dugout watching the first major-league game he had ever seen—until Chicago fell behind and acting manager Eddie Collins sent him in to pitch the final inning. "When I walked out on the mound, I felt enclosed," he recalled. "You see, I'd been used to playing on pastures, where when somebody hit a ball you had to stop it from rolling. Well, this field had fences around it. And of course in those days the Browns had big crowds, because they were usually contenders, so there was a lot of noise."[4] He retired the side in order. He pitched eight more times that year with a 6.35 ERA. His only victories came on the same day, when he relieved in both games of a doubleheader.

In 1924 Lyons split his time between starting and relieving, but was not impressive: a 4.87 ERA in 216 1/3 innings. For the next six seasons, 1925-1930, he blossomed into one of the American League's best pitchers, twice leading the league in victories while winning more than 20 games three times and losing 20 once. He accounted for 30 percent of his team's wins and finished in the top 10 in ERA four times. But the Sox rose no higher than fifth place.

On September 19, 1925, Lyons held the Washington Senators hitless until two were out in the ninth. Even the Washington fans were rooting for him, but pinch-hitter Bobby Veach lofted a looping single over the first baseman's head.

Less than a year later, on August 21, 1926, Lyons started against the Red Sox at Fenway Park. The lead-off hitter, Jack Tobin, walked on four pitches. When Lyons threw ball one and ball two to the next batter, manager Collins ordered a reliever to get warm. But Lyons retired that batter, then Baby Doll Jacobson lined to center. Johnny Mostil plucked the ball off his shoetops and doubled Tobin off base to end the inning. Lyons allowed only one more base runner, on an error, and finished his no-hitter by taking a toss from first baseman Earl Sheely and stepping on the bag for the final out.

He became friends with the erudite Princeton alumnus Moe Berg, a utility infielder for the Sox. Lyons said, "He makes up for all the bores in the world."[5] On August 6, 1927, Lyons was scheduled to face the Yankees' Murderers Row lineup. All three White Sox catchers were hurt, and they had just signed a replacement who arrived fat and out of shape. Lyons asked for Berg, who had served as the emergency catcher in only one major-league game. The Sox beat New York, 6-3, as Berg made a spectacular play to tag a runner at the plate.

The educated battery teamed up several more times. "In the years he was to catch me, I never waved off a sign," Lyons said.[6] As the possibly apocryphal story goes, whenever Lyons allowed a runner to reach second base, Berg would stop flashing signs and he and Lyons would speak Greek to call the pitches.[7] The pair later joined Lefty O'Doul on a visit to Japan, where they coached young players and laid the foundation for baseball's popularity in Asia.

Lyons also befriended Chuck Comiskey, the grandson of the Sox owner: "He was there when I was a kid bouncing around the ballpark. He was like a father to me. He was a very moral and high-class man."[8] Years later Comiskey recalled, "I never knew anyone who disliked him or said an unkind word about him."[9]

Following the lead of his manager, Jimmy Dykes, Lyons was a raucous bench jockey and prankster. He and Red Sox outfielder Doc Cramer would try to sneak up on each other so they could smash an egg on the other man's head. Lyons entertained teammates and fans with a never-ending fund of stories. Many of them involved his own (imagined) feats as a hitter. "One day there were two out in the ninth and I hit a pop fly so high that the fans got tired of waiting for it to come down. So they all went home and listened to it drop by turning on the radio."[10] He claimed to have played in an exhibition game at Joliet state prison until the warden ordered him to the bench because his line drives were punching huge holes in the prison wall. In real life, the switch-hitter was considered one of the best-hitting pitchers of his time, with a .233 batting average.

Fortunately for those around him, he was usually good-natured. At 5-foot-11 and 200 pounds, he was a powerful man who roughhoused like an overgrown boy, hoisting teammates and opponents off the ground. The Senators' Buddy Lewis said, "He was probably the strongest man I knew in the big leagues. He could pick me up by the shirt and just shake my damn teeth out."[11] Lyons and Lou Gehrig liked to test their muscles by arm-wrestling. According to Chuck Comiskey, the wrestling matches stopped when Lyons noticed that he was winning too easily. Lyons told Jimmy Dykes, "You can't see it when he's at the plate, but something's wrong with him."[12] (It's not clear whether this happened in 1939, when Gehrig was obviously ill, or the previous year, when the first signs of his physical decline went largely unnoticed.)

Despite his physique, Lyons was not a power pitcher. He struck out only two or three per game; his strikeout rate is the lowest of any Hall of Fame pitcher whose career started after 1920. His money pitch was a sailing fastball that he gripped along the seams and gave a twist as he released it. Today it would be called a cut fastball. The old-time pitching star Ed Walsh, a White Sox coach, encouraged him to use his slow curve as a change-up, and he became a master at changing speeds to keep batters off stride. In his early years he tried to fool hitters with a "pump handle" windup, swinging his arms above his head once, twice, or three times before delivering the ball.

Above all, he knew how to put the ball where he wanted it and seldom walked a batter.

When he lost 20 games in 1929, one of them was historic. On May 24 the White Sox hammered Detroit starter George Uhle for 10 hits and 5 runs in the first five innings. The Tigers battled back against Lyons to tie the score at 5-5 after seven. It stayed that way until the 21st. Lyons pitched 13 consecutive scoreless innings, although he was often in trouble. Uhle was even better, holding the Sox scoreless for 15 rounds and giving up only seven more hits.

Uhle led off the top of the 21st with a bad-hop grounder to second base. He legged it out for his fourth hit of the day, but was gasping when he reached first and was replaced by a pinch-runner. The Tigers went on to score the go-ahead run on Charlie Gehringer's sacrifice fly.

Detroit reliever Lil Stoner held the lead in the bottom of the 21st to make Lyons the loser in a 21-inning complete game. He gave up 24 hits and faced 85 batters. He and Uhle are major-league baseball's last marathon men. No pitcher since has worked 20 or more innings in a game.

During his six-year run as the Sox ace, Lyons carried a heavy workload. He led the AL in complete games and innings pitched twice, and pitched the second-most innings two other times. The load apparently caught up with him in 1931. At age 30 he came down with a sore shoulder and started only 12 games all season. The pain eventually diminished, but the injury changed his career.

"I lost the good stuff on my fastball," Lyons said. "I had to come up with something to keep me in the league. The knuckler rescued me then."[13] He had thrown a knuckleball occasionally before his injury; after 1931 he relied on it more heavily, though he was never a pure knuckleball pitcher. He reinvented himself as a junkball artist, mixing in his slow curve and what was left of his fastball.

Lyons returned to form in 1932 with a 3.28 ERA, although he finished 10-15 for a team that lost 102 games. From 1932-1934 he pitched more than 200 innings every year, but his workload shrank each season as his ERA rose. In 1935 manager Dykes began giving him six days' rest between starts, and he rebounded with a 15-8 record and a 3.02 ERA, his best in eight years.

Dykes designated him as the Sunday pitcher who would start one game of that day's doubleheader. "When I was a kid my mother wouldn't let me play ball on Sunday," Lyons said. "Then for [several] years that's the only day I played."[14] He thrived on the lighter schedule, usually contributing a dozen or more wins each season with a better-than-average ERA. In 1939 he lowered his ERA to 2.76, the best of his career so far, in 21 starts. He was chosen for his only All-Star team, but did not play. (The All-Star Game did not exist when Lyons was in his prime.)

The rookie Ted Williams asked his teammates about the White Sox veteran: "They'd say, 'Well, he's not real fast, but he's *sneaky* fast,' and 'His curve is hittable, but he gets it in good spots,' and 'You've gotta watch his change-up,' and 'He's got a knuckleball,' and 'The one thing you *can't* do, you can't guess with the son of a gun.'" Williams often named Lyons as the one of the toughest pitchers for him to hit: "Lyons was tough and he got tougher the more you faced him, because he'd learn about you by playing those little pitcher-batter thinking games, and he'd usually out-think you."[15] He refined his control even more and led the AL three straight times in fewest walks per nine innings.

"Sunday Teddy's" popularity grew as he grayed. In 1940, when he led the league with four shutouts, the White Sox staged "Ted Lyons Day" and fans lavished gifts and cash on their old favorite. Newsboys who peddled papers outside Comiskey Park pooled their earnings to buy him a $7 shirt. One of the boys, Peter Prevan, said, "The papers were two cents. Ted would buy a paper and give me a quarter. He'd give the other kids dimes for ice cream."[16]

In 1942, his 20th season in the majors, the 41-year-old completed all 20 of his starts, going 14-6 with a league-best 2.10 ERA. Then he joined the Marine Corps. He was too old for the military draft, but he was single without dependents. While he made no patriotic speeches about his decision to enlist, he had seen fellow players who had families sign up to do their part for the war effort. "So, take him away, marines," the *Chicago Tribune's* Irving Vaughn wrote, "but don't lose the return address."[17] Lyons was commissioned a second lieutenant and eventually was promoted to captain.

Contemporary accounts indicate that Lyons spent a fairly comfortable war serving as a physical fitness instructor while pitching for and managing Marine Air Corps baseball teams. Late in 1944 he joined service all-star teams made up mostly of major leaguers, including Ted Williams and Joe DiMaggio, that sailed to the Pacific to entertain the troops. After he faced DiMaggio in one of the games, he complained, "I left the country to get away from DiMaggio, and there he was."[18]

Lyons and Williams became friends during their stay in Hawaii—but only after he reassured the young slugger that, yes, he was as good a hitter as Babe Ruth. Williams also remembered Lyons' great strength: "When he grabbed you, you stayed grabbed."[19] Lyons saw the Cardinals' rising star Stan Musial playing for a Navy team in Hawaii, and said Musial's unique batting stance reminded him of "a kid looking around the corner to see if the cops are coming."[20]

When Lyons left the Marines in November 1945, he was closing in on his 45th birthday. He vowed to keep pitching until he was 50. On April 21, in the first Sunday doubleheader of the 1946 season, he spun eight shutout innings against the Browns, but lost when they scored two unearned runs in the ninth. The next Sunday he went the distance again to beat the Browns, 4-3, for his 260th big-league victory. It was his last. He started three more times and lost them all, though he was never hit hard. He had completed 28 consecutive games, a streak stretching back to 1941.

Poor pitching didn't finish Lyons' career; his new job did. On May 23, 1946, Jimmy Dykes resigned after 12 years managing the White Sox. Lyons was the surprise choice to replace him. He later said he never wanted to manage. Inheriting a seventh-place club with a 10-20 record, he removed himself from the active roster and hired Red Faber, who had won more games than any White Sox pitcher except Lyons, as a coach. He offered a coaching job to Moe Berg, but Berg declined. Lyons shook up the lineup and tutored left-handed pitcher Eddie Lopat, who was developing into a baffling junkballer like his manager. Lopat led the team with 13 victories and a 2.73 ERA. The White Sox went 64-60 under Lyons, but could not climb out of seventh place.

The Chicago franchise, once the strongest in the American League, was a wreck. The club had been mediocre to awful since the Black Sox were banned in 1920, achieving a winning record only seven times in 26 years. Every other AL team—even the St. Louis Browns—had won a pennant during that time. The roster was heavy with 30-something journeymen; the only star, Luke Appling, was 40. The Sox edged up to sixth place in 1947, though they lost four more games than the year before. That winter they traded Lopat, their best pitcher, to the Yankees for three more journeymen. In 1948 they sank to the cellar, losing 101 times.

The sole male heir to the Comiskey legacy, 22-year-old Charles A. Comiskey II, claimed his birthright and joined the front office as vice president in 1948. Despite his respect and affection for Lyons, he did what most owners of a last-place team would have done: He fired the manager. Comiskey announced that Lyons had quit. Lyons responded, "I've never quit at anything."[21]

Ted Lyons had been the face of the White Sox for a quarter-century. He held club records for wins, innings pitched, and complete games. (He still does.) The Sox had finished as high as third place only twice during his career; many sportswriters later said his 260 victories would have been 300-plus with a decent team. "Sure, you'd like to finish higher; it would have been more pleasant once in a while," he said later. "And if we could have won a pennant, just one, to see what it was like, it would have been nice. But I never regretted being with Chicago all those years. It's a wonderful town, with wonderful fans, and I can't say enough for them."[22]

Lyons had no trouble finding work. The new manager of the Detroit Tigers, Red Rolfe, hired him as a coach. Rolfe said, "Ted, I guess you sort of hated to leave the White Sox." Lyons replied, "Not at all. When I signed my first contract 25 years ago, they said the job might not be permanent."[23]

For the first time in his professional career, Lyons put on a different uniform in the spring of 1949. Since Rolfe had never managed in the minors or majors, he may have relied on Lyons' knowledge of other American League teams. Lyons stayed with Detroit for five years. Frank House, a bonus-baby catcher, remembered that "he was always the one who would buy the rookie pitchers a glove and a pair of shoes." House admired Lyons' watch, a new gadget equipped with an alarm. When House hit his first big-league home run, Lyons gave him the watch.[24]

With the Tigers on the way to the first last-place finish in their history, Rolfe was fired in the middle of the 1952 season. Lyons was offered the job, but turned it down. Pitcher Fred Hutchinson was named manager. Hutch said, "When I'm pitching Ted Lyons is the manager of the club." He gave Lyons the authority to pull him from the mound.[25] Lyons was let go when the Tigers shook up their coaching staff after the 1953 season.

Once more he quickly found a new job, this time as pitching coach for the Brooklyn Dodgers under rookie manager Walter Alston. After the 1954 season Alston was allowed to choose his own pitching coach, Joe Becker, and Lyons was released.

After 31 years in baseball, Lyons was out of the game for the first time in his adult life. But baseball was not through with him. He had been steadily gaining support in Hall of Fame elections since 1951; in 1954 he was named on 67.5 percent of sportswriters' ballots, close to the 75 percent required for election. The next year he went over the top, collecting 86.5 percent of the votes, second to Joe DiMaggio. Writers also elected another Chicago favorite, Cubs catcher Gabby Hartnett, and former Dodger pitcher Dazzy Vance. The Hall's Veterans Committee tapped Lyons' teammate Ray Schalk and old-time slugger Home Run Baker. At the induction ceremony in Cooperstown, Lyons thanked Schalk for helping him get started, and added "This is the greatest thing that can happen to a player after he ends his career."[26]

Lyons' 3.67 lifetime ERA is the second-worst among Hall of Fame pitchers, better than Red Ruffing's 3.80. However, his 118 adjusted ERA is equal to Tom Glavine's and superior to that of Steve Carlton, Nolan Ryan, and 19 other Hall of Famers. (Adjusted ERA equalizes different eras and ballparks. Put another way, Lyons' ERA was 18 percent better than the average pitcher's.) Using a more advanced metric, wins above replacement, Lyons' 58.8 WAR ranks 29th among Hall of Fame pitchers as of 2011, with 34 others behind him; by that measure he is a mid-level Hall of Famer.[27]

The Hall of Fame election brought another benefit: The White Sox hired Lyons as a scout and minor league pitching instructor. He continued scouting for 15 years. He never married, and lived with his sister Pearl on his rice farm in Vinton, Louisiana.

As he advanced into his 80s, Lyons' eyesight was failing and he had difficulty walking. In 1983 the White Sox wanted to retire his number 16 in a ceremony at the 50th-anniversary All-Star Game in Comiskey Park. Team chairman Jerry Reinsdorf offered to send a private plane to pick him up, but Lyons wouldn't go. Reinsdorf said, "I think he declined because he would think it would have been embarrassing for him to have someone help him walk onto the field."[28] Besides, Lyons said he didn't want his number retired; he wanted some young player to wear it.

Lyons' health continued to decline, and he died in a nursing home in Sulphur, Louisiana, on July 25, 1986, at age 85. The White Sox retired number 16 the following year.

## NOTES

1. Interview with *Baseball Magazine*, quoted in Eugene Murdock, *Baseball Players and Their Times: Oral Histories of the Game, 1920-1940* (Westport, Connecticut: Meckler, 1991), 229.
2. Donald Honig, *Baseball When the Grass Was Real*, reprinted in *A Donald Honig Reader* (New York: Fireside/Simon & Schuster, 1988), 89.
3. Ibid.
4. Ibid., 91.
5. Joseph A. Reaves, *Taking in a Game: A History of Baseball in Asia* (Lincoln: University of Nebraska Press, 2004), 67.
6. Nicholas Dawidoff, "Scholar, Lawyer, Catcher, Spy," *Sports Illustrated*, March 23, 1992, online archive.
7. Daniel Okrent and Steven Wulf, *Baseball Anecdotes* (New York: Oxford University Press, 1989), 95.
8. *Chicago Tribune*, July 27, 1986: C3.
9. Ibid., July 26, 1986: A3.
10. Wendell Smith, "Little White Lyons," *Baseball Digest*, May 1957: 20.
11. Rick Van Blair, "Opposing Pitchers Couldn't Stop Him, But a War Did," *Baseball Digest*, July 1994: 58.
12. *Chicago Tribune*, July 27, 1986: C3.
13. Jack Ryan, "Knuckle King Bans Knuckler," *Baseball Digest*, October 1946: 6.
14. Honig, *Reader*, 99-100.
15. Ted Williams with John Underwood, *My Turn at Bat: The Story of My Life* (New York: Fireside/Simon & Schuster, 1969, repr. 1988), 68.
16. *Chicago Tribune*, July 27, 1986: C3.
17. Ibid., October 15, 1942: 29.
18. Jimmy Cannon, "No Escape," *Baseball Digest*, May 1954: 20.
19. Williams, *My Turn At Bat*, 78.
20. *The Sporting News*, August 20, 1947: 13.
21. *Chicago Tribune*, October 5, 1948: B3.
22. Honig, *Reader*, 88-89.
23. *Chicago Tribune*, December 23, 1948: A1.
24. Rob Trucks, *The Catcher: Baseball Behind the Seams* (Indianapolis: Emmis Books, 2005), 146.
25. Harold Sheldon, "Mid-Year Hook Gets a Workout," *Baseball Digest*, September 1952: 70.
26. *The Sporting News*, August 3, 1955: 12.
27. WAR calculated by Sean Smith at http://www.baseballprojection.com/war/top500p.htm.
28. *Chicago Tribune*, July 26, 1986: A3.

# RUBE MARQUARD

## BY JOSEPH WANCHO

**IN SPORTS, COLLEGE OR PROFES-** sional, individual or team, nothing captures a fan's interest quite like a streak. This is especially true with baseball. Whether it is a team's winning or losing streak or a player's performance within the chalked lines, the fanfare and pressure may build each day. The fervent fan or even the uninformed follower of the national pastime may acknowledge that perhaps the greatest of all is Joe DiMaggio's hit streak. In 1941, the Yankee Clipper stirred up quite a bit of excitement with his 56-game hitting streak. It was a testament to DiMaggio's hitting prowess, and will always remain part of his lore.

But 29 years before Joltin' Joe was smacking the horsehide around American League parks, another one of the great players in Gotham set his own streak. And it was just as impressive. Rube Marquard, who was a pitcher on the 1912 New York Giants, put together a single-season winning streak that, like DiMaggio's, still stands. Beginning with his first start of the season, at Brooklyn on April 11, Marquard won 19 games in a row. He didn't lose until July 8. During the streak, left-handed pitcher Marquard had an earned-run average of 1.63.

If the same streak were played under the rules that are employed today, Marquard would have won 20 in a row. On April 20, against the Brooklyn Superbas, Marquard relieved Jeff Tesreau in the ninth inning. Tesreau had given up three runs and Brooklyn had taken a 3-2 lead over the New Yorkers. Marquard recorded all three outs in the ninth, and retreated to the dugout to watch the Giants score two in the bottom of the frame to win, 4-3. In those days, the win went to the pitcher who had pitched the most innings. In today's game, Marquard would get the win since he was the pitcher of record when the Giants took the lead.

Marquard credited Giants manager John McGraw for sticking with him during the early years of his career, when wins were hard to come by. Both McGraw and coach Wilbert Robinson echoed the same refrain to Marquard: "You've got it in you, if you can only find yourself."[1] But the pitcher also noted the other successful tactics he employed. "I suppose the great thing is to find the weaknesses of the batsmen you're pitching against," said Marquard. "Why, you've got to know 'em like your hand. I used to keep a book and watch each fellow like a hawk when he'd come up to the plate, and I'd mark down in that book just what he couldn't do. After a while, I'd find some of 'em couldn't hit a fastball. Then I'd write that down.

"Then players talk among themselves and swap experiences, for the one thing a ballplayer talks is shop. You never seem to talk anything else when you play ball. So you get to know the different players like an old pair of shoes. Then on a dark day, I blacken the ball."[2]

Asked what he meant, Marquard replied, "I chew tobacco so when I spit on the ball, it blackens up. Then I get it against my dark glove and a batsman can't see it."[3]

Richard William Marquard was born on October 9, 1886, in Cleveland, one of five children of Mr. and Mrs. Fred Marquard. Fred worked as the chief engineer for the City of Cleveland.

The elder Marquard believed that for a person to get anywhere in life, education was the key to unlock many doors of opportunity. Richard did not see the advantages of gaining a formal education, instead telling his father that he wanted to become a ballplayer. But Fred Marquard was steadfast in his stance against the career of a baseball player.

Marquard spent many of his days as a youth at League Park, serving as a batboy for the Cleveland Broncos, who eventually became the Naps when Nap Lajoie joined the team in 1902 from Philadelphia and became the manager in 1905.

According to Marquard, his friendship with Howard Wakefield, a catcher for the 1905 Naps, paved the way for a tryout with Waterloo of the Iowa State League. Marquard had no money to travel to Waterloo, and of course his father wouldn't provide it. According to Marquard, he made his way to Waterloo by stowing away on freight trains. After five days, Marquard found his way to Waterloo, and introduced himself to Charlie Frisbee, the Waterloo manager. Frisbee knew of Marquard through Wakefield, and decided to pitch Marquard the day after he arrived. According to Marquard, he begged for more time to get settled. He also requested a small advance on his salary so that he could get something to eat. But Frisbee held his ground, "Tomorrow or never, young fellow!"[4] Frisbee let Marquard believe that after he pitched, the advance would follow as well.

Marquard relented and defeated Keokuk the next day. But Frisbee wanted to see Marquard pitch one more time before he handed any money over to the young pitcher. A frustrated Marquard left Waterloo, hopping a train to head back to Cleveland. In 1907, Marquard went to work for the Telling Ice Cream Company and pitched for its baseball team in a semipro league. Sources vary, but he was paid about $25 a week.

Because of his fine work on the mound, Marquard was recommended to the Naps by the team's third baseman, Bill Bradley. The young pitcher met with team president John Kilfoyl with the hope of signing a contract. Wary of his experience in Waterloo, Marquard did not want to be taken advantage of again. When Kilfoyl offered $100 a month, Marquard balked. "I get that much from the ice cream company, and in addition, I get to eat all the ice cream I want."[5]

Marquard left with no contract. On his way home he stopped at a sporting-goods store in downtown Cleveland that was owned by Bradley and Charlie Carr. Carr, a first baseman on the Naps in 1904 and 1905, was now the manager and first baseman of the Indianapolis Indians of the American Association. Carr signed Marquard to a $200-a-month contract with Indianapolis. Marquard's father was not pleased. "Now listen," Fred said, "I've told you time and time

again that I don't want you to be a professional ballplayer. But you've got your mind made up. Now I'm going to tell you something: When you cross that threshold, don't come back. I don't ever want to see you again."[6] No matter. Richard headed west to Indy.

Indianapolis optioned Marquard to the Canton Chinamen of the Central League in 1907. He led the circuit with 23 wins. The next season, he joined the Indianapolis club. According to Marquard, it was here that he got the nickname Rube.[7] His sweeping delivery reminded a sportswriter at the *Indianapolis Star* of Rube Waddell. The star pitcher of the Philadelphia Athletics was also a southpaw and a future member of the National Baseball Hall of Fame.

Marquard gave a good account of himself at Indianapolis in 1908. He won his first six games, three of them shutouts on his way to a 28-19 record with a 1.69 ERA. On June 16, he threw a one-hitter, striking out nine, in a 4-0 win over Kansas City. Marquard's pitching ability reached the big leagues.

The Indianapolis club nearly traded Marquard to Detroit. The June 26 edition of the *Huntington Herald* reported that Marquard had been dealt to the Tigers for left-handed pitcher Ed Siever. The deal also included a sizable bonus for Siever, who balked about going to the minors. Siever was not exactly tearing it up in the AL, posting a 2-6, 3.50 ERA at the time of the deal. Marquard, on the other hand, sported a 17-6 record and had twirled six shutouts.[8]

In the end, Siever reported to the Indians, and Marquard stayed put in Indy as well. On June 30, Marquard pitched a three-hitter to defeat Louisville, 3-0, in a key game at Washington Park.

After the game, an auction was held, and the Indianapolis Indians were the hosts. The scene was described by the *Evening World*. "The Detroit club put in a claim for him and had the first call. Then John R. Brush, dipped in his oar. Garry Herrmann put in a bid, and even (Chicago owner Charles) Murphy of the Cubs took a hand in the game.

"Murphy bid as high as $5,000 over the long distance 'phone. When (Indianapolis owner W.H.) Watkins said there was nothing doing at that price, Murphy quit. Herrmann boosted the offer up to $6,500 and quit at the half-mile. President (Frank) Navin of the Tigers was the next highest bidder. He offered $7,500. Watty said $12,000 was his price, and Navin fainted. John T. Brush weighed in with a bid of $11,000, and Watkins, knowing he was getting the biggest price ever paid for a ballplayer, threw both arms around Brush and held him before there was a chance of him changing his mind and getting away."[9]

Marquard was immediately dubbed the "the $11,000 peach" by the Giants or "the $11,000 beauty" by others. "Whew, $11,000," he said, "you can't prove it by me that there is that much money in the world. Guess there must be, however, and I hope to have that and a little bit more one of these times. I am glad, naturally, that I have been sold to a first-class club, and I think I will be able to win my share of games."[10]

The Giants continued their spending, acquiring catcher Chief Meyers from St. Paul of the American Association for $6,000. The $17,000 paid for two players was a staggering amount for that period.

Marquard was to stay with Indianapolis until the completion of their season. On September 3, he pitched a no-hitter at Columbus.

Marquard reported to the Giants and made his major-league debut on September 25 against Cincinnati. The Giants lost 7-1, and Marquard gave up two earned runs. "I intend to get some good work out of Marquard and (Giants pitcher Bull) Durham," said manager John McGraw about the following season, "and I expect them to show some good speed in the race next year. You must not judge either of them by the showing they made in the doubleheader against Cincinnati toward the end of the season. They both have all the natural ability that is necessary to make a good pitcher. What they need is a little training with a major league club."[11]

But Marquard found the road a bit rocky. Never lacking confidence in his abilities, he started out in unfamiliar territory. He was losing more than he was winning. He went 9-17 in his first two seasons. The "$11,000 peach" was now being called the "$11,000 lemon." But McGraw told Marquard to ignore "the roasts" from the grandstand.

In 1911, McGraw and his coach Wilbert Robinson went to work on Marquard. When he joined the Giants, he used a side-arm delivery. McGraw got Marquard to change to pitching overhand. Robinson, a former catcher who was a teammate of McGraw's on the Baltimore Orioles, worked on getting Marquard to throw first-pitch strikes. Robby also tutored Marquard on how to mix his pitches. Marquard was soon throwing to a location, and improving on his control.

The results were immediate. Marquard posted a 24-7 record with a 2.50 ERA in 1911. He threw a pair of one-hitters three days apart, first beating St. Louis at the Polo Grounds on August 28, striking out nine, and then coming back on September 1 at the Baker Bowl in Philadelphia. Marquard struck out 10 Phillies on his way to the win.

Marquard led the National League with 237 strikeouts in 1911. The Giants won the pennant with a record of 99-54. Christy Mathewson won 26 games, and the two pitchers combined for more than half of the Giants' wins.

It was the first of three straight flags for the Giants, who broke the stranglehold the Cubs had for much of the previous few years. Those three pennants would be followed by three straight losses for McGraw's bunch in the World Series.

Against the Philadelphia Athletics in 1911, it was surely a battle of titans: McGraw vs. Connie Mack. They had gone up against each other previously in the 1905 Series with the Giants besting the A's in five games.

Christy Mathewson won three games in that 1905 Series, and he continued his mastery of the A's in 1911, winning Game One by a score of 2-1. The Game Two pitching matchup was Rube Marquard against Eddie Plank. The game was in a 1-1 tie until Frank Baker smacked a two-run home run, delivering a 3-1 verdict in favor of the Athletics. Marquard had been instructed by McGraw not to pitch fastballs to the power hitter. Baker, by the way, was not given the moniker Home Run Baker for no reason.

Marquard was to give Baker a steady diet of curveballs, and struck him out on three curves in the first inning. "In the fourth he caught the first pitch, a high out (curve) and pushed a weak grounder to (second baseman Larry) Doyle," said Marquard. "When he came up in the sixth, I fully intended to follow instructions and give him curveballs. After I had one strike on him and he refused to bite on another out-curve which was a little too wide, I thought to cross him by sending in a fast high straight ball, the kind I know he likes. Meyers had called for a curve but I could not see it and signaled for a high fastball. Either he knew the signal from (Eddie) Collins who was on second or he outguessed me, for he was waiting for that fast one and sent it over the fence."[12]

Baker's jolt was just the lift the Athletics needed, as they defeated the Giants in six games. Marquard, who also started Game Five, was victimized by another Rube in that game. Rube Oldring connected for a three-run homer against him. (All three runs were unearned.)

On July 8, 1912, Marquard's streak of 19 consecutive victories was snapped by the Cubs. Chicago won 7-2 at the West Side Grounds as Marquard was lifted from the game after giving up six runs—five earned. Beginning with that Cubs defeat, Marquard went 7-10 for the rest of the campaign to finish with a 26-11 record and an ERA of 2.57. The 26 wins were tops in the NL in 1912. He lost three straight from September 17 to October 1. But even his victories were hard to come by. In an 8-6 win over the Pirates at Forbes Field on August 22, Marquard won his 25th game of the season. But it was not without some difficulty as Pittsburgh collected 16 hits off him in the loss.

Marquard also found time around then to star in a short silent movie titled *Rube Marquard Wins*. The film depicts a tale of a baseball pitcher who is coerced by gamblers into throwing a baseball game. When Marquard refuses, he is kidnapped by the gamblers, but is saved by his girlfriend—just in time to win the game.[13]

The Giants won the 1912 NL pennant by 10 games over Pittsburgh. Their opponent in the fall classic was the Boston Red Sox. The Red Sox won the series in eight games (one was a tie). Marquard won two games for the Giants. On both occasions, he outdueled Red Sox righty Buck O'Brien.

Like many baseball players of the era, Marquard also took part in vaudeville acts. McGraw and Mathewson had also taken part in stage productions. It was a way to earn extra income, and many of baseball's biggest stars hammed it up for the audiences. Joe Kane, a veteran of the vaudeville stage, was seeking an athlete to pair with his wife, Blossom Seeley, for a show, and engaged Marquard. A real-life romance developed between Marquard and Seeley. Kane grew suspicious of their relationship and accused them of having an affair. At times, Kane became violent against his wife. He divorced Seeley and the pitcher and the actress married. Their union produced one son, Robert. The Marquard-Seeley affair was nationwide news; the tale of this love triangle was told in a book by Noel Hynd *Marquard & Seeley: A Scandalous Ragtime Romance*.

Marquard threatened to leave the Giants and stay in the acting biz. Of course it was just a ploy to get more money (maybe the acting did pay off after all). He inked his new deal with his bride by his side in late March of 1913. Marquard went out and pitched well for the Giants, posting his third consecutive year of 20 or more wins with a 23-10 record and a 2.50 ERA in 1913.

Marquard won nine games in a row from June 28 to July 27, lowering his ERA from 2.79 to 2.32. Rube pitched against Chief Bender in Game One of the World Series against the Athletics. The A's won, 6-4, and for the second time in three years kicked sand in the face of McGraw's boys.

The Giants lost their grip on the first-place mantle in 1914. The Boston Braves outdistanced the New Yorkers by 10½ games to take the NL pennant and the franchise's first world championship since 1898. Marquard did a reversal of his previous three seasons; he slumped to 12-22. A big part of that record occurred from August 8 to September 23 when Marquard lost 12 straight games. There were no games where he was given a no-decision. It was indeed 12 straight losses. A game that might be indicative of Marquard's season was played on July 17 at Forbes Field. Both starters, Marquard and the Bucs' Babe Adams, went the distance, 21 innings. The Giants won on Larry Doyle's two-run homer in the top of the 21st. But Marquard had to fight tooth and nail for one win, pitching over two games worth of innings to secure it.

As the 1915 season dawned, it appeared that many of the eight teams that made up the Federal League, a rival league to both the National and American Leagues established in 1913, were having financial problems. The clubs were feeling the pinch from paying players high salaries; building new ballparks and the cost of doing business were squeezing some clubs financially. The Indianapolis Hoosiers, for example, won the pennant in 1914 but because of low attendance were moved to Newark, New Jersey.

However, some clubs were still making attractive overtures to established major-league players. Robert Ward of the Brooklyn Tip-Tops waved a $10,000 contract under Marquard's nose. And Rube liked the aroma. He liked it so much that he swore out an affidavit stating that he was not under contract with the New York Giants, thus accepting a $1,500 bonus from Ward. In actuality, Marquard was under contract with the Giants for two years, and the stalemate as to his status carried on all winter. In the end, the Giants returned $1,500 to Ward, and Marquard grudgingly reported to spring training.[14]

Marquard started the 1915 season on the right foot. He tossed a no-hitter against the Brooklyn Robins on April 15 at the Polo Grounds. Rube struck out two and walked two in the 2-0 victory. Marquard backed his fine pitching performance with a single to right field in the seventh inning that scored Fred Merkle from second base.

The Giants, who had been on top for so long, were seeing some chinks in the old armor. Mathewson was not as effective and Marquard was running hot and cold, with a 9-8 record in late August. With the exception of Larry Doyle, who would lead the league in batting with a .320 average, Fred Merkle and Dave Robertson, the offense had fallen flat. The bench was not providing positive alternatives and the Giants, as well as McGraw, had lost their competitive fire. After the Giants lost four straight to the Cardinals, they were in unfamiliar territory: the cellar of the National League.

Marquard asked McGraw to trade him. McGraw replied, "Who would take you? You couldn't lick a postage stamp."[15] To prove his point, McGraw asked for waivers on Marquard, and everyone passed on him. Marquard contacted his old mentor Wilbert Robinson, now the manager of the Robins, and allegedly negotiated his own contract. Robby signed Marquard on August 31. In doing so, he paid the asking price of $7,500 to the Giants. Marquard was inserted into the second game of a doubleheader that same day against Pittsburgh. He pitched two scoreless innings in relief of starter Larry Cheney, who was acquired that day from the Chicago Cubs. Marquard was credited with the win as the Robins came from behind to win.

But Marquard was knocked around quite a bit in that final month of 1915. His record was 2-2, but his ERA was 6.20. In 24⅔ innings pitched, he gave up 17 earned runs. The 1916 season provided plenty of excitement for fans of the senior circuit. The Braves, Phillies, and Robins tussled all season for first place in the standings. After the Robins swept the Cubs in a three-game series, they opened a three-game set against the Phillies beginning on September 28. The Robins sat atop first place, ahead of the Phillies by 1½ games, Boston was in third place, 3½ games off the pace.

The Phillies won the first game, 8-4, as Pete Alexander won his 32nd game of the year. After an off day, the Robins and Phillies played a doubleheader on September 30. The Phillies took the opener 7-2, and now were in first place by themselves, a half-game ahead of Brooklyn. In the second game, Alexander, now 32-11, took the hill against Marquard. Marquard was equal to the task, going the distance in beating Philadelphia 6-1. Marquard struck out seven and scattered three hits. He supported his win with his first triple of the year, and scored a run. Brooklyn was now a half-game ahead in the standings. That was the last regular-season game Marquard would pitch in 1916. He finished 13-6 with a 1.58 ERA. He struck out 107 batters and walked 38 in 205 innings pitched.

Brooklyn closed the season against the Giants at Ebbets Field. The Phillies and Braves were scheduled for a six-game series at the Baker Bowl. But the Robins took three of four from New York and the Phils dropped four of six to the Braves. The Brooklyn Robins were headed to their first World Series.

There they would meet the Boston Red Sox. But the party was short-lived as Boston made quick work of their NL counterparts, winning the series in five games. Marquard lost Game One to Ernie Shore and Game Four to Dutch Leonard.

The Robins sank to seventh place in 1917, although Marquard led the club in victories, posting a 19-12 record with a 2.55 ERA. He also led the team in strikeouts with 117. The 1918 season was cut short, ending on Labor Day because the federal government's World War I "work-or-fight" order decimated major-league rosters. Marquard did his part, enlisting in the US Naval Reserve, serving for three months before he was discharged after the war ended in November.

The 1918 season was a role reversal for Marquard. He was 9-18 when the season came to a halt. He lost five of those games to last-place St. Louis. The 18 defeats tied him for the National League lead with Joe Oeschger of Philadelphia.

Marquard had an unfortunate ending to his 1919 season. In the fifth inning of a game on June 9 at Redland Field in Cincinnati, he was rounding second base on a hit when his spikes hooked into the bag. He fell heavily on his leg, and suffered a fracture in a small bone. He was lost for the rest of the season.

Burleigh Grimes was the anchor of the Brooklyn pitching staff. After coming over from Pittsburgh in 1918, Grimes had his first 20-win season in 1920, going 23-11 with a 2.22 ERA. Five other Brooklyn pitchers had double-digit wins, including Marquard, who posted a 10-7 record with a 3.23 ERA.

The Robins finished in first place in the NL and faced the Cleveland Indians. Marquard was chosen to start Game One, in part because he had experience pitching in the World Series, but also because he could neutralize Cleveland's left-handed hitters. Of course, Cleveland manager Tris Speaker countered that move with a right-handed-heavy lineup.

Stan Coveleski pitched for Cleveland and the Indians won the opener, 3-1. Marquard lasted six innings, giving up all of the Cleveland tallies.

The Robins won the next two games, at Ebbets Field. But it was what happened off the field in his hometown that cast Marquard in a questionable light. Marquard was arrested for scalping tickets. He was seized in a hotel lobby when he offered to sell eight box-seat tickets that cost $52.80 to a Cleveland police detective for $400. Marquard was released on his own recognizance and was to appear in court at the conclusion of the Series. The police released Marquard because they did not want to be accused of crippling Brooklyn's chances of winning the Series by holding the pitcher.[16]

Meanwhile, Cleveland took a commanding 4-2 lead in the Series (the World Series was a best-of-nine format that season). There was one more game to be played at League Park. "Beat? I should say we're not," said Robby. "We haven't been hitting and that's the only trouble. We're going out there tomorrow and smash into those Indians so hard they'll wish they'd never seen a world's series, and when we get back to

Brooklyn, Cleveland won't have a chance. I'll pitch either Rube Marquard or Burleigh Grimes and either one of them can stop Cleveland."[17]

Whether Robinson really considered Marquard to start Game Seven will never be known. His arrest before Game Four was a huge distraction to the Robins. His subsequent appearance in Common Pleas Court was a painful reminder as well. After Game One he was removed from the rotation and pitched out of the bullpen.

Cleveland wrapped up the title, the first for the franchise. For the game itself, the last thing it needed was controversy, coming on the heels of the 1919 Black Sox scandal. Eight Chicago players were indicted just before the 1920 season ended, and its memory was still fresh in the public's mind. And now there was Marquard with a ticket-scalping charge.

Although he got off with a $1 fine, Marquard was harshly criticized. "The scalping ordinance was gotten up for the benefit of people who have supported a baseball team all the year in order to protect them so they could get tickets at a reasonable price when a World Series or an important game comes up," said Cleveland Common Pleas Court Judge Samuel Silbert. "It is an unfortunate thing, because baseball is going through its test period. For fifty years baseball has been regarded as a clean sport, but now the effect of a sudden scandal has made people dubious."[18]

"I am through with him, absolutely," said Brooklyn President Charles Ebbets. "He hasn't been released, however, and if anyone wants him, he can have him. But Marquard will never again put on a Brooklyn uniform."[19]

True to Ebbets's word, the Robins traded Marquard to Cincinnati for pitcher Dutch Ruether on December 15, 1920. Marquard won 17 games (17-14, 3.39 ERA) for the Reds in 1921. But the Reds, who had just won the World Series in 1919, sank to the second division in the NL. Marquard, who had divorced Blossom Seeley, married Naomi Wigley from Baltimore in 1921.

Marquard got a real good sense for the second division the next four years. He was traded with infielder Larry Kopf to the Boston Braves for pitcher Jack Scott on February 18, 1922. In four years with the Braves, Marquard posted a 25-39 record and a 4.44 ERA. The Braves never finished higher than fifth place from 1922 to 1925, and were cellar dwellers for two seasons.

Rube's last season in the major leagues was 1925, when he won two games and lost eight. In 18 seasons, he compiled a 201-177 record and a 3.08 ERA. In 3,306⅔ innings pitched, he totaled 1,593 strikeouts and walked 858 batters. Marquard was an excellent control pitcher.

For the next several years, Marquard was a player or player-manager in the minor leagues. He managed Providence in the Eastern League in 1926, Jacksonville of the Southeastern League in 1929 and 1930, and Wichita-Muskogee of the Western League in 1933.

In 1932 Marquard was a coach for the Atlanta Crackers. He put out a 12-page pamphlet for youths titled "How to Pitch." His philosophy for a successful pitcher was control. "From my experience of 25 years in baseball," he wrote, "I have learned that control is 90 percent of successful pitching. If a pitcher has control, he has everything. The entire importance of pitching lies in ability to pitch to a 'spot' and put the ball where you want it.

"What I mean by control is not simply aiming the ball across the plate or splitting the middle, but pitching to a batter's weakness. Every batter has a weakness, no matter how good a hitter he may be. A smart pitcher soon discovers that."[20]

Marquard spent his later years working as a pari-mutuel clerk at racetracks in Maryland, New Jersey, Florida, and Rhode Island. He was inducted into the National Baseball Hall of Fame in Cooperstown on August 9, 1971, after being voted into the Hall by the Veterans Committee.

In 1966, Lawrence Ritter, an economist and a professor at New York University, wrote the book *The Glory of Their Times*. Each chapter contains an interview with a former player. Many of the players were from the Deadball Era and the book is widely considered a classic in baseball literature.

The first entry is of Rube Marquard. The interview has been considered by some as a fabrication by Marquard, or at least a story containing hyperbole. Sportswriter Joe Posnanski has questioned Marquard's place in the Hall of Fame. In his blog on March 27, 2014, Posnanski pointed to the Marquard chapter in Ritter's book as the reason for his enshrinement.[21]

Larry Mansch, who wrote a biography of Marquard for the SABR BioProject, also questioned the veracity of the facts. Mansch wrote: "Rube's recollection of some of the events of his life was circumspect; he shaved three years off his life, unnecessarily romanticized his hobo-style train trip to Iowa, and downplayed his scandalous affair with Blossom Seeley. Despite a few inaccuracies, his story seemed to capture the essence of the early days of baseball, and it was prominently featured as the first chapter of *Glory*."[22]

Marquard related to others in interviews that his real name was Richard LeMarquis. This fact was erroneously reported in *The Sporting News*'s obituary of Marquard in its June 21, 1980, edition. It is also mentioned in the book written by Noel Hynd. He said he changed his name to Marquard when he started to play professional baseball. A quick check of the US Census and Cleveland city directories of the late nineteenth century proves this untrue.

Richard "Rube" Marquard died on June 1, 1980, after a two-year battle with cancer.

One person whom Marquard held in high esteem was McGraw. Despite their differences, Marquard admired his former manager. "Take Mr. McGraw," he said. "What a great man he was! The finest and grandest man I ever met. He loved his players and his players loved him. Of course he wouldn't stand for any nonsense. When he laid down the law, you better abide by it."[23]

## NOTES

1. "A Talk With Marquard, Hero of Baseball Fans," *New York Sun*, July 14, 1912: 16.
2. Ibid.
3. Ibid.
4. Lawrence Ritter, *The Glory of Their Times* (New York: Macmillan and Company, 1966), 6.
5. Ritter, 9.
6. Ritter, 10.
7. Ritter, 12.
8. "The Sporting World," *Huntington* (Indiana) *Herald*, June 26, 1908: 4.
9. "Rube Marquard Was Turned Down by Naps," *Evening World*, July 27, 1908: 6.
10. "Marquard Will Get Big Sum as New York Giant," *Indianapolis News*, July 2, 1908: 12.
11. "McGraw Plans to Use Marquard and Durham," *Indianapolis News*, October 17, 1908: 8.
12. Norman L. Macht, *Connie Mack and the Early Years of Baseball* (Lincoln: University of Nebraska Press, 2007), 526.
13. "Marquard Is Hero of Moving Film Drama," *Pittsburgh Press*, August 23, 1912: 23.
14. Charles C. Alexander, *The Miracle Braves, 1914-1916* (Jefferson, North Carolina: McFarland, 2015), 98-99.
15. Charles C. Alexander, *John McGraw* (Lincoln: University of Nebraska Press, 1995), 187-188.
16. Arrest Marquard for Speculating, *New York Times*, October 9, 1920: 1.
17. "Robins Sure of Victory Today," *Cleveland Plain Dealer*, October 12, 1920: 18.
18. Marquard's Days With Robins Ended," *New York Times*, October 13, 1920: 21.
19. Ibid.
20. Marquard player file, National Baseball Hall of Fame.
21. joeposnanski.com/the-worst-pitcher-in-the-hall/.
22. Larry Mansch, Society for American Baseball Research, BioProject-Rube Marquard, accessed June 15, 2017. The Mansch biography is no longer available, having been replaced by this one.
23. Alexander, *John McGraw*, 151.

# "IRON MAN" JOE MCGINNITY

## BY DON DOXSIE

**ONE COULD MAKE A STRONG CASE** for McGinnity being the most durable pitcher in baseball history.

In just 10 seasons in the major leagues, "Iron Man" Joe McGinnity worked 3,441 innings and won 246 games. During the month of August in 1903, he pitched and won both ends of a doubleheader three times and he accomplished the feat two other times in his career. He pitched another 3,821 innings and won another 235 games in a minor-league career both before and after that one glorious decade in the majors.

And to his dying day in 1929, Joe McGinnity couldn't quite fathom why so many other pitchers weren't just as durable as he was.

In May of 1926, less than a year after throwing his final pitch in an organized game, he was serving as the pitching coach of the Brooklyn Dodgers and lamented the fact that major-league teams sometimes felt the need to have as many as 10 pitchers on their rosters. He thought they really only needed four or five.

"This policy has had a psychological effect upon the pitchers," McGinnity said in an interview with the United Press. "They have been influenced into the belief that they should not have to work without a long rest and that they can't be effective without that rest."[1]

McGinnity seldom rested for very long during his life. That applied not only to his baseball career but nearly every aspect of his life. He never stayed in one place or in one job for very long. His 6½-season stay with the John McGraw-led New York Giants was his lengthiest tenure in any location or with any team.

McGinnity, who was inducted into the Baseball Hall of Fame posthumously in 1946, was a living, breathing paradox in many ways.

Although he was one of the biggest men in the major leagues at the dawn of the twentieth century, at 5-foot-11 and 206 pounds, he was hardly a power pitcher. In his prime years, he relied almost exclusively on a baffling, rising curve ball that was so dear to him he gave it a nickname. He used a peculiar underarm pitching style but also sometimes threw a devastating sinker with a more conventional overhand motion. John McGraw often said he thought the use of two radically different pitching motions may have lessened the strain on his arm and contributed to making him so durable. He said when pitching his doubleheaders, McGinnity would sometimes throw one game overhand and work the other game with underarm motion. "It was as different as if two pitchers had been working," McGraw said.[2]

McGinnity also mixed in a healthy dose of guile and an almost unmatched understanding of how to manipulate batters. He occasionally blended in a spitball, was expert at using the quick pitch and never hesitated to brush back a hitter who stood too close to the plate. His 41 hit batsmen in 1901 are still the American League record.

He also loved to get inside the head and under the skin of opponents.

"He was a close second to McGraw when it came to needling players," Ed Burkholder once wrote in *Sport*. "When he was on the mound, an enemy baserunner was in a constant state of nerves, and his bantering with the batter in the box contributed much to his success."[3]

Legendary manager Connie Mack described simply described McGinnity as "a magician," noting that "he knew all the tricks for putting a batter on the spot."[4]

McGinnity received almost no formal schooling as a child growing up in the coalfields of Illinois, but he was one of the most cerebral players of his time, charting and chronicling the strengths and weaknesses of opposing batters long before it became the norm. He probably was the first pitcher to actually keep a "book" on opposing hitters. He had a ledger in his locker in which he wrote down observations about hitters almost every day so that he had his own systemized accounting of opponents' tendencies.

"It saves me a deal of trouble and unnecessary work, not to mention long chances," he said in a 1916 interview. "I don't have to try 'em out, like I'd have to if I didn't have the book. When you're trying a batter out to find his weakness you have to put a lot of stuff on the ball and tax your arm. The book saves me that trouble. It's all there in black and white, gathered from personal observation and experience for the most part. I don't trust to memory. Anyone is likely to forget, and a lapse of memory with three on in a tight game many times leads to a costly mistake."[5]

In another interview during the prime of his career, McGinnity added: "I ascribe a great deal of my success to my ability to judge the players as they come to bat. The first principle of a successful pitcher is to give his opponents what they don't want." In the same interview, he said he very seldom tried to strike out a batter, adding "Every pitcher has eight men on his club to help him out. The secret of successful pitching is to keep the batters from hitting 'em *hard*."[6]

McGinnity was a contradiction in at least one other way: Although he was a fairly stoic, easy-going man off the field, he had a simmering temper that occasionally got him into trouble on it. He undoubtedly was influenced by the combative McGraw and feisty John McCloskey, his first minor-league manager, and his career was littered with scuffles and scraps. In 1901, he was suspended for 12 days after physically assaulting umpire Tommy Connolly. He engaged in a wild, on-field fistfight with Pittsburgh's Heinie Peitz in 1906, for which he was briefly jailed and eventually suspended for 10 days. In a nomadic trek through the minor leagues following his major-league career, there were dozens of similar incidents.[7]

"McGinnity was always known as a fighter," the *Dubuque* (Iowa) *Telegraph Herald* reported. "When he entered a ballgame he had but one objective in mind — a victory. He was aggressive. He fought for his team and a player who did not show a disposition to fight for the club had no place in Joe's heart. There were times when many thought he went too far with his aggressiveness. But that was McGinnity's style of play and it won him ballgames. Off the field he was a different type of man, but once in that uniform he was all baseball, first, last and all the time."[8]

Pat Wright, an old friend of McGinnity's and his manager with Peoria in 1898, simply said he was "a hard player. He was a hard loser. He will fight to the last. He always did. He will not give up."[9]

If all that wasn't enough, McGinnity was a respectable hitter and was regarded by some as the best fielding pitcher of his era.

"I have never seen a pitcher with more confidence in himself than McGinnity had," Hughie Jennings said. "He was so cocksure of his fielding ability that he would take any sort of chance, throwing to any base under any circumstance, and this fielding ability lifted him out of many tight spots."[10]

He was born Joseph Jerome McGinnity on March 19, 1871, in Cornwall Township in Henry County, Illinois, to Peter and Hannah McGinnity. For more than a century, it was believed and widely reported that he had been born in Rock Island, but his birth actually took place about 30 miles east of there in a rural area covered with farmland and dotted with small coal mines.[11] His father was a Scottish immigrant and nomadic coal miner who moved his family around frequently to different areas.

When Joe was only 4, the family relocated to Shawneetown in the southeastern part of Illinois and it was there, in 1879, that tragedy struck the family. Peter McGinnity was working as a muleskinner, driving a wagon through the mine when he was crushed to death by a load of coal. His three oldest sons, including 8-year-old Joe, went to work in the mine in his place.[12]

The family continued to move around, seeking employment wherever new coal deposits were found. They moved to Springfield, Illinois, and then to Decatur, Illinois, which is where McGinnity was introduced to a leisure-time activity that would define his life. It was in Decatur that he first began playing baseball.

In 1889, McGinnity was on the move again, this time relocating to work the coal mines in McAlester in Indian Territory, which would later become the state of Oklahoma. He also continued to dabble in baseball, helping to found a town team that traveled around the region playing other teams in that corner of Oklahoma and even venturing into Texas and Arkansas.

He never really considered baseball as a career until yet another coal-mining tragedy occurred in the Osage Company's No. 11 mine in Krebs, just east of McAlester. More than 100 men died when an explosion ripped through the mine at the end of the work day on January 7, 1892. McGinnity had been among the last men to exit the mine before the mishap occurred. He escaped injury but many of his friends and co-workers perished in the incident. It made him begin to consider other career paths and he started to view baseball as something that could become more than just a way to spend his off hours.

He made some pocket money pitching for a team in Van Buren, Arkansas, and that led to him earning a professional contract with McCloskey and the Montgomery Colts of the Southern League in 1893.

He pitched well at times there, but went only 10-19 and in 1894 was signed by the Kansas City Blues in the Western League. He had his ups and downs there, too, and finally was released in mid-season, apparently at his own request.[13]

At the age of 23, his baseball career seemed to be over. He and Mary Redpath, a McAlester girl he had married the previous fall, moved back to Illinois and McGinnity spent the next three years there, doing a little mining, working as a bartender and playing as much baseball as he could for amateur and semipro teams in the Springfield/Decatur area.

He had always been a conventional power pitcher, throwing straight overhand with a good fastball and an adequate breaking pitch, but during those years back in Illinois he began working on something new. With Kansas City, he had seen a pitcher for the rival Grand Rapids team, Billy "Bunker" Rhines, baffle hitters with an unusual underarm throwing motion. He went to work trying to copy the motion and developed a rising curveball he nicknamed "Old Sal." He used the same grip as when he threw overhand but he swept his arm downward and released the ball from somewhere around his knees. It allowed him to throw one breaking pitcher after another with less snap in his wrist, reducing the wear and tear on his arm.

"The damn pitch never came straight at you," baseball historian Robert Smith wrote. "It started near Joe's shoes, for his fingers almost scraped the ground as he completed the pitch. And it appeared to be approaching crossways and upward, looking big enough to be broken in two, but always just escaping the full weight of the bat."[14]

Old Sal revived McGinnity's professional career. He signed to pitch for Peoria in the Western Association in 1898 and after compiling a 10-3 record, including a 21-inning, complete-game victory over St. Joseph, he signed to pitch for the Baltimore Orioles of the National League in 1899.

With Baltimore, McGinnity joined one of the most raucous and aggressive teams in the history of baseball and he immediately became the ace of the Orioles' staff, pitching 366 innings and winning

28 games. Perhaps more significantly, he made two new friends—a diminutive, scrappy, do-anything-to-win third baseman named John McGraw and a jovial, rotund catcher named Wilbert Robinson. Both became lifelong pals and all three men eventually ended up in the Baseball Hall of Fame.

It was Robinson who first recognized McGinnity's potential and encouraged McGraw to make him the team's top pitcher, and McGinnity often credited the man everyone called Uncle Robbie with polishing off some of his rough edges and teaching him some new tricks.[15]

Prior to the 1900 season, the National League condensed from 12 teams down to eight with Baltimore and Brooklyn, which had been owned by the same syndicate, being merged into one team. So, McGinnity suddenly found himself pitching for the Brooklyn Superbas (now Dodgers) that season.

He had spent the offseason working in a new profession, helping his father-in-law in an iron foundry back in McAlester, and when *Brooklyn Eagle* sportswriter Abe Yager interviewed him prior to the new season, McGinnity told him "I'm an iron man."[16] It became his new nickname although it eventually became more appropriate for other reasons.

He went 28-8 for Brooklyn as the Superbas won the NL pennant by 4½ games over Pittsburgh, but the Pirates weren't convinced that Brooklyn had the better team. The Pittsburgh Chronicle-Telegraph proposed a special postseason best-of-five series between the two teams with the winning team receiving a special 18-pound silver punch bowl as the prize.

All the games were played at Pittsburgh's Exposition Park, but Brooklyn had no trouble backing up what it had done in the regular season. It won the series in four games with McGinnity recording complete-game victories in the first and last games. When it was over, his teammates had the silver punch bowl engraved and presented it to him. He kept it for 20 years before giving it to the A.E. Staley Company of Decatur, which many years later gave it to the Baseball Hall of Fame.

In 1901, McGinnity found himself with yet another new team. McGraw and Robinson had jumped to the new American League and were heading up a new Baltimore Orioles team there. They convinced Iron Man to join them, signing him for $2,800 a season even though Brooklyn had offered him $5,000 to stay in the NL.

He went 26-20 for the Orioles in 1901 and led the new league in games pitched (48), complete games (39) and innings pitched (382). He also set modern-era AL records by allowing 412 hits and plunking 41 batters.

He was 13-10 for Baltimore in the middle of the 1902 season when he was on the move again. McGraw was constantly feuding with American League founder and president Ban Johnson, and he gained his release in the middle of the season and jumped to the New York Giants, maneuvering to take McGinnity and some of his other top players with him.

It was the start of something special. McGinnity went only 8-8 in the remainder of that season but over the next four years he posted records of 31-20, 35-8, 21-15 and 27-12 with the Giants, teaming with Christy Mathewson to form arguably the greatest 1-2 pitching tandem in the history of the sport. There have been only two instances in which two pitchers on the same team won 30 games in a season. Both times, it was McGinnity and Mathewson.

McGinnity deserves at least some credit for helping the younger Mathewson develop into one of the greatest pitchers who ever lived. Before McGraw and McGinnity arrived, the previous Giants management had been trying to convert Mathewson into a first baseman. McGinnity taught him how to throw a sinker, showed him how he scouted opposing hitters and gave him tips on fielding the pitching position. Mathewson also observed how McGinnity paced himself and made sure he had something left for tight spots.[17]

The Giants won NL pennants in 1904 and 1905, but it is the 1903 season for which McGinnity is most remembered. He started 48 games and worked 434 innings — both modern-day NL records — and in August became a veritable one-man pitching staff. On August 1 against the Boston Braves, he pitched and won both games of a doubleheader, 4-1 and 5-2, allowing just six hits in each game. He did it again a week later against Brooklyn and finished out the month on August 31 by again pitching and winning two games in the same day against Philadelphia.

McGinnity modestly insisted there was "never any great trick" to winning both ends of a twin bill. "I was pitching those games with my head, more than with my arm," he said. "An arm may not be able to go 18 innings in a day unaided, but it's different with the brain. A slow ball and a few good curves — that was all I had. But I guess it was enough."[18]

The Giants came up 6½ games short of winning the pennant that season despite the fact that McGinnity and Mathewson each won 30 or more games, but in 1904 they really began dominating the NL. McGinnity won 35 and Mathewson won 33 with Dummy Taylor adding another 21 wins for a team that clinched the NL pennant with 16 games remaining in the season.

It was the best year of McGinnity's career. Not only did he have a win total that only has been exceeded four times in baseball's modern era, he also led the National League with five saves although that statistic was not yet kept. He opened the season with a 14-game winning streak and ended it by winning 12 of his last 13 games. Along the way, there were nine shutout and 38 complete games. His final earned-run average was 1.61.

The World Series had been established the previous year with Pittsburgh playing the Boston Americans, but McGraw and Giants owner John T. Brush were still at odds with Ban Johnson, and they refused to play Boston in a postseason series.

But in 1905, after winning another pennant, the Giants finally agreed to play the Philadelphia Athletics in the World Series. They won it in five games with Mathewson performing the biggest heroics, hurling shutouts in Games One, Three, and Five. McGinnity was a tough-luck loser in Game Two and the winner in Game Four as the Giants became world champions. Philadelphia did not score an earned run in any of the five games.

McGinnity won 27 games in 1906 and was 18-18 in 1907, but it was apparent his skills were beginning to decline. He was only a part-time starter while going 11-7 in 1908 although he was involved in one last classic moment when the Giants played the Cubs in an important game late in the season.

The Giants appeared to have won the game, on September 23, when Al Bridwell singled in the winning run in the ninth inning. But rookie Fred Merkle, who was on first base at the time, did not go all the way to second base, veering off to run to the Giants' clubhouse as fans rushed the field. As Cubs second baseman Johnny Evers tried to get his outfielders to throw him the ball for a force-out at second that would negate the run, McGinnity, who was coaching third base for the Giants, intervened. There are dozens of conflicting accounts of what actually happened but all of them have McGinnity wrestling with various Cubs players to get possession of the ball and trying to throw it into the left-field seats. In the end, Merkle was called out and the game was ruled a tie. When the Cubs and Giants ended up tied for the pennant, they had to play a special playoff game at the Polo Grounds. The Cubs won and the infamous incident became known as the "Merkle Boner."

The playoff game was McGinnity's last as a major-league player. He gained his release from the team the following February and embarked on what would be a long and meandering voyage through the minor leagues as a player, manager and owner.

He and childhood friend H. Clay Smith started by purchasing the Newark team in the Eastern League and McGinnity took on the unlikely dual role of team president and star pitcher. He pitched more than 400 innings for Newark in both 1909 and 1910, winning 59 games in the two seasons combined. He did not pitch as well in 1911 and 1912, however, and the team began to flounder financially as well.[19]

Over the next six years, he owned and pitched for a string of teams in the Pacific Northwest in Tacoma, Butte, Great Falls, and Vancouver. He pitched well at times but his franchises almost always ended up falling on hard times financially, prompting another move. The *Montana Standard* newspaper in Butte noted in an editorial at the time of his death that "as a business man, McGinnity was a mighty good pitcher."[20]

After all those years of moving around the country, McGinnity welcomed an offer in 1919 from the A.E. Staley Company back in Decatur. The Staley Fellowship Club was beginning to form sports teams to be affiliated with its massive corn starch manufacturing operation and it hired McGinnity to head up its baseball team. It also brought in a young University of Illinois alumnus named George Halas to play the outfield for McGinnity's baseball team while also forming a football team. Within a few years, the football team originally known as the Decatur Staleys evolved into the Chicago Bears.

McGinnity, as always, just couldn't stay in one place for too long and he eventually was lured back into minor-league baseball by a team in Danville, Illinois. He was in his 50s by then but he wasn't content to just manage his team from the dugout. He still felt the urge to pitch and although he admitted his legs sometimes felt a bit wobbly, he thought his arm was as lively as ever.

"I don't feel old. Of course not," he said in one interview. "The idea seems absurd to me. I am able to take my regular turn on the mound and I expect to do that for many years yet. Baseball is too fine a game to give up, ever."[21]

He enjoyed one last glorious season as the player-manager with Dubuque in 1923, going 15-12 as a pitcher while managing the team to the Mississippi Valley League championship. After years of being criticized for his overbearing managerial style, in which he often fined players for the smallest indiscretions, he finally was vindicated with a pennant.

"Joe McGinnity was a leader," the *Dubuque Telegraph Herald* reported several years later. "He knew inside baseball and he was tricky. He never asked of his fellow players anything he couldn't do himself. That is the reason why he pulled over a pennant in 1923 with a club that hardly could be rated as the best all-around club in the league."[22]

It was his last hurrah. He threw his last pitch at the age of 54 with Springfield in the Three-I League in 1925.

His old friend, Wilbert Robinson, had become manager of the Brooklyn Dodgers and in 1926 he persuaded McGinnity to work with the team's pitchers, but he didn't even last a full season in the job. Mary McGinnity died in June of that year and Iron Man left the team. He spent the next few years living with his only daughter, Marguerite, in Brooklyn in a small house just a short walk from Ebbets Field.

He was diagnosed with bladder cancer in 1929 and underwent surgery in August for the removal of a tumor. As he was entering the operating room, he joked, "Well, I guess it's the ninth inning for me and I guess they're going to get me out."[23] Over the next few months, there were frequent reports that he was near death. He finally passed away on November 14 at the age of 58 and was buried alongside Mary at Oak Hill Cemetery in McAlester.

Not surprisingly, tributes flooded in from all over the country, from all the various communities in which he had lived for brief periods of time.

Perhaps the highest compliment came from Dick Kinsella, an old Springfield friend who served as a scout for the Giants. He said he thought McGinnity was the smartest pitcher in baseball history.

"He was what you might call a natural born baseball pitcher," Kinsella told the *Decatur Review*. "Although Christy Mathewson* was a wonder, I think Joe McGinnity knew more about baseball than Mathewson."[24]

## NOTES

1. United Press, "McGinnity's Novel Theory on Durability of Pitchers' Arms," May 5, 1926..
2. Walter Trumbull, "The Listening Post," *Richmond Times Dispatch*, November 16, 1929: 11.
3. Ed Burkholder, "McGinnity Was A Man of Iron," *Sport*, April 1954: 54
4. Connie Mack, *My 66 Years in the Big Leagues* (Philadelphia: Winston, 1950), 86.
5. "How M'Ginnity Tabbed His Batters," *Butte* (Montana) *Miner*, May 15, 1916.

## 20-GAME LOSERS

6   M.J. Sullivan, "The Men on Whom the Championships Depend," *Pearson's Magazine*, April 1905.

7   Don Doxsie, *Iron Man McGinnity* (Jefferson, North Carolina: McFarland Publishing, 2009), 61, 93-94.

8   *Dubuque* (Iowa) *Telegraph Herald*, November 14, 1929.

9   "Joe M'Ginnity, Ball Player," *Daily Illinois State Journal*, November 15, 1929: 6.

10  Hugh A. Jennings, "McGinnity Greatest Fielding Pitcher in Game, Says Jennings," *Philadelphia Evening Bulletin*, December 18, 1925: 38.

11  Doxsie, 5.

12  Ibid., 7.

13  Ibid., 31.

14  Benton Stark, *The Year They Called Off the World Series* (Garden City Park, New York: Avery Publishing, 1991), 83.

15  Doxsie, 44, 58.

16  "'Iron Man' Joe McGinnity," *Dubuque* (Iowa) *Telegraph Herald*, July 23, 1922.

17  Doxsie, 66.

18  James J. Corbett, "'Ol' Joe McGinnity, 50, Still Pitching Victories," *Philadelphia North American*, July 30, 1922.

19  Doxsie, 117-119.

20  "Iron Man Passes," *Montana Standard*, November 18, 1929.

21  Wilton Floberg, "On the Upper Side of Fifty," *Sporting Life*, August 1923: 9.

22  *Dubuque* (Iowa) *Telegraph Herald*, November 14, 1929. Associated Press, "Joe McGinnity's Condition Critical After Operation," *Dubuque Telegraph Herald*, August 27, 1929.

23  Associated Press, "Joe McGinnity's Condition Critical After Operation," *Dubuque Telegraph Herald*, August 27, 1929.

24  Howard V. Millard, "Joe McGinnity To Rest Beside Wife In Oklahoma," *Decatur* (Illinois) *Review*, November 15, 1929.

# PHIL NIEKRO

## BY TOM HUFFORD

**PHILIP HENRY NIEKRO JR. WAS BORN** in Blaine, Ohio, on April Fools' Day — April 1, 1939. That was appropriate, for he spent much of his career fooling batters with a pitch that most other pitchers wanted no part of.

The first of the Niekro family in America were Jozef Niekra, from Slodkow, Polish Russia, who had come to the U.S. in 1901, and Magdalena "Maggie" Mieszegr, from Blinow, Polish Russia. It isn't known if the two knew each other in Europe, but they were married in Monongah, West Virginia, where Jozef worked in the local coal mines, on February 9, 1903 — only 19 days after Maggie's arrival in America.[1]

Two daughters, Apolonia and Anna, were born to the couple before they moved about 75 miles north, to the small town of Blaine. It was in Blaine, in early 1913, that Jozef and Maggie had their only son — Philip Henry Niekro. "Actually, our name was spelled Niekra in Poland, but here, we got the 'o' on the end," said Phil many years later.[2] Life was not easy in the coal-mining community, but it was especially difficult for Philip — both of his parents died before his fifth birthday. The community saw to it that he was taken care of, and he attended elementary school and began high school before starting work in the mines at age 15. Philip married Henrietta "Ivy" Klinkoski, herself the orphaned daughter of Polish immigrants, in 1936, and they had their first child, a daughter, Phyllis, the next year. Two sons, Philip Henry Jr. and Joseph Franklin, would follow. By the early 1940s, the Niekro family had moved to nearby Lansing, Ohio, about seven miles west of Wheeling, West Virginia.

Phil Niekro Sr. played baseball on the sandlots of the coalfields, in the Mine Workers League. After arm trouble took away his fastball, a co-worker showed him the knuckleball. "A fellow named Nick McKay, who was in the minors for a while, showed me how to throw it. It was all I could throw," he told a writer.[3] In Lansing Phil Sr. would play catch with his children. He taught the knuckler to his oldest son, 8-year-old Phil Jr. Phil practiced all he could, with sister Phyllis as his backyard catcher. After a while, Phil found another catcher, his boyhood pal John Havlicek. John would go on to his own Hall of Fame career with the Boston Celtics of the NBA.

At Bridgeport High School, five miles east of Lansing, Phil played varsity baseball, basketball, and football. Over his four-year high-school mound career, he posted a 17-1 record, the only blemish being a 1-0 loss to Tiltonsville in 1954, his freshman year. The lone run in that game came on a home run by Bill Mazeroski, who signed with the Pittsburgh Pirates a few weeks later.[4]

Phil received athletic scholarship offers from several colleges, but turned them down, hoping for a future in professional baseball. The Pittsburgh Pirates and the Cleveland Indians were the two major-league teams closest to Lansing, but they showed little interest. Phil spent the summer after his high-school graduation pitching for local teams. The next July, he attended a Milwaukee Braves tryout camp in nearby Bellaire, Ohio. A Braves scout, Bill Maughn, was impressed enough to offer Phil a contract for $275 a month. Phil related, "My dad said, 'It's nice you want my son to play professional baseball but before he does, we have to sit down here and make a little deal.' I got $500 (as a signing bonus)."[5] "My greatest thrill in baseball was signing my first major-league contract in our kitchen, with my father and mother, my brother Joe, and my sister Phyllis present," Niekro said. "July 19, 1958 — I became a professional!"[6]

The Braves waited until the next spring to have Niekro report. He was assigned to the Braves' Class-D team in Wellsville, New York, where he got into 10 games, but his work was not impressive. One day, Phil went to the ballpark early and saw a big car parked on Main Street. "I recognized the driver from spring training in Waycross. He was a big-money guy. I thought to myself, 'Uh-oh, somebody's getting released today.'"[7]

In the clubhouse, manager Harry Minor called Phil into his office. "The Braves are sending us two new players," Minor said. "We're going to release you." Niekro recalled, "The first thing I thought about was that I was going to end up like my dad, in a coal mine. Or in a steel mill. I had my chance, and I screwed it up. So, I just sat there and finally said, 'I'm not going! Harry, I need to play, I just need to play!'"[8]

John Havlicek said, "He didn't want to go back to the mines, he didn't want to disappoint his dad. Phil says he'll shine shoes, cut grass, clean bases, anything to stay with the club. And the manager agreed to give Phil a second chance."[9]

The Braves sent Niekro to one of their other Class-D clubs, the McCook Braves in the short-season Nebraska State League, where he pitched in 23 games, all in relief. His work was a little better there; walked fewer batters in more innings, and his ERA was a more than respectable 3.12.

After making it through his first pro season, Niekro began climbing the ladder of the Braves system—Jacksonville, Austin, Louisville. In each city, he posted solid, but not spectacular, seasons, but he made progress at each stop.

Phil spent the 1963 season a little bit south of Louisville, at nearby Fort Knox, wearing the uniform of the US Army. "Of course, I pitched for the Fort Knox Army team and after that I pitched winter ball (in Venezuela), so it wasn't as though I sat out the whole year."[10]

Niekro arrived at camp in 1964 without much fanfare, but he quickly stood out and Milwaukee Braves manager Bobby Bragan decided to add him to his Opening Day staff. Niekro made his major-league debut in San Francisco, in the second game of the season. At last, the coal miner's son from Ohio could call himself a major leaguer!

NIekro saw regular work out of the bullpen for the first month of the season. On May 17, the club sent Niekro down to Triple-A Denver, with some new instructions—"be a starter." He finished the season in Denver, and his 172 innings pitched were by far the heaviest workload he had ever had.

With Warren Spahn having been sold to the Mets during the offseason, Niekro had every reason to think he might take over a starting spot in the Braves' 1965 rotation, but a strange thing happened in spring training. After succeeding as a starter the previous summer, the Braves moved him back to the bullpen.

On May 13 in Pittsburgh, Niekro was brought in to start the fifth inning and finished the game, during which the Braves rallied for a 5-4 win. Along with his first major-league victory, he also collected his first big-league hit.

Ten days later, on a United Airlines charter flight from Milwaukee to San Francisco, Niekro turned to his friend Gene Oliver and said, "I'm going to marry that girl." That girl happened to be Nancy Lee Ferrand, a stewardess from California. With more crew aboard than were needed, Nancy was told she could have the night off. She looked around and took one of the only available seats—next to Niekro. The two sat together and played gin rummy all the way to California. "One of us won two million dollars. I think it was Nancy," said Phil. Neither Phil nor Nancy remembered to get the other's address or phone number, but Nancy's mother suggested that she send Phil a letter, in care of the ballclub. She did, and they corresponded for 11 months, rarely seeing each other, until the middle of the next season.

When Phil reported to spring training in 1966, it wasn't with the Milwaukee team—the Braves had relocated to Atlanta. By Memorial Day, he had pitched only 20⅓ innings in 13 games, and in early June he was sent to the Braves' new Triple-A team in Richmond, Virginia.

Niekro appeared in 17 games for Richmond, four as a starter, and felt he was gaining even better control of his knuckler. He also accomplished something else on his agenda. When the US airlines went on strike in July, Nancy was stuck in California with no work. Phil suggested she buy a one-way train ticket and come to Richmond.

Back in Atlanta, the Braves were not showing any improvement. During the first week in August, they sent word for Niekro to rejoin the team at home. Phil made it back to Atlanta Stadium on August 8, in time to get into the last inning of a 10-9 Braves win over the Dodgers. The story in the next day's *Atlanta Journal* read "Niekro a Two-Timer," and said, "It's real funny the way things have been happening for me in pairs lately," grinned newlywed Niekro. "In the first place my wife and I were married twice over the weekend."[11] "We were married the first time Saturday night and the minister called Sunday morning and said he'd left something out of the ceremony so he came to the house that afternoon and married us again. Then we had to drive two cars down from Richmond because I promised Dick Kelley we'd bring his car to Atlanta for him. And tonight I make just two pitches and win a ball game. … And that's a dandy wedding gift."[12]

It may have been a dandy wedding gift for the Niekros, but the win didn't do much for Bobby Bragan. It was the last game of Bragan's major-league managerial career. The Braves fired him the next morning, and replaced him with coach Billy Hitchcock. For Niekro, however, that was the end of his minor-league career, and he never went back.

The Braves entered 1967 with high hopes, but while the team struggled to a 77-85 record Phil found himself back in the starting rotation by the middle of June. It was a breakout season for Niekro, and he ended the season with an 11-9 won-lost record, 10 complete games, 207 innings pitched, and a league-leading 1.87 ERA.

The other big story of 1967—especially to the Niekro family—was that of Phil's younger brother, Joe, making the Chicago Cubs Opening Day staff. But it wouldn't be until 1973, when Joe joined Phil in Atlanta, that Joe would take up the knuckleball in earnest.

Phil called the 1969 season "probably my best." The Braves finally got on track and won the Western Division championship by eight games over the Chicago Cubs, although they were swept in the National League Championship Series by the upstart New York Mets. Niekro's 23rd victory clinched the division crown for the Braves. Phil was named to the National League All-Star team, and finished second to Tom Seaver in the Cy Young Award voting. The July 26 issue of *The Sporting News* that season used a new nickname for Niekro for the first time—"Knucksie."

The next decade was pretty lackluster for the Braves, with the team posting winning records in only two seasons, and only Hank Aaron's pursuit of Babe Ruth's career home-run record adding much excitement. Two events stood out in the 1973 season for Niekro, however.

Everything fell into place on Sunday, August 5, when Niekro threw a 9-0 no-hitter at home against the San Diego Padres. Two days later, the Braves picked up brother Joe on waivers from the Detroit Tigers. Phil and Joe had always dreamed of playing on the same team together, and now their chance had come.

The 1977 club was the Braves' worst team in more than 40 years. An old adage says, "A pitcher has to be pretty good to lose 20 games!" Well, Phil *was* pretty good, going 16-20 to lead the league in losses, but he also led the National League in innings pitched, complete games, and strikeouts. After the season,

the Braves dismissed manager Dave Bristol, and, on the list of candidates to replace him, one name stood out—Phil Niekro. "They were looking for a manager. I knew the game and the players, so I threw my name in."[13] Instead, they handed the reins to Yankees coach and former Braves farmhand Bobby Cox, for his first major-league managerial job.

From 1977 through 1980, Niekro led the league in games started each year, with totals of 43, 42, 44, and 38. He went 19-18 in 1978, for a club that lost 93 games, but with a 1979 team that went 66-94, he managed to go 21-20. It was Phil's second 20-loss season in three years. Brother Joe, with his rejuvenated knuckleball career in Houston, also won 21 that year, to share the league lead with Phil. Phil became the first National League pitcher since 1905 to win and lose at least 20 games in the same season. Their dad, Phil Niekro Sr., summed up his sons' seasons in one concise sentence—"I'm proud of them and glad that they don't have to work for a living."[14]

After a 50-56 finish in the strike-interrupted 1981 season, Cox was let go, and Knucksie again expressed his interest in the position. "By that time, Ted Turner and I had become very close friends, and he made it known to me that I would someday be managing his team."[15] But it didn't happen. The job went to former Braves catcher Joe Torre, who had just been dismissed by the Mets.

The next season, 1982, was a bittersweet one. A spring-training injury caused Niekro to miss being a part of the Braves' terrific start, winning their first 13 games. He didn't make it onto the roster until game number 15. He finished the season at 17-4; his .810 winning percentage was the best in either league. The Braves passed the Dodgers during the last week of the season to capture the NL West flag. Niekro pitched two complete-game shutouts during that stretch, Knucksie's own two-run, eighth-inning home run against the Padres sealing the clinching game for the Braves.

Phil started Game One of the NLCS in St. Louis, and was ahead 1-0, but the game was called due to rain with two outs in the fifth inning. "We had to play it again from the beginning the next night. We ended up losing that game 7-0." Niekro then started Game Two, and led 3-2 after six innings. "I was pitching well in St. Louis. I had 'em where I wanted them, and Torre pinch-hits for me," said Niekro. The Braves ended up losing the game, 4-3, then moved back to Atlanta, where the Cardinals completed the three-game sweep. It was to be Niekro's last postseason chance with the Braves.

Niekro's record fell to 11-10 in 1983. His 201⅔ innings pitched were the fewest for a full season in his career, his walks were up and his strikeouts were down. The sentiment by many in the organization was that Phil was at the end of his career.

The headline in the *Atlanta Constitution* five days after the season ended screamed, "Niekro Leaving Braves." Sports editor Jesse Outlar wrote, "When Torre came back to manage the team that Niekro also would have liked to manage, there was speculation of friction. Though Niekro resented being pulled in the late innings by Torre, there was no verbal clash between them."[16] The next day, Chris Mortensen wrote, "Niekro confirmed that he had been encouraged to retire. He declined and was granted a request to put him on waivers for the purpose of giving him his unconditional release. While the decision had been unanimous at a September 25 staff meeting that Niekro should retire, it was primarily the decision of Torre and Bob Gibson, his pitching coach."[17]

Ted Turner, a longtime booster of Niekro, responded by telling the pitcher he could return as a player. "He said, 'Just tell me you want to pitch for the Braves and you've got a job.' I can't go back to the Braves under those conditions."[18] "It was a wonderful marriage for 24 years, but now we are divorced and neither one of us is unhappy. In brief, the Braves wanted me to retire, but I want to pitch another season or so."[19]

Braves fans were outraged. Joe Niekro, who would have welcomed Phil on his own Astros staff, was very outspoken: "It's Joe Torre," said Joe. "I think he thinks Phil is a threat to him; that's why he doesn't want Phil around anymore. He knows that if he messes things up worse than he did this year, Phil can step right in as manager."[20]

Knucksie may not have been the same pitcher he was a few years ago, but he was still just about the best that the Braves had.

Years later, Niekro related, "I was born a Brave, and I wanted to die a Brave. I had my mind set on that. And that was the longest damn day I had in my life. The most depressed day in my life was that day."[21]

Phil felt that he still had two or three years left, and that 300 victories were certainly within his reach—he already had 268.

Knucksie signed for 1984 with the New York Yankees. On August 6, an offday for the Yankees, the Braves saluted Niekro with a 40-minute pregame ceremony, in which his uniform number 35 was retired, and he was presented with a replica of the statue of himself that the team planned to erect outside the stadium. Ted Turner gave a speech in which he called Niekro "a shining light and influence on all Americans" and "a bright example to every young person and to every person in this whole country and in this whole world of ours."[22]

By season's end, Phil, at the age of 45, had led the Yankee staff in innings pitched and in wins with 16. The Braves finished under .500 in 1984; their top pitcher, Pascual Perez, won only 14 games; and manager Joe Torre was shown the door at the end of the season.

In 1985, Phil set his sights on repeating his 16-win total from the previous season—that would give him 300. But it wouldn't be easy. He won his 15th game of the season and 299th of his career on September 8, and knew that he had five more scheduled starts. On September 15, the Yankees made a trade with the Houston Astros, and brother Joe joined Phil in the Bronx.

The quest went down to the last game of the season, at Toronto, and Phil took the mound in Toronto, while thinking of his father, seriously ill in a Wheeling hospital. Phil didn't know that Yankees owner George Steinbrenner had hooked up a radio play-by-play of the game on the phone to Phil's mother at the hospital.

Phil decided to do something a little different—no knuckleballs. "Come the ninth inning, we're up 8-0. I had two outs and two strikes on Jeff Burroughs. I thought, 'I can't think of a better way to win 300 than with a knuckleball, what my dad taught me.' The only one I threw the whole ballgame. Jeff struck out and I had my 300th."

"Joe's the first one out to the mound to give me a hug. He says, 'Brother, I've gotta tell you something about Dad.' I'm expecting the worst. We go sit in the dugout and Joe said, 'Dad woke up in the seventh inning, looked at Mom and said, 'Boy, he's pitching a helluva game.' We fly to Pittsburgh the next day, and drive to the hospital to see him. I put that ball in his hand, and he's grinning from ear to ear!"[23]

With that victory, Phil Niekro became not only the 18th 300-game winner in major-league history, but also the oldest pitcher ever to record a shutout.

After returning home, and with the Braves once again looking for a skipper, Phil fully expected to hear from Ted Turner. "Ted's pledge that I would someday manage his ball club just kept rolling around inside my head," he said.[24] The Braves didn't say no; they didn't say anything. Phil never heard from the team, which chose to go with Chuck Tanner.

At this point, Phil turned his attention to working with brother Joe in passing Gaylord and Jim Perry in career victories by two brothers. Joe and Phil stood at 504, the Perrys at 529.

Although the Yankees signed Phil again for the 1986 season, and in spite of a good showing in spring training, he was released on March 28, the club citing his age as the reason.

Phil ended up signing with the Cleveland Indians, and his 11-11 record showed that he still had a little bit left. Joe picked up nine wins with the Yankees, their combined total of 524 still five short of the Perrys.

Another member of the Niekro family also joined the professional baseball family that summer, when the Indians drafted and signed left-handed pitcher Philip Dillmore, son of Phil and Joe's sister Phyllis.

June 1, 1987, turned out to be the magic date, as the Niekros finally passed the Perrys. Phil picked up a 9-6 win over Detroit, to notch victory number 530. Joe said, "I keep telling people that for us 530 wasn't just Phil and Joe, it was a Niekro record. The two of us accomplished it, but not without the strength and support of our family and people behind us."[25]

Finding themselves hopelessly out of the race, the Indians traded Niekro to the Toronto Blue Jays on August 9. He was back in a pennant race!

Phil knew this would most likely be his final chance to get to the World Series, but the storybook ending wasn't to be. Knucksie started three games for the Blue Jays, losing his first two starts and not making it out of the first inning in his final game. On August 31, Phil was released. "That's the third time I've been released," he said, "so it's nothing new. I just didn't do the kind of job that I'm capable of."[26]

Writers around the country paid tribute to Niekro, most surmising that his career was over, and lamenting that he never got a shot at the World Series. In Atlanta fans wondered if the Braves might sign Phil, giving him a chance to end his career with his original team. That was exactly the way Knucksie wanted to finish, but he was confused and a bit hurt by some of the negative reception that the idea received in the press.

Discussions with the Braves wavered back and forth for about two weeks, and on September 23 the team finally announced that it had signed Niekro to a $1 contract, and that he would start the final home game of the season.

On Sunday afternoon, September 27, 1987, the Braves unretired number 35, and Phil Niekro took the mound against the first-place San Francisco Giants. Things went well for three innings, but the top of the fourth was not kind to Phil. The Giants scored two runs and loaded the bases before manager Chuck Tanner came out to remove him. Niekro protested, to no avail, but the manager had already decided that he would not let Phil get into a position to lose the game. Tanner and Niekro walked off the field with the Braves holding a 5-2 lead.

Reliever Chuck Cary faced pinch-hitter Candy Maldonado, who homered to deep left-center field, giving the Giants a 6-5 lead. The final score was 15-6.

The next day Niekro said, "I'm not embarrassed by getting beat around. I've done that before. The most important thing was to wear the (Braves) uniform again."[27]

Phil and Joe finished their careers with a total of 539 wins.

In January 1993 Phil was on the Hall of Fame ballot for the first time, and his chances for election looked good. After all, every other 300-game winner had already been enshrined. When the ballots were counted, Niekro was named on 65.7 percent of the ballots, falling 40 votes short of being elected.

The baseball world was surprised in December 1993 when the Coors Brewing Company announced that it would sponsor an all-women's baseball team, the Colorado Silver Bullets, with Phil Niekro as their manager, and son John and brother Joe as coaches. "Women should have every opportunity to play competitive professional ball," he said. "I think we are going to surprise quite a few people with the ability of these athletes and the caliber of ball they can play."[28] Although the team was not a success on the field, it gained respect and recognition for its pioneering achievements. The Silver Bullets played for four seasons before Coors ended its sponsorship.

Phil was finally elected to the Baseball Hall of Fame in 1997, his fifth year of eligibility. He has been one of the more active and visible Hall of Fame members since his enshrinement, serving on the Hall's Board of Directors and as a member of the Veterans Committee. He has also been an ardent participant in the shrine's Hall of Fame Classic weekend, serving as one of the team managers for several seasons.

Niekro was chosen to receive the Lou Gehrig Memorial Award in 1979, and the Roberto Clemente Award for outstanding community service in 1980. He continued to be active in charitable endeavors in the Atlanta area.

Phil and Nancy moved to their retirement home on Lake Lanier, north of Atlanta, their three sons—Philip, John, and Michael—already grown. Phil remained active in baseball, and has become somewhat the "Godfather of the Knuckleball," mentoring such pitchers as Tim Wakefield, Steve Sparks, and R.A. Dickey. He also instructed his nephew, Lance, who gave the knuckler a trial in the minor leagues after spending parts of the 2003-2007 seasons as a first baseman with the San Francisco Giants.

"I had a great connection with my family," said Niekro. "My father was a coal miner. He took me fishing and hunting. There was a lot of love in our family. We went to church every Sunday together. I went to play bingo with my mother on Fridays. We did everything as a group. They supported me every step along the way."[29]

Years from now, someone walking through Saint Anthony's Cemetery in Blaine, Ohio, may wonder about the tombstone for Ivy and Phil Niekro Sr., the one with a baseball on the top, inscribed with the number 539. Anyone who knows the story will understand that it was truly a family affair.

## SOURCES

In addition to the sources cited in the Notes, the author also consulted:

*Books*

Atlanta Braves Media (Press) Guides 1966-2015.

Binette, Wilfrid. *Knuckler—The Phil Niekro Story* (Atlanta: Hallus, Inc., 1970).

Caruso, Gary. *The Braves Encyclopedia* (Philadelphia: Temple University Press, 1995).

Shatzkin, Mike. *The Ballplayers* (New York: Arbor House-William Morrow, 1990).

Thorn, John, Pete Palmer, Michael Gershman, David Pietrusza, and Dan Schlossberg. *Total Braves* (New York: Penguin Books, 1996).

Van Wieren, Pete, and Jack Wilkinson. *Of Mikes and Men* (Chicago: Triumph Books, 2010).

*Periodicals*

Fraley, Gerry. "Niekro Agrees to Start for Braves Against Giants," *Atlanta Constitution,* September 23, 1987: E-1.

Shaw, Bud. "The Most Important Thing Was to Wear the Uniform Again," *Atlanta Journal-Constitution,* September 28, 1987: D-1.

Smith, Claire. *New York Times,* January 8, 1997. nytimes.com/1997/01/08/sports/coal-miner-s-gift-is-treasured-by-son.html.

*Online Sources*

baseball-reference.com.

homemagazinenorthgeorgia.com (March-April 2012).

retrosheet.org.

YouTube.com - Phil Niekro, during his Induction Day speech at the National Baseball Hall of Fame, Cooperstown, New York (August 3, 1997).

*Archival Information*

US Census Records—1910, 1920, 1930, and 1940.

*Personal Correspondence*

Except where noted, all quotations are from the author's numerous conversations with Phil Niekro between 1987 and 2017.

## NOTES

1. Staatsarchiv Hamburg. *Hamburg Passenger Lists, 1850-1934* [database online]. Provo, Utah: Ancestry.com Operations Inc, 2008. Jozef Niekra, from Slodkow, Polish Russia, left Hamburg, Germany, bound for the United States, aboard the steamship Albano on August 28, 1901. On the ship's passenger list, Jozef's occupation was given as "arbeiter," which translates as "worker." Slightly more than a year later, 20-year-old Magdalena "Maggie" Mieszegr left her home in Blinow, Polish Russia, to go live with her brother Michal, near Fairmont, West Virginia, traveling from Bremen, Germany on the SS Brandenberg and arriving in New York on December 21, 1902.

2. "Phil Niekro Sr. Glad He Taught Sons the Knuckler," *Daytona Beach Morning Journal,* June 17, 1979.

3. Ibid.

4. Ohio Valley Athletic Conference, ovac.org/HallOfFame/Details/49.

5. Bill Madden, "Niekro a Hit at Hall, No Second Banana to Dodgers' Lasorda," *New York Daily News,* August 4, 1997.

6. National Polish-American Sports Hall of Fame polishsportshof.com/inductees/baseball/phil-niekro/.

7. Jack Wilkinson, *Game of My Life—Atlanta Braves* (Champaign, Illinois: SportsPublishingLLC.com, 2007), 47.

8. Ibid.

9. Curt Smith, *What Baseball Means to Me: A Celebration of Our National Pastime* (New York: Grand Central Publishing, 2002), 112.

10. Bob Wolf, "Phenom Foggy on His Name—Dazzler on Hill," *The Sporting News,* April 25, 1964: 19.

11. Phil and Nancy's marriage license was issued and signed by Thomas Royall Miller, clerk of the Hustings Court in Richmond. Miller had been an outfielder with the 1918-19 Boston Braves.

12. Wilt Browning, "Niekro a Two-Timer," *Atlanta Journal,* August 9, 1966: 16.

13. Wilkinson, 48.

14. "Phil Niekro, Sr. Glad He Taught Sons the Knuckler."

15. Phil Niekro and Tom Bird, *Knuckle Balls* (New York: Freundlich Books, 1986), 21.

16. Jesse Outlar, "Niekro Leaving Braves," *Atlanta Constitution,* October 7, 1983: 12.

17  Chris Mortensen, "Torre Ordered to Shun Niekro," *Atlanta Constitution,* October 8, 1983: 1-C.

18  Chris Mortensen, "Niekro Needed Gibson's Faith," *Atlanta Journal-Constitution*, October 8, 1983: 6-C.

19  "Torre Ordered to Shun Niekro."

20  Associated Press, "Niekro Cleaning Out Locker Today; Brother Joe Blames Joe Torre," *Augusta* (Georgia) *Chronicle*, October 7, 1983: 27.

21  Wilkinson, 52.

22  "Atlanta Braves Salute Phil Niekro, Retire Jersey," *Gainesville* (Florida) *Sun,* August 7, 1984: 3B.

23  Wilkinson, 56.

24  Niekro and Bird, 190.

25  Phil and Joe Niekro with Ken Picking, *The Niekro Files* (Chicago: Contemporary Books, 1988), 68.

26  "Phil Niekro Released," *New York Times*, September 2, 1987.

27  Dave Kindred, "One More Time Was Enough," *Atlanta Journal-Constitution*, September 28, 1987: D-1.

28  coloradosilverbullets.org/history.html.

29  "Hall of Fame Celebrates 75th Birthday With New Exhibits," MLB.com, June 13, 2014.

# HANK O'DAY

## BY DENNIS BINGHAM

**HANK O'DAY IS ONE OF THE FEW MEN** to have played, umpired, and managed at the major-league level. He was a World Series pitching hero. He had one of the greatest starts of any rookie manager in history. He was the home-plate umpire for 23 World Series games, as well as for four no-hitters in four different decades.[1] He was called "about as odd a character as the game ever produced."[2] He was the driving force behind rule changes that have dramatically transformed baseball. Yet, for all his influence in a remarkable career that spanned nearly half a century, O'Day is principally remembered for only one play.

Granted, that one play was indeed a biggie, in what has been characterized as "the most celebrated, most widely discussed, most controversial contest in the history of American sports."[3] O'Day was the home-plate umpire in the famous (or infamous) game in 1908 when Fred Merkle neglected to run to second base. Hank's historic ruling in nullifying the apparent winning run sent a shock wave through the baseball world, turning what was already the most exciting race of all time into the most tumultuous. That one decision became O'Day's legacy, defining his entire lengthy baseball career. It is even embossed on his Hall of Fame plaque.

Henry Francis O'Day was born in Chicago on July 8, 1859, the middle child of seven born to deaf parents James and Margaret (Loftus) O'Day, Irish immigrants.[4] His father operated a small farm, worked as a plumber, and then served as an engineer at a school. Hank grew to a height of 6 feet, weighed a hefty 180 pounds, sported a fashionable mustache, and probably spoke with a brogue.[5] Hank and his two older brothers spent their formative years playing baseball on the many open fields of Chicago in the city's thriving semipro leagues. Charles Comiskey, the same age as Hank, was a teammate. The O'Day brothers played under the name "Day" because their father disapproved of his sons playing the "frivolous pastime" of baseball.[6] For a while, Hank was a steamfitter's apprentice before giving it up and traveling to faraway California to play ball for St. Mary's College for three years.[7]

At age 22, in 1883, O'Day became a professional ballplayer when he joined the Bay City, Michigan, team of the Northwestern League as pitcher and center fielder for $125 a month. During that season, management of the financially strapped team realized it had to reduce its roster. They drew his name out of a hat and he was released, despite being the team's leading batter.[8] It was an appropriate beginning for Hank's career as a well-traveled journeyman pitcher.

The Toledo Blue Stockings, of the same minor league, picked up O'Day. At about the same time the team also signed catcher Moses Fleetwood Walker, who would later become the first African American in major-league history, 63 years before Jackie Robinson. *Sporting Life*, baseball's leading publication, was soon proclaiming O'Day and Walker as "one of the most remarkable batteries in the country."[9] With the addition of the talented twosome, Toledo quickly rose from fifth place to win the league championship. The team also fared quite well in exhibition games against major-league competition.

In 1884 O'Day became a major leaguer when the Blue Stockings, brimming with confidence after their great success, joined the American Association. Alas, when Toledo finished in eighth place, the team was dropped from the majors and O'Day was once again looking for another team. In his rookie big-league season, he pitched 326 innings, posting a 9-28 record and 3.75 ERA. He also displayed his versatility by playing 28 games at other positions. (In his major-league career, O'Day had spot starts at every position except catcher and second base.)

Veteran major-league catcher Deacon McGuire described O'Day's pitching style: "He was crafty and had a world of stuff, but he threw the heaviest and hardest ball I ever caught. It was like lead and it came at me like a shell from a cannon." To protect his hand whenever he caught O'Day, McGuire would insert a slab of raw meat into his thin catcher's glove.[10]

The year 1885 was a distressing one for O'Day personally. He was able to stay in the majors by signing with the AA's Pittsburg Alleghenys, but after missing several starts while visiting his dying father back in Chicago, he was released in midseason.[11] Unable to hook up with a major-league club after his father's death, O'Day pitched for Washington's minor-league club in the Eastern League. He rebounded with a sparkling 13-2 record and 0.74 ERA. This success was tempered with news that his 16-year-old brother Joseph had died after fracturing his skull in a fall from an amusement-park roller coaster in Chicago.[12]

In 1886 O'Day had an excellent year with Savannah (26-11, 1.03 ERA), prompting the Detroit Wolverines, hot contenders for the National League pennant, to pick him up late in the season. O'Day was overjoyed until he learned that Detroit had immediately sold him to the last-place Washington Nationals. He finally found some stability and remained with the Nationals for two full seasons, but it was a struggle pitching for a team with the worst hitting in the league. He started the 1888 season with a 0-9 record and one tie, thanks to his teammates scoring a total of nine runs in his first 10 starts. He was able to lead the league in a statistical category for the first and only time in his major-league career, but it was a dubious one — the most hit batsmen. O'Day was the team's workhorse with a combined 24-49 record, 657⅔ innings pitched, and a 3.52 ERA for the two seasons.[13] During his years with Washington, O'Day's catcher was the venerable Connie Mack.

O'Day would long remember the 1889 season, the most thrilling and satisfying of his playing career. He began the year still laboring for last-place Washington and at midseason had a 4.33 ERA and a 2-10 record. The New York Giants, fighting for the pennant, saw something special in O'Day and purchased him, with O'Day receiving a $200 cut. Being supported by a solid offense was a new experience. The Giants had four future Hall of Famers in their lineup, as well as two in their rotation.[14] However, it was O'Day who proved the difference by winning nine games down the stretch and leading the Giants franchise to their first NL championship. Baseball experts said that if the Giants "had not purchased O'Day from Washington at a critical period," New York would not have won the pennant.[15]

The Giants faced the Brooklyn Bridegrooms, winners of the American Association pennant, in a best-of-11 World Series to determine the best team in baseball. The Giants hitters were outstanding but their two aces, Tim Keefe and Mickey Welch, were pounded and New York found itself behind early in the Series. Giants manager Jim Mutrie turned to his two backup hurlers, Cannonball Crane and Hank O'Day, to pitch the rest of the games. They responded with a combined six consecutive wins to capture the crown for New York. "It was difficult to isolate a single hero in the Series," wrote author Jerry Lansche,

"but the logical choice was pitcher Hank O'Day."[16] He was dazzling in the pitcher's box. O'Day won the only two low-scoring games, one to tie the Series and the other the deciding contest, by limiting Brooklyn to three earned runs in 23 innings and holding their hitters to a microscopic .135 batting average.

There was a revolution in baseball in 1890. More than 150 players, finally fed up with their treatment by management over the years, formed their own major league, the Players League. Twelve members of the 1889 Giants, including Hank O'Day, became the nucleus of a "new" New York Giants team. O'Day finished the year with a 22-13 record, 329 innings pitched, and a 4.21 ERA. The Players League folded after only one season and the circuit's players scattered, most of them returning to their big-league club of the previous year. O'Day was not so lucky. It was his last major-league season as a player. The many innings he had hurled over the years had taken their toll and his right arm was dead.

Determined to extend his baseball life, O'Day toiled for four different teams in four minor leagues over the next three years (1891-1893).[17] In 1892 he suffered another personal tragedy when he learned of the death of his older brother James, 38, with whom he had played ball on the sandlots of Chicago. James was working for the Pinkerton Detective Agency when he suffered severe head injuries protecting Pennsylvania coal miners during a labor strike battle. Shortly thereafter, in a state of delirium, James committed suicide by jumping to his death from a moving train.[18]

In 1894 O'Day was at a crossroads in his life. A year earlier, baseball had increased its pitching distance to 60 feet 6 inches. He knew his playing career was over—nobody was looking for a has-been 35-year-old hurler with an ailing right arm—but he wanted to remain in the game he loved. He decided to take a crack at being an umpire (of which he had a little prior experience) and went to the Northwestern League to work some games. It would prove to be the wisest decision he ever made because it was a role he was born to perform.

A decade earlier, on September 11, 1884, while a rookie major-league pitcher with Toledo, O'Day had been selected to serve as the umpire when the regular arbiter had failed to show up. Despite having never done it before, O'Day performed his duties behind the plate "very acceptably."[19] He was a natural and would serve as a substitute umpire in another six games during his playing career. In O'Day's era, it was not unusual for an active player to serve as an umpire.[20] However, it is testament to his honesty, integrity, and talent that during his playing career no other active player was called upon to serve as "player-umpire" more than him.[21]

O'Day became an umpire during the profession's worst period. "It was hell to be an umpire in the 1890's; it's a wonder anyone would do it," wrote historian Bill James.[22] Larry Gerlach, the foremost umpire historian, aptly described the life of an arbiter during this violent decade on the diamond: "Umpires were routinely spiked, kicked, sworn at and spit upon by players, while fans hurled curses, bottles and all manner of organic and inorganic debris at the arbiters. Mobbings and physical assaults by players and patrons alike became commonplace; police escorts were familiar and welcome sights to the men in blue. … In short, a rough-and-tumble, no-holds-barred mentality dominated the game in the last past part of the 19th century."[23]

O'Day did not last long initially in the profession. In 1895 he quit umpiring, returned to Chicago, and took a job as a clerk in the City Recorder's Office. By taking his first job outside baseball, it is probable that he at that time had entirely given up the idea of remaining in the game in any capacity.[24] Fortunately for baseball, O'Day remained passionate about the game and would visit the old ballpark as often as he could.

On the overcast Sunday afternoon of July 7, 1895, Hank O'Day was sitting in the grandstand in a crowd of 9,000 awaiting the start of the game between the Chicago Colts and Cleveland Spiders. Chicago team owner James Hart noticed O'Day, approached him, explained that the regular umpire had not arrived, and pressed O'Day to take his place. O'Day agreed and the rest, in the oft-repeated cliché, is history.

During the spirited contest, "not even the semblance of a kick was registered by either team." Sitting in the stands with Hart were Spiders owner Frank Robison and New York Giants owner Andrew Freedman. The three magnates were so impressed with O'Day's work that they prevailed upon National League President Nick Young to immediately hire him as a full-time major-league umpire.[25]

O'Day quit his clerk position, signed a National League umpire contract, and two days later was calling balls and strikes for the Colts-Giants game in Chicago. For the remainder of the season, he traveled around the NL circuit, umpiring almost every day for a total 75 games.

One game illustrates what O'Day had to endure during his rookie season as a major-league umpire. "O'Day probably never had as narrow an escape from serious or death" as in the Cleveland-Washington game of August 20, reported the *Washington Post*. After the Nationals had lost the close contest, a crowd of about 1,000 irate fans surrounded O'Day, who "was so badly frightened … that his face blanched and his teeth chattered with a noise like castanets." Washington manager Gus Schmelz (for whom O'Day had once played for in the minors) pulled O'Day to safety into a dressing room, where he was guarded by a squad of police officers. When he later left with an armed escort, he was greeted by a shower of bricks. Hustled into a nearby hotel, he remained guarded by armed police until the outraged mob dwindled.[26] The next day the fearless O'Day was back at the same ballpark working a doubleheader behind the plate.

O'Day's first ejection involved Connie Mack, his old friend and former batterymate. Working alone, O'Day had hustled out to second base from behind home plate to make a close call of "safe" on a New York Giants batter-runner. Mack, manager of the Pittsburgh Pirates, uncharacteristically let loose a string of profanity that could be heard way up in the press box. O'Day ignored it until Mack "applied a name to him that was unprintable." O'Day walked up to the dugout and levied a fine of $100 on Connie, later upheld by the league president. Mack continued his tirade by "lashing him with language which could not be repeated in polite society." O'Day tossed Mack from the game and, when Mack refused to leave, summoned uniformed patrol officers to escort him from the park.[27] It was the first and only ejection of Mack's 66-year major-league career as a player and manager.

Needing more experience, O'Day spent the 1896 season umpiring in the Western League.[28] Ban Johnson, the minor league's imperious president, understood that baseball's frequent fistfights were eroding attendance and that if left unchecked would not only hinder the game's growth but might ultimately destroy it. Johnson insisted that strong security measures be employed in all his ballparks; that no profanity be allowed on the field or in the stands; and that players engaging in brawls be promptly suspended. Most importantly, Johnson gave his umpires total authority and supported them completely. Working full-time in the Western League was an epiphany for O'Day—this was the way baseball should and could be conducted.

Returning to the National League as a full-time umpire in 1897, O'Day was determined to do his part to reduce the game's excessive violence. It would prove to be one of his most immense contributions to baseball.[29] Employing full use of all the weapons an umpire has in enforcing discipline—warnings, imposing fines, ejections, threat of forfeit, and recommending suspensions—O'Day remained resolute, sending the clear message that he would not tolerate any disrespect of the game or his authority. In 1897 he ejected players and managers at a steady clip, mainly for fighting and bench-jockeying. The following season he even ejected a Chicago fan for using profane language.[30]

O'Day has the third highest ejection rate of any veteran umpire in major-league history.[31] Hall of Fame pitcher Christy Mathewson said, "It is as dangerous to argue with him as it is to try to ascertain how much gasoline is in the tank of an automobile by sticking down the lighted end of a cigar."[32] Although O'Day had a high ejection rate, he was not known to have a quick trigger. Being a former player himself, he understood that in the heat of competition tempers can flare. He would let players blow off a little steam, as long as they didn't go too far. "That is why I consider Hank O'Day the best in the business," wrote F.C. Lane. "He makes allowances for a man. ... Hank gives some leeway unless a player exceeds his bounds."[33]

"It is most important that an umpire not lose his temper," said O'Day. "As a matter of fact, he should not have a temper at all. He must not notice the little slurs." Nonetheless, when a player cheated or engaged in acts of unsportsmanlike conduct, "I order a player from the field promptly."[34] Stone-faced Hank O'Day, forever stoic, became known for never losing his cool. He also was recognized for never holding a grudge. O'Day would preach to young umpires the importance of having a short memory, to always strive to "forget all the little unpleasantness that has occurred on the field as soon as the game is over."[35]

When ejections weren't enough to restore order, O'Day would resort to forfeit. On June 22, 1900, in Philadelphia, the losing Phillies began making a mockery of the game by purposely walking batters and refusing to tag out runners in hopes that O'Day would call the game on account of darkness and have the score revert to the earlier inning. After several warnings, he forfeited the game to Brooklyn and was "nearly mobbed afterwards" by the enraged hometown fans.[36] A year later, on May 13, 1901, O'Day awarded another forfeit, this time against Brooklyn. In the top of the ninth with two outs, Brooklyn thought it had taken the lead when Bill Dahlen singled to left with the bags loaded, apparently driving in two runners. O'Day, however, would not allow the second run. He had noticed that the runner from second base had not crossed the plate before the runner from first had been thrown out at third base. It was a "time play," meaning the second run did not count. The Brooklyn players surrounded him, screaming in protest. An ejection, several warnings, and O'Day pulling out his watch and waiting three minutes did not restore the peace, so he awarded a forfeit win to New York.[37]

"During the formative era of major-league umpiring, no National League umpire was held in greater esteem for integrity and the ability to 'run the game' than O'Day," said Professor Larry Gerlach.[38] Far too often more than a few umpires of the era would make close calls in favor of the home team to avoid abuse from the local crowd. O'Day refused to be intimidated and continually made the right call as he saw it, regardless of the color of the player's uniform. Teams hated to see O'Day at their home games because they knew they would get no added advantage, but were delighted when he was assigned to their road games.[39]

Sportswriters, accustomed to bashing officials in their game accounts, praised O'Day for having the courage to make the right call, no matter how unpopular. One writer called him "the premier ump of all ages."[40] Another appreciated O'Day's talent of having "that wonderful knack of gauging that hairline width that separates a strike from a ball."[41] The words integrity, honor, and honesty became synonymous with the name Hank O'Day long before they were cemented by the call that would define his life.

On September 23, 1908, during the heat of a passionate pennant race, the Cubs and Giants were engaged in an intense game in New York's Polo Grounds. The umpires were Hank O'Day behind the plate and Bob Emslie on the bases. The score was tied in the bottom of the ninth with two outs and runners on first and third. The Giants' Al Bridwell hit a solid single to the outfield and Moose McCormick "scored" easily from third base. Hundreds of New York fans, believing their Giants had a walk-off victory, charged onto the field in celebration. However, rookie Fred Merkle, the baserunner on first base, had stopped halfway to second before running to the Giants' outfield clubhouse. It was a common practice of the day for players to run off the field to avoid fans entering the playing field after a game.

What followed next was pure pandemonium. As the fans swarmed the field, Cubs center fielder Solly Hofman continued to run after the batted ball. Johnny Evers, Cubs second baseman, stood on the bag screaming for Hofman to throw him the ball. Under the rules, if Merkle was forced out at second, the run would not count. Hofman threw the ball off the mark into the infield, where a Cubs player picked it up. Seeing what was happening, New York's Joe McGinnity wrested the ball from the player and threw it into a crowd of fans behind third base. Evers eventually got a baseball—if it was the actual game ball, nobody will ever know for sure—and stood on second base, declaring a force out.[42] Cubs shortstop Joe Tinker pleaded with base umpire Emslie to call the out; but Emslie said that in the chaos he did not see if Merkle had touched second base. O'Day, however, was watching everything. Hank conferred with his partner, told him that Merkle did not touch second base, and Emslie called the force out. O'Day then nullified the "winning" run and proclaimed the game a tie. The game did not continue into extra innings because O'Day determined that by the time the grounds were cleared of fans, it would have been too dark for further play.

The riotous mob of fans surrounding O'Day in the middle of the diamond "began pounding him on all available parts not covered by the protector, while the unfortunate attackers on the outside began sending messages by way of cushions, newspapers, and other missiles."[43] Police officers rushed in to rescue the umpires and escort them to the safety of their dressing room. National League President Harry Pulliam later denied all protests and upheld O'Day's decision. Despite scathing editorials and extreme pressure for O'Day and Pulliam to change their decision and award the win to New York, the two remained steadfast. O'Day's call was crucial because the Giants and Cubs finished the season in a dead heat with records of 98-55. The "Merkle Game" had to be replayed and the Cubs won, giving them the pennant by one game.

Merkle was saddled with the nickname "Bonehead" for the rest of his life. Pulliam committed suicide by shooting a bullet into his head. And O'Day umpired another 17 years, abuse being heaped upon him every time he entered the Polo Grounds by fans who believed he had robbed them of a championship.

The manner in which league presidents assigned O'Day to games is illustrative of how highly regarded he was as an umpire. O'Day usually worked alone but when he was a member of a two-man crew, he was generally assigned the more demanding plate position. In his first 1,000 games as a major-league umpire, he was behind the plate 90.4 percent of the time. A rookie umpire was often assigned to work with him so that the neophyte could learn from the master. When there was a particularly important series between contending teams, ones involving great pressure and large riotous crowds, O'Day was the man selected to work the games.

As durable as O'Day was, there are several gaps in his career explained by the many illnesses and injuries he suffered while umpiring. There were the many bruises and beatings he sustained from irate fans charging onto the field after one of his calls. Foul balls were particularly treacherous: One broke his toe, requiring two players to take his place as umpire; another one smashed through his mask, producing a nasty gash on his cheek and severely injuring his jaw; and yet another inflicted a head wound requiring an operation for removal of a piece of bone from behind his ear. He was seriously ill one entire season with recurring stomach problems brought on by stress. In other seasons, a robust case of influenza knocked him out for several weeks and an attack of appendicitis in St. Louis meant an ambulance trip to the hospital.

"World Series assignments clearly reveal the greatest umpires in any given era, as well as in baseball history," wrote Larry Gerlach.[44] And Hank O'Day's World Series record is truly astounding. When the first modern World Series was established in 1903, the two leagues were asked to send their best umpire to work the best-of-nine Series. The National League selected O'Day; the American League chose Tommy Connolly. What is extraordinary is that the two umpires did not alternate their positions during the Series. O'Day worked the plate for the first four games, with Connolly serving as the base umpire. O'Day's reputation was so great, he was so highly acclaimed for his ability to call balls and strikes, and he was so noted for his integrity, that the AL had no problem having the NL umpire working extra games behind the plate. For six of the first eight World Series games ever played, O'Day was the plate umpire.

O'Day was assigned to umpire four of the first five World Series (1903, 1905, 1907, and 1908), always working more plate games than his partner. When the World Series expanded to a four-man umpire crew in 1910, Hank was one of the two NL umpires selected. He would be chosen to umpire five more fall classics later in his career (1916, 1918, 1920, 1923, and 1926) for a total of 10 World Series, tied with Cy Rigler for the second-most ever behind Bill Klem. (O'Day would have had more World Series assignments had he not taken a break from umpiring to become a manager a couple of seasons.)

O'Day had other notable World Series "firsts" other than being the first plate umpire. In Game Two of the 1907 Series, he alertly called out Chicago Cub Jimmy Slagle, the only player in World Series history to become victim of the hidden-ball trick.[45] In that same game, Tigers manager Hughie Jennings was the first ever to be ejected from a World Series game—courtesy of Mr. O'Day. In Game Five of the 1920 Series, Bill Wambsganss executed the only unassisted triple play in the postseason; Hank was the second-base umpire making the three "out" calls in quick succession. (O'Day also worked the pressure-packed Game Seven of the 1920 World Series.)

One of the more intriguing periods of O'Day's long baseball career was his two stints as a National League manager. When O'Day was announced as the new skipper for the 1912 Cincinnati Reds, the baseball world was stunned. Even more surprising was when the rookie manager led the team to "one of the most sensational starts in major league history."[46] On May 12 the Reds were in first place with a 22-7 record, an amazing improvement from the team's sixth-place finish the year before. The Reds then slumped badly before making a surge toward the end to finish in fourth place with a 75-78 record. When O'Day heard that the Reds were going to replace him as manager with Joe Tinker, he quit before he was fired. The *New York Times* reported that "President Thomas J. Lynch and the National League Club owners would undoubtedly welcome O'Day back as an umpire."[47] The newspaper was correct; O'Day was back holding the indicator for the 1913 season.

O'Day then pulled off another surprise by agreeing to be the Chicago Cubs' new manager for the 1914 season. Although he did a decent job by leading the injury-riddled team to a winning record and a third-place finish, he was fired after the season. This time a sportswriter questioned whether O'Day would return to the NL as an umpire because he would be "no fit person to give unbiased decisions" to two teams he had once managed.[48] Ban Johnson attempted to sign baseball's best umpire for his American League, but O'Day remained loyal to the NL and was back behind the plate during the 1915 season. "That he was rehired twice after managing two National League teams speaks volumes as to his talent and integrity," said Larry Gerlach.[49]

As the game's dean of umpires, O'Day was instrumental in firmly establishing the use of umpire hand signals to communicate calls to fans and players, and improving mechanics for better officiating. At first he was opposed to umpires using signals because he believed an umpire should not be demonstrative. He soon came around because it was in the best interests of baseball. Surprisingly, the usually progressive O'Day also initially opposed the two-umpire system. He said an umpire "has more trouble working double than single, as in many cases he not only has to make his own decisions, but sometimes his mate's as well."[50] He said this not long after he had to help his partner make the call in the Merkle incident. O'Day, of course, understood that two umpires can cover and control a game much better than one and quickly became an avid supporter of the double-umpire system. He umpired long enough to see three and even four arbiters being assigned to regular-season games.

As influential as O'Day was in other areas, his most far-reaching impact concerned baseball rules. His contributions in the development of baseball have significantly helped the sport evolve into the great game it is today. Hank O'Day was the most prominent member of baseball's Joint Rules Committee in his time, with his vote and opinion carrying considerable weight. Whenever a new playing or scoring rule was proposed, or a question arose on how an established rule should be interpreted, baseball authorities would first turn to O'Day for advice and counsel. "His brain is an encyclopedia of all the rules of the game," said longtime baseball man Ted Sullivan.[51]

Hank was the originator of the "foul-strike rule," in which the first two foul balls struck by a batter are strikes; previously, an uncaught foul was essentially a "no pitch."[52] The rule, still in use today, has had a massive impact on the game. O'Day pushed for the rule requiring the catcher to remain directly behind the plate throughout an at-bat because it made for better officiating in the fair/foul and ball/strike calls. Previously, the catcher would stand far behind home plate when there were runners on base. (This rule also helped advance the development of safety equipment for catchers and umpires.) In 1910 baseball officials, concerned about the lack of offense in the game, were about to pass a new rule allowing four strikes for a strikeout until O'Day objected. Instead, he supported the introduction of a "lively ball" with a cork center. As a former pitcher, O'Day initially opposed the proposal to ban the spitball but, to provide needed offense to the game, he endorsed rules prohibiting the spitter and other "freak pitches." Throughout his career, O'Day pushed for the uniformity of the rules and regulations in both major leagues. He also helped quicken the game by allowing on-deck batters on the field.[53]

One scoring rule in which O'Day did not get his way is one we take for granted today. In 1920 sportswriter Fred Lieb proposed that whenever a player hits a game-winning home run out of the park (what we call a "walk-off" today), he should get credit for the home run and all the RBIs for any runners on base. Previously, for example, in a tie game in the bottom of the ninth with a runner on third base, a batter hitting a home run got credit for only a single on the theory that the game ended as soon as the baserunner from third scored. O'Day vociferously argued against this proposal, stating that the rule is "sacred and untouchable" that no run can be scored after the winning run has crossed the plate. When the measure was passed 5-1 by the Joint Rules Committee, he pounded on the table, shouting, "I'm telling you, it's illegal. You can't score runs after a game is over!"[54]

O'Day was renowned for his moral character as well as for being an odd character. "He was an umpire and nothing else," said NL President John Heydler.[55] Baseball consumed every fiber of his being, leaving little time for anything else. O'Day was described as "this strange character who lived in a shell, emerging only when he visited the field to render his decisions."[56] With no interest in anything but baseball, he rarely attended parties, the theater, movie houses, or any social event. He had no hobbies, other than relaxing at the race track.[57]

You could count the number of O'Day's friends on Mordecai Brown's right hand. "He preferred his own company," said Lieb. "He minded his own business and expected others to do the same."[58] One offseason, O'Day traveled from Chicago to Ontario to visit fellow umpire Bob Emslie, but O'Day's "idea of a good time was to sit for hours on Emslie's front porch in complete silence.[59]

A lifelong bachelor, O'Day never owned a home. He preferred to live in solitude in hotels and dine alone in restaurants. He would spend his winters working out so that he would be in proper shape to meet the demands of the long baseball season. In his off-hours he sat by himself in hotel lobbies reading nothing but baseball publications and the rulebook. If a player, fan, or sportswriter approached, he would wave them away unless they were there to talk baseball. A cheerful greeting from others would be met with a grumble.

O'Day's lack of a sense of humor contrasted equally to his towering sense of honor. "It is a National League tradition that Henry has never yet been known to smile," commented a *Baseball Magazine* reporter.[60] Christy Mathewson claimed to have seen O'Day laugh once, explaining that his "face acted as if it wasn't accustomed to the experience and broke out in funny new wrinkles."[61] Even some of his fellow umpires referred to him as "Groucho" behind his back.[62] Bill Klem called O'Day a "misanthropic Irishman" who "wouldn't speak a civil word to anybody."[63] O'Day's somber unsmiling face earned him the nickname "The Reverend."[64]

During an interview, NL President John Heydler talked about what it takes to be a great umpire: "The successful umpire must live the life of a hermit, apart from the friendships of the player and fans. He must be a man without a country, home or haunt in the world of baseball. He must be alone on the train. He must stay in a different hotel. He must keep aloof while in the baseball park and avoid all baseball assemblies. … Strength of character, courage of conviction, fixity of purpose and intelligence are necessary requisites for a successful umpire."[65] Although Heydler didn't mention Hank O'Day by name, everybody knew whom he was referring to.

It would take a skilled psychologist to determine why O'Day became such a sullen, secretive man both on and off the field. One explanation is that it was simply his nature, that "O'Day was born not liking people."[66] But accounts of his dour personality do not appear until after he became a full-time major-league umpire. A fan recalled that when O'Day was a pitcher in 1886, he was "a good-natured happy-go-lucky boy from the North, as full of fun as any other youngster on the Savannah team."[67] It is curious that the few friends O'Day had were all baseball men he had met as a younger man.[68] The many personal tragedies of his life may also have triggered the profound change in his personality.[69] There is yet another reason he was so unsociable: O'Day was so concerned that his integrity was beyond reproach that he had taken it to a ridiculous extreme. Fearful that even the slightest personal relationship might influence his calls on the field, he refused to get close to anyone.

All these factors no doubt contributed to O'Day's being so miserable, but the main one was likely the burden of being an umpire during his era. Umpire Silk O'Loughlin tried to persuade a young Bill Klem not to become an umpire by using O'Day as an example. "Look at O'Day," O'Loughlin told Klem. "One of the best umpires. Maybe the best today. But he's sour. Umpiring does that to you. The abuse you get from the players, the insults from the crowds, and the awful things they write about you in the newspapers."[70]

"O'Day served as a model to young umpires for courage, loyalty and a deep ingrained honesty," wrote Fred Leib.[71] O'Day encouraged Klem to make umpiring a career and, in 1904, introduced and recommended him to NL President Harry Pulliam.[72] When Klem made it to the majors, O'Day tutored and guided him. During his long career, O'Day was a mentor for countless umpires. "He told me a lot about umpiring, things to look for," said 24-year major-league veteran umpire Beans Reardon. "He was big and tough; guys didn't fool around with him. … And he told me, 'Hustle all the time. Be on top of every play, so you're in position to make the decision.' … He recommended me to the National League. I was very fortunate to learn from a great umpire like Hank O'Day. He was the best."[73]

On October 2, 1927, O'Day worked the Cubs-Cardinals game as the third-base umpire in a four-man crew. Nobody knew it at the time but the game featured the oldest man to ever umpire a major-league game. O'Day was 68 years and 86 days old. During the 1927 season, he had been behind the plate only a dozen times out of 147 games, quite a contrast to his younger days. At the end of the season, Heydler took O'Day off active duty, conferred him the title "umpire emeritus," and offered him a job as umpire scout. Grumbling, O'Day accepted it "with regret" because, in his heart, he wanted to continue umpiring.[74] He spent the next few years touring baseball's sandlots and minor-league parks, instructing and developing young umpires. O'Day umpired in 35 major-league seasons, particularly notable in an era when there were no unions and umpires signed one-year contracts.

In the early months of 1935, baseball fans read various reports of O'Day being seriously ill. In his final days, he was delirious, muttering about games he had umpired years earlier. He could go through a catalog of more than 4,000 games, each one with a different story, some thrilling, many routine, others amusing or trivial, and more than a few dangerous.

There was that game in 1898 when a fast-burning fire destroyed the old wooden Sportsman's Park in St. Louis. O'Day and players from both teams were heroes by creating a makeshift chute from the dugout benches for fans to slide down to the field to escape the burning grandstand, and then leading them to safety through an exit untouched by the flames.[75] Or that game when Luther Taylor, a deaf-mute, swore at O'Day with sign language only to be surprised when O'Day signaled back that he was ejected from the game. Taylor was unaware that O'Day, having had deaf parents, was fluent in American Sign Language. Maybe, as O'Day lay dying, he remembered his extended work on October 2, 1920, when he umpired the only twentieth-century major-league tripleheader with partner Peter Harrison.[76] O'Day may have recalled that time he learned that Giants shortstop Bill Dahlen was purposely getting ejected from games so that he could leave early and go to the race track, so O'Day refused to toss him despite being called "a big beer-soaked, fat-headed loafer and thief."[77] And, of course, there was that game when the zany Rabbit Maranville humiliated him when he stole second base by sliding between the umpire's legs.

On July 2, 1935, Hank O'Day died in Chicago of bronchial pneumonia, six days shy of his 76th birthday. To the end, he was still drawing pay as a NL "advisory umpire."[78] His funeral service, held in St. Jariath Catholic Church, was attended by many baseball dignitaries with major-league umpires serving as pallbearers.[79] He left no will; his sole heir was Henry McNamara, a nephew who had been named after him. O'Day was buried in Calvary Cemetery in Evanston, Illinois.

The *Chicago Tribune* ran a feature on the venerated arbiter, saying O'Day was "one of those blunt, rugged characters who seldom allowed his crusty exterior to reveal the really warm heart beneath. Hank O'Day's bark was worse than his bite. He was a great umpire, one of the game's greatest, courageous, honest, and with a thorough knowledge of the rule subtleties."[80]

In announcing O'Day's death, virtually every newspaper included in its headline the name Merkle. In one obituary, it was stated: "Hank is gone, but he'll not be forgotten."[81] Sadly, he would be forgotten for years when it came to being bestowed baseball's highest honor.

On July 28, 2013, Hank O'Day was inducted into the National Baseball Hall of Fame, 78 years after his death and 86 years after he had umpired his last ballgame.[82]

Why did it take so long for such an influential baseball figure to make it to Cooperstown?

The Hall of Fame held its first election in 1936 and, in the years following, many of the game's great players were properly honored, along with influential pioneers, executives, and managers. But what about the umpires, those dedicated men in blue who have had such a positive image on the game? It wasn't until Bill Klem died in 1951 that attention was brought to the fact that no umpire had ever been inducted. Two years later the legendary Klem was honored along with Tommy Connolly, the first umpires enshrined in the Hall of Fame. Why Connolly over O'Day? As fine an arbiter as Connolly was, O'Day had always been considered the greater umpire and more influential. Simply put, Connolly was an American League umpire while O'Day was a National League umpire. When the electors honored NL umpire Klem, they wanted an umpire representing the AL in the Hall of Fame.[83]

After Klem and Connolly, it would be another 20 years before another umpire was elected. Subsequently, six other outstanding umpires were inducted. O'Day, arguably the best of them all, was always overlooked. Baseball historian David Anderson endorsed O'Day and wondered why he had not already been bequeathed the big honor. "That he is not in the Hall of Fame is an oversight," Anderson wrote. "This is partly a function of the fact that he never married; baseball was his love, and he had no family to lobby for him. Conspiracy buffs may believe the oversight to be a measure of revenge by New York sportswriters for O'Day's decision in the infamous Merkle game, but more likely it is because O'Day was not known to be a particularly friendly person."[84]

Anderson is correct but ironically, the explanations for O'Day *not* having been honored are reasons why he *should* be honored. For O'Day, baseball was indeed his love, which came at the expense of not having the comfort of family and friends. He was also not "a particularly friendly person," but this was because he did not want to get close to anyone to ensure that his integrity as an umpire was never compromised. O'Day's credo was "I know no friends nor enemies on the field," an attitude that extended to his private life.[85] Nonetheless, it was through his forceful will and personality, at great personal sacrifice to him, that the game was enriched.

As for the Merkle incident, there is no better demonstration of O'Day's integrity, one of the criteria for the Hall of Fame.[86] That fateful day, it would have been easier to have just walked off the field when the "winning" run scored, but that would not have been the ethical thing to do.

Bill Klem's remarks also did not help O'Day's chances of reaching Cooperstown. He called the Merkle ruling "the rottenest decision in the history of baseball. ... It was bad umpiring."[87] On the contrary, it was a courageous decision and excellent umpiring. It was a betrayal by Klem of his former partner and the man who helped Klem become a major-league umpire. Of course, Klem waited until O'Day had been dead for 16 years before making his craven criticism.

Klem is universally recognized as "the greatest umpire in baseball history" and is much more celebrated than his contemporary Hank O'Day.[88] The two men had quite different philosophies regarding their profession. Klem was a showman and self-promoter; O'Day eschewed publicity. Klem enjoyed drinking and dining with players and managers; O'Day avoided all off-field contact with baseball people. Klem would make up his own baseball rules; O'Day insisted on the enforcement of the rules as written.[89] One could argue that O'Day, rather than Klem, should have been the first umpire inducted into the Baseball Hall of Fame.

Dennis McNamara, a retired Chicago police officer and O'Day's grandnephew, gave the induction speech at the posthumous Hall of Fame induction of the great umpire. "Uncle Hank was almost a mythic figure in our family and his example guided me as a policeman," McNamara said. "The lesson of Hank O'Day is: Do your best with honesty and integrity."[90]

## NOTES

1. When Ted Breitenstein (1898), Johnny Lush (1906), Hod Eller (1919), and Jesse Haines (1924) tossed their no-hit gems, Hank O'Day was calling the balls and strikes.

2. Lee Allen, *The Cincinnati Reds* (New York: G.P. Putnam's Sons, 1948), 99.

3. G.H. Fleming, *The Unforgettable Season* (New York: Holt, Rinehart and Winston, 1981), 243.

4. Personal information about Hank O'Day often conflicts because he always refused to talk about his private life. He was particularly thick-lipped about his age. Depending on the obituary or biography, his birth year varies widely. On his *Sporting News* umpire card, the year 1861 is crossed off and replaced with the handwritten "July 8, 1862." O'Day's birth certificate was lost in the Great Chicago Fire; however, census reports confirm that he was born in 1859. Hank's siblings were named Daniel, James Jr., Catherine (Kate), Margaret, Mary, and Joseph. His mother's name is often reported as Mary but it was actually Margaret. (Death notice, *Chicago Tribune*, March 14, 1895). Most sources contend that O'Day's middle initial is "M," including the National Baseball Hall of Fame; but prominent baseball historians, including Larry Gerlach, Norman Macht, and David Nemec, state that it is "F" for Francis. Dennis McNamara, O'Day's grandnephew, said Hank's parents were deaf. (YouTube website video entitled "Umpire O'Day Inducted Into Hall of Fame," posted December 11, 2013).

5. By the time O'Day became a full-time major-league umpire; he was much heavier and had shaved off his mustache. Hank would begin each baseball season weighing about 205 pounds, only to lose 30 pounds by October after hustling around the diamond in the hot sun all summer. "Not So Easy," *Sporting Life*, November 10, 1900: 5.

6. G.W. Axelson, *Commy: The Life Story of Charles A. Comiskey* (Chicago: Reilly & Lee Co., 1919), 21. The O'Day brothers, all pitchers, played for the semipro Libertys. Hank also played for the Spaldings, a team sponsored by Al Spalding. Publisher Alfred Spink was a teammate of the O'Day brothers, serving as their bare-handed catcher. Spink wrote: "The O'Day boys were all fine, brave fellows and Hank ... is perhaps the bravest and best of the lot." Alfred H. Spink, *The National Game* (St. Louis: The National Game Publishing Co. 1911), 371.

7. Chris Goode, *California Baseball: From the Pioneers to the Glory Years* (self-published, 2009), 17-18. Whether O'Day actually attended any classes at St. Mary or just played baseball is a good question. At the time there was an intense athletic rivalry between California colleges and many schools recruited ballplayers to serve as ringers. St. Mary's College must have had an excellent team in 1881-1883, when O'Day was a member, because the team had six players who would later become major leaguers.

8. "Hank O'Day, Picturesque Figure in National League History, Retires," *Pittsburgh Post-Gazette*, December 14, 1927. Although

9. David W. Zang, *Fleet Walker's Divided Heart: The Life of Baseball's First Black Major Leaguer* (Lincoln: University of Nebraska Press, 1995), 39. During his baseball career, Walker suffered much racial abuse from both teammates and opponents. Tony Mullane, self-admitted racist, and Curt Welch, open segregationist, were Walker's teammates. What was O'Day's relationship with Walker? Esteemed baseball historian Lee Allen wrote, "Neither O'Day nor Mullane liked Walker, and each did his best to throw the ball so hard the catcher would be injured, but they never succeeded in forcing him off the job." (Allen, *The Cincinnati Reds*, 100). If accurate, this is a large stain on O'Day's character. Allen is one whose view must be respected; however, his account is the only source that asserts that O'Day had any prejudicial tendencies. In his extensive research, David Nemec, the foremost authority on nineteenth-century baseball, "found nothing negative about (O'Day's) relationship with Walker" nor did he find "any reported derogatory incidents." (Email correspondence with author, January 2017) Additionally, according to Zang's well-researched biography, Walker had a cordial and successful partnership with O'Day.

10. Norman L. Macht, "Henry Francis 'Hank' O'Day," *Baseball's First Stars* (Cleveland: Society for American Baseball Research, 1996), 123.

11. "O'Day of the Pittsburgs Is in Chicago Attending a Very Sick Father," *Sporting Life*, July 7, 1885: 7.

12. "City Items," *Chicago Tribune*, September 4, 1885: 3.

13. Statistics are from Hank O'Day's minor-league page on Baseball-Reference.com. Typical of O'Day's hard-luck 1887 season was when he smashed a triple, "the longest hit of his career," and then scored on a wild pitch only to have the game called on account of darkness. The score reverted to the previous inning and Hank was deprived of his mighty hit and run scored. (Wm. A. Phelon, "Baseball Customs Past and Present," *Baseball Magazine*, October 1915: 55.)

14. O'Day's teammates and future Hall of Famers were Roger Connor, Buck Ewing, Jim O'Rourke, Monte Ward, Tim Keefe, and Mickey Welch.

15. "Championship vs. Exhibition Games," *Sporting Life*, November 6, 1889: 4.

16. Jerry Lansche, *Glory Fades Away: The Nineteenth-Century World Series Rediscovered* (Dallas: Taylor Publishing, 1991), 177.

17. In 1891-93, O'Day pitched for the Lincoln Rustlers, Columbus Reds, Marinette Badgers, and Erie Blackbirds, respectively in the Western Association, Western League, Wisconsin-Michigan League, and Eastern League. In leagues for which we have statistics, O'Day had a losing record every year despite recording decent earned-run averages.

18. David Nemec, *Major League Baseball Profiles, 1871-1900*, Vol. 1 (Lincoln: University of Nebraska Press, 2011), 145-146.

19. Ibid.

20. During this era and into the early years of the twentieth century, usually only one umpire was scheduled to work major-league games. Quite often he would fail to show up by game time because of travel disruptions, illness, or the fact that he had simply quit. Whenever this occurred, the two managers would each select one of their players to umpire the game, usually a pitcher on his offday or a catcher needing a day off. The selected player would have to be agreed upon by the opposing manager. The players would umpire the game in their baseball uniforms.

21. No fewer than 135 active players served as emergency substitute umpires during O'Day's seven-year major-league playing career (1884-1890), the vast majority of them umpiring only one game their entire career. O'Day was the exception. While an active player, Hank was called upon to serve as umpire for seven major-league games (three behind the plate), tied with pitcher Mickey Welch for the most during this period. While he served as a substitute umpire, O'Day's "team" lost four times; it is likely his teammates had some choice words for him in the clubhouse afterward.

22. Bill James, *The New Bill James Historical Baseball Abstract* (New York: Free Press, 2001), 53.

23. Larry R. Gerlach, "Umpire Honor Rolls," *Baseball Research Journal* (Cooperstown: Society for American Baseball Research, 1979): 82.

24. Before taking the job with the city, O'Day umpired some games in the Western League. Hank returned to Chicago in 1895 not only to find employment but also because his mother had died that year and his sister Margaret had died not much earlier ("Deaths," *Chicago Tribune*, March 14, 1895: 7). It is not known exactly why Hank, at this point, had foregone baseball as a career and had taken the security of a government job. It may have been because of the low salary of a minor-league umpire. As tough as O'Day was, it is unlikely that he gave up umpiring because of the profession's harsh demands.

25. Addie Joss, "Hank O'Day Got Job by Accident," *Pittsburgh Post-Gazette*, January 7, 1910: 7. Some details of Joss's account are inaccurate, such as stating that Thomas Lynch was the absent umpire. Joss wrote the article on the occasion of Lynch being appointed National League president in 1910, when O'Day was baseball's most famous umpire. It made for a good story that Lynch, O'Day's new boss, was the tardy umpire responsible for Hank becoming a major-league umpire 15 years earlier. Although Lynch was an NL umpire from 1888 to 1894, returning in 1896, he was not a full-time umpire in 1895. Research reveals that the absent umpire was likely Miah Murray, who worked the Giants-Cubs game on July 8, the day after O'Day had come to the rescue as arbiter. (Umpire pages for 1895, Retrosheet.org) Joss mentions that "there were three or four baseball magnates in the stands" that game; although

unusual, this rings true. The July 7 game was a makeup, with Cleveland traveling to Chicago for that one game. The Giants had played the Colts the previous day and would play them the next day, meaning the team (and their owner) were also in Chicago on July 7. Stanley Robison, part-owner of the Spiders, may also have been in the ballpark that day.

26  "Umpire's Close Call," *Washington Post*, August 21, 1895: 4.

27  Norman L. Macht, *Connie Mack and the Early Days of Baseball* (Lincoln: University of Nebraska Press, 2007), 118-119. Mack's ejection occurred on September 6, 1895; afterward, Connie still remained friends with O'Day.

28  On July 26, 1896, O'Day was called up from the minors to umpire one major-league game in Chicago that season.

29  Besides O'Day's strong actions, another influential factor in reducing the violence in baseball was Ban Johnson's minor league reaching major-league status in 1901 as the American League. Nonetheless, even with the forceful personalities of Johnson and O'Day, the game's culture of rowdiness was so embedded that it took several years before the problem was effectively curtailed. Meanwhile, the NL lost some excellent arbiters, like Jack Sheridan and Tommy Connelly, who jumped the senior circuit to umpire in the AL for its better working conditions. O'Day remained loyal to the NL, steadfastly working to rid the game of its violence. When the AL, in only its second season, outdrew the National League and continued to so for the rest of the decade, the older league eventually realized the importance of strict discipline and the wisdom of greater support of its umpires.

30  "Notes and Comments," *Sporting Life*, June 5, 1898.

31  Of the 81 major-league umpires who have worked more than 3,000 games (through 2017), the three with the highest rate of ejections are all National League umpires from the early twentieth century. Cy Rigler has the highest rate (an ejection every 17.2 games), followed by Bill Klem (17.9) and Hank O'Day (18.7).

32  Christy Mathewson, *Pitching in a Pinch* (New York: Grosset & Dunlap Publishers, 1912), 175.

33  F.C. Lane, "The Gamest Player in Baseball," *Baseball Magazine*, September 1913: 58.

34  "Live Talk About the Baseball Players," *St. Louis Republic*, March 20, 1904.

35  Ibid.

36  David Nemec and Eric Miklich, *Forfeits and Successfully Protested Games in Major League Baseball* (Jefferson, North Carolina: McFarland Publishers: 2014), 97.

37  Nemec and Miklich, 102.

38  E-mail correspondence with umpire historian Larry R. Gerlach, November 2012.

39  "Close Decisions: An Inside Study of the Life, the Work, the Difficulties and the Humor of a Baseball Umpire," *The American Magazine*, Volume 72 (New York: Crowell Publishing Company, 1911): 210.

40  "Notes of the Cubs," *Chicago Tribune*, July 16, 1909: 18.

41  Frederick G. Lieb, "Late Hank O'Day, Sphinx-Like, Fearless and Honest, Defied Wrath of McGraw in Merkle Decision," *The Sporting News*, July 11, 1935: 2.

42  As for the argument that Merkle should not have been called out because Evers did not have the right ball, O'Day later said the out would have been called regardless of what ball Evers was holding because of McGinnity's interference. "The Merkle Play," *Sporting Life*, October 24, 1914: 19.

43  *New York Herald*, September 24, 1908, account of game found in Fleming's *The Unforgettable Season*, 245.

44  E-mail correspondence with Gerlach.

45  John Snyder, *Cubs Journal* (Cincinnati: Clerisy Press: 2008), 141.

46  "Hank O'Day Resigns," *New York Times*, November 7, 1912. The Reds were so successful that a sportswriter joked that even their manager "Hank O'Day can smile these days without hurting his face." ("Around the Bases," *Chicago Defender*, May 18, 1912: 6).

47  "Hank O'Day Resigns."

48  "O'Day to Umpire American League," *Providence Evening News*, November 24, 1914: 4.

49  E-mail correspondence with Gerlach.

50  "Hank O'Day Is Unalterably Opposed to Proposed Double-Umpire System," *Pittsburgh Press*, October 16, 1908: 22.

51  Spink, 370.

52  For a fine description of the evolution of the foul-strike rule, see Peter Morris, *A Game of Inches: The Stories Behind the Innovations That Shaped Baseball* (Chicago: Ivan R. Dee, 2006), 84-89.

53  One of O'Day's rule proposals that never made the rulebook was actually not a bad idea. Hank wanted to install white rubber strips for the batter's box to prevent players from wiping away the chalk lines. ("Ump O'Day's Idea," *Sporting Life*, December 29, 1906).

54  Fred Lieb, *Baseball As I Have Known It* (New York: Coward, McCann & Geoghegan, 1977), 74-75.

55  David W. Anderson, *You Can't Beat the Hours: Umpires in the Deadball Era From 1901-1909* (North Charleston, South Carolina: CreateSpace Independent Publishing: 2013), 78.

56  Lieb, "Late Hank O'Day."

57  In honor of the great umpire, a thoroughbred race horse was named Hank O'Day. Dorothy Ours, *Man of War: A Legend Like Lightning* (New York: Macmillan Publishers: 2006), 77.

58  Lieb, "Late Hank O'Day."

59  Ibid.

60  "Short Lengths," *Baseball Magazine*, August 1913: 76.

## 20-GAME LOSERS

61  Mathewson, 168.

62  Lieb, "Late Hank O'Day."

63  William J. Klem and William J. Slocum, "I Never Missed One in My Heart," *Collier's Weekly,* March 31, 1951: 59.

64  Associated Press, "Umpire Hank O'Day Dies at Age of 74," *Boston Herald,* July 3, 1935: 17.

65  Associated Press, "To Be Successful Umpire, Official Must Be a Pariah," *Ludington* (Michigan) *Daily News,* April 9, 1924: 3.

66  Cait Murphy, *Crazy '08* (Washington: Smithsonian Books: 2008), 185. Murphy's work is a wildly entertaining account of the exciting 1908 season and the Merkle incident.

67  Lieb, "Late Hank O'Day."

68  O'Day played ball with Charlie Comiskey as a teenager; Connie Mack was a teammate; Bob Emslie was an opposing pitcher in Hank's playing days; and John Heydler was a fellow umpire in the early years. To psychoanalyze, socializing with these men may have brought back memories of happier times for O'Day.

69  When Hank was 12 years old, the Great Chicago Fire ignited about a block north of the O'Day home in 1871, a catastrophe he refused to ever talk about. Hank outlived his six siblings; all dying at relatively young ages, one by suicide and another in a tragic accident. He may have been closest to his younger sister Mary, with whom he had lived with for a short time. When Mary gave birth to a son on Hank's 40th birthday, she named the baby after her brother. Mary's death in 1924 must have hit Hank hard. ("Deaths," *Chicago Tribune,* February 18, 1924: 10).

70  Klem, "I Never Missed One in My Heart," 61.

71  Lieb, "Late Hank O'Day."

72  Bob Considine, "Foghorn," *Collier's Weekly,* April 13, 1940: 76.

73  Larry R. Gerlach, *The Men in Blue: Conversations With Umpires* (New York: Viking Press, 1980), 9-10.

74  *Pittsburgh Press,* December 16, 1927.

75  "Fire Ends the Game," *Chicago Tribune,* April 17, 1898. Hank lost clothes and personal effects when the umpire's dressing room burned down.

76  A.D. Suehsdorf, "The Last Triple-Header," *Baseball Research Journal* (Cooperstown: Society for American Baseball Research, 1980): 30-33.

77  "Close Decisions," *The American Magazine.*

78  George Kirksey, "Hank O'Day is Near Death; Merkle Boner Recalled," *Pittsburgh Press,* February 22, 1935: 39.

79  "Many Baseball Notables Attend O'Day Funeral," *Chicago Tribune,* July 6, 1935: 17. Among those in attendance were Commissioner Kenesaw Landis; Tom Connolly, supervisor of American League umpires; his protégé Bill Klem; and Bill Emslie and John Heydler, Hank's greatest admirers and closest friends.

80  "In the Wake of the News," *Chicago Tribune,* July 11, 1935: 21.

81  "Hank O'Day, Picturesque Figure," *Pittsburgh Post-Gazette.*

82  O'Day received 93.8 percent of the vote from the Hall of Fame's Pre-Integration Committee to earn induction. The 16-member committee consisted of Hall of Famers Bert Blyleven, Pat Gillick, Phil Niekro, and Don Sutton; baseball executives Roland Hemond, Bill DeWitt, Gary Hughes, and Bob Watson; and sportswriters and historians Jim Henneman, Steve Hirdt, Peter Morris, Phil Pepe, Tom Simon, Claire Smith, T.R. Sullivan, and Mark Whicker. They deserve praise for bestowing on O'Day the honor he had long deserved.

83  Another reason Connolly was elected to the Hall of Fame before O'Day was that his name was much better known at the time. In 1953 Connolly was still actively serving as the American League umpire supervisor at age 82; O'Day had been dead for 18 years. It was not the first time the Hall of Fame Veterans Committee had selected the wrong man. Years earlier, it had inducted the worthy Ban Johnson, the first American League president; at the same election, as a counterpart, the electors honored the forgettable Morgan Bulkeley, the first National League president, rather than the influential William Hulbert, the second NL president.

84  David W. Anderson, *More Than Merkle: A History of the Best and Most Exciting Baseball Season in Human History* (Lincoln: University of Nebraska Press, 2000), 98.

85  Lieb, "Late Hank O'Day."

86  Evidence that the Merkle decision was indeed a reason O'Day had not been inducted earlier is the newspaper headline reading: "Despite Call, O'Day Gets Call" (David Briggs, *Toledo Blade,* July 28, 2013).

87  William J. Klem and William J. Slocum, "Jousting With McGraw," *Collier's Weekly,* April 7, 1951: 31.

88  David Pietrusza, Matthew Silverman, and Michael Gershman, eds., *Baseball: The Biographical Encyclopedia* (New York: Total Sports Publishing, 2000), 613.

89  "Klem was a czar on the field. He made up his own rules," said veteran NL umpire Lee Ballanfant. (Gerlach, *Men In Blue*, 9). Authors David Nemec and Eric Miklich wrote, "Klem's infallibility is not even remotely true. Klem, in actuality, may have been involved in more overturned and controversial contests than any other umpire in history." (*Forfeits and Successfully Protested Games*, 212).

90  YouTube website video "Umpire O'Day Inducted Into Hall of Fame," posted December 11, 2013.

# OLD HOSS RADBOURN

## BY BRIAN MCKENNA

**CHARLES RADBOURN'S PITCHING** achievements were hailed by contemporaries and sportswriters for decades as some of the greatest feats of nineteenth century baseball. Little known today, many considered an 18-inning game in 1882 as the finest athletic contest ever seen on a baseball diamond. That game was won, not by the pitcher Radbourn, but by the batter Radbourn playing right field. After a scoreless 17 1/2 innings, he clubbed one over the left-field wall for the first walkoff home run in a 1-0 game in major-league history.

It was on the mound though that Radbourn truly shined. For decades, his winning 59 games in 1884 was viewed as the greatest of all pitching feats. Until recently, most references cited him with 60 wins, a discrepancy arising from determining who should be credited with the victory in his July 28 relief appearance. Throughout his lifetime and well into the career of Cy Young, Radbourn was hailed as the "King of Pitchers." He had an easy underhand motion from which he delivered a variety of pitches from varying arm angles. He was one of the first to truly dicker with his delivery day in and day out to keep hitters off balance, a trait expanded upon by Clark Griffith and Eddie Plank at the turn of the century.

Radbourn was a tireless worker who didn't seek the limelight. As one observer noted, he "never worked the press or catered to the grandstand, and was, in fact, so (in)different to applause or criticism that people who didn't know him well, regarded him as surly and capricious."[1] Year after year, he just took his turn in the rotation and produced what many of the era considered the finest career of all the hurlers.

Caroline (nee Gardner) Radbourn packed her possessions in the summer of 1851 and left Bristol, England with her daughter Sarah, headed for a new life in the United States. Her husband Charles had already relocated to America. Caroline and Sarah traveled with Charles' brothers James and George and his wife Emily and their children. They arrived in New York City on August 22, 1851 aboard the ship *Mary Ann Peter*. The families moved to Rochester where they stayed until 1855. There, Caroline gave birth to Charles on December 11, 1854.

In 1855, the families moved to McLean County, Illinois. Charles and Caroline, both born circa 1827, settled in the town of Martin while George and Emily settled in Bloomington. Soon, Charles and Caroline and family joined their kin in Bloomington, purchasing a farm on West Washington Road. In April 1856, Emily gave birth to George Radbourn, Charles' first cousin and also a future major leaguer. Initially, Charles, a butcher by trade, worked the family farm where his parents George and Sarah and his brother James also resided. In May 1857, he opened a meat market in town. In all, Charles and Caroline had eight children: Sarah, born circa 1848; Charles; John, born circa 1856; William, born circa 1858; Albert, born circa 1861; Selina, born circa 1862; Minnie, born circa 1856; May, born circa 1858.

Some sources claim that the younger Charles Radbourn's middle name was Gardner, his mother's maiden name. That may be but as a child he was usually referred to as Charles Jr. Radbourn attended local schools in Bloomington. In his late teens, he worked as a butcher in a slaughterhouse with his father and as a brakeman for the IB&W Railroad, traveling to Indianapolis and back. Contrary to rumors throughout his baseball career, Radbourn was not a veteran of the Civil War; in fact, he was only 10 years old when it ended.

Radbourn, a right-hander, loved to hunt and play baseball. He strengthened his arm as a teenager by repeatedly throwing the ball against a barn on his family's farm. At least by 1874, he was playing baseball for the main Bloomington nine, earning extra money on weekends and holidays. He also played some games as a ringer for Illinois Wesleyan University. With the

Bloomington squad, he predominantly played third base. His older cousin Henry was the pitcher. Of note, a game-fixing scandal rocked the Bloomington Reds in 1876.

In Bloomington on September 1, the Reds lost to Springfield 4-1. Radbourn went 1-for-4 and committed five errors in left field. In total, the club made 14 miscues, 10 of which were made between the left fielder and center fielder Gleason. Per the *Bloomington Pantagraph*, "The amount of betting that was done… was considerable."[2] Gamblers Edward Stahl, Edward Fifield and Jim Connors were present taking as many wagers as possible in favor of Springfield. At the end of the contest, a shouting match took place between the gamblers and fans, as many suspected that the contest was "set up." Henry Radbourn entered the fray, confronting the three men and accusing them of offering bribes. Later that night in fact, three players, Gleason, Roach, and Flynn, were seen at Connors' hangout having a "jolly good time" on the gambler's dime.

Later the *Pantagraph* interviewed Charlie Radbourn. He admitted to drinking heavily the night before the contest and to having a conversation with two gamblers at Schausten's Saloon. "He says he had a talk with these two, but can not remember distinctly what the talk was more than that it was in relation to throwing the game. After the talk Radbourn went over to two butchers in the saloon and told them about the talk. The butchers say that Charlie told them that Stahl and Connors offered him $25 if he would throw the game…He does not deny that he may have said that he would take the money, but, being drunk, was not responsible for his words."[3] Henry Radbourn, also at the bar, backed his story. Stahl approached Charlie again in the morning before the game, offering $75 total to the two Radbourns and catcher Sue Allen. "Charley having refused the offer told this at once to H. Radbourn who also declined."[4] On September 3, the stockholders met and expelled Gleason and Roach from the club. Flynn was exonerated as was the inebriated Radbourn.

Charles continued with the Bloomington club through 1877, the year he started pitching regularly. During this time, he played with future major leaguers Jack and Bill Gleason and Cliff Carroll. Radbourn's best friend growing up was Bill Hunter, a pitcher for the Bloomington team. One *Baseball Magazine* story claims that future major leaguer Dave Rowe, a resident of Illinois in the mid-1870s, taught Hunter and Radbourn how to throw a curveball, effectively launching Radbourn's career in the box.[5] Al Spalding regaled audiences with a description of his first meeting with Rad during an exhibition game in Bloomington around this time with his Chicago White Stockings. Radbourn relieved his cousin in the contest. As he warmed up, the Chicago players chuckled because the reliever twisted his body to face second base before delivering the ball to the plate. Spalding acknowledged that their smiles soon dissipated as Radbourn sent one batter after another back to the bench.

In 1878, a promoter named William Morgan organized an independent professional team in Peoria, less than 40 miles from Bloomington. The club, known as the Reds, was Peoria's first professional nine. It was captained by Tom Loftus and included several Bloomington-area favorites, including the Gleason brothers, Carroll and Radbourn, now 23 years old. Also on the club were Dave and Jack Rowe, William H. Taylor, and Henry Alveratta. Radbourn was paid $40 a month for the three-month period from July through September. At times, Peoria played exhibition games against National League clubs, racking up wins versus Milwaukee, Chicago, Hartford and Boston in the process. Radbourn played right field and change pitcher, the club's second pitcher. In 28 games he batted .299.

On April 1, 1879, Ted Sullivan, one of the game's foremost organizers, formed and ran the Northwest League which consisted of three clubs from Illinois—Davenport, Omaha, and Rockford, and Dubuque, Iowa. It was the first so-called minor league formed outside the east coast. Sullivan took steps to set a salary structure for the Northwest League and clearly subordinated the league to the National League, which to some establishes it as the first legitimate minor league. Sullivan ran the Dubuque team which was financed by Iowa's U.S. Senator William B. Allison and future Congressman and Speaker of the House David B. Henderson.

Before the season began, the Milwaukee National League team lost its charter and the club's best players *en masse* joined Rockford. Sullivan countered by signing many of the Peoria players. Radbourn signed up with Dubuque in March with Peoria teammates Loftus, the Gleason brothers, Alveratta, and Taylor. Also playing on the club were Charles Comiskey, Laurie Reis, Bill Lapham and Sullivan. Radbourn was paid $450 for the season, playing second base, the outfield and change pitcher. In one game on May 23, he made an incredible 15 putouts from second base. On August 4, he defeated the Chicago National League squad 1-0. Cap Anson later recalled, "in my fifteen years as premier batsman of the game, I never faced a pitcher who baffled me more completely with his curves than did Radbourn on the occasion of that memorable game in Dubuque...I do not hesitate to say that not one of the old school pitchers, or any of the later slabmen, could equal the famous Radbourn."[6]

That year, Dubuque was one of the top clubs in the country not associated with the National League. The club ran away with the Northwest League pennant. Per the *St. Louis Globe-Democrat*, Rad played in 47 games, placed 72 hits for a .337 batting average and scored 31 runs. By December, he was negotiating with Buffalo in the National League. The following appeared in the *Bloomington Pantagraph* on January 9, 1880: "Yesterday, Mr. Charley Radbourn received a letter from the secretary of the Buffalo base ball club, asking for his photograph and his record as a base ball player made last season; also to state the lowest salary for which he would play in the Buffalo nine during the coming season. He answered the letter, and in all probability an arrangement will be made during the next week. The Providence club some weeks ago offered Charley a place at $800 for the season of '80, but he declined the offer."[7]

During spring training in 1880, Radbourn strained his shoulder and never pitched for Buffalo. He made his major-league debut on May 5 in Cleveland, batting sixth and playing right field. He went 1-for-4 but Cleveland romped to a 22-3 victory. Unable to pitch, he was released after six games in May, three at second base and three in right field. Rad returned to the slaughterhouse in Bloomington believing that his baseball career was over.

Over the winter, he received several telegrams with baseball offers but ignored them. In January 1881, Bill Hunter answered a telegram from Providence pretending to be Radbourn and agreeing to join the club in the spring for the same money offered by Buffalo the previous year. Hunter then borrowed money from his father to send Rad to Hot Springs, Arkansas to get into shape. He also got Providence to advance $100 to cover the expenses. Somewhat reluctantly, Radbourn embarked on his major-league career. He officially signed on February 7. Providence finished in second place, nine games behind Chicago. Rad shared the pitching duties with Monte Ward through much of the season. He started 36 games and relieved in another five, amassing a 25-11 record and 117 strikeouts and finishing in the top 10 in most pitching categories including a league-leading win-loss percentage. He also played 25 games in the outfield and 13 games at shortstop.

Charles Radbourn, at 5-foot-9 and listed at 168 pounds, entered baseball during the underhand pitching era. There is some evidence that he threw overhand at least occasionally, as noted later. He was what was then known as a "strategic pitcher." In short, he used whatever assets he had to get batters out, not predominantly relying on speed. This is not to say that he wasn't a hard thrower; he was indeed. He threw a rising fastball, screwball, sinker, slow curve, and something Ted Sullivan described as a dry spitter. He tossed the ball from varying arm angles, possessed great control and changed speeds constantly. He was perhaps the most resourceful of all nineteenth century pitchers, something he passed on to fellow Bloomington resident Clark Griffith. Per Ted Sullivan, who considered Radbourn the greatest of all pitchers, "From the time I met Rad, he was continually inventing a new delivery and trying to get it under control. He had a jump to a high fastball, an in-shoot to a lefthanded batter, a drop ball that he did not have to spit on, and a perplexing slow ball that has never since been duplicated on the ball field. When he let fly with the high fastball, he threw it so hard he actually leaped off the ground."[8]

The *Cleveland Herald* believed the key to his success was the changeup: "A skillful change of pace is the most valuable item in a pitcher's work, as Radbourn's success—due chiefly to it—proves. The so-called 'drop' is either a ball started at the shoulder and slanting in its course, like (Hugh) Daily's, or a skillfully-delivered slow ball, dropping naturally through lack of speed, such as (Jim) McCormick and Radbourn use."[9] Some writers even printed later that Radbourn was the originator of the changeup. Of course this wasn't true but it's a testament to the respect his slow ball gathered.

He threw "a very short, sharp curve." The *Topeka State Journal* described his technique: "Charley Radbourn gets his curves without the use of his body. Having long fingers, he can get a firmer hold than most men, and then he never depends on wide curves, preferring to keep them so a batsman will hit out and get the ball on the end of his stick or close to the handle."[10]

Radbourn wasn't above doctoring the ball to gain an edge. He taught Griffith how to cut a ball with his spikes or any available object to gain a firmer hold for the sinker. He tried anything to stack the deck in his favor. As the *Milwaukee Sentinel* confirmed, "Radbourn was the first pitcher to introduce stepping around the box before delivering the ball. He also tried to work a new wrinkle by making the ball hit in front of the plate and bound over. It was legitimate, but the umpire would not allow it."[11] He wasn't above pitching around the top batters to face lighter hitters; in fact, it was a common ploy. A *Washington Post* article in 1883 claimed that, "Radbourn, pitcher of the Providence nine, can pitch either right or left handed."[12] There doesn't seem to be much supplementary evidence to support the claim, but it seems like something such a resourceful pitcher might try. In the era of no gloves, the batter wouldn't know which hand the delivery was coming from until the pitcher went into his windup.

A former infielder and outfielder, Rad was known as one of the top fielding pitchers of his era. He also controlled the pitch selection and gave his own signals throughout his career, even after it was common for catchers to give most of the signs. Typically, he only signaled for outside pitches, mainly the curve. Rad practiced with an iron ball, throwing it underhand to develop arm strength. He also long tossed to get his arm in shape before taking the mound. He babied his arm, soothing it with hot towels and getting frequent messages. As a result and despite racking up more innings than most, he was one of the few major-league pitchers prior to Cy Young to attain a good amount of success after age 30.

Radbourn appeared in 83 games for Providence in 1882, 54 of them on the mound totaling 474 innings. Either Monte Ward or Rad started every game, 32 and 52 respectively. Rad posted a 33-20 record with a league-leading 201 strikeouts and a second-place mark in victories. The Grays fell only three games short of the championship. On August 17, he played right field versus Detroit. There was no score for the first 17 1/2 innings. In the bottom of the 18th, Rad hit a home run over the left-field wall against Stump Wiedman to claim the victory. It was the first walk-off homer in major-league history in a 1-0 game. Surprisingly by today's standards, the contest only took 2 hours 40 minutes.

The American Association challenged the National League monopoly as a major league in 1882. By the end of the season, quite a few National League players were dissatisfied with their contracts. The AA seemingly was offering bigger paydays. In October, Radbourn signed with the St. Louis Browns in the AA, reuniting with the Gleason brothers, Charles Comiskey and Ted Sullivan. Providence teammates Art Whitney and Jerry Denny also signed with the Browns. Several other National Leaguers signed with Association clubs. In response, the National League threatened to blacklist the jumpers. Most, including Radbourn and the other Providence players, re-signed with their old clubs.

Providence fell to third place in 1883 but the word *fell* is misleading as they landed only five games out of first place. Rad tossed a no-hitter on July 25 versus Cleveland, an 8-0 win on the road. He took on the lion's share of Providence's pitching that season, appearing on the mound for 632 1/3 innings. Many know that Rad owns the single-season victory record with 59 in 1884 but few realize that he already owned the record. His 48 in 1883 set the major-league mark. The 300-strikeout mark was surpassed for the first time in '83. Rad amassed 315 along with Jim Whitney in the National League and Tim Keefe in the American Association. The new heights can be partially attributed to the expanded schedule, as each team played over 90 games for the first time. After the season, Radbourn joined Sullivan on a barnstorming trip through the south. The roster included Buck Ewing, Comiskey, Tony Mullane, and Pete Browning among others. In November, it was reported that Rad signed with Providence for $2,000. As the *Cleveland Herald* put it, "Radbourn has signed with Providence for about half of the $4000 called for…"[13] Obviously, he wasn't happy even before the new season started.

Eighteen eighty-four is often the main focus of Radbourn's career. Fifty-nine wins is hard to ignore. The pure numbers are staggering by today's standards. Rad took the mound in 75 different games. He started 73 of those and finished every one. He shut out opponents 11 times and that was one of the few figures that didn't lead the league. In 678 2/3 innings, he struck out 441 batters and posted a miniscule 1.38 ERA, a figure less than half the league average. Always impressive, Radbourn ceded fewer combined hits and walks than innings pitched. He won more than 83% of his decisions for a 59-12 won-loss record. Rad's success in '84 and his commitment to take the mound virtually every day towards the end of the season mark his campaign as perhaps the finest any pitcher ever entered into the books. The wear and tear would have a lasting consequence to the health of his right arm and his subsequent effectiveness.

The year started out on a somber note. On February 8, reports circulated out of Bloomington that the great Radbourn was shot in the thigh in a tiff with a female acquaintance. Luckily for baseball fans, it was actually one of Radbourn's cousins that suffered the injury. For the first time, the National League allowed pitchers to raise their arm above their shoulder, effectively legalizing the overhand delivery. The ruling sparked a great deal of controversy throughout the summer and into the following winter. Many feared that pitchers had gained too great an advantage. The American Association avoided the debate; their pitchers were still bound by the previous rules, which in truth were hard, if not impossible, to enforce. Pitchers always had and always would push the boundaries.

Radbourn's disgruntlement with his salary spilled over into spring training. Twenty-one-year-old Charlie Sweeney entered the season as Providence's other main starter. He pitched the lion's share of the games in the spring and was paid extra to do so which antagonized Radbourn, who also didn't care for the gushing plaudits that were being heaped on his young colleague. Once the season began, Radbourn took his place in the rotation. Through June, the pair started all but one of the club's 47 games, with Radbourn starting 24 of them. Sweeney, perhaps sore from the new overhand pitching style, fell out of the rotation on June 27. Radbourn was forced to fill in, starting and finishing 10 of the next 12 games. He wasn't happy about it, especially considering he didn't receive extra cash as Sweeney had during the preseason. It's obvious that Sweeney and Radbourn were having some sort of a running feud, as Rad pitched that many games straight at least twice the previous season without complaint. After a loss on July 12, a local newspaper, the *Providence Journal*, described the pitcher as acting "careless and indifferent."[14] It seems he was drinking heavier than usual during this time as well.

In those 10 games, Rad posted a so-so 6-4 record. On July 16, he lost to Boston 5-2 after becoming erratic and ceding a couple runs in the eighth after being called for a balk. Providence management immediately suspended him because of poor play. Per the *Boston Advertiser*, "There have been unpleasant reports of the dissatisfaction of Radbourne (sic), pitcher of the Providence club, current for some time. This evening the board of directors of the Providence association decided to summon him to appear before them tomorrow and answer certain questions regarding his conduct for the past three weeks."[15] Baseless accusations were even mounted that perhaps he was throwing games. The *Boston Globe* described his frame of mind; "Radbourn was in no condition, physically or mentally, to pitch."[16] He apparently snapped in the eighth in a dispute with the umpire and his catcher Barney Gilligan. The sloppy play included a walk, an error by Gilligan, a fumble by the third baseman and the balk call on an apparent third strike. "This seemed to break up Rad, and then he pitched the ball so wild that no man could hold it, and two men came home."[17]

Cyclone Miller started the next two games and Ed Conley the following. Sweeney relieved in two of the games and wasn't pleased about being pressed into action. The team wanted Sweeney to pitch on the 21st in an exhibition game in Woonsocket, Rhode Island. He wouldn't and the club scrambled to fill the role, using three pitchers including their backup catcher Sandy Nava. Sweeney did start the next day against Philadelphia. With a 6-2 lead after seven, manager Frank Bancroft pulled Sweeney, merely to give him some rest, and sent him to right field. He refused to go, cursed his manager, walked off the field, dressed and left the grounds. It seems Sweeney was doing a bit of drinking himself which added to his sour attitude. Providence, with only eight men on the field, yielded eight runs in the ninth and lost. That night, he tied one on again and refused to report the following day. Providence immediately expelled their only legitimate, eligible starter. It was later learned that Sweeney had been in consultation with the St, Louis club of the Union Association who happened to be playing in nearby Boston. Not coincidentally, he soon joined them.

The Providence directors met to decide how to proceed with the rest of the season, or if to proceed at all. Few viable starters were available on the market with rosters stretched thin with upwards of 33 clubs that season spread over three major leagues. Their record stood at 43-19-1, a mere 2 1/2 games behind first-place Boston in the standings and 5 1/2 games up on third-place New York. After falling so close to the pennant in previous seasons, all of Providence wanted the chance to seize first place. Bancroft consulted with Radbourn and the directors. Ultimately, Rad agreed to pick up much of the slack through the rest of the season for consideration. In his words, "I'll pitch every day and win the pennant for Providence, even if it costs me my right arm."[18] First, the reserve clause was stricken from his contract, allowing him to become a free agent at the end of the season. Second, his salary was raised substantially; in essence, Radbourn was paid the salary of two pitchers for the remainder of the season. Third, fearing that he was also in consultation with the Union Association, management gave him $1,000 according to newspaper accounts. In total, he made upwards of $5,000 in 1884, one of the highest figures in baseball history to date.

Of the remaining 51 games, Radbourn started 41 of them. In those starts, he put up an eye-popping 35-4-1 record, virtually single-handedly driving the club to the pennant. He won eighteen straight from August 7 to September 6, a new major league record, including an incredible 14 victories in August. He started all but one game between August 9 and September 24, amassing a record of 24-4 during the span. That August 7 victory put Providence in first place permanently. To be sure, the daily grind took its toll on the pitcher. Bancroft, who roomed with Radbourn in '84, later declared, "His showing was all the more remarkable and phenomenal when one knows that this great pitcher suffered untold agony in endeavoring to attain the goal for which he worked so hard and so pluckily. Morning after morning upon rising he would be unable to raise his arm high enough to use his hair brush. Instead of quitting he stuck all the harder to his task, going out to the ballpark hours before the rest of the team and beginning to warm up by throwing a few feet and increasing the distance until he could finally throw the ball from the outfield to home plate."[19] His arm was also being massaged nightly by Bancroft, teammates, porters, doctors or anyone available.

Providence won the pennant by 10 1/2 games over Boston; it was the club's only championship. In October, the club met the winners of the American Association, the New York Metropolitans, in an impromptu World Series, the first of its kind. Naturally, Radbourn started and finished each contest. After the first game the *New York Times* commented, "The curves of Radbourne (sic) struck terror to their hearts, and they fell easy victims to his skill."[20] He only ceded two hits "and one of these is doubtful."[21] The series lasted three games; Rad won each. In 22 innings, he struck out 17 and allowed only 17 hits and no walks.

The season was extended in 1884, about 15 games per team. Radbourn started 73 of the club's 114 games, plus exhibition contests and the World Series. Much is made of this heavy workload, and rightfully so, but it must be tempered slightly. For one, he pitched nearly as many innings in 1883, starting 68 of the club's 98 games. To kick off that season, he pitched the Grays' first 12 games and pulled off a similar 11-game streak in July. Secondly, 1884 wasn't that far removed from the era of one-man or one-man dominant rotations. Radbourn's 1883 season is an example of the latter. Pud Galvin (75 of 98) of Buffalo did much the same in '83, as did Jim McCormick (67 of 84) with Cleveland in 1882 and Jim Whitney (63 of 83) of Boston in 1881. The same could be said for McCormick (74 for 85), Mickey Welch (64 of 83), Lee Richmond (66 of 85), and Will White (62 of 83) in 1880.

As promised, Providence offered Radbourn his release after the season but they also extended him a new contract, a lucrative one. He slept on it and signed the next day, apparently all the ill-will had melted away. Part of his motivation to stay in the Providence area was a budding relationship with Caroline (Carrie) S. Stanhope from Newport, Rhode Island. National League opponents wanted to limit Radbourn's dominance and others that seemingly benefited from the rule permitting pitchers to extend their arms. At their November meetings, some executives pressured to have "pitchers to lower the arm to the shoulder. This, however, was opposed by the delegate from Providence. They were fearful that this would impair the effectiveness of their crack pitcher, Radbourne (sic), and fought stubbornly against it."[22] Note the inference here that Radbourn actually used an overhand delivery, at least as part of his arsenal. In the end, the league didn't adjust the rule but they did institute another measure pointed at Radbourn. The new regulation forced pitchers to keep both feet on the ground at the time of delivery. Ostensibly, the rule was instituted to protect base runners from tricky pickoff moves by pitchers. In truth, though, it was none too subtle slap at Rad who used a little hop during his delivery to get some extra oomph on the ball. It proved highly unpopular and impractical and was abandoned after a month into the following season.

Radbourn turned in a solid, if unspectacular, season in 1885 after coaching the pitchers at Brown University in the early spring. In 49 games he posted a 28-21 record with only 154 strikeouts. Providence dipped as well, finishing in fourth place with a sub-.500 record and 33 games out of contention. Rad butted heads with management once again at the end of the season. On September 11, he was hit hard, giving up 15 hits and three wild pitches in a 9-1 loss to New York. The club directors suspended him for "indifferent work." Said Radbourn, "I tried to pitch the best I could."[23] As the *New York Times* noted, that wasn't good enough for club management. "Director (J. Edward, 'Ned') Allen (of the Providence club) said that all his players would be summarily dealt with in the future, and he would compel them to play good ball or they would not play at all."[24] The charge of corruption was on the other foot this time though as the *New York Times* printed: "A dispatch from Providence says: "The published statement to the effect that the management of the Providence nine intended to throw games to Chicago in order to defeat New York in the fight for the pennant has caused much excitement and comment here. The management emphatically (denies) that they propose to favor Chicago as against New York. The latter may be true. The work, however, of releasing (Arthur) Irwin and suspending Radbourn and (Jerry) Denny, thus losing the services of the three strongest players of the team at a critical stage of the contest, affords food for conjecture."[25] Rad remained suspended through the rest of the season.

In truth, the suspension may have been financially motivated, a cost-cutting measure; soon after the season ended, Providence disbanded. Formally, the entire roster was transferred to league control. National League executives fought over the talent. President Arthur Soden of the Boston Beaneaters claimed Radbourn and catcher Con Dailey. Rad worked another solid year in '86, pitching in 58 games with a 27-31 record. After a bit of dickering, he signed with Boston for about of $4,800 in November, the highest figure in the game trailed by Fred Dunlap and King Kelly. He then spent the winter in Providence and supposedly married around this time; it was a common mistake as he actually just lived with his girlfriend.

Radbourn was still going strong in 1887, hurling in 50 games for a 24-23 record. His dominance was clearly waning though as evidenced by his mere 87 strikeouts. After doing so every year prior, he wouldn't fan 100 batters again. Some of this had to do with the shrinking of the pitcher's box by 18 inches prior to the season, effectively pushing the pitcher farther from the plate. Rad also liked to move around in the box as much as possible and took full advantage of every inch to intensify his delivery. His meager strikeout total in 1887 can also be explained by the fact that for that year only four strikes were required to retire a batter. His innings pitched would drop significantly after '87 as well. Through his first seven years in the majors, Radbourn amassed 3,481 innings, an average of nearly 500 per year. He would average about half that over his final four seasons. For some reason, Rad rarely used his famed drop ball in 1887. By August, he was openly discussing going into business in Bloomington and retiring from baseball.

The year ended on a sour note. On September 6, Rad lost 10-4 to Philadelphia. He walked five batters and bounced a wild pitch in the first inning. In total, he had seven base on balls, two wild pitches, two errors and hit two batters. At the time, the club only stood 7 1/2 games out of first place, but there were four tough teams higher in the standings. The Boston only had three more home games remaining and then would spend a month on the road to end the season. The club was headed for a western swing and Soden didn't feel the need to pay the travel expenses of a lackluster pitcher, in his opinion that is. So, he suspended Radbourn for "careless and slovenly play" or as another newspaper put it, "chronic poor play."[26] Soden made his announcement: "We have been played for flats long enough. Radbourn is paid over $600 a month to play ball. That sum ought to be enough to make him keep in condition to pitch good ball. I do not know whether it is poor condition, unwillingness, or what it is. But he has been doing the very worst of work. Today's game was the culmination point. If he cannot do any better work than he has done recently, he is not worth what we pay him."[27] Soden even went so far as to declare that the fans demanded the action, which was an obvious falsehood. It is true that Radbourn hadn't been shining in the box; he was 2-5 in his last seven starts. Of course, a suspension would also save the club the salary that Soden spoke of.

The suspension lasted 10 days before Soden relented on the 15th and summoned the pitcher to meet the club in Pittsburgh. Rad was none too happy to find his paycheck docked $200 for the time off. In November, Soden publicly offered Radbourn a mere $2,000 for 1888 with an incentive clause offering $100 for each victory. The pitcher cut off contact with the club, openly stating, "They have driven me out of the business. You will never see me in another game of ball."[28] The statement seemed all the more final when word leaked of a business opportunity.

In January 1888, he purchased a half-interest in a saloon and billiards pallor at 214 W. Washington Street beneath the Windsor Hotel, the largest hotel in Bloomington, renaming it Radbourn's Place; over the years, it attracted a great many sports fans. At the time it appeared that he would quit the game. The *Daily Inter Ocean* chimed in with its assessment of Rad's remaining potential on the diamond: "…his days of usefulness are about at an end. Radbourne's (sic) effectiveness lies in his command of the ball. He formerly brought the ball from over his head, but has given it up entirely, as it injures his arm."[29] Note another indication that indeed Radbourn threw the ball overhand at times, seemingly during the brief period between 1884 and '87.

The fact is Radbourn was still a useful pitcher and had been through this time an innings eater. The Boston club needed him to complement John Clarkson on the mound. April came and still no one heard from Rad. In the middle of the month, Soden declared, "We have heard absolutely nothing from Radbourne (sic). So far as we know he is still in Illinois and may remain there."[30] Boston management, known as the Triumvirs, was equally as stubborn, demanding that the pitcher join the club or face blacklisting by May 1. Behind the scenes though, the club was capitulating. They matched his salary from 1887, $4,800 and returned the $200 under contention. On April 17, Radbourn agreed to rejoin the team. On the 18th, he played first base for the local Bloomington club in an exhibition game against the St. Louis Whites, a Chris von der Ahe owned club. He wore his Boston uniform and went 3-for-4. That spring, he imparted some of his expertise onto a young Bloomington pitcher named Clark Griffith. Griffith in turn used every trick that Rad taught him and developed a few of his own to build a fine pitching career for a man standing only 5-foot-6 without a dominant fastball.

Boston fans and especially his teammates were thrilled to have Rad back. The club held a ceremony upon his arrival and gave him a gold-headed cane in appreciation with the inscription, "Presented to Charles Radbourn by the Boston Baseball Club, May 11th, 1888." On the 16th, he pitched his first game, a 2-1 win over Chicago. On June 27, he allowed only one hit in a 13-0 shutout of Washington. Radbourn's showing in '88 wasn't a success by any measure though. In 24 games he won only seven of 23 decisions. In December, he signed for another season in Boston.

Radbourn rebounded in 1889 to post a solid 20-11 record in 33 games. The year was contentious though. He had always had an issue with management and their dominance in player relations during the era. In truth, he had a problem with authority figures, managers, owners and umpires. He saw himself as a victim of the reserve clause, knowing full well that he would have made substantially more money if allowed to play in New York during his Providence days. He also felt the wrath of management in their indiscriminate use of suspensions and threat of blacklisting. In short, he was acclaimed as one of the top pitchers in the game, perhaps the greatest of the nineteenth century, and he was still treated poorly, in his opinion, by the businessmen that ran the game. In truth, that opinion wasn't far from the reality. Arthur Soden, for one, had little use for ballplayers outside their production. He firmly believed that labor served only one purpose—results - and had no use for the complications that employing human beings engendered. As a result, Radbourn was a strong supporter of Monte Ward's players union, the Brotherhood of Professional Baseball Players.

On November 13, Rad departed on a barnstorming tour with many of his Boston teammates organized by Chicago executive Jim Hart. He was one of the three pitchers along with Clarkson and Hugh Daily. King Kelly met the men in San Francisco. The union with some financial backers had established the Players League, which would operate as a third major league in 1890. Kelly was placed in charge of the new Boston franchise. He signed quite a few of the men to Players League contracts by the end of the year including Radbourn. On January 6, Rad left the west coast free from National League control. The Boston club, led by Kelly, Radbourn and Dan Brouthers captured the pennant by 6 1/2 games over Brooklyn. Rad chipped in a 27-12 record in 41 games, his most since '87. The season Radbourn became universally referred to as "Old Hoss" by the newsmen was 1987. The nickname, denoting his status as his team's workhorse, may have been used before this by his teammates.

Unfortunately, the Players League only lasted one season. Radbourn stuck with King Kelly who was hired to oversee the Boston club in the American Association. Kelly was then put in charge of a new Cincinnati franchise in the AA. He quickly sped off on a recruiting trip, stopping in Bloomington to ink Radbourn. Kelly left after signing the pitcher but received a shock when Rad signed with the National League Cincinnati entry on April 10. He was wooed by manager Tom Loftus, his first professional skipper back with Peoria, for $5,000 and a promise that he didn't have to pitch on Sundays. He was promptly blacklisted by the AA, which was of no consequence since it was in its final season anyway.

Radbourn was shelled in his first outing on April 25, one of his worst performances as a professional. He lost 23-7 to Cleveland, ceding 26 hits and 6 walks. By July, Rad was seriously contemplating retirement. He took his turn in the rotation until August 11 which proved to be his last major-league appearance. That day, he gave up 15 hits in an 8-6 loss to Brooklyn. For the season, he produced an 11-13 record over 26 games pitched. For his career, Radbourn completed 489 of his 503 starts for a 309-195 won-loss record which included 35 shutouts. He tossed a no-hitter and seven one-hitters, still a record for National League pitchers. Versatile, he also appeared in the outfield in 118 games and in the infield another 32 times. In nearly 2,500 at-bats, he hit .235 with 259 RBIs.

Rad asked for and was granted his release on August 23. Cincinnati signed Ed Crane as his replacement. Old Hoss officially retired at age 36 to tend to his saloon. There are some indications that Cincinnati was reneging on his salary payments which may have hastened his departure. At the time of his retirement, he was said to be worth $25,000 in real estate and bank stocks, a significant sum for the era. The money allowed him to spend much of his time away from the office. He spent countless hours hunting and fishing, passions he had indulged since childhood. He was skilled with a rifle by an early age and was a renowned field shooter as an adult, once issuing an open $1,000 challenge to the any and all comers, even national champions. Rad kept a kennel of "thoroughbred pointers" that honed their skills on long hunting trips.

He lived with his longtime girlfriend Carrie Stanhope whom he met during his time in Providence. Her maiden name was Clark and she had previously been married to Providence resident Charles Stanhope. The couple had a son, Charles Jr., born in 1875. The Stanhopes were separated by 1880; thus, Rad was not involved in their marital difficulties. Carrie, two years younger than Radbourn, was born in Ireland. Mother and son left Providence for good with Rad after the Grays' franchise folded. She assisted in the running of the Bloomington saloon, especially so after Radbourn's hunting accident. After his death, Radbourn's parents and seven siblings contested her claim to his estate. They were apparently unaware that Radbourn and Stanhope eventually did marry—on January 16, 1895 in Boston. The couple didn't have any children of their own.

A little bored, Radbourn considered coming out of retirement in 1893, but priced himself out of the market. The next season, he was a little more serious.

He contacted at least six managers including Chicago, Washington, Boston, St. Louis, and New York stating that he was in excellent condition and ready to pitch. No major-league club jumped at the opportunity so he signed with King Kelly's Allentown Colts, popularly known as Kelly's Killers, in the Pennsylvania State League. The team also included Mark Baldwin, Pete Browning, Mike Kilroy, Ted Larkin, and Sam Wise. The potential comeback ended before it began.

On April 13, 1894, Rad was accidentally shot in the face by a friend while hunting. He had stepped from behind a tree when his friend fired a shotgun. Radbourn lost sight in his left eye and received considerable damage to his face, including partial paralysis and some speech loss. Once a big, strong, good-looking athlete, his disfigurement weighed on him the rest of his life. Similar accidents weren't all that uncommon. Back in 1879, Rad's brother William shot himself in the left side and in both hands while hunting.

The ex-pitcher's waning years were unpleasant. Because of his face and ill-health, he became somewhat of a recluse at his apartment. He suffered from the effects of the paresis of the eye and other ailments and drank heavily. During at least his last year, Radbourn had severe cognitive troubles, perhaps brain damage from syphilis. He was also subject to convulsions and abnormalities with his nervous system. In 1895, it was falsely rumored to be dying of tuberculosis. He was ill though. As the *Boston Globe* described in December 1896, "Charley Radbourn…is now at his old home in Bloomington, Ill., a wreck of his former self, owing to sickness."[31] As his obituary in the local *Bloomington Pantagraph* described, he "…grew sick, lingered on from year to year as disease gnawed at his mental and physical being, robbing him of speech, feeling and locomotion long before the final day arrived."[32] The *Brooklyn Eagle* claimed that "his brain has been affected more or less for about a year."[33]

On February 3, 1897, Radbourn suffered another convulsion which ultimately left him in a comatose state. He never woke up, dying at age 42 around 2 PM two days later at his residence in the Windsor Hotel. He was buried at Evergreen Memorial Cemetery in Bloomington. The local newspaper kindly described him as "a great favorite in Bloomington. He was a sociable, humorous, good-natured man, and a charming story teller."[34] In 1939, he was elected to the National Baseball Hall of Fame in his proper slot among the first group of inductees.

## SOURCES

Special thanks for a valuable exchange of emails with Edward Achorn, author of *Fifty-Nine in '84: Old Hoss Radbourn, Barehanded Baseball and the Greatest Season a Pitcher Ever Had.*

Archivist/Librarian Bill Kemp at the McLean County Museum of History was especially helpful; in gathering information for this article, as was colleague Rochelle Gridley.

Bob LeMoine was of great help in tracking down citations to help document quotations in the original biography.

In addition to the sources cited in the Notes, the author also consulted:

Bell, David, *The Nineteenth Century Transaction Register*, SABR

Browning, Reed. *Cy Young: A Baseball Life* (Amherst: University of Massachusetts Press, 2000).

Ivor-Campbell, Frederick, Robert L. Tiemann and Mark Rucker. *Baseball's First Stars* (Cleveland: The Society for American Baseball Research, 1996).

Kahn, Roger. *The Head Game: Baseball Seen from the Pitcher's Mound* (New York: Houghton Mifflin Harcourt, 2001).

Leitner, Irving A. *Diamond in the Rough* (New York: Criterion Books, 1972).

Spatz, Lyle, ed. Society for American Baseball Research. *The SABR Baseball List and Record Book* New York: Scribners, 2007).

Kemp, Bill, "Famed 19th Century Ballplayer 'Old Hoss' Came from Bloomington," Pantagraph.com, April 6, 2008.

Ancestry.com, Baseball-reference.com, Retrosheet.org, and the following newspapers: *Alton (Illinois) Telegraph, Atchison (Kansas) Daily Globe, Bismarck Daily Tribune, Cincinnati Enquirer, Daily Bulletin* (Bloomington, Illinois), *Daily Evening Bulletin* (San Francisco), *Daily Iowa Capital, Daily Miner* (Reno, Nevada), *Daily Nebraska State Journal, Daily Northwestern* (Oshkosh, Wisconsin), *Daily Republican-Sentinel* (Milwaukee), *Decatur Daily Republican, Decatur Review, Dubuque Herald, Evening Gazette* (Sterling, Illinois), *Fitchburg* (Massachusetts) *Sentinel, Hamilton* (Ohio) *Daily Democrat, Hartford Courant, Iowa State Reporter, Janesville* (Wisconsin) *Gazette, Lincoln* (Nebraska) *Evening News, Logansport* (Indiana) *Journal, Logansport Pharos, Los Angeles Times, Milwaukee Journal, Newport* (Rhode Island) *Daily News, New York World, Oakland Tribune, Penny Press,* (Minneapolis), *Rocky Mountain News, San Antonio Light, Spirit Lake* (Iowa) *Beacon, Sporting Life, The Sporting*

*News*, *St. Louis Exchange*, *St. Paul Daily News*, and the *Weekly Gazette and Stockman* (Reno, Nevada).

## NOTES

1. E.E. Pierson, "'Old Hoss' Radbourne: The Famous Old Time Veteran Who Pitched Seventy-Two Games in a Single Season," *Baseball Magazine*, Vol.19 Issue 4 (August, 1917):423-424.
2. *Bloomington Pantagraph*, September 2, 1876: 3.
3. Ibid.
4. Per Archivist/Librarian Bill Kemp at the McLean County Museum of History.
5. E. E. Pierson, "'Old Hoss' Radbourn," *Baseball Magazine*, Vol. 19, Issue 4 (1917): 423.
6. Ibid.
7. *Bloomington Daily Pantagraph*, January 9, 1880: 3.
8. Alfred H. Spink, *The National Game: A History of Baseball, America's Leading Outdoor Sport, From the Time it was First played up to the Present Day, With Illustrations and Biographical Sketches*. (St. Louis: National Game Pub, 1911), 150, 152; Bill James and Rob Neyer, *The Neyer/James Guide to Pitchers: An Historical Compendium of Pitching, Pitchers, and Pitches* (New York: Simon and Schuster, 2004), 349-350.
9. *Cleveland Herald*, date unknown.
10. *Topeka State Journal*, May 1, 1891: 7.
11. *Milwaukee Sentinel*, date unknown.
12. "Outdoor Amusements," *Washington Post*, May 6, 1883: 8.
13. *Cleveland Herald*, date unknown.
14. *Providence Journal*, July 14, 1884.
15. "One More Victory for the Boston Club," *Boston Advertiser*, July 17, 1884: 8.
16. "A Good Clean Lead," *Boston Globe*, July 17, 1884: 4.
17. Ibid.
18. "Radbourne's [*sic*] Twirling Feat is Still Unrivaled; Won 63 Games and N.L. Pennant, 37 Years Ago," *St. Louis Post-Dispatch*, February 13, 1921:9.
19. "Old Providence Manager Tells Inside History of Old Hoss Radbourn Winning 26 out of 27 Games," *New Castle Herald* (Pennsylvania), July 7, 1908:2.
20. "The Baseball Field," *New York Times*, October 24, 1884: 2.
21. Ibid.
22. "No Deserters Wanted Back," *New York Times*, November 20, 1884:5.
23. "Notes of the Game," *New York Times*, September 13, 1885: 2.
24. Ibid.
25. "Notes of the Game," *New York Times*, September 24, 1885: 2.
26. *Tyrone Daily Herald* (Pennsylvania), September 9, 1887:1; "Base Ball Notes," *Indianapolis News*, September 7, 1887:3.
27. "Radbourn Indefinitely Suspended," *Hartford Courant*, September 7, 1887: 1.
28. "The Sporting World," *Cleveland Plain Dealer*, January 7, 1988: 5.
29. "Bat and Ball," *Daily Inter Ocean* (Chicago), January 2, 1888: Section 2: 12.
30. "Soden and Radbourne," *Inter Ocean*, April 18, 1888:2.
31. "Baseball Notes," *Boston Globe*, December 21, 1896: 7.
32. *Daily Pantagraph*, February 6, 1897: 7.
33. "Hurst and the Rules," *Brooklyn Eagle*, February 5, 1897: 10.
34. *Bloomington Pantagraph*, date unknown.

# EPPA RIXEY

## BY JAN FINKEL

WITHOUT HIS UNFORGETTABLE name, Eppa Rixey might be one of the more forgotten members of the Hall of Fame. His 266-251 won-lost record doesn't stand out, yet his win total stood as the National League record for left-handers until Warren Spahn surpassed it in 1959. Rixey greeted the moment with characteristic humor, saying he was glad Spahn had broken his record because it reminded everybody that he had set it. Conversely, his 251 losses are the most ever for a southpaw and ninth-most for all pitchers.

A tough competitor on the field but a gentleman and good teammate off it, Rixey was an anomaly. Whereas the average ballplayer of the era came from a farming, labor, and often immigrant background, Rixey's background was comparatively aristocratic. The Rixeys of Culpeper were Virginia gentility, descended from the Riccias of Italy, who had come to America by way of England, Scotland, and France. Eppa Rixey Sr., a banker, married the former Willie Alice Walton. Eppa Jr. was born May 3, 1891, the fourth of six children. Eppa attended school in Culpeper until he was 10, when the family moved to Charlottesville. Completing high school in Charlottesville, he entered the University of Virginia, graduating in 1912 with a bachelor's degree in chemistry.

The mainstay of Virginia's pitching staff, he also lettered in basketball, using his 6-foot-5 height and 210 pounds to advantage. He jumped directly from the university to the Philadelphia Phillies upon graduation but returned to Charlottesville in offseasons to earn two masters degrees (chemistry and Latin) with side trips into mathematics. During the winter he taught Latin at Episcopal High School in Washington, D.C. Rixey's background and education were enough to set him apart from the average ballplayer, but he went a step further, writing poetry in his spare time, particularly enjoying sonnets and triolets. Although ballplayers resented college men, he gained their respect by holding his ground when they initiated him.

Rixey jumped from the Virginia pitching staff to the Phillies through the efforts of National League umpire Charles (Cy) Rigler, who was moonlighting on the basketball and baseball staffs of the university. Rigler suggested the move to Rixey, who initially refused, saying he planned to be a chemist. Rigler sweetened the deal by promising to split equally with the young pitcher whatever finder's bonus he might receive from Philadelphia, which turned out to be $2,000. Rixey agreed because the United States was suffering an economic downturn in 1912, his father's bank was taking some losses, and he wanted to help his younger brother William (who became a physician) stay at Virginia. However, the league passed a rule prohibiting umpires from scouting for any individual team, and neither Rigler nor Rixey ever saw a dime. Nevertheless, Rixey joined Philadelphia in 1912 after graduating from Virginia.[1]

Eppa Rixey's career is a tale of two pitchers. As a Phillie, Rixie was inconsistent. His first two seasons were respectable (10-10 and 9-5), even promising given his youth, but his third (2-11, 4.37) was a disaster. His fourth season, with the Phillies winning their first pennant, was better in terms of ERA, but he was just 11-12 in wins and losses. A key to Rixey's improvement was new manager Pat Moran's confidence in him. Moran brought him into the third inning of the deciding fifth game of the World Series with Boston in relief of Erskine Mayer. Rixey was stung by home runs by Duffy Lewis and Harry Hooper, the latter bouncing into the center-field bleachers constituting what would be a ground-rule double under today's rules. He wound up taking the loss. In 1916 the Phillies improved their won-lost record but came in second to Brooklyn. Rixey, though, had perhaps his best season ever, going 22-10 with a microscopic 1.85

ERA and a career-high 134 strikeouts. He fell off in 1917, leading the league in losses with 21, but he had a good ERA (2.27) and threw four shutouts.

Rixey lost the 1918 season to the war, serving with the Chemical Warfare Division in Europe. His return from the military, marked by rustiness and dissatisfaction with Phillie managers Jack Coombs and Gavy Cravath, led to two abysmal seasons (6-12 and 11-22) with last-place teams. On February 22, 1921, he was happy to be traded to Cincinnati in exchange for Jimmy Ring and Greasy Neale. He was back playing for Pat Moran.

Rixey and Cincinnati were meant for each other, and he would pitch there for 13 seasons, finishing up in 1933 at the age of 42. He blossomed into an outstanding pitcher, winning a hundred games in his first five seasons and winning consistently for eight years. Even in his final campaign he still had enough, pitching mostly against Pittsburgh, to post a 6-3 record with a 3.15 ERA. He set a record in 1921 not likely to be equaled, serving up only one home run in 301 innings. He led the league in wins in 1922 with 25 and between July 24 and August 28, 1932, threw 27 consecutive scoreless innings.

Everything—except the nickname "Jeptha" that sportswriter William Phelon hung on him, which he tolerated but didn't like—was falling into place for Rixey. He became something of a bon vivant unable to take Prohibition seriously. From May 9 to May 18, 1922, a detective known only as "Operative No. 40" tailed Rixey all over Cincinnati. He noted that Rixey was sometimes alone but usually in the company of several different men and women, whom he described in detail. Some of the people were known, like teammates Rube Bressler and Greasy Neale, others not. Whatever circuitous route they took, they always wound up at the Foss-Schneider Brewing Company. After 10 days of observation of Rixey ("Subject") and his friends, Operative No. 40 came to a remarkable conclusion: "So I think if Subject is drinking, he is getting it at the brewery." Who engaged "Operative No. 40" is a mystery (presumably the Reds or the family of a prospective lady friend), but the bigger mystery is that anyone was surprised, shocked, or interested.[2]

Rixey settled down and on October 29, 1924, married Dorothy Meyers in St. Thomas Church in Terrace Park, a suburb of Cincinnati. They had two children, Eppa III and Ann. The Rixeys lived in the Cincinnati area, where Eppa worked during the winter in the insurance agency his father-in-law, Charles Meyers, had founded in 1888. Grandson Eppa Rixey IV was the chief operating officer of the Eppa Rixey Insurance Agency, whose motto was "Hall of Fame Performance for Your Insurance Needs" until 2003, when the company was acquired by Mark E. Berry and merged into the Berry Insurance Group.

To cap off his happy and prosperous life, the Veterans Committee elected Eppa to the Hall of Fame on January 27, 1963. He was the first Virginian to be so honored. Unfortunately, he was also the first honoree to die between election and induction, suffering a fatal heart attack on February 28. (Coincidentally, the second was fellow Virginian Leon Day in 1995.) Rixey is buried in Greenlawn Cemetery in Milford, Ohio.

Despite his size, Rixey was a finesse pitcher, working deep into the count to set up a hitter, never giving in, striking out few and walking even fewer, making the hitter hit the ball. A smart pitcher, he thought most hitters were dumb. Rube Bressler told Lawrence Ritter in *The Glory of their Times* that Rixey remarked upon his astonishment that on the 2-0 or 3-1 count almost every hitter in the league looked for his fast ball and never got it![3] He was durable, frequently working 280 or more innings. While surrendering more than a hit per inning, he didn't hurt himself with walks or home runs or errors; he fielded his position well, handling 108 chances without an error in 1917. And, like all good pitchers on generally weak teams, he suffered more than his share of losses. Similar southpaw contemporaries include Slim Sallee and Herb Pennock. Tom Glavine, although he walked and struck out more hitters more than did Rixey, pitched with the same mindset.

Rixey was the consummate Virginia gentleman, a fellow who took everything but losing (he could punish locker rooms or disappear for a day or two) and those who taunted his Southern heritage and thick drawl with renditions of classics like "Marching through Georgia" with gentle wit and self-deprecating humor. Visiting Cooperstown after he retired, he sent family and friends a post card with this message: "I finally made it!" Hearing he'd been elected to the Hall of Fame, he joked, "I guess they are really scraping the bottom of the barrel, aren't they?"[4]

A top-flight pitcher for many years, Eppa Rixey graced his team and enriched his community.

Note: An earlier version of this biography appeared in Tom Simon, ed. *Deadball Stars of the National League* (Washington, D. C.: Brassey's, Inc., 2004).

## SOURCES

In addition to the sources cited in the Notes, the author also consulted:

Fleitz, David L. *Ghosts in the Gallery at Cooperstown: Sixteen Little-Known Members of the Hall of Fame* (Jefferson, North Carolina, and London: McFarland, 2004).

Hoie, Bob, Carlos Bauer, et al, eds. *The Historical Register: The Complete Major & Minor League Record of Baseball's Greatest Players* (San Diego and San Marino: Baseball Press Books, 1998).

Sumner, Jim L. "Eppa Rixey, Southpaw: A Virginian in the Major Leagues." *Virginia Cavalcade* (Winter 1991): 133-142.

Swank, Bill. "Gavy Cravath." *Deadball Stars of the National League.* Tom Simon, ed. (Washington, D.C.: Brassey's Inc., 2004).

Thorn, John, Pete Palmer, and Michael Gershman, eds. *Total Baseball.* 7th ed. (Kingston, New York: Total Sports Publishing, 2001).

By far the most helpful source to me was a thoroughly enjoyable and informative telephone conversation with Eppa Rixey IV, the grandson of Eppa Rixey, during the fall of 2000. Without his kindness, many of the details of this article would be missing.

## NOTES

1. Martin Appel and Burt Goldblatt, *Baseball's Best: The Hall of Fame Gallery* (New York: McGraw-Hill, 1977), 323.
2. Operative No. 40's detailed 11-page report is in the Eppa Rixey Files at the National Baseball Hall of Fame and Museum in Cooperstown, New York.
3. Lawrence S. Ritter, *The Glory of Their Times: The Story of the Early Days of Baseball Told by the Men Who Played It* (New York: Macmillan, 1966), 200.
4. Adam Bell, "Eppa Rixey: A nostalgic and fanciful look back at a life in the game . . . of the University's very own member of the Baseball Hall of Fame," *The* [University of Virginia] *Cavalier Daily* (September 18, 1986). In Eppa Rixey Files at the National Baseball Hall of Fame and Museum in Cooperstown, New York.

# ROBIN ROBERTS

## BY C. PAUL ROGERS III

**FROM 1950 TO 1955, ROBIN ROBERTS** was the top right-hander in the National League while pitching for the Philadelphia Phillies. For most of the remainder of his 18-year career, he was a crafty veteran who had a remarkable resurgence with the Baltimore Orioles. Either way, he would go out, take his turn on the mound without saying a word, and throw strikes. The standing joke was that Andy Seminick and Stan Lopata, who caught Roberts with the Phillies, always took their rocking chairs with them when Roberts was pitching, in testament to his outstanding control. Robin Roberts was one of the last of a breed of pitchers who completed ballgames. In fact, he led the league in compete games five times and recorded 305 complete games in his career. From July of 1952 until June 1953 he completed a remarkable 28 games in a row. He also led the league in innings pitched five times, led by 346⅔ innings in 1953. From 1950 through 1955 Roberts averaged 323 innings pitched and 27 complete games while winning 20 or more games each year.

Roberts did not try to finesse the hitters; he dared them to hit the ball. When there were men on base, he reached back and burned the corners for strikes.[1] Roberts' slow, deliberate windup and delivery was so fluid that hitters could not wait for the pitch to come. It looked so easy; then the ball would explode over the plate, astonishing the hitters. "He's so close, you gotta watch him like an eagle," said umpire Jocko Conlan.[2] Hall of Famer Red Schoendienst once remarked that Roberts' fastball "seemed to skid across the strike zone as though it were on a sheet of ice."[3] Ralph Kiner, another Hall of Famer, said, "Probably the best fastball I ever saw was Robin Roberts'. His ball would rise around six or eight inches, and with plenty on it. And he had great control, which made him very difficult to hit."[4] Ernie Banks thought that Roberts in his prime was faster than Bob Gibson and the fastest pitcher he faced from 1953 to 1957.[5]

Robin Evan Roberts was born in Springfield, Illinois, on September 30, 1926, to Tom Roberts, a Welsh coal miner, and Sarah Roberts of England. His parents had two children when they immigrated to the United States in 1921.

Tom Roberts served in the British Army during World War I, and fought in the ferocious Gallipoli campaign in Turkey. After the war, he returned to the coal mines of Bolton in Lancashire, but was put out of work by a strike in 1921. A friend in Bolton informed Tom that he could find steady employment in American soft-coal fields around Springfield, Illinois.

But when Tom and his family reached Illinois, they found little prosperity—at one point the mines in Springfield operated only one day a week. The family lived in a two-room farmhouse that Tom gradually expanded as the family grew. In 1929, Tom left coal mining and farming and found a job with the Sangamo Electric Company as foreman in the plant's maintenance department.

Robin, known as Evan while growing up, was the fifth of six children, following Tom Jr., Nora, Joan, and John. After Robin came a younger brother, George. Tom Jr. was killed in a submarine accident in 1942, at the age of 21.

As a boy growing up on a family farm, Sarah Roberts remembered, Robin "never had a ball out of his hand." He hated farm work. When Robin deliberately broke one of his father's hoes to avoid farm chores, Tom Roberts paddled his son with a fly swatter, saying, "It doesn't hurt your hand and it don't mark the kid." But Robin went on playing, talking his three brothers into playing catch, using an old mattress propped against the garage door, hurling the ball into a hole in the middle for hours.[6]

Robin had his first exposure to organized sports when he entered the fifth grade in a two-room schoolhouse at East Pleasant Hill. C.B. Lindsay, a new teacher, had arrived at the school, and made learning fun with his energetic manner and enthusiasm. He encouraged his students to participate in sports, put on plays, and enter county competition in such areas as math, public speaking, and dramatic and humorous sayings. Lindsay's energy motivated Robin, who won blue ribbons in all those areas.

Robin and his brother George became avid Cubs fans. With the radio on an open window sill, they would go outside the house, imitating the ballplayers during the play-by-play. His mother would also listen to the Cubs games. In fact, she became so excited when Gabby Hartnett hit his famous "Homer in the Gloamin'" near the end of the 1938 season to catapult the Cubs into first place that she dropped a dish of potatoes while serving the family dinner. By the age of 12, Robin was playing baseball in a league the neighborhood kids organized. He was consumed by sports, particularly baseball. The local Springfield Browns played in the Class-B Three-I League and he went to the games whenever he could. Lou Novikoff of the rival Moline Plow Boys and Lou Gehrig became his first heroes. Later his favorites were Bill Nicholson of the wartime Cubs, later his teammate, and Otto Graham, the All-American quarterback at Northwestern, who also played in the band.

When Robin was in the eighth grade, Lindsay held a sports banquet and invited Hall of Fame pitcher Grover Cleveland Alexander to speak at the dinner. Alexander, an alcoholic who was living in a hotel in Springfield, gave a short, terse, speech: "Boys, I hope you enjoy sports, they are a wonderful thing. But I warn you about one thing: don't take to drink, because look what it has done to me." Then he sat down.[7]

Alexander's appearance foreshadowed a unique connection with Roberts. In 1950, Roberts became the first 20-game winner for the Phillies since Alexander won 30 games for the club in 1917. In 1958, Roberts won his 191st game for the Phillies, breaking the club record held by Alexander. And in 1976 Roberts became the first Phillies player elected to the Hall of Fame since Alexander.

Roberts began high school at Springfield High and went out for the varsity football team his sophomore year. He weighed about 125 pounds and was practice fodder, never getting to dress for a game. His mother wanted him to quit because he wasn't getting to play and had to take a crosstown bus home after practice, which meant not getting home until about 7:30. But he stuck it out all season, watching his team play from the stands after practicing all week.

Roberts also went out for basketball and was cut after the second practice. Instead, he played for an intramural team that got to the finals of the school tournament. The championship game was played before a varsity game and Robin led his team to victory, scoring 22 points. After the game, the varsity basketball coach asked him why he hadn't come out for the varsity. Robin said, "I did. You cut me on the second day."[8]

The school board changed the district boundaries after that year and Roberts transferred to Lanphier High, which was much closer to his home. He played varsity baseball, football, and basketball for Lanphier. Known for crying over losses but refusing to do chores, he told his mother, "Naw, Mom, I'm a ballplayer. You just wait until I get into the major leagues. Then I'll build you a house." Tom Roberts was impressed by his son's determination. In 1956, he said, "You just had to go along. He wouldn't do nuthin' else."[9]

World War II was going at full tilt when Roberts graduated from high school in 1944, so he enrolled in the Reserve Air Corps program, hoping to become a fighter pilot. The army sent him to Michigan State University, where he attended regular university classes and received initial military training. He was able to play a lot of pickup basketball and soon was asked to join the Spartan varsity for the winter quarter.[10] When the war ended, Roberts re-enrolled at Michigan State, eventually earning a Bachelor's degree in physical education with a minor in history.

Roberts was a fine basketball player for the Spartans. In 1946-1947 he captained the team and was its leading scorer. He was even named the Michigan Collegiate Player of the Year for 1947 by the *Detroit Free Press*, a signal honor considering about a dozen Michigan colleges fielded basketball teams.

In the spring of 1946, after his first basketball season at Michigan State, Roberts decided to try out for the baseball team. He showed up at practice unannounced. John Kobs, the baseball coach, who knew him only as a basketball player, asked him what position he played.

Roberts said, "What do you need?"

Kobs said, "I need pitching."

Although Roberts considered himself an everyday player, he said, "Well, I can pitch." Two years later, in 1948, Roberts would be pitching in the major leagues for the Philadelphia Phillies. He ended his first season with the Spartans with a 4-2 record, highlighted by a no-hitter against the Great Lakes Naval Training Station. It was the first no-hitter in Michigan State history. He lost the last game of the season, 2-0, to the University of Michigan, which was coached by former big-league pitcher Ray Fisher, who had toiled for the undistinguished New York Yankees from 1910 to 1917 and then for the world champion Cincinnati Reds in 1919.[11] Fisher was impressed with Roberts' raw talent and after the game invited him to join the summer semipro team he coached in Montpelier, Vermont, the Twin City Trojans in the Northern League. Thus in both 1946 and 1947, Roberts spent summers pitching in Montpelier for Fisher's Trojans.[12]

His first summer he compiled an 11-8 record and pitched a no-hitter against the Keene, New Hampshire, Yankees but lost 1-0 in a game that cost the Trojans the pennant.[13] In the summer of 1947, after winning 6 and losing 4 for Michigan State (including two wins against Fisher's University of Michigan squad), Roberts came into his own, amassing an 18-3 mark with a 2.33 earned-run average for the Trojans. He won 17 straight games and led his team to the Northern League title.

Based on that performance, Roberts started attracting major-league scouts. At least five teams pursued him, including the Boston Braves, the Phillies, the Red Sox, the Tigers, and the Yankees.

Phillies scout Chuck Ward had first noticed Roberts and followed him for over a year. Ward said, "To get one player like Roberts you look at 1,000 kids and sometimes it seems like 10,000."[14] Ward later told Roberts that he had been most impressed with him on a day in Vermont when Roberts did not have his best stuff and was being hit around a little. A runner on first tried to steal second and Roberts turned around after delivering the pitch to watch the play at second. The throw from the catcher, George Harms, hit Roberts squarely in the back of the head and knocked him out cold. When he came around he insisted on staying in the game and retired 12 in a row to win the game.[15]

After Roberts came home to Springfield from Vermont in 1947, the Phillies had him come to Wrigley Field in Chicago to work out. Babe Alexander, the Phillies traveling secretary, offered him a $10,000 bonus after the first day. He hesitated because he intended to return to Michigan State and play his final season of basketball and finish his degree. The following day the Phillies upped the ante to $15,000 and then after another workout the third day offered $25,000. Roberts said, "That would buy a pretty nice house, wouldn't it?" When Alexander said it would, he signed, knowing he could keep his promise to his mother.[16] Roberts later said, "When they got up to $25,000, I knew I was going to be able to buy a pretty good house for Mom, so I said yes. She really got a belt out of that house."[17]

And Roberts did just that, purchasing a $19,000 home for his mother and father, keeping his childhood promise. Robbie also bought a car and some new clothes with the remainder. At the time, Roberts was not aware of the income taxes on his earnings and wound up owing the Internal Revenue Service. His father loaned him the amount he needed. Roberts was finally able to pay back his father after he received his World Series check in 1950.[18]

Roberts also maintained his relationship with Fisher for many years. In 1955, for example, he stopped off after season's end in Ann Arbor and asked Fisher's permission to work out with the University of Michigan pitchers. Fisher granted permission, and watched Roberts uncork a few pitches. Right away Fisher saw that Roberts had replaced his three-quarters motion with a side-arm delivery, to favor a sore arm. "Robby, you've changed your delivery, haven't you?" Fisher asked. Roberts smiled in relief, saying, "That's what I wanted to know. You know, in Philadelphia, I'm Robin Roberts, and they won't tell me anything."[19]

In 1948, Roberts was invited to the Phillies spring training camp but reported late so that he could finish the winter quarter at Michigan State and complete his degree. After he arrived he immediately began having leg problems running on the soft, sandy turf while working out. After several days of dealing with muscle strains, Roberts happened to walk behind Phillies owner Bob Carpenter, unbeknownst to him. He overheard Carpenter say, "Well, it looks like I blew another $25,000." At that juncture Roberts hadn't even thrown a pitch.

Afterward, Roberts was down in the dumps in the locker room when veteran Phillies coach Cy Perkins came up to him and said, "They're on your ass, aren't they, kid?"

Roberts said, "Yes sir, they are all over me."

Perkins said, "Wait till they see you pitch. They won't be on your ass anymore." Perkins had been at Roberts' workouts in Wrigley Field the previous year. Roberts remembered someone saying, "Don't let that kid get out of the park." He now realized it was Perkins.

That began an important relationship that would last throughout Roberts' 18-year major-league career. Perkins, who had been a longtime catcher with Connie Mack's Philadelphia Athletics, had great confidence in Roberts and always knew when to say just the right thing to give him a boost. He never tried to tell Roberts how to pitch, simply saying, "Do it your way kid." In spring training in 1950 Perkins told Roberts, "I've been in baseball 35 years and the best five pitchers I've ever seen are Walter Johnson, Lefty Grove, Herb Pennock, Grover Cleveland Alexander, and you." At that time Roberts' big-league record was 22 wins and 24 losses. He went on, "I'm not kidding you. You've got the best delivery I've ever seen. You're our next 300-game winner."

Rarely did Perkins say anything to Roberts after a win. But he was always there after a loss, telling Roberts to remember that the guys on the other team were getting paid too, or, if Roberts had a particularly tough outing, recalling the time Lefty Grove got knocked out in the first inning.

After the Phillies let Perkins go after the 1954 season, saying he was too old, Roberts was so upset that he offered to pay Perkins' salary, to no avail.

When Roberts finally did pitch in his first spring-training game in 1948, he threw three scoreless innings against the St. Louis Cardinals B team, struck out four, and hit a triple. Afterward Roberts was sitting in front of his locker when he felt a tap on his arm. Roberts looked around and saw Perkins, who just gave him a wink and walked on by.[20]

After spring training, the Phillies sent Roberts to their Class-B farm club in Wilmington, Delaware, in the Eastern League. He did not linger long at Wilmington, compiling a 9-1 record in 11 starts. In his professional debut, on April 29, he struck out eight of the first 10 batters and finished with 17 strikeouts in a 19-1 victory over Harrisburg. He then struck out 14,

12, and 12 in his next three starts, all complete-game victories. On May 18, his fifth start, he pitched all 15 innings of a game that was called a 2-2 tie because of the league curfew, striking out 16. On June 5 he struck out 18 to tie the league record in a 4-1 win over Trenton. By the time he was called up by the Phillies on June 17, 1948, Roberts had recorded 121 strikeouts in 96 innings and compiled a 2.06 earned-run average.[21]

Roberts arrived at the Phillies clubhouse about 6:00 P.M. with about four hours of sleep on the day of his call-up and Phillies manager Ben Chapman asked how he felt. When Roberts said he felt fine, Chapman said, "You'll be pitching tonight." Two hours later he was on the mound against the Pittsburgh Pirates. Roberts was so nervous that he remembered walking leadoff hitter Stan Rojek on four pitches. Then he went to a deep count on Frankie Gustine before striking him out on a bad pitch. That ended his mound nervousness—for all time. He ended up allowing five hits in eight innings, but lost 2-0 to a five-hit shutout by Elmer Riddle.[22]

Roberts gained his first major-league victory in his very next start, on June 23, beating the Cincinnati Reds, 3-2 in a complete-game seven-hitter. He won his next two starts, throwing complete games against the Chicago Cubs and the Boston Braves before getting shelled by the same Braves on July 9.

Roberts quickly established a reputation for working quickly, peering in immediately for the sign after receiving the ball back from the catcher, trying to establish a rhythm. But the Phillies thought he was pitching too quickly, so coach Benny Bengough suggested a routine that Roberts followed for the rest of his career—hitch his pants, adjust the legs of his trousers, tug on the bill of his cap, wipe his brow, and then look in for the sign. He still was one of the quickest pitchers in baseball.[23]

Roberts pitched solidly if not spectacularly his first season, going 7-9. He pitched 146⅔ innings, gave up 148 hits, walked 61, and struck out 84, with a solid 3.19 earned-run average. He also took naturally to the intense and competitive environment of major-league baseball: Like his teammates, he was morose and silent after defeats, stared blankly out of bus and train windows, and killed time on road trips going to every movie in town. "I don't care what's playing. I like them all," he said.[24] While in Philadelphia Roberts, along with Richie Ashburn, Curt Simmons and Charlie Bicknell, stayed at a family-style boarding house run by Ashburn's parents.[25]

When Roberts came home after his rookie season, he asked his sister Nora if she knew any girls he might date. Through a mutual friend, Nora set him up with Mary Ann Kalnes, a grade-school teacher who had just graduated from the University of Wisconsin and had taken a job in Springfield because of her admiration of Abraham Lincoln. Roberts was immediately smitten and never went out with another girl. The running joke was that Roberts evidently had not made a very good first impression. Mary had attended a Michigan State-Wisconsin basketball game when Robin played for the Spartans, but didn't remember him.[26] They were married in December 1949 and would raise four boys.

Roberts finished with a 15-15 record in 1949, hurling 226⅔ innings, giving up 229 hits, walking 75, and striking out 95, with a 3.69 ERA. He started 31 games and completed 11 with three shutouts. Manager Eddie Sawyer even used him in relief 12 times and he had four saves.

After the season and their wedding, the Roberts family moved to Philadelphia's suburb of Meadowbrook, on Robin Hood Lane no less, right next door to teammate Curt Simmons and his family.[27]

The Phillies finished third in 1949, their best finish in many years. They finished with 19 wins in their last 30 games and were a young team coming together under Eddie Sawyer. Early in the 1950 season, Harry Grayson, sports editor of the Newspaper Enterprise Association, christened the young and talented Phillies the Whiz Kids.[28]

The Phils began the season with high hopes. On May 16 Roberts defeated Ewell Blackwell of the Cincinnati Reds 1-0 on a two-hitter. The Phillies got only three hits and scored the only run of the game in the first on two infield singles, a walk, and a double-play grounder. The game was pivotal to Roberts and signaled to him that, by beating one of the top pitchers in the league in such a close game, the Phillies were for real.[29] They took over first place for good in July as they won 13 of 18 during one stretch. In late July and early August Roberts contributed mightily by throwing three consecutive shutouts and 32⅔ consecutive scoreless innings.

In mid-September the Phillies held a 7½-game lead over the Dodgers, but things began to sour when Curt Simmons's National Guard unit was called to active duty because of the Korean War. The team also lost starting pitchers Bubba Church and Bob Miller to injuries and veteran reserve Bill Nicholson to illness. Down the stretch the club lost 9 of 12, including five in a row, to see their lead shrink to one game with one game left in the season.[30]

That game was on October 1 against the second-place Brooklyn Dodgers at Ebbets Field. The Dodgers would force a three-game playoff for the pennant if they won.

Eddie Sawyer selected Roberts to start against Don Newcombe of the Dodgers, in a clash of aces. Roberts had won 19 games but was making his third start in five days and his sixth attempt to win number 20. Newcombe was also after his 20th win.[31] Newcombe and Roberts started by pitching scoreless ball for five innings before the Phillies managed to get a run in the top of the sixth inning on singles by Dick Sisler, Del Ennis, and Puddin' Head Jones. In the bottom of the sixth, Roberts disposed of the first two Dodgers batters before Pee Wee Reese hit a fly that stuck on a ledge in right field, only 297 feet from the plate, for a game-tying homer.

The score was still tied at 1-1 when Cal Abrams led off the bottom of the ninth for the Dodgers by drawing a walk. After two failed bunt attempts, Reese lined a single to left field, moving the winning run to second with no one out and Duke Snider coming up. Ace reliever Jim Konstanty was warming up in the bullpen, but manager Eddie Sawyer stayed with Roberts.

Roberts and others figured that Snider, a powerful hitter, would attempt to bunt to get both runners in scoring position. But Snider crossed everyone up by lining the first pitch into center field. Richie Ashburn thought there was no way that Snider would bunt, and had moved in a couple of steps to be in better position to throw to the plate.[32] Ashburn fielded Snider's hit on the first bounce and came up throwing. He was reputed to have a weak throwing arm, and Dodgers third-base coach Milt Stock decided to test it by sending Abrams home. Ashburn's throw was strong and on the money, a one-hopper to catcher Stan Lopata, who tagged out Abrams 15 feet up the third-base line.

There was still only one out with men on second and third, and two dangerous batters coming up. Eddie Sawyer told Roberts to walk Jackie Robinson to set up a force at every base. The clutch-hitting Carl Furillo was the next hitter, but Roberts got him on a pop foul to first baseman Eddie Waitkus. Another slugger, Gil Hodges, was next and lifted a fly ball to Ennis in right field, the sun field at Ebbets Field. Ennis, battling it all the way, finally caught the ball by trapping it against his chest. After the game, Ennis showed where the seams of the ball had made an imprint on his chest.

The game went into the 10th inning and Sawyer let Roberts bat leadoff. He promptly bounced a single up the middle. Then Waitkus looped a single to center field, and the Phils had two men on base and no outs. Ashburn laid down a bunt, but Newcombe made a fine play, throwing out Roberts at third base. Sisler came to bat and found himself quickly in a hole, as Newcombe got ahead of him 0-and-2. Sisler battled, fouling off several pitches. He then timed a high fastball and ripped a low line drive to the opposite field in left that carried over the fence some 350 feet away to put the Phillies in the lead, 4-1, as his teammates surged out of the dugout to celebrate their sudden three-run lead.

Roberts quickly set down the Dodgers in order in the bottom of the 10th to clinch the Phillies' first pennant in 35 years (since 1915 when Grover Cleveland Alexander was their ace).[33] In leading the Whiz Kids to the pennant, Roberts went 20-11 with an ERA of 3.02 in 304⅓ innings

After Roberts' pitching career was over, he was amazed at the number of Brooklyn fans who would tell him how unhappy they were about the 1950 pennant race and Roberts' many confrontations with the Dodgers. Actors Danny Kaye and Eli Wallach seriously bemoaned the loss of the 1950 pennant to Roberts and the Phils. Historian Doris Kearns Goodwin wrote in her book *Wait Till Next Year* that as a little girl rooting for the Brooklyn Dodgers she was hoping that something would happen to Roberts so he would not be able to pitch against her beloved Bums.[34]

The Phillies then faced Casey Stengel's mighty New York Yankees in the World Series. The Yankees, whose lineup included Joe DiMaggio, Whitey Ford, Allie Reynolds, Yogi Berra, Bobby Brown, and MVP Phil Rizzuto, were prohibitive favorites to take the Series. Ace reliever Konstanty started the first game against the Yanks, hurling a masterful game, giving up only four hits and one run. But Vic Raschi was better, and the Yankees won 1-0. Roberts started the second game for the Phillies against Allie Reynolds. In the second inning, Roberts gave up a run to the New Yorkers on a walk and two singles. The Phillies finally broke through to score their first run of the Series in the fifth, knotting the score at 1-1. The Phillies then wasted opportunities in the seventh, eighth, and ninth innings as Reynolds kept them at bay.

Roberts went to the mound with the score tied 1-1 in the 10th inning. The first batter was DiMaggio, the Yankee Clipper. Four straight times Roberts had forced Joe to pop up. This time Roberts got behind in the count and threw DiMaggio a pitch his mentor Ray Fisher had told him he could hit, a high fastball out over the plate. DiMaggio lifted it onto the second deck of the left-field stands in Shibe Park, putting the Yankees up 2-1.

The Phillies threatened in the bottom of the 10th, on a walk to Jackie Mayo and a sacrifice bunt, but Reynolds then retired Ashburn and Sisler, putting the Phillies down 2-0 in the Series. The New Yorkers then wrapped up the Series with two straight wins, winning Game Three 3-2 and Game Four 5-2. The Phillies pitching was good, but their bats were silent, scoring only a total of five runs and batting only .203 in the four-game series. For their part, the Yankees hit only .222 as a team, but had a team earned-run average of just 0.73.

Spring training in 1951 found most Phillies fans expecting another run at the pennant. But it was not to be as the team floundered early and finished in fifth place, eight games under .500. Roberts was a workhorse, winning 21 while losing 15. He hurled 315 innings, walking only 64 while striking out 127, with an ERA of 3.03.

In 1952, Roberts had his best year, going 28-7, winning 20 of his last 22 starts and 17 of his last 18.[35] He also saved two games. His ironman ability allowed him to pitch 330 innings (the most innings any National League pitcher had thrown in 25 years), while allowing only 45 walks and striking out 148 to go with a 2.59 ERA. In a memorable game on September 6 against the Boston Braves, he pitched all 17 innings of a 7-6 win, shutting the Braves out the last nine innings. His 28 wins were 10 more than those of Sal Maglie, his closest competitor. Not surprisingly, *The Sporting News* voted him Major League Player of the Year and National League Pitcher of the Year. It seemed logical that Roberts would be voted the National League's Most Valuable Player, but Hank Sauer of the Chicago Cubs received that honor.[36]

A couple of years later Commissioner Ford Frick told Roberts at a dinner that he was going to create an award just for pitchers, since he did not think that pitchers got enough recognition.[37] Thus, in 1956, major-league baseball inaugurated the Cy Young Award, in large part because Roberts was snubbed for the MVP after his remarkable 1952 season.

For the next three years, Roberts was the picture of consistency. In 1953, he was 23-16, working 346⅔ innings, walking 61, and striking out 198, with an ERA of 2.75 for a third-place team. Roberts finished 23-15 in 1954, hurling 336⅔ innings while issuing 56 passes, striking out 185, and posting a 2.97 ERA as the Phillies finished in fourth place. In 1955, he recorded a 23-14 mark with a 3.28 ERA over 305 innings, and was rewarded with a second *Sporting News* Pitcher of the Year Award. For six consecutive years Roberts had pitched 300 innings or more while winning 20 games or more. His durability prompted Curt Simmons to observe, "He was like a diesel engine. The more you used him, the better he ran. I don't think you could wear him out."[38]

Roberts never pitched a no-hitter in the big leagues, but he came close several times. On April 29, 1954, he pitched a one-hitter to beat Warren Spahn and the Milwaukee Braves, allowing only a double to Del Crandall in the third inning. Two weeks later, pitching against Cincinnati at Connie Mack Stadium (Shibe Park having been renamed), Roberts gave up a leadoff homer to Bobby Adams and then proceeded to set down the next 27 batters in a row.

On Opening Day in 1955, Roberts took a no-hitter into the ninth inning, but with one out Alvin Dark singled to break it up.

In the midst of all this first-rate pitching, Roberts was gradually but steadily becoming involved in the economic, business, and political side of the game.

Between the 1951 and 1952 seasons Granny Hamner stepped down as the Phillies' player representative. His teammates elected Roberts to succeed him. Manager Eddie Sawyer advised him not to take the position because he thought it would interfere with Roberts' pitching. But Roberts believed that since his teammates had voted for him, he was obligated to represent them.

The first meeting Roberts attended as player representative for the Phillies, at the Broadmoor Hotel in Colorado Springs, was a lesson in baseball's labor relations. Walker Cooper, Terry Moore, and Ralph Kiner were among those in attendance. The player representatives' focus was to increase the value of their pension plan from distribution of the rapidly increasing television revenue. This resulted in plans for a meeting between American League player representative Reynolds, National League player representative Kiner, and Commissioner Ford Frick in Atlanta.

In Atlanta, the Players Association wanted attorney J. Norman Lewis to help them in their negotiations, but Frick vetoed the idea of having a lawyer present. Roberts argued that the players should go ahead with the meeting with the lawyer staying outside the room, making him available for consultation by the players. However, Roberts' position was voted down, and the meeting never took place.

Roberts learned from this experience that his assumption that the commissioner worked only in the best interests of baseball and the players were wrong. At the time of the aborted meeting, Roberts was unaware that the owners had not renewed Happy Chandler's contract as commissioner because of his pro-labor view of the players and their needs.[39]

After the events in Atlanta, Reynolds and Kiner hired Lewis to work with Hank Greenberg and John Kenneth Galbraith, who represented the owners, to hammer out a compromise deal. It was agreed that 60 percent or $1.8 million of the new TV revenue would go to the Players Association Pension Fund. Roberts now knew that a controversy would occur every time a new TV contract was written.

After the 1954 season, Kiner was traded to the Cleveland Indians of the American League and Roberts was elected to replace him as the National League's player representative.

Roberts resigned as the National League representative after the 1959 season, believing that his involvement was hurting his pitching. He also felt inadequate to accomplish what he believed needed to be done and advised the group to consider hiring an executive director to represent them.[40]

In the fall of 1964, with the World Series fast approaching, Roberts was aware that a new television contract was about to be agreed upon and a battle of how much revenue would go to the Players Association Pension Fund would ensue. With the consent of Bob Friend, by then the player representative for the National League, he spoke at a meeting of the Players Association and convinced them that they needed to hire a full-time executive director. Roberts later acknowledged that he was unaware at the time he advanced the idea of an executive director that it would result in radical changes with free agency and the reserve clause. All he wanted was for an executive director to ensure that the Players Pension Fund would be dealt with fairly and that the players' licensing rights would be protected.[41]

Backed by the players, Roberts and Jim Bunning (another Phillies pitching ace and Hall of Famer, and later a Republican senator from Kentucky) approached a veteran steel union economist and negotiator, Marvin Miller, and asked the longtime Brooklyn Dodgers fan to become executive director of the Players Association. At the time, its only asset to date was a single, battered filing cabinet. Miller said yes, provided the membership ratified his appointment.

Miller visited all the spring-training camps, and although opposed by the owners, was elected by the players as executive director in a 489-to-136 vote. Within 12 months, Miller had forced owners to raise the minimum major-league salary from $7,000 to $10,000 and make greater contributions to the pension fund. Doubtless Roberts' endorsement of Miller helped get him elected.

Roberts was very upset when Miller led the players out on their first strike in 1972. During their first interview before Miller was hired, he had said in response to a question from Roberts that he had no intention of ever engaging in a work stoppage with the players. In that first strike the issues were the players' benefits package including health insurance and the pension fund. When Roberts called Miller to remind him of his promise, Miller said, "Robin, I've been expecting your call."[42]

In 1956, Roberts' earnings from baseball peaked as he made $60,000 from the Phillies and various endorsements. But on the field he struggled much of the year. All the innings were starting to catch up to him and he had trouble extending his arm all the way. As a result, he lost some pop on his fastball. But heading into his last start, he still stood 19-17 and had a chance for his seventh straight 20-win season. It occurred on September 30, his 30th birthday, against the Giants in Connie Mack Stadium. He lost 8-3 to end his run, as the Phillies finished fifth with a 71-83 record.[43] Although he led the league with 22 complete games and allowed only 40 walks in 297⅓ innings, his earned-run average rose to an ominous 4.45.

Late in the 1956 season the Phillies and Cardinals talked seriously about a Robin Roberts-for-Stan Musial trade. It, of course, did not happen.

The next year, Roberts fell to 10-22 on a team that finished at .500, although his ERA fell slightly to 4.07. He rebounded in 1958, with a 17-14 record for a last-place team that finished 16 games under .500. In 1959, Roberts was 15-17 as the Phillies again finished in the basement with a 64-90 record. In 1960, he dropped to 12-16 with a team that was 59-95. On July 21, however, he pitched a memorable 3-0 victory against the San Francisco Giants at Candlestick Park, allowing only a very questionable hit in the fifth inning to Felipe Alou on a hard groundball right to the third baseman.[44]

But Roberts was having trouble shifting from pitching with power to pitching with finesse. The bottom fell out for both Roberts and the Phillies in 1961. The team lost 107 games, winning only 47. Roberts contributed to this ghastly record with a 1-10 season and an ERA of 5.85. Manager Gene Mauch criticized Roberts publicly on more than one occasion and the Phillies, figuring they could finish last without him, sold him to the Yankees on October 16, 1961.[45]

Thus in 1962, Roberts joined the reigning world champions. The Yankees figured that Roberts' experience would help, particularly with starters Ralph Terry and Bill Stafford vulnerable to military call-up. He went north with the team from spring training, but rain and offdays prevented him from making a regular-season appearance with the Yankees. Neither Stafford nor Terry was drafted, and Rollie Sheldon and rookie Jim Bouton emerged as solid starters. Manager Ralph Houk didn't need a 35-year-old finesse relief pitcher, so Roberts was released on April 25.

At this point, Roberts was prepared to quit baseball. He received a call from his friend Cy Perkins, who was always there when Roberts needed a lift. Perkins told Roberts not to quit, that he would be throwing shutouts at 40.[46] Shortly after his talk with Perkins, Roberts received a call from the Tokyo Giants asking him to play in Japan. But Roberts did not want to uproot his family and turned down their offer.

Roberts called Freddie Hutchinson, manager of the Cincinnati Reds, and arranged to work out with the team. Hutchinson liked what he saw and promised him 10 straight starts. But Roberts balked at the offered salary of $15,000 and said he would sign only if they matched his last salary of $35,000. The negotiations then fell apart, since no Reds player was making more than $30,000. Roberts then called Lee MacPhail of the Baltimore Orioles, who, after a workout, signed Roberts for his requested $35,000. Robbie was particularly happy about playing with the Orioles because Baltimore was close to Philadelphia and he could visit his family often.[47]

Roberts started his first game for the Orioles on May 27, 1962, against the Boston Red Sox. He pitched well, leaving after 7⅔ innings with a 2-2 tie. After that he was in the starting rotation. Roberts went 10-9 for the Orioles in 1962, throwing 191⅓ innings and posting a 2.78 ERA, second lowest in the American League. Moreover, in recognition of his career and life off the diamond, the Phi Delta Theta fraternity honored him with its Lou Gehrig Award.

In 1963 with the Orioles Roberts was 14-13 with a 3.33 ERA, starting 35 games and pitching over 250 innings. The next year he posted a 13-7 mark with a 2.91 ERA and four shutouts as the Orioles finished in third place with a 97-65 record, only two games behind the pennant-winning Yankees. Roberts was 38 years old as the 1965 season began and out of the rotation as the Orioles had a great young staff with the likes of Steve Barber, Dave McNally, Wally Bunker, and Milt Pappas.

They also had the 19-year-old bonus baby and future Hall of Famer Jim Palmer, who was just breaking in. The club asked Roberts to room on the road with Palmer, who was literally half his age. Late one night after a game in Los Angeles as they were trying to go to sleep, Palmer asked Roberts, "Old man, why don't you tell me about pitching?"

Roberts said, "Throw the hell out of the ball and go to sleep." Palmer later said that was some of the best advice he'd ever received.[48]

In May Roberts moved into the rotation to replace a sore-armed Pappas and threw four straight complete-game wins. He then did not win another game until July 5, going 1-7 with a 3.87 earned-run average over that span, leading the Orioles to release him on July 31. The Houston Astros, however, signed him five days later and Roberts broke in with a bang in the new Astrodome, hurling shutouts in his first two starts. He finished the season 5-2 for the Astros with a sparkling 1.89 earned-run average in 10 starts. His overall record for the year was 10-9 with a 2.78 ERA in 190⅔ innings.

After the season Roberts had elbow surgery to remove bone chips that had been bothering him for some time. He started on Opening Day for the 13th time in his career, replacing scheduled starter Dick Farrell, who came down with a sore arm. His elbow wasn't right and after mixed results, the Astros released him on Fourth of July. He was 3-5 with a shutout and a 3.82 ERA in 12 starts.

While Roberts was packing the station wagon to take his family home to Philadelphia, he got a call from the Chicago Cubs, who wanted him to replace pitching coach Fred Fitzsimmons, who had taken ill, as well as continue to serve on the active roster under manager Leo Durocher.[49] He signed and reeled off three quality starts for the Cubs before again running into problems to finish 2-3 with the Cubs in 11 appearances. Along the way he defeated the Atlanta Braves in relief for his 286th and last major-league win. In doing so he set a record, becoming the only pitcher in history with wins over the Boston Braves, the Milwaukee Braves, and the Atlanta Braves.

While with the Cubs, Roberts mentored another rookie pitcher who would become a Hall of Famer, Ferguson Jenkins, who always called Roberts his "idol."

The Cubs asked Roberts to come back in 1967 strictly as the pitching coach. Roberts, however, wasn't convinced that he was finished as a pitcher and didn't want all the travel away from his family if he were just coaching. As a result, he was released by the Cubs on October 4, 1966.

Instead, he worked out an arrangement with Bob Carpenter, owner of the Phillies, to pitch for Reading in the Double-A Eastern League to begin 1967. Reading was only an hour-plus commute for Roberts from his home in the Philadelphia suburbs. He wanted to pitch until June 15 for Reading; then, if no major-league club signed him, he would retire. He pitched well for Reading, winning five against three losses, tossing two shutouts and compiling a 2.48 earned-run average. His last game in Reading was on June 15 against Williamsport. He pitched eight innings, won 5-3 and said farewell to manager Frank Lucchesi. Since no organization had called, he headed home, his 20-year career in professional baseball over.

With his fluid, easy motion, Roberts had hoped to be able to pitch until he was 45, but it was not to be. On the drive home that evening, he thought of Cy Perkins, who had died in 1963. After the Yankees had released him in 1962, Perkins had told him he'd be throwing shutouts when he was 40. "Yes," Roberts thought, "but you didn't tell me it would be in York (Pennsylvania)."

Then Roberts recalled how Perkins had told him early in his career that he would be the next 300-game winner. He thought how Perkins had been correct about that one, too. He'd won nine games with Wilmington in 1948, 286 in the big leagues, and five with Reading in 1967 for exactly 300 victories. But he knew that wasn't exactly what Perkins had had in mind.[50]

For three months Roberts pondered what to do with the rest of his life. His main concern was how he was going to support his wife and four boys in private school. He believed he needed $40,000 a year to take care of his family properly.

He finally received a call from a friend, Jim Castle, who ran a small investment firm. When Castle offered Roberts a job with a salary of $25,000, he accepted. He was also offered a job with radio station WPEN in Philadelphia to do an early-morning sports show for $15,000 a year, so he had his $40,000.

He would arrive at the radio station at 6:30, do three sports shows and then head to the investment job. He worked in the investment business for 10 years, doing well enough not to need the sports show, but he missed baseball and hoped to get back in the game in some capacity.[51]

In 1972, Ruly Carpenter, the son of Bob Carpenter, succeeded his father as the Phillies president. As a youngster Ruly had always hung around the clubhouse and had become a close friend of Roberts. Roberts called Ruly to congratulate him. Roberts also told him that he would like to be considered for the Phillies' general-manager position, which was open. Ruly said he would talk to his father. At first Bob agreed but he later canceled the meeting.

Roberts later heard that Wister Randolph, the vice president of the Phils, had asked if there was a position for Roberts with the Phils. Bob Carpenter replied, "Who's going to take care of me when I'm old?" Roberts felt the remark was uncalled for and never again broached Carpenter about working for the Phillies.

It turned out, Roberts later learned, that Carpenter resented that he had been so deeply involved in the Players Association and the subsequent hiring of Marvin Miller as executive director.[52]

A few years later Ruly Carpenter did interview Roberts for the job of manager of the Phils, along with Andy Seminick, Richie Ashburn, Jim Bunning, and the man who got the job—Danny Ozark, then a coach with the Los Angeles Dodgers.[53]

In the early '70s Roberts, with his eldest son, Robbie, ran the Philadelphia Firebirds, a minor-league hockey team. Roberts then returned to the investment business, this time with Lehman Brothers, where he worked as a broker in the money-management division. The new job required his traveling to New York City three days a week. Though he did well financially, he still wanted to return to baseball.

He had kept his hand in baseball by coaching his sons Robbie and Danny in American Legion ball for two years and then for four years as volunteer baseball coach at Germantown Academy, where he coached sons Danny and Ricky.

In the fall of 1976, Roberts received a call from Dick Bowers, the athletic director at the University of South Florida in Tampa, about the baseball coaching position.[54] Roberts accepted the job and the family pulled up stakes and headed for Tampa with their youngest son, Jimmy. Roberts was elated about getting the coaching job at South Florida. Even though he would have a recruiting budget of only $5,000 a year, Roberts plowed ahead and coached for eight enjoyable years at South Florida.[55]

In 1982, Roberts coached his best club as South Florida went 45-13, won the Sun Belt Conference championship and went to the NCAA Regionals in Miami. There they defeated the University of Florida but lost to Miami and Stetson. Roberts' youngest son, Jim, was the first baseman on that South Florida team and made the all-conference team.

During his time there, USF developed a real rivalry against conference foe South Alabama, which was coached by his former big-league rival Eddie Stanky, who was known as "The Brat" in his playing days. The two teams often battled down to the wire for the conference title. Once when the two teams were playing in Mobile, Stanky became unhappy with the home-plate umpire's call of balls and strikes and yelled to him, "Just because he's in the Hall of Fame, you don't have to give him every pitch."[56]

When he coached, Roberts always said that he was a collector of ballplayers, not a teacher. Among other good ballplayers, he "collected" four players at South Florida who played in the big leagues.[57] They were Scott Hemond, a catcher and a first-round draft choice; infielder Tim Hulett; and southpaw pitchers Chris Welsh and Tony Fossas, who pitched in the big leagues past his 41st birthday.

In 1986, after eight years at USF, Roberts retired from coaching to relax and play more golf. Late in his playing career he had invested with old teammate Curt Simmons in the Limekiln Golf Course in suburban Philadelphia. With Simmons managing the course, it was now producing a nice income for both.

In his sixth year of eligibility, the Baseball Writers Association of America elected Roberts to the Baseball Hall of Fame in 1976 with 86.9 percent of the vote. During his induction speech, he promised to come back every year to the Hall of Fame weekend.[58] He fulfilled that promise, attending 35 induction ceremonies in a row. He also served several terms on the Hall's Board of Directors.

For his career, Roberts led the National League five times in complete games and 14 times made more than 30 starts in a season, once starting 41 games. Roberts was named *The Sporting News* Major League Pitcher of the Year four times and named to the All-Star Team seven times, starting for the National League five times. His career totals are 286 wins, 245 losses, a 3.41 ERA, 4,688⅔ innings pitched, 902 walks, 2,357 strikeouts, and 25 saves, with a winning percentage of .539.

Some have suggested that Roberts would have won far more games had he played for better teams, but Roberts himself scoffed at that notion. He pointed out that in his heyday in the early to mid-'50s, the Phillies were usually a first-division club and that his performance declined along with the team when it bottomed out in the late '50s and early '60s. He also noted that if he had pitched for the Yankees, for example, a club that had wanted to sign him, he might not have had the opportunity to pitch so much because their staff was so strong.[59]

Roberts was a two-pitch pitcher, fastball and curve, and mostly threw his fastball, delivering it with a pop of his wrist.[60] Cy Perkins always said that he threw faster easier than anyone he'd ever seen.[61] He had great control and his fastball had hop to it, creating a lot of fly balls. As he acknowledged, however, sometimes the fly balls had a little too much carry and ended up over the fence. In fact, he gave up 505 home runs during his career, the major-league record until it was broken by Jamie Moyer in 2010. But many of the home runs hit against him were solo shots with the game well in hand.[62]

Roberts' great control, especially for one who threw so hard and relied so heavily on his fastball, was also a key to his success. He was able to throw down and away and up and in and "paint the black." He rarely walked anyone, forcing the opposition to swing the bat. For example, in 1952 he walked only 45 batters in 330 innings.

Roberts was frequently criticized for not pitching inside and knocking hitters down, a common practice at the time.[63] In fact, some called him "the pitcher who was too polite."[64] Dizzy Dean, who broadcast television's *Game of the Week* during the 1950s, would often urge Roberts to brush hitters back. Even his pitching coach in the mid-'50s, Whitlow Wyatt, publicly criticized him for not throwing inside.[65] But it was just not in Roberts' nature to do so. He could remember intentionally throwing at a hitter only twice in his long career.[66]

Roberts was also criticized for refusing to learn another pitch when he lost something off his fastball and for not throwing a changeup or changing speeds. Cy Perkins had told him early in his career that throwing changeups interfered with a fastball pitcher's rhythm and since rhythm was very important to his success, he always resisted developing one, even late in his career.[67] He admitted to being stubborn about changing his way of pitching, but knew that if he hit his spots he would be successful, even after he didn't throw as hard as in his prime.[68] After his career was over, however, Roberts acknowledged that he wasn't sure if his stubbornness was responsible for his success or had perhaps led him to not take care of his arm as well as he might have.[69]

Roberts always took his losses very hard. If he lost at home, he knew he wasn't going to be very good company, so he would lie in his hammock in his back yard, sip a six-pack of beer, and watch the sun come up while brooding about the game.[70] On the road, he would walk back to the hotel and replay the game in his head over and over, focusing on what he'd done wrong. Maje McDonnell, the Phillies batting practice pitcher who became a coach, would often go with him. Once after a tough loss in Milwaukee in 1955, they walked back to the team hotel from County Stadium, a distance of seven miles.[71]

Jackie Robinson among others thought Roberts in his heyday was the best pitcher he'd ever seen.[72] Robinson said, "You can't hit him when it counts. There isn't a tougher competitor in the business."[73]

Stan Musial noted that with Roberts "there was no pretense, no trickery. He was going to come after you with that fastball of his that rose, hopped or slid. I never saw another fastball pitcher with such good control." Musial also marveled at how competitive Roberts was. "He enjoyed those tight spots, and had a unique ability to find something extra with the game on the line."[74]

When he pitched, Roberts had almost a unique ability to concentrate. He was able to focus intently on just the catcher and was totally oblivious to the crowed or any potential distractions. Once after a big game against the Dodgers he asked his wife, Mary, "Was there a big crowd tonight?" Mary responded that the stadium was jammed with more than 30,000 people. But not once warming up or during the game had Roberts even glanced into the stands.[75]

Hall of Fame umpire Al Barlick, who was from Roberts' hometown, once said that Roberts was so impassive on the mound that "he had the outward disposition of an oyster."[76]

Roberts used his strong legs to push off when he pitched, sometimes called a drop-and-drive delivery. He virtually dragged his right knee on the ground while finishing his delivery.[77] The delivery was very similar to the one Tom Seaver adopted. Also emulating the drop-and-drive delivery was Japanese pitcher Masaichi Kaneda, who as a 17-year-old saw Roberts pitch during a tour of Japan with the Eddie Lopat All-Stars. Kaneda became Japan's greatest pitcher with 400 victories.[78]

Noted author James Michener, a lifetime Phillies fan, was particularly fond of Roberts. They had become friends in the process of Michener's writing a book titled *Sports in America* in which Michener described the major role sports played in American society. Roberts was among the three people to whom he dedicated the book.[79]

Kaneda also became a successful manager in Japan after his playing career and invited Roberts and Mary to Japan in 1990 for his Lotte Orions spring training.[80]

Mary and Robin Roberts raised a family of four boys who collectively gave them seven grandchildren.

The Roberts's oldest son, Robbie, became the general manager of the Limekiln Golf Course north of Philadelphia. Danny, the second oldest son, was baseball coach of the United States Military Academy at West Point for 17 years, and later coached in the Phillies' minor-league system. Third son Ricky entered the restaurant business in Atlanta while Jimmy, the youngest, went into banking in Tampa.

Roberts' wife, Mary, died in Temple Terrace, Florida, on June 23, 2005, at the age of 77. Robin Roberts passed away almost five years later, on May 6, 2010, also in Temple Terrace. He was 83 years old.

Indulging in a bit of understatement, Tom Roberts, who had fought at Gallipoli and labored in the coal mines of Lancashire, Wales, and Illinois, summed up his talented son in 1956: "Ah, well, he could have done a lot worse."[81]

## SOURCES

In addition to the sources cited in the Notes, the author also consulted:

The National Baseball Library Archives, Cooperstown, New York.

Baumgartner, Stan, and Harry T. Paxton. "He Pitched the Phillies to the Pennant, *Saturday Evening Post*, January 13, 1951.

Brown, Hugh. "Did They Overwork Roberts?" *Sport*, February 1954.

_____. "Roberts Pitches to Win," *Baseball Yearbook*, 1953.

Clayton, Skip, and Jeff Moeller. *50 Phabulous Phillies* (Champaign, Illinois: Sports Publishing, 2000).

Fraley, Oscar. "Can Robin Roberts Win 300?" *Inside Sports*, March 1953.

Gordon, Robert. *Legends of the Philadelphia Phillies* (Champaign, Ilinois: Sports Publishing, 2005).

Hochman, Stan. "Robin Roberts Remembers the Whiz Kids," *Baseball Digest*, July 1972.

Honig, Donald. *A Donald Honig Reader* (New York: Simon & Schuster, 1988).

"How Roberts Does It." *Sport*, September, 1953.

Kelly, Gene. "Robin Roberts: The Pitcher Who Couldn't Pitch!" *Baseball Life Stories—1952*.

Lieb, Frederick G. "Best Since Matty: Robin Roberts," *Baseball Magazine*, September 1949.

Marazzi, Rich. "Robin Roberts," *Sports Collectors Digest*, October 20, 2000.

Newcombe, Jack. "Roberts Is the Phillies' Stopper," *Sport*, June 1952.

Orodenker, Richard, ed. *The Phillies Reader* (Philadelphia: Temple University Press, 1996).

Paxton, Harry. *The Whiz Kids—The Story of the Fightin' Phils* (New York: David McKay Company, Inc., 1950).

Peary, Danny, ed. *We Played the Game—65 Players Remember Baseball's Greatest Era, 1947-1964* (New York: Hyperion, 1994).

"The Phillies Pitching Pals," *Sport*, October 1953.

Reising, Robert, and C. Paul Rogers III. "Remembering Springfield's Hall of Fame Pitcher—Robin Evan Roberts," *Springfield Scene Magazine*, July/August 2016.

Roberts, Robin. "Pitching for Tomorrow," *Guideposts*, August 1956.

Ryczek, William J. *The Yankees in the Early 1960s* (Jefferson, North Carolina: McFarland, 2008).

Westcott, Rich. *A Century of Philadelphia Sports* (Philadelphia: Temple University Press, 2001).

Westcott, Rich, and Frank Bilovsky. *The New Phillies Encyclopedia* (Philadelphia: Temple University Press, 1993).

Williams, Edgar. "How Robin Roberts Wrestled His Way to a Comeback," *Baseball Digest*, December/January 1959.

_____. "Has Roberts Lost His Fastball?," *Baseball Digest*, January/February 1957.

_____. "His Control's Built In!," *Baseball Digest*, August 1953.

Yeutter, Frank. "Tale of Two Pitchers," *Complete Baseball*, February 1953.

## NOTES

1   According to teammate Bubba Church, Roberts would "reach back and get a little bit more and a little bit more and a little bit more" when the game was on the line. Gene Fehler, *When Baseball Was Still King* (Jefferson, North Carolina: McFarland, 2012), 155.

2   Dick Seamon, "The Whole Story of Pitching," *Time*, May 28, 1956: 62.

3   David Pietrusza, Matthew Silverman, and Michael Gershman, eds., *Baseball—the Biographical Encyclopedia* (New York: Total/Sports Illustrated, 2000), 949-50.

4   *The Hall—A Celebration of Baseball's Greats* (New York: Little Brown & Co., 2014), 88.

5   Bill Gleason, "2 Views of Roberts, All Good, of Course," *Chicago American*, August 10, 1966.

6   Seamon: 62.

7   Robin Roberts and C. Paul Rogers III, *My Life in Baseball* (Chicago: Triumph Books, 2003), republished as *Throwing Hard Easy—Reflections on a Life in Baseball* (Lincoln: University of Nebraska Press, 2014), 2-5; Hugh Brown, "Mr. Roberts—the Story of a Winner," *Sport*, August 1956: 59.

8   Roberts and Rogers, 6.

9   Seamon: 62. As a boy, Roberts had read that his hero Lou Gehrig had bought his mother a house, prompting him to make the same promise. Roberts and Rogers, 22; Brown, *Sport*.

10   In March 1945, after the 1944-45 college basketball season, Roberts was inducted into the Air Corps and sent to Sheppard Field in Wichita Falls, Texas, for basic training. But with the war nearing an end, preflight programs were filled, so Roberts was then assigned to sheet-metal school at Chanute Field in Illinois. He was discharged from the service on November 1, 1945, and headed back to Michigan State to resume his collegiate career. Roberts and Rogers, 13-14.

11   Roberts and Rogers, 14-15.

12   Wilbur (Bill) Kelly, "The Robin Roberts You Didn't Know!" *Baseball Magazine*, Spring 1953: 14-15, 51.

13   Roberts did not realize he had thrown a no-hitter until the public-address announcer gave the game totals after the game. The winning run scored on a walk, a stolen base and two infield groundouts. The opposing pitcher that day was Carl Braun, who went on to become an NBA All-Star with the New York Knicks. Roberts and Rogers, 16. Kelly, 51.

14   Chuck Ward, "How I Find Guys Like Robin Roberts," *Baseball Life Stories*, 1952: 44.

15   Ward told Roberts, "I wanted to sign you right then. I knew anybody with that hard a head would be a whale of a pitcher." Roberts and Rogers, 21.

16   The Phillies promised to keep Roberts' signing confidential and defer his signing bonus so that he could play basketball during his senior year at Michigan State. However, a week after Roberts returned to school the *Detroit Free Press* broke the story about Roberts' signing with the Phillies, making him ineligible to play basketball for the Spartans under the rules then existing. Roberts and Rogers, 23-24.

17   Roberts and Rogers, 22; Fay Vincent, *We Would Have Played for Nothing* (New York: Simon & Schuster, 2008), 208. Boston Braves general manager John Quinn had arranged for Roberts to work out with the Braves, who were following the Phillies into Wrigley Field to play the Cubs. He had also promised Roberts' parents a four-day vacation in Chicago at the Braves' expense. Thus, Robin's mother was initially disappointed when he wanted to sign with the Phillies, but Chuck Ward also promised the Roberts family a trip to Chicago after Robin signed. Milton Richmond, "Top Hurler in Baseball," April 1953: 74 (publication name unknown, copy of file with author).

18   Roberts and Rogers, 23.

19   Seamon: 65.

20   Roberts and Rogers, 28-30, Donald Honig, *Baseball Between the Lines* (New York: Coward, McCann & Geoghegan, 1976), 241-46. Other sources describe Roberts' first spring appearance as against the New York Yankees, where he reputedly struck out Joe DiMaggio and Phil Rizzuto. Lowell Reidenbaugh, *Cooperstown—Where Baseball's Legends Live Forever* (St. Louis: The Sporting News, 1983), 216; Frank Yeutter, "First Robin of Fling," *Baseball Digest* June, 1949: 4.

21   Al Cartwright, "Robin Roberts, (Blue) Rock of Ages," *The National Pastime*, 1999: 28. The Blue Rocks were in Hagerstown, Maryland, when Roberts was promoted. He was awakened at 10 A.M. by his manager, Jack Sanford, and told to come down to the lobby of the hotel. When Roberts got there, he was greeted by the entire team and presented with a pen and pencil set that was inscribed "Robin Roberts, Philadelphia Phillies." Roberts and Rogers, 35.

22   Roberts and Rogers, 35-37; Brown, *Sport*, August, 1956: 61; Cynthia J. Wilber, *For the Love of the Game* (New York: Morrow, 1992), 305.

23   Arthur Daley, "Everything's Under Control," *New York Times*, March 25, 1953; Rich Westcott, *Philadelphia's Top 50 Baseball Players* (Lincoln: University of Nebraska Press, 2013), 187.

24   Seamon: 65.

25   Harry T. Paxton, "The House Where the Ballplayers Live," *Saturday Evening Post*, September 10, 1949; Roberts and Rogers, 53-54.

26   Roberts and Rogers, 47.

27   For a number of years the Robertses' son Danny was the baseball coach at West Point and would bring his team to the Tampa area every year on their spring break to play games in the warm weather. When Mary stopped going to the West Point games, Danny asked her why. She said, "You throw to first base too much." Roberts and Rogers, 262.

28   Grayson was also the only baseball writer who picked the Phillies to win the 1950 pennant.

29   Roberts and Rogers, 69.

30   The press began referring to the team as "the Fizz Kids." Roger Kahn, *The Era: 1947-1957—When the Yankees, the Giants, and the Dodgers Ruled the World* (New York: Ticknor & Fields, 1993), 251.

31   During the 1950s aces Roberts and Newcombe would pitch against each other 23 times.

32   Robin Roberts and C. Paul Rogers III, *The Whiz Kids and the 1950 Pennant* (Philadelphia: Temple University Press, 1996), 315-16.

33   Roberts and Rogers, *The Whiz Kids and the 1950 Pennant*, 8-15, 311-38; Roberts and Rogers, 84-89.

34   Doris Kearns Goodwin, *Wait Till Next Year* (New York: Simon & Schuster, 1997), 107.

35   Art Morrow, "Robin Roberts—Baseball's Greatest Pitcher," *Inside Baseball*, March 1953: 20.

36   Sauer had led the league in home runs and runs batted in while hitting .270 for the fifth-place Cubs, who finished 10 games behind the fourth-place Phillies. The Athletics' Bobby

# 20-GAME LOSERS

      Shantz—24-7 with a 2.48 ERA—was the AL MVP, making Roberts' missing out on the award difficult to understand

37  Oscar Fraley, "Why They're Robbing Robin Roberts" (publication name unknown—copy on file with the author).

38  *The National Baseball Hall of Fame Almanac,* Durham: Baseball America, 2017 Edition), 370.

39  Roberts and Rogers, 215-16.

40  Roberts and Rogers, 217-18.

41  Roberts and Rogers, 218.

42  Roberts and Rogers, 224.

43  Roberts and Rogers, 153.

44  The ball was right at third baseman Joe Morgan, who fielded the ball but was off balance and fell backward with the ball in his glove. Roberts thought the official scorer might have called it an error if it had occurred later in the game. Robin Roberts as told to George Vass, "The Game I'll Never Forget," *Baseball Digest,* February 1976: 57-58.

45  Sandy Grady, "Split With Gene Mauch Hastened Robin Roberts' Exit," *Philadelphia Bulletin,* October 17, 1961.

46  Roberts and Rogers, 181.

47  Roberts and Rogers, 181-82; Vincent, 101.

48  Roberts and Rogers, 195.

49  Roberts and Rogers, 206.

50  Roberts and Rogers, 212-13.

51  Roberts and Rogers, 231-32.

52  Roberts and Rogers, 233.

53  Roberts and Rogers, 233-34.

54  Dick Bowers had first called Bobby Richardson, the former Yankees second baseman and then the coach of the University of South Carolina, about the position. Richardson declined, however, and suggested that Bowers call Robin Roberts, who had his degree from Michigan State and was qualified to coach baseball at the Division I level. Roberts and Rogers, 233-34.

55  Roberts and Rogers, 234-35.

56  Roberts and Rogers, 238.

57  Roberts would tell recruits, "If you can't play when you join me, you're not going to be able to play when you leave." Roberts and Rogers, 235-36; Vincent, 104.

58  Scott Gummer and Larry Shenk, *Phillies—An Extraordinary Tradition* (San Rafael, California: Insight Traditions, 2010), 189.

59  Honig, 235. In fact, during Roberts' heyday in the 1950s, the Yankees starters like Allie Reynolds, Vic Raschi, Ed Lopat, and Whitey Ford were throwing 100 (or more) fewer innings a year than Roberts.

60  According to Roberts, if he threw 115 pitches, 90 would be fastballs. Vincent, 93.

61  Roberts and Rogers, 29; Vincent, 82.

62  Roberts did have a sense of humor about all the homers he gave up, once saying, "They can accuse me of throwing home-run balls, but they can't accuse me of any prejudice. Just look over my record and you will find that I throw my home-run ball to everyone, irrespective of race or religion." Brown, *Sport,* August 1956: 56; Ed Pollock, "Robbie Is Pitching for Tomorrow," *Philadelphia Evening Bulletin,* July 16, 1956.

63  Seamon: 61; Brown, *Sport,* August, 1956: 56; Edgar Williams, "First Robin of Fling," *Baseball Digest,* January, 1953: 12.

64  Rich Marazzi and Len Fiorito, *Baseball Players of the 1950s* (Jefferson, North Carolina: McFarland, 2004), 329.

65  Edgar Williams, "Has Roberts Lost His Fastball?" *Baseball Digest,* January-February 1957: 9-10.

66  Once, in the mid-'50s, Roberts gave up home runs to Ted Kluszewski in Crosley Field his first two times up. Roberts decided that was enough of that and drilled Kluszewski in his very large right bicep his next time at bat. The ball dropped to Klu's feet, so he just picked it up and tossed it to Roberts as he jogged to first base. Thus, Roberts knew the pitch had not had the desired effect. Roberts and Rogers, 183, 263.

67  Vincent, 82.

68  Edgar Williams, "How Robin Roberts Wrestled His Way to a Comeback," *Baseball Digest,* December/January 1959: 37. When Roberts started his first game for the Astros in 1965, he met with his young catcher John Bateman to go over the signs. Bateman was incredulous that Roberts had only two pitches, fastball and curve. Roberts and Rogers, 199.

69  Anthony J. Connor, *Voices from Cooperstown—Baseball's Hall of Famers Tell It Like It Was* (New York: Collier Books, 1982), 289-90.

70  Honig, 241.

71  Roberts and Rogers, 40-41.

72  Jim Murray, "Roberts' Rules," *Los Angeles Times,* September, 20, 1962.

73  "Robin Roberts—So Good, You Can't Believe He's Real!" *Baseball Stars—1953:* 23.

74  Roberts and Rogers, ix, x; Harry T. Paxton, "Baseball's Biggest Winner," *Saturday Evening Post,* August 10, 1953: 98. Once in 1950 or 1951 the Cardinals loaded the bases against him in St. Louis. Sportsman's Park had a short right-field porch, but Roberts proceeded to strike out Red Schoendienst, Stan Musial, and Enos Slaughter, three future Hall of Famers, on 10 pitches. Bob Broeg, "Roberts Followed Alexander's Advice to Hall of Fame," *St. Louis Post-Dispatch,* August 8, 1976: 2C. In 1953 against the Chicago Cubs, he reputedly struck out the side on nine pitches after the Cubs loaded the bases with no outs on a hit and two infield errors. Gleason, *Chicago American,* August 10, 1966.

# 20-GAME LOSERS

75 Roberts and Rogers, 37; Honig, 233. Leo Durocher managed the Giants in the early 1950s and always coached third base, from where he would ride opposing players, including the opposing pitcher, mercilessly. Roberts could hear him when he was in the dugout on days someone else was pitching. When Roberts was on the mound, however, his focus was so intense that he never heard Durocher trying to razz him. Once when Roberts was walking off the mound toward the Phillies' third-base dugout, Durocher waited from him. When Roberts passed by, Durocher said, "Hey kid, I really bother you, don't I?" Roberts looked at Durocher and just kind of smiled as he walked by. Roberts and Rogers, 37.

76 "Robin Roberts—So Good You Can't Believe He's Real!": 21.

77 Marazzi and Fiorito, 328.

78 In 1967 Roberts received a call one day from his old Whiz Kids teammate Richie Ashburn, who was by then broadcasting the Phillies games. Richie said, "I saw you pitch last night." That was news to Roberts, who had retired a year before. It turned out Ashburn had seen the rookie pitcher Seaver throw for the New York Mets the night before. His delivery was a drop and drive very much like Roberts' delivery. Roberts and Rogers, 260.

79 Roberts and Rogers, 243-46.

80 Roberts and Rogers, 124-25.

81 Seamon: 62.

# RED RUFFING

## BY WARREN CORBETT

**HALL OF FAMER RED RUFFING'S** career is a reminder that you can't judge a pitcher by his wins and losses. The right-hander lost more than 20 games twice while pitching for the last-place Red Sox and won at least 20 for four straight years with the World Series champion Yankees.

Charles Herbert Ruffing was born in Granville, Illinois, on May 3, 1905, one of five children of German immigrants John and Frances Ruffing. He spent his childhood in nearby Coalton, attending schools in Nokomis. The nickname "Red" came from his hair color, but his family called him Charley and his wife called him Charles. He signed some autographs "Chas. 'Red' Ruffing."

Ruffing's father was a coal miner until he broke his back. He took a job in the company office and rose to be the mine superintendent. He also served as mayor of Coalton. Charley quit school and went into the mine when he was 13, working for three dollars a day. It was punishing physical labor, 600 feet underground, often swinging a pick while stooped over. And it was dangerous; he saw a cousin killed in an accident. At 15 Charley was working as a coupler, hooking coal cars together, when his left foot was crushed between cars. Doctors managed to save the foot, but he lost four toes.

He had been a hard-hitting outfielder and pitcher for the company baseball team, managed by his father. While he was on crutches recuperating from his accident, Doc Bennett, a former minor leaguer who managed a local semipro team, encouraged him to concentrate on pitching, since he would no longer be able to run well. When Ruffing was 18, Bennett arranged his first professional contract, with Danville, Illinois, just 140 miles from home in the Class-B Three-I League. After one season in Danville, he was sold to the Boston Red Sox. The 19-year-old was hit hard in six appearances and went back to the minors in July 1924. When Boston recalled him in September, he was in the big leagues to stay.

Ruffing joined the Red Sox just as the club plunged into the bleakest period in its history. Boston finished last in each of his five full seasons, losing more than 100 games three times. Sportswriter Stanley Frank wrote that owner Bob Quinn "was operating the Red Sox on a frazzled shoestring."[1] Quinn's predecessor, Harry Frazee, had traded or sold most of the team's best players. Several, including that Ruth kid, went to the Yankees.

Although Ruffing was the Red Sox' top pitcher, he showed no sign of greatness. Today he would be tagged with the backhanded compliment "inning eater." Relying primarily on a whistling fastball, he posted a better-than-average ERA only once, and then just barely better. His 39 victories and 96 losses gave him a .289 winning percentage, even worse than his team's sorry .344. After he batted .314 in 1928 while losing a league-leading 25 games, the Sox considered shifting him to the outfield, but found that his mangled foot slowed him down too much.

Owner Quinn faced one of his frequent financial crises in May 1930. Red Sox scout Pat Monahan recalled, "He was real worried. He said he'd have to raise $67,000 in 48 hours to make a payment. 'If I don't make it, Pat, they'll foreclose. I know they will.'" Quinn swapped the 25-year-old Ruffing to the Yankees for backup outfielder Cedric Durst plus $50,000 and, according to Monahan, an additional $50,000 loan from Yankees owner Jacob Ruppert.[2] The trade rated only a one-inch story in the *New York Times*, describing Ruffing as "an in-and-outer."[3]

The deal made Ruffing's career. The turnaround in his fortunes began the first time he took the mound for New York, when Babe Ruth slammed a first-inning home run. Ruffing gave up six runs to the Tigers, but knocked in the deciding runs himself with a single and two RBIs. Late in the season he

won six straight decisions. He sealed his place on the team with a two-hit shutout over the pennant-bound Philadelphia Athletics in September. He finished 1930 with a 15-5 record for the Yankees; his 4.14 ERA was better than average in the Year of the Hitter. He also batted a career-high .364 with four homers.

Bob Shawkey, a former pitcher who managed the Yankees in 1930, said he had noticed that Ruffing could dominate for four or five innings while he was with the Red Sox, but tired and lost his stuff because he was "pitching all with his arm." Shawkey revamped the pitcher's delivery.[4] That wasn't the only reason for the dramatic improvement; Joe McCarthy took over as manager the next year, and McCarthy consistently fielded strong defensive teams—a pitcher's best friend.

When Ruffing turned into a star in New York, some writers questioned whether he had been giving his best effort to the Red Sox. But he remembered, "We had kids just out of college, Class D players.

Nobody could win with them."[5] A young man in his early 20s could easily have become demoralized pitching for a hopeless team, then snapped out of it when he found himself backed by a lineup that included Babe Ruth and Lou Gehrig.

Twenty-two-year-old Lefty Gomez established himself at the front of the Yankees rotation in 1932 as McCarthy began retooling the aging club. With young catcher Bill Dickey, shortstop Frank Crosetti, and speedy outfielder Ben Chapman in the lineup, the Yankees romped to their first pennant in four years. Gomez won 24 games and Ruffing 18, with a 3.09 ERA, second-best in the AL. He led the league with 190 strikeouts.

Ruffing and Gomez gave the Yankees a pair of aces for a decade. Gomez, three years younger, was the better pitcher when healthy. He led the league in ERA twice and in strikeouts and shutouts three times, but suffered recurring bouts of arm trouble. Ruffing usually racked up more innings and complete games; he completed 62 percent of his career starts, while the average AL pitcher finished less than half. Yankee outfielder Tommy Henrich said, "You know, there wasn't that much difference between [Gomez] and Ruffing, but Ruffing was always looked upon as the ace."[6]

Joe McCarthy agreed; he chose Ruffing to start Game One of six World Series to Gomez's one. "Sure, he's the best pitcher around," the manager said.[7] McCarthy scheduled Ruffing's starts to match him against the Yankees' toughest challengers. He beat the Tigers 13 straight times from 1937 to 1939. Ruffing was the type of player McCarthy liked best: quiet, consistent, and durable. But the two were not close; Ruffing recalled, "Well, he said hello to me on the first day of spring camp and said good-by to me on the last day of the season. In between he just put the ball in my hand and that was all I wanted."[8]

Gomez was a clown and a quipster whose personality eclipsed the stoic Ruffing. (Gomez said the secret of his success was "clean living and a fast outfield.") One writer called Ruffing "the Coolidge of baseball," after the president who never spoke two words when one would do. McCarthy remarked, "If

Ruffing has nothing to say he doesn't bother to say it."[9] Ruffing's closest friends on the Yankees were his roommate, Tony Lazzeri, Frank Crosetti, and Bill Dickey, men who fit the stereotype of the "strong, silent type." His hometown, Nokomis, had put up a sign at the city limits welcoming visitors to the home of Jim Bottomley, the onetime Cardinal first baseman. When the Chamber of Commerce wanted to add Ruffing's name to the sign, he told them not to do it because "I might move."[10]

On October 6, 1934, Ruffing married a local girl, Pauline Mulholland, whom he had met when she was working in a candy store. He threw a raucous party after the wedding that kept most of the town up all night. Pauline usually attended his starts and heckled the opposition. When she criticized rookie third baseman Red Rolfe for making an error behind her husband, and Rolfe's wife overheard her, Ruffing told Pauline to apologize. He said, "Rolfe will help me win more games than he ever lost for me."[11]

After finishing second from 1933 through 1935, McCarthy assembled a juggernaut in 1936. With Babe Ruth retired, rookie Joe DiMaggio was anointed as the new face of the Yankees. The club won 409 regular-season games in the next four seasons and claimed the World Series championship every year, an unprecedented run of success.

During the Yankees' four years of dominance, Ruffing won at least 20 games and ranked in the top six in ERA each season. He developed a slider, then a new pitch. Umpire Bill Summers said, "[O]n account of Red Ruffing, the slider got to be the thing."[12] His career was peaking as he entered his mid-30s, an age when most pitchers began to fade. He shared his prescription for keeping fit: "Run, run, run…. Some of the young kids on the Yankees used to kid me about going to bed at 7:30 after running all day long. But as the years went by I noticed I was still up there while they were forgotten."[13] He kept his weight between 208 and 212 on a 6-foot-1 frame.

Ruffing gave the Yankees trouble only when it came time to sign his contract. He was a chronic holdout. After his first 20-victory season in 1936, he didn't sign until May 1937. With no spring training, he reeled off victories in his first four starts and went on to win 20 again.

By 1939 Ruffing's reported $28,000 salary was the second highest on the team, behind Lou Gehrig's $34,000. He won his first seven decisions, the last one the 200th of his career, as the Yankees were running away with their fourth straight pennant. But Ruffing's elbow was hurting. Without telling McCarthy or the trainers, he began having Pauline massage his arm with a vibrating machine. He said the secret treatment was all that kept him going.[14] He started only 28 games and sat out the last two weeks of the season. He finished with a 2.93 ERA, the best in any of his full seasons, and his second consecutive 21-7 record. And he was ready to start, and win, Game One of the World Series against Cincinnati.

In the opening game of the 1942 Series Ruffing held the St. Louis Cardinals hitless for seven and two-thirds innings until Terry Moore singled to right. St. Louis rallied for four runs in the ninth before Spud Chandler relieved to get the last out in the Yankees' 7-4 win. It was Ruffing's seventh World Series victory, a record that stood until another Yankee, Whitey Ford, broke it 18 years later. The Cardinals' ninth-inning rally was the turning point in the Series; they swept the next four games. Ruffing lost the decisive Game Five when he gave up a ninth-inning homer to Whitey Kurowski.

After the Series, with wartime draft calls growing, Ruffing took a job in a defense plant in Southern California, where he had moved. He was summoned for a draft physical, even though he was 37 years old, was missing four toes, and was married with dependents. He and Pauline had adopted a son, Charles Jr., who was called Chuck, and her mother lived with them.

The first doctors who examined him declared him unfit for military service, but an army doctor overruled them. Lieutenant Hal C. Jenkins said Ruffing could handle noncombat duty. Years later Ruffing grumbled, "He would have drafted any ballplayer."[15] At the time he said what was expected of a patriotic American: "There's only one way to feel. We've got a different battle on our hands."[16]

On his first day of basic training, as he told it, "A sergeant said to me, 'Ruffing, I understand you can pitch.'

"'That's right,' I answered. And the sergeant said, 'Okay, Buddy, let's see how fast you can pitch this tent.'"[17]

Ruffing's noncombat duty was pitching baseballs and leading soldiers' physical fitness training. He was stationed in California at the Long Beach Ferry Command on a team with big leaguers Max West, Harry Danning, Nanny Fernandez, and Chuck Stevens. In July 1943 he pitched a no-hitter against a Santa Ana Air Base lineup that included his civilian teammate Joe DiMaggio. He compiled a 20-2 record against fellow servicemen. In late 1944 he joined a team of military all-stars that sailed to Hawaii to entertain the troops. Some of the ballplayers went on to other Pacific islands, but Sergeant Ruffing sprained a knee and was sent back to the States. After Germany surrendered in May 1945, the War Department discharged all soldiers and sailors older than 40.

Ruffing took a short vacation with his wife and son before he reported to Yankee Stadium on June 9 to begin shedding some of the 20 pounds he had gained in the army. "I am like a kid with a new toy," the 40-year-old said. "I keep pinching myself and looking at my civilian clothes."[18] He made his first appearance in pinstripes on July 16 as a pinch-hitter and received a standing ovation. He delivered a single. In his return to the mound 10 days later, he held the Philadelphia Athletics scoreless for six innings before giving way to a reliever. He picked up the first of his seven victories and finished the 1945 season with a 2.89 ERA in 11 starts, capping his comeback year with a three-run homer in his final game. It was his 36th lifetime home run—34 of them as a pitcher, second in history to Wes Ferrell's 37 at that point. Ruffing was one of the best-hitting pitchers ever; opponents occasionally walked him to pitch to the Yankees' leadoff batter, Frank Crosetti. Ruffing pinch-hit 257 times in his career, hitting .258/.300/.316.

He opened the 1946 season as a spot starter and more than held his own against the other returning servicemen. By the end of June he was 5-1 with a 1.77 ERA when Philadelphia's Hank Majeski smashed a line drive that broke his kneecap. The Yankees released him in September. His career appeared to be over.

Not so fast. White Sox manager Ted Lyons, who had just retired from pitching at age 45, thought Ruffing, a mere lad of 41, still had value as a pitcher and pinch-hitter, and signed him for 1947. With 270 victories in his pocket, Ruffing said he wanted to catch Lefty Grove at 300. He didn't make it. A line drive hit him in the same knee during spring training, and he went on the disabled list. He returned in July for eight more starts, posting a 6.11 ERA, and was released at the end of the season. He finished with a 273-225 record; his 231 victories for the Yankees were a club record until Whitey Ford surpassed him. He probably would have gotten to 300 if he had not lost two-and-a-half seasons to military service.

The White Sox kept him on as a scout, then as manager of their Class-A farm club in Muskegon, Michigan. In 1950 he managed Cleveland's Class-D team in Daytona Beach, Florida. He spent the rest of the 1950s as a scout for the Indians and moved his family to the Cleveland area. In 1962 the expansion New York Mets, led by former Yankee general manager George Weiss and manager Casey Stengel, hired him as pitching coach. But he complained that the Mets' pitchers wouldn't listen to him, perhaps because of the noise of line drives ringing in their ears as they recorded a 5.04 ERA, the worst in the majors. He left after one season.

Ruffing drew as many as half of the Hall of Fame votes only once in his first dozen years on the ballot; 75 percent is required for election. In 1962 new Hall of Famer Bob Feller, writing for a popular magazine, *The Saturday Evening Post*, named Ruffing, shortstop Luke Appling, and Satchel Paige as players who deserved to be honored in Cooperstown.[19] Under the Hall's rules at that time, baseball writers voted only every other year; on the next ballot, in 1964, Appling was elected and Ruffing's support jumped to 70 percent. In 1967, his final year on the writers' ballot, he got 73 percent of the votes and was ushered into the Hall in a runoff. "It's a dream come true," he said.[20]

Many analysts regard Ruffing as a decent pitcher who rode to glory on the coattails of the Yankee dynasty. His reputation rests primarily on his 231 victories and four 20-win seasons as the ace of one of the most powerful clubs in history. His record was a bit better than the Yankees'; he compiled a .651 winning percentage, while the team went .630 with other pitchers.

Looking beyond wins and losses, Ruffing's 3.80 ERA is the worst by any Hall of Fame pitcher. He played in a high-scoring era and said he pitched to the score, coasting when, as often happened, the Yankees staked him to a big lead. His adjusted ERA, equalized for the era and ballparks in which he pitched, is 110, just 10 percent above average. More than 150 pitchers have done better (minimum 2,000 innings), although several Hall of Famers rank behind him, including Don Sutton and Catfish Hunter. Ruffing's stat lines show little "black ink," categories in which he led the league: once each in strikeouts, shutouts, complete games, and wins, and twice in strikeouts per nine innings and losses. He was never the equal of the dominant pitchers of his time—Lefty Grove, Carl Hubbell, and Dizzy Dean.

Ruffing's last years were hard. When he was 68 he suffered a stroke that paralyzed his left side, and had to use a wheelchair for the rest of his life. Pauline loaded him and his chair into their car to make the annual trip from Cleveland to Cooperstown for the Hall of Fame induction ceremonies. He contracted skin cancer and had part of an ear removed. Pauline cared for him while holding down a job at a nursing home to put food on the table. "He was truly a wonderful person," she said, "but he was so stubborn, sometimes he could be a trial. I brought a woman into the house a few times a week to help me with him, but he wouldn't let anyone touch him except me. Unless I fed him, he wouldn't eat."[21]

Ruffing died of heart failure on February 17, 1986, at a hospital in Mayfield Heights, Ohio. Pauline and their son Chuck survived.

In 2004 a plaque was placed in Yankee Stadium's Monument Park to honor the pitcher who was lucky to be a Yankee.

## NOTES

1   Stanley Frank, "As Good as He Has to Be," *Saturday Evening Post*, March 16, 1940: 86.

2   *The Sporting News*, March 4, 1967: 6.

3   *New York Times*, May 7, 1930: 31.

4   Donald Honig, *The Man in the Dugout* (Chicago: Follett, 1977), 178.

5   *Sporting News*, January 21, 1967: 27.

6   Honig, *When the Grass Was Real* in *A Donald Honig Reader* (New York: Fireside/Simon & Schuster, 1988), 257.

7   Frank, "As Good as He Has to Be," 90.

8   Bob August, "Slow Road to Recovery for Red Ruffing at 69," unidentified clipping in Ruffing's file at the National Baseball Hall of Fame library.

9   Ted Shane, "Big Red," *American Magazine*, August 1939: 44.

10  Richard J. Tofel, *A Legend in the Making* (Chicago: Ivan R. Dee, 2002), 54.

11  *Ibid.*, 74-75.

12  Bill James and Rob Neyer, *The Neyer/James Guide to Pitchers* (New York: Fireside, 2004), 368.

13  Paul Dickson, *Baseball's Greatest Quotations* (New York: Collins, 2008), 68.

14  Tofel, *A Legend in the Making*, 74.

15  William B. Mead, *Baseball Goes to War* (Repr., Washington: Broadcast Interview Source, 1993), 93. The book's original title was *Even the Browns*.

16  *New York Times*, December 30, 1942: 21.

17  Associated Press-*Christian Science Monitor*, January 13, 1943: 13.

18  *The Sporting News*, July 5, 1945: 4.

19  Bob Feller and Ed Linn, "The Trouble with the Hall of Fame." *Saturday Evening Post*, January 27, 1962.

20  *The Sporting News*, March 4, 1967: 5.

21  Milton Richman, "Red Ruffing Was a Winner on Mound and At Bat." *Baseball Digest*, August 1986: 78.

# AMOS RUSIE

## BY CHARLES F. FABER

**THE VELOCITY OF HIS FASTBALLS** earned him the nickname "The Hoosier Thunderbolt." Amos Rusie played long before the invention of the radar gun, so we don't know how fast his pitches were. John McGraw said of Rusie's fastballs, "You can't hit 'em if you can't see 'em."[1] Sportswriters of the day claimed that batters were so terrified of being hit by Rusie's pitches that they insisted the distance from the pitcher's box to the plate be increased.[2] As a pitcher for the New York Giants he was the biggest star on the biggest stage and he enjoyed life to the hilt.

Amos Wilson Rusie was born on May 30, 1871, in Mooresville, Morgan County, Indiana, a village about 20 miles southwest of Indianapolis. He was the second of the four children of Mary Elizabeth "Lizzie" Donovan and William Asbury Rusie. Amos's father must have been quite a man. Born in Mooresville in 1847, he joined the 33rd Indiana Volunteer Infantry on December 18, 1863, at the age of 16. During the war he lost his left leg above the knee. Available military records do not identify the battle in which he was wounded, but it was probably in Georgia or the Carolinas.[3] After his discharge William Rusie returned to Indiana and, despite the loss of his leg, worked for many years as a brick mason in Mooresville and Indianapolis. He died in a home for disabled veterans in 1925.

The Rusie family moved from Mooresville to Indianapolis during Amos's childhood. At the age of 16 Amos dropped out of school to work in a variety of jobs, including one in a factory and one as a varnisher in an Indianapolis furniture store. After working hours and on Sundays the teenager played for a number of amateur or semipro teams in the Indianapolis area. At first he played only in the outfield. One day when he was with the Grand River club in the City League, the regular pitcher was knocked out of the box, and Rusie relieved him. He found the position where he belonged, and he never played in the outfield again.[4] While pitching for an outfit called the Sturm Avenue Never Sweats in 1888, he shut out two touring National League clubs, the Boston Beaneaters and the Washington Nationals. After these stellar performances, John T. Brush, owner of the National League's Indianapolis Hoosiers signed Rusie to a professional contract.[5] At the start of the 1889 season, Frank Bancroft, manager of the Hoosiers, sent Rusie to Burlington, Iowa, for seasoning. He pitched four games for the Burlington Babies in the Central Inter-State League before being called up to Indianapolis. That was the extent of his minor-league career.

Amos Rusie made his major-league debut for the Hoosiers on May 9, 1889, at the age of 17. The 6-foot-1, 200-pound right-hander entered the game in relief of Jim Whitney in a 13-2 loss at Cleveland. He made his first start on June 15 at home as Indianapolis defeated Pittsburgh, 16-11. In his rookie season, he had a 12-10 record for the seventh-place Hoosiers. The Indianapolis club folded after the 1889 season. The National League distributed the Hoosiers players among other clubs in the league. Rusie was fortunate to be assigned to the New York Giants.

During his first month with the Giants, Rusie hooked up with Boston's Kid Nichols at the Polo Grounds in one of the great pitching duels of all time. On May 12 the two young hurlers each held their opponents scoreless for 12 innings. Going into the 13th, each pitcher had allowed only three hits. The Giants had elected to bat first. With one out in the top of the 13th, Mike Tiernan hit a tremendous line drive that cleared the fence in the deepest part of the Polo Grounds. Rusie quickly set the Beaneaters down in the bottom of the frame to claim a 1-0 victory. The game has been honored as one of the 100 greatest games of the 19th century.[6] Rusie became an instant celebrity in New York. Later he and Nichols were two of the three pitchers of the 1890s named to the National Baseball Hall of Fame. (Cy Young was the other.)

Rusie's star continued to shine brightly in New York. He won 29 games in 1890 and led the league in strikeouts. He started 62 games, pitched 56 complete games, and allowed the fewest hits per inning pitched of any hurler in the league. He also led the league in losses, walks, and wild pitches. He allowed 289 bases on balls, a major-league record that has never been broken and probably will never be approached. (The 208 walks given up by Bob Feller in 1938 is the closest to that number in the last 125 years.)

But it was Rusie's strikeouts that caught the fancy of the public. His 341 strikeouts in 1890 were the most in the decade of the 1890s. Only Bob Feller, Sandy Koufax, Randy Johnson, and Nolan Ryan have rung up more K's in a season since then. Rusie said it was not easy. "It took a lot of pitchin' to strike a man out in those days. The foul strike rule hadn't come in. A guy had to miss three of 'em clean before he was out."[7]

The Hoosier Thunderbolt became a sensation in the Big Apple. Restaurants named drinks after him, and vaudevilleans included skits about him in their acts. It was reported that Lillian Russell, the most famous Broadway star of the day, clamored to meet him. The young man lived it up. He enjoyed drinking and carousing in the big city, but the night life apparently did not interfere with his pitching. Sportswriter Sam Crane wrote, "Rusie went through his active pitching days as though on a continuous joy ride. He broke training whenever he felt like it and never looked upon life as a serious matter."[8]

Rusie's fastball was the stuff of legends. It was reputed to be the fastest pitch ever thrown up to that time. Outfielder Jimmy Ryan said, "Words fail to describe the speed with which Rusie sent the ball. … The giant simply drove the ball at you with the force of a cannon. It was like a white streak tearing past you."[9]

Connie Mack, whose major-league career spanned more than 60 years, saw all of the great fastball pitchers from Rusie to Feller. He batted against some and managed against the others. "Rusie was the fastest without a doubt," Mack said. "Maybe that is because I had to hit against him. And they looked like peas as they sailed by me. All I saw of them was what I heard when they went into the catcher's mitt."[10]

Dick Buckley, who had been Rusie's catcher in both Indianapolis and New York, tried inserting into his glove a sheet of lead, covered with a handkerchief and a sponge, to cushion the impact of the fastball.[11]

On November 8, 1890, Rusie married Susie May Smith in Muncie, Indiana. They had a daughter, Jeannette, born in 1897. At age 19 and enjoying the high life in New York City, Rusie at first was perhaps not an ideal husband. On January 9, 1899, May filed for divorce. The couple reconciled temporarily, but little more than a year later May filed for divorce again. On May 9, 1900, the court awarded May her divorce. Amos was devastated. He promised to stay sober and behave himself and agreed to leave the Giants and settle down in Indiana permanently. May had detested living in New York and hated what she perceived the city was doing to her husband's lifestyle.[12] Less than three months later the couple mar-

ried for the second time. Amos kept his word. This union lasted until May's death on October 7, 1942.

In 1891 Rusie won 33 games, the first of four consecutive seasons in which the fireballer posted more than 30 victories. On July 31, 1891, Rusie pitched a no-hitter, shutting down Brooklyn, 6-0. It was the first no-hitter ever pitched by a New York hurler. Year after year he was atop the leader board.

The Hoosier Thunderbolt led the National League in strikeouts five times, in shutouts four times, and in bases on balls five times.

Rusie's blazing fastball combined with his wildness intimidated batters. Some were so terrified at the prospect of being hit in the head by one of his thunderbolts that the league agreed in 1893 to move the pitcher's box farther from the plate. The change from 55 feet to 60 feet 6 inches instituted in1893 was the last alteration in the configuration of the baseball diamond.

The change in the location of the pitcher's box did not diminish Rusie's effectiveness. Although his strikeout numbers decreased, he still led the league in that category in 1893 and each the next two seasons. In 1894 Rusie had a career-high 36 victories and won the pitcher's Triple Crown by leading the National League in wins, strikeouts, and earned-run average.

At the end of the 1894 season William Temple, president of the Pittsburgh Pirates, proposed that a postseason series be played between the top two finishers in the National League. He donated an $800 cup, the Temple Cup, to be awarded to the winner of the best-of seven-series. The Baltimore Orioles had won the pennant, with the Giants second. Sparked by the pitching of Rusie and Jouett Meekin, the Giants swept the Temple Cup series in four straight games. The Hoosier Thunderbolt won Games One and Three by identical scores of 4-1, giving up only two runs, one of which was unearned, for an ERA of 0.50. Meekin pitched a shutout in Game Two, winning 9-0, and wrapped up the series by winning Game Four, 16-3. Both pitchers threw complete games in their starts; no other Giants pitchers appeared in the series.[13] A New York reporter wrote, "The alleged mighty hitters of the league's pennant winners are but putty in the hands of Rusie and Meekin."[14]

In the games of the Temple Cup series played at the Polo Grounds, which had no center-field fence, large crowds ringed the outfield. A rope was strung between posts to separate the fans from the playing field. Some patrons sat in carriages and viewed the game by looking over the heads of the standees.[15] Other horse-drawn vehicles were left unattended on Eighth Avenue below the field. In the eighth inning of Game Three, one of the horses bolted, climbed up the embankment, smashed the buggy, and charged into people standing around the rope. The horse ran through the crowd, jumped over the ropes, and charged onto the playing field. It headed straight across the field toward Giants left fielder Eddie Burke. A reporter wrote, "Burke had shown the Polo Grounds patrons some pretty fast running in his time, but he never equaled the sprint he made to get under the left field bleachers."[16] The runaway horse was caught; Rusie resumed pitching and finished his 4-1 victory.

In 1895 Giants owner Andrew Freedman deducted $200 from Rusie's pay. One hundred dollars was cut for allegedly being out after curfew one night and another hundred for "not trying hard enough" while pitching.[17] An irate Rusie protested the fines. Two hundred dollars was a very large chunk out of his $3,000 salary. He told Freedman he would not sign a contract for 1896 unless the fines were restored. The owner refused. Rusie sat out the entire 1896 season. Represented by a famous baseball personality and attorney, John Montgomery Ward, Rusie sued Freedman for $5,000 and release from his Giants contract. Owners of other National League clubs, worried that the courts might invalidate the reserve clause, gave Rusie $5,000 to drop the suit. Rusie agreed. "That $5,000 I got for not playing was almost $2,000 more than I would have been paid for playing all season," he said.[18] He remained a Giant, and Freedman paid him $3,000 for 1897.

Batters' fear of being hit by the Hoosier Thunderbolt's pitches was justified. Baltimore's Hughie Jennings, one of baseball's top shortstops, was hit in the head by a Rusie fastball in 1897. He was unconscious for four days.[19] Although he survived, his baseball-playing days were in jeopardy.

In 1898 Rusie suffered an injury that ended his effectiveness as a pitcher. He was pitching against the Chicago Cubs one day in August. Chicago's speedy outfielder Bill Lange was on first base. Lange had led the National League in stolen bases the previous year. Although his productivity was down in 1898, due to physical and attitude problems, he was still a threat on the basepaths.[20] Rusie resolved to pick the speedster off base. Instead of taking the usual step when throwing to a base, Rusie made a quick throw to first base without moving his feet. Something snapped in his shoulder. He got his out, but never regained his fastball. "My arm felt dead," Rusie said. "I finished the game throwing floating curves. The following day saw the start of a parade of doctors. Each examined my arm. Each had a different diagnosis The x-ray was unknown then, so their job wasn't an easy one."[21]

Rusie took five weeks off. "When I returned to the firing line, my arm felt okay," he said. "The zip in my fast one was still there; my curve crackled and snapped. For the rest of the season, everything was fine. But the following spring, when I tried to pitch, my arm felt dead. I took my turn on the hill, but every effort was followed by nights of torture, during which I walked the floor. So I had to hang up my glove."[22]

More than 40 years after his injury, Rusie put his hand on his shoulder and told an interviewer, "Even today I'm often bothered by twinges of pain here."[23]

After 1898 Rusie never won another game in the major leagues. He blamed his snap pickoff move for his downfall. He was quoted as saying, "I coulda lasted as long as Cy Young what with my strength and all. That's what happens when you try to act smart."[24]

The Hoosier Thunderbolt pitched nary a game in Organized Baseball in 1899 or 1900. He rested his arm for two years and used the time trying to repair his relationship with his estranged wife. On December 15, 1900, the New York Giants traded Rusie to the Cincinnati Reds for Christy Mathewson, in perhaps the most lopsided transaction in the entire history of baseball. One future Hall of Fame pitcher for another may not sound out of line, but it certainly was. Matty was a youngster on his way up; Rusie was all but finished as a pitcher. Mathewson went on to win 372 games for the Giants, the most any pitcher has ever won for any National League club. Rusie won no games for Cincinnati or anybody else.

At the time of the census in June 1900, Rusie was living with his widowed father in Indianapolis. The census taker listed him as a ballplayer, although he was playing no baseball that summer. May was living near Muncie with her brother Edward Smith. In less than two months Amos and May would be together again, this time 'til death did them part.

In 1901 Rusie started two games for the Reds and relieved in one. His record was 0-1, with an ERA of 8.59. He made his final major-league appearance on June 9, 1901, at the age of 30. The game was played at Cincinnati's League Park against Rusie's former team, the New York Giants. An overflow crowd of 17,000 fans surrounded the field and pushed toward the diamond. Balls that outfielders normally could have caught fell among the onlookers and went for two-base hits. In the bottom of the ninth inning the crowd overran the field and caused so much confusion that umpire Bob Emslie forfeited the game to the Giants.[25] The Giants were leading 25-13 at the time, and that was recorded as the official score. (Forfeited games are usually scored 9-0, but if the home team is at fault and visiting team is leading the actual score is recorded.)

After he retired from baseball, Rusie returned to his native Indiana. He worked at a pulp and paper mill in Muncie until the mill closed. He then moved to Vincennes, Indiana, where he worked as a laborer. He also did some pearling, that is, hunting for pearls in mollusks retrieved from the Wabash River or other bodies of water in the area. According to his obituary in *The Sporting News*, Rusie worked as a ticket taker at a Seattle ballpark in 1907 and 1908, and as a bottle layer in a bottle factory in Olean, Illinois, in 1910, and umpired in the Northwestern League for two weeks in 1911. The obituary contains several inaccuracies. His actual whereabouts in 1910 cannot be ascertained.

Neither he nor May can be located in 1910 census records released by Ancestry.com. Nor can he be found in available city directories for that year.

It is known that in 1911 Amos and May moved to Seattle, where he worked for 10 years as a gas fitter for a lighting company and as a steamfitter in a shipyard.

In 1921 John McGraw, now the manager of the New York Giants, brought Rusie back to New York, where he worked as a night watchman and later as superintendent of grounds at the Polo Grounds. Did he like the job? Accounts vary. In a SABR book published in 1996, Richard Puff wrote that he enjoyed the position.[26] Rusie's obituary in the *New York Times* stated that he didn't care much for the job.[27] Living in New York was difficult for May. She was partly paralyzed from an undisclosed cause and confined to a wheelchair. The couple moved back to Washington State in 1929.

Perhaps with help from McGraw, Rusie purchased a chicken ranch in Auburn, Washington, but it failed during the Great Depression. In July 1934 he was injured in an automobile accident that left him unconscious for four days. He suffered a brain concussion and several broken ribs. Unable to work, he fell behind on his house payments. In February 1935 a notice appeared in the Seattle newspapers announcing the mortgage foreclosure of the five-acre farm of Amos Rusie and wife in Auburn by the Home Owners Loan Corporation.

A moratorium loan on the little farm for $1,932.32 had been closed on November 29, 1933, and provided for interest payments of $8.05 in June 1934, and $17.87 monthly thereafter. Rusie was unable to make payments on the principal, interest, or taxes. The Rusies' income consisted of a $35 pension paid monthly to Amos by the Association of Professional Ball Players of America and a $28-a-month old-age payment for May.[28] The *Seattle Post-Intelligencer* instituted a fundraising campaign. Although unable to prevent the foreclosure, the paper, assisted by *The Sporting News*, raised enough money to provide the Rusies with an income for the rest of their lives and a little house in which to live.[29]

Because of their declining health, the Rusies stayed in the house only a few years. Before 1940 they moved in with their daughter Jeannette and her husband, Clarence E. Spaulding, an upholsterer in a Seattle department store.

May died on October 7, 1942. Amos suffered from chronic myocarditis, and two months after May's death, he died at Ballard General Hospital on December 6, 1942, at the age of 71. May and Amos were buried side-by-side in Acacia Memorial Park in the city of Lake Forest Park, just north of the Seattle city limits on the shores of Lake Washington.

In 1977 Rusie was elected by the Veterans Committee to the National Baseball Hall of Fame. The inscription on his plaque at Cooperstown reads:

AMOS WILSON RUSIE
"THE HOOSIER THUNDERBOLT"
INDIANAPOLIS N.L, NEW YORK N.L.,
CINCINNATI N.L. 1889-1895
1897-1898 AND 1901
GENERALLY CONSIDERED FIREBALL KING OF
NINETEENTH-CENTURY MOUNDSMEN. NOTCHED
BETTER THAN 240 VICTORIES IN TEN-YEAR
CAREER. ACHIEVED 30-VICTORY MARK FOUR
YEARS IN A ROW AND WON 20 OR MORE GAMES
EIGHT SUCCESSIVE YEARS. LED LEAGUE IN
STRIKEOUTS FIVE YEARS AND LED OR TIED
FOR MOST SHUTOUTS FIVE TIMES.

## SOURCES

In addition to those cited in the Notes, the most useful sources included Ancestry.com and Baseball-reference.com.

## NOTES

1   Richard Puff, "Amos Wilson Rusie," in Frederick Ivor-Campbell, Robert L. Tiemann, and Mark Rucker, eds.,

# 20-GAME LOSERS

1. *Baseball's First Stars* (Cleveland: Society for American Baseball Research, 1996), 143.
2. Ibid.
3. William Rusie was a private in Company C. See 33rdindiana.org/roster/c/warusi.html.
4. *The Sporting News*, December 28, 1939: 5.
5. Puff.
6. Peter Mancuso, "The Kid, the Bolt, and Silent Mike," in Bill Felber, ed., *Inventing Baseball*, (Phoenix: Society for American Baseball Research, 2013), 225-27.
7. Charles F. Faber, *Major League Careers Cut Short* (Jefferson, North Carolina: McFarland, 2011), 50.
8. the baseballpage.com/players/rusieam/01/bio.
9. baseball-reference.com/players//r/ryanji01.shtml.
10. *The Sporting News*, December 25, 1946: 5.
11. Puff, 143.
12. Findagrave.com.
13. Tom Schott and Nick Peters, *The Giants Encyclopedia*, 2nd ed. (Champaign, Illinois: Sports Publishing, 2003), 276.
14. *New York World*, October 7, 1894.
15. Philip J. Lowry, *Green Cathedrals* (New York: Walker, 2006), 150.
16. *New York World*, October 7, 1894.
17. Puff.
18. Ibid.
19. John Thorn, *Baseball in the Garden of Eden* (New York: Simon & Schuster, 2011), 250.
20. Bill Lamb, "Bill Lange," sabr.org/bio/proj.
21. *The Sporting News*, December 28, 1939: 5.
22. Ibid.
23. Ibid.
24. *New York Times*, December 7, 1942.
25. *New York Times*, June 10, 1901.
26. Puff, 144.
27. *New York Times*, December 7, 1942.
28. *The Sporting News*, April 15, 1937.
29. *The Sporting News*, June 3, 1937.

# BIG ED WALSH

## BY STUART SCHIMLER

**FROM 1907 TO 1912, "BIG ED" WALSH** tested the limits of a pitcher's endurance like no pitcher has since. During that stretch the spitballing right-hander led the American League in innings pitched four times, often by staggeringly large margins. He hurled a total of 2,248 innings, 300 more than any other pitcher in baseball. He started 18 more games than any other pitcher, and led the American League during that stretch in games finished and saves, though the latter statistic would not be tracked for another 60 years. His finest season came in 1908, when Walsh became the last pitcher in baseball history to win 40 games, and hurled an incredible 464 innings, 73 1/3 more than any other pitcher in baseball.

A fierce competitor, Walsh wanted the heavy workload the White Sox hoisted upon him. He also fielded his position with as much agility as any pitcher in the history of the game. During his six-year stretch of historic greatness, Walsh accumulated 963 assists, an amazing 344 more than any other pitcher in baseball. He fielded bunts like a territorial animal. Once, when a new third baseman came in for a bunt with a runner on second, Walsh got to the ball but couldn't make a play to third because it was uncovered. Walsh then reputedly turned to the third baseman and said, "If you do that again, I'll kill you. On bunts on that side of the field, you stay where you belong."[1] Though he finished his career with the lowest ERA (1.82) in baseball history, Walsh's arm couldn't withstand the overuse, and by 1913 the "Iron Man" pitcher was a shadow of his former self. Despite winning an impressive 182 games before his 32nd birthday, Walsh finished his career short of 200 wins.

Edward Augustine Walsh was born on May 19, 1882 (although census records place his year of birth variously as 1880 or 1881) in Plains, Pennsylvania, one of 13 children—10 boys and three girls—of Michael and Jane Walsh. Edward's father was a native of Ireland who immigrated to the United States in 1866, where he found work as a shoemaker and married Jane, a heavy-set Welsh immigrant who had crossed the Atlantic in 1854. Edward's mother was active in the local Catholic church choir, and often sang old Irish folk songs to her children. Ed attended parochial school until he reached the age of 12, when he began work as a slate-picker in the Plains mines for the Lackawanna Coal Company, earning 75 cents a day. For an additional $1.25, Ed also drove mule-drawn coal carts in the mines.

At age 18 he enrolled at Fordham University but left after only two days because he hated the wild students and grown men who were his roommates. Returning to Pennsylvania, Walsh began his baseball career as a pitcher for the Miner-Hillard Milling Company in Miners Mills, Pennsylvania, in 1901. In July 1902 Walsh signed his first professional contract, agreeing to terms with the Meriden Silverites of the Connecticut League for $150 per month. Walsh posted an impressive 16-5 record in Meriden before Wilkes-Barre of the Pennsylvania State League picked him near the end of the season. After winning only one of four decisions for Wilkes-Barre, Walsh was sold back to Meriden, where he spent the first part of the 1903 season before his skills caught the attention of Newark of the Eastern League. He finished out the 1903 campaign with Newark, notching a 9-5 record. After the season the Chicago White Sox purchased his contract for a mere $750.

Throughout his minor-league career, the 6-feet-1 193-pound Walsh—whose unusual height for his time earned him the moniker "Big Ed"—relied exclusively on a fastball and curve. During 1904 spring training with the White Sox in Marlin Springs, Texas, Walsh roomed with spitballer Elmer Stricklett, the same pitcher who had inspired Jack Chesbro to start experimenting with the pitch the year before. Stricklett taught Walsh the spitter, but the big right-hander did not start using the pitch for two years. As a spot starter and reliever for the White Sox in 1904 and 1905, Walsh went 14-6 with a solid 2.37 ERA. It was not until the 1906 campaign, when the White Sox captured their second American League pennant in six major-league seasons, that Walsh began to use the spitter on a regular basis. Although pitching with a weakened right arm for part of the season, Walsh put up his best regular-season numbers to date, posting a 17-13 record with a 1.88 ERA, seventh best in the league, and a league-leading 10 shutouts. But he saved his best work for the World Series, when he beat the cross-town Chicago Cubs twice in two starts, allowing only one earned run (and five unearned) in 15 innings of work, and striking out 17 batters, including a then-Series record 12 in a Game Three shutout.

On the heels of his World Series triumph, Walsh put together his first 20-win season in 1907. In a reflection of his competitive nature, he also began to change his approach on the mound. "Early in my career I eased up in the first few innings to save myself, but I found I couldn't get back into stride after once letting up," he later explained. "After that, I threw hard all the time. I threw my best to every hitter I faced and I found I had the strength to go all the way."[2]

In 1908 Walsh put together his masterpiece, compiling 40 wins against just 15 losses, a 1.42 ERA, including a league record-breaking 11 shutouts, and 464 innings pitched. Pushing himself to the limit, during one nine-day stretch Walsh pitched five times, including a four-hitter on October 2 that he lost to Addie Joss, who threw a perfect game. Walsh's pitching kept the White Sox in the American League's thrilling four-way pennant race until the last day of the season, and the club finished in third place, 1½ games behind the front-running Detroit Tigers. For the season, Walsh struck out 269 batters, a career best, and walked only 56 men, giving him the fourth lowest walk rate in the majors that year.

Not surprisingly, at the time Walsh's spitball was considered the most effective pitch in baseball. Walsh disguised the pitch by going to his mouth before every delivery, regardless of what he was going to

throw. When he did throw the spitter, according to Alfred Spink he moistened a spot on the ball between the seams an inch square. "His thumb he clinches tightly lengthwise on the opposite seam, and swinging his arm straight overhead with terrific force, he drives the ball straight at the plate," Spink wrote. "At times it will dart two feet down and out, depending on the way his arm is swung."[3]

In a 1913 article for *Baseball Magazine*, Walter Johnson called Walsh's delivery "about the most tantalizing in baseball" for the way it arrived at the plate "with such terrific speed, and unerringly dives just as if it knew what it was about and tried to dodge the hitter's bat…"[4] For all practical purposes, the pitch was the Deadball Era equivalent of the split-fingered fastball, and absolutely devastating to batters accustomed to seeing mostly fastballs and curves. "I think that ball disintegrated on the way to the plate and the catcher put it back together again," Sam Crawford later joked. "I swear, when it went past the plate it was just the spit went by."[5]

When batters did reach base, Walsh often picked them off with the game's most deceptive move to first base. In a motion that would probably be ruled a balk today, Walsh lifted his shoulder slightly, as if beginning his motion to throw home, before swinging around and firing the ball to first. Clyde Milan, one of the era's best base stealers, declared the move "at least a half balk" but Walsh got away with it anyway.[6]

In 1909, Walsh's numbers dipped as he recovered from the heavy workload he had sustained the year before. Starting in only 28 games, he finished the year with a 15-11 mark in 230 1/3 innings, less than half his 1908 total. Though his 1.41 ERA was nearly identical to his 1908 mark, Walsh's strikeout rate fell slightly while his walk rate nearly doubled. The cause of this sudden bout of "wildness" was that he was tipping his pitches. Specifically, the Cleveland Naps believed they had deciphered when he was going to throw the spitter, by noticing that he had a habit of ticking the bill of his cap prior to unleashing a wet one. Word spread quickly around the league, and hitters started to lay off the spitter, which usually dropped out of the strike zone. When Walsh learned what was happening, he changed his style. In 1910, Walsh finished with 18 wins against 20 losses, but the losing record was deceptive: Walsh's 1.27 ERA was the best of his career and also good enough to lead the league. In 1911 Walsh's ERA rose nearly a full run to 2.22, but he received better run support and won 27 games against 18 defeats in 368 2/3 innings pitched. In 1912 he again won 27 games, tossed six shutouts, collected a league-record 10 saves, and finished the year with a 2.15 ERA in 393 innings of work.

The first sign that his powerful right arm was about to give up on him occurred in the Chicago city series at the end of the 1912 season. In one outing against the Cubs Walsh took a line drive off his jaw. He went on pitching, but after the game his arm felt weak. Looking back, Walsh blamed himself for his sudden decline. "It was my fault I didn't continue in the majors longer than I did," Walsh said. "My arm was played out after the 1912 season—it needed a rest."[7] Instead, Walsh began the 1913 season still trying to fulfill the role as the staff's workhorse. He started 14 games, going 8-3 with a 2.58 ERA, but often required long periods of rest between starts. After lasting just five innings against the Philadelphia Athletics on July 19, Walsh was shelved indefinitely, and left the team to have his arm examined by Bonesetter Reese in Youngstown, Ohio. Reese looked over Walsh and declared that he had a "misplaced tendon" in his right shoulder. According to the *New York Times*, Reese fixed the pitcher in three minutes and declared he would be better than ever the following season.[8]

It didn't happen. Over the next three seasons Walsh pitched sparingly for the White Sox, starting only nine games from 1914 to 1916 and winning five. During that time he rejected a lucrative offer from the Federal League, and at one point contemplated becoming an outfielder. During the 1916 season Walsh appeared in only two games, pitching 3 1/3 innings. His most notable achievement came in late July, when he rescued two girls from drowning in Lake Michigan.[9] Let go by the White Sox at the end of the season, Walsh made a brief appearance with the Boston Braves in 1917, going 0-1 with a 3.50 ERA in 18 innings of work.

During World War I Walsh worked in a munitions factory. Thereafter he pitched briefly for Milwaukee of the American Association in 1919, Bridgeport (Connecticut) of the Eastern League in 1920, and finally with a semipro club in Oneonta, New York in 1921. He spent the first half of the 1922 season as an umpire for the American League. Walsh hated the job, mainly because he did not like calling strikes. "I remember when I wanted every pitch to be a strike," he said.[10] For the next several years he served as a coach for the White Sox, and after that was a battery coach at Notre Dame, where his son pitched. Ed Walsh, Jr. spent parts of four seasons in the major leagues, but his most notable achievement came in 1933, when as a pitcher for the Oakland Oaks of the Pacific Coast League he halted young Joe DiMaggio's 61-game hitting streak. Tragically, the younger Ed died suddenly of rheumatic fever in 1937. That same year, Ed's other son, Bob, also a graduate of Notre Dame, gave up baseball when he was almost hit with a line drive while playing for the Richmond club in the Piedmont League.

The Great Depression hit Walsh hard: his $14,000 investment in a show place on Hanover Road in Meriden went belly-up and for six years he worked for the Works Progress Administration, conducting a baseball school through the agency's recreational program. Toward the end of the decade Walsh became a chemical engineer and worked at a filtration plant for the Meriden municipal water department. When he wasn't working, Walsh indulged his love for golf, and became the course professional in Meriden.

To the end of his life, Walsh pushed for the spitball to be legalized. He once said, "everything else favors the hitters. Ball parks are smaller and baseballs are livelier. They've practically got pitchers wearing straitjackets. Bah! They still allow the knuckleball and that is three times as hard to control."[11]

Walsh was inducted into the Baseball Hall of Fame on July 21, 1947, and was the only one of that year's fifteen inductees to attend the ceremony, but he and his wife Rosemary struggled to make ends meet. By the late 1950s Walsh had contracted cancer. The disease impacted him greatly, as his weight dropped from 200 pounds to less than 100. To help pay his medical bills, the White Sox held an Ed Walsh Day at Comiskey Park in 1958, raising nearly $5,000 for his care. Ed Walsh died on May 26, 1959, two weeks after his 77th birthday (or 78th or 79th, depending on the source). He was buried in Forest Lawn Memorial Gardens in his adopted hometown of Pompano Beach, Florida.

Note

An earlier version of this biography originally appeared in David Jones, ed., *Deadball Stars of the American League* (Washington, D.C.: Potomac Books, Inc., 2006).

## SOURCES

Ed Walsh player file at the National Baseball Hall of Fame.

Broeg, Bob. "A St. Pat's Salute to Ed Walsh," *The Sporting News*, March 24, 1979: 40.

Holtzman, Jerry. "Big Ed Walsh, 77, Former White Sox Star, Gets day to Remember at Comiskey Park," *The Sporting News*, July 2, 1958: 7.

Keener, Sid C. "Walsh Weary," *Sporting Life*, July 12, 1913.

Meany, Tom. "Bid Ed Walsh's Fabulous Week," *Baseball Digest*, August 1959: 59-60.

Parker, Dan. "Big Ed Walsh Still Pitches a Fast One," *Daily Mirror*, January 30, 1946.

Peck, Howard H. "How 'Big Ed' Got the Spitball," *The Courant Magazine*, December 16, 1956: 4.

Smith, Red. "Views of Sport: Ed's One Bad Year," *New York Herald Tribune*, January 12, 1947.

"Big Ed Gave Game Many Transfusion: Walsh Rebuilding Huge frame to accept Baseball Honors," *Miami Herald*, June 19, 1958: 4-D.

## NOTES

1. Undocumented quotation.
2. Ed Walsh, "Pitching only 30 Pct. Now—Walsh," *The Sporting News*, January 9, 1957: 13.
3. Alfred Henry Spink, *The National Game* (St. Louis; National Game Publishing, 1910), 162.
4. Lawrence S. Ritter, *The Glory of Their Times* (New York: Harper Perennial, 2010), 56.
5. Ibid.
6. F.C. Lane, "Milan the Marvel," *Baseball*, May 1914: 101.
7. Undocumented quotation.
8. "Tendon in Walsh's Arm Adjusted," *New York Times*, August 20, 1913: 7.
9. "Ed Walsh Saves Two Girls," *Chicago Tribune*, July 28, 1916: 3.
10. "Bid Ed Walsh, Former Oneonta Baseball Manager, Dies at 78," *Oneonta Star*, May 27, 1959: 12.
11. "Walsh, Winner of 40 Games in One Season for White Sox, Dies at 78," *Cleveland Plain Dealer*, May 27, 1959.

# JOHN MONTGOMERY WARD

## BY BILL LAMB

**NO ESSAY-LENGTH BIOGRAPHY** could possibly do full justice to John Montgomery Ward. His life, both on and off the diamond, was entirely too eventful. His playing career was replete with notable achievements. When he joined the Providence Grays in 1878, an 18-year-old Ward was the National League's youngest player. During the 1880 season, he hurled the circuit's second perfect game after having been the NL's winningest pitcher the season before. When overuse and injury ruined his throwing arm, Ward, an exceptional athlete, transformed himself into a capable everyday player. He shortstopped the New York Giants to consecutive world championships in 1888-1889, and five years later led the Giants to a postseason Temple Cup triumph as player-manager. Nor did Ward abandon baseball after his retirement from playing in 1894. During his later years, he stood as a controversial candidate for the National League presidency; was club president and part-owner of the Boston Braves; and served in the front office of the Brooklyn franchise in the upstart Federal League.

As impressive as these achievements are, they are nonetheless overshadowed by Ward's contributions to the game as a trailblazer. Intelligent, well educated, and dynamic, Ward organized the first major-league players union in 1885 and was a tireless advocate for players' rights. He also authored the first popular How-To manual for youngsters wishing to take up the game. But first and foremost, Ward is remembered as the driving force behind the employee-controlled Players League, the audacious but short-lived challenger to the preeminence of the National League and American Association. Apart from all this, he also took an active role in the social and civic life of greater Gotham. At various times, Ward was a high-visibility Broadway bon vivant, a distinguished New York City attorney, a Long Island country squire and community pillar, and a major figure in Northeastern amateur golfing circles. Although there are other worthy contenders for the laurel, John Montgomery Ward may well have been the most accomplished man ever to play major-league baseball. And when it finally came in 1964, his posthumous induction into the National Baseball Hall of Fame was both well-deserved and long overdue.

The multifaceted Ward was born on March 3, 1860, in Bellefonte, Pennsylvania, a tranquil village located in the Nittany Valley, about 12 miles northeast of the Agricultural College of Pennsylvania (now Pennsylvania State University). He was the second of the three children born to James Ward (c.1806-1871), and his third wife, the former Ruth Hall (1826-1874).[1] The Ward clan was of English stock, descended from mid-1600s Connecticut settlers, while the Hall family was long-established in Bellefonte. James Ward and his brother Philoh (who married another Hall sister) were recent arrivals in Bellefonte, where they became the proprietors of a machine shop that produced threshers and other farming equipment. Unusual for a married woman of her time, Ruth Ward was also employed, teaching at a public elementary school in Bellefonte. In his youth, Monte,[2] as he was called by family and hometown acquaintances, was raised in a comfortable, pious Presbyterian household and attended village schools.

Tragedy struck the family in 1871. First, Monte's father died of consumption. Months later, his half-brother James Moore Ward, a divinity student, was killed in a railway accident. For a time, Ruth Ward, by now elevated to the post of school principal, managed. But in December 1874, she was stricken with pneumonia and died, orphaning her two sons. Older sibling Charles was taken in by his Uncle Philoh, but not Monte. At age 14, he was dispatched to Penn State, which, like many other colleges, also maintained a prep school for younger students. Here, as Johnny Ward, he first attracted public notice. In the spring of 1875, Ward, a member of Penn State's first baseball team, astounded several thousand onlookers on the Old Main Lawn by demonstrating that a thrown ball could actually be made to curve.[3] By then he was already an established pitcher in local circles, having begun as a youngster in Bellefonte, before graduating to an amateur club in Lock Haven. The following year, Ward's time at Penn State came to an abrupt halt. A midnight caper involving the theft of chickens from a nearby farm led to his expulsion from school.[4]

Now largely on his own, the youngster eked out an existence peddling nursery plants. His sales route took him through the Allegheny Mountains and included a stop in Renovo, Pennsylvania. There, Ward tried to supplement his meager salesman's wage by pitching for the borough's semipro team, the Resolutes. The club promised him $15 a month plus board, but ultimately stiffed him on payment.[5] That experience notwithstanding, Ward decided to pursue baseball as his calling. The 1877 season saw him in action for at least five clubs: an independent team in Williamsport, Pennsylvania, followed by League Alliance clubs in Philadelphia (the Athletic and the Philadelphias, aka Phillies), Janesville, Wisconsin, and Buffalo.[6] In most instances, the clubs disbanded shortly after Ward's arrival. Still, he remained undiscouraged, beginning the 1878 season with yet another League Alliance team: the Binghamton (New York) Crickets. Here, history repeated itself, as the Crickets folded in early July. Little statistical evidence of Ward's performance survives,[7] but he must have impressed. Days after the Binghamton club went under, 18-year-old Johnny Ward became a major leaguer, signing with the Providence Grays of the National League as a replacement for defecting pitcher Tricky Nichols.

Ward made his major-league debut on July 15, 1878, dropping a 13-9 decision to the Cincinnati Reds in a contest marred by slipshod defense on both sides. One game account stated: "Ward belongs to that class of pitchers who turn their backs to home plate and send in the ball after a quick turn. … His delivery is of questionable legality, his hand moving some distance above the hip in forward motion."[8] Whether strictly legal or not, right-hander Ward's sidearm slants were in regular use thereafter. He pitched every one of the 34 games remaining on the Providence schedule, posting a commendable 22-13 record, with a retroactive NL-leading 1.51 ERA in 334 innings pitched, for the third-place (33-27) Grays. Ward's batting (.196 BA), however, was a different matter and in need of improvement.

Baby-faced and still shy of his full adult stature (officially 5-feet-9/175 pounds, but probably smaller), Ward blossomed in his sophomore campaign. He posted a 47-19 record, pitching a herculean 587 innings. Ward led the National League in victories, winning percentage (.712), and strikeouts (239). He also played capably at third base and in the outfield when occasionally spelled in the box by Bobby Mathews (12-6). And his bat came to life, as well. Hitting from the right side,[9] Ward batted a solid .286, with 41 RBIs in 83 games. With shortstop-manager George Wright supplying leadership and the outfield duo of Paul Hines (.357) and Jim O'Rourke (.348) the offensive punch, Providence (59-25) captured the NL pennant by five games over runner-up Boston. That offseason, Ward remained in town managing a Providence sporting emporium. He returned to the Grays the following season, but Wright and O'Rourke had left the club. Early in the season, now 20-year-old Johnny Ward replaced Mike McGeary as manager, guided the Grays to an 18-13 record, and was then replaced himself by Mike Dorgan. Despite turmoil at the helm, Providence (52-32) made a respectable defense of its league crown, finishing second to a (67-17) Chicago juggernaut.

Key to Providence fortunes was the performance of pitching ace Ward. He posted a 39-24 record, with a sparkling 1.74 ERA in 595 innings pitched. Ward struck out 230 batters and posted a league-leading eight shutouts, as well. A personal highlight had occurred in a rare morning game on June 17. Ward retired all 27 Buffalo batters he faced in a 5-0 victory, registering only the second perfect game in big-league history.[10] But by now the overuse of his young right arm was beginning to take its toll, and Ward would never again approach these kinds of pitching heights. Nor, incidentally, would his appearance remain the same. Over the ensuing winter, Johnny began to cultivate the luxuriant mustache that would become a trademark for the rest of his life.

Beginning in 1881, Ward began transitioning into a position player. That year, he spent more time at shortstop and in the outfield (52 games) than he did in the pitcher's box (39), but was no great shakes at either. He batted a mild .244, while going 18-18 as a pitcher for another runner-up Providence club. The following season was pretty much the same. Ward split time between field positions and the pitcher's box, batting a soft .245 (only 14 of his 87 base-hits went for extra bases) and posting a 19-13 pitching log for the once again second-place Providence Grays. He seemed stuck in a rut, but fate was now about to smile on John Montgomery Ward.

Prior to the 1883 season, Ward was among the talented young players acquired by cigar manufacturer John B. Day for the clubs he was placing in the National League and its new rival, the American Association. Along with future Hall of Famers Buck Ewing, Roger Connor, and Mickey Welch, Ward was assigned to the NL Gothams (soon-to-be Giants).[11] By now, Ward had come a long way from the mischievous teenager cashiered from Penn State. He had matured into a serious man with serious ambitions—in baseball and beyond. And New York was the perfect fit for them.

To cure the deficiencies in his education and with his post-baseball future in mind, Ward began taking night and offseason classes at the prestigious Columbia College [now University] School of Law. Handsome, refined, immaculately tailored, and single, he also cut something of a figure in society, often spending evenings at the theater or in Manhattan drawing rooms. But for the short term, Ward still concentrated on playing baseball. During the 1883 season, he alternated between the outfield and the pitcher's box, batting .255 and going 16-13 as the club's number-2 starter behind Welch (25-23) for the sixth-place (46-50) Gothams.

The following season was a challenging one for Ward. An early-season injury to his right arm caused by a slide on the basepaths brought his pitching career irrevocably to its end.[12] To bolster his offensive output (and to lessen an admitted fear of being hit by pitches), Ward converted to batting left-handed. And he was spending more time in the infield than before (47 games at second base compared with 59 in the outfield). All the while, Ward was the club's field leader, having replaced Buck Ewing as New York captain (the first of many events that would strain the relationship between the two). By season's end, he was also the Gothams' manager, predecessor Jim Price having been dismissed from club employ after having been caught embezzling club funds for a second time.

The year 1885 was a watershed for Ward, as he began to transcend being just a ballplayer. On the field, Ward was one of the weaker offensive links (.226 BA) in a New York lineup fortified by the acquisition of another future Hall of Famer, Jim O'Rourke, and former Mets star Dude Esterbrook, obtained along with Mets pitching ace Tim Keefe via some rule-bending chicanery by Metropolitan Exhibition Company boss John B. Day.[13] Ward compensated for his poor bat by adapting successfully to the demanding position of shortstop and by heady field leadership. The Giants[14] soared to an 85-27 (.759) record, only to be outdone by the Cap Anson/King Kelly/John Clarkson Chicago White Stockings, who finished two games better.

The larger destiny that awaited Ward was augured by the law degree that he had received from Columbia in May. While he would not practice law for another 10 years, Ward promptly put his legal training to good use. Along with teammates Jim O'Rourke, Tim Keefe, Roger Connor, and Buck Ewing—all, like Ward, sober, intelligent men—and others, he founded the first serious ballplayers union, the Brotherhood of Professional Baseball Players. Over the next five years, Ward would use his keen intellect, legal understanding, and fluid pen to air union grievances about the one-sidedness of the club owner-ballplayer relationship. In time, these were embodied in a magazine article entitled "Is the Base-Ball Player a Chattel?," an incisive deconstruction of the Reserve Clause that gained widespread circulation.[15] Growing in public prominence and the subject of much sports-page ink, Ward became, in relatively short order, the most important player in major-league baseball, wielding power and influence over National League stars and journeyman players alike, almost all of whom had become members of the Brotherhood, which Ward led.[16]

Ward burnished his post-baseball resume with another academic degree, a Ph.B. in philosophy awarded by Columbia's School of Political Science in 1886.[17] But soon thereafter, Ward entered an entirely different venue—the world of celebrity culture, late-19th-century style. The vehicle: his courtship of the renowned stage actress Helen Dauvray. Born Ida Louise Gibson, Dauvray had been entertaining theater audiences since childhood, and was probably several years older than Ward. Small, buxom, ambitious, business-minded, and divorced, Helen was a great baseball fan and the donator of the Dauvray Cup, bestowed on the champion baseball teams of the late 1880s.[18] Ward and Dauvray were married in October 1887, but their union was a fragile one, jeopardized by their willful personalities, frequent profession-related separations, and Ward's infidelities.[19] The couple repeatedly quarreled, separated, and finally divorced in 1893. They had no children.[20]

Meanwhile, back at the Polo Grounds, Ward was maturing into a fine everyday player. Shortstop proved a congenial position, and he excelled there defensively. Ward's hitting also began to pick up. In 1886 he batted a solid .273, with a career-best 81 RBIs. The next season he skyrocketed to a walks-inflated .371 (later adjusted to a still-impressive .338),[21] with 114 runs scored and an eye-catching 111 stolen bases, then an NL record. He also played well in the field, his .919 fielding average being tops among NL shortstops. Notwithstanding Ward's contributions, the club was headed in the wrong direction, amid reports of internal strife involving its team captain. Cool and with an innate aura of superiority about him, Ward was respected, but never much liked by teammates. Several were reportedly not even on speaking terms with him. With New York on the way to an underachieving fourth-place finish, Ward was replaced or resigned—accounts differed—as Giants captain midway through the 1887 campaign, with Buck Ewing re-installed in the post. That off-season, Ward salved his pride by authoring the first popular instructional for budding baseball players, *Base-Ball: How to Become a Player, with the Origin, History and Explanation of the Game.*[22]

Ward remained at shortstop while the talent-laden Giants finally jelled. They captured consecutive National League pennants in 1888 and 1889, and bested the American Association champ in each postseason match to claim the title of world champions. Ward was at his offensive best during these series, batting .379 and .417, respectively. But all was not well in the baseball world, and John Montgomery Ward, predictably, was at the center of the unrest. As leader of the players union, Ward had long been sparring with NL club owners over the reserve clause. Hard feelings were exacerbated when the league adopted the player-classification plan proposed by Indianapolis owner John T. Brush. Under this scheme, players were assigned a classification (A through E) based upon subjective owner evaluation of their performance, value to the club, and deportment, with rigid and niggardly salary limits imposed for each classification. Perhaps not entirely coincidentally, the Brush plan had been crafted and adopted by the league while players union president Ward was out of the country and largely incommunicado as a member of the celebrated world tour arranged by Chicago White Stockings boss A.G. Spalding. Upon his return in March 1889, the classification plan was already in place, and there was little that Ward could do—for the time being. But he soon devised a radical remedy—creation of an entirely new baseball league, one controlled by its players.

A history of the Players League is beyond the scope of this biography. Suffice it to say that the circuit was almost entirely the product of Ward's energies. Among other things, he orchestrated the recruitment of financial investors in the Players League; found playing sites for its franchises; guided the members of his players union, almost all of whom jumped to the new league, onto their new clubs; arranged the Players League schedule, and dealt daily with the myriad organizational problems confronting the venture—all the while successfully fighting off National League efforts to suppress player movement toward the new circuit via enforcement of the reserve clause. Ward, Jim O'Rourke, Roger Connor, and others were hauled into court by Giants owner John B. Day, but in each instance, the court declined to enjoin the players from plying their trade elsewhere. The talent imbalance soon became obvious, as virtually all the NL stars, and a few prominent American Association players, as well, had joined a Players League team.

Nowhere was the situation more striking than in New York, where only Mickey Welch and outfielder Mike Tiernan remained with the NL Giants. The Players League Giants had O'Rourke, Connor, Tim Keefe, Buck Ewing, and the rest of 1889 world champs—save Ward. John M. (as he preferred to be called) placed himself across the East River as player-manager of the Brooklyn PL club. Competition at the gate was cutthroat, no more so than in New York, where the PL Giants ballpark (Brotherhood Park) was separated from the NL Giants ballpark (Polo Grounds II) by no more than a 10-foot alley. With three major leagues in operation simultaneously, there simply were not enough fans to go around, and clubs soon hemorrhaged red ink. Even before the 1890 season ended, NL Giants owner Day and his PL counterparts were in merger discussions. Thereafter, the hard-nosed A.G. Spalding hammered other PL backers into surrender, the protests of Ward, excluded from the negotiating table, being dismissed by NL and PL club owner alike.[23] Before the year was out, the Players League had expired, passing into baseball history.

Perhaps ironically, Ward had had his best all-around season in 1890, batting .335, with career-high marks in runs scored (134), on-base percentage (.393), and slugging (.426). He also stole 63 bases and led PL shortstops in assists (450). With the Players League dead and the American Association dying—the AA would fold at the close of the 1891 season—Ward rejoined the National League, but remained in Brooklyn, piloting the club to also-ran finishes during the 1891 and 1892 seasons. At times it was rumored that Ward, who had acquired a small stake in the Giants franchise, had his eye on ownership of the financially troubled New York club. But when he returned to the Giants in 1893, it was in the role of second baseman and manager. Upon arrival, Ward's first move stunned the New York faithful. He shipped Buck Ewing, an aging Giants icon with whom Ward had always had an uneasy relationship, to Cleveland in exchange for a promising outfielder-infielder named George Davis. The move would prove an astute one, as Ewing had only one outstanding season left in him, while Davis would provide New York with 10 seasons of brilliant offense and defense. Davis and Ward would also become good friends, but the relationship would prove the source of much grief for Ward in his post-baseball life.

Ward's final two major-league campaigns were filled with achievement. In 1893 he posted an outstanding .328/.379/.415 slash line, with 129 runs scored and 46 steals. The following year, he guided the Giants to an 88-44 second-place finish, and thereafter a four-game sweep of the pennant-winning Baltimore Orioles in the postseason Temple Cup match. He then announced his retirement. In 17 major-league seasons, John Montgomery Ward had been something of an anomaly: a good, if not great, performer as both a pitcher and a position player; only the incomparable Babe Ruth would surpass him as a combination pitcher-turned-everyday player. Ward had gone an impressive 164-103 (.614) as a hurler, with a 2.10 ERA in almost 2,500 innings pitched. He had been a competent .275 singles hitter (almost 84 percent of his 2,107 career base hits), an exceptional baserunner and run scorer, and a capable defender, particularly at the demanding position of shortstop. In six-plus seasons as a major-league player-manager, Ward guided his teams to a 412-320 (.563) mark, with a triumph in one postseason championship match. And almost singlehandedly, he had founded a bona-fide, albeit short-lived, major league. All in all, Ward had had a distinguished baseball career.

Approaching age 35, Ward embarked on the legal practice that he would maintain for the rest of his life. He began by clerking for a well-to-do-corporate lawyer named Austin Fletcher while he boned up for the New York bar examination.[24] Ward passed the exam and was licensed to practice in July 1895.[25] He set up his own law office in Brooklyn, and soon the connection to baseball supplied business to the fledgling barrister. First, second baseman Fred Pfeffer, and then fireballer Amos Rusie, engaged Ward to sue Andrew Freedman, the tempestuous new owner of the New York Giants.[26] These high-profile suits did much to establish Ward's credentials as an attorney, and his practice flourished.

When not building up his legal practice, Ward was consumed by a new passion: golf. Despite his age and relatively late start in the game, the athletically gifted John M. quickly developed into a links master, winning a local tournament in 1897.[27] By 1903, he was among the nation's top amateurs, runner-up in the North-South Tournament, then one of American golf's premier events.[27] That year also saw Ward's marriage to Katherine Waas, a vivacious Manhattan social worker some 17 years his junior. The couple had first met on the golf course, and were pronounced husband and wife within months. The union would prove a long-lasting and happy one, but childless. Another event that came to a head in 1903, however, would not prove such a felicitous one for Ward: the George Davis affair.

The matter is complicated. But in brief, Ward had counseled his friend Davis and entered modifications on the two-year contract that Davis had signed when he jumped to the Chicago White Sox after the 1901 season. A year later, Davis was back in the office seeking Ward's help to break that contract and jump back to the Giants. When Davis appeared in uniform for New York in early 1903, White Sox owner Charles Comiskey sought federal court intervention. At the ensuing proceedings, Ward offered the legal opinion that both the White Sox contract and the Giants contract were valid, and that Davis could take his pick as to which one to honor. To no great surprise, this kind of doublespeak did not play well in court. Worse yet was reaction in the court of public opinion, with baseball voices leading the chorus of disapproval. "Great is the power of the retaining fee over the legal mind," observed *The Sporting News*. "It can make black appear white and vice versa in a twinkling."[28] Chicago Cubs president James Hart characterized Ward's reasoning as 'trumped up" and liable to "ruin his standing with any reputable bar association,"[29] while American League President Ban Johnson denounced Ward as a "trickster" and "as crooked as any player who ever jumped his agreement."[30] In the end, the court ordered Davis's return to Chicago, where he was welcomed back by Comiskey and completed his Hall of Fame playing career there without incident. Not so fortunate was John Montgomery Ward, for whom the George Davis affair would produce long-term consequences.[31]

As he grew older, Ward became more conservative. Now instead of ballplayers, he sometimes represented the game's establishment, even defending in court the validity of the reserve clause that he had once reviled. But for the most part, Ward's practice gravitated toward the corporate world, with the Nassau Railway Company and public utilities being favored clients. Then in mid-1909, events thrust Ward back into the baseball limelight. The July 28 suicide of Harry Pulliam created an unexpected vacancy in the office of National League president, and John Montgomery Ward quickly emerged as a leading candidate for the post. Although he had no official role to play in the election, AL President Ban Johnson loudly intruded into the process, declaring that his league would not sit in council with the NL if Ward were its president. His conduct in the George Davis affair disqualified Ward from consideration for the NL presidency, in Johnson's opinion.[32] As it turned out, National League club owners did not give a hoot what Johnson thought, but the election vote repeated stalemated 4-4 between Ward and Louisville newspaperman Robert Brown over other issues. When NL umpiring chief Tom Lynch was finally proposed as a compromise candidate, Ward withdrew from the race gracefully, and endorsed Lynch's election.

Tom Lynch was unanimously elected NL president, but the matter did not rest there. Smarting from the public aspersion cast upon his character, Ward filed a $50,000 defamation suit against Ban Johnson. The action was tried in federal court, where Ward came off as the stereotypical shifty lawyer on the witness stand. Fortunately for him, Johnson was worse, a pompous blowhard who probably perjured himself during his testimony. In the end, the jury returned a modest $1,000 judgment in Ward's favor, but the suit had done little credit to the reputation of either party.[33] The unpleasantness notwithstanding, the episode seemed to rekindle Ward's interest in baseball, at least temporarily. In December 1911, he became part-owner and president of the National League Boston Braves. But less than a year later, Ward stepped down, citing the press of his legal practice. By doing so, he missed out on the glory of the Miracle Braves' improbable 1914 world championship. By then Ward was tending to his final baseball-connected job: business manager of the Brooklyn club in the upstart Federal League. His retirement from that post in April 1915 brought a near-40-year association with the game to an end.

Ward spent the final decade of his life as a gentleman farmer on Long Island, residing on the 200-acre tract in North Babylon where he and Katherine had lived since their marriage in 1903. The couple regularly attended Sunday services at St. Ann's Episcopal Church and were active in local social and civic affairs. As the years went by, John M. spent less and less time at his law office in Brooklyn and more time tending to the affairs of the ice company, fuel company, and newspaper (*Babylon Leader*) he had started. He also became a member of various fraternal orders, and served as a fishing conservation trustee. In addition, Ward was the founder and first president of the Long Island Golf Association, and continued to play the game at a high level until the end of his life, winning the Nassau County Championship at age 62.[34] He also hunted, fished, and traveled extensively. In March 1925, one such expedition preceded his demise. While on a hunting trip in Georgia, Ward was stricken by a recurrence of the pneumonia that had weakened his health for the previous three years. He died of acute lumbar pneumonia at a hospital in Augusta on March 4, 1925, the day after his 65th birthday. Following funeral services at St. Ann's Church, he was interred at Greenfield Cemetery in Hempstead, Long Island. The only immediate survivor was his wife, Katherine.[35]

When the Hall of Fame opened its doors in the late 1930s, John Montgomery Ward attracted negligible support (three votes in 1936). In 1946 Ward was among 39 major-league managers, executives, umpires, and sportswriters named to the Honor Rolls of Baseball, a second-class admission into Cooperstown that promptly receded into oblivion.[36] But in 1964—70 years after he had last played the game and nearly 40 since his death—Ward was a Veterans Committee choice for full enshrinement. Today, the Hall of Fame plaque for John Montgomery Ward lists his statistics and then states simply: "Played an important part in establishing modern organized baseball," better capturing in a phrase the legacy that this bio has taken some 6,000 words trying to memorialize.

## SOURCES

Sources for the biographical details provided herein include the John Montgomery Ward file maintained at the Giamatti Research Center, National Baseball Hall of Fame and Museum, Cooperstown, New York; biographies by Bryan DiSalvatore, *A Clever Base-Ballist: The Life and Times of John Montgomery Ward* (New York: Pantheon Books, 1999), and Dan Stevens, *Baseball's Radical for All Seasons: A Biography of John Montgomery Ward* (Lanham, Maryland: Scarecrow Press, 1998), and various of the newspaper articles cited below. Unless otherwise noted, statistics have been taken from Baseball-Reference and Retrosheet.

## NOTES

1. Ward's full siblings were Charles Lewis Ward (1855-1906) and a younger sister named Ida who died a week after her birth. He also had a half-sister named Mary Caroline (c.1840-1907), and a deceased half-brother named William, the children of his father's late first wife, Caroline (maiden name unknown). He also had a half-brother named James Moore Ward (1846-1871), the sole child of his father's late second wife, Ellen Moore. For more on the extended Ward family, including its distant connection to the famous retail entrepreneur A. Montgomery Ward, see DiSalvatore, 25-30.

2. In the 1870 US Census, Ward is listed as "Montgomery," a name he detested, according to biographer DiSalvatore. He tolerated "Monte," but that nickname was reserved for family and childhood acquaintances. "Monte" never appeared in newsprint during Ward's lifetime. In his early baseball years, teammates, fans, and the sporting press usually called him "Johnny Ward." As he matured and his stature grew in the game, he became "John Ward," and occasionally the grander "John Montgomery Ward" in newsprint. But the vast majority of the time, sports pages recorded the exploits of "John M. Ward," the name that Ward preferred and the one that he used for his signature. See DiSalvatore, 19-24.

3. As recounted by Geoff Rushton in "Did You Know: Baseball Pioneer Got His Start at Penn State," *Penn State Live*, June 20, 2006.

4. For more detail on the events that precipitated Ward's expulsion, see DiSalvatore, 56-58.

5. According to Hugh Manchester, "Bellefonte Claims 'Hall of Famer,'" *The (Bellefonte) Centre Democrat*, an undated circa 1959 news article contained in the Ward file at Cooperstown.

6. As per Sam Crane, "The Fifty Greatest Baseball Players in History: No. 29, John M. Ward," *New York Journal*, February 22, 1912. See also, "John M. Ward, Pitcher," *New York Clipper*, September 6, 1879.

7. Without specifics, one Ward biographer puts his overall pre-major-league pitching record at a pedestrian 28-28. See Stevens, 11.

8. *Cincinnati Daily Gazette*, July 16, 1878.

9. Baseball reference works invariably list Ward as a left-handed batter, but he did not become one until the 1884 season. For his first six major-league seasons, Ward batted as he threw: right-handed.

10. Only five days earlier, the first perfect game had been thrown by Worcester southpaw Lee Richmond.

11. Day had obtained Ewing, Connor, Welch, and Tim Keefe in the fire sale of the defunct NL Troy Trojans. For the time being, however, Keefe was assigned to Day's American Association club, the New York Metropolitans. Technically, both the NL Gothams and the AA Mets operated under the aegis of the Metropolitan Exhibition Company, Day's corporate alter ego.

12. Prior to the injury, Ward had gone 3-3, pitching in nine games.

13. The maneuvers that brought Esterbrook, Keefe, and Mets manager Jim Mutrie into the Gothams/Giants fold are described in the BioProject profile of John B. Day.

14. The nickname "Giants" traces to the 1885 season, and is customarily attributed to newly installed manager Jim Mutrie. The originator of the moniker, however, may well have been *New York Evening World* sportswriter P.J. Donahue. For more, see the BioProject profile of Mutrie.

15. First published in *Lippincott's Magazine*, August 1887.

16. The Brotherhood had concentrated on getting National League players to join. Few American Association players were in its ranks.

17. Ward later maintained that both his law and philosophy degrees came with honors, but a century later, officials at Columbia could not confirm this for the writer, as per email of Jody Armstrong, associate director, Arthur W. Diamond Law Library, Columbia University, dated February 26, 2008.

18. For more on Helen, Ward, and the long-missing Dauvray Cup, see John Thorn, "Baseball's Lost Chalice," in *Base Ball, A Journal of the Early Game*, Vol. 5, No. 2 (Fall 2011), 84-96.

19. For an entertaining, if fictionalized, account of Ward's dalliance with the actress Maxine Elliott (née Jessie Dermot), see James Hawking, *Strikeout: Baseball, Broadway and the Brotherhood in the 19th Century*, (Santa Fe, New Mexico: Sunshine Press, 2012), 191-193.

20. Interestingly, Tim Keefe, Ward's teammate and fellow union stalwart, married Helen Dauvray's sister, Clara Gibson Helm. That marriage, too, was childless and ended in divorce.

21. For the 1887 season only, walks were counted as base hits for batting-average purposes.

22. Released under the byline of John Montgomery Ward in 1888, the instructional was reprinted by SABR in 1993, and is now

available as a free e-book to SABR members. Biographer DiSalvatore maintains that the book represented the sole time that Ward consented to use of his disliked middle name by a publisher.

23  In response to vocal complaints by Ward about the merger of the two New York clubs, de facto PL Giants boss Edward J. Talcott tartly informed the press, "I don't propose to have Mr. Ward or anybody else criticize my business methods. Nor shall I allow Mr. Ward to tell me how my financial interests must be arranged. The fight cannot go on for another year, for baseball will become a dead sport. Ward can say what he likes but it cannot alter matters with us a particle." *Chicago Tribune,* November 7, 1890.

24  Per Stevens, 181.

25  As reported in the *New York Times,* July 20, 1895.

26  Freedman had acquired majority control of the Giants in late January 1895, an event often cited as the reason for Ward's retirement from the game. This is incorrect, as Ward had announced his intention to begin the practice of law months before Freedman's name surfaced as a bidder for the New York franchise. More to the point, Ward approved Freedman's entry into the game, selling him his small holding of club stock and endorsing Freedman's initial moves as Giants boss, particularly the naming of Ward protégé George Davis as Giants manager. Like A.G. Spalding, another future Freedman nemesis, Ward initially believed that the deep-pocketed Freedman was just the man the financially troubled New York franchise needed, and only soured on him later.

27  See Stevens, 199-200.

28  *The Sporting News,* April 18, 1903.

29  As quoted in *Sporting Life,* March 18, 1903.

30  *Sporting Life,* April 11, 1903.

31  A more expansive account of the George Davis affair is provided by the writer in "The Ward v. Johnson Libel Case: The Last Battle of the Great Baseball War," in *Base Ball, A Journal of the Early Game,* Vol. 2, No. 2 (Fall 2008), 50-52.

32  The Johnson broadside was first published in the *Chicago Tribune,* November 28, 1909, and reprinted in newspapers nationwide.

33  For more on the proceedings, see Lamb, 54-61.

34  As noted by Natalie A. Taylor in "Long Island's Gentleman Athlete: John Montgomery Ward," undated circa 1990 article from *The Nassau County Historical Society Journal* contained in the Ward file at Cooperstown. See also the *Babylon* (New York) *Leader,* March 6, 1925.

35  Katherine Waas Ward died in 1966, at 79. She was buried next to her husband.

36  For more on this long-forgotten laurel, see David L. Fleitz, "The Honor Rolls of Baseball," *Baseball Research Journal,* No. 34, 2005, 53-59.

# MICKEY WELCH

### BY BILL LAMB

### A FAR-FROM-GIANT GIANT, PITCHER

Mickey Welch formed a cornerstone of the celebrated National League franchise founded in New York. Generously listed in baseball reference works as 5-feet-8 and 160 pounds, the undersized right-hander pitched and won the Giants' [then Gothams'] inaugural NL game in 1883. Two years later, he compiled 17 consecutive pitching victories on the way to posting a 44-win season, still the all-time franchise record. By the time he departed the major league scene in early 1892, Welch had become only the third pitcher in big-league history to record 300 wins. He spent the remainder of his long life at the margins of the game, serving as a ballpark attendant at the Polo Grounds and Yankee Stadium, and regularly regaling New York sportswriters with tales from baseball's early years. Some three decades after his passing in 1941—and more than 80 years after he had appeared in his final major-league game—the memory of Mickey Welch was forever preserved by his induction into the National Baseball Hall of Fame.

Mickey Welch was born Michael Francis Walsh in the Williamsburg section of Brooklyn on July 4, 1859. He was the oldest of the three siblings surviving childhood born to horseshoer John Joseph Walsh (1835-1900) and his wife, Bridget (née Guinan, c.1833-1887).[1] The elder Walshes were Irish-Catholic immigrants from Tipperary about whom little else is known, except that by the time of the 1865 New York State Census, they had adopted, again for reasons unknown, the surname *Welch*.[2] Upon entering public life, Mickey would use that as his last name, rather than *Walsh*, whenever dealing with baseball club owners, sportswriters, and fans, as well with as government and local officials.[3]

Small but athletic, Mickey spent much of his youth on the sandlots of Brooklyn, a hotbed of the pioneer-era game and home of the champion Atlantic, Excelsior, and Eckford clubs. At age 18, he journeyed upstate to accept his first professional engagement, earning $45 per month as an outfielder-pitcher for the Volunteers club of Poughkeepsie, an independent professional nine. In the box, he reportedly went 16-6 in 23 games.[4]

Welch began the following season with a pro club in Auburn, New York, but departed early to join the Holyoke (Massachusetts) Shamrocks in faster competition.[5] He returned in 1879 to a Holyoke team upgraded by the acquisition of future Hall of Famer Roger Connor, and later major-league stalwarts Larry Corcoran, Fergy Malone, Jerry Dorgan, and Pete Gillespie. Appearing primarily as a pitcher, Welch used no windup for the mandated underhand delivery of a serviceable fastball and an effective array of breaking pitches, and fashioned a 23-14 record.[6] A highlight of the campaign was a 10-inning, 1-0 victory against Springfield, posted over opposing manager Bob Ferguson's protest that Welch's pitching motion was illegal. A competent batsman used as a backup outfielder, Mickey also hit .266 in 184 at-bats for the Shamrocks. A more enduring Welch highlight occurred off the diamond. On November 16, 1879, 20-year-old Mickey and his 18-year-old sweetheart, Mary Whelihan, were joined in marriage at St. Jerome Church in Holyoke. Their union would last 56 years and produce nine children.[7]

Suspect pitching motion notwithstanding, Welch had made a favorable impression on Bob Ferguson, and when the crusty veteran was appointed manager of the National League Troy Trojans in early 1880, he immediately acquired Mickey for his pitching staff. Welch was joining a middle-of-the pack club, but one loaded with young talent. No fewer than five Trojans (Buck Ewing, Tim Keefe, a hastily-released Dan Brouthers, Connor, and Welch) were destined for Cooperstown. But the club would have to endure its roster's growing pains. Welch's major league debut could not have gone much worse: a 13-1 loss to Worcester on May 1. Four days later, he broke into the win column, besting Worcester 3-1, and he soon justified Ferguson's faith in him. Appearing in 65 games total, Mickey logged a 34-30 record in a yeoman 574 innings pitched for the fourth-place (41-42) Trojans. Hitting from the right side, he also batted a solid .287 in 251 at-bats, third highest on the club. But standing in the pitcher's box a mere 45 feet from enemy batsman, Welch was shaky in the field, with a .841 fielding average.

Beginning in August, Welch occasionally was spelled in the box by a fellow rookie right-hander named Tim Keefe. Keefe went only 6-6 for Troy in 1880, but he and Welch had begun a decade-long collaboration as baseball's most dominant pitching duo. But first, the two would have to take some lumps. Troy headed for a (39-45) fifth-place finish in 1881. That season, Keefe assumed the number-one starter role that he would maintain for most of the partnership with Welch, getting the ball in 45 games (compared to Welch's 40 starts), but suffering an 18-27 record in 403 innings pitched. Mickey had more success, going 21-18 in 368 frames. The 2.67 Welch ERA was also better than Keefe's 3.24. The pattern continued in 1882. Keefe drew the starting assignment more often than Welch (42 times to 33), but posted the poorer record (Keefe: 17-26; Welch 14-16). But that season the win-loss records were misleading; Keefe (367 hits surrendered in 376 innings pitched) was far more difficult to hit than Welch (334 hits given up in only 281 innings pitched). But the disparity in their win-loss records was apparently dispositive to a future employer, and produced immediate consequences for Tim Keefe and Mickey Welch. And for major-league baseball in New York.

Since the expulsion of their clubs after the 1876 season, New York and Philadelphia, the nation's two largest cities, had been without a National League team. But in 1882, the death of NL commandant William Hulbert and the emergence of the American Association, a rival major league, prompted reconsideration of the circuit's structure. In short order, the NL liquidated the small-market franchises in Troy and Worcester, creating the needed vacancies for league reentry into New York and Philadelphia. Thereafter, both the NL and the AA began courting John B. Day, the well-heeled cigar manufacturer who controlled the New York Metropolitans, an independent, professional nine that had proved highly competitive in exhibition game play against NL and AA clubs. In time, the NL and AA each offered Day a place in their organization. Audaciously, Day accepted both offers, assigning the already-established Mets to the Association. His National League club was constructed from scratch, but built around player material acquired via the fire sale of the Troy Trojans. Day plainly intended his NL team, originally called the Gothams or simply the New-Yorks, to be the favored one, and stocked it with most of Troy's best ex-players: Buck Ewing, Roger Connor, Mickey Welch, and Pete Gillespie—but not Tim Keefe, who, in a painful misjudgment, was consigned to the Mets.

Keefe pitched brilliantly in 1883, going 41-27, with a 2.41 ERA and a league-leading 359 strikeouts in a staggering 619 innings pitched. And under the direc-

tion of wily manager Jim Mutrie, the Mets posted a more-than-respectable 54-42 record. Meanwhile, the Gothams got off to an auspicious start. With the Polo Grounds packed with 12,000 fans (including former president Ulysses S. Grant) for Opening Day, Mickey Welch pitched the home side to a 7-5 victory over Boston. But much to Day's chagrin, his pet club underperformed, posting a sixth-place (46-50) finish in NL standings. The individual matchup between Keefe and Welch came out much the same, with Mickey's stats, 25-23, with a 2.73 ERA and 144 strikeouts in 426 innings pitched, no way comparable to those of his old Troy comrade. The next season was more of the same—at least as far as the co-owned New York clubs went. With Keefe (37-17) and Jack Lynch (37-15) splitting hurling duties evenly, the 75-32 Mets captured the AA pennant handily. Meanwhile, the Gothams' improved 62-50 log was good for no better than fourth place in the senior circuit. But the imbalance in Mets-Gothams fortunes could no longer be attributed to Mickey Welch. Like Tim Keefe, he was entering the prime of his major-league career. For the 1884 season, he arguably outperformed Keefe, going 39-21, with a 2.50 ERA and 345 strikeouts in 557 1/3 innings pitched. In the process, he set a long-overlooked NL record that stood for nearly a century. On August 28, Welch began a game against Cleveland by striking out the first nine batters who faced him.[8] But Welch's standout individual performance did not lessen John B. Day's unhappiness about the Gothams mediocre standing in the NL, and drastic measures were about to be taken.

During the off-season, Day reassigned Mets manager Mutrie to the Gothams. Then, via some artful rule-bending, Tim Keefe and star third baseman Dude Esterbrook were transferred to the Gothams, as well.[9] With Cooperstown-bound John Montgomery Ward and Jim O'Rourke also in the New York lineup, the club was now the powerhouse Day desired.

The 1885 campaign found Mickey Welch at the zenith of his career. Sharing pitching duties with Keefe, Mickey went a franchise record-setting 44-11, with a 1.66 ERA and 258 strikeouts in 492 innings pitched, a performance punctuated by a 17-consecutive-game winning streak. Nor was Keefe a slouch that season, going 32-13, with a 1.58 ERA and 227 strikeouts in 400 innings. Both hurlers had successfully adapted to the rule changes of the mid-1880s (regarding balls and strikes; the lengthening of the pitching distance; the sanction of overhand pitching; etc.) by throwing from varying arm angles and adding put-away pitches to their repertoires: for Welch, the in-shoot (screwball), and for Keefe, the changeup. The two were also dead-earnest workers in the box, with a distinct aversion to losing.

But away from the field, Welch and Keefe were polar opposites. Keefe was a quiet, serious man, reserved, almost aloof in manner, and he sported the handlebar mustache near-ubiquitous among the ballplayers of the 1880s. In contrast, the clean-shaven Welch was a fun-lover. Although he reputedly refrained from tobacco, swearing, and hard liquor, Mickey was a fabled beer drinker, given to composing impromptu ditties about his favorite beverage.[10] He also frequently entertained teammates, companions, and other bar-goers with a fine Irish tenor singing voice. Notwithstanding their divergent personalities (and later differences over the Players League), Mickey Welch and Tim Keefe were good teammates and maintained a lifelong friendship.

For the 1885 campaign, the New York team performed up to expectations. But an exceptional 85-27 record was good for only second place that season, as the Chicago White Stockings, with Cap Anson, King Kelly, and John Clarkson at their playing peak, came in two games better in final NL standings. During the season, the New York team acquired the nickname that would accompany the club to later baseball glory: "Giants."[11] Star pitcher Welch also received an enduring sobriquet: "Smiling Mickey," a tribute to his even-temperedness in the pitching box—he never argued a call and was said to be the favorite pitcher of NL umpires—and the bemused grin that seemed plastered on his face.[12]

With an ever-growing family to support, Welch held out briefly during the offseason of 1885-1886, but club owner Day refused to yield to his "exorbitant" demands.[13] Welch later signed quietly, probably for about $3,000. He pitched well during the 1886 and 1887 seasons, but a nagging back and occasional arm miseries reduced his numbers: 33-22 in 500 innings pitched (1886), and 22-15 in 346 innings (1887). Meanwhile, Tim Keefe had gone a combined 75-39 in over 1,000 innings pitched, and had assumed the mantle of staff ace.

Following two also-ran finishes, the 84-47 Giants surged to the 1888 NL pennant, a full nine games ahead of second-place Chicago. Welch (26-19) ably seconded Keefe (35-12) during the season, and again assumed a support role when the Giants faced the AA champion St. Louis Browns in the post-season precursor of the modern World Series. With Keefe (4-0) going undefeated and Welch and right-hander Cannonball Crane splitting their four decisions, the Giants prevailed in the 10-game series, 6-4, and took home their first baseball championship.

The 1889 season was a virtual repeat. New York (83-43) nipped the Boston Beaneaters (83-45) at the wire for the NL crown, and then bested the AA Brooklyn Bridegrooms in the postseason. Although troubled by back problems, a thumb injury, and illness in the family, Welch pitched capably for the champions, going 27-12 in 375 innings pitched. But he was ineffective during the Series, being shelled by the Bridegrooms in his only outing. Keefe also went winless, being hit hard in his two post-season starts. Only unexpected pitching heroics by Crane (4-1) and Hank O'Day (2-0) allowed New York to prevail, 6-3.

While 1889 had seen the Giants successfully defend their world champions' crown, the season had been conducted amidst rising owner-player tension, with long-standing player resentment of the reserve clause in the standard major-league contract exacerbated by newly-adopted limitations on player salaries. Notwithstanding the fact that John B. Day was well-liked by his players, the New York Giants were the springboard of the coming insurrection, with union visionary John Montgomery Ward busily organizing a new, player-controlled major-league circuit for the 1890 season.

Although Welch had been a member of the Brotherhood of Professional Base Ball Players since its founding in 1885,[14] he did not join the exodus of Giants headed for the new league. Club owner Day, intent on holding onto at least a few members of his championship nine, tendered Welch a guaranteed, three-year contract at $4,000 per season, a pact which the Players League declined to match. Welch explained his decision to reject a lesser offer from the PL bluntly: "I am in the business for dollars and cents, and as the offer made by the old League was the better one, I accepted it."[15] Days later, he resigned from the Brotherhood.

In the end, only Welch and outfielder Mike Tiernan remained with the NL (Real) Giants. The rest joined Buck Ewing and the PL (Big) Giants. Fortified by an infusion of playing talent purchased from the defunct Indianapolis Hoosiers—Amos Rusie, Jack Glasscock, Jerry Denny, and others—the Real Giants fared better than expected on the field. The club's pitching mainstay was the 19-year-old Rusie, who went 29-34, with 341 strikeouts (and 289 walks) in 548 2/3 innings pitched. In more limited action, Welch chipped in a respectable 17-14 record, which included a 1-0 shutout of Pittsburgh on August 29. It was Welch's 300th major league win. In keeping with the times, the accomplishment went unnoted in the press.[16]

All things considered, the club's 63-68 final record was a relative triumph. But with the Big Giants playing their games next door to the Polo Grounds in newly erected Brotherhood Park, the competition for fans had been cutthroat, and both teams hemorrhaged red ink. Shortly after the financially ruinous season ended, the NL and PL Giants merged, heralding the demise of the Players League. Tim Keefe, Buck Ewing, Roger Connor, and Jim O'Rourke returned to the Giants fold for the 1891 season, but were now on the downside of storied careers.

So, too, was Mickey Welch. He appeared in only 22 games in 1891, going 5-9 with an inflated 4.28 ERA in 160 innings pitched, for a 71-61 Giants club.[17] In the final year of the guaranteed contract that he had signed in 1890, Welch returned to the club for the 1892 season. But his stay was short. Inactive for the first five weeks of the campaign, Mickey was handed the ball on May 17 for a game against the Baltimore Orioles. He lasted five innings, and was removed after surrendering nine runs. Shortly thereafter, the Giants released the 32-year-old Welch, bringing his major league career to an end.

In 13 seasons, Smiling Mickey Welch posted a 307-210 (.594) record, with a 2.71 career ERA. He pitched 4,802 innings, completing 525 of his 549 starts, while hurling 41 shutouts. In 4,802 innings pitched, he yielded 4,588 hits (.246 OBA), but his strikeouts (1,850) to walks (1,297) ratio was subpar. To counterbalance that, he had often helped himself with the bat. A modest .224 batting average included some pop: 121 extra-base hits, including 12 homers. Welch scored 268 runs, and drove in 202 more. He had also been an occasional position player, making 59 appearances in the outfield (albeit with a dismal .740 FA).

In all, Mickey Welch had been a ballplayer of the first rank. And he wanted to continue. Following his release by New York, Welch returned to familiar terrain, signing with the Troy Trojans, now a member of the Eastern League. In 31 EL games, he posted a 16-14 record, with a scintillating 0.87 ERA in 267 2/3 innings pitched. But with his family growing ever larger, Mickey desired to play closer to his home, in Holyoke. For 1893, he joined a local semipro club and, with hard feelings over the Players League forgotten, arranged a preseason exhibition game with the John Montgomery Ward-led New York Giants. Pitching for the first time from the newly established 60'-6" pitching distance, Welch was hammered, surrendering 11 runs before he could get out of the first inning. He then retreated to right field for the remainder of the 23-8 laugher.[18] That summer, Mickey toed the slab a few more times for the Holyoke club, before hanging his spikes up for good at season's end.[19]

His playing days now behind him, Welch gave his full attention to the Holyoke businesses, a hotel-saloon and a cigar shop that he had long owned an interest in. Later, he went into the milk production business with his sons.[20] In time, Welch found more reliable employment as steward of the Elks Lodge in Holyoke. Always trim and in good shape, he spent off-days hiking local hills. Or swapping yarns with Dirty Jack Doyle, a 17-year major-league veteran and long-time resident of Holyoke.[21] But his favorite leisure activity was taking in Boston and New York ball games, his enjoyment always enhanced on those occasions when he was seated with his old friend, Tim Keefe. One such trip, in 1912, resulted in a meeting with Giants manager John McGraw, and a new job as a night watchman at the Polo Grounds.[22] For the next 20 summers, Mickey and wife Mary would be summertime residents of Manhattan.

When Yankee Stadium was put into service in 1923, Welch doubled his ballpark duties, serving as a gatekeeper and press box attendant there. The latter position was a perfect fit for a storyteller like Mickey. On slow sports news days, reporters often filled column space with Welch reminiscences about a bygone baseball era, or his unshakeable opinion that the players of his day were the equal of, if not better than, the moderns, whose bashing offensive style of play Welch disdained. Late in his life, a delightfully eccentric Mickey Welch all-time team—Jack Doyle (not Lou Gehrig or Jimmie Foxx) at first; Ed Williamson over Honus Wagner at short; and an outfield with Hugh Duffy and Willie Keeler, but no Babe Ruth—was published in the New York press.[23] *New York Times* sportswriter John Kiernan, who often waxed nostalgic in print, described the now-elderly Welch as "hale and hearty and lively as a cricket."[24]

The passage of time may have been kind to Welch, but it was less so to his contemporaries. In April 1933, Mickey was saddened by the passing of Tim Keefe. He served as a pallbearer at the Keefe funeral. But the real blow came in October 1935 when his wife, Mary Welch, died unexpectedly at their new residence in Corona (Queens), New York. With his children long out of the house, Mickey was living on his own for the first time in decades. And when Dasher Troy—whose five errors at shortstop had nearly cost Welch the 1883 season opener—died in 1938, Mickey became the final survivor of the original New York Gothams/Giants.

By now, Welch's own days were numbered. Suffering from heart disease, he relocated to the home of grandson Bill Welch, Jr., in Nashua, New

Hampshire. In late-spring 1941, Mickey was removed to New Hampshire State Hospital in Concord, where doctors discovered that his left foot had become gangrenous.[25] He died there of congestive heart failure on July 30, 1941. Smiling Mickey Welch was 82. Returned to his Brooklyn birthplace for funeral services, the deceased reverted to being Michael Walsh, the name placed on his funeral card and inscribed on his gravestone. He was interred in the Walsh family plot at Calvary Cemetery in Woodside (Queens), New York.[26]

While Buck Ewing (1939) and Jim O'Rourke (1945) were early Hall of Fame inductees, the other early New York greats remained neglected until the mid-1960s. John Montgomery Ward and Tim Keefe received their due in 1964. And finally, in 1973, the call to Cooperstown was sounded for Mickey Welch.[27] At the enshrinement ceremony, his 84-year-old daughter Julia Welch Weiss acknowledged the plaque on behalf of the family. Long after his death, and more than 80 years after his final major-league game, Smiling Mickey Welch had become a baseball immortal.

## SOURCES

Sources for the biographical detail contained herein include the Mickey Welch file maintained at the Giamatti Research Center, National Baseball Hall of Fame and Museum, Cooperstown, New York; US and New York State Census data, family tree information accessed via Ancestry.com, and certain of the newspaper articles cited below. Unless otherwise noted, statistics have been taken from Baseball-Reference and Retrosheet.

## NOTES

1. The 1865 New York State Census lists Bridget *Welch* as the mother of seven children, with Michael (age 6), Mary (4), and infant Julia residing in Brooklyn with their parents.

2. See the 1865 New York State Census. A century later, Mickey's daughter advised the Hall of Fame that her father's correct surname was *Walsh*, and that the family had never legally changed it to *Welch*. See May 24, 1973 letter of Julia Welch Weiss to Cliff Kachline in the Mickey Welch file at the National Baseball Hall of Fame.

3. According to a respected baseball historian, "he was Michael Walsh off the field for the rest of his life. His friends called him Mike." See David L. Fleitz, *The Irish in Baseball: An Early History* (Jefferson, North Carolina: McFarland & Co., Inc., 2009), 29. When he erected a cemetery monument in his late parents' honor, Mickey commemorated them and other family members under the name *Walsh*, and he himself was later interred there as Smiling Mickey *Walsh*. See the posting with photo for Michael "Smiling Mickey" Welch on the Find-a-Grave website.

4. As per *Baseball's First Stars*, Frederick Ivor-Campbell, Robert L. Tiemann, and Mark Rucker, eds. (Cleveland: SABR, 1996), 170. See also Rich Westcott, *Winningest Pitchers: Baseball's 300 Game Winners* (Philadelphia: Temple University Press, 2002), 20.

5. The departure of Michael Welch from the Auburn club was noted in the *New York Tribune*, May 9, 1878. See also, the *Biographical Dictionary of American Sports: Q-Z*, David L. Porter, ed. (Westport, Connecticut: Greenwood Press, 1990), 1646, which maintains that Welch "began his pro career with Auburn in 1878," and an undated circa 1881 *New York Clipper* profile of Welch putting him with the Auburn club contained in the Hall of Fame's Welch file.

Baseball-Reference places Welch with the Pittsburg Alleghenys of the International League in 1878, with no stats provided. The only arguable Welch connection to that club found by the writer appeared in the *Boston Daily Advertiser*, May 6, 1878: "Welch, a young amateur belonging to the Lynn [Massachusetts] Emmets, pitched very well for the Alleghenys in place of Lafferty who is laid up with rheumatism." Whether this Welch was our subject or someone else, he lost to the Live Oak club, 10-1, although only three of the runs surrendered were earned. That our Mickey Welch spent the latter part of the 1878 season playing for Holyoke was reported by the *Cleveland Leader*, August 2, 1878, and confirmed by various published Holyoke box scores. See e.g., the *Worcester Daily Spy*, August 12, 1878.

6. As per *Baseball's First Stars*, 170. Baseball-Reference provides no won-loss record for Welch in 1879.

7. The Welch children were John (born c. 1880), Nora (1882), Mary (1885), William (1887), Julia (1889), Helen (1892), Lydia (c. 1893), Margaret Theresa (1895), and Mabel (c. 1897), as per the May 1973 letter of Julia Welch Weiss to Cliff Kachline, and various US Census reports.

8. Perhaps because the ninth Cleveland strikeout victim reached first base on a passed ball, the Welch record went unrecognized until after Mickey's death in 1941. See "An Overlooked Feat," an unidentified October 23, 1941 news item in the Mickey Welch file at the Hall of Fame. In the August 28, 1884 game, Welch struck out 14 Cleveland batters in all.

9. For more detail on the maneuvers that secured Mutrie, Keefe, and Esterbrook, see the SABR BioProject profile of John B. Day. The loss of the three gutted the pennant-winning Mets. In 1885, the club fell to seventh place in AA standings. The Mets were then sold to Staten Island entrepreneur Erasmus Wiman.

Two unsuccessful seasons later, the New York Metropolitans were disbanded.

10  The most remembered of these went: "Pure elixir of malt and hops, Beats all the drugs and all the drops."

11  Popularly attributed to Mutrie, the nickname "Giants" may actually have been coined by *New York Evening World* reporter P.J. Donahue. For more, see the SABR BioProject profile of James Mutrie.

12  The "Smiling Mickey" nickname is usually attributed to R.V. Munkittrick, a writer-cartoonist for the satirical magazine *Puck* and the *New York Evening Journal*.

13  As per *Sporting Life,* April 21, 1886. Welch had signed an improvident three-year deal in 1883, and had made only half of Tim Keefe's $3,000 salary for the 1885 season.

14  Noel Hynd, *The Giants of the Polo Grounds: The Glorious Baseball Days of the New York Giants* (New York: Doubleday, 1988), 26.

15  *New York Times,* January 14, 1890.

16  Welch was the third major-league pitcher to record 300 wins, preceded by Pud Galvin (in late 1888) and Tim Keefe (earlier in 1890).

17  Tim Keefe went 2-5 for the 1891 Giants before being released in July. He then signed with the Philadelphia Phillies. He retired after being cut loose by the Phillies in August 1893. Keefe's lifetime major-league record was 342-225.

18  *New York Times,* April 7, 1893.

19  David L. Fleitz, *More Ghosts in the Gallery: Another Sixteen Little-Known Greats at Cooperstown* (Jefferson, North Carolina: McFarland & Co., Inc., 2007), 148.

20  Ibid., 149.

21  Welch and Doyle enjoyed hoodwinking local reporters with an apocryphal tale about how the younger Doyle had caught Mickey's final major-league victory in 1892. See e.g., "Doyle Caught Welch in Mickey's Last Victory," *Holyoke* (Massachusetts) *Daily Transcript,* August 5, 1941. In fact, Mickey's last win was posted during the 1891 season, and he and Doyle were never members of the New York Giants at the same time.

22  McGraw had a soft spot for baseball old-timers, finding ballpark sinecures for Amos Rusie and Dan Brouthers as well.

23  Jimmy Powers, "Welch Omits Ruth in All-Time Team," *New York Sunday News,* April 2, 1939.

24  *New York Times,* January 25, 1938.

25  As per the death certificate in the Mickey Welch file at the Giamatti Research Center.

26  A color photo of the Calvary Cemetery headstone taken by SABR's Stew Thornley is posted on the Find-A-Grave website. Note should be taken, however, of second, erroneous Find-A-Grave posting that places the Walsh/Welch grave site in Lake Forest, California. Unhappily, this bogus California gravesite is the one listed by the Baseball-Reference entry for Mickey Welch.

27  Teammate Roger Connor had to wait until 1976 for his posthumous Hall of Fame induction.

# VIC WILLIS

## BY DANIEL R. LEVITT

**AS A ROOKIE IN 1898, VIC WILLIS WON** 25 games as a key member of the pennant-winning Boston Beaneaters, one of the top teams of the nineteenth century. Eleven years later in his penultimate season, Willis again won over 20 games as a member of the world champion Pittsburgh Pirates, one of the top teams of the Deadball Era. In between he pitched well enough to finish with 249 wins in only a 13-year career. A big man for his time at 6-foot-2, 205 pounds, Willis pitched with an overhand delivery and was known as a great strikeout pitcher. In 1995, nearly a century after his major-league debut, the Veterans Committee voted the hurler nicknamed the "Delaware Peach" into the Hall of Fame.

Victor Gazaway Willis was born on April 12, 1876 in Cecil County, Maryland. Soon afterward his family moved just across the state line to Newark, Delaware, where his father James supported the family as a carpenter, and his mother Mary ran the household. In Newark, Willis grew up playing baseball, starring on his school team at Newark Academy and later for Delaware College. By the time he was 18, Willis was playing semiprofessionally around the state of Delaware.

In 1895 as a 19-year-old Willis first entered organized baseball by joining the Harrisburg club in the nearby Pennsylvania State League. His workload piled up rapidly as he pitched in 16 of the team's 37 games. The Harrisburg club folded in June, but Willis had gained some recognition and quickly caught on elsewhere—less than two weeks later he signed with Lynchburg in the Virginia League.

Overall, Willis pitched capably in 1895 despite the forced midseason relocation, and the next year he moved up to Syracuse of the Eastern League for the 1896 season. Willis battled illness nearly the entire year, but fought through it for a while to achieve a record of 10-6 by late July. Eventually the illness got the better of him, and on July 31 he left the team for the rest of the season to recuperate.

He returned to Syracuse healthy in 1897 and finished the season 21-16 as Syracuse won the league championship. Syracuse realized they had a budding star and hoped to sell him for $2,000, a fairly high price for the time. They ultimately settled for $1,000 and catcher Fred Lake from Boston. The major-league club developed its interest in Willis from the recommendations of Providence manager Billy Murray and Syracuse catcher Jack Ryan, previously a catcher in Boston.

In 1898 Willis joined the National League's Boston Beaneaters, fresh off their fourth pennant in seven years. Willis was expected to help the team immediately, with one sportswriter commenting: "The 'Wolf' as he is termed ought to be a great winner for Boston," and he further described the big right-hander as having good control, a change of pace, and a sweeping curve.[1] The *Boston Sunday Journal* reported that "Willis has speed and the most elusive curves. His 'drop' is so wonderful that, if anyone hits it, it is generally considered a fluke."[2]

Willis saw his first action April 20 in a mopup role in Baltimore when he entered the game in the sixth with the Beaneaters behind, 10-3. Willis showed some first-game jitters and over the final three innings he gave up eight runs while walking three and hitting two Oriole batters. Nine days later, in his first start, Willis pitched better and won 11-4 in a complete game. Willis surpassed even his high spring expectations by following up this first victory to finish 25-13 for the pennant winning Beaneaters.

The 23-year-old Willis followed up his superb rookie campaign with one of the best seasons of his career. He won 27, lost only 8 and finished second in ERA while pitching 342 innings. That year he led the league in allowing the fewest hits per game; a feat helped by hurling his only no-hitter on August 7. In the sixth inning of that game Washington pitcher Bill Dinneen hit a ball that took a bad hop and just eluded Boston third baseman Jimmy Collins. Fortunately for Willis this ball was scored an error and his no-hitter was preserved. After the season in February 1900 Willis married Mary J. Minnis, a union that would lead to two children, a girl and a boy born 15 years apart.

Years later Boston first baseman Fred Tenney recollected the team's pitchers and fielders working in harmony, even if the outcome was not always as anticipated:

"I remember once Vic Willis was pitching for Boston and Jesse Tannehill was at the bat. Long [shortstop Herman] saw as Willis wound up that he was going to give Tannehill a low ball and Tannehill could wallop that kind. He was apt to paste them hard to right field.

"'No, no; don't give him that,' cried Long, but Willis was just letting the ball go and Long darted across the diamond in front of the second baseman as fast as his legs could carry him. He knew that Tannehill was apt to slam the ball to right field, and he wanted to head it off. There were two strikes on Tannehill, and as luck would have it he missed this one and struck out. Long described a circle, came up to Willis from the direction of first base, grabbed him by the hand and exclaimed, 'that's the way to pitch, old boy!'"[3]

Despite a subpar 1900 season, Willis was still regarded as a top hurler, and in 1901 Boston paid him a $2,400 salary. At the end of the nineteenth century the National League's magnates adopted a salary maximum of $2,400. For the top players, however, teams often supplemented this salary with additional payments, both above and below the table. Willis' teammate, star pitcher Kid Nichols earning $2,400, held out prior to the 1899 season after winning the 1898 pennant because the team offered only $235 per man as a championship bonus.

In 1901 the American League challenged the National as a major league, and the completion between the leagues for ballplayers bid up salaries. As some of his teammates were leaving for greener pastures in the AL, Willis reportedly agreed to jump to the American League's Philadelphia Athletics but soon changed his mind. Other star National League hurlers saw their salaries jump from the American League threat: Noodles Hahn leapt to $4,200, Christy Mathewson reportedly made $5,000, and Joe McGinnity $3,000. That year Willis turned in another good season with a 20-17 record and finished fourth in ERA while pitching over 300 innings.

In 1902 Willis responded sensationally to an incredible workload: he completed a league-high 45 games, the modern (since 1901) NL record; hurled 410 innings, the second-highest total in modern NL history; and led the league in strikeouts with 225. On May, 29 against New York Willis struck out a league-high 13 Giants; that only 450 spectators saw this game highlights how far this franchise had fallen in the new century from its recent championship days. Additionally, Willis was used in several key relief situations, and he has been retroactively credited with a league-high three saves.

The American League came calling again during the 1902 season. Detroit Tigers president Sam Angus met Willis in the Victoria Hotel and offered a large cash downpayment on a two-year contract of $4,500 per season. Naturally tempted by the cash and salary, Willis initially accepted, but again later reneged after Boston reportedly matched the offer. His services remained in dispute until after the season when he was awarded to Boston as part of the peace settlement between the two leagues.

Over the next three years Willis won only 42 games while toiling for the rapidly deteriorating Beaneaters. In 1904 when Willis finished with a league-high 25 losses, his 18 wins represented 33% of his team's 55 victories. He also proved an excellent fielder that year and recorded 39 putouts, a modern NL record that would stand for nearly a century. Willis, who years later would complain about the team's fielding ability, probably figured the only way to get some outs was to make them himself. His grandson remembered Willis saying: "those outfielders couldn't catch a flyball with a peach basket."[4]

Prior to the start of the 1905 season the now anemic Boston club offered a salary of only $2,400. Willis expressed displeasure with his drastic salary cut by threatening to jump to an outlaw league in Pennsylvania. He eventually rejoined the Beaneaters but may have wished he hadn't. In 1905, with the league's worst offense supporting him, Willis again led the league with 29 losses, the most ever in modern baseball. Not surprisingly, after this frustrating season Willis again flirted with the outlaw league.

This time, however, the Pirates rescued the Willis from the hapless Beaneaters. Pittsburgh owner Barney Dreyfuss surrendered three players in the trade for Willis: new third baseman Dave Brain, first baseman Del Howard and pitcher Vivian Lindaman. After the trade Willis sent a letter to Dreyfuss acknowledging his unhappiness on the Beaneaters and expressing his approval of the trade, and added: "Don't believe those tales you hear about my being all-in. Wait until you see me in action for your team and then form your opinion of my worth to your team. I assure you that I am delighted to be a Pirate and that I will do my best to bring another pennant to the Smoky City."[5] Dreyfuss reportedly restored Willis' $4,500 salary as well.

Willis started strongly for his new club pitching three straight shutouts early in the 1906 season. Now with a winning franchise again, Willis would win 21 to 23 games a year over his four years with the Pirates without ever losing more than 13 while consistently pitching around 300 innings a year. During his stint with the Pirates, Willis hurled the two one-hitters of his career.

The famous 1908 National League pennant race came down to the last game of the season for the Pirates. On Sunday October 4, the Pirates faced the Cubs in Chicago's old West Side Park in front of 30,247 fans, the most to have ever seen a baseball game up to that point and 6,000 more than had ever previously crowded into that park. A win for the Pirates and they would win the pennant; a loss and they would, for all intents and purposes, be eliminated.

Pirates manager Fred Clarke selected the well-rested Willis to start against the Cubs' Three-Finger Brown, another future Hall of Famer. Brown was on his way to an excellent 29-9 record but this would be his third game in six days. The Cubs jumped out to a 2-0 lead as the Pirates managed only three hits through the first five innings. The Pirates scored two in the sixth to tie the game. In the bottom of the sixth with two out Joe Tinker doubled and Willis and Clarke chose to intentionally walk catcher Johnny Kling to face Brown. Unfortunately for Willis and the Pirates, Brown singled in Tinker with the go ahead and winning run. The Cubs later added two insurance runs including another RBI from Brown and won the contest, 5-2.

In January of the following year, amid rumors of a salary dispute, Willis announced that he had decided to retire from baseball and claimed he could make more money back in his hometown of Newark, Delaware. By the time the season rolled around, however, Dreyfuss had brought Willis back into the fold

In mid-1909 Willis again pitched in one of the highest attended games to date—the grand opening of Forbes Field, one of the first concrete and steel stadiums. On June 30, amid great fanfare and the closing of many businesses at noon, 30,000 plus spectators including numerous baseball and Pennsylvania dignitaries packed the new stadium. The *Reach Guide* gushed on the unveiling: "Never, perhaps, in the history of the Old World or New—not excluding the assemblages in the Roman and Grecian amphitheaters and stadiums—was a scene more spectacular presented...."[6] Willis started for the Pirates, once again against the Cubs, and pitched a four hitter. But the team lost 3-2 in a game Dreyfuss obviously wanted very much to win: "What a shame we had to lose that one. I'd have given my share of the gate to have won on this day."[7]

Unlike the previous season, in 1909 the Pirates gave their opponents no opportunity for late season heroics by winning 110 games and outdistancing the second-place Cubs by 6 1/2 games. Willis played a key role by winning 22 and losing only 11, winning 11 consecutive games over one stretch during the season. In the World Series against the Tigers, Willis pitched in just two games, the only World Series appearances of his career. He relieved Howie Camnitz in the third inning of Game Two, and Ty Cobb promptly stole home. Willis gave up three runs over his 6 1/3 innings in relief as the Tigers won the game, 7-2.

With the Pirates up three games to two, Clarke gave Willis the Game Six start and a chance to win the Series. Despite being staked to a three run lead in the first inning, Willis could not hold the lead. Clarke pulled him after five innings with Detroit ahead, 4-3. Although the Pirates ended up losing Game Six, they came back to win Game Seven and the World Series two days later.

Despite his fine 1909 season, the Pirates waived Willis before the 1910 season amid allegations of disciplinary problems with manager Clarke during the previous summer and World Series. The chronically second-division St. Louis Cardinals claimed Willis, and *The Sporting News* reported that he "should have a year or two of high-class work left in him if he will behave himself."[8] Willis won only nine games for the seventh-place Cardinals, and just prior to the end of the season the team asked waivers on Willis.

During the offseason St. Louis sold Willis to the minor-league Baltimore Orioles of the Eastern League. Although some doubt existed whether Willis would report to the minors, he told the *Baltimore Sun*: "I feel very much satisfied to play in Baltimore."[9] Despite this apparent sale, both the Cubs and Reds put in a waiver claim for Willis. These waiver claims were ruled to be valid; St. Louis President Stanley Robison had mistakenly believed his waivers were good until the opening of the next season and consequently had to return Baltimore's check. Willis ended up being awarded to Chicago for the $1,500 waiver price, but elected to retire rather than report to the Cubs.

With his playing career now over, Willis retired to his hometown of Newark where he purchased and operated the Washington House Hotel. Willis remained active in baseball, managing semipro and coaching at the youth and college level. He also spent time enjoying golf and raising bird dogs. Vic Willis was 71 when he died in Elkton, Maryland, on August 3, 1947, the victim of a stroke.

## SOURCES

Many sources were consulted in preparing this biography. The most useful were *The Sporting News* (many issues), Harold Kaese's *The Boston Braves* (Putnam, 1948), Fred Lieb's *The Pittsburgh Pirates* (Putnam, 1948), Lois P. Nicholson's *Maryland to Cooperstown* (Tidewater, 1998), Stephen Cunerd's article, "Vic Willis: Turn of the Century Great," from SABR's 1989 *Baseball Research Journal*, several annual *Reach Guides*, Dennis DeValeria and Jeanne Burke DeValeria's *Honus Wagner* (Henry Holt, 1996), and Vic Willis's file at the National Baseball Hall of Fame library.

## NOTES

1. *The Sporting News*, February 12, 1898.
2. "Has Elusive Curves," *Boston Sunday Journal*, July 2, 1899.
3. "It's Done by Instinct," *Fort Wayne Daily News*, January 28, 1911.
4. Vin Mannix, "Persistence Pays Off for Grandson," *Florida News*, March 20, 1995.
5. *The Sporting News*, January 16, 1906.
6. "The National League's Showplace," The Reach Official American League Baseball Guide for 1910, (Philadelphia: A.J. Reach Company, 2010), 126.
7. Frederick G. Lieb, *The Pittsburgh Pirates* (Carbondale, Illinois: Southern Illinois University Press, 2003), 133.
8. *The Sporting News*, February 24, 1910.
9. "Sporting News in Tablet," *Fort Wayne Daily News*, January 12, 1911.

# CY YOUNG

## BY BILL NOWLIN AND DAVID SOUTHWICK

**CY YOUNG IS A NAME FAMILIAR TO** all but the most casual of baseball fans, well over 100 years after his pitching career ended. After all, he is the one the Cy Young Award is named after, the award given every year to the pitcher in each league. Young also holds numerous baseball records, including some that are unlikely to be broken, including both the most wins by any pitcher (511) and the most complete games (749).[1]

The years in which Young pitched in the major leagues (1890-1911) saw a number of significant changes in baseball, which included an increase in the distance from the pitcher's mound to home plate, and the introduction of the foul strike rule.[2] Fifteen times Young was a 20-game winner, and in five of those seasons he was actually a 30-game winner. There were even three seasons when he lost more than 20 games, but each time he came back and won as many as or more the following year.

He was present at the birth of the American League and threw the first pitch ever thrown in a World Series game. Winning three games in the 1903 World Series, Young also stands as the only pitcher to win a game in both the Temple Cup, the postseason championship series that had obtained in the National League in the years 1894-1897, and in the World Series, which began in the twentieth century.

Denton True Young was born on March 29, 1867, in Gilmore, Ohio, the oldest of five children of McKinzie Young Jr. and Nancy (Miller) Young. Gilmore was a small farming community about 100 miles south of Cleveland, and the Young family was raised on a farm owned by McKinzie's father, McKinzie Sr. "Dent's" education stopped after the sixth grade at the town's two-room school so he could help his parents with farming chores, but it was also at this time that he discovered the game of baseball. Encouraged by their father, who had been a private in the Union Army during the Civil War, the Young boys played baseball every chance they got. Developing into a better pitcher than hitter, Denton practiced throwing during lunch breaks from farm work ("I usta kill squirrels with a stone when I was a kid.")[3] Besides practicing and playing in recreational games, he organized his own team in Gilmore, then in the summer of 1884 he played on semipro teams in Newcomerstown, Cadiz, and Uhrichsville, Ohio.

Young did not enter professional baseball at a young age. Four years later, he was still playing semipro ball in Carrollton, Ohio, earning $1 a game.[4] In 1889 he played for Leesburg and New Athens, Ohio. Professional teams began to bid for his services.

Young hoped to one day marry the girl from the adjacent farm, Robba Miller, and he saw an opportunity to make money playing baseball. For $60 per month, he signed for the 1890 season with Canton, Ohio, of the Tri-States League. He was 23 years old.

It was in Canton during the preseason that Young picked up the moniker "Cyclone."[5] During the 14 weeks he played for Canton, he started 29 games and relieved in two. He was 15-15 for a team that finished last, but struck out 201 batters while walking only 33.[6] His final game for Canton was on June 25 at Pastime Park. He threw a no-hitter, and struck out 18 batters without walking a man.[7] A few days later, Young's contract was purchased by the National League's Cleveland Spiders for $300, and a few days after that, the Canton ballclub folded.[8]

Young's quick ascendancy to the majors was the result of the emergence of the ill-fated Players League, which forced National League teams to dig deep into the minor leagues for any available talent. Young's weight is listed as ranging from 170 pounds in his younger years to 210 pounds. He pitched his first major-league game on August 6, 1890, against Cap Anson's Chicago Colts. Before the game, Anson reportedly called Young "just another big farmer."[9] Young threw a three-hitter, beating the Colts 8-1.

He had his first big-league win. He won his next two starts as well. But the Spiders were a seventh-place team that year and finished 44-88, Young ended the season with a record of 9-7, by virtue of pitching and winning both games of a doubleheader on the final day of the season. He recorded a 3.46 earned-run average in that first partial season, striking out 39 and walking 30. He was the only Spider with a winning record.

In 1891 Young was the ace of the Spiders staff. The team finished fifth, but still with a losing record, 65-74. Young was a 20-game winner, however — in fact, a 27-game winner. He was 27-22 (2.85) in 55 games, 46 of them as the starter (he worked 43 complete games, throwing 423⅔ innings.) He was still doling out too many bases on balls, walking 140 opponents while striking out 140.

Though he had pitched a number of very good games, Young's first shutout came on April 15, 1892, when he beat Cincinnati 2-0. Fellow pitcher Nig Cuppy had an excellent 28-13 season, but Cy Young led the league in both wins and winning percentage (36-12), with a league-leading 1.93 ERA. His nine shutouts also led the league. The team finished in second place, but with two 35-game winners (Kid Nichols and Jack Stivetts, with identical 35-16 records, and a 22-game winner in Harry Staley to boot), the Boston Beaneaters were hard to beat. Boston finished 8½ games ahead of Cleveland. The two teams played a postseason "World Series" and the first game pitted Young against Stivetts. Neither pitcher gave up a run; the game ended 0-0 after 11 innings. Boston won the series.

After the 1982 season, Young married Robba Miller on November 8.

Between the 1892 and 1893 seasons, a significant change was implemented: the distance between the pitcher and batter was increased from 55 feet 6 inches to 60 feet 6 inches. Unsurprisingly, this helped the offense and thus did something of a number on Cy Young's ERA, which climbed to 3.36. Despite struggling to make the adjustment, pitchers still won games and lost them and Young was 34-16. He had finished strong, winning 16 of his last 20 decisions.

He walked one more batter than he struck out (103-102), but averaged only 2.2 walks per nine innings, best in the league. It was a statistic in which Young led the league 14 times. From 1893 through 1901, he led the league nine years in a row in a stat that one could argue best represented control. (In fact, his strikeouts-to-walks ratio of 0.99 was best in the league, too, among qualifying pitchers.)

In 1893 Young's ERA increased by 1.43 runs per game, and the league as a whole similarly saw an increase from 3.28 runs to 4.66 (1.38). And the next year (1894) the league ERA increased to 5.33. Young's went up, too, to 3.94, which we now see as the worst of his career. At one point, he lost seven decisions in a row. The 1894 Spiders dropped to sixth place; Young was 26-21.

In 1895 Young won 35 games and lost only 10. He struck out 121 and only walked 75. He brought his ERA down to 3.26, and the Spiders finished in second place, three games behind the Baltimore Orioles. The top two teams in the National League faced off in the best-of-seven postseason Temple Cup series. Young won Games One, Three, and the clinching Game Five.

He started slow in 1896, but then went on a 14-4 tear and on July 23 pitched a masterpiece, a no-hitter through 8⅔ innings, giving up a hit, then retiring the next batter to win the game. He was 28-15, with an ERA that was basically stable (3.24). His 140 strikeouts led the league. At some point during the season, Young started doing something he hadn't done before in his career—he started wearing a glove. Heretofore he had pitched without a glove on.

Young also did something else in 1896—he umpired in a game. In fact, he umpired in two games. If the umpire failed to turn up, teams typically agreed upon someone to perform the role. On June 19, something else happened. In the seventh inning, umpire Tom Lynch not only ejected Cleveland manager Patsy Tebeau but had to be physically restrained from assaulting him, held back by Chicago players. Lynch refused to umpire the rest of the game, so the teams decided to ask Young to umpire, along with the Chicago Colts' Con Daily.[10]

On July 29 in Cincinnati, Young umpired a second game when the scheduled arbiter didn't show up. The Cincinnati Reds provided Frank Foreman and the Spiders provided Young. In July 1903, Young umpired two games in the American League. Young played baseball at a fractious time, but was widely respected for his probity. Never once was he ejected from a ballgame.

Young's 1897 season saw him a 20-game winner for the seventh season in succession (21-19), but his ERA rose half a run to 3.78. One of his wins was his first no-hitter, on September 19, a 6-0 win over Cincinnati. The Reds batters, wrote the *Cleveland Plain Dealer*, "walked up to be slaughtered only because the rules required and not for the good it did them."[11] Cleveland finished in fifth place again. By the time the season was over, Young had 216 wins to his credit.

Young's ERA improved dramatically in 1898, more than a full run, from 3.78 to 2.53. He was 25-13 for another fifth-place club. In 46 games, including 40 complete games in 41 starts, he walked only 41 batters. It was his last year pitching for Cleveland.

This isn't the place to go into the story of how brothers Frank and Stanley Robison came to own not just the Cleveland club but also the St. Louis team, too—the Perfectos. With no prohibition against it, they concentrated their best players in St. Louis. On paper, it was simply a matter of assigning the player's contract from one team to the other. Young had another excellent year, for St. Louis: 26-16 (2.58), another 40 complete games, and only 44 walks in 44 games.

In 1900 St. Louis changed its name to the Cardinals. The National League contracted from 12 teams to eight, so any pitcher was inevitably facing a better array of hitters. After nine consecutive seasons of 20 or more wins—every season since his first, which was only a partial season—Young finished one win shy: 19-19. He actually thought he had won 20 games, and it was reported as such at the time in both *The Sporting News* and the *Spalding Guide* but, as Reed Browning explains, later reconstruction of the historical record (including regularizing scoring rules) deprived him of one victory. The count at the time showed Young with 20 wins, and had everyone believed he was one win short of the number, there were two opportunities that might have been handled otherwise and given him a shot to reach 20.[12]

When the syndicate of owners that controlled both the Cleveland and St. Louis franchises shifted Young to St. Louis in 1899, the pitcher's overpowering fastball began to lose some of its steam. His failure to win 20 games in 1900 resulted because a bruised rib suffered in a collision with the New York Giants' Ed Doheny caused him to miss significant playing time for the first time in his career. Additionally, as the summer progressed and Young suffered his share of tough losses, the normally quiet and reserved star uncharacteristically vented his frustration, charging into the stands on August 20 to confront a heckler who had accused him of quitting on the team. The Perfectos slumped into fifth place, 10 games below .500.

After the 1900 season, Young jumped to the nascent American League and won well over 20 games for each of the next four seasons, averaging more than 27 wins per year and twice topping 30 victories. Honus Wagner, who regularly faced Young in the National League toward the end of the decade, thought Young had the greatest fastball he had ever seen. "Walter Johnson was fast, but no faster than Rusie," Wagner observed. "And Rusie was no faster than Johnson. But Young was faster than both of 'em!"[13] Another contemporary, Cap Anson, observed that when the 6-foot-2, 210-pound Young unleashed his speed, it seemed as if "the ball was shooting down from the hands of a giant."[14]

After the 1900 season ended, several St. Louis players defected to the American League, including catcher Lou Criger, Young's batterymate, who signed with Boston. Though he was hounded by Boston's owner, Charles Somers, for several weeks, the cautious Young did not sign with the Americans until March 19, 1901. St. Louis owner Frank Robison had declined to match Boston's salary offer of $3,500, insisting that Young, about to turn 34, was just about all washed up.[15]

Along with that of Napoleon Lajoie, Young's defection to the American League in 1901 generated instant credibility for the upstart circuit. The winner of 286 games in his first 11 seasons, Young had established himself as a model of consistency and excellence, pitching more than 300 innings every year from 1891 to 1900 and ranking among the National League's top five in earned-run average six times during that span. Still, cracks were starting to show in the great pitcher's façade. At 34, Young had already entered the phase of his career when most pitchers start to break down. Indeed, in 1900, some opposing batters attested that Young was more hittable than ever, and newspaper reporters began routinely affixing the adjective Old in front of his name. By all appearances, then, when the Boston Americans signed Young, his agreement secured by a three-year contract, the acquisition might have been thought to represent more a public-relations coup than a legitimate pitching upgrade.

As it turned out, Boston, not to mention the rest of the American League, got much more than it could have expected. He demonstrated that he was far from washed up.

During his eight years with the Americans (later called the Red Sox), Young won 192 games, becoming the first major-league hurler to pitch effectively into his 40s.[16] In 1901, his first season with the Americans, one can argue that he had the advantage of facing competition watered down by the sudden addition of eight new major-league teams. Nonetheless, Young enjoyed one of the greatest pitching seasons in baseball history. Though he lost his first start, on April 30 he won the first game in Red Sox history, thanks to Buck Freeman's game-tying two-run homer in the ninth inning and two more Boston runs in the 10th. The 8-6 win was also the first extra-inning game in American League history.

On May 8, 1901, Young won the Americans' first home game, beating the Philadelphia Athletics, 12-4. He led the league in victories (33), strikeouts (158), and earned-run average (1.62), a feat now called pitching's Triple Crown. He also led the league in shutouts (5). In 371⅓ innings, he walked just 37 batters. Asked to explain his success, Young said, "I have almost perfect control of the ball this year, and I try to keep it bumping over the plate. If two or three men get on bases, I put on a little more steam and shoot 'em over as fast as I can—but I try all the time to keep 'em over."[17] *Sporting Life* suggested that Young was "like wine … better with age."[18] And, counting 1902, he still had five more 20-win seasons in him.

The many photos of Young that survive from this period portray a man advancing in years and gaining in weight. But as his girth expanded, his control sharpened; five times after 1900 he led the league in fewest walks per nine innings. And though his fastball lost some of its zip, the wily Young more than made up for it with a pair of curveballs, one thrown overhand with a sharp break, the other thrown sidearm with a sweeping arc. Both pitches were delivered from a variety of arm angles; occasionally Young even threw submarine-style to upset the batter's timing. In his continued mastery of opposing batters in the face of declining strength and advancing age, Young raised pitching to an art form, and earned his place in baseball's pantheon of all-time greats. "If I were asked who was the greatest pitcher the game ever knew, I would say Cy Young," sportswriter Francis Richter wrote in 1910, when Young was 43 years old. "Cy is now pitching as good ball today as he did twenty years ago."[19]

From late February into early April of 1902, Young even took a position as pitching coach of the Harvard baseball team.[20]

Over the next three seasons (1902-04), the American League's talent pool expanded vastly as more players made the jump to the junior circuit, but Young remained unfazed by the new arrivals. He led the league in victories in 1902 and 1903, and finished second in 1904. His 32-11 mark in 1902 was the fifth time he'd won more than 30 games (1892, 1893, 1895, and 1901 were the other seasons.)

In 1903, the American League adopted the "foul strike rule" that the National League had adopted in 1901. It's the same rule fans are familiar with ever since: The first two foul balls struck by a batter counted as strikes. Before that, fouls simply did not count. Needless to say, the rule was of benefit to pitchers. But pitchers still won and lost games, and Young won more than any of his counterparts.

Though he began to rely more exclusively on his assortment of breaking pitches, Young's control remained as sharp as ever: In 1904 he walked just 29 in 380 innings while striking out an even 200.

There was a remarkable road-trip stretch in 1903, when Young beat Detroit 1-0 on June 23, then beat St. Louis 1-0 on June 28, and beat Chicago 1-0 on July 1, in 10 innings. Throwing back-to-back-to-back 1-0 games had never been done before, and has never been done since.

In 1903, Young had his best season at the plate, batting .321 in 137 at-bats. Only outfielder Patsy Dougherty (.331) hit for a higher average on the Red Sox; the team average was .272 that year. Young's lifetime mark was .210, however, and he didn't get on base much more often than that. (Be had a .234 career on-base percentage.) He drove in 290 runs, and scored 325. He homered 18 times. As a fielder, working on rougher fields, Young had a major-league .939 fielding percentage.

Young's prowess on the mound helped the Americans win back-to-back pennants in 1903 and 1904, and though teammate Bill Dinneen stole the spotlight in Boston's best-of-nine victory over Pittsburgh in the first modern World Series (1903), Young aided the cause with a 2-1 record and a 1.85 ERA. He threw the first pitch in a modern World Series and, after giving up four runs in the first inning, suffered the first loss, 7-3.

In the best-of-nine Series, Young won Game Five in Pittsburgh, 11-2, preventing the Pirates from taking a four-games-to-one lead, and won Game Seven, 7-3, giving Boston a four-games-to-three edge and setting the stage for the triumphant clinching game back in Boston three days later, a 3-0 shutout for Dinneen.

Young's greatest achievement may have come on May 5, 1904, when at the age of 37 he pitched the first perfect game in American League history—just the third in the major leagues and the first from the 60-foot-6-inch pitching distance. Losing pitcher Rube Waddell of the Philadelphia Athletics, who had defeated Young in their previous encounter a week earlier, taunted the old pitcher, promising to beat him again. After Young pitched his masterpiece and Boston won, 3-0, Cy uncharacteristically returned fire, shouting to Waddell, "How did you like that one, you hayseed?"[21] It was Young's second career no-hitter (his first came in 1897); he would pitch a third in 1908, against the New York Highlanders.

Young's perfection against the Athletics came in the midst of a major-league record 24 consecutive innings in which the pitcher did not allow a single hit, as well as a scoreless innings streak that stretched to a then-record 45 innings.[22] "And they said Uncle Cy was all in, did they?" observed Boston catcher Duke Farrell of his 37-year-old teammate. "He fooled them, didn't he?"[23] Down the stretch, Young continued to impress, pitching shutouts in each of his last three starts to help the Americans to their narrow pennant victory over the Highlanders. In 1938, Johnny Vander Meer threw no-hitters in consecutive starts but even so, his streak of hitless innings topped out at 22.

Boston won the 1904 pennant, helped in good measure by Young throwing three consecutive shutouts (increasing his season total to 10) in his final three starts—October 2 (2-0), October 5 (3-0), and beating New York in Boston in the second game of an October 8 doubleheader, 1-0. After that win the two teams traveled to New York, and Boston won the pennant by winning the first game of two scheduled for October 10. The Americans would have gone on to play the New York Giants in the World Series, but the Giants refused to play them. Even the New York press fiercely mocked Giants owner John T. Brush for denying baseball fans the opportunity to see the top team in each league play a head-to-head postseason series.

Boston plunged in the standings in 1905, to fourth place, 16 games behind the Athletics, and then all the way to the cellar in 1906, an incredible 45½ games out of first. Their record was 49-105 (.318).[24] Only in 1932 (43-111, .279) did the team have a worse season.

Proving the point that it takes a team to win, Young lost one more game than he won in 1905 (18-19), despite a 1.82 ERA that was third in the league. In 1906 he was 13-21 with a 3.19 ERA, but his .382 winning percentage was still 64 points better than the team's. Remarkably, in both years, Young's FIP led the majors. Fielding Independent Pitching is a statistic designed to measure a pitcher's effectiveness at preventing home runs, walks, and hit batsmen, and in striking out opponents—four things that are within the control of the pitcher and not dependent on his fielders.

But 1906 was a year in which Young started the season 1-8 and failed to shut out the opposition even once.

Almost three-quarters of the way through the 1906 campaign, Chick Stahl had succeeded Jimmy Collins as manager of the 1906 Bostons. Near the end of 1907 spring training, however, he unexpectedly committed suicide. Young stepped in and managed the team for the few spring-training games that remained as well as the first six games of the regular season. The team was 3-3 when he handed the reins over to George Huff, the first of four managers for the 1907 team. Young returned to good form in 1907, with another 20-win season. He threw six shutouts and recorded a 1.99 earned-run average; he was 21-15 for the seventh-place team. In early September, he and his wife became parents for the first time, only to lose their daughter a few hours after she was born. On September 9, he pitched a 13-inning scoreless tie game against Rube Waddell, but he lost all four games he started after that.

The Boston Americans became the Boston Red Sox in 1908 and Cy Young had another superb season. He won his first four games by scores of 3-1, 8-1, 7-0, and 5-1. And on May 30, he threw a one-hitter, beating Washington 6-0 in the first game of a morning-afternoon doubleheader. On June 30 he topped that, throwing a no-hitter and a near-perfect game against the Highlanders. He walked the leadoff man, Harry Niles, but Niles was thrown out trying to steal second and Young disposed of the next 26 batters without a man reaching base. It was the third no-hitter of his career. The *Boston Journal* suggested that the walk had been a "gift of the umpire."[25] Young even drove in four of Boston's eight runs.

Young was 41 years old. At season's end, he had an ERA of 1.26 (second only to Addie Joss's 1.16) and a record of 21-11. The team finished fifth, at 75-79.

In the wake of Young's historic accomplishments, much of the baseball world began to acknowledge his unparalleled place in the pantheon of great pitchers. "Rusies have come and gone, in their turn, by Cy Young still pitches on," observed the *Detroit Tribune*. "Perhaps no ballplayer ever lived who paid stricter attention to business and who came out of a long series of honors showered on him with lesser opinion of himself and with such strict attention to temperate habits."[26] For his part, Young placed no special emphasis on his remarkable durability and longevity. He downplayed the significance of his offseason conditioning program, which consisted mostly of splitting wood at his Peoli, Ohio, farmhouse. "It isn't any secret," Young said, "just outdoor life, moderation, and a naturally good arm. I don't know that I take any better care of myself than any other pitcher does, it just happens, this thing of my lasting. It isn't the result of any system."[27] The farm featured corn, chickens, and sheep. Young apparently also raised hunting dogs and "constructed and sold large trunks, fashioned to meet the needs of traveling ballplayers and widely used in the major leagues."[28]

In an era when ballplayers were often regarded as dissolute, inveterate slackers, Young won praise for his clean living and moderate temperament. He prided himself on his work ethic, and reacted with indignation when accused of easing up with a big lead. "When you see me let any club make runs off my pitching on purpose," he snarled, "come around and I'll give you a brand new hundred dollar bill."[29] Easing up, he declared, placed the game "on the level with lawn tennis, tiddle-de-winks, or some other schoolgirl frivolity."[30] Later in life Young articulated a personal philosophy for playing the game the right way by enumerating five rules of conduct: 1) Be moderate in all things; 2) don't abuse yourself; 3) don't bait umpires; 4) play hard; and 5) render faithful service to your employer. Adhering to this creed, Young continued to enjoy success long after other pitchers had left the game. Thus, his unbreakable career records (511 victories, 7,354⅔ innings, 749 complete games) were the product not just of exceptional talent and good fortune, they were also the result of his own exacting standards.

Young won 477 complete games, fully 60 more than Walter Johnson. Only five times did he win a game that he had started but not completed.[31]

As Young approached and then passed his 40th birthday, he continued to rank among the game's best pitchers, thanks in large part to the wide assortment of breaking pitches and arm deliveries he employed to fool opposing batters. "If a right-hander crowded my plate," Young said after retiring as a player, "I sidearmed him with a curve, and then, when he stepped back, I'd throw an overhand fastball low and outside. I was fortunate in having good speed from overhand, three-quarter, or sidearm. I had a variety of curves — threw a so-called screwball or indrop, too — and I used whatever delivery seemed best. And I never had but one sore arm."[32] After enduring the worst season of his career in 1906, when he finished the year 13-21 for the woeful (49-105) Americans with a terrible 3.19 ERA, Young came back strong in 1907 and 1908, winning 21 games in each season and posting ERAs of 1.99 and 1.26, respectively. The 1906 season was the third year in which he'd lost 20 or more games; in 1891 he had been 27-22 and in 1894 he had been 26-21.

Lest we forget, pitchers and batters both lacked the analytic tools offered today by video and computers. They also typically worked without the kind of professional coaching that supports players a century later.

In February 1909 Young, then 42, was traded by Boston to the Cleveland Naps for Charlie Chech, Jack Ryan, and $12,500 cash. Back in the city where he had started his big-league career 19 years before, Young enjoyed one more solid season, going 19-15 with a 2.26 ERA. The first time he faced the Red Sox, on May 13 in Cleveland, he lost 8-1 but his first game pitching again in Boston was a two-hitter on June 11, a 3-1 win. He might have won 20 but for an injury on September 10. He finished the season with 497 victories.

The following year, Young started only 20 games, finishing with a 7-10 record. He won number 499 with a two-hitter on June 30 (no runner reached second base), and booked number 500 on July 19. In that one he allowed one hit through the first eight, but it took 11 innings to wrap it up, a win over Washington. The Senators held a 2-0 lead through eight, but the Indians tied it in the ninth and scored three times in the 11th.

Young then won four more in a row, but after August 9 didn't win any. He wasn't used in the last several weeks of the season. Still, he resisted calls for him to retire from the game. "Quit the game, well, I guess not," Young told a Cleveland reporter. "I'd be awfully lonesome, and you know this is a healthy game. I'll not quit until I have to."[33]

In 1911 the 44-year-old Young fared even worse, going 3-4 with a 3.88 ERA in seven starts before drawing his release on August 15. He was quickly picked up by the Boston Rustlers of the National League, who wanted him, according to one writer, "just to draw the crowd."[34] Young started 11 games for Boston down the stretch, going 4-5 with a 3.71 ERA. Despite much speculation that he would retire, Young attempted to hang on with the Rustlers (later the Braves) for the 1912 season, remaining with the team through spring training and warming the bench for the first month of the campaign. During spring training, *Sporting Life* had a little fun with Young's longevity: "The old boy is said to look better than any previous season since 1663, considered by many to be his best years since the Summer of 1169."[35]

But a chronically sore arm prevented Young from ever taking the field; when he attempted to do so, on May 23, he gave up after a brief warmup session, declaring, "It's no use. I'm not going on. These poor fellows have lost too many games already."[36] Finally Young's major-league career was officially over. He was 45 years old.

In 1913, the independent Federal League began play. The six-team league had franchises in Indianapolis, Cleveland, St. Louis, Chicago, Pittsburgh, and Covington, Kentucky. (The latter team relocated to Kansas City near the end of June.) Young managed the Cleveland Green Sox. They finished second, with a record of 64-54, 10 games behind Indianapolis. When the league reopened in 1914, it was as a third major league but Cleveland was not among the cities in the league.

In retirement, Cy returned to his home in Peoli, where he lived out a quiet retirement on his farm, growing potatoes and tending to his sheep, hogs, and chickens. He and his wife, Robba, did not raise any children; the death of their only offspring, a daughter, a few hours after her birth in 1907, left, in the words of Young biographer Reed Browning, "an almost inexpungeable hole" in their lives.[37] When Robba died in January 1933, a grieving Young sold his farm. "Somehow, after she died I didn't want to live there any more," he said.[38] Elected to the Baseball Hall of Fame in 1937, Young was inducted with the Hall's first class at the museum's opening in 1939.

Despite his frugal habits and status as a baseball legend, Young was beset by financial problems late in life. In 1935 he traveled to Augusta, Georgia, where he joined a group of baseball veterans looking to make some money during the Great Depression by playing exhibition games. When this venture failed, Young returned to Ohio, where he found work as a clerk in a retail store in Newcomerstown and lived with a local couple, John and Ruth Benedum. He was invited to, and attended, reunions of old-timers around the country. He was still living with the Benedums when he died of a coronary occlusion on November 4, 1955, at the age of 88. He was buried in Peoli Cemetery. The next year, baseball instituted the pitching award that bears his name.

Note: An earlier version of this biography originally appeared in David Jones, ed., *Deadball Stars of the American League* (Washington, D.C.: Potomac Books, Inc., 2006).

## SOURCES

In addition to the sources cited in the Notes, the author also consulted Baseball-Reference.com, Retrosheet.org, Baseballhalloffame.org, and the *Encyclopedia of Minor League Baseball*, as well as the *Boston Globe*, *Boston Post*, *New York Times*, and *Washington Post*.

The most indispensable source for Cy Young's life and career is Reed Browning's *Cy Young: A Baseball Life* (Amherst, Massachusetts: University of Massachusetts Press, 2003).

Other sources:

Ivor-Campbell, Fred, ed. *Baseball's First Stars* (Cleveland: SABR, 1996).

Masur, Louis P. *Autumn Glory:* Baseball's First World Series (New York: Hill & Wang, 2003).

## NOTES

1. Reed Browning the difficulty in determining accurately the number of Young's wins, suggesting that it may range from 508 to 513, but essentially agreeing that 511 is the number that researchers accept. Browning, 226-230.
2. We touch on these notes changes in the course of this brief biography.
3. Arthur Daley, *Times at Bat: A Half-Century of Baseball* (New York: Random House, 1950), 7.
4. This per a typed sheet in Young's player file at the National Baseball Hall of Fame.
5. *Canton* (Ohio) *Repository,* April 28, 1890, per Browning, 8.
6. Alvin K. Peterjohn, "First Year of Cyclone Young," *Baseball Research Journal* 5, 1976: 83-89.
7. "Couldn't Hit Young," *The Repository* (Canton), July 26, 1890: 3.
8. Peterjohn. The sum of $300 is reported by Browning, 10.
9. Browning, 12.
10. "His Fists," *Cleveland Leader*, June 20, 1896: 1.
11. "Young's Record," *Cleveland Plain Dealer*, September 19, 1897: 8.
12. Browning, 85-86.
13. Connie Mack, *My 66 Years in the Big Leagues* (Mineola, New York: Dover Publications, 2009), 91-92.
14. *Sporting Life*, July 18, 1891; quoted in Browning, 152.
15. Browning, 91.
16. His 192 wins for Boston remain a Red Sox franchise record, tied with Roger Clemens.
17. Unidentified newspaper clipping in Young's Hall of Fame player file.
18. *Sporting Life*, August 2, 1902: 11.
19. Francis Richter, unidentified 1910 newspaper clipping in Young's Hall of Fame player file.
20. "Baseball Coach Appointed," *Harvard Crimson*, February 10, 1902.
21. Browning, 144.
22. The current record (59) is held by Orel Hershiser.
23. Browning, 144.
24. It was not a good year for baseball in Boston. The National League's Boston Beaneaters (Braves) also won only 49 games, and lost 102.
25. "No Hit, No Run for 'Yanks' Off King Cy Young," *Boston Journal*, July 1, 1908: 1.
26. *Detroit Tribune*, quoted in "Cy Young's Life Is Simple Story," *Pittsburgh Weekly Gazette*, December 27, 1904: 7.
27. Alfred Henry Spink, *The National Game: A History of Baseball, America's Leading Out-door Sport, From the Time It Was First Played Up to the Present Day, with Illustrations and Biographical Sketches* (St. Louis: National Game Publishing Co, 1911), 166.
28. Browning, 97.
29. There were reports that both Lou Criger and Young had rebuffed very lucrative offers to throw games in the 1903 World Series. See Browning, 137-140.
30. *Sporting Life*, November 25, 1893.
31. Browning, 226.
32. Unidentified newspaper clipping in Young's Hall of Fame player file.
33. *Cleveland Leader*, August 21, 1910: 3, 1.
34. "Murnane Musings," Tim Murnane, *The Sporting News*, August 31, 1911: 3.
35. "National League News in Short Metre," *Sporting Life*, March 16, 1912: 11.
36. Arthur D. Hittner, *Honus Wagner: The Life of Baseball's "Flying Dutchman"* (Jefferson, North Carolina: McFarland, 1996), 212. Hittner was quoting the *Pittsburgh Gazette Times*.
37. Browning, 171. The baby girl's name, if indeed one had been chosen, did not appear in newspapers.
38. Browning found Young's remark in an unidentified clipping from 1944 in the Cy Young player file at the National Baseball Hall of Fame. More easily done in years gone by, there were apparently some impostors, or fanciful stories. A 1909 article in the *Oklahoma City Daily Oklahoman* reported the marriage of Miss Annie Dechman ("one of Oklahoma City's really popular society belles") to "well-known baseball pitcher" Cy Young. The newspaper did report skeptical reaction to the news from Dechman's friends: "It didn't sound probable, not even possible." Nonetheless, the young bride and whoever else was on the telephone both confirmed it. See "Young Wedding Is All a Surprise," *Daily Oklahoman*, November 20, 1909: 8.

# A TEAM WITH FOUR 20-GAME LOSERS

## BY BILL NOWLIN

**AS WE HAVE SEEN, THERE ARE LOTS** of different kinds of 20-game losers, even nearly two dozen of whom became Hall of Famers. We noticed that more than once there was a team that had two pitchers who each lost 20 or more games.

It was with some surprise, however, that we discovered a team with *four* 20-game losers—in the same year. It seems almost mathematically impossible. After all, that meant just those four pitchers alone accounted for 80 losses. Actually, it was worse than 80—although one was a 20-game winner, not one of the quartet lost as *few* as 20 games. The four pitchers collectively lost 94 games, and this was in the days of the 154-game schedule.

The 1905 Boston Beaneaters managed to achieve this distinction. We decided to give them their own section in this book.

The four pitchers were:

Irv Young (20-21)

Chick Fraser (14-21)

Kaiser Wilhelm (3-23)

… and the future Hall of Famer in the group, Vic Willis (12-29).

Willis's biography we have included in the section on Hall of Famers. The other three are presented here.

The Beaneaters finished with a 51-103 record in 1905, but they didn't finish in last place. The Brooklyn Superbas (48-104) were marginally worse despite boasting only two 20-game losers, Mal Eason (5-21) and Harry McIntire (8-25).

As it happens, the 1906 Boston National League team managed to surpass (if that is the word) the 1905 team. They did manage to finish last—66½ games out of first place, the first year in franchise history that the team placed last. They have four 20-game losers, too. For the record, the four in 1906 were:

Big Jeff Pfeffer (13-22)

Vive Lindaman (12-23)

Gus Dorner (8-25), and our returning friend from 1905 back for more:

Irv Young (16-25)

That totals 95 losses, topping the 1905 crew by one. It's impossible for a pitcher to win a game if his team fails to score even one run. The 1906 Boston Doves (as they were called) were shut out 28 times. In nine starts, Young saw the team shut out. Lindaman lost eight shutouts, Dorner lost seven, and Pfeffer lost four

The 1907 Doves had only one 20-game loser: Irv Young, for the third year in a row.

Enjoy the three bios in this section, and find Vic Willis among the Hall of Famers.

# CHARLES "CHICK" FRASER

BY MIKE LYNCH

**CHICK FRASER SPENT HIS ENTIRE LIFE** in baseball as a pitcher, coach, scout, and minor-league manager, and though his playing career wasn't especially successful it was certainly unique. He went 175-212 over 14 seasons, lost at least 20 games in a season five times, including three straight from 1904-1906, and ranks second all-time with 219 hit batters. He's one of only three pitchers with fewer than 200 wins but more than 200 losses and is the only modern-era pitcher to lose 20 games three years in a row with three different teams.

Charles Carrolton Fraser was born on August 26, 1873, in Chicago to Alexander and Agnes (Sturrock) Fraser, both of whom were born in Scotland.[1] Alexander Fraser (1846-1902) worked as a stationary engineer in Chicago. His wife, Agnes (1838-1908), had three children with him, Charles's older brother David dying in 1878. It's not clear when Fraser began playing baseball or where he got his nickname, but by the time he was 14 in 1887 he was reportedly a "star slabman" for the West End Juniors, for whom he pitched through his teenage years.[2]

*Sporting Life* editor Francis Richter saw Fraser allow 27 runs in a game as a 17-year-old and though he called the young twirler "hard-working and enterprising," Richter had doubts that Fraser would make good as a major leaguer.[3]

He declared that the Chicago native "was not counted anything above the scores of other boys who were twirling on the lots," and he "never expected to see him rise above mediocrity."[4] He credited Fraser for having success at the 50-foot distance before the mound was moved back to 60 feet 6 inches in 1893, but also lamented that the pitcher was "all speed and no head."[5]

In 1891 Fraser's presence on the Garden Citys team of the City League caused controversy when an opponent filed a protest, claiming that Fraser was a professional.[6] According to Richter, Fraser did in fact play professionally in Burlington, Iowa, but it's not known whether that was before or after he joined the Garden Citys.[7] Regardless, he became a professional in 1894 when he pitched for the Milwaukee Brewers and Minneapolis Minnies of the Western League. His 12-18 record at the age of 20 foreshadowed most of his career.

Fraser shouldered a huge workload in 1895 when he tossed a combined 413 innings en route to a 23-20 record with Minneapolis and a 3-3 mark with San Francisco in the California Winter League. The National League St. Louis Browns were so impressed that they were prepared to offer third baseman Ike Samuels, pitcher Bill Kissinger, and minor-league catcher John Rappold to Minneapolis for Fraser, but he ended up with the Louisville Colonels instead.

Fraser started the first game of the 1896 season against Cap Anson's Chicago Colts and lost 4-2. It was all downhill from there. The 22-year-old went 12-27 for a team that went 38-93 and finished last in the NL, and only two pitchers lost more games. Fraser led the league with 166 walks and 27 wild pitches, and only one pitcher hit more batters than Fraser's 29. The Colonels improved in 1897 and finished in 11th place with a 52-78 record, and Fraser paced the squad with 15 wins, but also led the league again with 22 wild pitches, and finished among the five worst in walks and hit batsmen.

Fraser began to wear out his welcome in 1898 despite another improvement under manager Fred Clarke, who was in his first full campaign as skipper and arguably the team's best player. The Colonels went 70-81 and finished in ninth place, but lost 10 of Fraser's first 12 assignments, including an embarrassing 16-2 drubbing in Fraser's hometown on April 29 in which his team committed eight errors, while the hurler walked seven and hit one batter.

In early July, Clarke married Fraser's wife's sister, Annette B. Gray, solidifying an already strong bond between the two men that often had Fraser spending winters at Clarke's ranch in Akron, Kansas, where they would hunt, fish, and lasso steer owned by Clarke's brother.[8] But that didn't stop Fraser from voicing his desire to leave Louisville. *Sporting Life* insisted Clarke couldn't get the best out of Fraser and that if Fraser were able to pitch for a different manager he'd be a "star of the first magnitude."[9]

Things finally came to a head in early August when Fraser claimed to have a sore arm not long after being removed from a game against Brooklyn. Rumors, however, were that the only thing hurt was his pride and the lame arm was a ruse.[10] Fraser finally got his wish and was sold to the Cleveland Spiders in early September for approximately $500. With Cleveland he went 2-3 to finish the year at 9-20.[11] Despite a then-career-low 245 innings, Fraser managed to hit 29 more batters, good for second worst in the NL.[12]

An unnamed Louisville official thought Fraser hadn't been pitching to win and that only his relationship with Clarke had kept the club from shipping him out sooner. Francis Richter even went so far as to claim that Fraser was one of the two most unpopular players in Louisville's history.[13] Clarke explained that one reason they parted with his brother-in-law was his disposition: "He doesn't get sore when he loses a hard game."[14]

Fraser was returned to Louisville at the end of the season, prompting him to consider retirement to become a full-time electrician, but he was sold to the Philadelphia Phillies in December and changed his mind. Fraser enjoyed a surprisingly successful season, going 21-12 with a 3.36 ERA, and allowed only one home run in 270⅔ innings.

The Phillies went 94-58 and finished third, nine games off the pace, and Fraser was one of three 20-game winners on the staff, joining Wiley Piatt (23 wins) and Red Donahue (21). His wildness continued—he finished second in the league in wild pitches—but for the first time he wasn't among the 10 worst in walks.

Not surprisingly, with success came plaudits; Fraser went from being unpopular in Louisville to "clever" in Philadelphia.[15] Perhaps not clever enough. Prior to the 1900 season, Fraser bet Clarke a suit of clothes that the Phillies would finish higher than the Pirates, who had moved from Louisville to Pittsburgh.[16] Pittsburgh went 79-60 and finished in second place, Philadelphia went 75-63 and finished in third. It wasn't Fraser's fault, though, as he anchored the staff with a team-best 3.14 ERA and tied for the team lead in wins with 15.

The 1901 season proved controversial and Fraser found himself right in the middle of it when he jumped to the Philadelphia Athletics of the newly formed American League for $2,500.[17] The AL raided the NL of many of its best players, including Phillies teammate and superstar second baseman Nap Lajoie, beginning a war that lasted for two years before the two settled many of their differences in January 1903.

In 1901 Fraser led the A's in wins with 22 while tossing a team- and career-high 331 innings, but also led the league in walks and hit batters with a career-worst 32. In 1902 Phillies owner John I. Rogers was awarded an injunction by the Pennsylvania Supreme Court that barred Fraser, Lajoie, and Bill Bernhard from playing with any team but the Phillies.

Fraser went back to the Phillies, for whom he toiled for the next three years, going 38-54 from 1902 to 1904. Arguably his career highlight came on September 18, 1903, when he threw a no-hitter against the Colts in Chicago. Otherwise it was another poor season in which Fraser went 12-17 with a 4.50 ERA in a league that averaged 3.26. His 14-24 showing in '04 began a streak of 20-loss seasons that has yet to be broken and probably never will be.

The Phillies lost 100 games in 1904 for the first time in franchise history, a total that would stand as the franchise's worst until 1921, and Fraser bore the brunt of the squad's terrible play, although he didn't help himself by finishing among the 10 worst in walks, wild pitches, and ERA. On December 20 Fraser was traded along with third baseman Harry Wolverton to the Boston Beaneaters for pitcher Togie Pittinger.

As if things couldn't get worse, the Beaneaters lost 103 games and finished a staggering 54½ games out

**CHARLES FRASER**
PITCHER OF THE PHILADELPHIA (N. L.) CLUB

of first place. They boasted a pitching staff with four 20-game losers, including Fraser, who went 14-21 and once again led the league in walks, this time with 149. Earlier in the season, Honus Wagner claimed Fraser invented the spitball, prompting *Sporting Life* to quip, "If that is so Fraser didn't know its value, or made poor use of it."[18]

Fraser refused to sign with Boston after the season so the Beaneaters sent him to the Cincinnati Reds for pitcher Gus Dorner on May 4, 1906.[19] The new Reds hurler was involved in an interesting, albeit not rare incident in Brooklyn on Sunday, June 17, when he and four others were arrested for playing ball on the Sabbath. Blue Laws at the time prohibited games from being played on Sunday and many arrests were made over the years with charges either being dropped or players receiving fines.

The Brooklyn Superbas ignored the law and played seven Sunday games during the first half of the 1904 season before team President Charles Ebbets tired of players being arrested. The following seasons were much the same, however; games played in Brooklyn on Sunday resulted in arrests or charges being filed, but Brooklyn continued to host games on Sundays regardless. On June 17, 1906, Superbas pitcher Mal Eason threw only two pitches before police officers arrested Eason, Ebbets, Brooklyn manager Patsy Donovan, Reds manager Ned Hanlon, and Fraser.

Ebbets knew arrests would be made but insisted he did nothing illegal, that he didn't charge an admission fee, and that fans voluntarily dropped donations into contribution boxes on their way into Washington Park.[20] The men were held on $500 bail, which was paid immediately and they were released. Magistrate John Naumer ruled in favor of the defendants, citing that no admission fee had been charged and no one had complained about noise or a disturbance.[21]

That would be one of the few highlights of the 1906 season for Fraser. The Reds went 64-87 and finished 51½ games behind the pennant-winning Cubs. Fraser went 10-20, losing 20 games for the third straight year and the fifth time in 11 seasons. Among twentieth-century pitchers, Fraser is one of only three to lose 20 games three years in a row and is the only one to do it with three different teams.[22]

The ink on the season's records had barely dried before Fraser announced that he was considering retirement to tend to his rapidly growing poultry business. "It's a big paying proposition," he told reporters, "and I believe that the returns will soon justify me in giving up baseball."[23] Fraser's comments prompted writers to take shots at his work ethic. "It evidently doesn't require much energy to run the poultry business," wrote the *Washington Post*.[24] And Ralph Davis of the *Pittsburgh Press* claimed Fraser "doesn't like work any too well" and would be a bad fit on a team loaded with hard workers.[25]

On November 19, 1906, it was reported that the Chicago Cubs were interested in acquiring Fraser and that team President Charles Murphy had been in talks with Reds President Garry Herrmann.[26] A week later the Reds put Fraser and a handful of others on waivers and the Cubs claimed him, setting off a series of contentious negotiations.[27] On December 16, Fraser was sent to the Cubs, although Herrmann wouldn't release him until Murphy had decided to part with players or buy Fraser outright.[28]

In January the Reds acquired outfielder Henry "Doc" Gessler in exchange for Fraser, but the deal hit a snag when Herrmann heard that Gessler had retired to practice medicine in Pennsylvania. The Reds magnate accused Murphy of trying to hand him a "gold brick" and swore that he never agreed to a deal for Gessler.[29] Gessler had received his M.D. degree from Baltimore Medical College, but had no intention of quitting baseball and mailed his contract to Cincinnati.[30] Murphy finally settled the matter by sending Herrmann a check for $1,500.

Fraser was reported to be "exceedingly jubilant, tickled to death and elated" about going to the Cubs, but the *Wilkes-Barre Record* warned fans not to get too excited. "Just wait till some hot day when Chick begins to give one of those famous exhibitions of that tired feeling of his. Then Chicago fandom is likely to rise up and smite the twirler with a vociferous vocabulary."[31] But Fred Clarke thought Fraser would thrive with the Cubs. "At that, the Chicken has plenty of nerve and, under Frank Chance, he will pitch great ball without doubt."[32]

Fraser was on his seventh team in 12 years, but was said to be a "fine fellow, well-liked by all who know him, and will fit in nicely with the [Cubs]."[33] Chicago manager and first baseman Frank Chance was excited to have the veteran right-hander on his staff, calling Fraser a "real pitcher with a strong team to back him."[34] Indeed. The Cubs were coming off seasons in which they won 93, 92, and a record 116 games, respectively, from 1904-1906.

*Sporting Life's* W.A. Phelon was effusive in his praise for Fraser, claiming he was "an easy-going fellow, who seldom tries to pitch his arm off, which is probably the reason he has lasted so long, and is hardly ever thought of as an old-timer."[35] He also wrote that Fraser "looks young and is strong and happy."[36]

Fraser made his first start of the 1907 campaign on April 23 against the Reds in Chicago and exacted a measure of revenge with a 4-3 win. Those who thought he would flourish with a great team behind him were right; he won five of his first six assignments and tossed shutouts in two of his first three starts. But the Cubs had a problem that every team loves to have—too much pitching—and Fraser was the low man on the rotation's totem pole, which resulted in career lows in games (22), starts (15), and innings (138⅓).

Still, thanks in part to using a spitball later in the season, Fraser had success, going 8-5 with a nifty 2.28 ERA for a team that won 107 games and easily won the World Series over the Detroit Tigers. Alas, the men ahead of Fraser in the pitching pecking order—Mordecai Brown, Orval Overall, Carl Lundgren, Jack Pfiester and Ed Reulbach—were so good, combining for a 1.43 ERA in almost 1,100 innings, that he wasn't needed in the fall classic.

Fraser would have another opportunity in 1908, however. Off the field, his business ventures were expanding—he owned a 20-acre plantation in Cuba and an 80-acre alfalfa ranch near Jerome, Idaho—but he wanted to continue playing ball.[37] He returned to the Cubs and helped them to their third straight pennant, going 11-9 with a 2.27 ERA as the fifth starter behind Brown, Reulbach, Pfiester, and Overall, who won 80 games between them and posted a combined 1.84 ERA.

Fraser's last chance to pitch in a World Series came and went after Chance went with his four best starters in a Series against the Tigers that went only five games before the Cubs secured their second straight championship.

After another holdout, Fraser signed his contract with the Cubs in early March of 1909 and made his first appearance of the season on May 3 in a 9-2 loss to the Pittsburgh Pirates. He threw three innings of relief after Andy Coakley was knocked from the box. It proved to be Fraser's last hurrah. He allowed no earned runs on two hits, but walked four and fanned only one in his final major-league game. Soon after, the 35-year-old was released to the New Orleans Pelicans of the Class-A Southern Association. He wouldn't go quietly.

In June, Fraser complained to the National Commission that the Cubs failed to pay his travel expenses to New Orleans, violating Rule 45 of the Commission's code, and that therefore he should be declared a free agent.[38] Charles Murphy was apoplectic, calling Fraser "an ingrate in every sense of the word," and claiming that Fred Clarke was using Fraser to "raise trouble in the ranks of the Cubs to promote the interests of the Pirates in the championship race."[39]

The National Commission rejected Fraser's claim and he threatened to sue Murphy, then joined the Chicago West Ends of the Chicago League, prompting Murphy to file a protest in 1910 on the grounds that Fraser's presence in the CL made it an outlaw league.[40] The pitcher helped lead the West Ends to a league championship and capped off his season with a one-hitter on September 24, but was suspended from the major leagues and fined $200 for failing to report to New Orleans.[41]

He would report to the Pelicans in 1911, but not before serving as a witness at a murder trial. On March 20, Fraser testified that he, his wife, and five other couples, including Charles and Theresa Schenk, had been celebrating Fraser's 14th wedding anniversary into the morning of March 18 with whiskey, champagne, wine, and dancing at the Schenk residence when Mrs. Schenk became dizzy and was put to bed. After the party, Theresa claimed to be awakened by burglars so she grabbed a revolver and went to the top of the stairs. Upon seeing a man at the bottom of the stairs, she shot and killed him.[42]

The man turned out to be her husband, Charles. Despite her claims of innocence, that it was an accidental shooting, a witness stated that he heard *two* gunshots about a minute apart.[43] Indeed, police found a second bullet on the second floor and surmised that the couple had argued in their upstairs bedroom, she fired the first shot there, he fled down the stairs, and she fired the fatal shot from atop the staircase.[44] A month later, Theresa Schenk was cleared of all charges due to a lack of motive.[45]

Fraser started 11 games for New Orleans and went 4-6 with a 3.89 ERA before being released and, at 38, finished his career in 1912 with Decatur of the Three-Eye League, for whom he went 6-6 with a 3.03 ERA in 15 games while also serving as manager. His playing career over, Fraser repaired to his farm in Idaho before beginning his second career in 1914 as the Pirates' pitching coach under his brother-in-law and pal, Fred Clarke. He also served as a scout with Pittsburgh, for whom he worked until he was released in December 1930. It was during this time that Fraser's father died on November 1, 1916, after living in a Chicago sanatorium for six years.

Fraser managed the Peoria Tractors of the Three-Eye League in 1931 before returning to the big leagues in 1934. That year, Casey Stengel earned his first big-league managing job, with the Brooklyn Dodgers, and almost immediately added Fraser to his staff, where he served as coach during the spring, much to the chagrin of the players, and as a scout until October.

Fraser used a drill called "high-low" to keep his players in shape, in which he "tossed a ball repeatedly—high, low, inside, outside, and everywhere—and the bending and twisting required to catch the pellet had the boys asking for mercy."[46] The players called the drill "Murder" and tried to keep their distance from the coach for fear that he'd make them play his "game."[47] He also delighted in belting fungos just out of their reach, forcing them to run long distances at top speed. He was so adept at gauging each man's abilities that he was said to be able to put a fly ball exactly where the player thought he had a chance to catch it before coming up a step short.[48]

The *Brooklyn Daily Eagle* claimed that Fraser returned to his Idaho farm every offseason and "there plots insidious methods of unusual exercise calculated to make the boys sleep well on March and April nights."[49]

In 1939, Fraser became a scout for the New York Yankees and was assigned the Northwest region of the country, but in April 1940, he was admitted to a hospital in Wendell, Idaho, not far from his Jerome home and was said to be in a "critical state."[50] A blood infection forced doctors to amputate Fraser's right leg and, not long after, his left leg just below the knee.[51]

On May 8, Fraser died of kidney disease at the age of 66.[52] He is buried in Jerome Cemetery in Jerome, Idaho.

## NOTES

1. Idaho Death Certificate; The *Chicago Tribune* listed Fraser's father as "Alexander" on November 2, 1916, after he died on November 1.
2. W.A. Phelon, "Taylor Case Still Worrying Lakeside Fans—Chance For a Big Misunderstanding All Around—Scramble in Cubs Outfield—News of the Game," *Sporting Life*, January 28, 1905: 7. Fraser was known as Chick as early as 1891, when he was 18. *Sporting Life* reported in May 1906 that Fraser was running a chicken farm outside Chicago while he was holding out for more money from Boston, so it's possible he'd been around chickens most of his life. But that's just speculation.
3. Francis Richter, "An Excellent Programme Laid Out For Himself—Two Virginia League Graduates—About a Couple of Young Players—Anson's Theatrical Hit," *Sporting Life*, December 21, 1895: 6.
4. Francis Richter, "Something About Fraser, the Pitcher Whom St. Louis is Angling For—The Drawback to Playing in the Virginia League, Etc." *Sporting Life*, November 30, 1895: 8.
5. Francis Richter, "An Excellent Programme Laid Out For Himself—Two Virginia League Graduates—About a Couple of Young Players—Anson's Theatrical Hit," *Sporting Life*, December 21, 1895: 6.
6. "Garden Citys and Whitings a Tie: On an Even Footing for the City League Championship," *Chicago Tribune*, September 28, 1891: 6.
7. Francis Richter, "Something About Fraser, the Pitcher Whom St. Louis is Angling For—The Drawback to Playing in the Virginia League, Etc." *Sporting Life*, November 30, 1895: 8.
8. "National League News," *Sporting Life*, October 3, 1903: 9; "Pitcher Fraser Expert With Lasso," *St. Louis Post-Dispatch*, July 22, 1906: 13.
9. Francis Richter, "Minor Mention." *Sporting Life*, August 6, 1898: 19.
10. Francis Richter, "Louisville Lines. The Team Now in Good Shape Though a Good Third Baseman is Still Desired—Players Left at Home—General News and Gossip," *Sporting Life*, August 20, 1898: 15.
11. Francis Richter, "The Colonels Still Playing Fast Ball—What the Recent Team Changes Import—The Outlook For Next Year, Etc.," *Sporting Life*, September 17, 1898: 7.
12. Cy Seymour led the National League with 32 hit batters, but faced 459 more batters than Fraser. Vic Willis tied Fraser's 29, but faced 211 more batters.
13. Francis Richter, "The Colonels Still Playing Fast Ball."
14. *St. Louis Post-Dispatch*, January 11, 1907.
15. Francis Richter, "Local Jottings," *Sporting Life*, October 21, 1899: 8.
16. "The Phillies Spring Traning Place Settled, Charlotte, N.C., Will Again Be Their Stamping Ground—The Club Looking For a Third Baseman—Lauder Likely to Leave the Team," *Sporting Life*, January 20, 1900: 7.
17. Baseball-Reference.com
18. "National League News," *Sporting Life*, May 13, 1905: 5.
19. Wm. F.H. Koelsch, "Helped Fraser's Deal," *Sporting Life*, May 26, 1906: 2.
20. "Brooklyn Shut Out by Reds 3 To 0," *New York Tribune*, June 18, 1906.
21. "Sunday Baseball O.K., So Naumer Concludes," *Brooklyn Daily Eagle*, June 19, 1906: 2.
22. Casey Patten had three straight 20-loss seasons with the Washington Senators from 1903-1905 and Irv Young had three straight with the Boston Beaneaters/Doves from 1905-1907.
23. Ralph S. Davis, "Sox Again Down the Nationals," *Pittsburgh Press*, October 12, 1906: 22.
24. "Echoes of the Diamond," *Washington Post*, February 1, 1907: 8.
25. Ralph S. Davis, "Charley Murphy Busy," *Pittsburgh Press*, December 2, 1906: 20.
26. "Favors a Longer Series," *Chicago Inter Ocean*, November 19, 1906: 9.
27. "Player Trade Rumored," *Wilkes-Barre Record*, November 26, 1906: 9.
28. "Chicago Gets Chick Fraser," *Pittsburgh Daily Post*, December 16, 1906: 17.
29. "Murphy Answers 'Garry' Herrmann," *Chicago Tribune*, January 15, 1907: 6.
30. "Gessler's Name on List," *Chicago Tribune*, February 23, 1907: 10.
31. "To Stop Betting at Base Ball Games," *Wilkes-Barre Record*, December 24, 1906: 11.
32. Bat Masterson, "Jimmy Collins Is in St. Louis," *St. Louis Post-Dispatch*, January 11, 1907: 7.
33. "'Chick' Fraser Will Help Cubs' Staff," *Belvidere* (Illinois) *Daily Republican*, January 17, 1907: 2.
34. W.A. Phelon, "Chas. Comiskey Has Something Under His Hat," *Sporting Life*, December 8, 1906: 9.
35. Ibid.
36. Ibid.
37. John B. Foster, "National League News," *Sporting Life*, February 15, 1908: 5; A.R. Cratty, "National League News," *Sporting Life*, November 7, 1908: 3.

38 "Fraser Fractious," *Sporting Life*, June 19, 1909: 9.

39 Ibid. If Murphy's accusations were true, and I highly doubt they were, Clarke and Fraser did a terrible job upending the Cubs. In the two seasons in which Fraser pitched for them, the Cubs won the World Series. Although he was a troublemaker in 1909 and caused some problems during spring training, he wasn't around long enough to be much of a disruption. Not to mention that the Pirates won 110 games, which still ranks second all-time among National League teams and is tied for fifth all-time. The Cubs won 104 games in 1909, but I doubt Fraser was the reason they couldn't top the Pirates.

40 "Pitcher Fraser Not Satisfied With His Commission Turn-Down," *Sporting Life*, July 3, 1909: 1; "After Chick Fraser," *Los Angeles Times*, April 17, 1910: VII8.

41 "Seek to Reinstate Fraser," *Chicago Tribune*, March 23, 1911: 19.

42 "Mrs. Schenk Is Ordered Held," *Boston Globe*, March 21, 1911: 9.

43 Ibid.

44 Ibid.

45 "Clears the Name of Mrs. Schenk," *Chicago Tribune*, April 25, 1911: 3.

46 Roscoe McGowen, "Vigorous Session Staged by Dodgers," *New York Times*, March 6, 1934: 31.

47 John Lardner, "Brooklyn's Rookies Balk at 'Murder,'" *Hartford Courant*, March 11, 1935: 3.

48 Tommy Holmes, "Fraser Keeps Dodgers Hopping Despite 'Unusual' Weather," *Brooklyn Daily Eagle*, March 10, 1936: 16.

49 Ibid.

50 "Chick Fraser in Critical State," *Ogden* (Utah) *Standard-Examiner*, April 25, 1940: 14.

51 "Chick Fraser Condition 'Grave,'" *Idaho Falls* (Idaho) *Post-Register*, May 2, 1940: 12.

52 "Chick Fraser of Yankees Dies at Wendell," *Idaho Falls Post-Register*, May 8, 1940: 13.

# IRVIN "KAISER" WILHELM

## BY GREGORY H. WOLF

**FEW NAMES IN EARLY TWENTIETH-** century America incited as much animosity and vitriol as Kaiser Wilhelm II, the emperor of Germany. After assuming the throne in 1888, the bombastic and often tactless leader inaugurated an aggressive foreign policy program that antagonized nations and directly led to World War I, in 1914. No wonder Ohio-born Irvin Wilhelm abhorred the nickname Kaiser. A journeyman right-handed spitballer in the Deadball Era, Wilhelm debuted in 1903 and posted a lackluster 56-105 record in parts of nine big-league seasons, most notably with the Boston Beaneaters and Brooklyn Superbas. Early in Wilhelm's career, bellicose fans hoped to unnerve him on the mound by shouting the invective "Kaiser!" Gradually, the press took up the moniker, and forever thereafter Wilhelm was known as Kaiser Wilhelm despite his vehement protestations, especially during his short stint as manager of the Philadelphia Phillies (1921-1922). All but forgotten, Wilhelm's name was revived in 2004 when research led by SABR's Ray Nemec determined that he held (as of 2015) the minor-league record for most consecutive scoreless innings, an eye-popping 72.[1]

Irvin Key Wilhelm was born in Wooster, a small town in northeastern Ohio about 50 miles south-southwest of Cleveland. Although sources agree on the date (January 26) of his birth, there is disagreement about the year. Most commonly cited is 1874; however, according to multiple US census reports Wilhelm was born in 1877 (the date this biography uses).[2] In a longstanding tradition among ballplayers, Wilhelm also subtracted a few years from his birth during his playing days, and listed 1879 as his birth date on his World War I draft card.[3] His parents were Joseph H. and Celia P. (DeMiller) Wilhelm, both native Ohioans, whose parents had migrated from Pennsylvania. They married around 1869 and raised three children, Charles, Edith, and Irvin.[4] The elder Wilhelm had a number of jobs, including blacksmith, painter, and house decorator.

Wilhelm got his start in baseball on the sandlots in Wooster and Wayne County. He attended Wooster High School in the 1890s, though no baseball team was fielded, and by 1894 hurled for town teams as far away as Mansfield, about 35 miles west of Wooster. Wilhelm, just 18 years old, began his career in professional baseball in 1895 when he signed with the Mansfield Kids in the inaugural season of the unclassified Interstate League. The *Mansfield News* reported that Wilhelm was "known in Mansfield as a good pitcher," and "signed on his own terms."[5] One of his teammates was 21-year-old Honus Wagner, who also inaugurated his professional career that year. In Wilhelm's first start, on May 9, he walked 11 batters.[6] By late summer he had left the team to continue his education at the College of Wooster, where according to *Sporting Life*, Wilhelm "picked up the art of pitching."[7]

Wilhelm resumed his professional baseball career in 1901 when he signed with the Birmingham Barons in the inaugural season of the Class-B Southern Association. According to the *Age-Herald* of Birmingham, manager Sam Mills signed the 24-year-old hurler "who comes highly recommended by Charley Zimmer, the veteran catcher of the Pittsburg, Pa. club."[8] Zimmer, a native Ohioan who had played for the Cleveland Blues in the American Association (1887-1888) and the National League Cleveland Spiders (1889-1899) was well aware of Wilhelm's reputation as a hard thrower. *Sporting Life* reported that Wilhelm became a "prime favorite" of the Birmingham fans, while *The Sporting News* opined that "his record … was phenomenal considering the circumstances under which he pitched."[9] Wilhelm (15-18) was the shining light on a poor Barons team (45-70).[10] They were even worse in 1902 (39-80 in the reclassified Class-A league), but Wilhelm was characterized as a "star" and "invincible" en route to a 14-9 record and 247 innings.[11] In June he replaced Frank Haller as player-manager; the latter, who also scouted for the Pittsburgh Pirates, returned to the Smoky City and encouraged Pirates owner Barney Dreyfuss to purchase the hurler.[12] "I like the play of Wilhelm," wrote sportswriter A.R. Cratty. "He is a neat ball player and gets over the ground."[13] After the Pirates acquired Wilhelm, Haller made a bold statement: "There is no doubt in my mind as to the big fellow's future. He will stay in the league."[14]

The Pirates had finished with an astounding 103-36 record in 1902 to finish in first place for the second straight season, but were dealt a serious blow when their star pitchers Jack Chesbro (28-6) and Jesse Tannehill (20-6) jumped to the American League New York Highlanders after the season.[15] Pittsburgh manager Fred Clarke hoped that Wilhelm and another acquisition, 23-year-old Cy Falkenberg, would join stalwarts Deacon Phillippe and Sam Leever to stabilize the staff. Before donning a Pirates uniform, Wilhelm suffered a serious case of food poisoning (supposedly from a can of pineapple), but was in good health as the season commenced.[16] "[Wilhelm] is no phenomenon, but a cool, calculating pitcher, has everything and knows how to use them," opined *Sporting Life*; however, Wilhelm (5-3) made just nine starts (completed seven) and tossed 86 innings for the pennant winners.[17] The highlight of his season was a five-hit shutout of the Boston Beaneaters at Pittsburgh's Exposition Park on June 4.[18] In a surprising move, Clarke released Wilhelm in late August. The decision perplexed beat reporter A.R. Cratty. "Wilhelm is no cub, but a mature man. He perhaps should give some reasons for the actions of his employers," he wrote, and suggested that "management did not like the twirler because he was not given to getting the ball 'there in tight places.'"[19] Several years later, *Sporting Life* wrote "[Manager] Clarke balls out men savagely at times," and suggested that the skipper jettisoned Wilhelm because "he wouldn't heed his commander's orders to cover first base."[20]

In the offseason the 6-foot, 160-pound Wilhelm signed with the Boston Beaneaters, coming off a sixth-place finish (58-80) in 1903. Local sportswriter J.C. Morse, excited by the acquisition, thought Wilhelm would join Togie Pittinger and Vic Willis to build one of the best staffs in the league. "The pitching force is a mighty good one, and ought to get good results with such a corps of pitchers," wrote Morse, who then offered a dig at the Pirates owner. "If Barney Dreyfuss had this Boston bunch he could win the pennant in a canter."[21] Wilhelm won his first start, defeating the Philadelphia Phillies, 8-7, in a slugfest at the Baker Bowl on April 16.[22] He subsequently hurled impressive victories over the Phillies (3-1 on April 26) and the Cincinnati Reds (2-1 on May 16) to earn Morse's praise ("he's done some good work").[23] But manager Al Buckenberger's squad was a far cry from the Boston teams that posted 14 consecutive winning seasons and captured five pennants from 1887 to 1900. They scored the fewest runs in the league and surrendered the second most, contributing to a seventh-place finish (55-98). Wilhelm (14-20) completed 30 of 36 starts and logged 288 innings; he formed with Willis (18-25) and Pittinger (15-21) the league's only trio of 20-game losers.

While the Beaneaters slogged through a horrendous season (51-103) to finish in seventh place for new skipper Fred Tenney in 1905, Wilhelm suffered one of the worst seasons in big-league history. After he tossed a two-hitter to defeat the Pirates, 2-1, on April 19, the bottom fell out.[24] Wilhelm finished the season with a 3-23 record; his ERA (4.53) in 242⅓ innings was the second highest in the NL. With Wilhelm, Irv Young (20-21), Vic Willis (12-29), and Chick Fraser (14-21), Boston set a dubious record by becoming the first team in NL history to have four 20-loss hurlers. Nonetheless, beat reporter J.C. Morse could not fault Wilhelm alone. "Wilhelm would have done far better had he a battling team behind him," he wrote. "Again and again the Boston pitchers would hold a team down for a spell and then the game would go to the other team because there was no hitting."[25]

Though one cannot definitely state when Wilhelm acquired the epithet Kaiser, an incident on April 14, 1905, is noteworthy. In front of a record crowd, estimated at between 28,000 and 40,000, at the Polo

Grounds, the New York Giants battered Wilhelm on Opening Day. Giants beat reporter William F.H. Koelsch wrote in *Sporting Life* that "facetious fans" dubbed Wilhelm "the Kaiser."[26] Up to this time, newspapers had referred to Wilhelm as Irvin or Irving, a misspelling the pitcher dealt with his entire life. Beginning in 1905, the sobriquet Kaiser gradually crept into stories about the hurler.

After the 1905 season, Wilhelm was sold to the Rochester Bronchos in the Class-A Eastern League, and subsequently sent to Birmingham. In his first year back in the South, Wilhelm went 22-13, pitching a perfect game against the Montgomery Senators on July 9, for the pennant-winning Barons.[27] "[Wilhelm] was a big factor in [Birmingham's] capture of the Southern League title," wrote *Sporting Life*.[28] The Barons dropped to fifth place in 1907, but Wilhelm sparkled with a league-leading 23 victories (14 losses). One of those wins was a 15-inning complete game against the Memphis Egyptians on July 15.

Wilhelm concluded the 1907 season in spectacular fashion by tossing shutouts in both games of a doubleheader against the Shreveport Pirates in Birmingham on September 14. "Including eighteen innings on this day," wrote *Sporting Life*, "he had gone fifty-nine consecutive innings without allowing a run. Pitcher [Walter] Johnson, of Washington, is believed to have held the record heretofore, having gone through six successive games in the Idaho State League without allowing a run."[29] In subsequent decades, Wilhelm's streak was misidentified as 56 innings. This clerical mistake became a hot topic in 2004 when Brad Thompson of the Nashville Smokies (Double-A Southern Association) tossed 57 consecutive scoreless innings to set what was believed to be a new minor-league record.[30] Soon thereafter, researchers not only discovered the mistake, but SABR's Ray Nemec determined that Wilhelm (who pitched in the big leagues in 1908-1910), hurled 13 scoreless innings to begin the 1911 season with Rochester. With 72 consecutive scoreless innings, Wilhelm extended his record for the longest such streak in minor-league baseball history.

Purchased by the Brooklyn Superbas after the 1907 season, Wilhelm got off to a contentious start with team owner Charles Ebbets. A religious man, Wilhelm informed the cantankerous owner that he did not want to pitch on Sundays, to which Ebbets responded bluntly, "We can use players only who play seven days a week."[31] Sportswriter Ren Mulford Jr. sympathized with the player. "You can bet if his name was Brown, and he has Mordecai's record to back him," he wrote, "Brooklyn would find enough games for him to work in on weekdays only."[32] Furthermore, Wilhelm refused to report until the National Commission clarified his contract situation. According to his personal correspondence with Garry Herrmann, chairman of the National Commission, and *Sporting Life*, Wilhelm thought he had had a non-reserve contract and demanded a portion of his acquisition price.[33] The committee ultimately determined that Birmingham had not promulgated Wilhelm's contract (a common practice also called pigeonholing); Wilhelm was awarded $350, while Birmingham was fined $150 and permitted to keep the remaining $500.[34]

Notwithstanding his various squabbles, Wilhelm's debut with the Superbas on April 17 at Washington Park in Brooklyn was a resounding success; he tossed a three-hitter to defeat Boston 3-2. The *Brooklyn Daily Eagle* was enamored with the good-natured hurler, whom it affectionately called Little Eva, one of Wilhelm's nicknames with the Barons. "Wherever the Superbas went on their spring trip, the wonderful work of Wilhelm was shouted from the rooftops," wrote the paper about his popularity down south. "If Irving (*sic*) had had press agents in every city, he couldn't have capped a bigger send off."[35] The daily was equally gushing about Wilhelm's hurling, noting his "great control of his spitball as well as his curves and slants."[36] In Wilhelm, skipper Patsy Donovan and Ebbets found an ideal successor to Elmer "Spitball" Stricklett, who had jumped the team to join the Pacific Coast League. Fulfilling *Sporting Life's* prediction that he'd be a "prize" if he pitched regularly, Wilhelm unexpectedly emerged as one of the best pitchers in the NL.[37] With his "mystic spitters" thrown with a side-arm delivery and a "fine little jump which he throws into the ball," Wilhelm set career highs in victories (16), innings (332, fourth in the league), complete games (33, trailing only Christy Mathewson), ERA (1.87), and shutouts (6).[38] He also lost 22 games for the weak-hitting Superbas, who finished in seventh place (53-101).

Named Opening Day starter in 1909, Wilhelm collected the signature victory of his big-league career, 3-0 in 13 innings over the New York Giants on April 16. In what was described by the *New York Times* as "one of the most hotly contested pitching battles ever witnessed" at the Polo Grounds, Giants starter Red Ames held the Superbas hitless through nine innings while Wilhelm surrendered his first safety in the eighth inning and finished with a three-hit shutout.[39] Wilhelm posted only two more victories all season (to go along with 13 losses), eventually lost his spot in the rotation, and sported a high ERA (3.26) in 163 innings. Said New York sportswriter John B. Foster, "If [Wilhelm] is good, nobody can do much with him, and if he isn't good, there is no reason why he cannot be battered as hard as any man in the business."[40] Brooklyn, which had captured pennants in 1899 and 1900, finished with a losing record for the sixth consecutive season. "Brooklyn's poor showing was due to inferior pitching, inconsistent hitting and erratic fielding," wrote *Sporting Life* in stinging fashion and added, "Wilhelm did poorly."[41]

Wilhelm suffered from typhoid fever for most of the 1910 season and was limited to a 3-7 record and a 4.74 ERA in just 68⅓ innings.[42] In the offseason he was sold to Rochester. Over the next three seasons, Wilhelm once again established his reputation as a rubber-armed pitcher, capable of starting and relieving. From 1911 to 1913, he posted records of 14-7, 16-10, and 18-7, and averaged 47 appearances and 228 innings. After capturing the Eastern League pennant in 1911, Rochester was one of eight charter members of the newly established International League in 1912. Renamed the Hustlers, Rochester was runner-up in the newly reclassified Double-A league in 1912 and 1913.

Throughout his baseball career, Wilhelm was described in the press as a popular fan favorite. And by all accounts, he was a likeable, articulate teammate whose college education and "good personality" harkened back to a time when baseball was played by amateur gentlemen and not rough-and-tumble, uncouth professionals.[43] Prior to signing with the Pirates in 1903, Wilhelm married Louis Ellen Motter, a divorcee with a son, Avery; they lived in Wooster in the offseasons. Eventually they divorced, and Wilhelm married Alice R. Sullivan, from Rochester, in the early 1910s. According to several newspapers, Wilhelm was an avid hunter, raised beagles, dabbled in real estate in both Ohio and New York, and was "reputed to have amassed a modest little fortune."[44]

The launch of the Federal League in 1914 revived Wilhelm's big-league aspirations. Along with two Rochester teammates, batting champion Hack Simmons and Fred Jacklitsch, Wilhelm jumped to the Baltimore Terrapins. At 37 years of age, Wilhelm served as skipper Otto Knabe's trusted "rescue man," starting 27 of a team-high 47 games, completing 11 of them, and logging 243⅔ innings.[45] Seemingly finding the fountain of youth, Wilhelm tossed two 10-

inning complete-game victories, against the St. Louis Terriers on May 26 and against the eventual pennant-winning Indiana Hoosiers on July 29. On the final day of the season, Wilhelm earned his 12th victory of the season (and what proved to be the last in his big-league career) in the second game of a doubleheader on October 10 by tossing a stellar seven-hitter against the Terriers to record his 12th career shutout. He also lost 17 times for the third-place club.

According to *Sporting Life*, Wilhelm was injured in 1915 and was "practically no use at all," making only one appearance for the Terrapins. However, the actual reason for his inactivity was a contract dispute. In an effort to develop its own farm system, the Federal League entered into an agreement with the Class C Colonial League under which all eight teams in the Federal League agreed to send the league six players each. Wilhelm refused to report, and was ultimately appointed an umpire in the Federal League by President James A. Gilmore, in July.[46] It was not Wilhelm's first professional umpiring experience. According to Norman Macht, Wilhelm was pressed into service as an ump for one game in 1904 and 1905.[47] Wilhelm subsequently filed a lawsuit against the Terrapins, claiming breach of contract for not permitting him to pitch.[48]

Not ready to hang up his spikes after the Federal League folded, Wilhelm joined the Class B Elmira Colonels in the New York State League, posting records of 14-19 and 17-16 respectively in 1916 and 1917. The league's closure after the '17 season seemingly signaled the end of the 40-year-old player's professional career. According to his World War I draft card, Wilhelm worked as an assemblyman at the Curtiss Aeroplane Company in Hammondsport, New York.[49] He also pitched in semipro leagues, and participated in baseball tournaments throughout central and western New York in 1918 and 1919.[50]

In 1920 Wilhelm made an unlikely comeback at the age of 43 by signing with the Jersey City Skeeters of the International League. Save for a teammate, 23-year-old Alex Ferguson (21-13), Wilhelm was the club's best hurler, splitting his 24 decisions and ranking 10th in the league in innings pitched (236) for a poor team (62-91). According to one report, Wilhelm tossed complete games to defeat the Syracuse Stars in both games of a doubleheader on September 12.[51] Wilhelm became friends with his manager, Wild Bill Donovan, a former big-league hurler with 185 wins and ex-manager of the New York Yankees (1915-1917). Donovan helped Wilhelm realize his dream by getting back to the majors, but not necessarily how the latter anticipated.

When Donovan was named skipper of the Philadelphia Phillies in 1921, he brought along Wilhelm as a coach and scout. In an unusual development, Phillies owner William Baker fired Donovan in late July. The episode commenced when Donovan was summoned to Chicago to testify in Commissioner Kenesaw Mountain Landis's ever-expanding investigation of the Chicago White Sox scandal in 1919. Baker, claiming that his skipper must have known the gamblers or about the betting, axed him. Not implicated in the scandal, Donovan was completely exonerated. Wilhelm took over as manager of the lowly, last-place Phillies (25-62) on July 26. Philadelphia sportswriter James C. Isaminger applauded Wilhelm's determination: "He must get credit for working hard. He is out on the coaching line hustling every day."[52] Under Wilhelm's stewardship, the Phillies went 26-41 to finish in the cellar for the third straight season.

The aging hurler also made the last four of his 216 big-league appearances in 1921. In parts of nine seasons, Wilhelm posted a 56-105 record, started 158 contests, completed 118 of them, and carved out a 3.44 ERA in 1,432⅓ innings.

Isaminger lauded Wilhelm as a "good baseball leader" but warned that "he is not a miracle worker and must have financial support" to be successful.[53] The latter comment was a clear indictment of William Baker, whose tightfisted control of the team, including the sale of star hurler Grover Cleveland Alexander after the 1917 season, began a streak of 14 consecutive losing seasons (1918-1931). Wilhelm, whom the Philadelphia press tabbed Kize or Irv in light of the manager's disdain for the name Kaiser, achieved a minor miracle in 1922 when he led the

Phillies to a seventh-place finish (57-96). "Wilhelm must deserve full credit," wrote Isaminger. "He made the most out of a team low in quality."[54] Nonetheless, Wilhelm was fired shortly after the season.

Wilhelm remained close to baseball for the remainder of his life. In 1923 and 1924 he served as pitching coach and scout for skipper George Stallings' Rochester Tribe of the International League. He also made his final professional baseball appearance as a player in 1923. He managed the Bridgeport (Connecticut) Bears of the Class-A Eastern League in 1925, and the Class-B Syracuse Stars/Hazleton Mountaineers in the New York Penn League in 1929; in 1928 he scouted for the Montreal Royals (International League).[55] Wilhelm coached baseball at the University of Rochester beginning in 1930.

On May 25, 1936, Wilhelm died at the age of 59 in Rochester and was buried in Wooster. In his obituaries, he was referred to as Irvin, Irving, Irv, Kaiser, and Kize; and indicative of the uncertainty of his birth year, his age was listed variously as 53, 57, and 58.[56] There was no confusion, however, about Wilhelm's love for the game and his tireless dedication to play, teach, and promote the sport. Preceding an exhibition game between semipro teams from Buffalo and Rochester on September 17, 1936, to benefit Wilhelm's widow, the *Rochester Journal* paid humble tribute to the hurler. "[Wilhelm] stood out as one of Rochester's most illustrious contributions to the national pastime. After his retirement from the majors, he was largely instrumental in the development of young baseball talent here."[57]

## SOURCES

In addition to the sources listed in the notes, the author consulted Irvin Kaiser's player file, National Baseball Hall of Fame, Cooperstown, New York.

## NOTES

1. J.J. Cooper, "Scoreless Innings Record Grows," *Baseball America*, May 21, 2004.
2. BaseballReference.com gives the date 1874; the 1900 US Census gives the year, 1877. See Ancestry.com.
3. Draft registration card available on Ancestry.com
4. According to the 1900 US Census, they had another child who died.
5. "New Men For Mansfield," *Mansfield* (Ohio) *News*, May 9, 1895: 4.
6. "Wilhelm Was Wild," *Mansfield* (Ohio) *News*, May 10, 1895: 5.
7. *Sporting Life*, September 21, 1907: 15.
8. "Approach of the Baseball Season," *Age-Herald* (Birmingham, Alabama), February 3, 1901: 5.
9. *Sporting Life*, February 8, 1902: 5; *The Sporting News*, January 18, 1902: 1.
10. Wilhelm pitched in 33 games and posted a 15-18 record for Birmingham in 1901. See *Reach's Official Base Ball Guide 1902* (Philadelphia: A.J. Reach, 1902), 190.
11. *Sporting Life*, July 5, 1902: 22; and June 14, 1902: 23.
12. *Sporting Life*, June 28, 1902: 5.
13. *Sporting Life*, August 9, 1902: 4.
14. *Sporting Life*, October 11, 1902: 4.
15. Even before the season ended, rumors of Chesbro's and Tannehill's jump to the American League circulated.
16. "Poisoned by Pineapple," *Pittsburgh Weekly Gazette*, March 11, 1902: 7.
17. *Sporting Life*, November 28, 1903: 5.
18. "Great Are the Champion Boys," *Pittsburgh Daily Post*, June 5, 1903: 10.
19. *Sporting Life*, November 28, 1903: 5.
20. *Sporting Life*, December 5, 1908: 10.
21. *Sporting Life*, May 14, 1904: 4.
22. *Sporting Life*, April 23, 1904: 6.
23. Sporting Life, May 7, 1904: 4; May 28, 1904: 6; and May 21, 1904: 4.
24. *Sporting Life*, April 29, 1905: 4.
25. *Sporting Life*, December 2, 1905: 8.
26. *Sporting Life*, April 22, 1905: 3.
27. *Sporting Life*, July 28, 1906: 24.
28. *Sporting Life*, September 21, 1907: 15.
29. *Sporting Life*, September 28, 1907: 13.
30. Jim Luttrell, "Baseball: Minor League Report; Scoreless Innings Streak Ends at 57," *New York Times*, May 21, 2004.
31. *Sporting Life*, February 22, 1908: 2.
32. Ibid.
33. Wilhelm's letter to Garry Herrmann, chairman of the National Commission, dated March 5, 1908. Player's Hall of Fame file.
34. *Sporting Life*, March 7, 1908: 4.

35 "Wilhelm Makes Brilliant Debut: Superbas Bat Bostons Again," *Brooklyn Daily Eagle*, April 18, 1908: 20.

36 Ibid.

37 *Sporting Life*, May 30, 1908: 9.

38 "Superbas Beat Quakers In a Whirlwind Inning," *Brooklyn Daily Eagle*, June 3, 1908: 4; *Sporting Life*, May 23, 1908: 20.

39 "30,000 See Giants Lose to Superbas," *New York Times*, April 16, 1909: 7.

40 *Sporting Life*, May 1, 1909: 6.

41 *Sporting Life*, June 22, 1910: 3.

42 *Pittsburg* (Kansas) *Daily Headlight,* September 1, 1910: 7.

43 *The Sporting News*, September 8, 1921: 1.

44 Many news articles mention this information; one is his obituary in the *Brooklyn Daily Eagle*. "Irvin Wilhelm, 57, Famous Pitcher of Brooklyn, Dies," May 23, 1936: 11.

45 *Sporting Life*, May 9, 1914: 13.

46 *Sporting Life*, August 2, 1915: 8.

47 Norman Macht, "Kaiser Wilhelm. Unlucky Phils Manager Of the 1920s," *Phillies Report*, May 29, 1991.

48 "Wilhelm To Sue Baltimore Feds," *Evening Tribune* (Providence, Rhode Island), August 15, 1915.

49 Draft registration via Ancestry.com.

50 "Big Games For These Semi-Pros," *Buffalo Commercial*, June 7, 1919.

51 International League Chronology, *Rochester Evening Journal and Post Express*, September 12, 1924: 14.

52 *The Sporting News*, August 25, 1921: 3.

53 *The Sporting News*, September 8, 1921: 1.

54 *The Sporting News*, October 5, 1922: 1.

55 "'Kize' Wilhelm Scout for Montreal," *Rochester Evening Journal and Post Express*, August 22, 1928: 11.

56 Wilhelm's age was listed as 53 in Associated Press, "Ex-Pitcher of Brooklyn is Dead," *New York Times*, May 24, 1936; he was 57 according to the *Brooklyn Daily Eagle*, "Irvin Wilhelm, 57, Famous Pitcher of Brooklyn Dies," May 23, 1936: 11; and 58 according to *The Sporting News*, May 28, 1936: 2.

57 "Crack Bison Nine In Benefit Game," *Rochester Journal*, September 17, 1935: 25.

# VIC WILLIS

Vic Willis is featured twice in this book. He appears amongst the list of Hall of Famers who are 20-game losers. He was also one of the four pitchers on the 1905 Boston Beaneaters who each lost 20 or more games in that unhappy season. His biography appears earlier in this volume.

# IRV YOUNG

## BY WILL ANDERSON AND BILL NOWLIN

**IRVING MELROSE "CY THE** Second"/"Young Cy" Young was born on July 21, 1877, and raised in Columbia Falls, Washington County, Maine, in the state's "Downeast" area. His father, William Wallace Young (1844-1911), worked as a farmer at the time of the 1880 census, and he and his wife, (the former Syldania French), raised six children—Rowland, Orie, Minerva, Sewall, Mabel, and their youngest, Irving.

Around 1894, William, Syldania, and family moved to Concord, New Hampshire, where William took a position as a woodworker in a car shop, helping make railroad cars. At the time of the 1900 census, Irving was listed as a fireman on the Boston & Maine Railroad, perhaps better work than serving as a lumberjack in the Maine woods.[1] Although he worked 60 hours a week on the railroad, Irv managed to find time to pitch for the YMCA and other local amateur clubs on weekends. He later took up work at a hosiery mill in Concord.[2] In 1904, at the rather advanced age of 26, Irv turned pro, joining Concord in the New England League.[3] There the young left-hander won 18 games (losing 14) and caught the eye of scout Billy Hamilton. Hamilton strongly recommended him to the Boston Beaneaters (the National League team later known as the Braves), who bought his contract for $500. (There was a brief problem that cropped up in June 1905, when the Concord club complained that it had yet to receive its final $250, but that was apparently resolved quickly enough.)[4]

Young was 5-feet-10 and listed at 170 pounds.

At age 27 in 1905, Irv Young had his shot at the major leagues. He made the most of it. He led the league in three categories: most innings pitched (378), most games started (42), and most complete games (41). He was second in the league in shutouts with seven (only the immortal Christy Mathewson, with eight, had more) and fifth in strikeouts. His earned-run average was 2.90, respectable in any league. And he won 20 games. Yet, alas, he lost 21. But let's discount that. Irv Young, in playing for manager Fred Tenney and the 1905 Beaneaters, was playing for one of the more inept teams in baseball's long history. Let's concentrate—and celebrate—on the fact that he won 20 games. As a rookie.

All these years later, Young's 1905 total of 378 innings pitched and 41 complete games are still major-league records for a rookie. Needless to say, in this day and age of almost incessant relief pitching, they are records that will most likely last forever. And that's a long, long time. Irv's total of seven shutouts was also a long-standing rookie high, tied by Pete Alexander in 1911 and by Jerry Koosman in 1968, and eventually broken by Fernando Valenzuela in 1981.

Young's banner season started well. He appeared in relief, pitching the final four innings of the Beaneaters' April 14 Opening Day game before a crowd of 40,000 at the Polo Grounds. And he pitched effectively, holding the soon-to-become World Champion McGrawmen to but four hits and two runs. He also knocked in Boston's only run in the eighth inning. Four days later he started the club's home opener, gaining his first major-league win in a 4-2 performance over Brooklyn. He limited the Superbas to seven hits and walked only one. According to the *New York Times*, the man whose nicknames compared him to the legendary Cy Young "made an excellent impression, striking out six men and keeping the Brooklyn hits well scattered."[5] On the 28th, Irv pitched the first of his seven shutouts of the year, holding the Phillies to three hits in a 2-0 Boston win. "Inability to hit Young's delivery was responsible for the home team's defeat today by Boston" was the rather quaint way the *Bangor Daily News* explained the game's outcome.

On May 6, Irv bested Christy Mathewson in a 2-1 cliffhanger. The Giants managed but seven hits off the Boston southpaw. Irv picked up his second shutout on May 11, scattering 10 Chicago hits in a 5-0 match. South Bridgton, Maine, native Wirt Virgin "Rip" Cannell—who played all 154 games in the outfield for the Beaneaters that year—got the game's only extra-base hit, a double.

Other highlights in Cy the Second's steady march toward becoming Maine's first 20-game winner of the century[6] include:

May 15—Beats Reds, 2-1, on a nine-hitter.

May 23—Tosses a five-hit shutout over the Pirates, 1-0.

May 27—Tosses another shutout in three-hitting the Phillies, 3-0.

June 3—Hurls yet another shutout—again a three-hitter—against John McGraw's Giants, 2-0. Writes the *New York Times*, "Young 'Cy' Young gave the champion New Yorks a sample of his pitching powers in the first game of a double header in this city to-day by allowing them only three hits during the entire nine innings."[7]

At that point, the *Boston Journal* featured a large photograph of Young under the heading "Find of the Year," noting that he had won eight of his first 11 games.[8] The paper added that he had gained deserved popularity in Boston, and was "as modest as he is skilful and it is a pleasure to see him work."[9]

Young's efforts attracted attention across the land, not only in the state of Washington but in Biloxi, Mississippi, where the local paper noted his "meteoric" rise from the sandlots of Whitefield, New Hampshire, and Tenney's being "jubilant." In late August, it was noted that Young "has won more games than any two of the other Boston twirlers" and that in four of his games he hadn't walked a batter.[10]

June 24—Loses a heartbreaker, 2-1, to the Giants in 12 innings. Again the *Times*: "Young, one of the sensational pitchers of the year, who had worsted the champions on the Polo Grounds this season, and who subsequently shut them out at Boston, proved just as effective as upon the other occasions, only two hits being made off his delivery up to the ninth inning."[11]

July 10—Defeats the Phillies, 3-2.

July 13—Five-hits the Reds in a 6-1 Boston win.

July 24—Tosses four-hitter vs. Pittsburgh in an 8-1 win.

August 21—Allows five hits and strikes out seven in downing St. Louis, 1-0.

September 1—Tops Brooklyn, 4-2, on an eight-hitter.

September 7—Again shuts out the Giants, allowing but four hits. Highlight of the game is a catch in center field by Rip Cannell in the sixth inning. The *Times* terms it "astonishing."[12]

September 13—Six-hits the Phillies in a 3-2 win (while also getting two hits and scoring a run).

September 20—Defeats Brooklyn, 6-5, with a bases-loaded triple by Cannell the big blow.

What's amazing is the number of games Irv Young could have—and probably should have—won in 1905. If he had come away victorious in all the games he lost by one run—mostly all by scores of 2-1 or 3-2—he could well have been a 30-game winner. Wouldn't that have put Columbia Falls on the map!

The truth is that the Beaneaters were terrible. They won but 51 games the entire season (while dropping slightly more than twice that many, 103). Young Cy's 20 wins, therefore, constituted virtually 40 percent of the team's victories. With any kind of run production behind him—the team's anemic .234 batting average was the lowest in the league—Young would have easily had another eight or ten games in the win column. Ironically, Young Cy's namesake—the winningest pitcher in baseball history and the man for whom the Cy Young Award is named—had a very similar season. Pitching for Boston's American League entry (the team we know now as the Red Sox), he also lost one game more than he won. His record for the year was 18-19.

In late September, the Pirates offered to purchase Young for the then-hefty price of $7,500. But Boston management would have none of it. The *Bangor Daily News*, in a September 29 article, put the area's many Beaneaters fans at ease. The paper reported Boston management as emphatically stating that "Such a deal will not be thought of"—Irv was just too valuable to the team.

That the offer was not accepted, however, was most unfortunate for Cy the Second. With the Pirates he would have been with a winner. With Boston he was destined to forever pitch for a loser.

In 1905, the Boston Nationals had not just one, but four 20-game losers. Joining Young in ignominy were:

Chick Fraser (14-21, 3.28); Kaiser Wilhelm (3-23, 4.53); and Vic Willis—later inducted into the Baseball Hall of Fame—at 12-29 (3.21).

A trade sent Willis to Pittsburgh, where he won more than 20 games in each of the next four seasons, 1906-09.

There was a moment in October 1905 when Cy Young and Young Cy faced off against each other. That year, the Boston Americans and Boston Nationals faced off in a postseason best-of-seven exhibition city series, all of the games played at the Huntington Avenue Grounds. The Nationals won the first game. In the second game, played on October 10 in front of nearly 8,000 spectators, the two Youngs went head-to-head. Cy Young himself was said to have been "out to make his showing against the much-touted National League star."[13] The Americans prevailed, 3-1, with Cy Young allowing just two hits, walking no one, and striking out 15 (including the Nationals pitcher three times). Young Cy yielded eight hits (one to the Americans' pitcher), while walking one and striking out four. Even though the Americans won Games Two through Five, the two teams played out the seven-game series, the result being that the Americans won two more games as well, taking the series six games to one.

In 1906 the Beaneaters were even more futile than the year before. Tenney was still at the helm. Their batting average dropped to .226; their won-lost record to 49-102; their starting catcher batted .189; their

second baseman hit .202; and reserve outfielder Gene Good—a sometimes actor/sometimes ballplayer who weighed in at 126 pounds—stroked a lowly .151. The team made 11 errors in one game in June. They were the doormat of the league, and almost nothing Young did was going to change that.

As in 1905, Young had kicked off the 1906 season brilliantly, throwing a one-hit, 2-0 shutout in Brooklyn on Opening Day, April 12. He walked no one. The only hit was a first-inning double to left field by Harry Lumley, who then got himself thrown out trying to stretch it into three bases. Boston committed three errors, one of them by Young (who also struck out three times).

In that second season in the bigs, 1906, Irv again led the National League in innings pitched (358⅓), games started (41), and complete games (37). He was fifth in the league in strikeouts and his earned-run average remained virtually unchanged at 2.91. Yet with the club worse than ever—the Beaneaters lost 19 games in a row during one especially dismal stretch in May and June—our man from Down East saw his record drop to 16-25. Just as in 1905, Young was one of four 20-game losers on the team. In 1906, the other were:

Gus Dorner (8-25, 3.65); Vive Lindaman (12-23, 2.43); and Big Jeff Pfeffer (13-22, 2.95).

The entire rest of the staff together lost only seven games. (The 1905 staff had lost nine games other than those by the four principal starters.)

John McGraw—recognizing talent when he saw it—offered $10,000 for the southpaw, only to be turned down.[14] Boston management clearly liked Irv Young. So did his teammates: When he got married in September, they bought a brass bed for the new bride and groom. On September 12 in Boston, Young married Elizabeth C. Myers of Boston, "a young social favorite of the Dorchester district"; the pair had met two years earlier, when Elizabeth, a baseball enthusiast, was vacationing and saw Young pitch for the Concord team.[15] The couple had one child, a daughter named Syldania, born in 1909.

Also reported as bidding to buy Young's contract were the Chicago Cubs, in October 1906.[16] And Barney Dreyfuss and the Pirates were still after him, more than doubling what they had reportedly offered a year earlier. A report in December 1906 claimed the Pirates would offer $15,000—and 21 ballplayers! All 21 had been placed on waivers. New Beaneaters co-owner John Dovey replied, "I'm not looking for quantity, but for quality in players. I'll tell you what I'll do. I'll trade even if you'll give me Hans Wagner, Fred Clark [sic], and Tommy Leach for Cy. Otherwise there is nothing doing."[17]

Before the start of the 1907 season, the futile ballclub's ownership changed hands. The new owners were a Pittsburgh theatrical man named John Harris and two brothers, George and John Dovey from Kentucky. The Doveys ran the team and, in their honor, the club's nickname was changed to the Doves. It was an appropriate appellation: On the field the team was almost invariably the personification of peace. Young was, however, the last to sign. "Better late than never," he said.[18] They finished seventh, 47 games behind the front-running Cubs. Still under Tenney, their record had improved to 58-90. But the toll of constantly losing was having its effect on Cy the Second. His earned-run average jumped to 3.96; his won-lost record fell to a most disheartening 10-23.

For the third year in a row, Young had lost more than 20 games. This year he held that distinction alone; no other pitcher lost more than 16.

President George Dovey had been willing to deal Young, something he had made clear as early as July 1907, if he could strengthen the team in doing so. Though his goal was to improve the team, he apparently was fond of Young. "Mr. Dovey has only the most kindly feeling toward Young," the Boston Globe wrote, "and it is partly on the latter's account that he is willing to let him go, as he may be able to do better with another club than he has done this season with Boston."[19]

Young started 1908, his last year in the National League, with the Doves. He was 4-9 for them and struggling a bit. "Young has not actually lowered in ability in any way," wrote one observer, "but the National league batsmen have solved his delivery. He cannot deceive them as successfully as before."[20]

On June 18, Young was traded to the Pirates for two other pitchers, Tom McCarthy and Harley Young (who, ironically, was nicknamed Cy the Third). Appearing in 16 games for Pittsburgh, Young Cy was 4-3. He pitched one truly spectacular game, a 17-inning complete-game shutout of the Dodgers on August 22 at Pittsburgh's Exposition Park, beating Sunny Jim Pastorius when he singled and came around to score for the 1-0 win. He was said to have "sat down on first base" after his long hit to center field, "reeled to second like a drunken man" on a following base hit, then—after an intentional walk loaded the bases—"lurched to home plate and fell on it" for the winning run.[21]

For the entire season, Young was 8-12 with his lowest-ever ERA, 2.42. It was not good enough.

In the offseason, Young worked in Boston for the National Express freight company, hauling freight and—when necessary—wielding an iron bar as leader of the company's ice-breaking gang. It was a way to keep in shape while helping put bread on the table.[22]

In 1909, the southpaw found himself with the Minneapolis Millers in the American Association. The Pirates dealt him to the Millers on April 13.[23] Early on, he made a strong impression. Indeed, as Stew Thornley wrote, "That summer, fans witnessed the greatest single-day mound performance in the history of the Millers. Tied for first with Milwaukee, Minneapolis faced the Brewers in a doubleheader at Nicollet Park July 13. Irving (Young Cy) Young held the Brewers to four hits in the first game to win, 1-0. Young also homered in the fifth for the game's only run. So impressive was Young that [manager Jimmy] Collins stuck with the southpaw in the nightcap; this time Young Cy held the Brewers hitless until the ninth, finishing with a one-hitter and 5-0 victory. The double shutout put the Millers two games in front of Milwaukee. The two teams scraped for the lead the next two months, but both faded in the final week, allowing Louisville to sneak into first as the season ended."[24]

Young had an excellent season, winning 23 games (23-18), with a 2.31 ERA. It was enough to earn him one last shot in the bigs. Charlie Comiskey, owner of the Chicago White Sox, picked up his contract for 1910.

For the White Sox, Young pitched effectively, sporting a 2.72 ERA. Again, however, he was with a weak club. Poor Irv was forever with bad clubs: in the two years he toiled for the Chisox, the best that can be said is that their record improved from 17 games under .500 to three games over .500. The 1910 White Sox won 68, lost 85, and finished sixth. In 17 starts, Young Cy was 4-8. It is worthy of note that all four victories were shutouts.

The year 1911 was Irv Young's last in the major leagues, and the team was 77-74. His record was 5-6, but his ERA leapt to a career-high 4.37. With a week left to go in the season, the White Sox released him back to Minneapolis.[25] He won a key game against Toledo on September 24.[26] The Millers finished first in the standings.

Young remained in the American Association, pitching for both Minneapolis and later the Milwaukee Brewers, through mid-1916. His teams finished first four years in succession—in 1911, 1912, 1913, and 1914. He was 16-14 for Minneapolis in 1912. His combined record for the two clubs in 1913 was 15-10. In both 1914 and 1915 he was a 20-game winner for the Brewers (20-16, 2.87) and 20-18 (2.62), respectively. He threw a league-leading seven shutouts in 1915, six of them before July 1.[27] In 1916, he was 0-3 in 16 appearances.

Young later played and coached in the Southern League. Later still, while living in Orrington, Maine, he played a bit and coached there, too.

By 1918, Young was back in Columbia Falls, working in a canning factory that September at the time he registered for the military draft during the World War. Two years later, he is listed as farming—a general farm, living with Elizabeth and their daughter.

Young's career record in the majors sees him 63-95, but with a 3.11 earned-run average that would be the envy of almost any pitcher in the past 100 years.

As a batter, he hadn't helped his teams much. He hit for a .126 batting average at the plate with a .148 on-base percentage in 496 major-league plate appearances. He drove in 18 runs in his 209 big-league games, and scored 21 times. As a fielder, he had a .958 fielding percentage (22 errors in 527 chances.)

Young lost his wife in 1926. He himself suffered a heart attack and died unexpectedly at the home of nephew Howard Young in South Brewer, Maine, on January 14, 1935, just across the Penobscot River from Bangor.[28] A rather small death notice appeared toward the back of the *Bangor Daily News* two days later. He was survived by his daughter, Mrs. William Hughes; a grandson, William Hughes Jr.; his sister, Minerva; and several nephews and nieces. He had been a member of the Brotherhood of Locomotive Firemen and the Tuscan Lodge of the Free and Accepted Masons.[29]

One can only suspect that if Irv Young had toiled for the Giants or the Cubs or the Pirates—the powerhouse, run-scoring teams of his National League heyday — rather than the lowly Beaneaters/Doves, his passing would have instead been front-page stuff.

Young is buried in Ruggles Cemetery in Columbia Falls.

## SOURCES

A brief version of this biography originally appeared in Will Anderson's self-published 1992 book *Was Baseball Really Invented in Maine?* and is presented here with the author's permission. Bill Nowlin has added new material, expanding on the original biography.

Thanks to Elizabeth Stevens of the Bangor Public Library for assistance.

## NOTES

1. United States Census, 1900; and Harold Kaese, *The Boston Braves, 1871-1953* (Boston: Northeastern University Press, 2004), 111.
2. "Young Cy 'Find' Of Season," *Tacoma* (Washington) *Daily News;* August 12, 1905: 17.
3. Young's earlier history in New England was described in "Irving Young, Pitcher of Concord, N.H. Baseball Team, Has Enviable Record," *Boston Herald*, July 4, 1904: 5.
4. "It Wants 'Young Cy,'" *Boston Globe*, June 13, 1905: 11.
5. "National League: Brooklyns Make Good Start, but Are Finally Beaten by Boston," *New York Times*, April 19, 1905: 12.
6. Bill Swift, from South Portland, Maine, won 21 games for the 1993 San Francisco Giants. This occurred after the original author's article was written.
7. "National League: New Yorks Could Not Hit Young, but Landed on Willis and Won," *New York Times*, June 4, 1905: 22.
8. "Find of the Year," *Boston Journal*, June 5, 1905: 4.
9. Ibid.
10. "Sports and Athletics," *Biloxi* (Mississippi) *Daily Herald*, August 25, 1905: 3.
11. "Winning Run Scored in Twelfth Inning," *New York Times*, June 25, 1905: 9.
12. "New Yorks Shut Out, Then Beat Boston," *New York Times*, September 8, 1905: 7.
13. "'Old Cy' Stacks Up Against 'Young Cy,'" *Boston Globe*, October 11, 1905: 2.
14. See, for instance, "Giants After 'Young Cy,'" *Boston Globe*, July 17, 1906: 8.
15. "'Young Cy' Young Weds Enthusiast," *Boston Herald*, September 13, 1906: 13.
16. "Murphy Controls Chicago 'Cubs,'" *Rockford* (Illinois) *Morning Star,* October 18, 1906: 2.
17. "After Young Cy Young," *Hartford Courant*, December 18, 1906: 9.
18. "'Young Cy' Climbs On to Tenney Wagon," *Boston Herald*, March 1, 1907: 9.
19. "Young 'Cy' May Go," *Boston Globe*, July 22, 1907: 5.
20. Ben Tavis, "Why Able Baseball Pitchers Sometimes Lose Their Cunning," *Lexington* (Kentucky) *Leader*, June 14, 1908: 5.
21. "Great Victory for Young Cy," *Los Angeles Times*, August 23, 1908: VI1.
22. "Famous Pitcher Hustles Freight to Prepare for Next Campaign," *Daily Illinois State Journal* (Springfield), February 7, 1909: 9.
23. "White Sox Will Get Four A.A. Players," *Kalamazoo Gazette*, April 14, 1909: 6.
24. Stew Thornley, *On to Nicollet: The Glory and Fame of the Minneapolis Millers* (Minneapolis: Nodin Press, 1988), 27.
25. "Olmstead and Young to Minneapolis," *Daily Illinois State Journal,* September 24, 1911: 14.
26. "Minneapolis 6, Toledo 1," *Omaha World-Herald*, September 25, 1911: 4.
27. Sam Weller, "Cy Young Leads in Using Brush," *Chicago Tribune,* October 31, 1915: B4.
28. Hilda Noyes McLean, "I Remember ... Baseball's 'Young Cy' Young," *Down East Enterprise* (Camden, Maine), November 1971: 98.
29. "Irving Young," *Bangor Daily News*, January 16, 1935: 10.

# 20-GAME LOSERS IN THE MINOR LEAGUES

## BY BILL NOWLIN

**WERE THERE MORE OR THEM OR** fewer of them? There are many more minor-league teams than there are major-league teams, and the pitchers at the minor-league level are there for a reason—though perhaps developing on their way to the big leagues. On the other hand, minor-league seasons tend to be shorter. A minor-league pitcher might be lucky to get 25 starts in a season, as opposed to maybe 33 for a pitcher in the major leagues. There would thus be fewer opportunities to lose 20.

Just as in the big leagues, though, for a pitcher to be kept on the team long enough to lose 20 games, that would likely have to be a pretty good pitcher. Otherwise, he might get cut, or sent to a lower level—unless the team was truly in a bind and simply had to keep someone on for lack of another pitcher as a replacement.

Right now, I unfortunately can't recall who first drew Tim Smith to my attention. He was a member of the New Britain Red Sox in 1992, and finished the season with a record of 3-20. That's quite a record, a .130 winning percentage.

But there are twentieth-century major-league pitchers who won a smaller percentage of their games. You'll find some of them in this book. Jack Nabors of the 1916 Philadelphia Athletics was 1-20 (.048), Joe Harris of the 1906 Boston Americans was 2-21 (.087), Kaiser Wilhelm of the 1905 Boston Beaneaters was 3-23 (.115), and Don Larsen of the 1954 Baltimore Orioles was 3-21 (.125).

Going back into the nineteenth century, one must acknowledge Jim Hughey of the 1899 Cleveland Spiders, who was 4-30 (.118) and John Cassidy, who was 1-21 (.045) with the 1875 Brooklyn Atlantics—despite having a 3.03 earned-run average.

It turns out that in recent years there have not been many 20-game losers either in the majors or the minors. Tim Smith was the last minor leaguer to lose 20, and that was 25 years ago, in 1992. The last major-leaguer to lose 20 was the Detroit Tigers' Mike Maroth (9-21 in 2003).

The last major leaguer prior to Maroth was Brian Kingman of the 1980 Oakland A's—23 years earlier. And the last minor leaguer prior to Tim Smith was George Angel with the 1964 York White Roses of the Double-A Eastern League, some 28 years earlier. Between Angel and Smith, there were 22 major-league pitchers who lost 20 or more games, leading to a sense that it might indeed be more frequent that pitchers lose 20 in the majors than in the minors.

Let's look by decade, though, and see if there are differences over time. We do indeed see that from 1961 through 1980 there were 30 major-league pitchers who lost 20 or more games in a single season as compared with only 3 minor leaguers. Before that, however, the trend was clearly the other way around. Many more minor leaguers were left in despite mounting loss totals during the course of a given season.

### Number of 20-Game Losers, 1901-2016

| Decade | # major-league pitchers with 20 or more losses | # minor leaguers* |
| --- | --- | --- |
| 1901-10 | 77 | 441 |
| 1911-20 | 35 | 219 |
| 1921-30 | 17 | 191 |
| 1931-40 | 21 | 73 |
| 1941-50 | 13 | 56 |
| 1951-60 | 10 | 30 |
| 1961-70 | 15 | 3 |
| 1971-80 | 15 | 0 |
| 1981-90 | 0 | 0 |

| 1991–2000 | 0 | 1 |
| 2001–10 | 1 | 0 |
| 2011–16 | 0 | 0 |

*Includes all levels of minor-league play, as well as some independent or leagues which were not affiliated. The Pacific Coast League, for instance, was sometimes designated as Open classification.

The year 1904 stands out as a banner year for 20-game Losers. There were 55 pitchers that year who lost 20 or more games in the course of the one season. Thirteen of them were major leaguers and 42 were minor leaguers.

These totals derive from data compiled by Sean Lahman. Emmet Nowlin helped with fact-checking.

Now, back to Tim Smith, the only minor league in the past half-century (52 years, to be precise, since George Angel in 1964). Tim was born in Melrose, Massachusetts, on August 9, 1968. A right-hander, he was drafted by the Boston Red Sox in 1990, and signed by Red Sox scout Bill Enos, but it wasn't that he was predestined for a professional baseball career.

"I hadn't really pitched much in high school," he said in an interview on March 30, 2017. "I pitched my senior year. I had a no-hitter in high school, so there was something there. I liked baseball. I liked hitting. I'm 6-4 so I had a pitcher's body. I had a good sinker." He attended Boston College and played baseball but he walked onto the team. "I tried out for the Cape League and made the team for Brewster in my sophomore and junior year."

And then he was drafted by the Milwaukee Brewers at the end of his junior year. BC's baseball coach was Bill Travers. He had pitched in the big leagues for the Brewers from 1974 through 1980. There's a good chance that Travers had something to do with Smith being drafted in the 31st round of the June 1989 amateur draft. Smith declined the opportunity to sign, intent on completing his education and graduating with his class at BC.

The very next year, the Red Sox drafted him, this time in the 24th round.

"And even then I was surprised," he said. "I wasn't expecting that. I would have good outings and bad outings. Well, I wouldn't say bad outings. I had a good sinker. I had some success. I think I had more success as a reliever. I was like .500 as a starter. I had a lot of success in the Cape League as a reliever. I would come in and throw strikes. Which is good and bad."

After graduation, he was assigned to the Elmira Pioneers in the Class-A New York-Penn League to pitch for the remainder of the season. He appeared in 23 games, two as a starter, and had a decent record (4-6, 3.68) but pitched a bit better than the stats show. "I had a good year at Elmira," he says, "but I had one bad outing where I gave up eight or nine runs, and I think I got like one out. He left me out there to dry."

The next year, Smith was made a starter with the Lynchburg (Virginia) Red Sox in the Carolina League, also Class A. He had a very good year, going 12-9 in 25 starts with a 2.16 ERA and eight complete games. But he almost certainly was worked too hard. "I hadn't pitched a ton [before Lynchburg], but then all of a sudden, I hurt my shoulder when I pitched that season. I was never really the same after that.

"I just did not want to come out of games. If you look, I threw 170-plus innings. Plus spring training. Plus getting ready for it. They do a lot of those pitch counts now, and inning counts. They slowly notch people up. If you put me in the bucket of the example of what not to do … really, my arm was popping out of the socket at the end of the year."

He went to see Dr. Arthur Pappas of the Boston Red Sox and was put on a physical therapy program. He feels now that he should have taken the next year off—the 1992 season. "I couldn't pitch the same. I didn't have the same pitches."

Smith was assigned to New Britain in the Double-A Eastern League, and that's the year he lost 20 games.

"That 20 losses pops out at you now, but it was all gravy at the end of the day for me. Just being there. You don't want to lose that many games. Some of the games I was terrible and some of the games we lost were close games, but it is what it is.

"My velocity was way down. I didn't have my second pitch, my slurve pitch. During that year, I started to develop a changeup which I then starting using the next year. The next two years I started off like 6-2 and then it just … my arm couldn't sustain it for the season. It's a long season."

The March 30 interview was about 10 days after I first reached out to Tim to request an interview. Thanks to the alumni folks at Boston College athletics for making the connection. In the interim, he had done some looking around at pitchers who had lost 20 games.

"That one year … after you first reached out to me I looked up 20-game losers, and there was a category of people that had good years and then had bad years. It might be that when you have a good year, you pitch a lot.

"I think it's a lot harder to do [lose 20 games] in the minors, because you don't get as many starts. You don't start 33 or 35 games. I pretty much had a decision in every start. I was trying to get better. I was leading the game in my last start when I came out, and still took the loss."

When he was at 19 losses, no one spoke to him about taking the rest of the season off, neither manager Jim Pankovits nor pitching coach Rick Wise. If they'd asked, he says, "I wouldn't have done that. When you're a minor leaguer, you've got to do everything you can to be seen. I was just so bullheaded, and that's part of the reason I wouldn't come out of games."

New Britain finished in last place, 58-82. "We were in last place and I contributed to that. You could say we didn't score as many runs, and there were better teams. And if I had pitched the way I did on another, maybe it would have been different but I definitely contributed to that.

"In some of the games [in 1992] I pitched lousy in the beginning of the game and then got better. And there was one game, I think I lost in 11 innings. Complete game. Sometimes my pitch counts were low, because I was a groundball pitcher, but just getting up and throwing. …

"If you look back and analyze it, the biggest thing for me was that injury. I just never should have pitched that year. The best thing for me would have been to strengthen and rest.

"If I was healthy, I wouldn't have been in that situation. I just should not have started the season. I should have just rehabbed and not even have gotten ready for spring training. Knowing what we know now about pitch counts and innings. … I pitched 175 innings in Lynchburg and the year before I only had 66."

Smith was brought back again in 1993 and 1994, pitching both years for New Britain, appearing in 28 games each year, with all but two appearances as a starter. He lowered his ERA to 3.79 in 1993 (but had a 7-13 record on a team that did worse than the year before, 52-88). In 1994, he was 6-14 as New Britain finished last (still under Pankovits) for the third year in a row.

"At the end of that last season, I was ready to quit. Ready to move on with my life. And I got traded to Seattle, out of nowhere, for Lee Tinsley. My girlfriend at the time was like, 'Well, what are you going to do?' I went to spring training and they really worked with me. I started throwing a lot harder. They changed my motion. Where I was usually high 80s, now I'm hitting low 90s. But I just mentally was not … I was ready to move on."

Smith works as a technology recruiter now. He's raising a family. He looks back on his 20-loss season still pleased with having given baseball a try.

"I played those years. I did my best. It's all good, the way I look at it. Baseball was all gravy. A little bit of gravy burned a little bit on the side there. A 20-loss season. I didn't plan on that but I knew I was a lot better than that."

# 20-GAME LOSERS

**Minor Leaguers with the Lowest Winning Percentage**

| Year | Player | League | Team | Record |
|---|---|---|---|---|
| 1950 | Charles Rogers | Longhorn League (Class D) | Ballinger Cats | 1-20 (.048) |
| 1939 | Douglass Ivey | Florida State League (Class D) | Palatka Azaleas | 3-22 (.120) |
| 1931 | Paul Duing | Middle Atlantic League (Class C) | Jeannette Jays/Altoona Engineers/Beaver Falls Beavers* | 2-20 (.091) |
| 1925 | Lee Wilson | Michigan-Ontario (Class B) | Flint Vehicles/Kitchener Colts** | 3-22 (.120) |
| 1920 | Rube Kroh | Texas League (Class B) | Houston Buffaloes/Shreveport Gassers/Galveston Pirates*** | 3-21 (.125) |
| 1915 | Dan Keller | Three-I League (Class B) | Dubuque Dubs/Freeport Comeons**** | 3-20 (.130) |
| 1914 | James Wainwright | Texas League (Class B) | Austin Senators | 3-22 (.120) |
| 1911 | Ralph Davie | Ohio-Pennsylvania League (Class C) | New Castle/Sharon** | 1-20 (.048) |
| 1906 | Peter Hansen | Northern-Copper Country League (Class C) | Fargo Trolley Dodgers | 3-23 (.115) |
| 1906 | Arch McCarthy | Eastern League (Class A) | Toronto Maple Leafs | 2-21 (.087) |
| 1905 | Glenn Liebhardt | Western League (Class A) | Omaha Rourkes/St. Joseph Saints** | 4-26 (.133) |
| 1902 | Walter Deaver | Southern League (Class B) | Nashville Volunteers/Birmingham Barons***** | 4-24 (.143) |
|  | George Haddock | International Association (unclassified) | Troy Trojans | 3-25 (.107) |

*The team moved twice during the course of the season. It finished with a record of 32-96.

**Player moved from one team to another during the season.

***Kroh, a former major leaguer, played for three different teams in the league in 1920.

****These franchises moved from one city to another during the season.

*****Deaver was 0-1 for Nashville, and 4-23 for Birmingham.

# CHRIS ARCHER
## Nearly A 20-game Loser in 2016

### BY BILL NOWLIN

**BACK WHEN CHRIS ARCHER WAS AT** 17 losses on the season, the *Boston Globe*'s Nick Cafardo wrote in his Sunday Notes column: "It says here that the Rays will not allow Chris Archer to lose 20 games. He's at 17 right now. The Rays, who are considered to be on the cutting edge of pitching, don't want their star pitcher being forever known for losing 20. The last pitcher to lose 20 was Mike Maroth, a former Red Sox farmhand who did it with the Tigers in 2003, when he went 9-21. That was the year [current Red Sox GM] Dave Dombrowski started working for the Tigers. 'We discussed [shutting him down] in Maroth's case, but he wanted to continue to pitch,' said Dombrowski."[1]

When he was at 17 losses, Bill Nowlin asked Archer about the possibility in an August 29 interview. "If you get to the point where you're at 18 or 19 losses, do you think someone will have a talk with you? Will you just keep on?" Archer's response, expressing surprise at the question: "What would there be to talk about? Am I going to take the ball if I have 18 or 19? Yeah. You take the ball."

NESN analyst Jerry Remy during the September 23 television broadcast as Archer was on tap to perhaps lose his 19th game (he did, by the score of 2-1), about him possibly going for a 20th loss. "They're not going to let him do that. They're a last place team and they're not going anywhere. They'll take him out of the rotation."

Archer hadn't had the best record against the Red Sox, in any event. Through the 23rd, he was 1-11 vs. Boston (and 0-5 in 2016 alone.)

Remy was wrong. Archer did start the game, in Chicago, on September 29. He pitched 6 2/3 innings, giving up three runs, and earned the win in the 5-3 game. He finished the season 9-19. But let it be known that Rays manager Kevin Cash and pitching coach Jim Hickey were willing to put Archer out there, in a position to lose 20, and Archer willingly took the ball. We're not in a position to know what conversations may or may not have taken place before the game.

### NOTES

1. Nick Cafardo, "MLB Must Address September Roster Expansion," *Boston Globe*, August 27, 2016.

# 19-GAME LOSERS, 1961-2016

## COMPILED BY CARL RIECHERS AND WARREN CORBETT

Source: baseball-reference.com

**Protected**
**Total: 13.** These pitchers did not start again after their 19th defeat, skipping at least one turn.
1961 Art Mahaffey, Phillies, record 11-19.
1961 Bob Friend, Pirates, 14-19.
1962 Jay Hook, Mets, 8-19.
1963 Don Rudolph, Senators, 7-19.
1974 Paul Splittorff, Royals, 13-19.
1974 Jim Bibby, Rangers, 19-19.
1974 Wilbur Wood, White Sox, 20-19.
1978 Rick Wise, Indians, 9-19.
1990 Tim Leary, Yankees, 9-19.
1991 Kirk McCaskill, Angels, 10-19.
2000 Omar Daal, Diamondbacks-Phillies, 4-19.
2003 Jeremy Bonderman, Tigers, 6-19.
2004 Darrell May, Royals, 9-19.

**Not Protected**
**Total: 39.** These pitchers made one or more additional starts after their 19th defeat.
1961 Pedro Ramos, Twins, 11-20.
1962 Roger Craig, Mets, 10-24.
1962 Al Jackson, Mets, 8-20.
1962 Dick Ellsworth, Cubs, 9-20.
1962 Turk Farrell, Astros, 10-20.
1963 Roger Craig, Mets, 5-22.
1963 Orlando Pena, Athletics, 12-20.
1964 Tracy Stallard, Mets, 10-20.
1964 Jack Fisher, Mets, 8-24.
1965 Larry Jackson, Cubs, 14-21.
1965 Al Jackson, Mets, 8-20.
1966 Dick Ellsworth, Cubs, 8-22.
1966 Mel Stottlemyre, Yankees, 12-20.
1969 Clay Kirby, Padres, 7-20.
1969 Luis Tiant, Indians, 9-20.
1970 Steve Carlton, Cardinals, 10-19.
1971 Denny McLain, Senators, 10-22.
1972 Steve Arlin, Padres, 9-19.
1973 Stan Bahnsen, White Sox, 18-21.
1973 Steve Carlton, Phillies, 13-20.
1973 Wilbur Wood, White Sox, 24-20.
1973 Clyde Wright, Angels, 11-19.
1973 Gaylord Perry, Indians, 19-19.
1974 Bill Bonham, Cubs, 11-22.
1974 Randy Jones, Padres, 8-22.
1974 Steve Rogers, Expos, 15-22.
1974 Mickey Lolich, Tigers, 16-21.
1974 Clyde Wright, Brewers, 9-20.
1974 Frank Tanana, Angels, 14-19.
1975 Wilbur Wood, White Sox, 16-20.
1977 Jerry Koosman, Mets, 8-20.
1977 Phil Niekro, Braves, 16-20.
1977 Vida Blue, Athletics, 14-19.
1979 Phil Niekro, Braves, 21-20.
1980 Brian Kingman, Athletics, 8-20.
1987 Mike Moore, Mariners, 9-19.
1993 Scott Erickson, Twins, 8-19.
2003 Mike Maroth, Tigers, 9-21.
2016 Chris Archer, Rays, 9-19.

**Season ended before next start.**
**Total: 15.**
1964 Galen Cisco, Mets, 6-19.
1966 Sammy Ellis, Reds, 12-19.
1967 George Brunet, Angels, 11-19.
1969 Bill Stoneman, Expos, 11-19.
1970 Mickey Lolich, Tigers, 14-19.
1971 Steve Arlin, Padres, 9-19.
1974 Bill Greif, Padres, 9-19.
1974 Lerrin LaGrow, Tigers, 8-19.
1977 Wayne Garland, Indians, 13-19.
1985 Jose DeLeon, Pirates, 2-19.
1985 Matt Young, Mariners, 12-19.
1990 Jose DeLeon, Cardinals, 7-19.
2001 Albie Lopez, Devil Rays-Diamondbacks, 9-19.
2001 Bobby J. Jones, Padres, 8-19.
2016 James Shields, Padres-White Sox, 6-19.

# THE PROTECTION MYTH

## Most Pitchers Don't Duck the Risk of 20 Losses

### BY WARREN CORBETT

**CHRIS ARCHER TOOK THE MOUND** for the Tampa Bay Rays at Chicago's U.S. Cellular Field on September 29, 2016, in a meaningless game between two teams slogging to the end of disappointing seasons. But a defeat would make Archer the majors' first 20-game loser in a dozen years.

That didn't matter to him—or so he said. He didn't believe a pitcher's won-lost record was a true measure of his value. The 28-year-old right-hander was a rising star suffering through a miserable season. Personable and outgoing, he was a fan and media favorite, and a tireless off-the-field worker on behalf of children.

The first half of 2016 had been a disaster. After the Rays' ace lost his first four games, his ERA stood at 7.32 and the sports talkers were asking, "What's wrong with Archer?" He had turned it around, holding opposing batters to a .260 on-base percentage after the All-Star break.

Archer's 19th defeat came on September 23 when Boston beat him, the 11th straight time he had lost to the Red Sox. The score, 2-1, was typical of his season; the last-place Rays had scored no more than two runs in 12 of his losses.

In his final start he shut out the White Sox until the sixth, and his teammates gave him a 5-1 lead at the seventh-inning stretch. In the bottom of the seventh, Chicago's light-hitting second baseman, Carlos Sanchez, slammed a two-run homer to narrow the margin to 5-3. That was also typical of Archer's season; it was the 30th home run he had allowed. Relievers Brad Boxberger, Erasmo Ramirez, and Alex Colome pitched scoreless ball the rest of the way to preserve the victory, only Archer's ninth of the year.

He insisted he hadn't worried about a 20th loss: "Honestly, I never let those type of things creep into my mind because it's pointless to think about negatives."[1]

*Tampa Bay Times* columnist Martin Kennelly said that if he had been Archer, "I would have come up with a stomach flu or something, anything."[2] The comment reflects the widespread belief that pitchers will hide in their lockers to avoid the stigma of a 20-loss season.

It ain't so, Joe. It is not at all common for a pitcher to dodge the risk of a 20th defeat. In 56 seasons of baseball's Expansion Era, since 1961, pitchers have lost 19 games 67 times (some more than once). The majority, 39, took their chances in at least one more start. For most it was a bad, if brave, bet; 31 of them were charged with a 20th defeat.

Two days after Archer's last start of 2016, the White Sox' James Shields lost his 19th decision. It came in Chicago's 161st game, so Shields didn't pitch again. That was the case with 15 of the pitchers who have lost 19 games in the Expansion Era: The season ended before they had a chance to lose number 20.

Just 13 of the 67 19-game losers were protected from a 20th defeat by either their managers or their own choice. Here are three typical examples:

In 2003 Detroit's Jeremy Bonderman lost his 19th in the club's 153rd game. His teammate Mike Maroth had already lost 21 as the Tigers staggered to the worst record in their history, 43-119.

Manager Alan Trammell was protecting Bonderman, a 20-year-old rookie right-hander who was one of the Tigers' bright hopes for the future. He had been dropped from the starting rotation in September because he was getting battered; he finished with a 5.56 ERA. After his 19th defeat in his only start in the last four weeks of the season, Bonderman said, "I don't care what happens, I just want to play."[3] Trammell put him into two more games as a reliever, in situations when the Tigers had big leads so he wasn't at risk of being charged with a loss.

In some cases managers made it clear that they didn't want their man to lose again. When the Cardinals' Jose DeLeon was knocked out in the second inning of his 19th defeat in 1990, his catcher, Tom Pagnozzi, said, "Not only was it not a good day, but it was not a good year." It was DeLeon's 14th loss in his last 15 decisions. What's more, he had suffered through a 2-19 season with Pittsburgh five years earlier.

Cardinals manager Joe Torre said DeLeon's confidence was shot: "He has to start over and not even know this year existed."[4] As it happened, DeLeon developed arm trouble the following year and was never a frontline starter again.

Some pitchers quietly disappeared after a 19th defeat. In 1990 Tim Leary lost his 19th in the Yankees' 149th game and didn't pitch again. Leary didn't deserve his 9-19 record; his adjusted ERA of 96 was just slightly worse than league-average. The club was in last place, going nowhere but home. The Yankees made no announcement, but they were negotiating a new contract with Leary and evidently decided to save him from embarrassment.

Only seven other Expansion Era pitchers have done what Archer did. Like Ted Williams chasing a .400 batting average on the last day of the 1941 season, they chose to face failure and stared it down. They avoided the dreaded 20th loss.

In 1993 Minnesota's Scott Erickson lost his 19th, his fourth straight defeat, in the club's 149th game. Taking his regular turn, Erickson started twice more. He didn't discuss his decision; he wasn't speaking to the media. A "mystery man" who dressed in black but couldn't sing like Johnny Cash, the right-handed sinkerballer had been a 20-game winner during the Twins' worst-to-first run in 1991, but had fallen on hard times.

His next start almost became his 20th loss. After he left the game in the seventh with two men on, reliever Carl Willis allowed both to score, putting Boston up, 4-3, with Erickson in line to be the losing pitcher. The Twins rallied to tie, taking him off the hook. In his final appearance he worked seven innings against the Angels and sat down with a 2-1 lead. Again Twins relievers blew the lead and the game, leaving Erickson with no decision. He finished 8-19 with a 5.19 ERA.

Right-hander Mike Moore spent the first seven years of his career with the 1980s Seattle Mariners, so he had plenty of losing experience. In 1987 he lost for the 19th time on September 20, in the Mariners' 149th game. He started twice more and won them both, although he gave up six earned runs in his final start, to finish at 9-19. Two years later Moore was traded to Oakland, won 19 games, and wound up pitching in two World Series with the A's.

Oakland's Vida Blue, a three-time 20-game winner, lost his 19th in the Athletics' 152nd game of 1977. With the club headed for last place in the AL West, he took his next turn and pitched nine innings without a decision. "I was glad not to lose 20, but it's no big deal," he said.[5] He skipped his final start, pleading a tired arm after 279⅔ innings. Blue was traded to the Giants after the season; he would happily have swum across the bay to get away from the sinking, stinking A's.

Frank Tanana was the rookie phenom of 1974 when he joined the Angels' rotation. (He had started four games the previous September.) But he lost seven straight decisions in June and July to fall to 4-13 with a 4.05 ERA.

After the All-Star break the 20-year-old left-hander looked like a different pitcher. "I said to myself, 'Hey, if I don't turn myself around I'm going to [Triple-A] Salt Lake City,'" he explained. "I buckled down."[6] He began missing bats and dramatically cut down his walks and home runs allowed.

The Angels were no help; they settled at the bottom of the AL West. Despite a 2.13 ERA in the second half, Tanana was charged with his 19th loss in Game 155. "He's going to be a damn good pitcher," manager Dick Williams said. "We wouldn't care if he had 10 more shots at losing that 20th."[7] Tanana made two more starts, both complete-game victories. He beat Minnesota, 3-2, and then, with three days' rest, shut out first-place Oakland, striking out 10. *The Sporting News* named the 19-game loser the AL Rookie Pitcher of the Year.

Tanana's September promotion a year earlier probably saved teammate Clyde Wright from 20 losses. When Wright lost for the 17th time in 1973, a little girl named Debbie Wright, not related, gave him a rabbit's foot. He won his next two games, but the rabbit's good luck soon died. Clyde (and Debbie) were victims of weak run support; the Angels scored no more than two runs in 13 of his starts.

After the veteran lefty lost his 19th in Game 135, with nearly a month left in the season, Tanana replaced him in the rotation as the team tried out some prospects. Wright pitched once in mop-up relief, then made two spot starts with a victory and a no-decision to finish at 11-19. The Angels traded him to Milwaukee, where he lost 20 the next year.

Unlike Tanana, Gaylord Perry was an established ace coming off a Cy Young Award when he lost 19 with Cleveland in 1973. He started 41 times that year and worked a career-high 344 innings for the last-place Indians. Perry's 19th defeat came in Game 143. After that he took the ball every fourth day and won four in a row, the last a 1-0 shutout of Boston, to square his record at 19-19. Perry's turn came around again on the final day of the season. He could have finished as a 20-game winner or a 20-game loser. Instead he went home to North Carolina, saying in effect, "Who cares?"

Twenty-four-year-old Steve Carlton had blossomed into an elite pitcher in 1969, when his 2.17 ERA was second in the National League. But in 1970 his ERA ballooned by 1.56 runs and his strikeout rate declined on the way to 19 defeats. "My control hasn't been as good and I haven't been getting my pitches down as well as last year," he said.[8] (He had not yet stopped talking to reporters.)

After losing number 19 in the Cardinals' 148th game, Carlton didn't run away. He started twice more, pitching seven innings without a decision and then ending his season with a complete-game victory over Montreal.

To recap:

19-Game Losers 1961-2016
| | |
|---|---|
| Made at least one more start | 39 |
| Season ended before next start | 15 |
| "Protected" from 20 losses | 13 |

These findings show that the round number 20 in the loss column is a bigger deal for sportswriters and fans than for pitchers. Major-league pitchers are competitive men. Most don't want to be seen as quitting on the team or playing for their own statistics.

So when another pitcher loses number 19, watch what he does next.

## SOURCES

Statistics from Baseball-reference.com and its Play Index.

## NOTES

1. Mark Topkin, "Rays' Archer Tops 200 Innings, Avoids 20 Losses in Win Over White Sox," *Tampa Bay Times*, September 29, 2016. tampabay.com/sports/baseball/rays/rays-manager-cash-says-record-wont-define-archer/2295899, accessed November 8, 2016.
2. Martin Fennelly, "Rays' Chris Archer, the 20-Loss Stigma and The Measure of This Pitcher," *Tampa Bay Times*, September 29, 2016. tampabay.com/sports/baseball/rays/rays-chris-archer-the-20-loss-stigma-and-the-measure-of-this-pitcher/2295755, accessed November 8, 2016.
3. Associated Press, "Twins Maintain AL Central Lead," *Fort Myers* (Florida) *News-Press*, September 20, 2003: 31.
4. Rick Hummel, "Torre Looking for Changes in DeLeon in 1991," *St. Louis Post-Dispatch*, September 29, 1990: 4C.
5. "Vida Happy It's Over," *San Mateo* (California) *Times*, September 29, 1977: 19.
6. Dick Miller, "Brash Tanana Wins Frosh Hill Prize," *The Sporting News*, November 26, 1974: 44.
7. Dan Hafner, "Angels Win 3-2 on Pinch Single," *Los Angeles Times*, September 28, 1974: III-5.
8. Associated Press, "Major Leagues," *Chillicothe* (Missouri) *Constitution-Tribune*, September 9, 1970: 21.

# CONTRIBUTORS

**NIALL ADLER** has been paid to watch sports (and sometimes theatre) since 1998. Everything from diving to swimming, water polo, Aussie Rules, horse racing, hockey, futbol and gridiron, and… baseball on four continents and at two of the top collegiate programs, Long Beach State and Stanford. He's even judged a demolition derby. Educated at the University of San Francisco and farther South in Melbourne, Australia, he's worked some larger events like BCS Bowl Games, the Australian Open, Pan American Games and the Melbourne Cup.

**WILL ANDERSON**, who died in March 2015, wrote nine books on beer but is noted in baseball circles as a 2002 inductee into the Maine Baseball Hall of Fame and member of the committee to bring the Portland Seadogs to Maine. He also wrote about roadside architecture, baseball, and 1950s Rock and roll, and was honored with the Maine Historic Preservation Award for his "diligent and dedicated service in support of Maine's historic and cultural heritage." He authored the 1992 book which was a precursor of SABR's "team books"— *Was Baseball Really Invented in Maine?* He followed that work with *The Lost New England Nine (2003)*, by which time the Tom Simon-edited *Green Mountain Boys of Summer* (2000) had also been published.

**BOB BAILEY** has been contributing to SABR Publications since 1988. He has writing extensively on the Nineteenth Century Louisville Colonels and the Junior World Series of the twentieth century. In 2013 he was one of the Associate Editors of SABR's *Inventing Baseball*. He has published two books on baseball topics. "*History of the Junior World Series* was a finalist for the 2004 Casey Award and *Baseball Burial Sites* cataloged over 8,000 burial locations for players and others associated with baseball. For the past 10 years he has edited "Nineteenth Century Notes," the newsletter of SABR's Nineteenth Century Committee.

**CHARLIE BEVIS** is the author of six books on baseball history, most recently *Tim Keefe: A Biography of the Hall of Fame Pitcher and Player-Rights Advocate*. A member of SABR since 1984, he has contributed more than four dozen biographies to the SABR BioProject as well as several to SABR books, including *The 1967 Impossible Dream Red Sox*. He is an adjunct professor of English at Rivier University in Nashua, New Hampshire, and lives in Chelmsford, Massachusetts.

**DENNIS BINGHAM** served as a writer, editor, and historian for the Chicago Police Department for three decades and now works free-lance. A longtime umpire, he works more than 150 games a year in the Chicagoland area at various levels. His passions include reading, attending White Sox games, and the study of baseball rules. In 1988, he co-founded SABR's Umpires and Rules Committee with Larry Gerlach and Bob McConnell. He lives with wife Diane on Chicago's south side; both are delighted whenever the cutest grandson in the word visits them. Their sons Sean, Kevin, and Rocky have all escaped the household with Sean, a United States naval officer, recently being deployed overseas.

**CHUCK CAREY** is a retired computer consultant who joined SABR in 1976. He was born and grew up in Southern California, attending games of the PCL Angels and Stars. He graduated from UCLA and served in the U. S. Navy and Foreign Service. His father was a second cousin of pitcher Walter Johnson, and Chuck regrets never having met the great pitcher. He did, however, meet Walter's daughter Carolyn and grandson, Henry Thomas, and was proud to have done a small part of the research which Thomas used in his book, *Walter Johnson, Baseball's Big Train*.

**ALAN COHEN** has been a SABR member since 2011, serves as Vice President-Treasurer of the Connecticut Smoky Joe Wood Chapter, and is the datacaster (stringer) for the Hartford Yard Goats. He has written more than 35 biographies for SABR's bio-project, and has contributed to several SABR books. He has expanded his research into the Hearst Sandlot Classic (1946-1965), an annual youth All-Star game which launched the careers of 88 major-league players. He graduated from Franklin and Marshall College with a degree in history. He has four children and six grandchildren and resides in West Hartford, Connecticut with his wife Frances, one cat (Morty) and two dogs (Sam and Sheba).

**WARREN CORBETT** is the author of *The Wizard of Waxahachie: Paul Richards and the End of Baseball as We Knew It*, and a contributor to SABR's BioProject.

**PAUL E. DOUTRICH** is a professor of American History at York College of Pennsylvania. Among the courses he teaches is one entitled Baseball History. He has written numerous scholarly articles and books about the revolutionary era in America and has curated several museum exhibits for the state of Pennsylvania. For the past fifteen years his scholarship has focused on baseball history. He has contributed manuscripts to various SABR publications and is the author of *The Cardinals and the Yankees, 1926: A Classical Season and St. Louis in Seven*. He has been a Red Sox fan since 1962 when he spent an afternoon with Ted Williams.

**DON DOXSIE** has been a sports reporter, columnist and editor for newspapers in Illinois and Iowa over the past 41 years, working for the past 33 years for the Quad-City Times in Davenport, Iowa. He has won dozens of state and national writing awards, including first place in the Associated Press Sports Editors contest for enterprise reporting in 2000. He first joined SABR in 1981 and has authored two books, *Iron Man McGinnity* and *Iowa Baseball Greats: Sixteen Men Who Were in the Game For Life*. A native of the Chicago area, he is a lifelong Cubs fan, an avid genealogist and the proud father of two and grandfather of two.

**ALEX DRUDE** is the author of *26 In a Row: The 1916 New York Giants and Baseball's Longest Winning Streak*. He also writes about various subjects for SporadicSentinel.com. For many years he was a TV sports anchor and reporter in Oregon getting paid to cover cool things like the Rose Bowl and the Track and Field Olympic Trials. He is currently a freelance TV sports producer in the San Francisco Bay Area and his favorite Beatles album is *Rubber Soul*.

**JEFF ENGLISH** is a graduate of Florida State University and resides in Tallahassee, Florida with his wife Allison and twin sons, Elliott and Oscar. He is a lifelong Cubs fan and serves as secretary of the North Florida/Buck O'Neil SABR chapter. He has contributed to multiple SABR projects.

**CHARLES F. FABER** was a native of Iowa who lived in Lexington, Kentucky, until his passing in August 2016. He held degrees from Coe College, Columbia University, and the University of Chicago. A retired public school and university teacher and administrator, he contributed to numerous SABR projects, including editing *The 1934 St. Louis Cardinals*. Among his publications are dozens of professional journal articles, encyclopedia entries, and research reports in fields such as school administration, education law, and country music. In addition to textbooks, he wrote 10 books (mostly on baseball) published by McFarland. His last book, co-authored with his grandson Zachariah Webb, was *The Hunt for a Reds October*, published by McFarland in 2015.

**JEFF FINDLEY** is a native of Eastern Iowa, where he did the logical thing growing up in the heart of the Cubs/Cardinals rivalry—he embraced the 1969 Orioles and became a lifelong fan. An informational security professional for a large insurance company in Illinois, he compiles a daily sports "Pages Past" column for his local newspaper.

A retired English professor, **JAN FINKEL** lives on Deep Creek Lake in the western mountains of Maryland. He joined SABR in 1994 and has contributed to the *Baseball Research Journal*, *NINE*, and the Biography Project. He served for 13 thoroughly enjoyable years as chief editor of the Biography Project.

**DAVID FLEITZ** is a writer, baseball historian, and computer systems analyst from Troy, Michigan. A 1976 graduate of Bowling Green State University in Ohio, David pursued a teaching career for 10 years before entering the business world. While working in the information technology field, David wrote numerous freelance articles for magazines and newspapers before turning his attention to writing books. Since 2001, he has written nine books on baseball history, including biographies of Shoeless Joe Jackson, Louis Sockalexis (the first Native American major league player), and 19th-century star Cap Anson. His latest work, *Rowdy Patsy Tebeau and the Cleveland Spiders: Fighting to the Bottom of Baseball, 1887-1899*, was published by McFarland in 2017.

David is a member of the Society for American Baseball Research (SABR), and is a three-time winner of SABR's annual national baseball trivia championship.

**ERIC FROST** lives in the Houston area, where he is a neonatal intensive care nurse and a clinical instructor in pediatric nursing for a local university. Eric has been interested in win-loss oddities since 1987, when his childhood hero, Nolan Ryan, led NL pitchers in ERA and still lost 16 of his 24 decisions.

**CHARLES HAUSBERG** is an attorney in Spokane, Washington and lifelong Yankee fan. His most memorable baseball experience was attending Jim Abbott's no-hitter in 1993.

**PAUL HOFMANN** is the Associate Vice President for International Programs at Sacramento State University. He is a native of Detroit, Michigan and lifelong Detroit sports fan. His research interests include 19th century and pre-World War II Japanese baseball. He is also an avid baseball card collector. Paul currently resides in Folsom, California.

**TOM HUFFORD** was one of the 16 Founding Members of SABR at Cooperstown, NY in 1971, and was President of the Braves 400 Club in 1991 and 1992. An architect/engineer by profession, he was a consultant to the Atlanta Braves during the design and construction of Turner Field.

**BILL LAMB** is a retired New Jersey state/county prosecutor and the editor of The Inside Game, the quarterly newsletter of the Deadball Era Committee. He now resides with family in Meredith, New Hampshire.

**BOB LEMOINE**'s Little League career saw him involved in far more losses than wins, so he holds a special place in his heart for 20-game losers. Originally from Maine and now living in New Hampshire, Bob spends much of his time researching and writing for SABR, squeezing in his real job as a high school librarian when he can. With an interest in Boston and nineteenth century baseball, Bob was co-editor with Bill Nowlin on SABR's *Boston's First Nine: the 1871-75 Boston Red Stockings* in 2016.

**LEN LEVIN** is a retired newspaper editor who is now the "grammarian" of the Rhode Island Supreme Court. (That means he edits their decisions.) He also spends a lot of time going to baseball games and editing for SABR publications.

**DAN LEVITT** is the author of several baseball books and numerous essays. He is a longtime SABR member and a recipient of the Bob Davids Award and the Chadwick Award. His books have won the Larry Ritter Book Award, the Sporting News-SABR Baseball Research Award, and have twice been finalists for the Seymour Medal.

SABR member and Massachusetts native **MIKE LYNCH** is the founder of Seamheads.com and author of five books, including *Harry Frazee, Ban Johnson and the Feud That Nearly Destroyed the American League*, which was named a finalist for the 2009 Larry Ritter Award and nominated for a

Seymour Medal. His most recent work includes a three-book series called *Baseball's Untold History* and several articles that have appeared in SABR books and on The National Pastime Museum's website. He lives in Roslindale, Massachusetts with the love of his life.

**BARB MANTEGANI** is a Manchester, New Hampshire native and a lifelong Red Sox fan who has written biographies for several other BioProject books. One of her fondest baseball memories was attending her first game at Fenway Park and seeing all of the green as she walked up the tunnel for the first time. She lives in McLean, Virginia, and enjoys attending Washington Nationals games with her husband and BioProject co-author David Raglin, where they always keep score using their custom scorebooks.

A lifelong Red Sox fan, **WAYNE MCELREAVY** lives off the grid in the hills of New Hampshire.

A Baltimore native, **BRIAN MCKENNA** has contributed over 50 works to SABR's Biography Project. His full-length projects include a biography of Clark Griffith and an analysis of the premature endings of baseball careers. Recently, he researched and wrote the first comprehensive look at the beginning of the sport in Baltimore, 1858-1872. It is available through SABR's Baltimore chapter.

**JUSTIN MCKINNEY** lives in Ottawa, Ontario and writes about strange baseball history including that time Rube Waddell got bit by a lion at medium.com/@baseballobscura. He is an active contributor to the SABR Pictorial History Research Committee and has located images of 68 previously missing players and counting for the Player Image Index. Growing up in Calgary, he attended numerous Calgary Cannons games and became a Baltimore Orioles fan thanks to their cool logo and Cal Ripken Jr. He still laments the loss of the Montreal Expos.

**BARRY MEDNICK** is a software engineer specializing in customer support and quality control. He has also taught at the college and high school level and currently tutors prospective teachers. Mednick holds a BS and MS from Columbia University's School of Engineering where he majored in operations research. He has been active in the Society for American Baseball Research since 1983 and has published several articles on baseball.

**CHAD MOODY** is a nearly lifelong resident of suburban Detroit, where he has been a fan of the Detroit Tigers from birth. An alumnus of both the University of Michigan and Michigan State University, he has spent 25 years working in various administrative capacities in the automotive industry. Chad's first foray into baseball research occurred at age 17, when his letter on pitchers who have homered in the World Series was published in a 1984 issue of *Baseball Digest*. From that humble beginning, he has since become a contributor to the SABR BioProject and several upcoming SABR publications. Chad and his wife, Lisa, live in Northville, Michigan, with their children, Jacob and Jessica, and their feisty dog, Daisy.

**SKIP NIPPER** is a retired New Era Cap sales representative and resides with his wife Sheila in Mt. Juliet, Tennessee. A graduate of Memphis State University, he is author of *Baseball in Nashville* (2007, Arcadia Publishing) and is a contributing author to SABR's Biography Project. He serves as secretary of the Nashville Old Timers Baseball Association and is a member of the Grantland Rice-Fred Russell (Nashville) SABR chapter. An avid researcher of local baseball history, he was called on by the Nashville Sounds to assist in the placement of historical images throughout First Tennessee Park prior to the ballpark's opening in 2015. He publishes his findings at www.sulphurdell.com and blogs at www.262downright.com on a regular basis.

**BILL NOWLIN** has never lost even one major-league game. A member of SABR's board of directors since 2004, he has written or edited more than 60 books, mostly on baseball, and is a co-founder of Rounder Records.

A new contributor to SABR, **EMMET NOWLIN** currently resides in Cambridge, Massachusetts. Although somewhat interested in managing the first space hotel, he does not intend to pursue the venture, or ever travel to space.

**ARMAND PETERSON** is a retired engineer and manager, living in Maple Grove, Minnesota. He's been hooked on baseball since he saw some cousins play a town team game on a hardscrabble field in eastern South Dakota when he was nine years old. He was a Yankees and Mickey Mantle fan in his youth—thanks to indoctrination by his baseball-playing cousins—but switched his allegiance to the Minnesota Twins when the Senators moved to Minnesota in 1961. Since retirement he has co-authored *Town Ball: The Glory Days of Minnesota Amateur Baseball*, and written several SABR biographies.

**DAVID RAGLIN** has been a SABR member for 32 years and has edited two SABR BioProject books with Mark Pattison, *Sock It To 'Em, Tigers* and *What a Start! What a Finish!* He has also contributed biographies for several other BioProject books and co-authored three other books on the Tigers. David is a native of Rochester, Michigan, and lives in McLean, Virginia, with his wife and BioProject co-author, Barb Mantegani, whom he met at a SABR event.

**CHRIS RAINEY** was introduced to SABR in the mid-1970's by one-time President Eugene Murdock. He helped to transcribe oral interviews that Murdock collected over the years. Rainey enjoyed a 35-year teaching career in Yellow Springs, Ohio where he coached baseball for 18 seasons. Over that time the teams made one regional appearance and won one league title. He now resides in Oxford, Ohio with his adorable wife, Janelle.

**STEPHEN V. RICE**, Ph.D., hails from Detroit, Michigan, and lives in Collierville, Tennessee. During his childhood he pored over statistics in the baseball encyclopedia and wondered about the players. The numbers don't say much about the players; they don't tell us who they were or what they were like. Now he writes biographies for the SABR BioProject, to help tell their stories. In his day job, he is a software architect in the Computational Biology department at St. Jude Children's Research Hospital in Memphis.

**CARL RIECHERS** retired from United Parcel Service in 2012 after 35 years of service. With more free time, he became a SABR member that same year. Born and raised in the suburbs of St. Louis, he became a big fan of the Cardinals. He and his wife Janet have three children and is the proud grandpa of two.

**JOEL RIPPEL**, a Minnesota native and graduate of the University of Minnesota, is the author or co-author of nine books on Minnesota sports history and has contributed as an editor or writer to several books published by SABR.

**PAUL ROGERS** is co-author of several baseball books including *The Whiz Kids and the 1950 Pennant* (Temple University Press, 1996) with boyhood hero Robin Roberts, and *Lucky Me: My 65 Years in Baseball* (SMU Press 2011) with Eddie Robinson. Paul is president of the Ernie Banks - Bobby Bragan DFW Chapter of SABR and a frequent contributor to the SABR BioProject, but his real job is as a law professor at Southern Methodist University, where he served as dean of the law school for nine years. He has also served as SMU's faculty athletic representative for 30 years.

**STUART SCHIMLER** is a historian specializing in America's cultural history. He is a contributing author to the books *Deadball Stars of the National League* (Potomac Books, 2004) and *Deadball Stars of the American League* (Potomac Books, 2004). Mr. Schimler writes extensively about presidential campaign songs, including an article for the encyclopedia *Music in American Life* (Greenwood, 2013). He holds a BA in history from the University of California, Berkeley.

**STEVEN D. SCHMITT** is author of *A History of Badger Baseball—The Rise and Fall of America's Pastime at the University of Wisconsin*. He has written SABR biographies on John DeMerit and Hawk Taylor in *That's Joy in Braveland—The 1957 Milwaukee*

*Braves* and individual biographies on Ty Cline, Steve Ridzik, Ken Johnson, and Johnny Gerlach for BioProject. His "Chicago Showdown" article is included in SABR's *A Pennant for the Twin Cities—The 1965 Minnesota Twins*. Schmitt is a former radio news reporter and play-by-play announcer for Wisconsin radio stations and former newspaper reporter for daily and weekly newspapers in southern Wisconsin. Schmitt has bachelor's and master's degrees from the University of Wisconsin—Madison School of Journalism and Mass Communication and resides in Madison, Wisconsin.

**JOE SCHUSTER** is the author of the novel *The Might Have Been* (Ballantine Books), which was a finalist for the CASEY Award for the best baseball book of 2012, as well as the short nonfiction book, *One Season in the Sun* (Gemma Open Door), which focuses on ballplayers whose major league careers lasted a few weeks or less. A member of the faculty of Webster University in St. Louis, he writes frequently for the Cardinals *Gameday* magazine. He is married and the father of five rabid Redbird fans.

**DAVID E. SKELTON** developed a passion for baseball early on when the lights from Philadelphia's Connie Mack Stadium would shine through his bedroom window. Long since removed from Philly, he now resides with his family in central Texas but remains passionate about the sport that evokes many of his earliest childhood memories. Employed for over 30 years in the oil and gas industry, he became a SABR member in early 2012 after a chance—and most fortunate—holiday encounter with a Rogers Hornsby Chapter member. Researching Dick Ellsworth for SABR's BioProject led to the peculiar findings that occasioned his 2013 article for the *Baseball Research Journal*.

**DAVID C. SOUTHWICK** is former publicity coordinator of the Boston Chapter of SABR. He conceived and initiated SABR's first team book for BioProject, on the 1975 Red Sox: *'75: The Red Sox Team That Saved Baseball*. When his beloved Red Sox are out of season, he is a dedicated follower of his alma mater's sports teams, the North Quincy (Massachusetts) High School Red Raiders. David presently resides in Dorchester, Massachusetts.

**GLEN SPARKS** grew up in Santa Monica, California. He has fond memories of listening to Vin Scully and Jerry Doggett broadcast Dodgers games on the radio and television. Glen has a bachelor's degree in journalism from the University of Missouri and worked in the newspaper world for many years. He lives with his wife, Pam, in Cardinals country, but he still stays tuned to Dodgers baseball and enjoys reading about the team's history, both in Brooklyn and Los Angeles. His biggest thrill? Watching a hobbled Kirk Gibson knock Dennis Eckersley's backdoor slider into the right-field pavilion at Dodger Stadium in Game One of the 1988 World Series. Glen writes for both the SABR Biography Project and the Games Project. This is his first piece for a SABR book.

**MARK S. STERNMAN** works in Boston and, though a diehard fan of the New York Yankees, holds a partial season-ticket plan for the Boston Red Sox. A SABR member since 1990, he has enjoyed writing for various SABR outlets about Tommy Beals, Ben Cardoni, Scotty Ingerton, Fred Tenney, and Sam Wise, players who like Buster Brown toiled for Boston's National League entry. He has also written game recaps for SABR books on Braves Field, the 1914 Boston Braves, 1967 Red Sox, and 1975 Boston Red Sox.

**JOHN STRUTH** lives in Ludlow, Massachusetts and is employed as an area psychologist with the Department of Developmental Services. He has been a member of SABR since 2006. A Mets fan, he grew up partial to fellow southpaw, Jerry Koosman, Interests include the pre-Negro League Black experience, and 19th Century baseball. He has previously written a bio on Alejandro Oms for the SABR book, *Cuban Baseball Legends*. He also presented a paper on the 1889 Cuban Giants at the Jerry Malloy conference in Newark several years back.

**COSME VIVANCO** is a Chicago-based writer who received his Masters of Fine Arts in Creative Writing from Columbia College in 2010. As a small child, he developed an incredible passion for baseball history. His other areas of interest are politics and music. This is his first contribution to the SABR Bioproject.

**JOE WANCHO** resides in Westlake, Ohio and is a lifelong Cleveland Indians fan. He has been a SABR member since 2005 and is the chair of the Minor League Research Committee.

**PHIL WILLIAMS** lives in Oreland, Pennsylvania, and has been a SABR member since 2007. He has contributed numerous articles to SABR's BioProject on Deadball Era figures, with a soft spot for Athletics and Phillies who were cheered (or jeered) by his Philadelphia baseball ancestors.

A lifelong Pirates fan, **GREGORY H. WOLF** was born in Pittsburgh, but now resides in the Chicagoland area with his wife, Margaret, and daughter, Gabriela. A Professor of German Studies and holder of the Dennis and Jean Bauman Endowed Chair in the Humanities at North Central College in Naperville, Illinois, he edited more than half a dozen books for SABR books while hard at work on several more.

# SABR BioProject Team Books

In 2002, the Society for American Baseball Research launched an effort to write and publish biographies of every player, manager, and individual who has made a contribution to baseball. Over the past decade, the BioProject Committee has produced over 6,000 biographical articles. Many have been part of efforts to create theme- or team-oriented books, spearheaded by chapters or other committees of SABR.

*THE 1986 BOSTON RED SOX:*
*THERE WAS MORE THAN GAME SIX*
One of a two-book series on the rivals that met in the 1986 World Series, the Boston Red Sox and the New York Mets, including biographies of every player, coach, broadcaster, and other important figures in the top organizations in baseball that year. .
**Edited by Leslie Heaphy and Bill Nowlin**
$19.95 paperback (ISBN 978-1-943816-19-4)
$9.99 ebook (ISBN 978-1-943816-18-7)
8.5"X11", 420 pages, over 200 photos

*THE 1986 NEW YORK METS:*
*THERE WAS MORE THAN GAME SIX*
The other book in the "rivalry" set from the 1986 World Series. This book re-tells the story of that year's classic World Series and this is the story of each of the players, coaches, managers, and broadcasters, their lives in baseball and the way the 1986 season fit into their lives.
**Edited by Leslie Heaphy and Bill Nowlin**
$19.95 paperback (ISBN 978-1-943816-13-2)
$9.99 ebook (ISBN 978-1-943816-12-5)
8.5"X11", 392 pages, over 100 photos

*SCANDAL ON THE SOUTH SIDE:*
*THE 1919 CHICAGO WHITE SOX*
The Black Sox Scandal isn't the only story worth telling about the 1919 Chicago White Sox. The team roster included three future Hall of Famers, a 20-year-old spitballer who would win 300 games in the minors, and even a batboy who later became a celebrity with the "Murderers' Row" New York Yankees. All of their stories are included in Scandal on the South Side with a timeline of the 1919 season.
**Edited by Jacob Pomrenke**
$19.95 paperback (ISBN 978-1-933599-95-3)
$9.99 ebook (ISBN 978-1-933599-94-6)
8.5"x11", 324 pages, 55 historic photos

*WINNING ON THE NORTH SIDE*
*THE 1929 CHICAGO CUBS*
Celebrate the 1929 Chicago Cubs, one of the most exciting teams in baseball history. Future Hall of Famers Hack Wilson, '29 NL MVP Rogers Hornsby, and Kiki Cuyler, along with Riggs Stephenson formed one of the most potent quartets in baseball history. The magical season came to an ignominious end in the World Series and helped craft the future "lovable loser" image of the team.
**Edited by Gregory H. Wolf**
$19.95 paperback (ISBN 978-1-933599-89-2)
$9.99 ebook (ISBN 978-1-933599-88-5)
8.5"x11", 314 pages, 59 photos

*DETROIT THE UNCONQUERABLE:*
*THE 1935 WORLD CHAMPION TIGERS*
Biographies of every player, coach, and broadcaster involved with the 1935 World Champion Detroit Tigers baseball team, written by members of the Society for American Baseball Research. Also includes a season in review and other articles about the 1935 team. Hank Greenberg, Mickey Cochrane, Charlie Gehringer, Schoolboy Rowe, and more.
**Edited by Scott Ferkovich**
$19.95 paperback (ISBN 9978-1-933599-78-6)
$9.99 ebook (ISBN 978-1-933599-79-3)
8.5"X11", 230 pages, 52 photos

*THE TEAM THAT TIME WON'T FORGET:*
*THE 1951 NEW YORK GIANTS*
Because of Bobby Thomson's dramatic "Shot Heard 'Round the World" in the bottom of the ninth of the decisive playoff game against the Brooklyn Dodgers, the team will forever be in baseball public's consciousness. Includes a foreword by Giants outfielder Monte Irvin.
**Edited by Bill Nowlin and C. Paul Rogers III**
$19.95 paperback (ISBN 978-1-933599-99-1)
$9.99 ebook (ISBN 978-1-933599-98-4)
8.5"X11", 282 pages, 47 photos

*A PENNANT FOR THE TWIN CITIES:*
*THE 1965 MINNESOTA TWINS*
This volume celebrates the 1965 Minnesota Twins, who captured the American League pennant in just their fifth season in the Twin Cities. Led by an All-Star cast, from Harmon Killebrew, Tony Oliva, Zoilo Versalles, and Mudcat Grant to Bob Allison, Jim Kaat, Earl Battey, and Jim Perry, the Twins won 102 games, but bowed to the Los Angeles Dodgers and Sandy Koufax in Game Seven
**Edited by Gregory H. Wolf**
$19.95 paperback (ISBN 978-1-943816-09-5)
$9.99 ebook (ISBN 978-1-943816-08-8)
8.5"X11", 405 pages, over 80 photos

*MUSTACHES AND MAYHEM: CHARLIE O'S THREE TIME CHAMPIONS:*
*THE OAKLAND ATHLETICS: 1972-74*
The Oakland Athletics captured major league baseball's crown each year from 1972 through 1974. Led by future Hall of Famers Reggie Jackson, Catfish Hunter and Rollie Fingers, the Athletics were a largely homegrown group who came of age together. Biographies of every player, coach, manager, and broadcaster (and mascot) from 1972 through 1974 are included, along with season recaps.
**Edited by Chip Greene**
$29.95 paperback (ISBN 978-1-943816-07-1)
$9.99 ebook (ISBN 978-1-943816-06-4)
8.5"X11", 600 pages, almost 100 photos

*SABR Members can purchase each book at a significant discount (often 50% off) and receive the ebook editions free as a member benefit. Each book is available in a trade paperback edition as well as ebooks suitable for reading on a home computer or Nook, Kindle, or iPad/tablet.*
*To learn more about becoming a member of SABR, visit the website: sabr.org/join*

# The SABR Digital Library

The Society for American Baseball Research, the top baseball research organization in the world, disseminates some of the best in baseball history, analysis, and biography through our publishing programs. The SABR Digital Library contains a mix of books old and new, and focuses on a tandem program of paperback and ebook publication, making these materials widely available for both on digital devices and as traditional printed books.

## Greatest Games Books

*TIGERS BY THE TALE:*
*GREAT GAMES AT MICHIGAN AND TRUMBULL*
For over 100 years, Michigan and Trumbull was the scene of some of the most exciting baseball ever. This book portrays 50 classic games at the corner, spanning the earliest days of Bennett Park until Tiger Stadium's final closing act. From Ty Cobb to Mickey Cochrane, Hank Greenberg to Al Kaline, and Willie Horton to Alan Trammell.
**Edited by Scott Ferkovich**
**$12.95 paperback (ISBN 978-1-943816-21-7)**
**$6.99 ebook (ISBN 978-1-943816-20-0)**
**8.5"x11", 160 pages, 22 photos**

*FROM THE BRAVES TO THE BREWERS: GREAT GAMES AND HISTORY AT MILWAUKEE'S COUNTY STADIUM*
The National Pastime provides in-depth articles focused on the geographic region where the national SABR convention is taking place annually. The SABR 45 convention took place in Chicago, and here are 45 articles on baseball in and around the bat-and-ball crazed Windy City: 25 that appeared in the souvenir book of the convention plus another 20 articles available in ebook only.
**Edited by Gregory H. Wolf**
**$19.95 paperback (ISBN 978-1-943816-23-1)**
**$9.99 ebook (ISBN 978-1-943816-22-4)**
**8.5"X11", 290 pages, 58 photos**

*BRAVES FIELD:*
*MEMORABLE MOMENTS AT BOSTON'S LOST DIAMOND*
From its opening on August 18, 1915, to the sudden departure of the Boston Braves to Milwaukee before the 1953 baseball season, Braves Field was home to Boston's National League baseball club and also hosted many other events: from NFL football to championship boxing. The most memorable moments to occur in Braves Field history are portrayed here.
**Edited by Bill Nowlin and Bob Brady**
**$19.95 paperback (ISBN 978-1-933599-93-9)**
**$9.99 ebook (ISBN 978-1-933599-92-2)**
**8.5"X11", 282 pages, 182 photos**

*AU JEU/PLAY BALL: THE 50 GREATEST GAMES IN THE HISTORY OF THE MONTREAL EXPOS*
The 50 greatest games in Montreal Expos history. The games described here recount the exploits of the many great players who wore Expos uniforms over the years—Bill Stoneman, Gary Carter, Andre Dawson, Steve Rogers, Pedro Martinez, from the earliest days of the franchise, to the glory years of 1979-1981, the what-might-have-been years of the early 1990s, and the sad, final days.and others.
**Edited by Norm King**
**$12.95 paperback (ISBN 978-1-943816-15-6)**
**$5.99 ebook (ISBN978-1-943816-14-9)**
**8.5"x11", 162 pages, 50 photos**

## Original SABR Research

*CALLING THE GAME:*
*BASEBALL BROADCASTING FROM 1920 TO THE PRESENT*
An exhaustive, meticulously researched history of bringing the national pastime out of the ballparks and into living rooms via the airwaves. Every play-by-play announcer, color commentator, and ex-ballplayer, every broadcast deal, radio station, and TV network. Plus a foreword by "Voice of the Chicago Cubs" Pat Hughes, and an afterword by Jacques Doucet, the "Voice of the Montreal Expos" 1972-2004.
**by Stuart Shea**
**$24.95 paperback (ISBN 978-1-933599-40-3)**
**$9.99 ebook (ISBN 978-1-933599-41-0)**
**7"X10", 712 pages, 40 photos**

## BioProject Books

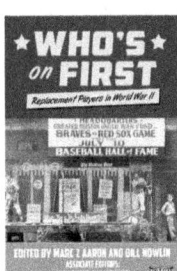

*WHO'S ON FIRST:*
*REPLACEMENT PLAYERS IN WORLD WAR II*
During World War II, 533 players made the major league debuts. More than 60% of the players in the 1941 Opening Day lineups departed for the service and were replaced by first-timers and oldsters. Hod Lisenbee was 46. POW Bert Shepard had an artificial leg, and Pete Gray had only one arm. The 1944 St. Louis Browns had 13 players classified 4-F. These are their stories.
**Edited by Marc Z Aaron and Bill Nowlin**
**$19.95 paperback (ISBN 978-1-933599-91-5)**
**$9.99 ebook (ISBN 978-1-933599-90-8)**
**8.5"X11", 422 pages, 67 photos**

*VAN LINGLE MUNGO:*
*THE MAN, THE SONG, THE PLAYERS*
40 baseball players with intriguing names have been named in renditions of Dave Frishberg's classic 1969 song, Van Lingle Mungo. This book presents biographies of all 40 players and additional information about one of the greatest baseball novelty songs of all time.
**Edited by Bill Nowlin**
**$19.95 paperback (ISBN 978-1-933599-76-2)**
**$9.99 ebook (ISBN 978-1-933599-77-9)**
**8.5"X11", 278 pages, 46 photos**

*NUCLEAR POWERED BASEBALL*
Nuclear Powered Baseball tells the stories of each player—past and present—featured in the classic Simpsons episode "Homer at the Bat." Wade Boggs, Ken Griffey Jr., Ozzie Smith, Nap Lajoie, Don Mattingly, and many more. We've also included a few very entertaining takes on the now-famous episode from prominent baseball writers Jonah Keri, Joe Posnanski, Erik Malinowski, and Bradley Woodrum
**Edited by Emily Hawks and Bill Nowlin**
**$19.95 paperback (ISBN 978-1-943816-11-8)**
**$9.99 ebook (ISBN 978-1-943816-10-1)**
**8.5"X11", 250 pages**

*SABR Members can purchase each book at a significant discount (often 50% off) and receive the ebook edtions free as a member benefit. Each book is available in a trade paperback edition as well as ebooks suitable for reading on a home computer or Nook, Kindle, or iPad/tablet.*
*To learn more about becoming a member of SABR, visit the website: sabr.org/join*

# SABR BioProject Books

In 2002, the Society for American Baseball Research launched an effort to write and publish biographies of every player, manager, and individual who has made a contribution to baseball. Over the past decade, the BioProject Committee has produced over 2,200 biographical articles. Many have been part of efforts to create theme- or team-oriented books, spearheaded by chapters or other committees of SABR.

THE YEAR OF THE BLUE SNOW:
THE 1964 PHILADELPHIA PHILLIES
Catcher Gus Triandos dubbed the Philadelphia Phillies' 1964 season "the year of the blue snow," a rare thing that happens once in a great while. This book sheds light on lingering questions about the 1964 season—but any book about a team is really about the players. This work offers life stories of all the players and others (managers, coaches, owners, and broadcasters) associated with this star-crossed team, as well as essays of analysis and history.
**Edited by Mel Marmer and Bill Nowlin**
**$19.95 paperback (ISBN 978-1-933599-51-9)**
**$9.99 ebook (ISBN 978-1-933599-52-6)**
**8.5"X11", 356 PAGES, over 70 photos**

THE MIRACLE BRAVES OF 1914
BOSTON'S ORIGINAL WORST-TO-FIRST CHAMPIONS
Long before the Red Sox "Impossible Dream" season, Boston's now nearly forgotten "other" team, the 1914 Boston Braves, performed a baseball "miracle" that resounds to this very day. The "Miracle Braves" were Boston's first "worst-to-first" winners of the World Series. Refusing to throw in the towel at the midseason mark, George Stallings engineered a remarkable second-half climb in the standings all the way to first place.
**Edited by Bill Nowlin**
**$19.95 paperback (ISBN 978-1-933599-69-4)**
**$9.99 ebook (ISBN 978-1-933599-70-0)**
**8.5"X11", 392 PAGES, over 100 photos**

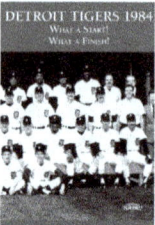

DETROIT TIGERS 1984:
WHAT A START! WHAT A FINISH!
The 1984 Detroit tigers roared out of the gate, winning their first nine games of the season and compiling an eye-popping 35-5 record after the campaign's first 40 games—still the best start ever for any team in major league history. This book brings together biographical profiles of every Tiger from that magical season, plus those of field management, top executives, the broadcasters—even venerable Tiger Stadium and the city itself.
**Edited by Mark Pattison and David Raglin**
**$19.95 paperback (ISBN 978-1-933599-44-1)**
**$9.99 ebook (ISBN 978-1-933599-45-8)**
**8.5"x11", 250 pages (Over 230,000 words!)**

THAR'S JOY IN BRAVELAND!
THE 1957 MILWAUKEE BRAVES
Few teams in baseball history have captured the hearts of their fans like the Milwaukee Braves of the 1950s. During the Braves' 13-year tenure in Milwaukee (1953-1965), they had a winning record every season, won two consecutive NL pennants (1957 and 1958), lost two more in the final week of the season (1956 and 1959), and set big-league attendance records along the way.
**Edited by Gregory H. Wolf**
**$19.95 paperback (ISBN 978-1-933599-71-7)**
**$9.99 ebook (ISBN 978-1-933599-72-4)**
**8.5"x11", 330 pages, over 60 photos**

SWEET '60: THE 1960 PITTSBURGH PIRATES
A portrait of the 1960 team which pulled off one of the biggest upsets of the last 60 years. When Bill Mazeroski's home run left the park to win in Game Seven of the World Series, beating the New York Yankees, David had toppled Goliath. It was a blow that awakened a generation, one that millions of people saw on television, one of TV's first iconic World Series moments.
**Edited by Clifton Blue Parker and Bill Nowlin**
**$19.95 paperback (ISBN 978-1-933599-48-9)**
**$9.99 ebook (ISBN 978-1-933599-49-6)**
**8.5"X11", 340 pages, 75 photos**

NEW CENTURY, NEW TEAM:
THE 1901 BOSTON AMERICANS
The team now known as the Boston Red Sox played its first season in 1901. Boston had a well-established National League team, but the American League went head-to-head with the N.L. in Chicago, Philadelphia, and Boston. Chicago won the American League pennant and Boston finished second, only four games behind.
**Edited by Bill Nowlin**
**$19.95 paperback (ISBN 978-1-933599-58-8)**
**$9.99 ebook (ISBN 978-1-933599-59-5)**
**8.5"X11", 268 pages, over 125 photos**

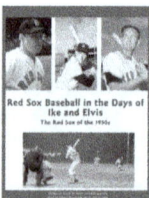

RED SOX BASEBALL IN THE DAYS OF IKE AND ELVIS: THE RED SOX OF THE 1950s
Although the Red Sox spent most of the 1950s far out of contention, the team was filled with fascinating players who captured the heart of their fans. In *Red Sox Baseball*, members of SABR present 46 biographies on players such as Ted Williams and Pumpsie Green as well as season-by-season recaps.
**Edited by Mark Armour and Bill Nowlin**
**$19.95 paperback (ISBN 978-1-933599-24-3)**
**$9.99 ebook (ISBN 978-1-933599-34-2)**
**8.5"X11", 372 PAGES, over 100 photos**

CAN HE PLAY?
A LOOK AT BASEBALL SCOUTS AND THEIR PROFESSION
They dig through tons of coal to find a single diamond. Here in the world of scouts, we meet the "King of Weeds," a Ph.D. we call "Baseball's Renaissance Man," a husband-and-wife team, pioneering Latin scouts, and a Japanese-American interned during World War II who became a successful scout—and many, many more.
**Edited by Jim Sandoval and Bill Nowlin**
**$19.95 paperback (ISBN 978-1-933599-23-6)**
**$9.99 ebook (ISBN 978-1-933599-25-0)**
**8.5"X11", 200 PAGES, over 100 photos**

*SABR Members can purchase each book at a significant discount (often 50% off) and receive the ebook editions free as a member benefit. Each book is available in a trade paperback edition as well as ebooks suitable for reading on a home computer or Nook, Kindle, or iPad/tablet.*
*To learn more about becoming a member of SABR, visit the website: sabr.org/join*

# THE SABR DIGITAL LIBRARY

The Society for American Baseball Research, the top baseball research organization in the world, disseminates some of the best in baseball history, analysis, and biography through our publishing programs. The SABR Digital Library contains a mix of books old and new, and focuses on a tandem program of paperback and ebook publication, making these materials widely available for both on digital devices and as traditional printed books.

## CLASSIC REPRINTS

*BASE-BALL: HOW TO BECOME A PLAYER*
by John Montgomery Ward
John Montgomery Ward (1860-1925) tossed the second perfect game in major league history and later became the game's best shortstop and a great, inventive manager. His classic handbook on baseball skills and strategy was published in 1888. Illustrated with woodcuts, the book is divided into chapters for each position on the field as well as chapters on the origin of the game, theory and strategy, training, base-running, and batting.
$4.99 ebook (ISBN 978-1-933599-47-2)
$9.95 paperback (ISBN 978-0910137539)
156 PAGES, 4.5"X7" replica edition

*BATTING* by F. C. Lane
First published in 1925, *Batting* collects the wisdom and insights of over 250 hitters and baseball figures. Lane interviewed extensively and compiled tips and advice on everything from batting stances to beanballs. Legendary baseball figures such as Ty Cobb, Casey Stengel, Cy Young, Walter Johnson, Rogers Hornsby, and Babe Ruth reveal the secrets of such integral and interesting parts of the game as how to choose a bat, the ways to beat a slump, and how to outguess the pitcher.
$14.95 paperback (ISBN 978-0-910137-86-7)
$7.99 ebook (ISBN 978-1-933599-46-5)
240 PAGES, 5"X7"

*RUN, RABBIT, RUN*
by Walter "Rabbit" Maranville
"Rabbit" Maranville was the Joe Garagiola of Grandpa's day, the baseball comedian of the times. In a twenty-four-year career that began in 1912, Rabbit found a lot of funny situations to laugh at, and no wonder: he caused most of them! The book also includes an introduction by the late Harold Seymour and a historical account of Maranville's life and Hall-of-Fame career by Bob Carroll.
$9.95 paperback (ISBN 978-1-933599-26-7)
$5.99 ebook (ISBN 978-1-933599-27-4)
100 PAGES, 5.5"X8.5", 15 rare photos

*MEMORIES OF A BALLPLAYER*
by Bill Werber and C. Paul Rogers III
Bill Werber's claim to fame is unique: he was the last living person to have a direct connection to the 1927 Yankees, "Murderers' Row," a team hailed by many as the best of all time. Rich in anecdotes and humor, Memories of a Ballplayer is a clear-eyed memoir of the world of big-league baseball in the 1930s. Werber played with or against some of the most productive hitters of all time, including Babe Ruth, Ted Williams, Lou Gehrig, and Joe DiMaggio.
$14.95 paperback (ISNB 978-0-910137-84-3)
$6.99 ebook (ISBN 978-1-933599-47-2)
250 PAGES, 6"X9"

## ORIGINAL SABR RESEARCH

*INVENTING BASEBALL: THE 100 GREATEST GAMES OF THE NINETEENTH CENTURY*
SABR's Nineteenth Century Committee brings to life the greatest games from the game's early years. From the "prisoner of war" game that took place among captive Union soldiers during the Civil War (immortalized in a famous lithograph), to the first intercollegiate game (Amherst versus Williams), to the first professional no-hitter, the games in this volume span 1833–1900 and detail the athletic exploits of such players as Cap Anson, Moses "Fleetwood" Walker, Charlie Comiskey, and Mike "King" Kelly.
**Edited by Bill Felber**
$19.95 paperback (ISBN 978-1-933599-42-7)
$9.99 ebook (ISBN 978-1-933599-43-4)
302 PAGES, 8"x10", 200 photos

*NINETEENTH CENTURY STARS: 2012 EDITION*
First published in 1989, *Nineteenth Century Stars* was SABR's initial attempt to capture the stories of baseball players from before 1900. With a collection of 136 fascinating biographies, SABR has re-released *Nineteenth Century Stars* for 2012 with revised statistics and new form. The 2012 version also includes a preface by **John Thorn**.
**Edited by Robert L. Tiemann and Mark Rucker**
$19.95 paperback (ISBN 978-1-933599-28-1)
$9.99 ebook (ISBN 978-1-933599-29-8)
300 PAGES, 6"X9"

*GREAT HITTING PITCHERS*
Published in 1979, *Great Hitting Pitchers* was one of SABR's early publications. Edited by SABR founder Bob Davids, the book compiles stories and records about pitchers excelling in the batter's box. Newly updated in 2012 by Mike Cook, *Great Hitting Pitchers* contain tables including data from 1979-2011, corrections to reflect recent records, and a new chapter on recent new members in the club of "great hitting pitchers" like Tom Glavine and Mike Hampton.
**Edited by L. Robert Davids**
$9.95 paperback (ISBN 978-1-933599-30-4)
$5.99 ebook (ISBN 978-1-933599-31-1)
102 PAGES, 5.5"x8.5"

*THE FENWAY PROJECT*
Sixty-four SABR members—avid fans, historians, statisticians, and game enthusiasts—recorded their experiences of a single game. Some wrote from inside the Green Monster's manual scoreboard, the Braves clubhouse, or the broadcast booth, while others took in the essence of Fenway from the grandstand or bleachers. The result is a fascinating look at the charms and challenges of Fenway Park, and the allure of being a baseball fan.
**Edited by Bill Nowlin and Cecilia Tan**
$9.99 ebook (ISBN 978-1-933599-50-2)
175 pages, 100 photos

*SABR Members can purchase each book at a significant discount (often 50% off) and receive the ebook editions free as a member benefit. Each book is available in a trade paperback edition as well as ebooks suitable for reading on a home computer or Nook, Kindle, or iPad/tablet.*
*To learn more about becoming a member of SABR, visit the website: sabr.org/join*

# Society for American Baseball Research

Cronkite School at ASU
555 N. Central Ave. #416, Phoenix, AZ 85004
602.496.1460 (phone)
SABR.org

## Become a SABR member today!

If you're interested in baseball — writing about it, reading about it, talking about it — there's a place for you in the Society for American Baseball Research. Our members include everyone from academics to professional sportswriters to amateur historians and statisticians to students and casual fans who enjoy reading about baseball and occasionally gathering with other members to talk baseball. What unites all SABR members is an interest in the game and joy in learning more about it.

SABR membership is open to any baseball fan; we offer 1-year and 3-year memberships. Here's a list of some of the key benefits you'll receive as a SABR member:

- Receive two editions (spring and fall) of the *Baseball Research Journal*, our flagship publication
- Receive expanded e-book edition of *The National Pastime*, our annual convention journal
- 8-10 new e-books published by the SABR Digital Library, all FREE to members
- "This Week in SABR" e-newsletter, sent to members every Friday
- Join dozens of research committees, from Statistical Analysis to Women in Baseball.
- Join one of 70 regional chapters in the U.S., Canada, Latin America, and abroad
- Participate in online discussion groups
- Ask and answer baseball research questions on the SABR-L e-mail listserv
- Complete archives of *The Sporting News* dating back to 1886 and other research resources
- Promote your research in "This Week in SABR"
- Diamond Dollars Case Competition
- Yoseloff Scholarships
- Discounts on SABR national conferences, including the SABR National Convention, the SABR Analytics Conference, Jerry Malloy Negro League Conference, Frederick Ivor-Campbell 19th Century Conference, and the Arizona Fall League Experience
- Publish your research in peer-reviewed SABR journals
- Collaborate with SABR researchers and experts
- Contribute to Baseball Biography Project or the SABR Games Project
- List your new book in the SABR Bookshelf
- Lead a SABR research committee or chapter
- Networking opportunities at SABR Analytics Conference
- Meet baseball authors and historians at SABR events and chapter meetings
- 50% discounts on paperback versions of SABR e-books
- Discounts with other partners in the baseball community
- SABR research awards

We hope you'll join the most passionate international community of baseball fans at SABR! Check us out online at SABR.org/join.

---

## SABR MEMBERSHIP FORM

|  | Annual | 3-year | Senior | 3-yr Sr. | Under 30 |
|---|---|---|---|---|---|
| **Standard:** | ❏ $65 | ❏ $175 | ❏ $45 | ❏ $129 | ❏ $45 |

*(International members wishing to be mailed the Baseball Research Journal should add $10/yr for Canada/Mexico or $19/yr for overseas locations.)*

| Canada/Mexico: | ❏ $75 | ❏ $205 | ❏ $55 | ❏ $159 | ❏ $55 |
| Overseas: | ❏ $84 | ❏ $232 | ❏ $64 | ❏ $186 | ❏ $55 |

Senior = 65 or older before Dec. 31 of the current year

### Participate in Our Donor Program!

Support the preservation of baseball research. Designate your gift toward:
❏ General Fund  ❏ Endowment Fund  ❏ Research Resources  ❏ _____
❏ I want to maximize the impact of my gift; do not send any donor premiums
❏ I would like this gift to remain anonymous.

Note: Any donation not designated will be placed in the General Fund.
SABR is a 501 (c) (3) not-for-profit organization & donations are tax-deductible to the extent allowed by law.

Name _____

E-mail* _____

Address _____

City _____ ST _____ ZIP _____

Phone _____ Birthday _____

* Your e-mail address on file ensures you will receive the most recent SABR news.

**Dues** $_____
**Donation** $_____
**Amount Enclosed** $_____

Do you work for a matching grant corporation? Call (602) 496-1460 for details.

If you wish to pay by credit card, please contact the SABR office at (602) 496-1460 or visit the SABR Store online at SABR.org/join. We accept Visa, Mastercard & Discover.

Do you wish to receive the *Baseball Research Journal* electronically? ❏ Yes  ❏ No
Our e-books are available in PDF, Kindle, or EPUB (iBooks, iPad, Nook) formats.

**Mail to: SABR, Cronkite School at ASU, 555 N. Central Ave. #416, Phoenix, AZ 85004**

www.ingramcontent.com/pod-product-compliance
Lightning Source LLC
Chambersburg PA
CBHW081331080526
44588CB00017B/2590